CONCISE
DICTIONARY
ENGLISH-
ENGLISH-HINDI

A Perfect Reference tool for Writers, Educationist,
Aspirants of Competitive Exams & Students

V&S PUBLISHERS

Published by

V&S PUBLISHERS

F-2/16, Ansari Road, Daryaganj, New Delhi-110002
☎ 011-23240026, 011-23240027 • *Fax* 011-23240028
Email info@vspublishers.com • *Website* www.vspublishers.com

Regional Office Hyderabad
5-1-707/1, Brij Bhawan (Beside Central Bank of India Lane)
Bank Street, Koti, Hyderabad - 500 095
☎ 040-24737290
E-mail vspublishershyd@gmail.com

Branch Office Mumbai
☎ 022-22098268
E-mail vspublishersmum@gmail.com

Follow us on

For any assistance sms **VSPUB** to **56161**

All books available at **www.vspublishers.com**

© **Copyright** *V&S PUBLISHERS*
ISBN 978-93-505713-7-8
Edition 2014

Printed at Param Offseters Okhla New Delhi-110020

Publisher's Note/प्रकाशकीय

A good response from dealers and commendable appreciation received from readers to our previously published dictionaries on science, commerce and language subjects has encouraged us to undertake yet another publication garnering high demand – An **English-English-Hindi-Dictionary**. The use of lexicographical techniques and latest compilation methods has further enhanced the utility of this dictionary. This edition will meet the requirements of students, researchers, travelers, scholars, translators, educationists, and writers. For better usefulness, 'Words or Terms' have been drawn from literature, science, geography, commerce & business etc. 'Terms' come tagged with explanatory meaning in English & Hindi both along with a sentence in English, for clear understanding for use both in speaking and writing.

'Terms' have been serialized in alphabetical order, *i.e.,* A-Z for ease in searching. To the extent possible, 'Terms' used in common parlance have been included, avoiding less frequent ones.

In the Appendices section, body parts, common ailments, apparel, cereals, fruit & vegetables, herbs & spices, and household items etc have been included for additional reference making it even more comprehensive.

We hope hoped that this dictionary will prove useful for student community besides others such as, educationists, writers, translators and common man.

We would be happy to have your views and comments for improving the content and quality of the book.

विज्ञान एवं वाणिज्य विषयों पर हमारे द्वारा प्रकाशित शब्द कोशों को बाजार से प्राप्त सराहना के फलस्वरूप हमने इस शब्दकोश को तैयार किया है जिसकी माँग उत्तरोत्तर बढ़ती जा रही है

इस शब्दकोश को कोशविज्ञान के सिद्धांतों और तकनीक को उपयोग में लाने के कारण यह शब्दकोश उपयोगिता में काफी व्यापक हो गया है। इस संस्करण से छात्रों, शिक्षाविदों, भ्रमणकारियों, शोधकर्ताओं, विद्वानों और लेखक की आवश्यकता की पूरी मदद मिलेगी। इस शब्दकोश में विभीन्न स्रोतों जैसे

अर्थशास्त्र, वाणिज्य, विज्ञान प्रोद्यौगिकी, प्रबंधन राजनीति भूगोल इत्यादि से आये शब्दों को भी शामिल किया गया है और साथ में उस शब्द के अर्थ को ठीक से समझने में मदद के लिये एक वाक्य भी दिया गया है अंग्रेजी भाषा में।

प्रत्येक अंग्रेजी शब्द या प्रविष्टि (एंट्री) का व्याकरण के साथ ही हिंदी और प्रविष्टियों को अल्फाबेटिकल (A – Z) रूप में प्रस्तुत किया गया है जिससे कि खोजना सरल एवं आसान है। केवल उन्ही प्रविष्टियों को शामिल किया गया है जो रोजमर्रा के बातचीत में प्रयोग में आती है। उपयोग में कम आने वाले शब्दों को विशेष रूप से सम्मिलित नहीं किया गया है।

पाठकों की सहूलियत हेतु शब्दकोश के अंत में अनेकों उपयोगी व अनिवार्य परिशिष्ट भी दिये गये हैं। शब्दकोश पर्यटकों, लेखकों, शिक्षाविदो और अनुवादों के लिये अत्यन्त उपयोगी साबित होगा।

हम पुस्तक की सामग्री और गुणवत्ता में सुधार लाने के लिये अपने विचारों और टिप्पणियों का स्वागत करेंगे।

Experiment Method/प्रयोग विधि

शीर्ष शब्द अंग्रेजी में स्थूल अक्षरों में दिये गये हैं।

Absorb/एबजॉर्ब *(verb)* – सोख लेना, चूसना soak up (liquid or another substance). *The Sponge Soaked up the liquid.*

शीर्ष शब्द का हिन्दी में उच्चारण भी स्थूल अक्षरों मे दिये गये हैं।

हिन्दी में उच्चारण के बाद व्याकरणित कोटि *(noun, adz. adv. prep.)* इत्यादि दिये गये हैं अग्रेंजी में तिर्यक अक्षरों मे दिया गया है।

Alive/एलाइव *(adj.)* – सजीव living, continuing in existence or use. *We are watching alive cricket match.*

adj., adv., prep., इत्यादि संक्षिप्त रूपों का पूर्ण रूप व्याकरण grammar पृष्ठ पर दिया गया है।

शीर्ष शब्द के अर्थ को हिन्दी में दिया गया है।

Baby/बेबी *(noun)* – बालक, बच्चा a child or animal that is newly or recently born. *Although adult, he behaves like a baby.*

शीर्ष शब्द का अर्थ अंग्रेजी में समझाने हेतु विस्तारपूर्वक से दिया गया है।

शीर्ष शब्द के अर्थ को उप्युक्त अग्रेंजी उदाहरण से स्पष्ट किया गया है। उदाहरण का वाक्य तिर्यक अक्षरों में किया गया है।

Boating/बोटिंग *(noun)* – नौका विहार water travel for pleasure. *Let us go for boating.*

शीर्ष शब्द का वाक्य में प्रयोग कर उसके अर्थ का स्पष्टीकरण किया गया है।

Label/लेबल

also	भी	*humorous*	हास्यकर
abbr.	संक्षिप्त रूप	*informal*	अनौपचारिक
chemistry	रसायन विज्ञान	*law*	कानूनी प्रयोग
compounds	यौगिक शब्द	*literary*	साहित्यिक
exclamation	विस्मयादिबोधक शब्द	*mathematics*	गणित
feminine	स्त्रीलिंग	*medical*	चिकित्सा
figurative	अलंकारिक	*music*	संगीत
formal	औपचारिक	*official*	आधिकारिक
geography	भूगोल	*philosophy*	दर्शन शास्त्र
geology	भूविज्ञान	*technical*	तकनीकी
geometry	रेखा गणित	*written*	लिखित
grammar	व्याकरण		

Grammar in Short/संक्षेप में व्याकरण

abbr.	abbreviation	संक्षिप्त
adv.	adverb	क्रियाविशेषण
adj.	adjective	विशेषण
conj.	conjunction	समुच्चयबोधक शब्द
det.	*determiner*	निर्धारक
excl.	exclamatory	विस्मयादिबोधक शब्द
noun	noun	संज्ञा
prep.	preposition	पूर्वसर्ग
pl.	plural	बहुवचन
verb	verb	क्रिया
[American English]	American English	अमेरिकन अंग्रेजी
[British English]	British English	ब्रिटिश अंग्रेजी

Table of Content/विषय-सूची

Aa

A/ए – अंग्रेजी वर्णमाला का पहला अक्षर the first letter of the English alphabet
(1) First note in music.
(2) First known quantity in Algebra.

Aback/एबैक *(adv.)* – पीछे की ओर [archaic] towards or situated to the rear. *The ship came into the harbour with all sails aback.*

Abaction/एबैक्सन *(noun)* – एक साथ बहुत से पशुओं की चोरी A large herd of cattle was stolen. *Police have registered a case of abaction.*

Abandon/एबैंडॅन *(verb)* – त्यागना give up (an action or practice) completely. *We abandoned the old car in an empty parking lot.*

Abase/एबेस *(verb)* – नीचा करना, मान घटाना belittle or degrade. *He was angry with his friend and abased him in public.*

Abash/एबैश *(verb)* – घबड़ा देना, संकुचित करना cause to feel embarrassed, disconcerted, or ashamed. *His father abashed him by criticizing him before his friends.*

Abashment/एबैशमेंट *(noun)* – लज्जा से आयी हुई विकलता felt feeling embarrassed due to modesty. *I left abashment as it was my first time to perform on stage.*

Abba/एब्बा *(noun)* – पिता, सबका पिता, ईश्वर (in the New Testament) God as father. *Abba will certainly listen to our prayers.*

Abbess/एबेस *(noun)* – महन्तिन a woman who is the head of an abbey of nuns. *He wanted the abbess to hear his confession.*

Abbey/एबे *(noun)* – मठ, गुरुद्वारा an establishment occupied by a community of monks or nuns. *Once there was an abbey here now the building is dilapidated and deserted.*

Abbot/एब्बॉट *(noun)* – मठाधिकारी, गुरुद्वारे का महन्त a man who is the head of an abbey of monks. *The abbot here is very popular he listen the grievances of all people.*

Abbreviate/एब्रीवियेट *(verb)* – छोटा करना, संक्षिप्त करना shorten (a word, phrase, or text).) *Etc. is an abbreviated form of etcetera.*

Abdal/एबडल *(noun)* – दरवेश a dervish. *He behaves like on abdal.*

Abdiel/एबडियल *(noun)* – ईश्वर का अनुचर, देवदूत an angel. *I hope that on abdiel will come for our help.*

Abdomen/एबडोमेन *(noun)* – मनुष्य का पेट या उदर the part of the body containing the digestive and reproductive organs; the belly. [zoology] the hinder part of the body of an arthropod. *His abdomen is flat because he does a lot of exercise.*

Abdominal/एबडोमिनल *(adj)* – उदर सम्बन्धी of or relating to or near the abdomen. *We took our brother to doctor as he complained of severe abdominal pain.*

Abduce/एबड्यूस *(verb)* – एक भाग से दूसरे को पृथक् करना advance audience for the criminal act of capturing and carrying away by force family member. *The problem was big but he soon abduced the conclusion.*

Abduct/एबडक्ट *(verb)* – बहका ले जाना take (someone) away illegally by force or deception. *Ashok's son has been abducted.*

Abduction/एबडक्सन *(noun)* – फुसलाकर किसी का अपहरण करना the carrying away of a person by fraud or violence. *Abduction of children has increased and the police have become active.*

Abecedarion/एबसेडेरियन *(noun)* – नवसिखुआ a novice. *He is an abecedarian learning the basics of computer.*

Abed/एबेड *(adv.)* – बिछावन पर [archaic] in bed. a state or condition markedly different from norm. *He was so tired that he went abed at once and slept.*

Aberrance/एबेरेन्स *(noun)* – धर्मनिष्ठा से विचलन deviation from rectitude. *Aberrance from the right path usually occurs in young age.*

1

A

Abet/एबेट *(verb)* – सहारा देना (abetted, abetting) (usu. In phr. Aid and abet) encourage or assist (someone) to do something wrong, in particular to commit a crime. *His wife died and police have arrested him for abetment to suicide.*

Abhor/एब्हॉर *(verb)* – घृणापूर्वक अविश्वास करना (abhorred, abhorring) detest; hate. *I abhor scenes of crime and violence.*

Abide/एबाइड *(verb)* – पालन करना (abide by) accept act in accordance with (a rule or decision). *We must abide by the rules of traffic.*

Ability/एबिलिटी *(noun)* – अधिकार, योग्यता the capacity to do something. *He has the ability of speaking five languages.*

Abject/एबजेक्ट *(adj.)* – अधम, नीच extremely unpleasant and degrading living in abject poverty. *He lives in abject poverty on footpath.*

Ablactate/एबलेक्टेट *(verb)* – छाती का दूध पिलाना to wean. *The mother got sick and the infant was ablactated.*

Ablactation/एबलॉक्टेशन *(noun)* – माता का दूध पिलाने की क्रिया the act of substituting other food for the mother's milk in diet of a child or young mammal. *Ablacation is usually advised by doctors when babies can't get mother's milk.*

Ablation/एब्लेशन *(noun)* – शरीर के क्लेशकर भाग का पृथक् करना the loss of solid material (especially ice) by melting or evaporation. The erosion of rock by wind action. *Exposed to strong winds over long periods even rocks undergo ablation.*

Ablative/एब्लेटिव *(adj.)* – अपादान करना [grammar] denoting a case indicating an agent, instrument, or source, expressed by 'by', 'with', or 'from' in English.

Ablaze/एब्लेज *(adj.)* – जलता हुआ, प्रकाशपूर्ण burning fiercely. *The bus was set ablaze by miscreants.*

Able/एबल *(adj.)*– 'योग्य' अर्थ का प्रत्यय जो संज्ञा Having the power, skill, or means to do something. *He is able to lift such a heavy weight.*

Ablepsy/एबलेप्सी *(noun)* – अन्धापन, दृष्टि शून्यता lowness of sight. *He suffers from ablepsy.*

Ablocate/एब्लोकेट *(verb)* – किराये पर देना to let out on hire. *He has ablicated his premises to an embassy.*

Abloom/एब्लूम *(adj.)*– फूलने की अवस्था में in the state of bloom. *The whole garden is abloom with flowers.*

Ablush/एब्लश *(adj.)* – लज्जित होते हुए having a red face from embarrassment, agitation or emotional upset. *She felt ablush when he expressed his love for her.*

Ablution/एब्ल्यूशन *(noun)* – कोई धार्मिक कार्य करने से पहले शरीर इत्यादि को शुद्ध करना the ritual of washing of a priest's hands or of sacred vessels. *Ablution is usually done by priests early in the morning.*

Ably/एब्ली *(adj.)* – योग्यता से, प्रवीणता से with competence. *He played ably and scared a centuary.*

Abnegate/एब्निगेट *(verb)* – त्याग करना [formal] renounce or reject (something desired or valuable). *Babar abnegated wine when Humayu was seriously sick.*

Aboard/एबोर्ड *(adv. & prep.)* – जहाज की छत पर, समीप On or into (a ship, train, or other vehicle). *He was aboard the ship in time.*

Abode/एबोड *(noun)* – क्रिया के भूतकाल का रूप formal or [poetic – literary] a house or home. *Residence: their right of adobe in Britain. Himalaya is the abode of gods.*

Aboil/एब्याल *(adv.)* – उबलता हुआ boiling. *The milk is aboil now put in rice.*

Abolish/एबॉलिश *(verb)* – हटा देना, नाश करना formally put an end to (a practice or institution). *Sati pratha was abolished during the British rule.*

Abolition/एबॉलिशन *(noun)* – घृणित, घिनौना the act of abolishing a system practice or invitation. *The credit to abolition of Sati pratha must go to Raja Ram Mohan Rai.*

Abominate/एबॉमिनेट *(verb)* – अति घृणा करना, द्वेष करना formal detest. *I abominate such rude behaviour.*

Aboral/एबॉरल *(adj.)* – मुँह की दूसरी ओर करना [zoology] furthest from or leading away from the mouth. *Remote from the mouth is called aboral.*

Aboriginal/एबोरिजिनल *(adj.)* - स्वदेशीय, आदि देशवासी An aboriginal inhabitant (Aboriginal) a person belonging to one of the indigenous peoples of Australia. *Aboriginal rituals are fascinating.*

Aborigines/एबओरिजिन्स *(noun)* - किसी देश के आदि निवासी an aboriginal person, animal, or plant. (Aborigine) an Australian aboriginal. *Aborigines of Australia are known all over the world.*

Abort/एबॉर्ट *(verb)* - गर्भपात होना Carry out or undergo the abortion of (a foetus). *She wanted to abort her child.*

Abound/एबाउन्ड *(verb)* - उमड़ उठना, भरपूर होना exist in large numbers or amounts. (abound in/with) have in large numbers or amounts. *This pond abounds in fish.*

About/एबाउट *(prep.&adv.)* - विषय में, निकट On the subject of; concerning. *I know nothing about him.*

Above/एबव *(prep.&adv.)* - ऊपर, शिखर पर At a higher level than. *High above the mountains a plane was flying.*

Abracadabra/एब्राकाडाब्रा *(noun)* - जन्त्र-मन्त्र exclamation a word said by conjurors when performing a magic trick. *The magician said Abracadabra and the lady disappeared.*

Abrade/एब्रेड *(verb)* - खुरच देना, नष्ट करना scrape or wear away by friction or erosion. *Strong winds abrade away the fertile earth.*

Abreast/एब्रेस्ट *(adv.)* - छाती से छाती मिलाते हुए Side by side and facing the same way. *While climbing over we found a huge rock abreast us.*

Abridge/एब्रीज *(verb)* - कम करना, संक्षेप करना Shorten (a text or film) without losing the sense. *This is the abridged edition of Mahabharata, you won't have to read the lengthy book now.*

Abrogate/एब्रोगेट *(verb)* - रद्द करना, तोड़ना formal repeal or do away with (a law or agreement). *I shall not abrogate this agreement.*

Abrupt/एब्रप्ट *(adj.)* - अचानक, खुड़बुड़ी Sudden and unexpected. *Her abrupt speech shocked me.*

Abruption/एब्रप्सन *(noun)* - एकाएक छूटने का कार्य [technical] the sudden breaking away of a portion from a mass. Medicine premature separation of the placenta from the wall of the womb during pregnancy. *The sudden abruption of the rock from the mountain was shocking.*

Abruptly/एब्रप्टली *(adj)* - एकाएक, तत्परता से quickly and actual warning. *He left the room abruptly.*

Abscess/एब्सेश *(noun)* - व्रण, शरीर के किसी भाग में मवाद भर जाना a swollen area within body tissue, containing an accumulation of pus. *After the accident an abscess formed on his left leg.*

Abscound/एब्सकॉन्ड *(verb)* - चुपके से भाग जाना Leave hurriedly and secretly to escape from custody or avoid arrest. *He absconded from the prison through a tunnel.*

Absence/एबसेन्स *(noun)* - किसी स्थान से अनुपस्थिति The state of being away from a place or person. *Her parents were worried because of the absence of their daughter from home.*

Absent/एबसेन्ट *(adj.)* - अनुपस्थिति Not present. *Many students were absent from the class.*

Absinth/एबसिन्थ *(noun)* - चिरायता The shrub wormwood. *He became an addict to absinth.*

Absolute/एबसल्यूट *(adj.)* - सम्पूर्ण not qualified or diminished in any way; total. not subject to any limitation of power; an absolute ruler. *A dictator is an absolute ruler.*

Absorb/एबजॉर्ब *(verb)* - सोख लेना, चूसना soak up (liquid or another substance). *The sponge soaked up the liquid.*

Abstain/एब्सटेन *(verb)* - पृथक् रहना, बचे रहना restrain oneself from doing something. *You are sick with an infection lungs so abstain from smoking.*

Abstenious/एबसटेनियस *(adj.)* - अटपाहारी, संयमी not self-indulgent, especially as regards eating and drinking. *He is an abstenious man and never touches alcohol.*

Abstention/एबसटेंशन *(noun)* - तटस्थ रहने की क्रिया an act of choosing not to vote either for or against. *Abstention is my preference in such cases.*

Absterge/एब्सटरेज *(verb)* - पापों को धो देना to purify, to purge. *I with to absterge now.*

Abstinent/एब्सटिनेन्ट *(noun)* - उपवास करने वाला, संयमी a person who refrains from drinking

A

intoxicating beverages. *My friends is an abstinent and he would never drink a beverage which has even the least alcohol.*

Abstract/एब्सट्रैक्ट *(adj.)* – भाववाचन, आदर्श theoretical rather than physical or concrete. *Love is an abstract idea.*

Absurd/एबसर्ड *(adj.)* – मूर्खतापूर्ण, निरर्थक wildly unreasonable, illogical or inappropriate. *It is an highly absurd theory nobody can make head or tail of it.*

Abundance/एबनडेन्स *(noun)* – प्रचुरता a very large quantity of something. plentifulness; prosperity. *This garden is famous for its abundance of flowers.*

Abuse/एब्यूज *(verb)* – गाली, दुर्व्यवहार use to bad effect or for a bad purpose. *During a fight the man abused one another a lot.*

Abut/एबट *(verb)* – मिलना (of land or a building) be next to or have a common boundary with. *My and my friend's houses are abutting.*

Acacia/अकासिया *(noun)* – गोंद उत्पन्न करने वाला बबूल का पेड़ a tree or shrub of warm climates which has yellow or white flowers and is typically thorny. [Genus Acacia: numerous species]. *The villages of India abound in Keeker (acacia) trees.*

Academy/एकेडेमी *(noun)* – पाठशाला, ज्ञानसमाज a place of study or training in a special field. [chiefly in names] US & Scottish a secondary school. *The academy of space of us is famous all over the world.*

Acarpous/एकारपस *(noun)* – अनुपजाऊ, बाँझ producing ne fruit. *This plant is acarpous as it produces no flower or fruit.*

Accelerate/एक्सीलरेट *(verb)* – जल्दी करना, चाल बढ़ाना begin to move more quickly. Increase in rate, amount, or extent. [physics] undergo a change in velocity. *If you accelerate highly the car will rush madly.*

Accentuation/एक्सेच्यूशन – अक्षरों पर दबाव डालकर उच्चारण the use or application of an accent. *Proper accentuation helps a lot in correct pronunciation.*

Accept/एक्सेप्ट *(verb)* – स्वीकार करना, सकारना consent to receive (something offered). *I'll accept this job offer.*

Acceptation/एक्सेप्टेशन *(noun)* – कृपापूर्वक स्वागत the accepted meaning of a word or phrase.

There is acceptation of many Hindi words into English language.

Access/एक्सेस *(noun)* – समीप में पहुँचना the means or opportunity to approach or enter a place. the right or opportunity to use something or see someone. *I have direct access to the minister office.*

Accession/एक्सेशन *(noun)* – राज्याभिषेक, चढ़ाव The attainment of position of rank. *He has gained accession to the rank of Admiral.*

Accidence/एक्सीडेन्स *(noun)* – व्याकरण का प्रत्यय विभाग dated the part of [grammar] concerned with the inflections of words.

Accidented/एक्सीडेन्टेड *(verb)* – असमतल, ऊँचे-नीचे धरातल पर An unfortunate accidented that happens unexpectedly and unintentionally. *The car accidented badly.*

Accipitral/एक्सीपिट्रूल *(adj)* – तीक्ष्ण दृष्टि वाला having acute vision. *Vulture is an accipitral bird.*

Acclaim/एक्लेम *(verb)* – जय-जयकार करना enthusiastic public praise. *His efforts were acclaimed.*

Acclamation/एक्लेमेशन *(noun)* – जय ध्वनि जय-जयकार Enthusiastic approval. *He received great acclamation for his speech.*

Acclivity/एक्लीविटी *(noun)* – पहाड़ की चढ़ाई, चढ़ाव an upward slope. *In the way, we went through an acclivity.*

Accommodate/एकोमोडेट *(verb)* – लोगों के कहीं बैठने या ठहरने की पर्याप्त सुविधा होना to adapt. *Each apartment can accommodate up to six people.*

Accompanier/एकॉमपेनियर – साथ देने वाला one who accompanies. *My friend is my accompanier in this journey.*

Accompany/एकॉमपेनी *(verb)* – साथ देना, सेवा करना go somewhere with. *My father accompanied me to my school.*

Accomplice/एकॉमप्लिस *(noun)* – अपराध में साथ देने वाला मनुष्य a person who helps another commit a crime. *He was my accomplice in the crime.*

Accord/एकार्ड *(verb)* – मिलना, समान होना give or grant someone (power or recognition). *His services have been accorded.*

According/एकॉर्डिंग *(adv.)* – अनुरूप (according to) as stated by or in. in a manner corresponding or in proportion to. *According to an announcement by the government petrol will be cheaper by two rupees.*

Accost/एकॉस्ट *(verb)* – बोलना, अशिष्टतापूर्वक, सम्भाषण करना approach and address boldly or aggressively.

Accouncheur/एकाउन्सर *(noun)* – प्रसूति-वैद्य a male midwife. *He is an accouncheur.*

Accouchement/एकॉचमेंट *(noun)* – बच्चे का जन्म [archaic] the action of giving birth.

Account/एकाउन्ट *(noun)* – गणना करना, हिसाब करना a description of an event or experience. *Your application has been taken into account.*

Accountship/एकाउन्टशीप *(noun)* – मुनीम का पद या कार्य the post of an accountant. *I am interested in accountship.*

Accredit/एक्रेडिट *(verb)* – विश्वास करना, मान्यता करना Give credit to (someone) for something. *He has been accredited with a lot of praise.*

Accrue/एक्रू *(verb)* – बढ़ना, लाभदायक होना (of a benefit or sum or money) be received in regular or increasing amounts.

Accumulate/एक्यूमुलेट *(verb)* – ढेर लगाना, इकट्ठा करना gather together a number or quantity of. build up. *He accumulated a lot of wealth.*

Accurate/एक्यूरेट *(adj.)* – अचूक, यथार्थ correct in all details. *Accurate shooting got him a gold in games*

Accusatory/एक्यूसेटरी *(adj.)* – दोष या अभियोग लगाने वाला one who accuses, accusing. *Out of anger she gave me black accusatory looks.*

Accuse/एक्यूज *(verb)* – अपराधी ठहराना charge with an offence or crime. claim that someone has done something wrong. *He was accused of murder. The court trial went on for 7 years.*

Accustom/एकस्टम *(verb)* – परिचय कराना, अभ्यास डालना make used to. (be accustomed to) be used to. *I am not accustomed to waiting for such long hours.*

Accentric/एक्सेन्ट्रीक *(adj.)* – केन्द्र में स्थित न रहने वाला without a centre; not centralized. *He was turned out of the meeting because of accentric behaviour.*

Acephalous/एसेफेलस *(adj.)* – बिना सिर का, बिना चौधरी का Without a head. *Worms who don't have a clear defined head are called acephalous.*

Acerbate/एसरबेट *(verb)* – कड़वाहट और तीखा करना cause to be bitter or resentful. *Insult noted out to him made him acerbated.*

Acerbic/एसरबिक *(adj.)* – खट्टा Sharp and forthright. *He was acerbic in his speech which angered many people.*

Acerbity/एसरबिटी *(noun)* – कटु वचन a rough and bitter manner. *Acerbity developed between two brothers on a land dispute.*

Acervate/एसरवेट *(adj.)* – गुच्छों में उगने वाला pertaining to a growth of fungi that forms a leaped-up mass. *This acervate may have medicinal properties.*

Acetic/एसेटिक *(adj.)* – सिरके के सदृश खट्टा relating to or containing acetic acid. *Thin object contains acetic acid let us give it a medical test.*

Acetify/एसेटिफाइ *(verb)* – सिरका बनाना, खट्टा करना make sour or more sour. *This solution has been acetified let's take it to the laboratory.*

Acetous/एसिटस *(adj.)* – खट्टा producing or resembling vinegar. *Producing or resembling vinegar.*

Acharnement/एकर्नमेंट *(noun)* – हत्या करने की लालसा [archaic] bloodthirsty fury or ferocity.

Achieve/एचिव *(verb)* – प्राप्त करना bring about or accomplish by effort, skill, or courage. *He has achieved a lot in such a short time*

Achromatic/एक्रोमेटिक *(adj.)* – बिना रंग का relation to or denoting lenses that transmit light without separating it into constituent colours. *These glass are achromatic. 2. without colour. Water is achromatic, i.e. it has no colour.*

Acid/एसिड *(noun)* – खट्टा, तीखा A substance (typically, a corrosive or sour-tasting liquid) with particular chemical properties including turning litmus red, neutralizing alkalis, and dissolving some metals. [Chemistry] any molecule able to donate a proton or accept electrons in reactions. *Some rowdy boys threw acid over a girl, her skin was burnt away.*

Acidification/एसिडिफिकेशन *(noun)* – अम्लीकरण the process of becoming acid or being converted into an acid. *Acidification of this liquid has taken place.*

Acidulate/एसिड्यूलेट *(verb)* – थोड़ा खट्टा करना make slightly acidic. *Don't worry this substance is only slightly acidulated.*

A

Aciform/एसिफॉर्म (adj) – सूई की आकृति के समान like the shape of a needle. *This aciform object is as sharp as a needle.*

Acme/एक्मि (noun) – शिखर the highest point of achievement or excellence. *He has become very rich and touched acme at last.*

Acne/एक्नि (noun) – मुहाँसा, डोड़सा a skin condition marked by numerous red pimples resulting from inflamed sebaceous glands. *In young age acne often appear on the face.*

Aconite/एकोनाइट (noun) – कुचला A poisonous plant bearing spiels of hooded pink or purple flowers. *Aconite is a plant used in homeopathic medicines.* [Genus Aconitum: many species, including monkshood.]

Acorn/एकॉर्न (noun) – शाहवलूत, जैतून के वृक्ष का फल the fruit of the oak, a smooth oval nut in a cuplike base. *This fruit is used in Ayurvedic therapy.*

Acoustic/एकॉस्टिक (adj.) – ध्वनि-सम्बन्धी relating to sound or hearing. (of building materials) used for soundproofing or modifying sound. (of an explosive mine) set off by sound waves. *The acoustic system of the auditorium failed and there was no performance for a long time.*

Acquaint/एक्वेन्ट (verb) – परिचित होना (acquaint someone with) make someone aware of or familiar with. *Why should you talk to me? I am not acquainted with you.*

Acquiesce/एक्विएज् (verb) – सन्तुष्ट होना, मौन, स्वीकार करना accept or consent to something without protest. *I acquiesce to your suggestion.*

Acquire/एक्वायर (verb) – प्राप्त करना, कमाना come to possess to obtain. to obtain, Learn or develop (a skill, quality etc.). *She has acquired great skill in designing clothes.*

Acquisition/एक्विजिशन (noun) – प्राप्ति, लाभ a recently acquired asset or object. *A painting by Picasso is his latest acquisition.*

Acquit/एक्विट (verb) – निर्दोष ठहराना Formally declare not guilty of a criminal charge. *He has been acquitted from the charge of murder.*

Acrid/एक्रिड (adj.) – तीखा unpleasantly bitter or pungent. *The food in this place smells acrid.*

Acrobat/एक्रोबैट (noun) – नट, रस्से नाचने वाला an entertainer who performs acrobatics. *Acrobats in the circus gave stunning performance.*

Acropolis/एक्रोपोलिस (noun) – दुर्ग a citadel or fortified part of an ancient. Greek city, built on high ground. *I visited an acropolis when I was in Greece.*

Across/एक्रॉस (prep. & adv.) – एक ओर से दूसरी ओर adverb from one side to the other of (something). Expressing movement over a place or region. On or towards the other side of. *He went across the room and opened the door.*

Act/एक्ट (verb) – कार्य करना . take action; do something. (act up) [informal] behave badly. *According to police the bomb explosion was an act of sabotage.*

Acting/एक्टिंग (noun) – नाटक का अभिनय the performance of a part or role in a drama. *His acting in the film was so powerful that it became an all time hit.*

Actinic/एक्टिनिक (adj.) – सूर्य की किरण सम्बन्धी [technical] (of light or lighting) able to cause photochemical reactions, as in photography, through having a significant short-wavelength or ultraviolet component.

Action/एक्सन (noun) – कार्य, कृति the process of doing something to achieve an aim. *If you don't take action in time things may go out of control.*

Actively/एक्टिवली (adj) – सक्रियता से in active way. *He actively helps the needy.*

Active/एक्टिव (adj.) – चंचल, चपल moving or tending to move about vigorously or frequently. (of a person's mind or imagination) alert and lively. *On account of his sharp mind and active imagination he has become a popular writer.*

Actor/एक्टर (noun) – अभिनेता a person whose perfession is acting. *He is a very fine actor he has always given powerful performances.*

Actual/एक्चुअल (adj.) – वास्तविक existing in fact. *The actual damage to the car was not as great as we had feared.*

Actuary/एक्चुअरी (noun) – मुंशी a person who compiles and analyses statistics in order to calculated insurance risks and premiums.

Acuity/एक्वीटी (noun) – तीक्ष्णता, बुद्धि की परीक्षा sharpness or keenness of thought, vision, or hearing. *He has great acuity that is why he is considered an authority over history.*

Aculeated/एक्यूलीटेड *(adj.)* - नोकीला तीक्ष्ण entomology denoting hymenopterans insects with stings, e.g. bees and wasps.

Acumen/एक्यूमेन *(noun)* - तेजी, बुद्धिकी सूक्ष्मता the ability to make good judgments and take quick decisions. *He has great business acumen that is why he is so successful.*

Acuminate/एक्यूमिनेट *(adj.)* - नुकीला biology (of a plant or animal structure) tapering to a point. *This acuminate plant has a sharp tapering point.*

Adage/एडेज *(noun)* - सूत्र, कहावत a proverb or short statement expressing a general truth. *There is an adage that as you sow so shall you reap.*

Adam/एडम *(noun)* - पुरुष, मनु *(old testament)* in Judaism-Christian mythology, the first man and the husband of Eve and the progenitor of the human race. *Adam ate the apple and sin entered his mind.*

Adamant/एडामंट *(adj.)* - हीरा, वज्र refusing to be persuaded or to change one's mind. *He is very adamant by nature and won't change his opinion about you.*

Adapt/एडैप्ट *(verb)* - नई परिस्थिति के अनुरूप व्यवहार करना make suitable for a new use or purpose. *Creatures who could not adapt to changing environment gradually died away.*

Add/एड *(verb)* - जोड़ना, अधिक करना join to or put with something else. Increase in amount, number, or degree. *If we add two and two it makes four.*

Addict/एडिक्ट *(noun)* - निरत होना, व्यसन होना a person who is addicted to something. *He is addicted to drugs.*

Addle/एडल *(adj.)* - सड़ा, बाँझ rotten, barren. *His addled behaviour surprised all people.*

Address/एड्रेस *(verb)* - निवेदन करना, अभिभाषण करना the particular of the place where someone lives or an organization is situated. *The president is addressing a meeting, he can't meet you.*

Adept/एडैप्ट *(adj.)* - प्रवीण, गुणी very skilled or proficient. noun a person who is adept at something. *He is adept at oil painting.*

Adequate/एडिक्वेट *(adj.)* - योग्य, पर्याप्त satisfactory or acceptable. *Children should be given adequate supply of milk.*

Adhere/एड:हियर *(verb)* - मजबूती से चिपकना, दृढ़ होना stick fast to. *I'll adhere to my words no matter what comes*

Adhesion/एडहीसन *(noun)* - चिपकने की प्रक्रिया the action or process of adhering. [physics] the sticking together of particles of different substances. medicine an abnormal union of surfaces due to inflammation or injury. *Adhesion to good habits always pays.*

Adhibit/एडहिबिट *(verb)* - नत्थी करना, लगाना, चिपकाना, संलग्न करना formal apply or affix to something else.

Adieu/एड्यू *(verb)* - नमस्कार, जाते समय का अभिवादन exclamatory chiefly [poetic – literary] goodbye. *When we had reached the airport I said adieu to my friend.*

Adit/एडिट *(noun)* - खान में आने-जाने का मार्ग an access or drainage passage leading horizontally into a mine. *We reached the mine through an adit.*

Adjacent/एड्जेसन्ट *(adj.)* - निकट या बगल next to or adjoining something else. *My house is adjacent to my school.*

Adjective/एडजेक्टिव *(noun)* - विशेषण, आश्रित [grammar] a word naming an attribute of a noun, such as sweet, red, or [technical]. *What adjective would you use to describe my home.*

Adjoin/एड्ज्वाइन *(verb)* - जोड़ना, लगाना verb be next to and joined with. *These two pieces of wood are adjoined together with a strong adhesive.*

Adjourn/एजर्न *(verb)* - विलम्ब करना, टालना break off (a meeting) with the intention of resuming it later. *The court is adjourned for today.*

Adjudge/एडजज *(verb)* - निर्णय करना consider or declare to be true or the case. *The witness was adjudged to be true*

Adjunet/एड्जंक्ट *(noun)* - मिला हुआ, जुड़ा हुआ an additional and supplementary part. *This person is my adjunct and will remain with me wherever I go.*

Adjuration/एज्यूरेशन *(noun)* - शपथ a solemnoath, mathematic the joining of two sets to form a large set.

Adjure/एज्यूर *(verb)* - शपथपूर्वक आज्ञा देना या कहना formal solemnly urge to do something. *He adjured to do sometime destructive*

A

Adjust/एडजस्ट *(verb)* – अनुकूल बनना, व्यवस्था करना alter slightly in order to achieve a correct or desired result. adapt or become used to a new situation. *I have adjusted to my new home.*

Adjutant/एज्यूटेंट *(noun)* – बड़े अफसर का सहायक a [military] officer acting as an administrative assistant to a senior officer. *He is an adjutant to the general.*

Adjuvant/एज्यूवेंट *(noun)* – सहायक पुरुष helping, assisting. *Adjuvant therapy has started and doctors are looking for complete recovery.*

Administer/एडमिनिस्टर *(verb)* – प्रबन्ध करना, सहायता देना, प्रशासन चलाना, देखभाल करना attend to the organization or implementation of. *The chemist administered the drug to me.*

Administrator/एडमिनिस्टेटर *(noun)* – शासक, प्रबन्धन कर्ता *My father is a good administrator and ably handled a flourishing business.*

Admirable/एडमायरेब्ल *(adj.)* – प्रशंसनीय-श्रेष्ठ deserving respect and approval. *You have done admirable work.*

Admissible/एडमिसिब्ल *(adj.)* – ग्राह्य, अंगीकार योग्य having the right to be admitted especially in acourt of [law]. *I am a lifelong member of this club and hence admissible to it any time.*

Admission/एडमिशन *(noun)* – स्कूल क्लास आदि में प्रवेश the process or fact of being admitted to a place. *These days it is very difficult to find admission in a good school.*

Admissive/एडमिशिव *(adj.)* – स्वीकारी, मानने वाला characterised by or allowing admission. *All children up to 14 are admissive to free education in government schools.*

Admix/एडमिक्स *(verb)* – मिश्रण करना, मिलाना [chiefly technical] mix with something else.

Admonish/एडमॉनिश *(verb)* – धीरे से झिड़कना, डाँटना, फटकारना reprimand firmly. earnestly urge or warn. *I admonished him for his rude behaviour.*

Adnominal/एडनॉमिनल *(adj.)* – संज्ञा से जुड़ा हुआ

Ado/एडू *(noun)* – कष्ट, उपद्रव trouble; fuss. *It was much ado about nothing.*

Adobe/एडोब *(noun)* – धूप में सुखाई हुई ईंट a kind of clay used to make sun-dried bricks. *Hermits build their adobe in jungle.*

Adolescence/एडोलसेंस *(noun)* – किशोरावस्था the time period between the beginning of puberty and adulthood. *The time period between adolescence (13-19 years) and adulthood is very critical from many angles.*

Adolescent/एडोलसेंट *(adj.)* – 13-19 की उम्र का किशोर लड़का या लड़की the process of developing from a child into an adult. noun an adolescent boy or girl. *Adolescents often remain confused if not properly guided.*

Adopt/एडॉप्ट *(verb)* – कानूनन गोद लेना legally take (another's child) and bring it up as one's own. *He adopted an attitude of innocence.*

Adorable/एडोरेबल *(adj.)* – आराध्य, पूजनीय inspiring great affection. *My mother is very adorable.*

Adore/एडोर *(verb)* – आराधना करना worship or venerate (a deity.) *I simply adore my English teacher.*

Adown/एडाउन *(prep.)* – नीचे, नीचे की ओर [archaic] down. *The liquid was poured adown his throat.*

Adrift/एड्रिफ्ट *(adj.&adv.)* – इधर-उधर तैरते हुए (of a boat) drifting without control. *This boat was found adrift in the sea.*

Adscript/एडस्क्रीप्ट *(adj. & noun)* – बाद मे लिखा हुआ, दास written after, a serf. *In order to complete the book he adscripted another character.*

Adult/एडल्ट *(noun)* – यौवन प्राप्त पुरुष, युवा adjective fully grown and development. or characteristic of adults. *He is an adult and can take his own decision*

Adulterant/एडल्टरन्ट *(noun)* – अपमिश्रक, मिलावट mixture. *Water is adulterant often mixed in milk.*

Adulterate/एडल्टरेट *(verb)* – मिलावट करना make food or drink less pure or of lower quality by adding.

Adust/एडस्ट *(adj.)* – जला हुआ, झुलसा हुआ [archaic] 1. burnt. 2. gloomy. *She looks adust.*

Adultery/एडल्टरी *(noun)* – व्यभिचार, पर पुरुष या पर स्त्री के बीच यौन सम्बन्ध voluntary sexual intercourse between a married person and a person who is not their spouse. *Adultery is crime and severely punished in Muslim countries.*

Advanced/एडवांस्ड *(adj)* – उन्नत move forwards. cause to occur at an earlier date than planned. *The work has completed before the advanced date.*

Advantage/एडवांटेज *(noun)* – लाभ या फायदे की स्थिति, महत्त्व a condition or circumstance that puts one in a favourable position. benefit; profit. *His being elected as a party candidate is of advantage to me.*

Adventure/एडवेन्चर *(noun)* – उत्तेजक, असाधारण an unusual, exciting, and daring experience. excitement arising from this. *We have planned great adventure in the jungles of east Africa.*

Adverb/एडवर्ब *(noun)* – क्रिया विशेषण [grammar] a word or phrase that modifies the meaning of an adjective, verb, or other adverb, or of a sentence. *She walked slowly. In this sentence slowly is an adverb.*

Adversary/एडवरसरी *(noun)* – प्रतिवादी, विरोधी an opponent. adjective another term for adversarila. *He is my adversary in estate business.*

Adversative/एडवरजेटिव *(adj.)* – विरोध-सूचक [grammar] (of a word or phrase) expressing opposition or antithesis. *This adversative attitude upset me.*

Adverse/एडवर्स *(adj.)* – विपरीत, प्रतिकूल harmful; unfavourable. *This medicine may have adverse effects.*

Advert/एडवर्ट *(verb)* – ध्यान दिलाना, संकेत करना formal refer to. *There was an advert in the newspaper regarding sale of summer clothes.*

Advertise/एडवर्टाइज *(verb)* – विज्ञापन देना, घोषित करना [archaic] notify. *If you want tenant, one way is to advertise in the newspaper.*

Advisability/एडविजेबिलिटी *(adj)* – शीघ्र होने की योग्यता *The chairman questioned the advisability of our plan.*

Advisable/एडवाइजेब्ल *(adj.)* – अनुमति योग्य, चतुर to be recommended; sensible. *It is an advisable step you took.*

Advice/एडवाइस *(verb)* – परामर्श देना, सलाह करना inform about a fact or situation. *I advise you to leave this place at once.*

Advocacy/एडवोकेसी *(noun)* – पक्ष का समर्थन, वकालत support. *This advocacy in the court was brilliant.*

Advocate/एडवोकेट *(noun)* – दूसरे के लिये बहस करने वाला, सिफारिश करना a person who publicly supports or recommends a particular cause or policy. *My father was a famous advocate.*

Adynamia/एडायनामिया *(noun)* – किसी रोग के कारण उत्पन्न हुई कमी lack of strength or vigour. *Adynamia in him is the result of long disease from which he is recovering.*

Adynamic/एडायनेमिक *(adj.)* – शक्तिहीन, निर्बल weak. *His adynamic speech thrilled everybody.*

Aeon/एवोन *(noun)* – युग, कल्प an indefinite and very long period. *Such astrological wonders among planets happen in aeons.*

Aeration/एअरेशन *(verb)* – वायु में मिलने का कार्य exposure to the action of air. *Aeration of clothes makes them dry.*

Aerial/एरियल *(noun)* – वायु सम्बन्धी, काल्पनिक, एंटिना a structure that transmits or receives radio or television signals. *If the aerial is in right direction TV transmits good pictures.*

Aeriferous/एरिफरस *(adj)* – वायु ले जाने वाला conveying air. *Bronchial tubes are aeriferous.*

Aeriform/एअरीफार्म *(adj.)* – वायु के समान, अवास्तविक resembling air or having the form of air. *Water is not as aeriform as wind.*

Aerify/एरीफाइ *(verb)* – भरना turn into gas. *This water has been aerified i.e. turned into gas.*

Aero/एअरो *(combining form)* – 'वायु' अर्थ का उपसर्ग of a relating to air: aerobic. *Aerobics keep you physically fit.*

Aesthetics/एस्थेटिक्स *(plural noun)* – सुन्दरता से सम्बन्धित, सौंदर्य शास्त्र a set of principles concerned with the nature and appreciation of beauty, especially in art. the branch of philosophy which deals with questions of beauty and artistic taste. *We should never lose sense of aesthetics.*

Aestival/एस्टीवल *(adj.)* – ग्रीष्म ऋतु सम्बन्धी [technical] belonging to or appearing in summer.

Aether/एथर *(noun)* – तेजो वह तत्व, आकाश variant spelling of ether (in senses 3 and 4). *Our earth is surrounded by aether.*

Afar/एफार *(noun)* – दूर से, दूर पर a member of a people living in Djibouti and NE Ethiopia.

Affable/एफबल *(adj.)* – सुशील, मिलनसार good-natured and sociable. *He is very affable by nature always laughing mixing and socializing.*

A

Affect/अफेक्ट *(verb)* – प्रभाव डालना, प्रेम करना have an effect on; make a difference to. touch the feeling of. *His words have affected me so much. I am going to apologize to him.*

Affectation/एफेक्टेशन *(noun)* – अहंकार, आडम्बर, ढोंग, दिखावा behaviour, speech, or writing that is artificial and designed to impress. a studied display of feeling. *His speech shows a lot of affectation these can't be his genuine feelings.*

Affected/अफेकटिड *(adj.)* – प्रभावित artificial, pretentious, and designed to impress. *His behaviour is clearly affected. He can't be gentle.*

Affection/एफेक्सन *(noun)* – प्रेम, अनुराग a feeling of fondness or liking. *I have great affection for my granddaughter.*

Affective/एफेक्टिव *(adj.)* – उत्तेजित करने वाला chiefly psychology relating to moods, feelings, and attitudes. *His affective cheerfulness touched all people.*

Afferent/एफरेंट *(adj.)* – अभिवाही, अन्तर्मुखी वाला relating to or denoting the conduction of nerve impulses or blood inwards or towards something. the opposite of efferent. noun an afferent nerve fibre or vessel.

Affiance/एफियान्स *(noun)* – वरदान, विवाह के लिए वचन देना [poetic – literary] be engaged to marry. *She is affiance with her boyfriend.*

Affidavit/एफिडेविट *(noun)* – शपथपत्र, हलफनामा [law] a written statement confirmed by oath or affirmation, for use as evidence in court. *I had to produce an affidavit in police station to the effect that I had lost my ID.*

Affiliate/एफिलिएट *(verb)* – गोद लेना, किसी बड़ी संस्था से मिलाना officially attach or connect to an organization. (of an organization) admit as a member. noun an affiliated person or organization. *This college is affiliated with Delhi University.*

Affined/एफाइन्ड *(adj.)* – संयुक्त, सम्बद्ध [mathematics] allowing for or preserving parallel relationships. *These two triangles are affined.*

Affinity/एफिनिटि *(noun)* – आत्मीयता, आकर्षण समानता, सम्बन्ध a spontaneous or natural liking or sympathy. a close relationship based on a common origin or structure. relationship by marriage. *I enjoyed great affinity with her and consequently I married her.*

Affirm/एफर्म *(verb)* – निश्चय के साथ कहना, दृढ़ता पूर्वक कहना state emphatically or publicly. [law] ratify (a judgment or agreement). [law] make a formal declaration rather than taking an oath. *I publicly affirmed that I had never seen that man before.*

Affirmative/एफर्मेटिव *(adj.)* – सकारात्मक स्वीकार या अंगीकार सूचक agreeing with or consenting to a statement or request. [grammar & logic] stating that a fact is so. Contrasted with negative and interrogative. *Unlike interrogative and negative sentences affirmative sentences show consent.*

Affix/एफिक्स *(verb)* – संयुक्त करना, जोड़ना attach or fasten to something else. noun [grammar] an addition to the base form or stem of a word in order to modify its meaning or create a new word. *Affix this stamp on the envelope and drop it into a letterbox.*

Afflict/एफ्लिक्ट *(verb)* – पीड़ा देना, कष्ट देना cause pain or suffering to. *He is afflicted with a terrible wound.*

Affluence/एफ्लूएन्स *(adj)* – धन की समृद्धि, अधिकता *His affluence carried a lot of weight and he became the President of the club.*

Affluent/एफ्लूएन्ट *(adj.)* – धनवान, परिपूर्ण, समृद्ध wealthy. *He is an affluent person and owns a chain of malls.*

Afford/एफोर्ड *(verb)* – कुछ करने या खरीद सकने के लिए पर्याप्त धन या समय निकाल सकना provide (an opportunity or facility). *I can't afford such a costly TV.*

Afforest/एफॉरेस्ट *(verb)* – जंगल लगाना convert (land) into forest for commercial exploitation. *The land mafia has afforested large chunks of land for commercial gain.*

Affray/एफ्रे *(noun)* – कलह noisy quarrel, dated a breach of the peace by fighting in a public place. *Affray near the cinema hall caused the police to intervene.*

Affright/एफ्राइट *(verb & noun)* – डराना, भय, ऊधम frighten. noun fright. *The lonely jungle in the night affrighted.*

Affront/अफ्रन्ट *(noun)* – सामना करना, अपमानित करना an action or remark that causes outrage or offence. verb offend the modesty or values of. *It was an affront on his part to insult his senior.*

Affuse/एफ्यूज *(verb)* – उड़ेलना, छिड़कना pour out. *I affused a lot of affection on her.*

Afield/एफिल्ड *(adv.)* – खेत में, या खेत पर in the field (in reference to hunting). *He was afield for hunting.*

Afire/एफायर *(adv.&adj.)* – जलती अवस्था में in flames. *The mob set afire the police jeep.*

Aflame/एफ्लेम *(adv.& adj.)* – आगे जलते हुए, चमकते हुए in flames. *The aeroplane went down aflame as it hit a mountain.*

Afloat/एफ्लोट *(adv.&adj.)* – बहता हुआ, जहाज पर floating in water. on board a ship or boat. There is nobody in the ship. *It must have been afloat for a long time.*

Afraid/एफ्रेड *(adj.)* – डरा हुआ, त्रस्त (often afraid of/to do) fearful or anxious. anxious about the well-being of. I am afraid that my father might not have another heart attack.

Afresh/एफ्रेश *(adv.)* – नये सिरे से in a new or different way. *He started afresh even after total bankruptcy.*

After/आफ्टर *(prep.)* – पीछे बाद मे, अनुसरण में in the time following (an event or another period of time). N. Amer. past (used in specifying a time). *I entered the house after my father had gone.*

Again/अगेन *(adv.)* – फिर, पुनः once more. *Again he won the trophy.*

Against/एगेन्स्ट *(prep.)* – प्रतिकूल in opposition to. to the disadvantage of. in resistance to. *I am totally against this project.*

Agamist/एगमिस्ट *(noun)* – विवाह-विरोधी me who is against marriage. *He is an agamist and will never marry nor will he encourage others to marry.*

Agape/अगेप *(adv)* – आश्चर्य से मुहँ खोले हुए (of a person's mouth) wide open. *The surprise news left him agape.*

Agate/अगेट *(noun)* – सुलेमानी पत्थर an ornamental stone consisting of a hard variety of chalcedony, typically banded in appearance.

Agenda/एजेंडा *(noun)* – विषयों की सूची, कार्यसूची a list of items to be discussed at a meeting. a list of matters to be addressed. *The chairman was given the agenda as soon as the meeting started.*

Agent/एजेंट *(noun)* – कार्यकर्ता, प्रतिनिधि, मुनीम a person that provides a particular service, typically one organizing transactions between two other parties. a person who manages financial or contractual matters for an actor, performer, or writer. *Travel and property agents are useful people.*

Agglutinate/एग्लूटिनेट *(verb)* – सरेस से जोड़ना या लगाना firmly stick or be stuck together to form a mass.

Aggravate/एग्रेवेट *(verb)* – (स्थिति को) बिगाड़ देना अधिक गंभीर बनाना [informal] annoy. *His drunken behaviour has aggravated an already bad situation.*

Aggregate/एग्रेगेट *(noun)* – एकत्रित करना, कुल जोड़ a whole formed by combining several disparate elements. *The aggregate of points gained by her in the match is very impressive.*

Aggress/एग्रेस *(verb)* – पहले छेड़छाड़ करना, अतिक्रमण करना, चढ़ाई करना *The army aggressed and went on offensive.*

Aggrieve/एग्रिव *(verb)* – दुःख देना characterized by or resulting from aggression. unduly forceful. *As he was attacked upon he is the aggrieved party.*

Aghast/एगास्ट *(adj.)* – भय से चकित, विस्मित filled with horror or shock. *I felt aghast at his cheap behaviour.*

Agile/एजाइल *(adj.)* – फूर्तिला, चपल, शीघ्र चलने वाला able to move quickly and easily. *Snake is an agile creature.*

Agist/एजिस्ट *(verb)* – कुछ धन लेकर चराने के लिए दूसरे के पशु लेना take in and feed (livestock) for payment. *My profession was to agist the cattle.*

Agitate/एजिटेट *(verb)* – आंदोलित करना, अशांति करना make troubled or nervous. *The news of accident agitated them.*

Agitation/एजिटेशन *(noun)* – व्याकुलता, घबराहट a mental state of extreme emotional disturbance. *In a state of agitation he attacked his opponent.*

Aglet/एग्लेट *(noun)* – चेन के किनारे पर लगाने की धातु की नोक a metal or plastic tube fixed tightly round each end of a shoelace. *The aglets of my shoes have become loose.*

Aglow/एग्लो *(adv)* – गरम, चमकता हुआ shining. *The palace was aglow with lights.*

A

Agnate/एग्नेट *(adj.)* – सगोत्र, पूर्वज related on the father's side. *We are agnate.*

Agnus/एग्नस *(noun)* – मेमना, भेड़ या बकरी का बच्चा a figure of a lamb bearing a cross or flag, as an emblem of Christ.

Agog/एगॉग *(adj.)* – गतिमान, आतुर very eager to hear or see something. *He was agog with excitement as he entered the movie hall.*

Agonic/एगोनिक *(adj)* – कोण न बनाने वाला, कोण रहित an imaginary line round the earth passing through both the north pole and the north magnetic pole, at any point on which a compass needle points to true north. *The needle is pointing to the North so it must be a point on the agonic.*

Agonist/एगोनिस्ट *(noun)* – योद्धा, लड़ाका biochemistry a substance which initiates a physiological response when combined with a part of the body directly. *He is an agonist in the field of boxing.*

Agonize/एगोनाइज *(verb)* – पीड़ा देना, कष्ट सहना, किसी कठिन समस्या पर लंबे समय तक सोचना undergo great mental anguish through worrying over something. *I was agonized to hear about his accident.*

Agony/एगोनी *(noun)* – यातना, अति शारीरिक पीड़ा, व्यथा extreme suffering. *I am far away from my family and thus living in great agony.*

Agoraphobia/एगोराफोबिया *(noun)* – भीड़ से डर लगना extreme or irrational fear of open or public places. *He is afraid of vast open space. Doctors say it is a disease named agoraphobia.*

Agrarion/एग्रेरियन *(adj.)* – कृषि या भूमि सम्बन्धी adjective of or relating to cultivated land or agriculture. relating to landed property. noun a person who advocates a redistribution of landed property. *Agrarian revolution in France is very famous.*

Agree/एग्री *(verb)* – अनुकूल होना have the same opinion about something. (of two or more parties) be in agreement. *I agree with you in this matter.*

Agrestic/एग्रस्टिक *(adj)* – ग्रामीण, देहाती rustic. *Rural people have agrestic simplicity.*

Agriculture/एग्रिकल्चर *(noun)* – खेती, कृषि धर्म the science or practice of farming, including the rearing of crops and animals. *Agriculture forms an important part of a country's economy.*

Aground/एग्राउण्ड *(adj.&adv.)* – अटका हुआ, धरती पर फंसा हुआ (with reference to a ship) on or on to the bottom in shallow water. *The ship ran aground and was damaged.*

Ague/एग्यू *(noun)* – जूड़ी, बुखार [archaic] malaria or some other illness involving fever and shivering, a fever or shivering fit.

Ahead/अहेड *(adv.)* – बढ़कर, आगे की ओर आगे further forward in space or time. in advance. in the lead. *America is far ahead than any other country in space science.*

Aheap/एहिप *(adj)* – ढेर में, डर से काँपता हुआ *The sheep felt panic and were aheap.*

Ahem/एहेम *(exclamatory)* – आश्चर्य या अविश्वास सूचक अन्यय, ध्यान आकर्षित करने के लिए एक अव्यय used to attract attention or express disapproval or embarrassment. *He didn't like the talks going on and to show his disagreement loudly said ahem.*

Aid/एड *(verb)* – सहायता करना, सहारा देना help or support. *The aided me in times of crisis.*

Aigrette/एग्रेट *(noun)* – सफेद सारस पक्षी, बाल का गुच्छा a headdress consisting of white egret's feather or other decoration such as a spray of gems.

Ail/एल *(verb)* – पीड़ा या व्यथा का होना [archaic] trouble or afflict in mind or body. *The ailing from TB.*

Aim/एम *(verb)* – लक्ष्य करना, प्रयत्न करना point (a weapon or camera) at a target. direct at someone or something. *I aimed my rifle at the wolf and shot him.*

Air/एअर *(noun)* – वायु, हवा the invisible gaseous substance surrounding the earth, a mixture mainly or oxygen and nitrogen. *Air surrounded earth if there were no air he won't be able to breathe and would die.*

Aisle/एजल *(noun)* – गिरजाघर का एक ओर का भाग a passage between rows of seat, pews, or supermarket shelves. *I walked through the aisle in the church and reached the pulpit.*

Ajar/एजार *(adj. & adv.)* – अधखुली दशा में adjective slightly open. *I left the door ajar to watch his activities.*

Akin/एकिन *(adj.)* – सगोत्र, सम्बन्धी नातेदार Of similar character. *He being my brother is akin to me.*

Alack/एलैक *(exclamatory)* – दुःख सूचक exclamatory [archaic] an expression of regret or dismay.

Alacrious/एलाक्रियस *(adj)* – प्रसन्न, खुश *His talk is so alacrious I enjoyed it greatly.*

Alacrity/अलैक्रिटी *(noun)* – प्रसन्नता, खुशी, उत्साह brisk and cheerful readiness. *The alacrity in his nature makes him good companion.*

Alolia/एलोलिया *(noun)* – बोली बन्द हो जाना *He is suffering from alolia and thus can't speak.*

Alamort/एलामोर्ट *(adj)* – अधमरा, उत्साहहीन, उदास *Every living thing is alamort.*

Alarm/एलार्म *(noun)* – संकेत, चेतावनी anxious or frightened awareness of danger. a warning of danger. *The news has set alarm bells ringing in my mind.*

Albeit/अलबीइट *(conj.)* – यद्यपि, ऐसा होते हुए भी, हालाँकि though. *He is poor albeit honest.*

Albert/एल्बर्ट *(noun)* – एक प्रकार जेब घड़ी की चेन brit. a watch chain with a bar at one end for attaching to a buttonhole.

Albino/एल्विनो *(noun)* – रंगहीन मनुष्य, वर्णहीन मनुष्य, सूरजमुखी मनुष्य a person or animal having a congenital absence of pigment in the skin and hair (which are white) and the eyes (which are usually pink). *A strong child was born to her having no colouring in eyes skin or hair it was an albino.*

Album/अलबम *(noun)* – चित्र, टिकट रखने की जिल्द a blank book for the insertion of photographs, stamps, with feathery leaves and plume-like flowers. *This album consists all my pictures of childhood.*

Albumen/एल्ब्यूमिन *(noun)* – गाढ़ा पदार्थ, अण्डे की सफेदी egg white, or the protein contained in it. *Albumen in the egg has lots of proteins.*

Alchemy/अलकेमी *(noun)* – रसायन विधा, कीमियागिरी the medieval forerunner of [Chemistry], concerned particularly with attempts to convert base metals into gold or to find a universal elixir.

Alcohol/अल्कोहल *(noun)* – शराब, बीयर आदि मादक पेय drinks, such as beer, wine etc. *Alcohol is an active agent in liquor or brew.*

Alcove/अल्कोव *(noun)* – घिरौची, मेहराबदार ताखा a recess, typically in the wall of a room. *I fitted my almirah in the alcove.*

Alee/एली *(adj.&adv.)* – आड़ में nautical on the leeward side of a ship, moved round to leeward.

Alegar/एलेगर *(noun)* – खट्टी शराब *This alegar made of sour ale won't suit your taste.*

Alert/एलर्ट *(noun)* – सावधान (often in phr. on the alert) the state of being alert. *This watchman is very alert you can't enter the compound without his permission.*

Algebra/एल्जेब्रा *(noun)* – बीजगणित the part of [mathematics] in which letters and other general symbols are used to represent numbers and quantities in formulae and equations. a system of this based on given axioms. *So far mathematics is concerned he is very weak in algebra.*

Algid/एल्जिड *(adj.)* – जड़ैया की शीत अवस्था का chilly. *In winter this room becomes very algid.*

Alias/एलिअस *(noun)* – उपनाम, कटिपत नाम a false or assumed identity. *Raj alias Raju was a notorious thug.*

Alien/एलिअन *(adj.)* – अन्य देश का, अन्य ग्रह का belonging to a foreign country. *He hails from USA. He is an alien.*

Alienate/एलिअनेट *(verb)* – चित्त हटाना, पराधीन करना cause to feel isolated. lose or destroy the support or sympathy of. *The father has legally alienated the rights of his property to his son.*

Alienist/एलिअनिस्ट *(noun)* – उन्माद रोग का विशेष चिकित्सक former term for psychiatrist. chiefly US a psychiatrist who assesses the competence of a defendant in a [law] court. *Alienists deal with mind.*

Aliform/एलिफॉर्म *(adj.)* – पर के आकार का wing-shaped. *An aliform kite flew in the sky.*

Alight/एलाइट *(verb)* – उतरना, नीचे से आना formal chiefly brit. descend form public transport. *He alighted from the moving bus.*

Alike/एलाइक *(adj.)* – सदृश, तुल्य similar. adverb in a similar way. *Both the brother are alike. They also behave alike.*

Aliment/एलीमेंट *(noun)* – पोषण, आहार, आश्रय nourishment. Scots [law] maintenance; alimony. *The judge fixed the aliment for the divorced women.*

Alimony/एलीमोनी *(noun)* – परित्यक्त पत्नी के भरण-पोषण का भत्ता, गुजारा, भरण-पोषण maintenance for a spouse after separation or divorce. *After the divorce he was ordered to pay a huge amount as alimony to his divorced wife.*

Aliquot/एलीक्योट *(noun)* – किसी पूर्ण विभाजक संख्या पर a portion of a larger whole, especially a sample taken for chemical analysis or other treatment. *When an aliquot of the river water was taken it was found to be contaminated.*

Alive/एलाइव *(adj.)* – सजीव living, continuing in existence or use. *We are watching alive cricket match.*

Alkali/ऐलकलाइ *(noun)* – क्षार a compound e.g. lime or caustic soda, with particular chemical properties including turning litmus blue and neutralizing or effervescing with acids. *This mixture seems to be alkaline.*

Alkaloid/अल्कलॉइड *(noun)* – वनस्पतियों का मूल तत्व [Chemistry] any of a class of nitrogenous organic compounds of plant origin which have pronounced physiological actions on humans. *Alkaloid compounds of a plant act physiologically on humans.*

Alkanet/एल्कानेट *(noun)* – रतनजोत a plant of the borage family with a hairy stem and blue flowers. *This blue flowered plant is called alkanet.*

All/ऑल *(pronoun)* – पूरा, कुल, समूचा predeterminer, determiner & pronoun the whole quantity or extent of. any whatever. the greatest possible. everything. *In all only ten students are present.*

Allay/एले *(verb)* – शांत करना, दमन करना, निराकरण करना alleviate (pain or hunger). *His talk allayed my fears.*

Allegation/एलिगेशन *(noun)* – आरोप, इल्जाम [law] a formal accusation against somebody. *The allegation against him is that of murder.*

Allege/अलेज *(verb)* – बिना प्रमाण के आरोप लगाना claim that someone has done something wrong, typically without proof. *It is alleged that he got drunk and hit his wife.*

Allegiant/एलिजिएण्ट *(adj)* – राजभक्त steadfast in devotion. *It is not possible to be allegiant to two masters.*

Allegoric/एलगोरिकल *(adj.)* – लाक्षणिक, रूपकमय used in or characteristic of or containing allegory. *In ancient times allegoric tales occupied an important place.*

Allegro/एलेग्रो *(adj.&adv.)* – प्रसन्न, प्रफुल्ल, आनन्द से at a brisk speed. noun an allegro movement, passage, or composition. *The allegro movement on women's rights succeeded in the end.*

Alleviate/एलीवियेट *(verb)* – छुटकारा देना, (पीड़ा को) कम करना make (pain or difficulty) less server. *The doctor's treatment alleviated my pain.*

Alley/एले *(noun)* – संकरी गली, उद्यानपथ a narrow passageway between or behind buildings. a path in a park or garden. *I saw two cats fighting in the alley.*

All Fours/ऑल फोर्स *(noun)* – ताश का एक खेल *In the card game all fours is very popular in clubs.*

Alliance/एलाइअन्स *(noun)* – नाता, रिश्ता, सन्धि a union or association formed for natural benefit. a relationship based on an affinity. the state of being joined or associated. Ecology a group of closely related plant associations. *There is alliance between the two states to preserve wild life.*

Alligate/एलिगेट *(verb)* – बाँधना या जोड़ना to join. *The two ends of the rope were alligated together to form a circle.*

Alligation/एलिगेशन *(noun)* – बन्धन की क्रिया process of joining. *Allegation between the two lasted a long time.*

Alligator/एलिगेटर *(noun)* – ग्राह, घड़ियाल a large semiaquatic reptile similar to a crocodile but with a broader and shorter head, native to the Americas and China. *Alligator looks like crocodile but there is some difference.*

Alliterate/एलिटरेट *(verb)* – एक ही अक्षरों से आरम्भ होने वाले शब्द का प्रयोग [poetry] use. *Alliteration as a form of poetry.*

Allocate/एलोकेट *(verb)* – भाग लगाना, हिस्से के रूप में बाँटना assign or distribute (resources or duties) to. *All person were allocated their duties by the election officer.*

Allocution/एलोक्यूशन *(noun)* – व्याख्यान a formal speech giving advice or a warning. *He was given an allocution before delivering the speech.*

Allograph/एलोग्राफ *(noun)* – दूसरे के लिए लिखा हुआ लेख a writing made by one person for another.

Allot/एलॉट *(verb)* – भाग देना, विभक्त करना, किसी काम के लिए समय तय करना apportion or assign (something) to someone. *I have been allotted a flat by DDA.*

Allotment/एलॉटमेंट *(noun)* – आवंटन, बाँटा गया, निर्धारित हिस्सा brit. a plot of land rented by an individual from a local authority, for growing vegetables or flowers. *Rupees one lakh was allotted by the centre to the flood hit areas.*

Allottee/एलॉटी *(noun)* – वह व्यक्ति जिसको या जिसके प्रति भाग दिया गया हो He is an allotte in the DDA lottery scheme.

Alloverishness/एलोवरीशनेश *(adj)* – अशक्तता, असुविधा a feeling of general discomfort. *She is suffering from alloverishness.*

Allow/अलाउ *(verb)* – कुछ करने की अनुमति देना admit as legal or acceptable. permit to do something. *Photography is not allowed inside the court*

Allowance/अलाउअन्स *(noun)* – अनुमोदन, वह मात्रा, राशि जिसे ले जाने की छूट मिली हो the amount of something allowed. a sum of money paid regularly to a person, typically to meet specified expenses. an amount of money that can be earned or received free of tax. house racing a deduction in the weight that a horse is required to carry in a race. verb [archaic] give a sum of money regularly as an allowance. *You'll get an allowance of Rs. 2000/- p.m. to run the house.*

Alloy/एल्लाय *(verb & noun)* – मिलावट करना a metal made by combining two or more metallic elements, especially to give greater strength or resistance to corrosion. an inferior metal mixed with a precious one.

Allspice/ऑलस्पाइस *(noun)* – एक प्रकार का मसाला, एक प्रकार का मसाला जिसमें लौंग दालचीनी, जायफल आदि की गंध होती है the dried aromatic fruit of a Caribbean tree, used as a culinary spice. *While visiting Caribbean island I ate the fruit allspice. It was very nice.*

Allude/एल्यूड *(verb)* – उद्देश्य करना, संकेत करना hint at. mention in passing. *While in restaurant I alluded at having an ice cream.*

Allure/एल्यूर *(verb)* – प्रलोभित करना, ललचाना [often as adjective alluring] powerfully attract.

Allusion/एल्यूजन *(noun)* – उद्देश्य, सूचना या संकेत the practice or device of making indirect or implicit references. a reference of this type.

Alluvial/एलुविअल *(adj)* – जलोढ़ कछारी, नदी के बहाव या बाढ़ से बना हुआ *The alluvial soil is greatly fertile.*

Alluvion/एलुवियन *(noun)* – कछारी भूमि, बाढ़ से जमी हुई मिट्टी [law] the formation of new land by deposition of sediment by the sea or a river. compare with avulsion. *Formation of alluvion land by deposition the sea or river of sedimentation has made this piece of land very fertile.*

Ally/एलाइ *(noun)* – मैत्री करना, जोड़ना a person or organization that cooperates with another. a state formally cooperating with another for a [military] or other purpose. the countries that fought with Britain in the first and second world wars. verb combine a resource or commodity with for mutual benefit. side with. *In 2nd World War America was an ally of France and UK.*

Almanac/एल्मानक *(noun)* – मन्त्र, जन्त्री, पंचांग an annual calendar containing important dates and statistical information such as astronomical data. an annual handbook containing information of general or specialist interest. *Let me consult the almanac to find an auspicious date for marriage.*

Almanographer/एल्मानोग्राफर *(noun)* – पंचांग बनाने वाला ज्योतिषी one who makes almanac. *Every year almanographers get busy in making the almanac.*

Almighty/ऑलमाइटि *(adj.)* – सर्वशक्तिमान, परमेश्वर omnipotent. *God is almighty.*

Almond/आल्मन्ड *(noun)* – बादाम फल, बादाम the oval edible nut-like kernel of the almond tree, growing in a woody shell. *It is said that five almonds in the morning everyday are greatly beneficial for health.*

Almoner/एल्मोनर *(noun)* – भिक्षा, वितरक, भिक्षा बाँटने वाला अध्यक्ष [historical] an official distributor of alms. *He is on the important part of almoner because he distributes alms.*

Almost/ऑलमोस्ट *(adv.)* – प्रायः, लगभग verb nearly. *He almost died of malaria.*

Alms/आल्म्स *(pl. noun)* – भिक्षा, धर्मदान (in [historical] contexts) charitable donations of money of food to the poor. *Alms have been distributed among the poor.*

Aloe/एलो *(noun)* – बोल, मुसब्बर a succulent tropical plant with a rosette of thick tapering

A

leaves and bell-shaped or tubular flowers on long stems. a strong laxative obtained from the bitter juice of various kinds of aloe. another term for century plant. *This bitter juice is that of aloe drink it is a good laxative, you'll get rid of your constipation also.*

Alone/एलोन *(adj.&adv.)* – एक, अकेला on one's own; by oneself. isolated and lonely. *Of all I alone supported him.*

Along/अलांग *(prep.&adv.)* – बराबर, साथ-साथ, एक सिरे से दूसरे सिरे तक या की ओर moving in a constant direction on (a more or less horizontal surface). *I went along the railing and soon reached the hall.*

Alopecia/एलोपेसिया *(noun)* – बालों का गंजापन medicine the absence of hair from areas of the body where it normally grows. *He suffers from alopecia and has lost a lot of hair.*

Aloud/एलाउड *(adv.)* – ऊँचे स्वर में, चिल्लाकर audibly. [archaic] loudly. *Please speak aloud I can't hear you.*

Alow/एलोव *(adv.)* – नीचे स्थान में [archaic] or dialect below; downwards. *Alow there is a lake.*

Alp/आल्प *(noun)* – ऊँचा पहाड़, पर्वत की चोटी a high mountain. the high range of mountains in Switzerland and adjourning countries. (in Switzerland) an area of green pasture on a mountain side. *When in Europe I tried to climb alps.*

Alpaca/ऐलपाका *(noun)* – एक प्रकार का चौपाया a long-haired domesticated south American mammal related to the llama. the wool of the alpaca, or fabric made from it. *When I went to South America I saw alpaca related to ilama.*

Alpha/अल्फा *(noun)* – वर्णमाला, का पहला अक्षर the first letter of the Greek alphabet transliterated as 'a'. denoting the first of a series of items or categories. brit. a first-class mark given for a piece of work. a code word representing the letter. A, used in radio communication. *Both English and Greek alphabet have a, as their first letter.*

Alphabet/अल्फाबेट *(noun)* – वर्णमाला, प्रथम सिद्धान्त a set of letters or symbols a fixed order used to represent the basic set of speech sounds of a language. *Without alphabet there can be no language.*

Alpinist/अल्पिनिस्ट *(adj.)* – ऊँचे पहाड़ पर चढ़ने वाला of or relating to high mountains. (in the names of plants and animals) growing or found on high mountains of or relating to the Alps. *This plant grows on alps hence we can call it alpinist plant.*

Already/ऑलरेडी *(adv.)* – पहले से, अभी before the time in question. as surprisingly soon or early as this. *I have already finished the book.*

Also/ऑल्सो *(adv.)* – और, सिवाय, भी in addition. *He is handsome and also intelligent.*

Altar/अल्टार *(noun)* – पूजा का ऊँचा स्थान, वेदी the table in a Christian church at which the bread and wine are consecrated in communion services. a table or flat-topped block used as the focus for a religious ritual. *Wine and bread were put on the altar in the church.*

Alter/ऑल्टर *(verb)* – बदलना change in character, appearance, direction, etc. North American & Austral, castrate or spay (a domestic animal). *He completely altered his appearance.*

Altercate/ऑल्टरकेट *(verb)* – विवाद करना *Don't altercate on this matter.*

Altered/ऑल्टर्ड *(adj)* – परिवर्तित, बदला हुआ (p.p. verb). *This character and appearance have been completely altered.*

Alternate/अल्टरनेट *(verb)* – एक अवस्था से दूसरी अवस्था में बदलना और पुन: पहली अवस्था में लौट आना occur or do in turn repeatedly. (of a thing) change repeatedly between two contrasting conditions. adjective 1. every other. other in a regular pattern. [Botany] (of leaves or shoots) placed alternately on the two sides of the stem.

Although/ऑल्दो *(conj.)* – यदि, यद्यपि in spite of the fact that. *Although he is a high class officer he has no manners.*

Altimeter/एल्टिमीटर *(noun)* – ऊँचाई नापने का एक प्रकार का यंत्र an instrument for determining altitude attained, especially a barometric or radar device fitted in an aircraft. *The altimeter fitted in the plane showed the altitude it was flying at.*

Altitude/अल्टीट्यूड *(noun)* – ऊँचाई, महत्त्व the height of an object or point in relation to sea level or ground level. Astronomy the apparent height of a celestial object above the horizon, measured in angular distance.

geometry the length of the perpendicular line from a vertex to the opposite side of a figure. *He dived into the sea from the altitude of 60 metres.*

Alto/अल्टो *(noun)* – स्त्री का निम्नतम और पुरुष का उच्चतम गान स्वर (especially in church music) the highest adult male singing voice. the lowest female singing voice; contralto. denoting the member of a family of instruments pitched second or third highest. *Do you hear the alto it is the high singing male voice and the low tone of the women singing together.*

Altogether/ऑल्टुगेदर *(adv.)* – सर्वथा, सम्पूर्ण रूप से completely. in total. on the whole. *Altogether the plan seems reusable.*

Alum/एल्यूम *(noun)* – फिटकरी [Chemistry] (also potash alum) a colourless astringent compound which is a hydrated double sulphate of aluminum and potassium, used in solution in dyeing and tanning. *The tanners use alum in solution for dyeing and tanning.*

Aluminium/एल्यूनियम *(noun)* – एक बहुत हल्की सफेद रंग की धातु a strong, light, corrosion-resistant silvery-grey metal, the chemical element of atomic number 13. *Aluminium is used in the manufacture of planes and window frames besides other material.*

Alumna/एल्यूम्ना *(noun)* – उपाधि प्राप्त विदुषी a former student of a school, college or university.

Alumnus/एल्यूमनस *(noun)* – विश्वविद्यालय या पाठशाला का विद्यार्थी a former pupil or student of a particular school, college, or university. *I have been an alumnus of K.M. college.*

Alveary/अल्विअरी *(adj)* – मधुमक्खी का छत्ता *This alveary is situated a great height it is very difficult to get it or break it.*

Alveolate/अल्विओलेट *(adj)* – मधुमक्खी के छत्ते के सदृश *This alveolate like object is full of cell like cavities may be it is an old honeycomb.*

Alvine/अल्वाइन *(adj)* – पेट या तोंद सम्बन्धी of or relating to the intestines. *He is suffering from alvine wounds and is on high antibiotics.*

Always/ऑल्वेज *(adv.)* – सदा, सर्वदा on all occasions. throughout a long period of the past. forever; repeatedly. *You always get what you deserve.*

Amain/एमैन *(adverb)* – बलपूर्वक, तुरन्त with great haste, at full speed. *The boys quickly ran away amain.*

Amalgam/एमैल्गम *(noun & verb)* – वस्तुओं का समिश्रण पारे से मिलाई हुई धातु a mixture or blend. *Don't amalgamate the various chemicals rashly it may explode.*

Amaranth/एमरेन्थ *(noun)* – अम्लान रंगीन पुष्प का पौधा a plant of a chiefly tropical family that includes love-lies-bleeding. *This tropical plant is used as a medicine.*

Amass/अमैश *(verb)* – संग्रह करना, ढेर करना accumulate over time. [archaic] (of people) gather together. *The fungus amassed overnight almost in no time.*

Amative/एमेटिव *(adj.)* – प्रेमशील, शृंगारप्रिय, कामोत्तेजकता inclined forward or displaying love. *During talks with her he suddenly became amative she didn't appreciate it.*

Amatorial/एमेटोरियल *(adj.)* – प्रेमी-सम्बन्धी, वासनात्मक pertaining to love. *This amatorial talk upset her.*

Amatory/एमेटोरी *(adj.)* – प्रेम उत्पन्न करने वाला relating to or induced by sexual love or desire. *He has an amatory character and has relation with many women.*

Amaurosis/एमारोसिस *(noun)* – थोड़ी या पूर्ण दृष्टि-हीनता medicine partial or total blindness without visible change in the eye, typically due to disease of the optic nerve, spinal cord, or brain. *His optical nerve was damaged and amaurosis occurred.*

Amaze/एमेज *(verb)* – विस्मित करना, चकित surprise greatly. *I was amazed at his sudden appearance after a long time.*

Amazon/एमेजन *(noun)* – स्त्री योद्धा, वीरांगना a member of a legendary race of female warriors believed by the ancient Greeks to exist in Scythia or elsewhere. a very tall, strong woman. *The legendary female warriors of Amazon are famous all over the world.*

Amabagious/एमाबेजियस *(adj.)* – द्विअर्थी, दुविधा पूर्ण, अनेकाअर्थी (of language) having more than one meaning. unclear because not distinguishing between alternatives. *You were amabagious in your speech mainly because you presented so many alternatives and your words had more than one meaning.*

Ambassador/एम्बैसडर *(noun)* - प्रतिनिधि, राजदूत a diplomat sent by a state as its permanent representative in a foreign country. a representative or promoter of a specified activity. *Many actors are brand ambassador of scents.*

Ambassadress/एम्बैसड्रस *(verb)* - राजदूत सम्बन्धी a women ambassader. *That lady over there in the thick of the party is an ambassadress. She is very glamorous and smart.*

Amber/एम्बर *(noun)* - अम्बर, तृणमणि hard translucent fossilized resin originating from extinct coniferous trees, typically yellowish in colour and used in jewellery. *Jewellers use amber to give yellow tinge to their jewellry.*

Ambidexter/एम्बीडेक्सटर *(adj.)* - दोनों हाथों से सहज में कार्य करने वाला of or relating to the immediate environs of something.

Ambient/एम्बियन्ट *(adj.)*- व्यापक, चारों ओर से घेरने वाला of or relating to the immediate environs of something. *Boats combined create an amalgam of an ambient landscape several and visionary.*

Ambiguity/एम्बिगुइटी *(noun)* - सन्देह an expression whose meaning cannot be determined from its contact. *His dialogues are full of ambiguity always having two meanings.*

Ambit/एम्बिट *(noun)* - परिधि चक्र, मण्डल the scope, extent, or bounds of something. *The sky has no ambit.*

Ambition/एम्बिशन *(noun)* - महत्त्वाकांक्षा, अभिलाषा, लालसा a strong desire to do or achieve something, desire for success, wealth, of fame. *His ambition is to become a doctor.*

Ambo/एम्बो *(noun)* - गिरजाघर का चबूतरा (in an early Christian church) an oblong pulpit with steps at each end. *The priest has started speaking from the ambo.*

Ambrosia/एम्ब्रोसिया *(noun)* - अमृत, अद्वितीय, पीयूष, सुधा, स्वाद का पदार्थ Greek & Roman Mythology the food of the gods. something very pleasing to taste or smell. *He is a very good cook. The food prepared by him tastes and smells of ambrosia.*

Ambsace/एम्बसैस *(noun)* - गुणहीनता *It was sheer ambsace that he lost the card game.*

Ambulance/एम्बुलेंस *(noun)* - चलता-फिरता फौजी अस्पताल a vehicle equipped for taking sick or injured people to and from hospital. *I'm eagerly awaiting the ambulance, my father is very sick.*

Ambulant/एम्बुलेंट *(adj.)* - बाहरी रोगी medicine able to walk about; not confined to bed. *He is ambulant quite mobile on his two feet.*

Ambulate/एम्बुलेट *(verb)* - इधर-उधर घूमना formal or [technical] walk; move about. *He ambulated from kitchen to the garden.*

Ambuscade/ऐम्बस्केड *(noun)* - छिपकर आक्रमण an ambush. verb [archaic] lie in wait; ambush. *He ambuscaded to attack his enemy by surprise.*

Ambush/एम्बुश *(noun)* - सिपाहियों का आक्रमण, घात लगाकर आक्रमण करने के लिये छिपे रहना a surprise attack by people lying in wait in a concealed position. verb attack in such a way. *Babar's army lay in ambush for surprise attack.*

Ambustion/एम्बशन *(noun)* - फफोला *He suffered an ambustion as he carelessly handled the gas.*

Ameliorate/एमेलिओरेट *(verb)* - सुधारना, उत्तम make better; reduce the undesirable effect of. *The medicine ameliorated the grip of disease.*

Amen/आमीन *(noun)* - ऐसा ही हो, एवमस्तु exclamatory said at the end of a prayer or hymn, meaning 'so be it'. *At the end of the prayer the priest said amen.*

Amenable/एमेनेबल *(adj.)* - उत्तरदायी, जिम्मेदार responsive to suggestion. (amenable to) capable of being acted on. *Go and talk to him he is an amenable fellow and will respond to you.*

Amend/एमेंड *(verb)* - संशोधन करना सुधारना make minor improvements to (a document, proposal, etc.). *I shall have to amend this speech, some fool has written it.*

Amenity/एम्निटी *(noun)* - सुविधा, सुख साधन a useful or desirable feature of a place. the pleasantness or attractiveness of a place. *The amentity of this place is appreciable.*

Amenorrhoea/एमेनेरोइया *(noun)* - स्त्रियों का मासिक धर्म बन्द होना an abnormal absence of menstruation. *This amenorrhoea is not to be taken lightly let's take her at once to the hospital and consult a gyno.*

Amerce → Amphibia

A

Amerce/अमर्स *(verb)*- दण्ड देना, जुर्माना करना punish with an arbitrary penalty; punish by a fine imposed arbitrarily by the direction of the court. *The court has amerced him. Let us arrange lonely for the fine.*

Amercement/एमर्समेंट *(noun)* – दण्ड English [law, historical] a fine. *Amercement imposed by the court is very huge.*

Amethyst/एमिथिस्ट *(noun)* – जामुनीमणी, कटैला *My watch shines in the night because it has fine particles of amethyst.*

Amiable/एमिअबल *(adj.)* – सर्वप्रिय, सबका प्यारा friendly and pleasant in manner. *He is an amiable fellow.*

Amid/अमिड *(prep.)* – मध्य में, बीच में surrounded by; in the middle of. *He was lost somewhere amid the huge crowd.*

Amidships/एमिडशीप *(adv.&adj.)* – जहाज के बीच में in the middle of a ship, either longitudinally or laterally. *As he stood amidships he was hit by a cannon.*

Amity/एमिटी *(noun)* – शुभ चिन्ता, बन्धुत्त्व, मंत्रिभाव friendly relations. *There is perfect amity between two friends.*

Ammeter/एमीटर *(noun)* – बिजली धारा शक्ति नापने का यन्त्र an instrument for measuring electric current in amperes. *Please bring the ammeter I have to measure the current.*

Ammonal/एमोनल *(noun)* – एक प्रकार का बारूद *Ammonal is the chief ingredient that terrorists use in making bombs.*

Ammonia/एमोनिया *(noun)* – चूने से बनी हुई क्षार a colourless, intensely pungent gas which dissolves in water to give a strongly alkaline solution. [NH_3] a solution of this, used as a cleaning fluid. *I am making a cleaning fluid with ammonia and water.*

Ammunition/एम्यूनिशन *(noun)* – गोली, बारूद, युद्ध-सामग्री a supply or quantity of bullets and shells. *The government does not allow civilians to live near ammunition depot because it is very dangerous.*

Amnesia/एमनेसिया *(noun)* – स्मृति-हीनता a partial or total loss of memory. *He has been suffering from amnesia for a long time.*

Amoeba/एमीबा *(noun)* – एक कोशिकीय जन्तु a single-celled animal which catches food and moves about by extending finger-like projections of protoplasm. *For reproduction purposes amoeba divides itself into two.*

Amoebean/एमोबियन *(noun)* – पारी-पारी से उत्तर देने वाला *To answer in amoebean has become his habit the answers all questions in poem or song.*

Amoral/एमॉरल *(adj.)* – अधर्मी, धर्मशून्य, अनैतिक lacking a moral sense; unconcerned whether something is right or wrong. *He is an amoral person not knowing what should be done and what shouldn't be.*

Amorist/एमोरिस्ट *(noun)* – कामुक, प्रेम करने वाला, श्रृंगारी a person who is in love or who writes about love. *He is a big amorist. He has written about a dozen books on love.*

Amorosa/एमरोसा *(adv.&adj.)* – प्यारा, पुंश्चली music in a loving or tender manner. *The music in the café was very amorosa.*

Amorous/एमॉरस *(adj.)* – कामी, कामुक, रसिक showing or feeling sexual desire. *He is very amorous by nature having many girl friends.*

Amortise/एमटॉइज *(verb)* – ऋण चुकाना gradually write off the initial cost of (an asset) over a period. reduce or cancel (a debt) by money regularly put aside. *The cost of your land has been amortised.*

Amount/अमाउन्ट *(noun)* – परिमाण होना, मात्रा रकम होना come to be (a total) when added together. *I have a large amount of money at my disposal and can buy anything I want.*

Amour/अमुर *(noun)* – गुप्त प्रेम भाव या अवैध प्रेम a love affair or lover; especially a secret one. *The amour was wounded in a sword fight.*

Amourette/एमॉरेट *adj)* – छोटा प्रेम विषय या प्रेमी *Lord Krishna in his childhood was a great amourette.*

Ampere/एम्पीयर *(noun)* – बिजली की धारा की नापने की इकाई the SI base unit of electric current, equal to a flow of one coulomb per second. *How many ampere of electricity have been used?*

Amphibia/एम्फिबिया *(adj)* –उभयचर, पृथ्वी और जल दोनों जगह में रहने वाले जन्तु [zoology] a cold-blooded vertebrate animal of a class (Amphibia) that comprises the forges, toads, newts, salamanders and caecilians, distinguished by an aquatic gill-breathing adult stage. *Frog etc. are amphibian animals which can live on both land and water.*

A

Amphibious/एम्फिबिअस *(adj.)* – स्थल या जल में रहने योग्य living in or suited for both land and water. *Many snakes are amphibious.*

Amphigory/एम्फिगरी *(noun)* – निरर्थक शब्द nonsensical writing. *All his work amounts to amphigory.*

Amphistomous/एम्फिसटोमस *(adj)* – दुमुँहा, दोनों मुँह ओर वाला *Leech is a amphistomous creature having a sucker at each end of the body to suck blood.*

Amphitheatre/एम्फीथियेटर *(noun)* – रंगभूमि round building consisting of tiers of seats surrounding a central space for dramatic or sporting events. a semicircular seating gallery in a theatre. *When I went to Rome I saw the famous amphitheatre there it is a round place which was built for games and athletic events.*

Amphora/एम्फोरा *(noun)* – दो हत्था कलश a tall ancient Greek or Roman jar or jug with two handles and a narrow neck. *I saw an amphora at a museum I would have loved to drink from it.*

Amplitude/एम्प्लिट्यूड *(noun)* – अधिकता, ऐश्वर्य, तरंगों के कंपन का अधिकतम आयाम [physic] the maximum extent or magnitude of a vibration or other oscillating phenomenon, measured from the equilibrium position or average value.

Amply/एम्प्ली *(adv)* – पर्याप्त रूप से in or ample manner. *The opinions of people were amply represented.*

Amputate/एम्प्युटेट *(verb)* – किसी अंग को काटना verb cut of (a limb) by surgical operation. *As gangrene set in the leg the doctors had to amputate it to save patient's life.*

Amuck/एमक् *(adv.)* – उन्मता variant spelling of amok. *The elephant ran amuck.*

Amulet/एम्यलिट *(noun)* – ताबीज an ornament or small place of jewellery thought to give protection against evil or danger. *I always wear an amulet given by a Sadhu.*

Amuse/अम्यूज *(verb)* – विनोद करना, मन बहलाना cause to laugh or smile. *I was amused by the pranks played by him.*

An/एन *(adj.)* – एक, कोई determine the form of the indefinite article used before words beginning with a vowel sound. *I saw a hen laying an egg.*

Anabaptism/एनाबैप्टिज्म *(noun)* – दुबारा, लामकरण the doctrine that baptism should only be administered to believing adults, held by a protestant sect of the 16th century. I am a non believer and as such I would never Anabaptism allow to be administered to me.

Anabasis/एनाबेसिस *(noun)* – फौज का आगे बढ़ना *He has gone on an unknown anabasis.*

Anacathartic/एनाकाथारटिक *(noun)* – कफ निकालने वाली औषधि *If you feel like vomiting take a sip of anacathartic it will cure you.*

Anachronism/एनक्रोनिज्म *(noun)* – काल-गणना का भ्रम, काल-दोष, तिथि व समय की अशुद्धता a thing appropriate to a period other than that in which it exists.

Anaclastic/एनाक्लास्टिक *(adj)* – किरण के तिरछेपन से सम्बन्ध रखने वाला *Look at the bottom of anaclastic glass the bottom seems to spring at you.*

Anaclisis/एनाक्लिसिस *(noun)* – चारपाई पर निरन्तर पड़े रहने से उत्पन्न फोड़ा [psychoanalysis] relationship marked by strong dependence on others. *He is suffering from anaclisis for which he is seeing psychologist.*

Anadem/एनाडेम *(noun)* – माला garland. *He was offered an anadem as he entered the city.*

Anaemia/एनिमिया *(noun)* – रक्तहीनता a condition in which there is a deficiency of red cells or hemoglobin in the blood, resulting in pallor and weariness. *He is suffering from anaemia. He should have checked hemoglobin.*

Anaesthesia/एनसथीसिया *(noun)* – शरीर के किसी अंग की चेतना शून्यता, शल्य चिकित्सा से पूर्व दवा द्वारा संवेदनहीनता उत्पन्न करने की प्रक्रिया insensitivity to pain, especially as artificially induced by the administration of gases or drugs before a surgical operation. *His body has been made insensitive to pain by anaesthesia because he is to undergo an operation.*

Anal/एनल *(adj.)* – पूँछ के नीचे का, गुदा के समीप of, relating to, or situated near the anus. *He had to undergo anal surgery to get rid of piles.*

Analeptic/एनालेप्टिक *(adj.)* – पुष्टिकर औषधि restorative, especially through stimulating the central nervous system. noun an analeptic drug. *It is an analeptic drug, it will stimulate your mind.*

A

Analgesia/एनलजेसिया *(noun)* – पीड़ाशून्य करने वाली दवा medicine relief of pain through administration of drugs or other methods. *Take an analgesia tablet to get relief from your pain.*

Analogical/एनालोजिकल *(adj.)* – सदृश, समान expressing composed of, or based on an analogy. *The two poems are analogical in content.*

Analogy/अनैलजि *(noun)* – समानता, तुल्यता a comparison between one thing and another made for the purpose of explanation or clarification. the process of making such a comparison. a thing regarded as analogous to another; an analogue. *There is a great analogy between the two brothers.*

Analysable/एनालाइजेब्ल *(adj.)* – सूक्ष्म परीक्षा capable of being partitioned. *This sentence is analysable.*

Analyse/एनलाइज *(verb)* – सूक्ष्म परीक्षा करना, विश्लेषण करना examine methodically and in detail the constitution or structure of. identify and measure the chemical constituents of. *If you analyse this chemical properly you will know its constituent.*

Analysis/एैलसिस *(noun)* – विघटन, विभाजन a detailed examination of the elements or structure of something. *Analysis of his DNA sample must be done as soon as possible.*

Analytical/एनलिटिकल *(adj.)* – विभाजन या विश्लेषण सम्बन्धी relating to or using analysis or logical reasoning. *Analytical discussion of a thing leads to its logical conclusion.*

Anamnesis/एनाम्नेसिस *(noun)* – पूर्व जन्म का स्मरण, अनुस्मृति recollection, especially of a supposed previous existence. *Anamnesis occurred to him at the age of eight and he remembered many facts of his past birth.*

Anarchic/एनारकिक *(adj.)* – नियम प्रतिकूल with no controlling rules or principles to give order. *The state was declared anarchic.*

Anarchy/एनार्कि *(noun)* – अराजकता, कुशासन a state of disorder due to lack of government or control. *Anarchy had spread all over the city.*

Anathema/एनैथमा *(noun)* – ईश्वर का शाप something that one vehemently dislikes: racism was anathema to her. *Casteism was anathema to her.*

Anatomy/एनाटमी *(noun)* – शरीर रचना विज्ञान the branch of biology and medicine concerned with bodily structure, especially as reveled by dissection. the body structure of a person, animal, or plant. *Anatomy interests me greatly.*

Anbury/एन्ब्यूरी – बैलों और घोड़ों की गिट्टी का एक रोग *You see this growth on this horse's back it is anbury which has to be surgically removed.*

Ancestor/एन्सेस्टर *(noun)* – पुरखा, पूर्वपुरुष, पूर्वज a person, typically one more remote than a grandparent, from whom one is descended. something from which a later species or version has evolved. *Our ancestor belonged to UP Kashipur.*

Anchor/एन्कर *(noun)* – लंगर, विश्वास का स्थान . a heavy object used to moor a ship to the sea bottom, typically having a metal shank with a pair of curved, barbed flukes. the brakes of a car. *The ship has dropped anchor and is secured firmly in a position.*

Anchorite/एन्कोराइट *(noun)* – संन्यासी, विरक्त [historical] a religious recluse. *He is an anchorite remaining alone and talking to body.*

Ancient/एन्सिएंट *(adj.)* – प्राचीन, पुराना belonging to or originating in the very distant past. chiefly humorous very old. *In ancient times there were very funny and dangerous animals.*

Ancillary/एन्सिलरी *(adj.)* – मुख्य गतिविधियों में सहायक providing support to the primary activities of an organization, additional; subsidiary. *This branch is an ancillary of the food department.*

Ancon/एन्कान *(noun)* – कुहनी (केहुनी) an elbow a console, typically consisting or two volutes, that supports or appears to support a cornice. *There is pain in my ancon.*

And/एण्ड *(conj.)* – और used to connect words of the same part of speech, clauses, or sentences. connecting two identical comparatives, to emphasize a progressive change. connecting two identical words, implying great duration or great extent. *Love and kindness are two great virtues.*

Andiron/एन्डिरॉन *(noun)* – अँगीठी के लोहे के सीकंचे a metal support, typically one of a pair,

A

for wood burning in a fireplace. It was very cold. *He put an andiron into the hearth for supporting fire logs.*

Anecdote/एनिक्डोट *(noun)* – कथा a short entertaining story about a real incident or person. an account regarded as unreliable or as being hearsay. *I'll tell you an anecdote about my brother.*

Anemograph/एनेमोग्राफ *(noun)* – वायु का वेग अंकित करने का यन्त्र an anemometer which records the speed, duration, and sometimes also the direction of the wind. *The anemograph shows that a strong wind is developing.*

Anemometer/एनिमॉमीटर *(noun)* – वायु की शक्ति नापने का यन्त्र an instrument for measuring the speed of the wind or other flowing gas. *According to the anemometer the speed of the wind is 200 kms an hour.*

Aneroid/एनेरोआएड *(adj.)* – एक प्रकार का निद्रव वायु, दाब मापक यन्त्र relating to or denoting a barometer that measures air pressure by the action of the air in deforming the elastic lid of an evacuated box. *This is an instrument called barometer or aneroid which tells us about the air pressure.*

Anew/एन्यू *(adv.)* – पुनः, फिर से नये सिरे से [chiefly poetic – literary] in a new or different way. once more; again. *Now that you have served your term you must start anew.*

Anfroctuous/एन्फ्रोक्टअस *(adj.)* – पेचीला, चक्करदार sinuous or circuitous. *Catacombs are always anfroctuous in construction.*

Angel/एन्जेल *(noun)* – देवदूत, फरिश्ता, सुन्दर या अबोध मनुष्य a spiritual being believed to act as an attendant or messenger of God, conventionally represented ad being of human form with wings. *You have proved yourself an angel by helping me in this hour of need.*

Anger/एन्गर *(noun)* – क्रुद्ध करना, कुपित करना a strong feeling of annoyance, displeasure, or hostility. verb provoke anger in. *By his behaviour he provoked anger in me.*

Angina/एन्गिना *(noun)* – गण्डमाला a condition marked by severe pain in the chest, arising from an inadequate blood supply to the heart. *Your father is holding his chest this seem angina pain. You should call a doctor at once.*

Angle/एन्गल *(noun)* – किसी विशिष्ट व्यक्ति या वर्ग को लक्ष्य करना a member of an ancient Germanic people that founded English kingdoms in Mercia, Northumbria, and East Anglia.

Angle/एन्गल *(noun)* – कोण the space (usually measured in degrees) between two intersecting lines or surfaces at or close to the point where they meet. a corner, especially an external projection or internal recess. a measure of the indlination of one line or surface with respect to another. *A triangle has three angles.*

Angler/एन्गलर *(noun)* – मछली पकड़ने वाला a scheming person; someone who schemes to gain an advantage. *He is an angler and has thousand tricks up in his sleeve so beware of him.*

Anglican/एंग्लिकन *(adj.)* – अंग्रेजी, इंग्लैंड के चर्च या अंग्रेजी भाषी देश के चर्च का सदस्य relating to or denoting the church of England or any church in communion with it. noun a member of any of these churches. *This church is Anglican as this in communion with the church of England.*

Angling/एन्गलिंग *(verb)* – मछली पकड़ रहा हैं fishing with a hook. *He has been angling for hours by the river side with a hook and line.*

Anglo/एंग्लो *(noun)* – इंग्लैंड या ब्रिटेन से सम्बन्धित a white English-speaking person, especially one of british or non-hispanic origin. *He is an Anglo descending from British race.*

Anglo-saxon/एंग्लो-सैक्सन *(noun)* – प्राचीन अंग्रेजी जाति का a Germanic inhabitant of England between the 5th century and the Norman conquest. a person of English descent. [chiefly North American] any white, English-speaking person. *Any white person speaking English chiefly north American comes under the category of Anglo Saxon.*

Angrily/एंग्रिली *(adv.)* – क्रोध से with anger. *She angrily shouted at him.*

Angriness/एंग्रीनेस *(noun)* – क्रोधावस्था the state of being angry. *In his angriness he couldn't think properly.*

Angry/एंग्री *(adj.)* – क्रुद्ध, कुपित feeling or showing anger. *This dog looks angry dangerous.*

Anguish/एंगविश *(noun)* – शारीरिक स्थिति या जीवन के बारे में चिंता, तीव्र वेदना extreme distress

A

of body or mind. *He caused me emotional anguish by his scandalous remarks.*

Angular/एनगुलर *(adj.)* – कोण वाला having angles of an angular shape. *This house is built in an angular shape and has lots of angles in it.*

Angulate/एनगुलेट *(verb)* – कोण से अनुरूप बनाया [technical] hold or bend (a part of the body) so as to form an angle or angles. skiing incline sideways and outwards during a turn. *We angulate our body a lot of time while doing yoga.*

Anil/एनिल *(noun)* – नील का पौधा और इसका रंग a blue dye obtained from plants or made synthetically. *I got my clothes dyed in anil blue.*

Anile/एनाइल *(adj.)* – बुढ़िया के समान like a feeble old woman. *He walked like an anile weak and trembling.*

Aniline/एनिलाइन *(noun)* – रंगो का रासायनिक आधार [Chemistry] a colourless oily liquid present in coaltar, used in the manufacture of dayes, drugs, and plastics. *We use aniline a colourless liquid in making dyes plastic drugs.*

Anility/एनिलिटी *(noun)* – वृद्धावस्था, बुढ़ापा dotage.

Animadvert/एनिमाडवर्ट *(verb)* – तिरस्कार करना formal criticize or censure. *He animadverted me before my friends and I felt insulted.*

Animal/एनिमल *(noun)* – जन्तु, पशु a living organism which is typically distinguished from a plant by feeding on organic matter; having specialized sense organs and nervous system, and being able to move about and to respond rapidly to stimuli. a mammal, as opposed to a bird, reptile, fish, or insect. *In contrast to tree animals can move.*

Animalcule/एनिमलक्यूल *(noun)* – अतिसूक्ष्म जन्तु या प्राणी [archaic] a microscopic animal.

Animalism/एनिमलिज्म *(noun)* – पाशविक प्रकृति, हैवानियत behaviour characteristic of animals; animality. *This animalism knows no bounds.*

Animality/एनिमलिटी *(noun)* – जीव-प्रदान, पाशविक प्रकृति behaviour or nature characteristic of animal, especially in being physical and instinctive. *The animality in him is too pronounced don't go near him.*

Animation/एनिमेशन *(noun)* – भरभूर जोश और उत्साह the state of being full of life or vigour. chiefly [archaic] the state of being alive. *Tom & jerry the various comics today especially historical films employ computer graphics and animation and give the images an illusion of movement of life.*

Animism/एनिमिज्म *(noun)* – ब्रह्मवाद, आत्मवाद the attribution of a living soul to plants, inanimate objects, and natural phenomena. *I believe in animism i.e. all plants and inanimate objects have a soul the whole universe was organized by a supernatural power.*

Animosity/एनिमॉसिटी *(noun)* – शत्रुता strong hostility. *I bear great animosity to this murderer, get him away from here.*

Animus/एनिमस *(noun)* – द्वेष, विरोधपूर्ण भावना या इच्छा hostility or ill feeling. *He has great animus and will become a successful man one day.*

Anise/एनीज *(noun)* – सौंफ का पौधा a mediterranean plant of the parsley family, cultivated for its aromatic seeds (aniseed). *I have great liking for the aroma of anise.*

Aniseed/एनिसीड *(noun)* – सौंफ का बीज the seed of the anise, used as a flavouring and in herbal medicine. *When once I was hurt in a village the local physician cured me with aniseeds.*

Ankle/एंकल *(noun)* – नली the joint connecting the foot with the leg. the narrow part of the leg between this and the calf. verb [informal], chiefly US walk. leave. *The water only came up to my ankles.*

Anklet/एंकलेट *(noun)* – नूपुर, पायजेब an ornament worn round ankle. *The American tourist wore anklets and the socks just up to her ankles.*

Anaa/एन्ना *(noun)* – एक आना a former monetary unit of India and Pakistan, equal to one sixteenth of a rupee. *Annas become obsolete currency.*

Annals/एनल्ज *(noun)* – पूर्वकथा, वार्षिक a record of the events of one year. a record of one item in a chronicle. *Let me consult the annals in the library. I may find something worthy.*

Annalist/एनालिस्ट *(noun)* – इतिहास-लेखक writer of history. *The retired professor of history was employed as an annalist by the college.*

Annex/एनेक्स *(verb)* – मिलाना, लगाना add as an extra or subordinate part. add to one's own territory by appropriation. noun 1. a building

A

joined to or associated with a main building. *Some years back Iraq wanted to annex some territory of Kuwait claiming it as its own.*

Annihilate/एनिहिलेट *(verb)* – पूरी तरह नष्ट या पराजित कर देना destroy utterly. [informal] defeat utterly. [physics] convert into radiant energy, especially by collision of a particle with an antiparticle. *During wars large chunks of territories are completely annihilated by bombarding.*

Anniversary/एनिवर्सरी *(noun)* – वार्षिकोत्सव the date on which an event took place in a previous year or in the past. *He celebrated his birth anniversary with great pomp and show.*

Annodomini/एनोडोमिनी *(adv.)* – ईसा मसीह के जन्म के पश्चात् का समय full form of AD. *I was born on 1938 Anno Domini i.e. after the birth of Christ.*

Annotate/एनटेट *(verb)* – व्याख्यात्मक टिप्पणियाँ देना add notes to (a text or diagram) giving explanation or comment. *Please annotate this paragraph.*

Announce/अनाउन्स *(verb)* – घोषणा करना make a formal public declaration about a fact, occurrence, or intention. make known the arrival of (a guest) at a formal social occasion. *Ladies and gentlemen I proudly announce the engagement of my daughter Tina with Anand.*

Annoy/एनॉय *(verb)* – दु:ख देना make a little angry. *I feel annoyed please don't repeat such silly mistakes in future.*

Annual/एन्युअल *(adj.)* – वार्षिक occurring once every year. *The school is celebrating its annual sports day.*

Annuitant/एन्वीटैंट *(noun)* – वार्षिक वेतन पाने वाला व्यक्ति formal a person who receives an annuity. *This farmer servant of my father is an annuitant, he gets fixed sum every year.*

Annuity/एन्वीटी *(noun)* – वार्षिक वेतन या भत्ता a fixed sum of money paid to someone each year, typically for the rest of their life. a form of insurance or investment entitling the investor to a series of annual sums. *Each year for the whole life I'll be paying annuity to the insurance company.*

Annular/एन्युलर *(adj.)* – गोल [technical] ring-shaped. *It is an annular object may be it is a ring of somebody.*

Anodyne/एनोडाइन *(noun & adj.)* – पीड़ानाशक unlikely to cause offence or disagreement but somewhat dull. noun a painkilling drug or medicine. *Please apply some anodyne on your ankle it will relieve your pain.*

Anoint/एनॉयन्ट *(verb)* – तेल लगाना, विलेपन smear or rub with oil, especially as part of a religious ceremony. ceremonially confer office on (a priest or monarch) by anointing. nominate as successor: his officially anointed heir. *Before being made monarch he was anointed by a priest.*

Anomaly/अनामली *(noun)* – अनियमितता, अव्यवस्था something that deviates from what is standard, normal, or expected. *The anomaly in his character didn't let him stick anywhere.*

Anon/एनॉन *(adv.)* – शीघ्र अभी [archaic] or [informal] soon; shortly. *He made a sign and anon a big crowd followed him.*

Anonymous/एनॉनिमस *(noun)* – जिस पुस्तक का नाम ज्ञात न हो, अनामक ग्रंथ an anonymous person or publication. *This book is written by an anonymous person it is clear that writer does not want to reveal his name.*

Anonymity/एनॉनिमिटी *(noun)* – अज्ञात होने की अवस्था, गुमनामी the state of being anonymous. *For years she has been able to retain her anonymity.*

Anosmia/एनाज्मीया *(noun)* – घ्राणशक्ति का नाश, सूँघने की शक्ति का नाश medicine the loss of the sense of smell, caused by head injury, infection, or blockage of the nose. *He has lost his sense of smell may be because of the blockage of the nose caused by anosmia.*

Another/अनदर *(pronoun)* – दूसरा पदार्थ या व्यक्ति one more; a further. *Another person is needed for help.*

Anserine/एन्सराइन *(adj.)* – बत्तख के समान, मूर्ख of or like a goose. *This egg is anserine.*

Answer/आन्सर *(noun)* – उत्तर, समाधान something said, written, or done as a reaction to a question, statement, or situation. *He answered all the questions in the paper.*

Ant/एन्ट *(noun)* – चींटी a small insect, usually wingless and with a sting, living in a complex social colony with one or more breeding queens. *Ants are very social and hard working insects.*

Antacid/एन्टासिड *(adj.)* – अम्लत्व-नाशक पदार्थ preventing or correcting acidity in the stomach. noun an antacid medicine. *You seem to suffer from acidity take an antacid.*

Antagonism/एन्टैगनिज्म *(noun)* – बैर, शत्रुता active hostility or opposition. *The English found a lot of antagonism in Indians.*

Antalkali/एन्टाल्कालि *(noun)* – क्षारत्व दूर करने वाला पदार्थ या औषधि *If you want to treat alkalosis take antalkali it neutralizes alkalis.*

Antarctic/एन्टार्कटिक *(adj.)* – दक्षिणी, दक्षिणी ध्रुववाली of or relating to the south polar region or Antarctica. *White bears are found in the Antarctic region.*

Ante/एन्टि *(noun)* – 'पूर्व' अर्थ का उपसर्ग a stake put up by a player in poker or brag before receiving cards. *This is the game of poker this player has already put an ante before receiving cards.*

Antecede/एन्टिसिड *(verb)* – समय से पूर्व घटित होना be earlier in time, go back further. *A antecedes the letter B.*

Antecedence/एन्टिसिडेंस *(noun)* – अगलापन, पूर्वत्व proceeding in time. *I enjoy the privilege of antecedence. All my brothers are younger.*

Antecedent/एन्टिसिडेंट *(noun)* – पूर्वगामी, पूर्वपद का a thing that existed before or logically precedes another. *For marriage purposes we have checked the antecedents of the boy.*

Antechamber/एन्टिचैम्बर *(noun)* – बाहरी दालान, उपकक्ष a small room leading to a main one. *Almost all the pyramids used to have a secret antechamber which led to main room or hall.*

Antedate/एन्टिडेट *(verb)* – पूर्वतिथि देना, स्थिर काल से पूर्व का समय come before in date. indicate that (a document or event) should be assigned to an earlier date. *There notes in this chapters should be antedate.*

Antelope/एन्टिलोप *(noun)* – एक प्रकार का हिरन या मृग, चिकारा a swift-running deer-like ruminant animal with upward-pointing horns, of a group including the gazelles, impala, gnu, and eland. *Once I went to Africa there I saw impala antelope etc. gracefully running.*

Antemeridian/एन्टिमिरिडियन *(adj.)* – आधी रात से दोपहर तक का समय before noon. *I'll see you tomorrow at 7 a.m. (antemeridian).*

Antemundane/एन्टिमन्डेन *(adj)* – पूर्वाह्न, सुबह दोपहर होने से पूर्व *We really know nothing or very little as to what happened in antemundane period.*

Anterior/एन्टिअरिअर *(adj.)* – शरीर का कोई अंग पूर्व या पिछला, पहले का chiefly [anatomy] & biology nearer the front, especially in the front of the body or nearer to the head. The opposite of posterior. [botany] situated further away from the main stem. *You need an anterior check up, a neurologist will be the best to consult.*

Anteroom/एन्टिरूम *(noun)* – गलियारा, दालान an antechamber, especially one serving as a waiting room. a large room in an officers mess adjacent to the dining room. *I waited in the anteroom to be called in the officer's mess.*

Anthelion/एन्थेलियन *(noun)* – बादलों के चारों ओर आकाश का मण्डल, प्रकाश चक्र a luminous halo round a shadow projected by the sun on to a cloud or fog bank. *Do you see that anthelion in the sky?*

Anthelmintic/एन्थेल्मिनिटिक *(noun & adj.)* – आँत के कीड़े निकालने की औषधि medicine of intestinal worm.

Anthem/ऐनथम *(noun)* – ईश्वर-स्तुति, भजन, देश, संगठन या पाठशाला के द्वारा अपनाया गया विशेष गान जो केवल विशेष अवसरों पर गाया जाता है a rousing or uplifting song indentified with a particular group or causes, a solemn patriotic song adopted as an expression of national identity, a musical setting of a religious text to be sung by a choir during a church service. *Our song of the nation i.e. National Anthem is Jan, gan, man.*

Anther/एन्थर *(noun)* – परागकेशर रखने वाला फुल का भाग the part of a stamen that contains the pollen. *You will find many insects sucking pollen at the anther.*

Anthology/एन्थोलोजी *(noun)* – गद्यावली, पद्यावली, संकलन a book that contains pieces at writing or poems often on the same subject by different authors.

Anthropoad/एन्थ्रोपायड *(adj.)* – केवल आकार में मनुष्य के सदृश्य resembling a human being in form. [zoology] relating to the group of higher primates including monkeys, apes, and humans. belonging to the family of great apes. [zoology] a higher primate. especially

A

an ape or apeman. *All apes and monkeys are anthropoads.*

Anti/ऐन्टि *(adj & adv)* – उपसर्ग जिसका अर्थ विपरीत समान में है opposed to, against. [informal] an opponent of something. *I am anti dictatorship.*

Antic/ऍन्टिक *(adj)* – अनोखा, विलक्षण [archaic] grotesque or bizarre. antico 'antique'. also 'grotesque'. *He bought an interesting antic from the bazaar of Morocco.*

Antichrist/ऍन्टिक्राइस्ट *(noun)* – ईसा-मसीह का शत्रु, शैतान, ईशा-विरोधी a postulated opponent of Christ expected by the early church to appear before the end of the world. *Antichrist will appear at the end of world.*

Anticipate/ऍन्टिसिपेट *(verb)* – आशा करना, पहले से विचार करना to expect to happen. *I don't anticipate such behaviour.*

Anticyclone/ऍन्टिसाइक्लोन *(noun)* – प्रति चक्रवात वायु a weather system with high barometric pressure at its centre, around which air slowly circulates. *The storm is coming we should put an anticyclone at the centre.*

Antidote/ऍन्टिडोट *(noun)* – प्रतिविष, विषनाशक, औषधि a medicine taken to counteract a particular poison. *If a snake bites you the doctors will inject an antidote and save you.*

Antilogy/ऍन्टिलॉजी *(noun)* – विरोधाभास [archaic] a contradiction in terms or ideas. *There is great antilogy between us so why talk?*

Antimony/ऍन्टिमॅनी *(noun)* – सुरमा the chemical element of atomic number 51, a brittle silvery-white semimetal. *In old times people used a piece of antimony to cure showing cuts.*

Anti-national/ऍन्टी नेशनल *(adj.)* – देशद्रोही against nation. *His ideas are antinational.*

Antinomy/ऍन्टिनोमी *(noun)* – अधिकार-विरोध a paradox. *It is an antinomy that my long last friend was living in my neighbourhood and I didn't know.*

Antipathetic/ऍन्टिपैथेटिक *(adj)* – विरुद्ध स्वभाव का of different nature. *Antipathic reaction, are expected from this drug.*

Antipathic/ऍन्टिपैथिक *(noun)* – विरुद्ध, विपरीत a deep-seated feeling of aversion. *I have developed deep antipathy towards my cousin. I don't know, why?*

Antipathy/ऍन्टिपैथी *(noun)* – घृणा, अनिच्छा a deep-seated feeling of aversion. *I have antipathy towards her.*

Antiphlogistic/ऍन्टिफ्लोजिस्टिक *(adj.)* – सूजन घटाने वाली contracting inflammation. *This is an antiphlogistic medicine. It will reduce your inflammation.*

Antiphonal/ऍन्टिफोनल *(noun)* – पारी-पारी से गाया हुआ another term for antiphonary. *Hymns are being sung in church in an antiphonal way.*

Antiphony/ऍन्टिफोनी *(noun)* – प्रतिध्वनि, प्रतिगान antiphonal singing, playing, or chanting. *I daily practice antiphony in the morning.*

Antipodes/ऍन्टिपोड्स *(pl. noun)* – प्रतिलोम Australia and Newzealand (used by inhabitants of the northern hemisphere). *Newzealand and Australia are directly opposite one another they are called antipodes.*

Antipyretic/ऍन्टिपायरेटिक *(adj.)* – ज्वर हटाने वाली औषधि used to prevent or reduce fever. noun an antipyretic drug. *This is an antipyretic drug take it and your fever will come down.*

Antiquarian/ऍन्टिक्वेरिअन *(adj.)* – प्राचीन पदार्थों का संग्रह करने वाला relating to or studying antiques. rare books, or antiquities. noun a person who studies or collects antiques or antiquities. *He is an antiquarian studying antiques rare books etc.*

Antiquated/ऍन्टिक्वेटड *(adj.)* – प्राचीन old-fashioned or outdated. *This expression is no longer in use it is antiquated.*

Antique/ऍन्टीक *(adj.)* – पुराना, प्राचीन ढंग का valuable because of its age. *Today I went to see the race of antique cars. It was fantastic.*

Antiseptic/ऍन्टिसेप्टीक *(adj.)* – अपवित्रता-नाशक relating to or denoting substances that prevent the growth of disease-causing micro-organisms. *Before operation doctors use strong antiseptics so as to kill various micro organisms.*

Antisocial/ऍन्टिसोशल *(adj.)* – समाज विरोधी ontrary to the customs of society and causing annoyance to others. psychiatry sociopathic. *Most of the antisocial elements have been arrested by police during a special drive.*

Antitheist/ऍन्टिथेइस्ट *(noun)* – अनिश्वरवादी *He is an antitheist. He doesn't believe in God.*

Antitheism/एन्टिथेइज्म *(noun)* – नास्तिकता one who doesn't believe in god. *I have read many books on antitheism but none appealed to me.*

Antithesis/एन्टिथेसिस *(noun)* – अर्थ के विपरीत a person or thing that is the direct opposite of another. a contrast or opposition between two things. *There is perfect antithesis between the two brothers. One is cool and other is hot tempered.*

Antitoxin/एन्टिटॉक्सिन *(noun)* – विषमारक, अतिविष, रोग के विष का हटाने वाला एक तत्व physiology an antibody that counteracts a toxin. *We must eat food rich in antitoxins so that they can counteract the toxins.*

Antler/एन्टलर *(noun)* – बारहसिंगे की शाखादार सींग a branched horn on the head of an adult deer. one of the branches on an antler. *I saw an antler in the sanctuary of South Africa. It was so thrilling.*

Antonym/एन्टोनिम *(noun)* – विपरीत अर्थ का शब्द, विलोम a word opposite in meaning to another. *Cruelty is the antonym of kindness.*

Antrum/एन्ट्रम *(noun)* – अस्थि कोटर a natural chamber or cavity in a bone. *As the zoologist looked into the antrum he found something stuck into it.*

Anus/एनस *(noun)* – गुदा, मलद्वार the opening at the end of the alimentary canal through which solid waste matter leaves the body. *Piles is a disease of anus.*

Anvil/एन्विल *(noun)* – निहाई, स्थूणा a heavy iron block on which metal can be hammered and shaped. *Blacksmiths shape iron by hammering it on the anvil.*

Anxiety/एन्जाइटी *(noun)* – चिन्ता, आकुलता a feeling of being anxious. psychiatry a nervous disorder marked by excessive uneasiness. *He suffers from anxiety disorders and is consulting a psychiatrist.*

Anxious/एन्कशस *(adj.)* – व्याकुल, चिन्तिन very eager and concerned to do something. *I am very much anxious about my son's fate. He never succeeds anywhere*

Any/एनी *(pron)* – कोई– किसी used to refer to one or some of a thing or number of things, no matter how much or how many. *Any of you is interested in taking part in debate.*

Aorta/एओरटा *(noun)* – महाधमनी the main artery of the body, supplying oxygenated blood from the heart to the circulatory system. *If due to any reason aorta is cut off, the patient will at once die.*

Apace/एपेस *(adv.)* – शीघ्रता, जल्दी से [poetic literary] swiftly; quickly. *I went to the accident spot apace.*

Apart/अपार्ट *(adv.)* – अलग separated by a specified distance. no longer living together or close emotionally. *Apart from being friends they are colleagues also.*

Apartment/अपार्टमेंट *(noun)* – किसी मकान में कमरों का समूह [chiefly North American] a suite of rooms forming one residence; a flat. a block of apartments. *These city people prefer to live in apartments.*

Apathetic/एपैथेटिक *(adj.)* – उदासीन, निरुत्साह not interested or enthusiastic. *He was apathetic to her miseries.*

Apathy/एपथि *(noun)* – अनिच्छा, जड़ता, उदासीनता lack of interest or enthusiasm. *He developed total apathy to his friend who didn't give up his bad habits.*

Apepsy/एपेप्सी *(noun)* – पाचन शक्ति की दुर्बलता *Besides other malfunctions he also suffer from apepsy.*

Aperient/एपेरियन्ट *(adj.)* – मल को ढीला करने वाली औषधि used to relieve constipation. noun an aperients drug. *Take this aperient. It will relieve you in the morning.*

Aperture/एपरचर *(noun)* – छेद, मोखा, झरी chiefly [technical] an opening, hole, or gap. the variable opening by which light enters a camera. *The sun light creeping through an aperture filled the room with light.*

Apetalous/एपेटैलस *(adj.)* – दलहीन [botany] having no petals. *Do you see this plant it is without petals and is called apetalous.*

Apex/एपेक्स *(noun)* – शिखर, चोटी the top or highest part of something, especially one forming a point. [botany] the growing point of a shoot. *The apex court gave a landmark judgment.*

Aphasia/अफेजिया *(noun)* – वागरोध, बोली बन्द होना, वाचाघात medicine inability to understand or produce speech as a result of brain damage. *He can't hear or talk because he is suffering from aphasia.*

A

Aphelion/एफीलियन *(noun)* – अपसौर, किसी ग्रह का सूर्य से सबसे दूर का स्थान linguistics omission of the initial sound of a word, as when he is is pronounced he's. *Aphelion is getting very popular these days.*

Aphorism/एफरिज़म *(noun)* – कहावत, वचन a pithy observation which contains a general truth. *A bird in hand is better than two in the bush is a popular aphorism.*

Aphrodisiac/ऐफ़्रोडिजीऐक *(noun)* – कामोत्तेजक, कामोद्दीपक औषधि a food, drink, or drug that stimulates sexual desire. *It is believed that a rhino's horn is a great aphrodisiac.*

Apiary/एपिअरी *(noun)* – मधुमक्खियों के पालने का स्थान a place where bees are kept. *He must be in the apiary. He has a lot of bees there.*

Apical/एपिकल *(adj.)* – शिखर-सम्बन्धी [technical] relating to or denoting an apex. *R is an apical letter.*

Apiculture/एपिकल्चर *(noun)* – मधुमक्खियों को पोसना, मधुपालन [technical] term for beekeeping. *He is an expert in apiculture.*

Apiece/अपीस *(adv.)* – एक-एक करके, प्रत्येक के लिए to, for or by each one. *The trench was dug apiece.*

Apocryphal/अपाक्रीफल *(adj.)* – झूठा, असत्य, संदिग्ध प्रमाण of or belonging to the apocrypha. *This document is apocryphal its authenticity can't be doubled.*

Apollo/अपोलो *(noun)* – यूनान के सूर्य देव a large creamy-white butterfly with black and red spots, found chiefly in the mountains of Europe. *I chanced to catch an Apollo while in Europe.*

Apologetic/अपालजेटिक *(adj.)* – क्षमा योग्य, प्रार्थना योग्य, क्षमायाचक, शर्मिंदा, खेदपूर्ण constituting a formal justification of a theory or doctrine. *I am apologetic for my rude behaviour.*

Apologist/अपालजिस्ट *(noun)* – क्षमा प्रार्थना करने वाला a person who offers an argument in defence of something controversial. *He is an apologist and will soon offer an apology.*

Apologize/अपालजाइज *(verb)* – अपना दोष बताकर क्षमा माँगना express regret for something that one has done wrong. *I apologize for having hurt you.*

Apologue/ऐपलॉग *(noun)* – उपदेश पूर्ण कहानी a moral fable, especially one with animals as characters. *Children let me tell you an apologue of a can and monkey.*

Apology/अपॉलजि *(noun)* – खेदसूचक क्षमा-प्रार्थना a regretful acknowledgement of an offence or failure, a formal expression of regret at being unable to attend a meeting or social function. *Please accept my apology for the delay.*

Apophthegm/एपॉपथेम *(noun)* – सूत्र, नीतिवचन a concise saying or maxim. *So I'll tell you an apophthegm live and live.*

Apoplexy/एपप्लेक्सी *(noun)* – मूर्छा, मिरगी का रोग dated unconsciousness or incapacity resulting from a cerebral hemorrhage or stroke. *He had a stroke of apoplexy and hence can't speak.*

Apostacy/एपॉस्टैसी *(noun)* – स्वधर्मत्याग, अपने सिद्धान्त या दल का त्याग *His apostacy led to his ruin.*

Apostate/अपोस्टेट *(noun)* – स्वधर्म-त्यागी, विश्वास a person who renounces a belief or principle. adjective abandoning a belief or principle. *He is an apostate. He has renounced his faith*

Apostle/एपॉस्ल *(noun)* – भक्त each of the twelve chief disciples of Jesus Christ. an important early Christian teacher or missionary. *Judas was an apostle of Christ who betrayed him.*

Apostolic/एपॉस्टोलिक *(adj.)* – देवदूत सम्बन्धी of or relating to the apostics. *He will not change his apostolic decision.*

Apothecary/एपोथिकैरी *(noun)* – दवा बेचने वाला, अत्तार [archaic] a person who prepared and sold medicines. *You can buy medicines from him. He is an apothecary.*

Apotheosis/अपोथिओसिस *(noun)* – देवता-तुल्य, निर्माण, दैवीकरण the highest point in the development of something. *This is the apotheosis. You can dive from here.*

Appal/अप्पल *(verb)* – डराना . greatly dismay or horrify. *He spoke appalingly bad language.*

Apparel/अपरेल *(noun)* – कपड़ा, वस्त्र formal clothing. embroidered ornamentation on ecclesiastical vestments. verb US appareled, appareling [archaic] clothe. *The apparels of royalty used to be very costly.*

Apparent/अपेरेन्ट *(adj.)* – वास्तविक जैसा आभासी that seems to be real but may not be. *It is very apparent that he is telling a lie.*

Apparition/एपरिशन *(noun)* – पिशाच, प्रेत an image of a person who is dead.. a ghost.

Suddenly in the dead of night an apparition appeared before me.

Appear/एपिअर *(verb)* – दृष्टिगोचर होना, जान पड़ना come into sight. come into existence or use. be published. [informal] arrive. *It was a long voyage but ultimately the land appeared.*

Appease/अपीज *(verb)* – सान्त्वना देना, मनाना placate by acceding to their demands. *All the small animals appeased lion's demand.*

Appellant/एपेलन्ट *(noun)* – पुनर्विचार की प्रार्थना करने वाला [law] a person who appeals against a court ruling. *The appellant demands that the case be reopened.*

Appellation/एपलेशन *(noun)* – पदवी, उपाधि, नत्थी करना formal a name or title. *The royal child was conferred the appellation of Prince.*

Append/अपेन्ड *(verb)* – जोड़ना, लगाना, मिलाना, नत्थी करना add to end of a document or piece of writing. *This piece of writing should be appended properly.*

Appendix/अपेन्डिक्स *(noun)* – उण्डुक पुच्छ, परिशिष्ट, अतिरिक्त विषय जोड़ी हुई वस्तु a small organ inside your body near your stomach, [anatomy] a tube-shaped sac attached to the lower end of the large intestine. *He usually has pain in his appendix.*

Appendicitis/अपेन्डिसायटिस – आँत में एक प्रकार का फोड़ा *He has appendicitis because his appendix has swelling.*

Apperception/एपर्सेप्शन *(noun)* – चित्त का आत्मज्ञान, मानसिक बोध psychology assimilation into the mind of a new concept. *The psychologist put up a new apperception into his mind.*

Appetence/अपेटेन्स *(noun)* – अति उत्सुक, अभिलाषा [archaic] a longing or desire. *Since long he had cherished appetency.*

Appetite/एपेटाइट *(noun)* – अभिलाषा, इच्छा a natural desire to satisfy a bodily need, especially for food. *I have great appetite for non-veg food.*

Applaud/अप्लॉड *(verb)* – प्रशंसा करना, ताली बजाना show approval by clapping. praise or approve of. *The show was greatly applanded by people.*

Applause/एप्लॉज *(noun)* – प्रशंसा, स्तुति approval expressed by clapping. *He got huge applause for his acting as Shaheed Bhagat Singh.*

Apple/एपल *(noun)* – सेब the rounded fruit of a tree of the rose family, with green or red skin and crisp flesh. *I like apples a lot.*

Appliance/अप्लाएन्स *(noun)* – घरेलू उपयोग का उपकरण a device designed to perform a specific task. *Electrical appliances of Bajaj are famous all over India.*

Applicable/एप्लिकेबल *(adj.)* – उचित relevant; appropriate. *This law is not applicable in this land.*

Applicant/एप्लिकैंट *(noun)* – प्रार्थी, प्रार्थना करने वाला, आवेदक a person who applies for something. *All applicants must appear for interview at 10 a.m. in the office.*

Application/एप्लिकेशन *(noun)* – प्रार्थना पत्र . a formal request to an authority. *I have submitted an application for leave.*

Apply/अप्लाइ *(verb)* – सूचित करना, आरूढ़ होना make a formal request. put one self forward as a candidate for a job. *I have applied for several jobs.*

Appoint/अप्वाइंट *(verb)* – नियुक्त करना, स्थापित करना assign a job or role to. *You are appointed as a teacher in directorate of Delhi Education Deptt. Here is your appointment letter.*

Apportion/एपॉर्शन *(verb)* – भाग करना, बाँटना share out; assign. *Let me apportion you a tough task.*

Apposite/अपोजिट *(adj.)* – योग्य, संगत very appropriate; apt. *It is an apposite decision taken at the right time.*

Appraise/अप्रेज *(verb)* – मूल्य ठहराना assess the value, quality, or performance of. set a price on. *I have appraised the value of his piece of furniture.*

Appreciable/अप्रीशिबल *(adj.)* – जानने योग्य, प्रशंसा करने योग्य large or important enough to be noticed. *Your effort are appreciable.*

Appreciate/एप्रिशियेट *(verb)* – गुण जानना, मान करना recognize the value or significance of. be grateful for. *I appreciate your efforts.*

Apprehend/एप्रिहेन्ड *(verb)* – पकड़ना, गिरफ्तार करना intercept in the course of harmful or illicit action seize or arrest. *The thief was apprehended at the spot.*

Apprehension/एप्रिहेंश्न *(noun)* – पकड़, बुद्धि, भय समझ, अनुभव anxious or fearful anticipation. *I have apprehension that something will go wrong.*

A

29

A

Apprentice/एप्रेन्टिस *(noun)* – नवसिखुआ, प्रशिक्षु a person learning a trade from a skilled employer. verb employ as an apprentice. *He is an apprentice learning the trade under skilled guidance.*

Apprise/एप्राइज *(verb)* – सूचना देना, बतलाना inform; tell. *I apprised him of all the facts.*

Apprize/एप्राइज *(verb)* – गुण जानना, मूल्य आँकना [archaic] put a price on.

Approach/अप्रोच *(verb)* – समीप जाना, मूल्य लगाना . come near or nearer to in distance, time, or standard. [archaic] bring nearer. *I approached him boldly.*

Approbate/एप्रबेट *(verb)* – अनुमोदन करना accept as valid; approval or sanction officially. *His documents have been approbated.*

Approbation/एप्रवेशन *(noun)* – अनुमोदन approval; praise. *His work has received a lot of approbation.*

Appropriate/एप्रोप्रिएट *(adj.)* – उचित, उपयुक्त suitable; proper. *Appropriate action has been taken against the culprit.*

Approval/अप्रूवल *(noun)* – अनुमोदन, स्वीकृति the action of approving of something a favourable opinion. *Your scheme has my approval.*

Approximate/अप्रॉक्सिमेट *(adj.)* – अति समीप, लगभग, निकट fairly accurate but not totally precise. verb come close in quality or quantity. estimate Fairly accurately. *I have approximately 98% works.*

Appurtenance/अपर्टेनन्स *(noun)* – अनुलग्न, पूरक an accessory associated with a particular activity. *A space wheel is an appurtenance in a vehicle.*

Apricot/एप्रिकाट *(noun)* – खूबानी का फल an orange-yellow soft fruit. resembling a small peach. *Apricot is a useful dry fruit increasing the activity of brain.*

Apriori/एप्राइओराइ *(adj.&adv.)* – कारण से कार्य का तर्क based on theoretical deduction rather than empirical observation.

Apropos/अप्रोपो *(prep.)* – अनुरूप, अनुसार with reference to. *Apropros your article in the magazine let me ask you a question.*

Apse/एप्स *(noun)* – अर्ध-वृत्ताकार आला या झरोखा a large semicircular or polygonal recess with a domed roof, typically at a church's eastern end. *You see that domed roof in the church, it is called apse.*

Apt/एप्ट *(adj.)* – उचित, ठीक appropriate; suitable. *I gave him an apt answer he was happy and surprised.*

Aqua/एक्वा *(noun)* – तरल घोल, जल the colour aquamarine. *Mix this medicine in aqua.*

Aquarium/एक्वेरियम *(noun)* – जन्तुओं को पालने की पानी से भरी शीशे की टंकी a transparent tank of water in which live fish and other water creatures and plants are kept. *I saw an aquarium in Singapore. It was thrilling to see the huge and dangerous creatures so close.*

Aquarius/अक्वेअरिअस *(noun)* – कुम्भ राशि astronomy a large constellation (the water carrier or water bearer). said to represent a man pouring water from a jar. *Do you see that large sign in the sky? It is Aquarius.*

Aqueduct/एक्विडयूट *(noun)* – लहर, कृत्रिम जलमार्ग an artificial channel for conveying water, especially a [bridge] or viaduct carrying a waterway. *Water in this canal is being carried through aqueduct.*

Aqueous/एक्वेअस *(adj.)* – जलीय, जलयुक्त of, resembling, or containing water. *I have bought an aqueous jar.*

Aquiline/एक्विलाइन *(adj.)* – मुड़ा हुआ (of a nose) curved like an eagle's beak. *Two birds have an aquline nose. May be it is an eagle.*

Arab/अरब *(noun)* – अरब देशवासी a member of a Semitic people inhabiting much of the middle east and north Africa.

Arabian/एरेबिअन *(noun)* – अरब देश का an Arab horse. adjective of or relating to Arabia or its people. *He is an Arabian. It is clear from his features and complexion.*

Arabic/ऐरबिक – अरब देश की भाषा the Semitic language of the Arabs, spoken in many dialects in much of north Africa and the middle east and written from right to left in a cursive script also used for other languages such as Persian, Urdu, and Malay. *I am learning Arabic. It is an interesting language written from right to left like Urdu.*

Arable/ऐरब्ल *(adj.)* – जोतने-बोने योग्य भूमि suitable for growing corps. (of corps) able to be grown on such land. noun arable land or crops. *The land that I have bought is quite costly but then it is arable.*

Arbiter/आरबिटर *(noun)* – मध्यस्थ a person who settles a dispute. *An arbiter has been appointed to solve the case between two brothers.*

Arbitrary/आर्बिट्ररी *(adj.)* – स्वच्छन्द, बिना तर्क के based on random choice or personal whim. *It is arbitrary decision. It isn't fair and I'll not abide by it.*

Arbitrate/आर्बिट्रेट *(verb)* – पंचायत करना act between parties with a view to reconciling differences. *I am going to arbitrate between the two parties to settle their old dispute.*

Arboreal/आरबोरियल *(adj.)* – वृक्ष सम्बन्धी of, relating to, or living in trees. *Birds are arboreal creatures.*

Arc/आर्क *(noun)* – चाप, कमान, वृत्तखण्ड a curve forming part of the circumference of a circle or other figure. a curving trajectory. [mathematics] indicating the inverse of a trigonometrically function: are cosine. *The gates of this building are arc shaped.*

Arcade/आर्केड *(noun)* – खम्भों पर बनी हुई मेहराबें a covered passage with arches along one or both sides. chiefly a covered walk with shops along one or both sides. architecture a series of arches supporting a wall. *I found him in the amusement arcade.*

Arcadia/आर्केडिया *(noun)* – ग्रीक देश का पर्वतीय इलाका a native of arcadia, a mountainous region of southern Greece. *He lives in Southern Greece he is an Arcadian.*

Arch/आर्क *(adj.)* – प्रधान, महत्त्वपूर्ण self-consciously playful or teasing. *The arch villain of the show is Ravana in Ramlila.*

Archaeology/आरकियोलॉजी – पुरतत्व the branch of anthropolgy that studies prehistoric people and thur ....through their material remains. *He is an archaeologist and often visits prehistoric or historic setes.*

Archbishop/अर्च्बिशप *(noun)* – प्रधान, पादरी *St. Thomas was the archbishop of Conterbury.*

Arch-enemy/आर्कएनेमी *noun)* – प्रधान-शत्रु, शैतान a chief enemy. *Devil is the archenemy of human race.*

Archfiend/आर्कफियन्ड – प्रधान-भूत *Devil has been described by Christian as archfiend.*

Archer/आर्चर *(noun)* – धनुष से बाण चलाने वाला a person who shoots with a bow and arrows. *There were many fine archers in king Richard's army.*

Archetype/आर्किटाइप *(noun)* – मूल रूप से आदर्श a very typical example. *Every man carries in his unconscious mind an archetype of his early ancestors.*

Architect/आर्किटेक्ट *(noun)* – शिल्पकार a person who designs buildings and supervises their construction. *He is a renowned architect who is designing this hospital.*

Archlike/आर्कलाइक *(adj.)* – मेहराब के सदृश बना हुआ *People built an archlike gate to welcome their leader.*

Archway/आर्कवे *(noun)* – मेहराब के नीचे का मार्ग a curved structure forming a passage or entrance. *I saw an old archway in a dilapilated building.*

Arctic/आर्क्टिक *(adj.)* – उत्तरी of or relating to the regions around the north pole. living or growing in such regions. *The cold is almost arctic*

Arcuate/आर्क्यूएट *(adj.)* – धनुष के आकार का [technical] curved.

Ardent/आर्डेन्ट *(adj.)* – प्रचण्ड, उत्साही, तीव्र very enthusiastic or passionate. *He is an ardent lover of mine.*

Ardour/आर्डर *(noun)* – उत्कण्ठा, व्यग्रता great enthusiasm or passion. *He has great ardour to become an IAS officer.*

Arduous/आर्डुअस *(adj.)* – कठिन, परिश्रमी, दुष्कर difficult and tiring. *The mountain climbing proved very arduous for me.*

Area/एरिया *(noun)* – क्षेत्रफल, समतल a region of an expanse or surface. a space allocated for a specific use. *It is an area reserved for airport.*

Areca/एरिका *(noun)* – सुपारी का वृक्ष *It is an areca. Would you dare to climb it and pluck a nut.*

Arefaction/अरिफैक्शन *(noun)* – सुखाने का कार्य *Arefaction has set in these plants and they are fast drying.*

Arefy/एयरीफाइ *(verb)* – सुखाना *The sun will arefy clothes.*

Arena/एरीना *(noun)* – अखाड़ा, रंगस्थली a level area surrounded by seating, in which public events and entertainments are held. *In circus public sit circularly and in the middle is round shaped arena where events take place.*

Arenaceous/एरिनेशस *(adj.)* – बालू के समान geology consisting of sand or sand-like particles. biology living or growing in sand. *This area is arenaceous full of sands and plants.*

A

Argent/आर्जेंट *(adj. & noun)* – चाँदी के रंग का [poetic – literary] & heraldry silver. *This piece of writing is argent.*

Argil/आरगिल *(noun)* – एल्यूमिना an artist clay. *The clay models are made of argil.*

Argue/आर्ग्यू *(verb)* – बहस करना, दलीले पेश करना, सिद्ध करना exchange diverging or opposite views heatedly. *To argue is to completely miss the point of discussion.*

Arguing/आर्ग्यूइंग *(noun)* – तर्क a contentious speech act; a dispute where there is strong disagreement. *The members of committee went on arguing for hours but there was no result because all had different views.*

Argument/आरगुमेंट *(noun)* – तर्क-वितर्क a heated exchange of diverging or opposite views. *Heated argument were exchanged among the club members but to no avail.*

Argute/आरग्यूट *(adj.)* – तीखा, कर्कश rare shrewd. *He is an argute person.*

Arid/एरिड *(adj.)* – गर्मी से झुलसा हुआ very dry; having little or no rain. *It is an arid and vast desert.*

Aries/एरीज *(noun)* – मेष राशि astronomy a small constellation said to represent the ram whose golden fleece was sought by Jason and the Argonauts. *Your sign in Aries that is what your date of birth says and the coming times are very good for you.*

Aright/एराइट *(adj.)* – ठीक dialect correctly; properly. *He entered the hotel turned aright.*

Arise/एराइज *(verb)* – उठना formal of poetic/ [literary] get or stand up. *With the arise of women emancipation movement in England many countries joined it.*

Arista/एरिस्टा *(noun)* – अन्न सा घास की बाल bristle like process near the tip of the antenna of certain files. *This is a strange fly called arista. It has bristle like growth near its antenna.*

Aristocracy/एरिस्टोक्रैसी *(noun)* – शिष्टजन, उच्चवर्ग the highest class in some societies, comprising people of noble birth with hereditary titles. a form of government in which power is held by the nobility. *Government controlled aristocracy is out of vogue.*

Aristocrat/एरिस्टोक्रैट *(noun)* – अभिजात, रईस a member of the aristocracy. *He is an aristocrat having lots of money and power.*

Aristophanic/एरिस्टोफेनिक *(adj.)* – हँसमुख, चतुर *The aristophanic poems make us laugh.*

Arithmetic/अरिथमेटिक *(noun)* – अंकगणित the branch of [mathematics] concerned with the properties and manipulation of numbers. the use of numbers in counting and calculation. adjective of or relating to arithmetic. *He is very intelligent in Arithmetic.*

Ark/आर्क *(noun)* – तिजोरी, बड़ा जहाज, पोत a boat built by noah to save his family from the flog.

Arm/आर्म *(noun)* – बाहु, भुजा, शाखा each of the two upper limbs of the human body from the shoulder to the hand. a limb of an octopus, starfish, or other animal. *Arms are very important limbs of human body.*

Armament/आर्मामेंट *(noun)* – शक्ति, बल, युद्ध करने की सामग्री [military] weapons and equipment. *The armament comprising of Jawans big guns anti air guns truck jeeps etc. crawled along the Mountainous area.*

Armature/आर्मेचर *(noun)* – विद्युत उपकरण the rotating coil or coils of a dynamo or electric motor. any moving part of an electrical machine in which a voltage is induced by a magnetic field. a piece of iron acting as keeper for a magnet. *The armature of this motor is burnt out, send it to the mechanic for winding.*

Armistice/आर्मिस्टिस *(noun)* – युद्ध-विराम, संधि a truce. *Orders for armistice were given by the general.*

Armless/आर्मलेस *(adj)* – बिना बाँह का without an arm. *I saw an armless beggar.*

Armlet/आर्मलेट *(noun)* – बाजूबन्द, समुद्र की शाखा an ornament worm around the arm for decoration. *Her armlet is very beautiful.*

Armorial/आर्मोरिअल *(adj.)* – कवच सम्बन्धी of or relating to heraldry or heraldic arms. *The coach had armorial bearing.*

Armour/आर्मर *(noun)* – कवच, अनुत्राण the metal coverings formerly worn by soldiers to protect the body in battle. *The metal armour worn by soldiers in old times used to be very heavy.*

Army/आर्मी *(noun)* – सैन्य, सेना an organized [military] force equipped for fighting on land. *Indian army is very strong and brave.*

Arose/एरोज – उठा past of arise. *He arose late in the morning.*

Around/एराउन्ड *(adv & prep)* – चारों ओर, बाहरी ओर located or situated on every side. *That old building must be somewhere around here.*

Arouse/एराउज *(verb)* – जागृत करना, उत्तेजित करना evoke (a feeling or response). provoke to anger or strong emotions. excite sexually awaken from sleep. *His behaviour aroused my anger.*

Arraign/अरेन *(verb)* – दोष लगाना, कलंक लगाना call before a court to answer a criminal charge. *The police arraigned for charge of murder.*

Arrange/अरेन्ज *(verb)* – स्थिर करना, क्रम मे रखना, व्यवस्थित करना put in a neat, attractive, or required order. *I have arranged everything in the room.*

Arrangement/एरेन्जमेंट *(noun)* – प्रबन्ध, क्रम से स्थापन the action, process, or result of arranging. *The arrangement in the hotel was superb.*

Arrant/एरैन्ट *(adj.)* – कुख्यात, अत्यन्त utter; complete: what arrant non-sense! *What arrant stupidity!*

Array/एरे *(noun)* – सजाना, सजना an impressive display or range of a particular thing. *The array of flowers was impressive.*

Arrear/एरिअर *(pl. noun)* – बकाया, अवशेष payments or debts that are outstanding and due. *My arrears along with invest are worth Rs. 1 lakh which are payable by the government.*

Arrest/अरेस्ट *(verb)* – बन्दी करना, गिरफ्तार करना seize by legal authority and take them into custody. *He was arrested by police and detained in the lock up.*

Arrival/एराइवल *(noun)* – आगमन someone and something that arrives *The arrival of train created a commotion on the platform.*

Arrive/एराइब *(verb)* – पा लेना, पहुँचना reach a destination. *The train has arrived.*

Arrogance/एरोगैंस *(noun)* – गर्व overbearing pride evidenced by a superior manner toward inferiors. *All kings used to have arrogance.*

Arrogate/एरोगैट *(verb)* – किसी की वस्तु पर अन्याय से अधिकार प्रकट करना take or claim for oneself without justification. *He arrogated that he had promoted her brother.*

Arrow/एेरो *(noun)* – बाण, तीर a stick with a sharp pointed head, designed to be shot from a bow. a symbol resembling this, used to show direction or position. verb more swiftly and directly. *He shot the arrow and hit the bull's eyes.*

Arse/आर्स *(noun)* – नितम्ब, चूतड़ a person's buttocks or anus. verb 1. behave in a stupid way, not to be bothered to do something. *I am going to hit his fat arse.*

Arsenal/आर्सेनल *(noun)* – हथियार-घर a store of weapons and ammunition. a [military] establishment where weapons and ammunition are made and stored. *A suspicious man was arrested from near the military arsenal.*

Arsenic/आर्सेनिक *(noun)* – संखिया, विष the chemical element of atomic number 33, a brittle steel-grey semimetal with many highly poisonous compounds. *Arsenic is a highly fatal chemical. It can kill you in second.*

Art/आर्ट *(noun)* – कला, कौशल the expression or application of creative skill and imagination especially through a visual medium such as painting or sculpture. works produced in this way.

Arterial/आर्टेरिअल *(adj)* – धमनी-सम्बन्धी of, involving or contained in the arteries. *The arterial system must be thoroughly understood and any defect should be soon done away with.*

Arteriotomy/आरटेरिओटॉमी *(noun)* – धमनी को काटने की क्रिया *The surgeon conducted an arteriotomy to let out some blood.*

Artery/आरटरी *(noun)* – धमनी any of the muscular-walled tubes forming part of the circulation system by which blood is conveyed from the heart to all parts of the body. *Blood must keep flowing through the arteries.*

Artful/आर्टफुल *(adj.)* – चतुर, धूर्त cunningly clever or skilful. *He is very arful at telling lies.*

Arthritis/आरथराइटिस *(noun)* – जोड़ो की सूजन a disease causing painful inflammation and stiffness of the joints. I suffer from arthritis. *I cannot bend my knees they are also painfully swollen.*

Artichoke/आर्टिचोक *(noun)* – चुकन्दर, हाथी चक a plant with large, theistic-like flower heads. *Jerusalem Artichoke is a plant famous for its peculiar flower head.*

Article/आर्टिकल *(noun)* – साहित्यिक लेख a particular object. *I have finished writing article for the magazine.*

A

Articular/आर्टिकुलर *(adj.)* – जोड़ सम्बन्धी, संधि [anatomy] of or relating to a joint. *Relating to the joints of body.*

Articulate/आर्टिकुलेट *(adj.)* – स्पष्ट, जुड़ा हुआ, अपने विचारों को स्पष्ट रूप से व्यक्त करने में कुशल fluent and clear in speech. *He is very articulate in his speech.*

Articulation/आर्टिकुलेशन *(noun)* – अभिव्यतीकरण the action of articulating. music clarity in the production of successive notes. phonetics the formation of a speech sound by constriction of the air flow in the vocal organs. *In this music show articulation is superb.*

Artifice/आर्टिफिस *(noun)* – चालाकी, साधन, छल

Artificial/आर्टिफिसियल *(adj.)* – कृत्रिम, बनावटी made as a copy of something natural. *She is wearing artificial jwellery.*

Artillery/आर्टिलरी *(noun)* – तोप इत्यादि चलाने वाले सैनिक large-caliber guns used in warfare on land. a branch of the armed forces trained to use artillery. *The artillery moved slowly with large calibre guns.*

Artisan/आर्टिजन *(noun)* – शिल्पकार, कारीगर a skilled worker who makes things by hand. *A potter is an artisan.*

Artist/आर्टिस्ट *(noun)* – ललित-कला मे निपुण, कलाकार a person who paints or draws as a profession or hobby a person who parctise or performs any of the creative arts. *There are many fine artists in our country who either draw or paint.*

Artistic/आर्टिस्टिक *(adj.)* – निपुणता का, कलात्मक relating to or characteristic of art or artists. *This artistic background helped him to gain admission in the music academy.*

Artless/आर्टलेस *(adj.)* – निष्कपट, सच्चा without guile or pretension. *He is a artless rather clumsy guy don't you suspect him on any account.*

Arts/आर्ट्स *(noun)* – कला, शिल्प the activity or skill of producing things such as painting, designs. *Arts provide us with general knowledge and intellectual skills.*

As/एज *(conj.)* – समान, जब used to indicate simultaneous occurrence. *He is as tall as his brother.*

Asafoetida/एसाफोइटिडा *(noun)* – हींग a fetid resinous gum obtained from the roots of a herbaceous plant, used in herbal medicine and Indian cooking. *Put a little asafoetida in dal it will make it tasty.*

Asbestos/ऐस्बेसटस *(noun)* – अदह a highly heat-resistant fibrous silicate mineral able to be woven into fabrics, used in brake linings and in fire-resistant and insulating materials. *I am wearing asbestos woven fabric it'll save me from fire.*

Ascend/असेन्ड *(verb)* – सवार होना, चढ़ना, उन्नति करना go up; climb or rise. *He has ascended to the post of Principal.*

Ascension/असेन्शन *(noun)* – उद्गम, अधिरोहण, चढ़ाव the action of ascending in status. *His ascension to the post of PM filled him with glory.*

Ascent/असेन्ट *(noun)* – चढ़ाव या अवरोहण an instance of ascending. a climb to the summit of a mountain. an upward slope. *The ascent to this mountain is very difficult.*

Ascertain/एसर्टेन *(verb)* – निश्चय करना find out for certain. *I want to ascertain if I have succeeded or not.*

Ascetic/एसेटिक *(noun)* – संन्यासी, तपस्वी characterized by the practice of severe self-discipline. noun an ascetic person. *Saints are ascetic persons.*

Ascribable/एस्क्राइबेब्ल *(adj.)* कारण बतलाने योग्य capable of being assigned or created to.

Ascribe/एस्क्राइब *(verb)* – आरोपण करना attribute something to (a particular cause, person or period). regard a quality as belonging to. *He ascribed his success to his friend.*

Aseptic/एसेप्टिक *(adj.)* – जो सड़ने योग्य न हो free of or using methods to keep free of pathological microorganisms. *Aseptic surgical methods are employed during operations.*

Ash/ऐश *(noun)* – राख tree with compound leaves, winged fruits, and hard pale wood. used in names of other trees, e.g. mountain ash. *Mountain ash is very beautiful and wonderful tress.*

Ashamed/अशेम्ड *(adj.)* – संकुचित, लज्जित feeling embarrassed or guilty. *I felt ashamed at having been so rude to her.*

Ashen/एशेन *(adj.)* – धूसर, पीला (of a person's face) very pale with shock, fear, or illness. *His face grew ashen as he looked at something in the dark.*

Ashore/एशोर *(adj.)* – किनारे पर, तीर पर to or on the shore or land from the direction of the sea. on land as opposed to at sea. *I reached ashore after a long voyage.*

Ashy/एशाइ *(adj.)* – धूसर of a light grey. *This piece of cloth looks ashy.*

Asiatic/एशियाटिक *(adj.)* – एशिया-सम्बन्धी relating to or deriving from Asia. *Features of Asiatic people are different from those of Europeans.*

Aside/एसाइड *(noun)* – एक ओर, दूर the side of a pop single regarded as the main one. *He sang aside the great pop singer.*

Asinine/एसिनाइन *(adj.)* – मूर्ख extremely stupid or foolish. *He is an asinine person.*

Ask/आस्क *(verb)* – पूछना, प्रार्थना करना say something in order to obtain an answer or some information. enquire about the well-being of. *I asked him about his father's health.*

Askew/आस्क्यू *(adj.&adv.)* – तिरछी दृष्टि से (कटाक्ष) not in a straight or level position. *He looked at me askew.*

Aslant/एस्लैंट *(adv.)* – तिरछी दृष्टि से at a slant. preposition across at a slant. *The child slipped and went aslant on the slope.*

Asleep/एस्लिप *(adj.&adv.)* – निद्रा में, सोते हुए in or into a state of sleep. not attentive or alert. *My father was fast asleep when I reached home.*

Aslope/अस्लोप *(adj.&adv.)* – ढलान की भाँति, ढालू दशा में [poetic – literary] in a sloping position. *The ship went aslope and then sank down.*

Aspect/आस्पेक्ट *(noun)* – छवि, भाव, आकृति a particular part or feature. a particular appearance or quality. *I didn't pay attention to this aspect of situation.*

Asperate/एस्परेट *(verb)* – रूखा करने या होने की क्रिया *I asperated the smooth surface of the stone slab.*

Asperity/अस्पेरिटी *(noun)* – रूक्षता, तीव्रता, कठिनाई, कायरता harshness of tone or manner. harsh qualities or conditions. *This asperity hurt me.*

Asperse/एस्पर्स *(verb)* – निन्दा करना, कलंक लगाना rare cast aspersions on. *People aspersed her but she remained undaunted.*

Aspersion/एस्पर्सन *(noun)* – निन्दा, कलंक an attack on someone's character or reputation.

They cast aspersions on him but he answered all their questions fearlessly.

Asphodel/एस्फोडेल *(noun)* – एक प्रकार की कुमुदिनी a plant of the lily family with long, slender leaves and flowers borne on a spike. *Thank you for this rare plant of asphodel.*

Asphyxia/एस्फाइक्सिया *(noun)* – किसी की साँस रोक देना या दम घुटना a condition arising when the body is deprived of oxygen, causing unconsciousness or death. *This man's death has been due to asphyxia.*

Aspirant/ऐस्परन्ट *(adj.)* – आकांक्षी, प्रार्थी अभ्यर्थी aspiring towards a particular achievement or status. noun a person who has such aspirations. *He is an aspirant for the job of director.*

Aspirate/एस्परेट *(verb)* – एक श्वास से उच्चारण करना phonetics pronounce (a sound) with an exhalation of breath. pronounce the sound of h at the beginning of a word. *Please aspirate the sound h in this word as in horse!*

Aspiration/एस्परेशन *(noun)* – लालसा a hope or ambition. *My aspiration is to become an army officer.*

Aspirator/एस्पीरेटर *(noun)* – वात शोषक यंत्र medicine an instrument or apparatus for aspirating. *Bring an aspirator to draw out the air from lungs.*

Aspire/एस्पायर *(verb)* – उत्कट इच्छा करना direct one's hopes or ambitions towards achieving something. *I aspire to be a business tycoon.*

Aspirin/एस्पिरिन *(noun)* – पीड़ा-नाशक एक औषधि a synthetic compound used to relieve pain and reduce fever and inflammation. *Take an aspirin and your fever will come down.*

Ass/ऐस *(noun)* – गर्दभ, गदहा an animal of the horse family which is smaller than a horse and had longer ears and a braying call. (in general use) a donkey. *He is an ass by means.*

Assail/एसेल *(verb)* – आक्रमण करना, चढ़ाई करना, चोट करना make a concerned or violent attack on. *A bad feeling assailed me in the morning.*

Assassin/एसैसिन *(noun)* – घातक, हत्यारा a person who assassinates. *This is the assassin who shot the president.*

Assault/एसॉल्ट *(noun)* – चढ़ाई, धावा, अचानक हमला a violent attack. [law] an act that threatens physical harm to a person, whether or not actual harm is done. *He assaulted me at a public place.*

A

Assemble/एसेम्बल *(verb)* – एकत्रित करना come or bring together. *I assembled the different parts of the machinery together.*

Assembly/एसेम्बली *(noun)* – मण्डली, सभा, विधानसभा a group of people gathered together. a group having legislative or decision-making powers. a regular gathering of teachers and pupils in a school. *All the MLA's were asked to assemble at the assembly at 10 a.m. Sharp for voting.*

Assent/असेन्ट *(noun)* – स्वीकृति देना, सहमत होना the expression of approval or agreement. verb express assent. *I expressed my assent to the proposal.*

Asseentient/असेन्सियन्ट *(noun)* – स्वीकृति देने वाला *He was in an assentient mood.*

Assert/एसर्ट *(verb)* – दृढ़तापूर्वक स्वीकार करना state a fact or belief confidently and forcefully. *I asserted my belief in God.*

Assertion/एसरशन *(adj.)* – निश्चित घोषणा having or showing a confident and forceful personality.

Assertive/एसरटिव *(adj.)* – निश्चित बात करने वाला having or showing a confident and forceful personality. *This statement was so assertive that none could doubt it.*

Assess/एसेस *(verb)* – मूल्य निर्धारित करना, राय बनाना evaluate or estimate the nature, value, or quality of. set the value of a tax, fine, etc. for (a person or property) at a specified level. *The bank will assess the value of your property before giving you loan.*

Assiduity/एसिड्यूटी *(noun)* – उद्योग, तत्परता constant or close attention to what one is doing. [archaic] or [poetic – literary] constant attentions to someone. *This assiduity for work is well known.*

Assiduous/एसिड्अस *(adj.)* – परिश्रमी adjective showing great care and perseverance. *His assiduous care soon cured him.*

Assign/एसाइन *(verb)* – निरूपण करना, स्थिर करना allocate (a task or duty) to someone. appoint to a particular task. *I assigned him the task of bringing money from the bank.*

Asunder/एसन्डर *(adj.)* – पृथक्, भिन्न [archaic] or [poetic – literary] apart. *I tore the file asunder.*

Asylum/असाइलम *(noun)* – आश्रय, राजनीतिक शरण the protection granted by a state to someone who has left their native country as a political refugee. shelter or protection form danger. *The diplomat was granted asylum by the state.*

At/एट *(prep.)* – पास, ओर में, से expressing location or arrival in a particular place or position. *I'll meet you at the railway station.*

Atelier/एटेलिअर *(noun)* – चित्रालय, शिल्पशाला a studio especially for an artist or designer. *Students are learning art in the atelier.*

Atheism/एथेइज्म *(noun)* – ईश्वर-निन्दा, नास्तिकवाद the theory or belief that god does not exist. *He believes in atheism for him there is no God.*

Athirst/एथर्स्ट *(adj.)* – प्यासा, उत्सुक extremity desirous. *He is athirst for money.*

Athlete/एथलीट *(noun)* – खेलकूद प्रतियोगिताओं में भाग लेने वाला a person who is proficient in sports, especially one who competes in track and field events. *There is no dearth of good atheletes in our country.*

Athwart/एथ्वार्ट *(noun)* – पार, आर-पार from side to side of; across. *The swan flew athwart the river.*

Atlantic/अटलैंटिक *(noun)* – अन्ध महासागर-सम्बन्धी of or adjoining the Atlantic Ocean. *Cold wind blew over the Atlantic.*

Atlas/ऐटलस *(noun)* – मानचित्र की पुस्तक a book of maps or charts. *Hear open this atlas and you will find all the countries and cities in it.*

Atoll/एटॉल *(noun)* – मूँगे का वृत्ताकार पहाड़, प्रवालद्वीप a ring-shaped reef or chain of islands formed of coral.

Atom/एटम *(noun)* – अणु, परमाणु the smallest particle of a chemical element, consisting of a positively charged nucleus (containing protons and typically also neutrons) surrounded by negatively charged electrons. *The present moment is so fleeting and atomic.*

Atomizer/एटमाइजर *(verb)* – हाथ की पिचकारी convert (a substance) into very fine particles or droplets. *We use atomizer to convert any substance into fragments.*

Atomy/एटमी *(noun)* – परमाणु, ठठरी [archaic] a skeleton or emaciated body. *I took pity at his atomy like body.*

Atone/अटोन *(verb)* – प्रायश्चित करना make amends or reparation for. *I went to church to atone for my sins.*

Atop/एटॉप *(prep. & adv.)* – शिखर पर, उँचाई पर on the top of. *The bird sat atop the tree.*

Atrophy/एट्राफी *(verb)* – योग्य आहार के बिना शरीर का क्षय होना (of body tissue or an organ) waste away, especially as a result of the degeneration of cells, or become vestigial during evolution. *Atrophy of muscles is very common in an old age.*

Attach/एटैच *(verb)* – बाँधना, कुर्क करना . fasten; join. include (a condition) as part of an agreement. *Please find attached my biodata with the application.*

Attack/एटैक *(verb)* – आक्रमण करना, धावा करना . take aggressive action against. act harmfully on. *He attacked me in open daylight.*

Attain/एटेन *(verb)* – प्राप्त करना, पूर्ण करना succeed in accomplishing. *I succeeded to attain my goal.*

Attainder/एटेन्डर *(noun)* – अपराध के कारण माल का जब्त होना [historical] the forfeiture of land and civil rights suffered as a consequence of a sentence of death for treason or felony. *He was an attainder so his property was attached and he was executed.*

Attaint/एटेन्ट *(verb)* – अपमानित करना [historical] subject to attainder.

Attar/एटार *(noun)* – अतर, इत्र a fragrant essential oil, typically made from rose petals. *I have used special attar see how good it smells.*

Attempt/एटेम्प्ट *(verb)* – प्रयत्न करना make an effort to achieve or complete. try to climb to the top of (a mountain). noun an act of attempting. a bid to kill someone. *He attempted to climb the mountain and succeeded.*

Attend/एटेन्ड *(verb)* – उपस्थित होना, भाग लेना be present at. go regularly to (a school, church, or clinic). *I'll certainly attend the class.*

Attendant/एटेन्डेन्ट *(noun)* – नौकर, अनुचर a person employed to provide a service to the public. an assistant to an important person. *I am attendant to the secretary.*

Attender/एटेन्डर *(noun)* – सेवा करने वाला परिचर someone who listens attentively. *He is an attender and regularly attends the lectures.*

Attention/एटेन्सन *(noun)* – ध्यान the mental faculty of considering or taxation. a person's behaviour to another as an indication of affection or sexual interest. *Don't pay any attention to him he is a fool.*

Attentive/एटेन्टिव *(adj.)* – सावधान paying close attention. *I am attentive to you.*

Attest/एटेस्ट *(verb)* – शपथ देना, अनुप्रमाणित करना provide or serve as clear evidence of. *I have my document attested from a gazetted officer.*

Attire/एटायर *(noun)* – वेश, वस्त्र, सजाना clothes, especially fine or formal ones. verb be dressed in clothes of a specified king. *He appeared in the fancy show in the attire of a king.*

Attitude/एटिट्यूड *(noun)* – स्थिति, रवैया a settled way of thinking or feeling. a position of the body indicating a particular. *Doesn't he behave funny? He must have same attitude problem.*

Attorney/एटॉर्नी *(noun)* – प्रतिनिधि, मुख्तार, न्यायविद a person, typically a lawyer, appointed to act for another in legal matters. chiefly us a qualified lawyer. *I have hired an attorney to fight my case.*

Attract/अट्रैक्ट *(verb)* – आकर्षित करना, मोहना draw or bring in by offering something of interest or advantage. *Full moon attracts the sea water.*

Attractor/एट्रैक्टर *(noun)* – आकर्षक, मोहक, लुभावना an entertainer who attract large audiences. *The hero is an attractor in the film.*

Attribute/एट्रिब्यूट *(noun)* – धर्म, उपाधि, गुण a quality or feature regarded as characteristic or inherent. *I attribute my whole success to my mother.*

Attrite/एट्राइट *(verb)* – रगड़ से घिसा हुआ [informal] wear down by sustained action. *His body attrited due to a long disease.*

Attrition/एट्रिशन *(noun)* – रगड़, घिसावट the action or process of gradually wearing down through sustained attack or pressure. *He travelled long through' the jungle and his body was in a condition of attrition.*

Auburn/ऑबर्न *(noun)* – सुनहरा भूरा रंग a reddish-brown colour. *I got my hair coloured auburn.*

Auction/आक्शन *(noun)* – नीलाम a public sale in which goods or property are sold to the

A

highest bidder. *He was deeply in debt so his house was auctioned.*

Audacious/ऑडेशस *(adj.)* – साहसी, ढीठपन recklessly daring. *He is an audacious fellow and will never see sense.*

Audible/ऑडिबल *(adj.)* – कर्णगोचर able to be heard. noun [American football] a change of playing tactics called by the quarterback at the line of scrimmage. *He has an audible and clear voice.*

Audibly/ऑडिब्ली *(adv.)* – स्पष्ट रुप से, सुनने में अन्य *She spoke audibly to listeners and they understood her.*

Audience/ऑडियन्स *(noun)* – सुनाई, श्रोतागण a gathering of spectators or listeners at a performance. *The audience was disturbed.*

Audiometer/आडिओमीटर *(noun)* – श्रवण शक्ति की परीक्षा करने का यन्त्र *Here is an audiometer whereby you can measure the sensitivity of hearing.*

Audiophone/अडिओफोन *(noun)* – बहरे मनुष्यों को सुनने में सहायता देने वाला यंत्र *As he is hard of hearing he uses an audiophone.*

Audit/ऑडिट *(verb)* – हिसाब की जाँच करना conduct an audit of. *Audit is going on so I can't attend to you please come tomorrow.*

Audition/ऑडिशन *(noun)* – परीक्षण हेतु गायन अभिनेता का लघु प्रदर्शन an interview for a musician, actor, etc, consisting of a practical demonstration of the candidate's suitability and skill. *Next is my turn for audition and I'm feeling a bit nervous.*

Auditive/ऑडिटिव *(adj.)* – श्रवण-सम्बन्धी of or relating to the process of hearing. *This problem is auditive.*

Auditor/ऑडिटर *(noun)* – लेखा-परीक्षक a person who conducts an audit. *He is the auditor who is going to audit the company accounts.*

Auditorial/ऑडिटोरिअल *(adj.)* – हिसाब की जाँच के सम्बन्ध का relating to an audit. *This is an auditorial mistake.*

Auditorium/ऑडिटोरिअम *(noun)* – सभा-मण्डप, सिनेमा, रंगशाला आदि the part of a theatre or hall in which the audience sits. *The auditorium was full of people who had come to see the famous drama.*

Auditory/ऑडिटोरी *(adj.)* – श्रवण या कान सम्बन्धी of or relating to the sense of hearing. *This is something that relates to auditory defect.*

Augean/ऑजीअन *(adj.)* – कठिन, गन्दा, मलिन extremely filthy from long reflect. *The old place smelled and was augean.*

Augur/ऑगर *(noun)* – बरमा a tool resembling a large corkscrew, for boring holes. *Take this augur it is tool for boring holes.*

August/अगस्त *(noun)* – अंग्रेजी का 8वाँ माह, प्रतापी, पूजनीय, महान the eight month of the year. *August is the 8th month of the year.*

Aulic/ऑलिक *(adj.)* – राजदरबार सम्बन्धी *Sometimes I would like to see an aulic festival where there will be royal person.*

Aunt/ऑन्ट *(noun)* – बुआ, मौसी, चाची the sister of one's father or mother or the wife of one's uncle. *One of my aunts is a director of this company.*

Aural/ऑरल *(adj.)* – श्रवण सम्बन्धी of or relating to the ear or the sense of hearing. *He had aural infection.*

Aureola/ऑरिओला *(noun)* – दैवी मुकुट, प्रभा मण्डल a radiant circle surrounding a person's head or body as a way of representing holiness. *You'll find an aureole around the head of saints.*

Auric/ऑरिक *(adj.)* – सोने का of or relating to an aura. *The halo around the sun is auric.*

Auriferous/ऑरिफरस *(adj.)* – सुवर्ण मिश्रित adjective (of rocks or minerals) containing gold. *These rocks are auriferous they contain gold.*

Auriform/ऑरिफार्म *(adj.)* – कान की आकृति का harming a shape resembling an ear. *I saw a tree leaf which was almost auriform like an ear.*

Aurilave/ऑरिलेव *(noun)* – कान खोदनी ear-pick. *All ear specialists have an aurilave to clean ear.*

Aurora/ऑरोरा *(noun)* – तड़का, अरुणोदय the northern lights or southern lights a natural phenomenon characterized by the appearance of streamers of coloured light in the sky near the earth's magnetic poles and caused by the interaction of charged particles form the sun with atoms in the supper atmosphere. *At aurora I was half awake and saw a strange dream.*

Aurum/ऑरम *(noun)* - सुवर्ण, सोना of gold. *This is an aurum necklace.*

Auspicate/ऑस्पिकेट *(verb)* - भविष्य बतलाना *He auspicated his trip by going to the temple.*

Auspice/ऑस्पिस *(noun)* - रक्षा, शरण में [archaic] an omen. *Seeing an owl is not a good auspice.*

Auspicious/ऑस्पिशस *(adj.)* - अच्छे, शकुन का indicating a good chance of success; favorable. Today is my brother's marriage. *It is an auspicious day.*

Austere/आस्टिअर *(adj.)* - कठोर, तीखा servere or strict in appearance or manner. *My father is very austere. I'm afraid of even speaking to him.*

Austerity/ऑस्टेरिटी *(noun)* - कठोरता, आत्मसंयम the trait of great self-denial. *Many saints preach austerity.*

Austral/आस्ट्रल *(adj.)* - दक्षिणी, दक्षिण का [technical] of the southern hemisphere. *This man seems austral in appearance, must be from Australia.*

Authentic/अथेंटिक *(adj.)* - सच्चा, यथार्थ, वास्तविक of undisputed origin or veracity; genuine. *These papers are authentic. I have shown them to a lawyer.*

Authenticity/अथेन्टिसिटी *(noun)*- सत्यता, प्रामाणिकता the property of being genuine or valid. *The authenticity of this document is beyond doubt.*

Author/ऑथर *(noun)* - लेखक, प्रवर्तक a writer of a book, article, or report. *He is an author of many novels.*

Authority/अर्थॉरिटी *(noun)* - अधिकार, देना, प्रमाणित करना the power or right to give orders and enforce obedience.

Authorize/ऑथराइज *(verb)* - अधिकार देना, प्रमाणित करना give official permission for or approval to. *I authorized him to attend the meeting on my behalf.*

Autobiography/ऑटोबायोग्राफी *(noun)* - आत्मकथा an account of a person's life written by that person. *Almost all great men write their autobiography.*

Autocracy/ऑटोक्रैसी *(noun)* - निरंकुश राज्यशासन a system of government by one person with absolute power. *Autocracy is not popular these days.*

Autocrat/ऑटोक्रैट *(noun)* - निरंकुश शासक a ruler who has absolute power. *Autocrats usually meet tragic ends.*

Autograph/ऑटोग्राफ *(noun)* - किसी प्रसिद्ध व्यक्ति के हस्ताक्षर a celebrity's signature written for an admirer. *I have with me autograph of Amitabh Bachchan he has wished me and signed it.*

Autogyro/ऑटोगायरो *(noun)* - एक प्रकार का वायुयान जो बिना दौड़ लगाये सीधे ऊपर को उठता है *For once I would like to sit in an autogyro which is a new kind of plane.*

Automatic/ऑटोमैटिक *(adj.)* - यंत्र से चलने वाला working by itself with little or no direct human control. self-loading and able to fire continuously. *These days automatic devices and machines are in Vogue with little human intervention.*

Automobile/ऑटोमोबाइल *(noun)* - मोटरगाड़ी [chiefly North American] a motor car. *I would like to sit in a racing automobile.*

Autonomous/ऑटोनामस *(adj.)* - स्वराज्य के अधीन not controlled by outside forces; existing as an independent entity. *Judiciary is an autonomous body.*

Autonomy/ऑटोनॉमी *(noun)* - स्वराज्य the possession or right of self-government. *People enjoy autonomy in democracy.*

Autumn/ऑटम *(noun)* - पतझड़ the season when the leaves full from the frees. *Trees shed their leaves in autumn.*

Auxiliary/अक्जिलिअरी *(adj.)* - सहायक, उपकारी providing supplementary or additional help and support. noun an auxiliary person or thing. *The flood victims were provided auxiliary help.*

Avail/एवेल *(verb)* - सहायता देना, उपकारी होना use or take advantage of. *When the opportunity comes avail yourself of it.*

Avale/एवेल *(verb)* - नीचे उतरना to get down. *I avaled from the horse.*

Avarice/एवाराइस *(noun)* - लोभ, धन का लालच extreme greed for wealth or material gain. *He suffers from avarice for wealth.*

Avenge/एवेन्ज *(verb)* - बदला लेना, दण्ड देना inflict harm in return for (an injury or wrong). inflict retribution on behalf of (a wronged person). *I avenged myself upon him as he had dishonored me.*

Avenue/एवेन्यू *(noun)* – द्वार, मार्ग a broad road or path, especially one lined with trees. *We had to walk along a long avenue before reaching the house.*

Average/एवरेज *(noun)* – औसत the result obtained by adding several amounts together and then dividing the total by the number of amounts. *We calculate average in arithmetic.*

Avert/एवर्ट *(verb)* – हटाना, टालना turn away (one's eyes or thoughts). *He averted his eyes from me.*

Aviary/एविअरी *(noun)* – चिड़ियाखाना, पक्षीशाला a large enclosure for keeping birds in. *I have built an aviary for birds.*

Aviation/एवियेशन *(noun)* – विमानन the activity or business of operating and flying aircraft. He has flew a lot of planes. *He is an expert at aviation.*

Avid/एविड *(adj.)* – किसी कार्य के प्रति अति उत्साह, उत्सुक keenly interested or enthuslastic. *He has an avid interest in music.*

Aviette/एवीट *(noun)* – हाथ या पैर से चलने वाला वायुयान

Avocation/एवोकेशन *(noun)* – व्यापार, उद्यम auxiliary activity. *Besides his hardware business his avocation is breeding dogs.*

Avoid/एवॉइड *(verb)* – कुछ करने से रोकना, बच जाना keep away or refrain from. prevent form doing or happening. [law] repudiate, nullity, or render void. *I always avoid him because he is a non-stop talker.*

Avulsion/एवल्शन *(noun)* – अलगाव, तोड़फोड़ [chiefly medicine] the action of pulling or tearing away. *The avulsion of the tissue from its wound is not a good sign.*

Await/एवेट *(verb)* – प्रतीक्षा करना, आशा करना Wait for. *I'll await you here.*

Awake/एवेक *(verb)* – जगाना, सचेत करना stop sleeping. *He has long been awake.*

Awaken/एवेकेन *(verb)* – जगाना stop or cause to stop sleeping. *I awakened him from sleep.*

Award/एवार्ड *(verb)* – अर्पण करना, देना give or grant officially as a prize or reward. noun something awarded. *He was given an award for his performance in athletic events.*

Aware/अवेयर *(adj.)* – सचेत, सावधान having knowledge or perception of a situation or fact. *I am aware that he is a good hero.*

Away/अवे *(adj. & adv.)* – दूर, हटजा to or at a distance. at a specified future distance in time. *He left his home and went far away.*

Awe/ऑ *(noun)* – भय, श्रद्धायुक्त भय a feeling of reverential respect mixed with fear or wonder. verb inspire with awe. *I looked at the big man with awe.*

Awful/ऑफुल *(adj.)* – भयंकर, डरावना very bad or unpleasant. *It was awful to be in such a dirty place.*

Awhile/एह्वाइल *(adj.)* – क्षण भर के लिये for a short time. *For awhile she was with her mother but soon she came back.*

Awkward/ऑकवार्ड *(adj.)* – भद्दा, कुरूप, अनाड़ी hard to do or deal with. *He is such an awkward fellow he never fits in any place.*

Awl/ऑल *(noun)* – मोची का टेकुआ a small pointed toll used for placing holes. *A shoe maker sews shoes with an awl.*

Awoke/अवोक – जगा past of awake. *I awoke late yesterday.*

Axe/एक्स *(noun)* – कुल्हाड़ी, कुठार, सूआ a heavy-bladed tool used for chopping wood. *Woodcutter cut wood with an axe.*

Axial/एक्सिअल *(adj.)* – केन्द्र, धुरी का अक्षीय forming, relating to, or around and axis. *The earth moves round the imaginary line namely axial. Which is around the axis.*

Axilla/एक्सिला *(noun)* – काँख, बगल [anatomy] an armpit, or the corresponding part in a bird or other animal. *Axilla itching is very common during summer.*

Axillary/एक्जिलरी *(adj)* – काँख-सम्बन्धी [anotomy] of or relating to the armpit. *If there is an axillary growth a doctor should be consulted at once.*

Axiom/ऐक्सिअम *(noun)* – सिद्धान्त, स्वयं सिद्ध an accepted statement or proposition regarded as being self-evidently true. *In mathematics we can't do without axioms.*

Axis/एक्सिस *(noun)* – अक्ष रेखा an imaginary line about which a body rotates or with respect to which it possesses rotational symmetry. *Our earth rotates round an imaginary line called axis*

Axle/एक्सल *(noun)* – धुरा जिस पर कोई पहिया घूमता है। noun a rod or spindle passing through the centre of a wheel or group of wheels. *Both the cart wheels are rotating on spindle like axle.*

Aye/ऐं *(adv.)* – सर्वदा exclamatory [archaic] nautical a response accepting an order. i assent. noun an affirmative answer, especially in voting. *Aye! We are moving ahead increase speed of your boat.*

Ayes/आइज *(noun)* – किसी प्रस्ताव का समर्थन करने वाले supporter of a proposal. *The passing boat asked some question I said 'Aye' i.e. answered in affirmative and rowed on.*

Azure/एज्योर *(adj.)* – आकाश के समान नीला, आसमानी bright blue in colour like a cloudless sky. heraldry blue. noun a bright blue colour. *She wore an azure coloured suit which looked smashing.*

A

B b

B/बी – अंग्रेजी वर्णमाला का दूसरा अक्षर the second letter of the English alphabet
(1) The seventh note in music.
(2) The second known quantity in Algebra.

Baa/बा *(verb)* – मिमियाने का शब्द – (of a sheep or lamb) bleat. noun the cry of a sheep or lamb. *The lamb cried baa and the shepherd became alert.*

Babble/बैब्ल *(verb)* – बड़बड़ाना, रहस्य या भेद खोलना – talk rapidly and continuously in a foolish, excited, or incomprehensible way. reveal something secret. *She babbled away the secret.*

Babe/बेब् *(noun)* – शिशु, बच्चा – [poetic/literary] a baby. *Hey babe you look special today.*

Babel/बेबेल *(noun)* – कोलाहल, खलबली – a confused noise made by a number of voices. *I couldn't hear him clearly in that babel.*

Baboon/बैबून *(noun)* – एक प्रकार का बड़ा बंदर, लंगूर – a large ground-dwelling social monkey with a long doglike snout and large teeth. *In Africa I saw herds of baboons dwelling on ground.*

Baby/बेबी *(noun)* – बालक, बच्चा a child or animal that is newly or recently born. *Although adult he behaves like a baby.*

Baccate/बैकेट *(adj.)* – जामुन या बेर की आकृति का Resembling a berry. *This seems to be the baccate that bears berries.*

Bacchanal/बकैनल *(noun)* – शराबी, मधुप्रिय an occasion of wild and drunken revelry. *Today's rave parties remind us of bacchanal parties given in honour of Bacchus the god of wine in old times.*

Bachelor/बैचलर *(noun)* – अविवाहित पुरुष a man who is not and has never been married. *People cast strange glances at bachelors.*

Bacillary/बैसलरी *(adj.)* – सूक्ष्म जीवों से सम्बन्ध रखने वाला [biology] relating to or produced by or containing bacilli.

Bacilliform/बैसिलीफॉर्म *(adj.)* – बेलन सरीखे सूक्ष्म जीवों के आकार का chiefly [biology] rod-shaped. *These Bacilliformed objects are germs of disease.*

Backbite/बैकबाइट *(verb)*– चुगली खाना to speak evil of a person in his absence. *He backites in my absence.*

Backbone/बैकबोन *(noun)* – रीढ़ की हड्डी, प्रधान आश्रय the spine. *I have pain in my backbone.*

Background/बैकग्राउण्ड *(noun)* – चित्र में पीछे का दृश्य, पृष्ठभूमि part of a scene, picture, or description that forms a setting for the main fighters, events, etc. *I have made enquiries about his background.*

Backhand/बैकहैंड *(noun)* – टेनिस में उल्टे हाथ का प्रहार, हथेली को अन्दर की तरफ रखकर किया प्रहार (in tennis and other racket sports) a stroke played with the back of the hand facing the direction of the stroke, with the arm across the body. verb strike with a backhanded blow or stroke. *Boris Becker was famous for his back hand shots.*

Backing/बैकिंग *(noun)* – सहारा, सहायता, समर्थन support. a layer of material that forms, protects, or strengthens the back of something. *You have my backing go on and fight.*

Backside/बैक्साइड *(noun)* – किसी पदार्थ का पिछला भाग [informal] a person's buttocks or anus. *I am not fond of seeing the backsides of people.*

Backslide/बैकस्लाइड *(verb)* – पीछे हट जाना, पतित होना, डिगना relapse into bad ways. *After remaining away a long time from alcohol he backslided and took to drinking again.*

Backward/बैकवर्ड *(adj.)* – पिछड़ा हुआ, पीछे directed behind or to the rear. *As he advanced the other man began to inch backward.*

Backwards/बैकवाईस *(adj.)* – पीछे की ओर in the direction of one's back. *I moved backwards as the animal came forward.*

Bacon/बेक्न *(noun)* – खाने योग्य सुअर का मांस cured meat from the back or sides of a pig. *He is fond of eating bacon meat from the side or back of the pig such meat is very nourishing he says.*

Bacteria/बैक्टिअरिया (noun plural) – वायु, जल इत्यादि के सूक्ष्म जीवाणु form of bacterium. *Bacteria are everywhere good bacteria bad bacteria.*

Bad/बैड् (adj.) – बुरा, दुष्ट, खराब of poor quality or a low standard. *This is in bad condition.*

Badge/बैज (noun) – चिह्न, लक्षण a small piece of metal, plastic, or cloth bearing a design or words, typically worn to indentify a person or to indicate support for a cause. *All scouts wear a badge.*

Badger/बैजर (noun) – बिज्जू a heavily built omnivorous nocturnal mammal of the weasel family, typically having a grey and black coat and a white-striped head. verb repeatedly and annoyingly ask (someone) to do something. *Beware of this animal it is badger and belongs to weasel family. Its size frightened me.*

Badly/बैड्लि (adv.) – बुरे प्रकार से in a Bad manner. *He was badly beaten.*

Baffle/बैफ़ुल (verb) – चकरा देना, उलझन में डाल देना restrain or regulate (a fluid, a sound, etc.) noun a derive used to restrain the flow of a fluid, gas, or loose material or to prevent the spreading of sound or light in a particular direction. *I baffled the already loud sound by turning the knob.*

Baft/बैफ्ट (noun) – मोटा सस्ता सूती कपड़ा coarse fabric, typically of cotton. *I have bought a piece of bafta cloth although coarse it is durable.*

Bag/बैग (noun) – कागज या कपड़े से बनी थैली a flexible container with on opening at the top. a piece of luggage. *Let us put all these things into one bag.*

Bagasse/बैगेश (noun) – चीनी बनाने मे गन्ने की सीठी the dry pulpy residue left after the extraction of juice from sugar cane. *I wonder in what way they use bagasse may be manure but it seems useless.*

Baggage/बैगेज (noun) – यात्री की सामग्री personal belonging packed in suitcases for travelling. *All my personal belongings are in this baggage.*

Bagman/बैगमैन (noun) – व्यवसायी यात्री brit. [informal], dated a travelling salesman. *He is a very successful bagman.*

Bagpipe/बैगपाइप (noun) – मसक बाजा a musical instrument with reed pipes that are sounded by the pressure of wind emitted from a bag squeezed by the player's arm. *He is expert at playing bagpipe.*

Bail/बेल (noun) – जामिन, प्रतिभूति the temporary release of an accused person awaiting trial, sometimes on condition that a sum of money is lodged on guarantee their appearance in court. *The judge granted him bail against the security of 50,000 rupees.*

Bailee/बेली (noun) – धरोहर जिसके पास कोई धरोहर रखी गयी हो [law] a person or party to whom goods are delivered for a purpose, without transfer of ownership. *I have arranged rupees 20,000 for his bail.*

Bailer/बेलर (noun) – जमानतदार, जमानत देने वाला he purchased our own bailer becouse almost everything comes in boxes.

Bailiff/बैलिफ (noun) – सहकारी अमीन An officer of the court who is employed to execute writs and processes and make arrests etc. *Yesterday a bailiff came to my friend's house to arrest him.*

Bait/बेट (noun) – चारा देकर ललचाना food used to entice fish or other animals as prey. *Fisherman use a bait to catch fish.*

Baize/बैज (noun) – मोटा ऊनी वस्त्र a coarse felt-like woolen material that is typically green used chiefly for covering billiard and card tables. *Cover the billiard and card tables with baize so they do not get damp or dirty.*

Bake/बैक (verb) – पकाना, कड़ा करना cook by dry heat without direct exposure to a flame, typically in an oven. *Biscuits are baked in the oven.*

Balance-wheel/बैलन्स-ह्वील (noun) – घड़ी को स्थायी गति से चलाने वाला पहिया another term for balance. *Things are weighed in a balance.*

Balancing/बैलन्सिंग (noun)- समतोलन, सन्तुलन *Circus people do hair raising balancing acts.*

Balcony/बैल्कनि (noun) – छज्जा a platform enclosed by a wall or balustrade on the outside of a building. *I usually stand in my balcony and look at the sea.*

Bald/बाल्ड (adj.) – गंजा, सिर पर बाल के बिना having a scalp wholly or partly lacking hair. feathers. *He is a bald man having no hair on his head.*

Balderdash/बॉल्डर्डैंस (noun) – खुराफात, बकवास, निर्थक बातचीत, खुराफात, बकवास senseless talk or writing. *All his talk and writings are balderdash.*

Baldric/बालड्रिक (noun) – तलवार लटकाने की पेटी [historical] a belt for a sword or other piece of equipment, worn over one shoulder

B

and reaching down to the opposite hip. *In old times soldiers wore their swords on a baldric.*

Bale/बेल *(noun)* – गट्ठर a large wrapped or bound bundle of paper. hay, or cotton. *Bales of cotton paper and they were being downloaded from the truck.*

Baleen/बेलीन *(noun)* – ह्वेल मछली की हड्डी whalebone. *This large bone must be baleen.*

Bale fire/बेल-फायर *(noun)* – चिता, होली a large open-air fire. *A strange soul of bale fire spread in some cities of a country.*

Baling press/बेलिगं-प्रेस *(noun)* – दबाकर बण्डल बनाने की मशीन

Balk/बाल्क/बाक *(verb & noun)* – बाधा, रुकावट, खींचना, निराश करना *(verb&noun)* [chiefly US] variant spelling of baulk. *As we travelled we saw a big baulk lying in our way.*

Ball/बॉल *(noun)* – गेंद, तोप का गोला round object that is hit or thrown or kind in game.

Ballad/बैलड *(noun)* – विरहा, आल्हा a poem consisting of one or more triples of stanzas with a repeated refrain and an envoy. *The old blind man was singing a ballad.*

Ballet/बैलेट *(noun)* – रंगमंच पर नाच गाना, नृत्य नाटक an artistic dance form performed to music. using precise and formalized set steps and gestures. *In India we rarely get an opportunity to see live ballet in London and Paris you can see a lot.*

Balista/बैलिस्टा *(noun)* – बड़े-बड़े पत्थर फेंकने का यन्त्र a catapult used in ancient warfare for hurling large boulders. *In old time the soldiers used balista to throw big stones.*

Balloon/बैलून *(noun)* – गुब्बारा a small rubber objectwhich is inflated and used as a child's toy or a decoration. a rounded outline strip of cartoon are written. *Children like balloons very much.*

Ballot/बैलट *(noun)* – चुनाव के लिये प्रयुक्त टिकट a procedure by which people vote secretly on an issue. the total number of votes cast in such a process. *These days people cast their vote by ballot.*

Balm/बाम् *(noun)* – मलहम, सुगन्धित औषधि a fragrant ointment used to heal or soothe the skin. something that has a soothing or restorative effect. *If you have headache you can use this balm it will be very helpful.*

Balmoral/बैल्मारल *(noun)*– एक प्रकार की छोटी कुर्ती, जूते around bramless hat with a cockade or ribbons attached, worn by certain scottish regiments. *Why not wear balmoral? It is strong walking boot.*

Balsam/बाल्सम *(noun)* – गुलमेंहदी, पीड़ा हरने वाली औषधि an aromatic resinous substance exuded by various trees and shrubs, used as a base for certain fragrances and medical preparations. a tree or shrub which yields balsam. *Balsam extracted from trees or shrubs is also of medicinal use.*

Balustrade/बैलुस्ट्रेड *(noun)* – जँगला, कटघरा a railing at the side of a stairccase to prevent people from falling.

Bam/बाम *(noun)*– झूठ, कपट falsehood, a hoax.

Bamboo/बैम्बू *(noun)*– वंश लोचन a giant woody grass with hollow jointed stems, grown chiefly in the tropics for use in furniture and implements. *Bamboo is largely used in furniture.*

Bamboozle/बैम्बूजल *(verb)* – छल करना, धोखा देना [informal] cheat or mystify. *I have been bamboozled by a fellow and thus lost a heavy amount of money.*

Ban/बैन *(verb)* – प्रतिरोध करना, शाप देना officially or legally prohibit. noun an official or legal prohibition. *It is banned for heavy vehicles to enter this street by order magistrate.*

Banana/बनाना *(noun)* – एक प्रकार का प्रसिद्ध पेड़ a long curved fruit which grows in clusters and has soft pulpy flesh and yellow skin when ripe. *I daily eat two bananas in my breakfast.*

Band/बैण्ड *(noun)* – चारों का समूह, बन्धन, तस्मा a flat, thin strip or loop of material used as a fastener, for reinforcement, or as decoration. a belt or strap transmitting motion between two wheels or pulleys. [north American] ornithology a ring of metal placed round a bird's leg to identify it. *I came across a band of robbers and they robbed me.*

Bandit/बैंडिट *(noun)* – चोर, डाकू, लुटेरा a violent robber or outlaw belonging to a gang.

Bandog/बैन्डॉग *(noun)* – सिक्कड़ में बँधा हुआ शिकारी कुत्ता a fighting dog bred for its strength and ferocity. *Don't go near house. There is bandog it is very ferocious.*

Bandoleer/बैन्डोलियर *(noun)* – करतूस रखने के लिए खानेदार पेटी a brood cartridge belt women over the shoulder by soldiers.

Bandy/बैन्डी *(adj.)* – हॉकी का खेल (of a person's legs) curved outwards so that the knees are wide apart.

Bang/बैंग *(noun)* – बंदूक के धमाके जैसी आवाज करने वाली a sudden loud, sharp noise. a sudden painful blow. *There was a loud bang and the gun went off.*

Bangle/बैंगल *(noun)* – कड़ा, चूड़ी, पहुँची a rigid ornamental band worn around the arm or wrist for decoration. *It is customary for Indian women to wear glass bangles.*

Banyan/Banian/बैन्यन *(noun)* – बरगद का पेड़, बनियान a kind of tree. *A banyan tree is very huge.*

Banish/बैनिश *(verb)* – हटा देना, देश निकालना, निर्वासित करना send away, especially from a country, as an official punishment. *He was banished from his country and asked to leave it forever as an official punishment.*

Banjo/बैंजो *(noun)* – बेला की तरह का एक बाजा a stringed instrument of the guitar family, with an open-backed sound box of vellum stretched over a round hoop. *He plays banjo beautifully.*

Banker/बैंकर *(noun)* – बैंक का स्वामी, मैनेजर a person who manages or owns a bank or group of banks. the person running the table, controlling play, or acting as dealer in some gambling or board games. *My uncle is a banker he owns a chain of banks besides being the manager of one.*

Banking/बैंकिंग *(noun)* – बैंककर्मी the business conducted or services offered by a bank. *Some private banks offer excellent banking.*

Bankrupt/बैंकरप्ट *(adj.)* – दिवालिया declared in [law] unable to pay one's debts. *My uncle was unable to pay his debts so he was declared bankrupt.*

Banner/बैनर *(noun)* – दो डंडों पर लगा कपड़े का टुकड़ा जिस पर कुछ लिखा हो noun a long strip of cloth bearing a slogan or design. a flag on a pole used as the standard of a king, knight, or army. adjective [north American] excellent; outstanding. *The procession went on. A lot of them bearing placards and banners.*

Banquet/बैंक्विट *(noun)* – विशिष्ट उत्सव an elaborate and formal meal for many people. verb entertain with a banquet. *I went to the banquet hall in a marriage and ate my fill.*

Bantam/बैन्टम *(noun)* – नाटा पुरुष, एक प्रकार का चूजा a chicken of a small breed. *My brother rears bantams.*

Banter/बैन्टर *(noun)* – उपहास करना the playful and friendly exchange of teasing remarks. verb engage in banter. *Although I bantered my friend a lot he didn't mind it and rather bantered me in return.*

Bar/बार *(noun)* – डण्डा छड़ a long rigid piece of wood, metal, or similar material, typically used as an obstruction, fastening, or weapon. a sandbank or shoal at the mouth of a harbour or an estuary. brit. a metal strip below the clasp of a medal, awarded as an additional distinction. heraldry a charge in the form of a narrow horizontal stripe across the shield. *Let us put a heavy bar across the door so that it can not open easily.*

Barb/बार्ब *(noun)* – तीर के पीछे मुड़ी नोंक sharp projection near the end of an arrow, fish hook, or similar object, which is angled away from the main point so as to make extraction difficult. a barbel at the mouth of some fish. one of the fine hair-like filaments growing from the shaft of a feather, forming the vane. *Barbed wire was placed all around the school.*

Barbarian/बार्बेरियन *(noun)* – असभ्य (in ancient times) a member of a people not belonging to one of the great civilizations. *In ancient times many kings used to be barbarian, uncultured and brutish often they gave horrible punishment to law breakers.*

Barbaric/बार्बेरिक *(adj.)* – असभ्य, रूखा savagely cruel. *People helplessly looked at the barbaric punishment given to a thief.*

Barber/बार्बर *(noun)* – नाई, हजाम a person who cuts men's hair and shaves or trims beards as an occupation. verb cut or trim (a man's hair). *I am going to the barber for a haircut.*

Barbican/बार्बिकन *(noun)* – किले की रक्षा का बाहरी घेरा – the outer defence of a city or castle, especially a double tower above a gate or drawbridge. *In old times castles used to have barbican for defense.*

Bard/बार्ड *(noun)* – भाट, कवि [archaic] or [poetic/literary] a poet, traditionally one reciting epics. (the bard) Shakespeare. *Shakespeare was a bard who recited epics and wrote plays.*

Bare/बेअर *(adj.)* – नंगा करना, प्रकट करना (of a person or part of the body) not clothed or covered. without the appropriate or usual covering or contents. (bare of) without. *He plays appeared bare bodied no clothes.*

B

Bargain/बारगेन *(noun)* – सस्ता सौदा, तौलमोल an agreement between two or more people as to what each will do for the other. *I struck a bargain with the trader and bought the blankets at almost + the price.*

Barge/बार्ज *(noun)* – भारी बोझ ले जाने की बड़ी नाव a long flat-bottomed boat for carrying freight on canals and rivers. a long ornamental boat used for pleasure or on ceremonial occasions. *The barges ply in rivers or canals and carry loads.*

Barium/बेरियम *(noun)* – एक श्वेत धातु the chemical element of atomic number 56, a soft white reactive metal of the alkaline earth group, medicine a mixture of barium sulphate and water, opaque to X-rays, which is swallowed to permit radiological examination of the stomach of intestines. *For a medical test I had to drink barium before X-ray.*

Barker/बारकर *(noun)* – छाल उतारने वाला [informal] a tout at an auction or sideshow who calls out to passers-by to attract custom. *He is a barker attracting the attention of passers-by for the show.*

Barm/बार्म *(noun)* – शराब का फेन, खमीरा the froth on fermenting malt liquor. *Barm (yeast) is good for health.*

Barman/बारमैन *(noun)* – वारमैन या साकी [chiefly brit.] a man serving behind the bar of a public house. *The Barman served me the drink I ordered.*

Barn/बार्न *(noun)* – खलिहान a large farm building used for storage or for housing livestock. *The cattle live in barn. It is used for storage also.*

Barometer/बैरोमीटर *(noun)* – वायु-भार मापक यन्त्र an instrument measuring atmospheric pressure, used especially in forecasting the weather and determining altitude. *I have a barometer at my house it is fun it gives me information about atmospheric pressure weather altitude etc.*

Baronet/बैरोनेट *(noun)* – छोटा नवाब a member of the lowest hereditary titled british order. *A baronet is the lowest in British title order.*

Baroque/बरॉक *(adj.)* – टेढ़ी-मेढ़ी relating to or denoting a style of European architecture, music, and art of the 17th and 18th centuries characterized by ornate detail. highly ornate and extravagant in style. noun the baroque style or period. *Baroque style in 17th – 18th century was highly ornate and extravagant.*

Barouche/बारूच *(noun)* – भवन निर्माण करना, 17वीं-18वीं शताब्दी के दौरान यूरोप में प्रचलित अति अलंकृत शैली सम्बन्धित एक प्रकार की चौपहिया गाड़ी [historical] a four-wheeled horse-drawn carriage with a collapsible hood over the rear half. *Barouche was a popular mode of transport in old times.*

Barrack/बैरक *(noun)* – सिपाहियों के रहने का स्थान provide with accommodation. *There are some military barracks where jawans live.*

Barracoon/बाराकून *(noun)* – बन्दियों के रखने का बाड़ा [historical] an enclosure in which black slaves were temporarily confined. *In old time black slaves used to be confined in barracoons.*

Barrage/बैरॉज(ग) *(noun & verb)* – बाँध, किसी स्थान पर लगातार गोलियों की वर्षा a concentrated artillery bombardment over a wide area. an overwhelming number of questions or complaints delivered in rapid succession. *The media barraged him with questions.*

Barrel/बैरल *(noun)* – पीपा a cylindrical container bulging out in the middle, traditionally made of wooden staves enclosed by metal hoops. a measure of capacity for oil and beer, equal to 36 imperial gallons for beer and 35 imperial gallons or 42 US gallons for oil. *The captain of the ship ordered various barrels of rum and beer.*

Barren/बैरन *(adj.)* – बाँझ, शून्य too poor to produce much or any vegetation. (of a tree or plant) not producing fruit or seed. *The desert is a barren place.*

Barricade/बैरीकेड *(noun)* – आड़, रोक an improvised barrier erected to obstruct the movement of opposing forces. verb block or defend with a barricade. *The town people raised a barricade to obstruct the advance of enemy forces.*

Barrier/बैरियर *(noun)* – आड़, घेरा, सीमा a fence or other obstacle that prevents movement or access. an obstacle to communication, understanding, or progress: a language barrier. *She was from Russia. The language barrier prevented me from talking to her.*

Barring/बारिंग *(prep.)* – अतिरिक्त, को दौड़कर except for; if not for. *Barring a few distant all relatives were invited to the birthday party.*

Barter/बाटर *(verb)* – अदल-बदल का व्यापार exchange for other goods or services. noun the action or system of bartering. *In ancient*

B

times when there was no currency people bartered one thing for another.

Barton/बार्टन *(noun)* – रियासत, इलाका we have all ready lost three Pups in Borton and we do not want to lose any more.

Basalt/बैसाल्ट *(noun)* – एक प्रकार की भूरी चट्टान a dark fine-grained volcanic rock composed largely of plagioclase with pyroxene and olivine. *Basalt is a volcanic rock.*

Base/बेस *(noun)* – पेंदी, तल the lowest part or edge of something, especially the part on which it rests or is supported. architecture the part of a column between the shaft and pedestal or pavement. [botany & zoology] the end at which a part or organ is attached to the trunk or main part. *The base of this statue is made of teak wood polished black.*

Bash/बैश *(verb)* – कसकर घूँसा मारना strike hard and violently. criticize severely. *He bashed me on the head.*

Bashful/बैशफुल *(adj.)* – विनीत, भीरू shy and easily embarrassed. *He is rather bashful and can be easily embarrassed.*

Basial/बेसियल *(noun)* – चुम्बन सम्बन्धी an aromatic plant of the mint family, native to tropical Asia, used as a culinary herb, a similar European plant which grows in hedges and scrub. *Basial is used in cookery.*

Basil/बेसिल *(noun)* – तुलसी leaves of the common basil; used fresh or dried. *Basil is a very useful plant.*

Basin/बेसिन *(noun)* – नदी का संग्रहण क्षेत्र a large bowl or open container for washing in, preparing food, or holding liquid. *You can was your hands in the wash-basin.*Basis – noun the underlying support for an idea, argument, or process. the principles according to which an activity is carried on: she needed coaching on a regular basis. *This gentleman is the basis of my argument.*

Basis/बेसिस *(noun)* – मूल आधार, विचार धारा विश्वास का आधार the underlying support for an idea, argument, or process. *This gentleman is the basis of my argument.* the principles according to which an activity is carried on. *All our activities have some fundamental basis. This particular idea has very strong basis.*

Bask/बास्क *(verb)* – किसी स्थान पर बैठकर या लेटकर गरमाहट का आनंद लेना lie exposed to warmth and sunlight for pleasure. *She was basking in the sun.*

Basket/बास्किट *(noun)* – टोकरी, डलिया a container used to hold or carry things, made from interwoven strips of cane or wire. *Please take this basket and bring vegetables from the market.*

Bass/बेस *(noun)* – गायन में सबसे नीचा सुर the lowest adult male singing voice. *As the singing went as in the church I could hear the bass in music.*

Bassinet/बैसिनेट *(noun)* – बच्चों का पालना a child's wicker cradle. *The child was lying is a bassinet.*

Bastard/बास्टार्ड *(noun)* – अविवाहित माता-पिता की संतान, नाजायज [archaic] or derogatory an illegitimate person. *Don't ever trust him he is a bastard.*

Bastion/बैस्टियन *(noun)* – दुर्ग की रक्षा करने के लिए बना उमड़ा भाग a projecting part of a fortification allowing an increased angle of fire. *Heavy firing was coming from bastion.*

Bat/बैट *(noun)* – चमगादड़ पक्षी, बल्ला a mainly nocturnal mammal capable of sustained flight, with membranous wings that extend between the fingers and limbs. *Thousands of bats were hanging upside down in the dark cave.*

Batch/बैच *(noun)* – समुदाय, थोक, दल, टुकड़ी समूह a quantity or consignment of goods produced at one time. computing a group of records processed as a single unit. verb arrange in sets or groups. *A batch of one thousand shirts was made ready overnight.*

Bath/बाथ *(noun)* – स्नान an ancient Hebrew liquid measure equivalent to about 40 litres or 9 gallons. *Pour 40 baths of water into the tank.*

Batiste/बटिस्ट *(noun)* – महीन कपड़ा a fine, light linen or cotton fabric resembling cambric. *I would like to have a shirt made of batiste.*

Batman/बैटमैन *(noun)* – अधिकारी का नौकर dated (in the british armed forces) an officer's personal valet or attendant. *In British armed force an officer used to have an attendant called batman.*

Baton/बेटन *(noun)* – डण्डा, इस डण्डे से मारना, छड़ी रिले दौड़ की छड़ी a thin stick used by a conductor to direct an orchestra or choir. *The conductor moved his baton to direct the music.*

Batsman/बैट्समैन *(noun)* – बल्लेबाज a player who bats in cricket. *Virat Kohli is a fine batsman.*

B

Batten/बैटन *(noun & verb)* – तख्ता thrive or prosper at the expense of. *He is battening upon the expense of his uncle.*

Battery/बैटरी *(noun)* – तोपखाना, मारपीट, संग्रह a container consisting of one or more cells, in which chemical energy is converted into electricity and used as a source of power. *Charge your cell phone the battery must be running low.*

Battle/बैटल *(noun)* – युद्ध, संग्राम, लड़ाई a sustained flight between organized armed forces. *A fierce battle between the two countries went on for a long time.*

Battle-plane/बैटलप्लेन *(noun)* – युद्ध करने का बड़ा वायुयान a kind of plane. *India bought many battleplane.*

Bauble/बॉबल *(noun)* – अल्प मूल्य का आभूषण, क्रिसमस वृक्ष पर लटकाने का सजावटी गंदनुमा वस्तु a small, showy trinket or decoration. a decorative hollow ball hung on a Christmas tree. *A few baubles hung on the Christmas tree looked beautiful.*

Bawd/बॉड *(noun)* – कुटनी, वेश्या, स्त्रियों को बहकाकर कुकर्म करने वाली स्त्री [archaic] a women in charge of a brothel. *Arrest her! She is the bawd.*

Bawdy/बॉडी *(adj.)* – अश्लील, फूहड़ humorously indecent. noun humorously indecent talk or writing. *He is fond of cracking bawdy jokes.*

Bawl/बॉल *(verb & noun)* – चिल्लाकर बोलना, चिल्लाना, चीखना shout out noisily. reprimand someone angrily. *I heard a Bawl and became nervous.*

Bawn/बॉन *(noun)* – पशुशाला, बाड़ा Irish & Chadian an area of grassy land near a house; a meadow. *I have a bawn near my house where a lot of sheep graze.*

Bay/बे *(noun)*– एक प्रकार का वृक्ष, खाड़ी a broad curved inlet of the sea. *When I was in Calcutta I went to see bay of Bengal.*

Bayonet/बेअनट *(noun)* – किरच, संगीन a long blade fixed to the muzzle of a rifle for use in hand-to-hand fighting. *The soldier stabbed the enemy with the bayonet.*

Bay-window/बे-विन्डो *(noun)* – जालीदार उमड़ी हुई, खिड़की a window built to project outwards from a wall. *Look out of the bay window and you'll see a man.*

Be/बी *(verb)* – होना symbolic the chemical element beryllium. *'Be' is a symbol representing the chemical element beryllium.*

Beach/बीच *(noun)* – समुद्र-तट a pebbly or sandy shore at the edge of the sea or a lake. verb bring on to a beach form the water. become or cause to become stranded on a beach. *In Goa there are many beautiful beaches where people bathe in the sea.*

Beacon/बीकॉन *(noun)* – प्रकाश-स्तम्भ, आकाशदीप a fire lit on the top of a hill as a signal. *The ship saw the beacon interpreted the signal and turned left.*

Beadle/बीडल *(noun)* – गिरजे का पदाधिकारी brit. a ceremonial officer of a church, college, or similar institution. *He is a beadle, talk to him respectfully.*

Beady/बीडी *(adj.)* – दानेदार small, round, and observing things clearly. *Look at this animal how beady and sharp are its eyes.*

Beak/बीक *(noun)* – चोंच a bird's horny projecting jaws; a bill. a projecting jaw in some other animals. *The beak of an eagle is very different from that of a crow.*

Beaker/बीकर *(noun)* – काँच का चोंचदार पात्र british a tall plastic cup. a lipped cylindrical glass container for laboratory use. archaic or [poetic/literary] a large drinking container with a wide mouth. *We use beaker in chemistry labs.*

Beam/बीम *(noun)* – धरन a long sturdy piece of squared timber or metal used horizontally in building to support a load above. a narrow horizontal length of squared timber used for balancing exercises in gymnastics. *You see that long square beam it is supporting the roof.*

Bean/बीन – सेम, बोड़ा *(noun)* an edible kidney-shaped seed growing in long pods on certain leguminous plants. the hard seed of coffee, cocoa, and certain other plants. *I like beans a lot they are so tasty to eat.*

Beanfeast/बीनफिस्ट *(noun)* – भृत्यों को दिया हुआ भोज [British informal] a celebratory party with plentiful food and drink. *Come let us go to the beanfeast there will be a lot to eat.*

Bear/बिअर *(verb)* – सहन करना carry have as an attribute or visible mark. conduct oneself in a specified manner. *He bears himself in a dignified way.*

Bear/बिअर *(noun)* – ले जाना, भालू का बच्चा a large, heavy mammal which walks on the soles of its feet, having thick fur and a very short tail. *Bear is a dangerous animal.*

Bearable/बिअरेबल *(adj)* – सहने योग्य, सहन करने योग्य tolerable. *It is not bearable.*

Beard/बिअर्ड *(noun)* – दाढ़ी a growth of hair on the chin and lower cheeks of a man's face. an animal's growth or marking that is likened to a beard, such as the gills of an oyster. a tuft of hairs or bristles on certain plants. *I am thinking of keeping a French cut beard this time.*

Bearing/बेअरिंग *(noun)* – ढंग, छवि, व्यवहार a person's way of standing, moving, or behaving.

Bearish/बेअरिश *(adj.)* – रीछ के समान, फूहड़ resembling or likened to a bear. *He is a bearish man tall and fat.*

Bearskin/बिअरस्किन *(noun)* – भालू का चमड़ा a tall cap of black fur worn ceremonially by certain troops. *Cap of bearskin with black fur is worn by people in extreme cold.*

Beast/बीस्ट *(noun)* – पशु, चौपाया an animal, especially a large or dangerous mammal. a bovine farm animal. *Lion is a big and dangerous beast.*

Beat/बीट *(verb)* – पीटकर हिलाना, पीटना strike repeatedly and violently so as to hurt or punish them. strike repeatedly so as make a noise. flatten or shape by striking it repeatedly with a hammer. *The teacher beat the student as he had not done his homework.*

Beatify/बिटीफाई *(verb)* – प्रसन्न करना (in the roman catholic church) announce the beatification of. *The church has beatified the dead man. He is in a state of bliss.*

Beating/बिटिंग *(noun)* – मारपीट का दण्ड the act of overcoming or outdoing. *I cannot tolerate such beating*

Beatitude/बिअटिट्यूड *(noun)* – मोक्ष, परम गति supreme blessedness. the blessings listed by Jesus in the sermon on the mount. *He was in a state of supreme beatitude.*

Belle/बेल *(noun)* – छैला, बाँका, रंगीली, सुन्दरी a beautiful girl or woman. *That belle is my fiancée.*

Beau-ideal/बो-आयडियल *(noun)* – अपूर्व सुन्दरता a person or thing representing the highest possible standard of excellence in a particular respect. *Gandhi ji was a beau-ideal.*

Beautiful/ब्यूटीफुल *(adj.)* – सुन्दर, आकर्षक pleasing the senses or mind aesthetically. *My girl friend is very beautiful.*

Beautifully/बियूटीफली *(adv)* – सुन्दर, मनोहर, सुन्दर ढंग से in a beautiful manner. *She worked beautifully.*

Beaver/बिवर *(noun)* – ऊदबिलाव a large semi aquatic board-tailed rodent, noted for its habit of gnawing through trees to fell them in order to make lodges and dams. the soft light brown fur of the beaver. chiefly [historical] a hat made of felted beaver fur. a heavy woolen cloth resembling felted beaver fur. *The beaver has gnawed tho' the tree to make it fall.*

Becalm/बीकाम *(verb)* – शान्त करना leave (a sailing ship) of the typical rhythm of this music. *The ship was becalmed because of lack of wind.*

Became/बीकेम – हुआ past participle of become. *The sea became calm after sometime.*

Because/बिकॉज *(conj.)* – क्योंकि, इस कारण से for the reason that; since. *You can't take the exam because you haven't come in time.*

Beck/बेक *(noun)* – पहाड़ी नाला या नदी, छोटी नाली north English a stream. *Beck lowed through the forest.*

Becoming/बिकमिंग *(adj.)* – उचित, अनुरूप (of clothing) looking well on someone. *This shirt is becoming on you.*

Bed/बेड *(noun)* – पलंग, शय्या a piece of furniture incorporating a mattress or other surface for sleeping or resting on. a place for a patient in a hospital. [informal] used with reference to a bed as a place for sexual activity. *It is time for sleep. I am going to bed.*

Bedaub/बेडॉब *(verb)* – रंग लगाना, रंग पोतना [poetic/literary] smear or daub with a sticky substance. *The doctor bedaubed the wound with a disinfectant.*

Bedazzle/बिडैजल *(verb)* – चमक से चौंधियाना greatly impress with brilliance or skill. *The actress bedazzled the audience with her great beauty.*

Bedchamber/बेडचैम्बर *(noun)* – शयन-गृह [archaic] a bedroom. *This way leads to the bedchamber.*

Bedding/बेडिंग *(noun)* – शयन सामग्री bedclothes. straw or similar material for animals to sleep on. *The bedding must be washed today.*

Bed-fellow/बेड-फेलो *(noun)* – भार्या a person or thing that is closely connected with another. *We are great friends. He is my bedfellow.*

Bedstead/बेडस्टीड *(noun)* – चारपाई, खटिया the framework of a bed. *Mattresses are good but I don't like the bedstead. Have it changed.*

Bed-time/बेडटाइम *(noun)* – निद्रा का समय the usual time when someone goes to bed. *It is bed-time now all must go to sleep.*

B

B

Bee/बी *(noun)* – मधुमक्खी, भ्रमर a stinging social insect which collects nectar and pollen form flowers and produces wax and honey. [apis mellifera and other species.] *Honeybees are dangerous insects should you try to get their honey they will attack you.*

Beech/बीच *(noun)* – एक प्रकार का जंगली विशाल वृक्ष a large tree with smooth grey bark, glossy leaves, and hard, pale, fine-grained wood. [fagus sylvaticus and other species.] *Mussourie forests are full of beech trees.*

Beef/बीफ *(noun)* – गोमाँस the flesh of a cow, bull, or ox, used as food. farming a cow, bull, or ox fattened for its meat. [informal] flesh with well developed muscle. strength or power. the substance of a matter. *Hindus do not eat beef.*

Beefy/बीफी *(adj.)* – माँसयुक्त, ठोस मांसल *He is a beefy fellow with all muscles and power.*

Beehive/बीहाइव *(noun)* – मधुमक्खी का कृत्रिम घर 1. a structure in which bees are kept, typically in the form of a dome or box. *Bees are kept in a dome or box called beehive.*

Been/बिन – हो आना, रहना होना past participle of be. *He has been watching TV for two hours news.*

Beestings/बीस्टिंग *(plural noun)*– माँ का पहला दूध the first milk produced by a cow or goat after giving birth. *Would you like to taste Beestings.*

Beet/बीट *(noun)* – चुकन्दर a herbaceous plant cultivated as a source of food for humans and livestock, and for processing into sugar. *Eating beet root is good for health.*

Beeves/बीव्स – गाय, बैल आदि पशु plural form of beef (in sense 1 of the noun.) *A lot of Europeans eat beeves.*

Befall/बिफाल *(verb)* – आ पड़ना, बीतना [poetic/ literary] (especially of something bad) happen to. *A great misfortune befell him.*

Before/बिफोर *(prep., conj. & adv.)* – आगे, पहले during the period of time preceding. *Our ancestors were there before us.*

Befoul/बिफॉल *(verb)* – गन्दा करना, बदनाम करना make dirty; pollute. *He has befouled the whole atmosphere by his abusive language.*

Befriend/बिफ्रेंड *(verb)* – मित्र बन जाना act as or become a friend to. *Although you have talked ill of me I'll still befriend you.*

Began/बिगेन – आरम्भ किया past of begin. *He began to earn from the age of eight.*

Beget/बिगेट *(verb)* – उपजाना, जन्म देना [archaic] or [poetic/literary] produce (a child). *She Beget me a son.*

Begging/बेगिंग *(noun)* – याचना, प्रार्थना a solicitation of money or food (in the street by on apparently penniless person). *Begging is something in human.*

Beginner/बिगिनर *(noun)* – आरम्भ करने वाला someone new to a field activity. *He is a beginner in cricket.*

Begone/बिगॉन – दूर हट! अलग रह! exclamatory archaic go away at once! *No more talking begone!*

Begot/बिगॉट – पैदा किया past of beget. *I begot a son from her.*

Behalf/बिहाफ *(noun)* – किसी के लिए, किसी की ओर से (in phrase on behalf of or on someone's behalf) in the interests of a persons, group, or principle. *I am here on behalf of the director.*

Behave/बिहेव *(verb)* – आचरण करना, व्यवहार करना act or conduct oneself in a specified way. *Will you behave yourself?*

Behead/बिहेड *(verb)* – सिरकाट देना cut off the head of (someone), especially as a form of execution. *In old times execution was often done by beheading.*

Behest/बिहेस्ट *(noun)* – आज्ञा, आदेश [poetic/ literary] a person's orders or command. *The troops advanced on behest of their commander.*

Behold/बिहोल्ड *(verb)* – देखना [archaic] or [poetic/literary] see or observe. *Behold! Here is my son.*

Beholden/बिहोल्डन *(adj.)* – अनुगृहीत, कृतज्ञ indebted. *I am beholden to you for this favour.*

Behoof/बिहूफ *(noun)* – लाभ, सुविधा, उपकार [archaic] benefit or advantage. *He purchased this for his own behoof.*

Behove/बिहोव *(verb)* – योग्य, उचित होना, उपयुक्त होना formal it is a duty, responsibility, or appropriate response for someone to do something. *It would behove you to be respectful to your elders.*

Being/बिइंग *(noun)* – अस्तित्व, प्रकृति, वह जिसका अस्तित्व हो, जन्तु existence. living; being alive. *It is my being here that matters most.*

Belated/बिलेटिड *(adj.)* – बहुत देर में आने वाला, विलंबित offer the expected or usual time delayed. *I have received your belated birthday greetings.*

Belay/बिले (verb) - लपेटकर बाँधना fix round a rock, pin, or other object to secure it. *Rock climbers use belay for secure footing.*

Belch/बेल्च (verb) - ओकाना, डकारना vomit wind noisily form the stomach through the mouth. *He belched noisily and everyone looked at him.*

Beleguer/बिलिगर (verb) - घेर लेना lay siege to. *The army beleguered the town.*

Belfry/बेलफ्राइ (noun) - घण्टाघर the place in a bell tower or steeple in which bells are housed. *Huge bells are hung in towers in belfry.*

Belie/बिलाइ (noun) - असत्य बनाना, झूठा साबित करना an acceptance that something exists or is true, especially one without proof. a firmly held opinion or conviction. a religious conviction.

Believable/बिलिवेब्ल (adj.) - विश्वास के योग्य, विश्वसनीय capable of being believed. *I find your statement believable.*

Belike/बिलाइक (adv.) - कदाचित् with considerable certainty without much doubt.

Belittle/बिलिटल (verb) - छोटा करना, न्यून करना, महत्त्व घटाना dismiss as unimportant. *I belittled his importance by ignoring him.*

Belladonna/बेलाडोना (noun) - धतूरा, अंगूरशेफ्य, कंटालिका deadly nightshade. a drug made from this plant, containing atropine. *Belladonna is a famous homeopathy drug.*

Belle/बेल (noun) - सुन्दरी, रूपवती स्त्री a beautiful girl or woman. *That belle is my fiancée.*

Bellicose/बेलीकोस (adj.) - लड़ाका, लड़ने को तत्पर aggressive; ready to fight. *He is a very bellicose person ever ready to fight.*

Belligerent/बेलिजरेंट (adj.) - शत्रुतापूर्ण, आक्रामक hostile and aggressive. engaged in a war or conflict. noun a nation or person engaged in war or conflict. *This one is belligerent country it sure will pick up a fight with some other country.*

Bell-metal/बेलमेटल (noun)- मिश्र धातु जिनके मेल से घण्टे बनते है an alloy of copper and tin for making bells, with a higher tin content than in bronze. *Bells are made of two metals copper and tin.*

Bellow/बेलो (verb) - डकारना, गरजना emit a loud, deep roar, typically in pain or anger. shout or sing very loudly. noun a loud, deep shout or sound. *He bellowed in anger.*

Bellows/बेलोज (noun & plural noun) - भाथी, धौंकनी a device with an air bag that emits a stream of air when squeezed together with two handles, used for blowing air into a fire. a similar device used in a harmonium or small organ. *In old times bellows were used to blow air into the furnance.*

Belly/बेली (noun) - पेट, उदर the front part of the human truck below the ribs, containing the stomach and bowels. the stomach, especially as representing the body's need for food. a cut of pork from the underside between the legs. *My belly is only half full give me more food.*

Belong/बिलांग (verb) - किसी की सम्पत्ति होना be rightly placed in or assigned to a specified position. *I belong to Khan family and I am in my right belonging.*

Beloved/बिलव्ड (adj.) - प्रिय, इष्ट, प्यारा dearly loved. noun a much loved person. *She is my beloved.*

Belt/बेल्ट (noun) - पेटी, कमरबन्द, विशिष्ट गुणों वाला क्षेत्र a strip of leather or other material worn round the waist to support or hold in clothes or to carry weapons. a belt worn as a sign of rank or achievement, ishment of being struck with a belt. *The green belt around Delhi is increasing.*

Belvedere/बेल्विडिअर (noun) - दृश्य देखने का ऊँचा मंच a summer house or other building positioned to command a fine view. *I stood in the belvedere and looked down on the scene pleasant.*

Bemire/बिमाअर (verb) - कीचड़ पोतना [archaic] cover or stain with mud. *It was raining and my clothes got bemired.*

Bemoan/बिमोन (verb) - विलाप करना lament or express sorrow for. *I bemoaned the loss of my friend.*

Bemuse/बिम्यूज (verb) - उलझन में, स्पष्ट रूप से काम करने में असमर्थ confuse or bewilder. *I found him in a drunk and bemused condition.*

Bend/बेन्ड (verb) - मोड़ना, झुकना, टेढ़ा करना shape or force (something straight) into a curve or angle. (of a road, river, or path) deviate from a straight line. *I bend the branch and plucked the fruit.*

Beneath/बिनीथ (prep.& adv.) - नीचे, नीचे की ओर extending or directly underneath. *You are beneath me in rank.*

B

Benefaction/बेनिफैक्शन *(noun)* – धर्मदान, उपकार [informal] a donation or gift. *The rich man gave the orphanage a big benefaction.*

Benefice/बेनिफिस *(noun)* – पादरी की वृत्ति, धर्मवृत्ति a church office. typically that of a rector or vicar, for which property and income are provided in respect of pastoral duties. *The man sitting in the benefic is our vicar.*

Beneficence/बेनिफिसेंस *(noun)* – हित, दया, कृपा doing good, feeling beneficent.

Beneficiary/बेनिफिशरी *(noun)* – धर्मस्व प्राप्तकर्ता, किसी की मृत्यु के बाद धन या सम्पत्ति प्राप्त करने वाला a person who gains benefit from something, especially a trust or will. *His father left him a lot of money in his will that makes him a beneficiary.*

Benefit/बेनिफिट *(noun & verb)* – लाभ, सुविधा, प्राप्त करने वाला an advantage or profit gained from something. *I have benefited a lot from your friendship.*

Benevolence/बेनिवोलन्स *(noun)* – दया, कृपा, सुजनता disposition to do good; an inclination to do kind of charitable acts. *His benevolence earned him a lot of fame.*

Benevolent/बेनिवोलेन्ट *(adj.)* – शुभचिन्तक, उदार well meaning and kingly. *A benevolent person works more for charity than for profit.*

Benighted/बिनाइटेड *(adj.)* – अन्धकार से आच्छादित in a state of intellectual or moral ignorance. *He is a benighted person not knowing what is moral or intellectual.*

Benign/बिनाइन *(adj.)* – सौम्य या उदार, कृपालु, सुखप्रद genial kingly. *This tumour is not malign but benign.*

Benison/बेनीजन *(noun)* – वरदान, आशीर्वाद [poetic/ literary] a blessing. *He has received benison from the priest.*

Bent/बेन्ट – झुकाव, रुचि, मुड़ा, टेढ़ा past and past participle of bend. adjective. sharply curved or having an angle. *I saw a bent iron rod in the junkyard.*

Benzene/बेनज़ीन *(noun)* – दाग छुड़ाने का तेल chemistry a volatile liquid hydrocarbon present in coaltar and petroleum, having a hexagonal ring-shaped molecule which is the basis of most aromatic organic compounds. [C_6H_6]. *The molecule present in benzene is the basis of most organic compounds.*

Benzoin/बेनज़ोइन *(noun)* – लोहबान a fragrant gum resin obtained from certain East Asian storax trees. *I like the fragrant smell of benzoin.*

Bequeath/बिक्वीथ *(verb)* – वसीयत द्वारा सम्पत्ति छोड़ जाना leave to a person or other beneficiary by a will. hand down or pass on. *He bequeathed all his money to a charity institution.*

Bequest/बिक्वेस्ट *(noun)* – इच्छापत्र द्वारा छोड़ी हुई सम्पत्ति the action of bequeathing. something that is bequeathed. *The bequest of money took place when he was about to die.*

Bergamot/बरगामॉट *(noun)* – नारंगी की जाति का वृक्ष an oily substance extracted from a variety of Seville orange, used in cosmetics and as flavouring in Earl Grey tea. *The tree bergamot bears the fruit Seville orange.*

Beri-Beri/बेरी–बेरी *(noun)* – जलन्धर के प्रकार का एक रोग a disease causing inflammation of the nerves and heart failure, ascribed to a deficiency of vitamin B_1. *Due to deficiency of vitamin B_1 my uncle was affected with Beriberi.*

Berry/बेरी *(noun)* – एक प्रकार का बेर, सरस फल a small roundish juicy fruit without a stone. botany any fruit that has its seeds enclosed in a fleshy pulp, for example a banana or tomato. *I am fond of eating berries.*

Beryl/बेरल *(noun* – हरितमणि, बिल्लौर फीरोजा a transparent pale green, blue, or yellow mineral consisting of a silicate of beryllium and aluminum, sometimes used as a gemstone. *Jweller sometimes use beryl as a gemstone.*

Beside/बिसाइड *(prep.)* – पास, समीप at the side of; next to. compared with. *He sat beside me in the bus.*

Besides/बिसाइडज *(prep.)* – सिवाय, अतिरिक्त के साथ भी in addition to; apart from. adverb in addition; as well. used to introduce an additional idea or explanation. *Serve me lunch besides I would like a coffee.*

Besiege/बिसीज *(verb)* – सेना की सहायता से घेर लेना surround with armed forces in order to capture it or force its surrender. crowd round oppressively. *Town has been besieged by army.*

Besmear/बिस्मीर *(verb)* – लेप करना पोतना, गंदा करना [poetic/literary] smear or cover with. *He had a bullet wound and was besmeared with blood.*

Besmirch/बिस्मर्च *(verb)* – कीचड़ उछालना, गन्दा करना, अन्धकार करना damage (someone's reputation). *Even if you besmirch in public, his sound reputation will remain intact.*

Bespotter/बिस्पॉटर *(verb)* – अपमानित करना spatter. *He bespattered other religion.*

Bespeak/बिस्पीक *(verb)* – पहले से शर्त कर लेना be evidence of. *I bespeak you to reserve a seat for me in Rajdhani Express.*

Besprinkle/बिस्प्रींकल *(verb)* – छिड़कना [poetic/literary] sprinkle with liquid, powder, etc. *All the wedding guests were besprinkle with fragrant scent.*

Bestead/बिस्टेड *(verb)* – काम में लाना, सहायता देना to avail, to help. *I can bestead it.*

Bestir/बिस्टिर *(verb)* – चेष्टा करना exert or rouse oneself. *I woke up and bestirred myself.*

Bestow/बिस्टो *(verb)* – प्रतिपादन करना, देना, आदर व्यक्त करने के लिए confer (an honour, right, or gift). *The title was betowed on him by the parson.*

Bestrew/बेरट्रियू *(verb)* – छितरना, फैलाना [poetic/literary] scatter or lie scattered over (a surface). *Dry leaves were bestrewed all over the ground.*

Bet/बेट *(verb)* – दाँव लगाना risk a sum of money or other valued item against someone else's on the basis of the outcome of an unpredictable event such as a race or game. *This party team looks a good bet for victory.*

Beta/बिटा *(noun)* – ग्रीक वर्णमाला का दूसरा अक्षर the second letter of the Greek alphabet transliterated as 'b'. denoting the second of a series of items or categories. British a second-class mark given for a piece of work. *As in Greek alphabet 'B' is the second letter so it is in English language.*

Betake/बिटेक *(verb)* – आश्रय लेना, लगाना [poetic/literary] go to. *I have to betake here.*

Beteem/बिटीम *(verb)* – बहाना, उत्पन्न करना to bring forth. *She will beteem this in the drain.*

Betel/बिटृल *(noun)* – पान, ताम्बूल the leaf of an Asian evergreen climbing plant, which in the east is chewed and used as a mild stimulant. *Betel leave are chewed by people in Asia.*

Bethink/बिथिंक *(verb)* – विचारना, सोचना, याद करना [informal] come to think. *Bethink he has not come today.*

Betide/बिटाइड *(verb)* – आ पड़ना, होना [poetic/literary] in good time; early. *Woe betide that rascal.*

Betimes/बिटाइम्ज़ *(adverb)* – यथासमय, शीघ्र [poetic/literary] in good time; early. *We must be up betimes tomorrow.*

Betoken/बिटोकन *(verb)* – दरसाना, सूचना देना [poetic/literary] be a warning or sign of. *Those black clouds betoken rain.*

Betroth/बिट्राथ *(verb)* – वचन देना, सगाई होना विद्रोह formally engaged to be married. noun the person to whom one is engaged. *She is betrothed to that gentleman.*

Better/बेटर *(adj.)* – उच्चतर, श्रेष्ठतर, बेहतर more desirable, satisfactory, or effective. more appropriate, advantageous, or well advised. *You won't find a better coffee shop than this one.*

Betwixt/बिट्वीवस्ट *(prep.&adv.)* – अन्तर में archaic term for between. *Let this secret be hidden betwixt we two people.*

Beverage/बेवरिज *(noun)* – कोई पेय पदार्थ a drink other than water. *In beverages I like coca cola the most.*

Bewail/बिवेल *(verb)* – विलाप करना greatly regret or lament. *She is bewailing the loss of her husband.*

Beware/बिवेअर *(verb)* – सावधान होना, सचेत होना be cautious and alert to risks or dangers. *Beware of this dog. It is a bad tempered one.*

Bewilder/बिबिल्डर *(verb)* – उलझन में डालना, भरमाना perplex or confuse. *I was bewildered not to find my friend at home.*

Beyond/बिऑन्ड *(prep.&adv.)* – बाहर, अतिरिक्त, परे, दूर at or to the further side of. more extensive or extreme than. *The city we have to reach in beyond that jungle.*

Bezique/बिज़ीक् *(noun)* – ताश का एक प्रकार का खेल a trick-taking card game for two, played with a double pack of 64 cards, including the seven to ace only in each suit. the holding of the queen of spades and the jack of diamonds in this game. *He is an expert in the card game of bezique.*

Bi/बाइ – दोहरा, दुबारा symbolic the chemical element bismuth. *Bi the chemical elements of bismuth.*

Bias/बायस् *(noun)* – भार, पक्षपात, झुकाव inclination or prejudice for or against one thing or person. a systematic distortion of a statistical result due to a factor not allowed for in its derivation. *My boss is biassed against me.*

Biaxial/बाइएक्सीअल *(adj.)* – दो धुरा वाला having or relating to two axes. *All four wheelers are biaxial.*

B

Bib/बिब *(noun)* – छोटा कपड़ा जो बच्चों की छाती पर फिट होते है a piece of cloth or plastic fastened round a child's neck to keep its clothes clean while eating. a loose-fitting sleeveless garment worn for identification. e.g. by competitors and officials at sporting events. the part above the waist of the front of an apron or pair of dungarees. *This child is wearing a beautiful bib round its neck.*

Bibber/बिबर *(noun)* – पियक्कड़ one given to drinking, top part of an apron covering the chest.

Bible/बाइबल *(noun)* – ईसाइयों की धर्म पुस्तक the Christian scriptures, consisting of the old and new testaments. the Jewish scriptures, consisting of the torah or [law], the prophets, and the hagiographa or writings. *Bible is largest selling book in the world.*

Bibliographer/बिब्लीओग्राफर *(noun)* – साहित्यिक ग्रन्थों का इतिहास-लेखक someone trained in compiling bibliographies.

Bibliography/बिब्लीआग्राफी *(noun)* – पुस्तक विद्या, ग्रन्थ-सूची a list of sources referred to in a particular work. a list of the books of a specific author or on a specific subject. *Most books have bibliography at the end. Telling us which books or other material have been consulted.*

Bibulous/बिब्यूलस *(adj.)* formal excessively fond of drinking alcohol. *He is a bibulous man. Very fond of drinking.*

Bibulous/बिब्यूलस *(adj.)* – जल सोखने वाला (of a legislative body) having two chambers.

Bicameral/बिकैमरल *(noun)* – दोधरा, द्विगृही the two hundredth anniversary of a significant event. *This lawyer's office is bicameral.*

Bicentenary/बाइसेन्टिनरी *(adj.)* – दो सौ वर्ष पर होने वाला Mahatma Gandhis bicentenarywill be hold in 2069. *Bicentenary is celebrated of many big events.*

Bicephalous/बायसेफेलस *(adj.)* – दो सिर वाला having two heads. *These children's bodies are joined together and only a surgeon can separate them.*

Bicker/बिकर *(verb)* – बेकार की बात पर, कलह करना, वेग से बहना argue about petty and trivial matters. *He is always bickering about pocket money with his parent.*

Bicuspid/बिकस्पिड *(adj.)* – दो नोकों वाला दाँत having two cusps or points. noun a tooth with two cusps, especially a human premolar tooth. *Two of his teeth are bicuspid let us consult a dentist.*

Bid/बिड *(verb)*- आज्ञा देना, घोषणा करना offer for something, especially at an auction. (of a contractor) tender for work. *At auction I'll bid for this painting.*

Biddable/बिडेब्ल *(adj.)* – आज्ञा मानने वाला meekly ready to accept and follow instructions. *He is a biddable person and will do as you say.*

Bidder/बिडर *(noun)* – दाँव लगाने वाला someone who makes an offer. *He is a smart bidder.*

Bidding/बिडिंग – आज्ञा, आदेश *Bidding is a tricky and intelligent game.*

Bide/बाइड *(verb)* – रहना, ठहरना [archaic] or dialect remain or stay in a certain place. *You can bide with me while you are in town.*

Biennial/बाइएनीअल *(adj.)* – दो-दो साल में होने वाला, द्वैवार्षिक taking place every second year. compare with biannual. *It is a biennial plant and will die in two years.*

Bier/बायर *(noun)* – अर्थी, जनाजा a movable platform on which a coffin or corpse is placed before burial. *The dead body was carried on a bier to the crematorium.*

Bifacial/बायफेसियल *(adj.)* – दो चेहरे वाला having two faces, or two different faces. *A bifacial child was born to her.*

Bifurcate/बाइफर्केट *(verb)* – दो भागों में विभाजित करना divide into two branches or forks. adjective forked; branched. *This lengthy volume has been bifurcated.*

Bigamist/बाइगेमिस्ट *(noun)* – द्विविवाही some oine who marries one person while already legally *He is a bigamist having two wives.*

Bigamy/बाइगैमि *(noun)* – द्विपत्नीत्व the offence of marrying someone while already married to another person. *Practicing bigamy is against the law.*

Bight/बाइट *(noun)* – घुमाव, झूलन a curve or recess in a coastline or other geographical feature. *The bight was beautiful and many person bathed there.*

Bigot/बिगॉट *(noun)* – हठधर्मी, कट्टर a person who is prejudiced in their views and intolerant of the opinions of others. *He is a bigot it is impossible to convince him of anything other than his own belief.*

Bike/बाइक *(noun)* – बाइसिकिल शब्द का छोटा रूप a bicycle or motorcycle. verb ride a bicycle or motorcycle. *I have purchased a new bike.*

B

Bilateral/बाइलैटरल *(adj.)* – द्विपक्षीय having or relating to two sides. involving two parties. *It is a bilateral agreement.*

Bile/बाइल *(noun)* – पित्त a bitter greenish-brown alkaline fluid secreted by the liver and stored in the gall bladder, which aids digestion. *Bile helps digest food.*

Biliary/बिलिएरी *(adj.)* – पित्त सम्बन्धी, पैत्तिक medicine of or relating to bile or the bile duct. *His liver is not right so he is taking some biliary.*

Billingual/बाइलिङ्ग्वल *(adj.)* – दो भाषाओं से सम्बन्धित speaking two languages fluently. expressed in or using two languages. *He is bilingual and can speak Tamil and Hindi fluently.*

Bilious/बिलियस *(adj.)* – पैत्तिक, पित्तग्रस्त affected by or associated with nausea or vomiting. *He is feeling bilious may be he will vomit.*

Bilateral/बाइलैटरल *(adj)* – दो अक्षरों का, द्विपक्षीय, दोतरफा involving two groups of people or two counties. *It is a bilateral agreement.*

Bilk/बिल्क *(verb)* – धोखा देना, छलना, ठगना [informal] cheat or defraud. obtain fraudulently. *He has bilked me of Rs. One million. I am going to lodge an FIR.*

Billet/बिलेट *(noun)* – निजी आवास का भाग जब सैनिक अस्थायी रूप से टिकते है a civilian where soldiers are lodged temporarily. verb lodge in a civilian house. *Right now the troops are lodged in a billet soon may will move out.*

Billion/बिलियन *(noun)* – एक अरब की संख्या [cardinal number] the number equivalent to the product of a thousand and a million; 1,000,000,000 or 10^9. dated, chiefly British a million million. *He has got a billion rupees i.e. thousand millions.*

Billow/बिल्लो *(noun)* – तरंग, बड़ी लहर, लहराना a large undulating mass of cloud, smoke, or steam. *In the distance we could see a thick line of billows.*

Billy-goat/बिलिगोट *(noun)* – बकरा a male goat. *He has three Billy- goats and two she- goats.*

Bimetallic/बाइमेटलिक *(adj.)* – दो धातुओं से मिलकर बना made or consisting of two metals. [historical] of or relating to bimetallism. *This vase is bimetallic made of two metals copper and tin.*

Bimonthly/बाइमन्थली *(adj.&adv.)* – त्रैमासिक appering every two months. *This magazine is bimonthly.*

Binary/बायनरी *(adj.)* – दोहरा जोड़ा, युग्मक composed of, or involving two things. *This problem is i.e. twofold composed of two parts.*

Bind/बाइन्ड *(verb)* – बाँधना, कसना tie of fasten (something) tightly together. restrain by tying their hands and feet. wrap or encircle tightly. *Bind the two ends of the rope together.*

Binocular/बायनोक्युलर *(adj.)* – दोनों आँखों से देखने वाला दूरबीन an optical instrament designed for simultaneoues use by both eyes. *I looked at the distant object with a binocular.*

Biogenesis/बाइओजेनिसिस *(noun)* – जीव से जीव की उत्पत्ति का सिद्धान्त the synthesis of substances by living organisms. *According to biogenesis a living matter given rise to another living matter.*

Biography/बायोग्राफी *(noun)* – किसी व्यक्ति का जीवन-वृत्तान्त an account of someone's life written by someone else. *I have read the biography of Tolstoy. It is fascinating.*

Biological/बायलोजिकल *(adj.)* – जीव विज्ञान सम्बन्धी of or relating to [biology] or living organisms. containing enzymes to assist the process of cleaning. *They are his biological parents.*

Biology/बायोलॉजी *(noun)* – जीव विज्ञान the scientific study of living organisms. the plants and animals of a particular area. the features of a particular organism or class of organisms. *I have taken biology as a subject it fascinates me to no end.*

Biscope/बाइस्कोप *(noun)* – चलते-फिरते परदे पर चलचित्र a kind of early movie projector. *I want to see a film in bioscope.*

Biparous/बायपरस *(adj.)* – दो बच्चे एक साथ जनने वाले producing two offspring at a time.

Bipedal/बायपेडल *(adj.)* – दो पैर वाला having two feet.

Biplane/बाइप्लेन *(noun)* – दो पंखे वाला वायुयान an early type of aircraft with two pairs of wings, one above the other. *Early planes used to be called biplanes as they had one wing over the other.*

Bipolar/बाइपोलर *(adj.)* – द्विध्रुवीय having or relating to two poles or extremities. of or occurring in both polar regions. *He is an authority over bipolar animal life.*

Birch/बर्च *(noun)* – भोजपत्र a slender hardy tree which has thin, peeling, typically silver-grey or white bark and yields a hard, pale, fine-

B

grained wood. *There are a lot of birch trees in Mussourie.*

Birdlime/बर्डलाइम *(noun)* - चिड़िया पकड़ने का लासा a substance spread on to twigs to trap small birds. *People trap small birds by spreading birdlime over twigs once they sit over it they can't fly away.*

Bird's eye/बर्ड्स आई *(noun)* - विशालदर्शी ऊँचे स्थान से देखा हुआ seen from above. *I have taken a bird's eye view of the problem. We shall go in detail later.*

Birth/बर्थ *(noun)* - जन्म, आरम्भ the emergence of a baby or other young from the body of its mother; the start of life as a physically separate being. *My sister gave birth to a daughter.*

Biscuit/बिस्किट *(noun)* - बिस्कुट [British] a small, flat, crisp unleavened cake. [north American] a small, soft round cake like a scone. *Biscuits are very popular in European countries.*

Bisect/बाइसेक्ट *(verb)* - समद्विभाग करना divide into two parts. *Now I'll bisect this circle.*

Bisexual/बायसेक्सुअल *(adj.)* - द्विलिंगीय sexually attracted to both men and women. *He is bisexual by nature attracted sexually to both men and women.*

Bismuth/बिस्मथ - काँसा, फूल a heavy brittle aliamagnetic trivallent metallic etement.

Bison/बाइजन *(noun)* - जंगली साँड़ humpbacked shaggyharied wild ox. [Bison bison (the [north American] buffalo) and b. bonasus (Europe, now only Poland).] *Bison is a huge north American buffalo.*

Bisque/बिस्क *(noun)* - बिना पालिश किये हुए चीनी मिट्टी a rich soup made from lobster of other shelifish. *I very much like to drink in bisque.*

Bistoury/बिस्टॉरी *(noun)* - जर्राह की पतली छुरी a surgical knife with a straight or curved narrow blade. *Surgeon work with a bistoury.*

Bit/बिट *(noun)* - खण्ड, लगाम की मुखी, छोटा टुकड़ा a small piece, quantity, or extent of something. *Let me have a bit of bread.*

Bitch/बिच *(noun)* - सियारिन, कुतिया a female dog, wolf, fox or otter. *I have named my bitch Sophie.*

Bite/बाइट *(verb)* - कुतरना, डंक मारना, दंश use the teeth to cut into something. wound with a sting, pincers, or fangs. *I bit a loaf of bread.*

Bitter/बिटर *(adj.)* - तीता, कठोर, कड़वाहट having a sharp, pungent taste or smell; not sweet. *Bitter gourd is a bitter vegetable.*

Bitumen/बिट्यूमेन *(noun)* - सड़कों या छतों पर डाला जाने वाला गाढ़ा तारकोल डामर बिटुमन a black viscous mixture of hydrocarbons obtained naturally or as a residue from petroleum distillation, used for road surfacing and roofing. *We need more bitumen for road and roof surfacing.*

Bivalve/बाइवाल्व *(noun)* - दो कपाट वाला, द्विकपाटी an aquatic mollusc which has a compressed body enclosed withing two hinged shelles, such as an oyster, mussel, or scallop.

Bivouac/बाइवॉक *(noun)* - पड़ाव में ठहरना, पड़ाव a temporary camp without tents or cover. verb stay in such a camp. *We stayed in bivouac camp it was so exciting and funny.*

Bizzare/बिजार *(adj.)* - अनोखा, विचित्र strange; unusual. *Yes tonight I saw a bizarre dream.*

Blab/ब्लैब *(verb)* - बड़बड़ करना reveal secrets or confidential information.

Black/ब्लैक *(adj.)* - काला, स्याह, प्रकाशरहित of the very darkest colour due to the absence of or complete absorption of light. deeply stained with dirt. served without milk. *Black is the opposite of white.*

Black-guard/ब्लैगार्ड *(noun)* - दुराचारी, अधम a man who behaves in a dishonourable or contemptible way. verb disparage or denounce. *He has betrayed us. He is a blackguard.*

Blackmail/ब्लैकमेल *(noun)* - डरा-धमका कर अवैध रूप से लिया गया पैसा the action of demanding money from someone in return for not revealing discreditable information. the use of threats or unfair manipulating in an attempt to influence someone's actions. verb subject to blackmail. *His grandson was kidnapped and he was subjected to blackmail.*

Blackness/ब्लैकनेस *(adj.)* - कालापन darkness. *Blackness has surrounded the place.*

Bladder/ब्लैडर *(noun)* - मूत्राशय a muscular membranous sac in the abdomen which receives urine from the kidneys and stores it for excretion. *My bladder is almost bursting please show me the toilet.*

Blame/ब्लेम *(verb)* - निन्दा करना, दोष लगाना assign responsibility for a fault or wrong to. noun responsibility for a fault or wrong. *There was an accident and the blame fell on the truck driver.*

Blameless/ब्लेमलेस *(adj.)* – निर्दोष free of guilt not subject to blame. *I find him blameless so he is free to go.*

Blameworthy/ब्लेमवर्दी *(adj.)* – निन्दा के योग्य, कसूरवार *This fellow is blameworthy as he caused the accident.*

Blanch/ब्लांच *(verb & noun)* – भय से पीला पड़ जाना make or become white or pale. *The blanched potatoes were immersed in boiling water and then peeled.*

Bland/ब्लैंड *(adj.)* – नम्र, विनीत, कोमल, चिकना lacking strong features or characteristics and therefore uninteresting. lacking flavour or seasoning insipid. *He is a bland fellow lacking any features or characteristics. I have no interest in him.*

Blandish/ब्लैंडिश *(verb)* – मीठे वचन से चापलूसी करना [archaic] coax with kind words or flattery. *I blandished her a lot and she became happy.*

Blanket/ब्लैंकेट *(noun)* – कम्बल, धुस्सा a large place of woolen material used as a covering for warmth, as on a bed. *I bought a good quality blanket from the market.*

Blare/ब्लेअर *(noun & verb)* – चिल्लाकर बोलना, गरजना sound loudly and harshly. noun a loud, harsh sound. *A blare of trumpets welcomed the king.*

Blasphemy/ब्लासफेमी *(noun)* – ईश्वर-निन्दा करना speak irreverently about God or sacred things. *He talked ill of God and thus blasphemed.*

Blast/ब्लास्ट *(noun)* – आँधी, भभकन, विस्फोट a destructive wave of highly compressed air spreading outwards from an explosion. *Suddenly there was a bomb blast in the market.*

Blatter/ब्लैटर *(verb)* – बकझक करना [informal] move or strike with a clatter. *The warriors attacked each other with a clatter of swords.*

Blaze/ब्लेज *(noun)* – प्रभा, चमक a white stripe down the face of a horse or other animal. *Captain cook was a trail blazer. He was the first to reach North pole.*

Blazon/ब्लेजॉन *(verb)* – प्रचार करना, फैलाना, कुलचिह्न display or report prominently or vividly. *He reported the incident in a blazon way.*

Bleach/ब्लीच *(verb)* – धोना, सफेद करना, तिलांजित करना cause to become white or much lighter to a chemical process or by exposure to sunlight. *This shirt has been bleached that is why it is looking so light and white.*

Bleaching/ब्लीचिंग *(noun.)* – वस्त्र इत्यादि सफेद करने की कला *I have purchased a packet of bleaching powder. It is best for washing dirty white shirts.*

Blear/ब्लीअर *(noun)* – मन्द करना, चौंधा देना, a small silvery river fish of the carp family. *I am fond of the silvery blear.*

Bleb/ब्लेब *(noun)* – फफोला a small blister on the skin. [biology] a rounded outgrowth on the surface of a cell. *Doctors have discovered a bleb on the surface of one of my cells.*

Bleed/ब्लीड *(noun)* – रक्त बहाना, तरस खाना lose blood from the body as a result of injury or illness. *He was bleeding profusely after the accident.*

Blemish/ब्लेमिश *(noun)* – दोष, कलंक a small mark or flaw which spoils the appearance of something. *There is a blemish on this diamond which has spoiled its appearance.*

Blend/ब्लेंड *(verb)* – मिलाना mix and combine with something else. *Mixing two things means blending them.*

Blessed/ब्लेसेड *(adj.)* – धन्य, सुखी fortunate. *Blessed are the meek for they shall also enter heaven'.*

Blessing/ब्लेसिंग *(adj.)* – ईश्वर की कृपा, सौभाग्य, वरदान make holly; consecrated. a title preceding the name of a dead person considered to have led a holy life, especially a person formally beatified by the roman catholic church. *I am praying for God's favour and blessings.*

Bleast/ब्लेस्ट *(adj.)* – पवित्र [archaic] or [poetic/ literary] term for blessed.

Blether/ब्लेथर *(noun)* – बड़बड़ करना, बकवास chiefly Scottish another term for blater.

Blew/ब्ल्यू *(verb)* – बहा-उड़ा past of blow. *Wind blew away my clothes.*

Blight/ब्लाइट *(noun)* – पाला, गेरूई a plant disease, especially one caused by fungi such as mildews, rusts, and smuts. *The growth of this plant has been infected by blight.*

Blimp/ब्लिम्प *(noun)* – एक प्रकार का छोटा हवाई जहाज [informal British] a pompous, reactionary person. *He owned a blimp and was fond of flying it.*

Blind/ब्लाइण्ड *(adj.)* – अन्धा, नेत्र ज्योतिहीन हो जाना या कर देना unable to see because of injury, disease, or a congenital condition. *He is blind person he can't see anything.*

B

B

Blindfold/ब्लाइन्डफोल्ड *(verb)* – आँखो पर पट्टी बाँधना without seeing. *He blind folded his eyes.*

Blindly/ब्लाइन्डली *(adv.)* – टटोलते हुए, बिना देखे without seeing or looking. *He obeyed me blindly.*

Blindness/ब्लाइन्डनेस *(noun)* – अन्धता, अज्ञान the state of being blind or lacking sight. *Blindness occurred to him because of weak eye nerve.*

Blink/ब्लिंक *(verb)* – पलक मारना, मिचकाना shut and open the eyes quickly. *As he suddenly confronted bright lights he blinked his eyes.*

Bliss/ब्लिस *(noun)*– परम सुख perfect happiness. a state of spiritual blessedness. verb [informal] be in a state of perfect happiness, oblivious to everything else. *He has been meditating long and now he is in a state of bliss.*

Blister/ब्लिस्टर *(noun)* – छाला, फफोला a small bubble on the skin filled with serum and typically caused by friction or burning. *The sole of his feet got blisters as he walked barefooted in the desert.*

Blithe/ब्लाइद् *(adj.)* – प्रसन्नवदन, आनन्दित cheerfully or thoughtlessly indifferent. *She is a blithe child always happy and playful.*

Blizzard/ब्लिजार्ड *(noun)* – बर्फीली आँधी a severe snowstorm with high winds. *We were trapped in a blizzard.*

Blockade/ब्लॉकेड *(noun & verb)* – अवरोध, रोकना an act of sealing off a place to prevent goods or people from entering or leaving. *There is a police blockade on the road.*

Blockhead/ब्लॉकहेड *(noun)* – मूर्ख, मतिहीन मनुष्य a stupid person, used to express law opinion of someone.

Blockish/ब्लॉकिश *(adj.)* – मूर्ख, बुद्धिहीन bulky or crude in form. *He is a blockish fellow.*

Blond/ब्लांड *(noun)* – गोरा मनुष्य जिसके बाल हल्के रंग के हों a person with pair skin and hair.

Bloody/ब्लडी *(adj.)* – निर्दयी, हत्यारा covered with or composed of blood. *The dead body was too bloody.*

Bloom/ब्लूम *(noun)* – कली, फूल a mass of iron or steel hammered or rolled into a thick bar for further working. [historical] an unworked mass of puddle iron. verb make into such a mass.

Blossom/ब्लासम *(noun & verb)* – फूल, मंजरी विकसित होना produce blossom. *The flowers blossomed on the tree.*

Blot/ब्लॉट *(noun)* – दाग, धब्बा, निशान a dark mark or stain, especially one made by ink. *Here is a blot on this otherwise clean page.*

Blotch/ब्लॉच *(noun)* – चकत्ता, त्वचा, पौधों पर पड़ने वाला अस्थायी चकत्ता a large irregular patch or unsightly mark. verb cover or mark with blotches. *There was rain last night and the road is covered with blotches.*

Blouse/ब्लाउज *(noun)* – एक प्रकार की जनानी कुरती a woman's upper garment resembling a shirt. *She is wearing a low cut red blouse which goes well with her saree.*

Blow/ब्लो *(noun)* – हवा का बहना, चलना a powerful stroke with a hand or weapon. *I gave him a blow on the chin.*

Blowy /ब्लोवी *(adj.)* – हवादार windy or windswept. *This valley is very blowy.*

Bludgeon/ब्लजन् *(noun)* – लाठी या सोटे से मारना a thick stick with a heavy end, used as a weapon beat with a bludgeon. *He beat him with a bludgeon.*

Blue/ब्लू *(adj.)* – नीला, आसमानी of a colour intermediate between green and violet, as of the sky or sea on a sunny day. having fur of a smoky grey colour. *The sky seems to be of blue colour.*

Blue blood/ब्लू ब्लड *(noun)* – कुलीन व्यक्ति, अभिजात noble birth. *He is a man of blue blood.*

Blueing/ब्लूइंग *(noun)* – वस्त्र का नीला करना variant spelling of bluing.

Blue-stone/ब्लू-स्टोन *(noun)* – तूतिया a bluish or grey building stone. *I would like to use some blue stones on this wall.*

Bluff/ब्लफ – *(noun)* झांसा देना an attempt to deceive someone into believing that one can or will do something. verb try to deceive someone as to one's abilities or intentions. *He bluffed me into believing that he could give me loan easily.*

Bluish/ब्लूइश *(adj.)*– हल्का नीला having a blue tinge. *Your blazer has a bluish tinge. It works fantastic.*

Blunder/ब्लन्डर *(noun)* – बड़ी भूल, भद्दी या मूर्खतापूर्ण भूल move clumsily or as if unable to see. *I committed a blunder by delaying the loan payment.*

Blunt/ब्लन्ट *(adj.)* – धारहीन, मन्द lacking a sharp edge or point. having a flat or rounded end. *He was hit on head with a blunt object.*

B

Blur/ब्लर *(verb)* – धब्बा, अस्पष्ट वस्तु make or become unclear or less distinct. noun something that cannot be seen, heard, or recalled clearly. *My eye – sight was blurred as something hit me on the head.*

Blurt/ब्लर्ट *(verb)* – बिना समझे बोल उठना say suddenly and without careful consideration. *'Ah! Yes I have committed the crime he blurted out.*

Bluster/ब्लस्टर *(verb)* – गरजना, कोलाहल करना talk in a loud, aggressive, or indignant way with little effect. *He gave me a blustering talk which had little effect on me.*

Boa/बोआ *(noun)* – बिना जहर का भारी सर्प, अजगर a large snake which kills its prey by constriction and bears live young. and other species, family bodice. *I saw a boa in jungle it was crushing its prey to death.*

Boar/बॉर *(noun)* – नर सूअर a tusked wild pig from which domestic pigs are descended. *If you confront boar in the jungle it can be very dangerous.*

Board/बोर्ड *(noun)* – दफ्ती, मेज a long, thin, flat piece of wood used for floors or other building purposes. [informal] the stage of a theatre. *I'll need at least a dozen boards for the floor.*

Boarding/बोर्डिंग – भोजन और रहने का स्थान food and lodging. *She liked in a boarding house.*

Boast/बोस्ट *(noun & verb)* – अहंकार, गर्व talk with excessive pride and self-satisfaction about oneself. *He boasted a lot about his inherited wealth.*

Boat/बोट *(noun)* – नाव, नौका a small vessel propelled by oars, sails, or an engine. a vessel of any size. verb travel in a boat. frame port in a boat. *I crossed the river by boat.*

Boating/बोटिंग *(noun)* – नौका विहार water travel for pleasure. *Let us go for boating.*

Boatman/बोटमैन *(noun)* – नाविक a person who provides transport by boat. *The boatman propelled the oars and the boat moved.*

Bobby/बॉबी *(noun)* – पुलिस का सिपाही British, [informal], dated a police officer. *While in U.K. a bobby stopped me and asked me some questions.*

Bodice/बॉडिस *(noun)* – चोली, अंगिया, कुर्ती the part of a women's dress above the waist. a woman's sleeveless undergarment, often laced at the front. *She wore a perfectly fitting bodice.*

Bog/बॉग *(noun)* – दलदल an area of very soft wet muddy ground. ecology wetland with acid, party soil. *Frogs often live in bog.*

Boggle/बोगल *(verb)* – ठमकना [informal] be startled or baffled: the mind boggles at the spectacle. hesitate or be anxious at. *My mind boggled at the speed the train ran.*

Bogie/बोगी *(noun)* – रेलगाड़ी का लम्बा डब्बा [chiefly British] an undercarriage with four or six wheels pivoted beneath the end of a railway vehicle. Indian a railway carriage. *There are eight bogies in this train.*

Bogle/बोगल *(noun)* – प्रेत, पिशाच a phantom or goblin. *It is rumored that a bogle roams here in this forest.*

Bogus/बोगस *(adj.)* – जाली, बनावट, असली या ढोंग करते हुए बनावट not genuine or true. *This driving licence is bogus said the policeman.*

Bodkin/बॉडकिन *(noun)* – लम्बा मोटा सूजा a thick, blunt needle with a large eye, used for drawing tape through a hem. [historical] a long pin used to fasten women's hair. printing a pointed tool used for removing pieces of metal type for correction. *Women fasten their hair with a bodkin.*

Boil/बॉइल *(verb)* – उबाल reach or cause to reach the temperature at which it bubbles and turns to vapour. *Water boils at 100^0 c*

Boisterous/बॉइस्टरस *(adj.)* – प्रचण्ड, उधमी शोरगुल मचाने वाला noisy, energetic, and cheerful. *Boisterous waters raged into the city.*

Bold/बोल्ड *(adj.)* – शूर, साहसी, आत्मसाहसी, निडर confident and daring or courageous. dated audacious; impudent. *He is bold and will certainly succeed.*

Bole/बोल *(noun)* – तना, धड़ a tree trunk. *Some years ago I engraved some letters on this bole and they are here.*

Bolster/बोल्स्टर *(noun)* – मसनद a long, thick pillow. *Please bring me a bolster I want to relax thoroughly.*

Bolter/बोल्टर *(noun)* – दलद्रोही a person or animal that bolts or runs away. Austral, [historical] an escaped convict or absconder. *Deer are the best bolters the moment you make a noise they will run and disappear.*

Bomb/बम *(noun)* – बमगोला a container of explosive or incendiary material, designed to explode on impact or when detonated by a timing or remote-control device. nuclear weapons collectively. *The bomb blast killed many people.*

B

Bombard/बामबोर्ड (verb) – बमवर्षा करना या आक्रमण करना attack continuously with bombs or other missiles. *America bombarted the Taliban until surrendered.*

Bomber/बॉमर (noun) – बमवर्षक वायुयान an aircraft that drops bombs. *Planes were largely as bombers in 2nd World War.*

Bon/बॉन (noun) – अच्छा good a Japanese Buddhist festival held annually in august to honour the dead. *Many people go to Japan to attend bon.*

Bonafide/बोनाफाइड (adj.) – वास्तविक genuine; real. adverb chiefly [law] without intention to deceive. *It is a bonafide document and you can submit it in the court without hesitation.*

Bondage/बॉन्डेज (noun) – दासत्व the state of being a slave or serf. *He was held in bondage for a long time.*

Bodman/बॉडमैन (noun) – दासी a person who stands surety for a bond. *In the court you will find lots of bondmen willing to stand surely.*

Bone/बोन (noun) – हड्डी, अस्थि one of the hard part inside the body of a person or … that are covered with muscil. *The bones in our body are made of calcified material.*

Bonfire/बॉनफायर (noun) – आतिशबाजी a large open-air fire. *Let us camp here and light a bonfire.*

Bonny/बोनी (adj.) – सुन्दर, हृष्ट-पुष्ट physically attractive; healthy-looking. *He is a bonny child; I would also like to have one like that.*

Bonus/बोनस (noun) – पारितोषिक, लाभ, अतिरिक्त राशि a sum of money added seasonally to a person's wages for good performance. british an extra dividend or issue paid to shareholders. *In this firm employees get bonus on every Diwali.*

Boo/बू – असन्तोष जनक शब्द करना [exclamatory] said suddenly to surprise someone. *She said 'Boo'! in my ear and I was started.*

Booby/बूबी (noun) – मन्दबुद्धि, अनाड़ी, मूर्ख a large tropical. *No use talking to him, he is a booby.*

Boodle/बूडूल (noun) – नकली नोट, रिश्वत का पैसा [informal] money, especially that gained or spent dishonestly. *All money spent or won in gambling is boodle.*

Boohoo/बूहू – चिल्लाकर रोने का शब्द exclamatory representing the sound of someone crying noisily. *'Boohoo' she cried loudly as she wept over the loss of her jewellery.*

Book-binder/बुक बाइन्डर (noun) – जिल्दसाज a person who binds books. *My father binds books. He is a book-binder.*

Book-case/बुक केस (noun) – पुस्तक रखने की अलमारी an open cabinet containing shelves on which to keep books. *I have bought a book-case just to keep books in order.*

Booking/बुकिंग (noun) – टिकट बेचना the act of reseving or engaging the services of a person or group. *Booking is still open let us buy tickets for the movie.*

Book-keeper/बुक कीपर (noun) – मुनीम, व्यापार में बही खाता रखने वाला मनुष्य someone who records the transactions of a business. *He is a book-keeper in the office.*

Book-keeping/बुक कीपिंग (noun) – मुनीमी the activity of keeping records of financial affairs. *The job of book-keeping is not an easy one as it involves financial dealings.*

Booklet/बुकलेट (noun) – किसी विषय पर जानकारी देने वाली छोटे आकार की पुस्तक a small, thin book with paper covers. *I prefer booklets to books. I can finish them quickly.*

Book-maker/बुकमेकर (noun) – पुस्तक का संकलन कर्ता घुड़दौड़ में लगे दाँवों का हिसाब रखने वाला व्यक्ति a person whose job is to take bets, calculate odds, and pay out winnings. *A book-maker has an important place in a gambling house.*

Book-mate/बुकमेट – सहाध्यायी, साथ का पढ़ने वाला *I am his book-mate, we often exchange books.*

Book-post/बुकपोस्ट (noun) – डाक द्वारा कम कीमत पर भेजी गई पुस्तक इत्यादि *I have received a book by book-post.*

Book-seller/बुकसेलर (noun) – पुस्तक बेचने वाला the proprietor of a bookstore. *A proprietor of a book-store you will find any book from that book-seller.*

Book-worm/बुकवर्म (noun) – किताबों का कीड़ा [informal] a person who enjoys reading. *He is reading he is a book-worm.*

Boom/बूम (noun) – समृद्धि a loud, deep, resonant sound. verb make this sound. *The firing cannons made a sound of boom- boom.*

Boon/बून (noun) – लाभ, वरदान a thing that is helpful or beneficial. *His having become my partner in business was no less a boon.*

Boor/बूअर (noun) – असभ्य, अशिक्षित a rough and bad-mannered person. *No use expecting from him fine manners he is a boor.*

Boost/बूस्ट *(verb)* – संख्या, मूल्य या शक्ति में वृद्धि करना help or encourage to increase or improve. noun a source of help or encouragement. *My father having come to my help in bad times boosted my morals.*

Boot/बूट *(noun)* – पूजा, सुविधा a sturdy item of footwear covering the foot and ankle, and something the lower leg. *I purchased a pair of boots.*

Booth/बूथ *(noun)* – छानी, मेले की दुकान a small temporary structure used for selling goods or staging shows at a market or fair. *There were a lot of booths in fair.*

Boot-lace/बूट लैस *(noun)* – जूते की फीता a cord or leather strip for lacing boots. *Will someone find my boot-laces I have to tie up shoe?*

Bootless/बूटलेस *(adj.)* – बेकार, अकारथ [archaic] ineffectual; useless. *Ignore it. It is something bootless.*

Booty/बूटी *(noun)* – लूट का माल valuable stolen goods. *Let us divide the booty among ourselves before the police come.*

Booze/बूज *(verb)* – अधिक मदिरा पीना [informal] noun alcoholic drink. verb drink large quantities of alcohol. *He drank a lot of booze and was out.*

Borax/बोरैक्स *(noun)* – सोहागा a white mineral consisting of hydrated sodium borate, found in some alkaline salt deposits and used in making glass and as a metallurgical flux. *Here is some borax it will help us make glass.*

Border/बॉर्डर *(noun)* – किनारा, छोर a line separeating two countries or other areas. the boundary between northern boundary and adjoining districts between Scotland and England. *The border line between India and Pakistan is very long.*

Bore/बोर *(noun & verb)* – ज्वार की लहर, छेद करना a steep-fronted wave caused by the meeting of two tides or by a tide rushing up a narrow estuary. *Look this place is called bore where the tide rushes up the mouth of a large river.*

Borer/बोरर *(noun)* – छेदने का यन्त्र a worm, mollusc, or insect which bores into plant material or rock. *The worm called borer has eaten into our plants as well as the rocks around.*

Boric/बोरिक *(adj.)* – सोहागे के क्षार-सम्बन्धी chemistry of boron.

Boring/बोरिंग *(adj.)* – विनोदहीन so lacking in interest as to cause mental weariness. *He is a very boring person. You will soon get tired of him.*

Born/बॉर्न *(adj.)* – पैदा हुआ existing as a result of birth. *I was born in the year 1938.*

Borne/बोर्न – आया हुआ past participle of bear. *The weight was borne by him for a long distance.*

Borrow/बॉरो *(verb)* – अनुकरण करना take and use with the intention of returning it. take and use from a person or bank under agreement to pay it back later. *I went to my friend to borrow some money.*

Bort/बोर्ट *(noun)* – हीरे की कनी inferior diamonds used in cutting tools. *Please get me a bort I have to cut glass.*

Bosh/बॉस *(noun)* – वृथा वार्ता [informal] nonsense. *Oh! He is talking bosh.*

Bosky/बोस्की *(adj)* – झाड़ीदार [poetic/literary] covered by trees or bushes. *It is a bosky place let us rest here.*

Bosom/बूजम *(noun)* – मन, भीतरी भाग a woman's breast or chest. *A buxom bosom adds to the beauty of a women.*

Botanic/बॉटैनिक *(adj.)* – वनस्पति शास्त्र-सम्बन्धी of or relating to plants or botony. *This problem is botanic i.e. related with plant life so go and ask a botanist about it.*

Botanist/बॉटैनिस्ट *(noun)* – वनस्पति शास्त्र का पंडित a biologist specialising in the study of plants. *My brother is a botanist.*

Botany/बॉटनी *(noun)* – वनस्पति विज्ञान merino wool. *This sweater is made of merino wool the best available.*

Botch/बॉच *(verb)* – पैबन्द, फोड़ा carry out badly or carelessly. noun a badly carried out task. *He has botched up the plan.*

Botchy/बॉची *(adj.)* – पैबन्द से भरा हुआ full of botches. *No use acting upon this botchy scheme.*

Both/बोथ *(adj. & prep.)* – दोनों, बराबर से Predetermined, determined, pronoun two people or things, regarded and identified together. *Both the brothers took up the challenge.*

Bother/बॉदर *(verb)* – कष्ट देना take the trouble to do something. *The problem is still bothering me.*

B

Bottler/बॉटलर (noun) - बोतलों में शराब भरने वाला a manufacturer that makes and battles beverages.

Bottom/बॉटम (noun) - तल, सबसे भीतरी स्थान the lowest point or part of something. the furthest part or point of something. the lower half of a two-piece garment. *The bottom of the trousers is loose I'll give it to the tailor to tighter it.*

Boudoir/बूड्वार (noun) - स्त्री का गुप्त कमरा a lady's bedroom or private room.

Bought/बॉट (verb) - खरीदा past and past participle of buy. *I bought a shirt yesterday.*

Boulder/बोल्डर (noun) - पानी से घिसा हुआ चिकना बड़ा गोला पत्थर a large rock. *A boulder fell down and raced past me.*

Bouncer/बाउन्सर (noun) - झूठा, शेखीबाज a person employed by a nightclub or pub to prevent troublemakers entering or to eject them from the premises. *The bouncer stopped him from entering the club because he was too drunk.*

Bouncing/बाउंसिंग (noun) - पुष्ट, भारी rebounding from an impact. *The ball hit the wall and come back bouncing.*

Bound/बाउन्ड (noun & verb) - सीमा, किनारा, उछलना walk or run with leaping strides. noun a leaping movement towards or over something. *The leopard leapt and bounded gracefully.*

Boundary/बाउन्डरी (noun) - सीमा, मर्यादा a line marking the limits of an area. *There is a boundary around the play ground.*

Boundless/बाउन्डलेस (adj.) - असीम unlimited. *Sportsmen have boundless energy.*

Bounds/बाउन्ड्स (noun) - सीमा, मर्यादा line or plane indicating the limit or extent of something.

Bounteous/बाउन्टिअस (adj.) - उदारता से [archaic] bountiful. *He is very bounteous, his bounty knows no limits.*

Bountiful/बॉउन्टिफुल (adj.) - दानशील, उदार abundant. *He is bountiful person and donates generously.*

Bounty/बाउन्टी (noun) - उदारता a reward paid for killing or capturing someone. *He was given a bounty by authorities for catching an escaped convict.*

Bouquet/बुके (noun) - गुलदस्ता a bunch of flowers. *She received a bouquet from her best friend.*

Bourse/बुर्स (noun) - हाट, बाजार a stock market in a non-English speaking country, especially France. *When I went to France I visited bourse also.*

Bout/बाउट (noun) - काम की पारी, बीमारी का दौरा शक्ति-परीक्षा a short period of intense activity. an attack of illness or strong emotion. *I had a bout of malaria.*

Bovine/बोवाइन (adj.) - गाय, मन्दबुद्धि of, relating to, or resembling cattle. noun an animal of the cattle family. *A cow belongs to bovine family.*

Bovril/बोवरिल (noun) - गोमांस का सत्व an extract of beef. *She likes bovril.*

Bow/बो (verb) - घुमाव, कमान bend the head or upper body as a sign of respect, greeting, or shame. *I bowed before my master.*

Bowel/बावेल (noun) - आँत, अँतड़ी the intestine. *There is something wrong my bowels are troubling me.*

Bower/बावर (noun) - पर्णशाला, स्त्री की गुप्त कोठरी an anchor carried at a ship's bow. *Bower is placed in the front part of the ship.*

Bowl/बाउल (noun) - प्याला, कटोरा a round, deep dish or basin. a rounded, concave part of an object. geography a natural basin. [chiefly north American] a stadium for sporting or musical events. an American football game played after the season between leading teams. *The Faqir drank from his bowl.*

Bowler/बॉलर (noun) - गेंद फेंकने वाला cricket a member of the fielding side who bowls. *A good bowler is an asset for a winning team.*

Bow-wow/बो-वो - कुत्ते की भूँक exclamatory an imitation of a dog's bark. noun [informal] a dog. *He irritated the dog and said 'bow-wow!'*

Boxing/बॉक्सिंग (noun) - मुक्केबाजी fighting with the fists. *I am fond of seeing boxing matches.*

Boy/बॉय (noun) - बालक, शिशु a male child or youth. *He is a well mannered boy.*

Boyhood/बॉयहुड (noun) - लड़कपन the childhood of a boy. *Now, your boyhood is over.*

Boyish/बॉयिश (adj.) - लड़के के जैसा befitting or characteristic of young boy. *Although mature he behaves boyish.*

Brabble/ब्रैबल् (noun) - लड़ाई-झगड़ा argue over petty thing. *Don't brabble over petty things.*

Brace/ब्रेस (noun) - युगल, बन्धन British a pair of straps passing over the shoulders and fastening to the top of trousers at the front and back to hold them up. *She wears braces because her teeth are irregular.*

Bracelet/ब्रेसलेट *(noun)* – पहुँची, कंगन, बाजू an ornamental band or chain worn on the wrist or arm. *She bought a diamond bracelet to wear on her wrist*

Bracer/ब्रेसर *(noun)*– शक्ति-वर्धिनी औषधि [informal] an alcoholic drink taken to prepare one for something difficult or unpleasant. *1…. He needed a bracer to prepare that dangerous stunt.*

Bracing/ब्रेसिंग *(adj.)* – पुष्टिकर, शक्तिवर्धक fresh and invigorating. *This is a bracing drink.*

Brackish/ब्रैकिश *(adj.)* – खारा slightly salty, as in river estuaries. living in or requiring such water. *Some fish need brackish water to live in.*

Bradawl/ब्रैडॉल *(noun)* – छेदने का शस्त्र a tool for boring holes, resembling a screwdriver. *I need a bradawl to drill a hole.*

Brag/ब्रैग *(noun)* – आत्मश्लाघा करना, डींग मारना, शेखी बघारना a simplified form of poker; *He is a bragger. He brags all the time of his wealth, of his power, of his business ventures etc.*

Braid/ब्रेड *(noun)* – गोटा, लेस threads of silk, cotton etc. woven into a decorative band. *The braid she wore was made of silk and cotton woven finely into a band.*

Braille/ब्रेल *(noun)* – अन्धों के लिए उभरे अक्षरों में छपी पुस्तक जिसे ढक कर पढ़ा जाता है a written language for the blind. in which characters are represented by patterns of raised dots. verb print or transcribe in Braille. *This book has been typed in Braille so that the blind can read it.*

Brain/ब्रेन *(noun)* – मस्तिष्क, बुद्धि an organ of soft nervous tissue contained in the skull, functioning as the coordinating centre of sensation and intellectual and nervous activity. the substance of an animal's brain used as food. *This intellectual and nervous activities show that he has lots of brains.*

Brake/ब्रेक *(noun)* – झाड़ी [historical] an open horse-drawn carriage with four wheels. *He travelled a long way in brake.*

Bramble/ब्रैम्बल *(noun)* – कँटीला पौधा, फाली या लाल बेरी दाली जंगली झाड़ी a prickly scrambling shrub of the rose family, especially a blackberry. [chiefly British] the fruit of the blackberry. verb British gather blackberries. *The gardener is gathering blackberries from bramble.*

Bran/ब्रैन *(noun)* – भूसी, चोकर pieces of grain husk separated from flour after milling. *Bran is good for health.*

Branch/ब्रान्च *(noun)* – शाखा, टहनी, डाल a woody extending part of a tree which grows out from the trunk or a bough. *This branch of tree is full of fruits.*

Brand/ब्राण्ड *(noun)* – व्यापारिक चिह्न, तलवार a type of product manufactured by a company under a particular name. a particular name. a particular type of something: the finish brand of socialism. *It is a levis Philippe shirts a brand name known world over.*

Brandish/ब्रैण्डिश *(noun)* – घुमाना, चक्कर देना wave or flourish as a threat or in anger or excitement. *Brandishing his sword he attacked him.*

Brandy/ब्राण्डी *(noun)* – आसव, शराब a strong alcoholic spirit distilled from wine or fermented fruit juice. *If you have cough cold you may take a little brandy that will help.*

Bravado/ब्रॅवाडो *(noun)* – शेखी, धमकी boldness intended to impress or intimidate. *He has lot of bravado and creates impression by his boldness.*

Brave/ब्रेव *(adj.)* – निडर, ईमानदार showing courage. noun dated an American Indian warrior: *verb* endure or face with courage. *He proved to be a brave soldier.*

Bravo/ब्रावो – शाबाश वाह-वाह exclamatory used to express approval for a performer. noun a code word representing the letter B, used in radio communication. *Bravo cried the crowd as he hit a sixer.*

Brawl/ब्रॉल *(noun & verb)* – कलह करना, विवाद करना, झड़प a rough or noisy fight or quarrel. verb take part in a brawl. *Police found him indulged in a street brawl and arrested him the others ran away.*

Bray/ब्रे *(noun)*– गदहे का स्वर, रेंकना the loud, harsh cry of a donkey. verb make such a sound. *In the morning I heard a donkey's braying and woke up irritated.*

Braze/ब्रेज *(verb)* – पीतल के समान रंग करना form, fix, or join by soldering with an alloy of copper and zinc. noun a brazed joint. *This is a brazed joint.*

Brazen/ब्रेजेन *(adj.)* – धृष्ट, पीतल का बना हुआ bold and shameless. *Her brazen attitude irritated all in the party.*

B

Brazier/ब्रेजिअर *(noun)* – बोरसी, ठठेरा a burning coal pan, a worker in brass. *He works in a factory where copper joints are brazed.*

Breach/ब्रीच *(noun)* – नियम, समझौते की शर्तों का उल्लंखन an act of breaking a [law], agreement, or code of conduct. a break in relations. *To enter someone's house without permission is a breach of law.*

Bread/ब्रेड *(noun)* – रोटी, जीवनवृत्ति food made of flour, water, and yeast mixed together and baked. *Bread is not native Indian food.*

Breakable/ब्रेकेब्ल *(adj.)* – तोड़ने योग्य capable of being braken or damaged. *This stick is thin and surely breakable.*

Breakage/ब्रेकेज *(noun)* – टूटन the act of breaking something. *The young men who created a scene in restaurant had to pay for the breakage.*

Breakdown/ब्रेकडाउन *(noun)* – वाहन या मशीन का चलते-चलते बंद हो जाना, स्वास्थ नष्ट होना a failure or collapse. *The breakdown of the car occurred at an isolated place.*

Breaker/ब्रेकर *(noun)* – समुद्र की बड़ी लहर a heavy sea wave that breaks on the shore. *The breaker came and almost the whole ship shook.*

Breakfast/ब्रेकफास्ट *(noun)*– सुबह का नास्ता a meal eaten in the morning, the first of the day. verb eat this meal. *You must not miss your breakfast as it is the first meal of the day.*

Breakneck/ब्रेकनेक *(adj.)* – बहुत तेज और खतरनाक dangerously or extremely fast. *He drove the car at breakneck speed.*

Breakwater/ब्रेकवाटर *(noun)* – लहरों के आघात से सुरक्षा के लिए समुद्र के पानी में बनायी गयी दीवार a barrier built out into the sea to protect a coast or harbour from the force of waves. *This barrier in the sea is named breakwater as it protects the coast from the force of waves.*

Breast/ब्रेस्ट *(noun)* – स्तन, वक्ष-स्थल either of the two soft, protruding organs on the upper front of a woman's body which secrete milk after pregnancy. *Mammary gland are glands of a women which secrete milk for the baby after birth.*

Breast-bone/ब्रेस्टबोन *(noun)* – हृदय पर की बीच की हड्डी a thin flat bone running down the centre of the chest and connecting the ribs; the sternum. *He was hit hard on his breast-bone.*

Breath/ब्रेथ *(noun)* – मन्द पवन, जीवन, श्वास air taken into or expelled form the lungs. an inhalation or exhalation of air form the lungs. *His breath came slow.*

Breathe/ब्रीद *(verb)* – श्वास लेना, साँस take air into the laughs and then expel it as a regular physiological process. respire or exchange gases. *Breathing is necessary to maintain life.*

Breathing/ब्रीदिंग *(noun)* – श्वास, जीवित a sign in Greek indicating the presence of an aspirate or the absence or an aspirate at the beginning of a word.

Breathless/ब्रेथलेस *(adj.)* – हाँफता हुआ gasping for breath, typically due to exertion. feeling or causing great excitement, fear, etc. *I found him breathless with excitement.*

Breed/ब्रीड *(noun)* – पशु की विशेष नस्ल a breed of cattle dog.

Breed/ब्रीड *(verb)*– पैदा करना, जन्म देना mate and then produce offspring. cause to produce offspring. *Insects breed like anything.*

Breeder/ब्रीडर *(noun)* – प्रजनक, प्रजनन की दृष्टि से पालन करने वाला a person or animal that breeds. *We humans and animals are breeders if we were not so the races would have died.*

Breeding/ब्रीडिंग *(noun)* – पालन, शिक्षण good manner regarded as characteristic of the aristocracy and conferred by heredity. *See his aristocratic manners his breeding must have been high class.*

Breviary/बिविअरी *(noun)* – स्तोत्र-संग्रह a book containing the service for each day, to be recited by those in orders in the roman catholic church. *Roman Catholics daily recite from breviary which contains service for each day.*

Brew/ब्रियू *(verb)* – शराब बनाना, उत्पन्न करना make by soaking, boiling, and fermentation. *I would like to have a jug of brew.*

Bribe/ब्राइब *(verb)* – घूस, रिश्वत dishonestly persuade to act in one's favour by a payment or other inducement. noun an inducement offered in an attempt to bribe. *He gave me a bribe of ten thousand rupees to get his licence before due date.*

Bribery/ब्राइबरी *(noun)* – घूस लेने या देने का कार्य *Bribery is very common in our country.*

Brick/ब्रिक *(noun)* – ईंट a small rectangular block of fired or sun dried clay, used in building. bricks collectively as a building material. *Without bricks we cannot make a house.*

Bridal/ब्राइडल *(adj.)* – वैवाहिक, विवाह सम्बन्धी उत्सव of or concerning a bride or a newly married couple. *She is wearing bridal make up.*

Bride/ब्राइड *(noun)* – दुलहिन a woman on or just before her wedding day.

Bridegroom/ब्राइडग्रूम *(noun)* – दूल्हा, वर a man on his wedding day or juts before and after the event. *The bridegroom sat on a horse.*

Bridge/ब्रिज *(noun)* – पुल, सेतु a structure that carries a road or railway across river valley road.

Brief/ब्रीफ *(noun)* – संक्षिप्त या अल्पकालिक, कानूनी बहस के लिए तैयार किया गया विवरण *What I want say in brief is that you must leave tomorrow.*

Brier/ब्रायर *(noun)*– गोखरू, काँटेदार झाड़ी variant spelling of briar. *Be careful! It is a brier a wild rose shrub. Can you pluck a flower safely?*

Brigade/ब्रिगेड *(noun)* – सैनिकों की टुकड़ी या इकाई a subdivision of an army, typically consisting of a small number of battalions and forming part of a division. *Brigadier commands a brigade which is a sub- division of army.*

Brigadier/ब्रिगेडियर *(noun)* – छोटी पलटन का अफसर a rank of officer in the British army, above colonel and below major general. *A brigadier is high ranking office above the rank of colonel.*

Bright/ब्राइट *(adj.)* – चमकीला, प्रसिद्ध, प्रदीप्त giving out much light, or filled with light. *The room was bright with light.*

Brighten/ब्राइटेन *(verb)* – चमकना make lighter or brighter. *I brightened light in the room switching on all the lights.*

Brilliant/ब्रिलिएन्ट *(adj.)* – अति प्रकाशित, कुशाग्र very bright or vivid. *He is a brilliant student.*

Brim/ब्रिम *(noun)* – प्याला, गिलास आदि का ऊपरी किनारा, कंठ, किनारा the projecting edge around the bottom of a hat. *The brim of her hat is decorated with a band of flowers.*

Brimstone/ब्रिमस्टोन *(noun)* – गन्धक, गंधक तितली [archaic] sulphur. *I chanced to see a brimstone butterfly.*

Brindle/ब्रिंडल *(adj.)* – भूरा, चितकबरा (especially of a domestic animal) brownish or tawny with streaks of other colour. *It is a brindle coloured dog.*

Brine/ब्राइन *(noun)* – खारा पानी, आँसू water saturated or strongly impregnated with salt; seawater. technical a strong solution of a salt or salts. verb soak in or saturate with brine. *I am not fond of drinking brine water.*

Brinish/ब्रिनिश *(adj.)* – नमकीन *This water tastes brinish.*

Brinjal/ब्रिन्जल *(noun)* – बैंगन, भांटा Indian & South African an aubergine.

Brink/ब्रिंक *(noun)* – तट the extreme edge of land before a stee slope or a body of water. *He was on the brink of bankruptcy.*

Briny/ब्रिनी *(adj.)* – नमकीन of salty water or the sea; salty. noun British [informal] the sea. *This is a briny drink and I don't like it.*

Brisk/ब्रिस्क *(adj.)* – तीव्र, चपल active and energetic. *They set off at a brisk.*

Brisket/ब्रिस्केट *(noun)* – पशु की छाती का मांस meat from the breast of a cow. *Bring me a plate of brisket.*

Bristle/ब्रिसल *(noun)* – सूअर के कड़े बाल a short, stiff hair or an animal's skin or a man's face. a bristle, or a man-made substitute, used to make a brush. verb stand upright away from the skin, typically as a sign of anger or fear. *He has grown a bristle on his chin.*

British/ब्रिटिश *(adj.)* – अंग्रेज of or relating to great Britain or the united kingdom. *He is a British citizen.*

Briton/ब्रिटन *(noun)* – ग्रेट ब्रिटेन का निवासी a native or inhabitant of great Britain, or a person of British descent. *My brother is a Briton.*

Brittle/ब्रिटल *(adj.)* – कुरकुरा hard but liable to break or shatter easily. *An ice slab is brittle.*

Broach/ब्रोच *(verb)* – चर्चा चलाना, जिक्र छेड़ना raise for discussion. *I broached the bottle open.*

Broad/ब्रॉड *(adj.)* – चौड़ा, स्पष्ट having a distance larger than usual from side to side; wide. of a specified distance wide. *In monsoon the river becomes very broad.*

Broadcasting/ब्रॉडकास्ट *(noun)* – प्रसारण a medium that disseminates via telecommunication. *Broadcasting the issue from radio is one way to solve the problem.*

Broadly/ब्रॉडली *(adv.)* – मोटे तौर पर *Broadly speaking this is not a serious issue.*

Brocade/ब्रोकेड *(noun)*– किमखाब जरीदार या बूटेदार कपड़ा a rich fabric woven with a raised

B

pattern. usually with gold or silver thread. verb weave with this design. *I would like to have a brocade saree woven with gold and silver threads.*

Broccoli/ब्रॉकलि *(noun)* – फूलगोभी जैसी एक सब्जी a cultivated variety of cabbage with heads of small green or purplish flower buds, eaten as vegetable. *So far as vitamin A is concerned broccoli is far better than cabbage.*

Brochure/ब्रोशर *(noun)* – एक विवरण पुस्तक a small book or magazine containing pictures and information about a product or service. *I visited the office of a building company and asked for their brochure so that I could read all detail at my home.*

Broil/ब्रायल *(noun)* – झगड़ा, लड़ाई [archaic] a quarrel or a commotion. *There was a broil out somewhere.*

Broke/ब्रोक *(adj.)* – तोड़ा [informal] having completely run out of money. *Give me some money I am completely broke.*

Broken/ब्रोकेन *(adj.)* – टूटा हुआ, टूटा-फूटा spoken falteringly and with many mistakes, as by a foreigner. *The foreigner spoke in broken Hindi.*

Broker/ब्रोकर *(noun)* – दलाल a person who buys and sells goods or assets for others. *He is a very intelligent broker. I feel my money safe in his hands.*

Bromide/ब्रोमाइड *(noun)* – एक रासायनिक मिश्रण जो औषधि में प्रयुक्त होता है Chemistry a compound of bromine with another element or group: methyl bromide. *Sometimes back people used to drink bromide for sleeplessness.*

Bromine/ब्रोमीन *(noun)* – गहरी लाल, विषैली गैस the chemical element of atomic number 35, a dark red toxic liquid halogen with a choking irritating smell.

Bronchus/ब्रॉन्कस *(noun)* – वायु-प्रणाली के दो प्रधान कोष्ठों में से एक any of the major air passages of the lungs which diverge from the windpipe. *I suffer from bronchitis as my windpipe is swollen.*

Bronze/ब्रॉन्ज *(noun)* – काँसा, काँसे का a yellowish-brown alloy of copper with up to one-third tin. *India has won many bronze medal in international sport events.*

Brood/ब्रुड *(noun)* – पशु या पक्षियों के एक ही बार में जने बच्चे a family of young animals, especially birds, produced at one hatching or birth. *The hen went looking for food with her brood behind her.*

Brook/ब्रुक *(noun)* – स्रोत, छोटी नदी a small stream. *There are many brooks in this jungle.*

Broom/ब्रुम *(noun)* – झाड़ू, बुहारी a long-handled brush of bristles or twigs, used for sweeping. *A broom is used for cleaning the room.*

Brothel/ब्रायल *(Plural noun)* – वेश्यालय, रंडी का घर a building where prostitutes are available.

Brother/ब्रदर *(noun)* – भाई a man or boy in relation to other sons and daughters of his parents. *My brother is a famous sportsman.*

Brow/ब्रोव *(noun)* – मस्तक, ललाट, पहाड़ों का शिखर प्रदेश a ship's gangway or landing platform. *Suddenly a car came over the brow of hill.*

Brown/ब्राउन *(adj.)* – भूरा of a colour produced by mixing red, yellow, and blue, as of dark wood or rich soil. *Brown colour is my favourite.*

Brownie/ब्रॉवनि *(noun)* – एक प्रकार की परी a member of the junior branch of the guides association, for girls aged between about. 7 and 10. *Last night I imagined I saw an elf. She was in the house of Mrs. Smith.*

Brownie/ब्राउनी *(noun)* – गिरियुक्त बड़ा चाकलेट *Bring we two prownies at is so rich in chocolate.*

Brownish/ब्राउनिश *(adj.)* – कुछ भूरा of a colour similar to that of wood or earth. *I would rather favour a brownish pair of shoes.*

Browse/ब्राव्जी *(verb)* – सरसरी तौर पर देखना survey goods or text in a leisurely and casual way. computing read or survey via a network. *His favourite pastime is to browse on computer network.*

Bruise/ब्रुइज*(noun)* – आघात an injury appearing as an area of discolored skin on the body, caused by a blow or impact rupturing underlying blood vessels. *While fighting the robbers he received many bruises.*

Bruit/ब्रट *(noun)* – सूचना, झूठी खबर [archaic] a report or rumour. *It is a bruit that he has been murdered.*

Brunt/ब्रंट *(noun)* – प्रहार, चोट the chief impact of something bad. *I'll bear the brunt of going bankrupt.*

Brushwood/ब्रशवुड *(noun)* – घनी झाड़ी undergrowth, twigs, and small branches. *There was a lot of brushwood in the jungle.*

Brusque/ब्रस्क *(adj.)* – फूहड़, असभ्य abrupt or offhand. *He left me in an brusque manner.*

Brustle/ब्रसल *(verb)* – खड़खड़ाना to rustele, to crackle.

Brutal/ब्रूटल *(adj.)* – असभ्य, क्रूर savagely violent. *Last night there was a brutal attack on him.*

Brute/ब्रूट *(noun)* – पशु, कठोर नर, बड़े आकार का शक्तिशाली पशु a violent or savage person or animal. [informal] a cruel or insensitive person. *So far as manners are concerned he is a brute.*

Brutish/ब्रूटिश *(adj.)* – पशु के समान resembling a beast showing lack of human sensibility.

Bubble/बबल *(noun)* – बुलबुला, क्रूरतापूर्ण, निशंसतापूर्ण a thin sphere of liquid enclosing air or another gas. an air or gas-filled spherical cavity in a liquid or a solidified liquid such as glass. *The water was full of bubbles.*

Buccal/बकल *(adj.)* – गाल सम्बन्धी technical of or relating to the cheek or mouth. *This is a buccal disease.*

Buccaneer/बुकानिअर *(noun)* – जहाजी लुटेरा [historical] a pirate, originally one preying on ships in the Caribbean. *Captain cook was a notorious buccaneer of Caribbean.*

Buck/बक *(noun)* – हिरण, साबर, नर कुछ पशुओं के नर प्राणी, नर हिरण, नर खरगोश an object placed as a reminder in front of a poker player whose turn it is to deal. *He is to deal the cards so put the buck in front of him.*

Bucket/बकेट *(noun)* – डोल, बाटली a cylindrical open container with a handle, used to carry liquids. a compartment on the outer edge of a waterwheel. the scoop of a dredger or grain elevator, or one attached to the front of a digger or tractor. *You can bathe, the bucket is full of water.*

Buckle/बकल *(noun)* – बकसुआ a flat rectangular or oval frame with a hinged pin, used for joining the ends of a belt or strap. *verb* fasten or decorate with a buckle. *I must have the buckle of my belt changed it has become loose.*

Buckler/बकलर *(noun)* – छोटी ढाल, रक्षा [historical] a small round shield held by a handle or worn on the forearm. *In old times fighters used to wear buckler on their forearm.*

Buckshot/बकशॉट *(noun)* – बन्दूक की बड़ी गोली coarse lead shot used in shotgun shells.

Buckwheat/बकह्विट *(noun)* – मोथी नामक अन्न an asian plant of the dock family, producing starchy seeds used for fodder or milled into flour. *Seeds of buckwheat are milled into flour and eaten during festival when ladies break their fast.*

Bud/बड *(noun)* – अंकुर, कली a compact knob-like growth on a plant which develops into a leaf, flower, or shoot. *A bud in plant grows into a flower fruit or seed.*

Budge/बज *(verb)* – सरकना, खिसकना make or cause to make the slightest movement. [informal] make room for another person by moving. *I won't budge an inch from my stand.*

Budget/बजट *(noun)* – कोष, पूँजी an estimate of income and expenditure for a set period of time. a regular estimate of national revenue and expenditure put forward by a finance minister. *This year's budget does not suit the common man.*

Buff/बफ *(noun)* – घूँसा, भैंस या बैल का चमड़ा [informal] a person who is interested in and very knowledgeable about a particular subject. *He is a buff on Mughal history. Ask him and he will answer any question.*

Buffalo/बफलो *(noun)* – भैंस a heavily built wild ox with backswept horns. and genus bubalus. *Buffalo's milk is thicker than that of a cow.*

Buffet/बुफे *(noun & verb)* – थप्पड़, घूँसा मारना a blow. *He was buffeted heavily and consequently sent to hospital.*

Buffoon/बफून *(noun)* – विदूषक भाँड, ठिठोलिया a ridiculous but amusing person. *He amuses all by his buffoonery.*

Bug/बग *(noun)* – खटमल, उड्स entomology an insect of a large order having piercing and sucking mouthparts, including aphids, leafhoppers, cicadas, and many other insects. [informal] any small insect. *As I slept in the open I found the bugs all over me they bit like me anything.*

Buggy/बग्गी *(noun)* – पालकी गाड़ी बग्घी a small motor vehicle with an open top. *In old times people used to travel in buggy.*

Bugle/ब्यूगल *(noun)* – विगुल, सिंगी an ornamental tube-shaped bead on clothing. *She has a bugle over her Kurta.*

Build/बिल्ड *(verb)* – निर्माण करना, रचना करना construct by putting parts or materials together. incorporate something as a permanent part of. *I am going to build my house on this plot.*

B

Built/बिल्ट – निर्मित, बना हुआ past and past participle of build. adjective of a specified physical build: a slightly built woman. *This lady is slightly built.*

Bulge/बल्ज *(noun)* – सूजन, फूलना a rounded swelling distorting a flat surface. *Do you see that raised portion on the flat land. We are going to play on that bulge.*

Bulginess/बल्जिनेस *(noun)* – फूलन The property possessed by a rounded convexity.

Bulk/बल्क *(noun)* – बोझ, परिणाम the mass or magnitude of something large. a large mass or shape. large in quantity: bulk supplier. *He is a supplier in bulk.*

Bull/बुल *(noun)* – साँड़ a papal edict. *This official order has been issued by the pope.*

Bullet/बुलेट *(noun)* – बन्दूक में चलाने की सीसे की गोली a projectile fired from a small firearm, typically metal, cylindrical and pointed. *He fired a bullet from his pistol and the bullet went past grazing me.*

Bulletin/बुलेटिन *(noun)*– संक्षिप्त सरकारी समाचार पत्र a short official statement or summary of news. a regular newsletter or report. *I just read the sports news in the bulletin.*

Bullion/बुलियन *(noun)* – चाँदी या सोने की ठोस ईंट gold or silver in bulk before coining, or valued by weight. *Bullion must be a sight to see the uncoined silver and gold.*

Bullock/बुलॉक *(noun)* – बरधा, बधिया किया हुआ बैल a castrated male bovine animal raised for beef. verb austral [informal] work very hard. *He works hard like a bullock.*

Bull's eye/बुल्स आई *(noun)* – निशाना लगाने का गोल बिन्दु the centre of the target in sports such as archery and darts. *Our Silverman Vijay Kumar hit the bull's eyes with pistol in rapid firing.*

Bully/बुली *(noun)* – दबंग, निर्दयी व्यक्ति a person who deliberately intimidates or persecutes those who are weaker. verb intimidate. *He is a school bully and intimidates weaker and smaller children.*

Bulwark/बलवर्क *(noun)* – कोट, सिद्धान्त a defensive wall. *We have created the bulwark against the enemy.*

Bumper/बम्पर *(noun)* – कोई असामान्य पदार्थ a horizontal bar across the front or back of a motor vehicle to reduce damage in a collision. *This year there was a bumper crop of wheat.*

Bumpkin/बम्पकिन *(noun)* – भद्दा गँवार मनुष्य an unsophisticated country person. *He is a bumpkin, a simple villager.*

Bumptious/बम्पशस *(adj.)* – अहंकारी, घमण्डी offensively self-assertive.

Bumpy/बम्पि *(adj.)* – उछलने वाला, कूदने वाला covered with or full of bumps.

Bunch/बन्च *(noun)* – गुच्छा, ग्रन्थि a number of things growing or fastened in which the hair is drawn into a tight cull at the back of the head. *I presented her with a bunch of flowers.*

Bundle/बन्डल *(noun)* – पोटली, गठरी a collection of things or quantity of material tired or wrapped up together. a set of nerve, muscle, or other fibers running in parallel close together. *He carried a bundle of sticks from the jungle.*

Bung/बंग *(noun)* – पीपे की डाट a stopper for a hole in a container. verb close with a bung. block something up. *I have closed the hole with a bung.*

Bunion/बुनियन *(noun)* – पैर के अँगूठे पर सुजन a painful swelling on the first joint of the big toe. *I have a painful swelling near the toe the doctor said it was a bunion and that I was not to worry.*

Bunk/बन्क *(noun)* – रेलगाड़ी की दीवार में लगी सोने के लिए पटरी a narrow shelf-like bed. verb [chiefly north American] sleep in a bunk or improvised bed in shared quarters. *Last night due to lack of space I slept on a bunk.*

Bunker/बन्कर *(noun)* – तलवार, बंकर, कोयला संग्रह करने का स्थान a large container or compartment for storing fuel. *During war soldiers live in bunkers and fight from there.*

Bunt/बन्ट *(noun)* – धक्का, अनाज की बीमारी the baggy centre of a fishing net or a sail. *Do you see that blown up centre in the sail it is called bunt.*

Bunting/बन्टिंग *(noun)* – झण्डी बनाने का कपड़ा या रंगीन कागज any of a large group of seed-eating song-birds related to the finches, typically with brown streaked plumage and a boldly marked head. and other genera, family emberizidae: numerous species. *Those singing and seed eating birds finches belong to bunting family.*

Buoy/बॉय *(noun)* – जहाज का मार्ग दिखलाने के लिए लंगर पर लगा पीपा keep afloat. *I can see a buoy let us moor there we can no longer keep afloat.*

Buoyancy/बॉयोएन्सी *(noun)* – उतराव, हल्कापन a sleeveless jacket lined with buoyant material, worn for water sports. *People wear buoyant jackets for water sports.*

Burble/बरबल *(verb)* – कष्ट देना make a continuous murmuring noise. *He has a bad habit of burbling.*

Bureau/ब्यूरो *(noun)* – दफ्तर, महकमा, सूचनाएँ उपलब्ध कराने वाली संस्था British a writing desk with drawers and an angled top opening downwards to form a writing surface. *I have purchased a bureau because I have to do a lot of writing work.*

Bureaucracy/ब्यूरियोक्रेसी *(noun)* – नौकरशाही a system of government in which most decisions are taken by state officials rather than by elected representatives. a state or organization governed according to such a system. *Bureaucracy has been the misfortune of our nation.*

Bureaucrat/ब्यूरॉक्रैट *(noun)* – कर्मचारी शासन-पद्धति का अनुयायी, नौकरशाह a government official perceived as being overly concerned with procedural correctness. *Bureaucrats are not a popular breed.*

Burette/ब्यूरेट *(noun)* – तरल पदार्थ की मात्रा मापने के लिए नली a graduated glass tube with a tap at one end, for delivering known volumes of a liquid. *We works with burettes in our chemistry labs.*

Burgeon/बर्जन *(verb)* – उगना, निकल आना grow or increase rapidly. *Some plants burgeon at very fast rate.*

Burgess/बर्गेस *(noun)* – नागरिक British archaic an inhabitant of a town or borough with full rights of citizenship. *He is a burgess and an important person in parliament.*

Burglar/बरग्लर *(noun)* – सेंध मारने वाला चोर a person who commits burglary. *He is a burglar has been sent many times to jail.*

Burial/बरियल *(noun)* – दफन the burying of a dead body. a funeral. *A lot of people were present at his burial.*

Burliness/बर्लिनेस *(noun)* – स्थूलता state of being burly.

Burly/बर्लि *(adj.)* – पुष्ट मोटा-ताजा large and strong. *He is a very burly person.*

Burn/बर्न *(noun)* – जल जाना, जलन Scottish & north English a small stream. *There are many burns in this forest.*

Burner/बर्नर *(noun)* – दीपक a part of a cooker, lamp, etc. that emits a flame. *The burner of this gas stove has become choked.*

Burnish/बर्निश *(verb)* – रगड़कर चमकाना polish by rubbing. noun the shine on a polished surface. *You see these vessels they are shining because they have been burnished vigorously.*

Burnt/बर्न्ट – जला हुआ past and past participle of burn. *This house has been burnt to ashes.*

Burrow/बरो *(noun)* – बिल खोदना, जमीन खोदना a hole or tunnel dug by a small animal as a dwelling. verb make a burrow. dig into or through something solid. *Rats have made a burrow here.*

Burst/बर्स्ट *(verb)* – फटन, धड़ाका, भीतरी दबाव से एकाएक फट जाना break or cause to break suddenly and violently apart. *He burst out in anger.*

Bury/बरी *(verb)* – जमीन में दफनाना put or hide underground. place in the earth or a tomb. *She want to be buried in the village grave yard*

Bush/बुश *(noun)* – झाड़ी, जंगल [British] a metal lining for a round hole, especially one in which an axle revolves. *The bushes of this mixer have to be changed they are worn out.*

Business/बिजनेस *(noun)* – व्यापार, कारोबार a person's regular occupation or trade. work to be done or matters to be attended to. *I run the business of export and import of clothes.*

Businesslike/बिजनेसलाइक *(adj.)* – नियमपूर्वक efficient and practical. *He is a business like efficient and practical person.*

Buskin/बस्किन *(noun)* – घुटने तक का जूता [historical] a calf-high or knee-high boot. a thick-soled laced boot worn by an ancient Athenian tragic actor to gain height. *Many Americans still wear buskin.*

Bustle/बस्ल *(verb)* – कार्य में लगना to be of people noise or activity. *He bustled about the kitchen making tea*

Busy/बिजि *(adj.)* – कार्य में निरत, लीन having a great deal to do. [chiefly north American] engaged. *Right now I am very busy please meet me tomorrow.*

Butcher/बुचर *(noun)* – कसाई a person whose trade is cutting up and selling meat in a shop. a person who slaughters and cuts up animals for food, *The butcher living in our street is very conscious of hygiene and is very efficient there is always a crowd of meat buyers around his shop.*

B

Butler/बटलर *(noun)* – भण्डारी, खानसामा a man who works in a very large house, whose main duty is to organise and serve food.

Butter/बटर *(noun)* – मक्खन a pale yellow edible fatty substance made by churning cream and used as a spread or in cooking.

Butterfly/बटरफ्लाई *(noun)* – तितली any of a large group of nectar feeding lepidopterist insects with two pairs of large, typically colourful wings, distinguished from moths by having clubbed or dilated antennae, holding their wings erect when at rest, and being active by day. *It is right to see coloured butterflies flying or sitting on a flower. I am against catching them.*

Butterine/बटरिन *(noun)* – बनावटी मक्खन, नकली मक्खन a kind of artificial butter. *I don't like butterine.*

Buttery/बटरी *(noun)* – मक्खन के समान चिकना British a room in a college where food is kept and sold to students. *Will you go to buttery and buy some food.*

Buttock/बटक *(noun)* – चूतड़, नितम्ब either of the two round fleshy parts of the human body that form the bottom. *I feel like kicking you on buttock.*

Buttony/बटनी *(adj.)* – अनेक बटनों वाला having several buttons. *This is a buttony coat.*

Buttress/बटूश *(noun)* – पुश्ता, आधार a projecting support of stone or brick built against a wall. *This wall is buttressed by a stone wall.*

Buzz/बज *(verb)* – भिनभिनाना a low, continous humming or murmuring sound, made by or simialr to that made by an insect. the sound of a buzzer or telephone. [informal] a telephone call. *Flies were buzzing all around me.*

By/बाइ *(prep. & adv)* – निकट में, साथ, के द्वारा through the agency or means of. indicating how something happens. *I went to Shimla by bus.*

Byblow/बाइब्लो *(noun)* – दोगला बच्चा, जारज सन्तान [British dated] a man's illegitimate child. *This child is a byblow because his father was living with another woman.*

Bye/बाइ – सलाम exclamatory [informal] goodbye. *Bye-Bye son! Come back soon.*

Byelection/बाइ-इलेक्सन *(noun)* – उपनिर्वाचन British the election of an MP in a single constituency of fill a vacancy arising during a government's term of office. *In the byelection. The candidate of democratic party won.*

Bygone/बाइगॉन *(adj.)* – बिगत, बीता हुआ belonging to an earlier time. *In the bygone era humans lived in caves.*

By-law/बाइलॉ *(noun)* – उपनियम, उपविधि या व्यवस्था British a regulation made by a local authority or corporation. *Houses should be built according to the bylaws of corporation.*

Byname/बाइनेम *(noun)* – चिढ़ाने का या अप्रधान नाम a sobriquet or nickname. *His byname is Tinku.*

Bypass/बाइपास *(verb)* – पगडण्डी, उपमार्ग a road that passes round the city. *Let us try to bypass the town centre.*

Byre/बायर *(noun)* – गोशाला [British] a cowshed. *Cows are tied in the Byre.*

Byroad/बाइरोड *(noun)* – सड़क जिस पर कम लोग चलते है a minor road. *A byroad goes inside the forest.*

Bystander/बाइस्टैन्डर *(noun)* – किसी घटना का मूक दर्शक [historical] a fine textile fibre and fabric of flax. *This cloth is made of bystander.*

Byword/बाइवर्ड *(noun)* – कहावत, व्यक्ति या वस्तु जो किसी विशेषता का प्रतिनिधि माना जाता है a person or thing cited as a notable example or embodiment of something. *This man is a byword of honesty. A limousim is a byword for luxury.*

Bywork/बाइवर्क *(noun)* – अवकाश के समय किया हुआ कार्य, उपकाम *It is my bywork.*

Cc

C/सी – अंग्रेजी वर्णमाला का तीसरा अक्षर the third letter of the English alphabet

(1) The first note in the natural major scale in music.

(2) An academic mark indicating the third highest standard.

Cabal/केबल *(noun)* – गुप्त षड्यंत्र रचना a secret political clique or faction. *Cabal was a much feared organization in Russia during cold war.*

Cabaret/कैबरे *(noun)* – सराय entertainment held in a nightclub or restaurant while the audience eat or drink at tables. a nightclub or restaurant where such entertainment is performed. *I went to a famous cabaret I dined there as well as enjoyed the dance performance on the stage.*

Cabbage/कैबिज *(noun)* – बन्दगोभी a cultivated plant eaten as a vegetable, having thick green or purple leaves surrounding a spherical heart or head of young leaves. *Of all the vegetables cabbage is my favourite.*

Cabin/केबिन *(noun)* – कुटी, छोटा कमरा a private room or compartment on a ship. *I am going to my cabin to sleep please don't disturb me.*

Cabinet/कैबिनेट *(noun)* – छोटा कमरा, दराजवाली संदूक, मंत्रिमंडल a cupboard with drawers or shelves for storing or displaying articles. a wooden box, container, or place of furniture housing a radio, television set, or speaker. *A wooden almirah which has various cabinets for radio TV etc.*

Cable/केबल *(noun)* – मोटा, पुष्ट रस्सा a thick rope of wire or hemp, typically used for construction, mooring ships, and towing vehicles. the chain of a ship's anchor. Architecture a moulding resembling twisted rope. *This is a cable for television. Please don't destroy it.*

Cabosse/कैबूस *(noun)* – जहाज या रेल का रसोईघर [north American] a railway wagon with accommodation for the train crew, typically attached to the end of the train. *A caboose has been attached to the end of of trains in which the train crew is travelling.*

Cacao/ककाव *(noun)* – कोकोआ का वृक्ष bean-like seeds. *Cacao is bean like seed, from which cacao, cacao butter and chocolates are prepared.*

Cache/कैश *(noun)* – गुप्त स्थान, नशीले पदार्थ या हथियारों का a hidden store of things. *You will find this item in cache which is a hidden store of things.*

Cachectic/कैकेक्टिक *(adjective)* – रोगी, रुग्ण medicine relating to or having the symptoms of cachexia. *She seems cachectic.*

Cachet/कैशे *(noun)* – मोहर prestige. *The MP's car carried a cachet.*

Cachexy/कैकेक्सी *(noun)* – मस्तिष्क की रुग्णावस्था, दुर्बलता, विकृति Any general reduction in vitality and strength of body and mind resulting from a debilitating chronic disease. *This chronic cachexy has weakened his body.*

Cachinnate/कैकिन्नेट *(verb)* – जोरों से हँसना [poetic/literary] laugh loudly. *Don't cachinnate here, please.*

Cachou/कैशू *(noun)* – कत्था dated a pleasant-smelling lozenge sucked to mask bad breath. *he uses cachouto hide his bad breath.*

Cackle/कैकल *(verb)* – भद्दे तरीके से हँसना give a raucous clucking cry. make a similar sound when laughing. *He laughed giving a cackle cry.*

Cactus/कैक्टस *(noun)* – थूहर, नागफनी a succulent plant of a large family native to arid regions of the new world, with a thick fleshy stem which typically bears spines, lacks leaves, and has brilliantly coloured flowers. *I have grand collections of cactus at home.*

Cad/कैड *(noun)* – अशिष्ट आचरण का मनुष्य, नीच पाजी dated or humorous a man who behaves

C

dishonorably, especially towards a woman. *He is a cad having a sense of humour and behaving indecently.*

Caddish/कैडिश *(noun)* – अभद्र, गँवार a small moth-like insect of an order having aquatic larvae that build protective cases of sticks, stones, etc. *I have seen caddish. It is an insect having a watery larvae which sticks to a stone.*

Cadence/कैडेन्स *(noun)* – स्वर, ताल, ध्वनि a modulation or inflection of the voice. *I was lost in the cadence of music.*

Cadet/कैडेट *(noun)* – सैनिक छात्र, सैनिक विद्यालय का विद्यार्थी, कनिष्ठ पुत्र a young trainee in the armed services or police, a secondary school pupil, younger son or daughter. a junior branch of a family. *I was an N.C.C. cadet.*

Cadge/कैज *(verb)* – भीख माँगते फिरना, फेरी लगाना [informal] ask for or obtain. (noun) falconry a padded wooden frame on which hooded hawks are carried to the field. *My uncle was carrying a cadge to fields. In the cadge were sitting hooded hawks.*

Cadmium/कैडमियम *(noun)* – टीन के समान एक धातु the chemical element of atomic number 48, a silvery-white metal resembling zinc. *Have you seen cadmium? It is silvery white metal resembling zink.*

Cadre/काडर *(noun)* – किसी संगठन के कुछ सदस्य जो किसी विशेष उद्देश्य के लिए चुने व प्रशिक्षित किये जाते हैं a small group of people trained for a particular purpose or profession. *Cadre in a group of activists is a communist organization.*

Cafe/कैफे *(noun)* – काफी गृह a small restaurant selling light meals and drinks. *A cafe suites me very well, there is light and the drink are excellent.*

Cage/केज *(noun)* – पिंजरा a structure of bars or worse in which birds or other animals are confined. *Do you see these caged birds? What a pity? Can a man be so cruel?*

Cain/कैन *(noun)* – हत्यारा, भ्रातृहंता [informal] create trouble or a commotion. *These four men are responsible for caining in the public.*

Cairn/केर्न *(noun)* – समाधि के ऊपर बैठाये हुए, टीला, स्तूप पत्थर a mound of rough stoned built as a memorial or landmark. a prehistoric burial mound made of stones. *See that cairn! It is prehistoric burial.*

Caisson/कैशन *(noun)* – बारूद की पेटी, गोला बारूद का बक्सा a two-wheeled military vehicle carrying artillery ammunition. *This vessel acts as a gale across entrains of a dry look.*

Caitiff/कैटिफ *(noun)* – डरपोक मनुष्य [archaic] a contemptible or cowardly person. *He is caitiff and I am not ready to talk to such people.*

Cajole/केजोल *(verb)* – खुशामद करना persuade to do something by sustained coaxing or flattery. *I cajoled him into going to see a movie with me.*

Cake/केक *(noun)* – मीठी रोटी an item of soft sweet food made from baking a mixture or flour, fat, eggs, sugar, etc. *I have never asked a more sweet cake.*

Calabash/कैलबाश *(noun)* – तुम्बा an ever-green tropical American tree which bears fruit in the form of large woody gourds. *Dried shell of the gourd of this fruit is used in many forms water container, tobacco pipe etc.*

Calamitous/कैलामिटस *(adjective)* – अभागा, दुखद, अनर्थकर (of events) having extremely unfortunate or dire consequences; bringing ruin. *The sudden expanding of volcano was calamitous.*

Calamity/कलैमिटी – दुःख, संकट *(noun)* an event causing great and often sudden damage or distress. *There was an earthquake and sudden calamity followed.*

Calcareous/कैल्केरीअस *(adjective)* – चूना मिला हुआ, चूनेदार containing calcium carbonate; chalky. *This substance is calcareous and contains calcium carbonate.*

Calcify/कैल्सिफाइ *(verb)* – चूने के प्रयोग से किसी वस्तु का कड़ा हो जाना या कड़ा कर देना harden by deposition of or conversion into calcium carbonate or some other insoluble calcium compounds. *When you calcify it, it is jammed when it is hardened by deposition of calcium carbonate.*

Calcium/कैल्सियम *(noun)* – चूने का तत्व या सार, दूध या पनीर जैसे खाद्य पदार्थों में पाया जाने वाला एक रासायनिक तत्व जो हड्डियों व दाँतों को मजबूत बनाने में सहायक होता है the chemical element of atomic number 20, a soft grey reactive metal of the alkaline earth metal group. *Calcium is necessary for bone.*

Calculate/कैल्क्युलेट *(verb)* – गणना करना determine mathematically. *I can calculate this sum easily.*

Calculation/कैल्क्युलेशन *(noun)* – गणना, पूर्व विचार, परिकलन a mathematical determination of quantity or extent. *Calculation of this sum is not possible.*

Calculator/कैल्क्युलेटर *(noun)* – गणना करने वाला इलेक्ट्रॉनिक यंत्र something used for making mathematical calculations, in particular a small electronic device with a keyboard and a visual display. *For quick calculation. There is an electronic device called calculation.*

Calculus/कैल्क्युलस *(noun)* – गणित की एक शाखा a type of [mathematics] that deals with rates of change for example the speed of a falling object. *My maths teacher taught calculus.*

Calender/कैलेन्डर *(noun)* – जन्त्री, पंचांग a chart or series of pages showing the days, weeks, and months of a particular year. *I have bought a beautiful calendar with important and events.*

Calendula/कैलेन्ड्यूला *(noun)* – एक प्रकार का फूल a plant of a genus that includes the common or pot marigold. *Calendula is a famous medicine.*

Calf/काफ *(noun)* – बछड़ा a young bovine animal, especially a domestic cow or bull in its first year. *The young one of bovine family is called calf.*

Calibre/कैलिबर *(noun)* – चरित्र-बल, किसी वस्तु का गुण quality of character or level of ability. the standard reached by something. *My company's employees are of (a) high calibre.*

Calico/कैलिको *(noun)* – दरेस, छींट [British] a type of plain white or unbleached cotton cloth. [north American] printed cotton fabric. *(adjective)* [north American] (of an animal, typically a cat) multicoloured or piebald. *I like to wear dresses made of calico cloth especially the printed ones.*

Calif/कैलिफ *abbreviation* – of California. *California is my favorite city.*

Calix/कैलिक्स *(noun)* – पुष्पकोश variant spelling of CALYX. *I love to see calix, the thing of leave that covers a flower bed.*

Calk/काक *(noun&verb)* – जूते में नाल जड़ना US spelling of CAULK. *If a mason is not available You can yourself take same calk a water dry substance and can fill the cracks and joints.*

Call/कॉल *(verb)* – नाम लेना cry out of in order to summon them or attract their attention. telephone. *I called out to my friend to stop.*

Call-boy/कॉल-बॉय *(noun)* – नाटक में पात्रों को बुलाने वाल लड़का *(noun)* a person in a theatre who summons actors when they are due on stage. *The call boy called out to cators when they had to be present is the stage.*

Calligraphy/कैलिग्राफी *(noun)* – सुन्दर लिखावट की कला decorative handwriting or handwritten lettering. the art of producing this. *If you wish to see the art of calligraphy visit the scribes near Jama Masjid.*

Callisthenic/कैलिस्थेनिक *(Plural noun)* – शक्ति सौन्दर्यवर्द्धक व्यायाम, शरीर की शक्ति और सुन्दरता बढ़ाने वाली gymnastic exercises to achieve bodily fitness and grace of movement. *I took up callisthenic to develop grace and fitness of the body.*

Callosity/कैलोसिटी *(noun)* – चमड़े का कड़ापन technical a callus. *This belt has callosity but cannot wrinkle.*

Callous/कैलस *(adjective)* – कठोर, हृदय insensitive and cruel. (noun) variant spelling of CALLUS. *This boy is simply callous.*

Callow/कैलो *(adjective)* – पंखहीन, अनुभवहीन inexperienced and immature. *He is a callow youth.*

Callus/कैलस *(noun)* – गाँठ, रगड़ से त्वचा पर पड़ा घट्टा a thickened and hardened part of the skin or soft tissue, especially one caused by friction. [medicine] the bony healing tissue which forms around the ends of broken bone. *I just fell down and this part has hardened callus.*

Calm/काम *(adjective)* – शान्त, चुपचाप, उत्तेजनाहीन not showing or feeling nervousness, anger, or other emotions. *His attitude was calm and cool.*

Calmative/कामेटिव *(adjective)* – शान्ति लाने वाली having a sedative effect. (noun) a calmative drug. *Many drugs are calmative by nature, they and calm you. You may even go to sleep.*

C

Calmly/कामली *(adverb)* – शान्तिपूर्वक in a calm manner. *He calmly took to my harsh call.*

Calomel/कैलोमेल *(noun)* – रसकपूर miraculous chloride, a white powder formerly used as a purgative. *If you take calomel it may remove constipations.*

Caloric/कैलोरिक *(adjective)* – थर्मल, गरम सम्बन्धी chiefly [north American] or technical of or relating to heat; calorific. *(noun)* [physics] a hypothetical fluid substance formerly thought to be responsible for the phenomenon of heat. *Caloric was previously thought to be rated to heat.*

Calorie/कैलोरी *(noun)* – ऊर्जा की इकाई the energy needed to raise the temperature of 1 gram of water through 1°C, equal to one thousand small calories and often used to measure the energy value of foods. *Don't eat fried food it has high calorie value.*

Calorimeter/कैलोरीमीटर *(noun)* – गर्मी की मात्रा नापने का यन्त्र an apparatus for measuring the amount of heat involved in a chemical reaction or other process. *The amount of heat generator in a chemical reaction can be measured by calorimeter.*

Caluminate/कैलमिनेट *(verb)* – निन्दा करना formal make false and defamatory statements about. *He caluminated me but I kept my calm.*

Calumny/कलम्नी *(noun)* – मिथ्या आरोप the making of false and defamatory statements about someone. *(verb)* formal calumniate. *The calumny he made against me made me furious and I slapped him.*

Calve/काव *(verb)* – जनना (गाय का) give birth to a calf. *The cow calved.*

Calx/काक्स *(noun)* – किसी धातु का भस्म [chemistry, archaic] a powdery metallic oxide formed when an ore or mineral has been heated. *The calx has been heated and the powder that had formed is called metallic oxide.*

Calyx/कैलिक्स *(noun)* – पुटचक्र, वाह्य दलपुंज botany the sepals of a flower, typically forming a whorl that encloses the petals and forms a protective layer around a flower or bud. *Calyx is a ring of leaves enclosing the bud.*

Cam/कैम *(noun)* – गति बदलने वाला पहिये का उभड़ा भाग a projection on a rotating part in machinery, designed to make sliding contact with another part while rotating and impart reciprocal or variable motion to it. *A rotating part of machine that sets in motion other part is called cam.*

Cambric/कैमरिक *(noun)* – महीन वस्त्र a lightweight, closely woven white linen or cotton fabric. *I always like to wear lightweight cambric shirts.*

Came/केम *(noun)* – आभा each of a number of strips forming a framework for enclosing a pane of glass, especially in a leaded window. *You see these strips forming a panework in this leaded window pane these are called came.*

Camel/कैमेल *(noun)* – ऊँट a large, long-necked, mainly domesticated ungulate mammal of arid country, with long slender legs, broad cushioned feet, and either one or tow humps on the back. *While in desert I rode a camel and enjoyed the ride.*

Camelopard/कैमेलोपार्ड *(noun)* – लकड़हरना [archaic] a giraffe. *Camelopard is a tall and very long necked animal.*

Cameo/कैमिओ *(noun)* – पत्थर में उभड़ी हुई नकाशी a peace of jewellery consisting of a portrait in profile carved in relief on a background of a different colour. *I would like to buy that cameo with the portrait in the profile.*

Camera/कैमरा *(noun)* – फोटो खीचनें का यंत्र a device for recording visual images in the form of photographs, cinema film, or video signals. *I have bought the latest digital camera with multiple devices.*

Camion/कैमिअन *(noun)* – तोप ले जाने की गाड़ी a large truck designed to carry heavy loads; usually without sides. *A conveyance used for transporting guns is called camion.*

Camisole/कैमिसोल *(noun)* – स्त्रियों की भीतरी पोशाक a women's loose-fitting undergarment for the upper body. *The camisole she is wearing is very colourful.*

Camouflage/कैमफ्लाज् *(noun)* – शत्रु को छलने के लिए कलापूर्ण विधि the disguising of military personnel and equipment by painting or covering them to make them blend in with their surroundings. The clothing or materials used for such a purpose. *The military men are wearing camouflaged uniform it helps them disappear in jungle.*

Camp/कैम्प *(noun)* – शिविर a place where people live in tents or simple building away from the usual house camp behaviour or style. *The climbers set up camp at the foot of mountain.*

Campaign/कैम्पेन *(noun)* – किसी विशेष उद्देश्य से नियोजित अभियान में भाग लेना, आंदोलन करना a series of military operations intended to achieve an objective in a particular area. *We campaigned for a special operation.*

Comphor/कैम्फर *(noun)* – कपूर a white volatile crystalline substance with an aromatic smell and bitter taste, occurring in certain essential oils. *This oil has pungent smell of camphor.*

Can/कैन *abbreviation* – Canada or Canadian. *Canada/Canadian. He is a Canadian.*

Canal/कैनल *(noun)* – नाला, नहर an artificial waterway allowing the passage of boats inland or conveying water for irrigation. *Over village has a very long canal and we are fond of bathing in it. It was made by U.P. government.*

Canard/कैनार्ड *(noun)* – कटिपत कथा an unfounded rumour or story. *It is a canard that he met with an accident. I am just coming after meeting him he is all right .*

Canary/कैनरी *(noun)* – पीले रंग की कैनरी चिड़िया a bright yellow finch with a melodious song, popular as a cage bird. *I have just bought a canary the bright yellow singing sweet thing. Come today and we shall hear her singing.*

Cancel/कैनसल *(verb)* – रद्द करना, निरस्त करना deicide that will not take place. annul or revoke: his visa had been cancelled. *The meeting has been cancelled.*

Cancellation/कैनसलेशन *(noun)* – रद्द करने की क्रिया *We had to make a last minute cancellation of our air tickets to Mumbai.*

Cancer/कैंसर *(noun)* – कर्क राशि, विस्फोट [Astronomy] a constellation said to represent a crab crushed under the foot of Hercules. *This month my cancer is strange and my financial condition will become good.*

Candle/कैन्डल *(noun)* – मोमबत्ती a cylinder of wax or tallow with a central wick which is lit to produce light as it burns. *I love to eat candle-light dinner with my girl friend.*

Candlemas/कैन्डलमास *(noun)* – कुमारी मेरी की स्मृति में दूसरी फरवरी की त्योहार February to commemorate the purification of the virgin marry and the presentation of Christ in the temple. *I joined candlemas last year*

Candour/कैन्डर *(noun)* – सरलता, सच्चाई, निष्कपटता the quality of being open and honest. *I like his candour character.*

Candy/कैन्डी *(noun)* – मिश्री [north American] sweets; confectionery. *Children love candies a lot.*

Cane/केन *(noun)* – बेंत the hollow jointed stem of tall reeds, grasses, etc., especially bamboo or the slender; pliant stem of plants such as rattan. a woody stem of a raspberry or related plant. *He was beaten with a cane as punishment.*

Canister/कैनिस्टर *(noun)* – टीन का पीपा a round or cylindrical container used for storing food, chemicals, rolls of film, etc. *We keep chemicall, film rolls, food etc. On round or cylindrical containers called canisters.*

Canker/कैन्कर *(noun)* – कीड़ी, घुन, पौधों का एक रोग destructive fungal disease of trees that results in damage to the bark. an open lesion in plant tissue caused by infection or injury. fungal rot in parsnips, tomatoes, or other vegetables. *You see this damaged bark of the tree. This is caused by a destructive fungal disease called canker.*

Cannon/कैनन *(noun)* – तोप a large, heavy piece of artillery formerly used in warfare. an automatic heavy gun that fires shells from an aircraft or tank. *Once for a way I saw artillery, an automatic heavy gun fire that fires shells from an aircraft or tank.*

Cannonade/कैननेड *(noun)* – निरन्तर गोला चलाना, गोलीबारी a period of continuous heavy gunfire. *(verb)* discharge heavy guns continuously. *There was cannonade and a heavy gun fire discharged continuously at the border.*

Cannula/कैन्यूला *(noun)* – धातु की जरही नली [surgery] a thin tube inserted into the body to administer medication, drain off fluid, or introduce a surgical instrument. *When my father was being operated upon cannula was inserted into his body.*

Canny/कैनी *(adjective)* – चतुर, चालाक, सावधान shrewd, especially in financial or business matters. *He is a canny fellow smart and shrewd in business and financial matters.*

Canoe/कैनू *(noun)* – डोंगी a narrow keelless boat with pointed ends. propelled with a paddle. *(verb)* travel in or paddle a canoe. *Once in a river in Africa I travelled in a canoe. It was great fun.*

Canon/कैनन *(noun)* – गिरजाघर की डिगरी, पादरी, कानून a member of the clergy on the staff of a cathedral, especially one who is a member of the chapter. *He is a canon Roman catholic clergy that lives like nuns and monks.*

Canonical/कैनानिकल *(adjective)* – नियमानुसार की डिगरी, प्रमाणिक, धर्म वैधानिक according to or ordered by canon [law]. *Please, follow canonical teaching.*

Canopy/कैनपि *(noun)* – चँदवा, आच्छादन a clothe covering over a throne, bed, etc. a roof-like projection or shelter. the expanding, umbrella-like part of a parachute. *The highest branches in the rainforest form a dense canopy.*

Canorous/कैनरस *(adjective)* – सुरीला rare melodious or resonant. *He has got a canorous voice.*

Cant/कैन्ट *(noun)* – कुभाषा, कपट की बात hypocritical and sanctimonious talk. *The report was wonderfully free of cant.*

Cantab/कैन्टब *abbreviation* – कैम्ब्रिज विश्वविद्यालय का सदस्य of Cambridge university. *Abbreviation of Cambridge university.*

Cantaloup/कैन्टलूप *(noun)* – एक प्रकार का बिलायती खरबूजा a small round melon of a variety with orange flesh and ribbed skin. *In taste I found cantaloupe better than ordinary melon.*

Cantankerous/कैन्टनकेरस *(adjective)* – लड़ाका bad-tempered, argumentative, and uncooperative. *He is a cantankerous fellow.*

Canteen/कैन्टीन *(noun)* – जलपान गृह a restaurant in a workplace or educational establishment. *I take lunch in my school canteen.*

Canter/कैन्टर *(noun)* – कदम चाल, घोड़े और घुड़सवार का मध्यम गति से दौड़ना a pace of a horse between a trot and a gallop, with not less than one foot on the ground at any time. a ride on a horse at such a speed. *(verb)* move at this pace. *I rode a cantering horse.*

Canticle/कैन्टिकल *(noun)* – छोटा गीत a hymn or chant forming a regular part of a church service. *A canticle was being sung in the church.*

Cantilever/कैन्टिलिवर *(noun)* – लकड़ी या धातु का लम्बा टुकड़ा जो दीवार से बाहर की तरफ निकला होता है और पुल या किसी अन्य ढाँचे को बल देता है, घोड़िया a long projecting beam or girder fixed at only one end, used chiefly in bridge construction. a bracket or beam projecting from a wall to support a balcony, cornice, etc. *(verb)* support by a cantilever or cantilevers. *This cantilever projecting from the wall is supporting this balcony.*

Canton/कैन्टन *(noun)* – प्रदेश, भाग a political or administrative subdivision of a country. a state of the Swiss confederation. *Canton is a state of the Swiss confederation.*

Cantonment/कैन्टॉनमेन्ट *(noun)* – छावनी, a military camp, especially a permanent military station in [British] India. *My uncle is a military officer, he stays in cantonment area which is a permanent military station.*

Canvas/कैनृवस *(noun)* – तिरपाल a strong, coarse unbleached cloth used to make sails, tents, etc. and as a surface for oil painting. a piece of canvas prepared for use as the surface for an oil painting. the floor of a boxing or wrestling ring, having a canvas covering. *I use canvas for oil painting.*

Canvass/कैनृवास *(verb)* – वोट माँगना, परीक्षा करना solicit votes from (electors). question in order to ascertain their opinion on something. *Canvassing for election is going at full speed.*

Canyon/कैनृयन *(noun)* – झरना, तीखे ढाल वाली गहरी घाटी a deep gorge, especially one with a river flowing through it. *Grand canyon of America is worth a visit.*

Cap/कैप *abbreviation* – टोपी, शिखर capacity. *I dan't have capacity for such hard work.*

Capability/कैपबिलिटि *(noun)* – योग्यता power or ability to do something. an undeveloped or unused faculty. *I have capability of speaking five languages.*

Capable/कैपेबल *(adjective)* – कार्य करने में सक्षम या समर्थ having the ability or quality necessary to do something. open to or admitting of something. *I am capable of crossing this river.*

Capacious/कैपेसस *(adjective)* – विशाल having a lot of space inside; roomy. *This building is quite capacious.*

Capacitate/कैपैसिटेट *(verb)* – गुणयुक्त करना formal or [archaic] make capable or legally competent. *He has been capacitated to become a first class lawyer.*

Capacity/कैपेसिटी *(noun)* – किसी पात्र की ग्रहणशक्ति the maximum amount that something can contain or produce. fully occupying the available space: a capacity crowd. the total cylinder volume that is swept by the pistons in an internal-combustion engine. *This glass is full of water. It has no more capacity.*

Cape/केप *(noun)* – बिना बाँहों के कंधों से लटकने वाला ऊपरी वस्त्र, अंतरीप the cape of good hope. *A piece of high land that sticks out into the sea the cape of good hope.*

Caper/केपर *(verb)* – उछल-कूद, कूद-फाँद, कूदना, फुदकना skip or dance about in a lively or playful way. *(noun)* a playful skipping movement. *She capered softly and lightly on the stage.*

Capillary/कैपिलरि *(noun)* – कोशिकानली, शरीर की सबसे छोटी रुधिर वाहिनियों में से एक कोशिकानली anatomy any of the fine branching blood vessels that form a network between the arterioles and venues. *Very small capillaries that join the arteries and veins.*

Capital/कैपिटल *(noun)* – राजधानी, मूलधन architecture the distinct, typically broader section at the head of a pillar or column. *New Delhi is the capital of India.*

Capitulate/कपिट्युलेट *(verb)* – किसी शर्त पर शत्रु के अधीन हो जाना cease to resist an opponent or an unwelcome demand; surrender. *The army capitulated before the enemy forces.*

Capon/केपन् *(noun)* – बधिया किया मुर्गा, मछली, पत्र a castrated domestic cock fattened for eating. *There is our fattened capon we intend to cut it today.*

Caprice/कैप्रिस *(noun)* – चपलता a sudden and unaccountable change of mood or behaviour. *As he is a man of caprice, it is difficult to deal with him.*

Capricious/कैप्रिशस *(adjective)* – चपल relating to or resembling a goat or goats. *He is capricious and cannot be trusted.*

Capricorn/कैप्रिकॉर्न *(noun)* – मकर राशि astrology the tenth sign of the zodiac which the sun enters at the northern winter solstice. *I was born under the sign of Capricorn.*

Caprine/कैप्रिन् *(adjective)* – बकरे या बकरे के समान relating to or resembling a goat or goats.

Capsicum/कैप्सिकम *(noun)* – शिमला मिर्च the fruit of a tropical American plant, of which sweet peppers and chilli peppers are varieties. *I am very fond of eating capsicum.*

Caprize/कैप्राइज *(verb)* – उलट देना be overturned in the water. *The boat capsized and sank into water.*

Captain/कैप्टन *(noun)* – नायक, कप्तान the person in command of a ship. the pilot in command of a civil aircraft. a rank of naval officer above commander and below commodore. *It is my ambition to become a captain either of a ship or of an aeroplane.*

Captions/कैप्सन *(noun)* – अनुशीर्षक, चित्र या फोटो के नीचे लिखित सूचना a title or brief explanation appended to an illustration or cartoon. a piece of text appearing on screen as part of a film or broadcast. *I enjoyed that Russian film simply because it had captions. The cartoon film was provided with captions.*

Captious/कैप्सस *(adjective)* – दोष ढूँढ़ने वाला formal tending to find fault or raise petty objections. *He is a man of captious nature.*

Captivate/कैप्टिवेट *(verb)* – मोहित करना attract and hold the interest and attention of; charm. *I found the film very captivating.*

Captive/कैप्टिव *(adj)* – बन्दी, कैदी, पिंजरे में बंद a person who has been taken prisoner or confined. *He has been captive.*

Captor/कैप्टर *(noun)* – बन्दी को पकड़ने या इनाम लेने वाला a person who imprisons or confines another. *She is so beautiful as to be my captor.*

Capture/कैप्चर *(verb)* – अधिकार या कब्जा करना take into one's possession or control by force.

C

make a move that secures the removal of (an opposing piece). *We captured the territories of enemy forces.*

Carocole/कैरोकोल *(noun)* – घोड़े की तिरछी चाल a half turn to the right or left by a horse. *(verb)* perform a caracole. *The horse was performing a caracole.*

Carat/कैरट *(noun)* – सोने की शुद्धता की माप की इकाई कैरट a unit of weight for precious stones and pearls, equivalent to 200 milligrams. *Maharaja jwellers are her favourite. She always buys in carat gold ornaments from them.*

Caravan/कैरवैन *(noun)* – काफिला, कारयुक्त बड़ा वाहन जिमें आमोद यात्रा के दौरान रहने, सोने, खाने, पीने आदि का प्रबंध होता है a vehicle equipped for living in, usually designed to be towed. *While in Rajasthan I came across a long colourful caravan.*

Carbide/कारबाइड *(noun)* – दूसरे तत्वों के साथ कार्बन का यौगिक [chemistry] a compound of carbon with a metal or other element: silicon carbide. *Carbide is a compound of carbon with a metal.*

Carbon/कार्बन *(noun)* – कोयला the chemical element of atomic number 6, non-metal which has two main forms occurs in impure form in charcoal, soot, and coal, and is present in all organic compounds. *Lots of writing problems have been solved by invention of carbon paper.*

Carbonic/कार्बनिक *(adjective)* – कार्बन सम्बन्धी of or relating to carbon or carbon dioxide. *Relating to carbon.*

Carbuncle/कारबंकल *(noun)* – रक्तमणि a severe abscess or multiple boil in the skin. *It is a carbuncle boil on year arm. You should at once consult a skin surgeon.*

Card/कार्ड *(verb)* – गत्ते या प्लास्टिक का कार्ड जिस पर सूचना होती है comb and clean with a sharp-toothed instrument to disentangle the fibres before spinning. *A sharp toothed comb to clean fibres before spinning is called card.*

Cardamom/कार्डमम *(noun)* – इलायची the aromatic seeds of a plant of the ginger family, used as a spice. *I like a bit of cardamom in my tea along with ginger.*

Cardiac/कार्डिआक *(adjective)* – हृदय सम्बन्धी of or relating to the heart. *He died of cardiac arrest.*

Cardinal/कार्डिनल *(noun)* – रोमन कैथोलिक चर्च का उच्च स्तरीय पादरी a leading dignitary of the roman catholic church, nominated by and having the power to elect the pope. *Nominated by pope, cardinal is a leading dignitary.*

Cardiograph/कार्डियोग्राफ *(noun)* – एक यन्त्र an instrument for recording heart muscle activity. *Doctors use cardiograph to measure heart activity.*

Care/केअर *(noun)* – किसी की देखभाल या देखरेख the provision of what is necessary for the health, welfare, maintenance, and protection of someone or something. [British] protective custody or guardianship provided for children by a local authority. *The adopled son was well taken care of.*

Career/करियर *(noun)* – नौकरी या पेशा an occupation undertaken for a significant period of a person's life, usually with opportunities for progress. the progress through history of an institution or organization. working with commitment in a particular profession: a career diplomat. pursuing a profession. *Without career, there is no life.*

Careful/केअरफुल *(adjective)* – सावधान, खबरदार taking care to avoid mishap or harm; cautious. protective of. prudent in the use of. *Be careful while driving lest you meet with an accident.*

Careless/केअरलेस *(adjective)* – असावधानी या लापरवाही not giving sufficient attention or thought to avoiding harm or mistakes. not concerned or worried about. showing no interest or effort; casual. *Don't assign any important work to him he is a careless fellow.*

Caress/केअरेस *(verb)* – लाड़-प्यार करना, प्रेम स्पर्श करना touch or stroke gently or lovingly. *(noun)* a gentle or loving touch. *I caressed her with love and affection.*

Caret/कैरिट *(noun)* – काकपद a mark placed below a line of text to indicate a proposed insertion. *Wherever you wish to in sort in text put a mark or caret under it.*

Cargo/कार्गो *(noun)* – विमान या जलपोत के द्वारा ढोया जाने वाला माल goods carried commercially on a ship, aircraft, or truck. *A cargo ship is different from passenger ship.*

Carking/कारकिंग *(adjective)* – कष्टकारक [archaic] causing distress or worry. *He is a carking fellow.*

Carl/कार्ल *(noun)* – नीच पुरुष, खेतिहर [archaic] a man of low birth. Scottish a man; a fellow. *He is a Carl and as such I don't want to have relations with him.*

Carline/कार्लाइन *(noun)* – डाइन any of the pieces of squared timber fitted fore and aft between the deck beams of a wooden ship to support the deck planking. *A fixture of the wooden squared timber fitted in a wooden ship from end to end.*

Carminative/कार्मिनेटिव *(adjective)* – बादी हटाने की दवा relieving flatulence. (noun) a carminative drug. *Carminative is a wind relieving drug in the stomach.*

Carmine/कारमाइन *(noun)* – लाल रंग a vivid crimson pigment made from cochineal. *It is a carmine pigment.*

Carnage/कानिज *(noun)* – संहार, सामूहिक हत्याकाण्ड the killing of a large number of people. *Carnage took place when Nadir Shah entered Delhi.*

Carnal/कारनल *(adjective)* – दैहिक, शारीरिक relating to physical, especially sexual, needs and activities. *Sexual needs are regarded as carnal.*

Carnation/कानेशन *(noun)* – सफेद गुलाबी या लाल सुगन्धित पुष्प a double-lowered cultivated variety of clove pink, with grey-green leaves and showy pink, white, or red flowers. *Carnation is a variety of clove.*

Carnival/कारनिवल *(noun)* – आनन्द उत्सव an annual period of public revelry involving processions, [music], dancing, etc. *in south America, Rio de Jenerio the annual carnival is celebrated with much fan fare. It is a tourist attrition as well.*

Carnivore/कारनिवोर *(plural noun)* – मांसभक्षी पशुओं की जाति [zoology] an order of mammals comprising the cats, dogs, bears, hyenas, weasels, civets, raccoons, and mongooses, having powerful jaws and teeth adapted for tearing and eating flesh. *Lion belongs to carnivore order of mammals.*

Carnivorous/कारनिवोरस *(adjective)* – मांसाहारी feeding on flesh. *Lion is a carnivorous animal.*

Carol/कैरॅल *(verb)* – ईसाइयों का धार्मिक भजन जो क्रिसमस पर गाया जाता है, गीत, स्तोत्र sing carols in the streets. *We sang carols happily in the streets.*

Carouse/कैराउस *(verb)* – अधिक मदिरा पीना drink alcohol and enjoy oneself with others in a noisy, lively way. *(noun)* a noisy, lively drinking party. *We arranged a party shortly some other friends also joined and soon we were carousing.*

Carp/कार्प *(verb)* – मीठे पानी की एक मछली complain or find fault continually. *Don't carp in the morning and make my day horrible.*

Carpal/कार्पल *(adjective)* – कलाई की आठ छोटी हड्डियाँ में से एक Any of the eight small bones in the wrist. *As she fell down, she felt her carpal strained.*

Carpenter/कारपेन्टर *(noun)* – बढई a person who makes wooden objects and structures. *(verb)* make by shaping wood. *He is a carpenter by profession.*

Carpet/कारपेट *(noun)* – कालीन, गलीचा a floor covering made from thick woven fabric. a large rug. *I bought a wall to wall carpet.*

Carpus/कार्पस *(noun)* – कलाई, मणिबंध the group of small bones between the main part of the forelimb and the metacarpus, forming the writs in humans. *She strained her carpus.*

Carriage/कैरिज *(noun)* – परिवहन a four-wheeled passenger vehicle pulled by tow or more horses. a wheeled support for moving a heavy object such as a gun. *In old times horse driven carriages were very popular.*

Carrier/कैरिअर *(noun)* – यात्रियों का समान ढोने वाली कंपनी a person or thing that carries, holds, or coveys something. *He carried the news to me. He is a news carrier.*

Carriole/कैरिओल *(noun)* – छोटी खुली गाड़ी [historical] a small open horse-drawn carriage for one person. a light covered cart. *In old time there used to be single person driven covered carriages called carrioles.*

Carry/कैरी *(verb)* – ले जाने की स्थिति संभालना, उठा रखना, किसी वस्तु या व्यक्ति को हाथों बाँहों आदि में थामकर एक स्थान से दूसरे स्थान तक ले जाना move or transport form one place to another. have on one's person wherever one

C

C

goes. conduct; transmit. be infected with and liable to transmit it to others. *I carried and delivered the parcel to him.*

Cartilage/कार्टिलेज *(noun)* – कोमलास्थि a firm, whitish, flexible connective tissue which is the main component of the articulating surfaces of joints and of structures such as the larynx and respiratory tract and the external ear. *He is suffering from as to arthritis as the cartilage of both his knees has dried.*

Cartographer/कार्टोग्राफर *(noun)* – नक्शा बनाने की कला, नक्शानवीस, मानचित्रकार a person who maps makes. *My brother is a cartographer.*

Cartography/कार्टोग्राफी *(noun)* – नक्शा खींचने की कला, नक्शानवीसी the science or practice of drawing maps. *Cartography is an art.*

Carton/कार्टन *(noun)* – सामान रखने का गत्ते या प्लास्टिक का डिब्बा a light cardboard container. *The new fridge I bought was enclosed in a big carton.*

Cartouche/कार्टूश *(noun)* – कारतूस रखने का बक्सा a carved tablet or drawing representing a scroll with rolled-up ends, used or name tally or bearing an inscription. a decorative architectural feature resembling a scroll. an ornate frame around a design or inscription. *If you look at Egyptian hieroglyphs bearing the name and title of a monarch, you will usually find them enclosed in an oval or oblong cartouche.*

Cartridge/कार्ट्रिज *(noun)* – कारतूस, किसी मशीन में प्रयुक्त सामग्री को रखने का बंद पात्र, इस पुर्जे को निकाला व पुनः भरा जा सकता है a container holding a spool of photographic film, a quantity of ink, or other item or substance, designed for insertion into a mechanism. *I have some space cartridges. You can keep your film spools into them.*

Caruncle/कारंकल *(noun)* – मांसग्रन्थि [zoology] a fleshy outgrowth, such as a bird's wattles or the red prominence at the inner corner of the eye. *This fleshy outgrawht is called caruncle.*

Cascade/कैस्केड *(noun)* – छोटा झरना a small waterfall, especially one in a series. *There is a cascade, we can take a bath here.*

Case/केस – *(noun)* घटना, स्थान a container designed to hold or protect something. the outer protective covering of a natural or manufactured object. *Here is a case for your spectacles. It is strong enough to protect your glasses.*

Casement/केसमेन्ट *(noun)* – खिड़की का कब्जेदार पल्ला a window set on a vertical hinge so that it opens like a door. *Please open the window casement and you will have a nice view of the sea.*

Caseous/कैसिअस *(adjective)* – पनीर के सदृश [medicine] characterized by caseation. *It is cheese like medicine. It seems caseous.*

Cash/कैश *(noun)* – रोकड़, नकद, नकदी [historical] a coin of low value from china, southern India, or SE Asia. *This coin seems to be cash either from China or India.*

Cashier/कैशिअर *(noun)* – रोकड़िया person handling payments and receipts in shop, bank, or business. *My father is a cashier in the bank. He handles payments and receipts.*

Cashmere/कश्मीरी *(noun)* – पशमीनें का दुशाला fine soft wool, originally that from the Kashmir goat. *I am wearing a cashmere sweater. It is very warm.*

Casing/केसिंग *(noun)* – ढकना a cover or shell that protects or encloses something. *The glass pane of the window is enclosed in a metallic casing.*

Casino/केसिनो *(noun)* – ऐसा स्थान जहाँ खेल-खेलकर पैसा जीता या हारा जा सकता है, जुआघर, कैसीनो an establishment where gambling games are played. *I visited a casino abroad. There a lot of gambling games were being played.*

Cask/कास्क *(noun)* – पीपा a large barrel-like container for the storage of liquid, especially alcoholic drinks. *My uncle has a cask full of rum.*

Casket/कासकिट *(noun)* – गहने रखने की सजावटी संदूकची a small ornamental box or chest for holding valuable objects. [British] a small wooden box for cremated ashes. chiefly [north American] a coffin. *My aunt keeps all ornaments in a casket.*

Casque/कास्क *(noun)* – फौजी टोपी [historical] a helmet. *Soldiers used to wear a casque while going to war.*

Cassia/कैशीअ *(noun)* – दालचीनी a leguminous tree or plant of warm climates, producing senna and other valuable products. *A lot of cassia trees (cinnamon) grew in our country.*

Cassock/कैसॉक *(noun)* – चोंगा a long garment worn by some Christian clergy and members of church choirs. *I have seen Christian clergy wearing cassocks.*

Cast/कास्ट *(noun)* – किसी नाटक आदि के समस्त कलाकार the actors taking part in a play or film. *(verb)* assign a part to (an actor). allocate parts in (a play or film). *The cast of the film is impressive.*

Caste/कास्ट *(noun)* – वर्ग, जाति each of the hereditary classes of Hindu society, distinguished by relative degrees of ritual purity of pollution and of social status. *Casteism has been the curse of India.*

Castigate/कास्टिगेट *(verb)* – ताड़ना देना, फटकारना reprimand severely. *I was castigated by my father for bunking the school.*

Cast-iron/कास्ट आयरन *(noun)* – कान्ती लोहा, ढलवा लोहा a hard, relatively brittle alloy of iron and carbon which can be readily cast in a mould. *my father deals in cast-iron business.*

Castle/कासल *(noun)* – किला दुर्ग the chaice of actors to play poarticular roles in a play or movie. *In old times kings used to live in castles.*

Castor-oil/कास्टर आयल *(noun)* – रेडी (अरंडी) का तेल a pale yellow purgative oil obtained from the seeds of an African shrub. *I took a close of castor-oil as I was suffering from constipation.*

Casual/कैजुअल *(adjective)* – आकस्मिक, अचानक relaxed and unconcerned. made, done, or acting without much care or thought. *He takes everything casually.*

Casuist/कैसुइस्ट *(noun)* – प्रलाप a person who uses clever but false reasoning. *He is a casuist and as such I don't like him.*

Cat/कैट *(noun)* – बिल्ली a catalytic converter. *We have a device in our cares exhaust system for converting pollutant gases into less harmful ones.*

Cata/केटा *prefix* – पीछे down; downwards; catadromous.

Cataclysm/कैटक्लिज्म *(noun)* – प्रलय, पानी की बाढ़ a violent upheaval or disaster. *The earthquake caused cataclysm.*

Catacomb/कैटकोम *(noun)* – मुर्दा रखने का, कब्रों का तहखाना an underground cemetery consisting of a gallery with recesses for tombs. *He was lost in the dark and frightening catacomb.*

Catalepsy/कैटलेप्सी *(noun)* – अपस्मार, मिरगी रोग a medical condition characterized by a trance or seizure with a loss of sensation and consciousness accompanied by rigidity of the body. *She suffered from catalepsy and at that time she appeared dead.*

Catalogue/कैटलॉग *(noun)* – वर्णक्रमानुसार सूचीपत्र a complete list of items arranged in alphabetical or other systematic order. *Please give your catalogue, I would like to know what you have got into your shop.*

Catamaran/कैटमरैन *(noun)* – दो पाटों वाली तीव्र गति नौका a yacht or other boat with twin hulls in parallel. *I was offered a ride in catamaran and enjoyed it.*

Cataplasm/कैटाप्लाज्म *(noun)* – फोड़े आदि पर बाँधने की पुलटिस [archaic] a plaster or poultice. *You should apply a cataplasm on your injury.*

Cataract/कैटरैक्ट *(noun)* – मोतियाबिन्द, जल का बड़ा प्रपात a large waterfall. *You have cataract in both of your eyes. I think you should consult aneye surgeon.*

Catarrh/कैटार – सर्दी, जुकाम *(noun)* excessive discharge of mucus in the nose or throat. *You are suffering from catarrh. Take some medicine.*

Catastrophe/कैटास्ट्रॉफी *(noun)* – आकस्मिक बड़ी आपत्ति, दुर्गति an event causing great damage or suffering. *The excursive floods brought great catastrophe.*

Catch/कैच *(verb)* – पकड़ना, थामना intercept and hold (something which has been thrown, propelled, or dropped). seize or take hold of. Cricket dismiss by catching the ball before it touches the ground. *Dravid caught a brilliant catch.*

Catching/कैचिंग *(adj)* – संक्रामक, आकर्षक in fectious, attractive. *It was an eye catching view.*

C

C

Catchy/कैची *(adj.)* – आकर्षक छलने वाली likely to attract attention. *It is a catchy song.*

Catechism/कैटकिज्म *(noun)* – ईसाई चर्च की मान्यताओं को सिखाने वाली प्रश्नोत्तरी a summary of the principles of Christian religion in the form of question and answers, used for teaching. *Principles of Christion religion are taught pen catechism.*

Catechize/कैटकाइज *(verb)* – प्रश्नोत्तर विधि से पूछताछ करना instruct by means of question and answer; especially by using a catechism. *Students are instructed by using catechizing method .*

Catechu/कैटिचू *(noun)* – कत्था, खैर a vegetable extract containing tennis, chiefly obtained form an Indian acacia tree and used for tanning and dyeing. *For tanning and dyeing a vegetable extract is used which is obtained from Indian tree acacia.*

Categorical/कैटेगोरिकल *(adjective)* – सुनिश्चित, सुस्पष्ट unambiguously explicit and direct. *The answer was a categorically no.*

Category/कैटगॅरी *(noun)* – समानवर्ग, व्यक्ति या वस्तुओं का वर्ग a class or division of people or things having particular shared characteristics. *So far as social status is concerned we belong to the same category.*

Cater/केटर *(verb)* – आवश्यकताओं की पूर्ति करना [chiefly British] provide food and drink at a social event. *Don't worry a lot of people are here to cater to your needs.*

Caterpillar/कैटरपिलर *(noun)* – कीड़ा, झिंगा the larva of butterfly or moth. *Caterpillars are beautiful to look at.*

Cathectic/कैथेक्टिक *(adjective)* – रेचक, विरेचक psychoanalysis of or relating to cathexis. *This powder is cathectic.*

Cathedra/कैथेड्रा – पादरी का सिंहासन *(noun)* a throne that is the official chair of a bishop.

Cathedral/कथीड्रल *(noun)* – बड़ा गिर्जाघर the principal church of a diocese. *The main church of a diocese where the bishop has his throan.*

Catheter/कैथिटर *(noun)* – पेशाब कराने की नलकी [medicine] a flexible tube inserted through a narrow opening into a body cavity, particularly the bladder, for removing fluid. *My friend could pass urine so they inserted catheter in his body through a thin opening and took out the fluid.*

Catholic/कैथलिक *(adjective)* – उदारचित, सहिष्णु including a wide variety of things. *My friend is of Roman catholic faiths.*

Catling/कैटलिंग *(noun)* – जर्राही छुरी, नश्तर double edged knife uesd to amputation. *Doctors use catling for amputation.*

Catoptric/कैटोट्रिक *(adjective)* – दर्पण या प्रतिबिम्ब सम्बन्धी [physics] of or relating to a mirror or reflection. *In own student days we had done lots of catoptric experiments.*

Cat's eye/कैट्स आई *(noun)* – लहसुनिया रत्न a semi-precious stone, especially chalcedony, with a chatoyant lustre. *My friend wears cat's eye. It suits him well.*

Cattle/कैटल *(plural noun)* – गाय, मवेशी large ruminant animals with horns and cloven hoofs, chiefly domesticated for meat or milk or as beasts of burden; cows and oxen. *This person has the greatest herd of cattle.*

Caudal/कॉडल *(adjective)* – पूँछ का, पूच्छीय of or like a taill. at or near the tail or the posterior part of the body. *Caudal growth in man disappeared a long time ago.*

Caught/कॉट – पकड़ा past and past participle of catch. *He was caught off mid wicket.*

Caul/कॉल *(noun)* – खवेड़ी, शीर्षावरण, भ्रूण झिल्ली the amniotic membrane enclosing a foetus. part of this membrane occasionally found on a child's head at birth, thought to bring good luck. *The child has a caul of it around it in the womb.*

Cauldron/कॉल्ड्न *(noun)* – कड़ाही a large metal pot, used for cooking over an open fire. *The vegetables for the wedding guests are being cooked in a cauldron.*

Cauliflower/कॉलिफ्लावर *(noun)* – फूलगोभी a cabbage of a variety which bears a large immature flower head of small creamy-white flower buds, eaten as a vegetable. *I like cauliflower.*

Causal/कॉजल *(adjective)* – हेतुक, कारण बताने वाला of, relating to, or acting as a cause. *The causal effect or rain was heavy floods.*

Causility/कॉजिलिटी *(noun)* – कारणत्व the relationship between cause and effect. *Without causility there can be no effect.*

Causation/कॉजेशन *(noun)* – कारण उपस्थित करने का कार्य the action of causing something. *The cause of his illness was being bitten by dangerous mosquitoes.*

Causative/कॉजटिव *(adjective)* – कारण सूचित करने वाला, कारण वाचक, प्रेरणार्थक acting as a cause. *The cause of his illness was being bitten by dangerous mosquitoes.*

Cause/कॉज *(noun)* – ध्येय, अभिप्राय a person or thing that gives rise to an action, phenomenon, or condition. reasonable grounds for a belief or action. *Heavy clouds are the cause and rain its effects.*

Causeless/कॉजलेस *(adj.)* – अकारण, निरुद्देश्य having no justifying cause or reason. *This attack seems to be causeless.*

Causeway/कॉजवे *(noun)* – बाँध a raised road or track across low or wet ground. *There is a causeway here, you can softly drive your car.*

Caustic/कॉस्टिक *(adjective)* – रासायनिक क्रिया द्वारा वस्तुओं को जला देने में सक्षम, ताना भरा able to burn or corrode organic tissue by chemical action. *Her caustic remarks upset him.*

Caution/कॉशन *(noun)* – चौकस, विशेष सावधानी care taken to avoid danger or mistakes. *Be cautious while taking that mud road.*

Cautionary/कॉशनरि *(adjective)* – सचेत करने के रूप में दिया हुआ serving as a warning. *There is a cautionary warning on the board.*

Cavalier/कैवलियर *(noun)* – घुड़सवार [historical] a supporter of King Charles I in the English civil war. *Cavaliers were soldiers fighting under a king.*

Cavalry/कैवलरी *(noun)* – घुड़सवार लोग, घुड़सवार सेना [historical] soldiers who fought on horseback. modern soldiers who fight in armoured vehicles. *These are the cavalry soldiers who fought on a horseback.*

Cave/केव *(noun)* – गुफा large natural underground chamber. *As students we looked for caves and often went in.*

Cavern/कैवर्न *(noun)* – कन्दरा, मांद a large cave, or chamber in cave. *We were thrilled to explore a cavern.*

Cavil/कैविल *(verb)* – बाल की खाल निकालना झूठी निन्दा करना make petty or unnecessary objections. *(noun)* an objection of this kind. *Women usually cavil.*

Cavity/कैविटी *(noun)* – कंदरा, कोटर, गुहिका an empty space within a solid object. a decayed part of a tooth. *Cavities decay a tooth.*

Caw/कॉ *(noun)* – काँव-काँव करना the harsh cry of a rook, crow, or similar bird. *The crow was cawing harshly.*

Cayenne/काइपन *(noun)* – बहुत तीता लाल मिर्चा a pungent, hot-tasting red powder prepared from dried chillies. *Some people have a fondness for too much chilli.*

Cease/सीज *(verb)* – अन्त होना, रूकना बंद करना come or bring to an end; stop. *When the rain ceased I stepped out of the house.*

Ceaseless/सीजलेस *(adjective)* – निरन्तर, लगातार constant and unending. *Ceaseless rain fell and nobody could go anywhere.*

Cedar/सिडार *(noun)* – देवदार का वृक्ष a tall, elegant coniferous tree yielding typically fragment, durable wood. Cedrus libani and other species in the genera cedrus and Thuja. *I would like to have a cedar in my compound.*

Cede/सीड *(verb)* – परित्याग करना give up (power or territory). *He ceded his lands to enemy forces.*

Ceil/सिल *(verb)* – कमरे की ऊपरी छत बनाना [archaic] line or plaster the roof of (a building). *The mason is ceiling.*

Ceiling/सिलिंग *(noun)* – घर की भीतरी छत the upper interior surface of a room. *The ceiling of my room is white coloured.*

Celebrate/सेलिब्रेट *(verb)* – उत्सव मनाना mark (a significant time or event) with an enjoyable activity. engage in festivities. *We all took part in Holi celebration.*

Celebrity/सेलिब्रिटी *(noun)* – कोई प्रख्यात व्यक्ति a famous person. *Most film stars are celebrities.*

Celerity/सिलेरिटी *(noun)* – शीघ्रता, वेग [archaic] swiftness of movement. *He acted avid amazing celerity.*

Celeste/सिलेस्ट *(noun)* – आकाश के समान नीले रंग का a musical instrument consisting graduated steel plates that are struck by hammers activated by keyboard.

Celestial/सिलेस्टियल *(adjective)* – दिव्य, स्वर्गिक positioned in or relating to the sky or outer space. *One day we may begin to live on a celestial planet.*

Celibacy/सेलिबेसी – कुँआरापन, शारीरिक सम्बन्धों से परहेज रखने वाला धार्मिक कारणो से बह्माचर्य an unmarried status, abstaining from sexual relations. *Saints and faqirs often observe celibacy.*

Celibate/सेलिबेट *(adjective)* – कुँआरा abstaining from marriage and sexual relations for religious reasons.

Cell/सेल *(noun)* – कोशिका, तहखाना a small room in which a prisoner is locked up or in which a monk or nun sleeps. a small compartment in a larger structure such as a honeycomb. [historical] a small monastery dependent on a larger one. *Prisoners are locked in cells .*

Cellar/सेलर *(noun)* – भूमि के भीतर का घर, तहखाना a storage space or room below ground level in a house. a stock of wine. *A stock of wine is usually kept in the cellar.*

Cellular/सेल्युलर *(adjective)* – जालीदार of, relating to, or consisting of living cells. *Cellular phones have becomes so popular these days.*

Celluloid/सेलुलाइड *(noun)* – कचकड़ा a transparent flammable plastic made in sheets from camphor and nitrocellulose, formerly used for cinematographic film. the cinema as a genre. *Today we use celluloid for making toys make up material and toilet articles.*

Cellulose/सेल्युलोज *(noun)* – कोशमय, वनस्पितयों की कोशिकाभित्तियों को बनाने वाला एक प्राकृतिक पदार्थ an insoluble substance which is a polysaccharide derived from glucose and is the main constituent of plant cell walls and of vegetable fibres such as cotton. *Cellulose forms the solid framework of plants.*

Cemetery/सेमट्रि *(noun)* – कब्रिस्तान a large burial ground. *His body was buried in the cemetery.*

Cense/सेंस *(verb)* – धूप देना ritually perfume with burning incense. *The grandmother burnt incense in the temple and it gave out aromatic smell.*

Censer/सेन्सर *(noun)* – धूपदानी a container in which incense is burnt. *We keep a censer in which incense is burnt.*

Censor/सेन्सर *(noun)* – पुस्तक, फिल्म आदि से उन आपत्तिजनक अंशों को हटाना जो किसी की भावनाओं को ठेस पहुँचाने की संभावना रखते हों an official who examines material that is to be published and suppresses parts considered offensive or a threat to security. psychoanalysis an aspect of the superego which prevents certain ideas and memories from emerging into consciousness. *Censor is responsible for reaming any part of fiction or film which is objectionable to society.*

Censeorious/सेन्सोरीअस *(adjective)* – दोष निकालने वाला severely critical. *He is very strict almost censorious.*

Censorship/सेन्सरशीप – लाइसेन्स देने वाला पद deleting parts of publications, correspondence or theatrical performances. *Censorship is a must even if it is a democratic country.*

Censure/सेन्सर *(verb)* – निन्दा, अनुचित काम के लिए भर्त्सना करना express severe disapproval of; formally reprove. *My father censured me over my rude behaviour.*

Census/सेन्सस *(noun)* – जनगणना an official count or survey of a population. *Who live in a country, including information about their age job etc.*

Cent/सेंट *(noun)* – एक सिक्का a monetary unit equal to one hundredth of a dollar or other decimal currency unit. *I have so many cents but no dollars.*

Centenarian/सेन्टेनरीअन *(noun)* – सौ वर्ष का वृद्ध पुरुष a person a hundred or more years old. *My grandfather is a centenarian.*

Centenary/सेन्टीनरी *(noun)* – शतवर्षीय समारोह [chiefly British] the hundredth anniversary of a significant event. *After 100 years we celebrate the centenary of many events of people.*

Centennial/सेंटेनिअल *(adjective)* – सौवीं वर्षगाँठ, शताब्दी of or relating to a hundredth anniversary. *When 100 years are complete of any event.*

Center/सेंटर *(noun)* – कमर की पेटी US spelling of centre etc. *Ceiling fan was fixed in the center of the ceiling.*

Centesimal/सेंटेसिमल *(adjective)* – सौ-सौ करके गिना हुआ of or relating to division into hundredths. *These bundles are centesimal.*

Centigrade/सेंटिग्रेड *(adjective)* – सौ अंशो में विभाजित of or denoting a scale of a hundred degrees, in particular the Celsius scale of temperature. *Water boils at 100°C.*

Centigramme/सेंटिग्राम *(noun)* – एक ग्राम का सौवाँ भाग *One 100th part of a gram is called centigramme.*

Centipede/सेंटिपीड *(noun)* – कनखजूरा an arthropod with a flattened, elongated body composed of many segments, most of which bear a pair of legs. *I am extremely afraid of centipedes.*

Central/सेन्ट्रल *(adjective)* – प्रधान in or near the centre of something. *In the crowd the heroine was of central attraction.*

Centralize/सेन्ट्रलाइज *(verb)* – केन्द्र में करना concentrate under a single authority. *In a dictatorship power is centralized in the hands of the dictator.*

Centre/सेन्टर *(noun)* – मध्य भाग a point in the middle of something that is equally distant form all of its sides, ends, or surfaces. the middle player in some team games. a kick, hit, or throw of the ball from the side to the middle of field. *A centre forward player is the most important one.*

Centrifugal/सेन्ट्रिफ्यूगल *(adjective)* – केन्द्र से हट जाने वाली [physics] moving away from a centre. *Centrifugal is the force which is tending to move away from the centre.*

Centripetal/सेन्ट्रिपिटल *(adjective)* – केन्द्र की ओर जान वाली [physics] moving towards a centre. *A force which is moving towards the centre.*

Centuple/सेन्ट्यूपल *(verb)* – सौगुना multiply by a hundred. *100 is reduced to zero if multiplied by zero.*

Century/सेन्चुरी *(noun)* – शताब्दी a period of one hundred years, in particular each of a number of such periods from the date of the birth of christ. *Sachin has made so many centuries.*

Cephalic/सेफालिक *(adjective)* – मस्तक सम्बन्धी of, in, or relating to the head. *It is something cephalic and has nothing to do with other body parts.*

Ceramics/सेरामिक्स *(adjective)* – मिट्टी से बना आग में पकाया हुआ made of clay that

is permanently hardened by heat. *I bought a ceramics plate.*

Cereal/सिअरिअल *(noun)* – अन्न सम्बन्धी, अन्य (चावल, गेहूँ आदि) a grain used for food, for example wheat, maize, or rye. a grass producing such grain, grown as an agricultural crop. *Cereals make carbohydrates in our body.*

Cerebral/सेरिब्रल *(adjective)* – प्रधान मस्तक सम्बन्धी, प्रमस्तिष्कीय of the cerebrum of the brain. intellectual rather than emotional or physical. *Cerebral part of his brain is very active.*

Cerebrum/सेरिब्रम *(noun)* – मस्तिक का प्रधान भाग anatomy the principal part of the brain, located in the front area of the skull and consisting of left and right hemispheres. *Cerebrum is the main part of the brain.*

Ceremonial/सेरिमोनियल *(adjective)* – विधि पूर्वक, रीति सम्बन्धी, औपचारिक, संस्कार relating to or used for ceremonies. *Marriage is a ceremonial affair.*

Certain/सरटेन *(adjective)* – निस्संदेह, पक्का able to be firmly relied on to happen or be the case. *I am certain that he will come.*

Certainly/सरटेन्ली *(adverb)* – अवश्य, निश्चित रूप से definitely; undoubtedly. yes; by all means. *I'll certainly go to Shimla this summer.*

Certificate/सर्टिफिकेट *(noun)* – प्रमाणपत्र an official document attesting or recording a particular fact or event, a level of achievement, the fulfillment of a legal requirement, etc. *I have all my certificates enclosed in a file.*

Certify/सर्टिफाइ *(verb)* – प्रमाण देना formally attest or confirm. *It is certified that he has passed his 12th grade.*

Certitude/सर्टिट्यूड *(noun)* – दृढ़, निश्चित होने का भाव a feeling of absolute certainty. something considered with certainty to be true. *I have the certitude that he will pass the exam first class first.*

Cerumen/सेरूमेन *(noun)* – कान का खूँट technical term for earwax. *The ear specialist took out a lot of cerumen from the ear.*

Ceruse/सेरूज *(noun)* – सफेदा [archaic] term for white lead. *Ceruse is the carbonate of lead.*

C

Cervical/सरवाइकल *(adjective)* – ग्रीवा सम्बन्धी anatomy of or relating to the cervix. *His cervical pain has increased.*

Cervine/सरवाइन *(adj.)* – हिरण के समान relating to or resembling deer. *Cervine is an animal resembling a deer.*

Cess/सेश *(noun)* – कर लगाना (in Scotland, Ireland, and India) a tax or levy. *Heavy cess has been imposed on traders.*

Cessation/सशेसन *(noun)* – समाप्ति the fact or process of ceasing. *Cessation of the war brought peace.*

Cession/सेशन *(noun)* – परित्याग the formal giving up of rights, property, or territory by a state. *Cession by the defeated state ended the battle.*

Chaff/चैफ *(noun)* – भूसा, हँसी उड़ाना the husks of grain or other seed separated by winnowing or threshing. chopped hay and straw used as fodder. *Chaff is mainly used on fodder.*

Chaffer/चैफर *(verb)* – सौदा करना haggle. *It is the habit of ladies to chaffer.*

Chagrin/शैग्रिन *(noun)* – तीव्र निराशा annoyance or shame at having failed. *(verb)* feel annoyed or ashamed. *She felt chagrined at having failed.*

Chain/चेन *(noun)* – जंजीर, सिकड़ी a connected flexible series of metal links used for fastening, pulling, etc., of in jewellery. a restricting force or factor. *The chain of my cycle is broken.*

Chair/चेयर *(noun)* – कुर्सी, सभापति a separate seat for one person, typically with a back and four legs. *I have bought an easy chair today.*

Chairman/चेयरमैन *(noun)* – सभापति a person in charge of meeting, committee, company, or other organization. *He is the chairman of our company.*

Chaise/शेज *(noun)* – गाड़ी, आनन्द की सवारी chiefly [historical] a horse-drawn carriage for one or two people, especially one with an open top and two wheels. *Chaise was very popular.*

Chalice/चैलिस *(noun)* – प्याला [historical] a goblet. *He drank from the chalice.*

Chalk/चॉक *(noun)* – खड़िया मिट्टी a white soft earthy limestone formed from the skeletal remains of sea creatures. a similar substance and used for drawing or writing. *Teachers write with chalk on the blackboard.*

Challenge/चैलेंज *(noun)* – माँग, दावा, चुनौती a call to someone to participate in a contest or fight to decide who is superior. a demanding task or situation. an attempt to win a sporting contest. *He threw me a challenge for a boxing match.*

Chamber/चैम्बर *(noun)* – कमरा a large room used for formal or public events. *The meeting was held in a chamber.*

Chamberlain/चैम्बरलिन *(noun)* – राज महल का प्रधान कर्मचारी an officer who managed the household of a monarch or noble. *He looks after the affairs of the noble man.*

Chameleon/कमीलियन *(noun)* – गिरगिट a small slow-moving lizard with a prehensile tail, long extensible tongue, protruding eyes, and the ability to change colour. *Chameleons can change their colour according to the environments.*

Chamois/केमोआयस *(noun)* – साबर, जंगली पहाड़ी हिरन an agile goat antelope with short hooked horns, found in mountainous areas of southern Europe. *I have seen many chamois.*

Champ/चैम्प *(verb)* – आवाज करते चबाना munch enthusiastically or noisily. make a noisy biting or chewing action. *He champed a lot while eating.*

Champion/चैम्पिअन *(noun)* – वीर, योद्धा, विजेता [law] an illegal agreement in which a person with no previous interest in lawsuit finances it with a view to haring the disputed property if the suit succeeds. *He is a champion into entering illegal lawsuits.*

Chance/चांस *(noun)* – दैवयोग a possibility of something happening. *You may succeed by chance who knows.*

Chancel/चैंसल *(noun)* – गिरजाघर का पूर्वी भाग the part of a church near the altar, reserved for the clergy and choir, and typically separated from the nave by steps or a screen. *The clergy is speaking from the chancel.*

Chancellor/चान्सलर *(noun)* – कुलपति a senior state or legal official of various kinds. the head of the government in some European countries, e.g. Germany. [chiefly British] the non-resident honorary head of a university. US the presiding judge of a chancery court. an officer of an order of knighthood who seals commissions. *He is our chancellor in Germany.*

Chancery/चैंसरी *(noun)* – उच्च न्यायालय, दीवानी की बड़ी अदालत [law] the lord chancellor's court, a division of the high court of justice. *Right now the case is in chancery.*

Chancy/चांसी *(adj & noun)* – सन्देह जनक, अनिश्चित, जोखिम भरा [informal] uncertain; risky. *It is highly chancy that you will win this gambling game.*

Chandler/चैंडलर *(noun)* – जहाज के समान बेचने वाला, मोमबत्ती बनाने एवं बेचने वाला a dealer in supplies and equipment for ships and boats. *He is a chandler and deals in ship equipment.*

Change/चेंज *(noun)* – परिवर्तन, रूपान्तर make or become different. arrive at a fresh phase; become new. *There was a sudden change in the plan.*

Changeable/चेंजेबल *(adjective)* – परिवर्तनशील, ढुलमुल liable to unpredictable variation. *'Don't worry, this currency note is changeable.*

Changelling/चेंजलिंग *(noun)* – बदला बच्चा a child believed to have been secretly substituted by fairles for the parents' real child in infancy. *This child in a changelling.*

Changing/चेंजिंग *(verb)* – बदलने वाला altering. *The weather is changing fast.*

Channel/चैनल *(noun)* – स्रोत, नाला a length of water wider than a strait, joining two larger areas of water, especially two seas. the English channel. a navigable passage in a stretch of water otherwise unsafe for vessels. *English channel joins two seas.*

Chant/चैंट *(noun)* – गीत, भजन a repeated rhythmic phrase, typically one shouted or sung in unison by a crowd. *People were chanting in a rhythmical and ritual way a mantra.*

Chanter/चैंटर *(noun)* – वाद्ययन्त्र गायक [music] the pipe of a bagpipe with finger holes, on which the melody is played. *Scotsmen were playing on chanter.*

Chanticleer/चैन्टक्लीर *(noun)* – पाला हुआ मुर्गा poetic a name given to a domestic cock, especially in fairly tales. *In my dreams I saw fairies and chanticleer.*

Chanty/शैंटी *(noun)* – मल्लाह गीत, मांझी गीत a rhythmical work song originally sung by sailors. *I like chanty very much.*

Chap/चैप *(noun)* – दरार, फटा होना crack and become sore, typically through exposure to cold weather. cause to crack in this way. *(noun)* a chapped area. *In winters her lips chap.*

Chape/चेप *(noun)* – टोपी में का बन्द [historical] the metal point of a scabbard. *The chape of my buckle is broken.*

Chapel/चैपल *(noun)* – ईसाईयों का छोटा गिरजाघर a small building for Christian worship, typically one attached to an institution or private house. a part of a large church or cathedral with its won altar and dedication. [British] a place of worship for nonconformist congregations. *I prayed in a chapel.*

Chaplain/चैपलेन *(noun)* – पादरी a member of the clergy attached to a private chapel, institution, regiment, etc. *I know a chaplain who is attached to a chapel.*

Chapman/चैपमैन *(noun)* – घूम-घूमकर बेचने वाला व्यापारी, फेरीवाला [archaic] a pedlar. *He is a poor chapmen.*

Chapter/चैप्टर *(noun)* – अध्याय a main division of a book. an act of parliament numbered as part of a session's proceedings. *I closed the chapter of my book as my mother called me.*

Characterise/कैरक्टराइज *(verb)* – गुण व दोष बतलाना be characteristic of what characterises a venetian painting? *Can you characterise this painting?*

Characteristic/कैरेक्टरिस्टिक *(adjective)* – अनोखा, विचित्र typical of a particular person, place, or thing. *(noun)* a feature or quality typical of a person, place, or thing. *I don't know its characteristics.*

Charade/कैरेड *(noun)* – शब्द अनुमान करने की पहेली an absurd pretence intended to create a pleasant impression. *I and my friend plagued charade and enjoyed it.*

Charcoal/चारकोल *(noun)* – लकड़ी का कोयला a porous black form of carbon obtained as a residue when wood or other organic matter is heated in the absence of air. a stick of this used for drawing. *I drew a picture with charcoal stick of dark grey colour.*

C

C

Charge/चार्ज *(verb)* – दाम माँगना demand as a price for a service rendered or goods supplied. *He charged me fifty rupees for carrying the luggage.*

Charger/चार्जर *(noun)* – बड़ी रकाबी, बैटरी आवेशित करने का विद्युत यन्त्र A device for charging a battery or battery powered equipment. *Please find my charger.*

Charitable/चैरिटबल *(adjective)* – धर्मात्मा, परोपकारी, दानी of or relating to the assistance of those in need. officially recognized as a charity. generous in giving to those in need. *This is a charitable dispensary.*

Charity/चैरिटी *(noun)* – सहायतार्थ संस्था, दीन-दुखियों की सहायता करने वाली संस्था an organization set up to provide help and raise money for those in need. *He gives a lot in charity.*

Charlatan/शार्लटन *(noun)* – जानकार होने का पाखंड करने वाला व्यक्ति, मायावी, छली a person falsely claiming to have a special knowledge or skill. *He is a charlatan and claims to possess knowledge which he doesn't have.*

Charlock/चारलॉक *(noun)* – जंगली सरसों a wild mustard with yellow flowers. *The yellow flower of the charlock is worth seeing.*

Charming/चार्मिंग *(adjective)* – रोचक, आकर्षक very pleasing or attractive. *He carries a magical charm with him.*

Charnel-house/कारनेलहाउस *(noun – कब्रिस्तान)* [historical] a building or vault in which corpses or bones are piled. *I happened to see a charnel house. I was horrified to see so many corpse and bones there.*

Chart/चार्ट *(noun)* – घटना या प्रगति की सूचना, रेखाचित्र a sheet of information in the form of a table, graph, or diagram. a weekly listing of the current best-selling pop records. *The records of Rihana have topped the chart this year.*

Charter/चार्टर *(noun)* – शासन पत्र, अधिकार पत्र, किसी संगठन या व्यक्ति समुदाय के अधिकारों, विश्वासों और उद्देश्यों का लिखित दस्तावेज a written grant by a sovereign or legislature, by which a body such as a university is created or its rights and privileges defined. *Universities are created from the written charter of monarch.*

Chary/चेअरि *(adjective)* – सावधान cautiously or suspiciously reluctant: leaders are chary of major reform. *I am chary of going to his home. Recently we had a fight.*

Chase/चेज *(verb)* – किसी का पीछा करना, पीछ-पीछे भागना pursue in order to catch or catch up with. *The police chased the thief.*

Chassis/चेसिस *(noun)* – किसी वाहन का धातु निर्मित चौखटा जिस पर अन्य पुरजे लगे होते है the base frame of a motor vehicle, carriage, or other wheeled conveyance. *The chassis of my car broke down.*

Chaste/चेस्ट *(adjective)* – सती, सादा, सीमित यौन सम्बन्ध abstaining from extramarital, or from all, sexual intercourse. *She is a chaste lady, keeping away from sex.*

Chastise/चेस्टाइज *(verb)* – दण्ड देना, पीटना reprimand severely. dated punish, especially by beating. *His father chastised him for running from stool.*

Chastity/चेस्टिटी *(noun)* – सतीत्व, संयम, शुचिता purity. *Chastity is a virtue.*

Chat/चैट *(noun & verb)* – बकवाद करना used in names of various songbirds with harsh, chattering calls, e.g. stonechat. *Some birds are named chat which have a harsh chattering call.*

Chateau/चैटेउ *(noun)* – देहात का मकान, फ्रांस में एक बड़ा महल या घर a large French country house or castle. *For some time I was guest in a chateau with a French friend of mine.*

Chatter/चैटर *(verb)* – वृथा की बकवाद, तेज गति से या निरर्थक किसी मामूली विषय पर बात करना talk rapidly or incessantly about trivial matters. *He chattered rapidly at a high pitch about small matters without stopping.*

Chatty/चैटी *(adjective)* – बड़ा बकवादी fond of chatting. *He is lively and fond of chatting.*

Chauffeur/शोफर *(noun)* – दूसरों के लिए उसकी कार की नौकरी करने वाला, मोटर हाँकने वाला a person employed to drive a car. (verb) drive as a chauffeur. *I have tried a new chauffeur for my car.*

Cheap/चीप *(adjective)* – सस्ता, कम कीमत low in price. charging low prices. inexpensive because of inferior quality. *It is cheap low priced jewellery, imitated and of poor quality.*

Cheapen/चीपेन *(verb)* – सस्ता करना reduce the price of. *He cheapened the price so.*

Cheat/चीट *(verb)* – छल, धूर्त act dishonestly or unfairly in order to gain an advantage. deprive of something by deceitful or unfair means. *Don't get intimate with him, he is a cheat.*

Check/चेक *(noun)* – एक रंगबिरंगी वर्गाकृतियों का पैटर्न a pattern of small squares. (adjective) (also checked) having such a pattern. *He wore a coat of check cloth.*

Checker/चेकर *(noun)* – जाँच करने वाला a person or thing that checks. *There are so many checkers at metro stations.*

Checkmate/चेकमेट *(noun)* – मात, शतरंज की अंतिम चाल जिसमें हार होती है chess a position of check from which a king cannot escape. *I made a move on the chess board and cried, 'checkmate'.*

Cheek/चीक *(noun)* – गाल, कपोल, धृष्ट होना either side of the face below the eye. *he has reddish cheek.*

Cheep/चीप *(noun)* – सीटी बजाना a shrill squeaky cry made by a young bird. *The young bird cried 'cheep.'*

Cheer/चिअर *(noun)* – खुश होना shout in praise or encouragement. preside or encourage with shouts. *These days in cricket matches you will usually find cheer-girls.*

Cheerless/चिअरलेस *(noun)* – मन्द, उदास, खिन्नतापूर्वक gloomy; depressing. *He is a sad silent cheerless fellow.*

Cheerly/चिअरली *(adverb)* – प्रसन्नता से, खुशी से [archaic] heartily. *He laughed cheerly.*

Cheery/चिअरी *(adj)* – मगन, प्रसन्न *He is an ever smiling cheery fellow.*

Cherub/चेरब – देवदूत, सुन्दर बालक a sweet innocent baby. *My little nephew looks like a cherup.*

Chess/चेस *(noun)* – शतरंज a board game of strategic skill for two players, the object of which is to put the opponent's king under a direct attack, leading to checkmate. *The two my uncle and father are busy playing chess and they would not get up till there is checkmate.*

Chest/चेस्ट *(noun)* – वक्ष:स्थल, सीना, पेटी, तिजोरी the front surface of a person's or animal's body between the neck and the stomach. the whole of a person's upper trunk. *There is birth mark on my chest.*

Chesterfield/चेस्टरफिल्ड *(noun)* – लंबी गद्दीदार चारपाई a sofa with padded arms and back of the same height and curved outwards at the top. *I have bought a chesterfield sofa.*

Chestnut/चेस्टनट *(noun)* – अखरोट का फल या वृक्ष a glossy hard brown nut which develops within a bristly case and can be roasted and eaten. *I have a chestnut tree in my compound and I daily enjoy the roasted nuts.*

Chevalier/शेवलियर *(noun)* – महाबीर, बहादुर, वीर पुरुष, घुड़सवार [historical] a knight. a member of certain orders of knighthood or of modern French orders such as the legion of honour. *Many great men have been awarded French orders of knighthood such as the legion of honour.*

Chew/चिउ *(verb)* – दाँतो से चबाना, निरंतर डाँटकर झुँझला देना bite and work in the mouth to make it easier to swallow. *We should bite small chew long so that the food digests easily.*

Chic/चिक *(adjective)* – सुरुचि सम्पन्न, आकर्षक elegantly and stylishly fashionable. *I saw a chic young girl.*

Chicane/शिकेन *(noun)* – चालाकी, दोहरा मोड़ a sharp double bend created to form an obstacle on a motor-racing track. *As I looked down there has a wide chicane under me.*

Chicken/चिकेन *(noun)* – मुर्गी का बच्चा a domestic fowl kept for its eggs or meat, especially a young one. *My grandmother has so many chickens.*

Chide/चाइड *(verb)* – डाँटना या झिड़कना scold or rebuke. *The teacher chided me on coming late.*

Chief/चीफ *(noun)* – नेता, सरदार, प्रधान पुरुष a leader or ruler of a people. the head of an organization. *He is the chief of our organization.*

Chieftain/चीफटन *(noun)* – सेनापति, मुखिया, कबीला का सरदार the leader of a people or clan. *He is the chieftain of a clan.*

Chiffon/शिफॉन *(noun)* – बारीक कपड़ा a light, transparent fabric typically made of silk or nylon. *My sister is fond of wearing chiffon sarees.*

C

C

Chilblain/चिलब्लेन *(noun)* – हाथ या पैर की बिवाई, ठंड के कारण हाथ-पैर आदि पर बना दर्दीला चकत्ता a painful, itching swelling on a hand or foot caused by poor circulation in the skin when exposed to cold. *He is suffering from chilblain.*

Child/चाइल्ड *(noun)* – बालक a young human being below the age of full physical development. a son or daughter of any age. *I am fond of children.*

Children/चिल्ड्रेन *(plural)* – बच्चे plural form of child. *Children are making a lot of noise.*

Chill/चिल *(noun)* – सिहरन, ठंड, an unpleasant feeling of coldness. *He has been caught by chill.*

Chilli/चिली *(noun)* – सूखी लाल मिर्चा a small hot-tasting pod of a variety of capsicum, used in sauces, relishes, and spice powders. *This vegetable is very chilli my mouth is burning please bring some water.*

Chilly/चिलि *(adjective)* – बहुत ठण्डा और कष्टकर unpleasantly cold. *It is ice all around. I am feeling chilly.*

Chimera/किमीरा *(noun)* – असम्भव कल्पना creek mythology a fire-breathing female monster with a lion's head, a goat's body, and serpent's tail. *I hoped to buy a car but I found it a chimera.*

Chimpanzee/चिम्पैंजी *(noun)* – अफ्रीका देश का वनमानुष an anthropoid ape with large ears, mainly black coloration, and lighter skin on the face, native to west and central Africa. *Chimpanzee are a lot of fun to see in the zoo.*

China/चाइना *(noun)* – चीन देश का, चीनी a fine white or translucent vitrified ceramic material. household tableware or other objects made from china. *I have just bought some China crockery.*

Chinese/चायनीज *(noun)* – चीन देशवासी, चीनी the language of China. *He speaks Chinese well.*

Chink/चिंक *(noun)* – झरोखा, दरार [informal], offensive a Chinese person. *He is a chink and I look down upon such people.*

Chintz/चिंट *(noun)* – छींट, फूलों के प्रिंट वाला चमकीला सूती कपड़ा printed multicolored cotton fabric with a glazed finish, used

especially for curtains and upholstery. *Chintz is used for curtains and upholstery.*

Chippy/चिप्पी *(noun)* – अरोचक [British] a fish and chip shop. *I went to a chippy to buy a fish.*

Chips/चिप्स *(noun)* – भुने आलू का टुकड़ा strips of potato fried in deep fat. *Many people are fond of chips.*

Chirography/किइरोग्रफि *(noun)* – हाथ की लिखावट handwriting, especially as distinct from typography. *His chirography is very good.*

Chirology/किइरोलजि *(noun)* – हस्तरेखा विद्या telling fortunes by lines on the palm of the hand. *He is an expert in chirology.*

Chiromancer/किइरोमैंसर *(noun)* – हस्तरेखा शास्त्री fortuneteller who predicts your future by the lines on your palms. *I don't know any chiromancer.*

Chirpy/चर्पी *(adjective)* – बकवादी [informal] cheerful and lively. *She is chirpy always talking and laughing.*

Chirr/चर्र *(verb)* – चर-चर का शब्द करना make a prolonged low trilling sound. *The bird mode a loud chirr sound.*

Chisel/चिजल *(noun)* – छेनी, रूपानी a long-bladed hand tool with a beveled cutting edge, struck with a hammer or mallet to cut or shape wood, stone, or metal. *Carpenters use chisel for cutting wood.*

Chit/चिट *(noun)* – छोटे कागज के टुकड़े पर संक्षिप्त लिखित टिप्पणी [derogatory] an impudent of arrogant young woman. *Do you think I am going to talk to that chit of a girl.*

Chitchat/चिटचैट *(noun)* – गपशप inconsequential conversation. *We indulged in chitchat for a long time.*

Chitty/चिटी *(noun)* – बच्चे के समान [British informal] term of chit. *She is sure a chitty gril.*

Chivalric/शिवैलरिक *(adj)* – शिष्ट, विनीत characteristic of the time of chivalry and knighthood in the middle Ages. *He is chivalric as well as handsome.*

Chivalrous/शिवेलरस *(adj)* – शूर-वीर के समान *Everybody knows about his being chivalrous.*

Chivalry/शिवेलरी *(noun)* – वीरता, शूरवीर के गुण the medieval knightly system with its religious, moral, and social code. *Chivalry is a custom of past now.*

Chloride/क्लोराइड *(noun)* – क्लोरीन मिश्रित एक यौगिक [chemistry] a compound of chlorine with another element or group: sodium chloride. *We daily take sodium chloride i.e., salt.*

Chlorine/क्लोरीन *(noun)* – साँस घुटाने वाली एक गैस the chemical element of atomic number 17, a toxic, irritant, pale green gas of the halogen group. *Chlorine is a toxic chemical.*

Chloroform/क्लोरोफार्म *(noun)* – बेहोश करने की एक प्रसिद्ध तरल औषधि a volatile sweet-smelling liquid used as a solvent and formerly as a general anaesthetic. [CHCl$_3$] *(verb)* make unconscious with this substance. *Before operations chloroform is given to patients so that they come unconscious thus insensitive to the pain of operation.*

Chock/चॉक *(noun)* – लकड़ी का टुकड़ा a wedge or block against a wheel or rounded object to prevent it from moving or to support it. *Chock is placed against a wheel to prevent it from moving.*

Chocolate/चॉकलेट *(noun)* – कोको के बीजों से बनी भूरी मिठाई जिसे खाद्य पदार्थों को विशेष स्वाद देने के लिए भी प्रयुक्त किया जाता है, चीनी a food made from rested and ground cacao seeds, typically sweetened and eaten as confectionery. a sweet covered with chocolate. *Chocolate or chocolate drink is much liked by children as well as adults.*

Choice/च्वाइस *(noun)* – चुनाव, छँटाव an act of choosing. the right or ability to choose. *I made the right choice between house work and job.*

Choir/क्वाइअर *(noun)* – नाचनें वाली की मण्डली an organized group of singers, especially one that takes part in church services. *Choir song was going on when we reached the church.*

Choke/चोक *(noun)* – दम घुटना या घोंटना the inedible mass of silky fibres at the centre of a globe artichoke. *Ths gas choked us.*

Choler/कॉलर *(noun)* – पित्त, क्रोध one of the four bodily humours, identified with bile, believed to be associated with a peevish or irascible temperament. *He is choleric by nature.*

Cholera/कॉलरा *(noun)* – हैजा an infectious and often fatal bacterial disease of the small intestine, typically contracted from infected water supplies and causing severe vomiting and diarrhoea. *He died of cholera.*

Choleric/कॉलरिक *(adjective)* – पित्तज, क्रोधी bad-tempered or irritable. *He has a choleric temperament.*

Choose/चूज *(verb)* – चुन लेना pick out as being the best of two or more alternatives. *He chose a wrong career for himself.*

Chopper/चॉपर *(noun)* – छोटी कुल्हाड़ी [British] a short axe with a large blade a machine for chopping. *He bought a chopper to kill his enemy.*

Choral/कोरल *(adjective)* – गायक, मण्डली के एक साथ गाने से सम्बन्धित of, for, or sung by a choir or chorus. *Choral songs were being sung in the church.*

Chord/कॉर्ड *(noun)* – वृत्त या वक्ररेखा के दो बिन्दुओं को मिलाने वाली रेखा, ताँत, चापकर्ण a group of notes sounded together in harmony. *The chord was struck and music rose up in harmony.*

Chorion/कोरिअन *(noun)* – गर्भ की बाहरी झिल्ली embryology the outermost membrane surrounding the embryo of a reptile, bird, or mammal. *He took up research work in embryology.*

Chorister/कोरिस्टर *(noun)* – गाने वाली मण्डली का सदस्य a member of a choir, especially a choir boy or choirgirl. *A beautiful chorister is leading the congregation.*

Choroid/कोरॉइड *(adjective)* – आँख की पुतली के भीतरी की झिल्ली resembling the chorion, particularly in containing many blood vessels. *The pigmented vascular layer of the eyeball between the retina and the sclera is called choroid.*

Chortle/कॉरटल *(verb)* – जोर से शब्द करना laugh in a gleeful way. *He chortled when he heard the joke.*

Chorus/कोरस *(noun)* – गायक दल a large group of singers, especially one performing with an orchestra. *He sings in chorus.*

Chrism/क्रिज्म *(noun)* – मलहम, पवित्र तेल a consecrated oil used for anointing in the catholic, orthodox, and Anglican churches. *In church I was anointed with consecrated chrism.*

C

Christ/क्राइस्ट (noun) – ईसा मसीह the title, also treated as a name, given to Jesus, exclamatory an oath used to express irritation, dismay, or surprise. *Christ! What is that huge bloody thing.*

Christian/क्रिश्चियन (adjective) – क्रिस्तानी of, relating to, or professing Christianity or its teachings. *I have many Christian friends and I love all of them.*

Christmas/क्रिसमस (noun) – ईसामसीह का जन्म दिन, बड़ा दिन the annual Christian festival celebrating Christ's birth, held on 25th December. *I took part in the National Christian festival which takes place on 25th December.*

Chromatic/क्रोमेटिक (adjective) – चमकीले रंग से पूर्ण [music] relating to or using notes not belonging to the diatonic scale of the key of a passage. ascending or descending by semitones.

Chrome/क्रोम (noun) – पीला रंग, अन्य धातुओं पर चढ़ाने वाली एक चमकदार धातु chromium plate as a decorative or protective finish.

Chromium/क्रोमियम (noun) – एक धातु-विशेष the chemical element of atomic number 24, a hard white metal used in stainless steel and other alloys. *Do you know chromium a while hard metal is used in making stainless steel.*

Chronic/क्रॉनिक (adjective) – दीर्घस्थायी पुराना persisting for a long time. *He is a chronic patient of asthma.*

Chronicle/क्रानिकल (noun) – ऐतिहासिक घटनाओं का कालानुक्रमित लिखित ब्योरा, इतिहास, वर्णन a written account of important or [historical] events in the order of their occurrence. *I went to the library to read some British Chronicle.*

Chromograph/क्रोमोग्राफ (noun) – सूक्ष्म रीति से समय नापने का एक यन्त्र an instrument for recording time with great accuracy. *Chronicles are recorded with the help of chronograph to help keep time accuracy.*

Chronological/क्रोनोलोजिकल (adj.) – कालक्रम के अनुसार relating to or arranged according to temporal order. *A chronological record follows the order in which things occurred.*

Chronology/क्रोनोलोजी (noun) – काल-निण्यि-विद्या the study of records to establish the dates of past events. *Professor consult chronology to find out in which order events followed.*

Chronometer/क्रोनोमीटर (noun) – ठीक-ठीक समय बतलाने वाली छोटी घड़ी an instrument for measuring time accurately in spite of motion or variations in temperature, humidity, and air pressure. *Chronometer is very useful for weather specialists.*

Chronometry/क्रोनोमिट्री (noun) – वैज्ञानिक रीति से समय की नाप the science of accurate time measurement. *Some people study chronometry.*

Chrysanthemum/क्राइसथेनमम (noun) – गुलादरऊदी का फूल a plant of the daisy family with brightly coloured ornamental flowers. *I am very much fond of chrysanthemum.*

Chrysolite/क्राइसोलाइट (noun) – चन्द्रकान्त a yellowish-green or brownish variety of olivine, used as a gemstone. *The gemstone that I am wearing is made of chrysolite.*

Chubby/चब्बी (adjective) – नाटा-मोटा plump and rounded. *What a beautiful and chubby child!*

Chuckle/चकल (verb) – मुँह बन्द करके हँसना laugh quietly or inwardly. *He chuckle at my joke.*

Chucklehead/चकलहेड (noun) – मूर्ख मनुष्य [informal] a stupid person. *He is a chucklehead.*

Chuckling/चकलिंग (adj) – मनोरंजक pleasing amusing. *It is a chuckling event.*

Chum/चम (noun) – पुराना मित्र a close friend. *You are my best chum.*

Chump/चम्प (noun) – मूर्ख [informal, dated] a foolish person. *He is a chump.*

Church/चर्च (noun) – गिरजाघर a building used for public Christian worship. *I go to church every Sunday as it offers public Christian worship.*

Churl/चर्ल (noun) – देहाती an impolite and mean-spirited person. [archaic] a miser. *He is a churl and miserable person I avoid him.*

Churn/चर्न (noun) – मक्खन बनाने का यंत्र a machine for making butter by agitating milk or cream. *Churn the milk well and you'll get butter.*

Chute/च्यूट (noun) – ढालु प्रणाल जिस पर वस्तुओं को सरकाया जा सकता है उन्हें उठाकर नहीं ले जाना पड़ता, वेग में जल का गिराव या उतार

a sloping channel or slide for conveying things to a lower level. a water slide into a swimming pool. *Water went down the chute.*

Cicatrize/सिकाट्राइज *(verb)* – सूज जाने वाले घाव का चिह्न heal by scar formation. *He has a cicatrize across his face.*

Ciolar/सिओलर *(noun)* – सेब की शराब [British] an alcoholic drink made from fermented apple juice. [north American] a cloudy unfermented drink made from crushed apples. *British people drink ciolar made by fermenting apple juice.*

Cigar/सिगार *(noun)* – चुरूट a cylinder of tobacco rolled in tobacco leaves for smoking. *Cigar is going out of fashion these days.*

Cigarette/सिगरेट *(noun)* – सिगरेट कागज में लपेटा हुआ तम्बाकू a thin cylinder of finely cut tobacco rolled in paper for smoking. *Cigarette smoking is very harmful.*

Cilia/सिलिया *(plural)* – बरौनी eye-lashes form of cilium. *She has beautiful cilia.*

Cilice/सिलाइस *(noun)* – भेड़-बकरी के रोवें का बना वस्त्र a garment of hair cloth. *In winter people wear cilice.*

Cinchona/सिनकोना *(noun)* – कुनैन का पेड़ a medicinal drug containing quinine and related compounds, made from the dried bark of various south American trees. *I had to eat malaria medicine cinchona for malaria fever.*

Cincture/सिंक्चर *(noun)* – किनारा, कमरपेटी a girdle border architecture a ring at either end of a column shaft. *I went to see a building being built. I found cinctures at either end of column shaft.*

Cinder/सिन्डर *(noun)* – भस्म a piece of burnt coal or wood that has stopped giving off flames but still has combustible matter in it. *We pulled out a cinder which seemed a piece of dead coal but it still had the combustible matter in it.*

Cingalese/सिंगलिज *(noun & adjective)* – सीलोन का निवासी [archaic] spelling of sinhalese. *Being a native of Ceylon.*

Cinnabar/सिनाबार *(noun)* – सिंगरिफ, सिन्दूर a bright red mineral consisting of mercury sup hide. *A married woman uses cinnabar.*

Cinnamon/सिनामॅन *(noun)* – दालचीनी, दालचीनी का वृक्ष an aromatic spice made from the fried and rolled bark of a SE Asian tree. *I am fond of taste of cinnamon.*

Cipher/साइफर *(noun)* – शून्य, गुप्त लिखावट a continuous sounding of an organ pipe, caused by a defect. *Your attainment of this year is cipher.*

Circa/सर्का *(preposition)* – लगभग, चारों ओर approximately about, around. *Born circa 150 B.C.*

Circlet/सर्कलेट *(noun)* – छोटा वृत्त, मण्डल a small circular arrangement or object. *I bought a beautiful circlet for wearing on my wrist.*

Circuit/सर्किट *(noun)* – चक्कर, परिभ्रमण a roughly circular line, route, or movement. *The circuit of this building is about a mile.*

Circuitous/सर्किटस *(adjective)* – कुटिल गतिवाला, चक्करदार longer than the most direct way. *It is a circuitous way leading out of the jungle.*

Circular/सर्कुलर *(adjective)* – गोल, समतल, वृत्ताकार, वर्तुलाकार having the form of a circle. *The circus animals moved in a circular path.*

Circulation/सर्कुलेशन *(noun)* – परिभ्रमण, प्रचार movement to and fro or around something. the continuous motion by which blood travels through the body. *The circulation of this paper has gone up.*

Circulative/सर्कुलेटिव *(adj)* – चक्कर देने वाली producing circulation.

Circulator/सर्कुलेटर *(noun)* – खबर फैलाने वाला one who spread news.

Circum/सरकम *(prep)* – चौकोर, चारों ओर *prefix* about; around within the word as an adverb as in circumambulate, or as a preposition as in circumpolar. *He has circumvented the difficulty.*

Circumference/सरकमफरेन्स – मण्डल परिधि the distance around something. *Circumference stance of this dish is 5".*

Circumscribe/सरकमस्क्राइब *(verb)* – घेरना, परिमित करना restrict; limit. *He has been circumscribed for crossing the limit.*

Circumsolar/सरकमसोलर *(adjective)* – सूर्य के पास या चारों ओर घूमने वाला moving or situated around the sun. *there are many in circumsolar stars in the galaxy.*

C

Circumspect/सरकमस्पेक्ट *(adjective)* – सावधान cautious or prudent. *He is a very circumspect person.*

Circumstance/सरकमस्टान्स *(noun)*– अवस्था a fact or condition connected with or relevant to an event or action. *His circumstance did not allow him to pay back the loan.*

Circumvent/सरकमवेंट *(verb)* – फँसाना, धोखा देना [archaic] outwit. *He circumvented his opponent.*

Circumvolution/सरकमवोल्यूशन *(noun)* – घुमाव a winding movement of one thing round another. *Many machines work on the basis of circumvolution.*

Circus/सरकस *(noun)* – सरकस, खेल का गोल मैदान a travelling company of acrobats, trained animals, and clowns, giving performances typically in a large tent. *The whole of our family went to see a circus show and we enjoyed it a lot.*

Cirrus/सिरस *(noun)* – बालों के गुच्छे की आकृति का बादल cloud forming wispy filamentous tufted streaks at high altitude. *I saw a cirrus it was around a mountain peak and had streaks of lightning.*

Cist/सिस्ट *(noun)* – कब्र, पत्थर का सन्दूक a stone chest a box for sacred utensils. *I keep all my sacred utensils in a cist.*

Cistern/सिस्टर्न *(noun)* – जलकुण्ड, जलाशय a water storage tank, especially as part of a flushing toilet. *I'll have to call a plumber because there is some problem with the cistern in the toilet.*

Citadel/सिटाडेल *(noun)* – दुर्ग a fortress protecting or dominating a city. *Old forts used to have a citadel against protection from enemy.*

Citation/साइटेशन *(noun)* – दृष्टांत, प्रमाण a quotation form or reference to a book or author. *Let me see a few citation of Mahatma Gandhis's autobiography.*

Cite/साइट *(verb)* – प्रमाण देना quote as evidence for an argument. *I will now cite a case to further strengthen my argument.*

Citizen/सिटिजन *(noun)* – नागरिक a legally recognized subject or national of a state or commonwealth. *I am a citizen of India.*

Citric/सिट्रिक *(adjective)* – नींबू की खटाई का derived from or related to citrus fruit. *Lemon juice is citric in nature.*

Citrine/सिट्रिन *(noun)* – निंबुअई, पीला a glassy yellow variety of quartz. *I am wearing a citrine ring.*

Citron/सिट्रन *(noun)* – जंभीरी नींबू, चकोतरा a shrubby Asian tree bearing large lemon-like fruits with thick fragrant peel. *This large lemon like fruit which is from citron tree will last at least a couple of days.*

City/सिटी *(noun)* – नगर, शहर a large town, in particular a town created a city by charter an containing a cathedral. [north American] a municipal centre incorporated by the state or province. *I live in Patna city.*

Civic/सिविक *(adjective)* – नगर या नगर से आधिकारिक रूप से सम्बन्धित नागरिक of or relating to a city or town. (noun) [informal] an elected, community-based body concerned with local government in a black township. *A city or township is called civic with a local government.*

Civil/सिविल *(adjective)* – जन सम्बन्धी, सभ्य of or relating to ordinary citizens, as distinct from military or ecclesiastical matters. *These are civil matter.*

Civilization/सिविलाइजेशन *(noun)* – सभ्यता an advanced stage or system of human social development. the process of achieving this. *As compared to old times, we are living in highly civilized society.*

Civilize/सिवलाइज *(verb)* – सुधारना bring to an advanced stage of social development. *He is a very social and civilized person.*

Clack/क्लाक *(verb)* – खड़खड़ाहट, कर्कश शब्द make or cause to make a sharp sound as of a hard object striking another. *There was a clacking sound as the hammer hit the iron.*

Claim/क्लेम *(verb)* – अपनी रकम माँगना assert that something is the case. *I claim this property to be mine.*

Clamant/क्लेमेंट *(adjective)* – आवश्यक noisy forcing itself urgently on the attention. *'Please, sir, I am clamant to your attention for a second'.*

Clamber/क्लाम्बर *(verb)* – कठिनता से चढ़ना climb or move in an awkward and laborious way. (noun) an act of clambering. *He clambered over the mountain.*

Clamour/क्लेमर *(noun)* – रटन, माँग, चिल्लाहट a loud and confused noise, especially of vehement shouting. a vehement protest or demand. *After the leader had spoken, there was a clamour noises in the crowd.*

Clamp/क्लैम्प *(noun)* – पाहू, शिकंजा a heap of potatoes or other root vegetables stored under straw or earth. *You will find a lot of potato's and other vegetables under this clamp.*

Clan/क्लान *(noun)* – जाति, दल a group of close-knit and interrelated families, especially in the Scottish highlands. *He is related with a monarchy clan.*

Clandestine/क्लैंडेस्टाइन *(adjective)* – गूढ़ गुप्त surreptitious. *I don't like his clandestine ways which are of secret nature.*

Clang/क्लैंग *(noun)* – झनझन का शब्द a loud, resonant metallic sound. *Iron clanged against iron and there was a metallic noise.*

Clank/क्लैंक *(noun)* – झनझन का शब्द a loud, sharp sound as of pieces of metal being struck together. *There was a clank as various machines started working.*

Clannish/क्लानिश *(adjective)* – जाति का pertaining to a clan. *I wanted to join their group but they acted clannish and kept me out.*

Clanship/क्लानशिप *(noun)* – गोत्रत्व, सजातीयता the system of clan membership or laity. *They are belong the same clanship.*

Clansman/क्लैन्समैन *(noun)* – सजातीय व्यक्ति a male member of a clan. *We had less clansman and no women.*

Clap/क्लैप *(noun)* – थप्पड़, ताली, गनोरिया, (यौन बीमारी) [informal] a venereal disease, especially gonorrhoea. *Don't clap here, please.*

Clapper/क्लैपर *(noun)* – ताली बजाने वाला the tongue or striker of a bell.

Claptrap/क्लैपट्रैप *(noun)* – प्रसन्न करने के लिये शब्दों का प्रयोग, प्रसन्न करने हेतु ताली बजाना nonsense. *Whatever you have talked so far is nothing but claptrap.*

Clarence/क्लैरेंस *(noun)* – चौपहिया बन्द गाड़ी [historical] a closed four-wheeled horse-drawn carriage, seating four inside and two outside. *In old days Clarence was a popular mode of transport.*

Clarification/क्लैरिफिकेशन *(noun)* – स्पष्टीकरण an interpretation that remove obstacles to understanding. *You owe me a clarification how did all this happen?*

Clarify/क्लेरिफाइ *(verb)* – स्पष्ट करना, मैल हटाना make more comprehensible. *Will you please clarify your stand?*

Clarity/क्लारिटी *(noun)* – स्वच्छता, सफाई the state or quality of being clear, distinct, and easily perceived or understood. *The clarity of his speech is appreciable.*

Clash/क्लाश *(verb)* – झगड़ना, टकराना विरोध करना come abruptly into violent conflict. have a forceful disagreement. *The two cars clashed head on.*

Clasp/क्लैप्स *(verb)* – बाँधना, लपेटना grasp tightly with one's hand. place around something so as to hold it tightly. hold tightly. press together with the fingers interlaced. *He clasped my hand warmly.*

Classic/क्लासिक *(adjective)* – प्रथम श्रेणी का judged over a period of time to be of the highest quality. of a simple, elegant, style not greatly subject to changes in fashion. *Some films and novels are classic. They do not fade with the passage of time.*

Classify/क्लासिफाइ *(verb)* – श्रेणी में रखना arrange in classes or categories according to shared qualities or characteristics. assign to a particular class or category. *Some official documents are classified as secret or top secret.*

Clatter/क्लैटर *(noun)* – झनझनाना, बकबक करना a loud rattling sound as of hard objects falling or striking each other. (verb) make or cause to make a clatter. fall or move with a clatter. *The swords of the two warriors clattered together.*

Clause/क्लॉज *(noun)* – कानून की उपवाक्य a unit of grammatical organization next below the sentence in rank, and in traditional [grammar] said to consist of a subject and predicate. *There is a clause in contract that none of us can resign till this particular job is completed.*

Clavicle/क्लॉविकल *(noun)* – हँसुली, हँसिया anatomy technical term for collarbone. *As he fell down, he broke his clavicle.*

C

C

Claviform/क्लैविफार्म (adjective) – गदा के आकार का another term of clavate.

Claw/क्लॉ (noun) – चंगुल, पंजा, नख a curved, pointed horny nail on each digit of the foot in birds, lizards, and some mammals. either of a pair of small hooked appendages on an insect's foot. *The claws of carnivorous birds are different from those of other birds.*

Clay/क्ले (noun) – मिट्टी, कीचड़ a stiff, sticky fine-grained impermeable earth that can be moulded when wet and baked to make bricks and pottery. *Bricks and pottery are made out of the clay.*

Claymore/क्लेमोर (noun) – दोधारी चौड़ी तलवार [historical] a type of two-edged or single edged broadsword used in Scotland. *They keep such swords in Scotland.*

Clean/क्लिन (adjective) – निर्मल, स्वच्छ, शुद्ध free from dirt, pollutants, or harmful substances. attentive to personal hygiene. *It is a clean place.*

Cleanse/क्लिन्ज (verb) – साफ करना make thoroughly clean. *She has been cleansed of her sins by a priest.*

Clearance/क्लियरंस (noun) – सफाई, रुकावट हटाना the action or process of clearing or of being dispersed. *Clearance sale! 30% rebate on every item.*

Cleat/क्लिट (noun) – फन्नी, डट्टा a T-shaped or similar projection to which a rope may be attached. *The cow was tied to this cleat.*

Cleft/क्लेफ्ट (noun) – फटन, दरार a fissure or split in rock or the ground. *You can put your foot into that cleft and climb upwards.*

Clemency/क्लेमेंसी (noun) – सरलता leniency and compassion shown to ward off enders by a person or agency charged with administering justice. *Please sir, I plead for clemency.*

Clergy/क्लर्जी (noun) – पादरी लोग the body of people ordained for religious duties in the Christian church. *He is the finest speaking clergy in the church.*

Clerical/कलेरिकल (adjective) – पादरियों का concerned with or relating to the routine work of an office clerk. *He was offered a clerical job which he refused.*

Clerk/क्लर्क (noun) – लेखक या मुंशी का पद a person employed in an office or bank to keep records or accounts and to undertake other routine administrative duties. *He is a clerk in an office.*

Clew/क्लॉ (noun) – पाल का कोना the lower or after corner of a sail. *If you go into a labyrinth, don't forget to carry a clew so that you can find your way back.*

Click/क्लिक (noun & verb)– खटका a short, sharp sound as of two metallic or plastic objects coming smartly into contact. a speech sound produced by sudden withdrawal of the tongue form the soft palate, front teeth, or back teeth and hard plate, occurring in some southern African and other languages. [computing] an act of pressing one of the buttons or become secured with such a sound: it clicked into place. [computing] press one of the buttons on a mouse. *She clicked her tongue as she saw the food on the table.*

Client/क्लाइन्ट (noun) – मुवक्किल, ग्राहक a person using the services of a professional person or organization. *He is our best client deal with him very carefully.*

Cliff/क्लिफ (noun) – चट्टान a steep rock face, especially at the edge of the sea. *Climbing cliffs is his favorites hoppy.*

Climate/क्लाइमेट (noun) – जलवायु, ऋतु the general weather conditions prevailing in an area over a long period. a prevailing trend or public attitude. *Climate of Africa is hot.*

Climax/क्लाइमेक्स (noun) – शिखर, चढाव the most intense, exciting, or important point of something. *As the climax scene of the film approached, I felt very tense and my heart beat has been increased.*

Climb/क्लाइम्ब (verb) – चढ़ना go or come up to a higher position. go up mountains as a sport. slope or lead up. grow up by clinging to or twining round it. *He is a professional mountain climber.*

Clime/क्लाइम (noun) – प्रदेश, देश, जलवायु [chiefly poetic/literary] a region considered with reference to its climate: jetting off to sunnier climes. *Summer climes in India are beautiful.*

Clinic/क्लिनिक *(noun)* – चिकित्सालय a place where specialized medical treatment or advice is given. *I went to doctor's clinic for a medical checkup.*

Clink/क्लिंक *(noun)* – झनझन शब्द a sharp ringing sound, such as that made when metal or glass are struck. (verb) make or cause to make a clink. *They clinked the glasses together and drank.*

Cloak/क्लोक *(noun)* – अँगरखा an over garment that hangs loosely form the shoulders over the arms to the knees or ankles. *I don't trust that man, he is covered in a cloak secrecy.*

Clock/क्लॉक *(noun)* – घड़ी, मोजे के ऊपरी भाग पर रेशमी कढ़ाई का काम an ornamental pattern woven or embroidered on the side of a stocking or sock near the ankle. *The ornamental patterns over your stockings is beautiful.*

Clod/क्लॉड *(noun)* – मूर्ख a lump of earth or clay. *He is a clod.*

Clog/क्लॉग *(noun)* – विघ्न a shoe with a thick wooden sole. *The engine of the car is clogged.*

Cloister/क्लायस्टर *(noun)* – मठ, विहार a covered, and typically colonnaded, passage round an open court in a convent, monastery, college, or cathedral. *He lives secluded cloister.*

Close/क्लोज *(noun)* – परिणाम, अन्त only a short distance away or apart in space or time. dense: close print. very near to being or doing something. *'God! I it was a close shave for me in the morning. As I was crossing the street a vehicle closely passed by me.'*

Closely/क्लोजली *(adv)* – गुप्त रूप से, ध्यान लगाकर attentively. *I watched his movement closely.*

Closeness/क्लोजनेस – छिपाव, समीपता *Too much closeness with anyone is unhealthy.*

Closet/क्लोजेट *(noun)* – गुप्त कोठरी a private or small room, chiefly [north American] a tail cupboard or wardrobe. *I have a closet made up of teak wood.*

Closure/क्लोजर *(noun)* – बन्द करने का कार्य an act or process of closing something. *The closure of the shop will be at 8 p.m.*

Clot/क्लॉट *(noun)* – थक्का, पिण्ड a thick mass of coagulated liquid, especially blood, or of material stuck together. *A clot of blood blocked his artery and he died.*

Clothe/क्लॉद *(verb & noun)* – ढाँपना put clothes on; dress. provide someone with clothes. *I put on best of my clothes and went to the wedding.*

Clotted/क्लॉटेड *(adj)* – घनीभूत with clots. *Clotted blood is a great danger.*

Cloud/क्लाउड *(noun)* – मेघ, बादल a visible mass of condensed watery vapour floating in the atmosphere, typically high above the general level of the ground. an indistinct or billowing mass of smoke, dust, or something consisting of numerous particles. an opaque patch within a transparent substance. *Clouds make the sky beautiful at dawn or sunset.*

Clough/क्लफ *(noun)* – कन्दरा, गुफा north English a steep valley or ravine. *The jungles was full of cloughs.*

Clove/क्लोव *(noun)* – लौंग any of the small bulbs making up a compound bulb of garlic, shallot, etc. *The oil of clove has many medical uses.*

Clown/क्लाउन *(noun)* – मसखरा, भाँड, असभ्य जन a comic entertainer, especially one in a circus, wearing a traditional costume and exaggerated make-up. *All children liked the performance of clowns in the circus.*

Club/क्लब *(noun)* – गदा, सफा a heavy stick with a thick end, used as a weapon. *Club was a favourite weapon of him.*

Clue/क्लू *(noun)* – विचारक्रम, सूत्र a fact or place of evidence serving to reveal a hidden truth or solve a problem. *Police found a clue and caught the gang of thieves.*

Clump/क्लम्प *(noun)* – गुच्छा, जोर से पैर पटकना a small group of trees or plants growing closely together. a compacted mass or lump of something. physiology an agglutinated mass of blood cells or bacteria, especially as an indicator of the presence of an antibody to them. *The wounded animal hid itself in a clump.*

Clumsily/क्लमसिली *(adv)* – फूहड़पन से in an awkward. *She behaved clumsily.*

Cluster/क्लस्टर *(noun)* – समूह (समुदाय), गुच्छा, भीड़ a group of similar things positioned or occurring closely together. *There was a cluster of ants around the piece of sweet.*

C

C

Clutch/क्लच *(verb)* – पकड़ना, जकड़ना grasp tightly. *Clutch the rope tightly, I am going to pull you up.*

Clutter/क्लटर *(noun & verb)* – कोलाहल things lying about untidily. an untidy state. *The entire floor of the room was cluttered with a lot of broken and useless things.*

Clyster/क्लाइस्टर *(noun)* – पेट में चढ़ाया जाने वाला पानी [archaic] term for enema. *Doctors used clysters to clean his intestines of all the excreta.*

Coach/कोच *(noun)* – शिक्षक an instructor or trainer in sport. *We still remember our hockey coach of college days.*

Coadjutor/कोएडजुटर *(noun)* – सहकारी, सहायक a bishop appointed to assist and often to succeed a diocesan bishop. *he is a coadjutor in a church.*

Coal/कोल *(noun)* – पत्थर का कोयला a combustible lack rock consisting mainly of carbonized plant matter and used as fuel. [British] a piece of coal. (verb) provide with or extract coal. *It was very cold and we burnt a lot of coals to heat the room.*

Coalition/कोअलिशन *(noun)* – संयोग, मेल a temporary alliance, especially of political parties forming a government. *Our today's governments is a coalition government.*

Coarse/कोअर्स *(adjective)* – सामान्य, घटिया, भद्दा rough or harsh in texture; unrefined. consisting of large grains or particles. *He seemed to be a country man. He was wearing coarse clothes.*

Coast/कोस्ट *(noun)* – सीमा, समुद्रतट the part of the land adjoining or near the sea. *There are some coasts very popular in European countries.*

Coat/कोट *(noun)* – मर्दाना कोट, ढपना a full-length outer garment with sleeves. a man's jacket. *He wore a blue coloured coat.*

Coating/कोटिंग *(noun)* – रंग की तह a thin layer or covering of something. *You have to give three coatings of paint to this room.*

Coax/कोक्स *(verb)* – फुसलाना, बहलाना persuade gradually or by flattery to do something. use such persuasion to obtain. manipulate carefully into a particular situation or position. *I coaxed my friend into going to a movie.*

Cob/कॉब *(noun)*– गोल डबल रोटी [British] a loaf of bread. *Many Christians first pray and then eat the cob.*

Cobalt/कोबाल्ट *(noun)* – गिलट के समान एक सफेद धातु the chemical element of atomic number 27, a hard silvery-white magnetic metal. *Cobalt in used in many alloys.*

Cobby/कॉबी *(adjective)* – पुष्ट, तीव्र of a horse or other animal stocky. *He is strong like a cobby.*

Cobra/कोब्रा *(noun)* – नाग, विषैला सर्प a highly venomous African or Asian snake that spreads the skin of its neck into a hood when disturbed. *We saw a cobra with its hood spread out. It looked ferocious but the snake charmer controlled it.*

Cobweb/कॉबवेब *(noun)* – मकड़े का जाल, महीन जाली a spider's web, especially an old or dusty one. *The room was dirty, untidy and full of cobwebs.*

Cocaine/कोकीन *(noun)* – कोकीन an addictive drug derived from coca or prepared synthetically, used as an illegal stimulant and sometimes medicinally as a local anesthetic. *Cocaine is used by many youngesters.*

Coccyx/कॉक्सिक्स *(noun)* – रीढ़ की सबसे नीचे की तिकोनी हड्डी a small triangular bone at the base of the spinal column in humans and some apes, formed of fused vestigial vertebrae. *It is the lowest small triangular bone at the end of spinal chord.*

Cochlea/कॉक्लिआ *(noun)* – कान के भीतर का घोंघे के समान कोष्ठ the spiral cavity of the inner ear containing the organ or corti, which produces nerve impulses in response to sound vibrations. *Inner part of the ear which responds to sound.*

Cock/कॉक *(noun)* – नर चिड़िया, मुर्गा dated a small pile of hay or other material, with vertical sided and a rounded top. *You can see many cocks with vertical piles of hey and dung.*

Cockboat/कॉकबोट *(noun)* – छोटी नाव a small boat towed behind a larger vessel. *My cockboat has being towed by a ship as it had developed some defect.*

Cockcrow/कॉकक्रो (noun) – अरुणोदय [poetic/literary] dawn. *He has the habit of rising at cockcrow.*

Cockerel/कॉकरेल (noun) – छोटा मुर्गा a young domestic cock. *Our backyard is usually full of cockerel.*

Cockpit/कॉकपिट (noun) – वायुयान में चालक कक्ष, मुर्गा लड़ने का अखाड़ा a compartment for the pilot and crew in an aircraft or spacecraft. the driver's compartment in a racing car. *When we were flying, I was very curious to see the cockpit but nobody was allowed there.*

Cockroach/कॉकरोच (noun) – झींगुर a beetle-like scavenging insect with long antennae and legs, some kinds of which are household pests. *I don't know why, but when I look a cockroach I feel like vomiting.*

Cockscomb/कॉक्सकम्ब (noun) – छैला the crest or comb of a domestic cock. *All male cocks have a cockscomb.*

Cocksure/कॉकस्योर (adjective) – पूर्ण निश्चित presumptuously or arrogantly confident. *He was cocksure to clear the interview but then nothing worked out. He failed.*

Coco/कोको (noun)– नारियल का पेड़ western Indian the root of the taro. *Our tropical tree is palm and it produces big nuts with water inside.*

Cocoon/कॉकून (noun) – रेशम का कौवा a silky case spun by the larvae of many insects for protection as pupae. something that envelops, especially in a protective or comforting way. *He found life so stressful that he sought the protective comfort of cocoon.*

Cod/कॉड (noun) – कॉड नाम की समुद्री मछली a large marine fish with a small barbel on the chin, important as a food fish. *My favourite fish is cod.*

Code/कोड (noun) – गुप्त भाषा, धर्म संहिता a system of words, figures, or symbols used to represent others, especially for the purposes of secrecy. a sequence of numbers dialed to connect t telephone with the exchange of the telephone being called. *While in school, we had our code words for almost everything.*

Codger/कोजर (noun) – झक्की वृद्ध पुरुष an eccentric old person. *He is a codger. Many people become like that in old age.*

Codicil/कोडिसिल (noun) – वसीयतनामे को तोड़ने का लेख an addition or supplement that explains, modifies, or revokes a will or part of one. *According to codicil, a part of the property will also go to deceased person's servant.*

Codifier/कोडिफायर (noun) – कानून बनाने वाला a codist, one who codifieds. *M.Ps are codifier.*

Codify/कोडिफाइ (verb) – कानून बनाना organize into a system or code. *His full information has been codified.*

Co-education/को-एडुकेशन (noun) – सहशिक्षा the education of pupils of both sexes together. *For a healthy development students should study in co-educational institutes.*

Coefficient/कोएफिशिअन्ट (noun) – गुणक [mathematics] a numerical or constant quantity placed before and multiplying the variable in an algebraic expression. *In 4xy, 4 is coefficient of xy.*

Co-equal/को-इक्वल (adjective) – बराबरी वाला having the same rank or importance. *I and my best friends are co-equals.*

Coerce/कोअर्स (verb) – रोकना विवश करना persuade to do something by using force or threats. *He coerced her into marrying him.*

Coexist/को-एक्जिस्ट (verb) – एक ही काल में होना exist at the same time or in the same place. exist in harmony. *In our society various members of the family coexist.*

Coextensive/को-एक्सटेंसिव (adjective) – एक ही स्थान या समय में व्यापक extending over the same area, extent, or time. *All people living today are coextensive.*

Coffee/कॉफी (noun) – कहवा, काफी a hot drink made from the roasted and ground bean-like seeds of a tropical shrub. the processed, roasted, and ground seeds used to make this drink. *My friend is so fond of a particular brand of coffee that he daily drinks four or five cups.*

Coffer/कॉफर (noun) – पेटी, कोष, तिजोरी a small chest for holding valuables. the funds or financial reserves of an institution. *The coffers of our government almost seem to be empty.*

Coffin/कॉफिन (noun) – बक्सा जिसमें शव रखा जाता है a long, narrow box in which a dead body is buried or cremated. *His dead body* *was placed in a coffin and carried to the crematorium.*

Cog/कॉग *(noun)* – पहिये का दाँता धुरकीली a broadly built medieval ship with a rounded prow and stern. *Cogs used to churn the water in medieval times.*

Cogence/कोजेन्स *(noun)* – निश्चित शक्ति, विश्वस्त convincing power. *He lacks cogence in this matter.*

Cogent/कोजेन्ट *(adjective)* – प्रबल clear, logical, and convincing. *His arguments were completely cogent.*

Cogitate/कोगिटेट *(verb)* – ध्यान देना, विचार करना formal meditate or reflect. *He is given to cogitate over things.*

Cognate/कॉगनेट *(adjective)* – सगोत्री linguistics having the same linguistic derivation as another. *Hindi is very much cognate to Urdu.*

Cognition/कॉगनिशन *(noun)* – अनुभव ज्ञान the mental action or process of acquiring knowledge. through thought, experience, and the senses. a perception, sensation, or intuition resulting form this. *We gain knowledge through cognition.*

Cognizable/कॉगनिजेब्ल *(adj.)* – विचार के योग्य [law] within the jurisdiction of court. *Your argument is perfect cognizable.*

Cognizance/कॉगनिजेन्स *(noun)*– ज्ञान, चेतना formal knowledge or awareness. [law] the action of taking judicial notice. *Law has taken cognizance of this fact.*

Cognizent/कॉगनिजेंट *(adj)* – सचेत having or showing knowledge or understanding or realization or perception. *How was cognizant of his opponent.*

Cohabit/कोहैविट *(verb)* – पति-पत्नी के समान सहवास करना live together and have a sexual relationship without being married. *Most of the couples cohabit instead of marriage these days.*

Cohesion/कोहीजन *(noun)* – संयोग, लगाव the action or fact or forming a united whole. [physics] the sticking together of particles of the same substance. *The group acted in cohesion.*

Cohesive/कोहेसिव *(adjective)* – एकता लाने वाला characterized by or causing cohesion. *This is a cohesive group of workers.*

Coif/कॉइफ *(noun)* – टोपी, टोप a woman's close-fitting cap, worn under a veil by nuns. [historical] a protective metal skullcap worn underarmour. *Nuns wear a coif which is a close cap covering top back and sides.*

Coil/कॉइल *(noun)* – चक्कर, गेंदुरी a length of something wound in a joined sequence of concentric rings. *I arranged the loose threads into a coil.*

Coin/कॉइन *(noun)* – मुद्रा, सिक्का a flat disc or piece of metal with an official stamp, used as money. money in the form of coins. *I have so many coins but no notes.*

Coincide/को-इन-साइड *(verb)* – समान या अनुरूप होना, सहमत होना, ठीक-ठाक बैठना occur at the same time or place. *We were together there at the same time by coincidence.*

Coir/कॉइर *(noun)* – नारियल की जटा fibre from the outer husk of the coconut, used in potting compost and for making ropes and matting. *I have some rugs and matting made of coir.*

Coition/कोइशन *(noun)* – मैथुन, रति another term for coitus. *Both the lovers indulged in coition.*

Coke/कोक *(noun)* – पत्थर के कोयले को ठोस बनाना [informal] term for cocaine. *Coke or cocaine is a dangerous drug.*

Colander/कोलेंडर *(noun & verb)* – चलनी में छानना a perforated bowl used to stain off liquid from food. *I am in need of a colander.*

Cold/कोल्ड *(adjective)* – जुकाम, सर्दी, ठंडा of or at a low or relatively low temperature. *I have caught cold.*

Colic/कॉलिक *(noun)* – उदर-पीड़ा severe pain in the abdomen caused by wind or obstruction in the intestines. *I have severe colic pain, please take me to a doctor.*

Collaborate/कोलेबोरेट *(verb)* – साथ-साथ काम करना work jointly on an activity or project. *I want to collaborate you in this project.*

Collapsible/कोलैप्सिब्ल *(adjective)* – सिकुड़ने या डूबने योग्य able to be folded down. *This sofa set is collapsible it can be folded and kept in a small place.*

Collapse/कोलैप्स *(noun & verb)* – क्षय, शक्ति ह्रास suddenly fall down or give way. fall inwards and become flat and empty. *The building suddenly collapsed.*

Collar/कॉलर *(noun)* – माला, कण्ठा a band of material around the neck of a shirt or other garment, either upright or turned over. *My shirts collar is usually too dirty.*

Collate/कोलेट *(verb)* – विस्तारपूर्वक तुलना करना collect and combine. compare and analyse. printing verify the number and order of the sheets of a book. *I worked in book binding shop and collated it.*

Colleague/कलीग *(noun)* – सहायक, साथी a person with whom one works in a profession or business. *Many colleagues work with me in the office.*

Collect/कलेक्ट *(verb)* – संग्रह करना accumulate. *His job in the office was to collect mail.*

Collected/कलेक्टेड *(adjective)* – शान्त not perturbed or distracted. *Throughout the proceeding, he remained calm and collected.*

Collection/कलेक्शन *(noun)* – समूह, संग्रह the action or process of collecting. *I have a big collection of newspaper photos regarding sport events.*

Collective/कलेक्टिव *(adjective)* – एकीकृत done by or belonging to all the members of a group. taken as a whole; aggregate. *(noun)* a cooperative enterprise. a collective farm. *A collective effort was done to clean the old temple.*

Collector/कलेक्टर *(noun)* – जिलाधीश a person who collects things of a specified type, professionally or as a hobby. *A tax collector collects taxes.*

Collet/कॉलेट *(noun)* – नगीने की बैठकी a segmented band put round a shaft and tightened so as to grip it. *I have got my gem set in a beautiful collet.*

Collide/कोलाइड *(verb)* – टक्कर खाना hit by accident when moving. *The train collided with a truck at the railway crossing.*

Collier/कोलियर *(noun)* – कोयला खोदने या ले जाने वाला a coal miner. *He is a collier by profession.*

Collinear/कोलिनिअर *(adjective)* – एक ही रेखा में [geometry] lying in the same straight line. *If point A and point B are joined by a straight line, they are called collinear.*

Collision/कॉलिजन *(noun)* – विरोध, टक्कर, मुठभेड़ an instance of colliding. *The two ships were moving on a course of collision.*

Collodion/कॉलोडिअन *(noun)* – तेजाबी रूई का चिपचिपा घोल a syrupy solution of nitrocellulose in a mixture of alcohol and ether, used for coating things, chiefly in [surgery] and in a former photographic process. *It is syrupy solution of nitrocellulose which if mixed with alcohol and ether is chiefly used in surgery.*

Colloquy/कॉलक्वि *(noun)* – बातचीत a formal conference or conversation. *The colloquy between the persons did not seem to come to an end.*

Collotype/कॉलोटाइप *(noun)* – फोटो का चित्र छापने की विधि a process for making high-quality prints using a sheet of light-sensitive gelatin. *My friend uses the collotype process for making high quality prints.*

Collude/कॉल्यूड *(verb)* – जाल रचना come to a secret understanding; conspire. *They colluded together to form a conspiracy to kill the king.*

Collusion/कॉल्यूजन *(noun)* – जाल, कपट secret or illegal cooperation in order to cheat or deceive others. *Both the bad characters were planning for collusion.*

Collyrium/कोलिरियम *(noun)* – काजल, सुरमा a kind of dark eye shadow, used especially in eastern countries. *Our women use collyrium for eye colouring.*

Colon/कोलोन *(noun)* – वृहदन्त्र, बड़ी आँत anatomy the main part of the large intestine, which passes from the caecum to the rectum. *Some persons develop ulcers in their colon.*

Colonel/कोलोनेल *(noun)* – सैन्यदल का अध्यक्ष a rank of officer in the army and in the US air force, above a lieutenant colonel and below a brigadier or brigadier general. *My father was a colonel in the army.*

Colonial/कोलोनिअल *(adjective)* – नई बस्ती का of, relating to, or characteristic of a colony or colonies. *She British had a big colonial empire.*

Colonist/कोलनिस्ट *(noun)* – नई बस्ती में रहने वाला a settler in or inhabitant of a colony. *In*

C

C

cities people usually live in colonies and can be called colonists.

Colonization/कोलोनाइजेशन (noun) – उपनिवेशन, नई बस्ती बसाने का कार्य the act or practice of colonizing. *Britain had done the most colonization.*

Colonize/कोलोनाइज (verb) – नई बस्ती बसाना establish a colony in a place. establish control over the indigenous people of a colony. *French, Dutch and Portuguese also tried to colonize India but the English men beat them to do it.*

Colonnade/कॉलोनेड (noun) – खंभों या वृक्षों की पंक्ति a row of evenly spaced columns supporting a roof or other structure. *There are 12 colonnades in this hall which support the roof.*

Colophony/कॉलफॉनि (noun) – रजन, राल another term for Resin. *It is a kind of resin.*

Coloration/कलरेशन (noun) – रंगने की कला का कार्य arrangement or scheme of colour; coluring. *There is something wrong with the coloration of this building, too bright colours.*

Colorific/कलरिफिक (adjective) – दूसरे पदार्थ मे रंग लाने योग्य able to give colour or tint to other bodies, rare having much colour. *This mixture of colours is rather colorific.*

Colossal/कॉलाजल (adjective) – बड़ा दीर्घकाय extremely large. sculpture at least twice life size. *This is a colossal problem.*

Colossus/कोलोसस (noun) – दीर्घकाय बड़ी मूर्ति a person or thing of enormous size, in particular a statue that is much bigger than life size. *The statue of colossus was giant sized.*

Colour/कलर (noun) – बहाना, आकृति, रंग the property possessed by an object of producing different sensations on the eye as a result of the way it reflects or emits light. one, or any mixture, of the constituents into which light can be separated in a spectrum or rainbow. the use of all colours, not only black and white, in photography or television. heraldry any of the major conventional colours used in any of the balls other than the white cue ball and the reds. *Almost all animals are colour blind.*

Colour-bar/कलर-बार (noun) – गोरे मनुष्यों का सामाजिक भेद *In British rule there used to be colour-bar, there is none now.*

Colouring/कलरिंग (noun) – रंगने का ढंग the process or art of applying colour. *M.F. Hussain was a master of colouring.*

Colourist/कलरिस्ट (noun) – रंगसाज an artist or designer who uses colour in special or skilful way. *My friend is a famous and great colourist.*

Colter/कॉल्टर (noun) – हल का फार US spelling of culter.

Co-mate/को-मेट (noun) – साथी, सहचर a fellow. *She is my co-mate. We live together.*

Comb/कोम (noun) – कंघी an instrument with a row of narrow teeth, used for untangling or arranging the hair. a short curves comb worn by women to hold the hair in place. *We should keep our combs clean.*

Combat/कम्बैट (verb) – भिड़ना take action to reduce or prevent. *The two forces were engaged in armed combat.*

Comber/कम्बर (noun) – बाल सँवारने वाला one who combs a long curling sea wave. *I got afraid when I saw the comber coming.*

Combine/कम्बाइन (verb) – मिलाना [chemistry] unite to form a compound. (noun) a group of people or companies acting together for a commercial purpose. *Various companies have combined to complete this project.*

Combustible/कमबस्टिबल (adj) – ज्वलनशील उत्तेजक capable of ignitigng and buring. *This mixture is highly combustible.*

Combustion/कमबसन (noun) – दाह, ज्वलन the process of burning. [chemistry] rapid chemical combination with oxygen, involving the production of heat and light. *Chemical combination with oxygen produces light and heat.*

Comedian/कॉमीडियन (noun) – हँसाने वाला an entertainer whose act is designed to arouse laughter. a comic playwright. *Charlie Chaplin was a great comedian.*

Comedy/कॉमेडी (noun) – सुखान्त नाटक entertainment consisting of jokes and sketches intended to make an audience laugh. a film, play, or programme intended to arouse laughter. *Most people prefer comedy to tragedy.*

Comeliness/कॉमलिनेस (noun) – सुन्दरता the quality of being good looking and attractive. *I like your comeliness.*

Comely/कमलि *(adjective)* – सुन्दर [archaic] typically of a woman pleasant to look at; attractive. *She is a comely women.*

Comer/कमअर *(noun)* – आने वाला a person who arrives. *He is a late comer.*

Comet/कॉमिट *(noun)* – पुच्छल तारा a celestial object which consists of a nucleus of ice and dust and, when near the sun, a diffuse tail, and typically follows a highly eccentric orbit around the sun. *I am so excited that tomorrow we shall see a comet. It is a bright celestial body with a long tail circling round the sun.*

Comfit/कमफिट *(noun)* – मिठाई [archaic] a sweet consisting of a nut, seed, or other centre coated in sugar. *I like comfits a lot.*

Comfort/कम्फर्ट *(noun)* – सुख a state of physical ease and freedom from pain or constraint. things that contribute to comfort. prosperity and a pleasant lifestyle. *I sat with comfort in the lounge.*

Comic/कॉमिक *(adjective)* – हास्यकर causing or meant to cause laughter. relating to or in the style of comedy. (noun) a comedian. *He had a very comic face which made us often laugh.*

Coming/कमिंग *(noun)* – पहुँच of the relatively near future. *This coming Thursday.*

Comity/कमिटि *(noun)* – शिष्टाचार an association of nations for their mutual benefit; the mutual recognition by nations of the laws and customs of others. *International comity is the need of the day.*

Comma/कॉमा *(noun)* – अँग्रेजी मे छोटे विराम का चिह्न a punctuation mark (,) indicating a pause between parts of a sentence or separating items in a list. *A long sentence must be separated with commas.*

Command/कमांड *(verb)* – आज्ञा देना give an authoritative or peremptory order. military be in charge of a unit. indicating or expressing authority; imposing. possessing or giving superior strength: a commanding lead. [archaic] control or restrain. *He is the commanding officer of this town's military.*

Commandant/कमांडेंट *(noun)* – किले का अधिकारी an officer in charge of a particular force or institution. *He is a commandant of the army.*

Commander/कमान्डर *(noun)* – नायक a person in authority, especially in a military context.

a rank of naval officer, above lieutenant commander and below captain. an officer in charge of a metropolitan police district an London. *He is a commander in military.*

Commanding/कमांडिंग *(adj)* – रोबदार He was *commanding troops in the battlefield.*

Commemorate/कमेमोरेट *(verb)* – स्मरणार्थ उत्सव मनाना honour the memory of as a mark of respect, especially with a ceremony or memorial. *Mahatma Gandhi is commemorated ejvry year on his birthday.*

Commence/कमेंस *(verb)* – प्रवृत्त होना begin. *The commonwealth games commenced at the scheduled time.*

Commend/कमेंड *(verb)* – प्रशंसा करना praise formally or officially. *He was commended for his high efficiency in the office work.*

Commensal/कमेंसल *(adjective)* – सहभोजी, एक ही पंगत में भोजन करने वाला relating to or denoting an association between two organisms in which one benefits and the other derives neither benefit nor harm. *Commensal is an organism or creature living in partnership with mother.*

Commensurable/कमेन्सुरेबल *(adj.)* – सदृश्य, अनुरूप सपरिमाण measurable by the same standard. *Their performances are not commensurable.*

Comment/कमेंट *(noun)* – टीका, समालोचना a remark expressing an opinion or reaction. discussion, especially of a critical nature, of an issue or event. an explanatory note in a book or other written text. *He passed a comment on my nature which I did not like.*

Commerce/कामर्स *(noun)* – वाणिज्य, व्यवसाय the activity of buying and selling, especially on a large scale. *Commerce between the two countries develops its relation.*

Commiserate/कोमिजरेट *(verb)* – दया करना, करुणा दिखाना express sympathy or pity; sympathize. *I commiserated with my friend when his relative died.*

Commissariat/कोमिसरियेट *(noun)* – सेना को रसद पहुँचाने का दफ्तर chiefly military a department for the supply of food and equipment. *Commissariat in military is an important unit.*

C

C

Commessary/कॉमिसरी *(noun)* – डिप्टी, रसद भेजने वाला आफिसर a deputy or delegate. a representative or deputy of a supply provisions. *He is a commissary who has come from UK to our country.*

Commissure/कोमिसर *(noun)* – दो पदार्थों का मिलन स्थान anatomy a seam between two bones. *The seam between the two bones has damaged, an operation is necessary.*

Commit/कमिट *(verb)* – समर्पण करना, सौंपना perpetrate or carry out. *I am committed to serve the nation.*

Committee/कमिटि *(noun)* – समिति a group of people appointed for a specific function by a larger group. a committee appointed by parliament to consider proposed legislation. the whole house of commons when sitting as a committee. *A committee appointed by a larger body does various works.*

Commodious/कमोडिअस *(adjective)* – सुविधा का, उपयुक्त formal roomy and comfortable. *It is a large and commodious room.*

Commodity/कमोडिटी *(noun)* – उपयोगी वस्तु a raw material or primary agricultural product that can be bought and sold. *I bought many commodities at home.*

Common/कॉमन *(adjective)* – साधारण, सबके लिए सामान्य occurring, found, or done often; not rare. without special rank or position; ordinary. of a sort to be generally expected: common decency. of the most familiar type. *We should all show common decency to one another.*

Commonalty/कॉमनल्टि *(noun)* – प्रजा लोग chiefly [historical] people without special rank or position, usually viewed as an estate of the realm. *The commonalty does not like corrupt leader.*

Commoner/कॉमनर *(noun)* – सामान्य मनुष्य one of the ordinary or common people, as opposed to the aristocracy or to royalty. *He looks glad, but he is neither an aristocrat nor a royalty, he is common like us.*

Commotion/कमोशन *(noun)* – कलह, हलचल a state of confused and noisy disturbance. *There was great commotion in crowd over the remarks of the speaker.*

Commove/कमूव *(verb)* – उत्तेजित करना cause to be agitated, excited, or roused. *Don't commove the public.*

Communal/कम्यूनल *(adjective)* – जातीय shared or done by all members of a community. involving the sharing of work and property: communal living. *Communal living is sharing the work and property.*

Commune/कम्यून *(noun)* – संस्था, फ्रांस का एक विभाग a group of people living together and sharing possessions and responsibilities. a communal settlement in a communist country. *Commune is a communal settlement in a communist country.*

Communicable/कम्यूनिकेब्ल *(adjective)* – प्रकाशित करने योग्य able to be communicated to others. *I have written a article which is communicable.*

Communicate/कम्यूनिकेट *(verb)* – कहना, देना share or exchange information or ideas. convey in a non-(verb)al way. pass on an infectious disease. transmit heat or motion. *We have been communicating through letters for a long time.*

Communication/कम्यूनिकेशन *(noun)* – कथन, व्यवहार the action of communicating. a letter or massage containing information or news. social contact. *There are so many means of communication-railways, phones, computers. All of us make use of them.*

Communion/कम्यूनिअन *(noun)* – साथ, सम्पर्क the sharing or exchanging of intimate thoughts and feelings. *An exchange of thoughts, sharing rituals, recognition and acceptance among between churches is called communion.*

Communique/कम्यूनिक *(noun)* – सरकारी विज्ञप्ति an official an(noun)cement or statement, especially one made to the media. *A communiqué was issued to the media by a party spokesman.*

Communism/कम्यूनिज्म *(noun)* – साम्यवाद a theory or system of social organization in which all property is vested in the community and each person contributes and receives according to their ability and needs. a theory or system of this kind derived from Marxism and established in the Soviet Union, China, and elsewhere. *I believe neither in socialism nor in democracy. I believe in communism* *where all property is vested in community and people give and receive according to their ability.*

Community/कम्यूनिटी *(noun)* – मण्डली, समुदाय a group of people living together in one place, especially one practising common ownership. a place considered together with its inhabitants: a rural community. the people of an area or country considered collectively; society. *Some people believe in community living sharing common interest and religion.*

Commutator/कॉम्यूटेटर *(noun)* – बिजली की धारा का कम बदलने का यंत्र an attachment, connected with the armature of a motor or dynamo, through which electrical connection is made and which ensures the current flows as direct current. *It is a device to reverse the direction of current.*

Commute/कम्यूट *(verb)* – अदल-बदल करना travel some distance between one's home and place of work on a regular basis. *We daily commute between our office and home.*

Compact/कम्पैक्ट *(adjective)* – सट्टा, संधि closely and neatly packed together; dense. having all the necessary components or features neatly fitted into a small space. *In the make up box, all the articles were compactly placed.*

Companion/कम्पेनियन *(noun)* – सहचर a person with whom one spends time or travels. a person employed to live with and assist someone old or unwell. *The railway journey was boring but luckily I found an interesting companion.*

Compare/कम्पेअर *(verb)* – उपमा करना, तुलना करना estimate, measure, or note the similarity or dissimilarity between. point out or describe the resemblances of something with; liken to. be similar to or have a specified relationship with another thing or person: salaries compare favourably with those of other professions. *By compare, our school is for better than that one.*

Comparison/कम्पीरिजन *(noun)* – उपमा, तुलना the action of comparing. the quality of being similar or equivalent. *I am comparing the two companies as to which to join.*

Compass/कम्पास *(noun)* – दिशा सूचक यंत्र an instrument containing a magnetized pointer which shows the direction of magnetic north and bearings from it. *In old times navigation was done with the help of compass.*

Compassion/कम्पैशन *(noun)* – दया sympathetic pity and concern for the sufferings or misfortunes of others. *We must have compassion for suffering of others.*

Compendious/कम्पेन्डियस *(adjective)* – परिमित, संक्षिप्त सार formal presenting the essential facts in a comprehensive but concise way. *His lecture was brilliant it was so compendious that if gave a long explanations in very short.*

Compendium/कम्पेन्डियम *(noun)* – संक्षेप, सार-संग्रह a collection of concise but detailed information about a particular subject. *I just bought a compendium I have so many friends to write to.*

Compensation/कम्पेन्सेशन *(noun)* – हरजाना something awarded to compensate for loss, suffering, or injury. something that compensates for an undesirable state of affairs. the action or process of compensation. *When my friend was injured in a hockey game being played at state level, he was compensated generously. All the expenses of hospital and medicine were borne by the state.*

Compensator/कम्पेनसेटर *(noun)* – क्षति चुकाने वाला *States and big companies for which the players play usually compensate for injury there.*

Compete/कम्पीट *(verb)* – स्पर्धा करना, बराबरी करना strive to gain or win something by defeating or establishing superiority over others. *I competed in the race and won.*

Compentence/कम्पीटेंस *(noun)* – योग्यता, गुण the quality or extent of being competent. *His competence in playing the football is excellent.*

Competent/कम्पिटेंट *(adjective)* – योग्य having the necessary ability or knowledge to do something successfully. efficient and capable. having legal authority to deal with a particular matter. *He is competent of sitting in the civil services examination.*

Competition/कम्पीटिशन *(noun)* – प्रतियोगिता the activity or condition of competing against others. ecology interaction between species or organisms which share a limited

C

environmental resource. *There is going to be a big sports competition and my brother in going to take part in it.*

Competitive/कम्पीटिटीव *(adjective)* – स्पर्धा करने के कार्य से सम्बन्धित relating to or characterized by competition. strongly desiring to be more successful than others. *He has a competitive nature always ready to competes. He wishes to prove that he is more desirable than others.*

Compile/कम्पाइल *(verb)* – संग्रह करना produce by assembling material from other sources. accumulate a specified score. *He is compiling a dictionary.*

Complacent/कम्पलेसमेंट *(adjective)* – सन्तुष्ट smug and uncritically satisfied with oneself or one's achievements. *He is a complacent smug and only irritatingly satisfied with himself.*

Complain/कम्प्लेन *(verb)* – शिकायत करना to express dissatisfaction or annoyance. *I'll complain against your behaviour to the Principal.*

Complaint/कम्प्लेंट *(noun)* – अभियोग an act or the action of complaining. a reason for dissatisfaction. [law] the plaintiff's reasons for proceeding in a civil action. an illness or medical condition, especially a relatively minor one. *I have received so many complaints against you. What have you to say?*

Complaisant/कम्प्लेसेंट *(adjective)* – अनुरोधी willing to please others or to accept their behaviour without protest. *He is a very complaisant person. He never minds the behaviour of others.*

Complement/कम्प्लीमेंट *(noun)* – सम्पूर्णता a thing that contributes extra features to something else so as to enhance or improve it. *I gave her a complement on her performance on the stage.*

Complete/कम्प्लीट *(adjective)* – पूर्ण, समाप्त having all the necessary or appropriate parts; entire. having as an additional part or feature. *I maintain complete abstinence from alcohol.*

Complex/कम्प्लेक्स *(noun)* – पेचीदा, जटिल consisting of many different and connected parts. *This is a complex machine complicate and intricate.*

Complexion/कम्प्लेक्सन *(noun)* – स्वभाव, रंग-रूप the natural tone and texture of the skin of a person's face. *Her complexions is something to be seen to believe.*

Complexity/कम्प्लेक्सिटी *(noun)* – जटिलता, पेचीदिगी the quality of being ritricate and compound. *He enjoyed the complexity of modern computer.*

Compliance/कमप्लायन्स *(noun)* – स्वीकृति accepting according to certain accepted standards. *There is no compliance in his characteristic.*

Compliant/कम्प्लायन्ट *(adjective)* – संकोची, आज्ञाकारी disposed to agree with others or obey rules, especially to an excessive degree; acquiescent. *My friend is very compliant. He will obey what ever is said to him.*

Compliment/कम्प्लीमेंट *(noun)* – अभिनन्दन के वचन politely congratulate or praise. *My friend has the habit of paying compliment to everyone on some point or the other. Consequently he is very popular among people.*

Comply/कम्प्लाई *(verb)* – स्वीकार करना act in accordance with a wish or command. *I'll comply with your wishers.*

Component/कम्पोनेन्ट *(noun)* – साधक, अंग a part or element of a larger whole, especially a part of a machine or vehicle. *A component of your machine is broken. It will take two hours to replace it.*

Comport/कम्पोर्ट *(verb)* – सहमत होना, व्यवहार करना another term for compote. *He comports in a very peculiar way.*

Compose/कम्पोज *(verb)* – टाइप बैठाना, रचना करना write or create a work of art, especially [music] or poetry. order or arrange in order to form an artistic whole. *His composition of music is excellent.*

Composition/कम्पोजिशन *(noun)* – बनावट, साहित्यक रचना, लेख the way in which a whole or mixture is made up; ingredients or constituents. a thing composed of various elements. a compound artificial substance. *A.R. Rehman is a great composer. His music composition won him an academy award.*

Compost/कम्पोस्ट *(noun)* – यौगिक खाद decayed organic material used as a fertilizer for growing plants. a mixture of compost with loam soil used as a growing medium. *These days farmers use compost as a fertilizer.*

Composure/कम्पोजर *(noun)* – शान्ति the state or feeling of being calm and composed. *Throughout the noise and quarrel he remained calm and composed.*

Compound/कम्पाउन्ड *(noun)* – सन्धि करना, मिलाना, मिश्रित करना a large open area enclosed by a fence, e.g. around a factory or within a prision. [south African] an area containing single-sex living quarters for migrant workers, especially miners. another term for pound. *The prisoners were free to move within the jail compound.*

Compounder/कम्पाउन्डर *(noun)* – औषधि बनाने वाला one who compound or mixes thing. *There are two compounder in this hospital.*

Comprehend/कम्प्रीहेंड *(verb)* – समझना grasp mentally; understand. *I have comprehended your answer to my question sir.*

Comprehensive/कम्प्रीहेंसिव *(adjective)* – समझने योग्य विस्तृत including or dealing with all or nearly all aspects of something. of large content or scope; wide-ranging. by a large margin. providing cover for most risks, including damage to the policyholder's own vehicle. *Lecture of the professor from science academy was comprehensive.*

Compress/कम्प्रेस *(verb)* – निचोड़ना, दबाना flatten by pressure; squeeze into less space. chiefly [biology] having a narrow shape as if flattened, especially sideways. squeeze or press together. (noun) a pad of absorbent material pressed on to part of the body to relieve inflammation or stop bleeding. *Doctors compressed on the wound an absorbent material so as to stop bleeding.*

Compromise/कम्प्रोमाइज *(noun)* – समझौता an agreement reached by each side making concessions. an intermediate state between conflicting opinions. *Instead of fighting a long legal battle they compromised out of the court.*

Comptroller/कम्पट्रोलर *(noun)* – हिसाब-नियन्त्रक a controller used in the title of some financial officers. *A comptroller is a financial officer.*

Compulsion/कम्पल्सन *(noun)* – अनुरोध, दबाव the action or state of compelling or being compelled; constraint. *You are under no compulsion to talk to me.*

Compulsive/कम्पल्सिव *(adjective)* – दबाव डालने योग्य resulting from or acting on an irresistible urge or compulsion. *He is a alcoholic so it becomes compulsive irresistible for him to buy the the wine.*

Compulsorily/कम्पलसरिली *(adv.)* – हठ से *It is compulsorily required by law not to drink or smoke in public.*

Compulsory/कम्पलसरी *(adjective)* – अनिवार्य required by [law] or a rule; obligatory. involving or exercising compulsion; coercive. *It is compulsory to keep to the left while driving.*

Compunction/कम्पक्सन *(noun)* – पश्चाताप a feeling of deep regret. *I felt great compunction for my behaviour.*

Computation/कम्प्यूटेशन *(noun)* – गणना, परिकलन the action of mathematical calculation. *He uses computer for the purpose of computation and study.*

Compute/कम्प्यूट *(verb)* – गणना करना, लेख करना reckon or calculate a figure or amount. *He compute all his tough calculations on computer.*

Comrade/कॉमरेड *(noun)* – मित्र, साथी a companion who shares one's activities or is a fellow member of an organization. *He is my comrade and we both belong to the same organization.*

Con/कॉन *(verb)* – कण्ठस्थ करना, धोखा देना deceive into doing or believing something by lying to them. (noun) a deception of this kind. *He is a conman. He takes everyone into confidence and deceives him.*

Conation/कॉनेशन *(noun)* – इच्छाशक्ति का प्रयत्न philosophy desire or will to perform in action; volition. *He willed to go abroad and by going abroad he performed his will into action/ conation.*

Concave/कॉनकेव *(adjective)* – नतोदर, खोखला having an outline or surface that curves inwards like the interior of a circle or sphere. compare with convex. *A concave mirror's surface curves inside like the interior of a circle.*

Conceal/कानसील *(verb)* – गुप्त रखना, छिपाना not allow to be seen; hide. keep secret; prevent from being known. *The thief concealed the goods into a pit.*

C

Concede/कनसीड *(verb)* – स्वीकार करना finally admit or agree that something is true. admit in a match or contest. *I must concede that you are speaking the truth.*

Conceivable/कन्सीवेब्ल *(adjective)* – विचारणीय capable of being imagined or understood. *His wishes are conceivable.*

Conceive/कन्सीव *(verb)* – गर्भधारण करना become pregnant with a child. *She has conceived and all the members of the family are very happy.*

Concentrate/कन्सेंट्रेट *(verb)* – एक केन्द्र में लाना, एकाग्र Christian church officiate jointly at a mass. *He is concentrated on his studies.*

Concentric/कन्सेंट्रिक *(adjective)* – एक केन्द्र का of or denoting circles, arcs, or other shapes which share the same centre. *He draw arcs and circles which concentric.*

Concept/कन्सेप्ट *(noun)* – सामान्य विचार an abstract idea. an idea to help sell or publicize a commodity. *I have a concept which will increase the sale of our commodity.*

Concern/कन्सर्न *(noun)* – व्यापार relate to effect. *Nokia is big concern.*

Concert/कन्सर्ट *(noun)* – योग, मेल योग, संगीत a musical performance given in public, typically of several compositions. *A music concert was held in Kala Bhawan.*

Concession/कन्सेशन *(noun)* – सुविधा प्रदान, छूट a thing that is conceded. a gesture made in recognition of a demand or prevailing standard. *The company amended 30% concession on its garments.*

Conciliate/कन्सिलियेट *(verb)* – शान्त करना placate; pacify. act as a mediator. formal reconcile. *I acted as a conciliator and pacified the two quarrelling friends.*

Concise/कन्साइज *(adjective)* – संक्षिप्त अल्प giving a lot of information clearly and in few words. *His information was concise and to the point.*

Concision/कन्सीजन *(noun)* – खतना, मुसलमानी *Concision is the religious act of Muslim.*

Conclave/कन्क्लेव *(noun)* – गुप्त बैठक या सभा, स्थान a private meeting. *A conclave was being held regarding the election of a pope.*

Conclude/कन्क्लूड *(verb)* – समाप्त करना bring or come to an end. formally settle or arrange a treaty or agreement. *The meeting was concluded on a note of harmony.*

Concluding/कन्क्लूडिंग *(adj)* – अन्तिम, आखिरी find. *This line is concluding line.*

Conclusion/कन्क्लूजन *(noun)* – समाप्ति the end or finish of something. the summing-up of an argument or text. the setting of a treaty or agreement. *I have reached the right conclusion.*

Conclusive/कन्क्लुसिव *(adjective)* – निर्णायक decisive or convincing. *It is conclusive that I will not sell my land.*

Concomitance/कन्कमिटैंस *(noun)* – समन्वय the fact of existing or occurring with something else. *Now there is concomitance between the two families.*

Concord/कनकॉर्ड *(noun)* – एकता formal agreement harmony. a treaty. *A concord was signed between the two countries.*

Concourse/कॉनकोर्स *(noun)* – समूह a large open central area inside or in front of a public building. *A big concourse gathered in the ground.*

Concrescence/कन्क्रेसेंस *(noun)* – सहवृद्धि [biology] the coalescence or growing together of separate parts.

Concretion/कन्क्रेशन *(noun)* – ठोस पदार्थ a hard solid mass formed by accumulation of matter.

Concubinage/कन्क्यूबिनेज *(noun)* – वेश्यापन chiefly [historical] the practice of keeping or the state of being a concubine. *Concubinage is when a state is given a lesser importance.*

Conculate/कन्क्यूलेट *(verb)* – पैरों से कुचलना to crush. *The elephant conculate the man.*

Condemn/कंडेम *(verb)* – निन्दा करना express complete disapproval of. *I condemn your words.*

Condensation/कन्डेन्सेशन *(noun)* – जमाव water form humid air collecting as droplets on a cold surface. *In our [chemistry] lab, we used to convert vapour or gas into a liquid.*

Condense/कन्डेन्स *(verb)* – घना करना make denser or more concentred. thicken by heating it to reduce the water content. express in fewer words; make concise. *What I say will be condensed.*

Condole/कन्डोल *(verb)* – दुःख में सहानुभूति प्रकट करना express sympathy for. *I condoled him on his sickness.*

Conduce/कन्ड्यूस *(verb)* – प्रवृत्त करना, उत्पादन करना formal help to bring about. *I conduced my friend in getting well.*

Conduct/कन्डक्ट *(noun & verb)* – निर्वाह, व्यवहार, आचरण the manner in which a person behaves. *He conducts himself gracefully.*

Conduit/कन्ड्इट *(noun)* – जल-प्रणाली a channel for conveying water or other fluid. *I bought a conduit pipe from the market.*

Cone/कोन *(noun)* – शंकु an object which tapers from a circular or roughly circular base to a point. a plastic cone-shaped object used to separate off sections of a road, a cone-shaped water container in which ice cream is served. the peak of a volcano. *Traffic cones are usually placed on busy roads.*

Coney/कोनी *(noun)* – एक प्रकार का खरगोश [British & heraldry] a rabbit. *They have gone out to hunt a coney.*

Confection/कन्फेक्शन *(noun)* – मिठाई an elaborate sweet dish or delicacy. *I am very fond of confection.*

Confideracy/कन्फिडरेसी *(noun)* – सन्धि a league or alliance, especially of confederate states. the confederate states of the US. *US is made up of confideracy.*

Confer/कन्फर *(verb)* – देना, प्रतिपादन करना, सलाह करना grant. *He was conferred the title of 'sir'.*

Conference/कन्फरेंस *(noun)* – सम्मेलन meeting for discussion. *many conferences took place in Delhi.*

Confess/कन्फेस *(verb)* – स्वीकार करना admit to a crime or wrongdoing. acknowledge reluctantly: I must confess that I was surprised. *The priest heard the confession as he declared his sins to him.*

Confidant/कन्फिडेंट *(noun)* – विश्वासपात्र a person in whom one confides. *I always confide in my sister, she is my confidant.*

Confide/कन्फाइड *(verb)* – रहस्य करना tell someone about a secret or private matter in confidence. *Let me confide in you what I have gone through.*

Confidence/कन्फिडेंस *(noun)* – आशा the belief that one can have faith in or rely on someone or something. a feeling of self-assurance arising from an appreciation of one's own abilities. *I have full confidence in you.*

Confiding/कन्फायडिंग *(adj)* – विश्वस्त trustworthy. *US has so many confiding agents.*

Confidential/कन्फिडेंसिअल *(adjective)* – गुप्त, विश्वास intended to be kept secret. *It is a confidential file, keep it in locker.*

Confine/कन्फाइन *(noun & verb)* – सीमा-प्रान्त keep or restrict someone or something within certain limits of space, scope, or time. be unable to leave due to illness or disability. dated of a woman remain in bed for a period before, during, and after giving birth. *He was confined to four walls of jail.*

Confirm/कन्फर्म *(verb)* – प्रमाणित करना establish the truth or correctness of. state with assurance that something is true. reinforce someone in an opinion or feeling. *I confirmed his statement.*

Confiscate/कन्फिस्केट *(verb)* – जब्त करना take or seize with authority appropriate to the public treasury as a penalty. *His whole property was confiscated by order of magistrate.*

Conflict/कन्फ्लिक्ट *(noun)* – युद्ध, विरोध a serious disagreement or argument. a prolonged armed struggle. an incompatibility between opinions, principles, etc. (verb) be incompatible or at variance with. *The two friends had conflict of opinion and they separated.*

Conflux/कन्फलक्स *(noun)* – संगम, भीड़ another term for confluence. *At Allahabad Sangam there is a conflux of holy rivers.*

Conformity/कन्फॉरमिटी *(noun)* – समानता compliance with conventions, rules, or laws. [British, chiefly historical] compliance with the practices of the church of England. *I live in conformity with the law of land.*

Confraternity/कन्फ्रैटरनिटी *(noun)* – भाईचारा, बंधुत्व a brotherhood, especially with a religious or charitable purpose. *We have formed a confraternity for a charitable purpose.*

Confuse/कन्फ्यूज *(verb)* – व्याकुल करना, घबराना, भ्रमित cause to become bewildered or perplexed. *He is a confused man who does not know what to speak.*

Confusion/कन्फ्यूजन *(noun)* – व्याकुलता uncertainty. a situation of panic. a disorderly jumble. *There was confusion in the entire meeting.*

C

Confute/कन्फ्यूट *(verb)* – असिद्ध करना, झूठा सिद्ध करना formal prove to be wrong. *I was confuted in the meeting.*

Conge/कन्ज *(noun)* – विदाई an unceremonious dismissal or rejection. *He had to face conge.*

Congeal/कन्जील *(verb)* – गाढ़ा करना become semi-solid, especially or rejection. *The blood flowing from his wound soon congealed.*

Congener/कांजिनर *(noun)* – समान, राजनीति a person or thing of the same kind as another. an animal or plant of the same genus as another. *Both plants are congener i.e. of the same category.*

Congenial/कन्जेनिअल *(adjective)* – सहानुभूति, स्वास्थ्यकर या वंश pleasant because of qualities or interests similar to one's own. suited to one's taste or inclination. *I find this wine very congenial.*

Congenital/कन्जेनिटल *(adjective)* – जन्मजात exosting from birth, having a particular trait form birth or by established habit. *He cannot walk properly, it is something congenital.*

Conglomerate/कनगलोमरेट *(adj)* – एक पिण्ड something consisting of a number of different and distinct things. a large corporation formed by the merging of separate firms. *We have many corporations in India which are conglomerated by a merger of separate firms.*

Conglutinate/कन्ग्लूटिनेट *(verb)* – सरेस से चिपकाना या बैठाना to stick together with glue. *These two pieces are conglutinated.*

Congratulate/कांग्रेचुलेट *(verb)* – धन्यवाद देना, बधाई देना express pleasure at the happiness or good fortune of. praise for an achievement. feel pride or satisfaction. *I congratulated my friend on his success.*

Congregate/कांग्रेगेट *(verb)* – एकत्रित करना gather into a crowd or mass. *A big crowd congregated in the hall.*

Congruent/कांग्रूएन्ट *(adjective)* – योग्य, अनुरूप in agreement or harmony. *These two pictures are not congruent.*

Conjoin/कन्जोवाइन *(verb)* – संयुक्त करना formal join; combine. *All of us conjoined to form a meeting.*

Conjugate/कन्जुगेट *(verb)* – विवाह करना, सम्भोग करना [biology] of bacteria or unicellular orbanism become temporarily united in order to exchange gentic material. *These couples are not conjugated.*

Conjunct/कन्जंक्ट *(adjective)* – संयुक्त joined together, combined, or associated. *An adverbial clause is conjuncted to the main clause by conjunction.*

Conjunctiva/कन्जक्टाइवा *(noun)* – आँख के भीतरी भाग की झिल्ली anatomy the mucous membrane that covers the front of the eye and lines the inside of the eyelids. *There was some trouble with my conjunctiva so I consulted a doctor.*

Conjunctive/कन्जंक्टिव *(adjective)* – जोड़ने वाला of, relating to, or forming a conjunction. involving the combination or co-occurrence of two or more things. (noun) [grammar] a conjunction. *A conjunctive joins two or more sentences.*

Conjuncture/कन्जक्टर *(noun)* – संयोग, घटना, अवसर a combination of events. *There is a conjuncture among the event of various companies.*

Conjure/कन्ज्योर *(verb)* – निष्ठापूर्वक अनुरोध करना cause to appear as if by magic. call to the mind. call upon to appear by means of a magic ritual. *The magician conjures up a ghost.*

Connect/कनेक्ट *(verb)* – संयुक्त मिलाना bring together so as to establish a link. be related in some aspect. join together so as to provide access and communication. put into contact by vide access and communication. put into contact by telephone. *We two friends are connected together by means of chatting over computer.*

Connivance/कनाइवेंस *(noun)* – उपेक्षा collusion. *It was a robbery committed with the connivance of police.*

Connive/कनाइव *(verb)* – आँख मारना secretly allow a wrongdoing. conspire. *We connived against the leader of the opposition group.*

Connote/कॉनोट *(verb)* – अर्थ सूचित करना imply or suggest, imply as a consequence or condition. *The word tropics connotes heat.*

Conquer/कॉन्कर *(verb)* – विजय करना overcome and take control of by military force. *Babur conquered a state of India.*

Conquest/कॉन्क्वेस्ट *(noun)* – विजय, बलपूर्वक किसी देश के अधीन करना the action of conquering. a territory gained in such a way. *The conquest of Everest was a historial events.*

Conscience/कॉन्-शन्स् *(noun)* – अन्त:करण, विवेक a person's moral sense of right and wrong. *He is a man of high conscience.*

Conscious/कॉन्-शस् *(adjective)* – सचेत aware of and responding to one's surroundings. *I was conscious that someone was following me.*

Consecrate/कन्सिक्रेट *(verb)* – संस्कार करना make or declare sacred. make into the body and blood of Christ. *After being consecrated he was ordained a bishop's life.*

Consecutive/कन्सेक्यूटिव *(adjective)* – निरन्तर following contin-uously. in sequence. *Adverbial clause of consequences shows result.*

Consensus/कनसेंसस *(noun)* – एकमत, अनुकूलता general agreement. *A consensus was reached in the general meeting.*

Consent/कन्सेंट *(verb)* – सहमत होना permission. verb give permission. agree to do something. *She has consent in this matter.*

Consentient/कन्सेंटियन्ट *(adjective)* – एकचित [archaic] in agreement. *She has no consentient opinion.*

Consentingly/कन्सेंटिंग्ली *(adv)* – सम्मति पूर्वक *She consentingly looked at him.*

Consequent/कन्सिक्बेंट *(adjective)* – अनुयायी following as a consequence. [archaic] logically consistent. *His consequent efforts brough success to him.*

Conservation/कन्जरवेशन *(noun)* – सुरक्षित रखने का कार्य preservation or restoration of the natural environment and wildlife. preservation and repair of archaeological, [historical], and cultural sites and artifacts. *Conservation of wildlife and trees is a must today.*

Conservative/कन्जरवेटिव *(adjective)* – स्थिति पालक, लकीर का फकीर averse to change or innovation and holding traditional values. sober conventional. *My granddad is very conservative. He is averse to everything new.*

Conservator/कन्जरवेटर *(noun)* – रक्षक पालक a person involved in conservation. *He has vowed himself to to conservative work.*

Conserve/कन्जर्व *(noun)* – अचार, मुरब्बा protect from harm or destruction. prevent the wasteful overuse of. preserve with sugar. *My father preserves most things. He protects things from harm or destruction.*

Consideration/कन्सिडरेशन *(noun)* – विचार-विमर्श careful thought. a fact taken into account when making a decision. *After much consideration I have decided to join your party.*

Considering/कन्सिडरिंग *(prep)* – समझते हुए taking into consideration. adverb [informal] taking everything into account. *Considering her wishes, I took her to a fivestar hotel.*

Consign/कन्साइन *(verb)* – सौंपना, देना deliver to someone's custody. send by a public carrier. put someone or something in order to be rid of them. *My consignment from Hong Cong is to arrive by the end of the month.*

Consist/कन्सिस्ट *(verb)* – रहना, होना, मिलना be composed of. have as an essential feature. *Tea consists of sugar milk and tea leaves.*

Consolation/कन्सोलेशन *(noun)* – आश्वासन, ढाढस comfort received by someone after a loss or disappointment. a source of such comfort. *My friend and many people consoled me over my loss.*

Consolatory/कन्सोलेटरी *(adj)* – सान्त्वना देने की प्रवृत्ति वाला tending to console. *He is a man of consolatory nature only.*

Console/कन्सोल *(verb)* – ढाढस देना to soothe, to comfort. *I consoled to my friend for best result.*

Consonance/कन्सोनैन्स *(noun)* – अविरोध agreement or harmony. *He always do his work with his consonance.*

Consonant/कन्सोनैट *(adj)* – अनुरूप a speech sound in which the breath is at least partly obstructed and which can be combined with a vowel to form a syllable. a letter representing such a sound. *There are five vowels and 21 consonants in English alphabet.*

Consort/कॉन्सॉर्ट *(noun)* – संगी, साथी a wife, husband, or companion, in particular the spouse of a monarch. *There are many consorts in the parl.*

Conspecific/कन्सपेसिफिक *(adjective)* – एक जाति का belonging to the same species. *Apes and monkeys belong to the same conspecific.*

C

Conspectus/कन्सपेक्टस *(noun)* – सामान्य दृश्य general view, synopsis. *The professor gave a long conspectus.*

Conspicuous/कन्सपिक्यूअस *(adjective)* – प्रत्यक्ष clearly visible. attracting notice or attention. *He was conspicuous by his absence.*

Conspiracy/कन्सपिरेसी *(noun)* – कपट-प्रबन्ध a secret plan by a group to do something unlawful or harmful. the action of conspiring. *When some people plan to do something bad is called conspiracy.*

Conspirator/कन्सपिरेटर *(noun)* – राजद्रोही a member of a conspiracy. *Cassius was the main conspirator against Cancer.*

Constable/कन्सटेबल *(noun)* – पुलिस का सिपाही [British] a police officer. a police officer of the lowest rank. *a police officer of the lowest rank.*

Constancy/कन्सटैन्सी *(noun)* – स्थिरता the quality of being enduring and free from change or variation. *He has the quality of constancy.*

Constant/कॉन्सटैंट *(adjective)* – स्थिर occurring continuously. *He is very constant in his work.*

Constellation/कन्सटिलेशन *(noun)* – नक्षत्र मण्डल a group of stars forming a recognized pattern and typically named after a mythological or other figure. *Do you see that constellation in the sky you can locate it any time because it retains its fixed pattern these are seven stars named after a Rishi.*

Constipate/कन्स्टिपेट *(verb)* – अवरोध करना affect with constipation. *He is suffering from constipation as such he has to take a laxative.*

Constituency/कन्सीच्यूअन्सि *(noun)* – निर्वाचन क्षेत्र a body of voters in a specified area who elects a representative to a legislative body. [chiefly British] the area represented in this way. *He is a constituency member and has great power.*

Constituent/कन्सीट्यूएन्ट *(adjective)* – रचने वाला, निर्वाचक being a part of a whole. *A state is governed by its constituent it has the power to appoint or elect.*

Constitute/कंस्टीट्यूट *(verb)* – नियुक्त करना, स्थापित करना, निर्माण करना a body of fundamental principle or established precedents according to which a state or organization is governed. [historical] a decree, ordinance, or [law]. *It does not constitute according to law.*

Constitutive/कन्सीट्यूटिव *(adjective)* – आवश्यक, संगठन सम्बन्धी having the power to establish something. *Having the power to constitute.*

Constrict/कन्सट्रिक्ट *(verb)* – दबाना to compress to contract. *He constricted the doors bell.*

Constringe/कन्सट्रिंजे *(verb)* – सिकोड़ना to draw, to frame. *I constringed my clothes.*

Construct/कन्सट्रक्ट *(verb)* – खींचना build or erect. *My friend has constructed a huge building.*

Construe/कन्सट्रयू *(verb)* – परिच्छेद करना, व्याख्या करना interpret in a particular way. dated analyse the construction of a text, sentence, or word. dated translate word for word. *My friend construed a piece of English from word to word in Hindi.*

Consul/कन्सल *(noun)* – वाणिज्य दूत a state official living in a foreign city and protecting the state's citizens and interests there. *If you have any problem, consult your consul.*

Consult/कॅन्सल्ट *(verb)* – सूचना प्राप्त करना seek information or advice from someone, especially an expert or professional. seek permission or approval from. engaged in the business of giving advice to other in the same field: a consulting engineer. *At once consult a doctor for your disease.*

Consumption/कन्जम्प्शन *(noun)* – उपभोग the action or process of consuming. an amount consumed. *That man consumed a lot of food.*

Contact/कन्टैक्ट *(noun & verb)* – सम्पर्क, संयोग, लगाव the state or condition of physical touching. the state or condition of communicating or meeting. caused by or operating through physical touch: contact dermatitis. *I will contact you soon.*

Contagion/कंटेजन *(noun)* – छूत का रोग the communication of disease form one person to another by close contact. dated a disease spread in such a way. *Close contact is responsible for contagion which is disease of spread by communication.*

Contagious/कन्टेजिअस *(adjective)* – स्पर्श से रोग फैलाने वाली spread by direct or indirect contact of people or organism. having a contagious disease. *People suffering from contagious disease spread this directly or indirectly.*

Contain/कन्टेन *(verb)* – रखना, धरना, बराबर होना have or hold within. *My medicines are contained in this box very carefully.*

Contaminate/कन्टैमिनेट *(verb)* – दूषित करना make impure by exposure to or addition of a hostile country or influence. *Flies contaminate food.*

Contemn/कण्टेम् *(verb)* – घृणा करना [archaic] treat or regard with contempt. *I look at him with contemn.*

Contemplate/कन्टेम्प्लेट *(verb)* – विचार करना, चिन्तन करना contem poraneity. *To anticipate, to intent, to medicate. I contemplated this exercise for understanding.*

Contemporaneous/कन्टैम्पोरेनियस *(adjective)* – समकालीनता existing at or occurring in the same period of time. *Lord Mohan's and Buddha were contemporaneous.*

Contemporary/कन्टेम्पोरैरी *(adjective)* – समकालिक living, occurring or originating at the same time. *Gandhiji and Vinoba Bhave were contemporaries.*

Contempt/कन्टेम्प्ट *(noun)* – तिरस्कार, अनादर, अपमान the feeling that a person or a thing is worthless or beneath consideration. *The judge said it is contempt of court and gave suitable punishment to the offender.*

Contemptuous/कन्टेम्टयूअस *(adjective)* – घृणित, तिरस्कार युक्त showing contempt. *I had nothing but contempt for him.*

Content/कन्टेन्ट *(adjective)* – सन्तुष्ट, प्रसन्न in a state of peaceful happiness or satisfaction. *I am content with my state of offers.*

Contention/कन्टेन्शन *(noun)* – विवाद heated disagreement. *A contention took place between the two friends.*

Contest/कॉण्टेस्ट *(noun)* – प्रतिस्पर्धा an event in which people compete for supremacy. a dispute or conflict. *There was a boxing contest between the two boxers.*

Context/कन्टेक्स्ट *(noun)* – प्रकरण, संदर्भ the circumstances that form the setting for an event, statement, or idea, and in term of which it can be fully understood. the parts that immediately precede and follow a word or passage and clarify its meaning. *After the event the provident said in this context that more such friendly matches will be hold.*

Continence/कन्टिनेन्स *(onun)* – संयम, आत्मनियंत्रण self commands restraint of passion. *Continence is a must.*

Continent/कन्टिनेन्ट *(noun)* – महाद्वीप any of the world's main continuous expanses of land. *India is a big continent.*

Contingency/कन्टिन्जेन्सी *(noun)* – आकस्मिक घटना a future event or circumstance which is possible but cannot be predicted with certainty. a provision for such an event or circumstance. *You are going to face a contingency friend but it will do you good.*

Contingent/कन्टिजेन्ट *(adjective)* – संदिग्ध subject to chance. dependent on. that can be anticipated to arise if a particular event occurs. *A contingent of police was sent to help a larger group.*

Continual/कन्टिन्यूअल *(adjective)* – सतत constantly or frequently occurring. *He is continually late.*

Continuator/कन्टिन्यूएटर *(adj)* – दूसरे की आधी लिखी पुस्तक को समाप्त करने वाला one who writes in continuation of author's work.

Continue/कन्टिन्यू *(verb)*– जारी करना persist in an activity or process. remain in existence, operation, or a specified state. *I'll continue carrying on in the same direction till I find the old temple.*

Continuity/कन्टिन्यूइटी *(noun)* – निरन्तरता होने की अवस्था the unbroken and consistent existence or operation of something. a connection or line of development with no sharp breaks. *The film was good but it lacked continuity.*

Continuous/कन्टिन्यूअस *(adjective)* – लगातार without interruption. forming a series with no exceptions or reversals. [mathematics] of which the graph is a smooth unbroken curve. *Yuvraj hit six sixers continuously.*

Contour/कॉन्टूर *(noun)* – पर्वत, समुद्र तट आदि की परिधि की रेखा an outline, especially one representing or bounding the shape or form of something. a line on a map joining points of equal height above or below sea level. a line joining points on a diagram at which some property has the same value. *The clay was given a definite contour and it looked beautiful.*

C

C

Contraception/कन्ट्रासेप्सन *(noun)* – गर्भ अवरोध the use of artificial methods or other techniques to prevent pregnancy. *There are so many contraceptions available in these days.*

Contract/कन्ट्रैक्ट *(noun)* – संविदा a written or spoken agreement intended to be enforceable by [law]. *I have one year's contract with him more than I will be free.*

Contradistinction/कन्ट्राडिस्टिंक्शन *(noun)* – विपक्षता distinction made by contrasting the different qualities of two things. *If you compare and contrast the two players, the destination will become clear.*

Contrariety/कन्ट्राराइटी *(noun)* – प्रतिकूलता [logic] contrary opposition. *There is contrariety and inconsistency between the two matches.*

Contrariwise/कन्ट्रैरीवाइज *(adverb)* – विपरीत in the opposite way. on the other hand. *This team is good but contrariwise the batsmen of the other team are far superior.*

Contrary/कन्ट्रैरी *(adjective)* – प्रतिकूल opposite in nature, direction, or meaning. *I am contrary to his nature. So we can't become friends.*

Contrast/कन्ट्रास्ट *(noun)* – अन्तर the state of being strikingly different from something else in juxtaposition or close association. *Black is in sharp contrast to white.*

Contribute/कन्ट्रिब्यूट *(verb)* – सहायता देना give in order to help achieve or provide something. help to cause or bring about. *Others with Mahatma Gandhi contributed a lot to bring freedom.*

Contrite/कन्ट्राइट *(adjective)* – शोकार्त feeling or expressing remorse. *My friend has left for USA and I am feeling rather contrite.*

Contrivable/कन्ट्रीवेबल *(adj)* – निर्माण what may be contrived. *I am contrivable this building.*

Contrivance/कन्ट्राइवेन्स *(noun)* – आविष्कार the action of contriving something. *We can contrive the problem by putting a dam over the river. This contrivance is sure going to work.*

Control/कन्ट्रोल *(noun)* – निग्रह the power to influence people's behaviour or the course of events. the restriction of an activity. tendency, or phenomenon. *I have full control over events.*

Controllable/कन्ट्रोलेब्ल *(adj)* – वश में करने योग्य subject to control. *He was not controllable.*

Controller/कन्ट्रोलर *(noun)* – अध्यक्ष one who has authority to control. *He is the controller of this ship.*

Controversy/कन्ट्रोवर्सी *(noun)* – प्रतिवाद disagreement, typically when prolonged and public. *This is a controversy topic going on for a long time.*

Controvert/कन्ट्रोवर्ट *(verb)* – अस्वीकार करना deny the truth of. *I will not controvert the truth of this statement.*

Contuse/कन्ट्यूज *(verb)* – कुचलना to injure without breaking skin to beat and bruised. *He was contused by a car.*

Conundrum/कोनन्ड्रम *(noun)* – पहेली an extended urban area, typically consisting of several towns merging with the suburbs of a central city. *Delhi is a conundrum city.*

Convalesce/कन्वैलेस *(verb)* – पुन: स्वस्थ होना gradually recover one's health after an illness or medical treatment. *He has just recovered he is a convalescent.*

Convection/कनवेक्शन *(noun)* – बिजली की शक्ति का एक स्थान से दूसरे स्थान का संवाहन transference of mass or heat within a fluid caused by the tendency of warmer and less dense material to rise. *Convection current.*

Convene/कन्विन *(verb)* – बटोरना call people together for a meeting. assemble for a common purpose. *All you people have been called to convene in the hall.*

Convenience/कन्वेनियंस *(noun)* – आराम freedom from effort or difficulty. a useful or helpful device or situation. *It is for your convenience, please.*

Conventicle/कन्वेंटिकल *(noun)* – धर्मसभा [historical] a secret or unlawful religious meeting, typically of nonconformists. *Non conformists need to hold such conventicle in old times.*

Convention/कन्वेन्शन *(noun)* – सभा a way in which something is usually done. socially acceptable behaviour. *It is a convention in our country to touch our elders' feet.*

Conventual/कन्वेन्युअल *(adjective)* – मठ-सम्बन्धी relating or belonging to a convent. relating to the less strict order of the Franciscans, living in large convents. *My sister lives in a convent. She is a nun.*

Conversable/कन्वर्सेब्ल *(adj)* – वार्ता करने योग्य easy in conversation fit for social inter course. *It is conversable matter.*

Conversant/कन्वर्सेंट *(adjective)* – परिचित familiar with or knowledgeable about something. *We were conversant together where he interfered.*

Conversation/कन्वरसेशन *(noun)* – बातचीत an [informal] spoken exchange of news and ideas between two or more people. *A conversation between the two leaders is going on.*

Converse/कन्वर्स *(verb)* – सम्भाषण करना engage in conversation noun [archaic] conversation. *I will converse with you after the office hours.*

Conversion/कन्वर्सन *(noun)* – रूपान्तर the process or action of converting or of being converted. *Conversion has taken place in this building.*

Convert/कन्वर्ट *(verb)* – बदलना change or cause to change in form, character, or function. change into others of a different kind. adapt to make it suitable for a new purpose. *Hydrogen and Oxygen can be converted into water.*

Convex/कन्वेक्स *(adjective)* – उन्नतोदर having an outline or surface curved like the exterior of a circle or sphere, compare with concave. *Convex mirrors are often used in transport vehicles.*

Convey/कन्वे *(verb)* – पहुँचाना transport or carry to a place. *I have conveyed your message to your friend.*

Conviction/कन्विक्शन *(noun)* – दोषसिद्धि an instance of being convicted the action or process of convicting someone. *He has been convicted to 10 years of imprisonment.*

Convince/कन्विन्स *(verb)* – निश्चय कराना cause to believe firmly in the truth of something. persuade to do something. firm in one's belief with regard to a particular cause: a convinced pacifist. *I told him that one must follow the rules of the land after some argument he was convinced.*

Convivial/कन्वाइवल *(adjective)* – उत्सव-सम्बन्धी friendly, lively, and enjoyable. cheerful and sociable. *He is convivial fellow.*

Convocation/कन्वोकेशन *(noun)* – समागम a representative assembly of clergy of the province of Canterbury or York. [British] a legislative or deliberative assembly of a university. [north American] a formal ceremony for the conferment of university awards. *He got the university award at convocation.*

Convoke/कन्वोक *(verb)* – पुकारना to call together. *I convoke him.*

Convolve/कन्वल्व *(verb)* – लपेटना rare roll or coil together. *He convolved the roll together into a ball.*

Convoy/कन्वॉय *(verb)* – सुरक्षित ले जाना (to escort). *I call him to convoy this cloths.*

Cony/कोनी *(noun)* – खरहा the rabbit. *I saw a cony.*

Coo/कू *(noun)* – कबूतर की तरह गुटकना make a soft murmuring sound. *She cooed into my ear and I loved it very much.*

Cook/कूक *(noun)* – रसोइया prepare by mixing, combining, and heating the ingredients. be heated so as to reach an edible state. *She is an expert cook and the credit goes to her for preparing some new dishes also.*

Cook-house/कूक-हाउस *(noun)* – घर के बाहर की पाकशाला a building used for cooking, especially on a ranch, military camp, etc. *let's go to cook house to eat something.*

Cool/कूल *(adjective)* – शीतल, शान्त of or at a fairly low temperature. keeping one from becoming too hot. *His behaviour was cool and unenthusiastic.*

Coolie/कूली *(noun)* – मजदूर dated an unskilled native labourer in India, china, and some other Asian countries. *Call that coolie he will carry our bag and baggage.*

Coop/कूप *(noun)* – मुर्गी के ढाँकने की टोकरी a cage or pen for confining poultry. *All poultry is confined in this rather small coop.*

Cooper/कूपर *(noun)* – नाद बनाने वाला a maker or repairer of casks and barrels. *Coopers make or repair casks and barrels.*

Co-operant/को-ऑपरेंट *(adj)* – मिलकर काम करने वाला co-operating. *I am with a co-operant.*

Co-operate/को-आपरेट *(verb)* – साथ-साथ काम करने वाला work jointly towards the same end. assist someone or comply with their requests. *We both are going to co-operate to complete this mission.*

C

Co-ordinate/को-ऑरडिनेट *(adj)* – समान पद का bring the different elements of into a harmonious or efficient relationship. *We all shall co-ordinate with another so as to reach the desired result.*

Coot/कूट *(noun)* – मूर्ख व्यक्ति, जल पक्षी an aquatic bird of the rail family with black plumage and a white bill that extends back on to the forehead as a horny shield. *He is a coot a typically old eccentric person.*

Copal/कोपल *(noun)* – वार्निश के प्रयोग की जाने वाली राल resin from any of a number of tropical trees, used to make varnish. *Copal obtained from this tree is used to make varnish.*

Coparcenary/कोपरसिनरी *(noun)* – अविभक्त जायदाद का संयुक्त उत्तराधिकारी joint heir to undivided property. *He is my coparcenary*

Co-partner/को-पार्टनर *(noun)* – अंश भागी a partner or associate, especially an equal partner in a business. *We are both equal partners in this firm.*

Cope/कोप *(noun)* – पादरियों का लम्बा चोंगा deal effectively with something difficult. *He coped the crisis skilfully.*

Coper/कोपर *(noun)* – घोड़ो का व्यापारी horse dealer. *He is the coper.*

Copier/कोपिअर *(noun)* – नकल करने वाला a machine that makes exact copies of something. *I am going to buy a photocopier machine.*

Copious/कोपिअस *(adj)* – प्रचुर plentiful, profuse. *We have capious of gold.*

Copper/कॉपर *(noun)* – ताँबा [British informal] a police officer. *British in formal 'cop' or police office.*

Copperas/कॉपरस *(noun)* – तूतिया green crystals of hydrated ferrous sulphate, especially as an industrial product. *Copperas is blue vitriol.*

Coppice/कॉपिस *(noun)* – जंगल an area of woodland in which the trees or shrubs are periodically cut back to ground level to stimulate growth and provide wood. (verb) cut back in this way. *This areas is called coppice. Trees and stubs are out here to stimulate their growth.*

Copra/कॉपरा *(noun)* – नारियल की गरी का गोला dried coconut kernels, form which oil is obtained. *Dry coconut copra from which oil is obtained.*

Copula/कोपुला *(noun)* – बन्धनी [logic] & grammar] a connecting word, in particular a form of the (verb) be connecting a subject and complement. *In grammar it connects a subject and complement.*

Copulate/कोपुलेट *(verb)* – मैथुन करना have sexual intercourse. *To have sexual inter course.*

Copulative/कॉपुलेटिव *(adjective)* – संभोगकारी [grammar] connecting words or clauses linked in sense. connecting a subject and predicate. *They were found in a copulative position.*

Copy/कॉपी *(noun)* – प्रतिलिपि a thing made to be similar or identical to another. *Will you please stop copying my notes.*

Copyhold/कॉपीहोल्ड *(noun)* – पट्टा लिखाई हुई जमीन [British historical] tenure of land based on manorial records. *According to manorial record, this land is copyhold.*

Copying-press/कॉपिइंग प्रेस *(noun)* – प्रतिलिपि छापने का यंत्र a machine for making an exact color of a menu script. *It is a copying-press.*

Copyist/कॉपिइस्ट *(noun)* – लेखक, प्रतिलिपि लेखक a person who makes copies. *He is a copyist. He imitates the art of other people.*

Coquettish/कोक्वेटिश *(adj)* – चोचला दिखलाने वाली a flirt woman. *She is a coquettish woman who is given to flirting.*

Coral/कोरल *(noun)* – प्रवाल a hard stony substance secreted by certain colonial marine animals as an external skeleton, typically forming large resets. precious red coral. *Hard substance consists of skeletons of certain animals.*

Corbel/कॉरबेल *(noun)* – ताखा a projection jutting out from a wall to support a structure above it. *Keep these things on the corbel.*

Cord/कॉर्ड *(noun)* – डोरी long thin string or rope made from several twisted strands. a length of such material. *The pieces of wood were tied with a cord.*

Cordate/कॉडेट *(adjective)* – हृदय के आकार का botany & [zoology] heart-shaped. *Heart shaped according [zoology] and botany.*

Cordial/कॉर्डीयल *(noun & adj)* – मित्रवत warm and friendly. *He is a very cordial and polite man.*

Core/कोर *(noun)* – हृदय the tough central part of various fruits, containing the seeds. *The core of coconut is very sweet.*

Co-religionist/को-रिलिजनिस्ट *(noun)* – एक ही धर्म का अनुयायी an adherent of the same religion as another person. *We both friend belong to Hindu religion.*

Co-respondent/को-रिस्पॉडेन्ट *(noun)* – किसी मुकदमे में सहकारी मुद्दालेह a person cited in a divorce case as having committed adultery with the respondent. *In this divorce case I will cite a case of person as having committed adultery with the accuser.*

Coriander/कोरियन्डर *(noun)* – धनियाँ an aromatic Mediterranean plant of the parsley family, the leaves and seeds of which are used as culinary herbs. *There are many types of corianders prepared in different states of India.*

Cork/कॉर्क *(noun)* – काग the buoyant, light brown substance obtained form the outer layer of the bark of the cork oak. *The cork was so hardly pressed into the both that-it-took all our efforts to take it out.*

Cormorant/कार्मरण्ट *(noun)* – पेटू मनुष्य a large diving seabird with a long neck, long hooked bill, short legs, and mainly black plumage. *Cormorant is a bird worth looking at.*

Corn/कॉर्न *(noun)* – दाना, पैर का गोखरू a small, painful area of thickened skin on the foot, especially on the toes, caused by pressure. *There was a thickened skin on my too. I went to a skin surgeon and had it removerd.*

Cornea/कॉरनिया *(noun)* – कनीनिका the transparent layer forming the front of the eye. *There is nothing wrong with the cornea of your eye.*

Corner/कॉर्नर *(noun)* – कोना, कोण a place or angle where two or more sides or edges meet. a place where two streets meet. *A man was hiding in a corner he appeared a thief to me.*

Cornet/कार्निट *(noun)* – एक बाजा a brass instrument resembling a trumpet but shorter and wider. *He plays cornet very well.*

Cornice/कॉरनिस *(noun)*– दीवार का साज an ornamental molding round the wall of a room just below the ceiling. *The cornice of this room is beautifully decorated.*

Corollary/कोरोलरी *(noun)* – अनुमान [logic] a proposition that follows from one already proved. *My friend argued brilliantly and cited a corollary that followed logically from another.*

Coronal/कोरोनल *(noun)* – किरीट of or relating to the crown or corona of something. *The coronal ceremony was held on grand scale.*

Coronation/कोरोनेशन *(noun)* – राजतिलक the ceremony of crowning a sovereign for a sovereigns' consort. *I had the good fortune to attend the coronation ceremony of the king.*

Coronet/कोरोनेट *(noun)* – माला a small or simple crown, especially as worn by lesser royalty and nobles. a circular decoration for the head. *At a royalty show that some lesser royalties were wearing smaller coronet.*

Corporal/कॉर्पोरल *(adj)* – कायिक, देह–सम्बन्धी a rank of non-commissioned officer in the army, above lance corporal or private first class and below sergeant. *An NCO above corporal and below sergeant.*

Corporate/कॉरपोरेट *(adjective)* – संयुक्त of or relating to a large company or group. *The corporate office of this company is in Delhi.*

Corporation/कॉरपोरेशन *(noun)* – मण्डली a large company or group of companies authorized to act as a single entity and recognized as such in law. *Urban Development Corporation works for urban development.*

Corporeity/कॉरपोराइटी *(noun)* – शरीरत्व rare the quality of having a physical body or existence.

Corps/कोर् *(noun)* – सेना का भाग a main subdivision of an army in the field, consisting of two or more divisions. a branch of an army assigned to a particular king id work. a body of people engaged in a particular activity. *Subdivision of army having two or more divisions assigned to a particular work.*

Corpse/कॉर्प्स *(noun)* – शव a dead body, especially of a human, (verb) theatrical slanged spoil a piece of acting by forgetting one's lines or laughing uncontrollably. *Corpses were lying all over the battle field.*

Corpulence/कॉपुलेन्स – मोटापन obesity. *He is a corpulent fat old man.*

C

Correct/करेक्ट *(verb)* – सुधारना free from error; true; right. chiefly [north American] conforming to a particular political or ideological orthodoxy: environmentally correct. *My friend wrote an all correct essay.*

Correlate/कोरिलेट *(noun)* – परस्पर सम्बन्धी वस्तुएँ have a relationship or connection in which one thing affects or depends or another. establish a correlation between.

Correspond/करेस्पॉन्ड *(verb)* – पत्र-व्यवहार करना, अनुरूप होना have a close similarity; match or agree almost exactly. be analogous or equivalent. *Each month we two friends correspond by letters.*

Corridor/कॉरिडॉर *(noun)* – बरामदा a long passage from which doors lead into rooms. [British] a passage along the side of a railway carriage giving access to compartments. *While is college, we used to spend a lot of time in the corridor.*

Corroborate/कराबॅरेट *(verb)* – पुष्ट करना confirm or give support to a statement or theory. *I corroborated his statement in the court.*

Corrode/करोड *(verb)* – धीरे-धीरे क्षय होना destroy or damage slowly by chemical action. be destroyed or damaged in this way. gradually weaken or erode. *The long action of water has corrode a deep gash in the rock.*

Corrosion/करोजन *(noun)* – क्रम से क्षय a state of deterioration in metals caused by oxidation or chemical reaction. *In this chemical reaction, corrosion will take place.*

Corrosive/कोरोसिव *(adjective)* – खाने वाला tending to cause corrosion. (noun) a corrosive substance. *Wind and water are great corrosive agents.*

Corrugate/कारूगेट *(verb)* – सिकोड़ना contract into wrinkles or folds. *The old man's face had contracted into wrinkles.*

Corrupt/करप्ट *(adjective)* – भ्रष्ट willing to act dishonestly in return for money or personal gain. evil or morally depraved. *He is a very corrupt officer. He won't favour you without money.*

Cortage/कॉरटेज *(noun)* – नौकर-चाकरों की श्रेणी a solemn procession, especially for a funeral. *I joined the cortage procession of my friend.*

Coryza/कॉराइजा *(noun)* – जुकाम [medicine] catarrhal inflammation of the mucous membrane in the nose, as caused by a cold. *I have been suffering form coryza since yesterday.*

Cosignatory/कोसिग्नेटरी *(noun & adj)* – दूसरे के साथ हस्ताक्षर करने वाला a person or state signing a treaty or other document jointly with others. *Many persons and states sign a mutual treaty and other documents.*

Cosmetic/कॉस्मेटिक *(noun)* – अंगराग relating to treatment intended to improve a person's appearance. *My friend underwent cosmetic surgery of the face. Now he looks much younger and smart.*

Cosmic/कॉस्मिक *(adjective)* – जगत सम्बन्धी of or relating to the universe or cosmos, especially as distinct from the earth. *Scientists have yet to know about a lot of cosmic mysteries.*

Cosmogony/कॉस्मोगनी *(noun)* – विश्व की उत्पत्ति का सिद्धान्त the branch of science concerned with the origin of the universe, especially the solar system. *My friend's hobby is cosmogony.*

Cosmos/कॉसमॉस *(noun)* – क्रमबद्ध संसार an ornamental plant of the daisy family, which bears single dahlia-like flowers and is native to Mexico and warm regions of America. *A Mexican plant that bears a single dahlia-like flower.*

Cost/कॉस्ट *(noun)* – मूल्य require the payment of in order to be bought or obtained. cause or require the expenditure or loss of. [informal] be expensive for; it'll cost you. *Please tell me the cost of this diamond.*

Costard/कॉस्टार्ड *(noun)* – एक प्रकार का बड़ा सेव [British] a cooking apple of a large ribbed variety. *I didn't like the taste of this kind of costard.*

Coster/कॉस्टर्ड *(noun)* – ठेले पर लादकर घूमकर फल बेचने वाला [British] short for costermonger. *The costar was selling fish, fruit and vegetables.*

Costive/कॉस्टिव *(adjective)* – वद्धकोष्ठ, मल रोकने वाला constipated. *This man appears costive.*

Costly/कॉस्टली *(adjective)* – महँगा causing suffering, loss, or disadvantage. *It is rather costly item. Haven't you something of modest price?*

Costume/कॉस्ट्यूम *(noun)* – वेश a set of clothes in a style typical of a particular country or [historical] period. a set of clothes worn by an actor or performer for a role. [British] dated a woman's matching jacket and skirt. *(verb)* dress in a particular set of clothes. *This is a special costume that belongs to 18th century.*

Cot/कॉट *(noun)*– पालना, झोपड़ी [British] a small bed with high barred sides for a baby or very young child. a plain narrow bed. [north American] a camp bed. nautical a bed resembling a hammock hung from deck beams, formerly used by officers. *A small bed barred on side for baby or very young child.*

Cote/कोट *(noun)* – बाड़ा a shelter for mammals or birds, especially pigeons. *Pigeons live in cotes.*

Co-tenant/को-टेनैंट *(noun)* – साझीदार a joint tenant. *These two boys are co-tenant in this room.*

Coterie/कोटेरी *(noun)* – सामाजिक संघ a small exclusive group of people with shared interests or tastes. *We few friends belong to a club with commonly shared interests and tastes.*

Cottage/कॉटेज *(noun)*– पर्णशाला a small simple house, typically one in the country. *A monk lives in this cottage.*

Cotton/कॉटन *(noun)* – सूती कपड़ा a soft white fibrous substance which surrounds the seeds of the cotton plant and is used as textile fiber and thread for sewing. *Cotton is packed into bales and has many uses.*

Couch/काउच *(noun)* – खटिया a coarse grass with long creeping roots. *In jungle we rolled on nature made couches.*

Cough/कफ *(verb)* – खाँसना, कास expel air from the lungs with a sudden sharp sound. *My friend kept on coughing loudly, so we took him to doctor.*

Council/कौंसिल *(noun)* – विचार सभा a formally constituted advisory, deliberative, or administrative body. a body elected to manage the affairs of a city, county, or district. *My friend resigned from the council due to some difference.*

Counsellor/काउन्सेलर *(noun)* – वकील a person trained to give guidance on personal, social, or psychological problems. *He is a counsellor and trained to give guidance on various issues.*

Countenance/काउन्टेनन्स *(noun)* – आकार a person's face or facial expression. *My friend has a very impressive countenance.*

Counteract/काउन्टरएक्ट *(verb)* – हराना, रोकना act against in order to reduce its force or neutralize it. *My friend counteracted when some absurd questions were asked from him.*

Counterchange/काउन्टरचेंज *(verb)* – अदला-बदली करना poetic chequer with contrasting colours. heraldry interchange the tinctures of with that of a divided field.

Countercharge/काउन्टरचार्ज *(noun)* – नालिश a change brought against accuser. *There are countercharges in this case.*

Counter-claim/काउन्टर-क्लेम *(noun)*– मुकदमे में प्रतिवादी की माँग a claim made to rebut a previous claim. [law] a claim made by a defendant against the plaintiff. *(verb)* [chiefly law] make a counterclaim. *He made a counter-claim for his lost bag and baggage.*

Counterfeiter/काउन्टरफिटर *(noun)* – जालसाज a forger, a cheat. *He is a counterfeiter.*

Counterfoil/काउन्टरफॉइल *(noun)* – नकल [chiefly British] the part of a cheque, ticket, etc. that is kept as a record by the person issuing it.

Countermand/काउन्टरमांड *(verb)* – प्रतिकूल आदेश देना revoke declare voting invalid. *It was declared that the voting was countermand.*

Counterpoise/काउन्टरपॉइज *(noun)* – पसँघा a factor or force that balances or neutralizes another. [archaic] a state of equilibrium. a counterbalancing weight. (verb) have an opposing and balancing effect on. bring into contrast. *A force that neutralizes the others.*

Countersign/काउन्टरसाइन *(verb)* – सांकेतिक शब्द add a signature to a document already signed by another person. (noun) [archaic] a signal or password given in reply to a soldier on guard. *I didn't countersign the check.*

Countervail/काउन्टरवेल *(verb)* – सम करना [offset] the effect of by countering it with something of equal force.

Countless/काउन्टलेस *(adjective)* – बेगम too many to be counted; very many. *A lot of crowd had gathered in the ground.*

Country/कन्ट्री (noun) – देश a nation with its own government, occupying a particular territory. *A nation with its own territory currency. Government and wild territory.*

Coup/कू (noun)– चोट a sudden violent seizure of power from a government. *A coup is sudden violent seizure of power from a government.*

Couple/कपल (noun) – युगल two individuals of the same sort considered together. *Two people of the age are considered for marriage.*

Couplet/कपलेट (noun) – श्लोक a pair of successive lines of verse, typically rhyming and of the same length. *Kaka Hathrasi was a master of couplets.*

Courage/करेज (noun) – सहारा the ability to do something that frightens one. strength in the face of pain or grief. *My friend has courage to face any danger, pain or grief.*

Courier/कोरिअर (noun) – हरकारा a messenger who transports goods or documents. *There are many courier agencies operating in the city.*

Course/कोर्स (noun) – पीछा करना [British] a textbook designed for use on a particular course of study. *My course of commerce consists of many textbooks.*

Court/कोर्ट (noun) – दरबार, कचहरी a body of people before whom judicial cases are heard. the place where they meet. *In a court of law judicial cases are heard.*

Courtesan/कोरटिजन (noun) – वेश्या, रण्डी a prostitute, especially one with wealthy or upper-class clients. *I met a courtesan who belonged to a rather richer and upper class.*

Courtesy/कर्टसी (noun) – विनय courteous behaviour. a polite speech or action, especially one required by convention.

Courtly/कर्टली (adjective) – सुशील very polite and refined. *My friend moves in royal circles. His courtly behaviour is liked by all.*

Courtship/कोर्टशीप (noun) – विवाह के निमित्त आराधना a period of courting, especially with a view to marriage. the courting behaviour of male birds and other animals. *Since my friend is courting a girl he is rather facing risky situations.*

Courtyard/कोर्टयार्ड (noun) – घर के बाहर का सहन an open area enclosed by walls or buildings, especially in a castle or large house. *Instead of open, we would rather play in our courtyard.*

Covenant/कॉवनेन्ट (noun) – पण, सौदा a solemn agreement. theology an agreement held to be the basis of a relationship of commitment with god. *My friend is a covenant member of church. He has agreed to pay by covenant.*

Coverlet/कवरलेट (noun) – चदरा a bedspread. *It is a beautiful coverlet.*

Covert/कॉवर्ट (adjective) – गुप्त not openly acknowledged or displayed. (noun) a thicket in which game can hide. *It is something covert to be displayed nor to be acknowledged.*

Covet/कॉवेट (verb) – लालच करना yearn to possess. *I covet that piece of jewellery. I wish it were mine.*

Covey/कॉवि (noun) – तीतरों का झुण्ड a small flock of birds, especially partridge. *There is a group of coveys, let's go and catch them.*

Cow/कॉउ (noun) – गाय a fully grown female animal of a domesticated breed of ox. an animal of this type which has borne more than one calf. compare with HEIFER. the female of certain other large animals, e.g. elephant, rhinoceros, or whale. *The cow is a household pet animal. It is domesticated.*

Cower/कॉवर (verb) – दबकना crouch down in fear. *There appeared a lion and the priest crouched down in great feer.*

Co-worker/को-वर्कर (noun) – दूसरे के साथ काम करने वाला one who works with another. *We are friends as well as co-workers.*

Coze/कोज (verb) – बकवाद करना to have chat [informal, archaic or North American] cousin.

Cozen/कोजेन (verb) – ठगना [poetic/literary] trick or deceive.

Cozy/कोजी (adjective) – सुखकर US spelling of cosy.

Crackle/क्रैकल (verb) – कड़ाके का शब्द करना a pattern of minute surface crackes. *There is crackling sound in the jungle.*

Cracknel/क्रैकनेल (noun) – कुरकुरा बिस्कुट a light, crisp, savoury biscuit. *Cracknels are my favorites.*

Cracksman/क्रैक्समैन (noun) – चोर, ठग [informal], dated a safe-breaker. *Police has caught a cracksman. He has looted many safes.*

Crafty/क्राफ्टी *(adj)* – कपटी cunning or deceitful. *He is a crafty fellow and not to be trusted at all.*

Crambo/क्रैम्बो *(noun)* – तुकबन्दी का खेल a game in which a player gives a word or line of verse to which other players must find a rhyme. *We are playing crambo and it is a very exciting game.*

Crane/क्रेन *(noun)* – सारस a large wading bird with large legs. *The crane is eating a fish.*

Cranny/क्रैनी *(noun)* – छिद्र a small, narrow space or opening. *He went down the narrow space and emerged at the other end.*

Crashing/क्रैशिंग *(noun)* – प्रचण्ड शब्द a loud resonant repeating noise. *A violent sound is called crashing.*

Crass/क्रैस *(adjective)* – अनाड़ी showing a grossly insensitive lack of intelligence. *He is stupid and crass, not an ounce of intelligence in him.*

Crate/क्रेट *(noun)* – टोकरी a slatted wooden case used for transporting goods. a square container divided into small individual units for holding bottles. *The wooden crate is ready for transportation.*

Crater/क्रेटर *(noun)* – ज्वालामुखी पर्वत का मुख large bowl-shaped cavity, especially one caused by an explosion or impact or forming the mouth of a volcano. *The volcano has a big crater.*

Crave/क्रेव *(verb)* – माँगना feel a powerful desire for. *My crave for her has just crossed all limits.*

Craving/क्रेविंग *(noun)* – लालसा an intense desire for some particular thing. *I have no craving at all.*

Craw/क्रा *(noun)* – पक्षियों का सिर या गला या पेट dated the crop of a bird or insect. *A pouch in bird's throat where food is prepared for digestion.*

Crawl/क्रॉल *(verb)* – रेंगना move forward on the hands and knees or by dragging the body close to the ground. move slowly along a surface. move at an unusually slow pace. *He crawled at Guruji feet.*

Creak/क्रिक *(noun & verb)* – कर्कश शब्द make a harsh high-pitched sound when being moved or when pressure is applied. *The bridge creaked under our weight.*

Crease/क्रिज *(noun)* – चुनन a line or ridge produced on paper or cloth by folding, pressing, or crushing. a wrinkle or furrow in the skin, especially of the face. *He is an old man. His face creased all over.*

Creation/क्रिएशन *(noun)* – सृष्टि निर्माण, उपाधि प्रदान the action or process of creating. a thing which has been made or invented, especially something showing artistic talent. *The universe is God's creation.*

Creative/क्रिएटिव *(adjective)* – उत्पादक relating to or involving the use of imagination or original ideas in order to create something. *(noun)* a person engaged in creative work. *A painting is an creative act.*

Credence/क्रेडेंस *(noun)* – प्रमाण पत्र belief in or acceptance of something as true. the likelihood of something being true; plausibility. *I have given him a letter of credence.*

Credent/क्रेडेंट *(adj)* – विश्वास के योग्य having credit. *He is my credent.*

Credential/क्रेडेंटियल *(noun)* – विश्वास पत्र a qualification, achievement, etc., especially when used to indicate suitability. *Excuse me sir, the principal would like to see your credentials.*

Credible/क्रेडिब्ल *(adjective)* – विश्वसनीय able to be believed; convincing. *His statement sounds credible.*

Creditor/क्रेडिटर *(noun)* – महाजन a person or company to whom money is owing. *I owe a lot of money to my creditors.*

Credulity/क्रेडुलिटी *(noun)* – विश्वासशीलता, सहजता tendency to believe readily. *There is no credulity in him.*

Creed/क्रीड *(noun)* – धर्म a system of religious belief; a faith. a formal statement of Christian beliefs. *Christianity is a wide spread creed.*

Creek/क्रीक *(noun)* – खाड़ी a small inlet on a seacoast a small houstness. *There was a creek.*

Creep/क्रीप *(verb)* – रेंगना move slowly and carefully, especially in order to avoid being heard or noticed. move or progress very slowly and steadily. grow along the ground or other surface by extending stems or branches. *To move very carefully and slowly so as not to be noticed.*

Cremate/क्रिमेट *(verb)* – दाह करना dispose of by burning it to ashes. *It is Hindu tradition to cremate the dead bodies.*

C

Creosote/क्रेयोसोट *(noun)* – लोहबान का तेल a dark brown oil containing various phenols and other compounds distilled from coal tar, used as a wood preservative. *Prepared from various things, it is a wood preservative. Also it is a an antiseptic.*

Crepitate/क्रेपिटेट *(verb)* – कड़कड़ शब्द करना make a crackling sound. *There was a crepitating sound as the wood burnt in the hearth.*

Crept/क्रेप्ट – रेंगा past and past participle of creep. *Past and past participle of creep.*

Crest/क्रेस्ट *(noun)* – मुकुट a comb or tuft of feathers, fur, or skin on the head of a bird or other animal. a plume of feathers on a helmet. *A plume of feathers on a helmet, fur on the head of the bird.*

Crew/क्रयू *(noun)* – जत्था a group of people who work on and operate a ship, boat, aircraft, or train. such a group other than the officers. *A group of people working on a ship, boat aircraft. Often termed derogatory.*

Crib/क्रू *(noun)* – पालना chiefly [north American] child's bed with barred or latticed sides; a cot. a manger. [British] a model of the nativity of Christ. *A child's bed with barred sides.*

Cricket/क्रिकेट *(noun)* – क्रिकेट, झींगुर an open-air game played on a large grass field with bat and ball between teams of eleven players, the batsmen attempting to score runs by hitting the ball and running between the wickets. *Cricket is a game popular throughout the world.*

Cricoid/क्रिकाइड *(adj.)* – गोलाकार anatomy the ring-shaped cartilage of the larynx. *My friend underwent cricoids operation of the cartilage of throat.*

Crier/क्राइअर *(noun)* – पुकारने वाला an office who makes public an (noun) cements in a court of justice. *My name was called out in the court by crier.*

Criminal/क्रिमिनल *(adjective)* – फौजदारी of, relating to, or constituting a crime. *He is a criminal and he spent 10 years in jail.*

Crimp/क्रिम्प *(verb)* – तह बनाना, सिकोड़ना compress into small folds or ridges. connect by squeezing together. make waves in with a hot iron. *She is crimping her saree.*

Crinoid/क्रिनॉइड *(noun)* – कुमुदिनी का पौधा [zoology] an echinoderm of a class that comprises the sea lilies and feather stars.

Cripple/क्रिपल *(noun & verb)* – लंगड़ा, लंगड़ाकर चलना [archaic] or offensive a person who is unable to walk or move properly through disability or injury. (verb) make unable to move or walk properly. cause severe and disabling damage to. *He is a cripple and drags along the street begging.*

Crisp/क्रिस्प *(adjective)* – भंगुर firm, dry, and brittle, especially in a way considered pleasing. having tight curls, giving an impression of rigidity. *These biscuits are fresh and crisp.*

Critic/क्रिटिक *(noun)* – समालोचक a person who expresses an unfavourable opinion of something. *He is a famous film critic.*

Criticism/क्रिटिसिज्म *(noun)* – समालोचना the expression of disapproval of some-one or something based on perceived faults or mistakes. *Criticism of a work of art carries a lot of weight with public.*

Critique/क्रिटिक *(noun)* – समालोचना a detailed analysis and assessment. (verb) evaluate in a detailed and analytical way. *A critique evaluates a work of an art in a detailed and analytical way.*

Croak/क्रोक *(noun)* – कौवे का काँव-काँव a characteristic deep hoarse sound made by a frog or a crow. *There is a croak in the park.*

Crocodile/क्रोकोडाइल *(noun)* – मगर a large predatory semi aquatic retile with long jaws, long tail, short legs, and a horny textured skin. *Once I saw a live crocodile in the river.*

Croesus/क्रोसस *(noun)* – धनी a small spring-flowering plant of the iris family, which grows from a corm and bears bright yellow, purple, or white flowers. *I specially like the yellow purple flowers of the Croesus plinth.*

Croft/क्रॉफ्ट *(noun)* – छोटी खेती a small rented farm, especially in Scotland, having a right of pasturage held in common with other such farms. *A small enclosed field in Scotland typically attached to a house.*

Crony/क्रॉनी *(adjective)* – परम मित्र [informal] unfit, unsound, or fraudulent. *He is crony-unfit any fraud.*

Crook/क्रूक *(noun)* – झुकाव a shepherd's hooked staff. a bishop's crozier. *A hooked staff is used by shepherds, bishops.*

Crooked/क्रूक्ड *(adjective)* – बदसूरत bent or twisted out of shape or position. *He is a crooked and criminal person and has been jail to many times.*

Croon/क्रून *(noun)* – भनभनाना hum, sing, or speak in a soft, low voice. *(noun)* a soft, low voice or tone. *She crooned melodiously in my car.*

Croquet/क्रोकेट *(noun)* – लकड़ी के गेंद और हथौड़ी से खेलने वाला खेल a game played on a lawn, in which wooden balls are driven through a series of square-topped hoops by means of mallets. an act of croqueting a ball. *(verb)* drive away by holding one's own ball against it and striking one's own. *A game played in a lawn in which wooden balls are used.*

Crore/क्रोर *(noun)* – एक करोड़ की संख्या *cardinal number* Indian ten million; one hundred lakhs. *This person must have at least crore of rupees z.e. ten million or one hundred lakh.*

Crotchet/क्रॉचेट *(noun)* – झक [music, chiefly British] a musical note having the time value of a quarter of a semibreve or half a minim. *A perverse or unfounded belief.*

Croton/क्रॉटन *(noun)* – कोटन एक प्रकार का पौधा a strong-scented tree, shrub, or herbaceous plant, native to tropical and warm regions. *A plant native to tropical and warm regions.*

Crouch/क्रोच *(verb)* – झुकना, नम्रतापूर्वक पाँव पड़ना, विनय करना adopt a position where the knees are bent and the upper body is brought forward and down. bend over so as to be close to. (noun) a crouching stance or posture. *All the persons crouched before the deity.*

Crow/क्रो *(noun)* – कौवे A large black bird. *This is a crow.*

Crowd/क्राउड *(noun)* – समूह, गण fill almost completely, leaving little or no room for movement. move or come together as a crowd. *Once I saw a crowd a crowd so huge and dense that one couldn't move an inch. It was a crowd of rather derogatory people.*

Crown/क्राउन *(noun)* – मुकुट a circualr ornamental headdress worn by a monarch as a symbol of authority. the monarchy or reigning monarch. a wreath of leaves or flowers, especially that worn as an emblem of victory in ancient Greece or Rome. *Crowns are circular metal headdresses are worn by monarchs.*

Crow-quill/क्रो-क्विल *(noun)*– महीन निब की कलम A fine steel pen used in sketching.

Crucial/क्रूसियल *(adjective)* – प्रामाणिक decisive or critical, especially in the success or failure of something. *Waiting for the result was a crucial moment either I will fail or I will pass.*

Cruciferous/क्रूसिफरस *(adjective)* – क्रॉस से आभूषित botany relating to or denoting plants of the cabbage family with four equal petals arranged in a cross. *Plants of the cabbage family.*

Crucifix/क्रूसिफिक्स *(noun)* – ईसा मसीह की मूर्ति a representation of a cross with a figure of Christ on it. *I wear a crucifix round my neck both as respect and love for Christ.*

Cruciform/क्रूसीफॉर्म *(adjective)* – क्रास के आकार का having the shape of a cross. *Many people wear ornaments in the form of cruciform.*

Cruel/क्रूएल *(adjective)* – दयाहीन disregarding or taking pleasure in the pain or suffering of others. causing pain or suffering. *Cruel people take delight in pain or suffering of others.*

Cruet/क्रूएट *(noun)* – तेल रखने की ढकनेदार शीशी a small container for salt, pepper, oil, or vinegar for use at a dining table. [British] a stand holding such containers. a small container for the wine or water to be used in the celebration of the Eucharist. *A small container for the wine or water to be used in celebrations.*

Cruise/क्रूइज *(verb)* – समुद्र में इधर–उधर यात्रा करना sail, travel, or move slowly around without a smoothly at a moderate or economical speed. *I cruised round thinking something may be I'll find a sexual partner.*

Crump/क्रम्प *(adj)* – ऐंठा टेढ़ा a loud thudding sound, especially one made by an exploding bomb or shell. *There was a sudden crump and all of us ran helter skelter.*

Crumpet/क्रम्पेट *(noun)* – रोटी, बाटी a thick, flat, savoury cake with a soft, porous texture, made from a yeast mixture cooked on a griddle and

C

eaten toasted and buttered. *A thick soft cake made from yeast and eaten with butter. It is one of my favourites.*

Crumple/क्रम्पल *(verb)* – पीसना crush or become crushed so as to become creased and wrinkled. *The piece of cloth was badly crimpled. It took me several efforts to smooth it out.*

Crusade/क्रूसेड *(noun)* – ईसाइयों का धर्मयुद्ध any of a series of medieval military expeditions made by Europeans to recover the holy land from the Muslims. a war instigated for alleged religious ends. *European efforts of war undertaken to recover holy land from Muslims.*

Cruse/क्रूस *(noun)* – मिट्टी का बर्तन [archaic] an earthenware pot or jar. *An earthen ware pot or jar.*

Crush/क्रस *(verb)* – नष्ट करना deform, pulverize, or force inwards by compressing forcefully. crease or crumple. *In the accident of two cars one car was completely crushed.*

Crust/क्रस्ट *(noun)* – छिलका the tough outer part of a loaf of bread. a hard, dry scrap of bread. *A layer of pastry covering a pie.*

Crutch/क्रच *(noun)* – बैसाखी a long stick with a crosspiece at the top, used as a support by a lame person. *I saw a lame man walking with the help of crutches. The crutch was a long stick with a crosspiece at the top.*

Cryogen/क्रिग *(noun)* – हिम a substance used to produce very low temperatures. *A substance used to produce very low temperature.*

Crypt/क्रिप्ट *(noun)* – गुफा an underground room or vault beneath a church, used as a chapel or burial place. *I visited a chapel under a church. I was rather frightened there.*

Cryptography/क्राइप्टोग्राफी *(noun)* – गुप्त लेखन की विधा the art of writing or solving codes. *Art of writing on solving codes.*

Crystalline/क्राइस्टलाइन *(adjective)* – बिल्लौर के समान स्वच्छ having the structure and form of a crystal. *The water of the stream was crystal clear.*

Cub/कब *(noun)* – लोमड़ी the young of a fox, bear, lion, or other carnivorous mammal. [archaic] a young man. *The young one of a lion bear or fox.*

Cubeb/कबेब *(noun)* – कवाबचीनी a pungent shrub used in [medicine]. *Cubeb is shrub of pungent berries.*

Cubicle/क्यूबिकल *(noun)* – छोटा शयनगृह a small partitioned-off area of a room. *I share a cubicle with my room mate.*

Cubiform/क्यूबिफार्म *(adjective)* – घनाकार technical cube-shaped. *His office is in a cube shaped room.*

Cukold/ककोल्ड *(noun)* – व्यभिचारिणी स्त्री का पति the husband of an adulterous regarded as an object of derision. *He is a married man but a cuckold an object of laughter.*

Cuckoo/ककू *(noun)* – मूर्ख, कोयल a grey or brown bird known for the far carrying two-note call of the male and for the habit of laying its eggs in the nests of small songbirds. used in names of other birds of the same family. *A brown bird which lays her eggs in the nest of small song birds.*

Cucumber/ककम्बर *(noun)* – खीरा a long, green-skinned fruit with watery flesh, eaten raw in salads. *A long, green skinned fruit eaten raw in salads.*

Cucurbit/ककरबिट *(noun)* – कोहड़ा chiefly [north American] a plant of the gourd family which includes melon, pumpkin, squash, and cucumber. *A plant of ground family-melon, pumpkin, squash.*

Cuddy/कडी – मूर्ख मनुष्य *(noun)* chiefly Scottish a donkey. *A cuddy, a stupid person.*

Cudgel/कजेल *(noun)* – गदका a short thick stick used as a weapon. *The thief beat the man with a cudgel.*

Cuff/कफ *(noun)* – आस्तीन का अगला भाग the end part of a sleeve, where the material of the sleeve is turned back or a separates band is sewn on. chiefly [north American] a trouser turn-up. *I asked my men to attach a cuff to the end part of my sleeve.*

Cuisine/क्विजिन *(noun)* – पकाने की विधि a style or method of cooking, especially as characteristic of a particular country or region. food cooked in a certain way. *I very much like cuisine good cooked in a certain way of the century.*

Culinary/कुलिनरी *(adjective)* – पाकशाला सम्बन्धी of or for cooking. *She has great culinary stalls.*

Culet/कुलेट *(noun)* – दुबारा गलाने के लिये काँच के टुकड़े recycled broken or waste glass used in glass-making. *Broken glass recycled in glass making.*

Culminant/कल्मिनेंट *(adjective)* – उच्चतम स्थान पर at or forming the top or highest point. *As the culmination of picture arrived I began to seat.*

Culminate/कल्मिनेट *(verb)* – परम कोटि को प्राप्त करना reach or be a climax or point of highest development. *As the debate between the two persons culminated I began to be excited.*

Culpable/कलपेब्ल *(adjective)* – दोषी deserving blame. *He was arrested for culpable homicide.*

Culprit/कल्प्रिट *(noun)* – अपराधी a person who is responsible for a crime or other misdeed. *The culprit was arrested by the police.*

Cult/कल्ट *(noun)*– उपासना की विधि a system of religious devotion directed towards a particular figure or object. a relatively small religious group regarded by others as strange or as imposing excessive control over members. *A small religious group directed to an object or person.*

Cultrate/कल्ट्रेट *(noun)* – छूरी के धार के समान बना हुआ shaped like the edge of a knife. *It is suave like cultrate.*

Culture/कल्चर *(noun)* – जोताई, संस्कृति the arts and other manifestations of human intellectual achievement regarded collectively, a refined understanding or appreciation of this. *They belong to different culture.*

Culvert - *(noun)* a tunnel carrying a stream or open drain under a road or railway. *There are so many culverts in the city.*

Cunning/कनिंग *(noun)* – चातुरी ingenious. *He is a cunning fellow charming and attractive. Don't fall under his trap. He can make you do whatever he wants.*

Cup-board/कप-बोर्ड – अलमारी *(noun)* a piece of furniture or small recess with a door and usually shelves, used for storage. *I had a storage of storing place. So I have just bought a cupboard.*

Cupid/क्यूपिड *(noun)* – कामदेव, मदन the Roman god of love. *The people of Rome worship cupid.*

Cupidity/क्यूपिडिटि *(noun)* – कामुकता, अति लोभ greed for money or possessions. *He suffers from cupidity he needs a lot of many other possessions.*

Curative/क्यूरेटिव *(adjective)* – सहायक able to cure disease. (noun) a curative [medicine] or agent. *Many diseases these days are curative which were not in old times.*

Curcuma/करक्यूमा *(noun)* – हल्दी a tropical Asian plant of a genus that includes turmeric and other species yielding spices, dyes, and medicinal products. *An Asian plant that yields turmeric and many other herbs.*

Curd/कर्ड *(noun)* – दही a soft, white substance formed when milk coagulates, used as the basis for cheese. a fatty substance found between the flakes of poached salmon. *Curd is my favourite dish, specially when I mix sugar with it.*

Curl/कर्ल *(verb)* – घुँघराला बाल form or cause to form a curved or spiral shape. *My fiancée has curly hair which I like very much.*

Curnudgeon/कर्नजन *(noun)* – कृपण a bad-tempered or surly person. *He is a curnudgeon and I won't even talk to him.*

Currant/क्यूरेंट *(adjective)* – दाख, सूखा अंगूर a body of water or air moving in a definite direction through a surrounding body of water of air in which there is less movement. *I like currant very much.*

Currency/करेंसी *(noun)* – मुद्रा the metal or paper medium of exchange that is presently used. *Rupee is currency of India.*

Current/करेंट *(adj)* – सामान्य, वर्तमान happening or being sued or done now. in common or general use. *The current of water was too strong for me to swim.*

Curricle/क्यूरिकल *(noun)* – टमटम [historical] a light, open, two-wheeled carriage pulled by two horse side by side. *The curricle were very popular in 18th century.*

Currier/करिअर *(noun)* – चर्मकार a person who curries leather. *A person who grooms a horse with a curry comb.*

Curry//करि *(noun)* – कढ़ी, शोरबा chiefly [north American] groom with a curry comb. *To groom with a curry comb.*

Curse/कर्स *(noun)* – शाप a solemn appeal to a supernatural power to inflict harm on someone or something. a cause of harm or misery. *I was so angry and felt such contempt that I cursed him with all my heart.*

C

Curt/कर्ट *(adjective)* - असभ्य ढंग से rudely. *He was rough and rude to me. He spoke in a curt way.*

Curtail/कर्टेल *(verb)* - नाटका का संक्षेप करना reduce in extent or quantity. *The powers of director were curtailed.*

Curtain/कर्टेन *(noun)* - पर्दा a piece of material suspended at the top to form a screen, typically movable sideways and found as one of a pair at a window. a screen of heavy cloth or other material that can be raised or lowered at the front of a stage. a raising or lowering of such a screen at the beginning or end of an act or scene. *There was a curtain between the stage performers and audience, upside down or sideways.*

Curtilage/कर्टिलेज *(noun)* - घर के बाहर का मैदान, बाग इत्यादि an area of land attached to a house and forming one enclosure with it. *A piece of land is attached to our house that has only one curtilage.*

Curvature/कर्वेचर *(noun)* - घुमाव the fact of being curved or the degree to which something is curved. [geometry] the degree to which a curve deviates from a straight line, or a curved surface deviates from a plane. *A curved object or a curved line on paper.*

Curve/कर्व *(noun)* - झुकाना, मोड़ना a line or outline which gradually deviates from being straight for some or all of its length. a line on a graph whether straight or curved showing how one quantity varies with respect to another. baseball a delivery in which the pitcher causes the ball to deviate from a straight path by imparting spin. (verb) from or cause to form a curve. *He formed a curve on the paper.*

Cusp/कस्प *(noun)* - शिखा each of the pointed ends of a crescent, especially of the moon. architecture a projecting point between small arcs in gothic tracery. *Cane shaped prominence on the surface of the tooth.*

Custodial/कस्टोडियल *(adj)* - संरक्षकता-सम्बन्धी pertaining to guarding ship. *There are so many custodial death is India.*

Custom/कस्टम *(noun)* - आचार रीति a traditional and widely accepted way of behaving or doing something that is specific to a particular society, place, or time. [law] established usage having the force of [law] or right. *It*

is a custom with us that we touch the feet of our elders.*

Cutaneous/क्यूटेनियस *(adjective)* - चर्म-सम्बन्धी of, relating to, or affecting the skin. *It is a cutaneous disease, you should have it treated.*

Cutis/क्यूटिस *(noun)* - भीतरी त्वचा anatomy the true skin or dermis. *This doctor is a specialist in the true skin or dermis.*

Cutlet/कटलेट *(noun)* - माँस का पकाया हुआ टुकड़ा a portion of meat, especially a lamb or veal chop from just behind the neck served grilled or fried. a flat croquette of minced meat, nuts, or pulses. *Nonveg cutlets are my favourites.*

Cutpurse/कटपर्स *(noun)* - गिरहकट [archaic] term for pickpocket. *He is a pickpocket by profession.*

Cut-throat/कटथ्रोट *(noun)* - हत्यारा a murderer or other violent criminal. *He is a ruthless cut-throat person.*

Cutting/कटिंग *(noun)* - टुकड़ा a piece cut off from something. [British] an article or other piece cut from a newspaper. a piece cut from a plant for propagation. *I specially looked for a sports magazine, so that I could show the desired cutting to the teacher.*

Cuvette/कवेट *(noun)* - सूखी खाई के बीच में खोदा हुआ गड्ढा a straight-sided container for holding liquid samples in a spectrophotometer etc. *a container for holding liquid samples.*

Cyanosis/सायोनोसिस *(noun)* - एक प्रकार रोग जिसमे शरीर नीला होता है [medicine] a bluish discoloration of the skin due to poor circulation or inadequate oxygenation of the blood. *A bluish medicine was applied on my cut because I have a poor circulation of blood.*

Cycloid/सायक्लायड *(noun)* - वृत्तजात [mathematics] a curve traced by a point on a circle being rolled along a straight line. *A curve on a point being rolled straight.*

Cyclone/सायक्लोन *(noun)* - बवंडर meteorology a system of winds rotating inwards to an area of low barometric pressure; a depression. another term for tropical storm. *There are some such daredevils that they actually go very near cyclone for scientific study.*

Cyclosis/सायक्लोसिस *(noun)* - शरीर में रुधिर का संचालन the circulation of cytoplasm within a cell. *There is no cyclosis in a dead body.*

Cyclostyle/सायक्लोस्टाइल *(noun)* – हाथ की लिखावट को छापने की कला an early device for duplicating handwriting, in which a pen with a small toothed wheel makes a stencil in a sheet of waxed paper. *An early device for duplicating handwriting.*

Cylindrical/सिलिंड्रिकल *(adj)* – बेलन के आकार का having the form of a cylinder. *It is cylindrical in shape.*

Cynic/सिनिक *(noun)* – निन्दाशील a person who believes that people are motivated purely by self-interest. a sceptic. a member of a school of ancient Greek philosophers founded by Antisthenes, characterized by an ostentatious contempt for wealth and pleasure. *My friend is a cynic.*

Cynosure/सायनोस्योर *(noun)* – ध्रुवतारा a person or thing that is the centre of attention or admiration. *Almost all film stars are cynosures.*

Cypher/सायफर *(noun)* – शून्य variant spelling of cipher. *Zero or cipher.*

Cystic/सिस्टिक *(adjective)* – मूत्राशय-सम्बन्धी chiefly [medicine] of, relating to, or characterized by cysts. *Medicine for cyst which may be a cavity or say filled with liquid usually in gall bladder.*

C

Dd

D/डी *(noun)* – अंग्रेजी वर्णमाला का चौथा वर्ण, आकारिक निर्माण the fourth letter of the English alphabet.
1. Denoting the fourth in a set of items, categories, sizes, etc.
2. Music the second note of the diatonic scale of C major.
3. The roman numeral for 500. [understood as half of CI, an earlier form of M.]

Dab/डैब *(noun)* – थपकी, हल्का, स्पर्श a small, commercially important flatfish found chiefly in the north Atlantic. *A dab of glue is enough to stick the pages together.*

Dabble/डैबल *(verb)* – किसी काम में हल्की फुल्की रुचि रखना move around gently in water. move the bill around in shallow water while feeding. *Riya is not serious about modelling. She only dabbles in it occasionally.*

Dace/डेस *(noun)* – मीठे पानी की एक प्रकार की छोटी मछली a freshwater fish related to the carp, typically living in running water. *The dace's beautiful blue-green body sparkled in the sunlight.*

Dacoit/डेकॉइट *(noun)* – डाकू a member of a band of armed robbers in India or Burma. *The dacoit was hiding in the bushes waiting to attack any travellers passing by.*

Daft/डैफ्ट *(adjective)* – बेवकूफ, मूर्ख [informal, chiefly British] silly; foolish. *Julian was scolded by his father for asking a very daft question.*

Daily/डेली *(adj & adv)* – दैनिक, प्रतिदिन done, produced, or occurring every day or every weekday. *The watchman was doing his daily rounds when he noticed the burglar trying to sneak into the house.*

Dainty/डैन्टी *(adjective)* – भोजन विशेष, छोटा और सुन्दर delicately small and pretty. delicate and graceful in build or movement. *Ballet dancers are very dainty in their movements.*

Dairy/डेअरि *(noun)* – दुग्धशाला, दुध, मक्खन बेचने वाली कंपनी a building or room for the storage, processing, and distribution of milk and milk products. *John's father runs a successful dairy business.*

Dais/डेस् *(noun)* – चबूतरा, मंच a low platform for a lectern or throne. *The professor stood on the dais while lecturing to the students.*

Daisy/डेजि *(noun)* – गुलबहार a small grassland plant with composite flowers having a yellow disc and white rays. used in names of other plants of the same family, e.g. michaelmas daisy. *Daisies bloom in the warm summer months.*

Dale/डेल *(noun)* – दर्रा, घाटी a valley, especially in northern England. *The dale is covered with flowers in the spring.*

Dally/डैली *(verb)* – खेलना, क्रीड़ा करना act or move slowly. *She was cruelly dallying with Jack's emotions.*

Dam/डैम *(noun)* – बाँध something that holds back water, or the body of water that is being held. *Hoover dam is built on the Colorado River in America. There is a need to build a dam across the river.*

Dame/डेम *(noun)* – गृहिणी, विशेष उपलब्धि पर किसी महिला को दी गयी उपाधि given to a woman with the rank of knight commander or holder of the grand cross in the orders of chivalry. *She was awarded the title of dame due to her aristocratic connections.*

Damn/डैम् *(verb)* – शाप देना be condemned by god to suffer eternal punishment in hell. be doomed to misfortune or failure. *Don't damn me, please.*

Damnation/डैम्नेशन *(noun)* – नरक-दण्ड condemnation to eternal. punishment in hell. exclamatory expressing anger or frustration. *He was cursed with eternal damnation for his misdeeds.*

Damned/डैम्ड *(adjective)* – नरका क [informal] used to emphasize one's anger or frustration. used to emphasize the surprising nature of something. *The town was better known as the town of the damned because of the misdeeds of its inhabitants.*

Damming/डैमिंग *(adjective)* – शाप देने वाला strongly suggestive of guilt or error. *His nervousness proved to be damning against him.*

Damp/डैम्प *(adjective)* – सीलनभरा slightly wet, moisture in the air, on a surface, or in a solid, typically with detrimental or unpleasant effects. [archaic] damp air or atmosphere.*His clothes got damp after he was caught in the rain.*

Damsel/डैम्जेल *(noun)* – युवती, कुमारी कन्या [archaic or poetic/literary] a young unmarried woman. *The damsel smiled prettily and thanked the boy for his help.*

Damson/डैमजन *(noun)* – आलूचा, आलूबुखारा a small purple-black plum like fruit. *The damson tree was laden with ripe fruit.*

Dance/डांस *(verb)* – नाचना, नृत्य करना move rhythmically to music, typically following a set sequence of steps. perform a particular dance or a role in a ballet. *She has quickly picked up the dance steps of salsa.*

Dancer/डांसर *(noun)* – नर्तकी to move the body and feet in rhythm, ordinarily to music. *Jane is a professional dancer.*

Dandelion/डैन्डेलियन *(noun)* – पीले फूल का एक प्रकार का पौधा a widely distributes weed of the daisy family, with large birth yellow flowers followed by globular heads of seeds with downy tufts. *The field was full of yellow dandelions swaying in the breeze.*

Dandiacal/डन्डियाकल *(adjective)* – ठाट-बाटवाला relating to a dandy, dandish. *This dandiacal man is very cruel in the heart.*

Dandle/डैन्डल *(verb)* – लाड़ करना move a baby or young child up and down in a playful or affectionate way. *Mr. Williams was dandling his grandson and playing with him.*

Dandruff/डैन्ड्रफ *(noun)* – बालों की रूसी small pieces of dead skin among a person's hair. *Dandruff is a disease where white pieces of dead skins accumulate on a person's head.*

Dandy/डैन्डी *(adjective)* – छैला, बाँका [informal, dated] an excellent thing of its kind. [informal, chiefly north American] excellent.

Tom is quite a dandy when it comes to his appearance.

Dane/डेन *(noun)* – डेनमार्क देश का निवासी a native or national of Denmark, or a person of Danish descent. *The famous writer of fairy tales, Hans Christian Anderson was a Dane.*

Danger/डैन्जर *(noun)* – भय, संकट, खतरा the possibility of suffering harm or injury. a cause of harm or injury. *Children must be warned of the danger of playing with sharp objects.*

Dangle/डैंगल *(verb)* – लटकाना, झुलाना, झूलना hang or cause to hang so as to swing freely. *The bungee jumpers were dangling from the end of the rope.*

Danish/डेनिश *(noun)* – डेनमार्क की भाषा the Scandinavian language spoken in Denmark. *Danish is the official language of Denmark.*

Dank/डैन्क *(adjective)* – तर, गीला damp, cold, and musty. *The house felt dank after being shut for many months.*

Dap/डैप *(verb)* – जल में थोड़ा-सा डुबाना, कूदना to dip lightly, to bounce. *He dapped the ball.*

Dapper/डैपर *(adjective)* – तेज, साफ-सुथरा neat and trim in dress and appearance. *Jim looked quite dapper at the wedding in the suit.*

Dapple/डैपल् *(noun)* – चितकबरा होना mark with spots or rounded patches. *The sunlight dappled on the curtains creating mysterious shadows.*

Dare/डेअर *(verb)* – साहस करना have the courage to do something. used to express indignation. used to order someone threateningly not to do something. *How dare you challenge him for a duel?*

Daring/डेअरिंग *(adjective)* – साहसी, शूरवीर, बहादुर adventurous or audaciously bold. *He is quite daring for a boy of his age.*

Dark/डार्क *(adjective)* – प्रकाश का अभाव, अंधेरा of a deep or somber colour. *One of the bandits was a tall dark ugly looking person.*

Darken/डार्केन *(verb)* – अंधेरा छा जाना make or become dark or darker. of something unpleasant cast a shadow over; spoil. *Sarah's mood darkened after hearing the bad news.*

Darkish/डार्किश *(adjective)* – अंधेरे में almost black. *The rug is darkish blue in colour.*

D

Darling/डार्लिंग (noun) – प्रियतम, प्रिय व्यक्ति के संबोधन के रूप में प्रयुक्त used as an affectionate form of address. a lovable or endearing person. a favourite of a certain group: the darling of labour's left wing. *Jane is her father's darling.*

Darn/डार्न (verb) – रफू करना mend by interweaving yarn across it with a needle. embroider with a large running stitch. *Sarah mended the tear in the shirt by darning it before it got bigger.*

Dart/डार्ट (noun) – बर्छी a small pointed missile thrown of fired as a weapon. a small pointed missile with a flight, used in the game of darts. *A dart is a small pointed missile with feathers at the rear which is used in target practice.*

Darter/डार्टर (noun) – बर्छी फेंकते रहना a long-necked bird which spears fish with its long pointed bill. *The darter was catching fish with the help of its long beak.*

Darwinism/डार्विनिज्म (noun) – विकासवाद the theory of the evolution of species by natural selection, advanced by the English natural historian Charles Darwin (1809-82). *The followers of Darwinism refuse to accept any other theory of evolution.*

Dash/डैश (verb) – धावा, दिखावट, पटकना, पटक देना move with sudden speed. *Why would he like to dash your hope for promotion?*

Dasher/डैशर (noun) – मथानी [informal] a flamboyant or stylish person. *It is important to operate the dasher properly while making cream in a churn.*

Dashing/डैशिंग (adjective) – साहसी, जोशीला, स्फूर्तिमय attractive in a romantic, adventurous way. stylish. *Bill looked quite dashing in his new clothes.*

Dastard/डैस्टर्ड (noun) – डरपोक मनुष्य, कायर [dated or humorous] a dishonourable or despicable person. *He was a dastard person.*

Dative/डेटिव (adjective) – सम्प्रदान कारक denoting a case of nouns and pronouns indicating an indirect object or recipient. *Dative case is called an indirect object.*

Datum/डेटम (noun) – स्वीकृत तत्त्व piece of information. *Datum of a place is a position from which elevations and depths are measured in surveying.*

Daub/डॉब (verb) – लीपना-पोतना coat or smear with a thick substance carelessly or liberally. spread on a surface in such a way. *The interior chimney hood was in silver colour with brown daub finish.*

Daughter/डॉटर (noun) – कन्या, पुत्री a girl or woman in relating to her parents. a female descendant. *John and Kate have two daughters.*

Davit/डेविट (noun) – क्रेन जहाज पर नाव लटकाने का यंत्र a small crane on a ship, especially one of a pair for lowering a lifeboat. *The lifeboat was lowered into the water with the help of the davit when the ship was sinking.*

Dawdle/डॉडल (verb) – विलम्ब करना, सुस्ती से चलना waste time. move slowly and idly. *Jack is very efficient time conscious and does not believe in dawdling.*

Dawn/डॉन (noun) – उषाकाल, बड़े सवेरे the first appearance of light in the sky before sunrise. *The rising sun appears on the horizon at dawn.*

Dawning/डॉनिंग (noun) – तड़के, अरुणोदय का समय [poetic/literary] dawn. *I like dawning.*

Daze/डेज (verb) – घबड़ा देना, स्तब्ध करना make unable to think or react properly. *To daze means unable to think in an orderly way.*

Dazzle/डैजल (verb) – चौंधिया देना of a bright light blind temporarily. *She came under the spell of dazzle by so many lights coming on suddenly.*

Deacon/डीकन (noun) – छोटा पादरी an ordained minister of an order ranking below that of priest. in some protestant churches a lay officer assisting a minister. *Deacon is the person who oversees church charities.*

Dead/डेड (adjective) – मृतक लोग, मृत, निर्जीव complete; absolute: dead silence. *He spoke in a cold and emotionless voice as if he were dead.*

Deaden/डेडेन (verb) – मन्द करना, पीड़ा कम कर देना make a noise sensation less strong or intense. make insensitive. *The pain had deadened her sensitivity to the problems of others.*

Deal/डील (noun) – व्यापारिक सौदा an agreement. fir or pine wood as a building material. *I made a deal with her promising to finish homework each night in exchange for one hour of television.*

Dealer/डीलर (noun) - व्यापारी a person who buys and sells goods. a person who buys and sells shares or other financialassets as a principal rather than as a broker or agent. *Jim's father is a dealer of cotton garments.*

Dealing/डीलिंग (noun) - आचरण, सम्बन्ध, लेन-देन (व्यापार में) way of acting towards others. *Dealing with customer complaints can sometimes be challenging, but there is always a solution that can be reached.*

Dean/डीन (noun) - गिरजाघर का अध्यक्ष, अभाव, अकाल variant spelling of dene. *Mr. Harris is the dean of the college.*

Dearth/डर्थ (noun) - दुष्काल a scarcity or lack of something. *There is a dearth of good workers these days.*

Death/डेथ (noun) - मरण, मृत्यु the action or fact of dying or being killed. an instance of a person or an animal dying. *The death of his pet dog came as a blow to Harry.*

Debar/डिबार (verb) - निषेध करना exclude or prohibit from doing something. *Having a criminal record will not debar you from doing voluntary work.*

Debase/डिबेस (verb) - गुणवत्ता या महत्त्व कम कर देना, पदवी घटाना lower the quality, value, or character of. *I admit, I did debase myself by reading her personal letter.*

Debatable/डिबेटेबल (adjective) - विवाद योग्य open to discussion or argument. *The benefits of the medicine were debatable.*

Debate/डिबेट (noun) - झगड़ना, वाद-विवाद में भाग लेना a formal discussion in a public meeting or legislative assembly. an argument, especially one involving many people. *A debate is a discussion of the opposing sides of a specific subject.*

Debauchery/डिबाचरी (noun) - लम्पट, व्याभिचारिता, अनैतिक a bout of excessive indulgence in sensual pleasures. *People with traditional beliefs dislike debauchery of any kind.*

Debilitate/डेबिलिटेट (verb) - दुर्बल करना make very weak and infirm. *A virus can completely debilitate your computer and potentially cause the loss of entire information.*

Debility/डेबिलिटी (noun) - कमजोरी, दुर्बलता the state of being weak in health or body especially from old age. *In old age, people suffer from physical debility.*

Debris/डेब्रिस (noun) - मलबा, दुर्घटना में नष्ट वस्तु के टुकड़े scattered rubbish or remains. loose natural material, e.g. broken rocks. *The market site was littered with debris after the bomb blast.*

Debt/डेट (noun) - उधार, कर्ज, ऋण money or services owed or due. *It is advisable to pay off one's debts on time.*

Debtless/डेटलेस (adj.) - कर्ज से बरी free from debt. *One can stay debtless if one learns to live within one's means.*

Debtor/डेटर (noun) - देनदार, कर्जदार ऋणी a person who owes money. *Being a debtor can be a horrible experience.*

Debus/डिबस (verb) - मोटर गाड़ी से उतरना या सामान उतारना [British, chiefly military slang] unload or alight from a motor vehicle. *The team was asked to debus from the vehicle as soon as they reached the camp.*

Decade/डिकेड (noun) - दस वर्ष का समय a period of ten years. *He ruled the movie world with his performance for more than a decade.*

Decadence/डिकाडेंस (noun) - क्षय, नाश the process, period, or manifestation of moral or cultural decline. *The Roman Empire came to an end due to sheer decadence of their lifestyle.*

Decagon/डेकागन (noun) - दस भुजा a plane figure with ten straight sides and angles. *The students were asked to create a model of a decagon.*

Decalogue/डेकालॉग (noun) - ईसा मसीह के दस आदेश the ten commandments. *There were decalogue boards behind the altar.*

Decant/डिकैंट (verb) - पसाना, निथारना, निस्तारण करना gradually pour form one container into another, typically in order to separate the liquid form the sediment. *It is time to decant the oil into another container to preserve it.*

Decapitate/डिकैपिटेट (verb) - सिर धड़ से अलग कर देना cut off the head of. *Mercenaries don't hesitate to decapitate anyone caught spying.*

Decease/डिसीस (noun & verb) - मरण, मृत्यु, मरना [archaic] to die. *Some folklore says that the spirits of the deceased are supposed to be watching over us.*

D

131

Deceit/डिसीट *(noun)* – धोखाधड़ी, फर्जीवाड़ा, कपट, छल the action or practice of deceiving. a deceitful act or statement. *Lying to someone is an act of deceit.*

Deceive/डिसीव *(verb)* – धोखा देना deliberately mislead or misrepresent the truth to. give a mistaken impression: the area may seem to offer noting of interest, but don't be deceived. *I knew she could easily deceive him.*

December/दिसम्बर *(noun)* – अंग्रेजी साल का अन्तिम महीना the last (12th) month of the year. *December comes after November.*

Decency/डिसेन्सी *(noun)* – मर्यादा moral or correct hehaviour. *You lack decency.*

Decent/डिसेन्ट *(adj)* – विनीत socially or conventionally correct; refined or virtuous. *She has decent behaviour.*

Deception/डिसेप्शन *(noun)* – माया a misleading falsehood.

Deceptive/डिसेप्टिव *(adj)* – धोखा देने वाला causing one to believe what is not true or fail to believe what is true. *I dislike her deceptive nature.*

Decadence/डेसाडेंस *(noun)* – पतन, पतनकाल the state of being degenerate in mental or moral qualities. *Your decadence will come soon.*

Deciduous/डेसिडुअस *(adj)* – पतनशील shedding foliage at the end of the growing season. *These are deciduous plants.*

Deck/डेक *(noun & verb)* – जहाज की छत, ढाँकना a floor of a ship, especially the upper, open level. *There was a big thud when I hit the deck of the ship.* a similar floor or platform, as in a bus or car park. *The ship was furnished with a deck.*

Declarant/डिक्लरेंट *(noun)* – कानूनी प्रतिज्ञा करने वाला मनुष्य [chiefly law] a person or party who makes a formal declaration. *A declarant is a person who signs a legal statement.*

Declaration/डिक्लरेशन *(noun)* – किसी विषय में अधिकारिक घोषणा a formal or explicit statement or announcement. [British] a public official announcement of the votes cast for candidates in an election. [law] a plaintiff's statement of claims in proceedings. *They made the declaration in front of the whole town.*

Declare/डिक्लेअर *(verb)* – सूचित करना, घोषित करना, उद्घोषणा करना, कोई बात अधिकारिक रूप से घोषित करना announce solemnly or officially; make clearly known. openly align oneself for or against a party or position. *The company is about to declare a final dividend on the ordinary shares.*

Declension/डिक्लेन्सन *(noun)* – क्षय, अवनति, ह्रास the variation of the form of a noun, pronoun, or (adjective), by which its grammatical case, number, and gender are identified. the class to which a noun or adjective is assigned according to this variation. *Sensual and carnal worship entering the gospel temple is often an evidence of spiritual declension.*

Declination/डिक्लाइनेशन *(noun)* – नीचे को झुकाव astronomy that angular distance of a point north or south of the celestial equator, north. *Declination the angle formed by a magnetic needle with the line pointing to the geographical North Pole.*

Declivity/डिक्लिवटी *(noun)* – ढाल, उतार a downward slope. *Declivity of these mountain's slopes down till the sea coast.*

Decoct/डिकॉक्ट *(verb)* – काढ़ा बनाना, उबालना [archaic] extract the essence from by heating or boiling it. *Please decoct by boiling if you want to extract the essence of the medicinal herb.*

Decontrol/डीकन्ट्रोल *(verb)* – विनियंत्रण करना, सरकारी नियन्त्रण हटाना release from controls or restrictions. *The government must decontrol the sale of petrol and diesel.*

Decorum/डेकोरम *(noun)* – मर्यादा, शिष्टता, शिष्टाचार behaviour in keeping with good taste and propriety. prescribed behaviour; etiquette. *The children were strictly asked to maintain decorum of the house.*

Decoy/डिकॉइ *(noun & verb)* – प्रलोभन, लुभाना किसी को मनचाहे ढंग से फंसाना a bird or mammal, or an imitation of one, used to lure game. *A duck used by a hunter to try to attract other ducks is an example of a decoy. (verb)* lure by means of a decoy. *The police caught the robber by using his family as a decoy.*

Decree/डिक्री *(noun)* – डिग्री, निर्णय an official order issued by a ruler or authority that has the force of [law]. a judgment or decision of certain [law] courts. *He was retired from government service on 31 December 2011 by a presidential decree.*

Deity/डेइटी *(noun)* – ईश्वर a god or goddess especially in a polytheistic religion. the creator and supreme being. *Krishna is worshipped as a deity by the Hindus.*

Delay/डिले *(noun)* – विलम्ब करना, रोकना a period of time by which something is late or postponed. *Unexpected problems led to delay in timely start of the function.*

Delegacy/डेलीगेसी *(noun & verb)* – प्रतिनिधि के रूप में नियुक्ति a body of delegates; a committee or delegation. *The Chinese delegacy is in town for the seminar.*

Delegate/डेलीगेट *(noun)* – प्रतिनिधि a person sent or authorized to represent others, in particular a representative sent to a conference. a member of a committee.*He is a delegate representing Russia.*

Delete/डिलिट *(verb)* – लिखित अंश को मिटाना remove or erase. *She was asked to delete all the files from the computer.*

Deliberation/डिलिबरेशन *(noun)* – विस्तृत विचार-विमर्श long and careful consideration. *The matter must be given enough deliberation before a decision is reached.*

Delicacies/डेलिकेसीज *(noun)* – स्वादिष्ट भोजन Delicacy refers to the state of being fragile, frail, soft or subtle, or refers to a gourmet food. *That night they ate the local delicacy and stayed in a 5-star hotel - the Hotel Taj!*

Delicate/डेलिकेट *(noun)* – नाजुक garments made for delicate fabric. *The vase was very delicate and on falling broke easily.*

Delicious/डिलिक्सिशस *(adjective)* – स्वादिष्ट या सुगन्धित highly pleasant to the taste. *Mango is a delicious fruit.*

Delict/डेलिक्ट *(noun)* – नियमोल्लंघन [law] a violation of the [law]; a tort. *It is an utter delict.*

Delight/डिलाइट *(noun)* – अति सुखी होना, अत्यन्त प्रसन्नता great pleasure. a cause or source of great pleasure. *Anne took great delight in singing.*

Delinquent/डेलिक्वेन्ट *(adjective)* – पाप करने वाला typically with reference to young people showing or characterized by a tendency to commit crime. *The programme deals with the group of ageing delinquents.*

Delirious/डिलिरीअस *(adjective)* – बेसुध, अचेत suffering form delirium. *Delirious with happiness that I am back at home after two years.*

Delocalize/डिलोकेलाइज *(verb)* – केन्द्रीभूत करना detach or remove form a particular location. *It was necessary to delocalize the sap before planting it in another nursery.*

Delude/डिलूड *(verb)* – मोहित करना, किसी को भ्रमित करना impose a misleading belief upon. *She tried to delude him into thinking that he could trust her.*

Delusion/डिलूशन *(noun)* – मोह, भ्रम आभास, भ्रांति, धोखा an idiosyncratic belief or impression that is not in accordance with a generally accepted reality. *He suffered from the delusion that he could write well.*

Demagnetize/डिमैग्नेटाइज *(verb)* – विचुम्बकित करना remove magnetic properties from. *Research is being done on whether it is possible to demagnetize iron.*

Demagogue/डेमागॉग *(noun)* – जनसमुदाय का नेता a political leader who seeks support by appealing to popular desires and prejudices rather than by using rational argument. *Demagogues played an important role in ancient Greece and Rome.*

Demand/डिमाण्ड *(verb)* – प्रबल अनुरोध या ओदश ask authoritatively or brusquely. insist on having. require; need. *The kidnappers made a ransom demand late at night.*

Demarcation/डीमार्केशन *(noun)* – किन्हीं दो वस्तुओं को पृथक् करने वाली सीमा रेखा the action of fixing boundaries or limits. a dividing line. *The demarcation between the rich and the poor was quite obvious.*

Demerit/डिमेरिट *(noun)* – अवगुण a feature or fact deserving censure. *The student earned a demerit for his actions.*

Demesne/डिमीन् *(noun)* – जमींदारी, भूसंपत्ति [historical] land attached to a manor and retained by the owner for their own use. [archaic] a domain. *I have demesne in my village.*

D

Demise/डिमाइस *(noun)* – समाप्ति या विफलता the end or failure of something. *In a way, ideals of democracy led to the demise of Soviet communism.*

Demolish/डिमॉलिश *(verb)* – ढाहना pull or knock down. *It has been decided to demolish the old house to make way for a new apartment building.*

Demon/डिमन् *(noun)* – दानव, राक्षस, असुर an evil spirit or devil. *It is usually the superstitious people who believe in demons.*

Demonetize/डिमोनेटाइज *(verb)* – धातु के सिक्कों का मूल्य घटना, मुद्राकरण करना, विमुद्रीकृत deprive a coin or precious metal of its status as money. *The twenty-five paise coins have been demonetized a long time ago.*

Demonstrate/डिमॉन्स्ट्रेट *(verb)* – प्रमाणित करना clearly show the existence or truth or. give a practical exhibition and explanation by giving proof.*The teacher demonstrated the experiment to the class.*

Demoralize/डिमॉरलाइज *(verb)* – उत्साह भंग करना, किसी का मनोबल गिराना cause to lose confidence or hope. *The caustic remarks by the management may demoralize the team after their defeat.*

Demurrage/डिमरेज *(noun)* – माल की समय से अधिक रूकावट का हर्जाना, बिलम्ब शुल्क [law] a charge payable to the owner of a chartered ship in respect of delay in loading or discharging. *Demurrage is a fine a transporter imposes on a customer for not taking delivery of goods within stipulated time.*

Den/डेन *(noun)* – कन्दरा या खोह, माँद a wild beast's lair. *It is dangerous to enter a lion's den.*

Denaturalize/डीनैचरलाइज *(verb)* – विकृति करना, स्वाभाविक गुण बदलना make unnatural. *America threatened to denaturalize Ryan of citizenship for want to documents.*

Dengue/डेंगू *(noun)* – लंगड़ा ज्वर, डेंगू बुखार a debilitating tropical viral disease transmitted by mosquitoes, causing sudden fever and acute pains in the joints. *The health authorities are afraid of a possible dengue outbreak.*

Denigrat/डेनीग्रेट *(verb)* – बदनाम करना, अलोचना करना, नीचा दिखाना criticize unfairly; disparage. *Why denigrate Jill in front of everyone if it wasn't her fault?*

Denote/डिनोट *(verb)* – बतलाना, किसी बात का द्योतक होना be a sign of; indicate. stand as a name or symbol for. *Use red ink to denote important points that need explanation.*

Dense/डेन्स *(adjective)* – घना, गहन, बहुत सी वस्तुओं या व्यक्तियों के जुटाव वाला closely compacted in substance. crowded closely together. *The jungle is dense to the point that in places, it is almost impenetrable.*

Dent/डेन्ट *(noun)* – छिद्र, गड्ढा a slight hollow in a hard even surface made by a blow or pressure. *From a minor dent to a full scale repair, we provide the best quality repair in the city.*

Denture/डेन्चर *(noun)* – कृत्रिम दाँतो की पंक्ति a removable plate or frame holding one or more artificial teeth. *Denture wearers are the most affected group along with people who have difficulties keeping their mouths clean.*

Denude/डिन्यूड *(verb)* – नंगा करना, कपड़ा उतार देना strip of covering or possessions; make bare. *The rains washed away the soil denuding the area around the tree.*

Denunciation/डिनन्सियेशन *(noun)* – किसी की तीखी सार्वजनिक भर्त्सना the action of denouncing someone or something. *The denunciation of the horrible practice resulted in everyone being relieved.*

Deodorize/डियोडॅराइज *(verb)* – निर्गन्धीकरण करना, गन्धहीन करना remove or conceal an unpleasant smell in. *Room freshener was used to deodorize the room.*

Decontology/डिकॉन्टोलोजी *(noun)* – धर्मशास्त्र philosophy the study of the nature of duty and obligation. *She is learning Decontology.*

Depart/डिपार्ट *(verb)* – प्रस्थान करना, रवाना होना leave, especially in order to start a journey. *They were supposed to depart at 5 o'clock to catch the train.*

Depasture/डिपास्चर *(verb)* – चरने के लिए पशुओं को बाहर निकालना, रवानगी, प्रस्थान किया [British] put to graze on pasture. *It is my duty in the morning to depasture the cattle.*

Depend/डिपेन्ड *(verb)* – भरोसा करना, निर्भर करना have faith and confidence. *Children depend on their parents for everything when they are young.*

Depict/डिपिक्ट *(verb)* – दर्शाना, चित्रित करना represent by a drawing, painting, or other art form. portray in words. *The government will take action if you depict women in a derogatory manner.*

Depletion/डिप्लीशन् *(noun)* – रिक्तिकरण erosion. Loss of vegetation *The continuing depletion of the earth's natural resources could prove very dangerous.*

Deplorable/डिप्लोरेबल *(adjective)* – शोचनीय, निंदनीय deserving strong condemnation; shockingly bad. *His actions were announced as being horribly deplorable.*

Deploy/डिप्लॉइ *(verb)* – सेना या हथियारों को संभावित लड़ाई के लिए तैयार रखना bring or move into position for military action. bring into effective action. *The government will deploy military to defend its frontiers.*

Depolarize/डिपोलराइज *(verb)* – विद्युत धारा का क्रम हटाना physics reduce or remove the polarization of. *Depolarize the circuit, please.*

Deponent/डिपोनेन्ट *(noun)* – गवाह, बयान देने वाला grammar denoting verbs which are passive or middle in form but active in meaning. *Deponent's name, address, age and occupation should be mentioned at the head of his deposition.*

Depopulate/डिपाप्युलेट *(verb)* – जनसंख्या कम करना substantially reduce the population of an area. *Countries facing a huge population explosion must come up with policies to depopulate.*

Deport/डिपोर्ट *(verb)* – देश से बाहर निकालना, निर्वासन expel a foreigner or immigrant from a country. *It was considered important for one to deport oneself with dignity in the old times.*

Deposit/डिपाजिट *(noun)* – धरोहर, जमा a sum of money placed in a bank or other account. *You may also have to pay a deposit which is normally refunded at the end of your stay.*

Deprave/डिप्रेव *(verb)* – कलुषित करना, बिगड़ना corrupt morally. *To behave in such a depraved manner can only lead to disaster.*

Depreciate/डिप्रीसिएट *(verb)* – एक अवधि के बाद किसी वस्तु का मूल्य घट जाना diminish in value over a period of time. reduce the recorded value of an asset over a predetermined period. *Some assets only depreciate over time.*

Depress/डिप्रेस *(verb)* – उदास करना, निपटारा करना, हताश करना deny a person or place the possession or use of something. *He was quite depressed after his pet died.*

Deprive/डिप्राइव *(verb)* – छीन लेना, किसी को किसी से वंचित करना deny a person or place the possession or use of something. *She was deprived of the love of both her parents.*

Depth/डेप्थ *(noun)* – गहराई the distance from the top or surface to the bottom of something or to a specified point within it. distance from the front to the back of something. the apparent existence of there dimensions in a two-dimensional representation. *It is important to study a subject in depth to excel in it.*

Deputation/डेप्युटेशन *(noun)* – नियुक्ति a group of people who undertake a mission on behalf of a larger group. *The deputation performed the task on behalf of their seniors very well.*

Deputy/डेप्युटि *(noun)* – प्रतिनिधि a person appointed to undertake the duties of a superior in the superior's absence. *He was recently appointed as deputy to the minister.*

Deracinate/डेरासिनेट *(verb)* – जड़ से उखाड़ लेना, उन्मूलन करना tear up by the roots. *The young sap was deracinated and planted where water was in abundance.*

Derby/डर्बी *(noun)* – एक प्रसिद्ध घुड़दौड़ an annual flat race at Epsom in surrey for three-year-old horses, founded in 1780 by the 12th earl of derby. a similar race or other important sporting contest. *The Derby is one of the most popular races in the world.*

Derelict/डिरेलिक्ट *(adjective)* – त्यक्त, परित्यक्त, परित्याग वस्तु in a very poor condition as a result of disuse and neglect. *The house has been in a derelict condition for a long time.*

Derivation/डिराइवेशन *(noun)* – मूल शब्द की व्युत्पति the deriving of something from a source or origin. *New words are derivations of old words and terms.*

Derive/डिराइव *(verb)* – किसी से कुछ प्राप्त करना obtain something from a specified source. base something on a modification of: *Marx derived his philosophy of history from Hegel.*

D

Derris/डेरिस *(noun)* – कीटनाशक an insecticide containing roten one, made from the powdered roots of a tropical plant. *Derris is a woody East Indian plant whose roots are used to manufacture insecticide.*

Dervish/डर्विश *(noun)* – दरवेश, फकीर a member of a Muslim fraternity vowed to poverty and known for their wild rituals. *Whirling is one of the rituals practised by the Dervish fraternity.*

Descant/डेस्कैंट *(noun)* – द्रुत उतार-चढ़ाव के साथ गाना music an independent treble melody sung or played above a basic melody. [archaic or poetic/literary] a melodious song. *The angels, we could say, sang the descant to creation's chorus.*

Describable/डिस्क्राइबेब्ल *(adjective)* – वर्णनीय capable of being described. *Happiness is a describable emotion.*

Describe/डिस्क्राइब *(verb)* – व्याख्या करना give a detailed account in words of. *She was asked to describe her experience in a few sentences.*

Description/डिस्क्रीप्सन *(noun)* – वर्णन a spoken or written account of a person, object, or event. the process of describing. *Thanks to the graphic facial features, the police arrested the thief in no time.*

Desert/डेजर्ट *(verb)* – त्याग देना callously or treacherously abandon. *The house was deserted when the police finally arrived.*

Desert/डेजर्ट *(noun)* – निर्जन, शून्य, रेगिस्तान, मरुस्थल a large area of land; usually covered with sand that is not and has very little water and very few plants. *Sahara is pamous desert in the world.*

Deserve/डिजर्व *(verb)* – अधिकार रखना, अच्छे या बुरे फल का पात्र होना do something or show qualities worthy of a reward or punishment as appropriate. *He certainly deserved the punishment for his misdeeds.*

Deshabille/डेजाबिये *(noun)* – गन्दा कपड़ा the state of being only partly or scantily clothed. *It was not a sad thing to be caught in a state of deshabille in the old days.*

Desiccate/डेसिक्केट *(verb)* – सुखाना remove the moisture from. *Please desiccate a slice of banana and put in a food dehydrator.*

Desire/डिजायर *(noun)* – इच्छा, कामेच्छा, कामवासना a strong feeling of wanting to have something or wishing for something to happen. strong sexual feeing or appetite. *I confess that I have never had a burning desire to go to England.*

Desirous/डिजायरस *(adjective)* – इच्छुक, आकांक्षी, अभिलाषी desiring. *He is particularly desirous of visiting Andaman & Nicobar islands. Those desirous of success must work hard.*

Desk/डेस्क *(noun)* – मेज a piece of furniture with a flat or sloped surface and typically with drawers, at which one can read, write, or do other work. *The front desk of the hotel was made of marble.*

Desolate/डेसोलेट *(adjective)* – सुनसान, निर्जन और अवसादपूर्ण, एकाकी, उदास giving an impression of bleak and dismal emptiness. utterly wretched and unhappy. *Finally we reached a desolate place devoid of people except for some grazing sheep.*

Despair/डेस्पेअर *(noun & verb)* – पूर्णनिराशा the complete loss or absence of hope. *Well, don't despair, help is at hand and we will be escorted back safely.*

Desperate/डेसपरेट *(adjective)* – अत्यधिक निराशा के कारण दुस्साहसी feeling, showing, or involving despair. tried in despair or when everything else has failed. *Desperate situations may lead some people to act in a risky manner.*

Despise/डिस्पाइज *(verb)* – घृणा करना, तिरस्कार करना feel contempt or repugnance for. *Due to his behaviour, he was thoroughly despised by the whole society.*

Despite/डिस्पाइट *(adv)* – के बावजूद without being of affected by the thing mentioned. *Anita was determined to do well despite her handicap.*

Despond/डिस्पाण्ड *(verb)* – निराश होना [archaic] become dejected and lose confidence. *We must not despond in bad days.*

Destine/डेस्टिन *(verb)* – स्थिर करना, ठहराना, नियत करना be intended or chosen for a particular purpose or end. *He was destined to become an IAS officer.*

Destiny/डेस्टिनी *(noun)* – भाग्य, नियति the events that will necessarily happen to a particular person in the future. the hidden power believed to control this; fate. *It is his destiny to act as saviour.*

Destroy/डिस्ट्रॉइ *(verb)* – नष्ट करना, किसी वस्तु को इस प्रकार हानि पहुँचाना कि वह इस्तेमाल न हो सके put an end to the existence of something by damaging or attacking it. ruin emotionally or spiritually. *The whole village was destroyed in the hurricane.*

Destructibility/डिस्ट्रक्टिबिलिटि *(adj.)* – ध्वंसता that can be destroyed. *John had not calculated the power of destructibility of the hurricane while designing his house.*

Destruction/डिस्ट्रक्शन *(noun)* – नाश, ध्वंस, तोड़फोड़ the action or process of causing so much damage to something that it no longer exists or cannot be repaired. a cause of someone's ruin. *The complete destruction of the school in the earthquake was terrible.*

Desultory/डेसल्टरी *(adjective)* – असंगत, अनियमित lacking purpose or enthusiasm. *They were engaging in a desultory conversation unwillingly.*

Detail/डिटेल *(noun)* – एक तथ्य या सूचना, ब्योरा a small individual feature, fact, or item. a small part of a picture reproduced separately for close study. *Please give me the detail of his business.*

Detain/डिटेन *(verb)* – किसी व्यक्ति को देरी कराना, व्यक्ति को किसी स्थान से नहीं जाने देना keep from proceeding by holding them back or making claims on their attention. *He was detained at the airport for more than three hours.*

Detect/डिटेक्ट *(verb)* – पता लगाना, ऐसी बात को खोज लेना जिसे जानना कठिन हो discover or identify the presence or existence of. *He could detect that something was not quite right.*

Detent/डिटेन्ट *(noun)* – किसी यन्त्र की गति स्थिर करने का खटका a catch in a machine which prevents motion until released. a catch that regulates striking. *This detent is meant to regulate motion of the machine.*

Detention/डिटेन्शन *(noun)* – किसी व्यक्ति को रोकने की प्रक्रिया the action or state of detaining or being detained. *Harry was sent to detention centre after school for being naughty.*

Deter/डिटर *(verb)* – किसी को कोई काम करने से रोकना, संभावित दुष्परिणामों को देखते हुए discourage from doing something by instilling fear of the consequences. prevent the occurrence of. *No amount of social work was going to deter her from studying to achieve her goals.*

Deteriorate/डिटेरिओरेट *(verb)* – क्षय होना, बदतर होना become progressively worse. *Jim's condition kept deteriorating even after he was treated at the hospital.*

Determinant/डिटर्मिनेन्ट *(noun)* – स्थिर, निर्धारण a factor which determines the nature or outcome of something. *Y-chromosome is the determinant of the birth of a boy or girl.*

Determinate/डिटरमिनेट *(adjective)* – निर्धारित having exact and discernible limits or form. *Determinate counsel of god means god determined the course of action.*

Detonate/डिटोनेट *(verb)* – धड़ाका करना, बम विस्फोट होना या करना explode or cause to explode. *No one was allowed to go near the place before the bomb was detonated.*

Detrain/डिट्रेन *(verb)* – रेलगाड़ी से उतारना या उतरना leave or cause to leave a train. *The whole family detrained as their plans got cancelled at the last moment.*

Detriment/डेट्रिमेंट *(noun)* – हानिकारक, नुकसानदेह the state of being harmed or damaged. *The action backfired to their detriment.*

Devil/डेविल *(verb)* – दानव [informal, dated] act as a junior assistant for a barrister or other professional. *Some people believe that the devil exists.*

Devilish/डेविलिश *(adjective)* – अति दुष्ट या उपद्रवी of, like, or appropriate to a devil in evil and cruelty. mischievous and rakish. very difficult to deal with or use. *He behaved in a devilish sort of way.*

Devious/डीवियस *(adjective)* – दोषी skillfully using underhand tactics to achieve goals. *Huma acted in a devious way to get the promotion.*

Devise/डिवाइज *(verb)* – उपाय या युक्ति निकालना plan or invent a complex procedure or mechanism. *He devised a plan to bring them to our home quickly.*

D

D

Devitalize/डिवाइटलाइज *(verb)* – निर्जीव करना deprive of strength and vigour. *The entire team was feeling devitalized after trekking for more than six hours.*

Devolution/डिवोल्यूशन *(noun)* – विकेन्द्रीकरण the devolving of power by central government to local or regional administration. *The school authorities practised devolution of power to make decision making more effective.*

Devolve/डिवॉल्ब *(verb)* – to deliver over किसी की मृत्यु के पश्चात् उसकी संपत्ति अधिकारी को सौंपना devolved, devolving to transfer or pass on (duties, responsibilities, etc. to another or others. *Devolve decision-making from central government to the people of the region.*

Devote/डिवोट *(verb)* – समर्पित करना give time or resources to a person or activity. *The teacher told Mukesh to devote more time to studies in order to score better marks.*

Devotion/डिवोशन *(noun)* – धर्मनिष्ठा, समर्पणभाव love, loyalty, or enthusiasm for a person or activity. *Scoring high marks in exams requires a lot of devotion from the student.*

Devour/डिवावर *(verb)* – भूख से मारे जल्दी-जल्दी खाना eat food or prey hungrily or quickly. consume destructively. *Anil devoured food at the restaurant like he was eating after a long time.*

Devout/डिवाउट *(adjective)* – अत्यधिक धार्मिक having or showing deep religious feeling or commitment. *James is a devout Christian.*

Dew/ड्यू *(noun)* – तुषार, ओस a liquid that condenses during the night on surfaces and plants when warm air touches a cool surface. *An example of dew is the liquid that drips off of blades of grass in the morning.*

Dexterity/डेक्सटेरिटी *(noun)* – निपुणता skill in performing tasks, especially with the hands. *Mathews showed great dexterity in the fine arts competition.*

Diabetes/डायबिटिज *(noun)* – मधुमेह a disorder of the metabolism causing excessive thirst and the production of large amounts of urine. *Doctors say diabetes is increasing at an alarming rate.*

Diadem/डायडेम *(noun)* – मुकुट a jewelled crown or headband worn as a symbol of sovereignty. *The diadem is a symbol of adornment.*

Diagonal/डायगोनल *(adjective)* – कर्ण denoting a straight line joining opposite corners of a rectangle, square, or other figure. straight and at an angle; slanting. mathematics denoting a matrix with non-zero elements lower right. *Do not use diagonals or right to left words.*

Diagram/डाइअग्रैम *(noun)* – आकृति, रेखाचित्र a simplified drawing showing the appearance or structure of something. *A diagram is a chart showing how all the departments within an organization are related.*

Dial/डायल *(noun)* – घड़ी का गोलाकार भाग जिस पर समय की इकाइयाँ अंकित होती है a disc marked to show the time on a clock or indicate a reading or measurement by means of a pointer. a disc with numbered holes on a telephone, turned to make a call. a disc turned to select a setting on a radio, cooker, etc. *This wall clock has a very large dial.*

Dialect/डायलेक्ट *(noun)* – प्रकृत भाषा, उपभाषा a form of a language which is peculiar to a specific region or social group. *I did not understand the dialect of the Bengal region.*

Dialogic/डायलोजिक *(adjective)* – वार्तालाप सम्बन्धी relating to or in the form of dialogue. *Your dialogical statement is not appreciable.*

Dialogue/डायलाग *(verb)* – बातचीत [chiefly north American] take part in dialogue. provide a film or play with dialogue. *Smith does not want to indulge in any dialogue with Jerry.*

Diamantiferous/डायमन्टिफरस *(adjective)* – हीरा उत्पन्न करने वाली producing or yielding diamonds. *These mines are diamantiferous.*

Diana/डायना *(noun)* – चन्द्रमा goddess of the hunt (Greek Mythology); *Diana is the name of the ancient Roman goddess of moon, hunt and chastity.*

Diaper/डायपर *(noun)* – बेलबूटा कढ़ा हुआ कपड़ा, अंगोछा [north American] a baby nappy. *Diaper is an absorbent cloth worn by babies.*

Diarist/डायरिष्ट *(noun)* – रोजनामचा रखने वाला a person who writes a diary. *Anne Frank was a diarist.*

Diarrhoea/डायरिया *(noun)* – अतिसार, दस्त की बीमारी a condition in which faces are discharged from the bowels frequently and in a liquid form. *James missed the school trip because he was suffering from diarrhoa.*

Diary/डायरी *(noun)* – रोजनामचा a book in which one keeps a daily record of events and experiences. a book with spaces for each day of the year in which to note appointments. *Writing a diary is a good habit.*

Dice/डाइस *(verb)* – पासे का खेल, वर्गाकार दाना जिस पर छ: बिंदिया होती है play or gamble with dice. *The player rolled the dice on the casino table.*

Dichotomy/डाइकाटामि *(noun)* – तर्क में किसी पदार्थ के दो विभाग a division or contrast between two things that are opposed or entirely different. *The dichotomy of the situation was that though he claimed to be an artist, he was unaware of Picasso's work.*

Dictaphone/डिक्टाफोन *(noun)* – बोले हुए शब्दों को टाइप में लिखने का यंत्र trademark a small cassette recorder used to record speech for transcription at a later time. *They recorded my speech on a dictaphone to play it at the function.*

Diction/डिक्शन *(noun)* – मुहावरा the choice and use of words in speech or writing. *Good diction is a pre-requisite for media persons.*

Dictum/डिक्टम *(noun)*– आदेश a formal pronouncement from an authoritative source. a short statement that expresses a general truth or principle. [law] short for obiter dictum. *He cited Augustine's dictum in his article.*

Did/डिड – किया past of do. *Did he go to school?*

Didactic/डिडैक्टिक *(adjective)* – उपदेशात्मक, शिक्षात्मक intended to teach, in particular having moral instruction as an ulterior motive in the manner of a teacher; patronizing or hectoring. *The speech given at the assembly was supposed to be didactic.*

Diddle/डिडल *(verb)* – बहकाना [informal] cheat or swindle. *Mom always said not to diddle away time.*

Die/डाइ *(verb)* – दम निकालना, मरना singular form of dice. *James can't stand to see anyone die.*

Diehard/डाइहार्ड *(noun)* – अन्त तक विरोध करने वाला a person who strongly opposes change or who continues to support something in spite of opposition. *She is a diehard fan of Tom Hanks.*

Diet/डाइट *(noun)* – भोजन, खुराक food, food prescribed by a doctor. *One should consume a balanced diet to stay healthy.*

Difference/डिफरेंस *(noun)* – मतभेद, असहमति, विवाद a way in which people or things are different. the state or condition of being different. *He couldn't explain the difference between the two portraits.*

Different/डिफरेंट *(adjective)* – पृथक, असमान not the same as another or each other; unlike in nature, form, or quality. *One should understand that sex and gender are two different things.*

Differentia/डिफरेंसिया *(noun)* – भेद का चिह्न a distinguishing mark or characteristic. chiefly philosophy an attribute that distinguishes a species of thing from other species of the same genus. *The birth spot is the differentia between the twins.*

Difficult/डिफिकल्ट *(adjective)* – कठिन, मुश्किल needing much effort or skill to accomplish, deal with, or understand. *The questions in final exam were very difficult.*

Diffidence/डिफिडेन्स *(noun)* – अविश्वास lack of self-confidence. *Don't put diffidence in this matter.*

Diffident/डिफिडेंट *(adjective)* – अविश्वस्त, आत्महीन modest or shy because of a lack of self-confidence. *He is a very diffident person.*

Diffract/डिफ्रैक्ट *(verb)* – टुकड़े करना to break into part, physics cause to undergo diffraction. *That effect is caused due to diffraction of light.*

Diffuse/डिफ्यूज *(adjective)* – छितराना spread out over a large area; not concentrated. not localized in the body. *Sugar diffuses in the tea on stirring.*

Dig/डिग *(verb)* – गड्ढा खोदना [informal, chiefly British] lodgings. *Please dig into your books and find the answer to this question. They went to dig the ground in search of dinosaur bones.*

Dight/डाइट *(verb)* – सजाना [poetic/literary] make ready; prepare. *Please dight for the competition.*

Dignify/डिग्निफाइ *(verb)* – सत्कार करना make something seem worthy and impressive. give an impressive name to someone or something unworthy of it. *He felt dignified in the company of leading writers.*

Dignitary/डिग्निटरी *(noun)* – उच्च पद का पादरी a person holding high rank or office. *He is a dignitary at the office.*

Dignity/डिग्निटी *(noun)* – गौरव, शान्त और गम्भीर आचरण the state or quality of being worthy of honour or respect. *One should carry oneself with dignity and pride.*

Digress/डायग्रेस *(verb)* – मुख्य विषय को छोड़कर भटकना leave the main subject temporarily in speech or writing. *Kindly be precise and do not digress from the topic.*

Dilapidate/डिलैपिडेट *(verb)* – नाश करना [archaic] cause to fall into someone in power without popular consent. *For want of repairs, the house was in a dilapidated condition.*

Dilate/डायलेट *(verb)* – चौड़ा करना become or make wider, larger, or more open. *Capillaries were dilated to allow the excess heat to be removed by blood flow.*

Dilettante/डिलेटैन्टि *(noun)* – कलानुरागी a person who cultivates an area of interest, such as the arts, without real commitment or knowledge. *He is a dilettante in the field of religion.*

Diligence/डिलिजेन्स *(noun)* – उद्योग, कर्मठता, परिश्रम careful and persistent work or effort. *One should show diligence towards one's work.*

Dill/डिल *(noun)* – मधुरिका लता a medicinal plant, austral [[informal] a naive or foolish person. *He is such a dill that everyone takes him for granted.*

Dilly-dally/डिली-डैली *(verb)* – टालमटोल करना [informal] dawdle or vacillate. *The government continues to dilly-dally on taking a decision on labour reforms.*

Dimension/डायमेन्सन *(noun)* – लम्बाई-चौड़ाई या ऊँचाई का मापन a measurable extent, such as length, breadth, or height. physics an expression for a derived physical quantity in terms of fundamental quantities such as mass, length, or time, raised to the appropriate power. *Dimension is the measurement of length, breadth and width.*

Dimidiate/डिमिडियेट *(verb)* – भागों में विभक्त करना heraldry so that only half of each is visible. having only one half depicted. *He has dimidiated the property amongst his sons.*

Diminish/डिमनिश *(verb)* – कम होना, छोटा होना या छोटा करना make or become less. *Objects appear to diminish in size as we go farther away from them.*

Diminution/डिमिन्यूशन *(noun)* – कमी a reduction. *Diminution means reduction in value of an individual.*

Diminutive/डिमिन्यूटिव *(adjective)* – अल्प heraldry a charge of the same form as an ordinary but of lesser size or width. *The meaning of diminution can be translated 'tiny', and diminutives are used frequently when speaking to small children. Harry is diminutive for Harold.*

Dimity/डिमिटि *(noun)* – सूती कपड़ा a hard-wearing cotton fabric woven with stripes or checks. *Could you buy me dimity from the market?*

Dimple/डिम्पल *(noun)* – गाल की तुड्डी की गड्ढा a small depression in the flesh, either permanent or forming in the checks when one smiles. *Dimple is a small depression some of us get on the cheeks while laughing or talking.*

Din/डिन *(noun)* – शोर-शराबा, हल्का-फुल्का a loud, continuous noise; confused clamour or uproar a loud. *The din created by loud speakers has made our life tough.*

Dingy/डिंजी *(adjective)* – गंदा और अंधेरा gloomy and drab. *That café was poorly lit, dingy and drab that we decided to come out of it immediately.*

Dinner/डिनर *(noun)* – दिन का मुख्य भोजन the main meal of the day, taken either without tails, typically one in honour of a person or event. *Let's have dinner at the restaurant tonight.*

Dint/डिन्ट *(noun)* – प्रहार, प्रयत्न an impression or hollow in a surface. *He succeeded in life by dint of hard study.*

Diocese/डायोसेस *(noun)* – पादरी का प्रदेश a district under the pastoral care of a bishop in the Christian church. *This area is the bishop's diocese.*

Dioxide/डायऑक्साइड *(noun)* – दो भाग ऑक्सीजन एवं एक भाग धातु का मेल chemistry an oxide containing two atoms of oxygen in its molecule or empirical formula. *Carbon dioxide is used to extinguish fire.*

Diphtheria/डिफ्थीरिया *(noun)* – कण्ठ का एक संक्रामक रोग a serious bacterial disease causing inflammation of the mucous membranes and formation of a false membrane in the throat which hinders breathing and swallowing. *He is suffering from diphtheria.*

Diplomacy/डिप्लोमेसी *(noun)* – अंतर्राष्ट्रीय कूटनीति the profession, activity, or skill of managing international relations. *One should talk with diplomacy on controversial topics.*

Dipper/डिपर *(noun)* – कल्छुल, सप्तऋषि, गोताखोर, जलपाख a stocky, short-tailed songbird frequenting fast-flowing streams and able to dive or walk under water to feed. *Dipper is a bird found in and around Mexico. Truck drivers use dipper at night.*

Dipterous/डिप्टरस *(adjective)* – केवल दो पंखों या पैरों वाला having two wings only, entomology of or relating to files of the order dipteral. botany having two wing-like appendages. *The birds having two wings only are called dipterous.*

Dire/डायर *(adjective)* – भयानक, गम्भीर, दारूण extremely serious or urgent. *There is a dire need to improve literacy in India.*

Direct/डायरेक्ट *(adj & verb)* – सीधा, ठीक, प्रत्यक्ष to order, going from one place to another without changing direction or stopping. astronomy & astrology proceeding from west to east in accord with actual motion. *He was directed to report to the head quarters immediately.*

Direction/डायरेक्शन *(noun)* – निर्देश a course along which someone or something moves, or which must be taken to reach a destination. a point to or from which a person or thing moves or faces. a trend or tendency. *Please move in the northern direction to reach the railway station.*

Director/डायरेक्टर *(noun)* – निर्देशक a person who is in charge of an activity, department, or organization. *She is the director of this prestigious organization.*

Dirge/डर्ज *(noun)* – मर्सिया, शोकगीत a lament for the dead, especially one forming part of a funeral rite. *The following is a dirge*

in remembrance of my uncle who expired yesterday.

Dirk/डर्क *(noun)* – एक प्रकार की कटार, छूरा a short dagger of king formerly carried by Scottish highlanders. *Use a dirk to fight the criminal.*

Disability/डिजैबिलिटी *(noun)* – अयोग्यता a physical or mental condition that limits a person's movements, senses, or activities. *He is suffering from mental and physical disability.*

Disabuse/डिसएब्यूज *(verb)* – ठीक करना, झूठे विचारों से छुटकारा पाना, भ्रम निवारण persuade that an idea or belief is mistaken. *(Don't disabuse innocent children.*

Disadvantage/डिसएडवांटेज *(noun)* – असुविधा, हानि, नुकसान an unfavourable circumstance or condition. *An example of a disadvantage is a team's star player having to sit out because of an injury.*

Disaffection/डिसएफेक्शन *(noun)* – घृणा, विरक्ति the feeling of being alienated from other people. *She had disaffection towards her husband.*

Disaffirm/डिसएफर्म *(verb)* – विरोध करना repudiate a settlement. *He disaffirmed that he ever signed a contract with that party.*

Disagree/डिसएग्री *(verb)* – सहमत न होना have a different opinion. *I disagree with you on your opinion.*

Disallow/डिसएलाउ *(verb)* – अस्वीकार करना refuse to declare valid. *Passengers holding ordinary tickets have been disallowed to board this coach.*

Disappear/डिसएपिअर *(verb)* – अदृश्य होना cease to be visible. cease to exist or be in use. go missing or be killed. *Thieves disappeared from the house before the security could arrive.*

Disappoint/डिसएप्वाइंट *(verb)* – नियुक्ति तोड़ना, निराश या हताश करना fail to fulfil the hopes or expectations of. prevent from being realized. *Do not disappoint your parents by indulging in bad deeds.*

Disapprobation/डिसएप्रोबेशन *(noun)* – अस्वीकृति strong disapproval, especially on moral grounds. *Disapprobation of smoking will not be lifted.*

D

Disapproval/डिसएप्रूवल *(noun)* – अस्वीकृति (बुरा होने के कारण) rejection, not approved. *Our request to let us in the hostel was met with stern disapproval by the warden.*

Disapprove/डिसएप्रूव *(verb)* – अस्वीकार करना, नापसंद करना have or express an unfavourable opinion. officially refuse to agree to. *I have disapproved your leave application.*

Disarm/डिसआर्म *(verb)* – हथियार ले लेना, निहत्था करना take a weapon or weapons away from. a country of force give up or reduce its armed forces or weapons. remove the fuse from a bomb. *The police disarmed the criminals.*

Disarrange/डिसअरेंज *(verb)* – क्रम हटाना, अव्यवस्थित करना make untidy or disordered. *Why did you disarrange the crockery?*

Disarray/डिसअरे *(noun)* – उलट-पलट, गड़बड़ a state of disorganization or untidiness. *The entire house is in disarray.*

Disaster/डिजास्टर *(noun)* – विनाश, तबाही a sudden accident or a natural catastrophe that causes great damage or loss of life. *The fire was a disaster at the wedding ceremony.*

Disastrous/डिजास्ट्रस *(adjective)* – नाशकारी causing great damage. *Dereliction of duty could prove to be disastrous for our aim.*

Disband/डिस्बैंड *(verb)* – सेना भंग करना या तोड़ना break up or cause to break up. *This company would be disbanded into small units for the operations.*

Disbelief/डिस्बिलिफ *(noun)* – अविश्वास inability or refusal to accept that something is true or real. lack of faith. *She stared at the TajMahal in disbelief.*

Disburden/डिस्बर्डेन *(verb)* – हल्का करना, बोझा उतारना relieve of a burden or responsibility. *Please disburden yourself regarding the sale of this property.*

Disburse/डिस्बर्स *(verb)* – धन देना, चुकाना, इकट्ठा किये हुए धन से पैसा देना pay out money from a fund. *The college disbursed grants to all who secured more than 75 percent marks.*

Discard/डिस्कार्ड *(verb)* – अलग करना get rid of as no longer useful or desirable. *Those not scoring runs would be discarded by the selectors.*

Discern/डिसर्न *(verb)* – कठिनाई से किसी वस्तु को देख या सुन पाना recognize or find out. distinguish with difficulty by sight or with the other senses. *I couldn't discern the difference between the shawls.*

Disciple/डिस्साइपल् *(noun)* – शिष्य, चेला, अनुयायी a personal follower of Christ during his life, especially one of the twelve apostles. *Seeta is a disciple of Gandhiji.*

Disciplinary/डिसिप्लिनरी *(adjective)* – अनुशासन सम्बन्धी having to do with discipline. *Disciplinary action was taken against those who failed to report in time.*

Discipline/डिसिप्लीन *(noun)* – अनुशासन the practice of training people to obey rules or a code of behaviour. controlled behaviour resulting from such training. *Discipline should be inculcated right from the time a child learns to speak.*

Disclaim/डिसक्लेम *(verb)* – अस्वीकार करना, मुकरना refuse to acknowledge. *Due to dispute, I disclaim his ownership of the house.*

Disclose/डिसक्लोज *(verb)* – किसी को कोई बात बताना या सार्वजनिक रूप से प्रकट करना make known. expose to view. *Do not disclose this information to anyone.*

Discolour/डिसकलर *(verb)* – मलिन करना, रंग बिगड़ना या बिगाड़ना become or cause to become a different, less attractive colour. *The dress I bought became discoloured after the very first wash.*

Discomfort/डिसकम्फर्ट *(noun)* – पीड़ा slight pain. slight anxiety or embarrassment. *I feel discomfort in his peresence.*

Discommode/डिसकमोड *(verb)* – कष्ट देना, सताना, परेशानी में डालना formal cause trouble or inconvenience to. *Do not discommode the guests.*

Discompose/डिसकम्पोज *(verb)* – अस्त-व्यस्त करना, अशांत कर देना disturb or agitate. *With your actions you are discomposing everybody present at the gathering.*

Disconcert/डिसकन्सर्ट *(verb)* – किसी के चित्त को विक्षुब्ध कर देना disturb the composure of. *Do not disconcert the boss.*

Disconnect/डिसकनेक्ट *(verb)* – पृथक् करना break the connection of or between. put out of action by detaching it from a power supply. *Please disconnect the phone connection from my house.*

Disconsent/डिसकन्सेंट *(verb)* – असहमत होना lack of contentment or satisfaction. a person who is dissatisfied. *I am disconsented with the company's performance.*

Disconsolate/डिसकन्सोलेट *(adjective)* – निराश, मायूस very unhappy and unable to be comforted. *He was very disconsolate after he heard the loss of his court case.*

Discontent/डिसकन्टेन्ट *(noun)* – असन्तोष lack of satisfaction. *Restless desire for something more or different led her to high levels of discontent.*

Discontinue/डिसकन्टिन्यू *(verb)* – रोक देना या बन्द कर देना stop doing, providing, or making. *He is discontinuing the job at the firm.*

Discount/डिसकाउन्ट *(noun)* – सामान्य से कम दाम, छूट a deduction from the usual cost of something. [finance] a percentage deducted from the face value of a bill of exchange or promissory not when it changes hands before the due date. *Enjoy a 30 percent discount on this product during this Diwali festival.*

Discourse/डिसकोर्स *(noun)* – सम्भाषण, किसी विषय पर गम्भीर चर्चा written or spoken communication or debate. a formal discussion of a topic in speech or writing. linguistics a text or conversation. *What's your discourse on this matter?*

Discourteous/डिसकर्टीअस *(adjective)* – असभ्य rude and lacking consideration for others. *One should not be discourteous to guests.*

Discover/डिसकवर *(verb)* – किसी नई बात का पता लगाना या खोज find unexpectedly or in the course of a search. become aware of a fact or situation. be the first to find or observe. *I will discover the truth behind the robbery.*

Discovery/डिसकवरी *(noun)* – आविष्कार the action or process of discovering or being discovered. a person or thing discovered. *The discovery of X-rays as a means to study bones was a great discovery.*

Discredit/डिसक्रेडिट *(verb)* – अपयश, बदनाम करना harm the good reputation of. cause to seem false or unreliable. *They have discredited him in the market by spreading false rumours.*

Discreet/डिसक्रीट *(adjective)* – विचारशील, विचारवान careful and prudent in one's speech or actions, especially so as to avoid giving offence or attracting attention. *Please be discreet about this information.*

Discrepancy/डिसक्रिपेन्सी *(noun)* – (दो बातों में) असंमति या अंतर an illogical or surprising lack of compatibility or similarity between two or more facts. *There is no discrepancy between the findings of the two projects.*

Discrete/डिसक्रीट *(adjective)* – अलग individually separate and distinct. *These are discrete pages.*

Discretion/डिसक्रीशन *(noun)* – विवेक, समझ-बूझ the quality of being discreet. *I will reveal this information only at your discretion.*

Discriminate/डिसक्रिमिनट *(verb)* – प्रभेद करना, किसी के प्रति भेदभाव करना या रखना recognize a distinction. perceive or constitute the difference in or between. *One must never discriminate against people as all are equals.*

Discussion/डिसकशन *(noun)* – अप्रासंगिक वार्ता, चर्चा विचार-विमर्श भाषण या लेखन an extended communication dealing with some particular topic.

Discussive/डिसकसिव *(adj)* – असम्बद्ध अगठित moving from one point to another without any strict structure.

Disdain/डिसडेन *(noun)* – तिरस्कार करना the feeling that someone or something is unworthy of one's consideration or respect. *Her voice was choked with disdain.*

Disease/डिजीज *(noun)* – रोग, व्याधि a disorder of structure or function in a human, animal, or plant, especially one that produces specific symptoms or that affects a specific part. *Cancer is a disease wherein malicious tumour develops in any part of the body.*

Disembark/डिसइम्बार्क *(verb)* – जलपोत या विमान पर से किनारे पर उतरना leave a ship, aircraft, or train. *He has disembarked from the ship.*

Disembarrass/डिसइम्बैरस *(verb)* – घबड़ाहट से मुक्त करना free oneself of a burden or nuisance. *I disembarrass myself from this situation.*

Disembroil/डिसइम्ब्रायल *(verb)* – आपत्ति से छुड़ाना, सुलझाना free from involvement or entanglement. *He disembroiled our dispute.*

D

D

Disenchant/डिसइन्चैट (verb) – जादू टोने के प्रभाव से छुड़ाना make disillusioned. *He refused to promote him because he disenchanted with his performance.*

Disengage/डिसइंगेज (noun) – अलगाना, छुड़ाना, सम्बन्ध तोड़ना fencing a disengaging movement. *Let's disengage from this conversation before we say something we'll regret later.*

Disentangle/डिसइंटैंगल (verb) – सुलझाना, किसी लिपटी हुई वस्तु से किसी व्यक्ति या वस्तु को मुक्त करना free from entanglement; untwist. remove knots or tangles from wool, rope, or hair. *Please disentangle this knot for me.*

Disfavour/डिसफेवर (noun) – विराग, अरुचि disapproval or dislike. *He is in disfavour of the prime minister.*

Disfigure/डिसफिगर (verb) – सौन्दर्य नष्ट करना spoil the appearance of.*Don't disfigure that statue by writing something on it.*

Disgorge/डिसगॉर्ज (verb) – उगलना discharge; cause to pour out. bring up or vomit. yield or give up. *The doctor gave an injection to help disgorge the food from the stomach.*

Disgrace/डिसग्रेस (noun) – अपमान, निरादर loss of reputation as the result of a dishonourable action. a person or thing regarded as shameful and unacceptable. *One mistake brought disgrace to the family.*

Disguise/डिसगाइज (verb) – छिपाना, भेष बदलना, रूप बदलना alter the appearance, sound, taste, or smell of so as to conceal the identity. conceal the nature or existence of a feeling or situation. *They disguised their faces before robbing the bank.*

Disgust/डिसगस्ट (noun) – घृणा, गुस्सा, चिढ़ strong revulsion or profound indignation. *I felt disgust after hearing of the crime he had committed.*

Dish/डिस (noun) – थाली, तश्तरी, रकाबी a shallow, typically flat-bottomed container for cooking or serving food. all the items that have been used in the preparation, serving, and eating of a meal. a shallow, concave receptacle: a soap dish. a bowl-shaped radio aerial. *I need a dish washer for my house.*

Disharmonize/डिसहारमोनाइज (verb) – बेसुरा करना cause to sound harsh and unpleasant. *Don't dishormonize your performance.*

Disharmony/डिसहारमनी (noun) – बेसुरापन, लयभंग lack of harmony. *The song is being played in disharmony.*

Dishearten/डिसहार्टेन (verb) – उत्साह भंग करना cause to lose determination or confidence. *Don't feel disheartened as there's always a second chance.*

Dishonest/डिसआनेस्ट (adjective) – बेईमान, धोखेबाज not honest, trustworthy, or sincere. *I didn't know he would turn out to be a dishonest man.*

Disinclination/डिसइनक्लानेशन (noun) – अरुचि a reluctance or unwillingness to so something. *He has disinclination towards his studies.*

Disinfect/डिसइन्फेक्ट (verb) – संक्रामक दोष दूर करना make clean and free from infection, especially by the use of a chemical disinfectant. *The sanitizer will disinfect you.*

Disingenuous/डिसइन्जेन्युअस (adjective) – कपटी, धूर्त not candid or sincere, especially in pretending that one knows less about something than one really does. *Don't go on his looks, he is very disingenuous.*

Disinherit/डिसइन्हेरिट (verb) – पैतृक सम्पत्ति से वंचित करना to deprive of inheritance. *The father disinherited his son from his property.*

Disintegrate/डिसइन्टिग्रेट (verb) – विखण्डित होना, टुकड़े-टुकड़े हो जाना break up into small parts as a result of impact or decay. *In nuclear fission, the nucleus breaks into two and the process continues.*

Disinter/डिसइन्टर (verb) – खोदना, किसी वस्तु को खोदकर बाहर निकालना dig up something that has been buried. *Let's not disinter past secrets.*

Disinterested/डिसइन्टरेस्टेड (adjective) – निष्पक्ष, तटस्थ not influenced by considerations of personal advantage; impartial. *He seems absolutely disinterested in this conversation.*

Disjoint/डिसज्वाइंट (adjective) – जोड़ पर से पृथक् करना, सम्बन्ध तोड़ना [Mathematics] having no elements in common. *Any disjointed effort will not achieve desired results.*

Disjunct/डिसजंक्ट (adjective) – असम्बद्ध, पृथक् किया हुआ disjoined and distinct from one another.*There seems to be great disjunct in his work.*

Dislike/डिसलाइक *(verb)* – नापसंद करना feel distaste for or hostility towards. *He disliked your brother.*

Dislocate/डिसलोकेट *(verb)* – अपने स्थान से हटना या हटा दिया जाना, उखड़ा जोड़, स्थान से हटाना disturb the normal arrangement or position of a joint in the body. *He fell while playing football and dislocated his elbow joint.*

Dislocation/डिसलोकेशन *(noun)* – स्थान भ्रष्टता the process or state of dislocating or being dislocated. *Poor policies of the government may lead to social dislocations in the society.*

Disloyal/डिसलॉइअल *(adjective)* – बेवफा, अविश्वासी not loyal or faithful. (never be disloyal to your work) *The books he wrote about his employer were so disloyal.*

Dismal/डिसमल *(adjective)* – शोकयुक्त, निराशाजनक causing or demonstrating a mood of gloom or depression; dreary. *They presented a totally dismal performance at the playground.*

Dismantle/डिसमैंटल *(verb)* – किसी वस्तु को टुकड़े-टुकड़े कर देना take to pieces. *Please dismantle this machine before transporting it to Mumbai.*

Dismast/डिसमास्ट *(verb)* जहाज का मस्तूल हटाना break or force down the mast or masts of a ship. *The ship has been dismasted.*

Dismember/डिसमेम्बर *(verb)* – खण्ड-खण्ड करना tear or cut the limbs from. *The train passed over and dismembered the body of the traveller.*

Disobedience/डिसुओबेडियन्स *(noun)* – अवज्ञाकारी, आज्ञा भंग non compliance *Gandhiji launched a Civil Disobedience Movement against British administration to make India a free nation.*

Disobey/डिसुओबे *(verb)* – आज्ञा, आदेश पालन से इनकार fail or refuse to obey. *Never disobey your parents or teachers.*

Disoblige/डिसुओब्लाइज *(verb)* – असन्तुष्ट करना offend by not acting in accordance with their wishes. *You are disobliging your guests.*

Disorganize/डिसऑर्गेनाइज *(verb)* – उपद्रव करना, अव्यवस्थित करना disrupt, upset, disarrange. *We had to go without food or water because the authorities were so disorganized.*

Disown/डिजॉन *(verb)* – त्यागना refuse to acknowledge or maintain any connection with. *That man disowned his daughter.*

Disparage/डिस्पैरिज *(verb)* – पद घटाना, बुराई करना, निंदा करना represent as being of little worth; scorn. *Don't try to pass disparaging remarks against anybody.*

Disparate/डिस्पर्एट *(noun)* – असमान, व्यक्ति या वस्तु आचरण या गुण में बेहद भिन्न हो things so different that there is no basis for comparison between them. *A strong leader can motivate a geographically disparate team to achieve agreed goals.*

Dispatch/डिस्पैच *(verb)* – किसी व्यक्ति या वस्तु को कहीं भेजना send off promptly to destination or for purpose. *The order was dispatched five minutes ago.*

Dispel/डिस्पेल *(verb)* – (शंका आदि) को दूर कर देना make doubt, feeling, or belief disappear. *The doubts, he has, must be dispelled.*

Dispensable/डिस्पेन्सेबल् *(adjective)* – अनावश्यक, अपरिहार्य able to be replaced or done without. *These items of my personal property are dispensable.*

Dispensation/डिस्पेन्सेशन *(noun)* – वितरण, बाँटना the action of dispensing. *I look forward to an early dispensation of my request.*

Dispense/डिस्पेन्स *(verb)* – बाँटना distribute to a number of people. supply or release a product. *Kindly dispense these blankets among all participants.*

Dispenser/डिस्पेन्सर *(noun)* – मशनी या डिब्बा जिससे आपको अभीष्ट वस्तु मिलती है distribute *A dispenser is a container so designed that the contents can be used in prescribed amounts.*

Disperse/डिस्पर्स *(verb)* – छितराना, बिखर जाना go or distribute in different directions or over a wide area. *The police fired water cannon shots to disperse the crowd.*

Dispersion/डिस्पर्सन *(noun)* – आबादी या चीजों के दूर-दूर तक फैलने की प्रक्रिया the action, process, or state of dispersing or being dispersed. *With the help of a prism, we can observe the dispersion of light into seven colours.*

Dispersive/डिस्पर्सिव *(adjective)* – फैलाने वाला spreading by diffusion. *This ia a dispersive prism which disperses the rays.*

D

Dispirit/डिस्प्रीरिट *(verb)* – उदास करना cause to lose enthusiasm or hope. *If you keep yourself away from the meet, the participants may feel dispirited.*

Displace/डिस्प्लेस *(verb)* – स्थान बदलना या स्थान छीन लेना shift from its proper or usual position. *Some workers have been displaced from their regular duty.*

Display/डिसप्ले *(verb)* – किसी वस्तु को ऐसे स्थान पर रखना कि लोग उसे देख सके place prominently so that it putter, television or cinema screen. *You are a public figure and your posture must display a positive attitude.*

Displease/डिसप्लीज *(verb)* – अप्रसन्न करना annoy or upset. *You should try not to displease any of your guests.*

Displeasure/डिसप्लेजर *(noun)* – किसी को नाराज करना a feeling of annoyance or dissatisfaction. *Never be a source of displeasure to your chairman.*

Disport/डिस्पोर्ट *(verb)* – आनन्द मनाना, दिल बहलाना enjoy oneself unrestrainedly; frolic. *She disported herself thoroughly with the massage at the spa.*

Disposable/डिसपोजेब्ल *(adjective)* – एक बार प्रयोग के बाद फेंकने योग्य intended to be used once and then thrown away. able to be dispensed with; easily dismissed. *I would like to be served my fruit drink in a disposable glass.*

Disposition/डिसपोजिशन *(noun)* – प्रवृत्ति, चरित्र a person's inherent qualities of mind and character. an inclination or tendency. *He can fight the lawsuit at his own disposition.*

Dispossess/डिसपॅजेस *(verb)* – अधिकार छीन लेना, निर्वासित कर देना deprive of land or property, people who have been dispossessed. *These people have been dispossessed of their houses.*

Dispraise/डिसप्रेज *(noun)* – निन्दा करना rare censure; criticism. *Never dispraise anybody's hard work.*

Disproof/डिसप्रुफ *(noun)* – खण्डन action or evidence that proves something to be untrue. *I have no evidence or disproof of his claims.*

Disproportion/डिस्प्रोपोरशन *(noun)* – अयोग्यता, विषमता a lack of proportion. *There is disproportion in the amount of water in these bottles.*

Disprove/डिस्प्रूव *(verb)* – खण्डन करना, किसी बात को असत्य सिद्ध करना prove to be false. *I can disprove her argument.*

Dispute/डिस्प्यूट *(verb)* – कलह करना argue about question whether a statement or alleged fact is true or valid. *China doesn't recognize McMohan Line as a frontier between India and China.*

Disqualify/डिसक्वालिफाइ *(verb)* – अयोग्य ठहराना pronounce ineligible for an office or activity because of an offence or infringement. make unsuitable for an office or activity. *We will disqualify any participant who fails to match up to our standards.*

Disquiet/डिसक्वायट *(verb)* – व्याकुल करना a feeling of anxiety. *Don't disquiet me, please.*

Disregard/डिसरिगार्ड *(nout & verb)* – उपेक्षा करना, किसी बात पर ध्यान नहीं देना pay no attention to; *His attitude reflects total disregard for her welfare.*

Disrelish/डिसरेलिश *(verb)* – अरुचि करना, नफरत करना regard with dislike or distaste. *There is never a time when I disrelish food.*

Disrepute/डिसरिप्यूट *(noun)* – अपयश the state of being discredited. *The fraud he committed has brought him great disrepute.*

Disrespect/डिसरिस्पेक्ट *(noun)* – अनादर, निरादर lack of respect or courtesy. *Showing disrespect to the national flag is an offence.*

Disrobe/डिसरॉब *(verb)* – वस्त्र उतारना, नंगा करना take off one's clothes; undress. *To disrobe at this public place is an offence, police will haul you.*

Disrupt/डिसरप्ट *(verb)* – बाधित करना disturb or interrupt. *Your sloppy behaviour is disrupting the normal proceedings of the day.*

Dissatisfied/डिससैटिस्फाइड *(adjective)* – असंतुष्ट not content or happy. *She is more often than not dissatisfied with her marks.*

Dissatisfy/डिससैटिसफाइ *(verb)* – असन्तुष्ट करना fail to satisfy or give pleasure to. *The poor quality of after-sales service has thoroughly dissatisfied me with the home music system.*

Dissemble/डिसेम्बल *(verb)* – छिपाना hide or disguise one's true motives or feelings. *He is very cunning and always dissembles his ulterior feelings to cheat.*

Disseminate/डिसेमिनेट *(verb)* – छितराना, फैलाना, प्रचार करना spread widely. *Kindly disseminate the following information among all the readers.*

Dissension/डिसेन्सन *(noun)* – विरोध, अनबन, झगड़ा disagreement that leads to discord. *There has been some dissension between the family members.*

Dissent/डिसेन्ट *(verb)* – मतभेद करना, सामान्य धारण से असहमति express disagreement with a prevailing view or official decision. disagree with the doctrine of an established or orthodox church. *There were many dissenting voices over the selection of the chairman.*

Disserve/डिसर्व *(verb)* – हानि पहुँचाना a harmful action. *Your selfish motives and other actions have been disserving this organization.*

Dissimulate/डिसिम्यूलेट *(verb)* – बहाना करना hide or disguise one's thoughts or feelings. *He should be open in his views and not dissimulate true feelings.*

Dissipate/डिसिपेट *(verb)* – नष्ट करना, गायब हो जाना be dispelled or dispersed, or cause to be so. *Unnecessary discussions will only dissipate your energy.*

Dissociate/डिसोसिएट *(verb)* – पृथक् करना disconnect or separate. *The company has dissociated with a few of its clients.*

Dissolve/डिजॉल्व *(verb)* – गलाना, घोलना, पिघलाना, भंग करना become or cause to become incorporated into a liquid so as form a so as to form a solution. *The President dissolved the parliament on the recommendation of the Prime Minister.*

Dissonance/डिसॉनन्स *(noun)* असंगति, बेसुरापन disagreeable sounds. *I dislike such dissonance.*

Distance/डिस्टैंस *(noun)* – अन्तर, दो स्थानों के बीच की दूरी the length of the space between two points. *Distance between Delhi and Mumbai is more than 1400 kilometres.*

Distant/डिस्टैंट *(adjective)* – दूरस्थ, समय या स्थान की दृष्टि से काफी दूर far away in space or time. at a specified distance: *The town lay half a mile distant.* faint or vague because far away. *He is a distant cousin of my friend.*

Distemper/डिस्टेम्पर *(noun)* – पीड़ा, रोग, व्यथा, विकार a viral disease of some animals, especially dogs, causing fever, coughing, and catarrh. *The paint made by mixing the pigment with water and a binder is called distemper. My dog is suffering from a viral infection known as canine distemper.*

Distend/डिस्टेन्ड *(verb)* – अंदरूनी दबाव के कारण फूलना या फुलाना swell or cause to swell because of pressure from inside. *The medical report showed the stomach to be grossly distended with a large food residue.*

Distensible/डिस्टेन्सिब्ल *(adjective)*- फुलाने योग्य capable of being distended; able to stretch and expand. *This bladder is distensible.*

Distinct/डिसटिंक्ट *(adjective)* – पृथक्, अलग तरह का स्पष्ट recognizably different in nature; individual or separate. *The twin brothers are pretty different from one another in nature.*

Distinguish/डिसटिंग्विश *(verb)* – पहचानना, भेद करना, दो वस्तुओं या व्यक्तियों में अंतर पहचानना recognize, show, or treat as different. perceive or point out a difference between. be an identifying characteristic of. *You must learn to distinguish between right and wrong.*

Distort/डिसटोर्ट *(verb)* – शक्ल या आवाज बिगाड़ना pull or twist out of shape. *This photograph has been taken from one corner and presents a distorted picture of the show.*

Distract/डिसट्रैक्ट *(verb)* – किसी व्यक्ति का किसी वस्तु से ध्यान भटकाना prevent from giving their full attention to something. divert from something. *Don't distract your sister from her studies by playing with her.*

Distraught/डिस्ट्राट *(adjective)* – व्याकुल, विक्षिप्त very worried and upset. *She has been very distraught about her family's well-being.*

Distress/डिस्ट्रेस *(noun)* – अत्यधिक पीड़ा और कष्ट extreme anxiety or suffering. *The captain of the ship sent out distress signals upon noticing the approaching hurricane.*

Distribute/डिस्ट्रिब्यूट *(verb)* – वितरण करना, बाँट देना hand or share out to a number of

D

D

recipients. *Kindly distribute these sweets among all children.*

District/डिस्ट्रिक्ट *(noun)* – जिला an area or part of a town or region. *A district is a kind of administrative region.*

Distrust/डिस्ट्रस्ट *(noun & verb)* – अविश्वास lack of trust. *Distrust politicians of all stripes.*

Disuse/डिसयूज *(noun)* – अप्रचार, अनुपयोग, अव्यवहार the state of not being used; neglect. *We have purchased a new toaster and the old one is in complete disuse now.*

Ditch/डिच *(noun)* – खाई, नाला a narrow channel dug to hold or carry water. *They started digging a six feet wide ditch around the building.*

Diuretic/डाइयूरेटिक *(adjective)* – मूत्रवर्धक causing increased passing of urine. *She has been prescribed diuretic medicines by the doctor.*

Diurnal/डाइअर्नल *(adjective)* – दैनिक of or during the daytime. *This trend is diurnal.*

Divagate/डिवगेट *(verb)* – इधर-उधर भटकाना, बहकना [poetic/literary] stray; digress. *Don't divagate from the subject.*

Dive/डाइव *(verb)* – गोता मारना, डुबकी लगाना plunge head first and with arms outstretched into water. *I am learning to dive in a swimming pool.*

Diverse/डायवर्स *(adjective)* – अनेक, विविध widely varied. *There is diverse variety of mugs available in the market.*

Diversion/डायवर्सन *(noun)* – दिशा परिवर्तन an instance of diverting. *The construction of the mall has necessitated diversion of traffic on the roads.*

Divert/डायवर्ट *(verb)* – किसी का दिशा परिवर्तन या मोड़ देना cause to change course or take a different route. *Reading self-help books can divert your mind from silly thoughts.*

Dives/डायवीज़ *(noun)* – रईस मनुष्य rich and luxurious person, [poetic/literary] a typical or hypothetical rich man. *That man seems a dives.*

Divest/डायवेस्ट *(verb)* – वस्त्रहीन करना, वंचित करना deprive or dispossess someone or something of. *Don't divest him of his self-earned assets.*

Dividend/डिविडेन्ड *(noun)* – कंपनी के शेयर धारकों को मिलने वाला लाभांश a sum of money that is divided among a number of people. such as the part of a company's profits paid to its shareholders or the winnings from a football pool. an individual's share of this money. *He has not received his dividend from the company yet.*

Dividing/डिवाडिंग *(verb)* – अलगाव, बाँटना, विभाजित करना separating *MacMohan Line is the dividing line between India and China.*

Divination/डिवाइनेशन *(noun)* – भविष्य कथन, दैविकला, शकुन the practice of divining or seeking knowledge by supernatural means. *To say nothing of the later practice of using divination to determine who was or wasn't a witch. She believes in divination.*

Divine/डिवाइन *(adjective)* – अपूर्व, दैविक, ईश्वरीय of from or like god or a god. devoted to god; sacred. *Only a divine grace can help me pass this examination.*

Divinely/डिवाइनली *(adverb)* – दिव्य रूप से godly, providence. *Some fake people claimed to possess divinely power.*

Divisibility/डिविजिबिलिटी *(noun)* – भाजकत्व quality of being divided *Scientists predict the divisibility of atoms into yet more smaller particles.*

Division/डिविजन *(noun)* – खण्ड, बँटवारा, वितरण the action or process of dividing or being divided. *Division of labour is central to our way of life.*

Divisor/डिवाजर *(noun)* – भाजक mathematic a number by which another number is to be divided. a number that divides into another without a remainder. *In the above question, 5 is the divisor.*

Divorce/डायवोर्स *(noun)* – तलाक the legal dissolution of a marriage. a legal decree dissolving a marriage. *Divorce produces insecurity among children.*

Dizzily/डिजिलि *(adverb)* – चक्कर से आक्रांत होकर in a light-hearted manner *After a few drinks, he was not steady and walked around dizzily.*

Dizzy/डिजि *(adjective)* – जिसे चक्कर आ रहा हो, चक्कर से आक्रांत, बहुत अधिक having a sensation of spinning around and losing one's balance. *She felt dizzy after going on that swing.*

Docile/डोसाइल *(adjective)* – विनीत ready to accept control or instruction; submissive. *She seems to be a very docile girl.*

Docker/डॉकर *(noun)* – गोदी (बंदरगाह) में काम करने वाला मजदूर a person employed in a port to load and unload ships. *We need to employ a docker to speed up loading the materials into the ship.*

Docket/डॉकेट *(noun)* – प्रमाण, दलील, सारांश [British] a document accompanying a consignment of goods that lists its contents, certifies payment of duty, or entitles the holder to delivery. *You should receive proof of purchase in the form of either a delivery docket or receipt from each of the shops you purchase from.*

Doctrinaire/डॉक्ट्रिनेअर *(adjective)* – कल्पना करने वाला मनुष्य, अव्यावहारिक seeking to impose a doctrine without questions or considerations. *Communist parties believe in the principles of doctrinaire. noun a doctrinaire person. He is a new doctrinaire of the party.*

Doctrinal/डॉक्ट्रिनल *(adj.)* – सैद्धान्तिक relating to or involving or preoccupied with doctrine. *They have doctrinal controversy.*

Doctrine/डॉक्ट्रिन *(noun)* – सिद्धान्त, राजनीतिक दल द्वारा प्रतिपादित मत a set of beliefs or principles held and taught by a church, political party, or other group. *Monroe doctrine led to the formation of the League of nations.*

Document/डॉक्युमेंट *(noun)* – दस्तावेज, कागजात a piece of written, printed, or electronic matter that provides information or evidence or that serves as an official record. *All legal documents have been sent to the lawyer.*

Dodder/डॉडर *(noun & verb)* – काँपना, डगमगाते हुए चलना be slow and unsteady. *This machine is a dodder.*

Dodge/डॉज *(verb)* – धोखा देना, बचकर निकलना, किसी से बचने के लिए तेजी से निकल जाना avoid by a sudden quick movement. move quickly to one side or out of the way. cunningly avoid doing or paying. *At the same time they often dodge the big decisions on things they do control.*

Doe/डो *(noun)* – मृगी, हिरणी, मादा खरगोश a female roe or fallow deer or reindeer. *I have seen many does and bucks in the forest.*

Doer/डूअर *(adjective)* – कर्ता करने वाला मनुष्य one who does. *But prove yourselves doers of the word, and not merely hearers who delude themselves.*

Doff/डॉफ़ *(verb)* – उतार कर रख लेना remove an item of clothing, especially a hat. *He doffed off his hat as a mark of respect for Don Bradman.*

Dogma/डॉग्मा *(noun)* – धर्ममत, निर्धारित सिद्धान्त जिन्हें प्रश्न किये बिना स्वीकार करना पड़ता है a principle or set of principles laid down by an authority as incontrovertible. *If necessary, you should discard any dogma and take practical steps to move ahead in life.*

Dogmatic/डॉग्मेटिक *(adj)* – हठधर्मी, हठधर्मिता पर आधारित मत represent as an incontro- vertible truth. *I dislike a dogmatic man.*

Doily/डॉयली *(noun)* – छोटा सुन्दर गमला a small ornamental mat made of lace or paper, put on a plate under sweet food. *We need to buy doily for the house.*

Doings/डूइंग्स *(noun)* – कार्यकलाप the activities in which someone engages. [informal chiefly British] things whose name one has forgotten. *Your doings are not beneficial to the society.*

Doit/डूइट *(noun)* – हालैंड देश का छोटा सिक्का [archaic] a very small amount of money. *His fraud concerned only a doit.*

Dole/डोल *(noun)* – भाग्य destiny [archaic]. *His dole is definitely good .*

Doleful/डोलफुल *(adjective)* – उदास या खिन्न sorrowful. *She looks doleful today.*

Doll/डॉल *(noun)* – गुड़िया, बच्चों का खिलौना a toy, toy in the form of a person. *A doll is a form of human being often used as a plaything for a child.*

Dollar/डॉलर *(noun)* – अमेरिका का सिक्का the basic monetary unit of the US, Canada, Australia, and certain countries in the pacific, Caribbean, SE Asia, Africa, and south America. *Dollar is the most acceptable currency in the world.*

Dolly/डॉली *(adj)* – नादान a child's word for a doll. *Dolly is a small platform with wheels to carry camera on it.*

D

Dolorous/डोलरस *(adjective)* – कष्टकारक, शोकपूर्ण [poetic/literary] feeling great sorrow or distress. *I feel dolorous after failing in my test.*

Dolour/डोलर *(noun)* – कष्ट, शोक, विषाद, क्लेश [poetic/literary] a state of great sorrow or distress *He is in a state of dolour after his break up with his girl friend.*

Dolphin/डॉलफिन *(noun)* – एक प्रकार की समुद्री मछली a small gregarious and intelligent toothed whale with a beak-like snout and a curved fin on the back. *Dolphins are very friendly mammals living in the sea.*

Dolt/डोल्ट *(noun)* – मूर्ख मनुष्य, मंद बुद्धि मनुष्य a stupid person. *Sherry can't take a decision, she is a complete dolt.*

Domain/डोमेन *(noun)* – प्रदेश, कार्यक्रम an area owned or controlled by a ruler or government. a sphere of activity or knowledge. *Spirituality is my domain.*

Dome/डोम *(noun)* – गुम्बद इमारत की गोल छत a rounded vault forming the roof of a building or structure. the revolving openable hemispherical roof of an observatory. *It is claimed that there are 100,000 geodesic domes in use around the world.*

Domestic/डोमेस्टिक *(adjective)* – घरेलू of or relating to a home or family affairs or relation. of or for use in the home. *Quarrels in the family are common domestic issues that need not be taken seriously all the time.*

Domesticate/डोमेस्टिकेट *(verb)* – (पौधों पशुओं आदि को) घरेलू बनाना, पालतू बनाना tame and keep it as a pet or for farm produce. humorous accustom to home life and domestic tasks. *Trying to domesticate wild animals should be prohibited.*

Domesticity/डोमेस्टिसिटी *(noun)* – पारिवारिक अभिरुचि, घरेलू चरित्र home or family life. *Fights are a part of domesticity. Activities characteristically performed at home fall within the purview of domesticity laws.*

Domicile/डोमिसाइल *(noun)* – गृह the country in which a person has permanent residence. [chiefly north American] a person's home. *Domicile is the name of the residence of your permanent home.*

Domiciliary/डोमिसिलियरी *(adjective)* – गृह सम्बन्धी concerned with or occurring in someone's home. *This is their domiciliary matter.*

Dominance/डॉमिनैन्स *(noun)* – प्रधानता, प्रभुत्व power and influence over others. *One should avoid the use of dominance to keep co-workers happy.*

Dominant/डॉमिनैंट *(adjective)* – प्रधान, most important, powerful, or influential. *His birthmark is very dominant on his face.*

Dominate/डॉमिनेट *(verb)* – अधिक सशक्त और प्रभावशाली होना have a commanding or controlling influence over. overlook. *There is no need for me to dominate over my workers.*

Domineer/डोमिनियर *(verb)* – अत्याचार करना behave in an arrogant and overbearing way. *The boss is such a domineering person.*

Dominical/डोमिनिकल *(adjective)* – प्रभु ईसा मसीह का सम्बन्धी of Sunday as the lord's day. *These beliefs are dominical.*

Dominion/डोमिनियन *(noun)* – राज्य, उपनिवेश the territory of a sovereign or government. [historical] a self-governing territory of the [British] commonwealth. *Prior to independence, India was a dominion of Britain.*

Don/डॉन *(verb)* – स्पेन देश की एक उपाधि ग्रहण करना, पहनना put on an item of clothing. *He donned a three-piece suit for the party.*

Donate/डोनेट *(verb)* – उपहार देना give for a good cause. *Please donate blood, it may save lives.*

Donation/डोनेशन *(noun)* – दान something that is given to a charity, especially a sum of money. *I would like to give my old clothes in a donation drive.*

Donative/डोनेटिव *(noun)* – उपहार रीति से प्राप्त, दान, उपहार given as a donation. [historical] given directly, not presentative. *This money has been exclusively earmarked for donative purposes.*

Done/डन *p.p. of do* – किया गया, समाप्त, पूर्ण cooked thoroughly. (used about food). *I have not done my homework.*

Donee/डोनी *(noun)* – जिस व्यक्ति को दान दिया जाता है a person who receives a gift. [law] a person who is given a power of appointment. *He is the donee of this gift.*

Donkey/डन्की *(noun)* – गधा a domesticated hoofed mammal of the horse family with long ears and a braying call, used as a beast of burden. *Donkeys are useful animal.*

Donor/डोनर *(noun)* – दाता a person who donates something. *He is a very gentle donor.*

Don't/डॉन्ट – डूनॉट का संक्षिप्त रूप contraction do not. *Don't mess with the beauty products kept on the dressing table.*

Doodle/डूडल *(verb)* – यूँ ही बिना ध्यान दिये रेखाएँ खींचना या चित्र बनाना to drawlines without thinking. *Don't doodle on the classroom walls.*

Doom/डूम *(noun)* – विनाश, कयामत death, destruction, or another terrible fate. [archaic] the last judgement. *The strict invigilation during examination spelled doom for many students..*

Doomsday/डूम्सडे *(noun)* – प्रलय का दिन the last day of the world's existence. the day of the last judgement. *They said 21st December 2012 would be doomsday for all living creatures on Earth.*

Door/डोर *(noun)* – कपाट, दरवाजा a hinged, sliding, or revolving barrier at the entrance to a building, room or vehicle, or in the framework of a cupboard. used to refer to a house: he lived two doors away. *The door handle of my drawing room is broken.*

Dope/डोप *(noun)* – (गैर कानूनी) मादक द्रव्य हेरोइन एक दवा जो एथलिट की सामर्थ्य बढ़ा देती है [informal] an illegal drug, especially cannabis or heroin. a drug used to enhance the performance of an athlete, racehorse, or greyhound. *There will be dope-test of all athletes.*

Doric/डोरिक *(adjective)* – देहाती यूनानी नगर डोरिस relating to or denoting a classical order of architecture characterized by a plain, sturdy column and a thick square abacus resting on a rounded moulding. *Doric was the popular dialect of ancient Greek.*

Dormant/डॉरमैंट *(adjective)* – कुछ समय के लिए निष्क्रिय not active for some time. *The voleanoes are dormant now-a-days.*

Dorsal/डोरसल *(adjective)* – पृष्ठीय, किसी पशु या मछली की पीठ anatomy of, on or relating to the upper side or back. compare with ventral. *Dorsal horn sensitisation reduces in line with tissue healing*

Dorsum/डोरसम *(noun)* – पीठ anatomy & zoology the dorsal part of an organism or structure. *Dorsum is the back side of the humans or the upper part of animals.*

Dose/डोज *(noun)* – दवा की खुराक a quantity of a medicine or radiation. time. an amount of ionizing radiation received or absorbed at one time. *Please consume the medicine according to the dose prescribed.*

Dot/डॉट *(noun)* – बिन्दु [archaic] a dowry from which only the interest or annual income was available to the husband. *All that the parents gave on their daughter's wedding was a dot.*

Dotage/डॉटेज *(noun)* – अत्यन्त अनुराग, सठियापा the period of life in which a person is old and weak. *Dotage means the slowing down of mental faculties of a person.*

Dotard/डोटार्ड *(noun)* – अतिवृद्ध an old person, especially one who is weak or senile. *He has very old, weak and dotard and has to depend on others for even small things.*

Dote/डोट *(verb)* – मूर्ख होना, स्नेह में डूबना be extremely and uncritically fond of. *He dotes on his daughter and believes she can do no wrong.*

Double/डबल *(adjective)* – दोहरा consisting of two equal, identical, or similar parts or things. designed to be used by two people. having two different roles or interpretations. having the same number of pips on each half. *The company has made double the profit compared to last year.*

Doubt/डाउट *(verb)* – सन्देह, अनिश्चय feel uncertain about. question the truth or fact of. disbelieve. *Please have no doubt about the instructions given.*

Douceur/डूसर् *(noun)* – नजराना a bribe. *He offered me douceur.*

Dough/डफ *(noun)* – गूँथा हुआ गीला आटा a thick, malleable mixture of flour and liquid, for baking into bread or pastry. *We need some dough for dinner tonight. Rotis were made out of soya dough.*

Doughty/डाउटी *(adjective)* – शूरवीर, हिम्मती, साहसी [archaic] or humorous brave and resolute. *He is a doughty person.*

Dove/डव *(noun)* – कबूतर a stocky seed- or fruit-eating bird with a small head, short legs, and a cooing voice, similar to but generally smaller and more delicate Than a pigeon. *Many doves were seen flying around this area last year.*

D

D

Dowager/डाउअजर् (noun) – मरे हुए व्यक्ति की संम्पति पाने वाली विधवा a widow with a title or property derived from her late husband. *I feel sorry for the dowager.*

Dowdily/डाउडिली (adv) – गंदे ढंग से in a dowdy fashionable manner. *She behaved dowdily in the party.*

Dowdy/डाउडि (adjective) – गंदा, भद्दा, फूहड़ unfashionable and dull in appearance. *The dress she wore at the party looked very dowdy.*

Down/डाउन (adv) – कछार, नीचे at a lower level or place. *Don't go down in the valley.*

Downfall/डाउनफॉल (noun) – नाश a loss of power, prosperity, or status. *They had a terrible downfall in business.*

Downpour/डाउनपोर् (noun) – मूसलाधार वर्षा a heavy fall of rain. *The city has been experiencing heavy downpour since morning.*

Downright/डाउनराइट (adjective) – पूर्णतया, पूरी तरह utter; complete: it's a downright disgrace. *The rejection of application was a downright disgrace to the family.*

Downstairs/डाउनस्टेअर्स (adjective) – सीढ़ी के नीचे पीड़ित, शोषित on or to a lower floor. *Please go downstairs and meet your friend.*

Down-trodden/डाउन-ट्रॉडेन (adjective) – पैर से कुचला हुआ oppressed or treated badly by people in power. *(Recent government steps are addressing the concerns of the down-trodden.*

Downward/डाउनवार्ड (adjective) – नीचे की ओर जाने वाला moving or leading towards or lower point or level. *The spacecraft descended downwards and splashed into the sea.*

Dowry/डाउरी (noun) – दहेज property or money brought by a bride to her husband on their marriage. *Asking for dowry is an offence in the eyes of the law.*

Doze/डोज (verb) – झपकी लेना sleep lightly. *She dozed off after immediately lunch. (noun)* a short light sleep. *I would like to have a doze after this tiring day.*

Dozen/डजन – दर्जन, बारह *(noun)* a group or set of twelve. *I went to buy a dozen of bananas from the grocery store.*

Dozer/डोजर (noun) – पिनक लेने वाला [informal] short for Bulldozer. *A dozer is an earth moving equipment to level the surface.*

Drab/ड्रैब (noun) – वेश्या a slovenly women. *Don't call any woman a drab.*

Drachm/ड्रैच्म (noun) – छोटा परिणाम [historical] a unite of weight equivalent to 60 grains or one eighth of an ounce. a liquid measure equivalent to 60 minims or one eighth of a fluid ounce. *We'll need 5 drachms of water for this homeopathic medicine.*

Draff/ड्राफ (noun) – खुद dregs or refuse. *It is draff of malt after brewing.*

Draft/ड्राफ्ट (noun) – प्रारूप, मसौदा a preliminary version of a piece of writing. a plan or sketch. *Every person above 18 is compulsorily drafted into the Israeli army.*

Draftsman/ड्राफ्ट्समैन (noun) – मसविदा बनाने वाला a person who drafts legal documents. *We urgently require the services of a draftsman in the office.*

Draggle/ड्रैगल (verb) – गन्दा करना make dirty or wet. hang untidily. *Don't draggle the clothes.*

Dragnet/ड्रैग्नेट (noun) – मछली फँसाने का जाल, महाजाल a net drawn through water or across ground to trap fish or game. *The police used a dragnet to catch the criminals.*

Dragon/ड्रैगन (noun) – अजगर, अग्ग उगलने वाला दैत्य a mythical monster like a giant reptile, typically with wings and claws and able to breathe out fire. used in names of various lizards. *A dragon is a ferocious looking mythical reptile.*

Dragoon/ड्रगुन (noun) – घुड़सवार, सिपाही a member of any of several [British] cavalry regiments. a mounted infantryman armed with a carbine. *The word dragoon originally meant infantry soldiers trained in the horse-riding.*

Drain/ड्रेन (verb) – मोरी, पानी निकलने से सूखा कर देना cause the water or other liquid in to run out, leaving it empty or dry. run off or out. carry off the superfluous water from an area. become dry as liquid runs off. drink the entire contents of. *The drains of this area are overflowing.*

Drake/ड्रेक (noun) – नर हंस a male duck. *Chinese restaurants prepare a variety of drake delicacies.*

Dram/ड्रैम (noun) – घूँट, छोटा परिमाण, ड्राम शब्द का छोटा रूप the basic monetary unit of Armenia, equal to 100 luma. *Dram is the currency of Armenia.*

Drama/ड्रामा *(noun)* – अभिनय a play. plays as a genre or literary style. *We have planned to enact three more dramas at this theatre this week. Let's not cause any more drama in this house.*

Drank/ड्रैंक – पीआ *past* of drink. *Socrates drank the cup of poison as soon as it was offered.*

Drape/ड्रेप *(verb)* – टाँकना arrange loosely on or round something. adorn or wrap loosely with folds of cloth. *She went to Rekha's house and taught her how to drape a sari properly.*

Draper/ड्रेपर *(noun)* – बजाज a person who sells textile fabrics. *We need to go to a draper to buy curtains for our house.*

Drapery/ड्रेपरी *(noun)* – बजाज का व्यवसाय cloth, curtains, or clothing hanging in loose folds. *The drapery set in this house is impeccably attractive.*

Drastic/ड्रैस्टिक *(adjective)* – तीव्र, अत्यधिक और भरपूर असरदार having a strong or far-reaching effect. *There has been a drastic change in her after the counselling.*

Draughtsman/ड्राफ्ट्समैन *(noun)* – चित्र बनाने वाला a person who makes detailed technical plans or drawings. an artist skilled in drawing. *We need to consult a draughtsman for the designs.*

Draughty/ड्राटी *(adjective)* – वायु के झोंके से पूर्ण cold and uncomfortable because of draughts of air. *The weather has become very cold and draughty for anyone to venture out.*

Drawback/ड्राबैक *(noun)* – कमी, असुविधा a disadvantage or problem. *His short height is a definite drawback in the basketball court.*

Drawee/ड्रावी *(noun)* – अदाकर्ता, हुण्डी की रकम लेने वाला the person or organization who has to pay a draft or bill. *He is the drawee of this bill.*

Drawer/ड्रावर *(noun)* – निकालने वाला आहर्ता a lidless box-like storage compartment made to slid horizontally in and out of a desk or chest. *I need a drawer to keep my belongings. He is the drawer of this cheque.*

Drawl/ड्रॉल *(verb)* – धीरे-धीरे बोलना, मंद उच्चारण लम्बी स्वर धमनियों में मंद-मंद बोलने की शैली speak in a slow, lazy way with prolonged vowel sounds. *Arun got irritated because his brother was drawling.*

Drawn/ड्रान *(adjective)* – दोनों पक्ष में समान, बराबरी, अनिर्णित looking strained from illness or exhaustion: *Cathy was pale and drawn.*

Dread/ड्रेड *(verb)* – भय anticipate with great apprehension or fear. *I dread the prospect of receiving thousands of emails.*

Dreadnought/ड्रेडनॉट *(noun)* – किसी से न डरने वाला व्यक्ति, एक प्रकार की लड़ाई का जहाज [historical] a type of battleship of the early 20th century, equipped entirely with large-caliber guns. *In 1857, the dreadnought was replaced with a larger hulk, HMS Caledonia (renamed dreadnought) which had 120 guns.*

Dream/ड्रीम *(noun)* – सपना या स्वप्न a series of thoughts, images, and sensations occurring in a person's mind during sleep, a state of mind in which someone is not fully aware of their surroundings. *He walked around in a dream.*

Drear/ड्रिअर *(adjective)* – मन्द उदास [poetic] dreary. *Drear days in winter when there is no transport of any kind for going to Laddakh.*

Dregs/ड्रेग्स *(noun)* – तलछट, डिब्बे में रखे गये द्रव पदार्थ की अंतिम बूँद जिसमें कूड़ा होता है the remnants of a liquid left in a container, together with any sediment. *Criminals are the dregs of society.*

Drench/ड्रेन्च *(verb)* – गीला करना wet thoroughly; soak. cover liberally with something: a sundrenched clearing. *We got drenched in the rain because we didn't have an umbrella.*

Dress/ड्रेस *(noun)* – स्त्री के कंधों से घुटने तक की पोशाक put on one's cloths. put clothes on someone. wear clothes in a particular way or of a particular type: *The way she dresses is very appropriate for a formal occasion.* dress in smart or formal clothes, or in a special costume. *The Anarkali dress is very popular among girls and women these days.*

Drew/ड्रियू *(verb)* – खींचा to draw past of draw. *She drew the window shade to prevent strong sun rays peeping into the room.*

Drib/ड्रिब *(noun)* – रिसाव, द्रव पदार्थ का बूँद-बूँद कर टपकना a very small amount. *A drib is a fine mist of water evaporating before it hits the ground.*

Dribble/ड्रिबल *(verb)* – चूना fall slowly in drops or a thin stream. allow saliva to run from the mouth. *She dribbles the basketball very well.*

Drily/ड्राइलि *(adverb)* – सूखे ढंग से in a matter-of-fact or ironically humorous way. *He commented drily on the text of my assignment.*

Drinker/ड्रिंकर *(noun)* – पियक्कड़ a person who drinks. *A drinker destroys his own health and family.*

Drinking/ड्रिंकिंग *(noun)* – मदिरा-पान a practice to drink wine. *He took to drinking as a way of forgetting hard blows suffered in everyday life.*

Drip/ड्रिप *(verb)* – रिसना, द्रव का बूँद-बूँद टपकना let fall small drops of liquid. fall in small drops. *You should put a bucket underneath to catch any stray drips.*

Drivel/ड्राइवल *(noun)* – निरर्थक बात nonsense. *Many journalists lap up any marketing drivel for want of something more interesting to write about.*

Driver/ड्राइवर *(noun)* – गाड़ी हाँकने वाला चालक a person or thing that drives something. *My chauffeur drives the car very slowly.*

Driving/ड्राइविंग *(adjective)* – वाहन चलने का कार्य having a strong and controlling influence: she was the driving force behind the plan. *Teachers are the driving force behind the success of their students.*

Drizzle/ड्रिज्जल *(noun)* – बूँदी-बाँदी होना, फूही पड़ना, वर्षा की फुहार light rain falling in very fine drops. *Drizzle didn't allow my cloths to dry out.*

Droit/ड्रायट *(noun)* – वैध अधिकार, सही a legal right. The history textbook has a chapter on droits. *France was the first country to introduce droit de suite in 1920.*

Droll/ड्रॉल *(adjective)* – विचित्र amusingly odd in a strange way. *He is a droll with a quiet tongue-in-cheek kind of humour.*

Droop/ड्रूप *(verb)* – लटकना bend or hang downwards limply. sag down from weariness or dejection. *The clothesline was drooping significantly after the clothes were hung for drying in the sun.*

Drop-scene/ड्राप-सीन *(noun)* – रंगभूमि का अगला पर्दा a drop curtain used as part of stage scenery. *A drop-scene is often used in the background in plays to eliminate need of actual erection of such costly scenes.*

Dropsy/ड्राप्सी *(noun)* – जलोदर a tip or bribe. *He offered me a dropsy to do his job.*

Dross/ड्रास *(noun)* – तलछट, मण्डूर scum on the surface of molten metal. *The speech the chairman delivered at the farewell was rubbish and totally dross.*

Drought/ड्राॅट *(noun)* – प्यास, अनावृष्टि a prolonged period of abnormally low rainfall; a shortage of water. thirst. *Gujarat is facing heavy drought this year.*

Drove/ड्रोव – झुण्ड past tense of drive. *We drove past your house last night.*

Drown/ड्राॅउन *(verb)* – डुबाकर मारना, डूबना die or kill through submersion in water. *Michael drowned in the swimming pool.*

Drowner/ड्राॅउनर *(noun)* – डुबाने वाला the person who drowns or the thing which drowns. *Heavy load on the boat acted as a drowner into the river.*

Drowse/ड्राउज *(noun)* – मन्द होना, झपकी लेना an instance of drowsing. a state of drowsiness. *Don't drowse in class while the teacher is teaching.*

Drowsy/ड्राउजी *(adjective)* – आलसी, नींद से भरा हुआ sleepy and lethargic. *I was feeling incredibly drowsy after a long day at work.*

Drub/ड्रब *(verb)* – बेंत से मारना पीटना beat up, defeat, hit or beat repeatedly. *He incessantly drubbed into the pole.*

Drudge/ड्रज *(verb)* – दासवृत्ति करने वाला मनुष्य, परिश्रम से काम do such work. *John was made to drudge at his previous job.*

Drug/ड्रग *(noun)* – दवा या औषधि a medicine or other substance which has a marked physiological effect when taken into the body. a substance with narcotic or stimulant effects. *The study of drugs results in formulation of medicines.*

Druid/ड्रुइड *(noun)* – इंग्लैंड की प्राचीन जाति का पुरोहित a priest, magician, or soothsayer in the ancient Celtic religion. a member of a present-day group claiming to be derived from this religion. *There lives a very famous druid near my house.*

Drunk/ड्रंक *(verb)* – शराब पिये हुए past participle of drink. affected by alcohol to the extent of losing control of one's faculties or behaviour. *Heavy drinking or getting drunk can damage your nerves.*

Dryad/ड्राइएड *(noun)* – जंगल की परी a nymph inhabiting a tree or wood. *Dryad was a nymph that lived on a tree according to Greek mythology.*

Dual/ड्अल *(adj)* – द्विवचन, दोनों, दोहरा a dual inflection. *America has agreed to supply technology that has dual-use.*

Dubiety/ड्यूबिटी *(noun)* – संदिग्धता, संदेह की भावना uncertainty. *I have dubiety on how this machine will function.*

Dubious/ड्यूबिअस *(adjective)* – अस्पष्ट सन्दिग्ध hesitating or doubting. *He is a very dubious man.*

Dubitation/ड्यूबिटेशन *(noun)* – सन्देह doubt; hesitation. *Please do not have any dubitation in your mind.*

Duchess/डचेस *(noun)* – ड्यूक की सुहागिन the wife or widow of a duke. a woman holding a rank equivalent to duke in her own right. *She is the duchess of Norfolk in England.*

Duck/डक *(noun)* – बत्तख a bird, a batsman's score of nought. *A duck is a bird that loves swimming. Sachin returned to the pavilion out on duck.*

Ducker/डकर *(noun)* – गोता लगाने वाला another name of duck *Ducker is a relatively small waterfowl with a flat bill, short neck and legs, and webbed feet.*

Ducking/डकिंग *(noun)* – गोता submersion, immersion. *The act of plumging into water is called.*

Duckling/डकलिंग *(noun)* – छोटा बत्तख a young duck. *We saw a duckling at the pond today.*

Ductile/डक्टाइल *(adjective)* – कोमल, नमनीय, तार खींचने योग्य able to be drawn out into a thin wire. *This connection requires the use of ductile wires.*

Ductility/डकटिलिटी *(noun)* – लचीलापन, मान लेने वाला the quality of being flexible *Not every flexible material has the property of ductility.*

Dud/डड *(noun)* – व्यर्थ, बेकार a thing that fails to work properly. an ineffectual person. *He is a complete dud, you can't really expect him to do a good job.*

Dude/ड्यूड *(noun)* – छैला, दोस्त a man. *He is quite popular among girls as a dude.*

Dudgeon/डज्-जन *(noun)* – क्रोध, रोष deep resentment. *The manager walked out in deep dudgeon.*

Duet/ड्एट *(noun)* – दो आदमियों को मिलकर गाने का गीत a performance by two singers, instrumentalists, or dancers. a musical composition for two performers. *A duet is a song sung by two singers.*

Duff/डफ *(noun)* – गूँथा हुआ आटा dough, a flour pudding boiled or steamed in a cloth bag. *We were asked to prepare a duff of the vegetables.*

Dug/डग *(verb)* – खोदा past and past participle of dig. *They dug into the history of the school.*

Dulcet/डल्सेट *(adjective)* – मीठा, आनंदकर sweet and soothing. *Shanon can comfort anyone for her behaviour is very dulcet.*

Dull/डल *(adjective)* – मन्द, जड़ lacking interest or excitement. *All work and no play may make you a dull person.*

Duly/ड्यूलि *(adverb)* – यथायोग्य, विधिवत in accordance with what is required or appropriate. as might be expected. *Please accept your payment duly sanctioned by the chief manager.*

Dumb/डम् *(adjective)* – गूँगा unable to speak, normally because of congenital deafness. unable to speak as a natural sate. temporally unable or unwilling to speak. *She was so dumb, she screwed her makeup.*

Dummy/डमी *(noun)* – मूढ़मति, नकली, कृत्रिम a model or replica of a human being. an object designed to resemble and serve as a substitute for the real one. [British] a rubber or plastic teat for a baby to suck on. *Dummy objects are used by military during firing practices.*

Dump/डम्प *(noun)* – उदासीनता *(verb)* फेंकना, अवांछित वस्तु से पिंड छुड़ाना a site for depositing rubbish or waste. a heap of rubbish left at a dump. [informal] an unpleasant or dreary place. *This is a dumping yard for biodegradable waste.*

Dumps/डम्प्स *(plural noun)* – उदासी, उदासीनता [informal] depressed or unhappy. *My life is not progressing, it is totally in the dumps.*

Dumpy/डम्पी *(adjective)* – नाटा-मोटा, थुलथुल short and stout. *Sherry is often called dumpy because of her looks.*

Dunce/डन्स *(noun)* – मूर्ख मनुष्य a person who is slow at learning. *People call Steve as dunce because he is slow to learn things.*

Dunderhead/डन्डरहेड *(noun)* – मूर्ख [informal] a stupid person. *He didn't know the table manners and was acting like a dunderhead at the dining table.*

Dune/ड्यून *(noun)* – किनारे पर बालू का टीला a mound or ridge of sand or other loose sediment formed by the wind, especially on the sea coast or in a desert. *During summers, the desert is covered with sand dunes.*

Dung/डंग *(noun & verb)* – खाद, गोबर, लीद defecate. *Cow dung is used as manure by farmers.*

Dungeon/डन्जन् *(noun)* – कालकोठरी a strong underground prison cell, especially in a castle. *It is difficult to live in that window-less poor-lit dungeon.*

Duodenum/ड्यूडेनम *(noun)* – पक्वाशय, छोटी आँत का पहला भाग the first part of the small intestine immediatelybeyond the stomach. *The doctors said that there was an infection in his duodenum.*

Dupe/ड्यूप *(noun)* – बेवकूफ बनाना *With his smooth talks he has deceived many gullible persons.*

Duplex/ड्यूप्लेक्स *(noun)* – फ्लैट या मकान जिसके दोनों मंजिलों पर कमरे सीढ़ियों द्वारा जुड़े हों [north American] a residential building divided into two apartments. *Jenny's living room is on the ground floor and bed room on the first floor in his duplex house.*

Duplicate/डुप्लिकेट *(adjective)* – नकल exactly like something else. *The stunt was played by the duplicate of Amitabh Bachchan.*

Duplicity/डुप्लिसिटी *(noun)* – कपट, छल deceitfulness. *Duplicity of documents is an offence. Duplicity is a deliberate deceptiveness in behaviour or speech.*

Duramater/डुरामैटर *(noun)* – मस्तिष्क की बाहरी झिल्ली anatomy the tough outer most membrane enveloping the brain and spinal cord. *He hurt his duramater in the accident.*

During/ड्युरिंग *(preposition)* – बीच में, के दौरान throughout the course or duration of. at a particular point in the course of. *There was a bomb explosion during the ceremony.*

Dust/डस्ट *(noun)* – धूल, मिट्टी fine, dry powder consisting of tiny particles of earth or waste matter. any material in the form of tiny particles: coal dust. [poetic] a dead person's remains. *Dust particles are a major contributor in the atmospheric pollution.*

Duster/डस्टर *(noun)* – झाड़न one that dusts *The teacher uses a duster.*

Dusty/डस्टी *(adjective)* – धूल धूसरित covered with or resembling dust. *The bed sheet is very dusty and needs washing.*

Dutch/डच *(noun)* – हालैंड की भाषा तथा वहाँ के निवासी the people of Holland. *Dutch culinary is very popular in Germany.*

Duteous/ड्यूटिअस *(adjective)* – भक्त [archaic] dutiful. *Cadbury has been a very duteous servant*

Dutiable/ड्यूटिएबल *(adjective)* – चुंगी लगने योग्य subject to import duty *All dutiable goods need to be cleared from customs department.*

Dux/डक्स *(noun)* – कक्षा में सबसे प्रथम बालक chiefly Scottish the top pupil in a school or class. *Ron is the dux of his class.*

Dwindle/ड्विन्डल *(verb)* – दुर्बल होना, क्रमिक रूप से क्षीण होते जाना diminish gradually. *The air plane dwindled in the sky.*

Dye/डाइ *(noun)* – वर्ण, रंग a natural or synthetic substance used to colour something. *Synthetic dyes are not good from environment's point of view.*

Dynamic/डिनेमिक *(adjective)* – ऊर्जा तथा नाना प्रकार के विचारों से पूर्ण शक्तिमान characterized by constant change or activity. full or energy and new ideas. *Only dynamic people go very far in life.*

Dynastic/डाइनैस्टिक *(adj)* – राजवंश-सम्बन्धी belonging to a line of kings, the branch of mechanics concerned with the motion of bodies under the action of forces. compare with kinematics statics. *He asked me to* correct the dynastics of the song. *Dynastics are the forces that stimulate development inside a process.*

Dynasty/डाइनैस्टी *(noun)* – राजवंश, वंश परंपरा a line of hereditary rulers. a succession of powerful or prominent people from the same family. *The Mughal Dynasty was very autocratic in character.*

Dysentric/डिसेन्ट्रिक *(adjective)* – आमतिसार-सम्बन्धी pertaining to dysentery (intestinal disease). *Doctors describe a person as dysenteric if he is suffering from inflammatory disorder of the lower intestine.*

Dyspepsia/डिस्पेपशिया *(noun)* – मन्दाग्नि indigestion. *The cause of most cases of functional dyspepsia is not known.*

Dysphagia/डिस्फेशिया *(noun)* – निगलने में कठिनाई medicine difficulty in swallowing, as a symptom of disease. *Any condition that weakens or damages the muscles and nerves used for swallowing may cause dysphagia.*

Dysphonia/डायफोनिया *(noun)* – मुख से शब्द निकलने में कष्ट difficulty in speaking due to a physical disorder of the mouth, tongue, throat, or vocal cords. *Spasmodic dysphonia may follow an infection of the respiratory tract, injury to the larynx or a period of excess voice use.*

Dysponea/डायसपोनिया *(noun)* – श्वासकृच्छ medicine laboured breathing. *Dysponea is a disease associated with pulmonary problems that includes both obstructive and restrictive lung disease and difficulty in breathing.*

Dysuria/डायसुरिया *(noun)* – मूत्रकृच्छ, मूत्र त्याग करने में कष्ट medicine painful or difficult urination. *In medicine, specifically urology, dysuria refers to pain in urination.*

D

Ee

E/इ *(noun)* – अंग्रेजी वर्णमाला का पाँचवाँ वर्ण the fifth letter of the English alphabet.
1. Denoting the fifth in a set.
2. Music the third note of the diatonic scale of C major. *It is the fifth letter in alphabet.*

Each/ईच *(adj)*– एक-एक, पृथक्-पृथक् every one of two or more people or things, regarded and identified separately. *Each battery has been kept in a separate room. They each have their own outlook.*

Eager/ईगर *(adjective)* – आतुर, उत्सुक strongly wanting to do or have. keenly expectant or interested. *I was so very eager to see the first show of the newly released film.*

Eagle/ईगल *(noun)* – गरुड़, बाज a large bird of prey with a massive hooked bill and long broad wings, renowned for its keen sight and powerful soaring flight. *I once had a chance to see an eagle a bird of prey. It had powerful wings and a big hooked beak.*

Eaglet/ईग्लेट *(noun)* – बाज का बच्चा a young eagle. *The eaglet is learning to fly.*

Ean/ईन – बच्चा जनना to yean, *suffix* forming adjectives and nouns such as antipodean. *Many Europeans come to visit India.*

Ear/इअर *(noun)* – कान the organ of hearing and balance in humans and other vertebrates, especially the external part of this. an organ sensitive to sound. *His ear drum had been perforated. So he went to an ear specialist for surgery.*

Earache/इअरऍक् *(noun)* – कान का दर्द pain inside the ear. *I have found earache to be one of the worst aches.*

Earl/अर्ल *(noun)* – इंग्लैण्ड के सरदारों की एक पदवी a British nobleman ranking above a viscount and below a marques. *Earl is a high ranking British nobleman.*

Earliness/अर्लीनेस *(noun)* – जल्दी Quality of coming early or earlier in time. *He is an early bird and always reaches any place the earliest.*

Early/अर्ली *(adjective)* – प्रातःकाल किसी कालावधि, कार्य आदि में जल्दी (पैसा) कमाना before the usual or expected time. *We ate an early dinner.*

Earn/अर्न *(verb)* – प्राप्त करना obtain in return for about or services. gain as interest or profit. gain as the reward for hard work or merit. *He has earned a lot of fame and money at such an early age.*

Earnest/अर्नेस्ट *(adjective)* – उत्सुक, गम्भीर या दृढ़ निश्चय वाला intensely serious. *He is an earnest police officer, never heard a complaint against him. He has been awarded for bravery as well.*

Earth/अर्थ *(noun)* – पृथ्वी the planet on which we live, the third planet of the solar system in order of distance from the sun. *The earth shook as the earthquake came.*

Earthen/अर्थेन *(adjective)* – मिट्टी का बना हुआ made of compressed earth. *I bought an earthen pot at a high price because it looked like a relic to me.*

Earthling/अर्थलिंग *(noun)* – मर्त्य a wood used by aliens to describe inhabitant of the earth. *This was perfectly normal earthling behaviour.*

Earthly/अर्थलि *(adjective)* – सांसारिक, पार्थिव of or relating to the earth or human life on the earth. material; worldly. *Human life on earth is millions of years old.*

Earthquake/अर्थक्वेक *(noun)* – भूकंप, भूचाल a sudden violent shaking of the ground as a result of movements within the earth's crust. *Suddenly the earth began to tremble and many houses collapsed. It was a severe earthquake.*

Earthwards – *(adverb)* towards the earth. *The spacecraft moved earthwards at the speed of 10,000 kmph.*

Earthworks/अर्थवर्क्स *(noun)* – नींव, खुदाई, मिट्टी का बाँध a large artificial bank of soil, especially one made as a defence in ancient times. *Earthworks used to be there in ancient times.*

Earthworm/अर्थवर्म *(noun)* – केंचुआ a burrowing annelid worm that lives in the soil. *A lot of earthworms can be seen during the rainy season.*

Earthy/अर्थी *(adjective)* – संसारिक, पार्थिव, स्वाभाविक resembling or suggestive of soil. *His approach to every problem is very earthy.*

Ease/ईज *(verb)* – सुख make or become less serious or severe. facilitate. *He does everything with great ease and grace.*

Easement/ईजमेंट *(noun)* – परभूमावधिकार, हकशफा का कानून law a right to cross or otherwise use another's land for a specified purpose. *He leads a life of easement.*

Easeful/ईजफुल *(adj)* – शान्त, आरामतलब, आरामदेह providing comfort. *Life was easeful at that time.*

Easiness/ईजीनस *(noun)* – आसानी, सरलता a feeling of refreshing tranquillity and an absence of tension or worry.

East/ईस्ट *(adj)* – पूरब situated in or facing or moving toward the east. *The sun rises in the east.*

Easter/ईस्टर *(noun)* – मार्च या अप्रैल के किसी रविवार को आने वाला पर्व जिसमें ईसाई लोग ईसा का पुनरुत्थान मनाते हैं a festival on a sunday in March or April when Christians celebrate Christendom to life. *Are you going away at easter?*

Easterly/ईस्टरली *(adj)* – पूर्व दिशा में towards or in the east. *They travelled in an easterly direction.*

Eastern/ईस्टर्न *(adj)* – पूर्वी in or from the east of a place. *Connected with the countries of the east.*

Eastward/ईस्टवार्ड *(adj)* – पूर्व दिशा की ओर toward the east. *The Ganga flows eastwards.*

Easy/ईजी *(adj)* – सुगम, सहज not difficult. *The maths is not easy.*

Eat/ईट *(verb)* – भोजन करना to put food into your mouth then bite or swallow. *Eat your dinner.*

Eatable/ईटेबुल *(adj)* – खाद्य पदार्थ article of food that can be used as food. *Wheat is an eatable.*

Eater/ईटर *(noun)* – किसी विशेष तरीके से खाने वाला a person who eats in a particular way. *Tiger is a big eater.*

Eating-house/ईटिंग हाउस *(noun)* – भोजनालय a building where people go to eat. *I had gone to an eating house.*

Eaves/ईब्स *(noun)* – ओरी the edge of a roof that stick out over the wall. *Naresh is an eavesdropper.*

Ebb/ईब *(verb)* – समुद्र जल का उतरना to flow away from the land. *The crowd enthusiasm began to ebb.*

Ebullience/अब्यूलिएन्स *(noun)* – प्रफुल्लित, उत्साहित, उफान, उबाऊ overflowing with eager enjoyment or approval. *There is an ebullience in the public.*

Eclectic/इक्लेक्टिक *(adj)* – चुनने वाला selecting what seems best of various styles or ideas. *He is an eclectic man.*

Economist/इकॉनॉमिस्ट *(noun)* – अर्थशास्त्री a person who studies or is an expert in economics. *He is an economist of the present times.*

Ecstasy/एक्सटेसी *(noun)* – अति आनन्द की भावना to be in ecstasy. a feeling or state or great happiness. *I feel ecstasy today.*

Ecstatic/एक्सटैटिक *(adj)* – अति प्रसन्न extremely happy. *You seem in ecstatic mood today.*

Eczema/एक्जिमा *(noun)* – खाज, खुजली एक प्रकार का चर्मरोग a disease which makes your skin red and dry so that you want to scratch it. *Eczema is a skin disease.*

Edacious/एडेशस *(adj)* – पेटू devouring or craving food in great quantities. *The beggar seems to be an edacious man.*

Edacity/इडेसिटि *(noun)* – अत्यधिक लालच excessive desire to eat. *I have edacity for tasty dishes.*

Eddy/एड्डी *(noun)* – भँवर a circular movement of water wind dust etc. *I saw an eddy in Ganga.*

Eden/ईडन *(noun)* – देवलोक any place of complete bliss and delight and peace. *The garaden of Adam and Eve is called Eden.*

Edge/एज *(noun)* – किनारा, चाकू आदि की धार the outside limit of an object, area, or surface.

E

an area next to a steep drop. *He sat on the edge of the rock.*

Edible/एडिबल *(noun)* – खाने योग्य items of food. *Don't worry, this fruit is edible.*

Edict/इडिक्ट *(noun)* – राजा की घोषणा, फरमान an official order or proclamation. *The edicts of Ashoka are famous all over the world.*

Edification/एडिफिकेशन *(noun)* – मानसिक उन्नति instruction for improvement. *A video was made for edification of fresh trainees.*

Edifice/एडिफिस *(noun)* – महल, भव्य भवन, बड़ी शानदार इमारत a building, especially a large, imposing one. *In early times, kings made a lot of edifices.*

Edition/एडिशन *(noun)* – प्रकाशन, पुस्तक का प्रकाशित रूप, संस्करण a particular form or version of a published text. the total number of copies of a book, newspaper, etc. issued at one time. a particular version or instance of a regular programme or broadcast. *This is the latest edition of the book.*

Editor/एडिटर *(noun)* – किसी पत्र का सम्पादक a person who is in charge of a newspaper, magazine, or multi-author book. *An editor's job is a tough job. He has to look after all the aspects of the magazine or the newspaper.*

Educate/एड्यूकेट *(verb)* – शिक्षा प्रदान करना give intellectual, moral, and social instruction to. train or give information on a particular subject. *He is a well educated man.*

Education/एड्यूकेशन *(noun)* – शिक्षा the process of educating or being educated. the theory and practice of teaching. information about or training in a particular subject. *Education is a must for every citizen.*

Educative/एड्यूकेटिब *(adj)* – शिक्षाप्रद educational. *It is a useful educative tool.*

Educator/एड्यूकेटर *(noun)* – शिक्षक a teacher. *This is the view of a professional educator.*

Educe/इड्यूस *(verb)* – खींचना, विकसित करना, निकाल देना formal bring out or develop (something latent or potential). *He educed the hidden talent in him.*

Effable/एफबल् *(adjective)* – कथनीय able to be described in words. *Her manner is very effable, which is what I like about her.*

Efface/इफेस *(verb)* – पोछना, मिटा देना या हटा देना erase from a surface. *Efface all the words from the blackboard.*

Effective/इफेक्टिव *(adjective)* – प्रभावोत्पादक, क्षमताशाली production a desired or intended result. *This rule is effective from today.*

Effectual/इफेक्चुअल *(adjective)* – समर्थ, असर पैदा करने वाला निश्चित effective. *The law of the land is always effectual.*

Effectuate/इफेक्चुएट *(verb)* – पूर्ण करना, कार्यान्वित करना formal put into force or operation. *The law has been effectuated since the 1ˢᵗ of this month.*

Effeminacy/एफ्फेमिनैसि *(noun)* – जनानापन, नामर्दी, स्त्रीत्व the trait of being effeminate. *His effeminacy is not tolerable.*

Effeminate/इफ्फेमिनेट *(adjective)* – डरपोक derogatory having characteristics regarded as typical of a woman. *He has an effeminate personality. People make fun of him.*

Effervesce/एफरवेश *(verb)* – बुदबुदाना be enthusiastic. *Supervisors are supposed to effervesce with praise and encouragement.*

Effete/इफ़ीट् *(adjective)* – थका हुआ, कमजोर affected, over-refined, and ineffectual. *He is an effete and thus useless for action.*

Efficacious/एफिकेशस *(adjective)* – समर्थ, लाभकारी formal effective. *It is an efficacious medicine.*

Efficacy/एफिकसि *(noun)* – गुण, प्रभाव ability to produce results. *There is little information on the efficacy of the new programme.*

Efficient/इफिशेन्ट *(adjective)* – कार्यकुशलता working productively with minimum wasted effort or expense. *He is an efficient worker.*

Effigy/एफ़िजि *(noun)* – प्रतिमा a sculpture or model of a person. *The effigies of Ravan, Meghnath and Kumbhkaran are burnt on Dhssehra.*

Effloresce/एफ्लोरेश *(noun & verb)* – फूलना lose moisture and turn to a fine powder on exposure to air. *The atomic plant is at effloresce.*

Effluence/एफ्लूएन्स *(noun)* – निकास प्रवाह a substance that flows out. *The effluence of sewage water could be seen clearly.*

Efflux/एफ्लक्स *(noun)* – वहि:स्रवण technical the flowing out of a substance or particle. *The efflux of rain water was very heavy.*

Effort/एफर्ट *(noun)* – प्रयत्न, मानसिक या शारीरिक प्रयास a vigorous or determined attempt. strenuous physical or mental exertion. *He put in great effort to clear the interview.*

Effrontery/ऍफ्रण्टरि *(noun)* – धृष्ठता, गुस्ताखी insolence or impertinence. *Effrontery close not pay in the end.*

Effusive/एफ्यूसिव *(adj)* – अधिक परिमाण में बहाने वाला uttered with unrestrained enthusiasm. *She was effusive in her praise.*

Egg/एग *(noun)* – अण्डा an almost round object with a hard shell that contains a young bird. *This object is like an egg.*

Ego/इगो *(noun)* – अहंकार, घमण्ड the good opinion that you have of yourself. *She has fragile ego.*

Egotistic/ईगटिस्टिक *(adj)* – अहंकारी characteristic of those having an inflated idea of their own importance. *I dislike her egotistic behaviour.*

Egress/इग्रेस *(noun)* – निर्गम, निकास the way out. *Rear seat entry and egress is better than average.*

Egyptian/इजिप्शन *(noun)* – मिस्र देश का निवासी a native or inhabitant of Egypt. *This man seems an Egyptian.*

Eh/ए *(exclamation)* – दूसरे को अपने से सहमत कराने के लिए प्रयुक्त used for asking to agree with you. *Did you like the files eh?*

Easel/ईजल् *(noun)* – तस्वीर खींचने या रखने का ठाठ an upright tripod for displaying something (usually an artist's canvas). *A wooden frame used to support a picture, blackboard is called an easel.*

Ejaculate/इजैक्यूलेट *(verb)* – वीर्य स्खलन करना to send out liquid (semen) from the male sexual organ (penis). *Don't ejaculate, control it.*

Elaborate/इलैबरेट *(verb)* – विस्तार से वर्ण करना to work out in detail. *Can you elaborate your idea?.*

Elapse/इलैप्स *(noun)* – बीत जाना pass by- come about. *Twenty seconds elapsed with nothing thrown.*

Elasticity/इलास्टिसिटी *(noun)* – लचीलापन, प्रत्यास्थता the quality that he has of being able to stretch and return to its original size and shape. *Rubber contains elasticity.*

Elate/इलेट *(verb)* – अतिप्रसन्न, प्रफुल्लित करना fill with high spirits; fill with optimism. *Don't try to elate me.*

Elbow/एल्बो *(noun & verb)* – कोहनी the place where the bones of your arm join and your arm bends. *Why are you elbowing me?*

Elder/एल्डर *(adj)* – आयु में बड़ा (परिवार के दो सदस्यों में) used of the older of two persons of the same name especially used to distinguish a father from his son. *He is my elder brother.*

Eldest/एल्डेस्ट *(adj)* – आयु में सबसे बड़ा oldest (three or more member in the family). *Her eldest child is a boy.*

Elect/इलेक्ट *(verb)* – मतदान द्वारा किसी प्रतिनिधि को चुन लेना to choice subject to have a particular job or position by voting for him/her. *He was elected in Punjab assembly.*

Electric/इलेक्ट्रिक *(adj)* – विद्युत उत्पन्न करने वाला, उत्तेजक an dctric current. *The atmosphere in the room was electric.*

Electrification/इलेक्ट्रिफिकेशन *(noun)* – विद्युतीकरण, विद्युतीकरण करना the act of providing electricity. *The electrification of the village is complete.*

Electrum/इलेक्ट्रम *(noun)* – गिलट, सोना-चाँदी की धातु an alloy of gold and silver. *Electrum is not useful for jewellery.*

Elegant/इलिगन्ट् *(adj)* – सुन्दर having a good or attractive style.

Elegiac/एलिजिआक *(adj)* – करुणामय resembling or characteristic of or appropriate to an elegy. *His poetry has an elegiac quality.*

Elegist/एलेजिस्ट *(noun)* – शोकगीत का लेखक an author of a mournful poem lamenting the dead. *Do you know any elegist in English.*

Elegy/एलजी *(noun)* – शोकगीत a mournful poem, typically a lament for the dead. *The elegy he recited was extremely mournful and moving.*

Element/एलिमेंट *(noun)* – प्रमुख तत्त्व a basic constituent part. an aspect: an element of danger. a group of a particular kind within a larger group: right-wing elements. *There was an element of danger in that place.*

Elementary/एलिमेंटरी *(adjective)* – मौलिक, सरल of or relating to the most rudimentary aspects of a subject; introductory. simple. *It is a very elementary problem, I'll solve it right away.*

Elemi/इलेमी *(noun)* – लाह an oleoresin obtained from certain tropical trees and used in varnished, ointments, and aromatherapy. *Product of certain tropical trees used in ointments and aromatherapy is called elemi.*

Elephantiasis/एलिफैंटाइटिस *(noun)* – फीलपाँव medicine a condition in which a limb becomes grossly enlarged due to obstruction of the lymphatic vessels, especially by nematode parasites. *He is suffering from elephantiasis. His foot has become very large and full of wounds.*

Elephantine/एलफैन्टीन *(adjective)* – हाथी का गज रूप of, resembling, or characteristic of an elephant, especially in being large or clumsy. *He is large and clumsy like an elephantine.*

Elevate/एलिवेट *(verb)* – उठाना, किसी व्यक्ति या वस्तु का ऊँचा उठाना lift to a higher position. raise to a higher level or status. hold up for adoration. military raise the axis of a piece of artillery to increase its range. *He is a great scientist and enjoys an elevated position in the science academy.*

Eleven/इलेवेन *(cardinal number)* – एकादश equivalent to the sum of six and five; one more than ten; 11. *There are eleven players in a cricket team.*

Elicit/एलिसिट *(verb)* – किसी से सूचना तथ्य आदि निकालना evoke or draw out a response or answer. *Although he was not a brilliant student still I managed to elicit an answer from him.*

Eligibility/एलिजिबिलिटि *(noun)* – निर्वाहन योग्यता the capability to be chosen. *His eligibility for the post cannot be questioned.*

Eligible/एलिजिबल *(adjective)* – उपयुक्त, ग्रहण करने योग्य satisfying the appropriate conditions. *Many high class young men are eligible backdoors.*

Eliminate/इलिमिनेट *(verb)* – अवांछित व्यक्ति या वस्तु को हटा देना completely remove or get rid of. reject or exclude from consideration or further participation. *All the anti-social elements have been eliminated from the party.*

Elision/इलिसन *(noun)* – स्वर का लोप the omission of a sound or syllable in speech. *The shortening of words or elision is quite popular.*

Elite/एलीट *(noun)* – सभ्रांत वर्ग a group of people considered to be superior in a particular society or organization. *He belongs to the group of elite people.*

Elixir/इलिक्सिर *(noun)* – रसायन a magical or medicinal potion, especially either one supposedly able to change metals into gold or supposedly able to prolong life indefinitely. *Ancient people believed in elixir which could prolong life and change base metal into gold.*

Elk/एल्क *(noun)* – एक प्रकार का बारहसिंघा a large northern deer with palmate antlers and a growth of skin hanging from the neck. called moose in north America. north American term for wapiti. *This kind of deer or moose is found in North America.*

Ellagic/इलैजिक *(noun)* – माजूफल सम्बन्धी chemistry a compound extracted from oak galls and some fruits and nuts, able to retard the growth of cancer cells to some extent. *An ellagic is a medicine somewhat effective against cancer.*

Ellipse/इलिप्स *(noun)* – अण्डवृत a regular oval shape, traced by a point moving in a point moving in a plane so that the sum of its distances from two other points is constant, or resulting when a cone is cut by an oblique plane which does not intersect the base. *A regular oval shape.*

Ellipsis/एलिप्सिस *(noun)* – अध्याहार, अर्थपूरक the omission of words from speech or writing. a set of dots indicating such an omission. *It is rare for an ellipsis to happen without any linguistic antecedent.*

Ellipsoid/एलिप्साइड *(noun)* – दीर्घ वृत्तज a three-dimensional figure sym-metrical about each of three perpendicular axes, whose plane sections normal to one axis are circles and all the other plane sections are ellipses. *A comparison in which an elliptical shape is described as ellipsoid.*

Ellipticity/एलिप्टिसिटी *(noun)* – दीर्घवृत्तीयता the property possessed by a round shape that is flattened at the poles. *The quality of being elliptic is called ellipticity.*

Elocution/एलोक्यूशन *(noun)* – वक्तृता व्याख्यान, श्रेष्ठ वक्तृत्व कला the skill of clear and expressive speech, especially of distinct pronunciation and articulation. a particular style of speaking. *He has the gift of elocution, being a leader, it makes things easy for him.*

Eloquence/इलोक्वेंस *(noun)* – वाक्पटुता fluent or persuasive speaking or writing. *His eloquence enables him to make things very clear. People love to hear him.*

Eloquent/इलोक्वेंट *(adjective)* – वाक्पटु, सार्वजनिक प्रसंग में वाणी का प्रयोग करने में दक्ष showing eloquence. *He is eloquent and always makes things very clear, never confused, never hesitating. His selection of words is excellent.*

Elucidate/इल्यूसिडेट *(verb)* – व्याख्या करना make clear; explain. *'Will you please elucidate the point?'*

Elysian/एलिजिअन *(adjective)* – अति सुखकर, स्वर्गिक of or relating to Elysium or the elysian fields, the place in Greek mythology where heroes were conveyed after death. of or like paradise. *It is an elysian room for us.*

Elysium/एलिजिअम – स्वर्ग, बैकुंठ a place or condition of ideal happiness. *An elysium is an imagenary place.*

Emaciated/इमैसिएटेड *(adjective)* – कृश, दुर्बल lean, wasted. *He is a an emaciated child, so thin and weak.*

Emanate/इमनेट *(verb)* – निकलना issue or spread out from a source. give out or emit. *Water emanated from a hole in the ground.*

Emancipate/इमैन्सिपेट *(verb)* – दास्त्वमुक्ति, मुक्त करना set free, especially from legal, social, or political restrictions. free from slavery law set free from the authority of its father or parents. *All the Negro slaves were emancipated after the civil war in America.*

Emasculate/ईमैस्कुलेट *(verb)* – प्रभवहीन, नपुंसक बनाना make weaker or less effective. *Many animals are emasculated by castration e.g. ox.*

Embank/ऍम्बैन्क *(verb)* – बाँध बाँधना protect or provide with an embankment. *In India many rivers cause havoc in rainy season. The government is trying to embank against those rivers.*

Embark/ऍम्बार्क *(verb)* – जलपोत पर सवार होना go on board a ship or aircraft. *He embarked on the ship in time.*

Embarrass/ऍम्बैरस् *(verb)* – लज्जित करना, व्याकुल करना cause to feel awkward, self-conscious, or ashamed. be caused financial difficulties. *I felt embarrassed when they talked of my poor economic condition in front of me.*

Embed/ऍम्बेड् *(verb)* – किसी वस्तु को मजबूती से बैठाना fix or become fixed firmly and deeply in the surrounding mass. *The idea got embedded in my mind.*

Embellish/ऍम्बेल्लिश् *(verb)* – सजाना adorn; decorate. *I embellished my bedroom.*

Ember/ऍम्बर् *(noun)* – अंगारा a small piece of burning or glowing material in a dying fire. *The burning coals looked like embers.*

Emblazon/ऍम्ब्लेजेन *(verb)* – सुशोभित करना, अलंकरण करना, चमकना conspicuously display on something. depict on something. *The brand name was emblazoned on the shirt.*

Emblem/ऍम्ब्लेम् *(noun)* – प्रतीक, चिह्न a heraldic device or symbolic object as a distinctive badge of a nation, organization, or family. a symbol or symbolic representation. *The three lions are the emblem of our country.*

Embodiment/ऍम्बॉडिमेन्ट *(noun)* – अवतार, मूर्ति रूप visible form of an idea or feeling. *He seems to be living form of embodiment of vitality.*

Embolism/ऍम्बॉलिज्म् *(noun)* – धमनी में रक्त संचालन का अवरोध occlusion of a blood vessel by an embolus (a loose clot or air bubble or other particle). *He was suffering from embolism.*

Embower/ऍम्बावर *(verb)* – ढाँकना poetic/literary surround or enclose. *His cottage was embowered by trees.*

Embrace/ऍम्ब्रेस *(noun)* – आलिंगन करना the act of clasping another person in the arms (as in greeting or affection).

E

163

Embroider/ऍम्ब्राइडर *(verb)* – कसीदा करनाsew decorative needlework patterns on. *His profession is embroidering sarees.*

Embroil/ऍम्ब्राइल *(verb)* – उलझाना, आपत्ति में डालना involve deeply in a conflict or difficult situation. archaic bring into a state of confusion or disorder. *After embroiling himself, he cried for help.*

Embryology/ऍम्ब्रिओलॉजि *(noun)* – भ्रूण-विज्ञान the branch of biology and medicine concerned with the study of embryos. *His article on embryology in the medical journal was worth reading.*

Emerge/इमर्ज *(verb)* – निकलना become gradually visible or apparent. become known. *The statue emerged slowly from the receding waters.*

Emergent/इमर्जेन्ट *(adjective)* – आकस्मिक in the process of coming into being; emerging. *I saw a calf emerging from its mother's body.*

Emersion/इमरर्शन् *(noun)* – प्रकट होना the process or state of emerging, especially from water. *The emersion of a large snake from the water scared me.*

Emetic/इमेटिक *(adjective)* – वमन, उबकाई causing vomiting. (noun) an emetic medicine or other substance. *I felt emetic when I saw the rotten corpse.*

Emigrant/ऍमिग्रैन्ट *(noun)* – अपना देश छोड़कर परदेश में बसने वाला a person who leaves their own country in order to settle permanently in another. *Many foreigners are now emigrants in America.*

Eminence/ऍमिनेन्स *(noun)* – श्रेष्ठता acknowledged superiority within a particular sphere. *He is an eminent scientist.*

Eminent/एमिनेन्ट *(adjective)* – श्रेष्ठ respected; distinguished. *He is an eminent eye specialist.*

Emission/एमिशन *(noun)* – प्रवाह, उत्सर्जन the action of emitting something, especially heat, light, gas, or radiation. a substance which is emitted. *The emission of smoke from the engine upset me.*

Emolument/एमॉल्युमेंट *(noun)* – पारिश्रमिक, लाभ formal a salary, fee, or benefit from employment or office. *My emoluments are not enough to be taxable.*

Emotion/इमोशन *(noun)* – भावना a strong feeling, such as joy, anger, or sadness. instinctive or intuitive feeling as distinguished from reasoning or knowledge. *I got emotional as I met my mother after a long time.*

Empanel/इम्पैनल *(verb)* – सूची में नाम लिखना variant spelling of impanel. *Five new members have been empanelled to the expert committee.*

Emperor/ऍम्परर *(noun)* – सम्राट the ruler of an empire. *Ashoka was a great emperor.*

Empire/ऍम्पायर *(noun)* – प्रभुत्व, एक देश द्वारा शासित देशों का समूह an extensive group of states ruled over by a singly monarch, an oligarchy, or a sovereign state. *The empire of Ashoka was wide spread.*

Emplane/ऍम्प्लेन *(verb)* – हवाई जहाज पर सवार होना go or put on board an aircraft. *He was late but he acted quickly and got emplaned for Londen.*

Employ/एम्प्लाय् *(verb)* – नियुक्त करना give work to and pay them for it. keep occupied. *I was employed throughout the day.*

Employer/एम्प्लॉअर *(noun)* – नियुक्त करने वाला a person that employs people. *That man over there is my employer, I drive his car.*

Empress/एम्प्रेस *(noun)* – महारानी, साम्राज्ञी a female emperor. the wife or widow of an emperor. *There have been many famous empresses in history.*

Emptier/ऍम्प्टिअर *(adj)* – खाली करने वाला one who empties. *Nothing can be emptier than an empty glass.*

Emptiness/ऍम्प्टिनेश *(noun)* – शून्यता, खालीपन state of containing nothing. *Through the window of an airplane you can see vast emptiness of space.*

Emulate/ऍम्युलेट *(verb)* – स्पर्धा करना attempt to much or surpass, typically by imitation. *He tried to emulate a famous actor but failed.*

Emulsion/इमल्शन *(noun)* – मिश्रित न होने वाले द्रवों का मिश्रण a fine dispersion of minute droplets of one liquid in another in which it is not soluble or miscible. *The emulsion technique has made my house look for batter than more point.*

Enable/एनेबल् *(verb)* – सामर्थ्य देना provide with the ability or means to do something. *My coaching enabled me to pass the exam with high marks.*

Enact/एनैक्ट् *(verb)* – कानून बनाना make a bill or other proposal law. *The proposal was enacted and made a law.*

Enamour/इनैमर *(verb)* – मोह लेना, आसक्त करना be filled with love or admiration for. *I was enamoured over her beauty.*

Encage/ऍनकेज *(verb)* – पिंजड़े में बन्द करना, डिब्बे में रखना to confine in or as in a cage. *Four little Australian birds were encaged in a metallic cage.*

Encamp/ऍनकैम्प *(verb)* – डेरा डालना settle in or establish a camp. *We encamped at a safe place in jungle.*

Encase/ऍनकेस *(verb)* – डिब्बे मे रखना enclose or cover in a case or close-fitting surround. *Please encase the sweets.*

Encash/ऍनकैश *(verb)* – हुंडी British convert a cheque, bond, etc. into money. *I have no money, I have to encash my cheque.*

Enchain/ऍनचेन *(verb)* – कसकर बाँधना bind with as if in chains. *The buffalo was taken into custody and enchained at the police station.*

Enchant/ऍनचैंट *(verb)* – जादू डालना delight; charm. *The place is so beautiful as if it is enchanted.*

Encircle/ऍनसर्कल *(verb)* – घेरना form a circle around; surround. *The thief was encircled by police.*

Enclose/ऍनक्लोज *(verb)* – घेरना surround or close off on all sides. *The tree was enclosed by herbs.*

Encompass/ऍनकम्पस् *(verb)* – घेरना surround and have or hold within. *The house was encompassed by a wall.*

Encore/आनकोर् *(noun)* – संगीत सभा के अंत में दर्शकों की फरमाइश पर प्रस्तुत अतिरिक्त कार्यक्रम a repeated or additional performance of an item at the end of a concert, as called for by an audience. exclamatory again! as called by an audience at the end of a concert verb call for an encore. demand an encore from a performer. *Her stage performance was so nice that public demanded an encore from her.*

Encounter/ऍनकाउन्टर *(noun)* – मुठभेड़, मुकाबला an unexpected or casual meeting. *I met a friend in a mall. It was a sudden encounter.*

Encourage/ऍनकरेज *(verb)* – प्रोत्साहित करना, सहायता देना give support, confidence, or hope to. help or stimulate the development of. *I encouraged him to study hard.*

Encroach/ऍनक्रोच *(verb)* – अतिक्रमण करना, सीमा को लांघना gradually and steadily intrude on a person's territory, rights, etc. advance gradually beyond expected or acceptable limits. *The enemy encroached upon its neighbour territory and then there was a war.*

Encrust/ऍनक्रस्ट *(verb)* – पपड़ी जमाना, जमना encrusted cover with a hard crust. *The bread was covered with a hard crust.*

Encumber/ऍनकम्बर *(verb)* – प्रतिबन्ध करना impede or burden. *I felt encumbered with the huge amount of homework.*

Encumbrance/ऍनकम्ब्रैन्स् *(noun)* – भार a burden or impediment. *I am facing some encumbrance in executing my scheme.*

Encyclopaedia/ऍन्साइक्लोपीडिया *(noun)* – विश्व-ज्ञानकोश a book or set of books giving information on many subjects or on many aspects of one subject, typically arranged alphabetically. *I have a set of encyclopedia at home. I can find anything in it.*

Endanger/ऍन्डेन्जर *(verb)* – व्यक्ति या वस्तु को खतरे में डालना put at risk or in danger. *He endangered his life when he went very near the cubs of tiger.*

Endear/ऍनडिअर *(verb)* – प्रियपात्र बनाना cause to be loved or liked. *I am endeared to you for the favour you have shown me.*

Endeavour/ऍन्डेवर *(noun)* – प्रयास an act of endeavouring; an enterprise. *I endeavoured to climb the mountain but failed.*

Endemic/एन्डेमिक *(adjective)* – स्थानिक regularly found among particular people or in a certain area. *Endemic a disease commonly found among people of certain area.*

Ending/एन्डिंग *(noun)* – परिणाम, अंत an end or final part. the final part of a word, constituting a grammatical inflection or formative element. *In the ending of film people were almost in tears.*

E

Endmost/एण्डमोस्ट *(adjective)* – सबसे दूर का nearest to the end. *The endmost part of the film was very exciting.*

Endorse/ऍन्डॉर्स *(verb)* – घोषणा या निर्णय का सार्वजनिकतौर पर समर्थन करना declare one's public approval of. *I have endorsed the document.*

Endow/ऍन्डाउ *(verb)* – किसी संस्था या विद्यालय को बड़ी धन राशि दान में देना give or bequeath an income or property to. establish a university pot, annual prize, etc. by donating funds. *I have endowed my property to my wife.*

Endue/ऍन्ड्यू *(verb)* – धारण करना poetic/literary endow with a quality or ability. *He is endued with great ability.*

Endurance/इन्ड्योरेन्स *(noun)* – सहन-शीलता the ability to endure difficult situations. *He has great endurance and can bear a lot of pain.*

Endure/इन्ड्योर *(verb)* – चुपचाप पीड़ा झेलना suffer and prolonged patiently. tolerate. *He endured the cancer pain for a long time.*

Endways/एण्डवेज *(adverb)* – खड़े बल with its end facing upwards, forwards the viewer. *The carpet covered the floor endways.*

Enema/ऍनिमा *(noun)* – वस्ति a procedure in which fluid is injected into the rectum, typically to expel its contents. *He suffered from severe constipation, so the doctor gave him enema.*

Energize/ऍनर्जाइज *(verb)* – क्रियाशील करना, उत्साहित और सतर्क करना give vitality. *The drink energized the boxers.*

Energumen/ऍनरग्यूमेन *(noun)* – पागल archaic a person believed to be possessed by the devil or a spirit. *That man is energumened see how wild he is acting, if possessed.*

Energy/एनर्जी *(noun)* – शक्ति, ऊर्जा the strength and vitality required for sustained activity. a person's physical and mental powers as applied to a particular activity. *He has great energy and can work hard for a long time without rest.*

Enface/एन्फेस *(verb)* – मुखाकंन करना facing forwards. *Enface means to write or stamp a bill on the face.*

Enfeeble/ऍन्फीबल *(verb)* – क्षीण बनाना weaken. *After the viral fever I felt very enfeebled.*

Enfold/एनफोल्ड *(verb)* – लपेटना, आलिंगन करना surround; envelop. *I enfolded the paper and made an envelope.*

Enframe/ऍन्फ्रेम – चौखटे में मढ़ना to set a picture in a frame. *The enframed photo looked life like.*

Engarland/ऍनगारलैंड – माला पहनाना to put a garland upon. *People engarlanded their leader.*

Engender/ऍन्जेन्डर *(verb)* – उत्पन्न करना give rise to. *The issue engendered continuing political controversy.*

Engineer/ऍन्जिनिअर *(noun)* – अभियन्ता a person qualified in engineering. *My father was an engineer and he made many machines.*

Engorge/इनगॉर्ज *(verb)* – लालच में ज्यादा खाना to devour greedily. *His stomach was engorged with water.*

Engraft/ऍन्गैफ्ट *(verb)* – संयुक्त करना another term for GRAFT. *Engraft as his liver was damaged only grafting another live tissue surgically could save his life.*

Engrain/ऍन्ग्रेन् *(verb)* – गहरा रंग चढ़ाना firmly fix, belief in a person. *He trivialized the struggle and further engrained the long standing attitudes.*

Engrave/इनग्रेव *(verb)* – धातु या पत्थर खोदना cut or carve a text or design on a hard surface. cut or carve a text or design on. cut a design as lines on a metal plate for printing. *His words were engraved in my mind for ever.*

Enhance/इनहांस *(verb)* – बेहतर दिखने के लिए वस्तु में सुधार आदि पर शब्द या आकृति खोदना improve the quality, value, or extent of. *As he enhanced his voice, people all over could hear him.*

Enigma/एनिग्मा *(noun)* – पेचीदा a mysterious or puzzling person or thing. *I could never understand that person, he is an enigma to me.*

Enjoin/ऍन्जॉइन् *(verb)* – रोक लगाना, निषेध करना instruct or urge to do something. law prohibit someone from performing an action by issuing an injunction. *He enjoined me to jump over the wall.*

Enlighten/ऍन्लाइट्न् *(verb)* – उपदेश देना, अपेक्षित जानकारी देते हुए किसी बात की समझ को बढ़ाना give greater knowledge and understanding to.

give spiritual insight to. rational, tolerant, and well-informed. *Lord Buddha enlightened many people.*

Enlist/ऍनलिस्ट *(verb)* – सेना में भर्ती होना toget help support etc. engage a person or their help. *He got himself enlisted in the army.*

Enmity/ऍनमिटी *(noun)* – शत्रुता, विरोध the state of being an enemy; hostility. *Now there is no enmity between us. Let us be friends.*

Ennoble/इनोबल् *(verb)* – प्रतिष्ठा बढ़ाना give a noble rank or title to. give greater dignity to; elevate. *He was ennobled to the rank of general.*

Ennui/आनन्वी *(noun)* – मानसिक थकावट, आलस्य, उदासी dissatisfaction arising from boredom. *Ennui got him as he felt extremely bored.*

Enormity/इनार्मिटि *(noun)* – किसी वस्तु की विशालटा प्रभाव की गंभीरता the large scale or extreme seriousness of something bad. great size or scale. *The enormity of the crime shocked me.*

Enough/एनफ *(adverb)* – प्रचुरता to the required degree or extent. *Enough is enough, now please be quiet.*

Enrapture/ऍनरैप्चर *(adjective)* – मंत्रमुग्ध होना give intense pleasure to. *I was enraptured by the view from the hill.*

Enrich/एनरिच *(verb)* – सुशोभित करना, गुणवत्ता बढ़ाना improve the quality or value of. *He was further enriched as his father left him all the money and property.*

Enrobe/ऍन्रोब *(verb)* – सुन्दर वस्त्र पहिनना formal dress in a robe or vestment. *He was dressed in a robe.*

Enroute/ऍनरूट *(adv)* – रास्ते में मार्ग द्वारा on the way while travelling. *This bus will go enroute Lady Shri Ram College, C.R. Park and Kalkaji.*

Enshroud/ऍन्श्राउड् *(verb)* – लपेटना to cover something completely. *The dead body was enshrouded for burial.*

Ensign/ऍन्साइन *(noun)* – ध्वज flag flown on a ship to show the nationality. *An ensign flew over the naval ship.*

Enslave/ऍनस्लेव *(verb)* – दास बनाना make a slave. cause to lose freedom of choice or action. *I was enslaved by her beauty.*

Ensnare/इनस्नेअर *(verb)* – बन्धन में डालना, जाल में डालना catch in or as in a trap. *The tiger was ensnared in a trap.*

Ensorcell/ऍनसॉरसेल *(verb)* – मोहित करना bewitch. *I was ensorcelled by the beauty of Kashmir.*

Enstamp/ऍनस्टाम्प *(verb)* – मोहर लगाना to impress eith a stamp. *The envelope was stamped at the post office.*

Ensue/ऍनस्यू *(verb)* – कुछ घटित होना (किसी के बाद या फलस्वरूप) happen or occur afterwards or as a result. *Bitterness ensued as the two friends quarrelled with one another.*

Ensure/एन्श्योर् *(verb)* – सुरक्षित करना सुनिश्चित करना make certain that something will occur or be so. make sure that a problem does not occur. *I will ensure that this kind of thing does not happen again.*

Entente/आन्टेन्ट *(noun)* – मित्रभाव a friendly understanding or informal alliance between states or factions. the understanding between Britain and France reached in 1904, forming the basis of Anglo-French cooperation in the first world war. *People hope that one day there will be entente between India and Pakistan.*

Entric/ऍटेरिक *(adjective)* – आँतो से सम्बन्धित of, relating to, or occurring in the intestines. *You are suffering from an enteric disease.*

Entering/इन्टरिंग *(noun)* – प्रवेश entrance. *Your entering is prohibited here.*

Enteritis/इन्टराइटिस *(noun)* – आँतो की सूजन medicine inflammation of the intestine, especially the small intestine, usually accompanied by diarrhoea. *Enteritis medicine is given in case of inflammation of intestine.*

Enterprising/एन्टरप्राइजिंग *(adjective)* – साहसी showing initiative and resourcefulness. *He is an enterprising fellow and will certainly succeed.*

Entertaining/ऍन्टरटेनिंग *(noun)* – मनोरंजक, दिलचस्प providing enjoyment. *An entertaining picture relieves our boredom.*

Enthrone/ऍन्श्रोन् *(verb)* – राजसिंहासन पर बैठाना, राज्याभिषेक करना install a monarch or bishop on a throne with due ceremony. treat with

E

honour and respect. *The king was enthroned with full pomp and show.*

Enthunder/ऍन्थण्डर *(verb)* – बादलों की गरज की तरह शब्द करना *The sky thundered and it began to rain heavily.*

Enthusiast/ऍन्थ्यूजिआस्ट *(noun)* – उत्साही a person who is full of enthusiasm for something. *He is an enthusiast by nature. These days he is full of enthusiasm for going to USA.*

Entice/ऍन्टाइस *(verb)* – मोहित करना, किसी को लालच देकर कुछ करने के लिए मनाना attract by offering pleasure or advantage. *Being enticed by her wealth, he married an elderly women.*

Entitle/ऍन्टाइटल् *(verb)* – नाम रखना give a right to. *He was entitled to this honour.*

Entity/ऍन्टिटी *(noun)* – अलग और स्वतंत्र अस्तित्व वाली वस्तु a thing with distinct and independent existence. *A star is an entity.*

Entoil/ऍन्टाइल् – जाल में फँसाना to entangle. *He entoiled a lot for his downfall.*

Entomb/ऍनटूम् *(verb)* – समाधि में गाड़ना bury in or under. *His dead body was entombed.*

Entomic/एनटॉमिक *(adj)* – कीड़े का pertaining to insects. *I purchased an entomic book.*

Entomology/ऍन्टामालॅजि *(noun)* – कृमि अध्ययन शास्त्र the branch of zoology concerned with the study of insects. *He is studying entomology and a lot of insects in jars can be seen in his laboratory.*

Entrails/ऍन्ट्रेल्स *(plural noun)* – आँत a person's or animal's intestines or internal. organs. *His entrails were severely damaged in an accident.*

Entrammel/ऍन्ट्रैम्मल *(verb)* – रोकना entrammeling; US untrammeled, entrammeling poetic/ literary entangle. *On his way home, he got entrammelled with his old enemy.*

Entrance/ऍन्ट्रेन्स *(noun)* – द्वार an opening allowing access. *I will meet her at the entrance of hospital.*

Entrant/ऍन्ट्रैन्ट *(noun)* – किसी व्यवसाय में प्रवेश करने वाला व्यक्ति a person who enters something. *All the entrants were gathered together at one place.*

Entreat/ऍन्ट्रीट/इन्ट्रीट् *(verb)* – प्रार्थना करना ask someone earnestly or anxiously. ask earnestly or anxiously for. *I entreat you to please pardon me.*

Entrench/ऍन्ट्रश/इन्ट्रेन्ब *(verb)* – खाई में घेरना, मोरचाबंदी करना establish firmly. *Congress party's firmly entrenched in power in India.*

Entrust/इन्ट्रस्ट *(verb)* – किसी का किसी काम का दायित्व सौंपना assign a responsibility to. put into someone's care. *I entrusted the child to the care of the mother.*

Envelop/इन्वेलप *(verb)* – लपेटना wrap up, cover, or surround completely. *I tore open the envelop and took out the contents.*

Envelope/एन्विलोप *(noun)* – लिफाफा a flat paper container with a sealable flap, used to enclose a letter or document. *A human figure appeared completely enveloped in a black dress.*

Envisage/इन्विसेज *(verb)* – भविष्य में संभावित स्थिति के बारे में सोचना regard or conceive of as a possibility. form a mental picture of. *I envisaged that I was flying in a plane.*

Envoy/इन्वॉय *(noun)* – दूत a messenger or representative, especially one on a diplomatic mission. *The envoy from U.K. met the foreign secretary.*

Envy/इन्वी *(noun)* – स्पर्धा, ईर्ष्या discontented or resentful longing aroused by another's possessions, qualities, or luck. a person or thing that inspires such a feeling. *My envy knew no bounds when I saw that my neighbour had bought a new and costly car.*

Enwrap/इनरैप *(verb)* – लपेटना warp; envelop. *I wrapped the gift in a shining paper.*

Eon/ईऑन *(noun)* – कल्प, युग, असीमित समय the longest division of geological time. *It will take an eon to change it.*

Ephemera/ऍफेमरा *(plural noun)* – अल्पजीवी कीट items of short-lived interest or usefulness. *I do not like things that are ephemera.*

Epicycle/एपिसाइकिल *(noun)* – छोटा वृत्त जिसका केन्द्र बड़े वृत्त की परिधि पर हो geometry a small circle whose centre moves round the circumference of a larger one. *The movement of the spring top resembles that of an epicycle.*

Epidemic/एपिडेमिक *(noun)* – व्यापक रोग, महामारी a widespread occurrence of an infectious disease in a community at a particular time. a sudden, widespread occurrence of an undesirable phenomenon. *(adjective)* relating to or of the nature of an epidemic. *When an epidemic like cholera spreads, lots of people die.*

Epidermal/एपिडरमल *(adj)* – बाह्य त्वचा सम्बन्धी related to outer covering. *This is an epidermal infection you must consult any skin specialist.*

Epigene/एपिजेन *(adjective)* – भूमितल पर बना हुआ geology taking place or produced on the surface of the earth. *All trees and crops are epigene.*

Epiglottis/एपिग्लॉटिस *(noun)* – घंटिका a flap of cartilage at the root of the tongue, which is depressed during swallowing to cover the opening of the windpipe. *There is some trouble with my epiglottis, I am going to a doctor.*

Epilepsy/एपिलेप्सी *(noun)* – मृगी का रोग a neurological disorder marked by sudden recurrent episodes of sensory disturbance, loss of consciousness, or convulsions. *Our neighbour has epilepsy, he often faints.*

Epilogue/एपिलॉग *(noun)* – नाटक का उपसंहार a section or speech at the end of a book or play serving as a comment on or a conclusion to what has happened. *Epilogues of some books are so brilliant that they make the whole concept clear.*

Epiphora/एपिफोरा *(noun)* – आँखों में आँसू इकट्ठा होने का रोग medicine excessive watering of the eye. *For his watering eyes doctor diagnosed epiphora and prescribed a medicine.*

Epistaxis/एपिस्टैक्सिस *(noun)* – बिनास फूटना medicine bleeding from the nose. *He often has epistaxis in the hot weather. He then lies down and applies ice to his nose.*

Epistle/इपिस्ल *(noun)* – साहित्यिक रचना formal or humorous letter. a book of the letters or literary work in the form of letters. *Just out of curiosity. I bought an epistle as I wanted to know how thoughts and emotions are expressed in the form of letters.*

Epistolary/एपिस्टोलरी *(adjective)* – पत्र सम्बन्धी relating to or denoting the writing of letters or literary works in the form of letters. *'Mind you, this novel is epistolary.'*

Epitaph/एपिटाफ *(noun)* – स्मरण लेख, समाधि लेख words written in memory of a person who has died, especially as an inscription on a tombstone. *I read some beautiful epitaphs when I visited a graveyard.*

Epithelium/एपिथेलियम *(noun)* – शरीर की बाह्य त्वचा anatomy the thin tissue forming the outer layer of the body's surface and lining the alimentary canal and other hollow structures, especially that part derived from the embryonic endoderm and endoderm. compare with endothelium. *The anatomy students asked the doctors many questions about epithelium.*

Epithet/एपिथेट *(noun)* – उपाधि an adjective or phrase expressing a quality or attribute of the person or thing mentioned. *The epithet of a 'gentleman', suited him perfectly.*

Epitome/एपिटमि *(noun)* – किसी बात का आदर्श उदाहरण a person or thing that is a perfect example of a quality or type. *She is an epitome of beauty.*

Equal/इक्वल *(adjective)* – समान being the same in quantity, size, degree, value, or status. evenly or fairly balanced: an equal contest. *It was an equal contest between the two boxers.*

Equality/इक्वलिटी *(noun)* – समानता the state of being equal. *There is great equality of intelligence between the two brothers.*

Equalize/ईक्वलाइज *(verb)* – बराबर करना make or become equal. level the score in a match by scoring a goal. *Our team scored a goal and we equalized with the rival team.*

Equator/इक्वेटर *(noun)* – भूमध्य रेखा a line notionally drawn on the earth equidistant from the poles, dividing the earth into northern and southern hemispheres and constituting the parallel of latitude 0°. astronomy short for celestial equator. *It is very hot near the equator eg. Africa.*

Equestrian/इक्वेसट्रिअन *(adjective)* – अश्वारोही of or relating to horse riding. *He is an equestrian champion.*

E

Equi/इक्वि *(prefix)* – यथा combine form equal; equally; equidistant. *The houses of both the friends are equidistant.*

Equipoise/इक्विपॉइज *(noun)* – संतुलन, पासंग balance of forces or interests. a counterbalance or balancing force. *(verb)* balance or counterbalance. *The armies of both the countries were equipoise.*

Equity/इक्विटी *(noun)* – निष्पक्षता न्यायनीति the quality of being fair and impartial. *He is a man known for equity in treatment.*

Era/एरा *(noun)* – युग a long and distinct period of history. geology a major division of time that is a subdivision of an aeon and is itself subdivided into periods. *The era of dinosaur was over even before man evolved.*

Eradicable/इरैडिकेबल् *(adj)* – निर्मूल करने योग्य destroyable completity. *Insurance companies accept eradicable diseases while computing premiums.*

Eradicate/इरैडिकेट *(verb)* – जड़ से उखाड़ना remove or destroy completely. *The plan of Nazi government of Germany was to eradicate Jews.*

Erase/इरेज *(verb)* – मिटाना rub out or obliterate; remove all traces of. *The pencil drawing was erased completely by an eraser.*

Erect/इरेक्ट *(adjective)* – सीधा खड़ा rigidly upright or straight. *Some body organs become erect due to excitement.*

Erectile/इरेक्टाइल *(adjective)* – सीधा होने लायक able to become erect. *The physician is trying to check the condition of erectile spies.* denoting tissues which are capable of becoming temporarily engorged with blood, particularly those of the penis or other sexual organs. relating to this process. *Many people suffer from erectile dysfunction.*

Erection/इरेक्शन *(noun)* – निर्माण करने योग्य या उसे सीधा खड़ा करने की क्रिया the action of erecting. *Erection of Taj Mahal look 22 years.*

Eremite/इरिमाइट *(noun)* – एकान्तवासी, संन्यासी a Christian hermit. *Many people become eremites.*

Eristic/इरिस्टिक *(adjective)* – वाद-विवाद सम्बन्धी of characterized by debate or argument. aiming at winning rather than at reaching the truth. *His eristic arguments were rather boring.*

Erode/इरोड *(verb)* – नष्ट करना, (समुद्र, मौसम आदि का) धीरे-धीरे करना with reference to the action of wind, water, etc. on the land gradually wear or be worn away. *The Fords on this coast continue to be eroded by sea.* gradually destroy an abstract quality or state. *Due to public humiliation his confidence is totally eroded.* [medicine] gradually destroy. *Acids erode the enamel that protect our teeth.*

Erosion/इरोजन *(noun)* – कटाव, अपक्षरण the process or result of eroding or being eroded. *Deserts have been formed as a result of erosion.*

Erosive/इरोसिव *(adjective)* – कटाक्ष सम्बन्धी erosion causing agents. *Acids have erosive qualities.*

Erotic/एरॉटिक *(adjective)* – कामुक, कामोत्तेजक of, relating to, or tending to arouse sexual desire or excitement. *Many ancient temples in India display erotic postures.*

Erratic/एरैटिक *(noun)* – भूगोल में हिमनद के दबाने के कारण अपने स्थान से हटी हुई चट्टान, अनिश्चित अस्थिर geology a large rock that differs from the surrounding rock, brought from a distance by glacial action. *The machine was defective and worked in an erratic way.*

Erratum/इरेटम *(noun)* – छापने की अशुद्धि an error in printing or writing. a list of corrected errors appended to a publication. *You will find the erratum at the end of the book.*

Erroneous/ए(इ)रोनियस् *(adjective)* – अशुद्ध, गलत सूचना पर आधारित wrong; incorrect. *His statement is erroneous.*

Error/एरर *(noun)* – दोष, गलती a mistake. *There are lots of spelling errors in this article.*

Erst/अर्स्ट *(adverb)* – पहले archaic long ago; formerly. *Erstwhile many big and strange animals become extinct.*

Eructate/ईरक्टेट *(noun)* – डकारना a reflex that expel gas noisely from the stomach through the mouth. *He is eructating too much.*

Erupt/इरप्ट *(verb)* – फटना forcefully eject lava, rocks, ash, or gases. *Suddenly the volcano erupted.*

Erysipelas/एरिसिपिलस *(noun)* – मुँहासा नामक रोग medicine a skin disease caused by a streptococcus and characterized by large raised red patches on the face and legs. *He is suffering from erysipelas and has gone to see a skin specialist.*

Eschew/एस्च्यू *(verb)* – त्यागना, छोड़ना abstain from. *He eschewed from drinking.*

Escort/एस्कॉर्ट *(noun)* – अनुचर a person or vehicle or group of these accompanying another to provide protection or as a mark of rank. *A large escort accompanied the king.*

Esculent/एस्क्युलेंट *(adjective)* – खाने योग्य, भक्षणीय fit to be eaten. *(noun)* an esculent thing. *This kind of food is not esculent.*

Esoteric/एसोटेरिक *(adjective)* – गोपनीय, गूढ़, रहस्यमय intended for or understood by only a small number of people with a specialized knowledge or interest. The opposite of exoteric. *This kind of meditation is esoteric.*

Espial/एस्पायल *(noun)* – निरीक्षण, जासूसी [archaic] the action or an instance of catching sight of something or of being seen. *He decided to withdrwa from his point of espial.*

Espionage/एस्पियनेज *(noun)* – जासूसी करने के तरीके the practice of spying or of using spies. *Russia and America were involved in a lot of espionage work against each other during the cold war.*

Esplanade/एस्प्लानेड *(noun)* – टहलने का नगर का खुला मैदान a long, open, level area, typically beside the sea, along which people may promenade. an open, level space separating a fortress from a town. *There is an esplanade road in Delhi opposite the Red Fort.*

Espousal/एस्पाउजल *(noun)* – सगाई the action of espousing. *His espousal of western ideas was not liked by village people.*

Espy/एस्पी *(verb)* – ताकना poetic/literary catch sight of. *I espied a rare bird in the forests of South America.*

Esquire/एस्क्वायर *(noun)* – महाशय British a polite title appended to a man's name when no other title is used, especially in a letter. north American a title appended to a lawyer's surname. *Noblemen training for knighthood were called esquires.*

Essay/एसे *(noun)* – निबंध a piece of writing on a particular subject. *He wrote a brilliant essay on 'Emancipation of Women.'*

Essence/इसेंस *(noun)* – सारतत्त्व, किसी वस्तु को मूलभूत और सर्वाधिक महत्त्वपूर्ण विशेषता the intrinsic nature of something the quality which determines something's character. philosophy a property or group of properties of something without which it would not exist or be what it is. *The essence of this paragraph is that man is not civilized as yet.*

Essential/एसेन्सियल *(adjective)* – आवश्यक fundamental; central. *It is essential that you catch today's flight.*

Estate/इस्टेट *(noun)* – जागीर, भूसंपत्ति a property consisting of a large house and extensive grounds. *My father has a large estate.*

Estimable/एस्टिमेब्ल *(adjective)* – आदरणीय worthy of great respect. *Mahatma Gandhi was an estimable person.*

Estimate/एस्टिमेट *(noun)* – मूल्य निरूपण an approximate calculation or judgement. a written statement indicated the likely price that will be charged for specified work. *At a rough estimate the government is recycling half of the paper used.*

Estop/इस्टॉप *(verb)* – अपने ही कार्य से रुकावट डालना [law] bar or preclude by estoppel. *The firm may be estopped from denying their statement.*

Estrange/इस्ट्रेंज *(verb)* – दूर रखना cause to feel less close or friendly; alienate. *He has no any connation with his estranged wife.*

Etcetra/एट्सेट्रा *(adv)* – इत्यादि used at end of a sentence to indicate that other similar items also exist. *If you are going to the market please bring some vegetables like potato, tomato, onion, cucumber etc.*

Eternity/इटरनिटी *(noun)* – अनंतकाल, पारलौकिक जीवन infinite or unending time. theology endless life after death. informal an undesirably long period of time. *We shall be loving each other till eternity.*

Ethics/एथिक्स *(plural noun)* – नीतिशास्त्र the moral principles governing or influencing conduct. *We should follow ethics strictly.*

E

Ethnic/एथनिक *(adjective)* – जाति सम्बन्धी of or relating to a group of people having a common national or cultural tradition. *Ethnic riots sometimes take place because of nationality and religious differences.*

Ethology/इथॉलजि *(noun)* – आचारशास्त्र the study of the characteristics of different peoples and the differences and relationships between them. *Persons who are interested in character sticks of different people and relationships among them must study ethology.*

Ethos/इथॉस *(noun)* – सामान्य प्रकृति the characteristic spirit of a culture, era, or community as manifested in its attitudes and aspirations. *The ethos of Indians has always been torching the feet of elders and worshipping natural objects.*

Ethyl/इथाइल *(noun)* – नशीली वस्तु का आधार chemistry of or denoting the alkyl radical. C_2H_5, derived from ethane. *A chemical derived from ethane is called ethyl.*

Etiology/इटिऑलजि *(noun)* – रोग निदान हेतु विज्ञान US spelling of aetiology.

Etiquette/एटिकेट *(noun)* – सदाचार, शिष्टाचार the customary code of polite behaviour in a society. *He is a man of perfect etiquette.*

Eucalyptus/यूकालिप्टस *(noun)* – मेंहदी की जाति का वृक्ष a fast-growing evergreen Australasian tree valued for its wood, oil, gum, and resin. the oil from eucalyptus leaves, chiefly used for its medicinal properties. *I would certainly like to have a eucalyptus tree is my garden. It is so beautiful and has so many uses.*

Eugenic/यूजेनिक *(plural noun & adj)* – सुन्दर संतति उत्पन्न करने के विषय का the science of using controlled breeding to increase the occurrence of desirable heritable characteristics in a population. *You should study eugenics if you want to know about controlled breeding in a population.*

Eulogist/यूलोजिस्ट – प्रशंसात्मक बातें बताने वाला one who praises. *He is a professional praise writer.*

Eulogy/यूलॅजी *(noun)* – प्रशंसा a speech or piece of writing that praises someone highly. *People often write eulogies about dead persons.*

Euphonic/यूफॉनिक *(adj)* – सुरीले स्वर वाला relating to characterized by euphony. *I like her euphonic trait.*

Euphony/यूफॉनी *(noun)* – सुस्वर the quality of being pleasing to the ear. *There is a great euphony in her speech.*

Euphorbia/यूफोर्बिया *(noun)* – कठिन शब्दों का प्रयोग करके लिखने की क्रिया a plant of a genus that comprises the spurges. *Euphorbia is a kind of tree.*

Eureka/यूरेका *(exclamation as noun)* – अपूर्व आविष्कार मैने पा लिया है, प्राप्ति की घोषणा a cry of joy and finding something unique by chance. *I cried 'eureka' when I found a rare plant which I had been long searching for.*

European/यूरोपियन *(noun)* – यूरोप देश का निवासी relating to Europe and its inhabitants. *You can see by the colour of his skin that he is a European and not an Asian.*

Evacuant/इवैक्एंट *(adjective)* – रेचक औषधि acting to induce some kind of bodily discharge. *A laxative is an evacuant medicine.*

Evacuate/इवैक्एट *(verb)* – लोगों को खतरनाक जगह से हटाकर सुरक्षित जगह पर ले जाना, शून्य करना remove from a place of danger to a safer place. leave a dangerous place. *As the flood came, the villagers were evacuated.*

Evade/इवेड *(verb)* – बचाना, बच निकलना escape or avoid, especially by guile or trickery. avoid giving a direct answer to a question. *At the party he said that he was a millionaire Industrialist and had been called specially. Thus he evaded paying anything.*

Evaporate/इवैपॅरेट *(verb)* – द्रव का भाप बन जाना turn from liquid into vapour. *The water evaporated as it boiled for too long a time.*

Eve/इव *(noun)* – संध्या the day or period of time immediately before an event or occasion. the evening or day before a religious festival. *There are a lot of festivals on Christmas eve.*

Evening/इवनिंग *(noun)* – साँझ, शाम the period of time at the end of the day, between late afternoon and bedtime. *Most often my friend came to have tea with me in the evening or also I went to his house.*

Event/इवेन्ट *(noun)* – घटना a thing that happens or takes place. a public or social occasion. *In event of my sudden death, please call the lawyer and have my will read.*

Ever/एवर *(adverb)* – किसी भी समय at any time. used in comparisons for emphasis. *'Darling, I am ever yours.'*

Eversion/एवर्शन – बाहर को उलटने का कार्य the position of being turned outward. *This is an act of eversion.*

Evert/एवर्ट *(verb)* – बाहर को उलटना [biology & physiology] turn outwards or inside out. *The hyena can evert its anal pouch.*

Evidence/एविडेंस *(noun)* – प्रमाण, सबूत information indicating whether a belief or proposition is true or valid. law information used to establish facts in a legal investigation or admissible as testimony in a law court. signs; indications. *What is the evidence that you did not commit the crime?*

Evince/इविन्स *(verb)* – दिखाना, व्यक्त करना formal reveal the presence of; indicate a quality or feeling. *I evinced that I was nervous.*

Evolution/इवल्यूशन *(noun)* – क्रमिक विकास उद्भव the process by which different kinds of living organism are believed to have developed from earlier forms, especially by natural selection. *The evolution of humans took bilions of years.*

Evolve/इवॉल्व *(verb)* – साधारण से क्रमश: विकसित होना या करना develop gradually. *Creatures on the earth evolved very gradually.*

Ewer/यूअर *(noun)* – घड़ा, कुम्भ a large jug with a wide mouth. *He used to drink water from an ewer.*

Exact/एक्ज़ैक्ट *(adjective)* – ठीक-ठीक, यथार्थ not approximated in any way; precise. accurate or correct in all details: an exact replica. tending to be accurate and careful about minor details. *What is the exact measurement of this room?*

Exaggerate/ऍग्जजरेट *(verb)* – बढ़ा-चढ़ाकर कहना represent as being larger or better than it really is. enlarged or altered beyond normal proportions. *He exaggerated the facts and nobody came to know the real facts.*

Examine/एक्ज़ामिन *(verb)* – परीक्षा करना inspect closely to determine the nature or condition of; investigate thoroughly. *As the police examined the case thoroughly, they came to know the culprit.*

Exanimate/एक्ज़ामिनेट *(verb)* – जाँच करना to test knowledge. *The teacher examinate the students answersheet.*

Exasperate/एक्ज़ैस्परेट *(verb)* – क्रुद्ध करना irritate intensely. *He was exasperated intensely by my repeated question.*

Excavate/एक्सकैवेट *(verb)* – खोदना make by digging. extract from the ground by digging. *A lot of excavation went on in Egypt when the pyramids were discovered.*

Exceed/एक्सीड *(verb)* – संख्या या मात्रा विशेष से अधिक हो जाना, अधिक होना be greater in number or size than. go beyond what is allowed or stipulated by a set limit, especially of one's authority. surpass. *He exceeded his time limit in speaking and thus lost marks in debate.*

Excel/एक्सेल *(verb)* – श्रेष्ठ होना be exceptionally good at an activity or subject. perform exceptionally well. *You want to excel everybody.*

Excellency/एक्सेलेन्सी *(noun)* – अन्य देश के प्रतिनिधि (राजदूत) आदि के लिए प्रयुक्त शब्द a title or form of address for certain high officials of state, especially ambassadors, or of the roman catholic church. *His Excellency the ambassador of Britain arrived in New Delhi today.*

Excellent/एक्सेलेंट *(adjective)* – उत्तम, उत्कृष्ट extremely good; outstanding. *He got excellent mark in English.*

Exception/एक्सेप्शन *(noun)* – अपवाद a person or thing that is excepted or that does not follow a rule. the action or state of excepting or being excepted. *Most people exaggerate and brag about their achievements he is an exception. He a quiet and polite man.*

Excise/एक्साइज *(noun)* – कुछ वस्तुओं और उत्पादन पर लगाया गया कर a tax levied on certain goods and commodities and on licenses granted for certain activities. *The rate of excise duty on petrol has been lowered to 8 per cent.*

Excision/एक्सिजन *(noun)* – उच्छेदन an omission that is made when the editorial change shortens a written passage. *The several excisions have destroyed the literary value.*

Excitant/एक्साइटैन्ट *(adj.)* – उत्तेजक [biology] a substance which elicits an active physiological or behavioural response. *The brain could become excited if chemical excitants flood into it.*

Excite/एक्साइट *(verb)* – उत्तेजित करना cause strong feelings of enthusiasm and eagerness in. arouse sexually. *I was very excited to see my favorite film star in person.*

Exciter/एक्साइटर *(noun)* – उत्तेजित करने वाला व्यक्ति या पदार्थ a thing that excites. *Elections act as exciters in an atom.*

Exciting/एक्साइटिंग *(adjective)* – उत्तेजक causing enthusiasm. *It is always exciting to see the finals of one day cricket matches.*

Exclaim/एक्सक्लेम *(verb)* – भावावेश में चिल्लाकर कुछ कहना cry out suddenly, especially in surprise, anger, or pain. *'An what a beautiful sea beach!' he exclaimed.*

Exclusion/एक्स्क्लुजन *(noun)* – निषेध, बाहर रखना exclusion the process or state of excluding or being excluded. *The insurance policy contains several exclusions.*

Exclusive/एक्सक्लुसिव *(adjective)* – केवल एक व्यक्ति रूप समूह के लिए excluding or not admitting other things. unable to exist or be true if something else exists or is true: mutually exclusive options. excluding all by what is specified. *This book is for exclusive sale in USA.*

Excogitate/एक्सकॉजिटेट *(verb)* – गौर से सोचना, विचारना formal thing out, plan, or devise. *I excogitated cleverly and won the chess match.*

Excrement/एक्सक्रिमेन्ट *(noun)* – विष्ठा, मल faeces. *In our villages excrement can be found lying extensively.*

Excreta/एक्सक्रेटा *(noun)* – मल-मूत्र आदि पदार्थ waste discharged from the body, especially faeces and urine. *In cities in every house there is a toilet for discharging excreta.*

Excruciate/एक्सक्रुसिएट *(verb)* – यातनाएँ देना, सन्ताप देना rare torment physically or mentally. *He excruciated her to no end, ultimately she left him and ran away.*

Exculpate/एक्सकल्पेट *(verb)* – निर्दोष सिद्ध करना formal show or declare to be not guilty of wrongdoing. *He was exculpated in the court.*

Excursion/एक्स्कर्शन *(noun)* – पर्यटन सैर a short journey or trip, especially one taken for leisure. *He has gone on an excursion on his return he will visit a bird sanctuary as well.*

Execrate/एक्सिक्रेट *(verb)* – शाप देना, घृणा करना feel or express great loathing for. *He execrated over the heinous crime.*

Executive/ऐक्ज़िक्यूटिव *(noun)* – शासन-सम्बन्धी, प्रशासक a person with senior managerial responsibility in a business organization. an executive committee within an organization. *He is a junior executive engineer in DDA.*

Executor/ऐक्ज़िक्यूटर *(noun)* – कार्यान्वित करने वाला, मृतक के इच्छापत्र का उत्तरसाधक law a person appointed by a testator to carry out the terms of their will. *Before his death, my father had already appointed an executor.*

Exemplar/एक्जेम्पलर *(noun)* – आदर्श प्रकार a person or thing serving as a typical example or appropriate model. *It was exemplary show of fashion designing.*

Exequies/ऐक्सिक्विज *(plural noun)* – अंतिम संस्कार, अन्त्येष्टि किया formal funeral rites. *When somebody dies it becomes necessary to perform exequies.*

Exhale/एग्ज़हेल् *(verb)* – साँस निकलना breathe out. *As he exhaled his breath, I could smell alcohol on it.*

Exhilarate/एग्ज़िलरेट *(verb)* – हर्षित करना, प्रमुदित करना cause to feel very happy or animated. *I was exhilarated to get first position in the class.*

Exhume/एक्ज्यूम *(verb)* – खोदकर भूमि से बाहर निकालना dig out something buried, especially a corpse from the ground. *On the orders of the judge a dead body was exhumed.*

Exigent/एक्सिजेंट *(adjective)* – अतिआवश्यक formal pressing; demanding. *You are taking a loan from him, remember he is a very exigent person. You will have to return back all his money in time.*

E

Exile/एक्जाइल *(noun)* – निर्वासन, देश-निष्कासन the state of being barred from one's native country. *The English exiled Bahadur Shah Zafar. He died in Burma.*

Exist/एक्जिस्ट *(verb)* – जीवित रहना, अस्तित्त्व होना have objective reality or being. be found: two conflicting stereotypes exist. *Somehow or other he exists in such great poverty.*

Exit/एक्जिट *(noun)* – निर्गम, बाहर निकलने का रास्ता a way out of a building, room, or passenger vehicle. a place for traffic to leave a major road or roundabout. *Sir, that is exit gate.*

Exogamy/एक्सोगैमी *(noun)* – जाति के बाहर विवाह-सम्बन्ध anthropology the custom of marrying outside a community, clan, or tribe, compare with endogamy. *Clan or tribal people seldom favour exogamy.*

Exorbitant/एक्जॉर्बिटैन्ट *(adj)* – अपरिमित much too high. *Despite exorbitant prices, people continue to buy onions.*

Exorcist/एक्सार्सिस्ट *(noun)* – ओझा a person who makes evil spirits leave a person or place. *He is an exorcist. He drives out evil spirit from a person or place.*

Exorcise/एक्सॉर्साइज *(verb)* – झाड़-फूँककर प्रेत हटाना drive out from a person or place. *He has exorcised the evil spirit.*

Exordium/एक्जार्डियम *(noun)* – प्रस्तावना, भूमिका formal the beginning or introduction of a discourse or treatise. *The exordium of the astronomer who was speaking on black holes in sky was brilliant.*

Expand/एक्सपैंड *(verb)* – बढ़ाना, फुलाना make or become larger or more extensive. *Scientist say that our universe is ever expanding.*

Expanse/एक्सपैंस *(noun)* – विस्तार, फैलाव a wide continuous area of something, typically land or sea. *The expanse of sea was vast.*

Expansion/एक्सपैंसन *(noun)* – वृद्धि, विस्तार देना the action or an instance of expanding. *Expansion of the bridge was nearing completion.*

Expansive/एक्सपैंसिव *(adjective)* – व्यापक, विस्तृत covering a wide area; extensive. *During the rainy season, rivers become expansive.*

Exparte/एक्सपार्टि *(adjective & adverb)*– एक तरफा, एक के पक्ष में law with respect to or in the interests of one side only. *The law gave an exparte decision.*

Expatiate/एक्सपेशिएट *(verb)* – विस्तारपूर्वक लिखना speak or write at length or in detail. *This time he expatiated about brain surgery.*

Expatriate/एक्सपैट्रिएट *(noun)* – देश से बाहर रहने वाला व्यक्ति निर्वासित व्यक्ति a person who lives outside their native country. *He is an expatriate settled in Canada.*

Expect/एक्सपेक्ट *(verb)* – आशा करना regard as likely to happen, do, or be the case. suppose or assume: *I expect I'll be late.*

Expectorate/एक्सपेक्टोरेट *(verb)* – थूकना, खखारना cough or spit out from the throat or lungs. *He expectorated phlegm.*

Expedient/एक्सपीडिएन्ट *(adj)* – उचित, स्वार्थ साधक पर नैतिक नहीं *The government decided that it was expediant not to increase taxes until after election.*

Expedition/एक्सपेडिशन *(noun)* – शीघ्रता a journey undertaken by a group of people with a particular purpose. *An expedition was sent to Himalayan mountains for the study of plants.*

Expense/एक्सपेन्स *(noun)* – अधिक खर्चीला cost incurred or required. costs incurred in the performance of a job or task. *The expenses of living in a metro city are very high.*

Expert/एक्सपर्ट *(noun)* – निपुण a person who is very knowledgeable about or skilful in a particular area. *He is an expert in flying helicopter.*

Expiration/एक्सपिरेशन *(noun)* – मृत्यु expiry. *Before buying please check the expiration date of the medicine.*

Expire/एक्सपायर *(verb)* – समाप्त होना come to the end of the period of validity. come to an end. *This medicine has expired.*

Explain/एक्सप्लेन *(verb)* – व्याख्या करना make clear by describing it in more detail. *The teacher took us to the planetarium and explained the planetary system.*

Explainer/एक्सप्लेनर *(noun)*- व्याख्या करने वाला one who makes an explanation. *My English teacher is a good explainer.*

E

Explanatory/एक्स्प्लैनेटरि *(adjective)* – स्पष्टीकरण serving to explain something. *He was asked to submit an explanatory note to why he was absent from office for three days.*

Explicate/एक्सप्लिकेट *(verb)* – व्याख्या करना, स्पष्ट करना analyse and develop in detail. analyse a literary work in order to reveal its meaning. *The professor explicated a few poems of William Blake.*

Explicit/एक्सप्लिसिट *(adjective)* – स्पष्ट, स्फुट clear and detailed, with no room for confusion or doubt. *His lecture on the properties of medicinal plants was so explicit that there was a thunderous applause.*

Explode/एक्सप्लोड *(verb)* – उड़ा देना, विस्फोट होना burst or shatter violently, especially as a result of rapid combustion or excessive internal pressure. *A bomb exploded and great damage was done.*

Exploit/एक्सप्लॉयट *(verb)* – अद्भुत कार्य (किसी का शोषण करना) make use of and derive benefit from a resource. *He exploited his rich clients to no end.*

Exploration/एक्सप्लोरेशन *(noun)* – अन्वेषण, जिज्ञासा the act of travelling through some place. *The exploration of pyramids of Egypt brought to light many strange facts.*

Explosive/एक्सप्लोसिव *(adjective)* – शीघ्रदाह able or likely explode. likely to cause an eruption of anger or controversy. *Police found out many explosives hidden in trash boxes.*

Export/एक्सपोर्ट *(verb)* – परदेश में माल भेजना send to another country for sale. spread or introduce to another country. *India exports high standard sugar, wheat and rice to many countries.*

Expositor/एक्सपॉजिटर *(noun)* – अर्थ-प्रकाशक a person or thing that explains complicated ideas or theories. *He is an expositor and will explain all these theories in an explicit way.*

Expostulate/एक्सपॉस्ट्यूलेट *(verb)* – तर्क करना express strong disapproval or disagreement. *He expostulated against the plan of action.*

Exposure/एक्सपोजर *(noun)* – प्रकाशकरण the state of being exposed to something harmful. a physical condition resulting from being exposed to severe weather conditions. *Exposure to cold made him fall sick.*

Expound/एक्सपाउन्ड *(verb)* – व्याख्या करना, समझाना present and explain (a theory of idea) systematically. *He expounded the theory lucidly.*

Express/एक्सप्रेस *(verb)* – ठीक, निश्चित convey in words or by gestures and conduct. *He expressed his disagreement by gestures.*

Expression/एक्सप्रेशन *(noun)* – कथन the action of expressing something. *The expression on his face was that of displeasure.*

Expulsion/एक्सपल्शन *(noun)* – बहिष्कार, निर्वासन, निस्कासन the action of expelling. *His expulsion from the class was a disciplinary action taken against him.*

Expunge/एक्सपंज *(verb)* – मिटाना obliterate or remove completely. *His name was expunged from the club as he frequently broke its rules and regulations.*

Expurgate/एक्सपर्गेट *(verb)* – परिष्कार करना remove matter regarded as obscene or unsuitable from (a text or account). *A lesson was expurgated from the textbook as it was historically untruly.*

Exquisite/एक्सक्विजिट *(adjective)* – सुन्दर, उत्कृष्ट of great beauty and delicacy. *She is a woman of exquisite beauty.*

Exsect/एक्सेक्ट *(verb)* – काट डालना [biology] cause to protrude. *You have to exsect the unruly weeds.*

Extant/एक्सटैन्ट *(adjective)* – वर्तमान still in existence. *Some ancient animals are still extant in some form or the other.*

Extend/एक्सटेंड *(verb)* – फैलाना make larger or longer in space or time. occupy a specified area or continue for a specified distance. *He extended the offer to him to join the party.*

Extensile/एक्सटेंसाइल *(adjective)* – फैलाने योग्य capable of being extended. *The area around is extensile.*

Extensive/एक्सटेंसिव *(adjective)* – चौड़ा, बड़ा covering a large area. large in amount or scale. *The tea shops are extensive in this area.*

Extent/एक्सटेंट *(noun)* – प्रसार, फैलाना, विस्तृत करना the area covered by something. the size or scale of something. *He can go to any extent to fulfil his ambition.*

Extenuate/एक्सटेन्युएट *(verb)* – अल्प करना, शक्ति कम करना lessen the seriousness of guilt or an offence by reference to mitigating factor. *The lawyer tried his best to extenuate the crime.*

Exterior/एक्सटिरियर *(adjective)* – बाहरी रूप, बाहरी भाग forming, situated on, or relating to the outside. outdoor. *The exterior of this building is done very exquisitely.*

Exterminate/एक्सटरमिनेट *(verb)* – जड़ से उखाड़ देना destroy completely; eradicate. *The termites were exterminated from the house by spraying chemicals.*

External/एक्सटरनल *(adjective)* – बाहरी belonging to, situated on, or forming the outside. *The external of this hotel is beautifully done.*

Extinct/एक्सटिंक्ट *(adjective)* – अप्रचलित having no living members. no longer in existence. not having reputed in recorded history. *Many species of plants and animals are getting fast extinct these days.*

Extinguish/एक्सटिंग्विश *(verb)* – बुझाना put out a fire or light. *All the candles were extinguished as the electricity was restored.*

Extirpate/एक्सटर्पेट *(verb)* – नाश करना, जड़ से उखाड़ना search out and destroy completely. *All the enemy hideouts were extirpated.*

Extort/एक्सटॉर्ट *(verb)* – छीनना, बलपूर्वक लेना obtain by force, threats, or other unfair means. *The mafia extorted a lot of money from shopkeepers.*

Extra/एक्स्ट्रा *(adjective)* – अधिक, अतिरिक्त added to an existing or usual amount or number. *All extra money he had was spent on his illness.*

Extraordinarily/एक्स्ट्राऑर्डिनरिलि *(adverb)* – अपूर्वता से, विलक्षणता से In a manner beyond ordinary. *He behaned extraordinarily in the court.*

Extraordinary/एक्स्ट्राऑर्डिनरी *(adj)* – असामान्य very unusual or remarkable. *He has extra-ordinary talent for writing fiction.*

Extravagance/एक्स्ट्रावैगेन्स *(noun)* – अतिशय, फिजूलखर्ची the act of spending more than necessary. *He is a reasonable man and does not indulge in extravagance.*

Extravagant/एक्स्ट्रावैगेन्ट *(adjective)* – लुटाऊ मुक्तहस्त lacking restraint in spending money or using resources. resulting from or showing this: extravagant gifts. *He is not extravagant but spends money wisely.*

Extreme/एक्स्ट्रीम *(adjective)* – यथासंभव अधिकतम, चरम very great. exceptional very severe or serious. *You must take extreme care when driving at night.*

Extremity/एक्सट्रीमिटी *(noun)* – सीमा the furthest point or limit. the hands and feet. *There is no extremity of his anger.*

Extricable/एक्सट्रीकेब्ल – विमुक्त करने योग्य that may be extricated. *It is an extricable matter.*

Extrinsic/एक्सट्रिंसिक *(adjective)* – बाहरी, अनावश्यक not essential or inherent. *This theory is a complex interplay of influence and extrinsic factors.*

Extrude/एक्सट्रूड *(verb)* – ढकेलना thrust or force out. *Ashes were being extruded from the volcano.* shape by forcing it through a die. *The wires being extruded from the iron rods.*

Exuberance/एक्सयूबरैंस *(noun)* – प्रचुरता, अधिक्य joyful enthusiams. full of energy. *They enjoyed the picnic with a youthful exuberance.*

Exult/एक्जल्ट *(verb)* – अति प्रसन्न होना show feel triumphant elation. show or feel triumphant. *Exulting in her escape, she closed the door behind her.*

E

Ff

F/एफ (noun) – अंग्रेजी वर्णमाला का छठा वर्ण the sixth letter of the English alphabet.
1. Denoting the next after E in a set of items, categories, etc.
2. Music the fourth note of the diatonic scale of C major.

F

Fabaceous/फेबेसियस (adjective) – सेम की तरह की of the pea family. *Leguminous Green-looking fabaceous plants are a good source of vitamins A, B and C.*

Fabian/फेबियन (noun) – दीर्घसूत्री a member or supporter of the Fabian society, an organization of socialists aiming to achieve socialism by non-revolutionary methods. *Members of the Fabian society aim to spread socialism in a gradual way.*

Fable/फेबल (noun) – कहानी a short story, typically with animals as characters, conveying a moral. a supernatural story incorporating elements of myth and legend. *Children like to read fables.*

Fabricate/फैब्रिकेट (verb) – निर्माण करना invent, typically with deceitful intent. *The evidence is totally fabricated.*

Fabulist/फैब्यूलिस्ट (noun) – मिथ्यावादी मनुष्य a person who composes fables. *Book publishers look for fabulists who can compose fables that interests children.*

Fabulous/फैब्यूलस (adjective) – मनगढ़न्त विस्मयकारी, प्रसिद्ध extraordinary, especially extraordinarily large. informal wonderful. *Her fabulous performances attracted everyone in the theatre.*

Face/फेस (noun) – मुख the front part of a person's head from the forehead to the chin, or the corresponding part in an animal. an aspect of something the unacceptable face of social drinking. *Face is the combination of eyes, ears, mouth and nose; Face is the part of the clock that displays the time.*

Facetious/फॅसीशॅस (adjective) – मसखरा joking, trying to joke at an inappropriate time, describes a joke made about something serious. *It is facetious trying to be humorous when the matter is serious.*

Facial/फेसियल (noun) – मुख-सम्बन्धी a facial is a beauty treatment that is designed to exfoliate, invigorate or treat the skin of the face. *A treatment done on your face that refreshes your skin is an example of a facial.*

Facile/फेसाइल (adjective) – सुगम appearing comprehensive only by ignoring the complexities of an issue; superficial. *Facile is winning a game against a team that isn't very good at that particular game.*

Facilitate/फॅसिलिटेट (verb) – सुगम बनाना make easy or easier. *You must facilitate to ensure that everyone's opinions are heard.*

Facing/फेसिंग (noun) – आवरण a piece of material sewn on the inside of a garment, especially at the neck and armholes, to strengthen it. the cuffs, collar, and lapels of a military jacket, contrasting in colour with the rest of the garment. *Facing is a name given to a piece of material sewn to the edge of a garment, such as a dress or coat, as lining or decoration. Facing is an outer layer or coating applied to a surface for protection or decoration.*

Facsimile/फैक्सिमली (noun) – प्रतिलिपि an exact copy, especially of written or printed material. *An exact copy that has been made of a cheque is an example of a facsimile. When you have an exact copy of a legal document, this is an example of a facsimile copy.*

Fact/फैक्ट (noun) – तथ्य, सत्य, वास्तविकता a thing that is indisputably the case. information used as evidence or as part of a report. chiefly [Law] the truth about events as opposed to interpretation. *In fact, he has gone to Delhi today.*

Faction/फैक्शन (noun) – दल, गुट, दलबंदी a small dissentient group within a larger one. *The youngsters have formed a faction within an otherwise peaceful political party.*

Factious/फैक्शस *(adjective)* – अराजक relating or inclined to dissension. *An example of something factious is a bunch of dissatisfied elements within a class.*

Factor/फैक्टर *(noun)* – गुणक, घटक, कारक a circumstance, fact, or influence that contributes to a result. [Biology] a gene that determines a hereditary characteristic. *An example of factor would be eye-witness accounts to a news report about a crime. 9 is a factor of 27.*

Factory/फैक्टरी *(noun)* – कारखाना a building or buildings where goods are manufactured or assembled chiefly by machine. *A factory is a building or group of buildings in which goods are manufactured.*

Factotum/फैक्टोटम *(noun)* – विश्वस्त अनुचर या सेवक an employee who does all kinds of work. *An employee or assistant who serves in a wide range of capacities is known as factotum.*

Facula/फैक्यूला *(noun)* – सूर्य पर का चमकता चिह्न astronomy a bright region on the surface of the sun, linked to the subsequent appearance of sunspots. *A large bright spot on the sun's photosphere is known as facula.*

Fad/फैड *(noun)* – धुन a craze. *A fad is any fashion that is taken up with great enthusiasm for a brief period of time.*

Fade/फेड *(verb)* – फीका पड़ना gradually grow faint and disappear. lose or cause to lose colour. become temporarily less efficient as a result of frictional heating. *When a colour begins to get lighter, this is an example of a time when the colour fades.*

Fading/फेडिंग *(noun)* – मंद, क्षीण, म्लानता A waning; a decline: *The match had to be stopped because of fading light.*

Faeces/फीसीज *(plural noun)* – विष्ठा waste matter remaining after food has been digested, discharged from the bowels. *The body eliminates faces through rectum.*

Fail/फेल *(verb)* – असफल होना be unsuccessful in an undertaking be unable to meet the standards set by a test. judge a candidate in an examination or test not to have passed. *When you get only 1 question correct out of 100 on the test, this is an example of a time when you fail.*

Fain/फेन *(adjective)* – प्रसन्नतापूर्वक, तैयार, उत्सुक pleased or willing under the circumstances.

An example of fain is a brilliant student who is eager to study with his friend who is not as sharp.

Fainting/फेन्टिंग *(noun)* – मूर्छा या बेहोशी unconsciousness. *She fell on the ground in dead fainting.*

Faith/फेथ *(noun)* – विश्वास complete trust or confidence. *Faith is belief in a person or thing that does not rest on logical proof or material evidence.*

Faithful/फेथफुल *(adjective)* – सच्चा remaining loyal and steadfast. remaining sexually loyal to a lover or spouse. *A Muslim who adheres strictly to the tenants of the Islamic religion is faithful.*

Faithless/फेथलेस *(adjective)* – अविश्वासी without religious faith. *How can you have faith in a person who is so faithless, treacherous and cruel?*

Fake/फेक *(adjective)* – बेईमान आदमी not genuine. *You are a fake person when you pretend to be sick when you aren't.*

Falcate/फैल्केट *(adjective)* – हँसुए की तरह घूमा हुआ curved like a sickle; hooked. *As we moved slowly toward the deep waters in the river a big fish arched its back, showing a strongly falcate fin.*

Falchion/फॉल्चन/फॉल्शन *(noun)* – कृपाण historical a broad, slightly curved sword with the cutting edge on the convex side. *A falchion is a short, broad sword with a curved cutting edge and a sharp point.*

Falciform/फैल्सीफार्म *(adjective)* – हँसुए के आकार का curved like a sickle; hooked. *Falciform ligament is a very rare anomaly and hardly any cases are reported.*

Falcon/फॉल्कन/फॉकन *(noun)* – बाज a fast-flying bird of prey with long pointed wings. falconry the female of such a bird, especially a peregrine, compare with tercel. *Falcon is a high flying bird that can spot its prey on ground from 5-6 kilometres above.*

Faldstool/फाल्डस्टूल *(noun)* – खेमे में रखने की छोटी तिपाई a folding chair used by a bishop when not occupying the throne or when officiating in a church other than his own. *Faldstool is a backless chair used by a bishop when officiating in any other church.*

F

Fallacious/फैलेसस (adjective) - मिथ्या containing a fallacy; erroneous: fallacious reasoning. *When you make an argument based on a mistaken belief, then the argument would be described as fallacious.*

Fallacy/फैलॅसि - अशुद्धि (noun) a mistaken belief. *An example of fallacy is the idea that the sun spins around the earth.*

Fallibility/फैलिबिलिटी (adjective) - भ्रमत्व capable of making a mistake or being deceived, liable to be erroneous or inaccurate. *If your analysis doesn't take all factors into consideration, you only increase your chance of fallibility.*

Fallible/फैलिबॅल (adjective) - भ्रमकारी capable of making mistakes or being erroneous. *We all human beings are fallible.*

Falling/फॉलिंग (noun) - गिरने वाला पदार्थ a dropping, descending, coming down, a coming down suddenly from a standing or sitting position, a hanging down, or a part hanging down, a downward direction or slope, a becoming lower or less, reduction in value, price, etc., a lowering of the voice in pitch or volume. *I saw a falling star.*

Falsification/फॉल्सिफिकेशॅन (noun) - कूटकरण any evidence that helps to establish the falsity of something. *He does deliberatey falsification of company's records.*

Falsify/फाल्सीफाई (verb) - कपट करना alter so as to mislead. *He made many attempts to falsify her statement.*

Falter/फॉल्टर (verb) - भचकना lose strength or momentum. move or speak hesitantly. *When facing an interview board, you must speak clearly, never falter.*

Faltering/फाल्टरिंग (adjective) - हीनता the act of pausing uncertainly. *Try to change your faltering behaviour.*

Fame/फेम (noun) - यश the state of being famous. *By dint of sheer labour, he made a name and fame for himself within a short span of time.*

Famulus/फैम्युलश (noun) - जादूगर का सहायक historical an assistant or servant, especially one working for a magician or scholar. *A private secretary or other close attendant, especially during medieval times, was known as famulus.*

Fanatic/फॅनैटिक (noun) - हठधर्मी a person filled with excessive zeal, especially for an extreme religious or political cause. informal a person with an obsessive enthusiasm for a pastime or hobby. *A fanatic is a person who has faith in a belief that is not supported by reason.*

Fanaticism/फनैटिसिज्म (noun) - धार्मिक हठ is extreme devotion or zeal. *An example of fanaticism is following a set of rules even to the extent of killing other individuals.*

Fancied/फैन्सिड (adjective) - कल्पना किया हुआ imaginary; imagined. *Despite knowing the opponent was a strong side, we fancied our chances of winning by scoring quick runs.*

Fanciful/फैन्सीफुल (adjective) - काल्पनिक over-imaginative and unrealistic. existing only in the imagination. *Examiners will give you marks only for knowledge, not for your fanciful writing style.*

Fanion/फैनियन (noun) - पैमाइश करने वालों का झण्डी a small flag used by surveyors or soldiers to mark a position. *Every army hoists a fanion to as evidence for a captured post or area.*

Farce/फार्स (noun) - प्रहसन a comic dramatic work or genre using buffoonery and horseplay and typically including ludicrously improbable situations. *The voting was farce since the supporters of the rival party were prevented from going near the polling booth.*

Farcical/फार्सिकॅल (adjective) - विनोदपूर्ण resembling farce, absurd or ridiculous. *When supporters of rival party are prevented from voting, the eulogy of democracy becomes totally farcical.*

Farina/फॅराइना (noun) - मैदा, मण्ड, माँड़ी flour or meal made of cereal grains, nuts, or starchy roots. *Farina is a wholesome meal made from different cereal grains, potatoes, nuts, etc. and eaten as a cooked cereal.*

Farm/फाम (noun) - खेत an area of land and its buildings used for growing crops and rearing animals. a farmhouse. an establishment for breeding or growing something, or devoted to a particular thing: a fish farm a wind farm. *A farm is a place where dairy cows are raised. A farm is a place where baby fish are raised; a fish farm. Nearly 80 percent* of agricultural lands is owned by state and collective farms.

Farmer/फाम(र) (noun) – किसान a person who owns or manages a farm. *A person who is primarily concerned with growing crops is called a farmer.*

Farrago/फरांगो (noun) – घालमेल, मिश्रण a confused mixture. *There was not one reasonable balanced statement in the whole farrago.*

Farrier/फैरिअर (noun) – नालबन्द a smith who shoes horses. *Make sure that your horses ' feet are regularly trimmed and shod, by a competent farrier, to prevent hoof cracks.*

Farrow/फैरो (noun) – सूअर पालना a litter of pigs. *Piggeries have a separate farrow house for production of litters even in winter.*

Fart/फाट (verb) – पादना emit wind from the anus. *Fart is the noise that gas makes when coming from the rear. Someone who constantly complains is known as a fart.*

Farthest/फाद्-इस्ट (adjective & adverb) – सबसे अधिक दूरी का variant form of furthest. *Within the Solar system, planet Neptune is farthest from the Earth.*

Fascicle/फैसिकल (noun) – पुस्तिका, पुलिन्दा, गुच्छा a separately published installment of a book. *The part of a book published prior to publication of complete book is called fascicule.In botany, a bundle of stems, flowers, or leaves is called fascicle.*

Fascinate/फैसिनेट (verb) – मोह लेना irresistibly attract the interest of. *With his acting ability Charlie Chaplin could fascinate a global audience for decades.*

Fascism/फासिज्म (noun) – फासीवाद, व्यक्तिगत स्वतन्त्रता के विरुद्ध सिद्धान्तवादी an authoritarian and nationalistic right-wing system of government.*The government led by Benito Mussolini in Italy was an example of fascism.*

Fast/फास्ट (verb) – उपवास करना abstain from food or drink, especially as a religious observance. A fast is a period of time during which you go without food. *An example of fast is not eating for twelve hours before having blood drawn.*

Fasten/फास्सन (verb) – जकड़ना close or do up securely. fix or hold in place. secure the end of a thread with stitches or a knot. *The*

airhostess announced to fasten seatbelt. These days traffic police will charge you if you don't fasten your seatbelt.

Fastidious/फास्टिडिअस (adjective)– दुस्तोषणीय very attentive to accuracy and detail. *I'm normally very fastidious about citing my sources on this blog.*

Fasting/फास्टिंग (noun) – उपवास abstaining from food. *I keep fasting on Tuesday.*

Fastness/फास्टनेस (noun) – स्थिरता a secure place well protected by natural features. *The colour has a smooth gloss finish whilst possessing superior light fastness. Reproduced using the latest technology, these beautiful prints have a potential light fastness of over 200 years.*

Fatal/फेटॅल (adjective) – प्राणनाशक causing death. leading to failure or disaster. *The shot in the head proved fatal.*

Fatalism/फेटलिज्म (noun) – भाग्यवाद the belief that all events are predetermined and therefore inevitable. a submissive attitude to events. *It's time to shake off the lazy fatalism that the poor will always side with us.*

Fatalist/फेटलिस्ट (noun) – भाग्यवादी Anyone who submits to the belief that they are powerless to change their destiny. *He is a fatalist because he believes in fate.*

Fatality/फेटलिटि (noun) – विपत्ति, कष्ट [pl. fatalities] fate or necessity; subjection to fate, something caused by fate, a strong likelihood of ending in disaster, a fatal quality; deadly effect; deadliness: the fatality of any specified disease, a death caused by a disaster, as in an accident, war, etc. *Any accidental fatality to a member of the workforce is unacceptable. 9 % of motorcyclist fatalities are over the drink drive limit.*

Fathom/फैदम (noun) – छ: फुट की नाप a unit of length equal to six feet. chiefly used in reference to the depth of water. *The engine shaft is sunk to a depth of130 fathoms. In short, scientists have not yet been able to fathom the nature of consciousness, its origins, or its role in nature.*

Fatally/फेटली (adverb) – सांघातिक रीति से as determined by fate; inevitably, so as to cause death or disaster; mortally. *He was fatally wounded in the racing car accident.*

F

Fatigue/फॅटीग *(noun)* – थकावट extreme tiredness, especially resulting from mental or physical exertion or illness. *An example of fatigue is what you feel after you run a half marathon.*

Fatiguing/फॅटिगुंइग *(adjective)* – थकाने वाला tiring. *It is very tenuous and fatiguing work.*

Fatty/फैटी *(adjective)* – चर्बीदार containing a lot of fat. *I saw a very fatty lady on the road.*

Fatuous/फैट्यूऑस *(adjective)* – ऊटपटांग, अनर्गल, बुद्धिहीन silly and pointless. *There was little point continuing that fatuous discussion.*

Faucet/फॉसिट *(noun)* – पीपे में लगी हुई टोंटी chiefly north American a tap. *Faucet is an American term for the British word tap.*

Faugh/फॉ – छि: छि: *(exclamatory)* expressing disgust. *Faugh! This place stinks.*

Fault/फॉल्ट *(noun)* – अपूर्णता an unattractive or unsatisfactory feature; a defect or mistake. a service of the ball not in accordance with the rules. *It's nobody's fault, it's just one of those things.*

Faultless/फॉल्टलेस *(adjective)* – निर्दोष without any fault or defect; perfect. *She was absolutely faultless at it, never ever making a mistake.*

Faulty/फॉल्टी *(adjective)* – दोषयुक्त having or displaying faults. *If goods are deemed faulty they will either be repaired or replaced. Faulty wiring could cause fires or electric shocks, which may end in disaster.*

Favour/फेवर *(noun)* – अनुग्रह approval or liking. overgenerous preferential treatment. *Please do them a favour by cleaning their home.*

Favourite/फेवरिट *(adjective)* – प्रिय preferred to all others of the same kind. *My favourite colour is blue as I like it more than any other colour.*

Favouritism/फेवरिटिज्म *(noun)* – पक्षपात the unfair favouring of one person or group at the expense of another. *Favoritism is an act of giving preferential treatment to someone or something.*

Fawn/फॉन *(noun & verb)* – चापलूसी give a servile display of exaggerated flattery or affection. show slavish devotion, especially by rubbing against someone. *The way a young girl acts approvingly towards a boy she likes is called fawn.*

Fay/फे *(noun)* – परी [poetic/literary] a fairy.

Fealty/फीऍलटि *(noun)* – निष्ठा historical a feudal tenant's or vassal's sworn loyalty to a lord. *I will permit you to till my land for free as long as you pledge fealty to my rule.*

Fear/फिअॅर *(noun)* – भय an unpleasant emotion caused by the threat of danger, pain, or harm. a feeling of anxiety concerning the outcome of something unwelcome happening. *Fear is a feeling of anxiety and worry caused by the presence or nearness of danger, evil, pain, etc.*

Fearful/फिअरफुल *(adjective)* – भयंकर, भयानक showing or causing fear. *I am fearful of that haunted house.*

Fearless/फिअरलेस *(adjective)* – नि:शंक brave or not scared. *An example of fearless is a fireman's attitude when fighting a fire.*

Feasibility/फीजॅबिलिटि *(adjective)* – संभाव्यता, औचित्य capable of being done or carried out; practicable; possible: a feasible scheme. *Feasibility studies indicate that the project is worthwhile and should be executed.*

Feasible/फीजॅबॅल *(adjective)* – सम्भव possible and practical to achieve easily or conveniently. *With deadline extended, it is now feasible to erect the plant shed.*

Feast/फीस्ट *(noun)* – प्रीतिभोज, दावत a large meal, especially a celebratory one. a plentiful supply of something enjoyable. *An example of a feast is a buffet-style meal.*

Feat/फीट *(noun)* – वीरता का कार्य, करतब, कमाल an achievement requiring great courage, skill, or strength. *Sachin Tendulkar is the only cricketer to have achieved the feat of scoring one hundred international centuries.*

Feather/फेदर *(noun)* – पंख any of the flat appendages growing from a bird's skin, consisting of a partly hollow horny shaft fringed with vanes of barbs. *Birds of the same feathers flock together.*

Feathery/फिदरी *(adjective)* – परदार resembling or suggesting a feather or feathers. *This jacket is feathery.*

Feature/फिचर *(noun)* – आकृति a distinctive attribute or aspect of something. a part of the face, such as the mouth, making a significant contribution to its overall appearance. *A feature is a distinct or outstanding part, quality, or characteristic of something.*

Febrile/फीब्राइल *(adjective)* – ज्वर-सम्बन्धी having or showing the symptoms of a fever. *Febrile describes a person who has a fever or has something caused by a fever.*

Feculent/फेक्यूलॅन्ट *(adjective)* – गन्दा of or containing dirt, sediment, or waste matter. *The article you have written is not original, it is rubbish and feculent.*

Fecund/फीकॅन्ड *(adjective)* – उपजाऊ highly fertile; able to produce offspring. *A woman who can get pregnant is an example of someone who would be described as fecund.*

Fecundate/फीकॅन्डेट *(verb)* – उपजाऊ बनाना [archaic] fertilize. [poetic/literary] make fruitful. *There are no insects to fecundate flowering plants.*

Fecundity/फीकॅनडिटि *(noun)* – उपजाऊपन The intellectual productivity of a creative imagination. The state of being fertile; capable of producing offspring. The quality of something that causes or assists healthy growth. *The fecundity of this land is the reason for its high price.*

Federal/फेडरेल *(adjective)* – संयुक्त having or relating to a system of government in which several states form a unity but remain independent in internal affairs. relating to or denoting the central government as distinguished from the separate units constituting a federation. *The constitution describes India as a unitary government with federal features.*

Federate/फेडरेट *(verb)* – एक संस्था मे सम्मिलित करना organize or be orgainzed on a federal basis. *To federate means to unite various parts by common agreement under a central authority.*

Federation/फेडरेशन *(noun)* – कई राज्यों का संघ a federal group of states. an organization within which smaller divisions have some degree of internal autonomy. *The United States is an example of federation.*

Federative/फेडरेटिव *(adjective)* – सन्धि united under a central government. *Indian states are federative in nature.*

Feeble/फीबॅल *(adjective)* – दुर्बल lacking physical strength. lacking strength of character. falling to convince or impress: a feeble excuse. *The doctors made feeble attempts to revive the poor patient.*

Feed/फीड *(verb)* – खिलाना give food to. provide an adequate supply of food for. *You should feed grams to horses.*

Feel/फील *(verb)* – महसूस करना perceive, examine, or search by touch. be aware of through physical sensation. give a sensation of a particular physical quality when touched: the wool feels soft. informal fondle someone for one's own sexual stimulation. *An example of feel is when you run your hand over a dress.*

Feeling/फीलिंग *(noun)* – स्पर्श ज्ञान an emotional state or reaction. emotional responses or tendencies to respond. strong emotion. *Feeling is the act of sensing that the surface of something is smooth because you touched it.*

Feign/फेन *(verb)* – बहाना करना pretend to be affected by a feeling, state, or injury. *Don't feign sickness in a feeble attempt to get your sister to mop the floor.*

Felicitate/फिलिसिटेट *(verb)* – अभिनन्दन करना rare congratulate. *I felicitate you on your marriage day.*

Felicitous/फिलिसिटॅस *(adjective)* – धन्य well chosen or appropriate: a felicitous phrase. pleasing. *The author writes felicitous lines that show a genuine poetic touch.*

Felicity/फिलिसिटी *(noun)* – आनन्द complete happiness. *Some seek their rest and happiness on earth, others eternal felicity in heaven.*

Feline/फिलाइन *(adjective)* – बिल्ली के समान or, relating to, or resembling a cat. *(noun)* a cat or other animal of the cat family. *A feline is an animal that belongs to the cat family.*

Fell/फेल *(verb)* – गिराना, काट गिराना To fell is to knock down. Fell is also the past tense of "fall" and means that you have fallen down. *When you are standing upright and then you fall down, this is an example of a situation where you fell.*

Feller/फेलर *(noun)* – वृक्ष काटकर गिराने वाला a person who fells trees. *He works as a feller under a contractor.*

Felony/फेलॅनि *(noun)* – महा अपराध a crime, typically one involving violence, regarded in the US and other judicial systems as more serious than a misdemeanour. *An example of felony is rape.*

Felspar/फेलस्पार *(noun)* – एक धातु विशेष variant spelling of felospar. *Felspar is an ore containing silicate of iron.*

Felt/फेल्ट *(noun)* – नमदा, कम्बल cloth made by rolling and pressing wool or another suitable textile accompanied by the application of moisture or heat, which causes the fibres to mat together. *We generally use felt in winter season.*

Female/फिमेल *(adjective)* – स्त्री जाति of or denoting the sex that can bear offspring or produce egg .relating to or characteristic of woman or female animal of a plant and or flower having a pistil but no stamens. *A female is a person of the sex that produces eggs and can bear young. Females are no more a weaker section.*

Feminine/फेमिनिन *(adjective)* – जनाना having qualities traditionally associated with woman, especially delicacy and prettiness. female. *Sewing and cooking are examples of hobbies that were traditionally described as feminine hobbies.*

Femininity/फेमिनिटी *(noun)* – स्त्रीत्व this girl always dresses like a boy. *I think she lacks feminity*

Feminize/फेमिनाइज *(verb)* – स्त्री बनाना make more feminine or female. *To feminize is to make or become feminine or effeminate.*

Femur/फेमर *(noun)* – जंघा पिण्डिका anatomy the bone of the thigh or upper hind limb. *The bone in your body that goes from your pelvis to your knee is known as femur.*

Fen/फेन *(noun)* – दलदल a low and marshy or frequently flooded area of land. flat low-lying areas of Lincolnshire, Cambridgeshire, and Norfolk, formerly marshland but now largely drained. ecology wetland with alkaline, neutral, or only slightly acid peaty soil. *Compare with bog. Low, flat, marshy and swampy land is known as fen.*

Fence – *(noun)* a barrier enclosing an area, typically consisting of posts connected by wire, wood, etc. a large upright obstacle in steeplechasing, showjumping, or cross-country. *An example of a fence is a two foot wooden barrier around a person's front yard.*

Fencing/फेन्सिंग *(noun)* – पटेबाजी the sport of fighting with blunted swords according to a set of rules in order to score points. *Fencing is a popular sporting event at Olympic games.*

Fenestra/फेनेस्ट्रा *(noun)* – खिड़की या छिद्र a small hole or opening in a bone, especially either of two in the middle ear. *Fenestra is a small opening in the inner wall of the middle ear.*

Fennel/फेनेल *(noun)* – सोया जाति का एक शाक an aromatic yellow-flowered plant of the parsley family, with feathery leaves used as culinary herbs or eaten as a vegetable. *Fennel is a tall herb with feathery leaves and yellow flowers whose foliage and aromatic seeds are used to flavour foods.*

Feral/फेरल *(adjective)* – जंगली, वन्य of an animal or plant in a wild state, especially after having been domesticated or cultivated. *A feral is an undomesticated cat that scratches and claws if you come near it.*

Ferment/फर्मेंट *(verb)* – खमीर उठना या उठाना undergo or cause to undergo fermentation. *Ferment is an agent or catalyst, such as, yeast, bacterium, mould, or enzyme that cause fermentation.*

Fern/फर्न *(noun)* – सुन्दर महीन पत्तियों का एक पौधा a flowerless vascular plant which has feathery or leafy fronds and reproduces by spores released from the undersides of the fronds. *I have seen many types of fern in wet areas.*

Ferocious/फेरोशस *(adjective)* – निर्दयी savagely fierce, cruel, or violent. *While in a zoo, you must be cautious against ferocious animals.*

Ferocity/फेरॉसिटि *(noun)* – क्रूरता the state of being wild or fierce. *The extreme and wild nature of a storm is an example of the ferocity of the storm.*

Ferriage/फेरिइज *(noun)* – नदी पार करने का भाड़ा charge for transportation by ferry. *What is the ferriage for crossing the river?*

Ferric/फेरिक *(adjective)* – लोहे का chemistry of iron with a valency of three; of iron. *Ferric oxide is one of the chemical compounds containing iron.*

Ferrous/फेरस *(adjective)* – लोहा सम्बन्धी chiefly or metals containing or consisting of iron. *Ferrous oxide is one of the chemical compounds containing iron.*

F

Ferrule/फेरूल *(noun)* – सामी a ring or cap which strengthens the end of a handle, stick, or tube. a metal band strengthening or forming a joint. *Ferrule is a metal or plastic ring or cap put around the end of a cane, tool handle, etc. to give added strength or for tightening a joint.*

Fertilize/फर्टिलाइज *(verb)* – उपजाऊ बनाना cause to develop a new individual by introducing male reproductive material. *To fertilize is to make the female reproductive cell fruitful by impregnating with the male gamete.Urea, phosphates and nitrates help fertilize soil for increased productivity.*

Ferule/फेरूल *(noun)* – बच्चों को मारने की छड़ी a flat ruler used for punishing children. *Ferule is an instrument, such as a cane, stick, or flat piece of wood, used in punishing children.*

Fervency/फर्वेन्सि *(noun)* – उत्सुकता feelings of great warmth and intensity. *He has fervency in his behaviour.*

Fervent/फर्वेन्ट *(adjective)* – गरम intensely passionate. *It is my fervent appeal to allow me 15 days leave.*

Fervid/फॉविड *(adjective)* – प्रचण्ड intensely enthusiastic, especially to an excessive degree. *He is a fervid patriot and won't mind dying for the good of the motherland.*

Fervour/फॉर्वर *(noun)* – उत्साह intense and passionate feeling. *Fervour is intense feelings or passion at a higher degree.*

Fester/फेस्टर *(verb)* – सड़ना of a wound or sore become septic. become rotten. *When food is left out for days to rot, the food festers and becomes unfit for consumption.*

Festival/फेस्टिवल *(noun)* – उत्सव a day or period of celebration, typically for religious reasons. *Deepawali is a festival of great pomp and show.*

Festivity/फेस्टिविटी *(noun)* – उत्सव-काल joyful and exuberant celebration. celebratory activities or events. *A week or so before Deepawali, the atmosphere acquires the look of festivity everywhere.*

Fetch/फेच *(verb)* – जाकर लाना To come or go after and take or bring back. *The puppy went to fetch the stick that we had tossed.*

Fetching/फेचिंग *(adjective)* – मोहक attractive: a fetching little garment. *She went for fetching a new hairstyle and a new garment.*

Fete/फेट *(noun)* – त्योहार British an outdoor public function to raise funds for a charity or institution, typically involving entertainment and the sale of goods. *An example of a fete is a school carnival.*

Feticide/फेटिसाइड *(noun)* – भ्रूणहत्या destruction or abortion of a fetus. *Cases of female feticide is on the rise in some parts of India.*

Fetid/फेटिड *(adjective)* – दुर्गन्धि-युक्त smelling unpleasant. *The spoiled food is an example of something that might be described as fetid.*

Fettle/फेटल *(noun)* – योग्यता condition: the horse remains in fine fettle. *Every jockey wants to keep his racing horse in fine fettle. She was in great fettle, bouncing all over the place.*

Fetus/फेटस *(noun)* – भ्रूण an unborn or unhitched offspring of a mammal, in particular an unborn human more than eight weeks after conception. *A baby that has been in its mother's stomach growing for 18 weeks is an example of a fetus.*

Feudal/फ्यूडल *(adjective)* – जागीरदारी according to, resembling, or denoting the system of feudalism. *Early developments were really about the maintenance of political power, essentially feudal in origin.*

Fever/फीवर *(noun)* – बुखार an abnormally high body temperature, usually accompanied by shivering, headache, and in severe instances, delirium. *He was running a temperature of 103 degree fahrenheit.*

Feverish/फीवरिश *(adjective)* – ज्वरात्, ज्वरग्रस्त someone whose temperature is too high, or someone who is greatly excited or has high energy. *A person who has a body temperature of 102 is an example of someone who is feverish. A crowd that is shouting and yelling because their team is winning is an example of a crowd that would be described as feverish.*

Fiasco/फिऐस्को *(noun)* – विशिष्ट असफलता a ludicrous or humiliating failure. *The party ended in a fiasco since the clown hired to entertain broke his leg and has threatened to sue the organizer.*

F

Fiat/फाइएट – आज्ञा fiat means an official order given by somebody in authority. *It is obligatory to follow the fiat of the commissioner.*

Fibril/फाइब्रिल *(noun)* – महीन रेशा [technical] a small or slender fibre. *Electron microscope is needed to observe the fibril formation.*

Fibrous/फाइब्रस *(adjective)* – रेशेदार consisting of or characterized by fibres. *When this dust is inhaled it can make the lungs gradually fibrous and lead to breathing problems.*

Fickle/फिकॅल *(adjective)* – अस्थिर changeable, especially as regards one's loyalties. *Children are very fickle minded and move to new toys because of their short attention span.*

Fiction/फिक्सन *(noun)* – उपन्यास prose literature, especially novels, describing imaginary events and people. *Publishers are coming out with fiction that is meant for children.*

Fictitious/फिक्टिशस *(adjective)* – झूठा not real or true, being imaginary or invented. *Many authors use fictitious names instead of their original ones.*

Fiddle/फिड्ल *(noun)* – सारंगी informal a violin. *The space in itself plays second fiddle to the lower gallery.*

Fiddler/फिड्लर *(noun)* – बजाने वाला musician who plays the violin. *A person who plays violin in a folk music is known as fiddler.*

Fidelity/फाइडेलिटि *(noun)* – स्वामी भक्ति continuing loyalty to a person, cause, or belief. *Fidelity is faithful devotion to duty or to one's obligations;*

Fidget/फिडगेट *(verb)* – बेचैन या अशान्त होना make small movements through nervousness or impatience. *He fidgeted with his notes while lecturing.*

Fie/फाइ *(interjection)* – धिक्! छी! छी! [archaic] or humorous used to express disgust or outrage. *Any exclamatory expression used to denote distaste or disapproval is known as fie.*

Fiend/फीन्ड *(noun)* – पिशाच an evil spirit or demon. a very wicked or cruel person. *He is so obsessed with crosswords that people call him a crossword fiend.*

Fiendish/फीन्डिश *(adjective)* – क्रूर, अतिदुष्ट extremely cruel or unpleasant. *Regular expressions can get quite fiendish to read at times.*

Fierce/फिअॅस *(adjective)* – खूँखार, हिंसक violent or aggressive, ferocious. intense: fierce opposition. of a mechanism having a powerful abruptness of action. *Fierce fighting broke out again between India and Pakistan.*

Fiery/फाइअॅरि *(adjective)* – उत्सुक resembling or consisting of fire. *He was high-spirited and had a very fiery temper, which led him at times to acts of cruelty.*

Fife/फाइफ *(noun)* – एक प्रकार की छोटी बाँसुरी a kind of small shrill flute used with the drum in military bands. *A small flute with a high, piercing tone, used mainly in military bands.*

Fifteen/फिफ्टीन *(cardinal number)* – पन्द्रह equivalent to the product of three and five; one more than fourteen; 15. classified as suitable for people of 15 years and over. *Fifteen is a sum of five and ten.*

Fifth/फिफ्थ *(cardinal number)* – पाँचवा constituting number five in a sequence; 5th. *The sum of two and three is five.*

Fight/फाइट *(verb)* – युद्ध करना take part in a violent struggle involving physical force or weapons. engage in a war or contest. quarrel or argue. defend oneself against an attack by someone or something. *Since independence, India and Pakistan have fought four wars.*

Fighter/फाइटर *(noun)* – लड़ाका a person or animal that fights. *India has decided to purchase fighter jets from France.*

Fighting/फाइटिंग *(noun)* – युद्ध combat, battle. Fighting broke out between rival forces. *Do you think fighting in the dressing room will help good performance on the field?*

Figment फिगमेंट *(noun)* – कल्पित वस्तु a thing believed to be real but existing only in the imagination. *Novels are nothing but the figment of an author's imagination.*

Figurative/फिग्युरॅटिव *(adjective)* – आलंकारिक departing from a literal use of words; metaphorical. *We haven't taken on new artists for some years, however mainly figurative artists would be considered.*

Figurine/फिगयूरीन *(noun)* – एक छोटी मूर्ति a small statue of a human form. *Figurines of* *a goddess have also been excavated by the archaeologists.*

Filament/फिलॅमॅन्ट *(noun)* – सूत, रेशा a slender thread-like object or fibre, especially one found in animal or plant structures. *A type of intermediate filament found in epithelial cells have been created in the laboratory.*

Filature/फिलॅचॅर – *(noun)* a place where silk thread is obtained from silkworm cocoons. *Filature is a reel of raw silk obtained from cocoons of silkworm.*

Filch/फिल्च *(verb)* – चुराना informal pilfer; steal. *The thief filched the purse and ran away into hiding.*

Filiform/फिलिफाम *(adjective)* – धागे की तरह [Biology] thread-like. *In botany, filiform is a term used to describe leaf-shapes.*

Filier/फिलियर *(noun)* – भरने वाला something used to fill a gap or cavity, or to increase bulk. an item serving only to fill space or time in a newspaper, broadcast, or recording. a word or sound filling a pause in an utterance or. *An item used to fill the space or time is known as filier.*

Filling/फिलिंग *(adj & noun)* – संतुष्ट करने वाला, भरावन a quantity or place of material that fills or is used to fill something. *I have got dental fillings done for rupees two thousand.*

Fillip/फिलिप *(noun)* – उत्साह a stimulus or boost. *The pep talk by the coach acted as a fillip to the team's sagging morale.*

Filly/फिलि *(noun)* – बछेड़ी, छिनाल a young female horse, especially one less than four years old. *He bought a lovely 3-year old filly with a view to train her for horse racing.*

Filmy/फिल्मी *(adjective)* – झिल्लीदार especially of fabric thin and translucent. *Filmy fern grows along the banks of the river Ravi as it runs through the hills.*

Filth/फिल्थ *(noun)* – गन्दगी, मैल disgusting dirt. obscene and offensive language or printed material. corrupt behaviour. *We simply didn't expect to see such filth at the family shopping store.*

Filthy/फिल्थी *(adjective)* – गन्दा disgustingly dirty. obscene and offensive. British informal very unpleasant. informal very disagreeable. *The language of these college students is pretty filthy.*

Filtrate/फिल्ट्रेट *(noun)* – निभारा हुआ तरल पदार्थ a liquid which has passed through a filter. *The liquid obtained after passing through the filter is known as filtrate. (verb)* rare filter. *Is this area watered out or are you producing mud filtrate?*

Fimbriate/फिम्ब्रिएट *(adjective)* – किनारीदार [Biology] having a fringe of fimbriae. *The wide portion of the fallopian tube near the fimbriated extremity is known as ampulla of uterine tube.*

Fin/फिन – मछली का सुफना *(noun)* a flattened appendage on the body of a fish or other aquatic animal, used for propelling, steering, and balancing. an underwater swimmer's flipper. *Fin is an organ attached to a fish's body that helps them in swimming under water.*

Final/फाइनल *(adjective)* – अन्तिम, समापन coming at the end of a series. reached as the outcome of a process: the final cost will run into six figures. *The final chapter of the book was quite absorbing.*

Finale/फिनाले *(noun)* – वित्त, अर्थ the last part of a place of music, an entertainment, or a public event. *The grand finale will end with a fabulous firework display over the stadium.*

Finance/फाइनेंस *(noun)* – धन, वित्त, इसका प्रबन्ध the management of large amounts of money, especially by governments or large companies. monetary support for an enterprise. the monetary resources and affairs of a state, organization, or person. *Finance minister of India has imposed a severe squeeze on the Indian economy.*

Finch/फिंच *(noun)* – एक प्रकार की छोटी चिड़िया a seed-eating songbird of a large group including the chaffinch, goldfinch, linner, etc., typically with a stout bill and colourful plumage. *Australian finches are very engaging little birds which can provide many hours of enjoyment.*

Finder/फाइन्डर *(noun)* – पता लगाने वाला a person that finds someone or something. *You can use the postcode finder for a wider scope.*

Fine/फाइन *(noun)* – आर्थिक दंड, सुन्दर, महीन a sum of money exacted as a penalty by a court of [Law] or other authority. *This restaurant is renowned for fine dining, shopping and cafés.*

F

Finery/फाइनरी *(noun)* – ठाट-बाट, अलंकार elaborate decoration (dress), historical a hearth where pig iron was converted into wrought iron. *Arrive in your own finery or choose from a wide selection of our costumes.*

Fingering/फिंगरिंग *(noun)* – छूने का काम handling with fingers, a manner or technique of using the fingers to play a musical instrument. *The main difficulty is that for a number of instruments there is no standard fingering.*

Finial/फिनियल *(noun)* – गाथिक इमारत में बना फूल a distinctive section or ornament at the apex of a roof, pinnacle, or similar structure in a building. an ornament at the top, end, or corner of an object. *Attach a narrow wrought iron curtain rod with decorative finials to the wall.*

Finical/फिनिकल *(adjective)* – तुनकमिज़ाज, अति कोमल *He is a finical person; his attitude is prone to change any moment.*

Finis/फिनिश *(noun)* – अन्त the end (printed at the of a book or shown at the end of a film). *Hem lines are elegantly long with the subtle tailoring and immaculate finis to the skirt.*

Finite/फाइनाइट *(adjective)* – मर्यादा युक्त limited in size or extent. *Although electricity travels fast, its speed is still finite and over a wire it is slower than in a vacuum.*

Fir/फर *(noun)* – देवदार an evergreen coniferous tree with upright cones and flat needle-shaped leaves. *Fir trees are extensively found in Kashmir.*

First/फर्स्ट *(ordinal number)* – मुख्य, प्रधान coming before all others in time or order; earliest; 1st. before doing something else specified or implied. for the first time. with a specified part o0r person in a leading position: it plunged nose first into the river. *Put child safety first. It happened in the first half of the 20th century.*

Fiscal/फिस्कल *(adjective)* – राजकर-सम्बन्धी of or relating to government revenue, especially taxes. *There is a fiscal deficit in the budget.*

Fish/फिश *(noun)* – मछली a flat plate fixed on a beam or across a joint to give additional strength. *You should try not to have more than two portions of oily fish a week.*

Fish-plate/फिश-प्लेट *(noun)* – रेल की पटरियों को जोड़ने की पट्टी a flat piece of metal used to connect adjacent rails in a railway track. *Fish-plates are used to strengthen railway tracks.*

Fission/फिजन *(noun)* – जीव कोशिकाओं का विभाजन the action of splitting or being split into two or more parts. *Nuclear fission is what powers all modern day reactors.*

Fissure/फिसर *(noun)* – दरार, फटन a long, narrow crack. *Many fissures are created in the society by religious differences.*

Fist/फिस्ट *(noun)* – घूँसा a person's hand when the fingers are bent in towards the palm and held there tightly. *He unclenched his fist to shake hands with the visitor.*

Fisticuffs/फिस्टिकफ्स *(plural)* – मुक्केबाजी fighting with the fists. *Fighting with the fists is called fisticuffs.*

Fistula/फिस्ट्युला *(noun)* – नासूर narrow passage, opening. *Patients who have a fistula can usually feel it "buzzing "slightly.*

Fitness/फिटनेस *(noun)* – उपयुक्तता the state of being fit. *Running, cycling, swimming etc can all raise your body fitness.*

Fitter/फिटर *(noun)* – यन्त्रों के अवयवों को यथास्थान बैठाने वाला one who fits, tailor. *All electrical appliances should be repaired by a qualified, registered electrical fitter.*

Fittings/फिटिंग *(noun)* – आवश्यक यंत्र an attachment. *This house comes with all fittings made of stainless steel.*

Five/फाइव *(cardinal number)* – पाँच equivalent to the sum of two and three; one more than four, or half of ten. *Twenty divided by four is five.*

Fix/फिक्स *(verb)* – स्थिर करना attach or position securely. direct or be directed unwaveringly toward: her gaxe fixed on jess. discover the exact location of by using radar, visual bearings, or astronomical observation. *Charges have been fixed in accordance with building regulations.*

Fixable/फिक्सेबल *(adjective)* – स्थिर करने योग्य can be fixed *All these appliances are fixable on any side of the wall.*

Fixation/फिक्सेशन *(noun)* – स्थिरीकरण the action or condition of fixating or being fixated. *Fixation of fractures is commonly used in many areas of trauma care.*

Fixactive/फिक्सेक्टिव *(noun)* – स्थिर करने वाला a substance used to fix, protect, or stabilize something. *Some people find that using a denture fixative in the early stages gives them extra security.*

Fixed/फिक्स्ड *(adjective)* – दृढ़ set firmly in place, protected. *Social systems are not fixed and unchanging, even when they are relatively stable. Fixed assets used by the charity should be briefly described, such as, make of desktop computer, or of motor vehicle.*

Fixity/फिक्सिटी *(noun)* – स्थिरता the state of being unchanging or permanent. *The fixity of his stave is unwavering.*

Fixture/फिक्सचर *(noun)* – दृढ़ता a piece of equipment or furniture which is fixed in position in a building or vehicle. articles attached to a house or land and considered legally part of it so that they normally remain in place when an owner moves, compare with fitting. *Provisional details of the forthcoming fixtures are listed below. It appeared to be constructed like today's plumbing fixtures.*

Fizzle/फिजल *(verb)*– फूत्कार शब्द करना make a feeble hissing or spluttering sound. end or fail in a weak or disappointing way. *Despite a hopeful beginning, Indian batting fizzled out weakly.*

Flageolet/फ्लैजॅलेट *(noun)* – मुरली, शहनाई a very small flute-like instrument resembling a recorder but with four finger holes on top and two thumb holes below. *A flageolet is a small flutelike instrument with a cylindrical mouthpiece, four finger holes, and two thumbholes.*

Flagon/फ्लैगॅन *(noun)* – सुराही a large container for serving or consuming drinks. a container used to hold the wine for Eucharist. a large bottle in which wine or cider is sold, typically holding 1.13 litres. *A flagon is a large vessel with a handle and spout and often a lid, used for holding wine or other liquors.*

Flagrant/फ्लेग्रन्ट *(adjective)* – ज्वलन्त conspicuous; blatant. *The draconian order issued is a flagrant misuse of bureaucratic power.*

Flail/फेअल *(noun)* – मूसल a threshing tool consisting of a wooden staff with a short heavy stick swinging from it. a similar device used as a weapon or for flogging. a machine having a similar action. *An example of a flail is a tool used to toss grain up in the air.*

Flair/फ्लेअर *(noun)*– प्रवृत्ति a natural ability or talent. *He possesses that natural flair for journalism without which no one will succeed in the news media.*

Flam/फ्लैम *(noun)* – छल, कपट in music one of the basic patterns of drumming, consisting of a stroke preceded by a grace note. *Flam is a double drumbeat where first note is a short and the second a long one.*

Flame/फ्लेम *(noun)* – अग्नि की ज्वाला a hot glowing body of ignited gas that is generated by something on fire. *Flame is a zone of burning gases and fine suspended matter associated with rapid combustion.*

Flamingo/फ्लेमिंगो *(noun)* – राजहंस a tail wading bird with mainly pink or scarlet plumage, long legs and neck, and a crooked bill. *In the wild, flamingoes breed in very large numbers on salt or soda lakes.*

Flange/फ्लेंज *(noun)* – निकला हुआ किनारा a projecting rim or piece. *I knew something was wrong when the brake drum and hub flange came off still attached to the wheel.*

Flank/फ्लैंक *(noun)* – पेट, मकान का किनारा the side of a person's or animal's body between the ribs and the hip. *Area between the ribs and hip of human or animal is known as flank.*

Flanker/फ्लैंकर *(noun)* – गढ़, किला rugby a wing forward. *Bhutia has played number eleven as open side flanker for most of the games.*

Flannel/फ्लैनॅल *(noun)* – फलालीन a kind of soft-woven woollen or cotton fabric that is slightly milled and raised. *I saw a grey flannel suit in that shop.*

Flannelette/फ्लैनलेट *(noun)* – सूती फलालीन a napped cotton fabric resembling flannel. *Flannelette is a soft cotton fabric with a nap.*

Flaring/फ्लेअरिंग *(adjective)* – जगमगाता हुआ burning, curving outward *Flaring of trousers at the bottom is no longer in fashion.*

F

Flash/फ्लैश *(verb)* – सहसा प्रकाशित होना burst forth into or as if into flame, give off light or be lighted in sudden or intermittent bursts, appear or occur suddenly *The image flashed onto the screen. Rescue flashed on us the time we got caught in the storm. The cars flashed by while we were waiting.*

Flashy/फ्लैशी *(adjective)* – चमकीला ostentatiously stylish. *I don't want anything too flashy like a Ferrari or a Bentley.*

Flask/फ्लास्क *(noun)* – बोतल, कुप्पी a narrow-necked conical or spherical bottle. *A thermos flask allows hot drinks to be carried.*

Flat/फ्लैट *(noun)* – एक खण्ड के कमरे chiefly British a set of rooms comprising an individual place of residence within a larger building. *High-rise flats were to be built in the inner zone.*

Flattish/फ्लैटिश *(adjective)* – कुछ चिपटा fairly flat. *The spinners were hammered for six and fours because of bowling a flattish deliveries.*

Flatulence/फ्लैटुलेंस *(noun)* – बाई, उदर–वायु accumulation of gas in the stomach, emptiness *Flatulence is the expulsion of mixed gases from the body, which are the byproduct of the digestion process.*

Flatus/फ्लेटस *(noun)* – अधोवायु formal gas in or from the stomach or intestines. *The medical term for mixture of gases formed as a byproduct of digestion process is known as flatus.*

Flaunt/फ्लॉन्ट *(verb)* – अकड़ना display ostentatiously. *There is no justification to flaunt your wealth among the poor people.*

Flavour/फ्लेवर *(noun)* – सुगन्ध the distinctive taste of a food or drink. *Flavoured coffees from around the world is available in this hotel.*

Flax/फ्लैक्स *(noun)* – पटुआ, सन a blue-flowered herbaceous plant that is cultivated for its seed and for textile fibre made from its stalks. textile fibre obtained from this plant.*Linen is made out of the natural fibre flax.*

Flay/फ्ले *(verb)* – चमड़ा उतारना, लूटना strip the skin from a body by carcass. *It is demoralizing for a person to be flayed in front of many people.*

Fledge/फ्लेज *(verb)* – परदार करना develop or allow to develop wing feathers that are large enough for flight. *The now fledged chicks have to undertake the first migration on their own. Then the vouchers would become fully fledged shares, traded on the stock market.*

Flee/फ्ली *(verb)* – भाग जाना run away. *They were fleeing from the country in fear of persecution.*

Fleece/फ्लीस *(noun & verb)* – पतला रेशा, ऊन, लूटना the wool coat of a sheep. *You want to fleece the poor labourers.*

Fleer/फ्लिअर *(verb)* – उपहास करना [poetic/ literary] laugh impudently or jeeringly. *Why fleer at someone who is yet to be trained for a new job?*

Flesh/फ्लेश *(noun)* – माँस the soft substance in the body consisting of muscle tissue and fat. *Future generations will scarcely believe such a person like Mahatma Gandhi ever walked in flesh and blood on this Earth. Flesh is the semi solid part of vegetables which breaks up during cooking.*

Fletcher/फ्लेचर *(noun)* – तीर बनाने वाला chiefly historical a person who makes and sells arrows. *Fletcher is a person who sells bows and arrows.*

Flex/फ्लेक्स *(verb)* – लचीला होना bend a limb or joint. *Exercise helps keep the muscles and joints flexed.*

Flexile/फ्लेक्साइल *(adjective)* – मुलायम [archaic] pliant and flexible. *Within these snow-beds the flexible fern occurs.*

Flexion/फ्लेक्शन *(noun)* – घुमाव the action of bending or the condition of being bent. *This exercise involves the flexion and extension of the lower back.*

Flexor/फ्लेक्सर *(noun)* – अंग के जोड़ को मोड़ने वाली माँसपेशी anatomy a muscle whose contraction bends a limb or other part of the body. *These exercises can make only a limited contribution to strengthening the flexors.*

Flexuous/फ्लेक्स्यूअस *(adjective)* – घुमावदा full of bends and curves. *Hundreds of miles of arteries and veins adjust inside the body because of their flexuous nature.*

Flick/फ्लिक *(noun)* – झटका a sudden smart movement up and down or from side to side. *Please flick the overdrive switch on.*

Flicker/फ्लिकर *(verb)* – फड़फड़ाना shine or burn unsteadily and fitfully. *Flicker of the burning candle was finally snuffed out.*

Flier/फ्लाइअॅर *(noun)* – विमानचालक उड़ने वाला person or thing which flies, a small advertisement *We have been distributing fliers all over the place. Bring your own kite or marvel at displays by the best fliers in the country.*

Flim-flam/फ्लिम-फ्लैम *(noun)* – बकवास insincere and unconvincing talk. *He is a 'real ' person to the poor people since he doesn't have any time for all that flim flam.*

Flimsy/फ्लिम्जी *(adjective)* – असार weak and insubstantial. *Don't come out with such flimsy reasons to stay away from the college.*

Flinch/फ्लिंच *(verb)* – पीछे हटना make a quick, nervous movement as an instinctive reaction to fear or pain. *Never flinch from your objective in the face of any difficulties.*

Flippancy/फ्लिपॅंसी *(noun)* – वाक्-चपलता quality or state of being flippant *You need to answer your absence with a little less flippancy this time.*

Flippant/फ्लिपैंट *(adjective)* – छिछोरा not showing a serious or respectful attitude. *How can you be so flippant about shattering people's lives and dreams?*

Flipper/फ्लिपर *(noun)* – मीनपक्ष a broad, flat limb, without fingers, used for swimming by sea animals such as seals, whales, and turtles. *Seals use their front flippers for moving on land and hind limbs for swimming in water.*

Flit/फिल्ट *(verb)* – उड़ जाना move swiftly and lightly. *A butterfly was flitting nearby and disturbing me during studies.*

Flitter/फ्लिटर *(verb)* – फड़फड़ाहट move quickly in a random manner. *The flittering of the butterfly around the table was disturbing my study.*

Float/फ्लोट *(verb)* – तैरना, उतराना rest or cause to rest on the surface of a liquid without sinking. *Helicopters have the capability to keep floating in the air without going forward.*

Flocule/फ्लोक्यूल *(noun)* – ऊन का छोटा झब्बा a small clump of material that resembles a tuft of wool. *Flocule is a small mass of matter resembling a soft tuft of wool.*

Floe/फ्लो *(noun)* – जल पर तैरता हुआ बरफ का टुकड़ा a sheet of floating ice. *Was the mass of ice that sank the Titanic actually an iceberg or a floe?*

Flog/फ्लॉग *(verb)* – बेंत से मारना beat with a whip or stick as a punishment. *If they are found by the police roaming suspiciously at night, they will be flogged.*

Flood/फ्लड *(noun)* – नदी, बाढ़ an overflow of a large amount of water over dry land. *The biblical flood brought by God upon the earth because of the wickedness of the human race.*

Flooring/फ्लोरिंग *(noun)* – कमरे का फर्श floor, *Laminated flooring has become very popular these days. Some house owners are choosing to fit laminated flooring in their homes.*

Flop/फ्लॉप *(verb)* – फटफटाना fall, hang, or collapse in a heavy, loose, and ungainly way. *The film failed to click with the audience and flopped.*

Floral/फ्लोरल *(adjective)* – पुष्प सम्बन्धी pertaining to flowers. *Floral tribute was sent on behalf of all the trust.*

Florescence/फ्लोरेंस *(noun)* – पुष्पन the process of flowering. *In the laboratory, you can use x-ray florescence to determine which metals are present in the sample.*

Floricultural/फ्लोरिकल्चरल *(adjective)* – फूलों की खेती से सम्बन्धित involving floriculture, flower gardening *Cultivation of flowers especially ones to be cut and sold is the business of floriculturists.*

Floriculture/फ्लोरिकल्चर *(noun)* – फूलों की खेती the cultivation of flowers. *Floriculture is a growing commercial venture in India.*

Florid/फ्लोरिड *(adjective)* – चमकीला, लाल having a red or flushed complexion. *The initials here are crisply engraved in a very florid style.*

Floridity/फ्लोरिडिटी *(adjective)* – फूलों की लाली flushed with red or pink; rosy; ruddy: said of the complexion *The complexion and dark eyes of the man seemed to glow with complete floridity.*

Floriferous/फ्लोरिफरस *(adjective)* – अनेक फूलों को उत्पन्न करने वाला of a plant producing many flowers. *Floriferous plants grow from*

F

early summer through to early winter and produce an abundance of flowers.

Florin/फ्लोरिन *(noun)* – दो शिलिंग के मूल्य का अंग्रेजी सिक्का a former British coin and monetary unit worth two shillings. *By 1550, the European trader had almost two thousand florins worth of debts.*

Florist/फ्लोरिस्ट *(noun)* – फूल बेचने वाला, माली a person who sells and arranges cut flowers. *Florists have a roaring business of selling flowers.*

Floss/फ्लॉस *(noun)* – पौधों की बोंडियों में के महीन रेशम के समान तन्तु the rough silk enveloping a silkworm's cocoon. A soft thread used to clean between the teeth. *Floss between the teeth by using a gentle rocking motion.*

Floatation/फ्लोटेशन *(noun)* – प्लवनशीलता, तिरने की क्रिया the action of floating or capacity to float. *Froth floatation process is used to remove impurities from extracted ore.*

Flotilla/फ्लोटिला *(noun)* – नावों का बेड़ा a small fleet of ships or boats. *Flotilla leader sent off a warning signal, to warn shipping. German torpedo flotillas attacked enemy main fleet at night.*

Flounder/फ्लाउन्डर *(verb)* – एक प्रकार की छोटी चिपटी मछली stagger in mud of water. *The first part seldom poses any problems but people often flounder when it comes to the second.*

Flourish/फ्लॉरिश *(verb)* – फलना-फूलना grow or develop in a healthy or vigorous way. be working or at the height of one's career during a specified period. *Maurya Dynasty flourished during the 3rd century B.C.*

Flout/फ्लॉउट *(verb)*– अपमान करना openly disregard a rule, [Law], or convention. *Those who flout the law would be dealt with severely.*

Flow/फ्लो *(verb)* – बहना move steadily and continuously in a current or stream. *A dam is built across the river to restrict the flow of water.*

Flower/फ्लाउअर *(noun)* – पुष्प, सार the seed-bearing part of a plant, consisting of reproductive organs typically surrounded by brightly coloured petals. and green sepals the calyx. *Rafflesia is the largest known flower in the world.*

Fluctuate/फ्लक्ट्युएट *(verb)* – लहराना rise and fall irregularly in number or amount. *Sensex has been fluctuating violently in value according to bulls or bear market.*

Flue/फ्लू *(noun)* – धुआँकश a duct in a chimney for smoke and waste gases. a channel for conveying heat. *A blocked flue can lead to carbon monoxide leaking into your kitchen and home. Make sure new water heaters in a bathroom are fitted to a balanced flue.*

Fluent/फ्लूएन्ट *(adjective)* – धारावाही speaking or writing easily and accurately, especially in a foreign language. used easily and accurately. *Universities in England will admit only those students who are fluent in English.*

Fluff/फ्लफ *(noun & verb)* – रोवाँ soft fibres accumulated in small light clumps. the flur or feathers of a young mammal or bird. *He brushed his collar to remove the fluff.*

Fluid/फ्लुइड *(noun)* – तरल पदार्थ a substance that has no fixed shape and yields easily to external pressure; a gas or especially a liquid. *Fluid mechanics is an important subject in engineering studies. All fluids when compressed under high pressure become solid.*

Fluke/फ्लूक *(noun)* – अनायास an unlikely chance occurrence, especially a stroke of luck. *You must work hard and don't depend to pass the exam by fluke.* (verb) achieve by luck rather than skill. *His success was largely attributed to fluke.*

Flummery/फ्लमरी *(noun)* – चापलूसी, लपसी empty compliments; nonsense. *Her flummery did not yield fruit.*

Flump/फ्लम्प *(verb)* – धड़ाके से गिरना fall, sit, or throw down heavily. *The heavy baggage slipped from his head and flumped to the ground with a loud thud.*

Flunkey/फ्लंकी *(noun)* – वर्दीधारी चपरासी chiefly derogatory a liveried manservant or footman. a person who performs menial tasks. *He works as a flunkey for the school manager.*

Fluorine/फ्लोरिन *(noun)* – एक अधातु तत्व the chemical element of atomic number 9, a poisonous pale yellow gas of the halogen series. *Fluorine is a fluid belonging to the Halogen family.*

F

Flurry/फ्लरी *(noun)* – हड़बड़ी a small swirling mass of snow, leaves, etc. moved by sudden gusts of wind. *Flurry of wickets however, meant that they were reduced from 95 for 1 to 96 for 5 within a space of 3 overs.*

Fluster/फ्लस्टर *(verb)* – घबड़ाना make agitated or confused. *Aron got a bit flustered under the glare of the camera.* *(noun)* a flustered state. *Flustered, excited man was talking to them.*

Flute/फ्लूट *(noun)* – बाँसुरी a high-pitched wind instrument consisting of a tube with holes along it, usually held horizontally so that the breath can be directed against a fixed edge. *Flute is an Indian musical instrument.*

Flutter/फ्लटर *(verb)*– व्याकुल करना fly unsteadily by flapping the wings quickly and lightly. *The flags flutter, the crowds cheer, and the legislatures meet to pass new constitution.*

Flux/फ्लक्स *(noun)* – बहाव, स्राव the action or process of flowing. *Do you want to clean the board to remove left over soldering flux?*

Flying/फ्लाइंग *(adjective)* – उड़ान capable or engaged in flying, brief, hurried *He made a flying visit to the neighbours' house. He took a flying glance at the report. The flying time between Delhi and Mumbai is two and a half hours.*

Foal/फोल *(noun)* – बछेड़ा a young horse or related animal. *The young of a horse is known as a foal.*

Fob/फाॅब *(noun)* – धोखा देना a chain attached to a watch for carrying in a waistcoat or waistband pocket. a small ornament attached to a watch chain. a small pocket for carrying a watch. a tab on a key ring. *Finally release the central locking button and press the fob to check the central locking operation. Don't fob your friends off with a sham gift!*

Focal/फोकल *(adjective)* – केन्द्रीय of or relating to a focus, in particular the focus of a lens. *Local centres are typically also focal points for the community life of their areas.*

Focus/फोकस *(noun)* – संगम the centre of interest or activity. an act of focusing on something. *Focus on these main issues of concern.*

Fodder/फाॅडर *(noun)* – चारा, भूसा food for cattle and other livestock. *Grass and haystack are the principal fodder for cattle.*

Foe/फो *(noun)* – शत्रु, बैरी formal an enemy or opponent. *The sniper rifle is dead accurate and one shot in the head is enough to kill almost any foe. Pakistan has considered India as its foe number one since independence.*

Foetus/फीटस *(noun)* – गर्भ unborn developing child inside the mother's womb *Last year, 40,000 female foetuses were aborted in Mumbai alone.*

Fogy/फोगी *(noun)* – पुराने विचार का मनुष्य variant spelling of fogey.

Foible/फाॅइबॅल *(noun)* – कमी, अवगुण a minor weakness or eccentricity. *Although Rita is very easy going person she does have a few foibles*

Foist/फाॅइस्ट *(verb)* – थोपना impose an unwelcome or unnecessary person or thing on. *Foisting unpopular policies is always resented by people.*

Fold/फोल्ड *(verb)* – परत bend something over on itself so that one part of it covers another. be able to be folded into a flatter shape. *The bedsheet was neatly folded.*

Folder/फोल्डर *(noun)* – पुस्तिका, फाइल a folding cover or wallet for storing loose papers. *Folders made of plastic have become very popular to carry important papers.*

Folderol/फोल्डराॅल *(noun)* – मूर्खता trivial or nonsensical fuss.

Foliage/फोलिएज *(noun)* – पत्ते plant leaves, collectively. *Foliage of all these trees would be collected and sent for incineration.*

Foliate/फोलिएट *(adjective)* – पत्तियों से पूर्ण foliated. *Foliate designs in linear patterns, derived from Khajuraho art were on show.*

Folk/फोक *(plural noun)* – जन-समूह [informal] people in general. *It is certainly a lovely place, populated by a friendly folks.* one's family, especially one's parents. *I am going to my hometown to meet my parents and other folks.*

Follower/फाॅलोवर *(noun)* – अनुचर a person who follows. *I am a devout follower of Hindu religion.*

Following/फाॅलोविंग *(adj.)* – निम्नलिखित coming after or as a result of. *Following articles matched your search criteria.*

F

Fondle/फॉन्डल *(verb)* – आलिंगन करना stroke or caress lovingly or erotically. *It is indecent to fondle someone in an inappropriate way.*

Foolhardy/फूलहार्डि *(adjective)* – दुःसाहसी, उजड्डड recklessly bold or rash. *It is foolhardy not to ask for discount when you can have it.*

Foolish/फूलिश *(adjective)* – बुद्धिहीन lacking good sense or judgment; silly or unwise. *It is foolish to ignore the guidelines regarding examination.*

Footing/फूटिंग *(noun)* – आधार secure placement of the feet, or something to allow stability *On a business level we are on a sound footing.*

Forage/फॉरिज *(verb)* – मवेशियों का भोजन search widely for food or provisions. obtain by searching. search so as to obtain food. *Cattle and livestock were foraging the plains looking for food.*

Foramen/फोरेमेन *(noun)* – रन्धक, रन्ध्र anatomy an opening, hole, or passage, especially in a bone. *Foramen are openings within the body which allow muscles, arteries, veins etc to connect with one another appropriately.*

Forasmuch/फॉर-ऐज-मच *(conjunction)* – चूँकि [archaic] because; since. *For as much as I know, he wouldn't come today.*

Foray/फॉरि *(noun)* – चढ़ाई a sudden attack or incursion into enemy territory. *The foray by the enemy forces was repulsed promptly.*

Forbade/फॉबेड – रोका past of forbid. *The police forbade onlookers to go near the damaged bridge.*

Forceps/फॉसेप्स *(plural noun)* – चिमटा a pair of pincers used in surgery or in a laboratory. a large instrument of such a type with broad blades, used to assist in the delivery of a baby. *Plastic forceps are ideal for removing laboratory specimens from liquids, such as, alcohol.*

Ford/फोर्ई *(noun)*– घाट *(verb)* पार करना a shallow place in a river or stream that can be crossed on foot or in a vehicle. *Use the third ford to cross the river because water at that point is shallow.*

Fore/फोर *(adjective)* – पहले का situated or placed in front. *Before you address the audience, please come to the fore so that they can see your face.*

Forecast/फोरकास्ट *(verb)* – अन्दाज लेना, भविष्यवाणी करना predict or estimate. *The meteorology department has forecasted a cold weather for the next 5 days.*

Foreclose/फोरक्लोज *(verb)* – मना करना, मार्ग बन्द करना take possession of a mortgaged property as a result of defaults in mortgage payments. *Banks have abolished the penalty imposed on customers if they foreclose their loan amount.*

Forefather/फोरफादर *(noun)* – पितर लोग an ancestor. *Leo Tolstoy was the forefather of modern Russian literature.*

Forefinger/फोरफिंगर *(noun)* – तर्जनी अगुँली the finger next to the thumb. *You hold a pen between your thumb and forefinger.*

Forefront/फोरफ्रंट *(noun)* – सबसे अगला भाग the leading position or place. *Mahatma Gandhi was always in the forefront during India's freedom struggle against the British.*

Forehead/फोरहेड *(noun)* – मस्तक the part of the face above the eyebrows. *The old man wiped the creased lines on his forehead with the back of his wrist and sat down.*

Foreign/फॉरिन *(adjective)* – विदेशी of, from, in, or characteristic of a country or language other than one's own. dealing with or relating to other countries. *All foreign nationals need to report at the immigration counter.*

Foreigner/फॉरिनॅर *(noun)* – अन्यदेशीय a person born in or coming from a foreign country. informal a stranger or outsider. *To marry a foreigner, permission must be obtained from the home ministry.*

Foreland/फोरलैंड *(noun)* – अन्तरीय an area of land in front of a particular feature. *Foreland basin near Broadway is another area where residential construction is very active.*

Foreleg/फोरलेग *(noun)* – पशु का अगला पैर either of the front legs of an animal with four legs *Kangaroos use both their forelegs and hind legs to run.*

Foremen/फोरमैन *(noun)* – चौधरी, प्रधान a worker who supervises other workers. *The foreman in charge of maintenance unit is very strict.*

Foremast/फोरमास्ट *(noun)* – जहाज का अगला निचला मस्तल the mast of a ship nearest the bow. *The foremast of the ship usually hoists the flag of the country where it is registered.*

Forenoon/फोरनून *(noun)* – मध्याह्न के पहले का समय north American or nautical the morning. *Americans call the period of time between morning and noon as forenoon.*

Forensic/फोरेन्सिक *(adjective)* – अदालती relating to or denoting the application of scientific methods and techniques to the investigation of crime. *There is the wide difference between crime studies and a purely forensic procedure.*

Fore-ordain/फोर्-आर्डेन *(verb)* – पहले से नियुक्त करना determine in advance, predetermine *He was foreordained by God to become a social leader.*

Fore-reach/फोर्-रीच *(verb)* – सामने तीर चलाना, आगे बढ़ जाना to overtake and pass. *The boat headed into the wind in order to forereach the jetty before another sailing vessel coming about.*

Foresee/फोर्-सी *(verb)* – सोचना be aware of beforehand; predict. *The coach could foresee a test cricketer in him, even though the trainee was just seven.*

Foreshadow/फोर्शैडो *(verb)* – पहले सूचित करना be a warning or indication of. *The design change in this new car foreshadows the launch of latest luxury cars in 2013.*

Foreshow/फोरशो *(verb)* – पहले से कहना [archaic] give warning or promise of. *The tussle for one-upmanship foreshows the battle of titans for political supremacy.*

Foresight/फोरसाइट *(noun)* – दूरदर्शिता the ability to predict or action of predicting the future. *He had the foresight to check that his escape route was clear.*

Forest/फॉरेस्ट *(noun)* – जंगल a large area covered chiefly with trees and undergrowth. historical an area, typically owned by the sovereign and partly wooded, kept for hunting and having its own laws. *Gir forest is the largest sanctuary for lions in India.*

Forestall/फोरस्टॉल *(verb)* – अनुमान करना prevent or obstruct by taking advance action. anticipate and prevent the action of. historical buy up before they come to market to profit from an enhanced price. *Cash transfer scheme* has been vigorously launched to forestall the opposition capturing power in the forthcoming general election.*

Forester/फॉरिस्टर *(noun)* – वनचर a person in charge of a forest or skilled in forestry. *Foresters are now designated as an officer under the government.*

Forethought/फोर्थॉट *(noun)* – पूर्वविवेक careful consideration of what will be necessary or may happen in the future. *With a little more forethought I should have used any copper utensil.*

Foreword/फोर्वर्ड *(noun)* – भूमिका a short introduction to a book, typically by a person other than the author. *This new edition carries a foreword by the Nobel laureate.*

Forfeit/फॉर्फिट् *(verb)* – जब्त करना lose or be deprived of as a penalty for wrongdoing. lose or give up as a necessary consequence. *She forfeited another hour in bed to muck out the horse. Prize winners who do not claim their prize within seven days will automatically forfeit their right to the prize.*

Forgather/फॉगैदर *(verb)* – परस्पर मिलना variant spelling of foregather.

Forgave/फॉगेव *(verb)* – क्षमा किया past of forgive. *They talked over their misunderstanding and forgave each other.*

Forgery/फोर्जरि *(noun)* – जालसाजी the act or legal offense of imitating or counterfeiting documents, signatures, works of art, etc. to deceive, anything forged *Anyone who commits forgery in that context is guilty of a criminal offence. The local police is investigating the case of document forgery.*

Forgo/फॉर्गो *(verb)* – त्याग देना go without something desirable. *I could happily forgo the chocolate, but not the crisp and salty snacks.*

Fork/फॉर्क *(noun)* – कांटा an implement with two or more prongs used for lifting or holding food. *The two-pronged fork is the ideal for eating fruits.* a farm or garden tool of larger but similar form used for digging or lifting. *Fork truck driver was forced to take leave off work suffering from stress.*

Forlorn/फॅर्लार्न् *(adjective)* – परित्यक्त pitifully sad and lonely. *The site has been almost entirely cleared leaving just the name of the station headquarters that looked rather forlorn.*

F

Formality/फॉर्मैलिटि (noun) – यथाविधि, आचार the rigid observance of rules or convention. a thing that is done simply to comply with convention, regulations, or custom. something done or happening as a matter of course. *Board members decided to observe the formality of reappointing the current auditor in order to meet the statutory mandate.*

Format/फॉर्मैट (noun) – पुस्तक का फर्मा the way in which something is arranged or presented. computing a defined structure for the processing, storage, or display of data. *The pdf file format opens in adobe acrobat reader.*

Formation/फॉर्मेशन (noun) – कृति the action of forming or the process of being formed. *Magnetic fields play very significant role in formation of star. Vitamin D works with calcium to help control bone formation.*

Formative/फॉर्मेटिव (adjective) – रूप देने या रचना की शक्ति serving to from something, especially having a profound influence on a person's development. *Better parental guidance is necessary during the formative years of a child.*

Former/फॉर्मर् (adjective) – प्राचीन, पहले वाला having been previously. of or occurring in the past. *Sharad Pawar is the former president of BCCI.*

Formica/फॉर्मिका (noun) – चींटी-सम्बन्धी trademark a hard durable plastic laminate used for worktops, cupboard doors, etc. *Formica is the trade name registered in the name of a company manufacturing plastic laminates.*

Formidable/फॉर्मिडेबॅल (adjective) – भयंकर inspiring fear or respect through being impressively large, powerful, or capable. *Australia is a formidable rival of India in the game of cricket.*

Forswear/फॅर्स्वेअर (verb) – सौगन्ध खाना agree to give up or do without. *He forswore not to break the community laws before being admitted back.*

Fort/फोर्ट् (noun) – किला a fortified building or strategic position. *Red fort is a historical building in Delhi.*

Forte/फॉर्ट् (noun) – प्रधान गुण a thing at which someone excels. *My personal secretary is Sheila whose main forte is internet research.*

Forth/फोर्थ (noun) – सामने, बाहर computer language *Forth is a stack-oriented computer programming language.*

Forthwith/फोर्थविथ (adverb) – तुरंत without delay. *You must cease to operate this programme forthwith.*

Fortitude/फॉटिट्यूड (noun) – धैर्य courage in adversity. *We pray to God to grant you fortitude to bear this grievous loss.*

Fortnight/फॉटनाइट (noun) – अर्धमास chiefly British a period of two weeks. informal two weeks from that day. *This magazine is published every fortnight, 24 issues each year.*

Fortress/फॉट्रिश (noun) – किला, गढ़ी a military stronghold, especially a strongly fortified town fit for a large garrison. *The Great Wall of China was primarily built to act as a fortress against marauding Mongols.*

Fortuitous/फॉट्यूइटस (adjective) – आकस्मिक happening by change rather than design. informal happening by a lucky chance. *It was a fortuitous meeting with the manager at the station that has got me the job.*

Fortuitously/फॉट्यूइटसलि (adv.) – अनायास happening by chance; accidental, bringing, or happening by, good luck; fortunate *The job I got could be attributed to my fortuitously meeting him at the club.*

Fortieth/फॉटिथ (noun) – चालीसवाँ the number forty in a series, fortieth part of forty equal parts *In ascending order, fortieth comes after thirty ninth.*

Forty/फॉर्टि (cardinal number) – चालीस the number equivalent to the product of four and ten; ten less than fifty; 40, *Forty is the number obtained by multiplying five with eight. Forty percent of the staff has been laid off.*

Forum/फोरम (noun) – अदालत a meeting or medium for an exchange of views. *The decision to hold election was decided last evening at the forum.*

Forwarding/फॉर्वर्डिंग (noun) – माल-असबाब भेजने का कार्य sending, forwarding, dispatching. *I am forwarding you details about the civil services examination.*

Found/फाउन्ड (verb) – स्थिर करना past & past participle of find; establish, discover, create, build, melt and mould. *The physician who*

F

found the elusive particle won the Nobel Prize. She found an interesting book at the bookstore last evening.

Founder/फाउन्डर *(noun)* – ढालने वाला, संस्थापक a person who founds an institution or settlement. *Raja Ram Mohun Roy was the founder of Bramho Samaj.*

Foundling/फाउन्डलिंग *(noun)* – पितृहीन शिशु infant that has been abandoned by its parents and is discovered and cared for by others. *The foster parents have got accustomed to foundling the infant found abandoned behind the playground two years back.*

Foundry/फॉउन्ड्रि *(noun)* – ढलाई करने का कारखाना a workshop or factory for casting metal. *In the brass foundry most of the work is cast from plate moulded patterns.*

Fount/फाउन्ट *(noun)* – उद्गम, झरना a source of a desirable quality. *My idea is to reach the founts of wisdom before I turn 18.*

Fourteen/फॉर्टीन *(cardinal number)* – चौदह equivalent to the product of seven and two; one more than thirteen, or six less than twenty; 14. *Fourteen is the number we get when ten is added to four.*

Fourth/फोर्थ *(ordinal number)* – चौथा constituting number four in a sequence; 4th. *The number succeeding third is known as fourth.*

Fovea/फोविया *(noun)* – शरीर में का गड्ढा anatomy a small depression in the retina of the eye where visual acuity is highest. *Fovea is any small cuplike depression or pit in the bone or organ in the body.*

Fowl/फॉउल *(noun)* – मुर्गा a domesticated bird derived from a jungle fowl and kept for its eggs or flesh; a cock or hen. any domesticated bird, e.g. a turkey or duck. used in the names of birds that resemble the domestic fowl, e.g. spurfowl. *Fowl is a bird used for food. A hen is an example of fowl. Chicken is an example of fowl.*

Fowler/फॉउलर *(noun)* – बहेलिया a bird hunter *Fowler is a person who hunts wild birds for food.*

Fowling/फाउलिंग *(noun)* – पक्षिवध की कला bird hunting *Fowling is a term that includes all forms of bird catching for meat, feather or any other part.*

Fra/फ्रा *(noun)* – एक उपाधि Fra, Friar, or Fray- a prefixed title. *Fra friar or sometimes even fray is a title often used in the former Spanish colonies such as, the Philippines or Southwest America.*

Fracas/फ्रैका *(noun)* – उपद्रव a noisy disturbance or quarrel. *The violent fracas between the rival factions didn't allow the function to proceed.*

Fractious/फ्रैक्शस *(adjective)* – लड़ाका easily irritated. *Fractious ethnic groups say they have little in common to oppose the enemy as a cohesive unit.*

Fracture/फ्रैक्चर *(noun)* – विदारण the cracking or breaking of hard object or material. a crack or break, especially in a bone or a rock stratum. *Skull fracture can have serious complications for the normal functioning of the body.*

Fragile/फ्रैजाइल *(adjective)* – मुलायम, भंगुर easily broken or damaged. *Glass is a highly fragile material.*

Fragment/फ्रैग्मन्ट *(noun)* – अंश a small part broken off or detached. an isolated or incomplete part. *Fragments of asteroids keep falling in one part or the other on earth nearly every day.*

Fragrance/फ्रैग्रॅन्स *(noun)* – सुगन्ध a pleasant, sweet, smell. a perfume or aftershave. *Now you can enjoy the calming effects of this lotion's lavender fragrance.*

Fragrant/फ्रैग्रॅन्ट *(adjective)* – सुगन्धित having a pleasant or sweet smell. *The delicately fragrant formula is speedily absorbed and leaves you feeling fresh.*

Frail/फ्रेल *(adjective)* – भंगुर, कमजोर weak and delicate. *She was an old frail lady yet carrying heavy bundles in her hands.*

Franc/फ्रैंक *(noun)* – फ्रान्स का दो पेन्स का सिक्का the basic monetary unit of France, Belgium, Switzerland, Luxemburg, and several other countries, equal to 100 centimes (replaced in France, Belgium, and Luxemburg by the euro in 2002) *Before emergence of Euro, Franc was the currency of France, Belgium and Luxemburg.*

Franchise/फ्रैन्चाइज *(noun)* – विशेषाधिकार an authorization granted by a government or

F

company to an individual or group enabling them to carry out specified commercial activities. a business or service granted such authorization. north American an authorization given by a professional leaguer to own a sports team. north American informal a team granted such authorization. *Whether you are an industry professional or new, a franchise is the perfect business opportunity for you.*

F

Frangible/फ्रैन्जिबॅल *(adjective)* – सहज में टूटने योग्य formal fragile; brittle. *These articles are frangible. Please handle with care.*

Fraught/फ्रॉट *(adjective)* – परिपूर्ण filled with something undesirable. *Proper care for sick and elderly remain fraught with legal uncertainty.*

Fray/फ्रे *(noun)* – कलह a situation of intense competitive activity. a battle or fight. *With five withdrawals, only two are left in fray for leadership of the party.*

Frazil/फ्रेज़िल *(noun)* – किसी जलाशय के तल की जमी हुई बरफ north American an accumulation of ice crystals in water that is too turbulent to freeze solid. *Frazil is a name given to those tiny, round or pointed ice crystals that are formed in super cooled waters and prevented from solidifying due to turbulence.*

Freckle/फ्रेकल *(noun)* – शरीर पर हल्का भूरा धब्बा a small light brown spot on the skin, often becoming more pronounced through exposure to the sun. *Freckles produce a sense of agedness in appearance.*

Freemason/फ्रीमेसन *(noun)* – प्रेमपूर्ण a member of an international order established for mutual help and fellowship, which holds elaborate secret ceremonies. *A member of a secret fraternal society named 'Free and Accepted Mason' advocating brotherly love and mutual love is known as a freemason.*

Freezing/फ्रीज़िंग *(adjective)* – जमाने वाला below 0°C. informal very cold. *The freezing of water is 0°C.*

Freight/फ्रेट *(noun)* – मालभाड़ा transport of goods in bulk, especially by truck, train, or ship. goods transported by freight. a charge for such transport. *Freight carried by rail, rather than road, produces at least 80 per cent less carbon dioxide.*

French/फ्रेंच *(adjective)* – फ्रान्स देश of or relating to france or its people or language. *Eiffel Tower is synonymous with the culture of French people.*

Frenetic/फ्रेनेटिक *(adjective)* – पागल fast and energetic in a rather wild and uncontrolled way. *Do some sincere thinking about youth force before life gets frenetic again.*

Frenzy/फ्रेन्ज़ी *(noun)* – उन्माद a state or period of uncontrolled excitement or wild behaviour. *Frenzy of excitement at ground since both teams were of equal standard.*

Frequency/फ्रिक्वेन्सी *(noun)* – तीव्रता the rate at which something occurs over a particular period or in a given sample. *Frequency of oscillations is more than nine million vibrations per second.*

Fretful/फ्रेटफुल *(adjective)* – शीघ्र कुपित होने वाला anxious or irritated. *There was little for them to eat, and the non-stop wailing of children made parents very fretful.*

Friable/फ्राइअॅबॅल *(adjective)* – जल्दी से बुकनी हो जाने वाला easily crumbled. *The property of a solid material to be broken into small pieces with little effort is known as friable.*

Friar/फ्राइअर *(noun)* – संन्यासी a member of any of certain religious orders of men, especially the four mendicant orders. *These building are occupied by friars.*

Friary/फ्राइऑरी *(noun)* – मठ a building occupied by friars. *Friar is sometimes used in former Spanish colonies, such as, the Philippines or Southwest America as a title.*

Friction/फ्रिक्शन *(noun)* – घिसाव the resistance that one surface or object encounters when moving over another. *We can't run fast on sand desert because of very high friction.* the action of one surface or object rubbing against another. *A mouse mat is normally used to reduce friction on a desk top computer.*

Friday/फ्राइडे *(noun)* – शुक्रवार the day of the week before Saturday and following Thursday. *Friday is the sixth day of the week and comes before Saturday.*

Friendless/फ्रेंडलेस *(adjective)* – मित्रहीन without friends. *His sermon-like lectures to anyone who comes to him has left him virtually friendless.*

Friendliness/फ्रेंडलिनेस *(adjective)* – मित्रत्व not hostile. *Our new neighbour has become very popular because of his simplicity and friendliness.*

Friendly/फ्रेंडलि *(adjective)* – दयालु kind and pleasant; of or like a friend. *We have published many child-friendly books.*

Friendship/फ्रेंडशिप *(noun)* – मित्रता the state of being friends, attachment between friends, friendly feeling or attitude; friendliness. *Through the group's social activities, you'd forge strong friendships which could last a lifetime. I have met many people during my holidays over the years, some of them having turned into lasting friendships.*

Frigate/फ्रिगेट *(noun)* – लड़ाई का जहाज a warship with a mixed armament, generally lighter than a destroyer. historical a sailing warship of a size and armament just below that of a ship of the line. *Indian Navy has built many frigates to defend the coastal waters of India.*

Fright/फ्राइट *(noun)* – भय, शंका a sudden intense feeling of fear. an experience causing fright; a shock. *Stage fright has always been a major problem with me.*

Frighten/फ्राइटेन *(verb)* – डराना cause to be afraid. drive someone away by fear. *Being alone, the lightning and thunder at the dead of the night frightened him no end.*

Frightful/फ्राइटफुल *(adjective)* – डरावना very unpleasant, serious, or shocking. *Frightful dreams, nonetheless they were only dreams and not a reality.*

Frigid/फ्रिजिड *(adjective)* – शीत, ठण्डा very cold. *He described her nature as extremely frigid, cold, dry and devoid of any cheering influence.*

Frill/फ्रिल *(noun)* – झालर a strip of gathered or pleated material sewn by one side only on to a garment or piece of material as a decorative edging or ornament. *She wore an expensive frilled shirt, pleated skirt and the long multi-coloured scarf.*

Fringe/फ्रिन्ज *(noun)* – किनारा a border of threads, tassels, or twists, used to edge clothing or material. *Fringe is the ornamental border consisting of loose hanging beads or threads in women's garments.*

Frippery/फ्रिपॅरी *(noun)* – आडम्बर showy or unnecessary ornament. *Most Smartphone and mobiles are actually getting larger, sprouting LED or LCD screens, card readers and all sorts of other frippery.* *(adjective)* [archaic] frivolous and tawdry. *She is an intelligent lady; don't go by her cheap clothing, imitated jewellery or other fripperies.*

Fritter/फ्रिटर *(verb)* – समय, धन या ऊर्जा व्यय करना waste, time, money, or energy on trifling matters. *Don't fritter away time over trivial matters.*

Frivol/फ्रिवल *(verb)* – आडम्बर करना, खिलवाड़ करना to spend foolishly. *Don't frivol your hard-earned money.*

Frivolity/फ्रिवॉलिटी *(noun)* – निरर्थक व्यापार light heartedness, foolishness *Take this project seriously and don't spend time over frivolities.*

Frizz/फ्रिज *(noun)* – लच्छे बनाना form into a mass of small, tight curls. *Please use a conditioner to bring new shine and lustre to hair as it controls the frizz.*

Frizzle/फ्रिजल *(verb)* – खदबदाना form into tight curls. *To frizzle, you must shallow fry the food until it curls and becomes crisp fry.* *(noun)* a tight curl in hair. *Ms. Frizzle with curled hair was a character in 'The Magic School Bus'.*

Fro/फ्रो *(adverb)* – दूर to and fro. *He is walking to and fro on the road.*

Frock/फ्रॉक *(noun)* – चोगा chiefly British a woman's or girl's dress. *Frock is one of the most comfortable dresses for girls.*

Frolic/फ्रॉलिक *(noun & verb)* – खेल, विहार play or move about in a cheerful and lively way. *You can expect to see festive frolics today involving our own picnic party.*

Frolicsome/फ्रॉलिकसम *(adjective)* – खिलाड़ी lively and playful. *Frolicsome children enjoy the thrill when it rains.*

Frond/फ्रॉन्ड *(noun)* – फूलने वाली झाड़ियों में पत्तियों का अंग the leaf or leaf-like part of a palm, fern, or similar plant. *Palm growers cut palm fronds, without harm to growing trees.*

Front/फ्रंट *(noun)* – ललाट the side or part of an object that presents itself to view or that is normally seen or used first. the position directly ahead the forward-facing part of

F

a person's body. *The front of his house is attractively designed and decorated.*

Frontage/फ्रन्टेज *(noun)* – घर का अग्रभाग the facade of building. *The frontage of the compound gave an appearance of a bungalow.*

Frontal/फ्रंटल *(adjective)* – ललाट सम्बन्धी of or relating to the forehead or front part of the skull: the frontal sinuses. *The doctor detected a legion in the frontal lobe.*

Frontlet/फ्रॅन्टलिट *(noun)* – मुकुट another term for phylactery. *Frontlet is an ornament or band worn on the forehead.*

Froth/फ्रॉथ *(noun)* – फेन, झाग a mass of small bubbles in liquid caused by agitation, fermentation, or salivating. impure matter that rises to the surface of liquid. *Froth flotation process is used to segregate impurities from the mineral ore.*

Frozen/फ्रोज़ेन – जमा हुआ past participle of freeze. *Due to very cold weather, water was frozen into ice.*

Fructification/फ्रक्टिफिकेशन *(noun)* – फल उपजाने की विधि [botany] a spore-bearing or fruiting structure, especially in a fungus. *Fructification is a name given to the structure of a fungus that is seed-bearing or spore-bearing.*

Fructify/फ्रक्टिफाइ *(verb)* – उपजाऊ बनाना formal make or become fruitful. *Your sincere studies will let it fructify into good result.*

Fructose/फ्रक्टोज़ *(noun)* – फलों में से निकाली हुई चीनी chemistry a sugar of the hexose class found especially in honey and fruit. *Fructose is a chemical compound.*

Fructuous/फ्रक्ट्अस *(adjective)* – उपजाऊ formal full of or producing a great deal of fruit. *His sincere studies have been very fructuous; he passed the examination with 90 per cent marks.*

Frugal/फ्रूगल *(adjective)* – कमखर्च sparing or economical as regards money or food. *Frugal way would be to save up and not take out a loan.*

Frugivorous/फ्रूजिवरस *(noun)* – फलाहार करने वाला one who eats fruits only. *I have seen many frugivorous saints.*

Fruitarian/फ्रूटेअरिअन *(noun)* – फलभोजी a person who eats only fruit. *It is difficult to stay energetic being just a fruitarian.*

Fruiterer/फ्रूइटरर *(noun)* – फल बेचने वाला chiefly British a retailer of fruit. *Fruiterer is a person, mainly in England and Australia, who retails fruits and vegetables.*

Fruitful/फ्रूटफुल *(adjective)*– सफल, उपजाऊ producing much fruit; fertile. *Make your ideas attractive, focus on the benefits and how you can make life more fruitful.*

Fruition/फ्रूइसन *(noun)* – सुख, स्वाद the realization or fulfilment of a plan or project. *International trade negotiations take a long time to reach fruition. The tree has begun to fruition and is likely to deliver better yield than last year.*

Fruitless/फ्रूटलेस *(adjective)* – फलहीन failing to achieve the desired results; unproductive. *For one reason or the other, my five attempts to speak to him on phone remained fruitless.*

Fruitlet/फ्रूटलेट *(noun)* – छोटा फल an immature or small fruit. [botany] another term for drupel. *A fruitlet is a small, yet to be fully grown fruit that is part of a multiple fruit.*

Fruity/फ्रूटि *(adjective)* – फल-सम्बन्धी of, resembling, or containing fruit. *My nose was filled with the smells of fruit because a number of baskets containing assorted fruits were kept in the car.*

Frustrate/फ्रस्ट्रेट *(verb)* – निराश करना prevent from progressing, succeeding, or being fulfilled. prevent from doing or achieving something. *Lack of money frustrated my desire to join a top ranked management school.*

Frustration/फ्रस्ट्रेशन *(noun)* – पराजय, उत्साहहीनता disappointment, depression, anxiety *Try to imagine the frustration, the boredom, and the anger that this desktop computer system creates.*

Frustrative/फ्रस्ट्रेटिव *(adjective)* – पराजयकारी, उत्साहहीनता करने वाला preventing attainment of a desire. *Constant traffic jams had been terribly frustrative in our plan to reach Delhi before night.*

Fry/फ्राइ *(verb & noun)* – भूनना, तलना plural young fish, especially when newly hatched. the young of other animals produced in large numbers, such as frogs. *Young of a variety of animals, including frogs and bees, are called a fry.*

F

Fucus/फ्यूकस *(noun)* – एक प्रकार का समुद्री सेवार a seaweed of a large genus of brown algae having flat leathery fronds. *This seaweed is called fucus.*

Fuddle/फॅडॅल *(verb)* – व्याकुल करना confuse or stupefy, especially with alcohol. *He is so cunning; he can befuddle you any day with his ingenuity.*

Fudge/फज *(noun)* – फज (टॉफी) अनर्थक वार्ता a soft crumbly or chewy sweet made from sugar, butter, and milk or cream. *This as a fudge ice cream sundae with all the chocolate toppings.*

Fuel/फ्यूअल *(noun & verb)* – ईंधन, ईंधन डालना any material that produces heat or power. *This car takes high fuel consumption. The plane is fuelled up and ready to go.*

Fug/फग *(noun)* – कमरे के अन्दर की दुर्गन्ध British informal a warm, stuffy atmosphere.

Fugacious/फ्यूगेशस *(adjective)* – क्षणिक [poetic/ literary] tending to disappear; fleeting. *In botany, fugacious is a term used to describe withering or dropping off early.*

Fugitive/फ्यूजिटिव *(noun)* – चंचल, अस्थिर a person who has escaped from captivity or is in hiding. *The police is on the lookout for the fugitive who was released on bail three days back.*

Fulcrum/फॅल्क्रॅम *(noun)* – आधार the point against which a lever is placed to get a purchase, or on which it turns or is supported. *Fulcrum is the point on which a lever is balanced when a force is exerted.*

Fulgent/फल्जेंट *(adjective)* – उज्ज्वल, चमकदार [poetic/literary] shining brightly. *Blazing sun, blinding headlights are some of the examples of fulgent dazzle.*

Fuller/फुलर *(noun)* – कपड़ा साफ करने वाला a grooved or rounded tool on which iron is shaped. *Fuller is a worker who cleanses wool by the process of fulling.*

Fulsome/फुलसम *(adjective)* – अति, बहुत, भरपूर flattering to an excessive degree. *Her stage performance received a fulsome praise from all quarters.*

Fumble/फम्बल *(verb)* – टटोलना use the hands clumsily while doing or handling something. do or handle something clumsily. move about clumsily using the hands to find one's way. fail to catch or field cleanly. *The ball was coming straight to him but he fumbled and dropped the catch.*

Fumigate/फ्यूमिगेट *(verb)* – सुगन्धित करना disinfect or purify with the fumes of certain chemicals. *This area is fumigated every fortnight to prevent breeding of mosquitoes.*

Fun/फन *(noun)*– क्रीड़ा, आनन्द light-hearted pleasure or amusement. *The picnic was a wholesome fun-filled pleasant trip.*

Funambulist/फ्यूनैम्ब्यूलिस्ट *(noun)* – रस्सी पर चलने वाला नट formal a tightrope walker. *The work of a funambulist is very risky.*

Fund/फण्ड *(noun)* – कोष, निधि a sum of money saved or made available for a particular purpose. *Funds have been earmarked to organize annual sports.*

Fundament/फन्डामेन्ट *(noun)* – चूतड़ the foundation or basis of something. *The whole fundament of this argument rested on conjecture.*

Fungus/फनगस *(noun)* – ककव, फफूँद any of a large group of spore-producing organisms which feed on organic matter and include moulds, yeast, mushrooms, and toadstools. *The discovery of penicillin has its origin in moulds.*

Funicle/फ्यूनिकल *(noun)* – रज्जुका, वृन्तिका, छोटी डोरी [botany] a filamentous stalk attaching a seed or ovule to the placenta. *The little stalk that attaches a seed to the placenta is known as funicle.*

Funicular/फ्यूनिक्यूलर *(adjective)* – रस्से से चलाया जाने वाला operated by cable with ascending and descending cars counterbalanced. *A 4-star hotel on a hill with wonderful panoramic views and linked by funicular to the central station.*

Funk/फंक *(noun)* – दुर्गन्ध a style of popular dance music of US black origin, having a strong rhythm that typically accentuates the first beat in the bar. *An example of funk is going to a party and feeling nervous about talking to new people.*

Furbish/फॅर्बिश *(verb)* – चमकाना, माँजना, चमक लाना give a fresh look to; renovate. *The hotel had furbished all rooms with new draperies*

F

and interiors for offering stunning views out to the sea.

Furcate/फॅकेट *(verb)* – फटे कोर का divide into two or more branches; fork. *The club has decided to furcate the entry and exit points.* *(adjective)* furcated; forked. *Entry and exit points have been furcated at the club.*

Furious/फ्युऑरिअॅस *(adjective)* – प्रचण्ड extremely angry. *He was furious at his staff for not completing the finding the important project.*

Furl/फॅल *(verb)* – लपेटना, समेटना roll or fold up neatly and securely. *The flag was taken down and furled properly and neatly.*

Furlough/फर्लो *(noun)* – गैर हाजिरी की छुट्टी leave of absence, especially from military duty. *He has rejoined duty after remaining on furlough for six months.*

Furnish/फॅर्निश *(verb)* – तैयार करना provide with furniture and fitting. *These flats are fully furnished 3 bedroom apartment with a community swimming pool.*

Furniture/फॅर्निचर *(noun)* – फर्नीचर, सज्जा-सामग्री the movable articles that are used to make a room or building suitable for living or working in, such as tables, chairs, or desks. *The hotel rooms are equipped with original antique furniture.*

Furor/फ्यूरॉर *(noun)* – विक्षेप, उन्माद, क्रोध an outbreak of public anger or excitement. *It is this photograph that caused much of the initial furor.*

Furrow/फॅरो *(noun)* – हल-रेखा, लीक, नाली a long, narrow trench made in the ground by a plough. *Each plot of land was divided from its neighbour by a deep furrow.*

Further/फॅदर *(adverb)* – आगे का at, to, or by a greater distance. *The sun lies much further from Mercury than that of earth.*

Furthest/फॅर्देस्ट *(adjective)*– स्थान में सबसे दूर का situated at the greatest distance. covering the greatest area or distance. *Furthest of the planets from the sun is a small icy rock of a planet.*

Furtive/फॅर्टिव *(adjective)* – गुप्त, चुराया हुआ characterized by guilty or evasive secrecy; stealthy. *Standing this side of the road, she gave a furtive look at the deserted shops on the opposite side of the road. Our first task as* trained professional is to document what goes on in this very furtive field.

Furuncle/फ्यूरन्कल *(noun)* – जहरबाद [technical] term for boil. *There may be white patches along the body side or raised furuncles on the skin.*

Fuse/फ्यूज *(verb)* – गलना a length of material along which a small flame moves to explode a bomb or firework. a device in a bomb that controls the timing of the explosion. *Fuse wire was trimmed to up to the length of the explosive device.*

Fusibility/फ्यूजिबिलिटी *(noun)* – द्रवशीलता that can be fused or easily melted *Fusibility of a material is the property of its melting when heat is applied.*

Fusible/फ्यूजिबल् *(adjective)* – द्रवशील able to be fused or melted easily. *Fusible metal plugs, which melt at known temperatures are placed across electric meters.*

Fusiform/फ्यूजिफॉर्म *(adjective)* – सूच्याकार [botany & zoology] tapering at both ends; spindle-shaped. *Fusiform cells have been identified on the control plants.*

Fusion/फ्यूजन *(noun)* – संगलन, द्रवण, गलन the process or result of fusing. *Fusion reactor is like a gas burner - the fuel which is injected into the system is burnt off.*

Fuss/फस *(noun)* – बतंगड़, आडम्बर a display of unnecessary or excessive excitement, activity, or interest. *Why is this fuss over the approval of a small loan?*

Fusty/फस्टि *(adjective)* – दुर्गन्धयुक्त smelling stale, damp, or stuffy. *This is a fusty room.*

Futility/फ्यूटिलिटि *(noun)* – असारता useless, worthless, triviality, vanity *We must now all accept the utter futility of trying to solve our border problems by war.*

Future/फ्यूचर *(noun)* – भविष्य time that is still to come. *Surf forecast websites to help you predict the future!* events or conditions occurring or existing in that time. *Future of mankind will become increasingly more sophisticated but highly individualistic.*

Fylfot/फिल्फॅट *(noun)* – स्वस्तिक swastika *Fylfot is an auspicious or lucky object, especially applied to mystic science.*

Gg

G/जी *(noun)* – अंग्रेजी वर्णमाला का सातवाँ वर्ण the seventh letter of the English alphabet.
1. Denoting the next after F in a set of items, categories, etc.
2. Music the fifth note in the diatonic scale of C major.

Gab/गैब *(noun & verb)* – गपशप, बकबक (करना) talk at length. *He was gabbing about his achivements at the previous job.*

Gabble/गैबल *(noun)* – बकबक talk rapidly and unintelligibly *She gabbled in a panicky way during the interview and was disqualified.*

Gabion/गेबियन *(noun)* – किलाबन्दी में उपयोग करने की मिट्टी भरी हुई खंचियाँ a cylindrical basket or container filled with earth, stones, or other material and used as a component of civil engineering works. *Gabion is a part and parcel of a civil engineer's work.*

Gable/गेबल *(noun)* – गृहशिखर the triangular upper part of a wall at the end of a ridged roof. *He tried to put a nail in the gable but failed as it was very high and hard.*

Gadfly/गैडफ्लाइ *(noun)* – गोमक्षिका, डाँस, कुकुरमाछी या दुष्ट बुद्धि वाला व्यक्ति a fly that bites livestock, especially a horsefly, warble fly, or botfly. *He is a very gadfly person beware of him.*

Gaff/गैफ *(noun)* – काँटेदार बरछा या भाला a stick with a hook or barbed spear, for landing large fish. *People catch fish specially big fish with gaff.*

Gaffer/गैफर *(noun)* – वृद्ध पुरुष [British informal] an old man. *He is a gaffer and we should respect him.*

Gag/गैग *(noun)*– मुख बन्धनी a piece of cloth put in or over a person's mouth to prevent him from speaking. *He is talking too much, they tied him up and put a gag into his mouth.*

Gage/गेज *(noun)* – जमानत, प्रतिभूति, बन्धक a valued object deposited as a guarantee of good faith. *Here is a diamond ring, keep it as a gage all your money will be returned.*

Gaggle/गैगल *(noun)* – बत्तख की तरह शब्द करना a flock of geese. *Look at the gaggle what a beautiful scene!*

Gaiety/गेइटि *(noun)* – आनन्द the state or quality of being light-hearted and cheerful. *I felt great gaiety as I looked at people dancing with abandon.*

Gaily/गेली *(adverb)* – प्रसन्नता से in a light-hearted and cheerful manner. *I gaily participated in the group dance.*

Gainer/गेनर *(noun)* – लाभ करने वाला मनुष्य a person or thing that going. *The brown horse came out as a gainer in the race.*

Gainful/गेनफुल *(adjective)* – लाभदायक serving to increase wealth or resources. *We should always try to indulge in gainful activities.*

Gainings/गेनिंग्स *(plural noun)* – प्राप्ति profits or earnings. *His gainings in the hardware business were great.*

Gainsay/गेनसे *(verb)* – विरोध करना formal deny or contradict; speak against. *The impact of good roads cannot be gainsaid. None could gainsay him.*

Gait/गेट *(noun)* – चाल a person's manner of walking. *She has a graceful gait.*

Gaiter/गेटर *(noun)* – पैर ढाँकने की पट्टी a covering of cloth or leather for the ankle and lower leg. *Girls usually wear gaiters in US.*

Galactic/गॅलैक्टिक *(adjective)* – मंदाकिनीय of relating to a galaxy or galaxies. *The galactic mystries are beyond man.*

Galea/गेलिया *(noun)* – टोप के आकार आकृति [botany & zoology] a structure shaped like a helmet. *This plant looks like a galea.*

Galipot/गैलिपॉट *(noun)* – कड़ी ताड़पीन से निकाली हुई राल hardened resin deposits formed on the stem of the maritime pine. *Galipots stuck to the trunk of the tree.*

Gallant/गैलॅन्ट (adjective) – सुन्दर brave; heroic. *He is a gallant officer.*

Galley/गैलि (noun) – लम्बी नाव, पोत, लम्बा ट्रे [historical] a low, flat ship with one or more sails and up to three banks of oars, chiefly used for warfare or piracy and often manned by slaves or criminals. *In old times criminals or slaves used to row galleys.*

Galliard/गैलिआर्ड (noun) – एक प्रकार का नृत्य a [historical] a lively dance in triple time for two people. *Galliards were in fashion in old times.*

Gallic/गैलिक (adjective) – फ्रान्स देश का of or characteristic of France or the French. *The gallic language is lovable.*

Gallinaceous/गैलिनेशस (adjective) – गृह कुक्कुट सम्बन्धी of or relating to birds of an order which includes domestic poultry and game birds. *The gallinaceous literature is very interesting.*

Gallipot/गैलिपॉट (noun) – मरतबान, चीनी मिट्टी का छोटा प्याला [historical] a small pot used to hold medicines or ointments. *Gallipots were used by a lot of people formerly.*

Gallium/गैलियम (noun) – एक रासायनिक तत्त्व the chemical element of atomic number 31, a soft, silvery-white metal which melts at about 30°C. *Gallium is a chemical element.*

Gallon/गैलन (noun) – तीन सेर दस छटाँक तरल पदार्थ की नाप a unit of volume for liquid measure equal to eight pints: in Britain, equivalent to 4.55 litres; in the US, equivalent to 3.79 litres. *He poured gallons of love on his beloved.*

Galloon/गॅलून (noun) – फीता a narrow ornamental strip of braid, lace, etc. used as a trim. *She is very fond of galloons.*

Gallop/गैलॅप (noun) – घोड़े की सरपट चाल the fastest pace of a horse or other quadruped, with all the feet off the ground together in each stride. *The gallop of the horses could be heard far away.*

Galore/गैलोर् (adjective) – अधिकता in abundance. *There were prizes galore.*

Galoshes/गलॉशिज (noun) – जूता के ऊपर रबर का जूता a waterproof rubber overshoe. *He wore galoshes to protect his trousers from muddy water.*

Galvanic/गैल्वैनिक (adjective) – उत्तेजक, प्रेरक relating to or involving electric currents produced by chemical action. *The actor received galvanic applause from the audience.*

Galvanism/गैल्वैनिज्म (noun) – रासायनिक क्रिया से उत्पन्न विद्युतशक्ति [historical] electricity produced by chemical action. *Galvanism has its own place in medical science.*

Galvanization/गैल्वॅनाइजेशन (noun) – बिजली से धातु चढ़ाने की क्रिया the process of covering metal with zink to protect it from rust.

Galvanize/गैल्वैनाइज (verb) – बिजली की सहायता से धातु चढ़ाना shock or excite into action. *The adverse circumstances galvanixed him into action.*

Galvanometer/गैल्वॅनॉमीटर (noun) – बिजली की धारा नापने का यन्त्र an instrument for detecting and measuring small electric currents. *Galvanometers are used in laboratories.*

Gam/गैम (noun) – हाथीदाँत [informal] a tooth or tusk. *He got hurt in his gam.*

Gamble/गैम्बल (verb) – दाँव लगाकर जुआ खेलना play games of chance for money; bet. *He gambles a lot for money and often loses.*

Gambler/गैम्बलर (noun)– जुआरी a person who gambes. *He is a gambler by habit, He does not believe in working for money.*

Gambling/गैम्बलिंग (noun) – जुआ an act of taking chance. *Gambling is a bad habit one should never indulge in it. It can be the ruin of anyone.*

Gamboge/गैम्बोज (noun) – गोंद के समान चिपकने वाला पीला रोगन a gum resin produced by certain east Asian trees, used as a yellow pigment and in medicine as a purgative. *Gamboge is used in medicine as a purgative.*

Gambole/गैम्बल (verb) – कलोल करना run or jump about playfully. *The horse gamboled around the playground.*

Gambrel roof/गैम्ब्रेल रूफ (noun) – दुढालू छत a roof having a shallower slope above a steeper one on each side. *Houses in China and Japan have gambrel hind of roof.*

Game/गेम (noun) – खेलकूद form of competitive activity or sport played according to rules, a meeting for sporting contests *Last Olympic Games were held in London in 2012.* athletics or sports as a lesson or activity at school *In order to be popular, you had to be good at games.*

Gamma/गामा *(noun)* – ग्रीक वर्णमाला की तीसरी अक्षर the third letter of the Greek alphabet. *Gamma is the third letter of the Greek alphabet.*

Gammer/गैमर *(noun)* – बुढ़िया [larchaic] an old woman. *She is a gammer. Don't mind her talk.*

Gammon/गैमॅन *(noun)* – सूअर की जाँघ ham which has been cured like bacon. *He is very fond of eating gammon, pig's bottom meat.*

Gamy/गेमी *(adjective)* – क्रीड़ापूर्ण having the strong flavour or smell of game, especially when it is high. *The room grew gamy as the meat cooked.*

Gander/गैण्डर *(noun)* – हंस a male goose. *A gander usually leads a flock.*

Gang/गैंग *(noun)* – मजदूरों की टोली an organized group of criminals or disorderly young people, [informal] a group of people who regularly associate together, *The gang of bank robbers was arrested by the police.*

Ganglion/गैंग्लिअॅन *(noun)* – नाड़ी ग्रन्थि anatomy a structure containing a number of nerve cells, often forming a swelling on a nerve fibre. a well-defined mass of grey matter within the central nervous system. *The doctor diagnosed ganglion but it was benign and not cancerous.*

Gangrene/गैंगरिन *(noun)* – अवसाद [medicine] localized death and decomposition of body tissue, resulting form either obstruected circulation or bacterial infection. *Gangrene set in the wound in his leg. Ultimately doctors amputed it.*

Gannet/गैनेट *(noun)* – एक प्रकार की समुद्री चिड़िया a large seabird with mainly white plumage, catching fish by plunge-diving. *When I had my first look at a gannet I was surprised to see how cleverly it caught the fish in the sea.*

Gantry/गैन्ट्री *(noun)* – सोपानी मंच a bridge-like overhead structure supporting equipment such as a crane or railway signals. a tall framework supporting a space rocket prior to launching. *The rocket fired into space from the gantry.*

Gaol/जेल *(noun)* – बन्दीगृह [British] variant spelling of jail. *Jail was formerly written as gaol.*

Gap/गैप *(noun)* – दर्रा, खाली जगह a break or hole in an object or between two objects. *He drove the car skilfully through the gap between two walls.*

Gape/गेप *(verb)* – मुँह बाना be or become wide open. *He stared at her with a gaping mouth.*

Garage/गैरॉज *(noun)* – मोटरखाना a building for housing a motor vehicle or vehicles. *This house has the facility of garage.*

Garb/गार्ब *(noun)* – पोशाक clothing or dress, especially of a distinctive or special kind. *In the fancy dress competition he came in the garb of a beggar.*

Garbage/गार्बेज् *(noun)* – गन्दगी rubbish or waste, especially domestic refuse. *I put the garbage by outside. The maid will take it away.*

Gargoyle/गार्गॉइल *(noun)* – परनाला a grotesque carved human or animal face or figure projecting from the gutter of a building, usually as a spout to carry water clear of a wall. *I was amused to look at the gargoyle which had a jackal like face and water sprouted out of it.*

Garish/गेरिश *(adjective)* – भड़कीला, चटकीला obtrusively bright and showy. *His choice is weird. He wears so garish clothes.*

Garland/गार्लॅण्ड *(noun)* – माला a wreath of flowers and leaves, worn on the head or hung as a decoration. *Indian people usually garland their guests.*

Garlic/गालिक् *(noun)* – लहसुन a strong-smelling pungent-tasting bulb, used as a flavouring in cookery. *Garlic is of great medicinal use. It also adds to the flavour of food.*

Garner/गानर *(verb)* – संग्रह करना gather or collect. *He garnered a lot of flowers from the garden.*

Garnet/गानिट *(noun)* – रक्तमणि a vitreous silicate mineral, in particular a deep red form used as a gem. *He is found of wearing garnet.*

Garnish/गानिश *(verb)* – अलंकृत करना decorate or embellish. *All the food containers in the marriage feast were garnished.*

Garniture/गानिचर *(noun)* – पहिनावा, सजावट a set of decorative vases. *I selected a garniture for giving as a gift.*

G

Garret/गैरेट (noun) – अटारी a top-floor or attic room, especially a small dismal one. *He lives in a garnet as he cannot afford to pay much rent.*

Garrison/गैरिसन (noun) – दुर्गरक्षक a body of troops stationed in a fortress or town to defend it. *The king ordered that the town should be provided with a garrison.*

Garron/गेरॉन (noun) – छोटा घोड़ा a small, sturdy workhorse of a breed originating in Ireland and Scotland. *Here is a garron and it can pull heavy load.*

Garrulity/गैरूलिटी (noun) – बकवाद taking a lot especially unimportant things. *She always indulged in garrulity.*

Garrulous/गैरूलस (adjective) – वाचाल excessively talkative. *He is a garrulous old man.*

Garter/गाटर (noun) – मोजा बाँधने का तस्मा a band worn around the leg to keep up a stocking or sock. [north American] a suspender for a sock or stocking. *She regularly wears garters.*

Garth/गाथ (noun) – मैदान [British] an open space surrounded by cloisters. *I have a garth at the back of my house.*

Gasconade/गैस्कनेड (noun) – शेखी tall talk. *Your gasconade will ruin you.*

Gash/गैश (noun) – गहरा घाव a long, deep slash, cut, or wound. *The gash in the forearm during fighting became infected.*

Gasket/गास्किट (noun) – पाल इत्यादि बाँधने की डोरी a sheet or ring of rubber or other material sealing the junction between two surfaces in an engine or other device. *Mechanics often use gasket to seal joints.*

Gasoline/गैसोलिन (noun) – मिट्टी के तेल से निकाला हुआ द्रव [north American] term for petrol. *The car needs gasoline so look out for a petrol pump.*

Gasometer/गैसोमीटर (noun) – गैस संचित रखने का पीपा a large tank in which gas for use as fuel is stored before being distributed to consumers. *'The petrol tanker has arrived, so open the lid of the gasometer.'*

Gasp/गैस्प (verb) – दम लेना catch one's breath with an open mouth, owing to pain or astonishment. strain to obtain by gasping. *He gasped with pain as he sprained his ankle.*

Gastronomy/गैस्ट्रॉनॉमि (noun) – उदर-सेवा the practice or art of choosing, cooking and eating good food. *He believes that gastronomy is a great way of life.*

Gaud/गॉड (noun) – तड़क-भड़क [larchaic] a showy and purely ornamental thing. *I dislike gaud.*

Gaudy/गॉडि (adjective) – भड़कीला extravagantly or tastelessly bright or showy. *He wears gaudy clothes.*

Gaul/गॉल (noun) – फ्रान्स देश का प्राचीन नाम a native or inhabitant of the ancient European region of Gaul. *Many labourers who worked in building pyramids lived in Gaul.*

Gaunt/गॉन्ट (adjective) – दुर्बल lean and haggard, especially through suffering, hunger, or age. *He is a gaunt old man.*

Gauntlet/गॉन्टलिट (noun) – लोहे का दस्ताना a stout glove with a long loose wrist. [historical] an armoured glove. *Gladiators wore gauntlet while fighting.*

Gave/गेव – दिया past of give. *He gave his son sufficient amount of money to start business.*

Gavel/गैवल (noun) – मुँगरी a small hammer with which an auctioneer, judge, etc. hits a surface to call for attention or order. *"See, this is the gavel which the judge hits on before calling order, order".*

Gawk/गॉक (verb) – मूर्ख या उल्लू की तरह ताकना stare openly and stupidly. *As she approached him, he gawked at her beauty.*

Gaze/गेज (noun & verb) – घूरना look steadily and intently.*His gaze disturbed her.*

Gazebo/गॅजीबो (noun) – बुर्ज या दूर का दृश्य देखने का मचान a small building, especially one in the garden of a house, that gives a wide view of the surrounding area. *I love living in a gazebo.*

Gazette/गॅजेट (noun) – गजट a journal or newspaper, especially the official one of an organization or institution. *The news of his appointment was published in the gazette.*

Gazetteer/गैजिटिअॅर (noun) – भूगोल-सम्बन्धी शब्दों का कोश a geographical index or dictionary. *'Look into the state gazetteer to find, this place.'*

Gearing/गिअरिंग *(noun)* – सामान, उपस्कर the set or arrangement of gears in a machine. *'Get the gearing checked by some mechanic.'*

Gecko/गेको *(noun)* – घरेलू छिपकली a nocturnal lizard with adhesive pads on the feet, found in warm regions. *'Look at this strange creature, it is a gecko.'*

Gelatine/जेलेटीन *(noun)* – जिलेटीन, सरेस a transparent sticky substance. *Gelatine is used to make jelly, film for camera etc.*

Gelatinous/जेलाटिनस *(adjective)* – चिपचिपा having a jelly-like consistency. of or like the protein gelatin. *This food is gelatinous.*

Gelation/जिलेशन *(noun)* – ठण्डा करके ठोस करने का कार्य technical solidification by freezing. *The process of gelation takes place as you put water tray in the freezer.*

Geld/गेल्ड *(verb)* – बधिया करना castrate a male animal. *An ox is a gelded animal.*

Gelid/जेलिड *(adjective)* – ठण्डा icy; extremely cold. *Siberia in Rusia is a gelid place.*

Gem/जेम *(noun)* – मणि, रत्न a precious or semi-precious stone, especially when cut and polished or engraved. *He is a gem of a person.*

Gemini/जेमिनि *(noun)* – मिथुन, जुड़वा astronomy a northern constellation the twins, said to represent the twins castor and pollex. *I am a Gemini and as such I'll do well today.*

Gemma/जेमा *(noun)* – पत्रकली a small cellular body or bud that can separate to form a new organism. *This gemma will fall into the earth and develop into a plant.*

Gender/जेन्डर *(noun)* – लिंग grammar a class into which nouns and pronouns are placed in some languages, distinguished by a particular infection. the property of belonging to such a class. *There are lot of difference between male and female gender.*

Genealogy/जिनिएलॅजि *(noun)* – वंश-परम्परा अन्वेषण करना line of descent traced continuously from an ancestor. *He is studying genealogy and willl be able to draw your family tree.*

Generalissimo/जेनरेलिसिमो *(noun)* – एक पद का नाम the commander of a combined military force consisting of army, navy, and air force units. *During war he was given the post of generalissimo.*

Generality/जेनॅरैलिटि *(noun)* – सामान्यता, अधिकांश a statement or principle having general rather than specific validity or force. the quality or state of being general. *Generality accepted him as a leader.*

Generalization/जेनॅरॅलाइजेशॅन *(noun)* – सामान्य अनुमान a general steatement. *Generalization of any commodity or rule helps people.*

Generalize/जेनरेलाइज *(verb)* – विशिष्ट उदाहरणों से साधारण नियम का अनुमान करना make a general or broad statement by inferring from specific cases. *He generalizes a lot and his friends are quite amused by it.*

Generally/जेनॅरलि *(adverb)* – बहुधा in most cases. *Generally speaking leaders do not fulfil their promises.*

Generalness/जेनरलनेस – सामान्यता the quality of being qeneral. *Generalness of his ideas appealed to people.*

Generate/जेनरेट *(verb)* – उपजाना cause to arise or come about. *He generates a lot of happiness wherever he goes.*

Generation/जेनरेशन *(noun)* – युग, पीढ़ी all of the people born and living at about the same time, regarded collectively. the average period in which children grow up and have children of their own. *Old and young generations can never adjust with each other.*

Generative/जेनरेटिव *(adjective)* – उत्पादक relating to or capable of production or reproduction. *All human beings are generative.*

Generator/जेनरेटर *(noun)* – जन्मदाता a person or thing that generates. *A generator creates electricity.*

Generic/जिनेरिक *(adjective)* – जातिगत referring to a class or group; not specific. *These clothes are generic but still good.*

Generosity/जेनरॉसिटि *(noun)* – उदारता the quality of being kind and generous. *I am overwhelmed by the sheer generosity of friends and neighbours.*

Genet/जिनेट *(noun)* – एक प्रकार की रोवें वाली बिल्ली a nocturnal catlike mammal with short legs and a long bushy ringed tail, found in Africa, SW Europe, and Arabia. *This zoo has received a genet. Let us go and see it.*

G

Genetic/जिनेटिक *(adjective)* - उत्पत्ति-सम्बन्धी of or relating to genes or heredity. of or relating to genetics. *This kind of behaiour is purely genetic.*

Genetics/जिनेटिक्स *(noun)* - उत्पत्ति-विषयक शास्त्र the study of heredity. *I find the science of genetics very interesting.*

Genie/जीनी *(noun)* - पिशाच a jinn or spirit, especially one imprisoned within a bottle or oil lamp and capable of granting wished when summoned. *The whole cosmos is like a genie you get whatever you want.*

Genitive/जेनिटिव *(adjective)* - सम्बन्ध-सूचक denoting a case indicating possession or close association. *The genitive forms of 'I' is my and mine.*

Geniture/जेनिचर *(noun)* - उत्पत्ति [larchaic] a person's birth or parentage. *I would like to know about this person's geniture.*

Genius/जीनिऑस *(noun)* - प्रतिभाशाली exceptional intellectual or creative power or other natural ability. *He is a genius. He has got 100% marks in maths.*

Genteel/जेन्टिल *(adjective)* - सुशील, सभ्य affectedly polite and refined. *He is a genteel person. Everybody likes him.*

Gentile/जेन्टाइल *(adjective)* - यहूदी से भिन्न जाति का, नास्तिक व्यक्ति not Jewish. *He is gentile and firmly believes in Christianity.*

Gentility/जेन्टिलिटि *(noun)* - शिष्टाचार socially superior or genteel character or behaviour. *He has great gentility and does not believe in hurting anybody.*

Gentilize/जेन्टिलाइज *(verb)* - शिष्ट बनाना to make gentle. *I tried to genttilize him but i failed.*

Gentle/जेन्टल *(noun)* - विनीत fishing a maggot, especially the larva of a blowfly, used as bait. *While fishing people generally use gentle.*

Gentleman/जेन्टलमैन *(noun)* - भद्र पुरुष a courteous or honourable man. *He is a thorough gentleman and you can always rely on him.*

Gentleness/जेन्टलनेस *(noun)* - कोमलता quality of being gentle. *'You are very rude, you should cultivate gentleness.'*

Gently/जेन्टली *(adv.)* - कोमलता से politely. *He gently asked her to go away.*

Genuine/जेन्यूइन *(adjective)* - यथार्थ truly what it is said to be; authentic. *It is a genuine document, even the court has admitted it.*

Geodesy/जीऑडिसी *(noun)* - भूमण्डल नापने का शास्त्र the branch of mathematics concerned with the shape and area of the earth or large portions of it. *He is a specialist is geodesy.*

Geography/जिऑग्रफि *(noun)* - भूगोल विद्या the study of the physical features of the earth and of human activity as it relates to these. *Geography is his favourite subject.*

Geomancy/जीओमैन्सि *(noun)* - मृत्तिका-शकुन विचार the art of setting buildings auspiciously. *He is an expert in geomancy.*

Geometry/जिऑमिट्रि *(noun)* - रेखागणित the branch of mathematics concerned with the properties and relations of points, lines, surfaces, solids, and higher dimensional analogues. *Some people find geometry very interesting.*

Geonomy/जिऑनॉमि *(noun)* - प्राकृतिक भूगोल natural geography. *He takes interest in reading books of geonomy.*

Geophagist/जिऑफैजिस्ट *(noun)* - मिट्टी खाने वाला one who eats soil. *His son is geophagist.*

Geophagy/जीऑफैजि *(noun)* - मिट्टी खाने का कार्य the practice in some tribal societies of eating earth. *Geophagy has no place in civilized and cultured societies.*

German/जर्मन *(noun)* - जर्मनी देश की भाषा a native or national of Germany, or a person of German descent. *I am learning German these day.*

Germanic/जर्मनिक *(adjective)* - जर्मनी सम्बन्धी relating to or denoting the branch of the indo-European language family that includes English, German, Dutch, Persion, and the Scandinavian language. relating to or denoting the people of ancient northern and western Europe speaking such languages *Germanic languages are widespread.*

Germicide/जॅर्मिसाइड *(noun)* - जीवाणुनाशी a substance which destroys bacteria etc. *His favourite field of study is germicide.*

G

Germinate/जर्मिनेट *(verb)* – बीज फूटना to start grawing. *Seeds germinate fast in rainy season.*

Germination/जर्मिनेशन *(noun)* – अँखुवा फूटने का समय *Germination of these seeds has taken place and no more water is needed.*

Gestation/जेस्टेशन *(noun)* – गर्भ धारण करने की स्थिति the process of carrying or being carried in the womb between conception and birth. *She has great capacity for gestation.*

Gesticulate/जेस्टिक्यूलेट *(verb)* – नाटक करना gesture dramatically in place of or to emphasize speech. *He gesticulated wildly and many people came to his help.*

Gesticulator/जेस्टिक्यूलेटर *(noun)* – हावभाव दिखाने वाला पुरुष one who gesticulates. *He is a greated gesticulator.*

Gesture/जेस्चर् *(noun)* – चेष्टा a movement of part of the body, especially a hand or the head, to express an idea or meaning. *He gestured me to follow him.*

Get-up/गेट-अप *(noun)* – बनावट [informal] a style or arrangement of dress, especially an elaborate or unusual one. *She came to the party in the get up of a princess.*

Gewgaw/ग्यूगा *(noun)* – खिलौना, नुमाइशी चीज a showy thing, especially one that is useless or worthless. *This gewgaw is worthless and useless.*

Geyser/गीजर *(noun)* – गरम पानी का झरना a hot spring in which water intermittently boils, sending a tall column of water and steam into the air. *There are many hidden geysers in the jungles of South America.*

Ghastly/गास्टलि *(adjective)* – भयंकर causing great horror or fear, macabre. *The ghastly accident took place on highway at 3 a.m.*

Ghost/गोस्ट *(noun)* – भूत an apparition of a dead person which is believed to appear to the living, typically as a nebulous image. [larchaic] a spirit or soul. *Ghost plays important roles in the plays of Shakespeare.*

Ghost-like/गोस्टलाइक *(adj)* – प्रेतवत् like a ghost. *The beggar's ghost like appearance frightened me.*

Giant/जाइअॅन्ट् *(noun)* – राक्षस an imaginary or mythical being of human form but superhuman size. *He has a giant like appearance being so tall and broad.*

Gibber/जिबर् *(verb)* – बड़बड़ाना speak rapidly and unintelligibly, typically through fear or shock. *He was so afraid that he gibbered instead of talking.*

Gibbet/जिबिट् *(noun)* – फाँसी देकर मृत्यु, टिकठी an upright post with an arm on which the bodies of executed criminals were left hanging as a warning or deterrent to others. *Criminals are taken to gibbet and hanged.*

Gibbon/गिब्बॅन *(noun)* – लंगूर a small, slender tree-dwelling ape with long, powerful arms, native to the forests of SE Asia. *Gibbons can be seen in plenty in jungles of SE Asia.*

Gibe/जाइब *(noun & verb)* – हँसी करना variant spelling of jibe. *He made a gibe against me and I was highly irritated.*

Gibus/जाइबस *(noun)* – उत्सव में पहनने की अँग्रेजी टोपी a kind of collapsible top hat. *He is fond of wearing gibus.*

Giddily/गिडिलि *(adverb)* – चपलता से disoriented. *He walked giddily and needed support.*

Giddiness/गिडिनेस *(noun)* – चपलता, चक्कर dizziness. *He suffers from giddiness and often falls down.*

Gift/गिफ्ट *(noun)* – उपहार a thing given willingly to someone without payment; a present. *I gave her a costly gift on her birthday.*

Gimantic/जाइमैन्टिक *(adj)* – विशाल extermely large. *This is a gigantic building.*

Gild/गिल्ड *(verb)* – सोने का मुलम्मा करना cover thinly with gold. *This is a gilded bracelet.*

Gill/गिल *(noun)* – गलफड़ा, गहरी कन्दरा the paired respiratory organ of fished and some amphibians, by which oxygen is extracted from water flowing over surfaces within or attached to the walls of the pharynx. *All fish have gills through which the inhale oxygen.*

Gilt/गिल्ट *(adjective)* – सुनहले रंग का covered thinly with gold leaf or gold paint. *Many artificial jewellery is gilt edged.*

Gimlet/गिम्लिट *(noun)* – छेद करने की बर्मी a small T-shaped tool with a screw tip for boring holes. *We need a gimlet to bore holes in the wall to fix clothes hanger..*

G

Ginger/जिंजर *(noun)* – अदरक a hot, fragrant spice made from the rhizome of a plant. *Ginger a root plant has many medicinal uses.*

Gingerly/जिंजरली *(adverb)* – धीरे से in a careful or cautious manner. *I gingerly touched the animal in the zoo.*

Gingham/जिंगम *(noun)* – धारीदार सूती कपड़ा lightweight plain-woven cotton cloth, typically checked. *I like to wear clothes made of gingham.*

Gingival/जिनजाइवल *(adjective)* – मसूड़े का medicine concerned with the gums. *I have bleeding gums and I need some gingival.*

Ginglymus/जिंग्लाइमस *(noun)* – शरीर का कब्जे के प्रकार का जोड़ anatomy a hinge-like joint such as the elbow or knee. *There is great pain in my ginglymus.*

Girandole/जिरॉन्डोल *(noun)* – आतिशबाजी की चरखी a branched support for candles or other lights. *Please bring a girandole I have many candles to light.*

Gird/गर्ड *(verb)* – घेरना make cutting or critical remarks. *(noun)* cutting or critical remark; a taunt. *He has a bad habit of girding and as such I dislike him.*

Girder/गर्डर *(noun)* – शहतीर a large metal beam used in building bridges and large buildings. *No large constructions can be done without girders.*

Girdle/गर्डल *(noun & verb)* – कमरबन्द, पेटी बाँधना Scottish and northern English term for griddle. *She has girdled her waist by a gorgeous belt.*

Girt/गर्ट *(noun)* – ऊपरी नाप old-fashioned term for girth. *He has a big girt as he eats too much.*

Girth/गर्थ *(noun)* – घोड़े की साज का पेटी, घेरा the measurement around the middle of something, especially a person's waist. *The tailor measured his girth, it was sixty inches.*

Gist/जिस्ट *(noun)* – भाव the substance or essence of a speech or text. *The gist of his talk is 'never give up'.*

Given/गिवेन *(adjective)* – दिया हुआ specified stated. *Given these hints you can find the solution to the problem.*

Giver/गिवर *(noun)* – दाता a person who gives something. *God is a giver of mercy.*

Giving/गिविंग *(noun)* – दान, अर्पण *Giving thanks is a good habit.*

Give/गिव *(verb)* – देना *He who gives, receives.*

Gizzard/गिजर्ड *(noun)* – पक्षियों तथा मछलियों का द्वितीय आमाशय a muscular, thick-walled part of a bird's stomach for grinding food, typically with girt. a muscular stomach of some fish, insects, molluces, and other invertebrates. *The bird was hit in gizzard.*

Glabrous/ग्लैब्रश *(adjective)* – बिना रोम का technical free from hair or down; smooth. *Her skin is glabrous and glowing.*

Glace/ग्लेस *(adjective)* – चमकदार सतह का having a glossy surface due to preservation in sugar. *It is a glace cherry.*

Glacial/ग्लेसिअल *(adjective)* – बर्फीला relating to ice, especially in the form of glaciers or ice sheets. *The glacial mountain floated slowly on the sea.*

Glaciated/ग्लेसिएटेड *(adjective)* – हिमानी से ढका हुआ covered or having been covered by glaciers or ice sheets. *A glaciated sea is highly dangerous for ships.*

Glacier/ग्लेसिअर *(noun)* – बरफ की धीरे-धीरे सरकने वाली चट्टान a slowly moving mass of ice formed by the accumulation and compaction of snow on mountains or near the poles. *A glacier collided with the ship.*

Glacis/ग्लैसिस *(noun)* – ढालुआँ किनारा a bank sloping down from a fort which exposes attackers to the defenders' missiles. *This glacis is very dangerous.*

Glad/ग्लैड *(adjective)* – खुश pleased; delighted. causing happiness: glad tidings. *I am glad to see you.*

Gladden/ग्लैडेन *(verb)* – खुश करना make glad. *He gladdens everybody he meets.*

Glade/ग्लेड *(noun)* – वनमार्ग an open space in a wood or forest. *Here is a glade we can fix our tents here.*

Gladly/ग्लैडली *(adverb)* – खुशी से willingly. *I will gladly do what ever you say.*

Gladness/ग्लैडनेस *(adjective)* – खुशी sense of happiness. *He radiates gladness wherever he goes.*

Gladstone-bag/ग्लैडस्टोनबैग *(noun)* – एक प्रकार का हल्का झोला a bag like a briefcase having two equal compartments joined by a hinge. *He is habitual of carrying a gladstone bag.*

Glamour/ग्लेमर *(noun)* – जादू an attractive and exciting quality, especially sexual allure. *The film world is a world of glamour.*

Gland/ग्लैण्ड *(noun)* – ग्रंथि an organ of the body which secretes particular chemical substances. a lymph node. *Our body has many glands that secrete different substances.*

Glandular/ग्लैण्डयूलर *(adjective)* – ग्रंथि-सम्बन्धी relating to or affecting a gland or glands. *This is a glandular disease.*

Glare/ग्लेअर *(verb)* – घूरना stare in an angry or fierce way. *The glare of the sun was very strong.*

Glaring/ग्लेअरिंग *(adj)* – देदीप्यमान *You have committed a glaring mistake.*

Glass/ग्लास *(noun)* – शीशा a hard, brittle, usually transparent or translucent substance made by fusing sand with soda and lime. ornaments and other articles made from glass. *The screen is made of glass. The top of this dining table is made of heavy black glass.*

Glaucoma/ग्लॉकोमा *(noun)* – आँख का एक रोग medicine a condition of increased pressure within the eyeball, causing gradual loss of sight. *He suffers from glaucoma and his eye sight is becoming dim.*

Glaucous/ग्लॉकॅस *(adjective)* – हल्के नीले रंग का technical or [poetic/literary] of a dull grayish-green or blue colour. *This is a glaucous cloth.*

Glaze/ग्लेज *(verb)* – शीशा लगाना fit panes of glass into a window frame or similar structure. enclose or cover with glass. *This house has a glazed balcony.*

Glazier/ग्लेजिअर *(noun)* – खिड़कियों में शीशा जड़ने वाला a person whose trade is fitting glass into windows and doors. *He is a glazier by profession. Call him to fix your window panes.*

Glazing/ग्लेजिंग *(noun)* – खिड़कियों आदि मे काँच बैठाने का कार्य the work of fitting panes. *Glazing is an art.*

Gleaming/ग्लीमिंग *(adj)* – चमकने वाला shining. *This is a brand new gleaming car.*

Glean/ग्लीन *(verb)* – लवन के बाद छुटा हुआ अन्न बटोरना collect gradually from various sources. *He gleaned information from the library to write a new article.*

Gleaning/ग्लीनिंग *(plural noun)* – बटोरने का कार्य things gleaned from various sources rather than acquired as a whole. *The act of gleaning is going on.*

Glebe/ग्लेब *(noun)* – मिट्टी [historical] a piece of land serving as part of a clergyman's benefice and providing income. *His glebe has sufficient income.*

Gleeful/ग्लीफुल *(adjective)* – आनन्दपूर्ण exuberantly or triumphantly joyful. *His gleeful talk charmed her.*

Gleet/ग्लिट *(noun)* – मवाद [medicine] a watery discharge from the urethra caused by gonorrhoeal infection. *Look at the gleet, this patient apperars to have a venereal disease.*

Glen/ग्लेन *(noun)* – कंदरा a narrow valley, especially in Scotland or Ireland. *The army was attacked when it was passing through a glen.*

Glib/ग्लिब *(adjective)* – चिकना articulate and voluble but insincere and shallow. *He is a glib fellow don't trust him too much.*

Glimmer/ग्लिमर *(verb)* – चमकना shine faintly with a wavering light. *The light glimmered and ultimately went out.*

Glimpse/ग्लिम्प्स *(noun)* – झलक see briefly or partially. *He had only a glimpse at the report and understood everything.*

Glint/ग्लिन्ट *(noun & verb)* – चमक, चमकना give out or reflect small flashes of light. *A glint of light told us that the tunnel was going to end.*

Glissade/ग्लिसेड *(noun)* – बरफ पर सरकना a slide down a steep slope of snow or ice, typically on the feet with the support of an outwards from the body and then takes the weight while the second leg is brushed in to meet it. *He performed nicely with the help of glissade.*

Glister/ग्लिस्टर *(verb)* – चमक sparkle; glitter. *The glow worms glistered in the dark of the night.*

Glitter/ग्लिटर *(verb)* – चमकना, प्रकाश फेंकना shine with a bright, shimmering reflected light. *All that glitters is not gold.*

G

211

Gloaming/ग्लोमिंग *(noun)* – सन्ध्या का मन्द प्रकाश [informal] fashionable people involved in show business or some other glamorous activity. *The faint light after the sets and before it rises is called gloaming.*

Gloat/ग्लोट *(verb)* – बुरी दृष्टि डालना [poetic/ literary] twilight; dusk. *He was gloating at his success in the interview.*

Globe/ग्लोब *(noun)* – पृथ्वी a spherical or rounded object. a golden orb as an emblem of sovereignty. *Look at the globe and find out at what longitude India is situated.*

Globular/ग्लोब्यूलर *(adjective)* – गोलाकार globe-shaped; spherical. *The earth is globural.*

Globule/ग्लोब्यूल *(noun)* – गोली a small round particle of a substance; a drop. *A globule of water fell down from the tree.*

Gloom/ग्लूम *(noun)* – अन्धकार partial or total darkness. *He strained his eyes peering into the gloom.*

Gloomy/ग्लूमी *(adjective)* – खिन्न poorly lit, especially so as to cause fear or depression. *These rooms are cold and gloomy I want to go in warm sunlight.*

Glorification/ग्लोरीफिकेसन *(noun)* – प्रशंसा to praise. *Her glorification made her a film star.*

Glorious/ग्लॉरिअश *(adjective)* – तेजस्वी worthy of bringing fame. *This is the most glorious victory of all time.*

Glossary/ग्लॉसरि *(noun)* – पारिभाषिक शब्द-कोश an alphabetical list of words relating to a specific subject, text, or dialect, with explanations. *Look at the glossary given at the end of the book to find out what does this word stand for.*

Glossiness/ग्लॉसिनेस *(noun)* – चमक attractive, shiny, smooth. *The glass top of the table has lost its glossiness.*

Glossy/ग्लॉसी *(adjective)* – चिकना shiny and smooth. *After the paint the wall has become very glossy.*

Glottis/ग्लॉटिस *(noun)* – घाटी the part of the larynx consisting of the vocal cords and the slit-like opening between them. *There is something stuck in his glottis he can't speak.*

Glower/ग्लोवर *(verb)* – तिरछी निगाह से देखना have an angry or sullen look on one's face; scowl. *He glowered at me and began to quarrel.*

Glow-worm/ग्लो-वर्म *(noun)* – जुगनू a soft-bodied beetle whose larva like wingless female emits light to attract males. *It is beautiful to look at glow-worm in the dark of the night.*

Glucose/ग्लूकोज *(noun)* – अंगूर से निकली हुई शक्कर a simple sugar which is an important energy source in living organisms and is a component of many carbohydrates. a syrup containing glucose and other sugars, made by hydrolysis of starch and used in the food industry. *Glucose is an important ingredient of diet.*

Glue/ग्लू *(noun & verb)* – सरेस an adhesive substance used for sticking objects or materials together. *The wood joints are being glued together.*

Glum/ग्लम *(adjective)* – मलिनमुख dejected; morose. *He is a glum looking fellow who rarely breaks his silence.*

Glut/ग्लट *(noun)* – आधिक्य an excessively abundant supply of something. *The glut of items in the market surprised the buyers.*

Gluten/ग्लूटॅन *(noun)* – लसलसा पदार्थ a substance present in cereal grains, especially wheat, which is responsible for the elastic texture of dough. *Wheat possesses gluten that is why we can knead it.*

Glyptography/ग्लिप्टॉग्राफी *(noun)* – रत्नों पर नक्काशी करने की विधा the art or scientific study of gem engraving. *He is an expert in glyptography.*

Gnarl/नार्ल *(noun)* – गाँठ a rough, knotty protuberance, especially on a tree. *Look at the gnarl, it is an old tree.*

Gnarled/नार्ल्ड *(adjective)* – ऐंठा हुआ knobbly, rough, and twisted, especially with age. *He is a gnarled old man.*

Gnat/नैट *(noun)* – मच्छर a small two-winged fly resembling a mosquito, typically forming large swarms. many other species, especially in the family culicidae. *This room is infested with gnats.*

Gnathic/नैथिक *(adjective)* – दाढ़ सम्बन्धी rare of or relating to the jaws. *I have gnathic pain.*

Gnaw/नॉ *(verb)* – कष्ट देना bite at or nibble persistently. *The worry gnawed at him.*

Gnome/नोम *(noun)* – बौना, कहावत a legendary dwarfish creature supposed to guard the earth's treasures underground. *Children like to imagine and talk about gnomes.*

Gnomic/नोमिक *(adjective)* – सूक्तिबद्ध in the form of short, pithy maxims or aphorisms. *His gnomic talk disturbed me.*

Gnostic/नॉस्टिक *(adjective)* – गूढ़वान-सम्बन्धी of or relating to knowledge, especially esoteric mystical knowledge. *He is a gnostic person maybe he will solve your problem.*

Gnosticism/नास्टिसिज्म *(noun)* – ब्रह्मज्ञान का सिद्धान्त a heretical movement of the 2nd-century Christian church, teaching that esoteric knowledge of the supreme divine being enabled the redemption of the human spirit. *Belief in Gnosticism was prevalent in 2nd century.*

Gnu/नू *(noun)* – अफ्रीका का बारहसिंगा a large African antelope with a long head, a beard and mane, and a sloping back. *Gnu can be seen in the jungles of Africa.*

Go/गो *(noun)* – एक जापानी खेल *(verb)* move from one place to another, travel *He went out to the shops she longs to go. We've a long way to go.* travel a specified distance *You have to go a few miles more to reach his house.* travel or move in order to engage in a specified activity *He used to go hunting quite often.* (go to) attend or visit for a particular purpose *We went to the cinema. He went to Cambridge University.* change in level, amount, or rank *Prices have gone up by 15 per cent.* [informal] said in various expressions when angrily or contemptuously dismissing someone *Go and complete all the pending jobs before you leave for home.*

Goad/गोड *(noun)* – अंकुश a spiked stick used for driving cattle. *The cowboys goaded their cattle across the field.*

Goal/गोल *(noun)* – गोल, अन्त, पहुँच a pair of posts linked by a crossbar and forming a space into which the ball has to be sent in order to score. *Both the football teams scored a goal against each other.*

Goat/गोट *(noun)* – अज, बकरा a hardy domesticated ruminant mammal that has backward-curving horns and a beard. a wild mammal related to this, such as the ibex, markhor, and tur. *The goats have a wonderful ability to climb rocky terrains.*

Gob/गॉब *(noun)* – थूक [British] a lump or clot of a slimy or viscous substance. [north American] a small, lump. *Don't touch it. It is a gob.*

Gobbet/गॉबेट *(noun)* – छोटा टुकड़ा a piece or lump of flesh, food, or other matter. *This gobbet looks rotten, throw it away.*

Gobble/गॉबॅल *(verb)* – शब्द करते हुए जल्दी-जल्दी खाना eat hurriedly and noisily. use a large amount of very quickly. *He gobbled the food down as he was very hungry.*

Gobbler/गॉब्लर *(noun)* – जल्दी से निगलने वाला a person who eats greedily. *He is a gobbler and makes a lot of noise while eating.*

Goblet/गॉब्लेट *(noun)* – कटोरा a drinking glass with a foot and a stem. [larchaic] a bowl-shaped metal or glass drinking cup. *He drank wine from a goblet.*

Goblin/गॉब्लिन *(noun)* – भूत, पिशाच a mischievous, ugly, dwarf-like creature of folklore. *Goblins often featured in early literature.*

Godown/गोडाउन *(noun)* – गोदाम a warehouse. *Most business house maintain a godown to stock their products.*

Goer/गोएर *(noun)* – जाने वाला a person who attends a specified place or event: a theatre-goer. *He is a thorough cinema goer.*

Goggle/गॉगॅल *(verb)* – आँख फाड़कर देखना look with wide open eyes, typically in amazement *He goggled at them incomplete disbelief.* (of the eyes) open wide or protrude *They were watching the circus show with their eyes goggling and their tongues hanging out.* *(adjective)* (of the eyes) protuberant or rolling *The lights were flashing so much that it was difficult to keep eyes from goggling.*

Goggles/गॉगल्स *(noun)* – धूप का रंगीन चश्मा a pair of glasses. *People generally use goggles in summer.*

Goitre/गॉइटॅर *(noun)* – गण्डमाला a swelling of the neck resulting from enlargement of the thyroid gland. *People suffering from goitre are put on special medicine.*

G

213

Golden/गोल्डॅन *(adjective)* – चमकीला made of, coloured like, or shining like gold. *It is a golden opportunity, don't let it go.*

Gone/गॉन *(adjective)* – बीता हुआ no longer present, departed *They were gone a long time. The bad old days are gone.* no longer in existence; dead or extinct *An aunt of mine, long since gone.* no longer available, consumed or used up *The food's all gone, I'm afraid.* in a trance or stupor, especially through exhaustion, drink, or drugs *He sat on a folding chair, half-gone.* beyond help, in a hopeless state *Spending time and effort on a gone car like old Ford.*

Gong/गॉन्ग *(noun)* – घड़ियाल a metal disc with a turned rim, giving a resonant note when struck. *As the gong struck all the courtiers stood up to receive the king.*

Goniometer/गोनिऑमीटर *(noun)* – गोनियाँ an instrument for the precise measurement of angles, especially the angles between the faces of crystals. *Crystals have many faces and goniometer is used to measure the angles.*

Goose/गूज *(noun)* – कलहंस a large water bird with a long neck, short legs, webbed feet, and a short, broad bill. the female of such a bird. *It is a flock of geese making sounds in the garden.*

Gooseberry/गूजबेरी *(noun)* – करौंदा around edible yellowish-green or reddish berry with a thin translucent hairy skin. *Pick up gooseberries among the thorns.*

Gopher/गॉफर् *(noun)* – एक प्रकार की गिलहरी a burrowing American rodent with fur-lined pouches on its cheeks. [informal north American] term for ground squirrel. in names of various burrowing reptiles: gopher tortoise. *In US a kind of rodents is called gopher.*

Gore/गोर् *(noun)* – गाढ़ा रक्त blood that has been shed, especially as a result of violence. *The sight of gore sickened me.*

Gorge/गॉर्ज् *(noun)* – ढालू तंग घाटी a steep, narrow valley or ravine. *He fell into a gorge and had to be pulled out.*

Gorget/गॉर्गेट *(noun)* – गुलूबन्द [historical] an article of clothing, a piece of amount covering the throat, a wimple. *Gorgets were in fashion in early times.*

Gorgon/गॉर्गन् *(noun)* – कुरूपा स्त्री Greek mythology each of three sisters with snakes for hair, who had the power to turn anyone who looked at them to stone. *Gorgon is a frightening creature.*

Gorilla/गॅरिला *(noun)* – बनमनुष a powerfully built great ape of central Africa, the largest living primate. *Gorillas are anthropoid creatures living in Africa.*

Gormandize/गॉर्मन्डाइज *(verb)* – भुक्खड़ की तरह भोजन करना variant spelling of gourmandize. *Don't gormandize please.*

Gory/गोरी *(adjective)* – रक्तरंजित, लहूलुहान involving or showing violence and bloodshed. *I feel horrified at such gory scenes.*

Gosling/गॉस्लिंग *(noun)* – हंस का बच्चा a young goose. *It is a gosling, let us play with it.*

Gospel/गॉस्पॅल *(noun)* – सुसमाचार the teaching or revelation of Christ. *We should study gospel if we want to know about Jesus Christ.*

Gossip/गॉसिप *(noun)* – बकवाद casual conversation or unsubstantiated reports about other people. *Almost all people are fond of gossip.*

Got/गॉट *(verb)* – पाया past and past participle of get. *He got past without noticing me.*

Gouge/गाउज *(verb)* – रुखानी से छेद या खाँचा काटना, निकालना make in a surface. *He attacked him desperately and almost gouged out his eye.*

Gourmand/गुऑर्मॅन्ड *(noun)* – खद्दूक a person who enjoys eating, sometimes to excess. *He is a gourmand and good food is his weakness.*

Gout/गाउट *(noun)* – वातरोग a disease in which defective metabolism of uric acid causes arthritis, especially in the smaller bones of the feet. *He is suffering from gout his uric acid is very high.*

Goutiness/गाउटिनेस् *(noun)* – गठियारोग a kind of arthritis. *Goutiness made him almost immobile.*

Gouty/गाउटि *(adj)* – वातरोग से ग्रस्त suffering from gout. *He is a gouty man and can't walk properly.*

Governability/गॅवॅनबिलिटि *(noun)* – शासन किये जाने की योग्यता policies, governance. *My governability was in question I had to prove that I was a good admistrator.*

G

Governable/गॅवॅर्नेबल *(adjective)* – शासनीय manageable. *It is small rebellion and therefore governable.*

Governance/गॅवॅर्नॅन्स *(noun)* – अधिकार the action or manner of governing. [larchaic] control. *There are different modes of governance all over the world.*

Governess/गॅवॅर्निस *(noun)* – गुरुआइन a woman employed to teach children in a private household. *I have at last found a good governess for my children.*

Gown/गाउन *(noun)* – चोंगा a long dress worn on formal occasions a protective garment worn in hospital by surgical staff or patients. a loose cloak indicating one's profession or status, worn by a lawyer, teacher, academic, or university student. the members of a university as distinct from the residents of a town. often contrasted with town. *Lawyers and doctors wear gowns as required by their profession.*

Grab/ग्रैब *(noun & verb)* – छीना-झपटी या छीनना seize suddenly and roughly. [informal] obtain quickly or opportunistically. grip the wheel harshly or jerkily. *I grabbed the thief by collar.*

Grabble/ग्रैबल *(verb)* – टटोलना [archaic] feel or search with the hands. *The officer grabbled my luggage but could find nothing objectionable.*

Graceful/ग्रेसफुल *(adjective)* – सुन्दर having or showing grace or elegance. *She is a very graceful lady.*

Graceless/ग्रेसलेस *(adj.)* – दुष्ट, भ्रष्ट bad impolite. *She is a graceless woman.*

Gracious/ग्रेशॅस *(adjective)* – दयालु courteous, kind, and pleasant. *Her gracious presence enchanted all people present.*

Gradate/ग्रॅडेट *(verb)* – सरियाना, स्तर के अनुरूप रखना to keep in order. *I have gradated all these books.*

Gradation/ग्रॅडेशन *(noun)* – उतार-चढ़ाव a scale of successive changes, stages, or degrees. *The gradation from harsh to soft tone took time.*

Grade/ग्रेड *(noun)* – क्रम, कोटि, श्रेणी a particular level of rank, quality, proficiency, or value. *He has got high grades in all subjects.*

Gradient/ग्रेड्यॅन्ट *(noun)* – उतार-चढ़ाव a sloping part of a road or railway. *Be careful the gradient is very steep here.*

Gradual/ग्रैड्युअल *(adjective)* – क्रमिक taking place in stages over an extended period. *Relax, the slope is gradual here.*

Graduate/ग्रैड्यूइट *(noun)* – स्नातक a person who has been awarded a first academic degree, or a high-school diploma. *He is a Delhi University graduate.*

Graduation/ग्रेड्युएशॅन *(noun)* – उपाधि प्राप्ति academic achievement. *He has completed his graduation from Bombay University.*

Graffito/ग्रफिटो *(noun)* – खोदकर बनाया गया चित्र drwaings] writings on walls. *The subway was covered in graffito.*

Graft/ग्राफ्ट *(noun)* – कलम, घूस [informal] bribery and other corrupt measures pursued for gain in politics or business. *Graft is spread all over our country.*

Grail/ग्रेल *(noun)* – पवित्र पात्र the cup or platter used by Christ at the last supper especially as the object of quests by knights. *In early times knights used to search for grail.*

Grain/ग्रेन *(noun)* – धान्यबीज wheat or other cultivated cereal used as food, a single seed or fruit or a cereal. *Wheat grain is our main cereal.*

Gram/ग्राम *(noun)* – ग्राम a metric unit of mass equal to one thousandth of a kilogram. *One thousand grams make a kilogram.*

Gram/ग्रैम *(noun)* – चना chickpeas or other pulses used as food. *Gram is a cereal rich in protein.*

Grammar/ग्रैमर *(noun)* – व्याकरण the whole system and structure of a language or of languages in general, usually taken as consisting of syntax and morphology. a particular analysis of this. *It is not easy to understand grammar of any language.*

Gramme/ग्राम *(noun)* – मेट्रिक माप में एक तौल variant spelling of gram.

Gramophone/ग्रैमॅफोन *(noun)* – ग्रामोफोन chiefly British old-fashioned term for record player. *A gramophone or record player can be a great source of entertainment.*

Granary/ग्रैनरि *(noun)* – कोठार, अन्न-भंडार a storehouse for threshed grain. *For an agricultural state, a granary is a must.*

Grandee/ग्रैन्डी *(noun)* – भद्र व्यक्ति a Spanish or Portuguese noble-man of the highest rank. a man of high rank or eminence. *A grandee commands respect.*

G

Grandeur/ग्रैन्ड्‌यर/ग्रैन्जॅर *(noun)* – महत्त्व splendour and impressiveness. high rank or social importance. *He is a man of grandeur hence respected by all.*

Grandiloquent/ग्रैन्डिलक्वॅन्ट *(adjective)* – रोब या घमण्ड से denoting cultivated plant varieties with large flowers. *Grandiloquent gardening is his hobby.*

Graniferous/ग्रॅनिफेरॅस *(adjective)* – अन्न उत्पन्न करने वाला botany producing grain or a grain-like seed. *It is a graniferous object, sow it and it will grow.*

Granite/ग्रेनाइट *(noun)* – ग्रेनाइट, इमारतों में प्रयुक्त होने योग्य कड़ा पत्थर a very hard, granular, crystalline igneous rock consisting mainly of quartz, mica, and feldspar. *Granite is very useful, it can be used in many ways.*

Granivorous/ग्रॅनिवॅरॅस *(adjective)* – अन्न के दाने खाने वाला [zoology] feeding on grain. *A lot of people are granivorous. Their main food is cereal and not meat.*

Granny/ग्रैनी *(noun)* – दादी [informal] one's grand-mother. *I love my granny she tells us a lot of nice stories.*

Grant/ग्रांट *(verb)* – स्वीकृति देना agree to give or allow to. give a right, property, etc. formally or legally to. *Don't worry, God will grant you your wish.*

Grantable/ग्रांटेबल *(adjective)* – उपहार के योग्य allowable. *This wish of yours is not grantable.*

Grantee/ग्रांटी *(noun)* – अनुदानग्राही one who receives grant. *I was a grantee in my college days.*

Granter/ग्रान्टॅर *(noun)* – दान देने वाला one who allows. *God is the granter of all our wishes.*

Granular/ग्रैन्यूलर् *(adjective)* – दानेदार resembling or consisting of granules. *This is something granular, polish its surface to make it smooth.*

Granule/ग्रैन्यूल *(noun)* – छोटा दाना a small compact particle. *A granule of sand can tell us a lot if studied under a microscope.*

Grape/ग्रेप *(noun)* – अंगूर a green, purple, or black berry growing to the distribution or measurement of grain sizes in sand, rock, or other deposits. *He is fond of eating black grapes.*

Grapery/ग्रेपरि *(noun)* – अंगूर का बाग a garden of grapes. *I like to visit grapery in Kashmir.*

Graphics/ग्रैफिक्स *(plural noun)* – लेखाचित्र कला the products of the graphic arts, especially commercial design or illustration. *Graphics have done wonders in the world of cinema.*

Graphite/ग्रैफॉइट *(noun)* – काला सीसा a grey, crystalline, electrically conducting form of carbon which is used as a solid lubricant, as pencil lead, and as a moderator in nuclear reactors. *Graphite is used in pencils to write.*

Grapnel/ग्रैप्नॅल *(noun)* – अनेक धारावाला छोटा लंगर a grappling hook. *He attacked the robber with a grapnel.*

Grapple/ग्रैपॅल *(verb)* – बाँधना, हाथापाई करना engage in a close fight or struggle without weapons. struggle to deal with. *He grappled bravely with the problem.*

Grass/ग्रास *(noun)* – घास vegetation consisting of short plants with long narrow leaves, growing wild or cultivated on lawns and pasture. ground covered with this. *The lawn has beautiful soft grass.*

Grassy/ग्रासी *(noun)* – हरा please gained from satisfaction of desire. *This is a barren land with grassy patches here and there.*

Grasshopper/ग्रासहॉपर *(noun)* – टिड्डा a plant-eating insect with long hind legs which are used for jumping and for producing a chirping sound. *It is a big swarm of grasshoppers and it will eat all the crop.*

Grateful/ग्रेटफुल *(adjective)* – कृतज्ञ feeling or showing gratitude. *I am grateful to you for the favour you have shown me.*

Gratification/ग्रैटिफिकेशन *(noun)* – संतोष please gained from satisfaction of desire. *I feel great gratification in serving the needy.*

Gratify/ग्रैटिफाइ *(verb)* – प्रसन्न करना give pleasure or satisfaction. *I gratified her by calling her to dinner.*

Grating/ग्रेटिंग *(adjective)* – कटु आवाज sounding harsh and unpleasant. *His grating voice upset me.*

Gratis/ग्रेटिस *(adverb & adjective)* – बेदाम free of charge. *The gratis entry to the function insisted many people.*

Gratitude/ग्रैटिट्यूड *(noun)* – कृतज्ञता thankfulness; appreciation of kindness. *I feel great gratitude for this kindness of yours.*

Gratuitous/ग्रैट्यूइटॅस *(adjective)* – ऐच्छिक done without reason, uncalled for. *This rude behaviour is gratuitous.*

Gratuity/ग्रट्यूअटि *(noun)* – उपहार formal a tip given to a waiter, porter, etc. *He paid 10% the fair as gratuity to the taxi driver.*

Gravely/ग्रेवली *(adverb)* – गम्भीरता से cause for alarm, seriousness. *He answered my questions gravely.*

Graveness/ग्रेवनेस *(noun)* – महत्व serious manner. *His graveness impressed me.*

Gravel/ग्रैबेल *(noun)* – कंकड़ a loose aggregation of small stones and coarse sand, often used for paths and roads. *The path to the garden was made of gravel.*

Graver/ग्रेवर *(noun)* – नक्काशी करने का औजार a burin or other engraving tool. *His name was engraved on the stone slab by a graver.*

Gravid/ग्रेविड *(adjective)* – गर्भवती technical pregnant. *She is a gravid lady.*

Gravitate/ग्रेविटेट *(verb)* – आकर्षित होना be drawn towards a place, person, or thing. *I felt gravitated to her.*

Gravitation/ग्रेविटेशन *(noun)* – आकर्षण-शक्ति movement, or a tendency to move, towards a centre of gravity. *Gravitation pulls down everything to earth.*

Gravy/ग्रेवी *(noun)* – मांसयूष the fat and juices exuding from meat during cooking. a sauce made from these juices together with stock and other ingredients. *The gravy is very tasty.*

Grayling/ग्रेलिंग *(noun)* – एक प्रकार की मछली an edible silvery-grey freshwater fish with horizontal violent stripes and a long high dorsal fin. *I would like to eat a grayling very much.*

Graze/ग्रेज *(verb)* – चरना eat grass in a field. feed on grass or grassland. *Cows graze in fields.*

Grazier/ग्रेजिअर *(noun)* – चरवाहा a person who rears or fattens cattle or sheep for market. *He is a grazier and sells fat sheep and cattle*

Grazing/ग्रेजिंग *(noun)* – चराई grassland suitable for pasturage. *This ground is good for grazing.*

Grease/ग्रीज *(noun)* – चरबी a thick oily substance, especially as used as a lubricant. *The machine is in need of grease.*

Greasy/ग्रीजी *(adjective)*– चरबीदार covered with or resembling grease. producing more body oils than average. containing or cooked with too much oil or fat. *This potato vegetable is very greasy, I can't eat it.*

Greatly/ग्रेटलि *(adverb)* – अत्यन्त very much. *He is greatly polite.*

Greaves/ग्रीव्ज *(noun)* – जंघात्राण [historical] a piece of armour for the shin. *The warriors used to wear greaves to protect lower body doing war.*

Greed/ग्रीड *(noun)* – लालच intense and selfish desire for wealth, power, or food. *Greed has been the ruin of many people.*

Greedily/ग्रीडलि *(adverb)* – अति लोभ से appetite for food or anything. *He greedily ate the food.*

Greediness/ग्रीडिनिश *(noun)* – लोभ selfish desire. *Greediness never pays.*

Greedy/ग्रीडि *(adjective)* – बहुभक्षक having or showing greed. *He is a greedy fellow hence never satisfied.*

Green/ग्रीन्स *(adjective)* – हरा, सब्जी green colour or pigment *Major roads are marked in red, yellow or green.* green clothes or material *The girls wore red and green dresses.* green foliage or vegetation *A lovely green canopy of pine trees can be seen in Kashmir.*

Greenish/ग्रीनिस *(adjective)* – थोड़ा हरा resembling green. *The greenish hue in this cloth is very attractive.*

Greenness/ग्रीननेस *(noun)* – हरापन freshness, refreshing. *The greenness of the valley attracted me.*

Greeny/ग्रीनि *(adverb)* – हरे रंग का green-like. *I like greeny vegetables.*

Gregarious/ग्रिगेऑरिअॅस *(adjective)* – यूथचारी fond of company; sociable. *He is a gregarious person.*

Grew/ग्रिउ *(verb)* – बढ़ा, उगा past of grow. *He grew tall very fast.*

Greyish/ग्रेइश *(adjective)* – थोड़ा भूरा resembling grey colour. *He likes grayish colour clothes.*

G

Grid/ग्रिड *(noun)* – छड़ लगा हुआ ढाँचा a framework of spaced bars that are parallel to or cross each other. *He got the front of his house covered with grid.*

Griddle/ग्रिडल *(noun)* – रोटी पकाने का तवा a circular iron plate that is heated and used for cooking food. *She cooked chapattis on griddle.*

Grievance/ग्रीवॅन्स *(noun)* – शिकायत a real of imagined cause for complain. *The officer patiently heard the grievance of the employee.*

Grieve/ग्रीव *(verb)* – दु:ख देना suffer grief. *The loss in business grieved him intensely.*

Grievous/ग्रीवस *(adjective)* – शोचनीय formal very severe or serious. *It is a grievous matter, listen carefully.*

Grill/ग्रिल *(noun)* – झँझरी variant spelling of grille. *His front door was covered with a grill.*

Grille/ग्रिल *(noun)* – लोहे के छड़ों की बनी हुई झँझरी a grating or screen of metal bars or wires. *A grille encircled the whole garden.*

Grim/ग्रिम *(adjective)* – डरावन, कुरूप very serious or gloomy; forbidding. black or ironic. *His grim look frightened me.*

Grimalkin/ग्रिमैल्किन *(noun)* – डाइन, बुड्ढी बिल्ली [larchaic] a cat. *She is a grimalkin.*

Grime/ग्राइम *(noun)* – जमी हुई मल या कीट dirt ingrained on a surface. *His shirt sleeves were covered with grime.*

Grimy/ग्रिमि *(adj)* – गन्दा *This kitchen cloth has become grimy, wash it.*

Grinder/ग्राइन्डर *(noun)* – पीसने वाला a machine used for grinding something. *With this set a coffee grinder comes free.*

Grip/ग्रिप *(verb)* – कसकर पकड़ना take and keep a firm hold of; grasp tightly. *He gripped his hand firmly.*

Gritty/ग्रिटि *(adjective)* – कंकड़ीला containing or covered with grit. *It is a rough and gritty road.*

Grizzle/ग्रिज़ल *(verb)* – चिल्लाना [informal, chiefly British] cry or whimper fretfully. *The child grizzled until its mother came.*

Groan/ग्रोन *(verb)* – कराहना make a deep inarticulate sound in response to pain or despair. *He groaned in pain.*

Groats/ग्रोट्स *(plural noun)* – भूसी निकाला हुआ अन्न hulled or crushed grain, especially oats. *Groats can be a good source of nourishment.*

Grocer/ग्रोसर *(noun)* – पंसारी a person who sells food and small household goods. *My uncle is a grocer and earns well.*

Grog/ग्रॉग *(noun)* – पानी मिली हुई शराब spirits mixed with water. [informal] alcoholic drink. *I want to have some grog.*

Grogginess/ग्रॉगिनेस *(noun)* – पियक्कड़पन habit of drinking. *This habitual grogginess will ruin your health.*

Groggy/ग्रागि *(noun)* – पियक्कड़ drunkard. *He is a inferior groggy. Don't follow him.*

Groin/ग्रॉइन *(noun)* – ऊरुसन्धि the area between the abdomen and the thigh on either side of the body. [informal] the region of the genitals. *The doctor prescribed him a medicine for itching in the groin.*

Groom/ग्रूम *(verb)* – खरहरा करना brush and clean the coat of a horse or dog. give a neat and tidy appearance to. *He was grooming the horse.*

Groove/ग्रूव *(noun)* – नाली a long, narrow cut or depression in a hard material. a spiral track cut in a gramophone record, into which the stylus fits. *There was a long groove along the hill.*

Grope/ग्रोप *(verb)* – अन्धे की तरह खोजना feel about or search blindly or uncertainly with the hands. *He groped for the way in dark.*

Grotesque/ग्रोटस्क *(adjective)* – विचित्र comically or repulsively ugly or distorted. *His grotesque appearance made all of us laugh.*

Grotto/ग्रॉटो *(noun)* – गुफा, कंदरा a small picturesque cave, especially an artificial one in a park or garden. *All children wanted to enter the grotto.*

Ground *(verb)* – past and past participle of grind. *The spices have been ground in the grinder.*

Grounding/ग्राउन्डिंग *(noun)* – पूर्ण रूप की प्रारम्भिक शिक्षा basic training or instruction in a subject. *Proper grounding is necessary before you train for anything.*

Groundless/ग्राउण्डलेस *(adjective)* – निराधार not based on any good reason. *These charges are groundless.*

Ground-nut/ग्राउण्डनट *(noun)* – मूँगफली another term for peanut. *I am fond of eating ground-nuts.*

Groundsel/ग्राउण्डसेल *(noun)* – डेहरी a plant of the daisy family with small yellow rayless flowers. *I have many groundsels in my garden.*

Groundwork/ग्राउण्डवक *(noun)* – मूल आधार preliminary or basic work. *Some groundwork is necessary before matter with a high official.*

Grout/ग्राउट *(noun)* – मसाला a mortar or paste for filling crevices, especially the gaps between wall or floor tiles. *I asked the mason to fill the gap with grout.*

Grove/ग्रोव *(noun)* – वृक्षवाटिका a small wood, orchard, or group of trees. *This a beautiful mango grove.*

Grovel/ग्रॉव्लॅ *(verb)* – उताने पड़ जाना crouch or crawl abjectly on the ground. *Some people grovel in temples before they reach their deity.*

Growable/ग्रोएबल *(adj)* – उगने योग्य *This plant is not growable.*

Grower/ग्रोवर *(noun)* – उपजाने वाला a person who grows. *He is a grower of vegetables.*

Growing/ग्रोइंग *(noun)* – बढ़ने वाला the act of developers. *The fast growing grass had to be cut.*

Grub/ग्रब *(noun)* – सूँड़ी the larva of an insect, especially a beetle. a maggot or small caterpillar. *This is a grub crawling on the branch of the tree.*

Grubble/ग्रबल *(noun)* – पैसे के लिए कुछ भी करने वाला a person who is determined to amass something, especially in an unscrupulous manner: a money-grubber. *He is a grubble and will do anything to get many.*

Grudge/ग्रज *(noun)* – दुर्भाव a persistent feeling of ill will or resentment resulting from a past insult or injury. *Although we have quarrelled, I bear no grudge against you.*

Gruff/ग्रफ *(adjective)* – कर्कश rough and low in pitch. *He spoke to me in a gruff voice.*

Grumble/ग्रम्बल *(verb)* – असन्तोष से बकना complain or protest in a bad-tempered but muted way. *He grumbled before his boss.*

Grumbling/ग्रम्बलिंग *(noun)* – विवाद complaint, protest. *By habit he is not given to grumbling.*

Grumpish/ग्रम्पिश *(adjective)* – क्रोधी sulking, grumpy. *He is a grumpish fellow always complaining.*

Guarantee/गारण्टी *(noun)* – जमानत a formal assurance that certain conditions will be fulfilled, especially that restitution will be made if a product is not of a specified quality. *I guarantee you the success of this project.*

Guava/ग्वावा *(noun)* – अमरूद a tropical american fruit with pink juicy flesh and a strong, sweet aroma. *Guava is a very tasty fruit.*

Guerdon/गॅर्डॅन *(noun)* – पारितोषिक a reward or recompense. *(verb)* give a reward to. *He received a guerdon for his social work.*

Guesswork/गेसवक *(noun)* – केवल कल्पना के आधार पर किया काम, अटकलबाजी the process or results of guessing. *Your guesswork didn't turn out to be correct.*

Guest/गेस्ट *(noun)* – अतिथि a person who is invited to visit someone's home or take part in a function. a visiting performer invited to take part in an entertainment. *We should entertain and respect our guests*

Guidable/गाइडेबल *(adj)* – मार्ग दिखलाने योग्य fit to guide. *This map is not guidable for us.*

Guidance/गाइडेंस *(noun)* – पथप्रदर्शक advice or information aimed at resolving a problem or difficulty. *We should give proper guidance to our children.*

Guideless/गाइडलेस *(noun)* – असहाय without guide. *We had been guideless in the valley.*

Guileful/गाइलफुल *(adjective)* – कपटी cunning, sly. *He is a guileful fellow, don't mix with him.*

Guileless/गाइललेस *(adjective)* – निष्कपट innocent. *He is guileless and innocent.*

Guilt/गिल्ट *(noun)* – अपराध the fact of having committed an offence or crime. *He has a strong sense of guilt about the wrong he has done.*

Guilty/गिल्टी *(adjective)* – अपराधी culpable of a specified wrongdoing. justly chargeable with a particular fault or error. *He is feeling guilty over the crime he has committed.*

Guise/गाइज *(noun)* – बहाना an external form, appearance, or manner of presentation. *He came to party in the guise of a king.*

G

G

Guitar/गिटार *(noun)* – गिटार a stringed musical instrument with a fretted fingerboard and six or twelve strings, played by plucking or strumming with the fingers or a plectrum. *He plays nice guitar.*

Gular/गलर *(adjective)* – ऊपरी कण्ठ-सम्बन्धी [zoology] of or relating to the throat, especially of a reptile, fish, or bird. *The gular disease of the bird in the zoo was treated by a doctor.*

Gulf/गल्फ *(noun)* – खाड़ी a deep inlet of the sea almost surrounded by land, with a narrow mouth. *He fell into the gulf and hurt himself.*

Gullet/गॅलिट्/गॉल्इट *(noun)* – गला the passage by which food passes from the mouth to the stomach; the oesophagus. *Something stuck in his gullet and a doctor had to be called.*

Gully/गॅलि *(noun)* – नाली a water-worn ravine. a gutter or drain. *The rain water flowed down the gully.*

Gulp/गल्प *(verb)* – निगलना, गटकना swallow quickly or in large mouthfuls, often audibly. *He gulped down the food.*

Gummy/गमि *(adjective)* – चिपचिपा, लिसलिसा viscous; sticky. *It's a gummy object and I don't like it.*

Gunner/गनर *(noun)* – तोप चलाने पर नियुक्त किया हुआ पुरुष a person who operates a gun. a British artillery soldier. *He is a gunner in the navy.*

Gunnery/गनरी *(noun)*– तोप बन्दूक की विधा the design, manufacture, or firing of heavy guns. *He is an expert of gunnery.*

Gunny/गॅनि *(noun)* – टाट, बोरा [chiefly north American] coarse sacking, typically made of jute fibre. *The stolen currency notes were found in a gunny bag.*

Gush/गश *(verb)* – वेग से बहना send out or flow in a rapid and plentiful stream. *The blood gushed out of his wound.*

Gusto/गस्टो *(noun)* – मजा, रुचि, चाव enjoyment or vigour. *He answered my questions with gusto.*

Gusty/गस्टि *(adjective)* – झोंकेदार, झोंकीला characterized by or blowing in gusts. *A gusty wind blew in the mountains.*

Gut/गट *(noun)* – उदर, साहस the stomach or belly. medicine & biology the intestine. entrails that have been removed or exposed. *I do not have the guts to face him.*

Gutter/गटर *(noun)* – जलमार्ग a shallow through beneath the edge of a roof, or a channel at the side of a street, for carrying off rainwater. technical a groove or channel for flowing liquid. *A foul smelling water flowed in the gutter.*

Guttle/गटल *(verb)* – भुक्खड़ की तरह खाना to eat hurriedly. *In the party, he guttled.*

Guttural/गटरल *(adjective)* – कण्ठ सम्बन्धी produced in the throat. *He made a guttural sound before he started speaking.*

Guy/गाइ *(noun)* – आदमी, लोग [British informal] as a form of address sir. *That guy over there is my cousin.*

Guzzle/गजल *(verb)* – लालची की तरह भोजन करना eat or drink greedily. *He has guzzled down many drinks.*

Guzzler/गजलर *(noun)* – लालची की तरह भोजन करने वाला drinking greedily. *He is a guzzler of tasty food.*

Gymnastic/जिम्नैस्टिक्स *(plural noun)* – व्यायाम, कसरत exercises involving physical agility, flexibility, and coordination, especially tumbling and acrobatic, feats. *She got first prize in gymnastics.*

Gypsum/जिप्सम *(noun)* – खड़िया मिट्टी, जिप्सम a soft white mineral like chalk. *Gypsum is used in makina plaster of paris.*

Gypsy/जिप्सी *(noun)* – कंजर जाति a member of a travelling people with dark skin and hair, speaking a language related to Hindi, and traditionally living by itinerant trade and fortune telling. *She is a gypsy and will tell you your fortune.*

Gyrate/जाइरेट *(verb)* – घूमना, चक्कर खाना move or cause to move in a circle or spiral. *She gyrated to the tune of the song.*

Gyre/जाइर *(verb)* – चक्रगति [poetic/literary] whirl; gyrate. *She gyred to the music.*

Gype/जाइप *(noun)* – बेड़ी [larchaic] a fetter or shackle. *The prisoner wore gype around his feet.*

Hh

H/एच – अंग्रेजी वर्णमाला का आठवाँ अक्षर the eight letter of the English alphabet
1. A symbol for hydrogen in Chemistry.

Ha/हा – आश्चर्य *exclamatory* expressing surprise, suspicion, triumph, etc. *Ha! I have finally learnt how to make a sentence.*

Haberdasher/हैबरडैशर *(noun)* – बिसाती A dealer in small items of dressing. *A retail dealer in men's furnishings, such as shirts, trousers, ties, and socks is known as haberdasher.*

Habergeon/हैबरजिअन *(noun)* – बिना आस्तीन का कवच – [historical] a sleeveless coat of mail or scale armour. *Habergeon was a sleeveless coat worn under the plated shirt during the 14th century.*

Habile/हैबिल *(adj.)* – निपुण skilful, dexterous, adroit. *People would call you a habile, if you can use both hands skilfully.*

Habiliment/हैबिलिमेंट *(noun)* – वस्त्र [archaic] clothing. *The clothes worn in a particular profession is known as the habiliment of that profession.*

Habilitate/हैबिलिटेट *(verb)* – योग्य बनाना (used with object) to clothe or dress, to make fit. *Get your poorly stitched dress habilitated by a draper so that it can fit you properly.*

Habitable/हैबिटेबॉल *(adj.)* – निवास योग्य suitable to live in. *Increasing volume of pollution each year is making the world less habitable to live than the previous year.*

Habitant/हैबिटेन्ट *(noun)* – निवासी an early French settler in Canada or Louisiana. *Dravidians were the original habitants of India.*

Habitat/हैबिटैट *(noun)* – जन्तु का प्राकृतिक वासस्थल the natural home or environment of an organism. *Forest is the natural habitat of wild animals.*

Habitation/हैबिटेशन *(noun)* – निवास्थान the state or process of inhabiting. *Wild animals prefer to live in the natural habitation of a forest.*

Habitual/हैबिचुअल *(adj.)* – स्वाभाविक done constantly or as a habit. *Students who are habitual of getting up early for studies generally score good marks in examinations.*

Habitually/हैबिचुअली *(adj.)* – यथारीति according to habit or custom. *He habitually keeps his main entrance door closed.*

Habituate/हैबिचुएट *(verb)* – अभ्यास करना [chiefly zoology] make or become accustomed to something. *You could harm yourself if you become habituated to self-medication.*

Habituation/हैबिचुएशन *(noun)* – अभ्यस्तता *(noun)* Being abnormally tolerant to and dependent on something that is psychologically or physically habit-forming (especially alcohol or narcotic drugs). *Habituation to regular use of a particular medicine reduces its efficiency on the body.*

Hack/हैक *(verb)* – काटना, मारना to cut or chop with repeated and irregular blows: *He hacked down the plants and saplings indiscriminately.*

Hackney/हैक्नि *(noun)* – घुड़सवारी का टट्टू a horse-drawn vehicle kept for hire. *In the19th century London, wealthy citizens used to sit in horse-driven hackneys to go from one place to another.*

Hackneyed/हैक्निड *(adj.)* – सामान्य much used, trite. *To write an impressive essay, avoid using hackneyed words that have become stale with overuse.*

Haddock/हैडॉक *(noun)* – एक प्रकार की समुद्री मछली a silvery-grey bottom-dwelling fish of north Atlantic coastal waters, popular as a food fish. *Haddock is a popular north Atlantic fish, which is usually eaten baked, roasted or fried.*

Hades/हेडीज *(noun)* – पाताल Greek mythology the underworld; the abode of the spirits of the dead. *Greek mythology describes hades as a place where the spirits of the dead live.*

Haematic/हीमैटिक *(adj.)* – रुधिर-युक्त relating to or containing or affecting blood, having the colour of, or containing blood. *The surgeon operated upon the person to remove the haematic cyst that looked like a ball of blood.*

Haematology/हीमैटॉलॅजी *(noun)* – रुधिर विधा the study of the [physiology] of the blood. *Doctors prescribe a number of haematological tests to determine the quality of blood of the patients.*

Haematuria/हीमैट्यूरिअ *(noun)* – मूत्रनली से रुधिर का स्राव medicine the presence of blood in the urine. *Haematuria is a disease of the urinary tract in which blood passes along urine.*

Haemoglobin/हीमोग्लोबिन *(noun)* – रक्त के कणों में के लाल परमाणु biochemistry a red protein containing iron, responsible for transporting oxygen in the blood in most invertebrates. *The red colour of the blood is due to haemoglobin which contains iron.*

Haemorrhage/हेमॅरिज *(noun)* – रक्त वाहिनियों से रुधिर का स्राव an escape of blood from a ruptured blood vessel. *Bleeding, medically known as haemorrhage is the loss of blood from the circulatory system.*

Haemorrhoids/हेमराइड्स *(noun)* – खूनी बवासीर a swollen vein or group of veins in the re-gion of the anus. *Haemorrhoids, also known as piles are swellings that can occur in the anus and lower rectum.*

Haggard/हैगॅर्ड *(adj.)* – रूक्ष आकृति का दुबला-पतला looking exhausted and unwell. *After the marathon race, he was completely exhausted and looked haggard.*

Haggle/हैगल *(verb)* – मोल-तोल करना, झगड़ना dispute or bargain persistently, especially over a price. *Women are better than men at bringing down prices by haggling with sellers.*

Haggler/हैगलर *(noun)* – मोलभाल करने वाला मनुष्य *He is a haggler by nature as he would haggle irrespective of the price quoted.*

Hagiographer/हैजिऑग्राफर *(noun)* – धर्मग्रन्थ का लेखक a writer of the lives of the saints. *Any person who writes about the lives of the saints, especially Christian, is known as a hagiographer.*

Hag-ridden/हैग-रिडेन *(adj.)* – दुःस्वप्न से ग्रस्त afflicted by nightmares or anxieties. *After visiting a haunted house, his expressions have become fearful and hag-ridden.*

Hail/हेल *(noun)* – ओला pellets of frozen rain falling in showers from cumulonimbus clouds. *We could not go out for picnic because of torrential rains and hail storms.*

Hair/हेअर *(noun)* – बाल any of the fine thread like strained growing from the skin of mammals and other animals, or from the epidermis of a plant. such strands collectively especially those on a person's head. *I go for hair cut every month.*

Hake/हेक *(noun)* – कॉड की तरह एक मछली a large-headed elongated food fish with long jaws and strong teeth. *Hake is a fish that resembles cod and found mostly in North America.*

Halberd/हैलबॅर्ड *(noun)* – एक प्रकार का गड़ासा [historical] a combined spear and battleaxe. *Halberd was a weapon with axe at one end and spear at the other used during 15th and 16th centuries.*

Halcyon/हैलॅसिअॅन *(adj.)* – रामचिरैया denoting a past time that was idyllically happy and peaceful. *Wouldn't you like to recall your halcyon days when you were happy and prosperous?*

Hale/हेल *(adj.)* – स्वस्थ strong and healthy. *If you maintain a balanced life, you would live a hale and hearty life.*

Haliography/हैलिऑग्राफि *(noun)* – समुद्र का वर्णन Description of the sea. *Old word for describing the sea. The word is no longer in use.*

Halt/हाल्ट *(noun & verb)* – पड़ाव, रोकना bring or come to an abrupt stop. *The police halted the march by the agitating protestors.*

Hatting/हैटिंग *(noun)* – एक तरह की टोपी A covering for the head, especially one with a shaped crown and brim. *British officers used to cover their head with a hatting made from coconut leaves to protect their head during Indian summer.*

Halter/हॉल्टर *(noun)* – बागडोर या पगहा a rope or strap placed around the head of an animal and used to lead or tether it. *The dog ran away after the leather halter tied around its neck broke.*

Halyard/हाल्यर्ड *(noun)* – पाल-रस्सी a rope used for raising and lowering a sail, yard, or flag on a ship. *In boats used for sailing, the rope used to hoist the sail is called halyard.*

Hamlet/हैम्लेट *(noun)* – छोटा गाँव a small village, especially one without a church. *Since hamlets are much smaller than villages, most people know one another.*

Hammock/हैमॉक *(noun)* – जहाज के कमरे की झूलन खटिया a wide strip of canvas or rope mesh suspended by two ends, used as a bed. *Since canvas-made hammock is wide and light in weight, people use it as a swing after tying its both ends to branch of trees.*

Hamper/हैम्पर *(noun)* – बाँस की पिटारी a basket with a carrying handle and a hinged lid, used for food, cutlery, etc. on a picnic, a box containing food and drink for a special occasion. *Hamper is a convenient multi-purpose basket to carry food and water when going on a picnic.*

Hamshackle/हैमशैकल *(verb)* – घोड़े के टाँग को उसके सिर से रस्सी बाँधना to hobble. *Hamshakle is a method of tying a rope around the head and one of the legs of the domestic animals if they become violent.*

Hamstring/हैमस्ट्रिंग *(noun)* – घुटने के पीछे की नस any of five tendons at the back of a person's knee. the great tendon at the back of a quadruped's hock. *Rafael Nadal lost in the Wimbledon tournament because his movement was severely restricted on the tennis court due to pulled hamstring.*

Hand/हैंड *(noun)* – हाथ the end part of the arm beyond the wrist, including the palm fingers, and thumb. western indian a persons' arm, including the hand. operated by or held in the hand. done or made manually. *We should wash our hands with soap before taking food. What time is it if both the small and the large hands of the watch is at two? How many hands have you employed to remove the garbage within two hours? To marry his girl friend, he met her parents asking for her hand in marriage.*

Handbag/हैंडबैग *(noun)* – थैला [British] a small bag used by a woman to carry everyday personal items. *She bought a new handbag so that her everyday personal items could be carried decently.*

Handbell/हैंडबेल *(noun)* – हाथ से बजाने की घण्टी a small bell, especially one of a set tuned to a flange of notes and played by a group of people. *The peon rushed inside the cabin, when the officer pressed the handbell kept on his table.*

Handbill/हैंडबिल *(noun)* – विज्ञापन पत्र a small printed advertisement or other notice distributed by hand. *A handbill is a form of paper advertisement and typically distributed within a locality.*

Hand-book/हैंडबुक *(noun)* – छोटी पुस्तक book giving brief information such as basic facts on a particular subject or instructions for operating a machine. *This hand-book introduces you to the rules and regulations of this club.*

Hand-cuff/हैंडकफ *(noun)* – लोहे की हथकड़ी a pair of lockable linked metal rings for securing a prisoner's wrists. *Thieves were hand-cuffed and taken to the police station.*

Handful/हैंडफुल *(noun)* – थोड़ा-सा a quantity that fills the hand. a small number or amount. *Despite wide publicity, only a handful of people came to watch the game.*

Handicraft/हैंडिक्राफ्ट *(noun)* – दस्तकारी a particular skill of making decorative domestic or other objects by hand. *Machine-made products have very nearly displaced the handmade handicrafts.*

Handiwork/हैंडिवर्क *(noun)* – हाथ से किया हुआ काम something that one has made or done, the making of things by hand. *Most carpets we see in the market are the handiwork of people living in Bhadohi in Uttar Pradesh.*

Handkerchief/हैंडकरचीफ *(noun)* – दस्ती, रूमाल a square of cotton or other material for wiping one's nose. *Wash your hands with soap and pat it dry with a handkerchief.*

Handler/हैंडलर *(noun)* – मूठ पकड़ने वाला a person who handles a particular type of article or commodity. *He is a baggage handler at the airport.*

Handling/हैंडलिंग *(noun)* – व्यवहार the action of one that handles something. *Every musical instrument needs careful handling.*

Handloom/हैंडलूम *(noun)* – हाथ से चलाने का करधा a loom worker by hand, a type of cloth. *Fabrics made of handloom shrink when washed and dried.*

H

Handmaid/हैंडमेड *(noun)* – दासी [archaic] a female servant, a subservient partner or element. *Wealthy people use the services of handmaids for cooking, washing, cleaning etc.*

Handmill/हैंडमिल *(noun)* – हाथ से चलाने की चक्की Domestic hand grinders. *These days most kitchens have a handmill to grind spices into fine powder.*

Handpress/हैंडप्रेस *(noun)* – हाथ से चलाने की छापे की कल a press worked by hand, to press down something by manual pressure. *Plastic granules can be converted into the shape of a glass with the help of a handpress.*

Handrail/हैंडरेल *(noun)* – सीढ़ी पर से चढ़ने-उतरने के सहारे का लकड़ी आदि का डँडहरा a rail fixed to posts or a wall for people to hold on to for support. *Handrails fixed along the staircase help people climb floors easily.*

Handsaw/हैंडसॉ *(noun)* – एक हाथ से चलाने की आरी woodcutting implement. *Carpenters use handsaw to cut wooden slabs to make a table.*

Handsome/हैंडसम *(adj.)* – मनोहर, सुन्दर good-looking. striking and imposing rather than conventionally pretty, well made, imposing, and of obvious quality, substantial. *He is a handsome person. Handsome bonuses have been given to all employees.*

Handwriting/हैंडराइटिंग *(noun)* – हस्तलेख writing with a pen or pencil rather than by typing or printing. a person's particular style of writing. *Good handwriting will help you get good marks in examinations.*

Handy/हैंडी *(adj.)* – सुलभ, पास, सुविधाजनक convenient to handle or use; useful. *Washing machines make washing clothes very handy.*

Hang/हैंग *(verb)* – लटकना, लटकाना suspend or be suspended form above with the lower part not attached. attach or be attached so as to allow free movement about the point of attachement: hanging a door. fall or drape in a specified way. paste to a wall. *She hanged the curtains beautifully. Hanging clothes in the sun speeds up drying.*

Hangar/हैंगर *(noun)* – विमानशाला a large building with extensive floor area, typically for housing aircraft. *Aircrafts are kept in the hangar for repair or when not flying.*

Hanger/हैंगर *(noun)* – खूँटी a shaped piece of wood, plastic, or metal with a hook at the top, for hanging clothes from a rail. *Clothes don't get crumpled or creased when hung on a hanger.*

Hanger-on/हैंगरऑन *(noun)* – अनुचर a person who associates sycophantically with another person. *People hanging around influential people are known as hanger-on.*

Hanging/हैंगिंग *(noun)* – फाँसी the practice of hanging condemned people as a form of capital punishment. *Many countries have abolished the practice of hanging the criminals.*

Hank/हैंक *(noun)* – लच्छा, अट्टी a coil or skein of wool, hair, or other material, a measurement of the length per unit mass of cloth or yarn. *In textile industry, a hank refers to a unit that is in coiled form.*

Hanker/हैंकर *(verb)* – लालायित होना feel a strong desire for or to do something. *He is always hankering for toffees and chocolates.*

Hapless/हैपलेस *(adj.)* – अभागा less fortunate. *The batsmen hit the hapless bowler for six boundaries in an over*

Happen/हैपॅन *(verb)* – घटित होना take place; occur. *The World Book Fair will happen every year in Delhi.*

Happening/हैपनिंग *(noun)* – घटना an event or occurrence. *There is a huge crowd here. What is happening?*

Happily/हैपिलि *(adj.)* – सुख से gladly, joyfully. *Both of them happily went back home.*

Happiness/हैपिनेस *(noun)* – सुख joy, glad. *Happiness is a mental state of well-being.*

Harangue/हरैंग *(verb)* – जोरदार भाषण देना criticize at length in an aggressive and hectoring manner. *Dishonest politicians harangue their honest rivals by speaking against them in public.*

Harass/हैरस *(verb)* – तंग करना, सताना torment by subjecting to constant interference or intimidation. *Don't harass this poor fellow. God will not forgive you.*

Harbinger/हार्बिंजर *(noun)* – हरकारा a person or thing that announces or signals the approach of something. *Beginning of India-Pakistan cricket matches could be a harbinger of good relations between them.*

Hard/हार्ड *(adj.)* – ठोस solid, firm, and rigid; not easily broken, bent, or pierced. not showing any signs of weakness; tough. high and stable; firm. *Iron is a very hard metal that can't be easily broken.*

Harden/हार्ड्न *(verb)* – कड़ा करना make or become hard or harder. *Boiling an egg hardens and solidifies its liquid material.*

Hardship/हार्डशिप *(noun)* – कष्ट, दु:ख severe suffering or privation. *In addition to pay, hardship allowance is also given to soldiers posted at Siachin.*

Hare/हेअर *(noun)* – खरहा a fast-running, long-eared mammal resembling a large rabbit, with very long hind legs. and other species. *Hare is a rabbit like animal mostly found in grassland.*

Harlequin/हार्लक्विन *(noun)* – विदूषक a mute character in traditional pantomime, typically masked and dressed in a diamond-patterned costume. [historical] a stock comic character in Italian commedia dell'arte. *Harlequin is a kind of joker or clown in Italian theatres.*

Harlot/हार्लट *(noun)* – वेश्या [archaic] a prostitute or promiscuous woman. *Women who sell their bodies for money are known as harlots.*

Harlotry/हॉरलट्री *(noun)* – वेश्यावृति prostit-ution. *Harlotry is one of the oldest professions where women sell their bodies for money.*

Harm/हार्म् *(noun)* – हानि physical injury, especially that which is deliberately inflicted. material damage. actual or potential ill effect. *I didn't mean to cause her any harm. This oil is unlikely to do much harm to the engine. There is no harm asking her.*

Harmful/हार्म्फुल *(adj.)* – हानिकारक causing or likely to cause harm. *Ultra-violet rays are very harmful for our skin.*

Harmfulness/हार्म्फुलनेस *(noun)* – सदोषता injuriousness, quality of being harmful. *No disease is less deadly than the other in harmfulness to the body.*

Harmless/हार्म्लेस *(adj.)* – अहानिकर not able or likely to cause harm. *You must tell jokes that are harmless to the self-esteem of a person.*

Harmonious/हार्मोनियस *(adj.)* – अनुरूप tuneful; not discordant. *The music was very harmonious.*

Harmonium/हार्मोनियम *(noun)* – हारमोनियम बाजा a keyboard instrument in which the notes are produced by air driven through metal reeds by foot-operated bellows. *Harmonium is one of the most important musical instruments to produce melodious notes.*

Harmonization/हार्मनाइजेशन *(noun)* – स्वर की एकता bringing into agreement. *Harmonization of relations within communities is essential for peace to prevail in the society.*

Harmonize/हार्मनाइज *(verb)* – शान्त होना music provide harmony for. *You can harmonize the area around with a soothing music.*

Harmony/हार्मनि *(noun)* – अनुरूपता the combination of simultaneously sounded musical notes to produce chords and chord progressions having a pleasing effect. *Pleasing musical notes produce peace and harmony to the mind.*

Harridan/हैरिडन *(noun)* – दुबली पतली जादूगरनी, डायन a strict, bossy, or belligerent old woman. *Despite belonging to the same gender, women employees resent strictness of harridans.*

Harrier/हैरिअर *(noun)* – एक प्रकार का बाज a hound of a breed used for hunting hares. *Harrier is a breed of hound dog used for hunting rabbits.*

Harry/हैरि *(verb)* – बर्बाद करना persistently carry out attacks on an enemy. *By attacking the US forces persistently, Talibani forces are harassing and harrying them no end.*

Harsh/हार्श *(adj.)* – कर्कश unpleasantly rough or jarring to the senses, cruel or severe. grim and unpalatable. *Judicial courts frown upon harsh treatment by teachers to students.*

Hart/हार्ट *(noun)* – लाल हरिण an adult male deer, especially a red deer over five year old. *More than five year old male deer are known as harts.*

Harum-scarum/हेरम्-स्केरम् *(noun)* – चंचल a reckless irresponsible person. *If you behave irresponsibly towards your family, people would call you a complete harum-scarum.*

Harvest/हार्वेस्ट *(noun)* – संग्रह किया हुआ अन्न the process or period of gathering in crops. the season's yield or crop. *Harvest time, when the crops are cut and processed, is a time of festivities in India.*

H

H

Harvester/हार्वेस्टर (noun) – फसल काटने वाला, फसल काटने की मशीन one who reaps, reaping machine. *Harvesters are huge machines that are used these days to harvest the crops to save time and labour.*

Hash/हैश (verb) – छोटे-छोटे टुकड़े करना make or chop into little pieces. *Many vegetables are hashed and cooked together to prepare the bhaji of pao-bhaji dish.*

Hasp/हास्प (noun) – कुण्डी, कुलाबा a latch, fastening. *The door could not be locked since the hasp was not there.*

Hastate/हैस्टेट (adj.) – बर्छी के आकार का botany having a narrow triangular shape like that of a spearhead. *Look carefully, it is a hastate.*

Haste/हेस्ट (noun) – वेग excessive speed or urgency of action. *Any work done in haste ends up as waste.*

Hasten/हेसन (verb) – जल्दी करना be quick to do something move quickly, cause to happen sooner than   anticipated. *The addition of a catalyst will speed up or hasten the chemical reaction.*

Hastily/हेस्टिली (adv.) – तुरन्त quickly. *Seeing the dog chaging at him, he hastily retreated back to his house.*

Hatch/हैच (noun) – छोटी खिड़की a small opening in a floor, wall, or roof allowing accesses from one area to another, in particular that in the deck of a boat leading to the cabin or lower level. a door in an aircraft, spacecraft, or submarine. *To come out of the submarine, sailors have to use the small hatch that serves both as entry or exit point.*

Hatchet/हैच्-इट (noun) – कुल्हाड़ी a small axe with a short handle for use in one hand. *Farmers often use a hatchet to make burrows in the field at the time of planting seeds.*

Hatching/हैचिंग (noun) – अण्डा सेने की क्रिया a newly hatched young animal/bird. *These days hatching of birds from eggs takes place in modern hatcheries.*

Hate/हेट (verb) – घृणा करना feel intense dislike for or a strong aversion towards. *If you don't like another person, please try your best not to hate him.*

Hateful/हेटफुल (adj.) – घृणित arousing or deserving of hatred. *Hateful attitude between two communities has never resolved any problem.*

Hater/हेटर (noun) – घृणा करने वाला पुरुष One who hates. *Don't carry such a cruel attitude towards others that people start calling you a hater.*

Hatred/हेट्-रेड् (noun) – शत्रुता intense dislike. *Hatred or ill-feeling towards others will not let you live in peace.*

Haughtily/हॉटिली (adv.) – गर्व से arrogantly, disdainfully. *He haughtily said no and didn't even bother to look at the poor man seeking alms.*

Haughty/हॉटि (adj.) – घमण्डी arrogantly superior and disdainful. *Haughty persons carrying an air of disdainful look are seldom liked by others.*

Haulier/हॉलर (noun) – जहाज को हवा के रुख पर चलाने वाला [British] a person or company employed in the commercial transport of goods by road. *A company that transports goods, especially in Britain, is popularly called a haulier.*

Haunch/हॉन्च (noun) – नितम्ब कूल्हा the buttock and thing considered together, in a human or animal. the leg and loin of an animal, as food. *The haunch of venison is a popular dish in Europe and America.*

Hautboy/हॉटबॉय (noun) – झड़बेर (स्ट्राबेरी) archaic form of hautbois. *Hautboy is a type of strawberry found in Central Europe and Asia.*

Haven/हैवेन (noun) – शरण-स्थान a place of safety or refuge. *A place to spend the night safely in a desert is as good as a haven.*

Haversack/हैवरसैक (noun) – सिपाहियों का सामान रखने का किरमिच झोला a small, stout bag carried on the back or over the shoulder, used especially by soldiers and walkers. *The kind of haversack used by soldiers has become very popular among school students to carry books and copies.*

Hawk/हॉक (verb) – फेरी लगाना carry about and offer for sale in the street. *These days hawkers use carts to hawk vegetables in the streets and lanes.*

Hawker/हॉकर (noun) – फेरी करके माल बेचने वाला व्यापारी a person who travels about selling goods. *These days hawkers use carts* to hawk daily utility wares in the streets and lanes.

Hawk-eyed/हॉकआइड *(adj.)* – सूक्ष्म दृष्टि वाला having a sharp eye to see distant objects. *Hawk-eyed machines have become very popular to determine whether the ball had touched the bat or not.*

Hawkish/हॉकिश *(adj.)* – बाज के सदृश advocating aggressive policies. *Trade unions generally resort to hawkish pronouncements against the managements.*

Hawser/ हॉजर – जहाज का बड़ा रस्सा a thick rope or steel cable used on a ship. *I saw a hawser lying on the ground near the bank of the river.*

Hawthorn/हॉथॉर्न *(noun)* – नागफनी a thorny shrub or tree with white, pink, or red blossom and small dark red fruits. *Hawthorn is an evergreen shrub.*

Hazardous/हैजर्डस् *(adj.)* – संकटमय risky; dangerous. *All chemicals prone to catch fire or cause health problems are known as hazardous.*

Hazel/हेजल् *(noun)* – जैतून के प्रकार का एक वृक्ष small tree or shrub. *Hazel is a small golden-brown coloured tree whose nuts are edible.*

Hazy/हेजि *(adj.)* – अस्पष्ट covered by a haze. *The cold winter morning was misty, foggy and hazy in which nothing could be seen clearly.*

Head-ache/हेड-एक *(noun)* – सिर की पीड़ा, सिरदर्द a continuous pain in the head. *I couldn't come to the office because of continuous headache since last night.*

Heading/हेडिंग *(noun)* – शीर्षक a title at the head of a page or section of a book. *The heading of this chapter is "Ways to sleep well".*

Headless/हेडलेस *(adj.)* – निर्मुण्ड without a head, incapacitated, leaderless. *This organization has remained headless ever since the chairman retired six months back.*

Headlong/हेडलांग *(adv.&adj.)* – बिना विचारे with the head foremost. *Don't recklessly headlong into doing anything without first giving sufficient thought.*

Headmaster/हेडमास्टर *(noun)* – प्रधान अध्यापक [chiefly British] a male head teacher. *The headmaster of this school is a strict disciplinarian.*

Headmost/हेडमोस्ट *(adj.)* – अगला [archaic] holding a position in advance of others; foremost. *The ship behind which all ships follow is known as the headmost.*

Headstrong/हेडस्ट्रॉंग *(adj.)* – हठी energetically wilful and determined. *He is so headstrong that he would sidestep every comfort to complete the job.*

Headway/हेडवे *(noun)* – आगे की ओर बढ़ाव Advance or progress. *Despite adequate help and support, he couldn't make any headway in finding the solution.*

Heady/हेडी *(adj.)* – नशा लाने वाली potent; intoxicating, having a strong or exhilarating effect. *Politicians behave in a heady and arrogant way because they have power and money in their hands.*

Heal/हील *(verb)* – व्याधि से मुक्त करना make or become sound or healthy again. *The doctor's concern should be to heal sick people.*

Healer/हीलर *(noun)* – पदार्थ one who heals, remedy. *Anyone who can heal the sickness of mind or body is a healer.*

Healing/हीलिंग *(noun & adj.)* – आरोग्यकर curing, restoring to health. *A motherly healing touch is necessary to restore the sick child to health.*

Healthily/हेल्थिली *(adv.)* – आरोग्य से in a healthy manner. *Children should be fed healthily so that they do well both in studies and games.*

Hearing/हिअरिंग *(noun)* – सुनवाई the faculty of perceiving sounds. the range within which sounds may be heard; earshot. *I couldn't understand the discussion because they conversed at a place that was out of my hearing range. Those hard of hearing are known as deaf.*

Hearsay/हिअर्से *(noun)* – सुनी बात information which cannot be adequately substantiated; rumour. *People, especially in villages, tend to easily believe in rumours or hearsays told by elders.*

Hearse/हर्स् *(noun)* – टिकठी a vehicle for conveying the coffin at a funeral. *Hearse is a vehicle to carry the dead to hospital for post-mortem.*

Heartburn/हार्टबर्न *(noun)* – हृदय-वेदना a form of indigestion felt as a burning sensation in the chest, caused by acid regurgitation into the esophagus. *Heartburn is a burning sensation in the chest caused by eating too much of acidic food.*

Heartless/हार्टलेस् *(adj.)* – क्रूर merciless, cruel. *In the face of heartless beating by policemen, the innocent man accepted his guilt.*

Hearth/हार्थ *(noun)* – अँगीठी the floor or surround of a fireplace. *They were sitting around the hearth to protect themselves from freezing cold.*

Heat/हीट *(noun)* – गरमी, ताप the quality of being hot; high temperature. *Heat is a form of energy arising from the random motion of the molecules of bodies.* technical the amount of heat needed for or evolved in a specific process. *When heat is given to a liquid, it turns into vapour.* a source or level of heat for cooking. *The heat of the sun gives us warmth.*

Heath/हीथ *(noun)* – वनभूमि an area of open uncultivated land, typically on acid sandy soil and covered with heater, gorse, and coarse grasses. *An open uncultivated land having small trees and evergreen grass is known as heath.*

Heavily/हेविली *(adv.)* – भारीपन in a weighty manner, clumsily. *He relied heavily on other's data to arrive at a solution.*

Heaviness/हेविनेस *(noun)* – भारीपन, नीरसता, उदासी condition of being heavy, weightiness. *The toys were crushed due to the heaviness of the steel box.*

Heavy/हेवि *(adj.)* – भारी of great weight; difficult to lift or move. *Objects that sank to the bottom of the sea quickly are quite heavy by weight.*

Hebetate/हेबिटेट *(verb)* – जड़ बनना या बनाना dull, blunt. *Unless the mental faculty is exercised regularly, chances are your intellectual ability will gradually hebetate.*

Hebraic/हिब्रेइक *(adj.)* – यहूदी भाषा का of Hebrew or the Hebrews. *Israeli people are very proud of Hebrew language, art or anything Hebraic.*

Hebraist/हिब्रेइस्ट *(noun)* – यहूदी भाषा का विद्वान a scholar of the Hebrew language. *Scholars of Hebrew language and literature are acknowledged as Hebraist.*

Hebrew/हिब्रू *(noun)* – यहूदी a member of an ancient people living in what is now Israel and Palestine, who established the kingdoms of Israel and Judah. *Hebrew is the official language of Israel.*

Hectic/हेक्टिक *(adj.)* – अत्यधिक व्यस्त full of incessant or frantic activity. *Hectic mopping of rain water became necessary in order to make the ground playable.*

Hecto/हेक्टो *prep.* – सौ का अर्थ सूचक one hundred; hectometre. *Hecto or hecta is a Greek word meaning one hundred.*

Hedge/हेज *(noun)*- row of bushes. *Hedge is a line of closely spaced shrubs and small trees to form a boundary or barrier.*

Hedonic/हेडोनिक *(adj.)* – सुखवादी, आनन्द pertaining to pleasure, pleasant sensations. *You are a hedonic if your sole aim is to seek sensual pleasure.*

Hedonism/हेडोनिज्म *(noun)* – सुखवाद the pursuit of pleasure; sensual self-indulgence, [philosophy] the ethical theory that pleasure is the highest good and proper aim of human life. *Hedonism is a philosophy that propagates that real pleasure comes only from sensual sensation.*

Hedonist/हेडोनिस्ट *(noun)* – आनन्दजीवी pleasure seeker. *A hedonist is a person who believes that sensual pleasure is the only real pleasure.*

Heedful/हीडफुल *(adj.)* – सचेत careful attentive. *Unless you are heedful in the class, you would miss the main points of the lecture.*

Heedless/हीडलेस *(adj.)* – असावधान showing a reckless lack of care or attention. *We know that heedless self-interest is bad morals for the society.*

Heehaw/हीहा *(noun)* – गदहे की तरह रेंकना the loud, harsh cry of a donkey or mule. *The harsh unpleasant cry of a donkey is called heehaw.*

Hefty/हेफ्टी *(adj.)* – बलवान large, heavy, and powerful. *Hefty sum of money is carried in vans secured with security guards.*

Height/हाइट *(noun)* – शिखर the measurement of someone or something from head to foot or from base to top. the quality of being tall or high. *To be eligible to apply for army, you must be at least 165 centimetres in height.*

Heighten/हाइटॅन *(verb)* – ऊँचा करना make higher, make or become more intense. *When alone, even the ticking of a wall clock heightens the perception of fear.*

H

Heinous/हीनस् *(adj.)* – घृणित utterly odious or wicked: a heinous crime. *To leave an injured person unattended is nothing short of a heinous crime.*

Heiress/एअरेश् *(noun)* – राजपुत्री a female heir, especially to vast wealth. *Paris Hilton is the heiress to the Empire of Hilton Hotels worldwide.*

Heirloom/एअॅलूम *(noun)* – जंगम द्रव्य, कुलागत वस्तु a valuable object that has belonged to a family for several generations. *The jewellery that has been passed down the generations is popularly known as heirloom.*

Heirless/ एअरलेस *(adj.)* – लावारिस lacking an heir, without successor. *The British government in India used to annex the properties of those Maharajas who died heirless.*

Heirship/एअरशीप *(noun)* – विरासत right to inheritance. *The state, character and priviledges of an heir is known as heirship.*

Held/हेल्ड *(past & past participle)* – रोक लिया गया participle of hold. *The senate held a meeting of executive members and decided to start a new 4-year degree course from the next session.*

Helianthus/हीलिएऽन्थॅस *(noun)* – सूरजमुखी का फूल Helianthus is a group of plants cultivated in Europe and America for use as food crops and decoration. *Helianthus is used for decoration.*

Helical/हेलिकल *(adj.)* – घुमौवा having the shape or form of a helix; spiral. *The Universe is helical in appearance as if coiled one over the other.*

Hell/हेल *(noun)* – पाताल a place regarded in various religions as a spiritual realm of evil and suffering, often depicted as a place of perpetual fire beneath the earth to which the wicked are consigned after death, a state or place of great suffering. exclamatory used to express annoyance or surprise or for emphasis. *Being sent to the solitary cell in a jail is nothing short of living in hell.*

Hell-cat/हेलकैट *(noun)* – कर्कशा स्त्री a spiteful, violent woman, a witch. *Women who are spiteful and violent in nature are known in the society as hell-cats.*

Helot/हेलॉट *(noun)* – प्राचीन स्पार्टा का दास a member of a class of serfs in ancient Sparta, intermediate in status between slaves and citizens. *Those Spartans who were not fully free as a citizen were known as helots.*

Help/हेल्प *(verb)* – सहायता make it easier to do something. improve to, assist to move in a specified direction. *He helped me to reach Connaught Place in the shortest possible way.*

Helper/ हेल्पर *(noun)* – सहायक a person who helps someone else. *The carpenter needed five more helpers to make the complete set of furniture.*

Helpful/हेल्पफुल *(adj.)* – उपकारक giving or ready to give help, useful. *I found his advice very helpful in passing the examination.*

Helpless/हेल्पलेस *(adj.)* – असहाय unable to defend oneself or to act without help. *The cubs were born blind and helpless.*

Helpmate/हेल्पमेट *(noun)* – पत्नी, बीबी या सहायक a helpful companion or partner. *My roommate is a true helpmate in all matters of study.*

Helter-skelter/हेल्टर स्केल्टर *(adj. & adv)* – अव्यस्थित अवस्था में, जल्दी में in disorderly haste or confusion. *Following shooting and arson in the area, everyone started running helter-skelter to find an escape route.*

Helve/हेल्व *(noun)* – किसी हथियार की मूठ the handle of a weapon or tool. *A helve is a handle attached to an axe or hammer.*

Hemisphere/हेमिस्फिअर *(noun)* – गोलार्द्ध a half of a sphere. *Equator divides the earth into two halves, northern hemisphere and southern hemisphere.*

Hemlock/हेमलॉक *(noun)* – धतूरा a highly poisonous plant of the parsley family, with fern-like leaves, small white flowers, and an unpleasant smell, a sedative or poisonous potion obtained from this plant. *Many allopathic medicines use hemlock as an ingredient, which otherwise is highly poisonous.*

Hemp/हेम्प *(noun)* – पटुआ the cannabis plant. the fibre of this plant, extracted from the stem and used to make rope, stout fabrics, fibrebouard, and paper. used in names of other plants that yield fibre, e.g. manila hemp. *Most of 50 and 100 kg bags used for packing wheat, rice and sugar are prepared from hemp.*

Hempen/हेम्पेन *(adj.)* – पटुवे का बना हुआ made of hemp. *This is hempen bag.*

H

Hem-stitch/हेमस्टिच (noun) – गोट लगाना a decorative stitch used especially along-side a hem, in which several adjacent threads are pulled out and the crossing threads are tied into bunches, making a row of small opening. *Skirts with hem-stitch are no longer fashionable.*

Hen/हेन (noun) – मुर्गी a female bird, especially of a domestic fowl, domestic fowls of either sex. used in names of various other birds, e.g. native hen. a female lobster, crab, or salmon. *The eggs laid by a hen are very popular as a breakfast item.*

Henbane/हेनबेन (noun) – एक जहरीला पौधा a poisonous plant of the nightshade family, with sticky hairy leaves and an unpleasant smell. Also known as stinking nightshade. *Henbane is a poisonous plant with narcotic properties.*

Henchman/हेन्चमैन (noun) – प्रधान सेवक chiefly derogatory a faithful follower or political supporter, especially one prepared to engage in crime or dishonest practices. *The gang leader and his henchmen creating nuisance were arrested by the police.*

Hendecagon/हेन्डेकागॅन (noun) – ग्यारह भुज की आकृति a plane figure with eleven straight sides and angles. *In geometry, a figure with eleven angles and sides is known as hendecagon.*

Henpecked/हेनपेक्ड (noun) – भार्या-शासित continually criticize and order about her husband. *His wife bullies him so much that he no longer takes any decision and has become a true henpecked.*

Hepta/हेप्टा – उपसर्ग जिसका अर्थ सात होता है a prefix meaning seven: having seven; heptathlon. *Hepta is a Greek word meaning seven.*

Heptad/हेप्टाड (noun) – सात का समुदाय technical a group or set of seven. *A group of seven is known as heptad.*

Her/हर (pronoun) – उस स्त्री का used as the object of a verb or preposition to refer to a female person or animal previously mentioned or easily identified. *She knew I hated her. I told Salina I would wait for her at the station.* referring to a ship, country, or other inanimate thing regarded as female. *The crew tried to sail her through a narrow gap.*

Herbarium/हर्बेरिअम् (noun) – वनस्पतियों का संग्रह a systematically arranged collection of dried plants. *Herbarium is a room where dry plants and herbs are stored.*

Herbivorous/हर्बिवॅरॅस (adj.) – शाकाहारी plant-eaters. *All plant-eating animals are herbivorous.*

Herby/हर्बि (adj.) – जड़ी-बूटी से परिपूर्ण of herbal. *If you want to buy herbs or herbal plants, please visit a herby dealer.*

Hereabout/हिअॅरॅएबाउट (adv.) – आसपास near this place. *His house is hereabout Delhi railway station area.*

Hereafter/हिअरआफ्टर (adj.) – इसके बाद in future. *All communications intended for the director will hereafter be addressed to the secretary.*

Hereby/हिअरबाइ (adv.) – एतद्द्वारा formal as a result of this document or utterance. *The order I sent yesterday is hereby withdrawn and you are to act as if it never existed.*

Hereditary/हिरेडिटरि (adj.) – पैतृक conferred by based on, or relating to inheritance. able to be passed on from parents to their offspring or descendants. *The only qualification for membership is intellect; other distinctions, hereditary or acquired, do not count.*

Heresy/हेरिसि (noun) – नास्तिकता belief or opinion contrary to orthodox religious doctrine. *The practice of following unorthodox religious philosophy is known as heresy.*

Heretic/हेरिटिक (noun) – पाखण्डी a person believing in or practicing heresy. *The person who renounces the orthodox religious doctrine is known as a heretic.*

Heritable/हेरिटॅबॅल (adj.) – वंशपरम्परा से प्राप्त होने योग्य able to be inherited. *This property is heritable among all three children.*

Heritage/हेरिटेज (noun) – विरासत valued things such as historic buildings that have been passed down from previous generations. of special value and worthy of preservation. *Taj Mahal is a world heritage site maintained by Archaelogical Survey of India.*

Heritor/हेरिटर (noun) – पूर्वजों की सम्पत्ति पाने वाला a person who inherits. *He willed his daughter as the heritor of all acquired properties after his death.*

H

Hermit/हर्मिट् *(noun)* – संन्यासी a person living in solitude as a religious discipline. a reclusive or solitary person. *Away from family members, he lives a reclusive life of a hermit as if he has renounced the worldly pleasures.*

Hermitage/हर्मिटेज *(noun)* – कुटी place where hermits live. *More than 50 hermits are living in this 500 year-old hermitage.*

Heroine/हीरोइन *(noun)* – नायिका a woman admired for her courage or outstanding achievements. a woman of superhuman qualities. *It is our moral duty to praise Rani Lakshmi Bai as heroine, who fought British forces in 1857.*

Heroism/हीरोइज़्म *(noun)* – पराक्रम characteristics of a hero, bravery. *Perhaps this love was kindling a new heroism in him.*

Heron/हेरॅन *(noun)* – सारस a large fish-eating wading bird with long legs, a long shaped neck, and a long pointed bill. *Pelicans and flamingoes, geese and ducks, storks and herons, ibises and cranes, flew in from all directions.*

Herpes/हर्पीज़ *(noun)* – जुलपित्ती नामक रोग a disease caused by a herpes virus, affecting the skin or the nervous system. *Herpes is a disease badly affecting the skin and nervous system.*

Herring/हेरिंग *(noun)* – एक प्रकार की पायी जाने वाली मछली a silvery fish which is most abundant in coastal waters and is an important food fish. *Herring is a popular edible fish mostly found in North America.*

Herself/हरसेल्फ *(pronoun)* – स्वयं स्त्री का used to refer to a thing or things belonging to or associated with a female person or animal previously mentioned. *She dressed herself with more than usual care, and came to meet visitors in her stormy beauty.*

Hesitant/हेजिटैन्ट *(adj.)* – हिचकने वाला slow to act or speak through indecision or reluctance. *Fearing loss of job, he looked hesitant to speak the truth in front of his employer.*

Hesitation/हेजिटेशन *(noun)* – सन्देह hesitating, faltering. *After slight hesitation she sat down, burying her face in her hands.*

Hesitative/हेजिटेटिव *(adj.)* – शंकाशील indecisive, hesitant. *This college doesn't admit students who are indecisive or hesitative by nature.*

Hesitator/हेजिटेटर *(noun)* – आगा-पीछा करने वाला मनुष्य one who hesitates, irresolute. *Because you don't explain your position, most people consider you a hesitator.*

Hesperian/हेस्पेरिअन *(adj.)* – पाश्चात्य western Greek mythology of or concerning the hesperides, a group of nymphs who guarded the garden of golden apples at the western extremity of the earth. *It is hesperian story.*

Hesperus/हेस्परस *(noun)* – सन्ध्या का तारा poetic the planet venus. *In Greek mythology, Hesperus is the evening star, the planet Venus in the evening.*

Heterodox/हेटरोडॉक्स *(adj.)* – नास्तिक not confor- ming with orthodox standards or beliefs. *A person who doesn't conform to the accepted religious beliefs is known as heterodox.*

Heugh/ह्यू *(noun)* – दर्रा a shaft in a coal pit. *Heugh is a shaft in a coal pit through which miners and ores move between the pit and the surface outlet.*

Heuristic/हियुरिस्टिक *(adj.)* – पता लगाने वाला enabling a person to discover or learn something for themselves. *Heuristic method involves finding a solution by trial and error or by rules that are only loosely defined.*

Hexa/हेक्सा *(combining form)* – उपसर्ग जिसका अर्थ छ: होता है six; having six. *Hexagon is an enclosed geometric form having six sides and angles.*

Hexagon/हेक्सागन *(noun)* – षट्कोण a plane figure with six straight sides and angles. *A geometric figure having six sides and angles is called hexagon.*

Hexameter/हेक्सामीटर *(noun)* – षट्पदी prosody a line of verse consisting of six metrical feet. *Hexameter is a verse consisting of six feet*

Hey/हे *(interjection)* – आनन्द सूचक exclamatory used to attract attention or to express surprise, interest, etc. *Hey! Where had you been for such a long time?*

Heyday/हेडे *(noun)* – हर्ष the period of one's greatest success, activity, or vigour. *During their heyday, no team could challenge the might of Brazilian football team.*

H

H

Hiatus/हाइएटस *(noun)* – स्वरविच्छेद a pause or gap in continuity, a break between two vowels coming together but not in the same syllable, as in the ear. *A small difference in pitch between two musical tones is known as hiatus.*

Hide/हाइड *(noun)* – खाल the skin of an animal, especially when tanned or dressed. *Hide of cow is considered most soft and light for footwear.*

Hideous/हिडिअस *(adj.)* – घिनौना, वीभत्स extremely ugly. extremely unpleasant. *They had hardly finished picnic before a hideous creature came towards them.*

Hie/हाइ *(verb)* – जल्दी से भागना move quickly. *Hie is an obsolete word meaning to move quickly.*

Hiemal/हाइमल *(adj.)* – शीत-ऋतु सम्बन्धी characteristic of or relating to winter. *Wearing an overcoat over a coat to protect one from biting cold signals the onset of hiemal.*

Hierarch/हाइअराकॉ *(noun)* – प्रधान पुरोहित a chief priest, archbishop; or other leader. *Persons holding a position of authority in a church are designated hierarch.*

Hierarchical/ हाइअँराकिॉकल *(adj.)* – प्रधान पुरोहित सम्बन्धी belonging to an hierarchy. *In the hierarchical order of precedence, the prime minister stands third only behind the president and vice president of India.*

Hierachy/ हायअँराकिॉ *(noun)* – पुरोहित का शासन a ranking system ordered according to status or authority. the upper echelons of a hierarchical system. an arrangement according to relative importance or inclusiveness. *In the hierarchy of Army, the general is the senior-most officer.*

Hiero/हाइअरो – पुरोहित-सम्बन्धी अर्थ का उपसर्ग combing form sacred; holy. *In ancient Greece, holy shrines and temples were known as hiero.*

Higgle/हिगल *(verb)* – फेरी करके बेचना [archaic] spelling of haggle, bargaining. *Unless you higgle hard, the vegetable seller wouldn't lower the price.*

High-born/हाइबॉर्न *(adj.)* – उच्च कुल का having noble parents. *This aristocratic club only admits high-born members.*

High-flier/हाइफ्लायर *(noun)* – साहसी पुरुष an adventurous person, racing horse. *A British thoroughbred racing horse is known as high-flier.*

High-flown/हाइ फ्लोन *(adj.)* – उन्नत pretentious, extravagant or grandiose. *The students couldn't understand the meaning of the high-flown talk on morality delivered by the speaker.*

High-handed/हाइ-हैन्डेड *(adj.)* – उद्धत domineering or inconsiderate. *They are your employees and shouldn't be treated in a high-handed manner.*

Highland/हाइलैण्ड *(noun)* – पहाड़ी प्रदेश an area of high or mountainous land. *The mountainous northern part of Scotland is popularly known as highland.*

Highly/हाइलि *(adv.)* – अति to a high degree or level, favourably. *A favourable action on my application would be highly appreciated.*

High-minded/ हाइ-माइन्डेड *(adj.)* – उदारचित having strong moral principles. *He is a high-minded person and on no account would compromise on his principles.*

High-priest/हाइ प्रिस्ट *(noun)* – प्रधान पुरोहित a chief priest of a non-christian religion, especially of historic judaism. the leader of a cult or movement. *The high-priest looked up in astonishment, as the disturbance in the church broke in on his studies.*

High-sounding/हाइसाउडिंग *(adj.)* – दिखावा pretentious. *The students couldn't understand the meaning of the high-sounding talk on morality delivered by the speaker.*

High-spirits/हाइस्पिरिट्स *(plural noun)* – साहसी lively and cheerful behaviour or mood. *After selection into the national team, the members were in high-spirits to do their best.*

High-time/ हाइटाइम *(verb)* – उचित समय in a manner of warning. *To be retained in the team, it is high time you start making runs.*

High-water/हाइवाटर *(noun)* – बाढ़ में जहाँ तक जल ऊपर होता है another term for high tide. *At the time of high-water, fishermen are advised not to go out into the sea.*

Hilarity/हिलैरिटि *(noun)* – प्रसन्नता cheerfulness, funniness *The attitude of hilarity can lighten the mood of any serious discussion.*

Hill/हिल *(noun)* – पहाड़ी a naturally raised area of land, not as high or craggy as a mountain. a heap or mound. *The Aravali hills rises in the western India and merges into the plains in Delhi.*

Hillock/हिलॉक *(noun)* – छोटी पहाड़ी a small hill or mound. *Hillock is a mound above the plains and lower than the hills.*

Hilly/हिलि *(adj.)* – पहाड़ियों से पूर्ण having many hills. *Shimla is an idyllic and hilly place surrounded by huge trees.*

Hilt/हिल्ट *(noun)* – मूठ handle of a sword, dagger, weapon, tool. *The sword had a costly hilt decorated with rubies and turquoises.*

Hindmost/हाइन्डमोस्ट *(adj.)* – सबसे पिछला especially of a bodily part hind. *Just then the horse stepped quickly around on his hindmost feet, and looked the professor in the face.*

Hindrance/हिन्ड्रैन्स *(noun)* – अवरोध a thing that hinders. *The hooligans were trying to create hindrance to prevent workers from going to the factory.*

Hindu/हिन्दु *(noun)* – हिन्दू a major religious and cultural tradition of the Indian subcontinent, including belief in reincarnation and the worship of a large pantheon of deities. *Hindu religion is one of the oldest religion in the world.*

Hinny/हिनि *(noun)* – खच्चर the offspring of a female donkey and a male horse, compare with mule. *A hinny is an offspring of a male horse and a female donkey.*

Hippodrome/हिप्पड्रोम *(noun)* – घोड़ो की दौड़ का मैदान a theatre or concert hall. *Hippodrome is an area where chariot race takes place.*

Hippology/हिपलॉजी *(noun)* – अश्वविद्या study of horses. *Hippology, the study of horses, helps one to learn how to breed thoroughbred racing horses.*

Hippopotamus/हिप्पॅपॉटॅमस *(noun)* – दरियाई घोड़ा a large thick-skinned semiaquatic African mammal, with massive jaws. *Hippopotamus is mostly found in Africa.*

Hircine/हर्साइन *(adj.)* – बकरे के समान [archaic] of or resembling odour of a goat. *A strong foul smell resembling that of a goat's odour is called hircine.*

Hireable/हाइअरेबल *(adj.)* – किराया के योग्य the act of hiring. *Children below 14 years are not hireable to work in any factory.*

Hireling/हायरलिंग *(noun)* – भाड़े का आदमी chiefly derogatory a person who is hired, especially for morally dubious or illegal work. *Mercenaries who fight on behalf of someone purely for money are called hirelings.*

Hirer/हाइअरर *(noun)* किराये पर देना one who hires. *The boss hired three more men for the job.*

Hirsute/हर्स्यूट *(adj.)* – रोयेंदार, रूखा formal often humorous hairy. *Their hirsute chests.*

Hiss/हिस *(noun)* – फुफकार sound like a escaping steam. *The sound made by angry snakes, cats or birds is called hiss.*

Hist/हिस्ट *exclamatory* – शान्त होकर सुनो [archaic] used to attract attention or call for silence. *Hist! Don't shout pere, please.*

Historian/हिस्टॉरिअन *(noun)* – इतिहास लिखने वाला an expert in or student of history. *Rudrangshu Mukherjee is a famous historian of India.*

Historicity/हिस्टॉरिसिटि *(noun)* – ऐतिहासिक प्रवृत्ति [historical] authenticity. *Historicity is the quality of being a part of recorded history as opposed to myth or legend.*

Hitherto/हिदरटू *(adv.)* – यहाँ तक until the point in time under discussion. *Things that had hitherto seemed impossible now came true.*

Hive/हाइब *(noun)* – मधुकोष a busy swarming place. *The bees live in a hive.*

Hoard/होर्ड *(noun)* – संग्रह a store of money or valued objects. *He rushed back to rescue his hoard of gold.* an amassed store of useful information. *The police discovered a hoard of secret information about their activities.*

Hoarse/होर्स *(adj.)* – रूक्ष of a voice rough and harsh. *His face looked tired, and his voice hoarse with shouting commands for hours.*

Hoax/होक्स *(noun)* – हँसी में छलना a humorous or malicious deception. *The evidence has been planted as part of elaborate hoax.*

Hobbledehoy/हॉबल्डिहॉय *(noun)* – भद्दा युवा पुरुष [informal dated] a clumsy or awkward youth. *That habbledehay is internally very nice fellow.*

H

Hobgoblin/हॉबगॉब्लिन *(noun)* – राक्षस a mischievous imp; a bogey. *A small creature that tricks people or causes trouble is called hobgoblin.*

Hobnob/हॉबनॉब *(verb)* – संग-साथ करना [informal] mix socially, especially with those of higher social status. *To appear influential, he would often go to parties and hobnob with senior bureaucrats.*

Hocus-pocus/होकॅस-पोकॅस *(noun)* – इन्द्रजाल meaningless talk used for trickery. *Please come to the point and not indulge in hocus pocus explanation that wastes time.*

Hod/हॉड *(noun)* – मसाला ढोने की कड़ाही a builder's v-shaped tray used for carrying bricks. *These days conveyors carry bricks and mortars in building upper floors instead of hods being used on head.*

Hodman/हॉडमैन *(noun)* – सुरखी चूना ढोने वाला आदमी a labourer carrying a hod. *A hodman carries bricks and mortars on his head during building construction.*

Hodge-podge/हॉज-पॉज *(noun)* – खिचड़ी [North American] variant of hotchpotch. *Hodge-podge is a word that describes a disorderly collection of things, items etc.*

Hoe/हो *(noun)* – कुदाली a long-handled gardening tool with a thin metal blade, used mainly for weeding. *You must use a hoe to dig up earth or plants. After just two doses of the hoe in the garden, the weeds entirely disappeared.*

Hog/हॉग *(noun)* – शूकर a pig, especially a castrated male reared for slaughter. *Hog is a term given to the pig that is reared for consumption.*

Hoggish/हॉगिस *(adj.)* – गन्दा coarsely gluttonous or greedy. *Fat-cheeked little boy and pot-bellied father displayed hoggish manners while eating at the dining table.*

Hoist/हॉइस्ट *(verb)* – उठाना, फहराना raise by means of ropes and pulleys. haul up. *A white flag was hoisted.*

Hold-all/होल्डऑल *(noun)* – बिस्तरा आदि बाँधने का बस्ता a large bag with handles and a shoulder strap. *Hold-all is a convenient carrying bag people use in packing sleeping materials during a train journey.*

Holdback/होल्डबैक *(noun)* – अवरोध restraint, hindrance, obstacle. *Don't put a holback to views when replying to psychologist's queries.*

Holdfast/होल्डफास्ट *(noun)* – काँटी a staple or clamp securing an object. *This staple pin will holdfast all papers in one place.*

Holland/हालैण्ड *(noun)* – एक प्रकार का मलमल, एक देश a kind of smooth, hard-wearing linen, used for soft furnishings. *Cotton and linen fabric used for window and book-binding still goes by the name Holland because the manufacturing started in the country by the same name.*

Hollow/हॉलो *(adj.)* – खाली, छूछा having a hole or empty space inside. *A hollow metal tube is required.* having a concave or sunken appearance. *Her cheeks were hollow and there were dark circles under her eyes.*

Holly/हॉलि *(noun)* – हरी रहने वाली काँटेदार झाड़ी an evergreen shrub, with prickly dark green leaves, small white flowers, and red berries. *Holly is an evergreen, deciduous plant with white flowers and green leaves.*

Holocaust/हॉलोकॉस्ट *(noun)* – सत्यानाश, पूर्ण आहुति complete destruction by fire, mass killing. *Holocaust is a name that surmises the slaughter of more than six million Jews by the Nazis during the Second World War.*

Holster/होल्स्टर *(noun)* – खोल, कबूर, पिस्तौल रखने के लिए चमड़े का बैग gun pouch, case in which pistol, revolver is carried. *He placed the pistol back into the holster and sped away.*

Holt/होल्ट *(noun)* – जंगल grove. *Holt is a name given to an area of woodland mainly made up of grove, bushes and small trees.*

Homage/होम्-ऍज् *(noun)* – श्रद्धांजलि honour or respect shown publicly. *Homage was paid by the visiting dignitary to Mahatma Gandhi, the father of the nation, at his Samadhi at Rajghat.*

Homily/हॉमिलि *(noun)* – प्रवचन, धार्मिक उपदेश a moralizing discourse. *Homily is a religious discourse given at a congregation for infusing morality.*

Hominy/हॉमिनि *(noun)* – दलिया coarsely ground corn used to make grits. *Hominy is peeled and dried kernels of corn.*

H

Homo/होमो *(noun)* – 'सदृश' अर्थ का उपसर्ग the genus of primates of which modern humans are the present-day representatives. *Homo is the genus that is composed of modern humans and species closely related to them.*

Homologous/हॉमोलॅगॅस *(adj.)* – तुल्य परिमाण का alike, equal, similar. *The forelimbs of humans and bats are homologous in make up or structures but they are used differently.*

Homonym/हॉमोनिम *(noun)* – एक ही रूप किन्तु भिन्न अर्थ वाले शब्द each of two or more words having the same spelling or pronunciation but different meanings and origins. *Words that have the same spelling or pronunciation but different meanings are known as homonyms.*

Honeymoon/हॅनिमून *(noun)* – विवाह के बाद दम्पति का आनन्द पूर्णमिलन a holiday taken by a newly married couple. *The young couple flew to Goa for honeymoon.*

Honk/हॉन्क *(noun & verb)* – भोंपू की आवाज, जंगली बत्तख का शब्द the sound of a car horn. *No honking please this is a silence zone.*

Honorific/ऑनरिफिक *(adj.)* – प्रतिष्ठा सूचक given as a mark of respect. (noun) a title or word expressing respect. *As a mark of respect, many universities offer the honorific title of doctorate to distinguished visiting dignitaries.*

Hoodwink/हूडविंक *(verb)* – धोखा देना to trick somebody. *I had been hoodwinked into buying a worthless cooker.*

Hooker/हूकर *(noun)* – वारांगना, वेश्या a prostitute, whore. *Hookers offer sensual pleasures to customers in return for money.*

Hooligan/हूलिगॅन *(noun)* – गुण्डा a violent young troublemaker. *Curfew has been imposed in the city to prevent hooligans from inciting further violence.*

Hopple/हॉपल *(verb & noun)* – घोड़े के पैरों को एक साथ बाँधना another term for bobble. *Hopple is a process of strapping the foreleg and hind leg together on each side (of a horse) in order to keep the like-sided legs moving in unison.*

Horde/हॉर्ड *(noun)* – झुण्ड chiefly derogatory a large group of people. *Until they reached the palace the hordes, so eager for booty, had completely refrained from plunder and pillage.*

Horizon/हॅराइजॅन *(noun)* – क्षितिज the line at which the earth's surface and the sky appear to meet. *The sun rose above the horizon.*

Horizontal/हॉरिजॉन्टॅल *(adj.)* – समतल parallel to the plane of the horizon. *Try to draw two lines parallel and horizontal to each other.*

Hormone/हॉर्मोन *(noun)* – हार्मोन, अन्त:स्राव treatment with oestrogens to alleviate menopausal symptoms or osteoporosis. *The doctor has suggested hormonal treatment can reduce problem of osteoporosis.*

Horner/हॉर्न्-अर *(noun)* – तुरही या भोंपू बजाने वाला a person who blows a horn. *A horner necessarily accompanies a music party to blow the horn.*

Hornless/हॉर्नलेस *(adj.)* – बिना सींग का without horns. *This cow has no horn on its head.*

Horology/हॉरॉलॅजि *(noun)* – घड़ी बनाने की विधा, ज्योतिष शास्त्र the study and measurement of time, the art of making clocks and watches. *Horology is the art and science of measuring time as well as of making clocks.*

Horoscope/हॉरॅस्कोप *(noun)* – जन्मकुण्डली a forecast of a person's future based on the relative positions of the stars and planets at the time of their birth. *Horoscope of both the boy and the girl is extensively matched before a marriage is settled in India.*

Horrible/हॉरॅबॅल *(adj.)* – डरावना causing or likely to cause horror. [informal] very unpleasant. *She felt that another little while in this heated, horrible place would drive her mad.*

Horribly/हॉरिबल् *(adj.)* – भयंकर रूप से awfully, terribly. *The news was harribly painful.*

Horribleness/हॉरिबल्नेस *(noun)* – डरावनापन awfulness, dreadfulness, repulsiveness. *This hotel is so filthy, it matches the horribleness to the previous one.*

Horrid/हॉरिड *(adj.)* – विकट causing horror. [informal] very unpleasant. *Was she awake or was she a prey to some horrid dream?*

Horrific/हॉरिफिक *(adj.)* – डराने वाला causing horror. *Horrific working conditions in the mining industry is simply disgusting.*

Horrify/हॉरिफाइ *(verb)* – डराना fill with horror. *I was horrified at the thought of being late for my interview.*

Horripilation/हॉरिपिलेशॅन *(noun)* – रोमांच poetic the erection of hairs on the skin due to cold, fear, or excitement. *This story is full of horripilation.*

H

Horror/हॉरर् *(noun)* – अति घृणा an intense feeling of fear, shock, or disgust. a thing causing such a feeling. intense dismay. *For the first time since the Revolution had begun, the horror of it and the meaning of it were brought home to him.*

Horticulture/हॉर्टिकॅल्चॅर *(noun)* – बागवानी the art or practice of garden cultivation and management. *Horticulture is the art of garden cultivation.*

Hose/होज *(noun)* – होज, रबर का नल या पाइप a flexible tube conveying water, used chiefly for watering plants and in firefighting. *The firefighters were using a large hose to spray water over the building on fire.*

Hosier/होजियर *(noun)* – मोजे का व्यापारी a manufacture or seller of hosiery. *Jockey is one of the largest manufacturer in the world engaged in trade in as a wholesale hosier.*

Hospice/हॉस्पिस् *(noun)* – सराय a home providing care for the sick or terminally ill. *Hospice is a name given to homes where sick travellers can stay and get treated medically.*

Hospitable/हॉस्पिटेबल् *(adj.)* – अतिथ्यकारी showing or inclined to show hospitality. pleasant and favourable for living in. *If you want to learn the art of pleasant, polished and hospitable manners of treating guests, please visit a five-star hotel.*

Hospital/हॉस्पिटॅल *(noun)* – अस्पताल an institution providing medical and surgical treatment and nursing care for sick or injured people. *Hospital is a place where sick and injured are fully taken care of with medicine and surgery.*

Hospitality/हॉस्पिटैलिटि *(noun)* – मेजबानी, मेहमानदारी the friendly and generous reception and entertainment of guests or strangers. *The poor man was received with the same hospitality by the king as that of any other rich person.*

Host/होस्ट *(noun)* – अतिथेय, मेजबान समुदाय a person who receives or entertains other people as guests. *The person you see standing there is the dinner-party host.* a person, place, or organization that holds an event to which others are invited. *London played host to the Summer Olympics in 2012.* the presenter of a television or radio programme: *The host for today's programme is Minni Mathur.*

Hostage/हॉस्टेज *(noun)* – प्रतिभू के रूप में शत्रु को प्रदत्त व्यक्ति a person seized or held as security for the fulfilment of a condition. *The hostages were to be released by the terrorists in exchange for five of their jailed friends.*

Hostel/हॉस्टल *(noun)* – सराय an establishment which provides cheap food and lodging for a specific group of people. *This private hostel is one of the best in the town to take care of food and lodging arrangements of students.*

Hostess/होस्-टेस् *(noun)* – अतिथि-सत्कार करने वाली स्त्री a female host. a woman employed to welcome and entertain customers at a nightclub or bar. a stewardess on an aircraft, train, etc. *Madhuri Dixit is the hostess of today's programme. Air hostesses take care of most individual needs of the flyers.*

Hostile/हॉस्टाइल *(adj.)* – विरुद्ध antagonistic; opposed. of or belonging to a military enemy. opposed by the company to be bought. *A warrior had succeeded in penetrating the hostile fort of the enemy unnoticed and killed the king with a sword.*

Hostility/हॉस्टिलिटि *(noun)* – विरोध animosity. *Hostility to foreign retail trade is likely to do more harm than good to Indian consumers.*

Hotly/हॉटलि *(adv.)* – क्रोध से excitedly, heatedly, angrily. *The hotly contested election went in favour of the ruling party by a thin margin.*

Hotchpotch/हॉचपॉच *(noun)* – खिचड़ी a confused mixture. *The coalition government ruling India is a hotchpotch of many political parties.*

Hotel/होटेल *(noun)* – होटल an establishment providing accommodation and meals for travellers and tourists. *Taj hotel is one of the best hotels in the world.*

Hound/हाउन्ड *(noun)* – शिकारी कुत्ता a dog of a breed used for hunting, especially one able to track by scent. *A hound is breed of dog mainly used for hunting in the jungles.*

Houri/हूरि *(noun)* – स्वर्गकन्या a beautiful young woman. *Really speaking, she is a houri on this earth.*

House/हाउस *(noun)* – घर, भवन a building for human habitation. chiefly a dwelling that is one of several in a building. *The house which he had taken up for his residence was not a very large one.*

H

Household/हाउसहोल्ड (noun) – कुटुम्ब, परिवार a house and its occupants regarded as a unit. *The household was, to all appearance, asleep at the unusually early hour.*

Houseless/हाउसलेस (noun) – गृहहीन without house. *Many people are houseless in India.*

Housewife/हाउसवाइफ (noun) – गृहिणी a married woman whose main occupation is caring for her family and running the household. *She is a housewife and doesn't work in any office.*

Housing/हाउसिंग (noun) – गृह, शरण houses and flats considered collectively. the provision of accommodation. *Housing societies are building attractive designer flats offering many options to buyers to choose.*

Hovel/हॉव्-एल (noun) – कुटी a small squalid or poorly constructed dwelling. *No bed in tent, hovel, or house was occupied; for everywhere the final packing was going on.*

Hover/हॉवर (verb) – हवा में घूमना, बहकना remain in one place in the air. *Army helicopters hovered over the area.* linger close at hand in an uncertain manner. *She hovered anxiously in the background.* remain at or near a particular level. *Inflation will hover around 6 percent this month.*

How/हाउ (adv.) – किस रूप से in what way or manner; by what means. *How does it work? She did not know how she ought to behave. She showed me how to adjust the focus of the camera.*

Howitzer/हाउइट्जर (noun) – एक प्रकार की छोटी बन्दूक a short gun for firing shells on high trajectories at low velocities. *Howitzer is a short barrelled-gun armies use to fire on enemies.*

Howler/हाउलर (noun) – भद्दी भूल [informal] a ludicrous mistake. *I regret my howler of throwing the banana and try to eat its skin.*

Howling/हाउलिंग (adj.) – चिल्लाहट [informal] great noise. *If you don't stop howling, I will report to the principal*

Hoyden/हॉयडन् (noun) – कुलटा स्त्री a boisterous girl. *This hoyden is too much dangerous.*

Hub/हब (noun) – धुरा the central part of a wheel, rotating on or with the axle, and from which the spokes radiate, the centre of an activity, region, or network. *Colombo is the shipping hub where ships from all countries unload and reload merchandise.*

Hubbub/हबब (noun) – कोलाहल a chaotic din caused by a crowd. a busy, noisy situation. *It was difficult to hear in the hubbub.*

Huckaback/हक्-अ-बैक् (noun) – तौलिया बनाने का मोटा रूखा कपड़ा a strong linen or cotton fabric with a rough surface, used for towelling and glass cloths. *Huckaback is a strong cotton fabric used for making towels.*

Huckster/हकस्टर (noun) – बिसाती a person who sells small items, either door-to-door or from a stall. *A huckster is a person who sells household items of daily use door-to-door.*

Huddle/हडल (verb) – सिमट जाना crowd together. *At last we reached the mouth of a ravine, and there we huddled ourselves under the streaming trees to relax.*

Hue/ह्यू (noun) – रंग छवि a colour or shade. technical the attribute of a colour, dependent on its dominant wavelength, by virtue of which it is discernible as red, green, etc. *Her face took on an unhealthy hue.*

Huff/हॅफ (verb) – शेखी करना blowout air loudly on account of exertion. *He was huffing under a heavy load. I was huffing and puffing to keep up with his speed.*

Hull/हल (noun) – जहाज का पेटा the main body of a ship or other vessel, including the bottom, sides and deck but not the superstructure, engines, and other fitting. *A hull is basically a foundation over which the ship construction takes place.*

Hullabaloo/हॅलॅबॅलू (noun) – शोरगुल [informal] a commotion or uproar. *In this hullabaloo of constant cross-talking, I can't lecture this class.*

Human/ह्यूमन (adj.) – मानव, मानवीय of, relating to, or characteristic of human-kind. of or characteristic of people human error. *To forgive is the highest form of human life. It's a human error.*

Humane/ह्यूमेन (adj.) – दयालु compassionate or benevolent. inflicting the minimum of pain. *Being compassionate to feelings of others is the best humane quality*

Humanism/ह्यूमनिज्म (noun) – मनुष्य जाति की सेवा rationalistic outlook or system of thought attaching prime importance to human rather than divine or supernatural matters. *Humanism is a reflection of respectful consideration for welfare of fellow human beings.*

H

Humanity/ह्यूमनिटि *(noun)* – मानवता human beings collectively. *Appalling crimes are being committed in Syria against humanity.* the state of being human. *No doubt our differences matter but our common humanity matters more.*

Humble/हॅम्बॅल *(adj.)* – नम्र having or showing a modest or low estimate of one's importance. *I felt very humble when meeting her.* (of an action or thought) offered with or affected by a modest estimate of one's importance. *My humble apologies for failing to attend the marriage ceremony.*

Humbly/हम्बलि *(adv)* – नम्रतापूर्वक simply, modestly, meekly. *He is very haughty but today surprisingly and very humbly he paid respect to all visitors.*

Humeral/ह्यूमरल *(adj.)* – स्कन्द सम्बन्धी of or relating to the humerus denoting plain vestment worn around the shoulders when administering the sacrament. *Humeral means relating to humerus.*

Humerus/ह्यूमरस *(noun)* – प्रगण्डास्थि anatomy the bone of the upper arm or forelimb, between the shoulder and the elbow. *Humerus is a bone of the upper arm.*

Humid/ह्यूमिड *(adj.)* – गीला marked by a relatively high level of water vapour in the atmosphere. *Due to heavy rain in this sea-resort, it has become very sultry and humid*

Humidity/ह्यूमिडिटी *(noun)* – गीलापन the state or quality of being humid. a quantity representing the amount of water vapour in the atmosphere or a gas. *Humidity is a term that defines the amount of water vapour in the air.*

Humility/ह्यूमिलिटि *(noun)* – दीनता a humble view of one's own importance. *Humility is the human property of being ego-less-ness.*

Humoral/ह्यूमॅरॅल *(adj.)* – त्रिदोष सम्बन्धी medicine of or relating to the body fluids, in particular involving the action of circulating antibodies. Often contrasted with cell mediated. *Humoral imbalance causes difficulties in the body.*

Humorist/ह्यूमरिस्ट *(noun)* – हँसी करने वाला मनुष्य a humorous writer, performer, or artist. *A humorist has the innate ability to act, speak or write in a way that gladdens the heart of everyone.*

Humorous/ह्यूमरस *(adj.)* – हँसी का causing amusement. having or showing a sense of humour. *Of all the books I have read, 'Bedtime Mailbox' has been the most humorous.*

Humour/ह्यूमर *(noun)* – मन की भावना the quality of being amusing or comic, especially as expressed in literature or speech. *His tales are full of humour.* the ability to appreciate or express humour. *The inimitable brand of humour was on show.*

Hunch/हन्च *(verb)* – कूबड़ raise and bend the top of one's body forward. sit or stand in such a position. *He sat with a forward bend in his body that looked almost like a hunch.* *(noun)* a feeling or guess based on intuition. *He has not informed me but I have a hunch that he is coming here today.*

Hung/हंग *(adj.)* – धातु का लटकाने के अर्थ में भूतकाल का रूप of an elected body having no political party with an overall majority. *Political pundits are predicting a hung parliament in the following elections.*

Hungrily/हंग्रिलि *(adj.)* – भूख की अवस्था में in a hungry manner. *No sooner the food was served, the visitor attacked it hungrily as if he had not had a morsel for a few days.*

Hungry/हंग्रि *(adj.)* – भूखा, दुबला feeling, showing, or causing hunger. *But I was not hungry any more, and did not care for food.*

Hunk/हंक *(noun)* – टुकड़ा, खंड a large piece cut or broken from something larger. *I like a hunk of cheese with bread.*

Hunting/हण्टिंग *(noun)* – आखेट the activity of hunting wild animals or game, especially for food or sport. *Hunting is a practice of pursuing a living wild animal for food, recreation or trade.*

Huntsman/हंट्स्मैन *(noun)* – शिकारी a person who hunts. a hunt official in charge of hounds. *A huntsman is a person who pursues a living wildlife, especially animals for food, recreation or trade.*

Hurdle/हॅर्ड्ल *(noun)* – बाधा, रुकावट one of a series of upright frames which athletes in a race must jump over. a hurdle race. *Hurdles are used for handling livestock, as decorative fencing and for horse-racing.*

Hurl/हर्ल *(verb)* – चक्कर देना, घूमाकर फेंकना throw or impel with great force. utter vehemently. *Javelin throwers try to hurl by* hand the long spear-like object farthest in order to win the competition.

Hurley/हर्लि *(noun)* – हॉकी की छड़ी a stick used in the game of hurling. *A stick which is used in hurling is called hurley.*

Hurrah/हुर्-र्-आ – आनन्दसूचक अव्यय *exclamatory* used to express joy or approval. *Hurrah! Our team has won the tournament for the third time in a row.*

Hurricane/हरिकेन *(noun)* – चक्रवात a storm with a violent wind, in particular a tropical cyclone in the Caribbean. *Hurricane is a name given to a tropical cyclone occurring in the Caribbean and characterized by strong winds and heavy rains.*

Hurry/हॅरि *(verb)* – आकुलता move or act quickly or more quickly. do or finish quickly. *It was necessary to hurry this matter to a close.*

Hurtful/हटफुल *(adj.)* – घातक causing mental pain or distress. *His attitude of not coming up to the door to welcome his poor friend was very hurtful.*

Hurtle/हर्टल *(verb)* – टकराना move or cause to move at great speed. *To enable the spacecraft escape the earth's gravitational pull, it is necessary to hurtle it at a speed more than 12 kilometres per second.*

Hush/हश *(verb)* – चुप या शान्त करना make or become quiet. *In a hushed tone he said goodbye.*

Husk/हस्क *(noun)* – छिलका the dry outer covering of some fruit or seeds. *Manufacturers are converting rice husk into edible oil.*

Husky/हस्कि *(adj.)* – भर्राया, भारी, भूसा भरा हुआ sounding low-pitched and slightly hoarse. *Because of cough and cold, her voice has become very husky.*

Hussar/हूजर् *(noun)* – घुड़सवार सिपाही a soldier in a light cavalry regiment which adopted a dress uniform modelled on that of the Hungarian hussars. *Those soldiers are called hussars.*

Husting/हस्टिंग *(noun)* – चुनाव का कार्यक्रम a meeting at which candidates in an election address potential voters. *Husting is a physical platform, usually in America, from which public representatives air their opinion to influence the voters.*

Hut/हट *(noun)* – झोंपड़ी a small single-storey building of simple or crude construction. *A hut is a single-storey dwelling unit mostly found in villages.*

Hutch/हच *(noun)* – सन्दूक, खाँचा a box or cage for keeping rabbits or other small domesticated animals. *Hutch is a box-like cage for keeping rabbits, guinea-pigs etc.*

Hyaena/हाइ-ईना *(noun)* variant spelling of hyena. *Hyaena is a carnivorous nocturnal animal that resembles a dog and found mostly in Africa*

Hybridize/हाइब्रिडाइज *(verb)* – वर्णसंकर पैदा करना cross-breed to produce hybrids. *To increase yields of food crops, only option left is to cross-breed or hybridize seeds.*

Hydrant/हाइड्रॅन्ट *(noun)* – पानी निकालने का बम्बा a water pipe with a nozzle to which a fire hose can be attached. *A hydrant consists of long rubber tubes attached to water support system and located at vantage point around large buildings to extinguish fires.*

Hydrate/हाइड्रेट *(verb)* – किसी पदार्थ का पानी में घोल cause to absorb or combine with water. *To hydrate the body, it is recommended to use a moisturising lotion over the exposed parts of the body while going out in the sun.*

Hydraulic/हाइड्रॉलिक *(adj.)* – भार से चालित denoting or relating to a liquid moving in a confined space under pressure, hydraulics. *To prevent accidents happening on the road, hydraulic brakes are attached in the vehicle in addition to the foot brakes.*

Hydro/हाइड्रो *(noun)* – 'जल' अर्थ का उपसर्ग [British] a hotel or clinic originally providing hydropathic treatment. *A hydro is a shortened name for a place offering cure through hydrotherapy.*

Hydrocele/हाइड्रोसिल *(noun)* – अण्डवृद्धि medicine abnormal accumulation of serous fluid in a sac in the body. *A morbid collection of fluid in the testicle is called hydrocele.*

Hydroelectric/हाइड्रोइलेक्ट्रिक *(adj.)* – जल-विद्युत relating to or denoting the generation of electricity using flowing water to drive a turbine which powers a generator. *To increase the availability of power, stations generating hydroelectric power must be installed.*

Hydrogen/हाइड्रोजन *(noun)* – हाइड्रोजन, उदजन a gel in which the liquid component is water. *Hydrogen and oxygen when mixed produce water.*

H

Hydrophobia/हाइड्रोफोबिया *(noun)* – जलत्रास extreme or irrational fear of water, especially as a symptom of rabies. *Hydrophobia is a disease in which the patient develops an abnormal fear of water.*

Hydroplane/हाइड्रोप्लेन *(noun)* – हवाई जहाज जो जल में चलकर हवा में उड़ता है a light, fast motor boat. *A hydroplane is a light motorboat designed to skim over the water at high speeds with the rear part of its hull touching the water.*

Hygiene/हाइजीन *(noun)* – स्वास्थ्य-विज्ञान conditions or practices conducive to maintaining health and preventing disease, especially cleanliness. *Hygiene is the art and practice for cleanliness, preservation of good health and prevention of illness.*

Hygrometer/हाइग्रोमीटर *(noun)* – आर्द्रतामापी an instrument for measuring humidity. *Hygrometer is an instrument to measure humidity in the atmosphere.*

Hymen/हाइमेन *(noun)* – विवाह के देवता, योनिच्छद a membrane which partially closes the opening of the vagina and whose presence is traditionally taken to be a mark of virginity. *The god of marriage is called hymen.*

Hymn/हिम *(noun)* – स्तुति a religious song of praise, typically a Christian song in praise of God. *Hymn is a song which is sung in the praise of God.*

Hyperbola/हाइपरबोला *(noun)* – अतिपरवलय mathematics a symmetrical open curve formed by the intersection of a cone with a plane at a smaller angle with its axis than the side of the cone. *Hyperbola is one of the four kinds of conic section, the others being, parabola, ellipse and circle.*

Hyperbole/हाइपरबोल *(noun)* – अतिशयोक्ति deliberate exaggeration not meant to be taken literally. *Hyperbole is the use of exaggeration as rhetoric to generate strong feelings and emotional bond, such as, comparing someone knowledge to Einstein.*

Hyperbolize/हाइपरबोलाइज *(verb)* exaggerate beyond truth. – अतिशयोक्ति पूर्वक वर्णन करना *The government has chosen to hyperbolize the benefits of foreign retailers offering goods at lower prices.*

Hypercritic/हाइपरक्रिटिक *(noun)* – सूक्ष्म छिद्रान्वेषी मनुष्य one who is critical beyond a reason. *Most opposition parties play hypercritic to any government's move to bring in foreign retailers.*

Hypertrophy/हाइपरट्रॉफी *(noun)* – किसी अंग की अधिक वृद्धि [physiology] enlargement of an organ or tissue resulting from an increase in size of its cells. *Hypertrophy is the abnormal increase in the volume of an organ due to the increase in the size of cells.*

Hypothecate/हाइपॉथिकेट *(verb)* – बन्धक रखना pledge by [law] to a specific purpose. *He decided to hypothecate his property to the bank to borrow money for his son's education.*

Hypothecation/हाइपॉथिकेशन *(noun)* – रेहन की क्रिया mortgaging. *Hypothecation is the practice where a borrower pledges a collateral as a guarantee to secure a loan.*

Hypothecator/हाइपॉथिकेटर *(noun)* – रेहन रखने वाला मनुष्य one who mortgages. *A hypothecator has signed over his personal property to the bank as security for the repayment of money borrowed.*

Hypothesis/हाइपॉथिसिस *(noun)* – अनुमान a supposition or proposed explanation made on the basis of limited evidence as a starting point for further investigation. [philosophy] a proposition made as a basis for reasoning. *The hypothesis that particles travel faster than light is difficult to verify on the available scientific instruments.*

Hypothetic/हाइपॉथेटिक *(adj.)* – माना हुआ theoretical, pertaining to hypothesis. *We have only gone as far as the Moon, it is only hypothetic to calculate the possibility of going to the Mars and come back to the Earth.*

Hypothesize/हाइपॉथेसाइज *(verb)* – कल्पना करना create a theory, form a hypothesis. *Since that hypothesis has been scientifically proved, there is no need for him to hypothesize again.*

Hysteria/हिस्टिरिआ *(noun)* – बदहोशी psychiatry a psychological disorder whose symptoms include selective amnesia, volatile emotions, and attention-seeking behaviour. *Hysteria is a state of mind characterized by unmanageable fear or emotional excesses.*

Hysteric/हिस्टेरिक *(adj.)* – मूर्छा-सम्बन्धी another term for hysterical. *A person suffering from uncontrolled emotional outburst is known as a hysteric.*

Ii

I/आइ *(noun)* – अंग्रेजी वर्णमाला का नौवाँ वर्ण the ninth letter of the Eglish alphabet.
  1. Denoting the next after H in a set of items, categories, etc.
  2. The roman numeral for one.

Iambic/आइम्बिक *adjective)* – गुरु अक्षर वाले पद से सम्बन्धित (prosody of or using iambuses. *The poem is known for its use of iambic pentameter.*

Ibex/आइबेक्स *(noun)* – पर्वत का जंगली बकरा a wild mountain goat with long, thick ridged horns and a beard. *Over those ice-covered mountains, we captured an ibex in camera.*

Ibidem/इबाइडेम *(avberb)* – उसी स्थान पर in the same source referring to a previously cited work. *This quotation by the author is from his book on philosophy, and the next quotation, ibidem.*

Ibis/आइबिस *(noun)* – सारस के प्रकार एक-एक पक्षी a large wading bird with a long down curved bill, long neck, and long legs. *We were amazed to see so many ibises, all at one place.*

Ice/आइस *(noun)* – बरफ frozen water, a brittle transparent crystalline solid. [chiefly British] an ice cream or water ice. *Mom asked John to place all the ice cubes in the jug containing juice.*

Ichneumon/इक्न्यूमॅन *(noun)* – एक प्रकार का नेवला a slender parasitic wasp with long antennae, which deposits its eggs in or on the larvae of other insects. *The biologist observed the larvae of ichneumon under microscope.*

Ichor/आइकॉर *(noun)* – पंछा, पूयरक्त देवताओं का रक्त Greek mythology the fluid said to flow like blood in the veins of the gods. *The witch prophesised that a man with ichor in his blood will be the next ruler of the kingdom.*

Ichthyoid/इक्थिऑइड *(adjective)* – मछली के आकर का मत्स्याभ having the form of a fish. *The aquatic animal had an ichthyoid body.*

Icicle/आइसिकल *(noun)* – बरफ की लटकती नुकीली चट्टान a hanging, tapering piece of ice formed by the freezing of dripping water. *The icicle shaped pieces were hanging from top of the wall.*

Icon/आइकॉन *(noun)* – प्रतिमा a devotional painting of Christ or another holy figure, typically on wood, venerated in the Byzantine and other eastern churches. *The lovely icon on the wall was making the devotees to bow with respect and surprise.*

Iconic/आइकोनिक *(adjective)* – मूर्ति-सम्बन्धी of, relating to, or of the nature of an icon. depicting a victorious athlete in a conventional style. *His style soon became iconic in the world of fashion.*

Iconoclast/आइक्नोक्लास्ट *(noun)* – मूर्ति तोड़ने वाला, मूर्तिभंजक a person who attacks cherished beliefs or institutions. *Raja Ram Mohan Roy was an iconoclast of his time as he stood against superstitions of all kind.*

Icosahedron/आइकॅसहेड्न *(noun)* – बीस फलक की ठोस आकृति a three-dimensional shape having twenty plane faces, in particular a regular solid figure with twenty equal triangular faces. *The chemistry teacher pointed to the icosahedrons figure on chart to explain the concept.*

Icy/आइसि *(adjective)* – बहुत ठण्डा covered with or consisting of ice. very cold. *The cave was dark and icy, so we could not enter it.*

Idea/आइडिअँ *(noun)* – कल्पना a thought or suggestion as to a possible course of action. a mental impression. a belief. *Backed by modern ideas, the country was able to bring necessary change in its social setup.*

I

Ideal/आइडिअॅल *(noun & adjective)* – आदर्श most suitable; perfect. *The room temperature was just ideal for doctors to perform surgery.*

Idealistic/आइडिअलिस्टिक *(adjective)* – आदर्शवादी characterized by idealism. unrealistically aiming for perfection. *An idealistic society is hard to conceive. She is an ideal candidate for this post.*

Ideality/आइडिएलिटि *(noun)* – आदर्शत्व formal the state or quality of being ideal. *Everyone wants to go with ideality when he begins some work.*

Idealize/आइडिअॅलाइज *(verb)* – आदर्श रूप में देखना या प्रस्तुत करना regard or represent as perfect or better than in reality. *In an idealized society, there are no crimes of any sort.*

Ideally/आइडियलि *(adverb)* – आदर्श रूप में preferably. in an ideal world. *Ideally you should exercise for 30 minutes every day. Ideally, you should take 20 mg of each tablet in the morning.*

Ideate/आइडिएट *(verb)* – कल्पना करना chiefly psychology imagine. form ideas. *His aim was to ideate a theory that could be proved rationally.*

Ideation/आइडिएशन *(noun)* – विचार-शक्ति the formation of ideas or concepts. *The scientist's ideation of psychological concept was too hard to believe.*

Idem/आइडेम *(avberb)* – वहाँ used in citations to indicate an author or word that has just been mentioned. *Marianne Elliot, Partners in revolution, 1982; idem, Wolfe Toe, 1989.*

Identical/आइडेन्टिकल *(adjective)* – अनुरूप exactly alike. developed from a single fertilized ovum, and therefore of the same sex and usually very similar in appearance. compare with fraternal. *Identical twins were born on July 8, to a woman in ward number 6.*

Identifiable/आइडेन्टिफाएबल *(adjective)* – पहचानने योग्य able to be recognized. distinguishable. *The bodies were so charred that they were no longer identifiable.*

Identification/आइडेन्टिफिकेशन *(noun)* – एकीकरण the action or process of identifying or the fact of being identified. *As soon as the identification process was over, we made an exit out of the office.* an official document or

other proof of a person's identity. *The police stopped the van and asked the driver to show his identification proof.*

Idiocy/इडिअॅसि *(noun)* – पागलपन extremely stupid behaviour. *He was ill-famed for his idiocy.*

Idiom/इडिअम *(noun)* – मुहावरा a group of words established by usage as having a meaning not deducible from those of the individual words. *A class on idioms was arranged for us, just a week before exams.*

Idiomatic/इडिअॅमैटिक *(adjective)* – मुहावरेदार using, containing, or denoting expressions that are natural to a native speaker. *She spoke fluent, idiomatic English. After 10 years of my stay in France, I am now used to Idiomatic French.*

Idiosyncrasy/इडिअॅसिन्क्रॅसि *(noun)* – प्रवृत्ति की विशेषावस्था a mode of behaviour or way of thought peculiar to an individual. a distinctive characteristic of a thing. *I could no longer stand his idiosyncrasies, therefore, I left.*

Idiot/इडिअॅट *(noun)* – निर्बुद्धि [informal] a stupid person. *What an idiot the biker was!*

Idiotic/इडिअॅटिक *(adjective)* – मूर्खतापूर्ण very stupid. *The girl rebuked the boys for their excessive idiotic behaviour.*

Idleness/आइडलनेस *(noun)* – बेकारी laziness. indolence. *He was punished for his idleness at school. Too much of an idleness can be boring enough.*

Idler/आइडलर *(noun)* – निकम्मा a person who idles. *I knew that my best friend was the biggest idler in the world.*

Idly/आइडलि *(adverb)* – आलस्य से with no particular purpose, reason, or foundation. *"What are your interests?" asked my fiancée.*

Idol/आइडॉल *(noun)* – प्रतिमा an image or representation of a god used as an object of worship. *The idols were adorned with jewels before being taken out on procession.*

Idolater/आइडॉलेटर *(noun)* – मूर्तिपूजक a person who worships idols. *The things grew worse at home when I refused to be an idolater.*

Idolatrous/आइडॉलट्रस *(adj)* – मूर्ति पूजन के समान relating to or practising idolatry. *The*

I

idolatrous behaviour is seen as contempt by many societies.

Idolatry/आइडॉलट्रि *(noun)* – मूर्ति-पूजा worship of idols. *In Hinduism, the roots of idolatry are very deep.*

Idolize/आइडॉलाइज *(verb)* – मूर्ति की भाँति पूजा करना revere or love greatly or excessively. *Don't idolize me as it would be of no use.*

Idolum/आइडोलॅम *(noun)* – कल्पना *While painting, he was taking a cue from his mental idolums.*

Idyll/आइडिल *(noun)* – पद्य में ग्रामीण जीवन का संक्षिप्त वर्णन a blissful or peaceful period or situation. *For the winter-lovers, Shimla stands out as an idyll destination.*

If/इफ *(conjunction)* – मानो अगर introducing a conditional clause: on the condition or supposition that. introducing a hypothetical situation. every time. *If you don't abide by rules, I would be forced to keep you out from this discussion.*

Igloo/इग्लू *(noun)* – हिमकुटी a dome-shaped Eskimo house, typically built from blocks of solid snow. *People living in Polar areas live in the houses called igloos.*

Igneous/इग्निअस *(adjective)* – आग्नेय, अग्निमय having solidified from lava or magma. *The area is all covered with igneous rocks.*

Ignis fatuus/इग्निस फैट्युअस – *(noun)* मिथ्या प्रकाश erratic movement. *The path that he chose proved to be an ignis fatuus and he ended up doing nothing.*

Ignite/इग्नाइट *(verb)* – आग लगाना catch fire or cause to catch fire. *As the sun set, the tribal people ignited the logs of wood.*

Ignition/इग्निशन *(noun)* – ज्वलन the action of igniting or the state of being ignited. *We kept standing there, watching the ignition of industrial waste.*

Ignoble/इग्नोबल *(adjective)* – नीच not honourable; base. *His bad deeds are really ignoble for society.*

Ignominious/इग्नॉमिनिअॅस *(adjective)* – घृणित, अधम deserving or causing public disgrace or shame. *His lustful acts brought him into an ignominious situation.*

Ignoramus/इग्नॅरॅमॅस *(noun)* – अज्ञानी, मूर्ख पुरुष an ignorant or stupid person. *Don't bring that ignoramus person before me.*

Ignorance/इग्नॅरॅन्स *(noun)* – अज्ञान lack of knowledge or information. *When minister was asked about the incident, he expressed ignorance.*

Ignorant/इग्नॅरॅन्ट *(adjective)* – अज्ञानी lacking knowledge or awareness in general. uninformed about or unaware of a specific subject or fact. *The students were ignorant of the changes made in their curriculum.*

Ignore/इग्नॉर *(verb)* – उपेक्षा करना disregard intentionally. fail to consider something significant. *In spite of all the efforts he made to approach me, I kept ignoring him.*

Iguana/इग्वॉना *(noun)* – पोह, एक प्रकार की छिपकली a large lizard with a spiny crest along the back. *The guide said, "Here, you will see a number of iguanas."*

Iliad/इलियड *(noun)* – होमर कवि का इस नाम का महाकाव्य a Greek epic poem in twenty-four books, traditionally ascribed to Homer, telling how Achilles killed Hector at the climax of the Trojan War. *Iliad by Homer is considered as one of the classic works of Greek literature.*

Illation/इलेशन *(noun)* – परिणाम, निष्कर्ष old-fashioned term for inference. *He could draw an illation from the facts that he had gathered.*

Illative/इलेटिव *(adjective)* – अनुमान करने योग्य, परिणामसूचक of the nature of or stating an inference. proceeding by inference. *The nature of his work is mostly illative.*

Illaudable/इलॉडबल *(adj)* – अग्रहणीय, अप्रशंसनीय *His every action and every decision was simply illaudable.*

Illegality/इलिगैलिटि *(noun)* – अन्याय गैर कानूनीपन contrary to or forbidden by law, especially criminal law. Illegality in consumption of drugs can't be overemphasized. *No one could dare stop all that illegality taking place in open.*

Illegally/इलीगलि *(adverb)* – अवैध (गैर कानूनी) ढंग से unauthorized by law. *Bob smuggled drugs into the country and then sold them illegally.*

I

Illegibility/इलेजिबिलिटि *(noun)* – अस्पष्टता not clear enough to be read. *Teachers were always scolding him for not paying attention to the illegibility in his written work.*

Illegible/इलेजेबॅल *(adjective)* – न पढ़े जाने योग्य not clear enough to be read. *The lawyer's writing was so illegible that we could not read a single thing.*

Illegitimacy/इलिजिटिमॅसि *(noun)* – हरामीपन not in accordance with accepted social standards. *It was surprising that such an illegitimacy was easily overlooked by ministers.*

Illegitimate/इलिजिटिमेट *(adjective)* – जारज not in accordance with the law or accepted standards. *The boy or girl born from the parents who are not married, is called an illegitimate.*

Illiberal/इलिबॅरॅल *(adjective)* – अनुदार, कड़ा अनुशासन opposed to liberal principles. *The policies of autocratic leaders were often illiberal and harsh.*

Illicit/इलिसिट *(adjective)* – अवैध forbidden by law, rules, or custom. *The two were having an illicit relationship, oblivious to everyone.*

Illimitable/इलिमिटेबल *(adjective)* – असीम, जिसकी सीमा न की जाये limitless. *A giant with illimitable powers emerged on the scene and destroyed everything.*

Illision/इलिजन *(noun)* – टक्कर dashing against. *His act of illision took everyone by surprise.*

Illiterate/इलिटरेट *(adjective)* – अशिक्षित, अनपढ़ unable to read or write. *A majority of people living in Indian villages are still illiterate.*

Illness/इलनेस *(noun)* – बीमारी a disease or period of sickness. *His mental illness grew day by day.*

Illumination/इल्यूमिनेशन *(noun)* – चमक lighting or light. *The illumination from the bright surface was directly falling in our eyes.*

Illuminative/इल्यूमिनेटिव *(adjective)* – प्रकाश करने वाला helping to explain or clarify. *The illuminative setting was created by a group of experts.*

Illumine/इल्यूमाइन *(verb)* – प्रज्वलित करना, प्रकाशित करना [poetic/literary] light up; illuminate. *In day, all the objects get illumined by the sun.*

Illusion/इलूशन *(noun)* – छल, भ्रम a false or unreal perception. a deceptive appearance or impression. a false idea or belief. *What he was looking at, was merely an illusion, not reality.*

Illusive/इलूसिव *(adjective)* – छली, भ्रमोत्पादक chiefly deceptive; illusory. *The man was trying to fool the police with his illusive looks.*

Illusory/इलूसरि *(adjective)* – मायावी, भ्रमित करने वाला based on illusion; not real. *The film was full of illusory scenes.*

Illustrate/इलॅस्ट्रेट *(verb)* – अलंकृत करना, चित्रात्मक व्याख्या provide with pictures. *"Could you illustrate your concept?" asked the student to his classmate.*

Illustration/इलॅस्ट्रेशन *(noun)* – चित्र, स्पष्टीकरण a picture illustrating a book or periodical. *All the children were looking at the illustrations with surprise and interest.*

Illustrative/इलॅस्ट्रेटिव *(adjective)* – दृष्टान्तयुक्त, चित्रयुक्त serving as an example or explanation. *He gave me a few illustrative examples for my better understanding of things.*

Illustrator/इलॅस्ट्रेटॅर *(noun)* – चित्रकार a person who draws or creates pictures for magazines, books, advertising, etc. *The man sitting there is a famous illustrator.*

Illustrious/इलसट्रिअस *(adjective)* – प्रसिद्ध well known and admired for past achievements. *When he looked back at his illustrious career, he felt good.*

Imageable/इमेजिएबल *(adjective)* – चित्त में धारण करने योग्य बिम्ब निर्माण that may be imaged. *The sheer beauty of the place is making it imageable.*

Imagery/इमेजरी *(noun)* – आकृति, बिम्ब, चित्रात्मकता figurative language, especially in a literary work. visual symbolism. *The English poets have used vivid imagery to impart beauty to their work.*

Imaginable/इमैजिनॅबल *(adjective)* – कल्पनीय, परिकल्पनीय possible to be thought of or believed. *The intensity of the pain suffered by the patients is not even imaginable.*

Imaginative/इमैजिनेटिव *(adjective)* – कल्पनापूर्ण having or showing creativity or inventiveness. *His imaginative thinking made him stand out of the crowd.*

I

Imagine/इमैजिन *(verb)* – विचार करना, कल्पना करना form a mental image or concept of. believe to exist. *In these days of technology, it is hard to imagine a life without computers and mobiles.*

Imago/इमेगो *(noun)* – कृमि की प्रौढ़ अवस्था entomology the final and fully developed adult stage of an insect. *Imago is the final stage of insect development cycle.*

Imbecile/इम्बेसाइल *(noun)* – अल्पमति [informal] a stupid person. *What an imbecile the person sitting on the sofa was!*

Imbecility/इम्बेसिलिटि *(noun)* – शरीर या मन की दुर्बलता stupid, idiotic. *The way he handled the task clearly indicated his imbecility.*

Imbibe/इम्बाइब *(verb)* – पी लेना, गटक जाना formal drink absorb. chiefly botany absorb into ultramicroscopic spaces or pores. *The water sprinkled quickly imbibed by the leaves.*

Imbroglio/इम्ब्रोल्यो *(noun)* – बिना क्रम का ढेर an extremely confused or complicated situation. *Despite of his best efforts, he soon found himself caught in an imbroglio.*

Imbrue/इम्ब्रू *(verb)* – धब्बा लगना archaic stain, especially with blood. *As soon as I entered the basement, he imbrued me with colours.*

Imbue/इम्ब्यू *(verb)* – दिल में बैठा देना, गहरे रंग में रंगना spread or diffuse through. *His speech imbued me so much that I started clapping.*

Imitable/इमिटॅबल *(adjective)* – अनुकरण करने योग्य copy or simulate. *The singer carries a unique style that is not imitable by anyone.*

Imitate/इमिटेट *(verb)* – अनुकरण करना follow as a model. *The actor had such a good comic sense that no one could imitate him.*

Imitation/इमिटेशन *(noun)* – अनुकरण the action of imitating. a copy. *Imitation is not everyone's cup of tea.*

Imitative/इमिटेटिव *(adjective)* – अनुकरणशील following a model. *Though he denies it all the time, his style is more or less imitative.*

Immaculate/इमैक्युलिट *(adjective)* – निर्मल perfectly clean, neat, or tidy. *The saint preferred immaculate surroundings for performing meditation.*

Immaturity/इमट्युअरिटि *(noun)* – अपरिपक्व अवस्था the state of being immature. *The immaturity of the immune system in very young children makes them especially vulnerable.*

Immeasurable/इम्मेजरेबल *(adjective)* – बहुत बड़ा too large, extensive, or extreme to measure. *The frustration that the people were facing at office had become immeasurable.*

Immediately/इमिडिएटली *(adv)* – तत्काल at once. *The passengers asked the driver to start the bus immediately.*

Immediateness/इमिडिएटनेस *(noun)* – समीपता occurring or done at once. *The boss ordered his team to show immediateness in completing the task.*

Immedicable/इम्मेडिकेबॅल *(adjective)* – अचिकित्स्य unable to be healed or treated, incurable. *In spite of all the efforts by the surgeons, the patient remained immedicable to the drugs.*

Immemorable/इम्मेमॅरेबल *(adj)* – विस्मरणीय not worth remembering. *The violent clashes made the event only immemorable.*

Immemorial/इम्मेमोरिअल् *(adjective)* – अति प्राचीन very old or long past. *From the times immemorial, our culture has rooted in traditions and customs.*

Immense/इमेन्स *(adjective)* – अमिट extremely large or great. *The sayings of the prophet had an immense effect upon my heart.*

Immensity/इमेंसिटी *(noun)* – अनन्तता extremely large or great, especially in scale or degree. *Seeing the immensity of the situation, the President cancelled his tour to Europe.*

Immerge/इमर्ज – तरल पदार्थ में डूबना to plunge into fluid. *As the water was not very cold, we decided to immerge in it.*

Immerse/इमर्स *(verb)* – डुबाना dip or submerge in a liquid. *The holy idol of the goddess was immersed by the devotees in water.*

Immersion/इमर्शन *(noun)* – निमज्जन the action of immersing or the state of being immersed. *The immersion ceremony was followed by chanting of hymns.*

Immethodical/इम्मेथॉडिकल *(adj)* – अव्यवस्थित not according to method. *The professor dismissed the idea as being impractical and immethodical.*

I

Immigrant/इमिग्रैण्ट *(noun)* – देशान्तर में बसने वाला a person who comes to live permanently in a foreign country. *The Asian country was not willing to grant all the rights to its immigrants.*

Immigrate/इमिग्रेट *(verb)* – देशान्तर में बसना या बसाना come to live permanently in a foreign country. *As the country was constantly under war, many of its residents decided to immigrate to the neighbouring land.*

Imminence/इमिनेन्स *(noun)* – समीपता the state of being imminent and liable to happen soon. *The imminence of a clash made the ministers avoid the rally.*

Imminent/इमिनेन्ट *(adjective)* – सन्निकटता about to happen. *With such a support from all the parties, a powerful change is imminent.*

Immiscibility/इमिसिबिलिटि *(noun)* – अघुलनशीलता (of liquids) not forming a homogeneous mixture when mixed. *The immiscibility of oil and water is the base of many chemical compounds.*

Immitigable/इमिटिगेबॅल *(adjective)* – कम न होने योग्य unable to be made less severe or serious. *The sacrifices of the martyrs remain immitigable.*

Immixture/इमिक्चर *(noun)* – शुद्धता the process of mixing or being involved with something. *There are several ways by which an immixture of substances can be separated.*

Immobile/इमोबाइल *(adjective)* – स्थिर not moving. incapable of moving or being moved. *The earthworm was crushed under leg and had turned immobile.*

Immobility/इमोबिलिटि *(noun)* – निश्चलता incapable of moving or being moved. *In an extremely old age, a person can face the immobility of joints.*

Immoderate/इमॉडरिट (इमॉडरेट) *(adjective)* – बेहद, अत्यधिक, अत्यन्त lacking moderation; excessive. *As per old scriptures, it is a sin to indulge in immoderate drinking and gambling.*

Immodest/इमॉडेस्ट *(adjective)* – अश्लील not humble, decent, or decorous. *His immodest behaviour was a cause of disturbance to everyone.*

Immodesty/इमॉडिस्टि *(noun)* – निर्लज्जता lacking humility or decorousness. *Client's immodesty forced the seller to put down the phone.*

Immolate/इमोलेट *(verb)* – बलिदान करना kill or offer as a sacrifice, especially by burning. *Sometimes, youngsters become so crazy in anger that they try to immolate themselves.*

Immolation/इमोलेशन *(noun)* – बलिदान kill or offer as a sacrifice, especially by burning: *Immolation is an act of cowardice and must be avoided in every situation.*

Immolator/इमोलेटर *(noun)* – बलिदान देने वाला kill by burning. *The immolator's life could not be saved due to grave injuries.*

Immoral/इमॉरॅल *(adjective)* – दुश्चरित्र not conforming to accepted standards of morality. *The public display of affection is considered an immoral activity by many.*

Immortal/इमॉर्टॅल *(adjective)* – अमर living forever. *As per legends, the gods drank nectar to become immortal.* deserving to be remembered forever. *His bravery on the battlefield has made him immortal in our hearts.*

Immovability/इमूवबिलिटि *(noun)* – स्थिरता not able to be moved. *The immovability of the joints causes extreme pain.*

Immune/इम्यून *(adjective)* – आक्रमण से मुक्त resistant to a particular infection owing to the presence of specific antibodies or sensitized white blood cells. biology of or relating to such resistance: the immune system. *His good health is attributed to his excellent immune system.*

Immunity/इम्युनिटि *(noun)* – उन्मुक्ति, प्रतिरक्षा the ability of an organism to resist a particular infection or toxin by the action of specific antibodies or sensitized white blood cells. *Immunity to malaria seems to have increased spontaneously.*

Immunize/इम्यूनाइज *(verb)* – मुक्त करना make immune to infection, typically by inoculation. *The doctor advised his patient to get immunized as soon as possible.*

Immure/इम्युअॅर *(verb)* – बन्द करना confine or imprison. *The dacoit kept the child immured for four days.*

Immutability/इम्यूटॅबिलिटि *(noun)* – नित्यता unchanging over time or unable to be changed. *Green vegetables raise the immutability of our body.*

Imp/इम्प *(noun)* – दुष्ट बालक, बाल राक्षस mischievous child. *The old man retorted, "Why don't you keep your imp under control?"a small, mischievous devil or sprite. The movie is based on the character of an imp who plays wicked all the time.*

Impacable/इम्पैकेबल *(adj)* – शान्त न करने योग्य not to be quieted. *The man is famous in office for his impacable nature.*

Impact/इम्पैक्ट *(noun)* – टक्कर, परिणाम, प्रभाव the action of one object coming forcibly into contact with another. *The impact was so huge that it produced a loud noise.*

Impaction/इम्पैक्शन *(noun)* – टक्कर the condition of being or process of becoming impacted. *Under the impaction of hammer, the nail got twisted.*

Impairing/इम्पेअरिंग *(noun)* – क्षति weaken or damage. *Keeping the mobile phone in close proximity to body can lead of impairing of cells.*

Impalpability/इम्पैल्पेबिलिटि *(noun)* – स्पर्श-ज्ञान शून्यता unable to be felt by touch. *The impalpability of our soul makes it all the more difficult to understand.*

Impanel/इम्पैनेल *(verb)* – निरीक्षक या पंच की सूची में दर्ज करना enrol a jury or enrol on to a jury. *A group of five judges were impanelled for the case.*

Imparadise/इम्पैराडॉइज *(verb)* – आनंदविभोर कर देना to bring into a state of extreme happiness. *The thought of going abroad was enough to imparadise me.*

Imparity/इम्पैरिटि *(noun)* – असमानता inequality. *Even in today's world, the poor are treated with imparity.*

Impart/इम्पार्ट *(verb)* – प्रदान करना communicate. bestow a quality. *As per the directions from the Principal, the teachers would be imparted technical knowledge during the training.*

Impartible/इम्पार्टिबल *(adj)* – भाग न करने योग्य not divisible. *According to the old theories, atoms are impartible.*

Impassible/इम्पैसिबल *(adjective)* – दुःखातीत incapable of feeling pain. *Years of devotion have made his heart impassable.*

Impassion/इम्पैशन *(verb)* – जोश दिलाना make passionate. *The guidance by his mentor impassioned him so much that he took the project right away.*

Impassive/इम्पैसिव *(adjective)* – भावना शून्य not feeling or showing emotion. *His impassive attitude was ridiculed by everyone.*

Impasto/इम्पेस्टो *(noun)*– रंग भरने की कला या ढंग art the process or technique of laying on paint or pigment thickly so that it stands out from a surface. *The beauty of the painting was aggravated by the lovely impasto work on it.*

Impatience/इम्पेशन्स *(noun)* – बेसब्री tendency of restlessness. *I want to work on my impatience.*

Impatient/इम्पेशॅन्ट *(adjective)* – व्यग्र having or showing a lack of patience or tolerance. *Your impatient nature is the root of all the problems.*

Impawn/इम्पॉन *(verb)* – बन्धक रखना to deposit as security. *The family had to impawn its cattle to get some money.*

Impayable/इम्पेएबल *(adjective)* – न देने योग्य priceless. *Whatever the man did for his country is totally impayable.*

Impeccability/इम्पेकेबिलिटि *(noun)* – निर्दोषता faultless highest quality. *The impeccability of the artist's work won him many applauds.*

Impendance/इम्पीडॅन्स *(noun)* – अवरोध the effective resistance to an alternating electric current arising from the combined effects of holmic resistance and reactance. See also acoustic impedance. *On the blackboard was written the formula for calculating electrical impedance.*

Impendent/इम्पेन्डेंट *(adj.)*- संकटासन्न imminent. *As they were advancing into the dark, the danger was becoming more impendent.*

Impending/इम्पेन्डिंग *(noun)* – आसन्न about to happen. *The impending danger was the reason for the cancellation of their plans.*

Impenetrable/इम्पेनिट्रेबल *(adjective)* – अथाह impossible to pass through or enter. impervious to new ideas or influence. *The extreme darkness had made the cave totally impenetrable.*

I

Imperative/इम्परेटिव *(adjective)* – आज्ञासूचक of vital importance. *The balance in ecosystem is imperative to man's existence.*

Imperator/इम्परेटर *(noun)* – सेनानायक Roman history commander a title conferred under the republic on a victorious general and under the empire on the emperor. *Soon after king's death, his young son was declared an imperator.*

Imperceptible/इम्परसेप्टिबॅलॅं *(adjective)* – अगोचर so slight, gradual, or subtle as not to be perceived. *Only an imperceptible change was noticed in the metabolic rate of the patient.*

Impercipient/इम्परसिंपिएन्ट *(adjective)* – अगोचर falling to perceive something. *His impercipient nature was attributed to his lack of experience in meta-physics.*

Imperfect/इम्परफेक्ट *(adjective)* – अधूरा, अपूर्ण faulty or incomplete. *All of us are born with imperfect minds.*

Imperialism/इम्पेरियलिज्म *(noun)* – राजाधिराज का शासन a policy of extending a country's power and influence through colonization, use of military force, or other means. *With the start of imperialism, the developed countries started expanding their territories.*

Imperialize/इम्पेरियलाइज *(verb)* – राजकीय या तेजस्वी बनाना imperial influence. *As the time passed on, the tendency to imperialize Asia increased among the western nations.*

Imperil/इम्पेरिल *(verb)* – खतरे में डालना put into danger. *It was not advisable to imperil the life of the child, so he was left at home.*

Impermanence/इम्परमानेंस *(noun)* – अस्थिरता not permanent. *The impermanence of life makes the man grateful to God.*

Impermanent/इम्परमानेंट *(adjective)* – अस्थायी not allowing fluid to pass through. *The application of wax over a surface makes it impermanent.*

Impermissible/इम्परमिसिबल *(adjective)* – अननुज्ञेय not allowed. *It was impermissible to enter without gate-pass.*

Impersonate/इम्पॉर्सनेट *(verb)* – भेष बदलना pretend to be for entertainment or fraud. *Throughout the investigation, the man impersonated as a cop.*

Impersonation/इम्पॉर्सनेशॅन *(noun)* – भेष या व्यक्तित्व परिवर्तन a representation of a person that is exaggerated for comic effect. *He thought that the impersonation as a saint would get him out of trouble, but it did not.*

Impersonative/इम्पर्सनेटिव *(adj)* – भेष (रूप) बदलने का pertaining to personating. *There was no use him being an impersonative.*

Impersonator/इम्पर्सनेटर *(noun)* – भेष बदलने वाला व्यक्ति someone who (fraudulently) assumes the appearance of another. *As an impersonator, he was a genius.*

Impertinence/इम्पर्टिनेंस *(noun)* – धृष्टता lack of respect. *My friend was punished badly for displaying impertinence to his teachers.*

Impetrate/इम्पिट्रेट *(verb)* – प्रार्थना करके प्राप्त करना to get by request. *When nothing worked for him, he tried to impetrate it by prayer.*

Impetration/इम्पिट्रेशन *(noun)* – प्रार्थना करने पर प्राप्त getting by request. *Their impetration fell on deaf ears.*

Impetuosity/इम्पिचुआसिटि *(noun)* – तीव्रता rash impulsiveness. *It is better to think before taking a step, instead of behaving with impetuosity.*

Impetus/इम्पिटस *(noun)* – प्रेरणा the force or energy with which a body moves. a driving force. *The fear of getting public rebuke was the impetus behind quick action by the officers.*

Impiety/इम्पाइअटि *(noun)* – अधर्म lack of piety or reverence. *In court, the peasant had to face king's impiety and cruelty.*

Impinge/इम्पिन्ज *(verb)* – टकराना have an effect. come into contact; encroach. *It is inappropriate to impinge on someone's privacy.*

Impious/इम्पायस *(adjective)* – पापी not showing respect or reverence. wicked. *People were surprised by his impious attitude towards them.*

Impiously/इम्पायसली *(adv)* – अधर्म से in an impious manner. *As he was behaving impiously, we left him alone.*

Impiousness/इम्पाइअसनेस *(noun)* – अधर्म unrighteousness by virtue of lacking respect for a god. *It was awkward to see saint's impiousness towards his religion.*

I

Impledge/इम्प्लेज *(verb)* – बन्धक या गिरवी रखना *At the oath ceremony, ministers impledged to take care of their responsibilities.*

Impletion/इम्प्लीशन *(noun)* – भराई *It was necessary to add impletion to the boxes before they could be transferred.*

Implicate/इम्प्लिकेट *(verb)* – फँसाना show to be involved in a crime. bear some of the responsibility for an action or process. *As he was naïve, it was easy to implicate him.*

Implication/इमप्लिकेशन *(noun)* – आशय, उलझन the implicit conclusion that can be drawn from something. a likely consequence. *The correspondent asked, "What are the implications of such a policy?"*

Implicative/इमप्लिकेटिव *(adjective)* – फँसाने वाला show someone to be involved in crime. *Nobody knew why he was giving implicative answers.*

Implore/इम्प्लोर *(verb)* – प्रार्थना करना beg earnestly or desperately [archaic] beg earnestly for. *The man without the licence implored before police to let him go.*

Imploringly/इम्प्लोरिंगलि *(adverb)* – साग्रह प्रार्थना के साथ beg someone for favour. *"Don't tell it to anyone." Said the man imploringly.*

Impolicy/इम्पालिसि *(noun)* – बुरी नीति a bad policy. *We were shocked to see the impolicy of the jury members.*

Impolite/इम्पोलाइट *(adjective)* – अविनीत not having or showing good manners. *"If you remain impolite to me, I shall not be able to help you", said the man to his neighbour.*

Impolitic/इम्पॉलिटिक *(adjective)* – अनुचित failing to possess or display prudence. *The minister was giving all the impolitic answers to the questions raised to him.*

Imponderable/इम्पॉन्डरबॅल *(adjective)* – बहुत हल्का very light, difficult or impossible to estimate or assess. *The time this issue takes to settle down is imponderable.*

Impone/इम्पोन *(verb)* – प्रभाव डालना to stake, to impose. *The man imponed the amount and went away immediately.*

Imponent/इम्पोनेन्ट *(adj.)* – प्रभाव डालने योग्य competent to impose obligation. *It was now* up to the imponent as who would be relieved from paying the duty.

Import/इम्पोर्ट *(verb)* – सूचित करना, आयात करना bring into a country from abroad. *All the goods imported into the country are of good quality.*

Importable/इम्पोर्टेबल *(adjective)* – देश में लाने योग्य bring into a country. *All importable goods in our country carry a special customs duty.*

Importation/इम्पोर्टेशन *(noun)* – आयात, किसी देश में पहुँचाना या ले जाना, बाहर से लायी हुई चीजे the process of importing. *The opposition was not happy with the importation process; so they walked out.*

Importance/इम्पोर्टेंन्स *(noun)* – महत्त्व the fact of being of value. *There are people that carry high importance in our lives.*

Important/इम्पोर्टेन्ट *(adjective)* – प्रभावशाली of great significance or value. *Our company has come out with some very important policies this year.*

Importunate/इम्पॉर्चुनेट *(adjective)* – हठी persistent or pressing. *His importunate habits were becoming annoying for others.*

Importune/इम्पॉर्चुन *(verb)* – आग्रह के साथ प्रार्थना करना harass with persistent requests. *I retorted, "Don't importune me. Give me some time."*

Importunity/इम्पॉर्चुनिटि *(noun)* – आग्रह bothering to the point of annoyared. *The man was always bothering us with his importunities.*

Impose/इम्पोज *(verb)* – थोपना force to be accepted, undertaken, or complied with. *As soon as the new rule was imposed, people started protesting.*

Imposing/इम्पोजिंग *(adjective)* – रोबदार grand and impressive. *The building looked magnificent with its imposing structure.*

Imposition/इम्पोजिशन *(noun)* *(noun)* – लगान action of imposing something or being imposed. *Tax imposition was prevalent even in ancient times.*

Impostor/इम्पॉस्टर *(noun)* – पाखण्डी pretending to be someone else to deceive. *After interrogation, it was clear that he was an impostor.*

I

Impoverish/इम्पॉवरिश (verb) – साधनहीन करना make poor. *The British rule impoverished Indian community to a great extent.*

Impracticable/इम्प्रैक्टिकेबल (adjective) – दुष्कर impossible in practice to do or carry out. *It is impracticable to listen to every employee and then take a decision.*

Imprecate/इम्प्रिकेट (verb) – शाप देना utter something bad. *It was his nature to imprecate everyone for all his problems.*

Imprecation/इम्प्रिकेशन (noun) – शाप formal a spoken curse. *His imprecations had no affect on my mind.*

Imprecatory/इम्प्रिकेटरी (adjective) – शापयुक्त spoken bad or poorly. *With time, his nature became more and more imprecatory.*

Impregnation/इम्प्रिग्नेशन (noun) – गर्भधारण saturate with a substance. *After repeated experiments, the biologists were, finally, successful in impregnation.*

Impression/इम्प्रेशन (noun) – प्रभाव an idea, feeling, or opinion. an effect produced or someone: her quick wit made a good impression. *The interviewee was able to create good impression on everyone.*

Imprimis/इम्प्राइमिस (adv) – सर्वप्रथम, पहले in the first place. *Imprimis, he is not required here.*

Imprison/इम्प्रिजन (verb) – कैद करना put or keep in a prison. *The culprit was imprisoned for five years.*

Improbability/इम्प्रोबेलिटि (noun) – अनहोनी unlikelihood. *There is improbability of raining heavily this year.*

Improperly/इम्प्रॉपर्लि (adverb) – अनुचित रीति से not according to acceptable standards. *Never go to an interview board improperly dressed.*

Impropriety/इम्प्रॉप्राइअटि (noun)– असभ्यता improper behaviour or character. *The lecturer said, "Such an impropriety would not be tolerated."*

Improver/इम्प्रूवर (noun) – व्यवसाय सीखने वाला make or become better. *He has played the role of an improver very well.*

Improvidence/इम्प्राविडॅन्स (noun) – अदूरदर्शिता not showing foresight, thoughtless. *Parents were worried about their children's improvidence.*

Improvisation/इम्प्राविजेशन (noun) – अचिन्तित रचना a creation spoken or written or composed extemporaneously. *Improvisation at writing has been my greatest strength.*

Imprudence/इम्प्रुडेंस (noun) – अविवेक not caring for consequence. *She displayed her imprudence by talking angrily to his boss.*

Impudence/इम्प्रुडेंस (noun) – ढिठाई impertinence. *The audience were shocked to see his impudence*

Impudicity/इम्प्युडिसिटि (noun) – अविनय formal lack of modesty. *His shouting at his juniors only showed his impudicity.*

Impugn/इम्प्यून (verb) – विपरीत बोलना dispute the truth, validity, or honesty of a statement or motive. *The lawyer was trying to impugn the statement given by the witness.*

Impugnment/इम्प्यूनमॅन्ट (noun) – विरोध calling into question, honesty, validity. *The impugnment of the statement was his only motive.*

Impuissance/इम्प्युसंस (noun) – नपुंसकता powerlessness revealed by an inability to act. *The knight exhibited his impuissance in the battlefield.*

Impulsion/इम्प्ल्सन (noun) – प्रेरणा a strong urge to do something. *His impulsion made him participate in the show.*

Imputation/इम्प्यूटेशन (noun) – दोषारोपण represent something undesirable. *He has always believed in imputation of failures to others.*

Imputatively/इम्प्यूटेटिवलि (adv) – कलंक से by imputation. *Their cause of woes has always been their boss working imputatively.*

Impute/इम्प्यूट् (verb) – दोष लगाना attribute to someone. *He has always imputed his awkward behaviour to laziness of his juniors.*

Inability/इनएबिलिटी (noun) – अयोग्यता the state of being unable to do something. *Her inability to perform well resulted in his expulsion from dance class.*

Inaccessible/इनएक्सेसिबल (adjective) – अप्राप्य unable to be reached. unable to be seen or used. *The presence of rugged mountains made the way to valley nearly inaccessible.*

I

Inaccessibly/इनएक्सेसिब्ली (adv) – न पहुँचनते हुए unable to be reached, used, unapproachable. *The jungle was located inaccessibly across the river.*

Inaccuracy/इनएक्यूरेसी (noun) – अशुद्धता the state of not being accurate. *The inaccuracy in his work irked his master.*

Inaction/इनएक्सन (noun) – आलस्य lack of action where some is expected or appropriate. *Police's inaction in the case has raised many eyebrows.*

Inactivity/इनएक्टिविटि (noun) – कार्य-हीनता idleness inactive. *The inactivity of the machines in the mill resulted in financial loss.*

Inadaptability/इनएडैप्टिबिलिटि (noun) – प्रबन्ध हीनता unable to adjust to new conditions. *The plants with inadaptability to the changing climate die early.*

Inaffable/इनएफेबल (adjective) – उदासीन not friendly, not easy to talk to. *We could not tolerate his inaffable manners.*

Inalterable/इनअल्टरेबल (adjective) – अपरिवर्तनीय unable to be changed. *Our boss has an inalterable nature.*

Inapplicable/इन्एप्लिकेबल (adjective) – अनुचित not relevant or appropriate. *This test is inapplicable to all those who are below 20 years of age.*

Inapposite/इनएपोजिट (adjective) – अयोग्य out of place; inappropriate. *I was finding my presence at the party totally inapposite.*

Inapprehensible/इनऐप्रिहेनिसबल – न समझने योग्य which cannot be understood. *The matter is inapprehensible to people living outside India.*

Inapt/इनऐप्ट (adjective) – अयोग्य not suitable or appropriate *His interference in our issues is inapt.*

Inaptly/इनऐप्टलि (adverb) – अयोग्यता से not suitable in the circumstances. *None of us could guess why she was behaving so inaptly.*

Inartistic/इन्आर्टिस्टिक (adjective) – फूहड़ having or showing a lack of skill or talent in art. *The poet was excellent in his work, yet he thought himself to be inartistic.*

Inattentive/इन्अटेन्टिव (adjective) – असावधान not paying attention. failing to attend to the comfort or wishes of others. *The inattentive students were rebuked by teachers.*

Inaudible/इनऑडिबल (adjective) – अकर्णगोचर unable to be heard. *The music was so loud that it was almost inaudible.*

Inaudibility/इनऑडिबिलिटि (noun) – अश्रव्यता unable to be heard. *While constructing an auditorium, the inaudibility factor is to be taken into account.*

Inaudibly/इनआडिब्लि (adv) – सुनाई न देते हुए in an inaudible manner. *He was speaking in an inaudibly loud manner.*

Inauguration/इन्आग्यूरेशन (noun) – उद्घाटन beginning of a system, policy, thing. *MLA was present at the time of inauguration of the library.*

Inauguratory/इन्आग्यूरेटरि (adverb) – उद्घाटन सम्बन्धी introduce a system, policy or period. *The minister's inauguratory speech was praiseworthy.*

Inborn/इनबॉर्न (adjective) – जन्म से existing from birth. natural to a person or animal. *Every person carries some inborn qualities.*

Inbreathe/इन्ब्रीद् (verb) – भीतर को श्वास लेना to inhale. *While working in factory, I inbreathed some foul gas.*

Inbred/इन्ब्रेड (adjective) – स्वाभाविक innate, produced by inbreeding. *Scientists are keen to experiment on inbred animals.*

Incarnate/इन्कार्नेट (adjective) – शरीरधारी embodied in flesh; in human form. *Man has always believed in the incarnate forms of God.*

Incarnation/इन्कार्नेशन (noun) – अवतार a living embodiment of a deity, spirit, or abstract quality. *Man believes in the incarnation of gods on earth.*

Incautious/इन्कॉशस (adjective) – धृष्ट, अचैतन्य Heedless of the potential problems. *His incautious nature brought much woe to his family.*

Incavation/इन्कैवेशन (noun) – पोला छिद्र a hollow hole. *The incavation was done by many engineers together.*

Incensory/इन्सेंसरी (noun) – धूपदानी another term for censer. *The incensory was placed inside the temple premises.*

I

Incentive/इन्सेन्टिव *(noun)* – प्रेरणा, प्रोत्साहन, प्रेरणा हेतु वस्तु a thing that motivates or encourages someone to do something. a payment or concession to stimulate greater output or investment. *The employees were expecting huge incentives at the end of the year.*

Inception/इन्सेप्शन *(noun)* – आरम्भ the establishment or starting point of an institution or activity. *The inception of the building took place in 1988.*

Inceptive/इन्सेप्टिव *(adjective)* – आदि का relating to or marking the beginning of something; initial. *The project is still in its inceptive stage.*

Inceptor/इन्सेप्टर *(noun)* – आरम्भ करने वाला beginner. *Many cells in body act as inceptors of signals from brain.*

Incertitude/इन्सर्टिट्यूड *(noun)* – अनिर्णय a state of uncertainty or hesitation. *It was the incertitude of the situation that he was unable to take a decision.*

Incessant/इन्सेसॅन्ट *(adjective)* – अनवरत, निरन्तर continuing without pause or interruption. *Over the years, the country has seen an incessant growth of population.*

Incestuous/इन्सेस्चुअस *(adjective)* – निकट सम्बन्धियों के साथ मैथुन से सम्बन्धित involving or guilty of incest. *Their incestuous relationship continued for many years.*

Incidence/इन्सिडेंस *(noun)* – घटना the occurrence, rate, or frequency of a disease, crime, or other undesirable thing. *The incidence of crimes has increased manifold in last few years.*

Incinerate/इन्सिनरेट *(verb)* – भस्म कर देना destroy by burning. *To get rid of the excessive garbage, it was incinerated.*

Incineration/इन्सिनरेशन *(noun)* – भस्मीकरण the act of burning something completely; reducing it to ashes. *The process of incineration continued for two days.*

Incinerator/इन्सिनरेटर *(noun)* – शव भस्म करने की चिता an apparatus for incinerating waste material, especially industrial waste. *All the garbage was put into the incinerator.*

Incise/इन्साइज *(verb)* – नक्काशी करना make a cut or cuts in a surface. cut a mark or decoration into a surface. *The surgeons incised patient's stomach and started operating.*

Incision/इन्सिजन *(noun)* – कटाव a surgical cut made in skin or flesh. *She was quite afraid of having incision done on her belly.*

Incisive/इन्साइसिव् *(adjective)* – काटने वाला Intelligently analytical and concise. *What he wanted was an incisive report of the project.*

Incisor/इन्सिजर *(noun)* – आगे का काटने वाला दाँत a narrow-edged tooth at the front of the mouth, adapted for cutting. *The incisors are meant for cutting the food bytes.*

Incite/इन्साइट *(verb)* – उत्तेजित करना encourage or stir up violent or unlawful behaviour. urge or persuade to act in a violent or unlawful way. *The crowd was incited by its leader to assemble there.*

Incivility/इन्सिविलिटी *(noun)* – असभ्यता rude or unsociable speech or behaviour. *We were surprised to notice the incivility of his nature.*

Inclemency/इनक्लेमेंसी *(noun)* – कठोरता unplesantly cold or wet weather. *Our boss believes in the inclemency of punishment.*

Inclement/इनक्लेमेंट *(adjective)* – प्रचण्ड unpleasantly cold or wet. *The tourists were not prepared for an inclement weather.*

Inclinable/इन्क्लाइनेबल *(adjective)* – अनुकूल, झुका हुआ favourable disposed towards something. *I am inclinable to get up late in the morning.*

Inclination/इनक्लिनेशन *(noun)* – झुकाव a natural tendency or urge to act or feel in a particular way. an interest in or liking for. *The man in black trousers has inclination to the Carnatic music.*

Incognito/इन्कॉग्निटो *(adjective & avberb)* – गुप्त having one's true identity concealed. *An incognito bar was running under the pretext of hair salon.*

Incognizant/इन्कॉग्निजंट *(adjective)* – अचेत formal lacking knowledge or awareness. *We were surprised to know about his incognizant attitude towards marriage.*

Incohesive/इन्कोहेसिव *(adj)* – असम्बद्ध not cohesive. *The writer took the pain of rewriting the incohesive paragraphs of the book.*

Incombustibility/इनकाम्बस्टिबिलिटि *(noun)* – अदाह्यता that can resist combustion. *While working on experiments ignition temperature, we came to know a lot about the incombustibility of substances.*

Incombustible/इनकाम्बसटिब्ल *(adjective)* – अदाह्य especially of a building material not inflammable. *We are going to make a list of incombustible substances that can be used in kitchen.*

Incomer/इनकमर *(noun)* – प्रवेश करने वाला [chiefly British] a person who has come to live in an area in which they have not grown up. *Many writers came to India as incomers and settled here.*

Incoming/इनकमिंग *(adjective)* – आने वाली in the process of coming in. being received rather than sent. *All his incoming calls were blocked by the authorities.* of an official or administration having just been elected or appointed to succeed another. *The incoming CEO has served the previous company for 15 years.*

Incomings/इनकमिंग्स *(noun)* – आमदनी income, revenue. *You must keep an account of all your incomings and outgoings.*

Incommensurable/इन्कमेंशरेबॅल *(adjective)* – अनियमित परिमाण का not able to be judged or measured by the same standards; having no common standard. *The difference in their experiences makes their performances incommensurable.*

Incommensurate/इन्कमेन्श्यूरेट *(adjective)* – अतुल्य out of keeping or proportion with. *The gravity of the situation is incommensurate with the steps taken by the government.*

Incommutable/इन्कम्म्यूटेबॅल *(adjective)* – अपरिवर्तनीय not capable of being changed or exchanged. *The wide difference in the prices of two books makes them incommutable.*

Incompatibility/इन्कम्पैटिबिलिटि *(noun)*– विभिन्नता *Incompatibility of a couple is the biggest factor responsible for a failed marriage.*

Incompatible/इनकम्पैटिबल *(adjective)* – बेमेल not able to exist or be used together. unable to live together harmoniously. *Their incompatible nature was always the reason behind their clashes.*

Incompetence/इन्काम्पिटन्स *(noun)* – अयोग्यता in ability to do something successfully. *No company is willing to hire a person with incompetence to perform tasks.*

Incomprehension/इन्काप्रिहेंशन *(noun)* – नासमझी failure to understand something. *"Can I know the reason behind your incomprehension of a simple concept?" asked the manager.*

Incomprehensive/इन्काम्प्रिहेन्सिव *(adjective)*– अपूर्ण not dealing with all aspects of something. *The books recommended by teacher are incomprehensive for perfect understanding of the concept.*

Incompressibility/इन्कम्प्रेसिबिलिटि *(noun)* – दबाब रोकने की शक्ति not able to be compressed. *Many uses of rubber are based on its amount of incompressibility.*

Incompressible/इन्कम्प्रेसिबल *(adjective)* – दबाने योग्य not able to be compressed. *The tyres used in vehicles must not be incompressible.*

Incomputable/इन्कमप्यूटेबल *(adjective)* – अगण्य rare unable to be calculated or estimated. *In spite of long hours spent, the problem remained incomputable.*

Inconceivability/इनकन्सिवेबिलिटि *(noun)* – अकल्पनीयता not capable of being grasped mentally. *The complex nature of the machine is the reason behind its inconceivability.*

Incondensable/इनकन्डेसॅबॅल *(adj)* – द्रव से ठोस के रूप में न जमाने योग्य *Despite all efforts, the problem has remained incondensable.*

Incondite/इन्कॉनडाइट *(adj)* – भद्दा *It was the incondite nature of the evidence that right judgment could not be delivered.*

Inconformity/इन्कॉन्फर्मिटी *(noun)v*– असमानता non-compliance with rules, laws regulations. *The new product failed to become popular, thanks to its inconformity to the quality standards.*

Incongruent/इन्कॉन्ग्रूएण्ट *(adjective)* – अयोग्य unsuitable. incongruous. *The two triangles shown in the diagram are incongruent.*

Incongruence/इनकॉन्ग्रूएन्स *(noun)* – विरोध incompatible. *The student was asked to prove the incongruence of the two triangles.*

Inconsequent/इन्कॉसिक्वंट *(adjective)* – अप्रस्तुत not connected or following logically; irrelevant. *The experiments on artificial intelligence remained inconsequent.*

I

Inconsequential/इन्कान्सिक्वेंशिअल *(adjective)* – अयुक्त not important or significant. *It was known from the beginning that the experiments were going to be inconsequential.*

Inconsequently/इनकन्सिक्वेंटली *(adv)* – तर्क–हीन ढंग से lacking consequence. *They continued inconsequently, without bothering about results.*

Inconsiderable/इन्कंसिडरेंबॅल *(adjective)* – कम मूल्य का of small size, amount, or extent. unimportant or insignificant. *There were particles on inconsiderable size present in the atmosphere.*

Inconsonant/इन्कॉन्सनॅन्ट *(adjective)* – बेसुरा rare not in agreement or harmony; not compatible. *As our theories were inconsonant, we could not agree with each other.*

Inconstancy/इन्कांस्टन्सि *(noun)* – चंचलता unfaithfulness by virtue of being unreliable or treacherous. *What bothers man about life is its inconstancy.*

Inconstant/इनकान्स्टंट *(adjective)* – चपल frequently changing; variable or irregular. *He was trying to confuse the jury members by giving inconstant answers.*

Incontaminate/इन्कॉन्टैमिनेट *(verb & noun)* – अदूषित, दूषित नहीं करना *The highest priority in this hotel is to provide incontaminate food.*

Incontestable/इन्कन्टेस्टेबल *(adjective)* – निर्विवाद not able to be disputed. *The authority of the manager in financial matters is incontestable.*

Incontinence/इन्कन्टिनेंस *(noun)* – असंयम lacking self-restraint uncontrolled. *The thing that he lags in is the incontinence of emotions.*

Incontinent/इन्कन्टिनॅन्ट *(adjective)* – असंयत, अपवित्र lacking voluntary control over urination or defection. *The patient had the problem of having incontinent urination.*

Inconvertibility/इन्कवर्टिबिलिटि *(noun)* – न बदलने जाने योग्य स्थिति not able to be changed in form, function. *The first problem that I faced in the foreign country was the inconvertibility of currencies.*

Inconvertible/इन्कन्वर्टबल *(adj)* – अपरिवर्तनीय, न बदलने योग्य used especially of currencies; incapable of being exchanged for or replaced by another currency of equal value. *This is an inconvertible currency.*

Incorrect/इन्करेक्ट *(adj)* – अनुचित, गलत not correct; not in conformity with fact or truth. *Your opinion is incorrect.*

Incorrupt/इन्करप्ट *(adjective)* – पवित्र not having undergone decomposition. *There are only a few countries in the world that can be called incorrupt today.*

Incorruptible/इन्करप्टिबल *(adjective)* – अशोध-नीय not susceptible to corruption, especially by bribery. *The CEO was bragging about the incorruptible nature of his employees.*

Incorruption/इन्करप्शान *(noun)* – शुद्धता incapability of being corrupted. *Today, incorruption is the biggest call of the day.*

Increasing/इन्क्रिजिंग *(adjective)* – बढ़ने वाला becoming bigger in size amount or degree. *The ever increasing population has posed new threats to the society.*

Incredibly/इन्क्रेडिब्ली *(adv)* – अविश्वास से not easy to believe. *The man in the movie was flying at an incredibly high speed.*

Incredulity/इन्क्रेडुलिटी *(noun)* – अविश्वास unable to believe something. *As they saw a giant bird in the sky, their eyes were wide opened with incredulity.*

Incremation/इन्क्रेमेशन *(noun)* – दाह कर्म burning. *With the setting of the sun, the incremation of the lady was over.*

Increment/इन्क्रिमेंट *(noun)* – बढ़ती an increase or addition, especially one of a series on a fixed scale. a regular increase in salary on such a scale. *I am expecting a good increment this year.*

Incrimination/इन्क्रिमिनेशन *(noun)* – अभियोग make someone appear guilty or of wrong-doing. *He did not know how to free her from the incrimination charges.*

Incrust/इन्क्रस्ट *(verb)* – पपड़ी चढ़ाना to cover with a crust, variant spelling of encrust. *The pot was incrusted with a metallic alloy.*

Inculcate/इन्कल्केट *(verb)* – शिक्षा देना To impress upon the mind of another by frequent instruction. *A good teacher inculcates good values in the minds of his students.*

Incubator/इन्क्यूबेटर *(noun)* - अंडे सेने की मशीन an apparatus used to hatch eggs or grow microorganisms under controlled conditions. *During our visit to the laboratory, we were allowed to see incubators.*

Inculpable/इन्कल्पेबल *(adj)* - दोष रहित faultless, unblamable. *The man was declared to be inculpable and was set free.*

Inculpate/इन्कल्पेट *(verb)* - दोष लगाना accuse, blame, or incriminate. *It was not fair to inculpate his colleague without any concrete proof.*

Inculpation/इन्कल्पेशन *(noun)* - निन्दा accuse, blame, incriminate. *His inculpation caused a stir in the film fraternity.*

Inculpatory/इनकल्पटरी *(adjective)* - निन्दासूचक attitude to blame, accuse. *An inculpatory system within the office was hard to bear.*

Incumbent/इन्कम्बेंट *(noun & adj)* - वृत्तिभोगी necessary for as a duty or responsibility. *The help that we were offering them was seen as incumbent on us.*

Incur/इनकर *(verb)* - कष्ट उठाना become subject to as a result of one's actions. *The company incurred huge losses during the last fiscal year.*

Incuriosity/इनक्यूरिऑसिटि *(noun)* - कुतुहल का अभाव not interested in knowing something. *The child's incuriosity to the objects around him worried his parents.*

Incurious/इन्क्यूरिअस *(adjective)* - अनुत्सुक not eager to know something; lacking curiosity. *After observing them for a long time, it was clear that they had incurious minds.*

Incursion/इन्करसन *(noun)* - चढ़ाई an invasion or attack, especially a sudden or brief one. *The kingdom had to face a sudden incursion from the neighbouring state.*

Incurve/इन्कर्व *(verb)* - भीतर मोड़ना curve inwards. *The bottles were incurved to give the desired shapes.*

Incuse/इन्क्यूज *(verb)* - ठप्पा लगाना an impression hammered or stamped on a coin. *All the old coins had incused designs on them.*

Indecent/इन्डीसेन्ट *(adjective)* - अश्लील not conforming with generally accepted standards of behaviour or propriety. *One should not tolerate any indecent behaviour at work place.*

Indecision/इन्डिसिजन् *(noun)* - दुविधा *My sister's indecision delayed her engagement.*

Indecisive/इन्डिसाइसिव *(adjective)* - अनिश्चित not able to make decisions quickly and effectively. *The indecisive Cabinet Ministers could not reach any agreement.*

Indeclinable/इन्डिक्लाइनेबॅल *(adjective)* - अव्यय, अविकारी [grammar] having no inflections. *What we were taught in the class was the perfect example of indeclinable words.*

Indecorous/इन्डेकॉरॅस *(adjective)* - अनुचित not in keeping with good taste and propriety; improper. *She hated indecorous remarks from his senior.*

Indecorum/इन्डिकॉरम *(noun)* - असभ्य व्यवहार failure to conform to good taste, propriety, or etiquette. *The indecorum at the award function raised a few eyebrows.*

Indeed/इनडीड *(avberb)* - सचमुच used to emphasize a statement, description, or response. *He was, indeed, a good friend of mine.*

Indefectible/इन्डिफेक्टिबॅल *(adjective)* - अचूक rare not liable to fail, end, or decay. *The company has guaranteed its products to be indefectible.*

Indefensible/इन्डिफेन्सिबल *(adjective)* - अरक्षणीय not justifiable by argument. *His case was an indefensible case.*

Indefinite/इन्डेफिनिट *(adjective)* - अनिश्चित not clearly expressed or defined; vague. lasting for an unknown or unstated length of time. *The workers have gone on an indefinite strike.*

Indeliberate/इन्डिलिबॅरिट *(adj)* - अविवेचित *What the employees were facing was the indeliberate result of the CEO's new plan.*

Indelibility/इनडेलिबिलिटि *(noun)* - अक्षयता that cannot be removed. *The indelibility of the scars was a source of everlasting torture to her.*

Indelicate/इन्डेलिकेट *(adjective)* - फूहड़ lacking sensitive understanding or tact. *The mother was criticized for her indelicate behaviour towards her children.*

I

I

Indemnification/इन्डेम्निफिकेशन *(noun)* – क्षतिपूर्ति compensate for loss or harm. *The process of indemnification was complete within a week.*

Indemnify/इन्डेम्निफाइ *(verb)* – बदला चुकाना compensate in respect of harm or loss. *Due to the pressure from victim's side, the authorities were forced to indemnify him.*

Indemnity/इन्डेम्निटी *(noun)* – जमानत security or protection against a loss or other financial burden; security against or exemption from legal responsibility for one's actions. *We did not know whether he should be provided with indemnity or not.*

Indenture/इन्डेंचर *(noun)* – इकारनामा A formal agreement, contract, or list, formerly one of which copies with indented edges were made for the contracting parties. *The two parties were given indentures of mutual agreement.*

Independence/इन्डिपेंडेंस *(noun)* – आजादी state of being free. *Some of the African countries got their independence very late.*

Independent/इन्डिपेन्डेन्ट *(adjective)* – स्वाधीन Free from outside control; not subject to another's authority. Self-governing. *The social committee set up last year works as an independent body.*

Indescribable/इन्डिसक्राइबॅबॅल *(adjective)* – अकथनीय too unusual, extreme, or indefinite to be adequately described. *The incident was so shocking that it remains indescribable for me till date.*

Indestructibility/इन्डिस्ट्रक्टिबिलिटि *(noun)*– अविनाशिता not able to be destroyed. *The original theory of the indestructibility of an atom was refuted by the later scientists.*

Indestructible/इन्डिस्ट्रक्टिबल *(adjective)*– अविनाशी not able to be destroyed. *The universe is indestructible.*

Indeterminable/इनडिटरमिनेबल *(adjective)* – अनिर्णय not able to be determined. *The insufficient data could only lead to indeterminable results.*

Indeterminate/इनडिटरमिनेट *(adjective)* – अनिश्चित Not exactly known, established, or defined. Mathematics having no definite or definable value. Medicine from which a diagnosis of the underlying cause cannot be made. *The underlying cause of his cancer remained indeterminate to doctors.*

Indifferent/इन्डिफरेन्ट *(adjective)* – उदासीन having no particular interest or sympathy; unconcerned. *The people at high positions usually have an indifferent attitude to their employees.*

Indigestion/इनडाइजेशन *(noun)* – स्वदेशीय pain or discomfort in the stomach associated with difficulty in digesting food. *I am suffering from indigestion from past several days.*

Indigestive/इनडिजेस्टिव *(adjective)* – अपच difficulty in digesting food. *Cellulose is indigestive to human intestines.*

Indignant/इनडिग्नॅन्ट *(adjective)* – रुष्ट, क्रुद्ध anger or annoyance at something unfair, unfair treatment. *The people were indignant over the killing of a young man.*

Indignation/इन्डिग्नेशन *(noun)* – रोष, क्रोध annoyance provoked by what is perceived as unfair treatment. *The residents showed their indignation over the killing incident.*

Indignity/इनडिग्निटी *(noun)* – अनादर, अपमान treatment or circumstances that cause one to feel shame or to lose one's dignity. *No woman can tolerate any type of indignity meted out to her.*

Indirect/इन्डिरेक्ट *(adjective)* – अप्रत्यक्ष Not direct. Source denoting a free kick from which a goal may not be scored directly. *There is an indirect connection between two power grids.*

Indirection/इन्डिरेक्शन *(noun)* – छलकपट indirect procedure or action. *It was due to his indirection that his team members remained confused.*

Indiscernible/इनडिसर्नॅबॅल *(adjective)* – अगोचर impossible to see or clearly distinguish. *The presence of fog was making the scenery indiscernible.*

Indiscipline/इन्डिस्प्लिन *(noun)* – अनुशासनहीनता lack of discipline. *Principal said, "No kind of indiscipline shall be tolerated within the school premises."*

Indiscrete/इन्डिस्क्रीट *(adjective)* – अभिभक्त rare not divided into distinct parts. *This novel does not have any indiscrete chapters.*

Indiscretion/इन्डिस्क्रेशन *(noun)* – अविचार the trait of being injudicious. *Indiscretion has always been his weakness.*

Indiscriminate/इन्डिस्क्रिमिनेट (adjective) – अव्यवस्थित done or acting at random or without careful judgement. *He is habitual to the indiscriminate use of pills.*

Indispose/इन्डिस्पोज (verb) – विमुख करना [archaic] make unfit for or averse to something. *Negative thinking can indispose a person of his sanity.*

Indisposition/इन्डिस्पोजिशन (noun) – अस्वस्थता, अरुचि a slight illness. *My mother was admitted to hospital when she complained of indisposition.*

Indisputable/इन्डिस्प्युटेबल (adjective) – निर्विवाद unable to be challenged or denied. *He thought that only he was the indisputable heir to the property.*

Indissolubly/इन्डिसोल्यूब्ली (adverb) – अविच्छेद्यता के साथ lasting unable to be destroyed. *The unions worked indissolubly to have their demands met.*

Indistinguishable/इन्डिस्टिंग्विशबॅल (adjective) – पृथक् न किये जाने योग्य not able to be identified as different or distinct. *There are animals that can change their colour to make their skin indistinguishable from their backgrounds.*

Indite/इन्डाइट (verb) – लिखना [archaic] write; compose. *The writer made it a habit to indite daily.*

Indivertible/इन्डायवर्टिबल (adj) – न हटाने योग्य *The heavy weight of the crane was making it almost indivertible.*

Individual/इन्डिविजुअल (adjective) – अकेला Single; separate. *It is not possible to take care of the individual needs of all the employees.*

Individually/इन्डिविड्यूअलि (adverb) – अलग-अलग singly, or by one separately. *The parents were supposed to meet the teachers individually.*

Indivisibility/इन्डिविजिबिलिटि (adjective) – अविभाज्यता unable to be divided or separated. *The indivisibility of atom was refuted by many scientists.*

Indo/इन्डो (combining form) – 'भारतीय' अर्थ का उपसर्ग Indian; Indian and...... indo-Iranian. Relating to India. *The Indo-Aryans came to settle in the country.*

Indocile/इन्डोसाइल (adjective) – अविनीत या अशिक्ष्य difficult to teach or discipline; not submissive. *Her husband's indocile nature caused many problems.*

Indocility/इन्डोसिलिटि (noun) – दुर्गमता difficulty in disciplining. *His indocility was a matter of concern to everyone.*

Indolence/इन्डोलेंस (noun) – सुस्ती laziness avoiding activities. *His mother said, "Your indolence will not take you anywhere."*

Indomitable/इन्डॉमिटेबल (adjective) – दुर्दमनीय impossible to subdue or defeat. *The king fortified his kingdom so well that it became indomitable by other states.*

Indubitable/इन्ड्यूबिटॅबल (adjective) – निश्चित impossible to doubt; unquestionable. *His sincerity towards work is indubitable.*

Induce/इन्ड्युस (verb) – बहकाना Succeed in persuading or leading to do something. *Workers were induced to extend their working hours.*

Induct/इन्डक्ट (verb) – प्रवेश कराना, भर्ती करना Admit formally to a post or organization. Formally introduce into possession of a benefice. US enlist for military service. *After an initial training for six months, the soldiers were finally inducted into the army.*

Inductor/इन्डक्टर (noun) – बिजली के यन्त्र का एक भाग A component in an electric or electronic circuit which possesses inductance. *We were attending a special class on inductors and their properties.*

Indulge/इन्डल्ज (verb) – लगना, प्रसन्न करना Allow oneself to enjoy the pleasure of. Become involved in an activity that is undesirable or disapproved of. *After his exams were over, he indulged himself in partying day and night.*

Indulgence/इन्डल्जेंस (noun) – आसक्ति the action or act of indulging, a thing that is indulged in; a luxury. *His indulgence into the luxuries of life took a toll of his bank balance.*

Indurative/इन्ड्यूरेटिव (adj) – ठोस बनाने वाला tending to harden. *The hot weather made the soil too indurative to plough.*

Industrial/इन्डस्ट्रियल (adjective) – उद्योग-सम्बन्धी of, used in, or characterized by industry. *There are many uses of the industrial oil.*

I

Industrious/इन्डस्ट्रियस *(adjective)* – उद्योगी active, laborious, diligent. *People living in mountainous areas are known to be very industrious.*

Industry/इन्डस्ट्रि *(noun)* – उद्योग, परिश्रम economic activity concerned with the processing of raw materials and manufacture of goods in factories. A particular branch of economic or commercial activity: the tourist industry. *There has been a big boom in fishery industry this year.*

Inebriety/इनीब्राइटि *(noun)* – मतवालापन, मस्ती inflected forms of inebriety. *He was carried to his home in the state of inebriety.*

Inedible/इन्एडिबल *(adjective)* – न खाने योग्य not fit for eating. *Some of the mushrooms are inedible.*

Inedited/इनएडिटेड *(adjective)* – अप्रकाशित, असम्पादित not edited. *The work by me remained inedited for a long time.*

Ineffable/इन्एफ़बल *(adjective)* – अवर्णनीय too great or extreme to be expressed in words: the ineffable natural beauty of the everglades. *We were thrilled to see the ineffable beauty of the nature.*

Ineffably/इन्एफ़ब्लि *(adverb)* – अवर्णनीय रूप में too extreme to describe in words, difficult to utter. *We were ineffably weak to say anything.*

Ineffaceable/इन-इफेसबल *(adjective)* – अमिट unable to be erased or forgotten. *The bad effects of pollution are almost ineffaceable.*

Inefficacious/इनएफिकेशस् *(adjective)* – निरर्थक not producing the desired effect. *The scientists' efforts had become inefficacious at that point of time.*

Inefficacy/इनएफिकॅसि *(noun)* – व्यर्थता not producing desired result. *The inefficacy of the old machines stalled the production rate.*

Inefficiency/इन्-एफिशंशि *(noun)* – अयोग्यता failing to make the best use of resources. *No company wants to hire people carrying inefficiency.*

Inefficient/इन्-एफिशन्ट *(adjective)* – अयोग्य not achieving maximum productivity; failing to make the best use of time or resources. *As the time passed, he came to know that his team is inefficient in delivery desired results.*

Inelastic/इन्-इलैस्टिक *(adjective)* – अनम्य, चीमड़ no elastic. *The spring was stretched so many times that it eventually became inelastic.*

Inelegance/इनएलिगॅन्स *(noun)* – सुन्दरता की कमी lacking refinement, physical grace and elegance. *The tourists were roaming about in a castle that had now acquired inelegance.*

Ineloquent/इनइलोक्वेंट *(noun)* – अवाग्मी not eloquent. *The girl was not happy to find that her groom was ineloquent.*

Ineptly/इनएप्टलि *(adverb)* – मूर्खता से showing no skill. *She handled the situation quiet ineptly.*

Inequality/इनिक्वालिटि *(noun)* – विषमता lack of equality. *During my visit to the foreign country, I noticed the inequality with which poor people were treated.*

Inequitable/इनइक्विटेब्ल *(adjective)* – न्याय विरुद्ध unfair; unjust. *None of us was happy with the inequitable distribution of company's profit.*

Inequity/इनइक्विटी *(noun)* – अन्याय lack of fairness or justice. *As a woman, she had to face the inequity of the justice.*

Inescapable/इनेस्केपेबल *(noun)* – न भागने योग्य unable to be avoided or denied. *The presence of heavy gases was making the balloon inescapable.*

Inessential/इनएसेन्सियल *(adjective)* – अनावश्यक not absolutely necessary. *After having repeated discussions, the topic is now inessential to be discussed again.*

Inestimable/इनएस्टिमॅबॅल *(adjective)* – अमूल्य not able to be measured; very great. *Calculating the exact age of the fossils is an inestimable thing.*

Inevitably/इनएविटब्लि *(adverb)* – अनिवार्य certain to happen. *Their end was inevitably coming.*

Inexact/इनिग्जैक्ट *(adjective)* – अवश्य, अयथार्थ not quite accurate. *The number of coins recovered from the site is still inexact.*

Inexecutable/एनिक्सेक्युटेबल *(adjective)* – जो पूर्ण न किया जा सके a programme not able to be run by computers. *There was a serious glitch that had made the programme inexecutable.*

I

Inexorably/इन्एक्सरब्लि *(adverb)* – कठोरता से impossible to prevent, unrelenting. *Most of the time, things were going on inexorably.*

Inexpectant/एन्-एक्सपेक्टैन्ट *(noun)* – निराश *It was inexpectant that he would arrive at such an odd hour.*

Inexepediency/इनएक्पेडिएन्सी *(noun)* – अयोग्यता unsuitableness. *What we were worried about was the inexpediency of the project.*

Inexpendient/इनएक्पेडिएन्ट *(adjective)* – अनुचित not practical, suitable, or advisable. *The proposal by the committee member seems to be inexpedient.*

Inexplosive/इनएक्सप्लोसिव *(adj)* – न भभकने योग्य not explosive. *It came to light that the material placed in the room was inexplosive.*

Inexpressive/इनएक्सप्रेसिव *(adjective)* – वर्णन न करने योग्य showing no expression. *The model was not fit for acting as she had an inexpressive face.*

Inextricable/इनएक्सट्रिकेबल *(adjective)* – न सुलझाने योग्य impossible to disentangle or separate. *He was trying to separate the inextricable wires.*

Infallible/इन्फैलिबल *(adjective)* – अमोघ incapable of making mistakes or being wrong. *His clever mind makes him an infallible guy.*

Infamize/इनफेमाइज *(verb)* – बदनाम करना to make infamous. *The allegation by the girl was enough to infamize the guy.*

Infamy/इनफेमी *(noun)* – कलंक well knwon for some bad quality. *To avoid facing infamy, he secluded himself from the society.*

Infant/इन्फैंट *(noun)* – शिशु a very young child or baby. *He was still an infant when his mother passed away.*

Infantile/इन्फैंटाइल *(adjective)* – शिशु-सम्बन्धी of or occurring among infants. *The doctor got his specialization in treating infantile diseases.*

Infantry/इन्फैंट्री *(noun)* – पैदल सेना foot soldiers collectively. *A huge infantry was prepared to take part in the war.*

Infeasible/इन्फिजिबल *(adjective)* – दुष्कर inconvenient or impracticable. *Though very useful, his plan seems to be infeasible.*

Infection/इन्फेक्शन *(noun)* – संक्रामक रोग the process of infecting or the state of being infected. *The infection was controlled by administering a set of antibiotics.*

Infelicitous/इन्फिलिसिटस् *(adjective)* – असुखकर liable to be transmitted through the environment. liable to speed infection. *The patients were susceptible to the infectious disease.*

Infelicity/इन्फिलिसिटि *(noun)* – अनुपयुक्तता an act or thing that is inapt or inappropriate, especially a remark or expression. *I had not expected such an infelicity from him.*

Inferable/इन्फरेबल *(adjective)* – तर्कसाध्य, अनुमेय deduce from evidence or reasoning. *The conclusion was inferable from the results of the experiment.*

Inference/इन्फरेंस *(noun)* – निष्कर्ष, अनुमान a conclusion reached on the basis of evidence and reasoning. *After much experimentation, the scientists, finally, reached upon an inference.*

Interiority/इन्फिरिआरिटि *(noun)* – हीनता a feeling of general inadequacy caused by actual or supposed inferiority, marked by aggressive behaviour or withdrawal. *After being rejected by all her friends, her inferiority made her live in reclusion.*

Infernal/इन्फर्नल *(adjective)* – नारकीय of or relating to hell or the underworld. *The place was so bad that it gave us the feeling of an infernal world.*

Inferno/इन्फर्नो *(noun)* – पाताल a large fire that is dangerously out of control. *Before the deadly inferno could be controlled, 5 shops were already gutted in it.*

Infertile/इन्फर्टाइल *(adjective)* – अनुपजाऊ unable to reproduce. *The infertile pigs were sent to the laboratory for some possible treatment.*

Infinite/इन्फिनिट *(adjective)* – अपरिमित limitless in space, extent, or size. very great in amount or degree. *Today, we are going to study about the infinite space that we live in.*

Infinitesimal/इनफिनिटेसिमल *(adjective)* – अतिसूक्ष्म extremely small. *The infinitesimal particles cannot be seen with naked eyes.*

Infinitive/इन्फिनिटिव *(noun)* – अपरिमित the basic form of a very, without an inflection binding it to a particular subject or tense normally occurring in English with the word to, as in to see, to ask. *Tomorrow, the English teacher will take class on infinitive clauses.*

Infinitude/इन्फिनिट्यूड *(noun)* – अपारता limitless. *The space is known for its infinitude.*

Infinity/इन्फिनिटि *(noun)* – अनन्तता the state or quality of being infinite. a very great number or amount. *The amount of food required to feed all the poor in the world amounts to infinity.*

Infirm/इन्फर्म *(adjective)* – दुर्बल not physically strong, especially through age. *With time, a person becomes more and more infirm.*

Infirmity/इन्फर्मिटि *(noun)* – दुर्बलता physical or mental weakness. *In old age, people have to deal with infirmity of their bodies and mind.*

Infix/इन्फिक्स *(verb)* – बैठाना implant or insert firmly in something. *After his fracture, a rod was infixed in his leg.*

Inflammation/इन्फ्लेमेशन *(noun)* – ताप, सूजन a localized physical condition in which part of the body becomes reddened, swollen, hot, and often painful, especially as a reaction to injury or infection. *To reduce the inflammation, he was kept on antibiotics.*

Inflator/इन्फ्लेटर *(noun)* – फुलाने वाला filling with gas or air. *An inflator was used to swell the balloons.*

Inflect/इन्फ्लेक्ट *(verb)* – मोड़ना [grammar] change or be changed by inflection. *The form of the word can be changed by inflecting it with affixes.*

Inflexibility/इन्फ्लेक्सिबिलिटि *(noun)* – कठोरता not able to bend, stiff unwilling to change. *The inflexibility of hours at work place is a cause of concern for many employees.*

Inflexibly/इन्फ्लेक्सिब्ली *(adverb)* – दृढ़ता से not willing to compromise hard. *He is comfortable to work inflexibly.*

Inflict/इन्फ्लिक्ट *(verb)* – दण्ड देना cause something unpleasant or painful to be suffered by someone else. *The criminals inflicted grave injuries to the victim.*

Infliction/इन्फ्लिक्शॅन *(noun)* – दण्ड inflicting painful or unpleasant. *He had no intention to cause infliction of any kind to anyone.*

Inflictor/इन्फ्लिक्टर *(noun)* – दण्ड देने वाला causing pain to some person. *After causing serious injuries to the victim, the inflictors ran away.*

Inflow/इन्फ्लो *(noun)*– भीतर के बहाव the action of flowing or moving in. *Many rivers have an inflow directed from west to east direction.*

Influence/इन्फ्लुअंस *(noun)* – प्रभाव, असर the capacity to have an effect on the character or behaviour of someone or something, or the effect itself. *Teachings of Swami Vivekananda have had a great influence on me.*

Infoliate/इन्फोलिएट *(verb)* – पत्तियों से ढाँकना to cover with leaves. *The area was first covered with soil and then infoliated.*

Inform/इन्फॉर्म *(verb)* – सूचित करना give facts or information to. *Why didn't you inform me about your ill health?*

Informal/इन्फॉर्मल *(adjective)* – अनौपचारिक relaxed and unofficial; not formal. *They decided to meet for an informal meeting.*

Informality/इन्फॉर्मैलिटि *(noun)* – अनौपचारिकता irregularity. *It was good that they gave consent to treat each other with informality.*

Informatory/इन्फॉर्मेटॅरि *adjective)* – सूचना युक्त information. *When everyone was gone, the CEO got engaged in an informatory talk with his manager.*

Infrequency/इन्फ्रिक्वेंसी *(noun)* – अनित्यता the state of being infrequent. *One thing for which he is known is the infrequency with which he comes to college.*

Infrugal/इन्फ्रूगल *(adj)* – अमितव्ययी not frugal. *Man's infrugal ways cost him dear.*

Infuriate/इन्फ्यूरिएट *(verb)* – क्रुद्ध करना make irritated or angry. *He infuriated his senior by being absent from the meeting.*

Infusion/इन्फ्यूजन *(noun)* – काढ़ा a drink, remedy, or extract prepared by infusing. *The hermit gave us an infusion to drink.*

Ingathering/इनगैदरिंग *(noun)* – खलिहान *An ingathering of people had blocked the way.*

Ingenious/इन्जीनिअस् *(adjective)* – विदग्ध, प्रवीण, उम्दा clever, original, and inventive. *His ingenious ways have always surprised us.*

I

Ingenuity/इन्जीन्युइटि *(noun)* – विदग्धता, पटुता the quality of being ingenious. *It is the ingenuity that makes a person stand out from the rest.*

Ingenuous/इन्जेन्युअस *(adjective)* – मायाहीन innocent, artless, and unsuspecting. *The cops were surprised to see how ingenuous the suspect was.*

Ingestion/इन्जेशन *(noun)* – अन्तर्ग्रहण take food, drink into the body. *The ingestion of food takes place in mouth cavity.*

Ingestive/इनजेस्टिव *(adj)* – पेट भरने योग्य taking food or other substance into the body by swallowing or absorbing it. *The ingestive process in plants takes place via roots.*

Ingoing/इनगोइंग *(adjective)* – भीतर प्रवेश करने वाला going towards or into. *The ingoing moth into the hole was injured.*

Ingrain/इनग्रेन *(verb)* – डुबोना, बोरना firmly fix or establish in a person. *The moral values were ingrained in his mind since childhood.*

Ingrained/इनग्रेन्ड *(adjective)* – गहरा, पक्का firmly established. *The ingrained values in a person help in shaping up his personality.*

Ingrate/इनग्रेट *(noun)* – कृतघ्न मनुष्य an ungrateful person. *He, being an ingrate, did not thank me for all the help that I provided.*

Ingredient/इनग्रेडिएण्ट *(noun)* – अंश any of the foods or substances that are combined to make a particular dish. *I used only a few ingredients to prepare the dish.*

Ingress/इनग्रेस *(noun)* – प्रवेश का अधिकार the action or fact or entering or coming in: the sides are sealed against the ingress of water, arrival of the sun, moon, or a planet in a specified constellation or part of the sky. *The prevention of the ingress of the infection into the wound was the main focus of the doctors.*

Ingurgitate/इन्गर्जिटेट *(adjective)* – लालच से भकोसना [poetic/literary] swallow greedily. *His habit to ingurgitate is very bad.*

Inherent/इन्ह़ीअरन्ट *(adjective)* – स्वाभाविक existing in something as a permanent or essential attribute. *There are too many traditions that are inherent in Indian culture.*

Inhospitality/इन्हॉस्पिटलिटि *(noun)* – अनादार difficult and harsh. *His inhospitality irks me.*

Inimical/इनिमिकल *(adjective)* – विरोधी tending to obstruct or harm; hostile. *Why is your behaviour so inimical all the time?*

Inimitable/इनिमिटेबल *(adjective)* – अनुपम impossible to imitate; unique. *The actor is known for his inimitable style.*

Iniquitous/इनिक्विटॅस *(adjective)* – अधर्मी, पापी unfair and morally wrong. *When he could not be successful in other tricks, he turned iniquitous.*

Iniquity/इनिक्विटी *(noun)* – दुराचार injustice or immoral behaviour. *We were not bothered by his iniquity.*

Initiation/इनिसिएशन *(noun)* – दीक्षा संस्कार admitting someone into a society, usually with a ritual. *On the very first day in college, we were called for an initiation session.*

Initiative/इनिसिएटिव *(noun)* – सूत्रपात the ability to initiate. the power or opportunity to act before others do. *Who will take the initiative now?*

Initiatory/इनिसिएटरि *(adjective)* – प्रारम्भिक cause to begin. *The project is still in its initiatory phase.*

Injudicious/इन्जुडिशस् *(adjective)* – विचारशून्य showing poor judgment; unwise. *We were not expecting such an injudicious act from him.*

Injure/इन्ज्योर *(verb)* – हानि पहुँचाना do or undergo physical harm to; wound. *Two people were badly injured in the accident.*

Injurious/इन्जूरिअस् *(adjective)* – हानि कारक causing or likely to cause injury. *Thriving on too much alcohol can be injurious to one's health.*

Injustice/इनजस्टिस *(noun)* – अन्याय lack of justice. *He had no idea how to deal with the injustice meted out to him.*

Inkling/इन्कलिंग *(noun)* – संकेत a slight suspicion; a hint. *I had not the slightest inkling that she would betray me at such an hour.*

Inland/इल्लैंड *(adjective & avberb)* – देश के भीतरी भाग का in or into the interior of a country. *We were thrilled to see a lovely inland there.*

I

Inly/इन्लाइ *(avberb)* – हृदय में [poetic/literary] inwardly. *Her inly feelings had gone strong.*

Inlying/इन्लाइंग *(adjective)* – पड़ा हुआ within or near a centre. *The inlying island was not very large.*

Inmate/इन्मेट *(noun)* – निवासी a person living in an institution such as a prison or hospital. *The inmates in my hospital room became life-long friends.*

Inmost/इनमोस्ट *(adjective)* – अतिप्रिय innermost. *She asked, "What is your inmost desire?"*

Innavigable/इन्नैविगेबल *(adj)* – अनौगम्य The flood in the river makes it innavigable at the time of rainy season.*

Innervate/इनर्वेट *(verb)* – उत्तेजित करना anatomy & zoology supply an organ or other body part with nerves. *The doctors were successful in innervating his legs.*

Innocent/इनोसेंट *(adjective)* – निर्दोष not guilty of a crime or offence. not responsible or directly involved: an innocent bystander. *The lad's innocent behaviour melted down my anger.*

Innocuous/इनोकुअस *(adjective)* – सीधा not harmful or offensive. *His intentions are not as innocuous as it seems.*

Innominate/इन्नामिनेट *(adjective)* – बिना नाम का not named or classified. *I was talking to an innominate man.*

Innovate/इन्नोवेट *(verb)* – नया सम्प्रदाय स्थापित करना make changes in something already existing, as by introducing new methods, ideas, or products. *As the students of mechanical engineering, we were expected to innovate the existing models of machines.*

Innovator/इनोवेटर *(noun)* – नयी रीति चलाने वाला introducer of new methods, ideas, products. *Albert Einstein was one of the best innovators of his times.*

Innumerable/इन्यूमरेबल *(adjective)* – अनगिनत too many to be counted. *I had innumerable berries in my lap.*

Innutrition/इन्यूट्रिशन *(noun)* – पोषण का अभाव lack of nutrition. *The child was suffering from innutrition since his birth.*

Inobservance/इन्अब्ज़र्वेन्स *(noun)* – ध्यानहीनता failure to notice intention. *Can't you mend your inobservance before initiating this project?*

Inodorous/इन्ओडॅरॅस *(adjective)* – गन्धहीन having no smell; odourless. *An inodorous gas present in the mine killed many workers.*

Inofficious/इन्अफिशॅस *(noun)*– अनैतिक contrary to moral duty. *He signed an inofficious will before dying.*

Inoperative/इन्आपरेटिव *(adjective)* – अकार्य-साधक not working or taking effect. *Half of the machines in the mill are inoperative.*

Inopportune/इन्ऑपॉर्ट्यून *(adj)* – कुसमय का occurring at an inconvenient time. *I was irritated by his inopportune arrival to my office.*

Inornate/इन्ऑरनेट *(adj)* – अविस्तृत not elaborate. *The building was an inornate one.*

Inpouring/इन्पोरिंग *(adj)* – भीतर की ओर गिरता हुआ the action of pouring something. *The inpouring water destroyed everything.*

Inquietude/इनक्वाइएट्यूड *(noun)* – बेचैनी, अशान्ति physical or mental unease. *My sister complaintd of inquietude after a hectic day.*

Inquire/इन्क्वायर *(verb)* – पता लगाना another term for enquire. *The police inquired the local residents about the accident.*

Inquiringly/इन्क्वायरिंगली *(adv)* – जाँचते हुए by way of inquiry. *He was asking inquiringly about the whole story.*

Inquisitor/इनक्विजिटर *(noun)* – जाँच करने वाला a person making an inquiry or conducting an inquisition, especially when regarded as harsh or very searching. *Everyone was annoyed by the irrelevant questions asked by the inquisitor.*

Inquisitorial/इनक्विजिटोरियल *(adj)* – तहकीकात सम्बन्धी of or like an inquisitor. *His inquisitorial behaviour irked us too much.*

Inrush/इनरश *(noun)* – भीतर की ओर तीव्र बहाव a sudden inward rush or flow. *The sudden inrush of water in the prison created frenzy everywhere.*

Insalubrity/इन्सैलुब्रिटी *(noun)* – अनारोग्य want of salubrity. *His insalubrity make him leave his job.*

Insanitary/इनसैनिटरी *(adjective)* – अस्वास्थ्यकर so dirty or germ-ridden as to be a danger to health. *Your insanitary habits put me off.*

Insanity/इनसैनिटी *(noun)* – उन्माद mentally ill. *The old man had bouts of insanity all day.*

Insatiable/इनसैटिएबल *(adjective)* – अति लोलुप difficult to satisfy. *I have an insatiable hunger to learn psychiatry.*

Insatiate/इनसैटिएट *(adj)* – असन्तुष्ट रहना never satisfied. *Desires of man can never be satiated.*

Inscribable/इनस्क्राइबेब्ल *(adjective)* – लिखने योग्य write on something as record purpose. *The wooden block is inscribable.*

Inscription/इन्सक्रिप्शन *(noun)* – लेख any character written on a monument. *King Asoka's inscriptions are etched on the pillars erected by him.*

Insectarium/इन्सेक्टेरियम *(noun)* – कीड़े-मकोड़े का पालने का स्थान a place where insects are kept, exhibited, and studied. *It was all fun to visit the insectariums.*

Insecticide/इन्सेक्टिसाइड *(noun)* – कृमिहत्या a substance used for killing insects. *The farmers were using excessive insecticides to prevent their crops from diseases.*

Insectivorous/इन्सेक्टिवॅरॅस *(adjective)* – कीट-भोजी feeding on insects worms etc. *The insectivorous animals play a crucial role in the biological cycle.*

Insectology/इन्सेक्टोलॅजि *(noun)* – कृमिशास्त्र the science of insects. *After passing out from school, she was looking forward to join a course on insectology.*

Insecure/इन्सिक्योर *(adjective)* – असुरक्षित not confident or assured. *We were talking about our insecure futures.*

Insecurity/इन्सिक्योरिटि *(noun)* – संकट uncertainty or anxiety about oneself. *I have no insecurities about my career.*

Inseminate/इन्सेमिनेट *(verb)* – बीजारोपण करना introduce semen into a woman or a female animal. *The goat was inseminated by a group of veterinary doctors.*

Insensate/इन्सेन्सेट *(adjective)* – ज्ञानरहित lacking physical sensation. *The patient's insensate limbs were showing a bit improvement.*

Insensible/इन्सेन्सिबल *(adjective)* – चेतनाहीन without one's mental faculties; unconscious. numb; without feeling. *I met an insensible man on my way to office.*

Insensitive/इन्सेन्सिटिव *(adjective)* – अचेतन showing or feeling no concern for others' feelings. *My senior's insensitive behaviou r towards me outs my mood off.*

Insentient/इन्सेन्श्यन्ट् *(adjective)* – जीवरहित incapable of feeling; inanimate. *The pig's insentient response was a cause of concern.*

Inseverable/इन्सेवरेबल् *(adj)* – अविभेद्य unable to be separated. *The two rocks had penetrated so deeply that they had become inseverable.*

Insheathe/इनशीद् *(verb)* – मियान लगाना to cover with sheath. *The rods were insheathed inside the covering of concrete.*

Inshore/इनशोर *(adjective)* – समुद्र के समीप at sea but close to the shore; operating near the coast: an inshore lifeboat. *In this region, inshore fishing is done on a large scale.*

Insight/इनसाइट *(noun)* – अन्तर्दृष्टि the capacity to gain an accurate and deep intuitive understanding of something, an understanding of this kind. *In order to understand complex human behaviours, we need to develop an insight.*

Insignificance/इन्सिग्नीफिकैन्स *(adj)* – तुच्छता too small or unimportant to be worth consideration. *Let's ignore our insignificant problems as of now.*

Insinuate/इन्सिन्युएट *(verb)* – धीरे-धीरे उसकाना suggest or hint in an indirect and unpleasant way. *The dacoit was insinuated by his master to do the killing.*

Insinuatingly/इनसिन्यूएटिंग्ली *(adv)* – उसकाते हुए *One of my cousins has the habit of talking insinuatingly in order to serve his means.*

Insipient/इनसिपिएण्ट *(noun)* – बुद्धिहीन wanting in sense or wisdom. *He was considered an insipient.*

Insistent/इन्सिस्टेंट *(adj)* – आग्रही, हठी insisting or very demanding. *Her insistent requests to do the appraisal were ignored by the authorities.*

I

Insobriety/इन्सोब्राइटी (noun) – असंयम drunkenness. *It is dangerous to drive while in the state of insobriety.*

Insolate/इन्सोलेट (verb) – धूप में सुखाना to dry in the sun. *During the day time, the damp clothes were insolated to ward off the moisture.*

Insolence/इन्सोलेन्स (noun) – अविनय rude behaviour. *Before I could tolerate more of his insolence, I left my job.*

Insolent/इन्सोलेन्ट (adjective) – ढीठ rude and disrespectful. *Her insolent answers created a bad impression on his seniors.*

Insoluble/इन्सोल्युबल (adjective) – अघुलनशील impossible to solve. *This is one of the insoluble riddles that I have ever come through.*

Insolvable/इन्साल्वेबॅल (adjective) – व्याख्या न करने योग्य insoluble. *The case's complexity has rendered it insolvable.*

Insolvency/इन्साॅल्वन्सि (noun) – दिवाला state of being insolvent. *Even in the state of insolvency, my friend was looking forward to the luxuries of life.*

Insolvent/इन्साॅल्वन्ट (adjective) – दिवालिया unable to pay debts owed. *The extravagancy turned the man into a pathetic insolvent.*

Insomnia/इन्सॉम्निआ (noun) – अनिद्रा habitual sleeplessness. *This girl suffers from insomnia and depression.*

Insomuch/इनसोमॅच (avberb) – यहाँ तक to the extent that. *We are addicted to the social networking sites insomuch that we feel pathetic without them.*

Insouciance/इन्सूस्यॅन्स (noun) – असावधानी the cheerful feeling you have when nothing is troubling you. *Insouciance on part of parents can make their children become detached.*

Inspect/इन्स्पेक्ट (verb) – परीक्षा करना look at closely. examine officially. *The microbiologist inspected the slide carefully.*

Inspection/इन्स्पेक्शन (noun) – निरीक्षण careful examination. *The quality manager was sent on a routine inspection to the godown.*

Inspector/इन्स्पेक्टर (noun) – निरीक्षक an official who ensures that regulations are obeyed. [British] an official who examines bus or train tickets for validity. *An inspector was on duty the day I joined the mill.*

Inspectorial/इन्सपेक्टोरियल (adjective) – निरीक्षक सम्बन्धी having to check compliance. *His inspectorial duties were assigned on the day of his joining.*

Inspirator/इन्स्पिरेटर – प्रेरणा देने वाला, श्वास लेने का यन्त्र *My father has been my greatest inspirator in my life.*

Inspiring/इन्सपायरिंग (adjective) – उत्तेजक having the effect of inspiring someone. *The children were listening to the inspiring stories narrated by their teacher.*

Inspirit/इन्सिपरिट (verb) – साहस देना encourage and enliven. *The saint inspirited our souls.*

Inspissate/इन्सपिसेट (verb) – गाढ़ा करना thicken or congeal. *The sugar solution was inspissated and added to the paste.*

Instability/इनस्टिबिलिटी (noun) – अस्थिरता lack of stability. *The instability of the wooden stand made me fall on the ground.*

Instable/इनस्टेबल (adj) – चंचल *A man with an instable mind was roaming on road.*

Installation/इन्स्टालेशन (noun) – प्रतिस्थापन, अभिषेक the action or process of installing or being installed. *The installation of electric wires took a week.*

Installed/इन्स्टाल्ड – स्थापित past of install. *The electrician said, "I have installed the electric meter."*

Instalment/इन्स्टालमेंट (noun) – किस्त a sum of money due as one of several equal payments for something, spread over an agreed period of time. *We have already paid this month's instalment of house rent.*

Instance/इनस्टांस (noun) – दृष्टान्त an example or single occurrence of something. a particular case. *It was the first instance that a child was presented as a witness to the case.*

Instancy/इन्स्टॅन्सि (noun) – जरूरत [archaic] urgency. *It was due to an instancy at office that we stayed there till midnight.*

Instantly/इन्स्टैन्टलि (adverb) – तुरन्त, तत्काल at once, immediately. *The student replied instantly, "I have completed the project."*

Instate/इन्स्टेट (verb) – स्थापित करना, रखना install or establish. *After intervention of authorities, the peace was instated in our area.*

I

Instead/इन्स्टेड *(avberb)* – बदले में as an alternative or substitute. in place of. *We were hoping promotions; instead, we were given performance bonuses.*

Instinct/इन्स्टिंक्ट *(noun)* – अन्तर्जात प्रवृत्ति an innate pattern of behaviour in animals in response to certain stimuli. a natural or intuitive way of acting or thinking. *To seek the company of others is the human's basic instinct.*

Institutor/इन्स्टिट्यूटर *(noun)* – आरम्भ करने वाला a person who introduces something. *The man in news is the institutor of Nano technology in our company.*

Instructor/इन्सट्रक्टर *(noun)* – अध्यापक, गुरु a teacher. north American a university teacher ranking below assistant professor. *My yoga instructor has left for the U.S.A.*

Instrumentality/इन्स्टिंमेंटैलिटि *(noun)* – कारणत्व the quality of serving as an instrument. *The instrumentality of the protests in amending juvenile law is appreciable.*

Instrumentally/इन्सट्रुमेंटलि *(adverb)* – विधि द्वारा serving as a means of pursuing an aim. *He has contributed instrumentally well for the two parties.*

Instrumentation/इन्सट्रुमेंटेशन *(noun)* – बाजे पर गीत का प्रबन्ध the instruments used in a piece of music. the arrangement of a piece of music for particular instruments. *The instrumentation of all the pieces was yet to be decided.*

Insubstantial/इन्सब्स्टैंशल *(adjective)* – अवास्तविक lacking strength and solidity. imaginary. *This proposal seems to be an insubstantial to our company.*

Insufferable/इन्सफरेबल *(adjective)* – घमण्डी intolerable. unbearably arrogant or conceited. *The man's saga of insufferable tortures moved me a lot.*

Insufficiency/इन्सफिसिएन्सी *(noun)* – कमी the condition of being insufficient. *Many parts of the country still have the insufficiency of food grains.*

Insufflate/इन्सफ्लेट *(verb)* – हवा भरना medicine blow or breathe into or through a body cavity. *An oxygen pump insufflated air into the mouth of the patient.*

Insulting/इन्सल्टिंग *(adjective)* – अपमानकारी disrespectful, abusive. *What an insulting remark he has made!*

Insuperable/इन्सपरेबल *(adjective)* – दुस्तर impossible to overcome. *The insuperable conditions forced us to leave the place.*

Insupportable/इन्सर्पोट्-एबल *(adjective)* – न सहने योग्य unable to be supported or justified. *He was banking on an insupportable theory.*

Insurable/इन्श्योरेबल *(adjective)* – बीमा कराने योग्य compersation in the event of damage or loss. *The house that I purchased recently is insurable.*

Insurant/इन्श्योरेन्ट *(noun)* – जीवन बीमा कराने वाला *All the insurants who had grievances gathered in the compound.*

Insure/इन्श्योर *(verb)* – नाश के निवारण के लिए बीमा करना arrange for compensation in the event of damage to or loss of property, life, or a person, in exchange for regular payments to a company. secure the payment of a sum in this way. protect someone against a possible contingency. *Our company insures employees against the loss of property and life.*

Insurgency/इनसरजेंसी *(noun)* – राजद्रोह a person or group fighting against government. *During insurgency, the government banned the use of social media sites.*

Insuregent/इनसरजेंट *(adjective)* – राजद्रोही rising in active revolt. *The insurgent attacks have turned more violent recently.*

Insurmountable/इनसरमाउंटेबल *(adjective)* – अविजेय too great to be overcome. *We are facing insurmountable problems at our work place.*

Insusceptible/इन्ससेप्टिबल *(adjective)* – विकारहीन not susceptible. *The Principal gave us an unsusceptible proposition.*

Intaglio/इंटैल्यो *(noun)* – नकाशी का काम an incised or engraved design. a gem with an incised design. a printing process in which the type or design is engraved. *What we were looking at were the fascinating designs of intaglios.*

Integral/इन्टिग्रल *(adjective)* – सम्पूर्ण necessary to make a whole complete; fundamental. included as part of a whole. having all the

I

parts necessary to be complete. *Democracy is integral to our nation.*

Integrator/इन्टिग्रेटर *(noun)* – पूरक, समाकलक that which completes. *In our higher classes, we were taught about integrator functions.*

Integrity/इन्टेग्रिटि *(noun)* – स्थिरता the quality of having strong moral principles. *He is truly a man of integrity.*

Intellection/इन्टिलेक्शन *(noun)* – विचारण, बुद्धि व्यापार the action or process of understanding. *The presentation of a concept makes the intellection an easy thing.*

Intellectual/इन्टेलेक्चुअल *(adjective)* – मानसिक बुद्धि सम्बन्धी of, relating to, or appealing to the intellect. having a highly developed intellect. *An interview tests your intellectual abilities along with the others qualities.*

Intellectuality/इन्टेलेक्चुअलिटी *(noun)* – बुद्धिमानी relating to intellect. *His intellectuality was put to test when he was asked to choose between two solutions.*

Intellectually/इन्टेलेक्चुअली *(adv)* – बुद्धिमानी से possessing a developed intellect. *If it is to be chosen intellectually, my vote would go to my reporting manager.*

Intelligibility/इन्टेलिजिबिलिटी *(noun)*– चतुराई the quality of being intelligible. *There are times where your intelligibility is put to test.*

Intemperance/इन्टेम्परैंस *(noun)* – असंयम lack of restraint excessive indulgence. *His intemperance to boozing has been his biggest weakness.*

Intend/इन्टेन्ड *(verb)* – इरादा करना have as one's aim or plan. plan that something should be or act as something. plan that speech should have a particular meaning. *My sister intends to clear IAS examination this year.*

Intendment/इन्टेन्डमेंट *(noun)* – अभिप्राय law the sense in which the law understands something. *The intendment of the new law was to benefit all the citizens.*

Intensity/इन्टेन्सिटी *(noun)* – तीव्रता the quality of being intense. *The rainfall's intensity has decreased over the years.*

Intensive/इन्टेन्सिव *(adjective)* – गहन, बलदायक very through or vigorous. *An intensive regime was suggested to him by his trainers.*

Intention/इन्टेन्शन *(noun)* – आशय an aim or plan. the action or fact of intending. a person's, especially a man's designs in respect to marriage. *He had no intention of marrying her.*

Intentional/इन्टेंशनल *(adjective)* – इच्छानुरूप deliberate. *All his flattering was intentional.*

Intently/इन्टेन्टलि *(adverb)* – निष्ठापूर्वक with eager attention. *We were listening to our teacher intently.*

Inter/इन्टर *(verb)* – गाड़ना place a corpse in a grave or tomb. *After all the rituals were over, he was interred.*

Interblend/इन्टर्ब्लेंड *(verb)* – परस्पर मिलाना *The painter interblended the four colours to form a unique shade.*

Interbreed/इन्टर्ब्रीड *(verb)* – भिन्न जातियों के पशु का जोड़ा मिलाना breed or cause to breed with an animal of a different race or species. *The scientists have been successful in interbreeding of species.*

Intercept/इन्टर्सेप्ट *(verb)* – अवरोध करना obstruct and prevent from continuing to a destination. *The criminals were intercepted to enter the office.*

Interception/इन्टर्सेप्शन *(noun)* – अवरोधन obstruct to prevent something from going further. *The interception of phone calls was initiated today.*

Interceptive/इन्टर्सेप्टिव *(noun)* – विघ्नकारक the system to prevent something from reacting destination. *The interceptive phone calls were the only way cops could reach him.*

Interchange/इन्टर्चेंज *(verb)* – परस्पर बदलना exchange with each other. put each of in the other's place. *Soon after the teacher ordered, the two friends interchanged their seats.*

Intercolonial/इन्टर्कलोनिअल् *(adjective)* – भिन्न प्रदेशों में रहने वाला existing or conducted between colonies. *With intercolonial discussions going on, people had to just wait and watch.*

Intercommunion/इन्टर्कम्यूनियन *(noun)* – आपस का मेल participation in holy communion by members of different denominations. *The discussions were going on to decide the place for the holy intercommunion.*

Intercourse/इन्टर्कोर्स *(noun)* – बीच में होने वाली घटना, कामक्रीड़ा communication or dealings between people. *It was at the end of the intercourse that the final decision was taken place.*

Intercurrence/इन्टर्करेंस *(noun)* – बीच में होने वाली घटना an intervening event. *The intercurrence of the events was a regular thing in that area.*

Intercurrent/इन्टर्करेन्ट *(adjective)* – रुक-रुक कर होने वाली medicine occurring during the progress of another. *The doctors were worried about the intercurrent disease that too had developed in her body.*

Interdependent/इन्टर्डिपेंडेन्ट *(adj)* – परस्पर आश्रयभूत होना mutually dependent. *It took a while for us to understand that the two factors were interdependent.*

Interdiction/इन्टर्डिक्सन *(noun)* – अवरोध a court order prohibiting a party from doing a certain activity. *The court ordered for the interdiction of illicit drugs.*

Interdictory/इन्टर्डिक्टरी *(adjective)* – निषेध करने वाला court order preventing someone from doing something. *The interdictory order prevented them from participating in future sacraments.*

Interested/इन्टरेस्टेड *(adj)* – दिलचस्पी लेने वाला having or showing interest; especially curiosity or fascination or concern. *Are you still interested in this work?*

Interesting/इन्टरेस्टिंग *(adjective)* – रुचिकर arousing curiosity or interest. *The movie was an interesting combination of action and comedy.*

Interference/इन्टरफिअरेंस *(noun)* – विघ्न the action of interfering or process of being interfered with. *His constant interference in my matters always puts me off.*

Interferer/इन्टरफिअरर *(noun)* – बाधा डालने वाला, दखल देने वाला come between so as to be hindrance or obstacle. *What an interferer he is!*

Interfering/इन्टरफिअरिंग *(adj)* – टाँग अड़ाने वाला intrusive in a meddling or offensive manner. *I don't like her because she is an interfering busy body.*

Interfluent/इन्टर्फ्लुएन्ट *(adj)* – मध्यस्रावी flowing into each other. *The directions in which the two rivers flow eventually makes them interfluent.*

Interfuse/इन्टफ्यूज *(verb)* – परस्पर मिलाना [poetic/literary] join or mix together. *The writer interfused his two articles.*

Intergrowth/इन्टर्ग्रोथ *(noun)* – एक साथ उत्पत्ति growing together, a thing produced by intergrowth in rocks. *The microbiologist noticed a green intergrowth in the algae.*

Interim/इन्टरिम *(noun)* – बीच का समय the intervene time. *Today, the interim budget was presented in the parliament.*

Interior/इन्टिरिअर *(adjective)* – भीतरी situated within or inside; inner. chiefly technical situated further in or within. *A lovely interior made me buy this house.*

Interjacent/इन्टर्जेसेंट *(adj)* – बिचला *The Interjacent Island was a place worth seeing.*

Interject/इन्टर्जेक्ट *(verb)* – बीच में टोकना, बोलना say abruptly, especially as an interruption. *The man interjected and stopped us from any further discussion.*

Interjection/इन्टर्जेक्शन *(noun)* – विस्मयादिबोधक शब्द an exclamation, especially as a part of speech. *Lately, I am working on interjections.*

Interjectional/इन्टर्जेक्शनल *(adj)* – उद्गार सम्बन्धी an abrupt remark, especially as an interruption. *I was asked by my teacher to avoid using too much of interjectional words.*

Interlinear/इन्टर्लिनिअर *(adjective)* – पंक्तियों के बीच में लिखा हुआ written between the lines of a text. *Look at the interlinear sentences and try to understand their relation to the text.*

Interlink/इन्टर्लिंक *(verb)* – कड़ियों से जोड़ना join or connect together. *The mechanic interlinked a series of small chains to form a long one.*

Interlocution/इन्टर्लोक्यूशन *(noun)* – वार्तालाप, संवाद a person who takes part in conversation interlocution of a person is required when two people not knowing each other's language talk. *The land is an interlocution between the two islands.*

Intermeddle/इन्टरमेडल *(verb)* – हस्तक्षेप करना interfere in other's matters. *One of the worst habits that one can have is to intermeddle.*

Intermediate/इन्टरमीडिएट *(adjective)* – बिचवई coming between two things in time, place, character, etc. *The best option was to stop at some intermediate place before travelling any further.*

Intermediation/इन्टरमेडिएशन *(noun)* – मध्यस्थता the act of intervening for the purpose of bringing about a settlement. *It was his maturity and experience that he was chosen for intermediation.*

Interment/इन्टरमेन्ट *(noun)* – मुर्दा गाड़ना the burial of a corpse in a grave or tomb. *As the king reached there, the interment had already taken place.*

Intermigration/इन्टरमाइग्रेशन *(noun)* – दो प्रदेशों के निवासी का स्थान परिवर्तन *An intermigration of the tribes resulted in mixing of their cultures.*

Intermingle/इन्टरमिंगल *(verb)* – मिलाना mix or mingle together. *As time passed on, the cultures intermingled and exchanged their traditions.*

Intermission/इन्टरमिशन *(noun)* – रुकावट a pause or break. an interval between parts of a play or film. *During the intermission, my friend went out for ordering some food for us.*

Intermittence/इन्टरमिटेंस – अंतर्विराम the quality of being intermittent; subject to interruption or periodic stopping. *What bothers them is the intermittence of the money inflow.*

Intermittent/इन्टरमिटेंट *(adjective)* – सविराम या अँतरिया occurring at irregular intervals. *The intermittent flow of money does not allow him to be extravagant.*

Intermix/इन्टरमिक्स *(verb)* – आपस में मिलना या मिलाना mix together. *All the pastes were intermixed in a bowl.*

Intern/इन्टर्न *(noun)* – अंतरंग डाक्टर [chiefly north American] a recent medical graduate receiving supervised training in a hospital and acting as an assistant physician or surgeon. a student or trainee who does a job to gain work experience or for a qualification. *I am looking for a company where I can get training as an intern.*

Internee/इन्टर्नि *(noun)* – नजरबन्द a person who is interned. *Every internee was ready for his portfolio.*

Internment/इन्टर्नमेंट *(noun)* – सीमित स्थान में नजरबन्दी confinement during wartime. *After finishing my internment, I am planning to settle abroad.*

Internal/इन्टर्नल *(adjective)* – आन्तरिक of or situated on the inside. inside the body. existing within an organization. relating to affairs and activities within a country. *The internal affairs of the company are to be kept secret.*

International/इन्टरनैशनल *(adjective)* – अन्तर्राष्ट्रीय existing or occurring between nations. agreed on by all or many nations used by people of many nations. *The United Nations works at an international level.*

Internationalize/इन्टरनैशनलाइज *(verb)* – अन्तर्राष्ट्रीय बनाना make international. *There was no need to internationalize this news.*

Internecine/इन्टर्नीसाइन *(adjective)* – परस्पर विनाशकारी destructive to both sides in a conflict. of or relating to conflict within a group. *For years, the countries were part of internecine wars.*

Interosculate/इन्टरआस्क्यूलेट *(verb)* – परस्पर मेल कराना to intermingle. *The biologists have made extensive researches to understand why many plants interosculate.*

Interplace/इन्टरप्लेस *(verb)* – बीच में रखना to place between. *A table was interplaced between two beds.*

Interplay/इन्टरप्ले *(noun)* – दो पदार्थों की पारस्परिक क्रिया the way in which two or more things affect each other. *I am trying to understand the interplay of the musical instruments.*

Interposition/इन्टरपोजिशन *(noun)* – व्यवधान the action of interjecting or interposing an action or remark that interrupts. *Doctors are working on the interposition of a chip between two valves.*

Interpret/इन्टरप्रेट *(verb)* – मतलब बताना explain the meaning of words, actions, etc. translate orally the words of a person speaking a different language. *What he interpreted was not very correct.*

I

Interpretation/इंटर्प्रिटेशन *(noun)* – व्याख्या the act of interpreting. *I am in need of an interpretation of this page.*

Interpreter/इंटर्प्रेटर *(noun)* – व्याख्या करने वाला a person who interprets foreign speech orally. *An interpreter was hired to translate from German into English.*

Interpretress/इंटर्प्रेटेश – व्याख्या करने वाली स्त्री a lady interpreter. *She is an interpretess of German to English.*

Interregnum/इंटर्रेग्नम *(noun)* – राज्य का राजा से खाली रहने का काल a period when normal government is suspended, especially between successive reigns or regimes. *The news about an interregnum in the state was no surprise to me.*

Interrelation/इंटर्रिलेशन – पारस्परिक सम्बन्ध mutual or reciprocal relation or relatedness. *What is the interrelation between two concepts?*

Interrogate/इन्टरॉगेट *(adjective)* – प्रश्न करना having the force of a question. [grammar] used in questions, contrasted with affirmative and negative. *The teacher asked us to frame an interrogative sentence.*

Interrogative/इन्टरॉगेटिव *(adj)* – प्रश्नार्थक relating to verbs in the so-called interrogative mood. *It is your interrogative gesture/remark.*

Interrupt/इन्टरप्ट *(verb)* – रोकना stop the continuous progress of. stop person who is speaking by saying or doing something. *The way he was interrupting us again and again forced us to send him away.*

Interrupted/इन्टरप्टेड *(adj)* – रुका हुआ discontinued temporarily. *The execution of the programme got interrupted due to a wrong instruction.*

Interrupter/इन्टरप्टर *(noun)* – विघ्न डालने वाला a person or thing that interrupts. *I had to act as an interrupter to stop their argument.*

Interruption/इन्टरप्शन *(noun)* – अवरोध an act of delaying or interrupting the continuity. *The regular interruption of the programme has spoiled my mood.*

Interruptive/इन्टरप्टिव *(adjective)* – विघ्न कारक the action of braking the continuity. *The interruptive ways of the person cost him dear.*

Intersect/इंटर्सेक्ट *(verb)* – दो टुकड़े करना divide by passing or laying across it. cross or cut each other. *A pole was erected at the place where the roads intersected each other.*

Intersection/इंटरसेक्शन *(noun)* – कटाव a point or line common to lines or surfaces that intersect, a point at which two or more things, especially roads, interacts. *Just reach the intersection and turn left.*

Interspersion/इन्टरस्पर्सन *(noun)* – छितराने का कार्य the act of combining one thing at intervals among other things. *The farmer was busy doing interspersion of the seeds in his fields.*

Interstice/इंटरस्टिस् *(noun)* – छिद्र a small intervening space. *The dust particles were passing easily through the interstice in door.*

Interstitial/इंटॅस्टिशॅल *(adjective)* – बीच का of, forming, or occupying interstices. *The interstitial space was allowing the sun rays to enter the room.*

Intertwine/इंटरवाइन *(verb)* – उलझना twist or twine together. *As I visited the garden again, I saw that the two branches had intertwined.*

Intertval/इन्टरवल *(noun)* – अवकाश an intervening time or space. *We used to chat a lot during interval time.*

Intervene/इन्टर्वीन् *(verb)* – विघ्न करना come between so as to prevent or later something. occur as a delay or obstacle to something being done. interrupt. *Please don't intervene in my personal affair.*

Intervener/इन्टर्वीनर *(noun)* – बाधा डालने वाला, हस्तक्षेप करना get involved, so as to alter or hinder an action, or through force or threat of force. *Despite his lack of experience, he was chosen as the intervener to settle matters.*

Intervening/इंटर्वीनिंग *(adj)* – मध्यवर्ती occurring or falling between events or points in time. *In the intervening months to come, she decided to join a linguistic course.*

Intervention/इंटर्वेन्शन *(noun)* – बिचवई the action or process of intervening. interference by a state in another's affairs. *In spite of the intervention by a third country, the two nations kept on fighting.*

Interview/इन्टरव्यू *(noun)* – साक्षात्कार a conversation between a journalist or broadcaster and a person of public interest. *The interview of the minister continued for two hours.*

Intervolve/इन्टर्वॉल्व – एक में दूसरा लपेटना to roll up with each other. *The mechanic intervolved two coils.*

Interweave/इन्टर्वीव *(verb)* – मिलाना, जोड़ना weave or become woven together. *The old lady was interweaving threads of three different colours.*

Intestate/इन्टेस्टेट *(adjective)* – जिसने इच्छापत्र न लिखा हो not having made a will before one dies. *The intestate case is still under discussion.*

Intimate/इन्टिमेट *(adjective)* – आत्मीय closely acquainted; familiar. having an [informal] friendly atmosphere. *An intimate atmosphere was created to welcome the guests at party.*

Intimate/इन्टिमेट *(verb)* – सूचना देना to inform. *I have already intimated him but he did not care.*

Intimation/इन्टिमेशन – सूचना an indirect suggestion. *Could you give me an intimation of how to solve the problem?*

Intimidate/इन्टिमिडेट *(verb)* – डराना frighten or overawe. *His terrible mask was intimidating every one.*

Into/इन्टू *(preposition)* – भीतर expressing motion or direction to a point on or within. *His entry into the room was prohibited.*

Intolerable/इन्टॉलरेबल *(adjective)* – न सहने योग्य unable to be endured. *Every time I meet her, she shows an intolerable behaviour.*

Intolerance/इन्टॉलरन्स *(noun)* – असहिष्णुता unwillingness to accept views beliefs opinion behaviour. *The two countries are trying to lessen the intolerance to each other.*

Intolerant/इन्टॉलरन्ट *(adjective)* – असहनशील not tolerant. *My uncle's intolerant behaviour keeps everyone annoyed.*

Intoleration/इन्टालरेशन *(noun)* – असहनशीलता *Too much of an intoleration is not good for anyone.*

Intomb/इन्टूम *(verb)* – कब्र में गाड़ना to deposit in a tomb. *Her body was intombed in the castle itself.*

Intoxicant/इन्टाक्सिकॅन्ट *(noun)* – मादक an intoxicating substance. *He used to stupefy his victims by using intoxicants.*

Intoxicate/इन्टॉक्सिकेट *(verb)* – मतवाला करना cause to lose control of their faculties. *He gas intoxicated the girl and she fell on ground.*

Intractable/इन्ट्रैक्टेबल *(adjective)* – हठीला, उद्धत hard to control or deal with. stubborn. *That person is ill-famed for his intractable behaviour.*

Intransient/इन्ट्रान्जिएन्ट *(noun)* – स्थिर *The final compound formed after this process is intransient.*

Intrant/इन्ट्रैन्ट *(noun)* – सभा में प्रवेश करने वाला one who enters a college or assembly etc. *Everyone was looking at the intrant.*

Intricacy/इन्ट्रिकेसि *(noun)* – गहनता the quality of being intricate. *The intricacy of the life cycle makes it more beautiful.*

Introduction/इन्ट्रॅडक्शन *(noun)* – परिचय the action of introducing or being introduced. a thing, such as a product, plant, etc., newly brought in. *With the introduction of new species, scientists are hoping to raise the production.*

Introductive/इन्ट्रॅडक्टिव *(adj)* – प्राथमिक introductory. *The first session was only introductive.*

Introspection/इन्ट्रॉस्पेक्शन *(noun)* – अन्तरावलोकन the examination of one's own thoughts or feelings. *We should spare a little time to do introspection.*

Introspective/इन्ट्रॉस्पेक्टिव *(adj)* – आत्मविचार-सम्बन्धी given to examining own sensory and perceptual experiences. *He was good at explaining the introspective concepts.*

Introversion/इन्ट्रोवर्शन *(noun)* – अन्तर्मुखता the condition of being folded inward or sheathed. *My master took the task of my introversion in his hands.*

Introvert/इन्ट्रोवर्ट *(noun* – अन्तर्मुखी a shy, reticent person. psychology a person predominantly concerned with their own thoughts and feelings rather than with external things. Compare with extrovert. *I am quiet introvert by nature.*

Intrude/इन्ट्रूड *(verb)* – टूट पड़ना come into a place or situation where one is unwelcome or uninvited. introduce into or enter with adverse effect. *The thief intruded the house at midnight.*

Intrusion/इन्ट्रूजन *(noun)* – बिना आज्ञा प्रवेश the action of intruding. a thing that intrudes. *The intrusion of the army can take place at any time.*

Intrusive/इन्ट्रूसिव *(adjective)* – बिना अधिकार के प्रवेश करने वाला intruding or tending to intrude. *He is known to be intrusive by nature.*

Intuition/इन्ट्युइशन *(noun)* – सहजज्ञान the ability to understand something immediately, without the need for conscious reasoning. *Recently , I have developed an intuition that our neighbours will leave their place.*

Intuitive/इन्ट्युटिव *(adjective)* – अन्तर्ज्ञान से प्राप्त instinctive. *In many people, intuitive abilities are well formed.*

Intumesce/इन्ट्युमेस *(verb)* – फूल जाना rare swell up. *The raisins intumesced after they were placed in water.*

Intwist/इन्ट्विस्ट *(verb)* – मिलाकर बुनना He took two strings and intwisted them.

Inumbrate/इनम्ब्रेट *(verb)*– छाया डालना *The painter inumbrated the portion below eyes in the portrait of a lady.*

Inunction/इनन्क्शन *(noun)* – मालिश करना chiefly medicine the rubbing of ointment or oil into the skin. *It was due to inunction that the burned part did not swell too much.*

Inundate/इनन्डेट *(verb)* – जलमग्न कर देना fill quickly beyond capacity; as with a liquid. *During rainy season, all the rivers got inundated.*

Inurbane/इनअरबेन *(noun)* – असभ्य rough. *The new fellow from the countryside is inurbane in his manners.*

Inutile/इन्यूटिल *(adj)* – व्यर्थ not worth using. *The mixer at home has become inutile.*

Invade/इन्वेड *(verb)*– चढ़ाई करना enter as or with an army so as to subjugate or occupy it. enter in large numbers, especially intrusively. attack and spread into an organism or bodily part. *When the neighbouring country invaded, our soldiers fought back with bravery.*

Invader/इन्वेडर *(noun)* – आक्रमण करने वाला someone who enters by force in order to conquer. *A bunch of invaders attacked from the North-West frontier.*

Invaginate/इन्वैजिनेट *(verb)* – अन्तर्वलित करना turned inside out or folded back to form a cavity. *The secret letter was invaginated in a box.*

Invalid/इन्वैलिड *(noun)* – बलहीन a person made weak of disabled by illness or injury. *In spite of breaking his legs, he does not consider himself an invalid.*

Invalidate/इन्वैलिडेट *(verb)* – दुर्बल करना deprive make or prove an argument. *His license was invalidated by the company.*

Invalidation/इन्वैलिडेशन *(noun)* – रोगी होने से नौकरी के अयोग्य करने का कार्य prove erroneous, deprive of legal validity. *The process of invalidation took only a week.*

Invaluable/इन्वैल्यूअॅबॅल *(adjective)* – बहुमूल्य extremely useful. *I have a box of invaluable jewellery that was gifted to me by my mother.*

Invar/इन्वार *(noun)* – फौलाद और गिलट की मिश्र धातु trademark an alloy of iron and nickel with a negligible coefficient of expansion. *Invar is an alloy of iron and nickel.*

Invariable/इन्वरिएबल *(adj)* – सदा एक-सा, अचल not liable to or capable of change. *There are both variable and invariable quantities in Physics.*

Invasion/इन्वेजन *(noun)* – चढ़ाई an instance of invading. the action or process of being invaded. *Our country is ready to face any type of invasion.*

Invasive/इन्वेसिव *(adjective)* – चढ़ाई करने वाला tending to invade or intrude. involving the introduction of instruments or other objects into the body or body cavities. *The invasive intentions of the neighbouring country are well known.*

Invective/इन्वेक्टिव *(noun)* – निन्दा strongly abusive or critical language. *I want to avoid his invective talks.*

Inveigle/इन्वेग्ल *(verb)* – ललचाना persuade by deception or flattery. *She was able to easily inveigle men.*

I

Invent/इन्वेंट *(verb)* – आविष्कार करना create or design a new device, process, etc. make up especially as to deceive. *Alva Edison invented electric bulb.*

Inventive/इन्वेंटिव *(adjective)* – आविष्कार करने योग्य having or showing creativity or original thought. *With an inventive brain like him, no one could think of winning the competition.*

Inventor/इन्वेंटर *(noun)* – अविष्कारक one who invents. *Our country has produced many a great inventors.*

Inventory/इन्वेंटरी *(noun)* – चल सम्पत्ति की विवरण सहित सूची a complete list of items such as goods in stock or the contents of a building. a quantity of goods in stock. the entire stock of a business, including materials and finished product. *I was asked to prepare an inventory of the things to be used in shopping.*

Inveracy/इन्विरैसिटि *(noun)* – असत्य untruthfulness lie. *I am fed up of his inveracity.*

Inverse/इन्वर्स *(adjective)* – उलटा opposite in position, direction, order, or effect. *A ball from inverse direction was about to collide with another ball.*

Inversion/इन्वर्सन *(noun)* – उलट-पुलट the action of inverting or the state of being inverted. reversal of the normal order of words, typically for rhetorical effect. music an inverted interval, chord, or phrase. *The inversion can change the state of an object.*

Invert/इन्वर्ट *(verb)* – उलटना, उलटाना to turn upside down. *Please invert this tin full of mustart oil.*

Investigate/इन्वेस्टिगेट *(verb)* – अनुसंधान करना carry out a systematic or formal inquiry into so as to establish the truth. carry out research into a subject. make a search or systematic inquiry. *A private agency has been investigating the case since last one year.*

Investigation/इन्वेस्टिगेशन *(noun)* – अनुसंधान an inquiry into unfamiliar or questionable activities. *As long as investigation is going on, media is prohibited from interfering into the matters.*

Investiture/इन्वेस्टिचर *(noun)* – प्रतिष्ठापन the action of formally investing a person with honours or rank. a ceremony at which this takes place. *The man was standing tall when his investiture going on.*

Investor/इन्वेस्टर *(noun)* – धन लगाने वाला a person or body that puts in money somewhere for profit. *The builder has invited many investors for his new project.*

Inveterate/इन्वेटिरेट *(adjective)* – हठी having a long-standing and firmly established habit or activity. firmly established. *No one is able to change his inveterate truthfulness.*

Invigilate/इन्विजिलेट *(verb)* – परीक्षा में विद्यार्थियों का निरीक्षण करना [British] supervise candidates during an examination. *In spite of the invigilation going on, students were copying from one another.*

Inviolate/इन्वॉअलेट *(adjective)* – पवित्र free from injury or violation. *No one has the guts to disturb his inviolate state of mind.*

Invisible/इन्विजिबल *(adjective)* – अदृश्य unable to be seen, either by nature or because concealed. treated as if unable to be seen; ignored. *An invisible gas was present in the mines.*

Invitation/इनविटेशन *(noun)* – बुलावा a written or verbal request inviting someone to go somewhere or to do something. the action of inviting. *When I rejected his invitation, he got very angry.*

Invitatory/इनविटेटॉरि *(adj)* – न्योता सम्बन्धी conveying an invitation. *He sent me an invitatory message in mail.*

Invocate/इन्वोकेट *(verb)* – स्तोत्र रूप से प्रार्थना करना to invoke in prayer. *She invocated evil spires.*

Involuntarily/इन्वॉलन्टरिलि *(adv)* – अनिच्छा से against your will. *They had, involuntarily, saved the boy's life.*

Involuntary/इन्वॉलन्टरि *(adjective)* – इच्छारहित done without conscious control. concerned in bodily processes that are not under the control of the will. *We have no control over the involuntary actions of some of our organs.*

Involution/इन्वॅल्यूशॅन *(noun)* – पेचीदगी physiology the shrinkage of an organ in old age or when inactive. *As a man grows old, involution of his organs starts taking place.*

Invulnerable/इन्वॅलनॅरेबॅल *(adjective)* – अमोघ impossible to harm or damage. *No one can disturb his invulnerable state of mind.*

Inwards/इन्वार्ड्स *(avberb)* – आन्तरिक towards the inside. into or towards the mind, spirit, or soul. *As he used to practise meditation, his thought process was more inclined inwards.*

Inweave/इन्वीव *(verb)* – ऐंठना weave together into a fabric or design. *The workers at textile mill were inweaving the threads.*

Inwork/इन्वर्क *(verb)* – भीतरी काम करना to work within. *The company want employees who can inwork.*

Inwrap/इन्राप *(verb)* – समाप्त करना [archaic] spelling of enwrap. *I am about to inwrap this work.*

Iodine/आइअडीन *(noun)* – औषधि में प्रयुक्त एक अँग्रेजी अधातु तत्व the chemical element of atomic number 53, a halogen forming black crystals and a violet vapour. an antiseptic solution of this in alcohol. *Doctors advise to apply iodine solution over infections.*

Ion/आइअन (आयॅन्) *(noun)* – आयन, विद्युतशक्ति उत्पन्न करने वाला परमाणु an atom or molecule with a net electric charge through loss or gain of electrons, either positive or negative. *Exchange of ions takes place in a chemical reaction.*

Irascible/इरैसिबल *(adjective)* – उत्तेजक hot-tempered; irritable. *People with irascible nature find it hard to work with colleagues.*

Ireful/आयरफुल *(adj)* – क्रोधी feeling or showing extreme anger. *I am not going to bear his ireful attitude all the time.*

Irefully/आयरफुली *(adv)* – रोष से in an angry manner. *He always behaves irefully.*

Iridescent/आयरिडिसेंट *(adjective)* – रंग बदलने वाला showing luminous colours that seem to change when seen from different angles. *The party hall was glowing with iridescent lights.*

Iris/आयरिश *(noun)* – इन्द्रधनुष a flat, coloured, ring-shaped membrane behind the cornea of the eye, with an adjustable circular opening in the centre. *Iris is an important of our eyes.*

Irksome/अर्कसम *(adj)* – दुःखदायी so lacking in interest as to cause mental weariness. *He was making irksome remarks on the fellow passengers.*

Iron/आयरन *(noun)* – लोहा a strong, hard magnetic silvery-grey metal, the chemical element of atomic number 26, used in construction and manufacturing. *Iron vessels are still used for cooking in our country.*

Irradiate/इरैडिएट *(verb)* – चमकना expose to radiation. *Some of the cancers are treated using irradiation.*

Irradiation/इरैडिएशन *(noun)* – प्रदीपन, किरणन the process or fact of irradiating or being irradiated. *The cancer patient was exposed to irradiation.*

Irradicate/इरैडिकेट *(verb)* – बोना, छितराना expose to radiation. *The seeds were irradicated into the soil.*

Irrational/इरैशनल *(adjective)* –अविवेकी not logical or reasonable. *We need to shed our irrational attitude in order to make progress.*

Irreclaimable/इरिक्लेमेबल *(adjective)* – अनुद्धार्य not able to be reclaimed. *They were shocked to learn that their money was irreclaimable.*

Irrecognizable/इरेकॅग्नाइजेबॅल *(adj)* – अनभिज्ञेय that connot be recojnised. *He had changed so much that his face was simply irrecognizable to us.*

Irreconcsilable/इरेकॅन्साइलेबॅल *(adj)* – अशाम्य incompatible. *He knew from the very beginning that his nature was irreconcilable with his wife.*

Irrecoverable/इरिकॅवरेबॅल *(adj)* – अपूरणीय not able to be recovered or remedied. *My mother was suffering from an irrecoverable disease.*

Irredeemable/इरिडीमेबॅल *(adjective)* – कभी न सुधर सकने योग्य not able to be saved, improved, or corrected. *The accident has given him irredeemable injuries.*

Irreducible/इरिड्यूसिबल *(adjective)* – अखंडनीय, अपरिवर्तनीय not able to be reduced or simplified. *This complex theorem is irreducible.*

Irrefutable/इरेफ्यूटेबॅल *(adjective)* – अकाट्य impossible to deny or disprove. *The actor has been facing some irrefutable charges.*

Irregularity/इरेग्यूलैरिटि *(noun)* – अनियमितता behaviour that breaches the rule or etiquette

I

or custom or morality. *The Commonwealth Games saw many irregularities.*

Irreligion/इरिलिजन *(noun)* – नास्तिकता the quality of not being devout. *What he hates most about me is my irreligion.*

Irreligious/इरिलिजस *(adjective)* – विधर्मी indifferent or hostile to religion. *People who are irreligious have to face many things in society.*

Irremissible/इरिमिसिबॅल *(adjective)* – अक्षम्य rare unpardonable. *His crimes are irremissible.*

Irremovable/इरिमूवेबॅल *(adjective)* – अस्थानान्तरीय incapable of being removed. *The cancer had spread to both the ovaries, thus making them irremovable.*

Irrepressible/इरिप्रेसिबॅल *(adjective)* – अदम्य not able to be restrained. *His irrepressible desires was making him crazy.*

Irreproachable/इरिप्रोचॅबॅल *(adj)* – निष्कलंक beyond criticism. *This great work is irreproachable.*

Irresolute/इर्रेजल्यूट *(adjective)* – अस्थिर uncertain. *In spite of his officer's faith in him, he was irresolute of his capabilities.*

Irresolution/इर्रेजल्यूशन *(noun)* – अदृढ़ता doubt concerning two or more possible alternatives or courses of action. *The constant irresolution on his part created a wrong impression on others.*

Irresolvable/इर्रिजॉल्वेबॅल् *(adjective)* – अविभाज्य करने योग्य impossible to solve. *I have some irresolvable differences with my boss.*

Irrespective/इर्रेस्पक्टिव *(adjective)* – पृथक् regardless of. *Irrespective of what I wanted, he continued doing dilly-dally.*

Irresponsible/इर्रेस्पान्सिबल् *(adjective)* – गैर जिम्मेदारी not showing a proper sense of responsibility. *Both the parents had an irresponsible attitude towards their kid.*

Irresponsive/इर्रेस्पान्सिव *(adjective)* – प्रतिवचन न देने वाला not responsive. *The newly born child was displaying an irresponsive behaviour.*

Irretentive/इर्टेन्टिव *(noun)* – न रोकने योग्य not retentive. *This soil has become irretentive to hold moisture.*

Irretrievable/इर्ट्रीवेबल *(adjective)* – बिना उपाय का not able to be retrieved. *The traces of the lost fossils are irretrievable.*

Irreverence/इर्रेवरेन्स *(noun)* – अपमान lack of respect for people or things that are generally respected. *He came there with irreverence in his heart.*

Irreverent/इर्रेवरेन्ट् *(adj)* – शक्तिहीन, अनादरकारी disrespectful. *It was very bad on his part to display irreverent attitude towards his elders.*

Irreverential/इर्रेवरेशल *(adjective)* – अपमान-सम्बन्धी state of disrespect for things or person that are generally respected. *Over the years, he has become irreverential to everyone.*

Irreversible/इर्रिवर्सिबल *(adjective)* – अपरिवर्तनीयता impossible to be reversed or altered. *Ageing is an irreversible process.*

Irrigable/इर्रिगबॅल *(adjective)* – सींचने योग्य to supply water for irrigation. *A large part of India's land is irrigable.*

Irrigate/इर्रिगेट *(verb)* – सींचना supply water to by means of channels. supply with water. *The farmers use rain water to irrigate this area.*

Irrigation/इर्रिगेशन *(noun)* – सिंचाई का काम the state of supplying water to land. *Irrigation is the main occupation of the villagers living in remote areas.*

Irrigator/इर्रिगेटर *(noun)* – सींचने वाला मनुष्य one who supplies water to fields. *Large irrigators are used for supplying water to the fields.*

Irritable/इरिटेबल *(adjective)* – शीघ्र क्रुद्ध होने वाला easily annoyed or angered. *Would you stop doing irritable talks?*

Irritably/इरिटेब्ली *(adverb)* – चिड़चिड़ाहट से tendency to become easily annoyed. *He said irritably, "Go away."*

Irritate/इर्रिटेट *(verb)* – क्रुद्ध करना make annoyed or angry. *She irritates me with her cribbing.*

Irritating/इर्रिटेटिंग *(adj)* – चिढ़ाने वाला exciting. *Would you stop irritating me?*

Islet/आइलेट *(noun)* – छोटा द्वीप a small island. *The water was surrounded by a number of islets.*

Isometric/आइसोमेट्रिक *(adjective)* – एक परिमाण का of or having equal dimensions. *The two triangles drawn here are isometric.*

I

Italicize/इटैलिसाइज *(verb)* – तिरछे अक्षरों में छापना *Please italicize the important words.*

Italics/इटैलिक्स *(noun)* – छापे का अक्षर जो दाहिनें ओर झुका होता है। the branch of indo-European languages that includes Latin and the Roman language. *Kindly note down the words that are printed in italics.*

Itch/इच् *(noun)* – खुजली an uncomfortable sensation or condition that causes a desire to scratch the skin. *The baby has developed itches on her back.*

Itchiness/इचीनेस *(noun)* – खुजली the condition of causing an itch. *The itchiness in summers is normal.*

Itchy/इची *(adjective)* – खुजली का having or causing an itch. *The powder was very itchy for my body.*

Item/आइटम *(noun)* – वस्तु an individual article or unit. a piece of news or information. an entry in an account. *Please make a list of all the items that you are going to buy.*

Iterative/इटरेटिव *(adjective)* – बारम्बार दोहराने वाला relating to or involving iteration, especially of a mathematical or computational process. *The program comprised of an iterative cycle.*

Itinerancy/इटिनरैन्सि *(noun)* – दौरा, भ्रमण the state of travelling from one place to another. *In ancient times, itinerancy was a common thing among traders.*

Itinerant/इटिनरन्ट *(adjective)* – घूमने वाला travelling from place to place. *A number of itinerants had gathered there.*

Itinerate/इटिनरेट *(verb)* – घूमना travel from place to place to perform one's professional duty. *He had to itinerate from place to place to do the trading.*

Itself/इटसेल्फ *(pronoun)* – स्वयं उसका used as the object of a verb or preposition to refer to a thing or animal previously mentioned as the subject of the clause. *The dog was so crazy that it bit itself.*

Ivory/आइवरी *(noun)* – हाथीदाँत a hard creamy white substance composing the main part of the tusks of an elephant, walrus, or narwhal. *Many jewels are made from ivory.*

Izard/इजर्ड *(noun)* – एक प्रकार का बारहसिंगा a chamois. *The wild life sanctuary had many izards living in it.*

I

Jj

J/जे *(noun)* – अंग्रेजी वर्णमाला का दसवाँ वर्ण the tenth of the English alphabet. *J is the tenth letter in the English alphabet.*

Jab/जैब *(noun)* – धक्का, चुभन, *(verb)* कोंचना, चुभाना *I have him a jab in his stomach. She jabbed at picture with her finger.*

Jabber/जैबर *(verb)* – बड़बड़ाना talk rapidly and excitedly but with little sense. *He jabbered and I failed to understand him.*

Jabot/जाबो *(noun)* – किनारी, झालर an ornamental ruffle on the front of a shirt or blouse. *She wore a jabot which looked very attractive.*

Jacinth/जैसिंथ *(noun)* – नारंगी रंग का रत्न a reddish-orange gem variety of zircon. *She wore a jacinth on her ring finger.*

Jackal/जैकाल *(noun)* – सियार a slender, long-legged wild dog that often hunts or scavenges in packs, found in Africa and southern Asia. *Jackal is a wild dog and scavenger found in Asia and Africa.*

Jackass/जैक्-ऐस् *(noun)* – मूर्ख, नर गदहा a stupid person. *You jackass! How dare you to speak to me like that.*

Jacket/जैकेट *(noun)* – जाकिट an outer garment extending to the waist or hips, with sleeves and a fastening down the front. *He wore a woollen grey jacket which suited him very well.*

Jacobin – *(noun)* [historical] a member of a radical democratic club established in Paris in 1789, in the wake of the French revolution. *He was questioned for being a Jacobin.*

Jaconet/जैकॅनेट *(noun)* – एक प्रकार का सूती कपड़ा a lightweight cotton cloth with a smooth and slightly stiff finish. *He bought two metres of jaconet for his shirt.*

Jactitation/जैक्टिटेशन *(noun)* – शरीर की ऐंठन [medicine] restless tossing or twitching of the body. *He suffers from jactitation and is taking medicines.*

Jag/जैग *(verb)* – बेंध देना, चट्टान का नुकीला भाग slab, pierce, or prick. *A thorn jagged his skin.*

Jail/जेल *(noun)* – बन्दीगृह a place for the confinement of people accused or convicted of a crime. *He was lodged in central jail.*

Jalap/जैलप *(noun)* – एक प्रकार की रेचक a purgative drug obtained [chiefly] from the tuberous roots of a Mexican climbing plant. *You can take a dose of jalap for constipation.*

Jam/जैम् *(noun)* – मीठा अचार [chiefly British] a conserve and spread made from fruit and sugar. *Children like mixed fruit jams a lot.*

Jangle/जैंगल *(verb)* – कर्कश शब्द करना make or cause to make a ringing metallic sound. *The bells jangled in the temple.*

Janitor/जैनिटर *(noun)* – द्वारपाल, लिफ्टचालक [chiefly north American] a caretaker of a building. *Janitor was appointed after careful investigation. A janitor sometimes acts as a liftman.*

January/जैन्युऑरी *(noun)* – जनवरी the first month of the year. *Visitors to Delhi found it to be a very cold in January.*

Jape/जेप *(noun)* – हँसी a practical joke. *I was angry because he had played a very funny jape on me.*

Jar/जार *(noun)* – झगड़ा, धक्का, बर्तन a wide-mouthed cylindrical container made of glass or pottery. *He took out some pickle from the jar.*

Jargon/जार्गन *(noun)* – अनर्थक वचन, शब्दजाल words or expressions used by a particular profession or group that are difficult for others to understand. *He talked a lot of political jargon which left nobody wiser.*

Jasper/जैस्पर *(noun)* – एक प्रकार का रत्न an opaque reddish-brown stone. *Jasper being a precious stone is put to many use.*

Jaundice/जॉन्डिस *(noun)* – कामला रोग [medicine] yellowing of the skin due to an excess of bile pigments in the blood. *He has been hospitalized because of advanced case of jaundice.*

Jaunty/जॉन्टी *(adjective)* – बाँका, ज़िन्दादिल having a lively and self-confident manner. *He is a jaunty fellow and hence liked by all.*

Jay/जे *(noun)* – नीलकण्ड पक्षी a bird of the crow family with boldly patterned plumage, typically with blue feathers in the wings or tail and a harsh chattering call. *Here is a jay sitting in the tree, see how beautiful it looks.*

Jazz/जाज *(noun)* – शोरगुल का नाच-गाना a type of music of black American origin characterized by improvisation, syncopation, and a regular rhythm, and typically played on brass and woodwind instruments. *Jazz is my favourite music.*

Jealousy/जलॅसि *(adjective)* – डाह showing envious resentment. *Jealousy consumed her as she saw her boy friend with another girl.*

Jeer/जिअर *(verb)* – उपहास करना make rude and mocking remarks at someone. *The crowd jeered at the speaker.*

Jejune/जिजून *(adjective)* – फीका, नीरस naïve and simplistic. *He is a jejune fellow and after alone.*

Jelly/जेलि *(noun)* – मीठी चटनी chiefly British a dessert consisting of a sweet, fruit-flavoured liquid set with gelatin to form a semi-solid mass. a small sweet made with gelatin. *The dinner was followed by jelly.*

Jemmy/जेमि *(noun)* – सेंध मारने की सबरी a short crowbar. *The thieves forced open the door with a jemmy.*

Jenny/जेनि *(noun)* – मादा, गधी a female donkey or ass. *It is a jenny grazing over there.*

Jeopardize/जेपॅडाइज *(verb)* – खतरा में डालना put into a situation in which there is a danger arising from being on trial for a criminal offence. *He jeopardized his career by trying to bribe a clerk.*

Jeopardous/जेपर्डॅस *(adj)* – आपत्तियुक्त exposed to danger. *He followed a jeopardous path thereby endangering himself.*

Jeopardy/जेपर्डि *(noun)* – शंका danger of loss, harm, or failure. *The peace procese is jeopardy.*

Jerk/जर्क *(noun)* – झटका a quick, sharp, sudden movement. *A jerk near the tree attracted his attention.*

Jersey/जर्सी *(noun)* – कुर्ती a knitted garment with long sleeves, worn over the upper body. *He wore a thick woollen jersey as it was bitter cold.*

Jess/जेस *(noun)*– चमड़े का पतला तसमा a short leather strap that is fastened round each leg of a hawk, to which a leash may be attached. *The hawk is wearing jesses.*

Jest/जेस्ट *(noun)* – हँसी a joke. *Forget it man, I said it in jest.*

Jester/जेस्टर *(noun)* – विदूषक [historical] a professional joker of fool at a medieval court. *There used to be court jesters in medieval times.*

Jestful/जेस्टफुल *(adjective)* – ठिठोलिया entertaining. *He spoke in a jestful manner.*

Jestingly/जेस्टिंग्लि *(adverb)* – हँसी में in a humorious manner. *He teased her jestingly.*

Jet/जेट *(noun)* – फुहारा a rapid stream of liquid or gas forced out of a small opening. *A jet of water drenched me.*

Jetty/जेटि *(noun)* – घाट a landing stage or small pier. *Let us walk over the jetty, it is beautiful to be surrounded with water.*

Jewel/जूऑल *(noun)* – जवाहिर, रत्न a precious stone, especially a single crystal or a cut and polished piece of a lustrous or translucent mineral. pieces of jewellery. a hard precious stone used as a bearing in a watch, compass, etc. *it is a very precious jewel and I am unable to buy it.*

Jeweller/जूऑलर *(noun)* – जौहरी a person or company that makes or sells jewels or jewellery. *He is a jeweller by profession.*

Jezebel/जेजॅबल *(noun)* – ढीठ स्त्री a shameless or immoral woman. *She is a jezebel and as is out most of the nights.*

Jibe/जाइब *(noun)* – ताना, हँसी an insulting or mocking remark. *Her jibes insulted him.*

Jiffy/जिफी *(noun)* – क्षण [informal] a moment. *He left in a jiffy.*

Jig/जिग *(noun)* – एक प्रकार का नाच a lively dance with leaping movements. a piece of music for jig, typically in compound time. *She jigged around him in the dance hall.*

J

Jiggle/जिगल *(verb)* – झुलाना move or cause to move lightly and quickly from side to side or up and down. *The forest was full of jiggling monkeys.*

Jingle/जिंगल *(noun)* – टनटनाहट a light, loose ringing sound such as that made by metal objects being shaken together. *The jingle of bells could be heard from far.*

Jobber/जॉबर *(noun)* – छोटा कार्य करने वाला a principal or wholesaler dealing only on the stock exchange with brokers, not directly with the public. north American a wholesaler. *He is a jobber, and doesn't sell in retail.*

Jobbery/जॉबरी *(noun)* – दलाली the practice of using a public office or position of trust for one's own gain or advantage. *He has been accused of jobbery and an enquiry is set up against him.*

Jockey/जॉकी *(noun)* – घुड़दौड़ का सवार a professional rider in horse races. *He is a skilful and well-known jockey.*

Jocose/जोकोस *(adjective)* – खिलाड़ी formal playful or humorous. *He is a jocose fellow and liked by all.*

Jocular/जाक्युलर *(adjective)* – परिहासिक fond of or characterized by joking; humorous. *He is a jocular character.*

Jocund/जॉकन्ड *(adjective)* – प्रमुदित formal cheerful and light-hearted. *He is jocund by nature.*

Jogger/जॉगर *(noun)* – धीरे-धीरे चलने वाला a person who jogs. *He is a daily jogger in the park.*

Jogtrot/जॉगट्रॉट *(noun)* – धीमी समान गति a slow trot. *The horse went on a jogtrot.*

Johney/जॉनी *(noun)* – ठाटदार मनुष्य a man. *Hey Johnny! Come here and take your money.*

Joinder/जाइन्डर *(noun)* – मिलाव, प्रतिशेष law the action of bringing together. *The court ordered the joinder of both witnesses.*

Joiner/जॉइनर *(noun)* – बढ़ई, जोड़ने वाला a person who constructs the wooden components of a building. *He is a joiner by profession.*

Joining/ज्वाइनिंग *(verb)* – संगम, जोड़ने की क्रिया to link to conhect. *Joining army was his main aim.*

Jointly/जॉइन्टलि *(adverb)* – एक साथ मिलकर together in association. *We jointly stood against the injustice.*

Joke/जोक *(noun)* – उपहास, चुटकुला a thing said to cause amusement. a trick played for fun. *He cut a joke and all laughed.*

Joker/जोकर *(noun)* – मसखरा, विदूषक a person who is fond of joking. [informal] a foolish or inept person. *Children are highly amused by jokers in the circus.*

Jokingly/जोकिंगलि *(adverb)* – मसखरेपन से in a lighter vein. *I said it jokingly, please don't wind.*

Jollily/जॉलिलि *(adverb)* – आनंद से cheerful, happy. *He jollily said all this.*

Jolliness/जॉलिनेस् *(noun)* – प्रमोद, प्रभुदितावस्था joviality. *His jolliness is infectious.*

Jonquil/जॉनक्विल *(noun)* – एक प्रकार का नरगिस a narcissus with small fragrant yellow flowers and cylindrical leaves. *I have a few jonquils in my garden.*

Jordan – *(noun)* name of a country. *Jordan is a country situated in the middle-east.*

Josser/जॉसर *(noun)* – मूर्ख मनुष्य British a man, typically one regarded with contempt: an old josser. *He is an old josser and talks in coherently.*

Jostle/जॉसल *(verb)* – धक्का देना push or bump against roughly. struggle or compete forcefully for. *The crowd jostled to reach the famous actor.*

Jot/जॉट *(verb)* – संक्षेप में लिखना write quickly. *He jotted down the notes.*

Jotting/जॉटिंग *(noun)* – यादगार a brief note. *As he read the jotting he became upset.*

Jounce/जाउन्स *(verb)* – झटकारना jolt or bounce. *The ball jounced high.*

Journalist/जर्नलिस्ट *(noun)* – सम्पादक a person who writes for newspapers or magazines or prepares news to be broadcast on radio or television. *He is a journalist by profession.*

Journalize/जर्नलाइज *(verb)* – पत्रिका में लिखने का कार्य करना, समाचारपत्रीय बनाना dated enter in a journal. *This article has been journalized by a famous reporter. He has journalized all the events date wise.*

Journey/जर्नी *(noun)* – यात्रा an act of travelling from one place to another. *He has gone on a long journey.*

Jove/जोव *(noun)* – बृहस्पति नक्षत्र used for emphasis or to indicate surprise. *By jove! You are really a tall man.*

Jovian/जोविअन *(adjective)* – बृहस्पति-सम्बन्धी of or like the god jove. *A search robot will be sent for Jovian exploration.*

Jowl/जॉउल *(noun)* – गाल the lower part of a cheek, especially when fleshy or drooping. north American the cheek of a pig as meat. the dewlap of cattle or wattle of birds. *Some people develop jowls in old age.*

Joyless/जॉयलेस *(adjective)* – उदास not giving or feeling pleas me. *He is a joyless and miserable fellow.*

Joyful/जॉयफुल *(adjective)* – हर्षित feeling or causing joy. *He leads a joyful life.*

Jubilate /जूबिलेट – *(verb)* show great happiness. *It's time to senj and jubilate aloud before God.*

Jubilant/जूबिलेन्ट *(adjective)* – प्रसन्न happy and triumphant. *He was jubilant after having won the race.*

Jubilee/जुबिली *(noun)* – महोत्सव a special anniversary, especially one celebrating twenty-five or fifty years of something. *He recently celebrated the silver jubilee of his marriage.*

Judge/जज *(noun)* – न्यायाधीश a public officer appointed to decide cases in a law court. a person who decides the results of a competition. a personable or qualified to give an opinion: a good judge of character. *He has recently been appointed a judge.*

Judgeship/जजशिप – *(noun)* the person qualified and give opiniom. *To be eligible for judegeship, a lawyer must have 10 years of practice in a law court.*

Judicature /जुडिकेचर – *(noun)* the administration of justice. *Our constitution says that the legislature is separate from the judicature.*

Judicial/जुडिसियल *(adjective)* – अदालती of, by or appropriate to a law court or judge. *He has been sent to 10 days judicial custody.*

Judiciary/जुडिसिअरी *(noun)* – न्यायाधीशों का समुदाय the judicial authorities of a country. *The judiciary of a country must be impartial.*

Judicious/जुडिशॅस *(adjective)* – उचित having or done with good judgement. *It was a judicious division.*

Jug/जग *(noun)* – जलपात्र [British] a cylindrical container with a handle and a lip, for holding and pouring liquids, [north American] a large container for liquids, with a narrow mouth. *He has ordered a jug of juice.*

Jugful/जगफुल– *(noun)* contents in a jug. *She gave us jugful of water.*

Juggins/जगिन्स – *(noun)* [British informal, dated] a simpleton. *You silly juggins, why did you listen to him?*

Juggle/जॅगॅल *(verb)* – बाजीगरी करना, धोखा देना continuously toss into the air and catch a number of objects so as to keep at least one in the air at any time. *He juggles balls faultlessly.*

Juggler/जॅगलॅर *(noun)* – मायावी one who balances several activites at once. *He is a barman as well as a juggler.*

Jugular/जूग्यूलर *(noun)* – गरदन या कण्ठ सम्बन्धी of the neck or throat. *The murderer cut his jugular vein.*

Juice/जूस *(noun)* – फल या सब्जी का रस the liquid present in fruit or vegetables. a drink made from this. *He is fond of fruit juice.*

Juicy/जूसि *(adjective)* – रसीला full of juice. *It is a cent per cent juicy drink.*

Julep/जूलेप *(noun)* – शर्बत a sweet drink made from sugar syrup, sometimes containing alcohol or [medicine]. *You seem to be tired, you need a drink of julep.*

July/जुलाइ *(noun)* – जुलाई the seventh month of the year. *It is hot in July in Delhi.*

Jumble/जम्बल *(noun)* – घालमेल an untidy collection of things. *Things are in a jumble in this place, sort them out.*

Jump/जम्प *(verb)* – कूदना push oneself off the ground using the muscles in one's legs and feet. pass over by jumping. get on or off quickly. *The cat jumped over the wall.*

Jumping/जम्पिंग – *(verb)* push oneself off a surface. *He is jumping with joy. He is a good dancer and is called jumping jack.*

J

Junction/जंक्शन *(noun)* – संगम a point where two or more things, especially roads or railway lines, meet or are joined. *He was found wandering on a railway junction.*

Juncture/जॅन्क्चर *(noun)* – समय a particular point in time. *You must start doing things at this juncture.*

Junior/जूनिअर् *(adjective)* – अल्पवयस्क of, for, or denoting young or younger people. British of, for, or denoting school children aged 7-11. *All juniors should gather here.*

Juniority/जूनिआरिटी *(noun)* – छोटापन denoting young. *Juniority or seniority matters a lot in a job.*

Junket/जंकेट *(noun)* – ज्योनार a dish of sweetened and flavoured curds of milk, often served with fruit. *He often goes to junkets and spends a lot of money.*

Junta/जन्टा *(noun)* – गुप्त मण्डली a military or political group ruling a country after taking power by force. *Many countries are still ruled by military junta.*

Jupiter/जूपिटर *(noun)* – बृहस्पति ग्रह the largest planet in the solar system, fifth in order from the sun and one of the brightest objects in the night sky. *Astronomers are a lot interested in the planet Jupiter.*

Jural/जूरॅल *(adjective)* – विधिक, वैधिक formal of or relating to the law. *It is a jural matter and advice must be sought from an expert.*

Jurisprudence/जुरिस्प्रूडेन्स *(noun)* – विधिशास्त्र the theory or philosophy of law. *Jurisprudence must be fair in delivering fair openion.*

Jurist/जूरिस्ट *(noun)* – विधिशास्त्री an expert in law. *He is a famous jurist.*

Juror/जूरर् *(noun)* – प्रमाण-पुरुष a member of a jury. *He is a juror and a party to a many decision makings.*

Just/जस्ट *(adjective)* – धार्मिक morally right and fair. appropriate or deserved. well founded. *Just a moment let me speak.*

Justice/जस्टिस *(noun)* – न्याय just behaviour or treatment. the quality of being just. *Justice must be done.*

Justiciable/जस्टिशिअबल् *(adjective)* – न्याय-योग्य law subject to trail in a court of law. *We sijned the agreement justicable under Indian Courts.*

Justiceship/जस्टिसशिप – *(noun)* just and fair treatment. *Indian justiceship is renowned for slow but fair treatment.*

Justly/जस्टली *(adverb)* – न्यायपूर्वक ठीक-ठीक fairly, morally. *I justly believe in the action.*

Justness/जस्टनेस *(noun)* – यथार्थता justifiable opinion. *The justness of the sentence is unquestionable.*

Jute/जूट *(noun)* – जूट, पटुआ rough fibre made from the stems of a tropical plant, used for making rope or woven into sacking. *Ropes among many other things are made from jute fibre.*

J

Kk

K/के (noun) – अंग्रेजी वर्णमाला का ग्यारहवाँ अक्षर the eleventh letter of the English alphabet.
1. Denoting the next after J in a set of items, categories, etc.

Kail/केल (noun) – एक प्रकार की बन्दगोभी, करमसाग a vegetable. *Kail or kale is a kind of cabbage with large leaves and no compact round head.*

Kaiser/कैजर (noun) – जर्मनी उपाधि [historical] the German emperor, the emperor of Austria, or the head of the holy roman empire. *Kaiser was the emperor of Austria, Germany.*

Kale/केल (noun) – बन्दगोभी a hardy cabbage of a variety which produces erect stems with large leaves and no compact head. *Leaves of the kale cabbage are edible.*

Kaleidoscopical – (adjective) ability to changs patterns. *The movement of dances was almost kaleidoscopical.*

Kalium – (noun) an element. *Kalium is the Latin name for potassium.*

Kangaroo/कैनगारू (noun) – कंगारू a large plant eating marsupial with a long powerful tail and strongly developed hind limbs that enable it to travel by leaping, found only in Australia and New Guinea. *Kangaroo is the national animal of Australia.*

Kaolin/केओलिन (noun) – चीनी मिट्टी a fine soft white clay, used for making porcelain and china and in medicinal absorbents. *Kaolin clay is used for making china and porcelain.*

Keenly/किनली (adverb) – उत्सुकता से showing eagerness or enthusiasm. *He is keenly interested in Maths.*

Keenness/कीननेस (noun) – तीखापन eagerness. *She had great keenness to join dance classes.*

Keener/कीनर (noun) – तेज, चतुर enthusiastic. *He is keener than his brother.*

Keeper/कीपर (noun) – रक्षक a person who manages or looks after something or someone. *He has employed a housekeeper.*

Keeping/कीपिंग (noun) – रक्षा the action of keeping something. *In keeping with my dad's desire, I have taken sports as my career.*

Keepsake/किपसेक (noun) – स्मरणार्थक चिह्न a small item kept in memory of the person who gave it or originally owned it. *This locket is a keepsake of my mother.*

Keg/केग (noun) – कठरा a small barrel, especially one of less than 10 gallons or 30 gallons. *He is fond of keg beer.*

Kemp/केम्प (noun) – ऊन के मोटे रेशे a coarse hair or fibre of wool. *Please throw this bunch of Kemp out.*

Ken/केन (noun) – दृष्टिविषय one's range of knowledge or sight. *He has great ken of this rocky terrain.*

Kennel/केनेल (noun) – जलमार्ग या कुन्ताघर a small shelter for a dog. *The dog is sleeping in its kennel.*

Kept/केप्ट – रखा, कीप क्रिया का भूतकाल का रूप past and past participle of keep. *He has kept his promise.*

Kerchief/करचीफ (noun) – सिर ढाँपने का चौकोर कपड़ा a piece of fabric used to cover the head. *He always carries a handkerchief.*

Kernel/कर्नेल् (noun) – गरी, गिरी a softer part of a nut, seed, or fruit stone contained within its hard shell. the seed and hard husk of a cereal, especially wheat. *The kernels of most nuts are edible.*

Kerosene/केरोसीन (noun) – मिट्टी का तेल a light fuel oil obtained by distilling petroleum; paraffin oil. *Kerosene stoves are still used by people who don't have cooking gas.*

Kestrel/केस्ट्रल (noun) – बाज पक्षी a small falcon that hunts by hovering with rapidly beating wings. *Many people living in mountains keep kestrels or pets.*

K

Ketchup/केचअप *(noun)* – चटनी a spicy sauce made chiefly from tomatoes and vinegar, used as a relish. *Chilly tomato ketchups are quite popular.*

Kettle/केटॅल *(noun)* – पतीली, केतली a metal or plastic container with a lid, spout, and handle, used for boiling water. *Tea is boiling in the kettle.*

Key/की *(noun)* – चाभी a small piece of shaped metal with incisions cut to fit the wards of a particular lock, which is inserted into the lock and rotated to open or close it or turning a screw, peg, or nut. a pin, bolt, or wedge inserted into a hole or between parts so as to lock the parts together. *I have lost my keys and I don't know how I shall open the door.*

Keyhole/कीहोल *(noun)* – ताली लगाने का छिद्र a hole in a lock into which the key is inserted. *He tried to look inside through the keyhole.*

Keynote/कीनोट *(noun)* – प्रधान राग a prevailing tone or central theme. setting out the central theme of a conference. *Read this keynote before you enter the conference room.*

Keystone/कीस्टोन *(noun)* – प्रधान सिद्धान्त a central stone at the summit of an arch, locking the whole together. *This is the keystone to the building.*

Kibble/किबल् *(verb)* – कूटना, पीसना grind or chop. *The meal has been kibbled into pellets.*

Kibe/काइब *(noun)* – बेवाय [archaic] an ulcerated chilblain. *Her both feet are full of kibes.*

Kibosh – *(noun)* [informal] put a decisive end to. *He decided to put the kibosh on the agreement.*

Kid/किड *(noun)* – बकरी का बच्चा a young goat. leather made from a young goat's skin. *Hey kid! Don't you mess with me, you have yet to grow.*

Kiddle/किड्डल *(noun)* – मछली पकड़ने के लिये नदी लगाया बाँध a dam or barrier in a river, with an opening fitted with nets to catch fish. *It is a kiddle here on the river with an opening to catch fish.*

Kiddy/किडि *(noun)* – छोटा बच्चा a young child. *Kiddies play here.*

Kier/किअर् *(noun)* – पात्र बर्तन container. *This is of no use, it is broken kier.*

Kill/किल *(verb)* – मार डालना cause the death of put an end to. stop. overexert oneself. yield a

specified amount of meat when slaughtered. *The goat has been killed for meat.*

Killer/किलर *(noun)* – हत्यारा a person or thing that kills. *A serial killer is on prowl.*

Killing/किलिंग *(noun)* – हत्या an act of causing death. *Killing animals is forbidden in some religions.*

Kiln/किल्न *(noun)* – आँवाँ, भट्ठा a large oven for baking clay and bricks. *He owns many brick kilns.*

Kilo/किलो *(noun)* – मेट्रिक नाप में एक हजार के लिए उपसर्ग measure of weight. *Give me a kilo of potato.*

Kilogram/किलोग्राम *(noun)* – एक हजार ग्राम measure of weight. *A kilogram of onions will cost you 30 rupees.*

Kin/किन *(noun)* – नातेदार one's family and relations. *All my kin live around here.*

Kind/काइन्ड *(noun)* – किस्म, प्रकार a class or type of people or things having similar characteristics. *The kind of people you mix with are not undesirable.*

Kindliness/काइनडलिनेस् *(noun)* – दयालुता quality of being kind, gentle. *I would be much abliged for your kindliness.*

Kindling/किन्डलिंग *(noun)* – आग जलाने की चैली small sticks or twigs used for lighting fires. *It is cold and dark, kindling a fire is necessary.*

Kindly/काइन्डलि *(adverb)* – उपकारी, कृपा करके in a kind manner. *He kindly asked me to have a seat.*

Kindness/काइन्डनेस *(noun)* – सहानुभूति, दयालुता the quality of being kind. *Kindness is a virtue.*

King/किंग *(noun)* – राजा, नरपति the male ruler of an independent state, especially one who inherits the position by right of birth. *He is a king and can order anything.*

Kingdom/किंगडम *(noun)* – राज, साम्राज्य a country, state, or territory ruled by a king or queen. *The kingdom of Ashoka spread far and wide.*

Kingless/किंगलेस *(adjective)* – नृपहीन male ruler of an independent state. *The state remained kingless for some time after the death of the king.*

Kinglet/किंगलेट *(noun)* – छोटा राजा [chiefly] derogatory a minor king. *He is merely a kinglet ruling a small state.*

Kinglike/किंगलाइक *(adjective)* – राजा के सदृश like a king. *His behaviour is kinglike and rather irritating.*

Kingly/किंगलि *(adjective)* – राजकीय typical of a king. *He visited his kingdom to perform his kingly duties.*

Kinless/किन्लेस् *(adjective)* – बिना परिवार का not having relative. *He wandered into a desert and for all practical purposes a kinless person.*

Kinsfolk/किन्सफोक *(plural noun)* – भाई-बन्धु a person's blood relations, regarded collectively. *Most of his kinsfolk live abroad.*

Kinship/किंशीप *(noun)* – नातेदारी blood relationship. *In the very first meeting, I felt a strange kinship with her.*

Kirk/कर्क *(noun)* – गिरजाघर Scottish & north English. a church. the church of Scotland. *During my stay in UK, I will visit the kirk.*

Kisser/किशर *(noun)* – चूमने वाला a person who kisses someone. *He is a great kisser.*

Kitchen/किचेन *(noun)* – रसोईघर a room where food is prepared and cooked. *Kitchen must be kept neat and clean.*

Kitchener/किचनर् *(noun)* – चूल्हों की पंक्ति [historical] a kitchen range. *The new flats come equipped with modern kitchener.*

Kloof/क्लूफ़ *(noun)* – सँकरी घाटी South African a wooded ravine or valley. *There are beautiful kloofs in South Africa.*

Knag/नैग *(noun)* – लकड़ी की गाँठ a short dead branch. *The trunk of this tree is full of knags.*

Knap/नैप *(verb)* – शिखर *(verb)* architecture & archaeology by striking ti, so as to make a tool or a flat stone for building walls. *This building is made of knapped stone and flint.*

Knapper/नैपर् *(noun)* – पत्थर तोड़ने वाला one who shapes stones. *He is an expert knapper capable of giving desired shape to 200 square stones.*

Knapsack/नैपसैक *(noun)* – चमड़े का बैग a soldier's or hiker's bag with shoulder straps, carried on the back. *He is a tourist and always carries a knapsack.*

Knave/नेव *(noun)* – धूर्त [archaic] a scoundrel. *He is a kvave and as such not to be trusted.*

Knavery/नेवरि *(noun)* – दुष्टता, बेईमानी an act of dishonesty. *Indulging in acts of knavery may land you in jail.*

Knead/नीड *(verb)* – सानना to work up into dough. *She is kneading wheat flour.*

Knee/नी *(noun)* – घुटना the joint between the thigh and the lower leg. a person's lap. *He has been hurt in his knee.*

Knell/नेल *(noun)* – अरथी के साथ बजने वाले घण्टे का शब्द the sound of a bell, especially when rung solemnly for a death or funeral. something regarded as a warning of disaster. *The knell of the village bell tells us that somebody had died.*

Knew/न्यू – जान लिया past of know. *I knew he wasn't a thief.*

Knife/नाइफ *(noun)* – चाकू a cutting instrument consisting of a blade fixed into a handle. *The robber had a knife in his hand.*

Knighthood/नाइट्हूड *(noun)* title, rank. *He was honoured with knighthood on his birthday.*

Knit/नीट *(verb)* – जोड़ना make by interlocking loops of yarn with knitting needles or on a machine. make in knitting. *My mother is knitting a sweater for me.*

Knob/नॉब *(noun)* – गाँठ a rounded lump or ball, especially at the end or on the surface of something. *He turned the knob and opened the door.*

Knobble/नॉबल *(noun)* – छोटी गाँठ [British] a small lump on something. *There is a knobble on the wall.*

Knotting/नॉटिंग *(noun)* – गठबन्धन the action or craft of tying knots in yarn to make carpets or other decorative items. the knots in such an item. *Carpets are made by knotting the yarn.*

Knotty/नॉटी *(adjective)* – पेंचदार full of knots. *It is a knotty rope.*

Knowable/नोएबल् *(adjective)* जानने योग्य becoming aware. *This idea is knowable to the core.*

K

Knowing/नोइंग *(adjective)* – ज्ञान being fully aware. *Today's society is too knowing too corrupt.*

Known/नोन *(adjective)* – सूचित recognized, familiar, or within the scope of knowledge. *He is a well-known person.*

Knuckle/नकल *(noun)* – अँगुली का जोड़, पोर a part of a finger at a joint where the bone is near the surface. *I have pain in my knnckles.*

Knurl/नर्ल *(noun)* – गाँठ a small projecting knob or ridge. *It is a knurl here and a very hard place.*

Kodak/कोडैक *(noun)* – फोटो उतारने का एक यन्त्र a brand of camera. *Kodak has caused manufacturing cameras.*

Kraal/क्राल *(noun)* – बाड़ा a traditional African village of huts, typically enclosed by a fence. *African villages of huts are called kraals.*

Kymograph/काइमोग्राफ *(noun)* – तरंगलेखी यन्त्र *an* instrument for recording variations in pressure, e.g. in sound waves or in circulating blood. *A kymograph is used for recording vibrations in circulating blood.*

K

Ll

L/एल – (noun) अंग्रेजी वर्णमाला का 12वाँ अक्षर the twelfth letter of the English alphabet. *L is the Roman numeral for 50.*
1. Denoting the next after K in a set of items, categories. etc.

La/ला *(noun)* – गायन में छठा स्वर the sixth note of the octave.

Labarum/लेबरम *(noun)* – रूमी रण-पताका a symbolic banner. *Labarum was Constantine's military symbol.*

Labefaction/लैबिफैक्शन *(noun)* – नाश [archaic] deterioration or downfall. *His labefaction occurred soon after his business collapsed.*

Label/लेबल *(noun)* – टिकट a small piece of paper, fabric, etc. attached to an object and giving information about it, a piece of fabric sewn inside a garment and bearing the brand name, size, or care instructions. *The label on the shirt reads 'Peter England' 42.*

Labial/लेबियल *(adjective)* – ओठ-सम्बन्धी [chiefly anatomy & biology] of or relating to the lips or a labium. *Any thing that is in some way concerned with lips is known as labial.*

Laboratory/लैबॉरेटरि *(noun)* – प्रयोगशाला a room or building for scientific experiments, research, or teaching, or for the manufacture of drugs or chemicals. *There was a cage of white mice in the science laboratory for experimental purposes.*

Laborious/लेबोरियस *(adjective)* – परिश्रमी requiring considerable time and effort, showing obvious signs of effort. *It was a laborious job and he did it well.*

Labour/लेबर *(noun)* – मेहनत, श्रमिक (वर्ग) work, especially hard physical work. *The labour was constantly working on the railway line.*

Laboured/लेबर्ड *(adjective)* – परिश्रम-सूचक done with great difficulty. *His laboured breathing could be heard from a distance.*

Labourer/लेबरर *(noun)* – कर्मकार, मजदूर a person doing unskilled manual work. *20 labourers were hired to clean the tank.*

Labourite/लेबरिट *(noun)* – मजदूर दल का सदस्य a member or supporter of a labour party. *He is a labourite and will not vote for any other party.*

Laburnum/लेबरनम *(noun)* – पीले फूल का एक पौधा a small hardwood tree with hanging clusters of yellow flowers followed by pods of poisonous seeds, from this grape. *I have a laburnum in my garden, don't eat its fruit.*

Labyrinth/लैबरिन्थ् *(noun)* – व्याकुलता a complicated irregular network of passages or paths. an intricate and confusing arrangement. *Once you enter this labyrinth underground, it will be very difficult for you to come out.*

Labyrinthine/लैबरिन्थाइन *(adjective)* – पेचीला, पेचीदा, अस्पष्ट like a labyrinth, especially in being complicated or twisted. *It is labyrinthine puzzle and very difficult to solve.*

Lac/लैक *noun)* – लाख (a resinous substance secreted as a protective covering by the lac insect, used to make varnish, shellac, etc. *Lac is an important ingredient of varnish.*

Lacerable/लैसरेब्ल *(adj)* – चीरा लगाने योग्य that may be lacerated. *It is not lacerable.*

Lacerate/लैसरेट *(verb)* – पीड़ा देना tear or deeply cut the flesh or skin. *The knife lacerated his skin.*

Laceration/लैसरेशन *(noun)* – विदारण cut or tear in skin. *He suffered lacerations to his face and hands.*

Laches/लैचेज *(noun)* – ढिलाई [law] unreasonable delay in making an assertion or claim, which may result in refusal. *Laches resulted into refusal of his claim.*

Lachrymal/लैक्रिमल *(adjective)* – अश्रु-सम्बन्धी formal connected with weeping or tears. *He has some lachrymal problem.*

Lack/लैक *(noun)* – अभाव, कमी absence or deficiency of something. *His lack of common sense often puts him in trouble.*

Lackadaisical/लैकेडेजिकल *(adj)* – व्यग्र दु:खी lacking enthusiasm and thoroughness. *His lackadaisical attitude was responsible for his failure in interview.*

Lackey/लैकी *(noun)* – दास a servant, especially a liveried footman or manservant. *He looks more like a lackey the master of this mansion.*

Laconic/लैकोनिक *(adjective)* – छोटा using very few words; terse. *Laconic speech has become his habit.*

Lactation/लैक्टेशन *(noun)* – स्तन्य-दान the secretion of milk by the mammary glands. *Lactation process starts soon after the birth of the baby.*

Lactic/लैक्टिक *(adjective)* – दुग्ध के गुण का of relating to, or obtained from milk. *This is lactic powder.*

Lactometer/लैक्टोमीटर *(noun)* – दूध की शुद्धता नापने का यन्त्र an instrument for measuring the density of milk. *A lactometer is used to find how watery is the milk.*

Lade/लेड *(verb)* – भार रखना put cargo on board. *The laden ship started its journey.*

Lading/लेडिंग *(noun)* – बोझ the action of loading a ship with cargo. *The labour were instructed to complete lading the ship in 6 hours.*

Ladle/लैडल *(noun)* – करछुल a large long handled spoon with a cup shaped bowl, used for serving soup or sauce. *The guests were served soup with a ladle.*

Lady/लेडी *(noun)* – गृहिणी a women. *She is a lady and as such you should respect her.*

Laggard/लैगार्ड *(adjective)* – मन्द slower than desired or expected. *He is a laggard and unlikely to succeed.*

Lagging/लैगिंग *(noun)* – लपेटन, परिवेष्टन material providing heat insulation for a boiler, pipes, etc. *You can buy lagging from this shop.*

Lagoon/लैगून *(noun)* – दलदल, समुद्र से बना झील a stretch of salt water separated from the sea by a low sandbank of coral reef. *What a beautiful lagoon, let us go and swim.*

Laid/लेड – लेटा हुआ past or past participle of lay. *The hen has laid an egg. The table has been laid, please come for dinner.*

Laird/लेअर्ड *(noun)* – जमींदार a person who owns a large estate. *He is a laird and as such a very rich man.*

Laity/लैइटि *(noun)* – जनसामान्य lay people. *He is a lay man and doesn't know much of anything.*

Lake/लेक *(noun)* – झील a large area of water surrounded by land. *Let us fish in this lake.*

Lame/लेम *(adjective)* – लँगड़ा disabled in the leg or foot. *He is a lame fellow and as such can't walk properly.*

Lamentable/लैमेंटेब्ल *(adjective)* – शोचनीय deplorable or regrettable. *There was lamentable atmosphere in the house after the news of accident.*

Lamentably/लैमेंटेब्ली *(adverb)* – शोक से very bad, deplorable. *She was lamentably ignorant.*

Lamentation/लैमेंटेशन *(noun)* – विलाप experssion of grief, sorrow. *The accident area presentated a scene of lamentation.*

Lamenter/लैमेंटर *(noun)* – विलाप करने वाला a grieving person. *Look ahead, don't be a lamenter worrying about the past.*

Laminate/लैमिनेट *(verb)* – तबक बनाना overlay with a layer of protective material. *He got his certificates laminated.*

Lamp/लैम्प *(noun)* – दीपक an electric, oil, or gas device for giving light. *Oil lamps are still burnt in villages without electricity.*

Lampoon/लैम्पून *(verb)* – आक्षेप publicly satirize or ridicule. *He was lampooned by journalists.*

Lamprey/लैम्प्री *(noun)* – एक प्रकार की मछली an eel like jawless fish, often parasitic, that has a sucker mouth with horny teeth and a rasping tongue. *The fisherman caught a lamprey in his net.*

Lance/लान्स् *(noun)* – बर्छी a long weapon with a wooden shaft and a pointed steel head, formerly used by a horseman in charging. *The knight was hit by a lance.*

Lancet/लान्सेट् *(noun)* – नश्तर a small, broad two-edged surgical knife or blade with a sharp point. *His skin was pricked with a lancet.*

Landau/लैन्डा *(noun)* – लण्डी गाड़ी a four-wheeled enclosed horse-drawn carriage with a removable front cover and a back cover that can be raised and lowered. *Royals in England used landau for travelling even in the 20th century.*

Landed/लैंडेड *(adjective)* – भूमि सम्पन्न owning much land, especially through inheritance.

L

consisting of or relating to such land. *He is inherited huge to have landed property.*

Landing/लैंडिंग *(noun)* – अवतरण the process of coming to or bringing something to land. *The landing time of the plane has come.*

Landlady/लैंडलेडी *(noun)* – जमींदारिन a woman who leases land or property. *She is our landlady and has come to collect rent.*

Landmark/लैंडमार्क *(noun)* – सीमा चिह्न an object or feature of a landscape or town that is easily seen and recognized from a distance. *Is there any landmark near your house whereby I can reach you easily?*

Landward/लैंडवार्ड *(adjective)* – पृथ्वी की ओर facing towards land as opposed to sea. *I have a house facing landwards as opposed to seawards..*

Languish/लैंग्विश *(verb)* – दुर्बल होना grow weak or feeble. [archaic] pine with love or grief. *He is languishing in jail.*

Lank/लैंक *(adjective)* – दुर्बल long, limp, and straight. *He is a lank fellow.*

Lantern/लैंटर्न *(noun)* – दीपक a lamp with a transparent case protecting the flame or electric bulb. the light chamber at the top of a lighthouse. *It is very dark outside, take a lantern with you.*

Lap-dog/लैपडॉग *(noun)* – छोटा कुत्ता a person who is completely under the influence of another. *He is a lap-dog always obeying his wife blindly.*

Lapis-lazuli/लैपिस-लैज्युलाइ *(noun)* – वैदूर्य a bright blue metamorphic rock consisting largely of laurite, used in jewellery. *Lapis-lazuli rock is used in jewellery.*

Lapse/लैप्स *(noun)* – अतिक्रम a brief failure of concentration, memory, or judgement. a decline from previously high standards. *He suffered from lapse of memory after the accident.*

Lard/लार्ड *(noun)* – सूअर की चर्बी fat from the abdomen of a pig, rendered and clarified for use in cooking. *The meat is being cooked in lard.*

Larder/लार्डर *(noun)* – माँस रखने का भण्डार घर a room or large cupboard for storing food. *All the wheat grain has been stored in the larder.*

Large/लार्ज *(adjective)* – विशाल of considerable or relatively great size, extent, or capacity. *This medicine has a large spectrum.*

Largely/लार्जली *(adverb)* – विशेष करके on the whole; mostly. *Largely speaking people avoid breaking social norms.*

Larva/लार्वा *(noun)* – डिंभक, इल्ली an active immature form of an insect or other animal that undergoes meta-morphosis, e.g. a caterpillar or tadpole. *Larva is an immortive form of inseet between the stages.*

Larynx/लैरिंक्स *(noun)* – हलक anatomy the hollow muscular organ forming an air passage to the lungs and containing the vocal cords. *Something has gone wrong with his larynx, he is unable to speak.*

Lashing/लैसिंग *(noun)* – मार a whipping or beating. *Her lashing tongue didn't spare anybody.*

Lassitude/लैसिट्यूड *(noun)* – थकावट physical or mental weariness; lack of energy. *He is suffering from lassitude and needs rest.*

Last/लास्ट *(adjective)* – अन्तिम coming after all others in time or order; final. lowest in importance or rank. the least likely or suitable. *He came last in the race.*

Lastly/लास्टली *(adverb)* – अन्त में in the last place; last. *Lastly, I would like to thank all who have come here.*

Latchet/लैचेट *(noun)* – फीता [archaic] a narrow thong or lace for fastening a shoe or sandal. *The latchets of my shoes are worn out.*

Lately/लेटली *(adverb)* – थोड़े दिन हुए recently; not long ago. *Lately he has been behaving in a strange way.*

Lateral/लैटरल *(adjective)* – बगल का of, at, towards, or from the side or sides. *Lateral roots help plants take up water.*

Latex/लैटेक्स *(noun)* – रस, दूध, दुधिया milky fluid found in many plants, notably the rubber tree, which coagulated on exposure to the air. *A synthetic product resembling latex is used to make paints.*

Lathe/लेद *(noun)* – खराद a machine for shaping wood or metal by means of a rotating drive which turns the piece being worked on against changeable cutting tools. *Square pieces are being shaped on the lathe for making legs of the table.*

Lather/लैदर *(noun)* – साबुन का फेन a frothy white mass of bubbles produced by soap when mixed with water. *He formed a thick layer of lather on his beard before shaving.*

L

Latin/लैटिन (noun) - प्राचीन रोमन सम्बन्धी, इनकी भाषा the language of ancient Rome and its empire. *He is a Latin American.*

Latitude/लैटिट्यूड (noun) - चौड़ाई, स्वच्छन्दता the angular distance of a place north or south of the equator. *That city is situated at an latitude of 50° North.*

Latterly/लैटरली (adverb) - थोड़े काल में recently. *Latterly there has been a lot of development in sports in India.*

Lattice/लैटिस (noun) - जाली, झँझरी a structure or pattern consisting or strips crossing each other with square or diamond-shaped spaces left between. *I have covered the window with a lattice.*

Laudable/लाडबॅल (adjective) - सराहने योग्य deserving praise and commendation. *His stage performance was laudable.*

Laudation/लाडेशन (noun) - स्तुति *His speech drew great laudation from audience.*

Laudatory/लाडेटरी (adjective) - प्रशंसक expressing praise and commendation. *The leader was surrounded by a laudatory crowd.*

Laughably/लाफेब्ली (adverb) - हास्यास्पद ढंग से worth laughing. *His actions on the stage were laughable pretensions.*

Laughing-stock/लाफिंग-स्टॉक (noun) - हँसी का पात्र a person subjected to general mockery or ridicule. *He is a henpecked husband and as such a laughing stock among friends.*

Launderer/लाउन्डरर (noun) - धोबी a person who washes clothes. *Your clothes are dirty, get them cleaned by a launderer.*

Laureate/लॉरिएट (noun) - प्रतिष्ठित a person given an award for outstanding creative or intellectual achievement: a nobel laureate. *Tagore was a nobel laureate.*

Lava/लावा (noun) - भूराल hot molten or semi-fluid rock heaped from a volcano or fissure, or solid rock resulting from cooling of this. *Lava came out of the crater of the exploding volcano.*

Lave/लेव (verb) - बहाना poetic wash or wash over. *Sea laved the rocks near the island.*

Laver/लेवर (noun) - समुद्री शैवाल an edible seaweed with thin reddish-purple and green sheet like fronds. *Some people are fond of eating laver products.*

Lawyer/लायर (noun) - वकील a person who practises or studies [law], especially a solicitor or a barrister or an attorney. *As he had to appear in the court he hired a lawyer.*

Lax/लैक्स (adjective) - शिथिल not sufficiently strict, severe, or careful. *He is lax in attitude and will not interfere with our scheme.*

Layer/लेअर (noun) - परत a sheet or thickness of material, typically one of several, covering a surface or body. *A layer of white paint covered the walls of the room.*

Lazar/लैजर (noun) - रोगी [archaic] a poor and diseased person, especially a leper. *A leper used to be called lazar in old times.*

Lazy/लेजी (adjective) - आलसी unwilling to work or use energy. *He is a lazy fellow and will keep on delaying for hours.*

Lea/ली (noun) - चरागाह poetic an open area of grassy or arable land. *Let us pitch our tent here in the lea.*

Leaderless/लीडरलेश (adjective) - बिना अगुआ का not having a person to command. *A leaderless crowd soon turns into a mob.*

Leadership/लीडरशीप (noun) - नायकत्व the action of leading a groop. *We gained freedom under the leadership of Mahatma Gandhi.*

Leafage/लीफेज (noun) - पत्तियों का समुदाय plant strcuture similar to leaves. *The leafage is very thick in this part of jungle.*

Leafless/लिफलेस (adj) - पत्ररहित having no leaves. *Leafless trees have their own beauty.*

Leafy/लिफी (adjective) - पत्तीदार having many leaves or much foliage. *Green leafy vegetables have a lot of vitamin A.*

Leaky/लीकी (adjective) - टपकने वाला having a leak. *This is a leaky roof and droplets of water keep on trickling down.*

Leal/लील (adjective) - ईमानदार [Scottish archaic] loyal and honest. *All these party men are leal.*

Leaning/लिनिंग (noun) - झुकाव tendency to subtend partiality to take sides. *This wall is not safe, a tree is leaning against it.*

Leanness/लिननेस (noun) - दुर्बलता thin, little reward. *Girls tend to follow the craze for leanness.*

Learned/लर्नेड *(adjective)* – विद्वान having or characterized by much knowledge acquired by study. *He is a highly educated and learned person.*

Learning/लर्निंग *(noun)* – ज्ञान knowledge or skills acquired through experience or study or by being taught. *Learning while earning is a good scheme to follow.*

Lease-holder/लीजहोल्डर *(noun)*– पट्टेदार owner of property by lease. *He is a lease-holder of this property.*

Least/लीस्ट *(pronoun)* – सबसे छोटा smallest in amount, extent, or significance. *The least you can do is to help me unpack.*

Leatherette/लेदरेट *(noun)* – कृत्रिम चमड़ा imitation leather. *It is a belt made of leatherette.*

Leathern/लेदर्न *(adjective)* – चमड़े का बना हुआ [archaic] made of leather. *A leathern foam covered his face.*

Leathery/लेदरी *(adjective)* – चिमड़ा having a tough, hard texture like leather. *This seems to be a leathery object.*

Leaved/लीव्ड *(adjective)* – पर्णयुक्त having a leaf or leaves of a particular kind or number. *It is a brown leaved plant.*

Leaven/लीवेन *(noun)* – खमीर a substance, typically yeast, added to dough to make it ferment and rise; dough reserved from an earlier batch in order to start a later one fermenting. *Leaven is added to dough to ferment and make it rise.*

Leavings/लीविंग्स *(plural noun)* – जूठन things that have been left as worthless. *Leavings covered the entire sea beach.*

Lecher/लेचर *(noun)* – लम्पट a lecherous man. *He is a lecher, always running after women.*

Lechery/लेचरी *(noun)* – कामुकता offensive sexual desire, lustfulness. *Don't indulge into lechery in this old age.*

Lecturer/लेक्चरर *(noun)* – उपदेशक a person who gives lectures, especially as a teacher in higher education. *He is a lecturer in English.*

Ledger/लेजर *(noun)* – लेखाबही a book or other collection of financial accounts. *Here is the ledger if you want you can check it.*

Leech/लीच *(noun)* – चिकित्सक a parasitic or predatory annelid worm with suckers at both ends, examples of which were formerly used in medicine for bloodletting. *Formerly leeches were used in medicine for blood letting.*

Leer/लिअर *(verb)* – कटाक्ष मारना look or gaze in a lascivious or unpleasant way. *He leered at her as she came in wearing shorts.*

Lees/लिज *(noun)* – मैल the sediment of wine in the barrel; dregs. *Wine bards contain a lot of lees.*

Legacy/लेगॉसि *(noun)* – उत्तरदान an amount of money or property left to someone in a will. *He left a big legacy for his son.*

Legal/लिगल *(adjective)* – कानूनी of, based on, or required by the [law]. *It is a legal offence to smoke here.*

Legality/लिगैलिटी *(noun)* – वैधता the quality or state of being legal. *Legality of this rule is in question.*

Legalization/लिगलाइजेशन *(noun)* – धर्म-व्यवस्था to make something legal. *Legalization of something is a matter of legislature.*

Leagalize/लिगलाइज *(verb)* – अधिकार देना make legal. *It has been legalized that smoking in public places is an offence.*

Legally/लिगली *(adverb)* – कानूनी ढंग से according to [law]. *Legally speaking same rule of law applies to everyone.*

Legatee/लिगेटी *(noun)* – दान पत्र पाने वाला a person who receives a legacy. *He is a legatee to all his father's estate.*

Legation/लिगेशन *(noun)* – दूतकर्म a diplomatic mission. *A legation has been sent to Pakistan.*

Legend/लिजेंड *(noun)* – अपूर्व कहानी a traditional story popularly regarded as historical but which is not authenticated. *There are many legends about ancient warriors.*

Legendary/लेजेन्डरि *(adjective)* – कहावती of, described in, or based on legends. *Amitabh Bachchan is a legendary figure.*

Leghorn/लेग्हॉर्न *(noun)* – एक प्रकार का घरेलू मुर्गा a kinf of domestic foul, fine plaited straw. a hat made of this. *He is found of wearing hats made of leghorn.*

Legible/लेजिबॅल *(adjective)* – पढ़ने लायक clear enough to read. *It is a legible handwriting.*

Legibly/लेजिब्ली *(adverb)* – स्पष्टता से readably clearly. *Try to write your notes legibly.*

L

Legislate/लेजिस्लेट *(verb)* – कानून बनाना make or enact laws. *The legislative body legislates.*

Legitimacy/लेजिटिमैसी *(noun)* – यथार्थता, असलियत में conforming to the [law]. *The legitimacy of this statement is doubtful.*

Legume/लेम्यूम *(noun)* – शिम्ब, फली a leguminous plant grown as a crop. *Legume is grown as a crop.*

Leguminous/लेग्यूमिनस *(adjective)* – फलीदार botany relating to or denoting plants of the pea family typically having seed in pods, distinctive flowers, and root nodules containing nitrogen-fixing bacteria. *Many plants are leguminous bearing seeds in pods.*

Leman/लेमन *(noun)* – प्रेमिका [archaic] a lover or sweetheart. *She is my leman.*

Lemon/लेमन *(noun)* – नींबू a pale yellow oval citrus fruit with thick skin and fragrant, acidic juice. a drink made from or flavoured with lemon juice. *Would you like to have some lemon juice.*

Lend/लेन्ड *(verb)* – उधार देना, उधारी grant to the use of something on the understanding that it shall be returned. *Could you lend me some money?*

Lendable/लेंडेबॅल *(adjective)* – उधार देने योग्य allow someone to use something. *He doesn't have any lendable assets.*

Lender/लेन्डर *(noun)* – महाजन a person or firm that lends money. *He is a money lender by profession.*

Length/लेंग्थ *(noun)* – सीमा दूरी, लम्बाई the measurement or extent of something from end; the greater or greatest of two or more dimensions of a body. the length of a horse, boat, etc., as a measure of the lead in a race. *The length of this bridge is five km.*

Lengthen/लेंग्थेन *(verb)* – बढ़ाना make or become longer. *The shadows lengthen as the sun sets.*

Lengthy/लेंग्थी *(adjective)* – लम्बा of considerable or unusual duration. *We arrived at the conclusion after a lengthy discussion.*

Leniency/लेनिएन्सी *(noun)* – दयालुता quality of being merciful. *Too much leniency with children often spoils them.*

Lenient/लेनिएण्ट *(adjective)* – दयावान merciful or tolerant. *He is lenient by nature.*

L

Lenity/लेनिटि *(noun)* – दया poetic kindness; gentleness. *One of his qualities is lenity.*

Lenten/लेन्टेन *(adjective)* – मितव्ययी related to Lent, of, in, or appropriate to Lent. *This food without meat is appropriate to Lent.*

Lentil/लेन्टिल *(noun)* – मसूर a high-protein pulse which is dried and then soaked and cooked prior to eating. *Lentil dal is full of proteins.*

Lentisk/लेन्टिस्क *(noun)* – मस्तगी का वृक्ष the mastic tree. *Lentisk is a mastic tree bearing gum.*

Leo/लीओ *(noun)* – सिंह, शेर का बच्चा, सिंह राशि astronomy a large constellation said to represent the lion slain by Hercules. *He is a leo as he was born on 25th of July.*

Leopard/लेपॅर्ड *(noun)* – चीता a large solitary cat that has a fawn or brown coat with black spots, found in the forests of Africa and southern Asia. *Leopards can be seen in zoo or jungles of Asia and Africa.*

Leper/लेपर *(noun)* – कोढ़ी a person suffering from leprosy. *These days there is treatment available for lepers.*

Leprosy/लेप्रॅसी *(noun)* – कोढ़ a contagious bacterial disease that affects the skin, mucous membrane, and nerves, causing discoloration and lumps on the skin and, in severe cases, disfigurement and deformities. *Once leprosy was incurable and was deemed as a result of evil deeds in past life.*

Lese-majesty/लीज्-मैजेस्टि *(noun)* – राज-विद्रोह the insulting of a sovereign; treason. *Lese-majesty resulted in his being hanged on scaffold.*

Lesion/लीजन *(noun)* – पीड़ा chiefly medicine a region in an organ or tissue which has suffered damage through injury or disease. *He suffers from lesion in right arm as a result of an accident.*

Less/लेस *(determine & pronoun)* – कम a smaller amount of; not as much. *The class has less students today.*

Lessen/लेसन *(verb)* – कम करना make or become less. *It lessened my anger when he begged pardon. Let me lessen your burden, give me those bags.*

Lest/लेस्ट *(conjunction)* – कदाचित् with the intention of preventing; to avoid the risk of. *Don't drive rashly lest you should have an accident.*

Lethal/लीथल् *(adjective)* – मृत्युकर sufficient to cause death. *A lethal overdose of sleeping pills took his life.*

Lethargy/लेथार्जि *(noun)* – आलस्य a lack of energy and enthusiasm. *He lives a lack lustre life as a result of lethargy.*

Lettuce/लेटूस *(noun)* – चुकन्दर a cultivated plant of the daisy family, with edible leaves that are eaten in salads. *Lettuce is an important part of salad.*

Leveret/लेवरिट *(noun)* – शशक a young hare in its first year. *I have caught a leveret and I'll make it a pet.*

Leviable/लेविएबल *(adjective)* – कर लगाने योग्य possibility of being taxed, fined. *Octroi tax is leviable on out of state products.*

Leviathan/लेवाइअथन *(noun)* – बड़ा दैत्य a sea monster. a very large aquatic creature, especially a whale. something very large or powerful. *Many leviathans can be seen in this part of sea.*

Levity/लेविटी *(noun)* – ओछापन the treatment of a serious matter with humour or lack of respect. *You are a highly qualified doctor and levity doesn't behove you.*

Levy/लेवि *(noun)* – कर लगाना the imposition of a tax, fee, fine, or subscription. a sum of money raised by such a levy. *This year the government has collected a huge levy.*

Lewd/ल्यूड *(adjective)* – कामुक crude and offensive in a sexual way. *His lewd remarks angered her.*

Lexicon/लेक्सिकन *(noun)* – शब्द-संग्रह the vocabulary of a person, language, or branch of knowledge. *This shop has a number of good lexicons.*

Liability/लाइअबिलिटि *(noun)* – जवाबदेही the state of being liable. *He is more of a liability than an asset.*

Liar/लाइ-अर *(noun)* – मिथ्यावादी a person who tells lies. *Don't believe him, he is a notorious liar.*

Libel/लिइबेल *(noun)* – अपमान-लेख [law] the publication of a false statement that is damaging to a person's reputation. compare with slider. such a statement; a written defamation. *This newspaper has published a libel and a case has been filed against its editor.*

Liberally/लिबरलि *(adverb)* – उदारता से in a generous way. *She liberally gifted all poor children.*

Liberate/लिबरेट *(verb)* – मुक्त करना set free, especially from imprisonment or oppression. free from social conventions, especially with regard to sexual roles. *Many prisoners were liberated on Independence Day.*

Liberation/लिबरेशन *(noun)* – मुक्ति setting free from oppression. *Liberation was granted to many African colonies by the British government.*

Liberator/लिबरेटर *(noun)* – मुक्ति देने वाला a person who liberates one from oppression. *He was seen as a liberator of persons working as bonded labourers.*

Libertine/लिबर्टिन् *(noun)* – कामुक a person who is freely indulgent in sensual pleasures. *He is a libertine and whole-heartedly enjoys life.*

Librate/लाइब्रेट *(verb)* – हिलाना oscillation of the moon. *Astrologers liberate the position at the time of birth to predict future.*

Libration/लाइब्रेशन *(noun)* – कम्पन astronomy an apparent or real oscillation of the moon, by which parts near the edge of the disc that are often not visible from the earth sometimes come into view. *Libration helps astrologers predict future of a person or thing or a country.*

Lid/लिड *(noun)* – ढकना a removable or hinged cover for the top of a container. *One of the lids of the containers is missing.*

Life/लाइफ *(noun)* – इच्छा से, जीवन the condition that distinguishes animals and plants from inorganic matter, including the capacity for growth, functional activity, and continual change preceding death. living things and their activity. a particular type or aspect of people's existence; school life. *Compared to plants and trees, there is apparently no life in stones.*

Lifelong/लाइफलांग *(adjective)* – जीवन पर्यन्त lasting or remaining in a particular state throughout a person's life. *Lifelong habits die hard.*

Lifetime/लाइफटाइम *(noun)* – जीवनकाल the duration of a person's life. the duration of a thing or its usefulness. *He didn't do even a single charitable act throughout his lifetime.*

L

Liftable/लिफ्टेबल *(adjective)* – उठाने योग्य quality of being lifted. *Mount arteries always carry easily liftable packs.*

Lightness/लाइटनेस *(noun)* – हल्कापन source of illumination. *The lightness of these shoes is remarkable.*

Likeable/लाइकेबल *(adjective)* – पसंद के लायक pleasant; easy to like. *He is a likeable person welcomed by all.*

Likelihood/लाइक्लिहुड *(noun)* – सम्भावना the state or fact of being likely. *In all likelihood, he will be arriving tomorrow.*

Liken/लाइकेन *(verb)* – सदृश करना point out the resemblance of someone or something to. *Casteism is likened to a deadly disease.*

Likeness/लाइकनेस *(noun)* – समानता resemblance. the semblance or outward appearance of. a portrait or representation. *Likeness between the father and son is remarkable.*

Likewise/लाइकवाइज *(adverb)* – और भी also; moreover. *He, likewise his brother is quarrelsome.*

Limitation/लिमिटेशन *(noun)* – मियाद a restriction. a defect or failing. *Every human being has his or her limitations.*

Limited/लिमिटेड *(adjective)* – सीमित restricted in size, amount, or extent. not great in ability. *It is a private limited company and not a government concern.*

Limn/लिम्न *(verb)* – चित्र रंगना poetic depict or describe in painting or words; suffuse or highlight with bright colour or light. *The painting was limned to attract customers.*

Limner/लिम्नर *(noun)* – चित्र रंगने वाला a painter of portraits. *He is a renowned limner having painted many portraits.*

Limp/लिम्प *(verb)* – लंगड़ाते हुए चलना walk with difficulty. *He walked limpingly.*

Limpness/लिम्पनेस *(noun)* – लगड़ापन state of walking with great difficulty. *His limpness caused him to walk slowly.*

Lineage/लिनिज *(noun)* – वंश, कुल ancestry or pedigree. *His lineage is royal.*

Lineal/लिनिअल *(adjective)* – पैतृक in a direct line of descent or ancestry. *The lineal crawl of ants is remarkable.*

Linger/लिंगर *(verb)* – विलम्ब करना be slow or reluctant to leave. spend a long time over. be slow to disappear or die. *He lingered on till he was firmly asked to leave.*

Lingerer/लिंगरर *(noun)* – दीर्घसूत्री one who is reluctant to leave. *He is a lingerer and wants go easily.*

Lingering/लिंगरिंग *(adjective)* – चिरकाल का leasting for a long time, slow to end. *His lingering figure caused disturbance to us.*

Linguist/लिंगविस्ट *(noun)* – भाषा प्रवीण a person skilled in foreign languages. *He is a well known linguist.*

Link/लिंक *(adj)* – सम्बन्धित *(noun)* relationship between two things or situations. *Police have found his name linked to a terrorist outfit.*

Linn/लिन *(noun)* – कन्दरा [Scottish archaic] a waterfall; the pool below a waterfall. a steep precipice. *Let's take bath in this linn.*

Liny/लाइनी *(adjective)* – रेखायुक्त [[informal]] marked with lines. *It is a liny piece of paper.*

Lion/लायन *(noun)* – शेर a large tawny-coloured cat of Africa and NW India, of which the male has a shaggy mane. *He fought like a lion in the battle.*

Lip/लिप *(noun)* – ओठ either of the two fleshy parts forming the edges of the mouth opening. another term for labium. *Beautiful lips make a face attractive.*

Liquefaction/लिक्विफैक्शन *(noun)* – गलाने का कार्य process to make liquid. *Liquefaction is the process to convert gas into liquids.*

Liquefier/लिक्विफायर *(noun)* – गलाने वाला means to make liquid. *Use of liquefier is necessary to change gases into liquids.*

Liquescent/लिक्वेसेंट *(adjective)* – गलाने योग्य poetic becoming or apt to become liquid. *Ice is liquescent.*

Liquidity/लिक्विडिटि *(noun)* – तरलता finance the availability of liquid assets to a market or company. liquid assets. *How much your liquid assets are worth?*

Liquidation/लिक्विडेशन *(noun)* – ऋण निस्तार process of liquidating a business. *The firm went into liquidation last year.*

Liquorice/लिकॉरिस *(noun)* – मुलेठी a sweet, chewy, aromatic black substance made from the juice of a root and used as a sweet and in medicine. *Liquourice has a sweet taste and is used in medicine.*

Listener/लिस्नर *(noun)* – सुनने वाला a person who listens. *I like him as he is a patient listener.*

L

Listless/लिस्टलेस *(adjective)* – उदासीन lacking energy or enthusiasm. *I found him listless and lying in bed.*

Literacy/लिटरेसी *(noun)* – साक्षरता the ability to read and write. *A literacy drive has been launched in the village.*

Literally/लिटरली *(adverb)* – यथाशब्द taking words in their usual or most basic sense without metaphor or allegory. free from distortion. [informal] absolute. *Literally speaking, the matter is leased, no more discussion.*

Litigation/लिटिगेशन *(noun)* – विवाद the process of taking legal action. *No firm wishes to go into litigation.*

Litigious/लिटिजियस *(adjective)* – अदालती tending to go to [law] to settle disputes. concerned with or disputable by litigation. *He is a litigious fellow always quarrelling and raising disputes.*

Liturgics/लिटर्जिक्स *(plural noun)* – कर्मकाण्ड विषय the study of liturgics. *Liturgics are often performed in set places e.g. mosques or temples.*

Liven/लाइव्वेन *(verb)* – प्रसन्न करना make or become more lively or interesting. *The atmosphere became livened as she sang melodiously.*

Livid/लिविड *(adjective)* – नीला पड़ा हुआ [informal] furiously angry. *He was livid with anger.*

Living/लिविंग *(noun)* – जीवन an income sufficient to live on, or the means of earning it. *He earns his living by working as a labourer.*

Lizard/लिजर्ड *(noun)* – छिपकली, बम्हनी a reptile that typically has a long body and tail, four legs, movable eyelids, and a rough, scaly, or spiny skin. *I find lizards very repulsive.*

Lo/लो *(exclamatory)* – अहा [archaic] used to draw attention to an interesting event. *Lo! here comes our esteemed guest.*

Load/लोड *(noun)* – दबाव a heavy or bulky thing that is being carried or is about to be carried. the total number or amount that can be carried in a vehicle or container: a carload of people. *The load is about to be moved in a truck.*

Loader/लोडर *(noun)* – बोझने वाला a machine or person that loads something. *About fifteen persons worked round the clock as loaders to load the cargo ship.*

Loan/लोन *(noun)* – ऋण a thing that is borrowed, especially a sum of money that is expected to be paid back with interest. the action of lending. short for loanword. *The bank gave him a loan of one lakh rupees.*

Loath/लोथ *(adjective)* – अनिच्छुक reluctant; unwilling. *I was loath to leave the party.*

Loathe/लोद *(verb)* – निन्दा करना feel hatred or disgust for. *She loathed his presence.*

Loathing/लोदिंग *(noun)* – अतिघृणा feeling of dislike. *He felt nothing but loathing for her.*

Loathsome/लोदसम *(adjective)* – घृणाजनक causing hatred or disgust. *I find centipedes loathsome.*

Labelia/लाबेलिया *(noun)* – एक फूल का पौधा a plant of the bellflower family, typically with blue or scariest flowers. *I have just bought a lobelia for my garden.*

Local/लोकल *(noun)* – स्थानिक, स्थानीय a local person or things. [British informal] a pub convenient to a person's home. [north American] a local branch of a trade union. *The local post office is quite near my house. It is a local infection on and can be treated in the dispensary. A local person told me your address.*

Locality/लोकैलिटी *(noun)* – प्रदेश the position or site of something; an area or neighbourhood. *Is there any cinema house in your locality?*

Locate/लोकेट *(verb)* – स्थापन करना discover the exact place or position of. *. I located his address with much difficulty*

Location/लोकेशन *(noun)* – स्थान निर्धारण a particular place or position. the action or process of locating. *The director was on look out for a suitable location to shoot his film.*

Lockage/लॉकेज *(noun)* – नहर का बाँध the construction or use of locks on waterways. the amount of rise and fall of water levels resulting from the use of locks. *This lockage system is quite difficult to understand.*

Locket/लॉकेट *(noun)* – छोटा ताला, लोलक a small ornamental case worn round a persons' neck on a chain and used to hold things of sentimental value. *He wears a locket which has his wife's photo.*

Lock-stitch/लॉक-स्टिच *(noun)* – दुहरी सियन a stitch made by a sewing machine by firmly linking together two threads or stitches. *These stitches are made by a lock-stitch machine.*

Lock-up/लॉक-अप (noun) – बन्दीगृह a jail, especially a temporary one. *He was put in lock-up for a hit and run case.*

Locomotor/लोकॉमोटर (adjective) – गति-सम्बन्धी [chiefly biology] of or relating to locomotion. *Locomotor modes of all creatures are different.*

Locust/लोकस्ट (noun) – टिड्डी a large, mainly tropical grasshopper which migrates in vast swarms and is very destructive to vegetation. *A big swarm of locust descended on the fields.*

Locution/लोक्यूशन (noun) – वाक्शैली a word or phrase, especially with regard to style or idiom; a person's style of speech. *His locution is unique.*

Lofty/लाफ्टि (adjective) – ऊँचा, उन्नुंग, अहंकारी of imposing height. *It is a lofty building.*

Loftiness/लॉफ्टिनेस (noun) – गर्व state of being noble. *His loftiness knew no bounds.*

Logarithm/लॉगरिथ्म (noun) – घात प्रमापक लघुगणक a quantity representing the power to which a fixed number must be raised to produce a given number. *Logarithm simplifies calculations.*

Logger/लॉगर (noun) – मूर्ख a person who fells trees for timber. *He is a logger whose profession is to cut trees for timber.*

Logician/लॉजिसियन (noun) – तार्किक one who justifies with logic. *He does good reasoning, he is a fine logician.*

Loiter/लॉइटर (verb) – देर करना stand around or move without apparent purpose. *He loitered round the place.*

Loiterer/लॉइटरर – आलसी waiting around without any reason. *He is a loiterer and does no work.*

Loitering/लॉइटरिंग (noun) – विलम्ब state of waiting without reason. *He was found loitering and police questioned him.*

Lollop/लॉलॉप (verb) – सुस्ती से घूमना move in an ungainly way in a series of clumsy bounds. *Some animals lollop.*

Lone/लोन (adjective) – अकेला having no companions; solitary. lacking the support of others. poetic unfrequented and remote. *He is a lone wolf, mixing with nobody.*

Loneliness/लोनलिनेस (noun) – निर्जनता without companion. *He began to suffer as loneliness surrounded him.*

Longevity/लान्विटि (noun) – दीर्घायु long life. *Longevity has been a matter of study for scientists since long.*

Longevous – (adjective) rare. *Tortoise is a longevous specie.*

Longish/लॉन्गिश (adjective) – दीर्घाकार great distance. *The railway platform was quite longish.*

Longitude/लॉंगिट्यूड (noun) – लम्बाई, देशान्तर the angular distance of a place east or west of a standard meridian, especially the Greenwich meridian. *Longitude lines are drawn on a map or globe for marking the distance of a place from Greenwich meridian.*

Looker-on/लुकरऑन (noun) – दर्शक a person who behaves more like a spectator than a participant. *The lookers-on stared at the two filthy persons in a public place.*

Looking/लुकिंग (noun) – दिखावट search, attention towards a particular direction. *Looking down I saw a man climbing stairs.*

Loom/लुम (verb) – अस्पष्ट रूप से देख गया appear as a vague form, especially one that is threatening. seem about to happen. (noun) a vague first appearance of an object seen in darkness or fog, especially at sea. *An iceberg loomed large over the ship.*

Loon/लुन (noun) – दुर्जन [informal] a silly or foolish person. *He is a loon and talks nonsense.*

Loophole/लुपहोल (noun) – बचाव का रास्ता an ambiguity or inadequacy in the [law] or a set of rules. *Lawyers are smart enough to find loopholes in the law.*

Loosely/लुजलि (adverb) – शिथिलता से frivolous. *People avoid him as he is in the habit of talking loosely.*

Looseness/लुजनेस (noun) – ढीलापन not fitting properly. *I couldn't wear the pants because of their looseness.*

Loosen/लुजेन (verb) – पृथक् करना make or become loose. make more lax; warm up in preparation for an activity. *I got my trousers loosened by a tailor as they were very tight.*

Lore/लोर (noun) – शिक्षा a body of traditions and knowledge on a subject: farming lore. *Lore is an important part of any social culture.*

Loser/लूजर (noun) – खोने वाला a person or thing that loses or has lost. [informal] a person who fails frequently. *He is a loser and will never amount to anything.*

Lotus/लोटस *(noun)* – कमल a large water lily, now or formerly regarded as sacred. *Lotus is regarded as sacred flower in India.*

Lounger/लाउंजर *(noun)*– आलसी a comfortable chair, especially an outdoor chair that reclines. *I intend to buy a lounger and relax on it.*

Lout/लाउट *(noun)* – ग्रामीण मनुष्य an uncouth or aggressive man. *He is a lout and sure to quarrel with you sooner or later.*

Loutish/लाउटिश *(adjective)* – अनाड़ी rude and aggressive person. *He is a loutish fellow. Don't mix with him.*

Love/लव *(verb & noun)* – प्रेम करना an intense feeling of deep affection. a deep romantic or sexual attachment to someone. a great interest and pleasure in something. affectionate greetings. *I love my granddaughter a lot.*

Loveliness/लवलिनेस *(noun)* – सुन्दरता state of being attractive. *Her loveliness is to be seen to be believed.*

Lovely/लवलि *(adjective)* – सुन्दर exquisitely beautiful. [informal] very pleasant. *She is a lovely woman*

Lowermost/लोअरमोस्ट *(adjective)* – सबसे नीचे का at the bottom. *Our body's lowermost parts are feet.*

Lowliness/लोलिनेस *(noun)* – विनय low manner, low status. *His lowliness almost reduced him to zero.*

Lowly/लोलि *(adjective)* – दर्पहीन low in status or importance. *He is a lowly employee of the company.*

Loyal/लॉयल् *(adjective)* – सच्चा showing firm and constant support or allegiance to a person or institution. *He is a loyal worker of the party.*

Loyalist/लॉयलिस्ट् *(noun)* – राजभक्त a person who remains loyal to the established ruler or government, especially in the face of a revolt. a supporter of union between great Britain and northern Ireland. *Congress loyalists keep attacking the opposition parties.*

Lozenge/लोजेंज *(noun)* – समचतुर्भुज, बर्फी, मिठाई a rhombus or diamond shape; a small sweet canady. *Take this lozenge, it will melt in your mouth and soothe your throat.*

Lubber/लबर *(noun)* – गँवार [archaic] or dialect a big, clumsy person. *He is a lubber and not smart enough to do this job.*

Lucent/ल्यूसेंट *(adjective)* – प्रकाशमान् poetic shining. *This is a lucent piece of writing.*

Lucidly/ल्यूसिडली *(adverb)* – स्पष्टता से in a simple manner. *The tough vocabulary of the text was lucidly explained by the teacher.*

Luckily/लकिलि *(adverb)* – भाग्यवश fortunately. *Luckily I won the lottery.*

Luckless/लकलेस *(adjective)* – भाग्यहीन unfortunate. *The luckless fellow passed through many difficulties in life.*

Lucre/ल्यूकर *(noun)* – लाभ poetic money, especially when gained dishonourably. *He is a miser and loves to hoard lucre.*

Luculent/ल्यूक्यूलेन्ट *(adjective)* – स्पष्ट rare. clearly expressed. *The luculent moon was a sight to see.*

Lues/लुईज *(noun)* – महामारी, गरमी syphilis. *He suffers from lues.*

Lumbago/लम्बेगो *(noun)* – कमर का दर्द pain in the lower back. *He has been diagnosed as suffering from lumbago.*

Luminary/ल्यूमिनरी *(noun)* – चन्द्रमा a person who inspires or influence others. *He is a luminary who does a lot of inspirational talking.*

Lumpish/लम्पिश *(adjective)* – भारी roughly or clumsily formed. *It is a lumpish pointing.*

Lumpishness/लम्पिशनेस *(noun)* – स्थूलता to behave in a rough manner. *Lumpishness is not a desirable trait.*

Lunancy/ल्यूनेसी *(noun)* – उन्माद insanity. *He suffers from lunacy.*

Lupine/लूपिन *(noun)* – शमीधान्य a plant of the pea family, with deeply divided leaves and tall colourful tapering spikes of flowers. *I have received a lupine as a gift from my friend.*

Lurcher/लर्चर् *(noun)* – चोर [British] a crow-bred dog, typically a retriever, collie, or sheepdog crossed with a greyhound originally used for hunting and by poachers. *A lurcher is a born hunter.*

Lustful/लस्टफुल *(adjective)* – कामातुर having strong feelings of sexual desire. *He is a lustful person, always alive and full of life.*

L

Lustiness/लस्टिनेस *(noun)* – कामुकता state of casting lewd glances. *Our society does not consider lustiness a desirable trait.*

Luteous/ल्यूटिअस् *(adjective)* – गहरे नांरगी रंग का biology of a deep orange-yellow or greenish yellow colour. *He is interested in the luteous study of yellow colour.*

Luxuriant/लक्जरिअंट् *(adjective)* – अत्यन्त rich and profuse in growth. *The plant should have luxuriant growth.*

Luxuriate/लक्जरिएट *(verb)* – आनन्द मचाना enjoy as a luxury. *He luxuriated in a five star hotel.*

Luxury/लक्जरी *(noun)* – विलासिता the state of great comfort and extravagant living. *He is a rich man and lives in great luxury.*

Lydian/लिडिअन् *(noun)* – कोमल, जनाने ढंग का a native or inhabitant of the ancient region of Lydia in western Asia minor. *I dislike his lydian hehaviour.*

Lying/लाइंग *(adjective)* – पड़े हुए present participle of 'lie', not telling the truth. *I can see very clearly that right now you are lying.*

Lymph/लिम्फ *(noun)* – शरीर में का पंछा [physiology] a colourless fluid containing white blood cells, which bathes the tissues and drains through the lymphatic system into the bloodstream; fluid exuding from a sore or inflamed tissue. *Lymph came out of the sore on his hand.*

Lynch/लिन्च *(noun)* – अन्याय युक्त दण्ड देना kill for an alleged offence without a legal trial, especially by hanging. *The thief was lynched by the mob.*

Lynx/लिन्क्स *(noun)* – बिल्ली के कुल का जंगली पशु a wild cat with a short tail and tufted ears. *We saw a lynx in the zoo.*

Lyre/लायर् *(noun)* – वीणा a stringed instrument like a small Unshaped harp with strings fixed to a crossbar, used especially in ancient Greece. *Ancient Greeks used to play lyre.*

Lyric/लिरिक *(noun)* – वीणा का, गायन सम्बन्धी the words of a song. *The poet wrote a beautiful lyric.*

L

Mm

M/एम *(noun)* – अंग्रेजी वर्णमाला का 13वाँ वर्ण the thirteenth letter of the English alphabet.
1. Denoting the next after L in a set of items, categories. etc.
2. The Roman numeral for 1000. *About 1M people participated in the protests.*

Ma/मा *(noun)* – मा informal one's mother. *Priyanka's Ma runs her own construction business.*

Ma'am/मैम *(noun)* – महोदया a respectful form of address for a woman, in particular for female royalty or any woman. *Nigar ma'am is an excellent teacher.*

Mab/मैब *(noun)* – परियों की रानी a fairy queen said to create and control men's dreams. *Sonya played the character of Queen Mab perfectly at the carnival yesterday.*

Mac/मैक *(noun)* – आ उपसर्ग [informal, chiefly north American] a form of address for man whose name is unknown to the speaker. *Hey there, brother Mac, could you please tell me the way to Sandy Street?*

Macaque/मॅकाक *(noun)* – अफ्रीका का लंगूर a medium-sized monkey with a long face and cheek pouches for holding food. *To study the habits of macaque monkeys, one needs to live close to their habitat.*

Macaroni/मैकॅरोनि *(noun)* – सेवई a variety of pasta formed in narrow tubes. *I remember my childhood days over a bowl full of macaroni and cheese that I often have for breakfast.*

Macaronic/मैकॅरॉनिक *(adjective)* – अनेक भाषाओं का मिश्रण denoting languages, especially burlesque verse, containing words or inflections from one language introduced into the context of another. *English is becoming macaronic by incorporating words from other languages.*

Macaroon/मकारून *(noun)* – बादाम a light biscuit made with egg white, sugar, and ground almonds or coconut. *Strawberry macaroons are Tom's favourite evening refreshment.*

Macassar-oil/मैकासर-आइल् *(noun)* – मकासर नगर का सुगन्धित तेल a kind of oil formerly used by men to give shine to their hair. *Ved explained the benefits of Macassar oil at the workshop.*

Macaw/मकॉ *(noun)* – तोता a longtailed parrot with bright plummage. *Its colourful plumage characterizes the Macaw species.*

Mace/मेस *(noun)* – गदा, जावित्री [historical] a heavy club with a metal head and spikes. *The robber used a mace to attack his victim.*

Machiavelli/मैकियावेली *(noun)* – धूर्त राजनीतिज्ञ a person who is prepared to use unethical means to gain power. *Machiavelli was a great political writer.*

Machinal/मैकिनल *(adj.)* – यन्त्रवत् like machines. *Monotony is often the consequence of a machinal lifestyle.*

Machinate/मैकिनेट *(verb)* – षड्यन्त्र करना engage in plots and intrigues; scheme. *The police found out that Sandy's own brother machinated his murder.*

Machination/मैकिनेशन *(noun)* – कूट प्रबन्ध a plot or scheme. *Nefertiti's political machinations brought her to control the whole of Egypt.*

Machine/मशीन *(noun)* – साधन an apparatus using or applying mechanical power and having several parts, each with a definite function and together performing a particular task; technical any device that transmits a force or directs its application. *A pulley is a simple machine.*

Machinery/मशीनरी *(noun)* – यन्त्रों का समूह machines collectively, or the components of a machine. *Mining requires the use of some heavy machinery.*

Mackerel/मैकॅरॅल – समुद्री मछली *(noun)* a surface-dwelling marine fish with a greenish-blue back, commercially important as a food fish. *Mackerel is a delicacy in some parts of the world.*

M

Mackintosh/मैकिन्टॉश (noun) – बरसाती कपड़ा British a full-length waterproof coat. *Sam put his mackintosh on to shelter himself from the heavy snowfall that came suddenly.*

Macrame/मॅक्रामि (noun) – गाँठ दी हुई झालर the craft of knotting cord or string in patterns to make decorative articles. *Tina surprised everyone with her talent of macramé at the summer camp.*

Macrocosm/मैक्रोकॉज्म (noun) – त्रिभुवन the universe, the cosmos. *Our solar system is just a small part of the macrocosm, which is a collection of several such solar systems.*

Macron/मैक्रॉन (noun) – दीर्घचिह्न a written or printed mark used to indicate a long vowel in some languages and phonetic transcription systems, or a stressed vowel in verse. *Tina learnt the importance of macrons in her phonetics class at the university today.*

Macula/मैक्यूला (noun) – धब्बा anatomy an oval yellowish area surrounding the fovea near the centre of the retina in the eye, which is the region of greatest visual acuity. *Rob hurt the macula of his eyes in an accident.*

Maculate/मैक्युलेट (adjective) – धब्बा लगाना spotted or stained. *The maculated cloth revealed the secret behind the murder crime.*

Maculation/मैक्यूलेशन (noun) – लांछन, धब्बा mark of spot. *Maculation on a leopard's body is a natural phenomenon.*

Mad/मैड (adjective) – पागल mentally ill; insane. extremely foolish or ill advised. *To challenge the authority and expecting it to bend its rules is a mad idea.*

Madden/मैडेन (verb) – पागल होना drive insane. *His love for her maddened him.*

Madder/मैडर (noun) – छबीला a plant related to the bedstraws, with roots that yield a red dye. a red dye or pigment obtained from this plant. *The madder plant is known for the red dye that it yields.*

Mademoiselle/मैडमॅजेल (noun) – कुमारी a title or form of address for an unmarried French-speaking woman. *Monsieur Heathcliff requested Mademoiselle Emma for a drink in the bar.*

Madhouse/मैडहाउस (noun) – पागलखाना [historical] a mental institution. [informal] a psychiatric hospital. *The state government employs the inmates of the Boston madhouse.*

Madly/मैडली (adverb) – पागलपन से in mad way. *Tom is madly in love with Rita.*

Madness/मैडनेस (noun) – पागलपन foolish behaviour, mental illness. *Playing with fire is an act of sheer madness.*

Madrigal/मैड्रिगल (noun) – देहाती गीत a 16th or 17th century part song for several voices, typically unaccompanied and arranged in elaborate counterpoint. *The Madrigal is an interesting form of music and lyrics that involves a group of people singing together or individually.*

Magazine/मैगजीन (noun) – शस्त्र, पत्रिका a periodical publication containing articles and illustrations. a regular television or radio programme comprising a variety of items. *Elle Décor is a good magazine to learn about the current trends in the market.*

Mage/मेज़ (noun) – पण्डित archaic or poetic a magician or learned person. *Sita knew that the heavily bearded man was a mage the moment she saw him meditating in the Himalayas.*

Maggot/मैगॉट (noun) – कृमि a soft-bodied legless larva, especially that of a fly or other insect and found in decaying matter. *The meat dish was infested with maggots.*

Maggoty/मैगॉटि (adjective) – कीड़ों से भरा हुआ full of maggots. *The rice dish turned maggoty after two days.*

Magi/मेजाइ (plural noun) – विद्वान् the three wise men from the east who brought gifts to the infant Jesus. *Karan told her son about the Magi who brought gifts for the infant Jesus on the eve of Christmas.*

Magical/मैजिकल (adjective) – जादू का containing magic. *Preeti says that her trip to Venice was absolutely magical.*

Magician/मैजिशियन (noun) – जादूगर a person with magical powers. a conjuror. *Tory invited a magician to delight the kids attending her son's birthday party.*

Magnanimity/मैग्नानिमिटि (noun) – उदारता generosity. *Monty's donations to the children's fund reflect his magnanimity.*

Magnate/मैग्नेट (noun) – रईस a wealthy and influential person, especially in business. *Lalit Mohan is a business magnate in the steel industry.*

M

Magnet/मैग्नेट *(noun)* – चुम्बक a piece of iron or other material, typically in the form of a bar or horseshoe, that has the property of attracting similar objects or aligning itself in an external magnetic field. *A magnet attracts all objects made out of iron.*

Magnetism/मैग्नेटिज्म *(noun)* – आकर्षणशक्ति a physical phenomenon produced by the motion of electric charge, which results in attractive and repulsive forces between objects. *Leela and Sam share a strong aura of magnetism that is not easily understood by others.*

Magnetization/मैग्नेटाइजेशन *(noun)* – आकर्षण संस्कार property of attraction. *The iron ore under the Earth's surface leads to its magnetization.*

Magnifiable/मैग्निफाएबल *(adj)* – बढ़ाने योग्य *Virus and bacteria are easily magnifiable with the help of a microscope.*

Magnification/मैग्निफिकेशन *(adverb)* – बृहत्तरकरण make something appear bigger than it actually is. *Viruses are visible only under high magnification.*

Magnificence/मैग्निफिसेंस *(noun)* – प्रताप the quality of being magnificent. *Nefertiti, the Egyptian queen, prided herself over the magnificence of her empire.*

Magnifico/मैग्निफिको *(noun)* – रईस powerful, or illustrious person. *The jury facilitated the illustrious magnificoes of the Bollywood industry.*

Magnifier/मैग्निफायर *(noun)* – बढ़ाकर दिखलाने वाला an equipment that used to to look things begger. *Biologists study microorganisms with the help of a magnifier.*

Magniloquence/मैग्निलोक्वेंस *(noun)* – प्रौढ़ भाषण use of flwery language. *The dowager Queen was known for her magniloquence throughout the kingdom.*

Magpie/मैग्पाइ *(noun)* – नीलकण्ठ पक्षी a long-tailed bird of the crow family, typically with pied plumage and a raucous voice. a black-and-white Australian butcher-bird with musical calls. *We saw a beautiful magpie at the bird sanctuary yesterday.*

Mahogany/महोगनी *(noun)* – महोगनी वृक्ष hard reddish-brown wood from a tropical tree, used for furniture. *Ben ordered new mahogany wood furniture for his new office.*

Maiden/मेडॅन *(noun)* – कुमारी कन्या [archaic or poetic] a girl or young woman. a virgin. *The fair maiden loved her village and never wanted to leave it.*

Mailable/मेलेबॅल *(adj)* – डाक से भेजने योग्य *Betty sent all the mailable documents to Veronica as soon as possible.*

Maintenance/मेन्टिनेन्स *(noun)* – जीविका the process or state of maintaining or being maintained. *The present government of Goa has ensured strict control over the maintenance of the state.*

Maize/मेज *(noun)* – मक्का [chiefly British] a cereal plant originating in central America and yielding large grins set in rows on a cob. *Maize forms an integral part of breakfast in the West.*

Major/मेजर *(adjective)* – प्रमुख, वयस्क important, serious, or significant, greater or more important, main. *Financial inadequacy is a major problem in developing nations.*

Make-believe/मेक-बिलिव *(noun)* – बहाना the action of pretending or imagining. *All the characters in the play are make-believe.*

Maker/मेकर *(noun)* – रचने वाला a person or thing that makes or produces something. *The maker of this chair is Sam.*

Makeshift/मेकशिफ्ट *(adjective)* – क्षणिक interim and temporary. *This house is a makeshift arrangement.*

Makeweight/मेकवेट *(noun)* – पसँघा धड़ा something put on a scale to make up the required weight. *The makeweight added by the vegetable vendor was faulty.*

Making/मेकिंग *(noun)* – रचना the process of making or producing something. *The making of a cake requires patience and precision.*

Maladjustment/मॉलएड्जस्टमेंट – बुरा प्रबन्ध *Rex is a maladjusted boy in his school.*

Malady/मैलडि *(noun)* – रोग a disease or ailment. *Depression is one of the most widespread maladies in the world.*

Malaise/मैलेज *(noun)* – शारीरिक क्लेश a general feeling of discomfort, illness, or unease. *Rita often experiences a sense of malaise at her workplace.*

Malapropos/मैलएऐप्रपो *(adverb)* – असमय में inopportunely; inappropriately. *He malapropos commented on his fellow colleagues.*

M

Malcontent/मैलकन्टेन्ट *(noun)* – अतृप्त a discontented person. *The malcontents are the first ones to create problems in a happy environment.*

Malefaction/मैलिफैक्शन *(noun)* – पाप, शाप a person who commits a crime or some wrong. *Unfortunately, politicians are allowed to commit crimes such as financial corruption and other such malefactions by the state apparatus.*

Malefactor/मैलिफैक्टर *(noun)* – पापी formal a person who commits a crime or some other wrong. *The malefactor involved in the murder is still missing.*

Malefic/मॉलिफिक *(adjective)* – हानिकर poetic causing harm. *His malefic words made him exercise control over all the workers.*

Maleficence/मॉलिफिसेन्स *(noun)* – अपकार most black magic originate out of male ficence. *Maleficence often leads to forced agreement in a given situation.*

Maleficent/मॉलिफिसेन्ट *(adjective)* – अपकारी state of cusing harm. *His maleficent eyes often led to the undoing of women.*

Malevolence/मॉलेवलॅन्स *(noun)* – द्रोह state of hostility. *Tina's eyes reflect her malevolence towards Rob.*

Malformation/मैल्फॉःमेशन *(noun)* – बुरी बनावट abnormality of shape or form in a part of the body. *Warts are a malformation by birth and need to be removed surgically.*

Malice/मैलिस *(noun)* – डाह the desire to do harm to someone; ill will. *Rita experiences unbearable malice towards men who molested her last year and seeks revenge.*

Malicious/मॅलिशस *(adjective)* – द्रोही पापाम्मा characterized by malice; intending or intended to do harm. *His malicious nature is the cause of his unethical behaviour.*

Malign/मॅलाइन *(verb)* – बदनाम करना *(adj.)* घातक speak ill of. *Tom's malign nature led to his dismissal from his workplace yesterday.*

Malignancy/मॉलिग्नैन्सी *(noun)* – द्रोह the state or presence of a malignant tumour; cancer. a cancerous growth. a form of cancer. *The biopsy revealed the nature of the malignancy.*

Malignity/मॉलिग्निटि *(noun)* – ईर्ष्या speaking in a spiteful manner. *Criminals often show signs of heinous malignity.*

Malignly/मॉलिग्नलि *(adverb)* – द्रोह से attitude of speaking ill of others. *All of Iago's dialogues with Othello are malignly planned.*

Malison/मैलिसन *(noun)* – शाप archaic a curse. *The onlookers screamed several malisons at the murderers.*

Mall/माल *(noun)* – ठण्डी सड़क a large enclosed shopping area from which traffic is excluded. *Rob likes grocery shopping at the mall on Sundays.*

Mallard/मैलॅई *(noun)* – जंगली बत्तख the commonest duck of the northern hemisphere, the male having a dark green head and white collar. *Mallard is a delicacy in some parts of the world.*

Mallet/मैलेट् *(noun)* – मुँगरी a hammer with a large wooden head. *She murdered her abusive husband using only a mallet.*

Malodorous/मैलोडॅरॅस *(adjective)* – बदबूदार smelling very unpleasant. *She walked through malodorous alleys to reach the post office.*

Malpractice/मैल्प्रैक्टिस *(noun)* – बुरी चाल improper, illegal, or negligent professional activity or treatment. *The doctor lost his licence to practise medicine because of his malpractice.*

Malt/मॉल्ट *(noun)* – भिगोया हुआ जौ barely or other grain that has been steeped, germinated, and dried, used especially for brewing or distilling and vinegar-making. *Malt beer is a refreshing drink, especially during summers.*

Maltreat/मैल्ट्रीट *(verb)* – गाली देना treat cruelly or with violence. *Sam had been maltreating his wife since the day they got married.*

Mammary/मैमरि *(adjective)* – स्तन-सम्बन्धी denoting or relating to the human female breasts or the milk secreting organs of other mammals. *Rita realized that her mammary tumour had spread throughout her chest area.*

Mammon/मैमन *(noun)* – कुबेर wealth regarded as an evil influence or false object of worship. *Greeks worshipped Mammon for greater wealth.*

Mammoth/मैमथ *(noun & adj)* – महान्, विशालकाय a large extinct elephant of the Pleistocene epoch, typically hairy and with long curved tusks. *The Mammoth is an extinct animal.*

Manacle/मैनॅकॅल *(noun)* – हथकड़ी a metal band, chain, or shackle for fastening someone's hands or ankles. *Patients who have severe mental illness are often kept in manacles.*

Manage/मैनेज् *(verb)* – चलाना be in charge of; run. *She managed the entire fashion show on her own.*

Manageability/मैनेजिबिलिटी *(noun)* – व्यवस्था ability to control or deal without difficulty. *A person's ability to work in a stressful environment depends the manageability of various tasks.*

Manageable/मैनेजेबूल् *(adjective)* – प्रबन्ध करने योग्य able to control without difficulty. *All things are manageable once planned in an organized fashion.*

Management/मैनेजमेन्ट *(noun)* – अनुशासन the process of managing. *The management of any company depends on its team.*

Manager/मैनेजर् *(noun)* – प्रबन्धक a person who manages an organization or group of staff. *My Manager is a strict disciplinarian.*

Manageress/मैनेजरेश *(noun)* – प्रबन्धकर्त्री a female manager. *Deepika makes an intelligent and a competent mangeress.*

Managerial/मैनेजीरिअल् *(adjective)* – प्रबन्ध-सम्बन्धी relating to management. *Preeti fulfils her managerial duties in perfect order.*

Mandate/मैन्डेट *(noun)* – आदेश an official order or commission to do something. *All drivers are said to follow the state mandate of safe and slow driving.*

Mandatory/मैन्डेटरी *(adjective)* – आज्ञा-सूचक required by law or mandate. *Mandatory rules enforced by the government ought to be followed by all the citizens on a nation.* compulsory. *Wearing a vermillion mark on the forehead is mandatory for all married Hindu women.*

Manes/मानेज/मानीज *(plural noun)* – पितरों की आत्माएँ the defined souls of dead ancestors. *Some tribes still pray to their manes hoping that they would be rid of any diseases or misfortunes.*

Mangle/मैंगल *(verb)* – खण्ड-खण्ड करना [chiefly British] a machine having two or more cylinders turned by a handle, between which wet laundry is squeezed and pressed. *Mangles are used to dry and iron out clothes in large numbers.*

Mango/मैंगो *(noun)* – आम a fleshy yellowish red tropical fruit which is eaten ripe or used green for pickles or chutneys. the evergreen Indian tree which bears this fruit. *Mango is the king of fruits.*

Mangy/मेन्जि *(adjective)* – रूखा having mange. *The mangy dog was sent to the veterinarian.*

Mania/मेनिआ *(noun)* – उन्माद mental illness marked by periods of excitement, delusions, and overactivity. *Patients suffering from mania are often unable to control their anger.*

Maniac/मेनिअक् *(noun)* – पागल मनुष्य a person exhibiting extremely wild or violent behaviour. *Ginger is a maniac and is very aggressive.*

Manikin/मेनिकिन् *(noun)* – छोटा मनुष्य a very small person. *Dicken's fictional character or Uncle Scrooge is depicted as a manikin.*

Manipulation/मनिप्युलेशन *(noun)* – दस्तकारी the action of manipulating something in skilful manner. *Rob is a manipulative boss.*

Manner/मैनर *(noun)* – चाल a way in which something is done or happens. *Clive gives orders to his team in an unstoppable manner.*

M

Manse/मैन्स *(noun)* – पादरियों का घर the house occupied by a minister of a Scottish Presbyterian church. *Civilians visit the manse on Sunday.*

Mansion/मैन्सन *(noun)* – बड़ा भवन, हवेली, कोठी a large, impressive house. *Raman lives in a mansion in Mumbai.*

Mansuetude/मैनस्विट्युड *(noun)* – सीधापन archaic meekness; gentleness. *His wife takes advantage of his mansuetude.*

Mantelet/मैन्टॅलेट *(noun)* – बुरका variant spelling of mantlet. *Tia gave the poor beggar her mantelet on Christmas eve.*

Mantis/मैन्टिस *(noun)* – एक प्रकार का कीड़ा a slender predatory insect with a triangular head, typically waiting motionless for prey with its forelegs folded like hands in prayer. *Ned saw a Mantis on his way back home from work.*

Manually/मैन्युअली *(adverb)* – हाथ से करते हुए by human labour. *Some machinery ought to be operated manually.*

Manufactory/मैन्युफैक्टरी *(noun)* – कारखाना archaic a factory. *The carpenter's wife worked at the manufactory to earn a little extra.*

Manufacture/मैन्युफैक्चर *(verb)* – दस्तकारी make on a large scale using machinery. *Steel factories manufacture utensils.*

Mar/मार *(verb)* – हानि करना abbreviation March. *Spring season lasts from Mar-May.*

Marasmic/मरैज़्मिक *(adj)* – शरीरक्षय- सम्बन्धी undernourished children. *Nancy felt sorry for her marasmic child.*

Marasmus/मरैज़्मस *(noun)* – शरीर का क्षय medicine undernourishment causing a child's weight to be significantly low for their age. *Vicky's son suffers from Marasmus.*

Maraud/मॅराड *(verb)* – लूटना attack and steal; raid. *The invading army marauded the village.*

Marcescence/मारसेसॅन्स *(noun)* – मुरझाहट property of withering low remaining attached to the stem. *With the advent of winter, the crops in the village had started to marcescence.*

Marcescent/मारसेसॅन्ट *(noun)* – मुरझाने वाला botany withering but remaining attached to the stem. *The China Rose had become marcescent but had not lost its beauty.*

Mare/मेअर *(noun)* – घोड़ी the female of a horse or other equine animal. *Ruth loved to ride her mare during vacations.*

Margosa/मारगोसा *(noun)* – नीम का वृक्ष neem tree. *Margosa has healing and antiseptic properties.*

Marigold/मेरिगोल्ड *(noun)* – गेंदा a plant of the daisy family with yellow, orange, or copper-brown flowers, cultivated as an ornamental. used in names of other plants with yellow flowers, e.g. marsh marigold. *Marigold garlands are used to beautify the bride in Indian weddings.*

Marine/मॅरीन *(adjective)* – समुद्रीय of, relating to, or produced by the sea. *Vinit is a botanist who specializes in marine plants.*

Mariner/मैरिनर *(noun)* – नाविक formal or poetic a sailor. *Fawaz wants to become a mariner when he grows up.*

Maritime/मैरिटाइम *(adjective)* – समुद्रीय connected with the sea, especially in relation to seafaring commercial or military activity. *Cindy knows all the rules of maritime sailing.*

Marked/मार्कड *(adjective)* – चिह्नित having a visible mark. having distinctive marks on their backs to assist cheating. *All the victims of the holocaust were marked on their skin.*

Marker/मार्कर *(noun)* – गिनने वाला an object used to indicate a position, place, or route. a thing serving as a standard of comparison. *Promotion acts as a marker of success.*

Market/मार्किट *(noun)* – बाजार a regular gathering of people for the purchase and sale of provisions, livestock, and other commodities. an open space or covered building where vendors convene to sell their goods. *I go to the market in the morning to buy fresh vegetables.*

Marketable/मार्केटेबल *(adjective)* – बिक्री के योग्य able or fit to be sold or marketed. *Marketable goods often enjoy huge popularity.*

Marking/मार्किंग *(noun)* – परों की रंगाई an identification mark. a pattern of marks on an animal's fur, feathers, or skin. *The markings on a leopard are unique.*

Marksman/मार्क्समैन *(noun)* – निशानेबाज a person skilled in shooting. *Sam is an excellent marksman.*

Marmoreal/मार्मोरियल *(adjective)* – इसके सदृश poetic made of or likened to marble. *Rita has Marmoreal flooring in her attic.*

Maroon/मैरून *(noun)* – आतिशबाजी a member of a group of black people living in parts of Surinam and the West Indies, descended from runaway slaves. *Ben's ancestors belonged to the Maroon community.*

Marriageable/मैरिजेबल *(adjective)* – विवाह करने योग्य fit or suitable for marriage, especially in being wealthy or of the right age. *Geeta wants to be married to her lover once she attains the marriageable age.*

Mars/मार्स *(noun)* – मंगल ग्रह a small planet of the solar system which is fourth in order from the sun and the nearest to the earth. *Mars is the fourth planet in our solar system.*

Marsh/मार्श *(noun)* – दलदल an area of low-lying land which is flooded in wet seasons or at high tide, and typically remains waterlogged at all times. *Lotus plant grows in abundance in marshlands.*

Marshiness/मार्शिनेस *(noun)* – दलदली स्थिति proneness to water logging. *Tropical American land is known for its marshiness.*

Marshy/मार्शि *(adj)* – दलदली resembling a marsh. *Marshy areas are usually accident prone.*

Mart/मार्ट *(noun)* – हाट a trade centre or market. *Heena bought a new pair of shoes from the Mart yesterday.*

M

Martian/मार्श्यन् *(adjective)* - मंगल ग्रह का निवासी of or relating to the planet mars or its supposed inhabitants. *The Martian rock was being studied by the scientists.*

Martinet/मार्टिनेट *(noun)* - तीक्ष्ण शासक a strict disciplinarian, especially in the armed forces. *George was an excellent Martinet in the American army.*

Martingale/मार्टिंगेल *(noun)* - जेरबन्द a strap or set of straps running from the noseband or reins to the girth of a horse, used to prevent the horse from raising its head too high. *Gia fell from her horse when the Martingale broke.*

Martyr/मार्टर *(noun)* - शहीद a person who is killed because of their religious or other beliefs. *Shaheed Bhagat Singh was a martyr.*

Masher/मैशर *(noun)* - छैला a utensil for mashering food. *I want to buy a potato masher.*

Masked/मास्क्ड *(adjective)* - गुप्त cover with a mask. *Both the robbers were masked in order to hide their identities.*

Masker/मास्कर *(noun)* - नकाब डाले हुए Grub a thing used to conceal something. *Street writers were great maskers of good literature.*

Mason/मेसन *(noun)* - राजमिस्त्री a builder and worker in stone. *Fred's father is a mason.*

Masonry/मेसनरी *(noun)* - राजगीरी stonework. the work of a mason. *Dany says his talent lies in masonry.*

Masque/मास्क *(noun)* - कठपुतली का तमाशा a form of amateur dramatic entertainment, popular in 16th and 17th century England, which consisted of dancing and acting performed by masked players. *Several women writers such as Aphra Behn wrote plays that were dramatized as masques in the 18th century.*

Massacre/मैसेकॅ(र) *(noun)* - खूनखराबा an indiscriminate and brutal slaughter of people. *The Jallianwala massacre continues to haunt people till date.*

Massage/मैसाज् *(noun)* - अंगमर्दन the rubbing and kneading of muscles and joints of the body with the hands, especially to relieve tension or pain. *A good massage is a great way to relieve stress.*

Masseur/मैसॅर *(noun)* - मालिश करने वाला मनुष्य a person who provides massage professionally. *Michel hired a masseur for his wife after she fell from the stairs.*

Massy/मैसी *(adjective)* - ठोस, भारी massive. *I need to buy a massy bed for the kids.*

Mast/मास्ट *(noun)* - मस्तूल a tall upright post, spar, or other structure on a boat, in sailing vessels generally carrying a sail or sails. *The sailor fixed the mast before the ship sailed.*

Masterly/मास्टरली *(adjective)* - अद्वितीय performed or performing very skillfully. *Naved's masterly act made him a popular favourite with all his superiors at his workplace.*

Mastership/मास्टरशीप *(noun)* - ऐश्वर्य through knowledge. *A man's mastership is judged by his manners in front of his inferiors.*

Mastery/मास्टरी *(noun)* - अधिकार comprehensive knowledge or skill in a particular field. *Fred has mastery over all of Dickens' novels.*

Mastic/मैस्टिक *(noun)* - गोंद, लासा an aromatic gum or resin exuded from the bark of a Mediterranean tree, used in making varnish and chewing gum and as a flavouring. *Mastic has no side effects in the long run.*

Masticable/मैस्टिकेबल *(adj)* - चबाने योग्य chewable. *This food is easily masticable.*

Mastication/मास्टिकेशन *(noun)* - चबाने का कार्य state of chewing. *The mastication of food depends on the bacteria in the human gut.*

Masticate/मास्टिकेट *(verb)* - चबाना chew food. *George's mother bit her tongue while masticating her meal.*

Mastitis/मैस्टाइटिस् *(noun)* - स्तन की सूजन inflammation of the mammary giand in the breast or udder. *Mastitis is often seen as an early symptom of cancer.*

Matchable/मैचेबल *(adj)* - अनुरूप fit to be matched, suitable. *The matchable characteristics of aquatic plants are of great importance to marine biologists.*

Matchless/मैचलेस *(adjective)* - अनुपम unequalled; incomparable. *Cleopatra's matchless beauty is talked about even today.*

Materialism/मैटीरिअलिज्म *(noun)* - जड़वाद a tendency to consider material possessions and physical comfort as more important than spiritual values. *Materialism is a distinct characteristic of selfish individualism.*

M

Materiality/मैटेरिअलिटि *(noun)* – भौतिकत्व material existence. *The nuclear weapons explain the materiality of the developed nations.*

Materialize/मैटीरिअलाइज *(verb)* – भौतिक बनाना become actual fact; happen. appear or be present: the train failed to materialize. *The driver failed to materialize despite constant phone calls.*

Maternity/मैटरनिटि *(noun)* – मातृत्व motherhood. *Kareena is on her maternity leave till September.*

Mathematician/मैथेमेटिशिअन *(noun)* – गणितज्ञ *Anurag was a well-known mathematician in the University of Delhi.*

Mathematics/मैथेमेटिक्स *(noun)* – गणित-विद्या the branch of science concerned with number, quantity, and space, either as abstract concepts or as applied to physics, engineering, and other subjects. *Mathematics plays an important part in the study of planetary shifts in space.*

Matricidal/मैट्रिसाइडल *(adj)* – मातृहत्या-सम्बन्धी showing tendency to kill one's mother. *Tom is suspected to have matricidal tendencies after his mental illness.*

Matricide/मैट्रिसाइड *(noun)* – मातृहत्या the killing of one's mother. a person who kills his/her mother. *Matricide is a heinous crime.*

Matrimonial/मैट्रिमोनियल *(adj)* – विवाह-सम्बन्धी relating to marriage. *Sagar got his matrimonial pictures clicked by a professional photographer.*

Matrimony/मैट्रिमॅनि *(noun)* – विवाह-संस्कार the state or ceremony of being married; marriage. *Guneet and Avreen are enjoying a healthy state of holy matrimony as on date.*

Matting/मैटिंग *(noun)* – चटाई material used for mats, especially coarse fabric woven from a natural fibre. *Matting is a common practice in the villages of India.*

Mattock/मैटॉक *(noun)* – गैंती, फावड़ा an agricultural tool similar to a pickaxe, but with one arm of the head curved like an adze and the other like a chisel edge, used for breaking up hard ground, digging up roots, etc. *The farmer's daughter gifted him a mattock with her first salary.*

Mattress/मैट्रेस *(noun)* – गद्दा, तोशक a fabric case filled with soft, firm, or springy material used for sleeping on. *Prisoners are just given a mattress to sleep on in jail.*

Maturate/मैच्यूरेट् *(verb)* – मवाद पड़ना, पक जाना form pus. *The soldier's wounds maturated despite the timely medication.*

Maturity/मैट्युरिटि *(noun)* – परिपक्वता, सिद्धि the state, fact, or period of being mature. *The farmers wait a long time for the maturity of their crops.*

Maudlin/मॉडलिन *(adjective)* – भावुक self-pityingly or tearfully sentimental. *Betty is prone to sudden bouts of maudlin reactions.*

Maund/मॉन्ड *(noun)* – मन a measure of weight equal to 8 kilogram. *The Zamindar promised a maund of rice to every villager in his village.*

Maunder/मॉन्डर *(verb)* – बकना move, talk, or act in a rambling or aimless manner. *Sam is often seen maundering the streets after losing his job.*

Mausoleum/मॉसोलीॲम *(noun)* – मकबरा a building, especially a large and stately one, housing a tomb or tombs. *Shahjahan is a renowned Mughal emperor for building mausoleums in and around his territory.*

Mauve/मॉव् *(noun)* – चमकीला गुलाबी रंग a pale purple colour. *Mauve is my favourite colour.*

Maw/मॉ *(noun)* – उदर the jaws or throat, especially of a voracious animal. *The canine caught the neck of the mongoose in his maw.*

Maximize/मैक्सिमाइज *(verb)* – परम संख्या तक बढ़ना make as large or great as possible. *The key to a successful business is to minimize time taken and maximize profits.*

Maze/मेज *(noun)* – भूलभुलैया a network of paths and hedges designed as a puzzle through which one has to find a way. *The maze at the theme park is the most popular form of entertainment for people in Disneyland.*

Maziness/मेजिनेस *(noun)* – घबड़ाहट, व्यग्रता the state of being mazy. *The maziness of his thoughts drove people crazy.*

Mead/मीड *(noun)* – मध्वासव an alcoholic drink of fermented honey and water. *The men were drunk on mead.*

Meagre/मीगर *(adjective)* – दुर्बल lacking in quantity or quality. *These meagre offerings won't help the children.*

Mean/मीन *(verb)* – अर्थ होना या रखना intend to convey or refer to. have as its signification in the same language or its equivalent in another language. be of a specified degree of

M

importance to. *I mean that I will see you in two hours.*

Meander/मीएन्डर *(noun)* – गोमूत्रिका follow a winding course. *The river meandered through the forest.*

Meaning/मिनिंग *(noun)* – आशय what is meant by a word, text, concept, or action. *What is the meaning of this poem?*

Meaningly/मिनिंग्ली *(adverb)* – अर्थ सहित intended to communicate something. *He looked at her meaningly.*

Measles/मिजल्स *(noun)* – खसरा, मसूरिका an infectious viral disease causing fever and a red rash, typically occurring in childhood. *Each child must be vaccinated against measles.*

Measurable/मेजॅरॅबॅल *(adjective)* – नापने योग्य able or large enough to be measured. *Please give me a measurable quantity of milk.*

Measureless/मेजरलेस *(adjective)* – असीम having no limits. *My love for my parents is measureless.*

Measurement/मेजरमेंट *(noun)* – नाप the action of measuring. an amount, size, or extent as established by measuring. a unit or system of measuring. *The designer worked on incorrect measurements.*

Meat/मीट *(noun)* – मांस flesh of an animal. *The lion pounced upon the meat.*

Mechanical/मिकैनिकल *(adjective)* – बुद्धिरहित working or produced by machines or machinery. of or relating to machines or machinery. *The engine being demonstrated is mechanical.*

Mechanism/मेकॅनिज़्म *(noun)* – यन्त्र रचना a piece of machinery. *A very complex mechanism runs this car.*

Mechanization/मेकनाइज़ेशन *(noun)* – यन्त्रीकरण the act of making mechanical. *The mechanization of the process optimized the entire process.*

Meconium/मेकोनियम *(noun)* – गाढ़ा हरा पदार्थ the dark green substance forming the first faeces of a newborn infant. *The meconium had a bad smell.*

Meddler/मेडलर *(noun)* – विघ्न डालने वाला one who interferes. *He is such a meddler in everyone's business.*

Medial/मीडिअल *(adjective)* – बीच में का situated in the middle. *The medial line was a little slanted.*

Median/मीडिअन *(adjective)* – मध्यम, मध्यस्थ situated in the middle, especially of the body. *Median depth of the river is six feet.*

Medical/मेडिकल *(adjective)* – चिकित्सा-सम्बन्धी of or relating to the science or practice of medicine. *He is a medical practitioner.* *(noun)* an examination to assess a person's state of physical health or fitness. *The boss has gone for his annual medical.*

Medicaster/मेडिकास्टर – ढोंगी वैद्य a quack. *Don't go to a medicaster at any cost.*

Medicinal/मेडिसिनल *(adjective)* – औषधि-सम्बन्धी having healing properties. relating to medicines or drugs. *The herb has medicinal use.*

Medicine/मेडिसीन *(noun)* – औषधि the science or practice of the diagnosis, treatment, and prevention of disease. *The child wants to study medicine when he grows up.*

Mediocre/मीडिओकर *(adjective)* – सामान्य of only moderate or average quality. *His mediocre performance failed to impress the critics.*

Mediocrity/मीडिऑक्रिटि *(noun)* – सामान्यता the quality of being just average. *I am tired of all the mediocrity.*

Meditate/मेडिटेट *(verb)* – सोचना, मनन करना focus one's mind for a period of time for spiritual purposes or as a method of relaxation. *I meditate for a few minutes every day.*

Meditation/मेडिटेशन *(noun)* – चिन्तन the action or practice of meditating. *Meditation gives you peace.*

Meditative/मेडिटेटिव *(adjective)* – ध्यानतत्पर absorbed in deeper thoughts. *His stance was very meditative.*

Mediterranean/मेडिटरेनियन *(adj)* – भूमध्य-सागरीय of or characteristic of the Mediterranean sea, the countries bordering it, or their inhabitants. *The Mediterranean climate does not suit me.*

Meed/मीड *(noun)* – इनाम [archaic] a deserved share or reward. *He was happy to have reserved his meed.*

Meek/मीक *(adjective)* – विनीत quiet, gentle, and submissive. *At times, his meek demeanour looks quite fake.*

Meeting/मिटिंग *(noun)* – सभा an assembly of people for a particular purpose, especially for formal discussion. an organized event at

M

which a number of races or other sporting contests are held. *The meeting failed to cause any breakthrough.*

Meetness/मीटनेस *(noun)* – योग्यता suitable or proper. *In spite of his meetness for the job, his profile was rejected.*

Megrim/मेग्रिम *(noun)* – झक [archaic] low spirits. *Snap out of your megrim.*

Melancholia/मेलन्कोलिया *(noun)* – विषाद रोग melancholy. dated a mental condition marked by persistent depression and ill-founded fears. *Her melancholia threatened to turn into something serious.*

Melancholic/मेलन्कॉलिक *(adjective)* – विषादपूर्ण sadness. *The melancholic poem touched many a solitary hearts.*

Melancholy/मेलन्कॉलि *(noun)* – उदासीनता a deep and long lasting sadness. another term for melancholia condition. *I wish my friend would get out of the melancholy.*

Melee/मेली *(noun)* – संकुल संग्राम a confused crowd or scuffle. *I was dying to get out of the melee.*

Meliferous/मेलिफरस *(adjective)* – मधु उत्पन्न करने वाला yielding or producing honey. *Bee is a meliferous insect.*

Mellifluence/मेलिफ्लूएंस *(noun)* – मीठापन pleasing to listen. *The mellifluence of the beautiful music touched my heart.*

Mellivorous/मेलिवरस *(noun)* – मधुभक्षी eating honey. *Bear is a mellivorous animal.*

Melodic/मिलॉडिक *(adjective)* – सुरीला of, having, or producing melody. pleasant sounding. *His melodic voice won him a nomination.*

Melodious/मिलॉडिअस् *(adjective)* – सुरीला pleasant sounding tuneful. relating to melody. *The melodious music echoed in the church.*

Melodist/मेलॉडिस्ट *(noun)* – गाने वाला a composer of melodies. *The melodist has done a wonderful job.*

Melody/मेलॉडि *(noun)* – लय a sequence of single notes that is musically satisfying. the principal part in harmonized music. *The melody was beautiful.*

Melon/मेलॉन *(noun)* – तरबूज the large round fruit of a plant of the gourd family, with sweet pulpy flesh and many seeds. *I love melons.*

Membral/मेम्ब्रल *(adj.)* – अंग सम्बन्धी pertaining to limbs. *Please collect all the membrals.*

Membrane/मेम्ब्रेन *(noun)* – झिल्ली, खाल a pliable sheet like structure acting as a boundary, lining, or partition in an organism or cell. *He had hurt his tympanic membrane.*

Memorize/मेमॅराइज *(verb)* – याद करना learn by heart. *The child has memorized the entire poem.*

Memory/मेमॅरि *(noun)* – यादगार the faculty by which the mind stores and remembers information. *He has a very sharp memory.*

Menace/मेनेस् *(noun)* – धमकी a threat or danger, a threatening quality. He is a menace to the society. *You cannot menace me.*

Mend/मेंड *(verb)* – मरम्मत करना restore to a sound condition, return to health. *The cobbler mended my shoes.*

Mendacious/मेंडेशस *(adjective)* – झूठा untruthful. *He is a mendacious person.*

Mendacity/मेन्डैसिटि – मिथ्यावादिता falsity. *I am tired of your mendacity.*

Mendancy/मेन्डिकॅन्सि – भिक्षावृत्ति beggary. *The family was reduced to mendicancy.*

Mendicant/मेन्डिकॅन्ट *(noun)* – भिक्षुक-भिखारी given to begging. of or denoting a religious order originally dependent on alms. *The mendicant roamed the streets.*

Menial/मीनिअल् *(adjective)* – ओछा requiring little skill and lacking prestige. domestic. *He started his career with menial jobs.*

Meniscus/मिनिस्कस *(noun)* – अर्द्धचन्द्राकार ताल the curved upper surface of a liquid in a tube. *The meniscus was turbulent.*

Mensal/मेन्सल *(adj)* – मासिक monthly. *This is a mensal occurrence.*

Menses/मेन्सीज *(noun)* – आर्त्तव blood and other matter discharged from the uterus at menstruation. *She went to the doctor to consult regarding the heavy menses.*

Menstruate/मेन्स्ट्रूएट *(verb)* – रजस्वला होना discharge blood and other material from the lining of the uterus at intervals of about one lunar month. *One can get stomach ache during menstruation.*

Mensurable/मेन्शरेबल् *(adjective)* – नापने योग्य able to be measured. *The results should be mensurable.*

Mensuration/मेन्सुरेशन *(noun)* – क्षेत्रमिति measurement. the part of geometry concerned with ascertaining lengths, areas, and volumes. *He scored full marks in mensuration.*

Mental/मेंटल *(adjective)* – मानसिक of, done by, or occurring in the mind. *The child performs mental calculations quickly.*

Mention/मेंसन *(verb)* – कथन refer to briefly. refer to by name. *Yes, she did mention you to me.*

Mentioned/मेन्शन्ड *(adj p.t. of mention)* – निर्दिष्ट *I mentioned you to my boss.*

Mentor/मेंटर *(noun)* – विश्वसनीय मन्त्री an experienced and trusted adviser. an experienced person in an institution who trains and counsels new employees or students. *I consider him as my friend and mentor.*

Mercantile/म:कॅन्टाइल *(adjective)* – व्यवसायी of or relating to trade or commerce. *His mercantile interests led him to take up business studies.*

Mercenary/मॅ:सिनरि *(adjective)* – स्वार्थी motivated primarily by the desire for gain. *The company entered India with apparent mercenary interests.*

Merchandise/मॅ:चॅन्डाइज *(noun)* – व्यापारी माल goods for sale. products used to promote a film, pop group, etc. *The store sold good quality merchandise.*

Mercurial/मर्क्यूरिअल् *(adjective)* – चंचल subject to sudden changes of mood or mind. *I am wary of his mercurial temper.*

Mercury/मर्करी *(noun)* – पारा a small planet that is the closest to the sun in the solar system. *There is no atmosphere on Mercury.*

Mercy/मर्सी *(noun)* – दया compassion or forgiveness shown towards an enemy or offender in one's power. *The government showed mercy towards the captured soldier.*

Mere/मिअर *(adjective)* – मात्र that is solely or no more or better than what is specified: mere mortals. *We are mere mortals, not Gods!*

Meretricious/मरिट्रिशस *(adjective)* – बनावटी शोभा का showily but falsely attractive. *The marriage party was full of meretricious people.*

Merge/मर्ज *(verb)* – मिला देना combine or be combined to form one. blend or cause to blend gradually into something else. absorb in another. *Please merge the two sentences.*

Merit/मेरिट *(noun)* – श्रेष्ठता excellence; worth. an examination grade denoting above average performance. *I completed my course with a merit.*

Merlin/मर्लिन *(noun)* – बाज a kind of falcon. *The two merlins were fighting for territory.*

Merman/म:मैन *(noun)* – दरियाई मर्द male of a mermaid. *Mermen are mythical creatures.*

Merriness/मेरिनेस *(noun)* – आनन्द cheerfullness, festivity. *We invited our neighbours to be a part of the merriment.*

Mesdames/मेडेम् *(noun)* – महाशया plural form of madam. *Mesdames, what will you have for lunch?*

Mesentery/मेसॅन्टॅरि *(noun)* – आन्त्रपेशी a fold of the peritoneum attaching the stomach, small intestine, and other organs to the posterior wall of the abdomen. *The professor pointed out the mesentery to the students during dissection.*

Mesmerist/मेस्मेरिस्ट *(noun)* – मूर्छित करने वाला one who hypnotises. *The mesmerist amazed the audience with his performance.*

Mesmerization/मेस्मेराइजेशन *(noun)* – मूर्छित करने का कार्य state of mesmerising. *The thief claimed that he was under the effect of mesmerization when he committed the crime.*

Message/मेसेज् *(noun)* – समाचार written, or recorded communication sent by one person to another. *I sent a message to all my friends to wish them a happy new year.*

Messenger/मेसेन्जर *(noun)* – दूत a person who carries a message. *The messenger handed me the envelope and rushed back.*

Messieurs/Messrs/मेसॅज/मेसये *(noun)* – महाशय लोग plural form of monsieur. *Messieurs, what would you like to order for lunch?*

Messuage/मसुविज् *(noun)* – गृहवाटिका a house with outbuildings and land. *The messuage was huge.*

Metabolism/मेटॉबॅलिज्म *(noun)* – चयापचय the chemical processes that occur within a living organism to maintain life. *She has a high rate of metabolism.*

Metabolize/मेटॅबॉलाइज *(verb)* – चयापचय करना process or undergo processing by metabolism. *The stomach metabolizes some types of food easily.*

M

Metacarpus/मेटॅकार्पस *(noun)* – हाथ की हथेली the group of five bones of the hand between the wrist and the fingers. *He hurt his metacarpus.*

Metallic/मेटलिक *(adjective)* – धातुरूप of relating to, or resembling mental. sharp and ringing. having the sheen or lustre of metal. *I like the metallic jewellery box.*

Metallist/मेटलिस्ट *(noun)* – धातु कर्मकार *The metallist worked hard to shape the hard metal.*

Metallography/मेटलॉग्राफि *(noun)* – धातुविद्या the descriptive science of the structure and properties of metals. *She is a student of metallography.*

Metallurgy/मेटलर्जि *(noun)* – धातुशोधन the branch of science concerned with the properties, production, and purification of metals. *He was interested in metallurgy.*

Metalogical/मेटलॉजिकल *(adj)* – न्याय-विरुद्ध beyond the scope of logic. *I love this metalogical discussion.*

Metamorphose/मेटमॉर्फोज् *(verb)* – रूप बदलना undergo metamorphosis. *The tadpole metamorphosed into a frog.*

Metamorphosis/मेटमॉर्फोसिस *(noun)* – रूपान्तरण zoology the process of transformation from an immature form to an adult form in two or more distinct stages. *I am fascinated by the process of metamorphosis.*

Metaphor/मेटॅफॅ(र) *(noun)* – रूपक a figure of speech in which a word or phrase in applied to something to which it is not literally applicable. a thing regarded as symbolic of something else. *The young poet did not like using metaphors.*

Metaphysical/मेटैफिजिकल *(adjective)* – आध्यात्मिक of or relating to metaphysics. based on abstract reasoning. transcending physical matter or the laws of nature. *I love metaphysical poems.*

Metaphysics/मेटैफिजिक्स *(noun)* – आत्मतत्वज्ञान the branch of philosophy concerned with the first principles of things, including abstract concepts such as being and knowing. *He likes discussing the concepts of metaphysics.*

Mete/मीट *(verb)* – सीमा dispense or allot justice, punishment, etc. *The jury meted out an appropriate punishment to the culprit.*

Meteor/मीटिअॅ(र) *(noun)* – उल्कापात a small body of matter from outer space that becomes incandescent as a result of friction with the earth's atmosphere and appears as a streak of light. *I love watching meteors fall from the outer space.*

Meteoroid/मीटिअरॉइड *(noun)* – उल्का के परमाणु astronomy a small body in the solar system that would become a meteor if it entered the earth's atmosphere. *The students discovered a new meteoroid.*

Meteorite/मीटिअॅराइट *(noun)* – उल्का an acrolite. *The scientists studied the meteorite.*

Meteorology/मीटिअॅरॉलॅजि *(noun)* – अन्तरिक्ष विद्या the study of the processes and phenomena of the atmosphere, especially as a means of weather forecasting. *With the introduction of new satellites, there have been considerable advances in meteorology.*

Meter/मीटर *(noun)* – नापने वाला a device that measures and records the quantity, degree, or rate of something. *The meter was faulty.*

Method/मेथॅड *(noun)* – रीति a particular procedure for accomplishing or approaching something. *The method to solve this mathematical problem is quite simple.*

Methodical/मिथॉडिकल *(adjective)* – यथाक्रम characterized by method or order. *He is very methodical in his approach.*

Methodize/मेथॅडाइज *(verb)* – व्यवस्था करना arrange in an orderly or systematic manner. *Please methodize the slides.*

Metrical/मेट्रिकल *(adjective)* – छन्दोवद्ध or, relating to, or composed in poetic meter. *The poet writes metrical poems.*

Mica/माइका *(noun)* – अबरक a silicate mineral found as minute shiny scales in granite and other rocks. *Little bits of mica shone through the sand.*

Mice/माइस – चूहे *plural* form of mouse. *The house is infested with mice.*

Microbe/माइक्रोब *(noun)* – जीवाणु a micro-organism, especially a bacterium causing disease or fermentation. *Many microbes are helpful to human beings.*

Microscope/माइक्रॉस्कोप *(noun)* – खुर्दबीन an optical instrument for viewing very small objects, typically magnifying by several hundred times. *The doctors studied the sample under a microscope.*

Mid/मिड *(adjective)* – बीच का of or in the middle part or position of a range. *The*

M

population of this state is in the mid of the range of populations of various states of the country.

Middle/मिडॅल *(adjective)* – बिचला at an equal distance from the extremities of something; central. placed so as to have the same number of members on each side. intermediate in rank, quality, or ability. *The chair in the middle is slightly misaligned.*

Midget/मिजिट् *(noun)* – बौना an extremely small person. extremely small. *The midget entertained the crowd.*

Mien/मीन *(noun)* – छवि, रंगढंग a person's look or manner. *We weren't comfortable with his mien.*

Miff/मिफ *(verb)* – मुहाँचाही [informal] offend or irritate. *I think I miffed him by my silence.*

Migration/माइग्रेशन *(noun)* – देशान्तरगमन movement animals, birds or people to new places. *The wild-beasts are about to start their annual migration.*

Migratory/माइग्रेटरी *(adjective)* – घूमने वाला animal or birds that move from one place to another. *Geese are migratory birds.*

Mike/माइक *(noun)* – माइक्रोफोन a microphone. *The mike stopped working while he was speaking.*

Milch/मिल्च *(adjective)* – दूध देने वाली denoting a domestic mammal giving or kept for milk. *This milch cow is very docile.*

Mild/माइल्ड *(adjective)* – दयालु gentle and not easily provoked. *He has very mild manners.*

Mile/माइल *(noun)* – मील a unit of measure equal to 1,760 yards. *I have travelled 7 miles today.*

Mileage/माइलेज *(noun)* – चली हुई दूरी a number of miles travelled or covered. *The car has good mileage.*

Milfoil/मिल्फॉइल *(noun)* – एक प्रकार का पौधा a kind of plant. *The milfoil is an abundant plant.*

Militancy/मिलिटंसी *(noun)* – लड़ाकापन adopting violent methods for some cause. *Militancy needs to be curbed at any cost.*

Militant/मिलिटॅन्ट *(adjective)* – युद्ध में लगा हुआ favouring confrontational methods in support of a cause. *The militant organization was banned in several countries.*

Militarism/मिलिटरिज़्म *(noun)* – सैनिक-शासन the belief that a country should maintain and readily draw on a strong military capability for the defence or promotion of national inferests. *Confrontations are common when two neighbouring countries favour militarism.*

Military/मिलिटरी *(adjective)* – फौजी of, relating to, or characteristic of soldiers or armed forces. *The military ways of life are very fascinating.*

Militia/मिलिसिया *(noun)* – रक्षक योद्धा a military force that is raised from that civil population to supplement a regular army in an emergency. a rebel force acting in opposition to a regular army, all able-bodied civilians eligible by law for military service. *Some countries consider it important to have a strong militia.*

Milk/मिल्क *(noun)* – दूध an opaque white fluid rich in fat and protein, secreted by female mammals for the nourishment of their young. the milk of cows as a food and drink for humans. the milk-like juice of certain plants, such as the coconut, a milk-like liquid with a particular ingredient or use: cleansing milk. *Milk is an important source of calcium for children.*

Milkiness/मिल्किनेस *(noun)* – कोमलता resembling milk in colour or quality. *The milkiness of her skin got her many admirers.*

Milky/मिल्कि *(adjective)* – दूधिया containing milk. *The chocolate is too milky for my liking.*

Mill/मिल *(noun)* – चक्की a building equipped with machinery for grinding grain into flour. a piece of machinery for grinding grain. *The mill runs for four hours every day.*

Millepede/मिलिपीड *(noun)* – गोजर very small invertebrates that live in socil and under stones. *I found a millepede in my bathroom.*

Millet/मिलेट् *(noun)* – बाजरा a cereal which bears a large crop of small seeds, used to make flour or alcoholic drinks. *She bought a sack of millet.*

Million/मिलिअन् *(cardinal number)* – दस लाख the number equivalent to the product of a thousand and a thousand; 1,000,000 or 10^6 *She needs to save 3 million dollars to buy the house she likes.*

Millionaire/मिल्यनेअ(र) *(noun)* – लखपति a person whose assets are worth one million pounds or dollars or more. *Her parents*

M

wanted her to marry a millionaire but she fell in love with me.

Milt/मिल्ट *(noun)* – मछली का पित्त the semen or sperm-filled reproductive gland of a male fish. *The fish stores its sperm in the milt.*

Mimicry/मिमिक्रि *(noun)* – विडम्बना, परिहासात्मक नकल skill of imitating something for entertainment or ridicule. *She is very good at mimicry.*

Minacious/मिनेशॅस *(adjective)* – डराने वाला menacing, threatening. *The students ran to the classroom when they saw the minacious principal coming.*

Minaret/मिनारेट *(noun)* – धरहरा, कोटा मीनार a slender tower, especially that of a mosque, with a balcony from which a muezzin calls Muslims to prayer. *The mosque has beautiful minaret.*

Mince/मिन्स *(verb)* – बनाकर बोलना, चबाकर बोलना cut up or shred into very small pieces. *I went to get the meat minced.*

Mind/माइन्ड *(noun)* – स्मृति-उत्सव the faculty of consciousness and thought. *At times, it is prudent to follow your mind.*

Minded/माइन्डेड *(adj)* – प्रवृत्त inclined to think in a particular way: liberal-minded scholars. *I love to spend time with like-minded people.*

Mindful/माइन्डफुल *(adjective)* – सचेत conscious or aware or responses planned for their psychological effect on another. *They are very mindful of the way they speak to each other in the presence of their children.*

Mine/माइन *(possessive pronoun)* – मेरा referring to a thing or things belonging to or associated with the speaker. possessive determine archaic used before a vowel my. *This pencil box is mine.*

Minerva/मिनर्वा *(noun)* – सरस्वती Roman goddess. *He wanted to name her baby girl Minerva.*

Mingle/मिंगल *(verb)* – एकत्र होना mix or cause to mix together. *The two liquids mingled well.*

Miniate/मिनिएट *(verb)* – सिन्दूर से रंगना to paint with vermilion. *The ladies miniated each other.*

Minify/मिनिफाई *(verb)* – छोटा करना to make small in size. *Don't minify his contribution in your success.*

Minimal/मिनिमल *(adjective)* – अतिसूक्ष्म of a minimum amount, quantity, or degree. *My expenditure on cosmetics is minimal.*

Minion/मिन्यॅन *(noun)* – भृत्य a follower or underling of a powerful person, especially a servile or unimportant one. *He is but a minion in the party.*

Ministerial/मिनिस्टेरिअल *(adjective)* – राजकीय relating to a government menister. *The ministerial convoy has just passed this way.*

Ministress/मिनिस्ट्रेस *(noun)* – प्रबन्धकर्त्री a woman who ministers. *The ministress governed her state very well.*

Ministry/मिनिस्ट्री *(noun)* – मंत्रालय a government department headed by a minister. *The ministry approved his proposal.*

Minor/माइनर *(adjective)* – छोटा having little importance, seriousness, or significance. *This is a minor issue.*

Minotaur/मिनॅटार् *(noun)* – नरवृषभ Greek mythology a creature who was half-man and half-bull, kept in a labyrinth on Crete by King Minos and killed by Theseus. *The movie had an excellent depiction of a minotaur.*

Minster/मिन्स्टर *(noun)* – बड़ा गिरजाघर a large or important church, typically one of cathedral status in the north of England that was built as part of monastery. *I visit the York Minster every Sunday.*

Minstrel/मिन्स्ट्रल *(noun)* – चारण, बन्दी a medieval singer or musician. *The minstrel was famous for his melodious voice.*

Mint/मिन्ट *(noun)* – पुदीना an aromatic plant with two-lipped, typically lilac flowers, several kinds of which are used as culinary herbs. the flavour of mint, especially peppermint. *Mint grows very easily.*

Mintage/मिन्ट्-ऍज् *(noun)* – सिक्का menting of coins. *The mintage of coins is a complicated process.*

Minute/मिनिट *(noun)* – मिनट, क्षण a period of time equal in sixty seconds or sixtieth of an hour. *It will take me 5 minutes to complete this task.*

Miracle/मिरॅकॅल *(noun)* – चमत्कार an extraordinary and welcome event that is not explicable by natural or scientific laws, attributed to a diving agency. a remarkable and very welcome occurrence. *Her recovery is nothing less than a miracle.*

M

Miraculous/मिरैक्युलस *(adjective)* – चमत्कारी having the character of a miracle. *The new medicine has produced miraculous results.*

Mire/मायर् *(noun)* – कीचड़ a stretch of swampy or boggy ground. soft mud or drill. ecology a wetland area or ecosystem based on peat. *The children keep away from the mire.*

Mirror/मिरर *(noun)* – दर्पण a surface, typically of glass coated with a metal amalgam which reflects a clear image. *I bought an ornate mirror for my house.*

Mirth/मर्थ् *(noun)* – प्रमोद amusement; laughter. *The party was full of mirth.*

Mirthless/मर्थलेस *(adj)* – आनन्दरहित without mirth. *She had a mirthless face.*

Misadvised/मिसएडवाइज्ड *(adjective)* – असदुपदिष्ट wrong recommendation. *Children should never be misadvised.*

Misalliance/मिसुएलायंस् *(noun)* – अयोग्य वैवाहिक सम्बन्ध an unsuitable or unhappy alliance or marriage. *Their marriage was a misalliance from the very beginning.*

Misapplication/मिसअप्लिकेशन *(noun)* – कुप्रयोग wrong application. *The company lost a lot of trust because of their misapplication of investor funds.*

Misapprehensive/मिसएप्रिहेन्सिव *(adj)* – भ्रम-पूर्ण misconceiving. *You are fighting with me because of our misapprehensive interpretations of my words.*

Misascribe/मिसएस्क्राइब *(verb)* – मिथ्यारोपण करना to ascribe wrongly. *Several works of literature are misascribed to wrong authors.*

Misbecome/मिसबिकम *(verb)* – अयोग्य होना to be unbecoming. *This dress is misbecoming on you.*

Misbegotten/मिसबिगॉटॅन *(adjective)* – दोगला, जारज badly conceived, designed, or planned. contemptible. *This is a misbegotten building.*

Misbehave/मिसबिहेब *(verb)* – दुराचार करना behave badly. *The bus conductor was fired because he misbehaved with children.*

Misbehaviour/मिसबिहेवियर *(noun)* – दुराचार bad behaviour. *The child was reprimanded for his misbehavior.*

Misbelief/मिसबिलिफ *(noun)* – मिथ्या विश्वास a wrong or false belief or opinion. *The misbelief led to a wrong decision.*

Miscarriage/मिस्कैरिज *(noun)* – गर्भपात the spontaneous or unplanned expulsion of a foetus from the womb before it is able to survive independently. *She was upset after her miscarriage.*

Miscarry/मिस्कैरी *(verb)* – विफल होना have a miscarriage. *She was admitted in the hospital when she miscarried.*

Miscellaneous/मिसिलेन्यॅस *(adjective)* – पंचमेल of various types. composed of members or elements of different kinds. *The boy had a huge collection of miscellaneous stamps.*

Miscellany/मिसेलनि *(noun)* – मिश्रण a mixture. a collection of pieces of writing by different authors. *The miscellany was published by a reputed publisher.*

Mischief/मिसचीफ *(noun)* – शरारत, हानि playful misbehavior or troublemaking. *The children's faces were full of mischief.*

Mischievous/मिसचिवॅस *(adjective)* – अपकारी causing or disposed to mischief. *The mischievous children were scolded every day.*

Miscite/मिसाइट *(verb)* – मिथ्या उद्धरण देना to quote wrongly. *He miscited Shakespeare in the conference.*

Misclaim/मिसुक्लेम *(verb)* – अनुचित दावा करना *He misclaimed the rights to the property.*

Misconceive/मिस्कन्सिव *(verb)* – उलटा समझना fail to understand correctly. *You misconceived what I was saying.*

Misconception/मिस्कन्सेप्शन *(noun)* – भ्रान्त धारणा a false or mistaken view or opinion. *I want to remove this misconception.*

Miscounsel/मिस्काउन्सेल *(verb)* – बुरी सलाह देना to advise wrongly. *The lawyer miscounselled the client.*

Miscount/मिस्काउन्ट *(verb)* – अशुद्ध गिनती करना count incorrectly. *I miscounted the number of pages that I had to read.*

Miscreant/मिस्क्रिएण्ट *(noun)* – बदमाश, पाजी a person who behaves badly or unlawfully. *The police caught the miscreant.*

Miscreated/मिस्क्रिएटेड *(adjective)* – विकृत created wrongly, misshapen. *The miscreated cow attracted a crowd.*

Misdeem/मिसडिम *(verb)* – झूठा अनुमान करना to judge wrongly. *I have misdeemed your abilities all this while.*

M

Misdemeanour/मिस्डिमिनर् *(noun)* – दुष्कर्म a minor wrongdoing. law a not-indictable offence, regarded in the US as less serious than a felony. *The judge let him go with just a warning as this was his first misdemeanour.*

Misdoing/मिस्डुइंग *(noun)* – कुकर्म a misdeed. *His mother reported his misdoing to his father.*

Misdoubt/मिस्डाउट *(verb)* – आशंका chiefly archaic have doubts about the truth or existence of. be suspicious about. *I have my misdoubts about the existence of the so-called monster.*

Miser/माइजर *(noun)* – कंजूस a person who hoards wealth and spends very little. *My uncle is a miser.*

Miserable/मिज़रॅबॅल *(adjective)* – दुःखी wretchedly unhappy or uncomfortable. causing unhappiness or discomfort. habitually morose. *My brother was miserable for days after losing his new ball.*

Miserliness/माइजलिनेस् *(noun)* – कृपणता extreme desire to save money. *My father was tired of his boss's miserliness.*

Misfire/मिस्फायर *(verb)* – आग न पकड़ना, गोली न चलना fail to fire properly. fail to ignite that fuel correctly or at all. *The rocket misfired.*

Misform/मिस्फॉर्म *(verb)* – कुरूप बनाना to put into a bad shape. *The misformed plans did not yield any results.*

Misfortune/मिस्फॉर्चुन *(noun)* – दुर्गति bad luck. an unfortunate event. *We condoled him for his misfortune.*

Misgiving/मिस्गिविंग *(noun)* – अविश्वास a feeling of doubt of apprehension about something. *I have my misgivings about this itinerary.*

Misguide/मिस्गाइड *(verb)* – बहकाना rare mislead. *The ignorant man misguided the tourists.*

Mishap/मिस्हैप *(noun)* – अनिष्ट, अनर्थ, दुर्घटना an unlucky accident. *It was nothing but a mishap.*

Mishmash/मिस्मैश *(noun)* – घालमेल, उपद्रव a confused mixture. *The platter looked more like a mishmash than edible food.*

Misjudge/मिस्जज *(verb)* – अन्याय करना form an incorrect opinion of. judge wrongly. *I misjudged the situation.*

Mislead/मिस्लीड *(verb)* – बहकाना, धोखा देना cause to have a wrong impression about someone or something. *Don't mislead the students.*

Mislike/मिस्लाइक *(noun)* – अप्रिय होना archaic dislike. *His mislike for her was written all across his face.*

Mismanage/मिस्मैनेज् *(verb)* – बुरा प्रबन्ध करना manage badly or wrongly. *The event management company mismanaged the birthday party.*

Misogamy/मिसॉगॅमि *(noun)* – विवाह-निन्दा rare hatred of marriage. *His misogamy was the reason that he never married.*

Misplace/मिस्प्लेस *(verb)* – गलत जगह में रखना put in the wrong place. *I misplaced my trust in you.*

Misprize/मिस्प्राइज *(verb)* – नीचा समझना rare undervalue. *The antique dealer misprized the cutlery collection.*

Misquotation/मिस्कोटेशन *(noun)* – अशुद्ध उद्धरण inaccurate quote. *The misquotation became a subject of mockery.*

Misquote/मिस्कोट *(verb)* – अशुद्ध उद्धरण देना quote inaccurately. *The news channel misquoted the politician.*

Misread/मिस्रीड *(verb)* – अशुद्ध पढ़ना read or interpret wrongly. *I misread the email and sent a wrong reply.*

Misrelation/मिसरिलेशन *(noun)* – अशुद्ध वर्णन wrong relation. *The misrelation changed the entire message of the play.*

Misreport/मिसरिपोर्ट *(verb)* – मिथ्या समाचार देना give a false or inaccurate report of. *The audit company was penalized for its misreport.*

Misrule/मिसरूल *(noun)* – कुशासन unfair or inefficient government. disorder. *The government's misrule plunged the country into turmoil.*

Miss/मिस *(noun)* – कुमारी कन्या fail to hit. *Miss Tate, can you please come here?*

Mis-shapen/मिस्शेपेन *(adjective)* – कुरूप not having the normal or natural shape. *No one bought the mis-shapen box.*

Missile/मिसाइल *(noun)* – प्रक्षेपणास्त्र an object which is forcibly propelled at a target. *The missile was very big.*

M

Mission/मिशन *(noun)* – लक्ष्य, शिष्टमंडल an important assignment, typically involving travel abroad. a group of people sent on a mission. an organization or institution involved in a long-term assignment abroad. a military or scientific expedition. *The spies were on a mission to save the country.*

Mis-spend/मिस-स्पेंड *(verb)* – अपव्यय करना spend time or money foolishly or wastefully. *I misspent my life's saving on useless investments.*

Mist/मिस्ट *(noun)* – कुहरा a cloud of tiny water droplets in the atmosphere at or near the earth's surface, limiting visibility to. a lesser extent than fog. a condensed vapour settling on a surface. a blurring of the sight, especially caused by tears. *The mist swirled across the landscape.*

Mistake/मिस्टेक *(noun)* – दोष, भूल a thing which is not correct. an error of judgement. *This entire idea was a mistake.*

Mistaken/मिस्टेकेन *(adjective)* – अशुद्ध wrong. based on a misunderstanding or faulty judgement. *It was a case of mistaken identity.*

Mister/मिस्टर *(noun)* – महाशय variant form of Mr., often used humorously. [informal] a form of address to a man. *Now look here Mister, you cannot get away with this.*

Mistress/मिस्ट्रेस *(noun)* – प्रेमिका a woman in a position of authority or control. chiefly British a female school teacher. the female owner of a dog, cat, etc. archaic a female head of a household. *The children respected the mistress.*

Mistrust/मिस्ट्रस्ट *(verb)* – शंका करना have no trust in. *The teacher mistrusted the students.*

Misusage/मिस्यूसेज् *(noun)* – दुर्व्यवहार archaic unjust treatment. *The public was protesting against the misusage of the victim.*

Mite/माइट *(noun)* – घुन, अल्प मात्रा a samll insect with four pairs of legs, several kinds of which are parasitic. *The house is infested with mites.*

Mitigable/मिटिगेबॅल *(adjective)* – शान्त करने योग्य making less severe, painful. *The situation is still mitigable.*

Mitigant/मिटिगॅन्ट *(verb)* – मृदु करने वाला make less serious, or painful. *He is a very good mitigant.*

Mitigate/मिटिगेट *(verb)* – शान्त करना make less server, serious, or painful. *He mitigated the argument between the neighbours.*

Mitigation/मिटिगेशन *(noun)* – शान्ति the action of reducing seriousness of something. *They had to go to the court for mitigation.*

Mitigatory/मिटिगेटरी *(adjective)* – शान्त करने वाला action of making pain less severe. *Their mitigatory moves were welcome.*

Mix/मिक्स *(verb)* – मिलाना combine or be able to be combined to form a whole. make by mixing ingredient's combine into one to produce a recording. *Please mix this powder in the milk.*

Mixture/मिक्सचर *(noun)* – मिश्रण a substance made by mixing other substances together. the process of mixing or being mixed. a combination of different things in which the components are individually distinct. the charge of gas or vapour mixed with air admitted to the cylinder of an internal-combustion engine. *The mixture was very tasty and nutritious.*

Mizzle/मिज़ॅल *(noun)* – झींसी light rain; drizzle. *The mizzle at this time of the year is beneficial for the crops.*

Moan/मोन *(noun)* – कराहना a long, low sound expressing suffering or sexual pleasure. a low sound made by the wind. *The little boy moaned because of pain.*

Moat/मोट *(noun)* – खाई a deep, wide defensive ditch surrounding a castle or town, typically filled with water. *The moat was full of crocodiles.*

Mobile/मोबाइल *(adjective)* – अस्थिर able to move or be moved freely or easily. accommodated in a vehicle so as to travel around. able or willing to move between occupations, places of residence, or social classes. *I love the concept of mobile libraries.*

Mobility/मोबिलिटि *(noun)* – चंचपता the ability to move or be moved easily. *The injury impacted his mobility.*

Mobilizable/मोबिलाइजेब्ल *(adjective)* – युद्ध-कार्य के योग्य one that can be moved or impressed. *This plan sounds mobilizable.*

Mocha/मोका *(noun)* – सुन्दर कहवा a fine quality coffee. a drink or flavouring made with this, typically with chocolate added. *I like having a mocha with my breakfast.*

M

Mock/मॉक *(verb)* – चिढ़ाना tease scornfully; ridicule. mimic scornfully or contemptuously. *The grown-up boys mocked the younger ones.*

Mode/मोड *(noun)* – प्रकार a way in which something occurs or is done, a way of operating a system, any of the kinds or patterns of vibration of an oscillating system, the character of a modal proposition. another term for mood. *I like this mode of working.*

Model/मॉड्ल *(noun)* – प्रतिरूप a three dimensional representation of a person or thing, typically on a smaller scale. a figure in clay or wax, to be reproduced in a more durable material. *The investors were impressed by the model of the new car.*

Moderate/मॉडरेट *(adjective)* – परिमित average in amount, intensity, or degree. *The moderate intensity storm is expected to hit the shore today.*

Moderateness/मॉडरेटनेस *(noun)* – हल्कापन quality of being moderate. *Not everyone appreciated his moderateness.*

Moderation/मॉडरेशन *(noun)* – किफायत the avoidance of excess or extremes, especially in one's behavior or political opinions. *Everything should be practised in moderation.*

Moderator/मॉडरेटर *(noun)* – सभापति an arbitrator or mediator. a presiding officer, especially a chairman of a debate. a Presbyterian minister presiding over an ecclesiastical body. *The moderator did his job well.*

Modern/मॉडर्न *(adjective)* – आधुनिक of or relating to the present or recent times. characterized by or using the most up to date techniques, equipment, etc. denoting a recent style in art, architecture, etc. marked by a departure from traditional styles and values. *The modern mobile phones are much more sophisticated than the older ones.*

Modernization/मॉडर्नाइजेशन *(noun)* – नवीनीकरण adoption of modern ideas, habits, equipments, methods. *Modernization has his benefits as well as drawbacks.*

Modest/मॉडेस्ट *(adjective)* – परिमित unassuming in the estimation of one's abilities. *He is a modest player.*

Modesty/मॉडेस्टि *(noun)* – विनय quality of being unassuming. *I was humbled by his modesty.*

Modifable/मॉडिफेब्ल *(adjective)* – परिवर्तनीय make partial changes. *The plan is still modifiable.*

Modification/मॉडिफिकेशन *(noun)* – रूपान्तरण the action of modifying a change made. *The modification of the plan led to its failure.*

Modulate/मॉड्युलेट् *(verb)* – आवश्यकतानुसार घटाना बढ़ाना exert a modifying influence on; regulate. *The new manager modulated the processes the team had been following.*

Modulator/मॉड्युलेटर *(noun)* – न्यूनाधिक करने वाला one who exerts a madifying inflvence. *The modulator malfunctioned.*

Modulus/मॉड्युलस *(noun)* – मापांक another term for. the position square root of the sum of the squares of the real and imaginary parts of a complex number. *I have always found calculating the modulus tiresome.*

Moist/माइस्ट् *(adjective)* – नम slightly wet; damp or humid. rainy. *The clothes were all moist in the morning.*

Moisten/माइस्टेन *(verb)* – भिगोना wet slightly. *The fumes moistened my eyes.*

Moistness/मॉइस्टनेस् *(noun)* – तरी slightly wet. *The moistness of her eyes made her look as if she'd been crying.*

Moisture/मॉइस्चर् *(noun)* – गीलापन water or other liquid diffused in a small quantity as vapour, within a solid, or condensed on a surface. *The moisture in the air encouraged moulding.*

Molar/मोलर *(noun)* – पीसने वाला a grinding tooth at the back of a mammal's mouth. *The dentist filled the cavity in her molar.*

Molasses/मोलैसेज् *(noun)* – खाँड़, गुड़, जूसी thick, dark brown juice obtained from raw sugar during the refining process. *Molasses is very useful in yeast production.*

Mole/मोल *(noun)* – छछूंदर, तिल, मस्सा a small burrowing mammal with dark velvety fur, a long muzzle, and very small eyes, feeding mainly on worms and grubs. *I saw a mole in my garden.*

Molecule/मोलेक्यूल *(noun)* – कण a group of atoms bonded together, representing the smallest fundamental unit of a compound that can take part in a chemical reaction. *It is possible to see molecules under the microscope.*

M

Molest/मॉलेस्ट *(verb)* – कष्ट देना pester or harass in a hostile way. assault or abuse sexually. *The culprits who molested the girl were sentenced to the harshest punishment.*

Mollification/मॉलिफिकेशन *(noun)* – शमन appeasement of anger or anxiety. *He is always successful in his mollification attempts.*

Mollify/मॉलिफाइ *(verb)* – मुलायम करना appease the anger or anxiety of. reduce the severity of; soften. *The government's attempts to mollify the indignant youth backfired.*

Molten/मोल्टेन *(adjective)* – गला हुआ liquefied by heat. *The molten lava flowed into the river.*

Moment/मोमेन्ट *(noun)* – क्षण a brief period of time. an exact point in time. *Wait a moment! I forgot something.*

Momentarily/मोमेंटरिलि *(adverb)* – क्षण भर के लिए for a very short time. *I was momentarily nervous before the speech.*

Momentariness/मोमेन्टरिनेस् *(noun)* – क्षणिकता lasting for a very short time. *The celestial event was missed because of its momentariness.*

Momentary/मोमेन्टरि *(adjective)* – अस्थायी brief. *There was a momentary interruption in the telecast.*

Momentum/मोमेन्टम् *(noun)* – गति, चाल the quantity of motion of a moving body, equal to the product of its mass and velocity. *The vehicle's momentum kept it going for a bit.*

Monachism/मानकिज्म *(noun)* – मठवाद monastic living. *The ways of monachism are an interesting subject of study.*

Monad/मॅनैड *(noun)* – इकाई a single unit; the number one. *The number 1 is called a Monad.*

Monarch/मॉनॅर्क् *(noun)* – राजा a sovereign head of state, especially a king, queen, or emperor. *The monarch was generous and just.*

Monarchy/मॉनॅर्कि *(noun)* – साम्राज्य government by a monarch. a state with a monarch. *A monarchy functions in a different way than a democracy.*

Monastic/मनैसूटिक *(adjective)* – वैरागियों का of or relating to monks, nuns, etc. or the buildings in which they live. resembling monks or their way of life. *The monastic way of life is very difficult.*

Monetary/मॉनिटरि *(adjective)* – मुद्रा-सम्बन्धी of or relating to money or currency. *Will there be any monetary benefit for me out of this work?*

Money/मॅनि *(noun)* – धन a medium of exchange in the form of coins and banknotes. formal sums of money, wealth. payment or financial gain. *Everyone wants to earn money.*

Mongrel/मांग्रेल *(noun)* – दोगला कुत्ता a dog of no definable type or breed. *The mongrel was dirty but cute.*

Monism/मॉनिज्म *(noun)* – वेदान्त philosophy & theology. a theory or doctrine that denies the existence of a distinction or duality, such as that between matter and mind, or god and the world. *He subscribes to the philosophy of Monism.*

Monk/मॅन्क *(noun)* – उदासी, मठवासी a member of a religious community of men typically living under vows of poverty, chastity, and obedience. *The monk spent his life studying theology.*

Monkey/मंकी *(noun)* – बन्दर a small to medium-sized primate typically having a long tail and living in trees in tropical countries. *Monkeys can be very destructive.*

Monological/मॅनलॅजिकल *(adj.)* – भाषण-सम्बन्धी a long speech by one actor. *Monological sequences depend a lot upon the acting skills of the actor.*

Monophobia/मॅनोफोबिया *(noun)* – अकेले रहने का भय morbid dread of being left alone. *She cannot stay alone because she has monophobia.*

Monotonous/मॅनटॅनस *(adjective)* – एक लय का dull, tedious, and repetitions. *I want to change my monotonous schedule.*

Monsieur/मॅन्स्यो *(noun)* – महाशय a title or form of address for a French speaking man, corresponding to Mr or sir. *Monsieur, what would you like to order?*

Monsoon/मॉन्सून *(noun)* – ऋतु-पवन a seasonal prevailing wind in the region of the Indian subcontinent and SE Asia, bringing rain when blowing from the south-west. *We wait eagerly for monsoon every year.*

Monstrosity/मॉन्स्ट्रॉसिटि *(noun)* – राक्षसीपन something very large and unsightly. a grossly malformed animal, plant, or person. *Some people show case of deformities in animals as monstrosities to earn money.*

M

Monstrous/मॉन्सट्रॅस *(noun)* – विकट very large and ugly or frightening. *The monstrous tree was centuries old.*

Montanic/मॉन्टैनिक *(adj)* – पर्वत पूर्ण pertaining to mountain. *The montanic landscape is spectacular.*

Monticle/मॉन्टिकल *(noun)* – छोटी पहाड़ी a hill or a small mountain. *The Church stood on the monticle.*

Monument/मॉन्युमेंट *(noun)* – यादगार a statue, building, or other structure erected to commemorate a notable person or event. *The monument is a popular tourist spot.*

Mood/मूड *(noun)* – चित्तवृत्ति a state of mind or feeling. an angry, irritable, or sullen state of mind. *I am in a good mood today.*

Moon/मून *(noun)* – चन्द्रमा the natural satellite of the earth, visible by reflected light from the sun. a natural satellite of any planet. *The Moon looks exceptionally bright today.*

Moonling/मूनलिंग *(noun)* – मूर्ख मनुष्य a foolish person. *Don't behave like a moonling.*

Moor/मूर *(noun)* – बंजर भूमि an open wasteland. *We went for a walk on the moors. The moor was actress.*

Mop/मॉप *(noun)* – कूँची an implement consisting of a bundle of thick loose strings or a sponge attached to a handle, used for wiping floors. an act of wiping with a mop. *The mop was very dirty and needed to be washed.*

Mopish/मॉपिश *(adjective)* – तेजहीन feel dejected. *Why are you in such a mopish mood?*

Moquette/मॉकेट *(noun)* – सन a thick pile fabric used for carpets and upholstery. *The moquette used in making this carpet is of a very good quality.*

Moralist/मॉरलिस्ट *(noun)* – नीतिज्ञ a person who moralizes, or who teaches or promotes morality. *Our class teacher is a moralist.*

Morality/मॅरेलिटि *(noun)* – नीति विद्या principles concerning the distinction between right and wrong or good and bad behaviour. a system of values and moral principles. *Some people need lessons in morality.*

Moralization/मॉरलाजेशन *(noun)* – नीति उपदेश comment on issues of right and wrong. *Moralization of some issues is simply uncalled for.*

Moralize/मॉरॅलाइज *(verb)* – धर्मोपदेश करना comment on issues of right and wrong, typically with an unfounded air of superiority. *The panel was attempting to moralize the crime.*

Morally/मॉरली *(adverb)* – नैतिक दृष्टि से principles of right or wrong behaviour. *Your argument is morally wrong.*

Morbid/मॉर्बिड् *(adjective)* – अस्वस्थ, रोगी, घिनावना characterized by or appealing to an abnormal and unhealthy interest in unpleasant subjects, especially death and disease. *Some writers enjoy writing morbid stories.*

Morbose/मॉर्बोस *(adj)* – अस्वस्थ unsound. *His weight has reached the morbose levels.*

Mordacious/मॉर्डेशस् *(adjective)* – तीव्र formal bitingly sarcastic or vituperative. *The mordacious article hurt many egos.*

Mordant/मॉर्डेन्ट् *(adjective)* – चरपरा sharp or critical; biting. *His mordant comments earned him many enemies.*

Moreover/मोरओवर *(adjective)* – सिवाय as a further matter; besides. *Moreover, you also owe me a treat.*

Morgue/मॉर्ग् *(noun)* – क्रोधी प्रकृति a haughty temper. *The student felt scared when he was in the morgue.*

Moribund/मॉरिबॉन्ड *(adjective)* – मरणासन्न at the point of death. *The moribund man asked for his lawyer.*

Morning/मॉर्निंग *(noun)* – सवेरा the period of time between midnight and noon, especially from sunrise to noon. sunrise. *I like waking up early in the morning.*

Moron/मॉ:रॉन *(noun)* – मंदबुद्धि [informal] a stupid person. *Don't brave like a moron.*

Morphia/मॉर्फिआ *(noun)* – अफीम का सत्व, मार्फिया dated morphine. *The patient was administered morphia before the surgery.*

Morrow/मॉरो *(noun)* – उत्तर दिवस, आने वाला कल archaic the following day. *I will contact my friend the first thing morrow.*

Mortalize/मॉर्टलाइज् *(verb)* – मर्त्य बनाना to make mortal. *The poor beggar's curse mortalized the deity.*

Mortgage/मॉर्गेज् *(noun)* – गिरवी the charging of property by a debtor to a creditor as security for

M

a debt, on the condition that it shall be returned on payment of the debt within a certain period. *The poor farmer offered his land as a mortgage to educate his children.*

Mosque/मॉस्क *(noun)* – मसजिद (मस्जिद) a Muslim place of worship. *The mosque has beautiful minarets.*

Mosquito/मॉस्कीटो *(noun)* – मच्छर variant spelling of miskito. *The mosquito buzzed around my ear all night.*

Mostly/मोस्टलि *(adverb)* – अत्यन्त as regards the greater part or number. *The results are mostly positive.*

Mot/मॉट *(noun)* – कहावत a compulsory annual test for safety and exhaust emissions of motor vehicles of more than a specified age. *My car failed the mot.*

Mote/मोट *(noun)* – धूलिकण a speck. *The plane was no bigger than a mote.*

Motely/मॉटलि *(adjective)* – विचित्र रंग का varied in appearance or character; disparate. *Her motley dress didn't suit the professional working atmosphere.*

Moth/मॉथ *(noun)* – कीट a chiefly nocturnal insect having two pairs of broad wings covered in microscopic scales, typically drably coloured and held felt when at rest, and lacking the clubbed antennae of butterflies. *The moth fluttered around the lamp.*

Mother/मदर *(noun)* – माता, जननी a woman in relation to a child or children to whom she has given birth. a woman who has care of a child through adoption. a female animal in relation to its offspring. *A mother's love is unconditional.*

Motile/मोटाइल *(adjective)* – गतियोग्य zoology & botany capable of motion. *Protozoans are motile microbes.*

Motion/मोशन *(noun)* – चेष्टा, व्यापार the action or process of moving or being moved. *Moving things remain in motion for a while before stopping.*

Motive/मोटिव *(noun)* – कारण, प्रेरक a factor inducting a person to act in a particular way. *One should be focussed in working towards a motive.*

Motor/मोटर *(noun)* – गाड़ी a machine, especially one powered by electricity or internal combustion, that supplies motive power for a vehicle or other device. *A large capacity generator needs a powerful motor.*

Motto/मोटो *(noun)* – आदर्श वाक्य a short sentence or phrase encapsulating a belief or ideal. *In order to be successful, everyone should have a clear motto.*

Mould/मोल्ड *(noun)* – साँचा a hollow container used to give shape to molten or hot liquid material when it cools and hardens. *The bakery shop near the market has lovely cake moulds.*

Moulder/मोल्डर *(verb)* – सड़ना slowly decay. *Food was mouldering due to breakdown of refrigerator.*

Mound/माउन्ड *(noun)* – ढूहा a raised mass of earth or other compacted material, especially one created for purposes of defence or burial. baseball a slight elevation form with for pitcher delivers the ball. *Soldiers hid behind the mound during attack from enemies.*

Mount/माउन्ट *(verb)* – पर्वत climb up or on to; ascend. *Stock prices mounted steadily.*

Mountable/माउन्टेबल *(adjective)* – चढ़ने योग्य ability of being climbed up. *He bought a set of mountable band pads.*

Mountebank/माउन्टिबैन्क *(noun)* – नीमहकीम, कठवैद्य a swindler. *The mountebank was exposed.*

Mounted/माउन्टेड *(adjective)* – घुड़सवार riding an animal, typically a horse. *Mounted riders were dressed in traditional gear.*

Mourn/मोर्न *(verb)* – विलाप करना feel deep sorrow following the death or loss of. express this sorrow through conventions such as the wearing or black clothes. *She mourned the loss of her pet.*

Mournful/मोर्नफुल *(adjective)* – दुःखी feeling, expressive, or inducing sadness, regret, or grief. *He played a mournful melody.*

Mouse/माउस *(noun)* – चूहा, मूस a small rodent that typically has a pointed snout, relatively large ears and eyes, and a long tail. *She has a pet mouse.*

Mouth/माउथ *(noun)* – मुख the opening and cavity in the lower part of the human face, surrounded by the lips, through which food and air are taken and vocal sounds are emitted. the corresponding opening through which an animal takes in food. *He filled his mouth with sweets.*

M

Mouthless/माउथलेस *(adjective)* – मुखहीन the opening through which food is taken or words spoken. *The box is mouthless.*

Movability/मूवेबिलिटि *(noun)* – चलनशीलता ability to be moved. *They were concerned about the movability of the display case.*

Movable/मूवेबॅल *(adjective)*– चलायमान capable of being moved. *They kept the costumes in an easily movable cupboard.*

Move/मूव *(verb)* – गति, कदम go or cause to go in a specified direction or manner. *He moved left to catch the ball.*

Movement/मूवमेन्ट *(noun)* – व्यापार, चाल an act of moving. *The dancers' movement was reflected in the mirror.*

Mower/मोअॅर *(noun)* – घास काटने का यन्त्र an equipment to cut grass. *He bought a new mower.*

Mowing/मोइंग *(noun)* – लवन, कटाई loose mown grass. *The mowings were kept neatly in a corner.*

Muchness/मचनेस् *(noun)* – बहुतायत the state of being much. [informal] very similar. *The performances appeared much of muchness.*

Mucous/म्यूकस *(adjective)* – श्लेष्मल mouldy, musty festering. *The mucous wound took a long time to heal.*

Mud/मड *(noun)* – कीचड़ soft, sticky matter consisting of mixed earth and water. *The kids are playing with mud.*

Muddle/मड्ल *(verb)* – गड़गड़ करना bring into a disordered or confusing state. confuse two or more things with each other. *He muddled up the piles.*

Muff/मफ *(noun)* – मफ, दस्ताना a short tube made of fur or other warm material into which the hands are placed for warmth. *She lost her muff.*

Muffler/मॅफ्लॅ(र) *(noun)* – गुलूबंद, मफलर a wrap or scarf worn around the neck and face for warmth. *The red muffler is his favourite.*

Mug/मग *(noun)* – जलपात्र a large cup, typically cylindrical and with a handle and used without a saucer. *The tea mug was empty.*

Mugginess/मगिनिस *(noun)* – गीलापन unpleasantly humid. *It was a warm and humid, full of mugginess.*

Muggy/मग्गी *(adjective)* – सूखा तथा तर unpleasantly warm and humid. *It's very muggy today.*

Mulberry/मॅल्बॅरि *(noun)* – शहतूत small deciduous tree with broad leaves. *There is a mulberry tree in our yard.*

Mulet – *(noun)* male mule. *He bought a young mulet for his barn.*

Mulish/म्यूलिश *(adjective)* – हठी stubborn like a mule. *He irritated everyone with his mulish behaviour.*

Muller/मॅलॅ(र) *(noun)* – बट्टा a stone used for grinding materials such as artists pigment. *The cat broke my muller.*

Mullock/म्यूलक *(noun)* – कूड़ा, गर्दा austral rubbish or nonsense. *Everyone avoids his mullock.*

Multangular/मूलटँगुलर *(adjective)* अनेक कोणों वाला having many angles.*He drew a multangular.*

Multifarious/मल्टिफेरिअश *(adjective)* – रंगबिरंगा having great variety and diversity. many and various. *The stall has a multifarious display.*

Multiform/मल्टिफॉर्म् – नाना रूप का existing in many forms or kinds. *They offer a multiform programme.*

Multilateral/मल्टिलैटरल *(adjective)* – बहुभुजी agreed upon or participated in by three or move parties. *They took multilateral decision.*

Multinomial/मल्टिनॉमियल *(adjective & noun)* – अनेक नामों वाला mathematics another term for polynomial. *They did an exercise on multinomials.*

Multiplex/मल्टिप्लेक्स *(adjective)* – अनेक नामों वाला consisting of many elements in a complex relationship. *They have a multiplex relation.*

Multiplicable/मल्टिप्लिकेबॅल *(adjective)* – गुणन करने योग्य able to be multiplied. *The numbers were multiplicable.*

Multiplicand/मल्टिप्लिकैंड *(noun)* – गुण्य a quantity which is to be multiplied by another the multiplier. *The multiplicand was written in blue.*

Multiplication/मल्टिप्लिकेशन *(noun)* – गुणन-क्रिया the process of multiplying. *He used a calculator for multiplication.*

Multiplier/मॅल्टिप्लाइअ(र) *(noun)* – गुणक a quantity by which a given number is to be multiplied. *He copied the multiplier wrongly.*

Multiply/मल्टिप्लाइ *(verb)* – गुणा करना obtain from another which contains the first number a specified number of times. *Children are learning to multiply and divide.*

Multitude/मल्टिट्यूड *(noun)* – झुण्ड large number of people or things. *A multitude of people supported the cause.*

Mumble/मम्बल *(verb)* – अस्पष्ट बोलना say something indistinctly and quietly. *He only mumbled his protest.*

Mummy/मॅमि *(noun)* – रक्षित मृतक शरीर a body that has been preserved for burial by embalming and wrapping in bandages. *We saw Tutankhamen's mummy in the museum.*

Mundane/मन्डेन *(adjective)* – संसारी lacking interest or excitement. *His teaching method was very mundane.*

Munificence/म्यूनिफिसेन्स *(noun)* – दानशीलता quality of being very generous. *They thanked him for his munificence.*

Munificient/म्यनिफिसेंट *(adjective)* – उदार very generous. *She is very munificent to her employees.*

Muniment/म्यूनिमेंट *(noun)* – अधिकार-पत्र chiefly law title deeds or other documents proving a person's title to land. *He kept the muniments safely in the drawer.*

Munition/म्यूनिशन *(noun)* – युद्ध-सम्बन्धी military weapons, ammunition, equipment, and stores. *They lost because of shortage of munitions.*

Mural/म्यूरल *(noun)* – भीत सम्बन्धी a painting executed directly on wall. *The murals on the temple walls are almost perfectly preserved.*

Murderer/मर्डरर् *(noun)* – हत्यारा a person who commits murder. *He was wrongly suspected to be a murderer.*

Murderous/मर्डरस् *(adjective)* – घातक capable of, intending, or involving murder or extreme violence. *It was a murderous rage.*

Mure/म्युअँ(र) *(verb)* – बन्द करना archaic confine in or as in a prison. *They were mured in because of heavy storm.*

Murk/मॅर्क *(noun)* – अँधेरा darkness or fog causing poor visibility. *The murk was making it difficult to drive.*

Murmur/मर्मर् *(noun)* – मन्द ध्वनि a low continuous backgroung noise. *The murmur of the class was very distracting.*

Murrain/मरेन् *(noun)* – पशुओं की महामारी on infectious disease affecting cattle or other animals. *His cow is suffering from murrain.*

Murrey/मरि *(noun)* – शहतूत के रंग का archaic, the deep purple-red colour of a mulberry. *She bought a murrey scarf.* Another term for sanguine. *He felt murrey.*

Muscle/मसल *(noun)* – मांसपेशी a band of fibrous tissue in the body that has the ability to contract, producing movement in or maintaining the position of a part of the body. *He pulled a muscle while running.*

Museum/म्यूजिऑम *(noun)* – अजायबघर a building in which objects of historical, scientific, artistic, or cultural interest are stored and exhibited. *The museum was reopened after major renovations.*

Mush/मॅश *(noun)* – गूदा a soft, wet, pulpy mass. *There was a mush outside the door.*

Mushroom/मॅश्रूम *(noun)* – कुकुरमुत्ता a spore producing fungal growth, often edible and typically having a domed cap with gills on the underside. *He loves mushrooms on his pizza.*

Mushy/मॅशि *(adjective)* – गूदेदार soft and pulpy. *She gifted the baby a mushy toy.*

Music/म्युजिक *(noun)* – सुर, राग the art or science of combining vocal or instrumental sounds to produce beauty of form, harmony, and expression of emotion. the sound so produced. *They play soothing music in the evening.*

Musician/म्युजिशियन *(noun)* – संगीतज्ञ a person who plays a musical instrument or is otherwise musically gifted. *She is a brilliant musician.*

Musk/मस्क *(noun)* – कस्तूरी, मृगमद a strong smelling reddish brown substance secreted by the male musk deer, used as an ingredient in perfumery. *The display showed raw musk along with the processed perfume.*

Musket/मस्केट् *(noun)* – फौजी सिपाही की बन्दूक an infantryman's light gun with a long barrel, typically smooth bored and fired from the shoulder. *The musket broke after it fell from the cliff.*

Muslin/मस्लिन *(noun)* – मलमल, तंजेब lightweight cotton cloth in a plain weave. *He hung the curd in a muslin cloth.*

Muss/मॅस *(verb)* – गड़बड़ी make untidy or messy. *He mussed the sketch.*

M

Must/मस्ट *(verb)* – होना be obliged to; should. expressing insistence. *The seal must be broken before trying to open the can.*

Mustard/मॅस्टॅर्ड *(noun)* – सरसों a hot tasting yellow or brown paste made from the crushed seeds of certain plants, eaten with meat or used as a cooking ingredient. *I loved mustard in sandwich.*

Musty/मस्टि *(adjective)* – सड़ा हुआ having a stale or mouldy smell or taste. *He found a musty bread in the store room.*

Mutable/म्यूटॅबॅल *(adjective)* – अस्थिर liable to change. inconstant in one's affections. *The audience response is very mutable.*

Mutation/म्यूटेशॅन *(noun)* – परिवर्तन the action or process of changing. a change. *The mutation of the structure was too rapid.*

Mute/म्यूट *(adjective)* - चुपचाप, मौन refraining from speech or temporarily speechless. *They were so shocked that they stayed mute for a minute.*

Mutilate/म्यूटिलेट *(verb)* – अंग-भंग करना injure or damage severely, typically so as to disfigure. *The doll was mutilated.*

Mutter/मटर *(verb)* – गुर्राना say in a barely audible voice. talk or grumble in secret or in private. *He muttered his unhappiness with the arrangements.*

Mutual/म्यूट्युअॅल *(adj)* – परस्पर experienced or done by each of two or more parties towards the other or others: mutual respect. having the same specified relationship to each other. *They had a mutual respect for each other's ritual.*

Muzzle/मॅज़ॅल *(noun)* - थूथन, बन्दूक का मुँह the projecting part of the face, including the nose and mouth, of an animals such as a dog or horse. a guard fitted over an animal's muzzle to stop it biting or feeding. *The child coloured crocodile's muzzle yellow!*

Muzzy/मॅज़ि *(adjective)* – तेजहीन confused. *He felt muzzy as he didn't get proper sleep the previous night.*

My/माइ *(possess. det.)* – मेरा belonging to or associated with the speaker. used with forms of address in affectionate, sympathetic, humorous, or patronizing contexrs. *My mother baked a cake for me.*

Myalgia/माइएल्जिआ *(noun)* – पेशीशूल pain in a muscle or group of muscles. *He is taking medicines to treat myalgia.*

Myalism/माइएलिज़्म *(noun)* – एक प्रकार का जादू a Jamaican folk religion focused on the power of ancestors, typically involving drumming, dancing, spirit possession, ritual sacrifice, and herbalism. *They spent the night discussing myalism beliefs.*

Myopia/माइओपिआ *(noun)* – निकटदृष्टि दोष short sightedness. *She suffers from myopia.*

Myriad/मिरिअॅड *(noun)* – दस हजार an indefinitely great number. *A myriad of colours were created by the glass work.*

Myriapod/मिरिअपॉड *(noun)* – गोजर a centipede, millipede, or other arthropod having an elongated body with numerous leg bearing segments. *They studied a myriapod sample in the lab today.*

Myrobalan/माइरॉबॅलॅन *(noun)* – आँवला another term for cherry plum. *They were asked to bring leaves of a cherry plum or myrobalan.*

Myrrh/मॅर *(noun)* – लोहबान a fragrant gum resin obtained from certain trees and used, especially in the near east, in perfumery, medicines, and incense. *Ancient Egyptians were very fond of myrrh.*

Myrtle/मर्टल *(noun)* – हिना an evergreen shrub with glossy aromatic foliage and white flowers followed by purple black oval berries. *The gardener planted four new myrtle in the garden today.*

Mysterious/मिस्टिरिअॅस *(adjective)* – गुप्त difficult to understand. *He disappeared under mysterious circumstances.*

Mystic/मिस्टिक *(noun)* – अप्रकट, गुप्त, गहन a person who seeks by contemplation and self surrender to attain unity with the deity or the absolute, and so reach truths beyond human understanding. *He is self-proclaimed mystic.*

Mysticism/मिस्टिसिज़्म *(noun)* – गूढ़ विद्या the belief or state of mind characteristic of mystics. *They discussed the popular ancient mysticism of the area.*

Mystify/मिस्टिफाइ *(verb)* – घबराना utterly bewilder. *The audience was mystified by his performance.*

Myth/मिथ *(noun)* – कल्पित कथा a traditional story concerning the early history of a people or explaining a natural or social phenomenon, and typically involving supernatural being or events. *Despite his*

M

education, he firmly believes in the Hindu myth of creation.

Mythical/मिथिकल *(adjective)* – काल्पनिक occurring in myths or folk tales. *She made a project on mythical monsters.*

Mythologer/माइथोलॉजर *(noun)* – पौराणिक one having a collection of myths. *He is famous mythologer.*

Mythology/मिर्थॅलजि *(noun)* – पौराणिक कथा a collection of myths, especially one belonging

to a particular religious or cultural tradition. *Indian mythology is very vast and varied.*

Mythonomy/मिथॅनमि *(noun)* – पुराण शास्त्र the laws which govern the evolution of myths. *I don't believe in your mythonomy.*

Mythoplasm/माइथोप्लाज्म *(noun)* – कथा-कहानी कथन

Mythus/माइथस *(noun)* – देवताओं की काल्पनिक कथा a myth or mythos. *He narrated a mythus.*

M

Nn

N/एन *(noun)* – अंग्रेजी वर्णमाला का 14वाँ वर्ण the fourteenth letter of the English alphabet.
1. Denoting the next after M in a set of items, categories, etc.

Nab/नैब *(verb)* – पकड़ना, बंदी बनाना catch doing something wrong. *The police nabbed the thief.*

Nacelle/नैसेल *(noun)* – हवाई जहाज का डिब्बा the outer casing of an aircraft engine. *The passengers here carried to the airship in a nacelle.*

Nag/नैग *(verb)* – कष्ट देना harass constantly to do something to which they are averse. *Disturbing nagged him day and night.*

Naiad/नाइऐड *(noun)* – जल देवता a nymph inhabiting a river, spring, or waterfall. *This story is a story of naiads.*

Nail/नेल *(noun)* – नख, कील a small metal spike with a broadened flat head, driven typically into join things together or to serve as a hook. *He drove nail in the wall.*

Naive/नेव *(adjective)* – सरल lacking experience, wisdom, or judgment. *Please forgive him, he is a naïve fellow.*

Name/नेम *(noun)* – नाम a word or set of words by which someone or something is known, addressed, or referred to. *His name is famous among novelists.*

Namkeen/नमकीन *(noun)* – नमकीन indian salty snack. *Indians usually serve guests namkeen and tea as refreshment.*

Nanny/नैनी *(noun)* – आया a person, typically a woman, employed to look after a child in its own home. *He hired a nanny for his baby.*

Nape/नेप *(noun)* – गर्दन का पिछला भाग the back of a person's neck. *The hair stood on his nape as he watched the horror film.*

Napery/नेपरी *(noun)* – मेजपोश [archaic] household linen, especially tablecloths and napkins. *I am going to wash the napery today.*

Naphtha/नेफ्था *(noun)* – शीघ्र जलने वाला खनिज तेल विशेष a flammable oil containing various hydrocarbon, obtained by the dry distillation or organic substances such as coal, shale, or petroleum. *Naphtha is a dangerous petroleum product.*

Napkin/नैपकिन *(noun)* – नैपकिन a square piece of cloth or paper used at a meal to wipe the fingers or lips and to protect garments. *Please wipe your fingers on a napkin.*

Napoleonic/नैपोलियोनिक *(adjective)* – प्रसिद्ध राजा नेपोलियन प्रथम के समान of, relating to, or characteristic of Napoleon I or his time. *It is a Napoleonic hat.*

Narcissus/नारसिसॅस *(noun)* – नरगिस a daffodil with a flower that has white or pale outer petals and a shallow orange or yellow centre. *I have a narcissus in my garden.*

Narcosis/नारकोसिस *(noun)* – मूर्छा medicine a state of stupor, drowsiness, or unconsciousness produced by drugs. *He has taken a strange drug and is under narcosis.*

Narcotic/नारकोटिक *(noun)* – बेहोश करने वाली दवा an addictive drug, especially an illegal one, affecting mood or behaviour. medicine a drug which induces drowsiness, stupor, or insensibility, and relieves pain. *He is under the influence of narcotic.*

Narcotize/नारकोटाइज़ *(verb)* – बेहोश करना, नशीला करना या बनाना affect with or as if with narcotic drug. *The robbers wanted to narcotize the family to rob with fear.*

Nard/नार्ड *(noun)* – एक पौधा (जटामासी, बालछड़) a Himalayan plant. *Some Ayurvedic medicines use nards during preparation.*

Narrate/नैरेट *(verb)* – वर्णन करना give a spoken or written account of. provide a commentary to accompany. *He narrated the incident very clearly.*

N

Narrative/नैरेटिव *(noun)* – कथा a spoken or written account of connected events; a story. the narrated part of a literary work, as distinct from dialogue. the practice or art of narration. *It was a brilliant piece of narrative.*

Narrowish/नैरोइश *(adverb)* – कुछ-कुछ सँकरा some what narrow. *The lane is narrowish.*

Narrowly/नैरोली *(adverb)* – कष्ट से by a small marging. *It was a bad accident he narrowly escaped death.*

Narrowness/नैरोनेस *(noun)* – संकोच limited in space, amount or scope. *Narrowness of mind is responsible for many foolish acts.*

Nasal/नेजल *(adjective)* – नासिका सम्बन्धी of or relating to the nose. *He sings in a nasal voice.*

Nascency/नसेंसी *(noun)* – उत्पादन का आरम्भ state of just coming into existence. *Indian space industry is 40 years old and is completely out of nascency.*

Nascent/नेसेंट *(adjective)* – उगने वाला – just coming into existence and beginning to display signs of future potential. *It is a nascent bud.*

Nasturtium/नैस्टर्शम् *(noun)* – एक प्रकार की रेंगने वाली या जमीन पर फैलने वाली लता a south American trailing plant with round leaves and bright orange, yellow, or red flowers, widely grown as an ornamental. *I have just purchased a nasturtium.*

Nasty/नेस्टी *(adjective)* – मलिन highly unpleasant or repugnant. *There was a nasty smell in the kitchen.*

Natal/नेटल *(adjective)* – जन्म-सम्बन्धी of or relating to the place or time of one's birth. *His natal sign is Gemini.*

Nates/नेटीज् *(plural noun)* – चूतड़ anatomy the buttocks. *She has well rounded nates.*

Nation/नेशन *(noun)* – राष्ट्र a large aggregate of people united by common descent, culture, or language, inhabiting a particular state or territory. a [north American] Indian people or confederation of peoples. *India is a multi-lingual and multi-cultural nation.*

National/नेशनल/नैशनल *(adjective)* – राष्ट्रीय of, relating to, or characteristic of nation. *Crimes against women have become a national issue.*

Nationalism/नैशनलिज्म *(noun)* – राष्ट्रीय स्वतन्त्रता की नीति patriotic feeling, principles, or efforts. an extreme form of this marked by a feeling of superiority over other countries. *Uncontrolled nationalism sometimes leads to dictatorship and war.*

Nationalize/नैशनलाइज *(verb)* – राष्ट्रीय बनाना transfer a major branch of industry or commerce from private to state ownership or control. *Big private companies are often nationalized in socialist countries.*

Native/नेटिव *(noun)* – देशवासी a person born in a specified place or associated with a place by birth. a local inhabitant. *He is a native of Australia.*

Nativity/नेटिविटि *(noun)* – ईसामसीह का जन्म दिन, जन्म पत्रिका the occasion of a person's birth. *The nativity of Jesus Christ is celebrated as festival of Christmas.*

Natron/नेट्रन् *(noun)* – सज्जी-खार a mineral salt found in dried lake beds, consisting of hydrated sodium carbonate. *Natron is a useful mineral.*

Nattily/नैटिलि *(adverb)* – स्वच्छता से smartly. *She turned out at the reception dresses nattily.*

Nattiness/नैटिनेश *(noun)* – स्वच्छता state of smartness. *She is well mannered and so is her nattiness with dress.*

Natty/नैटि *(adjective)* – चालाक small and fashionable. *Because of her fashionable style. She is known as the most natty girl in the college.*

Natural/नैचुरल *(adjective)* – स्वाभाविक existing in or derived from nature; not made, caused by, or processed by humankind. unbleached and undyed; off-white. *Oceans, mountains, trees, rivers etc. are natural objects.*

Naturalism/नैचुरलिज्म *(noun)* – प्राकृतिक नियमों के सिद्धान्त a style and theory of representation based on the accurate depiction of detail. *His writings have a lot of naturalism.*

Naturalist/नैचुरलिस्ट *(noun)* – पदार्थ शास्त्रज्ञ an expert in or student of natural history. *My brother is a naturalist and studies how certain animals and plants developed into present form.*

Naturalize/नैचुरलाइज *(verb)* – अभ्यस्त कराना admit a foreigner to the citizenship of a country. alter so that it conforms more closely to the phonology or orthography of

N

the adopting language. *He is a naturalized citizen of India and not so by birth.*

Naturally/नैचुरलि *(adverb)* - स्वभाव से in a natural manner. *Naturally we don't feel at case with strangers.*

Naturalness/नैचुरलनेस *(noun)* - यथार्थता quality of being natural. *He demonstrates naturalness that many others try hard to project on the stage.*

Naught/नॉट *(noun)* - शून्य [archaic] nothing. *All his efforts were brought to naught.*

Nausea/नॉसिया *(noun)* - मिचली, उबकाई a feeling of sickness with an inclination to vomit. *He had nausea in the foul smelling place.*

Nauseate/नॉसिएट *(verb)* - जी मिचलाना affect with nausea; offensive to the taste or smell. *He felt nauseated after eating the food.*

Nautical/नॉटिकल *(adjective)* - नाविक of or concerning sailors or navigation; maritime. *A nautical mile covered by ship is about 2,025 yards.*

Naval/नेवल *(adjective)* - नौसैनिक of, in, or relating to a navy or navies. *He is a high ranking naval officer.*

Nave/नेव *(noun)* - गिरजाघर का मध्य भाग, पहिये की नाभि the central part of a church building usually separated from the chancel by a step or rail and from adjacent aisles by pillars. *There were a lot of people present in the nave.*

Navel/नेवेल *(noun)* - नाभि a rounded knotty depression in the centre of a person's belly caused by the detachment of the umbilical cord after birth; the umbilicus. *She wears a diamond in her navel.*

Navicular/नैविक्युलर *(adjective)* - नाव के प्रकार का chiefly [archaic] boat-shaped. *He had a navicular bone fracture in an accident.*

Navigable/नैविगॉबॅल *(adjective)* - जहाज या नाव ले जाने योग्य of a waterway or sea able to be sailed on by ships or boats. *It is a stormy sea and not navigable at this time.*

Navigate/नैविगेट *(verb)* - जहाज चलाना plan and direct the route or course of a ship, aircraft, or other form of transport, especially by using instruments or maps. *The captain navigated the ship safely through ice-bergs.*

Navigation/नैविगेशन *(noun)* - नौविद्या the process or activity of navigating the passage of ships. *He has finished his training in navigation.*

Navigator/नैविगेटर *(noun)* - नाविक a person who navigates a ship, aircraft, etc. *he is an expert navigator and trusted by the captain.*

Navvy/नैवि *(noun)* - भूमि खोदने वाला या नहर खोदने वाला मजदूर [British dated] a labourer employed in the excavation and construction of a road, railway, or canal. *A navvy is usually hired on daily wages.*

Navy/नेवी *(noun)* - जहाजों का बेड़ा the branch of a state's armed services which conducts military operations at sea. poetic a fleet of ships. *The British navy is very powerful.*

Nawab/नवाब *(noun)* - नवाब a native governor during the time of the Mughal empire. *He lives lavishly like a nawab.*

Nay/ने *(adverb)* - नहीं or rather; and more than that. *He is foolish and nay ill-mannered as well.*

Neap/नीप *(noun)* - सबसे नीचे का a tide just after the first or third quarters of the moon when there is least difference between high and low water. *Trapped in a neap tide, the ship ran aground.*

Near/नियर् *(adverb)* - समीप at or to a short distance away. *My house is near a big super market.*

Nearness/नियरनेस् *(noun)* - समीपता proximity. *Too much nearness in any relation is not halting.*

Neat/निट *(adjective)* - सुन्दर in good order; tidy or carefully arranged. *The room was neat and clean.*

Neath/निथ *(preposition)* - 'नीचे' अर्थ का यह शब्द कविता में प्रयुक्त होता है chiefly beneath. *There is a cat sitting beneath the table.*

Neb/नेब *(noun)* - चोंच Scottish a nose, snout, or bird's beak. *The neb of a crocodile looks frightening.*

Nebula/नेब्युला *(noun)* - नीहारिका astronomy a visible cloud of gas or dust in outer space. old-fashioned term for galaxy. *You can see the nebula shining over there in the sky.*

Necessarian/नेसेसरिअन *(noun & adjective)* - दैववादी another term for necessitarian. *I am a staunch necessarian.*

N

Necessary/नेसेसरी *(adjective)* – आवश्यक required to be done, achieved, or present; needed. *It is something necessary, so do it.*

Necessitate/नेसेसिटेट *(verb)* – विवश करना make necessary as a result or consequence. force or compel to do something. *He was necessitated into selling his property.*

Necessitous/नेसेसिटस *(adjective)* – दीन, अकिंचन of a person poor, needy. *He is a necessitous person, give him some money.*

Necessity/नेसेसिटी *(noun)* – आवश्यकता the state or fact of being necessary. *Necessity is the mother of invention.*

Neck/नेक *(noun)* – ग्रीवा the part of a person's or animal's body connecting the head to the rest of the body. *She has a slim round neck.*

Necrology/नेक्रोलॉजी *(noun)* – मृत्यु-लेख an obituary notice. *His name does not appear in necrology.*

Necromancy/नेक्रोमैन्सी *(noun)* – जादू the supposed practice of communicating with the dead, especially in order to predict the future. witchcraft, sorcery, or black magic in general. *He practises black magic and is supposed to be indulged in necromancy.*

Necrophagous/नेक्रोफेगस *(noun)* – शव (मुर्दा) खाने वाला eating carrion. *Vultures are necrophagous creature.*

Necrophobia/नेक्रोफोबिया *(noun)* – मृत्यु का भय extreme or irrational fear of death or dead bodies. *He suffers from necrophobia.*

Necrosis/नेक्रॅसिस *(noun)* – हड्डी का निर्जीव होना medicine the death of most or all of the cells in an organ or tissue due to disease, injury, or failure of the blood supply. *The old man had an accident and died of necrosis.*

Nectar/नेक्टर *(noun)* – अमृत a sugary fluid secreted within flowers to encourage pollination by insects, collected by bees to make into honey. *Bees and insects collect nectar from flowers.*

Neddy/नेड्डी *(noun)* – खच्चर a child's word for a donkey. *He is a fine neddy and will certainly win the race.*

Need/नीड *(verb)* – अभाव requirement because it is essential or very important rather than just desirable. *If need be, I'll come to your house.*

Needful/नीडफुल *(adjective)* – आवश्यक formal necessary: requisite. *The needful must be done urgently to help the flood victims.*

Needle/नीड्ल *(noun)* – सूई a very fine slender piece of metal with a point at one end and a hole or eye for thread at the other, used in sewing. a similar, larger instrument used in crochet, knitting, etc. *Give me a needle and some black thread I have to darn the torn pocket of my shirt.*

Needless/निडलेस *(adjective)* – निरर्थक unnecessary; avoidable. *It is needless to observe these formalities here.*

Needs/नीड्स *(adverb)* – आवश्यक of necessity. *Let your needs be limited.*

Needy/नीडि *(adjective)* – दरिद्र lacking the necessities of life; very poor. *He is needy, so let us help him.*

Never/नेवर *(adverb)* – कभी नहीं at no time in the past or future. *Never use such abusive language again.*

Nefarious/निफेरिअश *(adjective)* – पापी criminal or antisocial. *He is a nefarious fellow and had been in jail many times.*

Negative/निगेटिव *(adjective)* – निषेधार्थक consisting in or characterized by the absence rather than the presence of distinguishing features. expressing or implying denial, disagreement, or refusal. grammar & logic stating that something is not the case. contrasted with affirmative and interrogative. *Don't talk to him, he is in a negative state of mind.*

Neglect/नेगलेक्ट *(verb)* – उपेक्षा करना fail to give proper care or attention to. fail to do something. *He spent a negative childhood.* *(noun)* the state or process of neglecting or being neglected. failure to do something. *He neglected his studies and failed in the class.*

Neglectful/नेग्लेक्ट्फुल – ध्यान रहित *(adjective)* not giving proper attention. *He is a neglectful parent.*

Negligence/नेगिलजेंस *(noun)* – उपेक्षा failure to take proper care over something. law breach of a duty of care which results in damage. *Negligence on the part of guard cost him his job.*

Negligent/नेगिलजेंट *(adjective)* – असावधान failing to take proper care. *He is a negligent worker and hence cannot be relied upon.*

N

Negligible/नेग्लिजिबल *(adjective)* – उपेक्षा करने योग्य so small or unimportant as to be not worth considering; insignificant. *He passed the exam with negligible margin.*

Negotiable/निगोशिअबल् *(adjective)* – बेचा-बिक्री करने योग्य open to discussion or modification. *This flat is for sale and the price is negotiable.*

Negro/नीग्रो *(noun)* – हब्शी a member of a dark-skinned group of people originally native to Africa south of the Sahara. *Many negroes were enslaved by European colonizers.*

Negus/नीगॅस *(noun)* – नीगस a ruler, or the supreme ruler, of Ethiopia. *He was the negus of a big African tribe.*

Neigh/ने *(noun)* – घोड़े का हिनहिनाना a characteristic high whinnying sound made by a horse. *The horse was disturbed and neighed as the stranger approached him.*

Neighbour/नेबर *(noun)* – पड़ोसी a person living next door to or very near to another. a person or place in relation to others next to it. *My neighbour is a nice fellow.*

Nemesis/नेमिसिस *(noun)* – प्रतिशोध, दण्ड the inescapable agent of someone's downfall, especially when deserved a downfall caused by such an agent. *His wife proved to be his nemesis.*

Neo/निओ *(combining form)* – 'नवीन' या 'आधुनिक' अर्थ का उपसर्ग new: neonate. *Neoclassical paintings are a lot attractive to look at.*

Neon/निऑन *(noun)* – निऑन the chemical element of atomic number 10, an inert gaseous element of the noble gas group. *Neon lights are spread all over metro cities.*

Neophyte/निओफाइट *(noun)* – नवदीक्षित, नया शिष्य a person who is new to a subject, skill, or belief. *He is a neophyte and it will take him some time to adjust.*

Neoplastic/निओप्लास्टिक *(adjective)*– नवनिर्मित या रचित medicine of or relating to a neoplasm or neoplasia. *It is a neoplastic building.*

Neoteric/निओटेरिक *(adjective)* – आधुनिक, नया recent; new; modern. *His neoteric views on religion are worth reading.*

Nephew/नेफ्यु *(noun)* – भतीजा a son of one's brother or sister, or of one's brother-in-law or sister-in-law. *This young man is my nephew.*

Nephology/नेफॉलजि *(noun)* – मेघ-अध्ययन-शास्त्र the study or contemplation of clouds. *Nephology interests me a lot.*

Nephritic/नेफ्रिटिक *(adjective)* – वृक्क सम्बन्धी renal. of or relating to nephritis. *He has a nephritic disease, take him to a hospital.*

Nepotism/नेपॉटिज्म *(noun)* – कुल पक्षपात the favouring of relations or friends, especially by giving them jobs. *Almost all political leaders practise nepotism.*

Neptune/नेप्ट्यून *(noun)* – समुद्र देवता a planet of the solar system, eighth in order from the sun. *Neptune is a very distant planet.*

Nerve/नर्व *(noun)* – ऊर्जा, शक्ति, बल, नस a whitish fibre or bundle of fibres in the body that transmits impulses of sensation between the brain or spinal cord and other parts of the body. *He sure had nerve to face the challenge.*

Nerveless/नर्वलेस *(adjective)* – निर्बल lacking vigour or feeling. *He is nerveless in the face of danger.*

Nervous/नर्वस् *(adjective)* – शीघ्र घबड़ा जाने वाला easily agitated or alarmed. apprehensive. resulting from anxiety or anticipation. *He is a very nervous fellow and gets frightened easily.*

Nest/नेस्ट *(noun)* – घोंसला a structure or place made or chosen by a bird for laying eggs and sheltering its young. a place where an animal or insect breeds or shelters. a snug or secluded retreat. a bowl-shaped object likened to a bird's nest. *This large tree has many nests in its branches.*

Nestle/नेसॅल *(verb)* – शरण लेना, चिपट जाना settle comfortably within or against something. *She nestled against me.*

Nestling/नेस्टलिंग *(noun)* – पक्षी का बच्चा, गेदा a bird that is too young to leave the nest. *She is a nestling and isn't ready to fly yet.*

Net/नेट *(noun)* – फन्दा a length of open-meshed material of twine, cord, etc. used typically for catching fish. a net supported by a frame at the end of a handle, used for catching fish or insects. *Many fish were caught in the net.*

Nether/नेदर *(adjective)* – नीचे lower in position. *He is nether in position to many employees.*

Nettle/नेटल *(noun)* – बिच्छू का पेड़ a herbaceous plant having jagged leaves covered with stinging hairs. used in names of plants of a similar appearance. *Don't touch this plant. It is a nettle.*

Neural/न्युअरल *(adjective)* – तंत्रिकीय, तंत्रिका of or relating to a nerve or the nervous system. *He underwent a neural.*

Neuritis/न्युअराइटिस *(noun)* – तंत्रिका शोथ medicine inflammation of a peripheral nerve or nerves. *He is suffering from neuritis.*

Neurosis/न्यूरॉसिस *(noun)* – एक प्रकार का पागलपन medicine a relatively mild mental illness not caused by organic disease, involving depression, anxiety, obsessive behaviour, etc. but not a radical loss of touch with reality. *He has neurosis and is consulting a psychologist.*

Neurotic/न्यूरॉटिक *(adjective)* – नाड़ी सम्बन्धी medicine having, caused by, or relating to neurosis. *His neurotic behaviour upset all.*

Neuter/न्यूटर *(adjective)* – नपुंसक of or denoting a gender of nouns typically contrasting with masculine and feminine or common. *'It' is a neuter gender.*

Neutral/न्यूट्रल *(adjective)* – उदासीन impartial. belonging to an impartial state or group. unbiased. *He is a neutral person, you can go and seek his advice.*

Never/नेवर *(adverb)* – कभी नहीं not ever. *Never before did he speak in such a way.*

Nevertheless/नेवरदलेस *(adverb)* – तथापि, तो भी in spite of that. *He is foolish, nevertheless honest.*

New/न्यू *(adjective)* – नया, नवीन not existing before; made, introduced, or discovered recently or now for the first time. not previously used or owned. *He has bought a new car.*

News/न्यूज *(noun)* – समाचार, वार्ता newly received or noteworthy information, especially about recent events. *This is the latest news you are hearing.*

Nexus/नेक्सस *(noun)* – बन्धन a connection a connected group or series. *The nexus between politicos and mafia is something highly undesirable.*

Nib/निब *(noun)* – कलम की नोक the pointed end part of a pen, which distributes the ink. a pointed or projecting part of an object. *The nib of pen is broken.*

Nibble/निबॅल *(verb)* – कुतरना take small bites out of. eat in small amounts. gently bite at. *Rats have nibbled the piece of bread.*

Nice/नाइस *(adjective)* – मनोहर pleasant; agreeable; satisfactory. good-natured; kind. *He is a nice man by nature.*

Nicely/नाइसलि *(adverb)* – सुन्दरता से in a pleasant manner. *The Job was nicely done.*

Niceness/नाइसनेस *(noun)* – सुन्दरता *The niceness of his behaviour impressed all.*

Niceties/नाइसेटिज *(noun)* – बारीकियाँ atractive things. *He observed all the niceties of behaviour.*

Nicety/नाइसेटि *(noun)* – सूक्ष्मता a fine detail or distinction. accuracy. a detail of etiquette. *His drawings had great nicety.*

Niche/निच *(noun)* – ताखा a shallow recess, especially one in a wall to display an ornament. *The golden statue was placed in a niche.*

Nicknacks/निकनैक्स *(noun)* – तुच्छ पदार्थ variant spelling of knick-knack. *She is fond of wearing knickknacks.*

Nicotiana/निकोटियना *(noun)* – तमाखू का an ornamental plant related to tobacco, with tubular flowers that are particularly fragrant at night. *The plant of nicotiana smells fragrant at night.*

Nicotine/निकोटिन *(noun)* – तमाखू का सत्व a toxic oily liquid which is the chief active constituent of tobacco. *He is addicted to nicotine.*

Niddle-noddle/निडॅल-नॉडल – हिलता हुआ, झूमता हुआ, डाँवाँडोल a man of wavering nature. *I don't like his niddle-noddle behaviour.*

Nidification/निडिफिकेशन *(noun)* – घोंसला बनाने का कार्य zoology nest-building. *In spring birds are busy in nidification.*

Niece/नीस *(noun)* – भतीजी a daughter of one's brother or sister, or of one's brother-in-law or sister-in-law. *Meet her, she is my niece.*

Nifty/निफ्टी *(adjective)* – बढ़िया, सुन्दर [informal] particularly good, skilful, or effective. stylish. *It is a nifty piece of an art.*

Niggard/निगर्ड *(noun)* – कंजूस a mean or stingy person adjective [archaic] niggardly. *He is a niggard, keep away from him.*

N

Niggardliness/निगर्ईलिनेस् *(noun)* – कृपणता mean and meagre. *The niggardliness the government's budget angered voters.*

Niggardly/निगर्ईलि *(adjective)* – लालची ungenerous. meagre. *(adverb)* [archaic] in a mean or meager manner. *He talked to me in a very niggardly way.*

Nigger/निगर् *(noun)* – हब्शी offensive a black person. *To call a black person nigger is to insult him.*

Niggle/निगल *(verb)* – तुच्छ बातों में समय नष्ट करना cause slight but persistent annoyance, discomfort, or anxiety. *She is quarrelsome and niggles her husband daily.*

Night/नाइट *(noun)* – रात the time from sunset to sunrise. this as the interval between two days. *It grew pitch dark at night.*

Night-bird/नाइटबर्ई *(noun)* – उल्लू another term for night owl. *Owl keeps awake at night and hence is called a night-bird.*

Night-blindness/नाइटब्लाइण्डनेस *(noun)* – रतौंधी less technical term for nyctalopia. *He suffers from night-blindness, as the night descends, he loses his vision.*

N

Night-fall/नाइटफॉल *(noun)* – सन्ध्याकाल dusk. *It is night-fall now and he hasn't returned as yet.*

Night-hawk/नाइटहॉक *(noun)* – चोर an American nightjar with pointed wings. *Owl is a bird of prey and is also called night-hawk.*

Nightlong/नाइटलॉन्ग *(adjective)* – रातभर throughout the night. *After the nightlong vigil, the police caught the culprit.*

Nightsoil/नाइटसॉएॅल *(noun)* – मल, विष्ठा human excrement collected at night from cesspools and privies, sometimes used as manure. *These persons collect the nightsoil.*

Nigrescent/नाइग्रेसेन्ट *(adjective)* – काला होने वाला rare blackish. *These negroes are nigrescent.*

Nil/निल *(noun)* – नहीं nothing; zero. *(adjective)* non-existent. *So his achievement is nil.*

Nimble/निम्बल *(adjective)* – चपल quick and light in movement or action. *Small birds are usually very nimble.*

Nimbus/निम्बस *(noun)* – प्रभामण्डल a large grey rain cloud. *The photos of saints have a nimbus around their heads.*

Nimrod/निर्मॉड *(noun)* – शिकारी a skilful hunter. *The ancient man was a nimrod.*

Nincompoop/निनकम्पुप *(noun)* – मूर्ख a stupid person. *What a nincompoop he is!*

Nine/नाइन *(cardinal number)* – नौ equivalent to the product of three and three; one less than ten. *There were nine muses in Greek mythology.*

Nineteen/नाइनटिन *(cardinal number)* – उन्नीस one more than eighteen; nine more than ten; 19. *He is only nineteen year old.*

Ninety/नाइनटि *(cardinal number)* – नब्बे equivalent to the product of nine and ten; ten less than one hundred; 90. *Ninety is the word for the digit 90.*

Ninny/निनि *(noun)* – मूर्ख मनुष्य [informal] a foolish and weak person. *He is a ninny don't expect anything wise from him.*

Niobium/निओबियम *(noun)* – एक प्रकार की धातु the chemical element of atomic number 41, a silver-grey metal used in superconducting alloys.

Nip/निप *(noun)* – नाखून या दाँत का कटाव nail or teeth biting, [informal], offensive a Japanese person. *He is a nip, you can't understand his language.*

Nippers/निपर्स *(noun)* – कतरनी [informal] a child. *Please bring me a pair of nippers.*

Nipple/निप्पल *(noun)* – चूचुक the small projection in which the mammary ducts of female mammals terminate and from which milk can be secreted. the corresponding vestigial structure in a male, [north American] the teat of a feeding bottle. *The baby sucked at the nipple of her mother.*

Nit/निट *(noun)* – लीख [informal] the egg or young form of a louse or other parasitic insect, especially the egg of a human head louse. *There are many nits in her hair.*

Nitre/नाइटर *(noun)* – शोरा potassium nitrate; saltpeter. *He brought a vial of nitre for some experiment.*

Nitric/नाइट्रिक *(adjective)* – शोरा का containing nitrogen with a valency of five. *Nitric acid is used in chemical experiments.*

Nitrify/नाइट्रिफाइ *(verb)* – शोरा बनाना chemistry an organic compound containing a cyanide group CN bound to an alkyl group. *To nitrify* means to convert ammonia into nitrates or nitrites.

Nix/निक्स *(exclamatory)* – कुछ भी नहीं expressing denial or refusal. *The government nixed the proposal to organise indo-pak cricket series.*

No/नो *(abbreviation)* of number – कोई भी नहीं US north. *The no.7 horse will win.*

Nob/नॉब *(noun)* – सिर [austral, informal] a shark. *I have just seen a nob near our boat.*

Nobble/नॉबल *(verb)* – बेईमानी से छीन लेना [British informal] to abtain by dishanesty, try to influence or thwart by underhand or unfair methods. tamper with to prevent it from winning a race. *Being at an influential post, he nobbled a lot of money.*

Nobility/नोबिलिटि *(noun)* – कुलीनता the quality of being noble. *He belongs to nobility and is a much respected man.*

Noble/नोबल *(adjective)* – महानुभाव belonging by rank, title, or birth to the aristocracy. *He is a noble man by birth and manners.*

Nock/नॉक *(noun)* – तीर के कोने का खण्ड archery a notch at either end of a bow or at the end of an arrow, for receiving the bowstring. *Every arrow has a nock at its end to fit the bow-string.* *(verb)* fit to the bowstring.

Nocturnal/नाक्टर्नल *(adjective)* – रात्रि सम्बन्धी done, occurring, or active at night. *Owl is a nocturnal bird.*

Nocturne/नॉक्टर्न *(noun)* – रात्रि का दृश्य या गीत music a short composition of a romantic nature. *I saw a nocturne in an art exhibition and bought it at quite a high price.*

Noddle/नॉडल *(noun)* – मस्तक [informal, dated] a person's head. *There was a holo around the holy person's noddle.*

Noddy/नॉडी *(noun)* – मूर्ख dated a silly or foolish person. *Sometimes he acts noddy but otherwise is quite intelligent.*

Node/नोड *(noun)* – गाँठ a point in a network at which lines intersect or branch. a piece of equipment, such as a computer or peripheral, attached to a network. mathematics a point at which a curve intersects itself. astronomy either of the two points at which a planet's orbit intersects the plane of the ecliptic or the celestial equator. *New leaves are growing from the node.*

Nodose/नोडोस *(adjective)* – गाँठदार technical characterized by hard or tight lumps; knotty. *The tree was quite old and had a nodose trunk.*

Nodule/नॉड्यूल *(noun)* – छोटी ग्रन्थि या गुल्म a small swelling or aggregation of cells, especially an abnormal one. *The doctor noticed a nodule on his hand.*

Noggin/नॉगिन *(noun)* – छोटा घड़ा या पात्र या प्याला brickwork in a timber frame. *The mason finished noggin in the wooden frame.*

Noise/नॉइज़ *(noun)* – शोरगुल a sound, especially one that is loud, unpleasant, or disturbing. continuous or repeated loud, confused sounds. *I can no longer stand this loud noise.*

Noiseless/नॉइज़लेस *(adjective)* – मौन silent very quiet. *The house was noiseless as nobody lived there.*

Noisily/नॉइज़िलि *(adv)* – उच्च स्वर से *He noisily made his entry on the stage.*

Noisy/नॉइज़ी *(adjective)* – कोलाहल करने वाला full of or making a lot of noise. *It was a noisy classroom.*

Nomad/नोमैड *(noun)* – बंजारा a member of a people continually moving to find fresh pasture for its animals and having no permanent home. a wanderer. *These are nomads and won't stay here for long.*

Nomadic/नोमैडिक *(adjective)* – भ्रमणकारी living a life of a nomad. *He is nomadic by nature, always wandering.*

Nominal/नॉमिनल *(adjective)* – नाम मात्र का existing in name only. relating to or consisting of names. *It is an outdated law and has only a nominal value.*

Nominally/नॉमिनलि *(adv)* – नाम मात्र से existing in name only *He was nominally in charge of the building.*

Nominate/नॉमिनेट *(verb)* – किसी पद के लिए निर्दिष्ट करना put forward as a candidate for election or for an honour or award. appoint to a job or position. *Party has nominated him as a candidate for the coming election.*

Nominative/नॉमिनेटिव *(adjective)* – कर्ता कारक grammar denoting a case of nouns, pronouns, and adjectives expressing the subject of a verb. *He is a nominative case in grammar.*

N

Nominee/नॉमिनि *(noun)* – नियुक्त पुरुष a person who is nominated. *He is a nominee to the leadership of the party.*

Non/नॉन *(prefix)* – अ, अन्, गैर अर्थ का उपसर्ग expressing negation or absence: non-recognition. not of the kind or class described: non-believer. expressing a neutral negative sense where in or un has a special connotation. *He is a non-believer in God. Certain species of insects have become non-existent.*

Nonagon/नॉनागन् *(noun)* – रेखागणित में नव कोण की आकृति a plane figure with nine straight sides and angles. *Nonagon is a geometrical figure with nine sides and angles.*

Nondescript/नानडिस्क्रिप्ट *(adjective)* – अपूर्व lacking distinctive or interesting characteristics. *He is a nondescript person, nobody takes interest in him.*

Nonentity/नॉनेन्टिटि *(noun)* – अस्तित्वहीनता an unimportant person or thing. *People hardly notice a nonentity.*

Non-existence/नान-इग्जिस्टॅन्स *(noun)* – सत्ता का न होना not real or present. *Non-existence of police led to riots.*

Non-plus/नॉनप्लस *(verb)* – व्याकुल करना surprise and confuse, flummox. *He became nonplussed as he saw the horrible accident.*

Non-resident/ननरेजिडेन्ट *(adjective)* – अपने स्थान पर न रहने वाला not living in a particular country or a place of work. not requiring residence at the place of work or instruction. *There are many non-resident Indians.*

Nonsense/नॉनसेन्स *(noun)* – व्यर्थ प्रलाप words that make no sense. *What nonsense! You shouldn't have behaved like that.*

Non-sequitur/नॉनसेक्विटर *(noun)* – निष्कर्ष या परिणाम जो अनुमान से नहीं निकलता है a conclusion or statement that does not logically follow from the previous argument or statement. *His non-sequitur did not impress anybody.*

Nonsuit/ननसूट *(verb)* – किसी मुकदमे का खारिजा subject to the stoppage of their suit on the grounds of failure to make a legal case or bring sufficient evidence. *His case was declared to be nonsuited.* *(noun)* the stoppage of a suit on such grounds. *The lack of efficient evidence resulted in nonsuit.*

Noodle/नूडल *(noun)* – नूडल, मूर्ख a very thin, long strip of pasta or a similar flour paste. *He is fond of eating noodles.*

Nook/नूक *(noun)* – कोना a corner or recess, especially one offering seclusion or security. *Many insects lived in the nooks of the deserted house.*

Noon/नून *(noun)* – मध्यकाल twelve o'clock in the day; midday. *His much awaited call came at noon.*

Noose/नूज *(noun)* – सरकने वाला फन्दा a loop with a running knot which tightens as the rope or wire is pulled, used especially to hang offenders or trap animals. *The noose tightened around the criminal's neck.*

Nor/नॉर *(conjunction & adverb)* – न तो and not; and not either: they were neither cheap nor convenient. neither: nor can I . *He cannot use such abusive language, nor can I.*

Norm/नॉर्म *(noun)* – नमूना the usual, typical, or standard thing. a required or acceptable standard: the norms of good behaviour. *He observes all norms of good behaviour.*

Normal/नॉर्मल *(adjective)* – यथाक्रम conforming to a standard; usual, typical, or expected. *Once his anger subsided he will behave normal.*

Normalcy/नॉर्मल्सी *(noun)* – प्राकृतिक दशा condition of being usual typical. *He regained normalcy of behaviour after the psychiatric treatment.*

Normality/नॉर्मैलिटि *(noun)* – विधिवत् the state of being normal. *Normality in every sphere of life is something desirable.*

Normalize/नॉर्मलाइज *(verb)* – नियम बाँधना bring to a normal or standard state. *His behaviour become normalized after a long time after accident.*

Normally/नॉर्मलि *(noun)* – विधिवत् in a normal manner; in the usual way. *Although angry, he behaved normally.*

Norman/नॉर्मन *(noun)* – नार्मंडी देश का निवासी a member of a people of mixed Frankish and Scandinavian origin who settled in Normandy in the 10th century; in particular, any of the Normans who conquered England in 1066 or their descendants. a native or inhabitant of modern Normandy. *He lives in Normandy and is called a Norman.*

N

Norse/नॉर्स *(noun)* – नार्वे देश की भाषा an ancient or medieval form of Norwegian or a related Scandinavian language. *Ancient Norwegians spoke Norse language.*

North/नॉर्थ *(noun)* – उत्तर the direction in which a compass meddle normally points, towards the horizon on the left-hand side of a person facing east. *Delhi is situated in the north of India.*

Northing/नार्दिंग *(noun)* – उत्तर की ओर जहाज की गति a figure or line representing northward distance to north Korea. *By convention, everything above 80 nothing is considered as positive.*

North-star/नॉर्थ-स्टार *(noun)* – ध्रुवतारा the pole star. *North-star is also called pole star.*

Northward/नॉर्थवई *(adjective)* – उत्तर की ओर in a northerly direction. *(adverb)* towards the north. *(noun)* the direction or region to the north. *The ship had hardly gone a few miles northward when a storm overtook it.*

Northwest/नॉर्थवेस्ट *(noun)* – पश्चिमोत्तर the point of the horizon midway between north and west. *Many cities are situated in the northwest of India.*

Nose/नोज *(noun)* – नाक the part projecting above the mouth on the face of a person or animal, containing the nostrils and used in breathing and smelling. *He has a long and prominent nose.*

Nosebag/नोजबैग *(noun)* – तोबड़ा a bag containing fodder, hung from a horse's head and into which it can reach to eat. *The horse was eating from the nosebag.*

Nose-ring/नोजरिंग *(noun)* – नथुनी metallic ring worn by women. *Most Indian women wear nose-ring.*

Nosing/नोजिंग *(noun)* – सीढ़ी के डण्डे का गोल किनारा rounded edge of a step or moulding. a metal shield for such an edge. *He put his foot on the nosing.*

Nostalgia/नॉस्टैल्जिया *(noun)*– घर पर पड़े रहने की बीमारी sentimental longing or wistful affection for a period in the past. *When idle he usually has nostalgia.*

Nostril/नॉस्ट्रिल *(noun)* – नथुना either of two external openings of the nasal cavity in vertebrates that admit air to the lungs and smells to the olfactory nerves. *We breathe through our nostrils.*

Nosy/नोजि *(adjective)* – कुतूहली [informal] showing too much curiosity about other people's affairs. *As he was too nosy, I asked him to mind his own business.*

Not/नॉट *(adverb)* – नहीं used chiefly with an auxiliary verb or be to form the negative. *He does not want to go to school.*

Notability/नोटेबिलिटि *(noun)* – ख्याति a famous or important person. *He is a notability among writers.*

Notable/नोटेबॅल *(adjective)* – प्रसिद्ध worthy of attention or notice. *This is the only notable part of an otherwise long speech.*

Notably/नोटेबुलि *(adverb)* – प्रसिद्धि से in particular. *This guide-book is very informative, notably in the third chapter.*

Notarial/नोटेरियल *(adjective)* – लिखित पत्रों को प्रमाणित करने वाले अफसर से सम्बन्धित something related to notaries. *To perform notarial works, you must be a law graduate.*

Notary/नोटरी *(noun)* – लिखित पत्रों को प्रमाणित करने वाला अफसर a person authorized to perform certain legal formalities, especially to draw up or certify contracts, deeds, etc. *This deed is to be certified by a notary.*

Notation/नोटेशन *(noun)* – गणना a system of written symbols used to represent numbers, amounts, or elements in a field such as music or mathematics. *Look carefully at the notation of this mathematical sum.*

Notch/नॉच *(noun)* – खाँच, खाँचा an indentation or incision on an edge or surface. each of a series of holes for the tongue of a buckle. a nick made on something to keep a record. a point or degree in a scale. *There are only four notches on this belt, I need at least two more.*

Noteless/नोटलेस *(adj)* – अप्रसिद्ध not attracting notice. *It is a blank and noteless diary.*

Notelet/नोटलेट *(noun)* – पुस्तिका a small folded sheet of paper with a decorative design on the front, for an [informal] letter. *He sent me a notelet, inviting me on his birthday.*

Notepaper/नोटपेपर *(noun)* – चिट्ठी लिखने का कागज paper for writing letters on. *Please bring me pad of notepapers I have some letters to write.*

N

Noteworthy/नोटवर्दी *(adj)* – विचार करने योग्य *It is something noteworthy that throughout the meeting he kept quiet.*

Nothing/नथिंग *(pronoun)* – शून्य not anything. something of no importance or concern. naught. *There is nothing good I see in him.*

Nothingness/नथिंगनेस *(noun)* – शून्यता the absence or cessation of existence. *The nothingness of many things can be seen clearly in old age.*

Noticeable/नोटिसेबॅल *(adjective)* – विचारणीय easily seen or noticed; clear. *The politeness of his behaviour was noticeable.*

Notifiable/नोटिफाइअबॅल *(adjective)* – सूचना देने योग्य denoting something, especially a serious infectious disease, that must be reported to the appropriate authorities. *The fast spreading disease is modifiable and authorities must be informed about it.*

Notification/नोटिफिकेशन *(noun)* – सूचना the action of notifying something. *A notification has been issued to the effect that everyone must be present in the office by 10 a.m. tomorrow.*

Notify/नोटिफाइ *(verb)* – सूचना देना inform, typically in a formal or official manner. report formally or officially. *All employees have been notified that no short leave will be given.*

Notion/नोशन *(noun)* – कल्पना a concept or belief. a vague awareness or understanding. *I have a notion that we shall soon find a solution to the problem.*

Notional/नोशनल *(adjective)* – मन से गढ़ा हुआ hypothetical or imaginary. *It is only a notional problem and hence no concrete answer is available.*

Notoriety/नॅटॅराइअॅटि *(noun)* – कुख्याति the state of being known for some bad deeds. *He soon gained notoriety as a gangster.*

Notorious/नॅटोरिअस् *(adjective)* – कुख्यात famous for some bad quality or deed. *He was a notorious smuggler.*

Nought/नॉट *(noun)* – शून्य the digit 0. *All his efforts were brought to nought because of bad luck.*

Noun/नाउन *(noun)* – संज्ञा a word used to identify any of a class of people, places, or things, or to name a particular one of these. *Noun is a naming word.*

Nourish/नॅरिश *(verb)* – पालना provide with the food or other substances necessary for growth and health. enhance the fertility of. *He nourishes a grudge against me.*

Nourishment/नॅरिशमेंट *(noun)* – पोषण the food necessary for growth, health and well-being. *Proper nourishment helps children grew fast and healthy.*

Novel/नॉवेल् *(noun)* – उपन्यास a fictitious prose narrative of book length. *He is a famous novel writer.*

Novelette/नॉवलेट् *(noun)* – छोटी कहानी a short novel, typically a light romantic one. *I finished reading the novelette in an hour.*

Novelist/नॉवेलिस्ट् *(noun)* – उपन्यास-लेखक a writer of novels. *Charles Dickens was a famous novelist.*

Novelty/नॉवेल्टि *(noun)* – कौतुक the quality of being novel. a new or unfamiliar thing or experience. denoting something intended to be amusing as a result of its originality or unusualness. *Exploring the ancient caves was a novelty.*

Novice/नॉविस *(noun)* – नवसिखिया, नवछात्र a person new to and inexperienced in a job or situation. *He is a novice and as such to be pardoned for the lapse.*

Noviciate/Novitiate/नॉविसिएट *(noun)* – नवशिष्यालय the period or state of being a novice. *Novices live in this novitiate.*

Now/नाउ *(adverb)* – अभी at the present time. at or from this precise moment. under the present circumstances. *It is late, I should leave now.*

Nowhere/नोह्वेअर *(pronoun)* – कहीं नहीं no place. *He is nowhere to be seen.*

Noxious/नॉक्सस *(adjective)* – हानिकारक harmful, poisonous, or very unpleasant. *The smoke arising here is noxious.*

Nozzle/नॉज़ॅल *(noun)* – फौब्बारे का अग्रभाग a spout at the end of a pipe, hose, or tube used to control a jet of liquid or gas. *The nozzle of the hose was blocked.*

Nuance/नूआंस *(noun)* – भाव तथा अर्थ इत्यादि में का सूक्ष्म अन्तर a subtle difference in or shade of meaning, expression, colour, etc. *The newspaper published his views but with a nuance.*

N

Nubile/न्यूबाइल *(adjective)* - विवाह करने योग्य youthful but sexually mature and attractive. *She is very nubile although quite young.*

Nubility/न्यूबिलिटि *(noun)* - विवाह-योग्यता girl old enough to be married. *Many lecherous employers try to take advantage of nobility of young secretaries.*

Nudge/नज *(verb)* - केहुनियाकर संकेत करना prod gently with one's elbow to attract attention. *He nudged her in the crowd.*

Nugatory/नुगेटरी *(adjective)* - व्यर्थ worthless. *The committee passed a nugatory and pointless observation.*

Nugget/नगेट् *(noun)* - बिना स्वच्छ किये हुए सोने का पिण्ड a small lump of gold or other precious metal found ready formed in the earth. *He found a number of nuggets while digging the earth.*

Null/नल *(adjective)* - व्यर्थ having no legal force; invalid. *The archaic law was declared null and void.*

Numb/नॅम *(adjective)* - गति-शून्य deprived of the power of sensation. *He became numb with grief.*

Numbly/नॅम्लि *(adverb)* - स्तब्धता deprive of feeling or responsiveness. *He numbly nodded his head.*

Numeral/न्यूमॅरॅल *(noun)* - संख्या सम्बन्धी a figure, word, or group of figures denoting a number. *I understand this numeral very well.*

Numeration/न्यूमरेशॅन *(noun)*- गिनती the action or process of numbering or calculating. a method of numbering or computing. *Numeration requires knowledge of arithmetic.*

Numeric - *(adjective)* relating to numbers. *The list has been prepared in numeric order.*

Numerical/न्यूमेरिकल *(adjective)* - संख्या-सूचक of, relating to, or expressed as a number or numbers. *Remember the symbol of this numerical.*

Numerous/न्यूमरस *(adjective)* - बहुत many. consisting of many members. *Numerous members attended the club meeting.*

Numismatic/न्यूमिस्मेटिक *(adjective)* - मुद्रा-सम्बन्धी of or relating to coins or medals. *He is deeply interested in numismatics, you should show him this old coin.*

Numskull/नमस्कल *(noun)* - बेवकूफ, उल्लू का पट्ठा variant spelling of numbskull. *The numskull didn't understand me and began to quarrel.*

Nuncio/नन्सियो *(noun)* - ईसाइयों के धर्माध्यक्ष का दूत a papal ambassador to a foreign government or court. *The nuncio met bishops and visited churches.*

Nunnery/नॅनॅरि *(noun)* - बैरागिनियों की कुटी a religious house of nuns. *She being a nun, lives over there in the nunnery.*

Nuptial/नॅप्शॅल *(adjective)* - वैवाहिक of or relating to marriage or weddings. *Nuptial bells rung in the church.*

Nutriment/न्यूट्रिमेंट *(noun)* - पुष्टि देने वाला आहार nourishment; sustenance. *Fruits have lots of nutriment.*

Nutrition/न्यूट्रिशन *(noun)* - आहार the process of ingesting and assimilating nutrients. food; nourishment. *The hungry man was immediately provided nutrition.*

Nutritious/न्यूट्रिशस *(adjective)* - पौष्टिक full of nutrients; nourishing. *A pomegranate is a nutritious fruit.*

Nutritive/न्यूट्रिटिव *(adjective)* - पुष्टिकर of or relating to nutrition. *The food served was high in nutritive value.*

Nuzzle/नॅज़ॅल *(verb)* - नाक लगाना rub or push against gently with the nose and mouth. *The child nuzzled against his mother.*

Nyctalopia/निक्टैलोपिया *(noun)* - रतौंधी a condition marked by inability to see in dim light or at night. *He suffers from nyctalopia and can't see at night.*

Nymph/निम्फ *(noun)* - अप्सरा a mythological spirit of nature imagined as a beautiful maiden. a beautiful young woman. *She is almost a nymph, I love her very much.*

N

Oo

O/ओ (noun) – अंग्रेजी वर्णमाला का 15वाँ वर्ण the fifteenth letter of the English alphabet.

1. Denoting the next after N in a set of items, categories, etc.
2. A human blood type lacking both the A and B antigens. *My blood group is O.*
3. Zero in a sequence of numerals, especially when spoken. *My telephone nubmer is six O triple five.*

Oh – (noun) exclamation. *Oh! such a lovely place.*

Oaf/ओफ (noun) – जड़मति a stupid, boorish, or clumsy man. *He is considered an oaf among his friends.*

Oak/ओक (noun) – सुन्दर बलूत वृक्ष a large tree which bears acorns and typically has lobed leaves and hard durable wood. used in names of other trees or plants resembling this, e.g. poison oak. *Oak trees are generally found in temperate forests.*

Oaken/ओकेन (adj) – बलूत वृक्ष का बना हुआ resembling properties of an oak tree. *The oaken smell indicated that there was some winery around.*

Oakum/ओकम (noun) – खण्डित रज्जु [chiefly historical] loose fibre obtained by untwisting old rope, used especially in caulking wooden ships. *Oakum is caulking purposes in ships.*

Oar/ओर (noun & verb) – नौका दण्ड a pole with a flat blade, used to row or steer a boat through the water. a rower. *We had to oar our boats ourselves as no man was available to do the same.*

Oarless/ओरलेस (adj) – बिना डाँड़े का lack of oars. *You can't take a rowing boat out to sea of totally oarless.*

Oarsman/ओर्समैन (noun) – मल्लाह a rower. *A new oarsman was hired for the boat that we were going to sit in.*

Oasis/ओएसिस (noun) – नखलिस्तान, मरूद्यान a fertile spot in a desert where the water table rises to ground level. *It was pleasant to see an oasis after spending hours in desert.*

Oast/ओएस्ट (noun) – शराब बनाने में हॉप के फल सुखाने की भट्ठी a kiln for drying hops. *A woman was placing hops in an oast.*

Oat/ओट (noun) – जई a cereal plant with a loose branched cluster of florets, cultivated in cool climates. *Oat plants are generally used for feeding animals.*

Oath/ओथ (noun) – सौगन्ध a solemn promise, often invoking a divine whiteness, as to the truth of something or as a commitment to future action. *The President is going to take his oath today.*

Oatmeal/ओटमिल (noun) – जई का दलिया, चूर्ण meal made from ground oats and chiefly used in porridge or oatcakes. *Oatmeal was the primary food for the tribes living in that area.*

Obduracy/आब्ड्यूरेसि (noun) – कठोरह्रदयता stubborn unyielding. *My brother's obduracy had made him unpopular in his friend circle.*

Obdurate/आब्ड्युरेट (adjective) – दुराग्राही stubbornly refusing to change one's opinion or course of action. *The leader was so obdurate that he refused to listen to anyone.*

Obeah/ओबिअँ (noun) – हब्शियों का जादू a kind of sorcery practised especially in the Caribbean. *The lady was an expert in practising obeah.*

Obedience/अबीडिएन्स (noun) – आज्ञापालन compliance with an order or law or submission to another's authority. *The student who were lacking in obedience were rusticated.*

Obedient/अबीडिएन्ट (adjective) – आज्ञाकारी willing to comply with order. *As a student, I was quite obedient to my teachers.*

Obedientiary/अबेडिएन्शरि (noun) – मठ का आज्ञाकरी सेवक (noun) holder of an authoritative position in a monastery. *Two monks were made obedientiaries by their seniors.*

O

Obeisance/ओबेसॅन्स *(noun)* – नमस्कार bow, courtesy, respect. *Every religion teaches us the lessons of obeisance and truthfulness.*

Obelisk/अॅबेलिस्क *(noun)* – सूच्याकार स्तम्भ a tapering stone pillar of square or rectangular cross section, set up as a monument or landmark. *Beside the pyramid was standing a tall obelisk.*

Obese/ओबीस *(adjective)* – स्थूलकाय grossly fat or overweight. *His seven year old child was quite obese.*

Obesity/ओबीसिटि *(noun)* – स्थूलता the state of being grossly overweight. *Obesity gives rise to a number of health problems.*

Obey/अॅबे *(verb)* – कहना मानना submit to the authority of. carry out a command or instruction. behave in accordance with a general principle, natural law, etc. *All the royal ministers were expected to obey to the command of the king.*

Obfuscate/अॉब्फस्केट *(verb)* – घबरा देना, धुँधला कर देना make unclear or unintelligible. *His action further obfuscated the situation.*

Obi/ओबि *(noun)* – जादू-टोना, जापानी रूमाल variant form of obeah. *Japanese women used to wear an obi over their kimonos.*

Obituarist/ओबिट्युअरिस्ट *(noun)* – मृत्युलेख लिखने वाला मनुष्य one who writes and releases in newspapers brief sketch of a departed soul. *That man has been an obituarist for many years.*

Obituary/ओबिच्यूरि *(noun)* – मृत्यु-समाचार a notice of a person's death in a newspaper or periodical, typically including a brief biography. *After a day of his death, we saw his obituary in the newspaper.*

Objectify/अॅबजेक्टिफाइ *(verb)* – प्रत्यक्ष रूप से उपस्थिति करना express in a concrete form. *His strength as a writer was to objectify emotions in words.*

Objection/अॅब्जेक्शॅन *(noun)* – विरोध the action of challenging or disagreeing with something. an expression of disapproval or opposition. *People raised an objection to the way voting was done in our area.*

Objectionable/अॅब्जेक्शनेबल् *(adjective)* – अनुचित arousing distaste or opposition. *The movie had many objectionable scenes in it.*

Objectivity/अॅब्जेक्टिविटि *(noun)* – स्थूलता the quality of being objective. *The editor said to author, "While creating this piece, you should employ objectivity."*

Objectless/अॅब्जेक्टलेस *(adj)* – निष्प्रयोजन an object that can't be seen or imagined. *His idea was rejected for being objectless.*

Objector/अॅब्जेक्टर *(noun)* – आपत्तिकर्ता one who objects to something. *No one had the slightest idea that the man would turn out to be an objector.*

Objuration/अॉब्ज्यूरेशन *(noun)* – शपथ *The newly elected minister was undergoing the process of objuration.*

Objurgation/अॉबजरगेशन *(noun)* – तिरस्कार to rebuke severely. *The party member could not bear the objurgation and left immediately.*

Objurgatory/अॉबजरगेटरि *(adj)* – तिरस्कार पूर्ण to scold severely. *We were shocked by the objurgatory remarks that he made that day.*

Oblate/अॉब्लेट *(noun)* – धर्म-कर्म में जीवन अर्पण करने वाला a person dedicated to a religious life, but typically not having taken full monastic vows. *The wife had no qualms about her husband being an oblate.*

Obligate/अॉब्लिगेट *(verb)* – किसी कार्य के लिए मनुष्य को बाध्य करना compel legally or morally. *As per the law, the criminal was obligated to sign the documents.*

Obligatory/अॉब्लिगेटरि *(adjective)* – आवश्यक compulsory. having binding force. *It was his obligatory duty to keep a check on the number of crimes in his area.*

Oblige/अॉब्लाइज *(verb)* – विवश करना compel legally or morally. *The teacher asked to make notes and the students obliged.*

Obligee/अॉब्लिजी *(noun)* – कृतज्ञ a person to whom another is bound by contract or other legal procedure. compare with obligor. *In that case, I was an obligee and the man had to comply with my terms.*

Obliging/अॉब्लाइजिंग *(adjective)* – सुशील, उपकारी willing to do a service or kindness; helpful. *His obliging ways earned him popularity among his mentors.*

O

Obligor/ऑब्लिगर *(noun)* – आभारी a person who is bound to another by contract or other legal procedure. compare with obligee. *The obligor had no choice but wait for the contract to end.*

Oblique/ऑब्लीक *(adjective)* – वक्र, तिरछा neither parallel nor at right angles; slanting. *The sun rays fall obliquely on earth's surface.*

Obliquely/अब्लीकलि *(adverb)* – कुटिल रीति से not being done in a direct way. *The sunrays fall on earth obliquely.*

Obliquity/अब्लीक्विटि *(noun)* – वक्रगति slanting. *The obliquity of the light rays determines their degree of hotness.*

Obliterate/ऑब्लिटरेट *(verb)* – नष्ट करना destroy utterly; wipe out. *An entire species of turtles got obliterated after the landslide.*

Obliteration/अब्लिटरेशन *(noun)* – लोप destructing or being destructed. *The obliteration of the entire army came as a shock to the king.*

Oblivious/ऑब्लिवियस *(adjective)* – भुलक्कड़ not aware of what is happening around one. *While doing work, I become oblivious of all the things happening around.*

Oblong/ऑब्लॉन्ग *(adjective)* – आयताकार having a rectangular shape. *The lady has an oblong face.*

Obloquy/ऑब्लक्वि *(noun)* – गाली strong public condemnation. *The minister is trying to become popular by using obloquy as a tool.*

Obmutescence/ऑब्म्युटेसेंश *(noun)* – मौन persistent silence *His obmutescence was an indication that he was not interested in our discussion.*

Obnoxious/ऑब्नॉक्शस *(adjective)* – घृणित extremely unpleasant. *The obnoxious presence of the criminal in the victim's family was angering many.*

Obnubilate/अब्न्युबिलेट *(noun)* – छिपाना darken as if covered with something. *Soon, the dark clouds obnubilated the entire sky.*

Obnubilation/अब्न्युबिलेशन *(noun)* – व्यग्र अवस्था making obscure, covering. *His act of obnubilation to hide his crime soon came to light.*

Oboe/ओबो *(noun)* – शहनाई a woodwind instrument of treble pitch, played with a double reed and having an incisive tone.

As we reached the hut, some natives were playing on oboes.

Obscene/अब्सीन/ऑब्सीन *(adjective)* – अश्लील offensive or disgusting by accepted standards of morality and decency. *I objected to the obscene remarks made by the man.*

Obscurant/ऑब्स्क्युअरॅन्ट *(noun & adjective)* – सुधार का विरोधी the act of deliberately preventing the facts. *We did not have the slightest idea of his obscurant activities.*

Obscuration/ऑब्स्क्युअरेशन *(noun)* – अँधेरा करने का कार्य keeping from being seen, conceal. *The lady's obscuration of the facts was taken in the bad light.*

Obsecrate/ऑब्सिक्रेट *(verb)* – प्रार्थना करना earnest pleading. *The man obsecrated for getting pardon.*

Obsequies/आब्सीक्विज *(pl. noun)* – अन्त्येष्टि funeral rites. *Her mother's obsequies were performed in wee hours.*

Obsequious/ऑब्सीक्विअस *(adjective)* – जीहुजूरिया, चापलूस obedient or attentive to an excessive or servile degree. *The employee's obsequious attitude gave him no benefits at the time of appraisals.*

Observable/अॅब्जॅर्वेबॅल *(adj)* – दृष्टिगोचर able to be noticed. *Despite being very far, the island was still observable from our ship.*

Observance/अॅब्जॅर्वॅन्स *(noun)* – रीति the practice of observing the requirements of law, morality, or ritual. *Our Principal expected from the students a thorough observance of rules.*

Observant/अब्जरवन्ट *(adjective)* – सावधान quick to notice things. *His observant eyes were able to locate the lost keys.*

Observation/ऑब्जर्वेशन *(noun)* – निरीक्षण the action or process of closely observing or monitoring. *The mentally unstable man was kept under a strict observation.*

Observationally/ऑब्जर्वेशनलि *(adv)* – विचार पूर्वक the process of observing something or someone. *In order to get details of an object, it is required to notice them observationally.*

Observe/ऑब्जर्व *(verb)* – देखना, अवलोकन करना notice; perceive. watch attentively. detect in the course of a scientific study.

I was observing the petri-dish with full concentration.

Observer/ऑब्जर्वर *(noun)* – प्रेक्षक a person who watches something. *What a keen observer he is!*

Observing/ऑब्जर्विंग *(adj)* – ध्यान से निरीक्षण करने वाला a person watching something. *Observing from far, he said, "The land is now not very far."*

Obsess/ऑबसेस *(verb)* – कष्ट देना preoccupy continually or to a troubling extent. *He is obsessed with social media networking.*

Obsession/ऑबसेशन *(noun)* – प्रेत-बाधा the state of being obsessed. *His obsession with food never seems to end.*

Obsolescence/ऑब्सॅलेसॅन्स *(noun)* – अप्रचलन becoming out of date, out of fashion. *The obsolescence of this technology is attributed to the new developments in the field.*

Obsolescent/ऑब्सॅलेसॅन्ट *(adjective)* – अप्रचलित becoming obsolete. *The introduction of electric engine rendered the steam locomotives obsolescent.*

Obsolete/ऑब्सलीट *(adjective)* – अप्रचलित no longer produced or used; out of date. *The water clocks have now become obsolete.*

Obstacle/आब्स्टैकॅल *(noun)* – विघ्न a thing that blocks one's way or hinders progress. *He was not deterred by the obstacles coming his way.*

Obstetrics/आब्स्टेट्रिक्स *(noun)* – प्रसव-कला of or relating to childbirth and the processes associated with it. *My sister is keen to study obstetrics as her field of specialization.*

Obstetrician/ऑब्सटेट्रिशन *(noun)* – प्रसव कराने में प्रवीण a physician or surgeon qualified to practice in obstetrics. *He recommended my wife to join the hospital as a qualified obstetrician in the city.*

Obstinate/ऑब्स्टिनेट *(adjective)* – हठी stubbornly refusing to change one's opinion or chosen course of action. *Her obstinate nature did not allow her to do idol worship.*

Obstreperous/ऑब्स्ट्रेपरस *(adjective)* – झगड़ालू noisy and difficult to control. *In spite of being a jury member, he could not control his obstreperous ways.*

Obstruction/ऑब्स्ट्रक्शन *(noun)* – रुकावट the action of obstructing or the state of being obstructed. *Many obstructions were placed in his way, yet he did not succumb to them.*

Obstructive/ऑब्सट्रक्टिव *(adj)* – प्रतिबन्धक causing a blockage or obstruction. *The path was too obstructive to drive a vehicle smoothly.*

Obtain/ऑब्टेन् *(verb)* – प्रवृत्त होना acquire or secure. *The students obtained their teacher's permission to visit the library.*

Obtest/ऑबटेस्ट *(noun)* – आग्रह करना to supplicate. *When the thief got caught, he obtested a lot before cops.*

Obtrude/ऑब्ट्रूड *(verb)* – इच्छा के विरुद्ध करना, लादना, थोपना become obtrusive. *We were annoyed as he obtruded on us.*

Obtruncate/ऑब्ट्रंकेट *(verb)* – मस्तक काटना (To deprive of a limb). *In a feat of anger, the villager obtruncated his brother.*

Obtrusive/ऑब्ट्रूसिव *(adjective)*– बलपूर्वक प्रवेश करने वाला noticeable or prominent in an unwelcome or intrusive way. *We loathed him due to his obtrusive way of behaving.*

Obtund/ऑब्टॅन्ड *(verb)* – निस्तेज बना देना deaden the sensitivity, blunt. *In summers, the monsoon rain obtunds hotness in air.*

Obturate/ऑब्टयुअरेट *(verb)* – रोकना to block, obstruct. *The rust on the surface obturated the machine from running smoothly.*

Obtuse/ऑब्टयूस *(adjective)* – मन्द, मूढ़ annoyingly insensitive or slow to understand. *The student was so obtuse that he could not get the concept even after three hours of lecture.*

Obtusion/ऑब्टयूजन *(noun)* – भुथरा करने का कार्य the act of making blunt. *Too much of disturbance resulted in obtusion of my mind.*

Obverse/आब्वर्स *(noun)* – विपरीत the side of a coin or medal bearing the head or principal design. *The archaeologist remarked, "Look at the obverse of this coin; there is a unique symbol on it."*

Obvert/ऑब्वर्ट *(verb)* – अभिमुख करना so as to infer another proposition with a contradictory predicate or to turn something so as to present another side or aspect of the view. *He obverted the plank and saw a cobweb in the corner.*

O

Obversion/ऑब्व्सन *(noun)*– अभिमुखीकरण alter a preposition so as to infer another preposition with an entirely different meaning. *The obversion of vision will help you the other aspects of the story.*

Obviate/ऑब्विएट *(verb)* – हटाना, प्रतिरोध करना remove. *She, very cleverly, obviated all the evidences related to the crime.*

Obvious/ऑब्विअस *(adjective)* – प्रत्यक्ष easily perceived or understood; clear. *What he was trying to say was indicated from his obvious speech.*

Ocarina/ऑकरीना *(noun)* – एक प्रकार का बाजा a small wind instrument with holes for the fingers, typically having the shape of a bird. *The lovely lady in the room was playing very well on ocarina.*

Occasion/ऑकेजन *(noun)* – अवसर a particular event, or the time at which it takes place. a suitable or opportune time. *He knew that this was the only occasion he could convey his feelings to her.*

Occasioned/अकेजन्ड – *(adverb)* particular time when something happened. *The resignation of the CEO occasioned the company to choose the senior most person to occupy the vacant place.*

Occipital/ऑक्सिपुट *(adj)* – मस्तक के पिछले भाग का relating to the back of the head. *The technician took an X-ray of the patient's occipital view.*

Occiput/आक्सिपेंट *(noun)* – मस्तक का पिछला भाग the back of the head. *The doctor examined his occiput and wrote remarks on the prescription.*

Occlude/ऑक्लुड *(verb)* – रोकना stop, close up, or obstruct. *His gigantic body was occluding the light from behind.*

Occlusion/ऑक्लुजन *(noun)* – रुकावट medicine the blockage or closing of a blood vessel or hollow organ. *An occlusion in her heart became the cause of her untimely death.*

Occultation/ऑकल्टेशन *(noun)* – छिपाव mystical powers, practice, phenomene. *In astronomy, the process of occultation is used to determine the presence of asteroids.*

Occultism/ऑकल्टिज्म *(noun)* – दैवी रहस्य practice of mystical powers. *Occultism is related to the study of supernatural phenomena.*

Occultist/ऑकलटिस्ट *(noun)* – जादूगर one who practices mystical supernatural powers. *The lady hired an occultist to know about her future.*

Occultly/ऑकल्टली *(adverb)* – छिपी रीति से in a manner of mystical supernatural powers. *Their occultly talk continued for hours.*

Occultness/ऑकल्टनेस *(noun)* – भेद in a manner of mystical powers without scientific explanation. *We could not ignore the factor of occultness while discussing about astrology.*

Occupancy/ऑक्युपॅन्सि *(noun)* – अधिकार में रखने वाला the action or fact of occupying a place. *The allotment of houses depends upon their current state of occupancy.*

Occupant/ऑक्युपन्ट *(noun)*– अधिभोक्ता a person who occupies a place at a given time. law a person holding property, especially land, in actual possession. *The occupants of this house are out on a tour.*

Occupation/आक्युपेशॅन *(noun)* – वृत्ति the action, state, or period of occupying or being occupied. *His occupation with his job left him with no spare time.*

Occupy/ऑक्युपाइ *(verb)* – अधिकार या भोग करना reside or have one's place of business in. take control of by military conquest or settlement. enter and stay in without authority, especially as a form of protest. *On reaching there, we saw that the room was already occupied by a couple.*

Occur/अॅकर् *(verb)* – घटित होना happen; take place. *When the incident occurred, the family was out of town.*

Occurrence/ऑकरेंस *(noun)* – घटना the fact or frequency of something occurring. *The rare occurrence of the event makes it all the more interesting.*

Occurrent/ऑकरेंट *(adjective)* – घटित होने वाला actually occurring or observable. *The long words are quite occurrent in this article.*

Ocean/ओशॅन् *(noun)* – महासागर a very large expanse of sea; in particular, each of the Atlantic, pacific, Indian, arctic, and Antarctic oceans. [chiefly north American] the sea. *The Pacific Ocean is the biggest ocean in the world.*

Oceanic/ओशऐनिक *(adjective)* – महासागरीय of or relating to the ocean. *There are a number* *of oceanic activities that keep on taking place from time to time.*

Ochlocracy/ऑक्लॉक्रसि *(noun)* – भीड़-तन्त्र formal government by the populace; mob rule. *The movement to establish ochlocracy was crushed very badly.*

Ochlocrat/ऑक्लॉक्रैट *(noun)* – अनियन्त्रित प्रजातन्त्र राज्य का अधिनायक government by popular, mob rule. *He refused to admit that he was an ochlocrat.*

Ochre/ओकर *(noun)* – एक प्रकार की मिट्टी an earthy pigment containing ferric oxide, varying from light yellow to brown or red. *In party, a lady was wearing an ochre coloured dress.*

O'clock/ओक्लॉक *(adverb)* – घड़ी में used to specify the hour when telling the time. *My sister reached the airport exactly at 5o' clock in the evening.*

Octad/आक्टैड *(noun)* – आठ का समुदाय a group or set of eight *In the practical test, we were shown an octad compound and were asked to write about its properties.*

Octagon/ऑक्टॅगॅन *(noun)* – अष्टभुज a plane figure with eight straight sides and eight angles. *It is easy to calculate area of an octagon.*

Octahedron/ऑक्टहेड्न *(noun)* – अष्टफलक ठोस आकृति a three-dimensional shape having eight plane faces, in particular a regular solid figure with eight equal triangular faces. *The compound that we were asked to test was an octahedron.*

Octangular/ऑक्टैन्ग्युलर *(adjective)* – आठ कोणों की आकृति वाला having eight angles. *An octangular shape is defined by the presence of eight angles.*

Octant/ऑक्टन्ट *(noun)* – वृत्त का अष्टमांश an arc of a circle equal to one eighth of its circumference, or the area enclosed by such an arc with two radii of the circle. *Our Mathematics teacher explained the method of calculating the area of an octant.*

Octave/ऑक्टेव *(noun)* – अष्टक music a series of eight notes occupying the interval between two notes, one having twice or half the frequency of vibration of the other. the interval between threes two notes. each of the two notes at the extremes of this interval. these two notes sounding together. *Our music teacher gave us good lessons on octave.*

Octavo/ऑक्टेवो *(noun)* – आठ परतों की a size of book page that results from folding each printed sheet into eight leaves. *An octavo is the size of the pages resulting from folding a printed page into eight leaves.*

Octennial/ऑक्टेनियल *(adjective)* – आठ वर्ष में होने वाला lasting for or recurring every eight years. *Through our telescope, we were looking at an octennial star in the sky.*

October/ऑक्टोबर *(noun)* – अंग्रेजी वर्ष का दसवाँ महीना (अक्टूबर) the tenth month of the year. *My sister's birthday falls on eighteenth of October.*

Octodentate/ऑक्टोडेंटेट *(noun)* – आठ दाँतों वाला having eight teeth. *An octodentate animal was standing before us.*

Octonocular/ऑक्टोनोक्यूलर *(adj)* – आठ आँखों वाला *"Have you ever seen an octonocular animal?" asked my friend.*

Octopod/ऑक्टोपॉड *(noun)* – आठ पैरों वाला an octopus. *Octopods are short animals with eight arms.*

Octroi/ऑक्ट्राइ/ऑक्ट्रुवा *(noun)* – चुंगी a duty levied in some countries on various goods entering a town or city. *The truck carrying the freight had to pay an octroi before entering the neighbouring city.*

Octuple/ऑक्ट्युपॅल *(adjective)* – आठगुना consisting of eight parts or things. *In college, our octuple group was famous for giving musical performances.*

Oddish/ऑडिश *(adjective)* – विचित्र different from what is normal. *He was doing everything in an oddish way.*

Oddly/ऑडलि *(adverb)* – विलक्षणता से different to what is usual. *Of late, he is behaving in an oddly manner.*

Odds/ऑड्स *(plural noun)* – विषमता, कलह the ratio between the amounts staked by the parties to a bet, based on the expected probability either way. *The odds on horse race are 14 to 3.*

Odious/ओडिअस् *(adjective)* – घिनौना extremely unpleasant; repulsive. *What an odious remark was passed by him!*

O

Odium/ओडिअॅम *(noun)* – द्वेष general or widespread hatred or disgust. *The recent killing of a girl has created odium among masses.*

Odontalgia/ऑडॉन्टैल्जिया *(noun)* – दाँतों का दर्द toothache. *The development of plaque was giving her an odontalgia.*

Odontoid/ऑडॉन्टाइड *(noun)* – दन्ताभ anatomy a projection from the second cervical vertebra on which the first can pivot. *He was feeling pain in his odontoid joint.*

Odontology/ऑडॉन्टालजि *(noun)* – दन्तशास्त्र the scientific study of the structure and diseases of teeth. *His avid interest in odontology made him go abroad and do specialization in it.*

Odorous/ओडॅरस *(adj)* – सुगन्धित having or giving off odour. *The fish tank was giving an odorous smell.*

Odour/ओडर *(noun)* – सुगन्ध a distinctive smell. a lingering quality or impression. *In order to avoid the bad odour, she sprayed room freshener.*

Oecology/ईकॅलॅजि *(noun)* – प्राणिशास्त्र की शाखा जिसमें प्राणियों पर वातावरण के प्रभाव का अध्ययन होता है a less common spelling of ecology *All the elements in an ecology should be in balance with one another.*

Oedipus/ईडिपस् *(noun)* – ईडिपस a person in Greek mythology. *As per the legend, Oedipus was the son of Laius and Jocasta.*

O'er/ओवर *(adverb & preposition)* – 'Over' का छोटा रूप [archaic] or poetic form of over. *O'er that hill, he met the princess of her heart.*

Oesophagus/ईसॉफॅगॅस *(noun)* – ग्रासनली the part of the alimentary canal which connects the throat to the stomach. *Any constriction in oesophagus does not let the food to pass to the stomach easily.*

Of/ऑव *(preposition)* – का, में, पर expressing the relationship between a part and a whole. *Of all the coaches in train, only three had passengers in them.*

Off/ऑफ *(abbreviation)* – दूर office. *His off is not very far from his house.*

Offal/ऑफॅल *(noun)* – कूड़ा the entrails and internal organs of an animal used as food. *As

the girl saw the man eating offal, she vomited at once.*

Offence/ऑफेन्स *(noun)* – अपराध an act or instance of offending. *Man's offence was too much to be given any kind of pardon.*

Offenceless/ऑफेन्सलेस *(adj)* – दोष-रहित unoffending. *The country was too weak and offenceless to retaliate.*

Offend/ऑफेन्ड *(verb)* – कष्ट देना cause to feel hurt or resentful. *By not succumbing to the demands of his master, he had offended him.*

Offensiveness/ऑफेन्सिवनेस *(noun)* – अपराध, अपकार acting aggressively. *When he could not find any other way to gather attention, he stooped to offensiveness.*

Offer/ऑफर *(verb)* – प्रस्ताव present or proffer. *He offered me job immediately after going through my curriculum vitae.*

Offerer/ऑफरर *(noun)* – प्रस्तावक one who offers something or some proposal. *The offerer presented us with new plans.*

Offering/ऑफरिंग *(noun)* – अर्पण a thing offered, especially as a gift or contribution. something offered as a religious sacrifice or token of devotion. *As soon as he entered the temple premises, we knew that he had come with some offering.*

Office/ऑफिस *(noun)* – कार्यालय, दफ्तर a room, set of rooms or building used as a place of business for non-manual work. *Recently, we have been shifted to a brand new office.*

Officer/ऑफिसर *(noun)* – अधिकारी a person holding a position of authority, especially a member of the armed forces who holds a commission or a member of the police, civil, or ecclesiastical office. *The officer on duty did not pay any attention to the ongoing protests.*

Official/ऑफिशल *(adjective)* – अधिकार-सम्बन्धी of or relating to an authority or public body and its activities and responsibilities. *As per the official notice, the employees submitted their income tax forms.*

Officially/ऑफिश्लि *(adverb)* – अधिकार पूर्वक in a formal way. *It is now known officially that some of the projects would be kept on hold till next announcement.*

O

Officiate/ऑफिशिएट *(verb)* – स्थानापन्न होना act as an official. *The manager officiated for the time when the Director was out of the city.*

Officinal/ऑफिसिनल *(adjective)* – औषधियों की जड़ीबूटियों से सम्बन्धित used in medicine. *We were not aware of the herb's officinal properties.*

Officious/ऑफिशस *(adjective)* – धृष्ट asserting authority or interfering in an annoyingly domineering way. *There was no other option but to sack him in order to get rid of his officious ways.*

Offing/ऑफिंग *(noun)* – किनारे से देख पड़ता हुआ दूर का समुद्र the more distant part of the sea in view. *We were looking at a ship in the offing.*

Offish/ऑफिश *(adjective)* – अलग रहने वाला [informal] aloof or distant in manner. *I abhorred his offish attitude towards me.*

Offset/ऑफसेट *(noun)* – अंकुर, प्रतिकरण a consideration or amount that diminishes or balances the effect of a contrary one. *The family of the victim was given monetary assistance as an offset against the job offer.*

Offside/ऑफसाइड *(adjective & adverb)* – दूर की दिशा occupying a position on the field where playing the ball or puck is not allowed, generally through being between the ball and the opponent's goal. *The coach was explaining to him the offside rule of the game.*

Offspring/ऑफस्प्रिंग *(noun)* – सन्तान a person's child or children, or the young of an animal. *The offspring of the mammal were too small and were kept under veterinary observation.*

Oft/ऑफ्ट *(adverb)* – बहुधा [archaic] or poetic often. *It would be oft that she crossed the barrier and go across the river.*

Ogive/ओजाइव *(noun)* – नुकीली कमानी की मेहराब architecture a pointed or gothic arch. *It was clear that some skilled craftsmen were involved in the construction of the ogive.*

Ogle/ओगल *(verb)* – आँखें लड़ाना stare at lecherously. *The shabby man used to ogle the ladies waiting for the train.*

Ogygian/ऑगिजिअन – अति प्राचीन समय का *The archeologists were working on an ogygian fossil found beneath the soil.*

Oh/ओह *(exclamatory)* – ओह expressing surprise disappointment, joy, or other emotion. *The girl exclaimed, "Oh! The poor man has not eaten since yesterday."*

Ohm/ओम् *(noun)* – विद्युत् प्रतिरोध की नाप the SI unit of electrical resistance, transmitting a current of one ampere when subjected to a potential difference of one volt. *The correct answer to the question was 4 ohms.*

Oil/ऑइल *(noun)* – तेल, फुलेल a viscous liquid derived from petroleum, used especially as a fuel or lubricant. petroleum. *The driver thought it would be better to fill the oil tank before he could run out of it.*

Ointment/आइन्टमेंट *(noun)* – लेप, मलहम a smooth oily substance that is rubbed on the skin for medicinal purposes or as a cosmetic. *Apply some ointment over the infected area.*

Olden/ओल्डेन *(adjective)* – पुराने समय का of a former age: the olden days. *In olden days, people used to travel a lot by boats.*

Oldish/ओल्डिस *(adj)* – कुछ पुराना of or belonging to the past. *Retorted the manager, "This idea is a bit oldish."*

Oldness/ओल्डनेस *(noun)* – बुढ़ापा of a certain age. *The oldness of the building is evident from its withered look.*

Oldster/ओल्डस्टर *(noun)* – युवा अवस्था से अतीत [informal chiefly north American] an older person. *The child was too happy to see the same oldster walking down the street.*

Oleaginous/ओलिएऐजिनेस *(adjective)* – चिकना oily or greasy. *Water had almost no effect over the oleaginous wood.*

Oleander/ओलिएंडर *(noun)* – करबीर a poisonous evergreen shrub grown in warm countries for its clusters of white, pink, or red flowers. *The oleanders were all boomed with lovely flowers.*

Oleic/ओलिइक *(adj)* – तेल-सम्बन्धी [chemistry] name of an acid. *Oleic acid is used in the manufacture of soaps.*

Olid/ऑलिड *(adj)* – दुर्गन्ध वाला foul smelling. *The garbage was so olid that no one of us could stand it.*

Oligarch/ऑलिगार्क *(noun)* – अल्पतन्त्र का सदस्य a ruler in an oligarchy. *It was the high time*

O

that an oligarch had to be selected among the group members.

Olivary/ऑलिवरि *(adjective)* – अण्डाकार anatomy relating to or denoting the nucleus situated in the olive of the medulla oblongata in the brain. *The olivary bodies are present on medulla oblongata.*

Olive/ऑलिव *(noun)* – जैतून का वृक्ष a small oval fruit with a hard stone and bitter flesh, green when unripe and blusih black when ripe, used as food and as a source of oil. *Olives were given to the patient in order to have his speedy recovery.*

Olympian/ओलिम्पियन *(adjective)* – श्रेष्ठ, शानदार associated with mount Olympus in NE Greece, traditional home of the Greek gods. resembling or appropriate to a god, especially in superiority and aloofness. *The prince's Olympian looks caught everybody's attention.*

Omega/ओमेगा *(noun)* – यूनानी वर्णमाला का अन्तिम अक्षर the last letter of the Greek alphabet, transliterated as 'O'. *Omega is the last letter of the Greek alphabet.*

Omen/ओमेन *(noun)* – शकुन an event regarded as a portent of good or evil. *Setting out on the journey was considered a bad omen by the astrologer.*

Ominous/ऑमिनॅस *(adjective)* – अशुभ giving the worrying impression that something bad is going to happen. *I had the ominous feeling about her going out, so I did not let her do so.*

Omissible/ऑमिसिबल *(adj)* – छोड़ने योग्य leave out or exclude. *Before working on the project again, he got rid of all the omissible data.*

Omission/ऑमिशॅन *(noun)* – चूक, भूल someone or something that has been left out. *The omission of data took about an hour.*

Omissive/ऑमिसिव *(adj)* – छोड़ने वाला less important. *He had no idea that he was wasting his time on the omissive details.*

Omit/ऑमिट *(verb)* – छोड़ देना leave out or exclude. fail to do. *As our syllabus was still pending, the teacher omitted two chapters from it.*

Omni/ऑम्नि *(combining form)* – सब प्रकार से all; of all things: omnifarious. in all ways or places: omnipresent. *The omnipotent gods were challenged by the demons for war.*

Omnifarious/ऑम्निफेरिअस *(adj)* – सब प्रकार का formal comprising or relating to all sorts

or varieties. *The book had omnifarious details about the growth and evolution of species.*

Omnific/ऑम्निफिक *(adj)* – सर्वोत्पादक all creating. *The Almighty is considered to have omnific powers.*

Omniform/ऑम्निफार्म *(noun)* – सब प्रकार के रूपवाला having every form. *Some of the microorganisms are omniform.*

Omnigenous/ऑम्निजिनस *(adj)* – सब जाति का consisting of all kinds. *Our database consists of omnigenous records.*

Omnipotence/ऑम्निपोटेंस *(noun)* – सर्व (अनन्त) शक्ति the quality of having great power. *The demon had grown arrogant over his omnipotence.*

Omnipotent/ऑम्निपोटेंट *(adj)* – सर्वशक्तिमान formal comprising or relating to all sorts or varieties. *The book depicted the giant to have omnipotent powers.*

Omnipresence/आम्निप्रजेन्स *(noun)* – विश्वव्यापकता to be present everywhere. *Every religious text talks about the omnipresence of God.*

Omnipresent/ऑम्निप्रेजेंट *(adjective)* – विश्वव्यापी present everywhere at the same time. *The priest said, "We should pay reverence to the omnipresent Almighty."*

Omniscience/ऑम्निश्यन्स् *(noun)* – सर्वज्ञान knowledge of everything. *He tried to convince of his omniscience, but no one believed him.*

Omniscient/ऑम्निश्येन्ट् *(adjective)* – त्रिकाल दर्शी knowing everything. *None of our deeds is hidden from the omniscient God.*

Omnivorous/ऑम्निवरस *(adjective)* – सर्वभक्षी feeding on a variety of food of both plant and animal origin. *The birds are known to be omnivorous creatures.*

Omoplate/ओमॅप्लेट *(noun)* – कन्धे पर की हड्डी shouder blade. *After the accident, he had to undergo surgery of his omoplate.*

Onagar/ऑनगर् *(noun)* – गोरखर an animal of a race of the Asian wild ass native to northern Iran. *Onagars are known to inhabitate in regions of northern Iran.*

Once/वन्स *(adverb)* – पहले एक बार on one occasion or for one time only. at all; on even

O

one occasion. *We were allowed to talk to the Minister only once.*

Oncoming/ऑनकमिंग *(adjective)* – पहुँच approaching from the front; moving towards one. *The driver could not notice the oncoming bus and hence, met an accident.*

One/वन *(cardinal number)* – कोई, एक the lowest cardinal number; half of two; 1, *We ordered only one plate of the main course menu.*

One-eyed/वन-आइड *(adj)* – काना blind of one eye. *The story about the one-eyed man is fascinating.*

Oneirocritic/ऑनाइअरॅक्रिटिक *(noun)* – स्वप्न का अर्थ बताने वाला *An experienced oneirocritic is called as a guest in a radio show.*

Oneness/वननेस *(noun)* – एकता, अकेलापन the state of being unified, whole, or in harmony. *Only by the oneness of the nation, we can expect to thwart our enemies.*

Onerous/अॅनरस *(adjective)* – कष्टसाध्य involving a great deal of effort. *I was pretty sure that hurdle race was going to be onerous job.*

Oneself/वनसेल्फ *(pronoun)* – अपने को स्वयं used as the object of a verb or preposition when this is the same as the subject of the clause and the subject is one. *How to neglect the promises that one is making to oneself?*

One-Sided/वन-साइडेड *(adj)* – पक्षपाती partial. *The police had heard only one-sided story till then; now it was the time for the other party.*

Onfall/ऑनफॉल *(noun)* – आगमन an approach of night. *With the onfall of summers, our literature classes were resumed.*

Onflow/ऑनफ्लो *(adverb)* – आगे की ओर बहाव the action of moving steadily. *Initially, the onflow was high, but later, it slowed down.*

Onion/अॅन्यॅन *(noun)* – प्याज an edible bulb used as a vegetable, having a pungent taste and smell and composed of several concentric layers. *There are many antimicrobial properties in onion.*

Oniony/अॅन्यनि *(adj)* – प्याज के गन्ध का having the smell of onion. *An oniony smell was emanating from kitchen.*

Onlooker/ऑनलूकर *(noun)* – दर्शक a non-participating observer; a spectator. *The onlookers were just standing there, without bothering to do anything for the victims.*

Onset/ऑनसेट *(noun)* – आक्रमण, प्रारंभ the beginning of something, especially something unpleasant. *With the onset of monsoons, the water-borne diseases become common.*

Onslaught/ऑनस्लॉट *(noun)* – प्रबल आक्रमण a fierce or destructive attack. an overwhelmingly large quantity of people or things. *The onslaught took lives of many innocent people.*

Ontological/ऑन्टॅलॉजिकल *(adj)* – दार्शनिक metaphysical, study of native of being. *More research is required in the field of ontological studies.*

Ontologist/ऑन्टोलॉजिस्ट *(noun)* – सत्त्व-विद्या का पण्डित one who studies the nature of being. *An ontologist deals with the study of metaphysics.*

Ontology/ऑन्टलॅजि *(noun)* – दर्शन या सत्व विद्या the branch of metaphysics concerned with the nature of being. *His inclination towards philosophy made him opt for a course on ontology.*

Onus/ओनस *(noun)* – उत्तरदायित्व a burden, duty, or responsibility. *As we were not ready to take the onus, another eligible person was chosen for the post.*

Onward/ऑनवर्ड *(adverb)* – आगे या सामने की ओर in a containing forward direction; ahead. forward in time. *From that time onward, the two companies decided to work together.*

Onymous/ऑनिमस् – गुमनाम नहीं (सनाम) (bearing in author's name) *The site did not allow the authors to post onymous articles.*

Onyx/ऑनिक्स *(noun)* – गोमेद रत्न a semi-precious variety of agate with different colours in layers. *Onyx is used as an ornamental stone.*

Oogenesis/ओअजेनिसिस *(noun)* – भ्रूण का बढ़ना biology the production or development of an ovum. *During oogenesis, female's body produces an ovum.*

Oology/ओअॅलजि *(noun)* – पक्षी के अण्डों का अध्ययन the study or collecting of birds' eggs. *I have an avid interest in oology.*

O

Ooze/ऊज (verb) – रिसना, चूना, टपकना slowly trickle or seep out. slowly exude or discharge. *Water was oozing out of the pore at the bottom of the pot.*

Ooziness/ऊजिनेस (noun) – टपकन the state of being oozy. *The bark was still out of its ooziness.*

Oozings/ऊजिंग्स (noun) – द्रव का टपकन flow of fluid in drops. *The oozing had stopped by then and the pore was no longer moist.*

Oozy/ऊजि (adj) – रिसने वाला slowly trickling out of something. *A hole in the gum bottle had rendered it oozy.*

Opacity/ओपैसिटी (noun) – धुँधलापन the condition of being opaque. *In Photoshop, to see the underlying layer, the opacity of the upper layer needs to be decreased.*

Opalescent/ओपॅलेसेन्ट (adjective) – पोलकी रत्न का showing many small points of shifting colour against a pale or dark gound. *With light shining directly over oil, its surface had turned opalescent.*

Opaline/ओपलाइन (adjective) – दूधिया opalescent. *What we were looking at was a beautiful opaline sky.*

Opalize/ओपलाइज – पोलकी के सदृश बनाना to make like opal. *The modern infrastructure has opalized the urban cities.*

Opaque/ओपेक (adjective) – अपारदर्शक not able to be seen through; not transparent. *An opaque object does not allow light to pass through its surface.*

Ope/ओप (adjective & verb) – खुलना [poetic or archaic] form of open. *Cool breeze was coming in the room through ope window.*

Openable/ओपेनेबल (adjective) – प्रकाशित करने योग्य allowing access. *As the bottle was placed in freezer for many days, its cap was no longer openable.*

Opener/ओपेनर (noun) – खोलने वाला a device for opening something. *To open the soda bottles, I needed an opener.*

Openly/ओपेनली (adverb) – दिल खोलकर without concealment, deception, or prevarication; frankly or honestly. *The model had no qualms to talk openly about her relationships.*

Openness/ओपेननेस (noun) – प्रकाशता unlock, to allow access. *It required a great deal of effort on leader's part to bring openness in the attitude of his workers.*

Opera/ऑपरा (noun) – संगीत नाटक a dramatic work in one or more acts that is set to music for singers and instrumentalists. a building for the performance of opera. *All of us were given the passes to the Opera, but two of us could not attend it.*

Opera-glass/ऑपराग्लास (plural noun) – नाटक देखने की दूरबीन small binoculars for use at the opera or theatre. *Sitting on rear seats, we had to put on the opera-glasses to see the happenings on the stage clearly.*

Operant/ऑपरंट (adjective) – कार्य करने की शक्ति रखने वाला involving the modification of behavior by the reinforcing or inhibiting effect of its own consequences. *The operant conditioning is based on the fact that the behaviour is based on the type of stimulus applied.*

Operate/ऑपरेट (verb) – कार्य करना function or control the functioning of. *As soon as the machine started operating, it developed some hitches.*

Operatic/ऑपरैटिक (adjective) – संगीत नाटक के सदृश of, relating to, or characteristic of opera. extravagantly theatrical. *Their operatic performances were worth applauding.*

Operative/ऑपरेटिव (adjective) – प्रयोजक functioning; having effect. having the most relevance or significance in a phrase. *The machine guns were put to test during their operative phase.*

Operator/ऑपरेटर (noun) – प्रवर्तक a person who operates equipment or a machine. a person who works at the switchboard of a telephone exchange. *The operator just put down the receiver without saying a word.*

Operetta/ऑपरेटा (noun) – छोटा संगीत नाटक a short opera, usually on a light or humours theme and having spoken dialogue. *The group members were thrilled when they were handed over the tickets of the operetta.*

Operose/ऑपरोस (adjecitve) – अति परिश्रमी involving much effort. *They could not allow their operose efforts to go in vain.*

O

Ophidion/ऑफिडिअन् *(adjective & noun)* – सर्प सम्बन्धी relating to reptile group, snake. *The fish belonged to the ophidion genus.*

Ophiology/ऑफिअलॅजि *(noun)* – सर्पविद्या (study of snakes) *Would you like to opt for Ophiology as your field of specialization?*

Ophthalmia/ऑफ्थल्मिया *(noun)* – आँख आना medicine inflammation of the eye, especially conjunctivitis. *The eye surgeon had many cases of opthalmia that day.*

Ophthalmology/आफ्थैल्मॅलॅजि *(noun)* – नेत्र-विज्ञान the branch of medicine concerned with the study and treatment of disorders and diseases of the eye. *His son is keen to go abroad and study ophthalmology.*

Ophthalmy/ऑफ्थैल्मि *(noun)* – आँखों की सूजन selling of eyes. *It was due to his recurrent ophthalmy that he could not work on computer for hours.*

Opine/ओपाइन *(verb)* – तर्क करना formal hold and state as one's opinion. *She opined on the country's poor security system for women.*

Opinion/ओपिनियन *(noun)* – अनुमान a view or judgement not necessary based on fact or knowledge. the beliefs or views of a large number of people: the changing climate of opinion. an estimation of quality or worth: he had a high opinion of himself. *Would you mind giving your opinion in this case?*

Opium/ओपियम *(noun)* – अफीम an addictive drug prepared from the juice of a poppy used illicitly as a narcotic and occasionally in medicine as an analgesic. *The illegal trading of opium from China into other Asian countries still continues.*

Opossum/ऑपास्सम् *(noun)* – अमेरिका देश का एक प्रकार का चौपाया an American marsupial which has a naked prehensile tail and hind feet with an opposable thumb. *The zoology chapter was entirely focused on the study of Opossums.*

Opponency/ऑप्पोनॅंसि *(noun)* – शत्रुता *The opponency, in this case, was so strong that they could not defend themselves.*

Opponent/ऑपोनॅंट *(noun)* – शत्रु a person who opposes. *In the tournament, she was going to face a strong opponent.*

Opportunism/ऑपर्ट्यूनिज़्म *(noun)* – सुलह, सन्धि *Sometimes, it becomes necessary to employ opportunism to further one's case.*

Opportunist/ऑपर्टयूनिस्ट *(noun)* – अवसरग्राही a person who takes advantage of opportunities as and when they arise, regardless of planning or principle. *What an opportunist he is!* adjective opportunistic. *The man was too naïve to employ any opportunistic tactics.*

Opportunity/ऑपर्ट्यूनिटि *(noun)* – अवकाश, सुअवसर a favourable time or set of circumstances for doing something. *An opportunity never comes twice.*

Opposability/अपोजबिलिटि *(noun)* – विरोधभाव *The opposability of the human thumb makes it easy to hold objects with ease.*

Opposable/ऑपोसेब्ल *(adjective)* – विरोध के योग्य zoology capable of facing and touching the other digits on the same hand. *Our opposable thumb has rendered us with many capabilities.*

Oppose/अपोज *(verb)* – विरोध करना disapprove of, resist, or be hostile to. compete with or fight. *When my turn came, I vehemently opposed the barbaric act.*

Opposer/अपोजर *(noun)* – विरोधक one who opposes. *Our own team member turned out to be our opposer.*

Opposing/अपोजिंग *(adjective)* – विरुद्ध काम करने वाला different from or in conflict with each other. *The two opposing forces clashed and the result was disastrous.*

Oppositely/ऑपोजिटलि *(adverb)* – विपरीत भाव से situated on the other side. *The two tables were placed oppositely.*

Opposition/ऑपोजिशन *(noun)* – विरोध, प्रतिकूलता resistance or dissent. a group of opponents. [British] the principal parliamentary party opposed to that in office. *The opposition is raising its voice against the recommendations proposed by the ruling party.*

Oppositional/अपोजिशनल *(adjective)* – विरोधी expressing dissent. *Their oppositional behaviour came in the way of coming out with a resolution.*

Oppression/अप्रेशन *(noun)* – उत्पीड़न cruel, unjust treatment. *The peasants raised their voice against the oppression of landlords.*

O

Oppressive/ऑप्रेशिव *(adjective)* – अत्याचारी harsh and authoritarian. *In order to get rid of his oppressive ways, I just ran away.*

Oppressor/अप्रेशर *(noun)* – निर्दयी a person who oppresses people. *A time came when the oppressor had to succumb to the demands of the peasants.*

Opprobrious/ऑप्रोब्रियस *(adjective)* – घृणित highly scornful. *He was staring at me with opprobrious looks.*

Oppugn/ऑप्यून *(verb)*- विरोध करना [archaic] dispute the truth or validity of. *In spite of giving assurance about positive results, his team mates oppugned the new strategy.*

Oppugnation/ऑपग्नेशन *(noun)* – विरोध Opposition: *I was too timid to face the oppugnation.*

Oppugner/अप्यूगनर् *(noun)* – विरोध करने वाला question the validity of. *In contrast to our expectations, he turned out to be an oppugner.*

Opsonic/आप्सोनिक *(adj)* – शरीर के भीतर के कृमियों पर प्रभाव डालने an antibody or other substance that binds with foreign their organisms inside the body. *An opsonic reaction became active as soon the foreign bodies entered the surface.*

Opsonin/ऑप्सोनिन *(noun)* – किसी रोगी के कृमियों को मारकर शरीर प्रवेश करने की biochemistry an antibody or other substance which binds to foreign micro-organisms or cells making them more susceptible to phagocytosis. *The body had not enough opsonins to fight against the attack of microorganisms.*

Optative/ऑटेटिव *(adjective)* – इच्छा सूचक grammar relating to or denoting a mood of verbs in Greek and certain other languages, expressing a wish, equivalent in meaning to English let's or if only. *She was talking in an optative mood that day.*

Optic/अप्टिक *(adjective)* – नेत्र-सम्बन्धी of or relating to the eye or vision. *An operation needed to be done on his optic nerve.*

Optical/ऑप्टिकल *(adjective)* – आँख का of or relating to vision, light, or optics. *The lecture was based on the use of optical devices.*

Optician/ऑप्टिसियन *(noun)* – चक्षुविद्या में निपुण a person qualified to prescribe and dispense glasses and contact lenses, and to detect eye diseases, or to make and supply glasses and contact lenses. *I went to the optician and he advised to use glasses as soon as possible.*

Optics/ऑप्टिक्स *(plural noun)* – दृष्टि-विज्ञान the branch of science concerned with vision and the behaviour of light. *Optics was a mandatory subject in our graduation course.*

Optimacy/ऑप्टिमैसि *(noun)* – शिष्टजन the nobility. *Her parents are searching a groom from the optimacy.*

Optimist/ऑप्टिमिस्ट *(noun)* – आशावादी person who expects good things to happen. *He was such an optimist that even during worst period of his life, he did not get discouraged.*

Option/ऑप्सन *(noun)* – रुचि a thing that is or may be chosen. the freedom or right to choose. *After hopping from job to job, I didn't have any options left.*

Optional/ऑप्सनल *(adjective)* – ऐच्छिक available to be chosen but not obligatory: optional extras. *I did no preparation of the optional subject, yet passed it with flying colours.*

Optophone/अप्टोफोन *(noun)* – अन्धों को पदार्थ दिखलाने में सहायता देने का यन्त्र *An optophone is a useful device for blind people for reading by hearing.*

Opulence/ऑपुलेंस *(noun)* – ऐश्वर्य using expensive materials. *We lived in opulence and spent extravagantly.*

Opulent/ऑप्यूलेंट *(adjective)* – सम्पन्न ostentatiously rich and luxurious wealthy. *The child was born into an opulent family.*

Or/आर् *(noun)* – अन्यथा, पहले gold or yellow, as a heraldic tincture. A logical operator *We were asked to write the truth-table of the logical operator 'OR'.*

Oracular/ऑरक्यूलर् *(adjective)* – देववाणी तुल्य of or relating to an oracle. *An oracular building was present at the centre of the city.*

Oral/ओरल *(adjective)* – मौखिक spoken rather than written. *One must take care of his oral hygiene.*

Orange/ऑरेंज *(adjective)* – सन्तरा of or relating to Orangemen or their order. *The Orange organization is based in Ireland.*

O

Orangery/ऑरेंजरि *(noun)* – नारंगी का बगीचा a building like a large conservatory where orange trees are grown. *An orangery was constructed within the botanical institute.*

Orant/ऑरैंट *(noun & adj)* – पूजक worshipper. *An orant gesture indicates worship in Christianity.*

Orate/ओरेट *(verb)* – व्याख्यान देना to make a speech. *The way he orates is quite impressive.*

Orator/ऑरेटर *(noun)* – सुवक्ता a proficient public speaker. an official speaking for a university on ceremonial occasions. *Being an orator, she was always encouraged to participate in discussions.*

Oratory/ऑरेटरी *(noun)* – वक्तृत्व-शक्ति a small chapel for private worship. *Only priest was allowed to enter the oratory.*

Orb/ऑर्ब *(noun)* – गोला a spherical object or shape. a golden globe surmounted by a cross, forming part of the regalia of monarch. *The orb present on king's crown was shimmering with light.*

Orbicular/आरबीक्यूलर *(adjective)* – गोल technical having the shape of a flat ring or disc. *I could not understand what that orbicular object was.*

Orbit/ऑर्बिट *(noun & verb)* – ग्रहपथ path an object takes to cericle another object. *Every planet revolves in its own orbit.*

Orchard/ऑर्चर्ड *(noun)* – फलों का बाग a piece of enclosed land planted with fruit trees. *We were fascinated by the presence of a lovely orchard near our new house.*

Orchestra/ऑरकेस्ट्रा *(noun)* – वादकवृन्द a group of instrumentalists, especially one combining string, woodwind, brass, and percussion sections. *Before orchestra could begin, one of the singers fell on the stage.*

Orchid/ऑर्किड् *(noun)* – रंग-बिरंगे फूलों वाले विचित्र पौधे a plant of a large family distinguished by complex showy flowers with a labellum and frequently a spur. *I am thinking of buying an orchid for my living room at my farm house.*

Orchitis/ऑर्कीइटिस् *(noun)* – अण्डकोष का शोथ medicine inflammation of one or both of the testicles. *The man got irritated by the constant orchitis, so he consulted a sexologist.*

Ordain/ऑर्डेन *(verb)* – निर्दिष्ट करना confer holy orders on. *The clergyman was ordained under the administration of a bishop.*

Ordainer/ऑर्डेनर् *(noun)* – संस्थापक one who passes orders. *The cleric was the ordainer in the holy ceremony.*

Ordainment/ऑर्डेनमेन्ट *(noun)* – आज्ञा order. *The ceremony of ordainment had to be interrupted in between.*

Ordeal/ऑर्डिअल् *(noun)* – कठिन परीक्षा official order. a prolonged painful or horrific experience. *I have been facing this ordeal from a very long time.*

Orderliness/ऑर्डरलिनेस् *(noun)* – सद्व्यवहार in a neat and methodical way. *The man vouched to bring orderliness in his institute.*

Orderless/ऑर्डरलेस् *(adj)* – क्रमहीन lacking organisation or order. *She had no idea that she would have to teach an orderless class.*

Orderly/ऑर्डरलि *(adjective)* – क्रम के अनुसार neatly and methodically arranged. *Everyone was impressed with the orderly way he used to do things.*

Ordinance/ऑर्डिनैंस *(noun)* – अध्यादेश formal. an authoritative order. [north American] a by-law. *The government, recently, passed an ordinance regarding vehicle parking.*

Ordinarily/ऑर्डिनरिलि *(adv)* – साधारण रूप से usually. *The Mathematics genius could solve all the problems ordinarily.*

Ordinariness/ऑर्डिनरिनेस् *(noun)* – सामान्यता no special or distinctive features. *We were surprised to see the ordinariness of his dress at the party.*

Ordinary/ऑर्डिनरी *(adjective)* – प्रचलित with no distinctive features; normal or usual. *In spite of her ordinary looks, she was able to garner the attention of boys.*

Ordinate/ऑर्डिनेट *(noun)* – क्रमानुसार mathematics a straight line from a point on a graph drawn parallel to the vertical axis and meeting the other; the y-coordinate, compare with abscissa. *The class on ordinate and abscissa was an interesting one.*

Ordination/ऑर्डिनेशन् *(noun)* – विधान the action of ordaining someone in holy orders. *The man was too adamant to follow the ordination.*

O

Ordnance/ऑर्डनैन्स *(noun)* – तोपखाना mounted guns; cannon. US munitions. *The army ordered for a whole new ordnance.*

Ordure/ऑर्ड्यूर *(noun)* – विष्ठा excrement; dung. *The street had a stench of ordure.*

Ore/ओर *(noun)* – बिना संस्कार की हुई धातु a naturally occurring solid material from which a metal or valuable mineral can be extracted profitably. *In our Chemistry class, we learned the process of extracting iron from its ore.*

Oread/ओरिड *(noun)* – पहाड़ की अप्सरा Greek a nymph believed to inhabit mountains. *Oread is a Greek mythological character.*

Orectic/ऑरेक्टिक *(adjective)* – इच्छा-सम्बन्धी technical, rare of or concerning desire or appetite. *His orectic manners clearly indicate that he had fetish for food.*

Organ/आर्गन् *(noun)* – शरीर का अंग a large musical instrument having rows of pipes supplied with air form bellows and arranged in ranks, each controlled by a stop, and played using a keyboard or by an automatic mechanism. a smaller instrument without pipes, producing similar sounds electronically. *He is dexterous at playing organ pipe.*

Organdie/ऑर्गन्डी *(noun)* – अरगन्डी a fine, translucent, stiff cotton muslin, used chiefly for dresses. *She was looking pretty in her dress made of organdie.*

Organic/ऑर्गैनिक *(adjective)* – जैव relating to or derived from living matter. [chemistry] relating to or denoting compounds containing carbon and chiefly or ultimately of biological origin. compare with inorganic. *The organic matter is biodegradable.*

Organization/ऑर्गनाइजेशन *(noun)* – सृष्टि संगठन the action of organizing. Systematic arrangement of elements. a systematic approach to tasks. *We work in an organization that works for social welfare.*

Organize/ऑर्गेनाइज *(verb)* – बनाना, संगठन करना arrange systematically, order. *As she saw the things scattered here and there, she started organizing them.*

Orgasm/ऑर्गैज्म् *(noun)* – क्षोभ the climax of sexual excitement, characterized by intensely pleasurable sensations canted in the genitals. *It was not the first time that he was not able to fully enjoy the orgasm.*

Orgastic/ऑर्गैस्टिक *(adjective)* – आवेग-सम्बन्धी relating to orgasm. *He could not hold his joy that he experienced during the orgastic activity.*

Orgy/ऑर्जि *(noun)* – रात्रि उत्सव a wild party characterized by excessive drinking and indiscriminate sexual activity. *Orgies are usually organized secretly.*

Orient/ओरिएन्ट *(noun)* – पूर्व दिशा poetic the countries of the east, especially east Asia. *The Orient is blamed for aping the West.*

Oriental/ओरिएन्टल *(adjective)* – प्राचीन relating to Asians. *There is no doubt about the oriental origin of the gibbons.*

Orientally/ओरिएन्टली *(adverb)* – प्राचीनता से characteristic of people of Asia. *It was clear that their mannerism was driven orientally.*

Orientate/ओरिएन्टेट *(verb)* – पूरब की ओर बनाना orient orientate is another term for orient. *It was her lack of her knowledge about Indian culture that she requested me orientate her.*

Origanum/ऑरिगेनम *(noun)* – एक फलवाला पौधा an aromatic plant of a genus that includes marjoram and oregano. *The aromatic properties of Origanum are used for various purposes.*

Origin/ओरिजिन *(noun)* – उद्गम the point where something begins or arises. anatomy the more fixed end or attachment of a muscle. *The origin of mankind has always remained a puzzle.*

Original/ओरिजिनल *(adjective)* – मौलिक existing from the beginning; first or earliest. *The original species of human had a close resemblance to the modern man.*

Originality/ऑरिजिनैलिटी *(noun)* – मौलिकता ability to think orginally. *The director was looking for originality in acting.*

Originally/ओरिजनली *(adv)* – पहले से from or in the beginning. *Originally, there were no wireless technology in the field of communication.*

Originate/ओरिजिनेट *(verb)* – प्रारम्भ होना have a specified beginning. create or initiate. *A few varieties of jute originated in India.*

Origination/ओरिजिनेशन *(adj)* – प्रारम्भ some of beginning. *India is attributed to be the origination place of many spices.*

Originatives/ओरिजिनेटिव्स *(adj)* – उत्पन्न करने वाला creating or initiating something new. *My son is gifted with an originative mind.*

Originator/ओरिजिनेटर *(noun)* – उत्पादक a person who creates something new. *Man is considered the originator of many innovations.*

Orion/ओरिअन *(noun)* – मृगशिरा नक्षत्र a constellation on the equator to the east of Taurus; contains Betelgeuse and Rigel. *Orion is a constellation that can be seen during winter season.*

Orison/ओरिसन *(noun)* – प्रार्थना [archaic] a prayer. *The devotees paid their reverence by saying an orison.*

Orleans/ऑर्लिअन्स *(noun)* – एक प्रकार का बेर a city in France. *Orleans is a city in France where Joan of Arc led French against England.*

Orlop/ऑर्लॉप *(noun)* – जहाज की सबसे नीची छत the lowest deck of a wooden sailing ship with three or more decks. *We saw captain sitting on an orlop.*

Ornament/ऑर्नामेंट *(noun)* – अलंकार an object designed to add beauty to something. decorative items collectively; decoration. music embellishments made to a melody. *Ornaments have been recovered from the excavation sites of Harappa civilization.*

Ornamental/ऑर्नामेंटल *(adjective)* – विभूषक serving or intended as an ornament. *The ornamental vessels have always been a part of Indian aestheticism.*

Ornamentalism/ऑर्नामेंटलिज्म *(noun)* – अलंकरण intended to be decorative item. *The fetish for ornamnetalism never ceases to exist.*

Ornamentalist/ऑर्नामेंटलिस्ट *(noun)* – सुशोभित करने वाला user of ornament as a decoration piece. *Today, I am going to meet a renowned ornamentalist from Israel.*

Ornamentally/ऑर्नामेंटली *(noun)* – सजाया हुआ in the manner of decoration. *The king's room was looking ornamentally beautiful.*

Ornate/आर्नेट *(adjective)* – सुशोभित elaborately or highly decorated. *The elephant was ornate with gold jewelry.*

Ornithology/आर्निथॅलॅजी *(noun)* – पक्षी विद्या the scientific study of birds. *Dr. Salim Ali did an excellent job in ornithology.*

Orphan/ऑर्फन *(noun)* – अनाथ a child whose parents are dead. *The business was keen to donate money for educating orphans in his society.*

Orphanage/ऑर्फनेज *(noun)* – अनाथालय residential utilities for care of orphans. *This orphanage has been blacklisted due to illegal practices carried in it.*

Orphic/ऑर्फिक *(adjective)* – सुरीला of or concerning Orpheus, a legendary Greece, said to have been based on poems by Orpheus, characterized by rites of purification, death, and rebirth. *The orphic rites and rituals were common in ancient Greece.*

Ort/ऑर्ट *(noun)* – जूठन remainder of food from meal. *After eating he left an ort and fed it to his cat.*

Orthodox/ऑर्थोडॉक्स *(adjective)* – शास्त्रानुसार सत्य धर्मावलम्बी conforming with traditional or generally accepted beliefs. *She belongs to an orthodox family.*

Orthoepy/ऑर्थोएपि *(noun)* – शुद्ध उच्चारण सिखलाने की विद्या the study of correct or accepted pronunciation. *Only a few people are interested in Orthoepy.*

Orthogonal/ऑर्थोगोनल *(adjective)* – समकोणाकार of or involving right angles; at right angles to each other. *The students were asked to calculate the area of the given orthogonal shape.*

Ortolan/ऑर्टलन् *(noun)* – बगेरी a small songbird formerly eaten as a delicacy, the male having an olive-green head and yellow throat. *A male ortolan was sitting over a tree branch.*

Oscillate/ऑसिलेट *(verb)* – झूलना move or swing back and forth at a regular speed. waver between extremes of opinion or emotion. *The pendulum of the clock oscillates back and forth repeatedly.*

O

Oscillation/ऑसिलेशन *(noun)* – दोलन back and forth movement in a regular rhythm. *Electro-mechanical oscillations take place in a microphone.*

Oscillating/ऑसिलेटिंग *(adj)* – इधर-उधर हिलता हुआ *The government is still oscillating over the decision to pass Jan Lokpal bill.*

Oscitant/ऑसिटैंट *(adjective)* – निद्रालु yawning. *The students were usually oscitant during the boring History lecture.*

Oscitate/ऑसिटेट *(verb)* – जँभाई लेना to yawn. *The teacher was aghast to see that the boys in punishment were oscitating.*

Oscular/ऑसक्यूलर *(adjective)* – चुम्बन का humorous of mouth or relating to kissing. *The doctor was going to operate oscular bone.*

Osculation/ऑस्क्यूलेशन *(noun)* – चुम्बन humorous kiss. *The two were lost in their act of osculation.*

Osmium/ओस्मियम *(noun)* – एक धातु the chemical element of atomic number 76, a hard, dense silvery-white metal. *Osmium is used in applications where durability of material is required.*

Ossicle/ऑसिकल *(noun)* – आस्थिक anatomy & zoology a very small bone, especially one of those in the middle ear. *Ossicle is a bone in man's middle ear.*

Ossification/ओसिफिकेशन *(noun)* – हड्डी बनने की क्रिया cease developing, became stony, stagnant. *As the time progressed, the society saw an ossification of the traditional beliefs.*

Ossify/ओसिफाई *(verb)* – कड़ा हो जाना turn into bone or bony tissue. *Osteoclasts are specialized cells that ossify and help in bone formation.*

Ostensible/ऑस्टेन्सिबल *(adjective)* – प्रकट, प्रत्यक्ष apparently true, but not necessarily so. *No one could doubt his ostensible purpose of charity.*

Ostensive/ऑस्टेन्सिव *(adjective)* – स्पष्ट linguistics denoting a way of defining by direct demonstration, e.g. pointing. *Teacher's ostensive way of teaching appealed all the students.*

Ostracism/आस्ट्रैसिज्म *(noun)* – देशनिकाला exclusion from a group or society. *The couple's ostracism from the society has raised a few eyebrows.*

Ostrich/ऑस्ट्रिच *(noun)* – शुतुरमुर्ग a large flightless swift-running African bird with a long neck, long legs, and two toes on each foot. *An ostrich lays the biggest eggs in the world.*

Otalgia/ओटैल्जिआ *(noun)* – कर्णशूल medicine earache. *I was suffering from an otalgia.*

Other/अदर *(adjective & pronoun)* – अन्य, दूसरा used to refer to a person or thing that is different from one already mentioned or known. alternative of two. those not already mentioned. *The other criminal is still out of the reach.*

Otherness/अदरनेस *(noun)* – परायापन the quality of fact of being different. *She had some sort of otherness in her and this made him fall in love with her.*

Otherwise/अदरवाइज *(adverb)* – अन्यथा in different circumstances; or else. *Do it now, otherwise I would report it to your manager.*

Otiosely/ओशिओसुलि *(adverb)* – सुस्ती से leisurely. *I do not appreciate his way of living otiosely.*

Otitis/ऑटाइटिस *(noun)* – कान की सूजन medicine inflammation of part of the ear, especially the middle ear. *Why don't you get your otitis get treated.*

Otology/ऑटॉलॅजी *(noun)* – कान (के रोगों) का शास्त्र the study of the anatomy and diseases of the ear. *I am going to take a course in Otology.*

Otter/ऑटर *(noun)* – जलमार्जार (ऊदबिलाव) a semi aquatic fish-eating mammal of the weasel family, with an elongated body, dense fur, and webbed feet. *What we were looking at was a large otter.*

Otto/ऑटॅ *(noun)* – इत्र another term for attar. *The sweet smell of otto had an intoxicating smell on me.*

Oubliette/ऊब्लिएट *(noun)* – गुप्त गुफा a secret dungeon with access only through a trapdoor in its ceiling. *The prince was hooked to a chain in the dark oubliette.*

Ought/ऑट *(modal verb)* – चाहिए modal used to indicate duty or correctness. used to indicate a desirable or expected state. used to give or ask advice. *You ought to carry this responsibility on your shoulders.*

Our/आवर *(possession determine)* – हम लोगों का belonging to or associated with the speaker and one or more others previously mentioned or easily indentified. belonging to or associated with people in general. *Our culture has many flaws that need to be corrected.*

Ousel/ऊज़ल् *(noun)* – भुजंगा a black bird, variant spelling of ouzel. *An ousel resembles a blackbird.*

Oust/आउस्ट *(verb)* – बाहर करना drive out or expel from a position or place. *We could no longer take his rubbish attitude, so he was ousted.*

Ouster/आउस्टर *(noun)* – बेदखली law ejection from a freehold or other possession; deprivation of an inheritance. removal from the jurisdiction of the courts. a clause that is or is claimed to be outside the jurisdiction of the courts. *His ouster from family business came as no surprise to us.*

Outbalance/आउटबैलेंस *(verb)* – प्रभाव में अधिक होना be more valuable or important than. *I have no idea of why the party is outbalancing the issue over other things.*

Outbid/आउटबिड *(verb)* – अधिक मूल्य लगाना bid more for something than. *The company outbid our local business to get the lucrative project.*

Outbrag/आउटब्रैग *(verb)* – सुन्दरता से बढ़ना to surpass in beauty. *My senior outbrags about his achievements as and when he gets the chance.*

Outburn/आउटबर्न *(verb)* – तीव्रता से जलना to burn with excess. *The flames were so high that the entire building got outburned.*

Outburst/आउटबर्स्ट *(noun)* – विस्फोट a sudden violent occurrence or release of something, especially angry words. *No one was amused to see her sudden outburst as soon as she had occupied her seat.*

Outcaste/आउटकास्ट *(noun)* – जाति से निकाला हुआ a person with no caste, or one expelled from their caste. *He was declared an outcaste after he confessed his love for the dalit woman.*

Outclass/आउटक्लास *(verb)* – बढ़ जाना be far superior to. *She outclassed her friends in her choice of sophisticated things.*

Outcry/आउटक्राई *(noun)* – पीड़ा का शब्द a strong expression of public disapproval. an exclamation or shout. *After the public outcry, the case was reopened.*

Outdare/आउटडेअर *(verb)* – ललकारना to defy. *She outdared her male competitors to save the child from the clutches of the leopard.*

Outdistance/आउटडिस्टेंस *(verb)* – आगे बढ़ जाना leave a competitor or pursuer far behind. *After only a mile was left, I outdistanced the person running in front of me.*

Outdoor/आउटडोर *(adjective)* – खुले मैदान का done, situated, or used outdoors. liking the outdoors. *We should encourage our children to pursue outdoor activities.*

Outer/आउटर *(adjective)* – बाहरी outside; external. further from the centre or the inside. *A line was drawn from the centre of the inner circle to the half of radius of outer one.*

Outermost/आउटरमोस्ट *(adjective)* – सबसे बाहरी furthest from the centre. *The outermost region of a candle flame is the coldest.*

Outfall/आउटफॉल *(noun)* – नदी का मुहाना the place where a river, drain, etc. empties into the sea, a river, or a lake. *The tourists were allowed to have the view of the outfall.*

Outfit/आउटफिट *(noun)* – (उपकरण) सामान a set of clothes worn together. *His outfit was apt for the occasion.*

Outfitter/आउटफिटर *(noun)* – सामग्री इकट्ठा करने वाला मनुष्य a shop selling men's clothing. *Why don't you visit a good outfitter in your area?*

Outfly/आउटफ्लाई *(verb)* – उड़ने में बढ़ जाना more agility. *It was thrilling to see how the jet aircraft was able to outfly its older counterparts.*

Outfool/आउटफूल *(verb)* – मूर्खता में बढ़ जाना to exceed in foolishness. *We were fully convinced that his outfooling himself was a thing done purposely.*

Outgate/आउटगेट *(noun)* – बाहर जाने का मार्ग passage for going out. *We made an exit from the outgate.*

Outgaze/आउटगेज *(verb)* – अधिक दूर तक देखना to gaze farther. *The man was outgazing and keeping an eye on our every single move.*

Outgive/आउटगिव *(verb)* – उदारता में बढ़ जाना to excel in liberality. *She always outgives, thanks to her philanthropic nature.*

O

Outgoing/आउटगोइंग *(adjective)* – बाहर जाना a going out, friendly and confident. *I wish I were a bit more outgoing.*

Outgrow/आउटग्रो *(verb)* – से बढ़ जाना grow too big for. *My son has outgrown of his teenage clothes.*

Outgrowth/आउटग्रोथ *(noun)* – अतिवृद्धि something that grow out of something else. *We noticed some green outgrowths on potatoes.*

Outguard/आउटगार्ड *(noun)* – दूर से रक्षा कार्य guarding at a distance. *A small outguard was positioned at about 2 kilometres from the army.*

Outhouse/आउटहाउस *(noun)* – घर के बाहर का छोटा मकान a smaller building built on to or in the grounds of a house. an outside toilet. *The guests had to be kept in the outhouse.*

Outlaw/आउटलॉ *(noun)* – दस्यु a fugitive from the law. *He being an outlaw can create problems for him.*

Outlay/आउटले *(noun)* – खर्च an amount of money spent. *Kindly give me an account of the outlay on arranging tours.*

Outleap/आउटलिप *(verb)* – आगे को कूदना *The deer outleapt and became invisible.*

Outlet/आउटलेट *(noun)* – निकास a pipe or hole through which water or gas may escape. *I forgot to close the gas outlet.*

Outline/आउटलाइन *(noun)* – खाका a line or lines enclosing or indicating the shape of an object in a sketch or diagram. the contours or bounds of an object. *The teacher drew an outline of human heart and asked us to draw its parts.*

Outlive/आउटलिव *(verb)* – अधिक जीना live longer than. survive or last beyond. *The husband outlived her wife by several years.*

Outlook/आउटलुक *(noun)* – चौकसी a person's point of view or attitude to life. *You should change your negative outlook of life.*

Outlying/आउटलाइंग *(adjective)* – दूर का remote. *The doctor had no qualms about working in an outlying village.*

Outmarch/आउटमार्च *(verb)* – आगे बढ़ना *We were able to outmarch the dacoits who came looking for us.*

Outmeasure/आउटमेजर *(verb)* – विस्तार में बढ़ना exceed in quantity or extent. *The imported rice outmeasured our needs.*

Outmost/आउटमोस्ट *(adjective)* – सबसे बढ़कर furthest away. *Pluto is the outmost planet of our solar system.*

Outname/आउटनेम *(verb)* – यश में बढ़ जाना to surpass in reputation. *The popularity of her novels has outnamed her failures in life.*

Outness/आउटनेस *(noun)* – बाहरीपन the state of being outside. *It is the outness of her nature that she has dozens of friends.*

Outnumber/आउटनम्बर *(verb)* – संख्या में बढ़ना be more numerous than. *The number of articles contributed by her has outnumbered the total articles written by anyone else.*

Outpace/आउटपेस *(verb)* – तेज दौड़ना go faster than. *My sister walks slow and can never outpace me.*

Outpart/आउटपार्ट *(noun)* – केन्द्र से दूर पर का हिस्सा a part remote from the centre. *Peel the outpart of the mango and throw it away.*

Outplay/आउटप्ले *(verb)* – खेल में हराना play better than. *The continuous practice on her part made her outplay other girls.*

Outpost/आउटपोस्ट *(noun)* – सीमा-चौकी a small military camp at a distance from the main army. a remote part of a country or empire. an isolated or remote branch of something. *After some time, he was stationed at the outpost.*

Outpower/आउटपॉवर *(verb)* – शक्ति में बढ़ना to excel in power. *In the story, the small boy overpowers the beast.*

Output/आउटपुट *(noun)* – घानी the amount of something produced by a person, machine, or industry. the process of producing something. the power, energy, etc. supplied by a device or system. *The farmers are expecting more output of grains this year.*

Outrage/आउटरेज *(noun)* – उपद्रव an extremely strong reaction of anger or indignation. a cause of outrage. *The delay in the murder case created an outrage in public.*

Outrageous/आउटरेजस *(adjective)* – उपद्रवी shockingly bad or excessive. *The minister was criticized for his outrageous comment on communalism.*

Outreach/आउटरीच *(verb)* – छलना reach further than. reach out. *There was no doubt that our team shall outreach theirs.*

O

Outride/आउटराइड *(verb)* – घुड़सवारी में आगे जाना ride better, faster, or further than. *With regular practice, he could outride everyone else.*

Outroot/आउटरूट *(verb & noun)* – जड़ से निकाल देना to root out. *The outroot of the dowry system requires more efforts on our part.*

Outrun/आउटरन *(verb)* – निकल भागना run or travel faster or further than. escape from. *Can you outrun me?*

Outset/आउटसेट *(noun)* – आरम्भ the start or beginning. *It was clear from the outset that he was unwilling to take the case in his hand.*

Outshine/आउटसाइन *(verb)* – चमकना shine more brightly than. *One of the vases in the shop was outshining others.*

Outsider/आउटसाइडर *(noun)* – परदेशी a person who does not belong to a particular group. a person not accepted by or isolating themselves from society. *They were not willing to accept an outsider like him in their group.*

Outsize/आउटसाइज *(adjective)* – सामान्य नाप से बढ़कर exceptionally large. *His outsized body required specially tailored clothes.*

Outskirt/आउटस्कर्ट *(plural noun)* – सरहद the outer parts of a town or city. *He stopped the car on the outskirts of the city.*

Outspoken/आउटस्पोकेन *(adjective)* – स्पष्ट कहा हुआ frank in stating one's opinions. *She is always condemned for her outspoken nature.*

Outspread/आउटस्प्रेड *(adjective)* – छितराया fully extended or expanded. *His outspread arms showed that he wanted to hug her.*

Outstanding/आउटस्टैंडिंग *(adjective)* – न चुकाया हुआ exceptionally good. *Her performance in the exams was outstanding.*

Outstep/आउटस्टेप *(verb)* – आगे को बढ़ना exceed. *Don't outstep the limits imposed on you.*

Outstretch/आउटस्ट्रेच *(verb)* – फैलाना extend or stretch out. *To grab the handle, he outstretched his arm.*

Outstrip/आउटस्ट्रिप *(verb)* – अतिक्रम करना move faster than and overtake. exceed. *The leopard outstripped the hyena and grabbed it.*

Outturn/आउटटर्न *(noun)* – तैयार माल the amount of something produced. *The outturn of the mill has exceeded the expectation.*

Outvalue/आउटवैलू *(verb)* – मूल्य से हराना to be of greater value than. *That the character outvalues all other virtues in man is a fact.*

Outvote/आउटवोट *(verb)* – अधिक वोट से हराना defeat by gaining more votes. *The independent candidate surprised everyone by outvoting his rival.*

Outwalk/आउटवाक् *(verb)* – अधिक तेज चलना walk faster. *No matter how fast I walk, I cannot outwalk my friend.*

Outwall/आउटवाल *(noun)* – घर की बाहरी दीवार the exterior wall of a building. *The outwall of the house badly needs a paint.*

Outward/आउटवार्ड *(adjective)* – बाहरी of, on, or from the outside. relating to the external appearance of something rather than its true nature. outer. *Don't get deceived by his outward appearance.*

Outwatch/आउटवाच *(verb)* – अधिक पहरा देना watch until it disappears. keep awake beyond the end of. *The child kept outwatching the train till it became invisible.*

Outwear/आउटविअर *(verb)* – पूर्ण रूप से थका देना to wear out completely. *The act of pushing cart outweared the man.*

Outweigh/आउटवे *(verb)* – भार या महत्त्व में बढ़ना be heavier, greater, or more significant than. *Being a highly experienced man, his decision outweighs many others.*

Outwind/आउटविंड *(verb)* – बन्धन ढीला करना to unclose. *Why don't you unwind yourself a bit?*

Outwit/आउटविट *(verb)* – बुद्धि द्वारा पराजित करना deceive by greater ingenuity. *It was due to his sharp mind that he outwitted everyone in the discussion round.*

Outwork/आउटवर्क *(noun)* – घर के बाहर किया हुआ कार्य an outer section of a fortification or system of defence. *The security level at the outwork is unsatisfactory.*

Ova/ओवा – अण्डे plural form of ovum. *The fertilization takes place when one of the ova fuses with one or more sperms.*

Oval/ओवल *(adjective)* – अण्डाकार having a rounded and slightly elongated outline; egg

O

shaped. *Her oval face makes her wear any type of makeup.*

Ovarian/ओवेरियन *(adjective)* – अण्डाशय सम्बन्धी of or relating to an ovary or the ovaries. *The risk of the ovarian cancer is higher in women who smoke heavily.*

Ovarious/ओवेरियस *(adj.)* – अण्डधारी consisting of eggs. *He was advised to change his ovarious diet.*

Ovary/ओवरी *(noun)* – अण्डाशय a female reproductive organ in which ova or eggs are produced. *Her left ovary has a cyst.*

Ovate/ओवेट *(adjective)* – अण्डाकार oval; egg shaped. *Yesterday, I bought an ovate lantern.*

Oven/ओवेन *(noun)* – चूल्हा an enclosed compartment, usually part of a cooker, for cooking food. *Why don't you purchase an oven?*

Overact/ओवरएक्ट *(verb)* – आवश्यकता से अधिक काम करना act a role in an exaggerated manner. *In almost every movie of hers, she has overacted.*

Overalls/ओवरआल्स *(adjective)* – ऊपरी ओढ़ना या वस्त्र total. taking everything into account. *The overall result of the discussion is that project should be completed by May this year.* *(adverb)* taken as a whole. *Overall, the meeting was quiet fruitful.*

Overawe/ओवरऑ *(verb)* – डराना subdue or inhibit with a sense of awe. *The speaker overawed the crowd by his inspiring speech.*

Overbalance/ओवरबैलेंस *(verb)* – अधिक भारी होना fall or cause to fall due to loss of balance. *Being drunk, she overbalanced and fell on ground.*

Overbear/ओवरवियर *(verb)* – वश में करना overcome by emotional pressure or physical force. *The traumatic incident was too much for her to overbear.*

Overbearing/ओवरबियरिंग *(adjective)* – अहंकारी unpleasantly overpowering. *The overpowering lad badly needs a lesson.*

Overblow/ओवरब्लो *(verb)* – फूलों से भरना to cover with flowers. *The musician was overblowing his flute to catch everyone's attention.*

Overboard/ओवरबोर्ड *(adverb)* – जहाज की छत पर from a ship into the water. *It was due to deadly waves that he was thrown overboard.*

Overbuild/ओवरबिल्ड *(verb)* – आवश्यकता से अधिक निर्माण करना put up too many buildings in. build too many of. build elaborately. *This city is overbuilt and needs a revamp.*

Overburden/ओवरबर्डेन *(verb)* – अधिक लाद देना burden excessively. *The rearing of four children has overburdened her.*

Overbusy/ओवरबिजी *(adjective)* – कार्य में अतिलीन excessively busy. *Where are you overbusy these days?*

Overcareful/ओवरकेअरफुल *(adjective)* – आवश्यकता से अधिक सावधान excessively careful. *Her overcareful attitude has been the subject of mockery among her colleagues.*

Overcast/ओवरकास्ट *(adjective)* – मेघाच्छन cloudy; dull. *The overcast sky looks so pleasing.*

Overcharge/ओवरचार्ज *(verb)* – अधिक मूल्य होना charge too high a price. *I rebuked the seller for overcharging.*

Overcoat/ओवरकोट *(noun)* – लबादा a long warm coat. *Before setting out, don't forget to wear an overcoat.*

Overcold/ओवरकोल्ड *(adj)* – बहुत ही ठण्डा cold to excess. *I am immune to the overcold weather.*

Overcostly/ओवरकॉस्टली *(adj)* – बहुत महँगा very costly. *An average man is unable to buy overcostly things.*

Overcrowd/ओवरक्राउड *(verb)* – बड़ी भीड़ जमाना fill beyond what is usual or comfortable. *Getting in of more passengers overcrowded the bus.*

Overdate/ओवरडेट *(verb)* – बाद की तारीख डालना to postdate. *While signing the papers, the manager overdated them.*

Overdose/ओवरडोज *(noun)* – अधिक मात्रा an excessive and dangerous dose of a drug. *Overdose of any pill can be dangerous.*

Overestimate/ओवरएस्टिमेट *(verb)* – अधिक आँकना form too high an estimate of. *The minister had overestimated his victory in the coming elections.*

Overestimation/ओवरएस्टिमेशन *(noun)* – अधिक मूल्य निरूपण approximate usage. *His overestimation of the things cost him dear.*

O

Overfeed/ओवरफिड *(verb)* – परिमाण से अधिक खिलाना feed too much. *Overfeeding the cattle can make them ill.*

Overfill/ओवरफिल *(verb)* – परिमाण से अधिक भरना fill to excess. *Our department is overfilled with employees.*

Overgrown/ओवरग्रोन *(adjective)* – अधिक बढ़ा हुआ grown over with vegetation. *Farmer was busy plucking out the overgrown grass.*

Overhang/ओवरहैंग *(verb)* – ऊपर लटकना hang over. *The branches of this tree are overhanging.*

Overhappy/ओवरहैप्पी *(adj)* – बहुत ही प्रसन्न *What is the reason of your being overhappy?*

Overhardy/ओवरहार्डी *(noun)* – अत्यधिक साहसी unduly doring. *The man is just pretending to be overhardy.*

Overhasty/ओवरहेस्टी *(adj)* – अधिक शीघ्रता करने वाला unduly hasty. *I have a habit of being overhasty in completing things.*

Overhaul/ओवरहॉल *(verb)* – जाँचना examine and repair it if necessary. *The driver stopped his jeep and overhauled the tyres.*

Overhead/ओवरहेड *(adverb)* – सिर पर above one's head; in the sky. *At that time, the sun was shining overhead*

Overhear/ओवरहिअर *(verb)* – छिपकर सुनना hear accidentally or secretly. *He was overhearing to the secret conversion.*

Overheat/ओवरहिट *(verb)* – अधिक गरम करना make or become too hot. *The cylinder overheated and then exploded.*

Overissue/ओवरइस्सू *(verb)* – चुकाने की शक्ति से अधिक हुंडी जारी करना issue beyond the authorized amount or the issuer's ability to pay. *An inadvertent error in software made the bank overissue the man.*

Overjoy/ओवरजॉय *(verb)* – अति प्रसन्न करना to fill too much joy. *I was overjoyed on getting through the bank exam.*

Overlabour/ओवरलेबर *(verb)* – आवश्यकता से अधिक काम करना to over-work. *Even overlabouring could not earn him a decent salary.*

Overlavish/ओवरलैविश *(adj)* – व्ययशील lavish to excess. *He has been living in an overlavish style.*

Overlaying/ओवरलेयिंग – कृत्रिम ढक्कन an artificial covering. *The skin overlaying was ruptured at many places.*

Overlie/ओवरलाइ *(verb)* – ऊपर पड़ना lie on top of. *The cucumbers were grated and made to overlay the lower piece of bread.*

Overload/ओवरलोड *(verb)* – बहुत लादना load excessively. *Don't overload your taxi with the unnecessary things.*

Overlong/ओवरलांग *(adjective & adverb)* – बहुत अधिक लम्बा too long. *This overlong street bends to the right.*

Overlook/ओवरलूक *(verb)* – उपेक्षा करना fail to notice. ignore or disregard. pass over in favour of another. *All my requests to redevelop the site were overlooked.*

Overlooker/ओवरलूकर *(noun)* – चौकसी रखने वाला a supervisor. *The company badly needs an overlooker for its godowns.*

Overlord/ओवरलार्ड *(noun)* – राजाधिराज a ruler, especially a feudal lord. *The farmer requested his overlord to lower the rent.*

Overmaster/ओवरमास्टर *(verb)* – अधीन करना overcome. *With patience and dedication, you can overmaster any difficulty.*

Overmeasure/ओवरमेजर *(verb)* – अत्यधिक परिमाण an amount beyond what is proper *The shopkeeper was in a habit of overmeasuring the commodities.*

Overmodest/ओवरमॉडेस्ट *(adj)* – अत्यधिक विनीत excessively modest. *There is no point in being overmodest to get the things done.*

Overmuch/ओवरमच *(adverb determine & pronoun)* – अत्यन्त too much. *The man has been practising overmuch.*

Overnice/ओवरनाइस *(adjective)* – नकचढ़ा dated excessively fussy or fastidious. *Don't try to be overnice with your boss.*

Overnight/ओवरनाइट *(adverb)* – अतीत रात्रि में for the duration of a night. during the course of a night. *Only an overnight and the government had lost its majority.*

Overpass/ओवरपास *(noun)* – पार करना a bridge by which a road or railway line passes over another. *As the train reached the overpass, we heard some noise.*

O

Overpeople/ओवरपिपॅल *(verb)* – अधिक जनसंख्या से भरना to fill with too many people. *The auditorium was overpeopled and there was no vacant seats left.*

Overplus/ओवरप्लस *(noun)* – वेशी a surplus. *An overplus was sent by the company to its shareholders.*

Overply/ओवरप्लाई *(verb)* – अत्यधिक शक्ति लगाना to exert too much force. *His overplying has exhausted him.*

Overpoise/ओवर्पॉइज *(noun)* – समतोलन से अधिक भार preponderant weight. *The lady was overpoising her husband's new ventures to the existing ones.*

Overpost/ओवरपोस्ट *(verb)*– अति शीघ्रता करना To leave out swiftly *After a heated argument, I overposted from the room.*

Overpower/ओवरपॉवर *(verb)* – हराना defeat with superior strength. overwhelm. *The king's huge army easily overpowered their enemy.*

Overpraise/ओवरप्रेज *(verb)* – अतिप्रशंसा to prais too highly. *There is no need to overpraise him for his single achievement.*

Overprize/ओवरप्राइज *(verb)* – मूल्य में बढ़ जाना to surpass in prize. *The business men have the tendency to overprize their products.*

Overproduction/ओवरप्रोडक्सन *(noun)* – सामग्री की माँग से अधिक पूर्ति more than normal. *With the overproduction of wheat, the prices have gone down.*

Overrate/ओवररेट *(verb)* – अधिक मूल्य लगाना rate more highly than is deserved. *This movie by Shyam Bengal is overrated.*

Overreach/ओवररीच *(verb)* – धोखा देना reach too far. try to do more than is possible. *I have no idea of why he is trying to overreach his goal.*

Overrent/ओवररेंट *(verb)* – बहुत ज्यादा किराया लेना to exact excessive rent. *The lady has overrented her apartment.*

Override/ओवरराइड *(verb)* – कुचलना use one's authority to reject or cancel. *With his power and influence, he could override any decision made by the community members.*

Overrule/ओवररूल *(verb)* – रद्द करना reject or disallow by exercising one's superior authority. *The judge overruled the objection raised by the lawyer.*

Oversea/ओवरसी *(adverb)* – समुद्र पार in or to a foreign country. *His business has seen a huge growth overseas.* adjective form, to, or relating to a foreign country. *The overseas treaty was signed by the two countries.*

Oversee/ओवरसी *(verb)* – चौकसी करना To supervise: *The inspector came to oversee the quality of the manufactured goods.*

Overseer/ओवरसिअर *(noun)* – निरीक्षक *He, being an overseer, was assigned the job of supervision.*

Oversell/ओवरसेल *(verb)* – बहुत महँगा बेचना sell more of than exists or can be delivered. *He used to dupe people by overselling their shares.*

Overset/ओवरसेट *(verb)* – नीचे गिरना upset emotionally. *The son's rude behaviour has overset his mother.*

Overshade/ओवरशेड *(verb)* – ढाँकना to throw shade over. *Big leaves of the tree were overshading the plants below.*

Overshadow/ओवरशैडो *(verb)* – छाया करना tower above and cast a shadow over. *The tall building has overshadowed the small house.*

Overshoot/ओवरशूट *(verb)* – लक्ष्य के बाहर मारना go past unintentionally. *As she remained utterly confused, she easily overshot her destination.*

Oversight/ओवरसाइट *(noun)* – भ्रम an unintentional failure to notice or do something. *Oversight should not be made an excuse every time.*

Overskip/ओवरस्किप *(verb)* – लाँघना to leapover. *My boss has the tendency to overskip anyone who is about to go up in the ladder.*

Oversow/ओवरसो *(verb)* – परिमाण से अधिक बोना to sow too much. *In order to save space, the farmer oversowed in the field.*

Overspent/ओवरस्पेंट – अधिव्यय p.t. of overspend. *After shopping was done, he realized that his savings have been overspent.*

Overstate/ओवरस्टेट *(verb)* – बहुत बढ़ाकर कहना state too emphatically; exaggerate. *My friend has the habit of overstating any incident or happening in the company.*

O

Overstay/ओवरस्टे *(verb)* – अधिक काल तक ठहरना stay longer than the duration or limits of. *The hotel is charging more money for overstay.*

Overstep/ओवरस्टेप *(verb)* – किसी कार्य में आगे बढ़ जाना go beyond a prescribed or generally accepted limit. *Don't overstep or I will have to do complain against you.*

Overstock/ओवरस्टॉक *(verb)* – अति संग्रह करना stock with more than is necessary or required. put more animals in than it is capable of supporting in terms of food or space. *Most of the godowns are overstocked this year.*

Oversupply/ओवरसप्लाई *(noun)* – माँग से अधिक पूर्ति an excessive supply. *The oversupply of food grains has led the prices to go down.*

Overtax/ओवरटैक्स *(verb)* – बहुत अधिक कर लगाना tax excessively. *In India, an average man is overtaxed.*

Overtly/ओवर्टली *(adverb)* – प्रत्यक्ष रूप से done openly. *This man is prone to talk with an overtly bold way.*

Overtone/ओवरटोन *(noun)* – फोटो के चित्र में गहरा रंग डालना a musical tone which is a part of the harmonic series above a fundamental note, and may be heard with it. *Overtone is a frequency that is more than the fundamental frequency.*

Overtrade/ओवरट्रेड *(verb)* – पूँजी से अधिक व्यापार करना engage in more trade than that can be supported by market or resources. *The businessman is inclined to overtrade to get more profits.*

Overturn/ओवरटर्न *(verb)* – नष्ट करना turn over or cause to turn over and come to rest upside down. *The driver hit the pole and his car overturned.*

Overvaluation/ओवरवैल्युशन *(noun)* – अधिक मूल्यांकन overestimate the importance of. *Overvaluation of anything or anyone does no good, so it should be avoided.*

Overvalue/ओवरवैलू *(verb)* – बहुत अधिक दाम लगाना overestimate the importance of. *Don't overvalue them too much.*

Overwatch/ओवरवाच *(verb)* – अधिक चौकसी करना to watch exceedingly. *He was assigned the duty to overwatch the activities of his neighbours.*

Overweight/ओवरवेट *(adjective)* – अधिक भारी above a normal, desirable, or permitted weight. *The overweight lady was finding it difficult to climb the stairs.*

Overworn/ओवरवर्न *(adj)* – बहुत थका हुआ worn out. *The overworn man fainted on the road.*

Overzeal/ओवरजील *(noun)* – बहुत अधिक जोश too zealons. *She was overzeal to go abroad.*

Ovicular/अविक्युलर *(adj)* – अण्डे से सम्बन्धित pertaining to an egg. *The teacher explained the ovicular mechanism at a great length.*

Ovine/ओवाइन *(adjective)* – भेड़ के समान of, relating to, affecting, or resembling sheep. *She was made fun due to her ovine facial features.*

Oviparous/ओविपरस *(adjective)* – अण्डों से बच्चे पैदा करने वाला producing young by means of eggs which are hatched after they have been laid by the parent, as in birds. compare with viviparous and oviparous. *Snake is an oviparous animal.*

Oviposit/ओविपॉजिट *(verb)* – अण्डा देना zoology lay an egg or eggs. *The hen was ovipositing at the time it was shifted to another cell.*

Owing/ओइंग *(adjective)* – दातव्य yet to be paid or supplied. *Please pay the owing amount.*

Owl/ऑउल *(noun)* – उल्लू nocturnal bird of prey with large eyes, a hooked beak, and typically a loud hooting call. *An owl is a nocturnal bird.*

Own/ओन *(adjective & pronoun)* – अपना belonging or relating to the person specified. done or produced by the person specified. particular to the person or thing specified; individual. *All the property that he has rented is his own*

Owner/ओनर *(noun)* – स्वामी a person who owns somethings. *The owner of this building lives in Canada.*

Ox /ऑक्स *(noun)* – बैल a domesticated bovine animal kept for milk or meat; a cow or bull, see also cattle. used in names of wild animals

O

related to or resembling this, e.g. musk ox. a castrated bull, especially as a draught animal. *The farmer has kept an ox that he uses as a draught animal.*

Oxford/ऑक्सफोर्ड *(noun)* – इंग्लैण्ड के प्रसिद्ध विश्वविद्यालय का नगर a type of lace-up shoe with a low heel. *He preferred wearing oxford on every occasion.*

Oxonian/ऑक्सोनियन *(adjective)* – ऑक्सफोर्ड विश्वविद्यालय का छात्र of or relating to oxford or oxford university. *The Oxonian degree keeps a high value.*

Oxygen/ऑक्सीजन *(noun)* – प्राणवायु the chemical element of atomic number 8, a colourless, odourless reactive gas that forms about 20 percent of the earth's atmosphere and is essential to plant and animal life. *All living beings require oxygen to live.*

Oxygenate/आक्सीजनेट *(verb)* – प्राणवायु से पूर्ण करना supply, treat, charge, or enrich with oxygen. *The dying plants in room need to be oxygenated.*

Oxygon/ऑक्सिगन् *(noun)* – दो न्यून-कोण का त्रिभुज an oxygon is a triangle with two acute angles. *Draw an oxygon on this paper.*

Oxyphonia/ऑक्सिफोनिया *(noun)* – कर्कश उच्चारण harshness of voice. *She used to sing with an irritating oxyphonia.*

Oyster/ऑइस्टर् *(noun)* – सीप, घोंघा a bivalve marine mollusk with a rough, flattened, irregularly oval shell, several kinds of which are farmed for food or pearls. *She is very fond of eating oysters.*

Ozone/ओज़ोन *(noun)* – बिजली पैदा करने वाले यन्त्र से उत्पन्न हुई ठोस प्राणवायु an unstable, pungent, toxic form of oxygen with three atoms in its molecule, formed in electrical discharges or by ultraviolet light. *The ozone layer developed a hole as it got exposed to the ultra-violet rays.*

O

Pp

P/पी *(noun)* – अंग्रेजी वर्णमाला का सोलहवाँ वर्ण the sixteenth letter of the English alphabet.

1. denoting the next after o in a set of items, categories, etc.

Pa/पा *(noun)* – बच्चों के बोली में पापा का संक्षिप्त रूप a single step taken when walking or running. *With each pace, we were nearing the gates of the haunted house.*

Pace/पेस *(noun)* – कदम, गति, विकास की गति a single step taken when walking or running. *With each pace, we were nearing the gates of the haunted house.*

Pacific/पैसिफिक *(adjective)* – शान्तिप्रिय peaceful in character or intent. *The pacific nature of the leaders is the reason behind justice prevailing in the State.*

Pacify/पैसिफाइ *(verb)* – शान्ति स्थापित करना quell the anger or agitation of. *Somehow we managed to pacify the angry crowd that had collected at his shop.*

Pack/पैक *(noun)* – बेचा हुआ सामान, डिब्बा, समूह a cardboard or paper container and the items contained within it. *The toys were rattling inside the pack noisily.*

Package/पैकेज *(noun)* – डिब्बा, पुलिन्दा, प्रस्ताव का मुह an object or group of objects wrapped in paper or packed in a box, a packet. *The package was nicely covered so no one could guess what was inside.*

Packet/पैकेट *(noun)* – डिब्बा, पुलिन्दा a paper or cardboard container. *They were trying to pack all the groceries into one packet.*

Packing/पैकिंग *(noun)* – डिब्बे में भरना material used to protect fragile goods in transit. *The instrument was covered with safe packing so it would reach safely.*

Pact/पैक्ट *(noun)* – समझौता a formal agreement between individuals or parties. *The countries drew a pact to work towards saving and nurturing the environment.*

Pad/पैड *(noun)* – सुरक्षा के लिए नीचे रखा साधन a thick piece of soft or absorbent material. *We covered the wound with a pad so it would heal fast.*

Paddle/पैडल *(noun)* – चप्पू चलाना a short pole with a broad blade at one or both ends, used to move a small boat or canoe through the water. *We were terrified when the paddles fell from our hands into the water.*

Paddy/पैडी *(noun)* – धान rice that has not been processed in any way and is still in its husk. *I like to see paddy crops in the field.*

Padlock/पैडलॉक *(noun)* – ताला लगाना a detachable lock hanging by a pivoted hook on the object fastened. *Ever since the thieves struck, we have been extra careful to lock the main doors with padlocks.*

Paediatrician/पैडियाट्रिसियन *(noun)* – बाल रोग विशेषज्ञ चिकित्सक medical practitioner specialishing in children another disease. *She took her baby to the paediatrician when the fever did not comedown with a tablet.*

Pagan/पैगन *(noun)* – विधर्मी a person holding religious beliefs other than those of the main world religions. *The Church declared him an atheist when he told them he was a pagan.*

Page/पेज *(noun)* – किताब, अखबार के पृष्ठ, सन्देश देना, परिचालक one side of a leaf of a book, magazine, or newspaper, or the material written or printed on it. *He folded page after page though he understood nothing of what was written there.*

Pageant/पेजन्ट *(noun)* – विशेष समारोह में शोभायात्रा an entertainment consisting of a procession of people in elaborate costumes, or an outdoor performance of a [historical] scene. *The group organized pageants in the* villages to educate them about the history of their country.

Pail/पेल् *(noun)* – बाल्टी, डोल a bucket. *Jack and Jill went up the hill to fetch a pail of water.*

Pain/पेन् *(noun)* – पीड़ा, वेदना a strongly unpleasant bodily sensation such as is caused by illness or injury. *She was already in immense pain by the time the doctor arrived.*

Painful/पेन्फुल *(adjective)* – पीड़ादायी affected with or causing pain. *She was a painful character to associate with.*

Painless/पेन्लेस *(adjective)* – पीड़ारहित not causing physical pain. *There is now a painless war in Iraq.*

Paint/पेंट *(noun)* – रंग, रंगना a substance which is spread over a surface and dries to leave a thin decorative or protective coating. *The fence required at least two coats of paint.*

Painter/पेंटर *(noun)* – रंगने वाला, चित्रकार an artist who paints pictures. *Though he is an engineer by profession, he is also an excellent painter.*

Painting/पेंटिंग *(noun)* – रंगाई the action or process of painting. *He sat in the garden all day painting the trees and birds around.*

Pair/पेअर *(noun)* – जोड़ा a set of two similar things considered as a unit. *I am in a need of a pair of shoes.*

Pal/पॉल *(noun)* – साथी a friend. *Dhanya was my best pal in school.*

Palace/पैलेस *(noun)* – महान् a large, impressive building forming the official residence of a sovereign, president, archbishop, etc. *The Buckingham Palace is indeed one of the greatest tourist attractions in UK.*

Palatable/पैलेटेबल *(adjective)* – स्वादिष्ट, रुचिकर pleasant to taste. *I suggested that she should add some more salt to her curry to make it palatable.*

Palate/पैलेट *(noun)* – तालु the roof of the mouth, separating the cavities of the mouth and nose in vertebrates. *Cleft palate is a common disability where the nose or lips do not form properly.*

Palatial/पैलेसियल *(adjective)* – विशाल, भव्य, महल जैसा resembling a palace, especially in being spacious or grand. *She owns a palatial house in Beverly Hills.*

Pale/पेल *(adjective)* – विवर्ण, निस्तेज, पीला चेहरा, खूँटा-खूँटी containing little colour or pigment; light in colour or shade. having little colour, typically as a result of shock, fear, or ill health. *She was pale with fever when the doctor came to see her.*

Palette/पैलेट *(noun)* – रंग पट्टिका, रंग मिलाने की तश्तरी an artist's tablet for mixing colours. *Browns greens and blues are typical of leonardo da vinci's palette.*

Pall/पाल *(noun)* – अरुचिकर हो जाना, कफन, काला आवरण a cloth spread over a coffin, hearse, or tomb. *The unappealing sight of his death seemed to have been turned into a beauty thanks to the exquisiteness of the pall spread on his coffin.*

Pallid/पैलिड *(adjective)* – बीमारी के कारण मंद पड़ना pale, especially because of poor health. *The pallid face of the invalid tore my heart.*

Pallor/पैलर *(noun)* – बीमारी या भय से पीला पड़ना an unhealthy pale appearance. *She stood in the driveway of our garage with swollen eyes, mangled hair and an eerie pallor on her face.*

Palm/पाम *(noun)* – हथेली, हाथ की सफाई, ताड़-खजूर के पेड़ an unbranched evergreen tree with a crown of very long feathered or fan-shaped leaves, growing in tropical and warm regions. *The beach was lined with beautiful palms.*

Palmist/पामिस्ट *(noun)* – हस्तरेखा विशेषज्ञ Fortuneteller who predicts your future by the lines on your palms. *Desperate to know if the astrologer's predictions were believable, we decided to take a second opinion from the palmist who lived across the street.*

Palpable/पैल्पेबल् *(adjective)* – सुस्पष्ट, जिसे देखा या अनुभव किया जाये able to be touched or felt. *The liver, spleen and kidneys are not palpable, said the doctor.*

Palpitate/पॉल्पिटेट् *(verb)* – कँपकँपाना, धड़कन तेज होना beat rapidly, strongly, or irregularly. *The air in the room seemed to palpitate with the deep fear that inflicted the children trapped there.*

Palsy/पॉल्जि *(noun)* – जोड़ों में दर्द, चलने में कठिनाई dated paralysis, especially when accompanied by involuntary tremors. *He could not finish the painting as his actions were frequently disturbed by his palsy.*

Paltry/पाल्ट्रि *(adjective)* – नगण्य, तुच्छ बहुत कम very small or meager. *Sadly, what she received as a reward was a paltry sum in comparison to the amount her rival received.*

Pamper/पैम्पर *(verb)* – अत्यधिक लाड़-प्यार indulge with a great deal of attention and comfort; spoil. *The younger sibling is always more pampered.*

Pamphlet/पैम्फलेट *(noun)* – पर्चा, पुस्तिका a small booklet or leaflet containing information or arguments about a single subject. *We had kept several pamphlets talking about the features of the product, at the counter.*

Pamphleteer/पैम्फलेटियर *(noun)* – पर्चा लिखना, पर्चा-पुस्तिका से प्रचार a native or inhabitant of the ancient region of pamphylia in southern Asia Minor. *The people of Pamphylia are called Pamphylians, and not Pamphleteers. Pamphleteers are those who distribute or prepare pamphlets.*

Pan/पैन *(noun)* – कड़ाह, कड़ाही, तसला, पलड़ा (उपसर्ग) a metal container for cooking food in. *She made the curry in a beautiful non-stick pan.*

Panacea/पैनेसिया *(noun)* – सब रोगों की दवा, रामबाण दवा a solution or remedy for all difficulties or disease. *Eating chocolates is no panacea for your mental issues.*

Pancake/पैनकेक *(noun)* – मैदा, दूध, अण्डा आदि मिलाकर बनाया पुआ a thin, flat cake of batter, fried and turned in a pan and typically rolled up with a sweet or savoury filling. *My aunt made chocolate and banana pancakes for tea.*

Panda/पन्डा *(noun)* – मटर जैसा सफेद और काले रंग का एक जानवर a large bear-like black-and-white mammal native to bamboo forests in china. *There was a time when China was the land of pandas.*

Pandemonium/पैन्डिमोनियम *(noun)* – हुड़दंग, हुल्लड़, कोलाहल, अफरा-तफरी wild and noisy disorder or confusion; uproar. *The sisters had created such a pandemonium, their neighbours were worried.*

Pander/पैन्डर *(verb)* – लोभवश – सहायता या प्रोत्साहन gratify or indulge. *He refuses to ponder to his boss's demand.*

Pane/पेन *(noun)* – जंगला का एक भाग, खिड़की का शीशा a single sheet of glass in a window or door. *He hit a flying sixer and the next moment we heard the crash of the window pane!*

Panel/पैनल *(noun)* – पल्ले का डिल्ला, पट्टी, नामित सूची a distinct section, typically rectangular, forming part of or set into a door, vehicle, garment, etc. a decorated area within a larger design containing a separate subject. *I suggested that the architect consider a separate panel on the wall to place the telephone and other accessories.*

Pang/पैंग *(noun)* – दर्द, टीस, कसक a sudden sharp pain or painful emotion. *I felt a sudden pang of guilt and pain in my heart when I heard her confession.*

Panic/पैनिक *(noun)* – भगदड़, अफरा-तफरी, तहलका sudden uncontrollable fear or anxiety. [informal] frenzied hurry to do something. *She panicked when the tremors started,* *(verb)* be affected by or cause to feel panic. drive someone through panic into hasty or rash action. *People fled in panic as the fire spread.*

Panorama/पैनॉरामा *(noun)* – बड़ा परिदृश्य an unbroken view of a surrounding region. *We were asked to climb to a certain point about 200 meters higher than our current altitude in order to get a panoramic view of the mountains.*

Pansy/पैन्जि *(noun)* – फूल, पौधा, गुलबकावली जैसा फूल a viola with flowers in rich colours, especially of a cultivated variety. *The garden was blooming with pansies of all kinds and colours.*

Pant/पैंट *(verb)* – हाँफना, साँस फूलना, एक वस्त्र breathe with short, quick breaths, typically from exertion or excitement. long for or to do something. *She came up the stairs, panting in excitement and stress, eager to see her brother waiting at the door.*

P

Panther/पैन्थर *(noun)* – तेंदुआ a leopard, especially a black one. *Bagheera is the name of the panther in The Jungle Book.*

Panties/पैन्टिज *(plural noun)* – स्त्रियों की जांघिया [informal] legless underpants worn by women and girls; knickers. *She had folded and kept her panties neatly in a pile in the drawer.*

Pantomime/पैंटोमाइम *(noun)* – नकल करना, मूक अभिनय, हास्य अभिनय के नकल British a theatrical entertainment involving music, topical jokes, and slapstick comedy, usually produced around Christmas. *The students organized a pantomime for their Annual School Day celebrations around Christmas.*

Pantry/पैन्ट्री *(noun)* – रसोई, रसोई भण्डार a small room or cupboard in which food, crockery, and cutlery are kept. *My father's hunger grew stronger at the mere sight of the delicious food being cooked in the pantry car next to his coach.*

Pants/पैंट्स *(plural noun)* – पतलून, निकर British underpants or knickers. *The kid's mother took him to the lavatory and instructed him to take off his pants on his own without her help.*

Papa/पापा *(noun)* – बच्चों द्वारा प्रयुक्त पिता के लिए सम्बोधन [north American] or dated one's father. *We wanted to wait for Papa to arrive, before we started dinner.*

Papaya/पपाया *(noun)* – पपीता a fruit shaped like an elongated melon, with edible orange flesh and small black seeds. *The doctor advised her to stick to a papaya diet to have a detox effect.*

Paper/पेपर *(noun)* – कागज, दस्तावेज, समाचार पत्र, प्रश्न material manufactured in thin sheets from the pulp of wood or other fibrous substance, used for writing or printing on or as wrapping material, sheets of paper covered with writing or printing; documents. officially documented but having no real existence or use: a paper profit. *When the document did not print, I checked the printer and realized that the printing paper had finished.*

Par/पार *(noun)* – अन्य के बराबर golf the number of strokes a first-class player should normally require for a particular hole or course. a score of this number of strokes at a hole. *They were late again, but that's par for the course.*

Parable/पैरबल् *(noun)* – दृष्टान्त, दृष्टान्त कथा, नीति कथा a simple story used to illustrate a moral or spiritual lesson. *We were all asked to narrate a parable each at the storytelling session.*

Parachute/पैराशूट *(noun)* – हवाई छतरी, हवाई जहाज से नीचे उतरने का साधन a cloth canopy which fills with air and allows a person or heavy object attached to it to descend slowly when dropped from a high position, especially in an aircraft. *We saw a parachute descending from a distance and realized it's a sky diver.*

Parade/परेड *(noun)* – सैन्य-प्रशिक्षण, जुलूस a public procession, especially one celebrating a special day or event. *The city was lit up and the colourful parade made its way from Central Park to the farthest corner of the city where it ends.*

Paradise/पैराडाइज *(noun)* – स्वर्ग, वाटिका, शान्ति स्थल heaven as the ultimate abode of the just. the garden of Eden. *The Father said there was a place for all of us in Paradise.*

Paradox/पैराडॉक्स *(noun)* – विरोधाभास, विरोधी गुण a seemingly absurd or self-contradictory statement or proposition that may in fact be true. an apparently sound statement or proposition which leads to a logically unacceptable conclusion. *He presented a paradoxical situation for us to evaluate, so we would know both extremes.*

Paraffin/पैराफिन *(noun)* – मिट्टी तेल, कोयले आदि से प्राप्त तेल a flammable waxy solid obtained by distilling petroleum or shale and used for sealing and waterproofing and in candles. *In the candle-making class, we were taught to work with paraffin wax.*

Paragon/पैरागन *(noun)* – आदर्श व्यक्ति या वस्तु a person or thing regarded as a model of excellence or of a particular quality. *He is a paragon of excellence for all of us to follow.*

Paragraph/पैराग्राफ *(noun)* – अनुच्छेद, लेख आदि का विभाजन a distinct section of a piece of writing. indicated by a new line, indentation, or numbering. *There were too many paragraphs in her prose. (verb)* arrange

P

in paragraphs. *The teacher asked us to paragraph these lengthy statements to make a single story.*

Parallel/पैरॅलल *(adjective)* – समानान्तर, समकक्ष, समतुल्य side by side and having the same distance continuously between them. *The roads were parallel to one another and hence reached simultaneously.*

Parallelogram/पैरॅलेलॅग्रैम् *(noun)* – समानान्तर चतुर्भुज a four-sided plane rectilinear figure with opposite sides parallel. *The mathematics teacher explained how to construct a parallelogram to the class.*

Paralyse/पैरालाइज *(verb)* – लकवा मारना cause to become incapable of movement. *The accident caused her to be paralysed below the waist.*

Paralysis/पैरालाइसिस *(noun)* – लकवा, पक्षाघात the loss of the ability to move part or most of the body. *Her paralysis, after the accident, brought down her self esteem.*

Paramilitary/पैरामिलिटरी *(adjective)* – अर्द्धसैनिक बल organized on similar lines to a military force. *The government ordered the paramilitary forces to act as a last resort attack against the terrorists.* *(noun)* a member of a paramilitary organization. *We were told that the late officer had served as a chivalrous soldier in the paramilitary during the 26/11 attacks.*

Paramount/पैरामाउन्ट *(adjective)* – अत्यधिक महत्त्वपूर्ण, सर्वोच्च more important than anything else; supreme. *Taking over the prime minister's seat was of paramount importance to him.*

Paranoia/पैरॅनीऑं/पैरानिआ *(noun)* – भ्रान्ति, मानसिक रोगी की क्षति a mental condition characterized by delusions of persecution, unwarranted jealousy, or exaggerated self-importance. *Post the accident, she had paranoia for a long time especially when she sat in a car.*

Parapet/पैरापिट *(noun)* – मुण्डेर, दोनों ओर की नीची दीवाल a low protective wall along the edge of a roof, bridge, or balcony. *The thief hid on the parapet all night which is why he could not be caught.*

Paraphernalia/पैराफर्नेलिआ *(noun)* – साज-समान, उपकरण miscellaneous articles, especially the equipment needed for a particular activity. *The photographers gathered their paraphernalia and moved to the next location.*

Paraphrase/पैराफ्रेज *(verb)* – अन्वय, कथन का शब्दान्तर express the meaning of using different words, especially to achieve greater clarity. *The editor asked me to paraphrase the poem to suit the author's tastes.* *(noun)* a rewording of a passage. *The write-up was actually a paraphrased version of a famous poem.*

Parasite/पैरासाइट *(noun)* – परजीवी, दूसरे पर भोजन हेतु आश्रित an organism which lives in or on another organism and benefits by deriving nutrients at the other's expense. *The disease is caused by single-celled parasites that multiply in the human blood stream.*

Paratroops/पैराटूप्स *(plural noun)* – वायुयान से कूदने हेतु सैनिक troops equipped to be dropped by parachute from aircraft. *The army instructed the paratroops to be released into the building slowly.*

Parcel/पार्शल *(noun)* – बँधा सामान, भेजा जाने वाला डिब्बा an object or collection of objects wrapped in paper in order to be carried or sent by post. *I received a parcel by courier this morning.*

Parch/पार्च *(verb)* – सूखना, झुलसना make or become dry through intense heat. roast lightly. *The earth was parched and so were we.*

Parchment/पार्चमेंट *(noun)*– लेखन-पत्र कागज के स्थान पर प्रयुक्त हेतु a stiff material made from the prepared skin of a sheep or goat, formerly used as a writing surface. *The sage had written a message in a parchment.*

Pardon/पार्डन् *(noun & verb)* – क्षमा, क्षमा करना, खेद प्रकट करना the action of forgiving or being forgiven for an error of offence. *The jury agreed in unison that the criminal should not be given pardon.*

Parent/पेरेन्ट *(noun)* – माता-पिता, जिससे अन्य उत्पन्न हों वे पेड़-पौधे a father or mother. an animal or plant from which younger ones are derived. *All the students were asked to inform their parents about the meeting.*

Parenthesis/पैरेन्थेसिस *(noun)* – वाक्यांश अलग करना, कोष्ठक a word or phrase inserted as an explanation or after-thought, in writing usually marked off by brackets, dashes, or commas. *We had to memorize the parenthesis along with the formulae for the exam.*

Pariah/पेरिआ *(noun)* – अछूत, चण्डाल an outcast. *As I left the village, I came across a group of pariahs waiting to see me.*

Parish/पैरिश *(noun)* – स्थानीय, चर्च और पादरी वाला गाँव a small administrative district with its own church and clergy. *All the members of the parish had gathered at the Church for the baptism ritual.*

Parity/पैरिटि *(noun)* – समानता, सममूल्यता equality or equivalence, especially as regards status, pay, or value. *The target to achieve parity could not be reached.*

Park/पार्क *(noun)* – उद्यान, सार्वजनिक उद्यान, वाहन स्थान a large public garden in a town, used for recreation. *The kids love playing in the park every evening.*

Parka/पर्का *(noun)* – टोपी सहित गरम वस्त्र a large windproof hooded jacket for use in cold weather. *She ensured that we were all wearing our parkas before skiing.*

Park/पार्क *(noun & verb)* – गाड़ी खड़ी करना, गाड़ी खड़ी करने का स्थान an area devoted to an specified purpose. *We saw the parking meters and parked our car there.*

Parley/पार्लि *(noun)* – सन्धि-बैठक, मैत्री सभा, सन्धिवार्ता a conference between opposing sides in a dispute, especially regarding an armistice. *Unfortunately, the parley yielded little results.* *(verb)* hold a parley. *The ministers finally decided to hold a parley to discuss all the issues.*

Parliament/पार्लियामेण्ट *(noun)* – संसद, संसद भवन the highest legislature, consisting of the sovereign, the house of lords, and the house of commons. the members of this legislature for the period between dissolutions. *The Parliament is in a constant state of chaos in our country.*

Parlour/पार्लर *(noun)* – विशेष सेवा या सामान की दुकान dated a sitting room in a private house. *We were asked to wait in the parlour for the VIP to arrive.*

Parochial/पैरोकिअल *(adjective)* – संकुचित, सीमित, सिकुड़ा हुआ of or relating to a church parish. *The parochial clergy was to be elected soon.*

Parody/पैरोडी *(noun)* – किसी कृति या व्यक्ति की नकल an imitation of the style of a particular writer, artist, or genre with deliberate exaggeration for comic effect. *The children had prepared a parody of the latest movie for the Annual Day function.*

Parole/पेरोल *(noun)* – अच्छे आचरण पर संक्षिप्त रिहाई the temporary or permanent release of a prisoner before the expiry of a sentence, on the promise of good behavior. *The town was living in fear ever since the news broke out of the criminal being out on parole.*

Parsimony/पार्सिमनि *(noun)* – मितव्यय, कम खर्च करना extreme unwillingness to spend money or use resources. *Such parsimony may help you cross this stage of financial crisis.*

Parsley/पार्सलि *(noun)* – पुदीना जैसा पौधा a plant with white flowers and crinkly or flat leaves used as a culinary herb and garnish. *You may garnish the pasta with some chopped parsley.*

Parsnip/पार्सनिप *(noun)* – गाजर-चुकन्दर जैसी सब्जी long tapering cream-coloured root with a sweet flavour. *We wanted Mother to make something with parsnip for dinner today.*

Parson/पार्सन *(noun)* – पादरी, ईसाई पुजारी a beneficed member of the Anglican clergy; a rector or vicar. [informal] any clergyman, especially a protestant one. *The parson was called to fix the date of the engagement and decide the availability of the Chapel.*

Part/पार्ट *(noun)* – हिस्सा, विभाग, टुकड़ा, भूमिका, अलग होना a piece or segment of something which combined with others makes up the whole. a component of a machine: aircraft parts. *All the parts combined make a whole.*

Partial/पार्सियल *(adjective)* – आंशिक, पक्षपात, पक्षपातपूर्ण existing only in part; incomplete. *A partial solar eclipse was visible in India.*

Participate/पार्टिसिपेट *(verb)* – भाग लेना, भागीदार बनाना, सहभागी take part. *Everybody had a chance to participate in the function.*

Participle/पार्टिसिपल् *(noun)* – कृदन्त प्रत्यय, क्रिया-रूप grammar a word formed from a verb and used as an adjective or noun or used to make compound verb forms. *We were asked to identify the participle in the given sentences in the exam.*

Particle/पार्टिकल *(noun)* – कण, अति लघु अंश a minute portion of matter. *The tiny particles floating in the air in the room made us sneeze constantly.*

Particular/पार्टिकुलर *(adjective)* – व्यक्ति विशेष से सम्बन्धित, सावधान denoting an individual member of a specified group or class. *It was a particular child in the class that she had been talking about for the past one hour, I finally realized.*

Parting/पार्टिंग *(noun)* – वियोग, अलगाव the action of moving away or being separated from someone. *To see the couple parting was a painful sight.*

Partisan/पार्टिजन *(noun)* – पक्का हिमायती, अन्ध भक्त an adherent of a party. *Most newspaper are politically partisan.*

Partition/पार्टिसन *(noun)* – विभाजन the action or state of dividing or being divided into parts. *The country's partition was the most tragic event in its history.*

Partner/पार्टनर *(noun)* – भागीदार a person who takes part in an undertaking with another or others, especially in a business or firm with shared risks and profits. *Both the husband and wife were equal partners in their family business.*

Partridge/पार्ट्रिज *(noun)* – तीतर a short-tailed game bird with mainly brown plumage. *I was surprised to see so many partridges in the farm.*

Party/पार्टि *(noun)* – दल, राजनीतिक दल, टोली a social gathering of invited guests, typically involving eating, drinking, and entertainment. *We decided to organize a surprise birthday party for our father.*

Pass/पास *(noun)* – बढ़ जाना, आगे बढ़ना, गुजरना, हाथों-हाथ देना, हस्तान्तरण, दूसरे की ओर बढ़ाना, दशा में परिवर्तन, समाप्त होना, परखकर स्वीकृत, अनुमोदन, स्वीकार करना, दर्रा a route over or through mountains. *The pass was closed owing to incessant snowing in the mountains.*

Passable/पासेबल् *(adjective)* – जिसे पार किया जा सके good enough to be acceptable. *The last of the ten points she kept was the only passable one.*

Passage/पैसिज *(noun)* – आर-पार का मार्ग, पार करने की प्रशंसा, पार गमन, गलियारा a riding movement in which a horse executes a slow elevated trot, giving the impression of dancing. *Black Beauty was known for performing the most superior passage in the whole series.*

Passbook/पासबुक *(noun)* – लेखा-पुस्तिका a book issued by a bank or building society to an account holder, recording transactions. *My passbook was overflowing with entries, so the officer issued another one.*

Passenger/पैसेन्जर *(noun)* – यात्री, दल में कामचोर व्यक्ति a traveller on a public or private conveyance other than the driver, pilot, or crew. *The passengers beat up the eve-teaser and kicked him out of the bus.*

Passing/पासिंग *(adjective)* – बहुत कम समय के लिए, गुजरने की प्रक्रिया going past. *The band was passing by the crowd and everybody cheered.*

Passion/पैशन् *(noun)* – आवेग, आवेश, तीव्र यौन-आकर्षण, उत्साह strong and barely controllable emotion. an outburst of such emotion. *He screamed at her passionately.*

Passionate/पैशनेट् *(adjective)* – कामुकता पूर्ण, कामुक, भावावेश पूर्ण showing or caused by passion. *She was very passionate about travelling.*

Passive/पैसिव *(adjective)* – आवेग का अभाव, निश्चेष्टा, निष्क्रिय accepting or allowing what happens or what others do, without active response or resistance. *We were urged to rise from our passive state and start acting!*

Passport/पासपोर्ट *(noun)* – पारपत्र, विदेश यात्रा का आदेश पत्र an official document issued by a government, certifying the holder's identity and citizenship and entitling them to travel abroad under its protection. *I showed the officer my passport so that I could board the flight fast.*

P

Password/पासवर्ड (noun) – अवरोध निवारक गुप्त शब्द a secret word or phrase used to gain admission to something. *I had written the password somewhere so that I do not forget it but I think I should have revealed it to my mother at least.*

Past/पास्ट (adjective) – अतीत, भूतकाल, बीता हुआ समय gone by in time and no longer existing. recently elapsed: the past twelve months. *I had been waiting for the past two hours.*

Pasta/पैस्टा (noun) – आटे, अण्डे और जल से बना एक खाद्य पदार्थ dough extruded or stamped into various shapes. for cooking in boiling water and eating, typically with a savoury sauce. *The chef prepared the best pasta I had ever had.*

Paste/पेस्ट (noun) – लेई, गीला आटा, मिश्रण, चिपकाना a thick, soft, moist substance, typically produced by mixing dry ingredients with a liquid. *We made a loose paste before adding coconut to it.*

Pasteboard/पेस्टबोर्ड (noun) – कोई सूचना चिपकाने की तख्ती thin board made by pasting together sheets of paper. *The pasteboard was full, so we needed another board.*

Pastel/पैस्टेल (noun) – मुलायम रंगीन खड़िया, हल्का कोमल रंग a crayon made of powdered pigments bound with gum or resin. a work of art created using pastels. *I bought her a packet of pastel colours as she loved art and colouring.*

Pasteurize/पैस्ट्युराइज (verb) – गरम करके कीटाणु रहित करना subject to a process of partial sterilization, especially by heating. *I have started ordering pasteurized milk.*

Pastime/पास्टाइम (noun) – आमोद-प्रमोद, मनोरंजन का समय an activity that someone does regularly for enjoyment; a hobby. *Television is not the best pastime for a child.*

Pastor/पास्टर (noun) – ईसाईयों के पुरोहित, पुजारी a minister in charge of a Christian church or congregation, especially in some non-Episcopal churches. *We felt blessed as our neighbour was a pastor!* (verb) be the pastor of. *He became the pastor of St Francis' Church shortly.*

Pastry/पेस्ट्री (noun) – गोल-लम्बा मीठा या नमकीन खाद्य a dough of flour, fat, and water, used as a base and covering in baked dishes such as pies. *Ma taught me how to bake the pastry-base for pie.*

Pasture/पास्चर (noun) – चरागाह, पशुओं का चरना land covered mainly with grass, suitable for grazing cattle or sheep. *The cows and buffaloes were having the time of their life in the pasture.*

Pastures/पास्चर्स (noun) – परिस्थितियाँ a persons situation in life. *She resigned the job for pastures new.*

Pasty/पेस्टी (noun) – चिपचिपा, चिपचिपाहट वाला [chiefly British] a folded pastry cake filled with seasoned meat and vegetables. *I loved the beef pasty she made for tea the other day.*

Pat/पैट (verb) – पीठ थपथपाना, सफलता पर प्रशंसा करना touch quickly and gently with the flat of the hand. *Dogs always love a pat on the head.*

Patch/पैच् (noun) – पैबन्द, जमीन का छोटा टुकड़ा, पैबन्द लगाना a piece of material used to cover a torn or weak point. a shield worn over a sightless or injured eye. a piece of cloth sewn on to clothing as a badge. an adhesive piece of drug impregnated material worn on the skin so that the drug may be gradually absorbed. [historical] a small black silk disc worn on the face, especially by woman in the 17th and 18th centuries. *She covered the injured eye with a patch of cloth.*

Patchwork/पैचवर्क (noun) – छोटे टुकड़े जोड़कर बनाया हुआ needlework in which small pieces of cloth in different designs are sewn together. *She made a patchwork bag and it looked quite cool.*

Patchy/पैची (adjective) – पैबन्द चुल, आसमान गुण या स्तर वाला existing or happening in small, isolated areas. *She had sewn me patchy trousers.*

Patent/पैटेन्ट (noun) – स्पष्ट, साफ, एकत्व अधिकार, एकत्व का अधिकार लेना a government license to an individual or body conferring a right or title for a set period, especially the sole right to make, use, or sell an invention. *She was*

P

an acclaimed scientist who had patents on six discoveries.

Paternal/पैटरनल *(adjective)* – पैतृक of or appropriate to a father. *His paternal instincts were aroused when he saw his child walking on the wrong track.*

Paternity/पैटरनिटी *(noun)* – पितृत्व the state of being someone's father. *He did not accept claims of his paternity easily.*

Path/पाथ *(noun)* – मार्ग, पथ, पगडण्डी a way or track laid down for walking or made by continual treading. *There was a well laid out walking path in the park.*

Pathetic/पैथेटिक *(adjective)* – दयनीय, कारुणिक arousing pity, especially through vulnerability or sadness. *The pathetic state of existence of the tramp brought tears to her eyes.*

Pathological/पैथलॉजिकल *(adjective)* – रोग-विज्ञान से सम्बन्धित, आधारहीन involving, caused by, or of the nature of a disease. *Her disease was diagnosed as pathological.*

Pathology/पैथलॉजी *(noun)* – रोग-विज्ञान the branch of [medicine] concerned with the causes and effects of disease. *The head of the pathology department is now voted to take over as the dean of the university.*

Pathos/पैथॉस *(noun)* – कारुणिकता a quality that evokes pity or sadness. *Khalil Gibran's writings involve a lot of pathos.*

Patience/पेसेंस *(noun)* – सहनशीलता, धैर्य, ताश का एक खेल the capacity to tolerate delay, trouble, or suffering without becoming angry or upset. *Living in those terrible conditions was testing my patience.*

Patient/पेसेंट *(adjective)* – मरीज, रोगी having or showing patience. *She has always been extremely patient with her son.* *(noun)* a person receiving or registered to receive medical treatment. *She has been a patient in this hospital for the last two weeks.*

Patriarch/पैट्रियार्क *(noun)* – परिवार या कबीले का मुखिया the male head of a family or tribe. an older man who is powerful within a family or organization. a founder. *He was the undefiable patriarch of the royal family.*

Patroit/पैट्रिअट *(noun)* – देशभक्त a person who vigorously supports his country and is prepared to defend it. *Shaheed Bhagat Singh was a patriot who laid down his life for the country.*

Patriotic/पैट्रिअटिक *(adverb)* – देशभक्ति पूर्ण one who is filled with sense of nationalism. *The patriotic song that my friend sang in the School Assembly aroused tears in everyone's eyes.*

Patrol/पट्रोल/पेट्रोल *(noun)* – गश्त लगाना a person or group sent to keep watch over an area, especially a detachment of guards or police. *The patrol kept watch over the hotel that was under hijack.*

Patron/पेट्रन *(noun)* – संरक्षक a person who gives financial or other support to a person, organization, cause, etc. *My brother has been a patron of our organization for several years.*

Patronage/पेट्रोनेज *(noun)* – संरक्षण और समर्थन the support given by a patron. *We thanked the president and the Trustee for their patronage to our institution.*

Patronize/पेट्रनाइज *(verb)* – संरक्षक बनना, नियमित ग्राहक बनना treat with an apparent kindness which betrays a feeling of superiority. *Though I was grateful for his contribution to our institution, I detested his patronizing attitude.*

Pattern/पैटर्न *(noun)* – ढंग, उदाहरण, आदर्श a repeated decorative design. an arrangement or sequence regularly found in comparable objects or events. *The sheriff recognized a definite pattern in the series of crimes that had been occurring in the town of late.*

Paucity/पॉसिटी *(noun)* – कमी, अभाव the presence of something in only small or insufficient amounts. *There was a paucity of resources in the city that is why they were demanding help from the Centre.*

Paunch/पॉन्च *(noun)* – तोंद a large or protruding abdomen or stomach. *Mother asked us to start exercising else we will soon have a paunch.*

Pauper/पापर *(noun)* – कंगाल penniless. *He died a pauper.*

Pause/पॉज *(noun)* – विराम without break. *He continued playing for so minutes without a pause.*

P

Pave/पेव (verb) – रास्ते में ईंट-पत्थर लगाना, पथराव करना cover with flat stones or bricks. *It was as if the path had been paved for her to walk on.*

Pavement/पेवमेंट (noun) – पदमार्ग, पैदल पथ British, a raised paved or asphalted path for pedestrians at the side of a road. *If we do not walk on the pavement, there is a risk we will get hit by a vehicle.*

Pavilion/पेविलियन (noun) – मैदान के पास खिलाड़ियों-दर्शकों के लिए भवन British, a building at a cricket ground or other sports ground used for changing and taking refreshments. *The sportsmen made their way to the pavilion to freshen up during the break.*

Paw/पॉ (noun) – पंजा an animal's foot having claws and pads. *We found paw prints in the garden, probably belonging to some wild animal.*

Pawn/पॉन (noun & verb) – ज्यादा, मुहरा, बन्धक रखना a chess piece of the smallest size and value. *Moving the pawn near his bishop was the only way out for her in the game.*

Pay/पे (noun & verb) – भुगतान देना, वेतन, वेतन देना something that remunerates. *Today is pay-day.*

Pea/पी (noun) – मटर a spherical green seed eaten as a vegetable. *Peas masala was my favourite curry.*

Peace/पीस् (noun)– शान्ति freedom from disturbance, tranquillity. *I went to the mountains in search of peace.*

Peaceable/पीसेबल् (adjective) – शान्तिदायक, शान्तिप्रद inclined to avoid war. *We should look for a peacable solution than resorting to war.*

Peaceful/पीसफुल (adjective) – शान्त, शान्तिप्रद free from disturbance; calm. *Her 11th storey balcony was indeed very peaceful.*

Peach/पीच (noun) – आडू, आड़ूबुखारा a round stone fruit with juicy yellow flesh and downy yellow skin flushed with red. *We decided to try and bake a peach cake.*

Peacock/पीकॉक (noun) – मोर, मयुर पक्षी a male peafowl, having very long tail feathers with eye-like markings that can be erected and fanned out in display. *There were almost twenty peacocks dancing in the rain in all their glory at the zoo.*

Peak/पीक (noun) – चोटी, शिखर, तीव्रता, पराकाष्टा a point in a curve or on a graph, or a value of a physical quantity, which is higher than those around it. the point of highest activity or achievement. *He showed in the presentation the time period when the sales of the company were at their peak.*

Peal/पील (noun) – घंटनाद, एकाएक होने वाली घनघोर आवाज a loud riming of a bell or bells. bell-ringing a series of changes rung on a set of bells. a set of bells. *There was a peal of bells when the priest came out of the sanctum sanctorum.*

Peanut/पीनट (noun) – मूँगफली, अतिन्यून राशि the oval seed of a [south American] plant, eaten as a snack or used for making oil or animal feed. *Having too many peanuts at a time came make you put on weight.*

Pear/पेअर (noun) – नाशपाती a yellowish or brownish green edible fruit, narrow at the stalk and wider towards the tip. *We decided to add some pears to the dessert.*

Pearl/पर्ल (noun) – मोती, मुक्ता, मोती के रंग का बहुमूल्य a hard, lustrous spherical mass, typically white or bluish-grey, formed within the shell of an oyster or other bivalve mollusc and highly prized as a gem, an artificial imitation of this. *He bought me a pearl necklace for our wedding anniversary.*

Peasant/पेजण्ट (noun) – खेतिहर, अज्ञानी व्यक्ति a poor smallholder or agricultural laborer of low social status. *The peasants were discussing a revolt against the capitalists who were trespassing into their area.*

Peasantry/पेजन्ट्रि (noun) – किसानवर्ग poor agricultural labourer. *The whole peasantry was revolting against the capitalists.*

Peat/पीट (noun) – खाद, सड़ी पत्तियों-पौधों से बना खाद partly decomposed vegetable matter forming a deposit on acidic, boggy ground, dried for use in gardening and as fuel. *The agriculturist advised the farmers to use peat as a form of fuel.*

Pebble/पेबल् (noun) – चिकना कंकड़ small stone made smooth and round by the action

P

of water or sand. *I love sitting quietly at the riverside, throwing an occassional pebble into the water. (adjective)* [informal] very thick and convex. *It was a pebble that could not be crushed.*

Peck/पेक *(noun & verb)* – दो गैलन की सूखी तोल, दाना चुगना, चोंच मारना a measure of capacity for dry goods, equal to a quarter of a bushel. *A peck of those items would be worthless for the price I was being offered.*

Peculiar/पिक्यूलिअर *(noun)* – विशिष्ट, विलक्षण, विशेष प्रकार का chiefly a parish or church exempt from the jurisdiction of the diocese in which it lies, though subject to the jurisdiction or the monarch or an archbishop. *People often discuss the peculiar jurisdiction of the Archbishop of Canterbury.*

Pedagogue/पेडागॉग *(noun)* – बालशिक्षक शिक्षक formal a teacher, especially a strict or pedantic one. *The pedagogues of yore have all been laid to rest*

Pedal/पेडल *(noun)* – साइकिल, नाव आदि चलाना each of a pair of foot-operated levers for powering a bicycle or other vehicle propelled by leg power. *The bike had colourful blue pedals.*

Pedantic/पेडांटिक *(adjective)* – पाण्डित्य पूर्ण, पण्डितादर excessively concerned with minor details. *It was a rather pedantic effort.*

Pedestal/पेडेस्टल *(noun)* – आधार-खम्भ, मंचिका, मूर्ति का आधार the base or support on which a statue, obelisk, or column is mounted. a position in which one is greatly or uncritically admired: you shouldn't put him on a pedestal. *My friend asked me not to put her up on a pedestal.*

Pedestrian/पिडेस्ट्रिअन् *(noun)* – पैदल यात्री, उत्साहहीन a person walking rather than travelling in a vehicle. *The pedestrians had crowded around the accident site. (adjective)* dull; uninspired. *What a pedestrian attitude she had.*

Pedigree/पेडिग्री *(noun)* – वंशावली the record of descent of an animal, showing it to be pure-bred. *She did not like the idea of making strays pets, so she bought a pedigree.*

Peddler/पेड्लर *(noun)* – फेरीवाला an itinerant, trader in small goods. *He had been unsuccessful in big businesses and eventually became a peddler of small articles.*

Pee/पी *(verb)* – पेशाब करना urinate. *She hurried to find a place to pee. (noun)* an act of urinating. *The gastroenterologist asked her to pee in a bottle for a urine test.*

Peek/पीक *(verb)* – झाँकना, ताक-झाँक करना look quickly or furtively. *She was peeking from the corner of the tree.*

Peel/पील *(noun)* – सब्जी, फल के छिलके उतारना to take the skin off a fruit or vegetable. *Could you peel the potatoes.*

Peep/पीप *(verb)* – चुपके से झाँकना, धीरे से उघारना look quickly and furtively. *She peeped from the hole in the wall.*

Peer/पिअर् *(verb)* – समान पद या योग्यता वाला, प्रतिद्वन्द्वी look with difficulty or concentration. *She was peering at the man who stood at a distance.* be just visible. *To peer at someone is impolite, my mother instructed.*

Peerless/पिअर्लेस *(adjective)* – अद्वितीय, अनुपम unequalled. *The princess's beauty was peerless.*

Peeved/पीव्ड *(adjective)* – नाराज, परेशान annoyed, irritated. *She was a bit peeved at him for his carelessness.*

Peevish/पीविश *(adjective)* – चिड़चिड़ा, बदमिजाज irritable. *On reviewing the conduct of the culprit, and examining his somewhat peevish and whimsical correspondence, the judge finally drew the sentence in the favour of the victim.*

Peg/पेग *(noun)* – खूँटी, मूल्यवृद्धि रोकना a short projecting pin or bolt used for hanging things on, securing something in place, or marking a position. a clip for holding things together or hanging up clothes. *The clothes, peg came off by itself a few days ago.*

Pelican/पेलिकन *(noun)* – एक प्रकार का पक्षी a large gregarious water bird with a long bill and an extensible throat pouch for scooping up fish. *The zoo has several seasonal birds including pelicans.*

P

Pellet/पेलेट (noun) – छर्रा, गोली, कागज का गोला a small, rounded, compressed mass of a substance. *A beetle was rolling a pellet of dung up a hill.*

Peil-mell/पेल-मेल (noun) – हड़बड़ी, अव्यवस्था disorder. *I dislike such pell-mell.*

Pelt/पेल्ट (verb) – ढेला फेंककर या गोली से मारना hurl missiles at. *The enemies were being pelted with missiles non stop.*

Pen/पेन् (noun) – कलम, लेखनी, लिखना an instrument for writing or drawing with ink, typically consisting of a metal nib or ball, or a nylon tip, fitted into a metal or plastic holder. writing as an occupation. an electronic device used in conjunction with a writing surface to enter commands or data into a computer. *My handwriting was most beautiful when I wrote with a fountain pen.*

Penal/पीनल् (adjective) – कानूनी दण्ड से सम्बन्धित of, relating to, or prescribing the punishment of offenders under the legal system. punishable by law. *I was told that her crime was punishable under the penal code.*

Penalty/पेनाल्टि (noun) – दण्ड, सजा, खेल-कूद का दण्ड a handicap imposed on a player or team for infringement of rules, especially a penalty kick. bridge points won by the defenders when the declarer fails to make the contract. *His only chance in the game was the penalty kick.*

Penance/पेनैन्स (noun) – तपस्या voluntary self-punishment as an open expression of repentance for wrongdoing. *The sage was known to have been through a lot of penance to attain this state.*

Pence/पेन्स (noun) – एक प्रकार का सिक्का plural form of penny. *The small magnet cost just a few pence.*

Pencil/पेन्सिल (noun) – लकड़ी में लगे पत्थर वाली लेखनी, लिखना, चित्र बनाना an instrument for writing or drawing, typically consisting of a thin stick of graphite enclosed in a long thin piece of wood or fixed in a thin cylindrical case. *She bought different kinds of pencils for her daughter's first day at school.*

Pendant/पेन्डैन्ट (noun) – लटकन, घर आदि में नीचे लटकने वाला a piece of jewellery that hangs from a necklace chain. *I gifted her a pendant on her birthday.*

Pendulum/पेंडुलम (noun) – लोलक, घड़ी का लगातार घूमता लोलक a weight hung from a fixed point so that it can swing freely, especially a rod with a weighted end that regulates the mechanism of a clock. *She bought a grandfather clock from the antique shop with a modified pendulum.*

Penetrate/पेनिट्रेट (verb) – प्रवेश, घुसना, आर-पार या अन्दर देखना force a way into or through. other sounds. *We tried hard to penetrate into the hole in the tree, but got stuck.*

Penguin/पेंग्इन् (noun) – एक प्रकार का पक्षी a flightless black and white seabird of the southern hemisphere, with wings used as flippers. *The advocates resemble penguins in their attire.*

Penicillin/पेनिसिलिन (noun) – एक प्रकार की औषधि an antibiotic produced naturally by certain blue moulds, now usually prepared synthetically. *We had to procure a certain dosage of penicillin as soon as possible to cure the patient.*

Peninsula/पेनिन्सुला (noun) – प्रायद्वीप, तीन तरफ से जल से घिरा हुआ a long, narrow piece of land projecting out into a sea or lake. *Our geography teacher explained the concept of peninsula.*

Penitent/पेनिटेंट (adjective) – पश्चाताप, पश्चाताप पूर्ण feeling or showing sorrow and regret for having done wrong. *What is the point of being penitent after making a mistake?* (noun) a person who repents his sins. a person who confesses his sins to a priest and submits to the penance that he imposes. *She made mistakes and was penitent at the end of the whole episode.*

Penitentiary/पेनिटेन्सियरी (noun) – कारागार [north American] a prison for people convicted of serious crime. *There was no other option but to send the criminal to a penitentiary institution.*

Penknife/पेननाइफ *(noun)* – छोटा जेबी चाकू a small knife with a blade which folds into the handle. *I tried cutting the fruits with my penknife.*

Penniless/पेनिलेस *(adjective)* – कंगाल without money; destitute. *After the grand party, she was left penniless.*

Penny/पेन्नी *(noun)* – एक प्रकार का सिक्का a British bronze coin and monetary unit equal to one hundredth of a pound. *We were taught by the British Academy how to exchage pennies and pounds at the Exchange Office.*

Pension/पेन्सन *(noun)* – सेवा निवृत्ति के बाद का विशेष वेतन a small hotel or boarding house in France and other European countries.*A pension had somewhat lesser to offer than a hotel.*

Pensive/पेन्सिव *(adjective)* – चिन्ता-मग्न engaged in deep thought.*Don't disturb you father when he is in a pensive mood.*

Pentagon/पेन्टागॉन *(noun)* – पंच भुजाकार a plane figure with five straight sides and five angles. *The geometry teacher taught us to draw a pentagon.*

Penthouse/पेन्टहाउस *(noun)* – बहुमंजिला इमारत के ऊपर ऊँचा कमरा a flat on the top floor of a tall building. typically luxuriously fitted and offering fine views. *The executive bought a plush penthouse in a posh locality downtown.*

Penultimate/पेनअल्टिमेट *(adjective)* – उप-अन्त, अन्तिम के पूर्व का last but one.*The penultimate line of the chemical series was difficult to learn.*

Penury/पिन्यूरी *(noun)* – दरिद्रता extreme poverty. *Unknown to the world, she lived in a state of penury.*

People/पीपुल् *(plural noun)* – आम स्त्री-पुरुष, आमलोग human beings in general or considered collectively. the mass of citizens in a country; the populace.*The people of the country were getting ready to revolt against the dictator.*

Pepper/पेपर् *(noun)* – काली मिर्च, गोल मिर्च a pungent, hot-tasting powder prepared from dried and ground peppercorns, used to flavor food. *I was growing pepper in my kitchen garden.*

Peppermint/पेपरमिंट *(noun)* – पुदीने जैसे पौधे से बनी मिठी गोली the aromatic leaves of a plant of the mint family, or an oil obtained from them, used as a flavouring in food. *Peppermint is a nice mouthfreshner to have after dinner.*

Per/पर *(preposition)* – प्रत्येक for each: *We bought the land for Rs 3000 per square feet.*

Perceive/परसिव *(verb)* – अनुभव करना, देखना, जानना become aware or conscious of. *I perceived his comments as a criticism.*

Percent/परसेंट *(adverb)* – प्रतिशत by a specified amount in or for every hundred.*We got 30 percent of the total distribution of the land.* *(noun)* one part in every hundred. the rate, number, or amount in each hundred.*The land was being distributed at 30 percent of its actual landspace.*

Percentage/परसेंटेज *(noun)* – प्रतिशतता a rate, number, or amount in each hundred. *She scored a bad percentage in the internal exams.*

Perceptible/परसेप्टिबल् *(adjective)* – इन्द्रियगोचर, स्पष्ट नजर आना able to be perceived.*Only 10 percent of space lies in the perceptible limit.*

Perception/परसेप्शन *(noun)* – प्रत्यक्ष ज्ञान, प्रत्यक्ष बोध the ability to see, hear, or become aware of something through the sense. the state of being or process of becoming aware of something in such a way. *She was amazed at the level of perception of the baby.*

Perceptive/परसेप्टिव *(adjective)* – सूक्ष्म दृष्टि, परखने में तेज having or showing acute insight. *She was more perceptive and receptive as a student, than others.*

Perch/पर्च *(noun)* – चिड़ियों का अड्डा a thing on which a bird alights or roosts. *The bird fluttered for a while and then settled itself precariously on a perch high above.*

Percolate/पर्कोलेट *(verb)* – रिसना, छनना filter through a porous surface or substance. *The liquid was percolating through the filter cloth.*

Percussion/पर्कशन् *(noun)* – तालवाद्य the action of playing a musical instrument by striking or shaking it. denoting musical instruments

P

played in this way. percussion instruments forming a band or section of an orchestra. *The percussion team was the star of the evening's performance.*

Peremtory/पेरम्टरी *(adjective)* – शीघ्र आदेश या देश पालन की अपेक्षा insisting on immediate attention or obedience; brusque and imperious. *The teacher spoke in a peremptory tone.*

Perennial/पेरेनिअल *(adjective)* – चिरस्थायी, बार-बार होने वाला lasting for a long time: enduring or continually recurring. continually engaged in a specified activity: a perennial student. *We were aiming at achieving perennial happiness.*

Perfect/परफेक्ट *(adjective)* – पूर्ण, परिपूर्ण, दोषरहित having all the required elements, qualities, or characteristics. *When the batter had reached that perfect consistency, we poured it into a tin and baked it.*

Perfection/परफेक्शन *(noun)* – पूर्णता, उच्चतम स्थिति या गुण the action, process, or condition of perfecting or being perfect. *Perfection of the invention took years.*

Perforate/पर्फरोट् *(verb)* – कागज में छोट-छोटे छेद करना pierce and make a hole or holes in. *We placed it in a tin perforated with round holes.* *(adjective)* [biology & medicine] perforated. *The paper needs to be perforated to make it easier to tear.*

Perform/परफॉर्म *(verb)* – कार्य करना, निर्देशित कार्य सम्पन्न करना carry out, accomplish, or fulfil. *She knew she had to perform in this exam.*

Performance/परफॉर्मेंस *(noun)* – प्रदर्शन, कार्य पूर्ण करने की योग्यता an act of performing a play, concert, or other form of entertainment. *There was a performance scheduled for the weekend.*

Perfume/परफ्यूम *(noun)* – सुगन्ध, इत्र a fragrant liquid typically made from essential oils, used to impart a pleasant smell to one's body or clothes. *Her clothes smell really good because of the perfume she uses.*

Perhaps/परहैप्स *(adjective)* – शायद, कदाचित् expressing uncertainty or possibility. *Perhaps it was this way or perhaps it was that.*

Peril/पेरिल *(noun)* – समाप्ति का संकट, गहरा संकट a genie or fairy. *She was divine, a peril indeed!*

Perimeter/पेरिमिटर *(noun)* – परिमिति, आकृति की बाहरी सीमा की लम्बा the continuous line forming the boundary of a closed geometrical figure. *I was trying to calculate the perimeter of the circle in the paper.*

Period/पिरिअड *(noun)* – निश्चित अवधि, रजस्वला का समय, पूर्ण विराम a length or portion of time *The country was going through a period of economic prosperity.*

Periodic/पिरिऑडिक *(adjective)* – निश्चित अवधि के बाद पुनरावृत्ति appearing or occurring at intervals. *The meteors appeared at periodic intervals.*

Periodical/पिरिऑडिकल *(adjective)* – साप्ताहिक, मासिक पत्र, पत्रिका occurring or appearing at intervals, published at regular intervals. *She had periodical fits of depression.* *(noun)* a periodical magazine or newspaper. *She had published in several periodicals.*

Periphery/पेरिफरि *(noun)* – क्षेत्र की सीमा, किनारा the outer limits or edge of an area or object. *The enemies had reached the periphery of the region.*

Periscope/पेरिस्कोप *(noun)* – समुद्र तल देखने का यन्त्र an apparent consisting of a tube attached to a set of mirrors or prisms, by which an observer typically in a submerged submarine or behind a high obstacle can see things that are otherwise out of sight. *Suddenly he saw a periscope rising from the water at a distance.*

Perish/पेरिस *(verb)* – नष्ट होना, नष्ट कर देना, गल जाना die, especially in large numbers. *Thousands had perished in the fire accident.*

Perjure/पर्जर् *(verb)* – सौगन्ध लेकर झूठ बोलने का अपराध law commit perjury. *The witness perjured herself when she denied knowing the defendant.*

Perk/पर्क *(verb)* – भत्ता, प्रसन्नता, प्रफुल्लित होना make or become more cheerful or lively. *She perked up as soon as she was shown a chocolate.* *(adjective)* dialect perky; pert. *You're in a perky mood.*

P

Perm/पर्म *(noun)* – केश को कृत्रिम ढंग से लहरदार बनाना a method of setting the hair in waves or curls and treating it with chemicals so that the style lasts for several months. *The Hollywood actress's perm was back.* *(verb)* treat in such a way. *She had her hair permed.*

Permanence/परमानेंस *(noun)* – स्थायित्व, पक्का the state of remaining unchanged in definitely. *There is no permanence to anything in this world.*

Permanent/परमानेंट *(adjective)* – स्थायी, चिरस्थायी lasting or remaining unchanged indefinitely, or intended to be so; not temporary. *Nothing in this world is permanent.* *(noun)* a perm for the hair. *Her hair colour was permanent.*

Permeate/परमिएट *(verb)* – फैल जाना, व्याप्त होना spread throughout; pervade. *A thinker once said, our thinking is permeated by our historical myths.*

Permissible/परमिसिब्ल् *(adjective)* – अनुमति योग्य allowable; permitted.*The minerals in our tap water were beyond the permissible limit*

Permission/पर्मिशन् *(noun)* – अनुमति authorization. *She asked for permission to leave at noon.*

Permissive/पर्मिसिव् *(adjective)* – अति स्वतन्त्रता allowing or characterized by freedom of behaviour. *You are lucky to have permissive parents.*

Permit/पर्मिट *(verb)* – स्वीकृति देना, अनुमति देना give permission to or for something. *They were denied permit to sell alcoholic beverages.*

Perpendicular/पर्पेन्डिक्युलर् *(adjective)* – लम्ब, सीधी खड़ी रेखा at an angle of 90 to a given line, plane, or surface. *The axes are perpendicular to each other.*

Perpetrate/पर्पिट्रेट् *(verb)* – अपराध या गलती करना carry out or commit. *He perpetrators of the crime will be punished.*

Perpetual/पर्पेचुअल् *(adjective)* – समाप्त न होने वाला, अनन्त never ending or changing. denoting or having a position or trophy held for life rather than a limited period. having no fixed maturity date. *She had opened a perpetual fixed deposit in the bank.*

Perpetuate/पर्पेचुएट *(verb)* – बनाये रखना cause to continue indefinitely. *The new library will perpetuate its founder's great love of learning.*

Perplex/पर्प्लेक्स *(verb)* – हैरान कर देना cause to feel baffled. *She looked perplexed when I asked her about her project.*

Perquisite/परक्विजिट *(noun)* – नियमित वेतन के अतिरिक्त लाभ [historical] a thing which has served its primary use and to which a subordinate or employee has a customary right. *Long distance calls at discount rates was one of the perquisites of the job.*

Persecute/परसिक्यूट *(verb)* – सताना, मुकदमा करना, लगातार प्रश्न करना subject to prolonged hostility and ill-treatment. *Jews were mercilessly persecuted in the former Soviet Union.*

Persevere/पर्सिविअर *(verb)* – कठिनाइयों के बाद भी कोशिश करते रहना continue in a course of action in spite of difficulty or with little or no indication of success. *To persevere is the only way to success.*

Persist/परसिस्ट् *(verb)* – लगातार करते रहना, बार-बार घटित continue firmly or obstinately in an opinion or a course of action in spite of difficulty or opposition. *Though I refused to buy her a chocolate, she continued to persist.*

Person/पर्सन् *(noun)* – व्यक्ति (स्त्री-पुरुष या बच्चा) a human being regarded as an individual. *Each one of us is an individual person whose rights ought to be guarded and respected.*

Personal/पर्सनल *(adjective)* – व्यक्तिगत affecting, or belonging to a particular person. involving the presence or action of a particular individual. *You have to take personal initiative to get this project done.*

Personality/पर्सनैलिटि *(noun)* – व्यक्तित्व the combination of characteristics or qualities that from an individual's distinctive character. *She had a charming personality.*

Personalize/पर्सनलाइज् *(verb)* – व्यक्तिगत करना design or produce to meet someone's

P

individual requirements. *The designer offered to get a personalized version of his product designed especially for the queen.*

Personify/पर्सॅनिफाई *(verb)* – जीवन देना, मानवीकरण करना represent by a figure in human form. *She personified the idol.*

Personnel/पर्सनेल *(plural noun)* – कर्मचारीगण, कार्यकर्ता वर्ग people employed in an organization or engaged in an organized undertaking. *Thousands of personnel had been employed at several points to make the fair a success.*

Perspective/पर्सपेक्टिव *(noun)* – परिदृश्य, विस्तृत क्षेत्र का चित्र the art of representing three-dimensional objects on a two-dimensional surface, so as to convey the impression of height, width, depth, and relative distance. *These drawings are difficult to comprehend from a certain perspective.*

Perspire/पर्स्पायर् *(verb)* – पसीना आना give out sweat through the pores of the skin as a result of heat, physical exertion, or stress. *She was perspiring heavily at the gym.*

Persuade/पर्स्वेड् *(verb)* – मना लेना cause to do something through reasoning or argument. *I tried my best to persuade her about the benefits of the scheme.*

Persuasion/पर्स्वेजन् *(noun)* – राजी करने का प्रयास the action of persuading someone to do or believe in something. *Three foremost aids of persuasion, according to me, are humility, concentration and gusto.*

Persuasive/पर्स्वेसिव् *(adjective)* – विश्वास दिलाने योग्य good at persuading someone to do or believe something. *She was quite persuasive in her beliefs.*

Pert/पर्ट *(adjective)* – उद्धत युवती attractively lively or cheeky. *She was pert in her conduct, smart and spontaneous.*

Pertain/पर्टेन *(verb)* – सम्बन्ध रखना, अपना होना be appropriate, related, or applicable. *The evidence that pertains to the accident was collected and saved.*

Pertinent/पर्टिनेन्ट *(adjective)* – उपयुक्त, युक्तिसंगत relevant; appropriate. *Her advice was quite pertinent to his situation.*

Perturb/पर्टर्ब् *(verb)* – घबड़ा देना make anxious or unsettled. *She was perturbed by his carelessness as it could lead to an accident some day.*

Peruse/पेरूज् *(verb)* – ध्यानपूर्वक पढ़ना formal read or examine thoroughly or carefully. *I sent the employer my project report for his perusal.*

Pervade/पर्वेड् *(verb)* – सर्वत्र फैल जाना, पूर्ण व्यक्ति spread or be present throughout; suffuse. *Corruption is like cancer that pervades every corner of society.*

Pervasive/पर्वेसिव *(adjective)* – व्याप्तिपूर्ण widespread. *The pervasive odour of garlic was irritating me.*

Perverse/पर्वर्स *(adjective)* – विकृत रुचि वाला, जानबूझकर गलत व्यवहार करने वाला showing a deliberate and obstinate desire to behave unacceptably. sexually perverted. *He took perverse satisfaction in foiling her plans.*

Perversion/पर्सवर्सन *(noun)* – सदाचार विमुख the action of perverting. abnormal or unacceptable sexual behaviour. *His perversion was met with strong repercussions.*

Pervert/पर्वर्ट *(verb)* – कदाचारी alter from its original meaning or state to a corruption of what was first intended. *It is an analysis that perverts the meaning of the poem.*

Pessimism/पेसिमिज्म *(noun)* – निराशावादिता lack of hope or confidence in the future. *Do not lie in a state of pessimism if you are unable to face your problems.*

Pessimist/पेसिमिस्ट *(noun)* – निराशावादी a tendency to see the worst aspect of things. *Do not be a pessimist and run from your problems.*

Pest/पेस्ट *(noun)* – कीड़े-मकोड़े a destructive insect or other animal that attacks crops, food, or livestock. *The crop was infested with pests this season.*

Pester/पेस्टर *(verb)* – सताना trouble or annoy with persistent requests or interruptions. *Do not pester your parents for sweets when they have just had a fight.*

Pesticide/पेस्टिसाइड *(noun)* – कीटनाशक a substance for destroying insects or other pests of plants or animals. *Thanks to the new pesticides, our crops were saved this year.*

Pestilence/पेस्टिलेन्स *(noun)* – महामारी, छूत का रोग [archaic] a fatal, epidemic disease, especially bubonic plague. *The government had planned strict actions against the pestilence.*

Pet/पेट *(noun)* – पालतू, दुलारा व्यक्ति a domestic or tamed animal or bird kept for companionship or pleasure. *I love animals and have always wanted to own a pet.*

Petal/पेटल *(noun)* – फूल की पँखुड़ी each of the segments of the corolla of a flower. *I took out the petals of the rose and spread them in the water.*

Peter/पिटर *(verb)* – शनै: शनै: समाप्त होना diminish or come to an end gradually. *The water that was gushing was now reduced to a peter.*

Petite/पेटिट *(adjective)* – कद में छोटी, देहयष्टि आकर्षक attractively small and dainty. *She had a petite figure.*

Petition/पिटिशन *(noun)* – औपचारिक अर्जी, याचिका a formal written request, typically signed by many people, appealing to authority in respect of a cause. an appeal or request. *I signed a petition in favour of the bill that was currently being discussed in the Parliament.*

Petrify/पेट्रिफाइ *(verb)* – स्तब्ध रह जाना paralyse with fear. *She was petrified at the sight of the thief in the house.*

Petrol/पेट्रोल *(noun)* – गैस तेल British refined petroleum used as fuel in motor vehicles. *We had to fill petrol in the car before we went on the road trip.*

Petroleum/पेट्रोलीअम *(noun)* – खनिज तेल a hydrocarbon oil found in suitable rock strata and extracted and refined to produce fuels including petrol, paraffin, and diesel oil; oil. *The different countries were fighting over petroleum extraction.*

Petticoat/पेटिकोट *(noun)* – स्त्रियों का अधोवस्त्र a woman's light, loose undergarment in the form of a skirt of dress. *Her petticoat seemed longer than her sari.*

Petty/पेटि *(adjective)* – नगण्य, तुच्छ trivial. *The children were fighting over petty issues.*

Pew/प्यू *(noun)* – लकड़ी की लम्बी कुर्सी a long bench with a back, placed in rows in churches for the congregation. [British informal] a seat. *The VIPs were seated in the front pews while the commoners behind.*

Phantom/फैन्टम *(noun)* – भूत-प्रेत, भ्रान्ति-छलावा chiefly [archaic] variant spelling of fantast. *She was paranoid and thought there was a phantom in the house.*

Pharmaceutical/फार्मस्यूटिकल *(adjective)* – औषधि निर्माण और वितरण of or relating to medicinal drugs, or their preparation, use or sale. *The drugs she was buying were purely for pharmaceutical use.* (noun) a compound manufactured for use as a medicinal drug. *I had to resort to pharmaceuticals as Yoga was not yielding any results.*

Pharmacy/फार्मेसी *(noun)* – औषधालय, दवा-विधि का अध्ययन a place where medicinal drugs are prepared or sold. *I rushed to the pharmacy to buy the medicines.*

Phase/फेज *(noun)* – अवस्था, चरण a distinct period or stage in a process of change or development. each of the aspects of the moon or a planet, according to the amount of its illumination. *We were asked to stay away from the sea when the moon's phase changes.*

Pheasant/फेजन्ट *(noun)* – बटेर a large long-tailed game bird native to Asia, the male of which typically has showy plumage. *There were lots of pheasants in the jungle.*

Phenomenal/फिनॉमिनल् *(adjective)* – असाधारण, चमत्कारिक extraordinary. *It was a phenomenal achievement to cross that border.*

Phenomenon/फिनामिनन् *(noun)* – इन्द्रियगोचर, उल्लेखनीय a fact or situation that is observed to exist or happen, especially one whose cause is in question. *We decided to study the phenomenon as it was a rare occurrence.*

Phew/फ्यू *(interjection)* – साँस लेने और छोड़ने की आवाज, घृणा सूचक शब्द *exclamatory* [informal] expressing relief. *Phew! Finally we are there!*

P

Phial/फाइअल् *(noun)* – काँच की छोटी शीशी a small cylindrical glass bottle, typically for medical samples or [medicines]. *She poured the tonic into a phial and handed it over to the customer.*

Philanthropy/फिलन्थ्रपि *(noun)* – दान आदि के द्वारा जरूरतमंदों की सहायता, उपकार [archaic] a philanthropist. *Bill Gates is known for being quite a philanthrope in his circle.*

Philately/फिलैटिलि *(noun)* – डाक टिकट संग्रह the collection and study of postage stamps. *He had an active interest in philately.*

Philology/फिललॅजि *(noun)* – भाषा विकास का अध्ययन the study of the structure, [historical] development, and relationships of a language or language. *She decided to study philology.*

Philosopher/फिलॉस्फर *(noun)* – दार्शनिक a person engaged or learned in [philosophy]. *India is known for its share of philosophers and spiritual gurus.*

Philosophy/फिलॉसफि *(noun)* – दर्शन the study of the fundamental nature of knowledge, reality, and existence. a set of theories of a particular philosopher. *I wanted to take up philosophy in my post graduation.*

Phlegm/फ्लेग्म *(noun)* – कफ, बलगम the thick viscous substance secreted by the mucous membranes of the respiratory passages, especially when produced in excessive quantities during a cold. *The doctor realized that his patient's lungs were filled with phlegm.*

Phlegmatic/फ्लेग्मेटिक *(adjective)* – शान्तचित, आसानी से क्रोधित न होना unemotional and stolidly calm. *He had a phlegmatic attitude.*

Phone/फोन *(noun)* – दूरभाष phonetics a speech sound. *I could hear different phones of music.*

Phonetic/फोनेटिक *(adjective)* – ध्वनिशास्त्र, भाषा ध्वनिशास्त्र phonetics of or relating to speech sounds. having a direct correspondence between symbols and sounds. of or relating to phonetics. *We were trying to analyse the phonetics of the musical note.*

Phoney/फोनि *(adjective)* – नकली not genuine. *It was a phoney affair. (noun)* a fraudulent person or thing. *He turned out to be a phoney guy.*

Phosphorus/फास्फोरस *(noun)* – सहज जलने वाला पीला पदार्थ the chemical element of atomic number 15, a poisonous, combustible non-metal which exists as a yellowish waxy solid which ignites spontaneously in air and glows in the dark and as a less reactive form used in making matches. *One can modify the lights in their house and use phosphorus lamps*

Photocopy/फोटोकॉपी *(noun)* – छाया प्रतिलिपि a photographic copy of something produced by a process involving the action of light on a specially prepared surface. *Ever since I bought a photocopy machine, all the college students have been flocking to my shop. (verb)* a photocopy of. *To photocopy her notes was the only way I could make up for the classes I missed.*

Photograph/फोटोग्राफ *(noun)* – चित्र, छायाचित्र a picture made with a camera, in which an image is focused on to film and then made visible and permanent by chemical treatment. *She has lots of photographs of our school days. (verb)* take a photograph of. *I wanted to take a photograph of my favourite actor with me.*

Phrase/फ्रेज *(noun)* – मुहावरा a small group of words standing together as a conceptual unit. an idiomatic or short pithy expression. *I had trouble understanding the phrases she used in her essay.*

Physical/फिजिकल *(adjective)* – दैहिक, शारीरिक, भौतिक of or relating to the body as opposed to the mind. involving bodily contact or activity: a physical relationship. *He shared a physical relationship with the girl next door.*

Physician/फिजिसियन *(noun)* – चिकित्सक a person qualified to practice [medicine], especially one how specializes in diagnosis and medical treatment as distinct from surgery. *We decided to approach a general physician to get a diagnosis.*

Physics/फिजिक्स *(noun)* – भौतिक शास्त्र the branch of science that studies nature and properties of matter. *She did a bachelors honours course in physics before going on to astronomy.*

P

Physiognomy/फिजिऑग्नमि *(noun)* – चेहरे के नाक-नक्श का अध्ययन a person's facial features or expression, especially when regarded as indicative of character or ethnic origin. *His physiognomy seemed different from the actual description the witness gave.*

Physiology/फिजिऑलॅजि *(noun)* – शरीर विज्ञान the branch of biology concerned with the normal functions of living organisms and their parts. the way in which a living organism or bodily part functions. *We were studying the physiology of aquatic animals.*

Physiotherapy/फिजिऑथेरपि *(noun)*– व्यायाम से चिकित्सा the treatment of disease, injury, or deformity by physical methods such as massage and exercise rather than by drugs or surgery. *The doctor advised three months of physiotherapy for the patient to recover completely.*

Physique/फिजिक *(noun)* – शरीर-सौष्ठव, शारीरिक गठन the form, size, and development of a person's body. *His powerful physique attracted quite a few proposals.*

Piano/पिआनो *(noun)* – एक वायु वाद्य a large keyboard musical instrument with a wooden case enclosing a soundboard and metal strings, which are struck by hammers when the keys are depressed. *The piano was the star in the entire orchestra.*

Pick/पिक *(noun & verb)* – गैंती, खोदनी, उठाना, चुनना, खुरेचना a tool headed by a curved bar with a point at one end and chisel edge or point at the other, used for breaking up hard ground or rock. *He owned a factory that makes picks.*

Picket/पिकेट् *(noun & verb)* – नोकदार छड़ (खूँटा), धरना देना a person or group of people standing outside a workplace trying to persuade others not to enter during a strike. *Let's go and picket the shop.*

Pickle/पिकल *(noun)* – अचार a relish consisting of vegetable or fruit preserved in vinegar, brine, or mustard. [north American] a cucumber preserved in this way. liquid used to preserve food or other perishable items. *Pickle with curd rice is a delicious combination.*

Picnic/पिकनिक *(noun)* – उद्यान-भोज a packed meal eaten outdoors, or an occasion when such a meal is eaten. *The school had planned a picnic for the children.* *(verb)* have or take part in a picnic. *The children were excited about participating in the picnic.*

Pictorial/पिक्टोरिअल *(adjective)* – सचित्री, चित्रमय of or expressed in pictures; illustrated. *The album was a pictorial description of the whole event.* *(noun)* a newspaper or periodical with pictures as a main feature. *She bought a pictorial often sold at the newspaper shop.*

Picture/पिक्चर *(noun)* – चित्र, चलचित्र a painting, drawing, or photograph. a portrait. an image on a television screen. *The pictures spoke for themselves.*

Picturesque/पिक्चरेस्क *(adjective)* – मनोरम दृश्यावली, मनोहर प्राकृतिक दृश्य visually attractive in a quaint or charming manner. unusual and vivid. *The hill station was picturesque and a photographer's paradise.*

Pie/पाइ *(noun)* – पके मांस का पुआ a baked dish of savoury or sweet ingredients encased in or topped with pastry. *I asked mother to bake an apple pie for tea.*

Piece/पीस *(noun)* – टुकड़ा, अंश, हिस्सा a portion of an object or of material produced by cutting, tearing, or breaking the whole. *I asked my friend to pass me a piece of her bread to taste.*

Piecemeal/पीसमिल *(adjective & adverb)* – खण्डित कार्य characterized by unsystematic partial measures taken over a period of time. *It was a piecemeal effort she made.*

Pierce/पिअर्स *(verb)* – छेदना, भेदना, बेधना make a hole in or through with a sharp pointed object. *The thorn had pierced through her skin.*

Piety/पाइ-इटि *(noun)* – धर्मपरायणता, श्रद्धा, धार्मिक the quality of being pious or reverent. a belief accepted with unthinking conventional reverence. *He impressed the gods with his piety.*

Pig/पिग *(noun)* – सूअर an omnivorous domesticated hoofed mammal with sparse bristly hair and a flat snout, kept for its meat.

P

a wild animal related to this, a hog. *The pig sty had not been cleaned in weeks.*

Piggery/पिगरी *(noun)* – सूअर खाना, सूअर का खोभाड़ a farm where pigs are bred. *The stench came from the piggery nearby.*

Pigeon/पिजन् *(noun)* – कबूतर a stout seed or fruit-eating bird with a small head, short legs, and a cooing voice, similar to but generally larger than a dove. *Two pigeons had built a nest in my terrace.*

Piggy bank/पिग्गि-बैंक *(noun)* – गोलक a money box;s especially one shaped like a pig. *I got a piggy bank as a gift on my ninth birthday.*

Pigheaded/पिगहेडेड *(adjective)* – जिद्दी, अड़ियल stupidly obstinate. *When I insisted stubbornly, mother asked me to stop being so pig headed.*

Piglet/पिग्लेट *(noun)* – सूअर का बच्चा a young pig. *The pigs in the sty had given birth to cute little piglets.*

Pigment/पिग्मेंट *(noun)* – रंग, रंजक the natural colouring matter of animal or plant tissue. *The leaves were unique as they had different pigments.* a substance used for colouring or painting, especially a dry powder which constitutes a paint or ink when mixed with oil or water. *We decided to use a different combination of pigment for the rest of the painting.*

Pigtail/पिग्टेल *(noun)* – गुच्छे में बँधे बाल a plaited lock of hair worn singly at the back or on each side of the head. *I like the girl with pigtails who sits at the back of the class.* a short length of braided wire connecting a stationary part to a moving part in an electrical device. *The pigtails were twisted and had to be repaired.*

Pile/पाइल *(noun)* – ढेर, एक ऊपर एक सजाना, बल्ली a heavy stake or post driven into the ground to support the foundations of a superstructure. *Pile is a form of deep foundation typically found in high rise buildings.*

Piles/पाइल्स *(plural noun)* – बवासीर, एक प्रकार का खूनी-बादी रोग haemorrhoids. *the doctor advised the piles patient to avoid eating spicy food.*

Pilgrim/पिल्ग्रिम *(noun)* – तीर्थयात्री a person who journeys to a sacred place for religious

reasons. *The facilities for pilgrims in our country need to improve dramatically.* *(verb)* [archaic] travel or wander like a pilgrim. *I shall pilgrim next year.*

Pilgrimage/पिल्ग्रिमेज *(noun)* – तीर्थ, तीर्थ यात्रा a pilgrim's journey. *Mecca is one of the most crowded and famous pilgrimage points in the world.* *(verb)* go on a pilgrimage. *My mother shall pilgrimage after retirement.*

Pill/पिल *(noun)* – दवा की गोली a small round mass of solid [medicine] for swallowing whole. a contraceptive pill. *The doctor prescribed sleeping pills to the insomniac.*

Pillage/पिलेज *(verb)* – सैनिकों द्वारा लूटमार rob or steal with violence, especially in wartime. *Pillage by a victorious army during war has been a common practice throughout recorded history.* *(noun)* the action of pillaging. *A bitter pillage followed the war.*

Pillar/पिलर *(noun)* – खम्भ, स्तम्भ a tall vertical structure, usually of stone, used as a support for a building or as an ornament or monument. *The pillars in the palace had been ornately designed.*

Pillion/पिलियन (पिल्यॉन) *noun* – पीछे सवारी के बैठने का स्थान a seat for a passenger behind a motorcyclist. *The pillion rider also needs to wear a helmet.* [historical] a woman's light saddle. a cushion attached to the back of a saddle for an additional passenger. *The horse nearly threw the rider and the pillion off its back.*

Pillow/पिलो *(noun)* – तकिया a rectangular cloth bag stuffed with feathers, wadding, or other soft materials, used to support the head when lying or sleeping. *He went hunting around the city for the best pillows to sleep on.* short for lace pillow. *Pillows add colour and style to the living room.* *(verb)* rest as if on a pillow. *My mother's lap is the best pillow I could sleep on.*

Pilot/पाइलट् *(noun)* – चालक, विमान चालक a person who operates the flying controls of an aircraft. *Its alarming to know some of the pilots sleep over the controls during a flight.* 2 a person with expert local knowledge qualified to take charge of a ship entering or leaving a harbor. a navigational handbook for

P

use at sea. [archaic] a guide or leader. *The Titanic would not have sunk if the pilots were more alert about the ice bergs.*

Pimple/पिम्पल *(noun)* – फुंसी a small hard inflamed spot on the skin. *Getting pimples may also be a sign of attaining puberty.*

Pin/पिन *(noun)* – मेख, सूई सी नुकीली, नत्थी करना a thin price of metal with a sharp point at ore end to fasten papers, cloth etc. *The girl used a safety pin to secure her handkerchief to the uniform.*

Pinafore/पिनाफोर *(noun)* – वस्त्र रक्षक ढीला वस्त्र a collarless, sleeveless dress worn over a blouse or jumper. *The children wore pinafores at nursery school.*

Pincer/पिन्सर् *(noun)* – सँड़सी a tool made of two pieces of metal bearing blunt concave jaws arranged like the blades of scissors, used for gripping and pulling things. *I screamed when the dentist brought an instrument that looked like a pincer close to my mouth.* a front claw of a lobster, crab, or similar crustacean. *When in danger, the crab uses its pincers as a deadly weapon.*

Pinch/पिन्च *(verb)* – चुटकी, चुटकी काटना grip tightly and sharply between finger and thumb. hurt by being too tight. tighten the lips or a part of the face, especially with worry or tension. *Pinching nerves in the neck can be very painful.*

Pine/पाइन *(noun)* – चीड़ का पेड़, अति दुःखी an evergreen coniferous tree having clusters of long meddle-shaped leaves, grown for its soft wood or for tar and turpentine. used in names of coniferous trees of other families, e.g. Chile pine. *Natural stands of scots pine can also be found in the Heathlands of southern England.*

Pineapple/पाइनएपल *(noun)* – अनन्नास/अनानास a larg juicy tropical fruit consisting of aromatic edible yellow flesh surrounded by a tough segmented skin and topped with a tuft of stiff leaves. *A diet based on pineapple fruit is said to work wonders for weight reduction.*

Ping-pong/पिंग-पौंग *(noun)* – एक प्रकार का खेल, गेंद [informal] term for table tennis. *The Asian teams tend to dominate Ping-Pong games at the Olympics.*

Pinnacle/पिनैकल *(noun)* – पराकाष्टा a high pointed piece of rock. *The islands are known to have a number of shallow reefs and coral pinnacles.*

Pinpoint/पिनपॉयेन्ट्/पिनपॉइन्ट् *(adjective)* – इंगित करना absolutely precise. *The new imaging software can pinpoint the area of impact to within a few millimetres.*

Pinprick/पिनप्रिक *(noun)* – सूई चुभाना, तंग करना a prick caused by a pin. *The tire of the bike had a small puncture much like a pinprick.* a very small dot or amount. *Here in our little community, a pinprick on the map of the five great continents of the world.*

Pint/पाइन्ट *(noun)* – एक माप a unit of liquid or dry capacity equal to one eighth of a gallon, in Britain equal to 0.568 litre and in the US equal to 0.473 litre. [British informal] a pint of beer. *Mix extracts, pour into a clean pan and boiling until the mixture measures 2 pint.*

Pioneer/पायनिअर *(noun)* – अग्रणी, अगुआ an innovator or developer of new ideas or techniques. *There is an exhibition in town that explains the work of the famous Yorkshire aviation pioneer, Robert Blackburn.* a member of an infantry group preparing roads or terrain for the main body of troops. *A pioneer from the Mid West Infantry was sent to perform engineering tasks, form roads, and dig trenches as the troop advances towards the border.*

Pious/पायस *(adjective)* – पवित्र, धर्मपरायण, भक्त devoutly religious. *He was revered by many as a saint because he was so pious.* making a hypocritical display of virtue. *The so called miracles enacted by many 'god' men in today's world need to be studied in detail before terming them as pious fraud.*

Pip/पिप *(noun)* – छोटे बीज, संकेत ध्वनि, असफल होना a small hard seed in a fruit. *The fibroid detected is as miniscule as a pip of an orange.*

Pipe/पाइप *(noun)* – नली, नल, नलिका, तम्बाकू a tube used to convey water, gas, oil, or other fluids. a cavity in cast metal. *The pipe in my bathroom needs to be replaced.* a device used for smoking tobacco, consisting of a narrow

P

tube with a bowl at one end in which the tobacco is burned, the smoke from which is then drawn into the mouth. *Cinema has often shown actors smoking a pipe on screen quite stylishly.*

Pipeline/पाइपलाइन *(noun)* – बड़ी नली, नलिका का प्रसार a long pipe for conveying oil, gas, etc. over long distances. *The proposed pipeline for gas between the two countries would run below the sea.* the hollow formed by the breaking of a large wave. *The Banzai pipeline is a surf reek break located in Hawaii.*

Piper/पाइपर *(noun)* – वायुवादक one who plays on pipe. *Whatever you do, at some point in time you have to pay the piper.*

Piping/पाइपिंग *(noun)* – नल की लम्बाई, सीटी की ध्वनि lengths of pipe. *A frequent failure of piping in air conditioning units is a concern that needs to be addressed.* thin lines of icing or cream, used to decorate cakes and desserts. *One has to learn modern piping techniques to make elegant and artistic decorations on the cake.*

Pirate/पाइरेट *(noun)* – जलदस्यु a person who attacks and robs ships at sea. *The threat of pirates in the Indian Ocean has brought the South Asian countries together to weed them out.*

Pisces/पिसीज़ *(noun)* – मीन, मीन राशि, मछली astronomy a large constellation said to represent a pair of fishes tied together by their tails. *Pisces is a constellation lying between Aquarius and Aries.*

Pistol/पिस्टॅल् *(noun)* – तमंचा a small firearm designed to be held in one hand. *The policeman ordered the robber to throw his pistol towards the door.*

Piston/पिस्टन *(noun)* – अन्य यन्त्रों को गतिशील करने वाला यन्त्र A disc or short cylinder fitting closely within a tube in which it moves up an down against a liquid or gas, used in an internal-combustion engine to derive motion, or in a pump to impart motion. *The mechanic realized that the car was not functioning as the piston in its engine was stuck.*

Pit/पिट् *(noun & verb)* – गड्ढा, खदान, गड्ढे बनाना the stone of a fruit. *You should remove the pit and eat the pulp of any fruit.*

Pitch/पिच *(noun)* – खेल का तैयार मैदान, तीव्रता, गिरने का स्थान, कोलतार a sticky resinous black or dark brown substance which hardness on cooling, obtained by distilling tar or turpentine and used for waterproofing. *(verb)* chiefly [archaic] cover or coat with pitch. *Applying pitch on the roof helped Anna keep her hut safe during the rains.*

Pitcher/पिचर *(noun)* – घड़ा, सुराही a large jug. *As the afternoon got on, the mother brought out a large pitcher of lemonade for the children playing outside.*

Pitchfork/पिचफॉर्क *(noun)* – पाँचा a farm tool with a long handle and two sharp metal prongs, used for lifting hay. *(verb)* lift with a pitchfork. *The police suspect that the murder was committed using the pitchfork they found lying near the body.*

Piteous/पिटिअस *(adjective)* – दयनीय, कारुणिक अवस्था deserving or arousing pity. *As the moon rose in the sky, the wolf let out a piteous cry.*

Pitfall/पिटफॉल *(noun)* – संकट, अनजाना संकट A hidden or unsuspected danger or difficulty. *The company's new CEO has a hard task of resurrecting the firm from the recent economic pitfall.*

Pith/पिथ *(noun)* – गुद्दा, महत्त्वपूर्ण अंश Spongy white tissue lining the rind of citrus fruits. Botany the spongy cellular tissue in the stems and branches of many higher plants. [archaic] spinal marrow. *The pith of the orange acts as a protective cover to the soft fruit within.*

Pitiable/पिटिएबल *(adjective)* – दयनीय Deserving or arousing pity. *Mary wanted to help the man who seemed to be in a pitiable condition.*

Pitiful/पिटिफुल *(adjective)* – दयाद्र, दया से भरा Deserving or arousing pity. [archaic] compassionate. *The baby let out a pitiful moan on seeing his mother.* very small or poor; inadequate: a pitiful attempt. *Saying that you do not get time to exercise is a pitiful excuse for escaping from the punishment.*

Pitiless/पिटिलेश *(adjective)* – दयाशून्य, निर्दयी showing no pity; harsh or cruel. *The warden at the hostel is a pitiless man.*

Pittance/पिटैंस *(noun)* – छोटी रकम a very small or inadequate amount of money. *Despite working hard for an entire year, he was given a pittance as salary.*

Pity/पिटि *(noun)* – दया the feeling or sorrow and compassion caused by the sufferings of others. *One feels great pity for the people who have no shelter of their own.*

Pivot/पिवॅट् *(noun)* – धुरी the central point, pin, or shaft on which a mechanism turns or oscillates. *You just need to adjust the pivot and the wheel will function effortlessly.*

Pixie/पिक्सी *(noun)* – परी के समान electronics a minute area of illumination on a display screen, one of many from which an image is composed. *The farther the object, you need smaller pixie to get a clearer image.*

Pizza/पिज्ज़ा *(noun)* – सब्जियों से लदी रोटी a dish or Italian origin, consisting of a flat, round base of dough of Italian origin, consisting of a flat, round base of dough baked with a topping of tomatoes, cheese, and other ingredients. *There are more than a dozen chains of this pizza making firm spread all across the country.*

Placard/प्लैकार्ड *(noun)* – प्रदर्शन (विरोध) हेतु तैयार नारे a printed paper for public display, either posted on a wall or carried during a demonstration. *(verb)* cover with placards. *The angry crowd outside the palace was holding placards against the royal family. To bring the point to the notice of the authorities, it is best to cover the topic with placards.*

Placate/प्लैकेट् *(verb)* – शान्त करना, सन्तुष्ट करना calm, pacify or appease. *It is not an easy task to placate a crying toddler.*

Place/प्लेस *(noun)* – स्थान, क्षेत्र, रखना a particular position or point in space; a location. [informal] a person's home. a point in a book reached by a reader at a particular time. *If you are searching for this place, you need to go straight and turn right at the intersection.*

Placid/प्लैसिड् *(adjective)* – शान्त, उत्तेजित न होने वाला not easily upset or excited; calm. *A strong individual is always placid in his heart.*

Plagiarize/प्लेजिअराइज़् *(verb)* – बातों, लेखन की नकल take the work or an idea of someone else and pass it off as one's own. *Imitation may be the best form of flattery but plagiarism is not appreciated by anyone.*

Plague/प्लेग *(noun)* – महामारी a contagious bacterial disease characterized by fever and delirium, typically with the formation of bosons and sometimes infection of the lungs. *The best way to avoid a plague epidemic is to keep the surroundings clean.*

Plain/प्लेन *(adjective)* – सीधा, साफ, स्पष्ट, समतल not decorated or elaborate; simple or ordinary. without a pattern; in only one colour. unmarked; without identification: a plain envelope. *I love the combination of a floral top with a plain skirt.* easy to perceive or understand; clear. not using concealment or deception; frank: he recalled her plain speaking. *Explaining the problem in plain words would avoid any confusion.* of a person having no pretension; not remarkable or special. not marked by any particular beauty; ordinary looking. *She may be a plain looking person but her resolve is made of steel.*

Plaintiff/प्लेन्टिफ *(noun)* – वादी law a person who brings a case against another in a court of law. compare with defendant. *The plaintiff and the judge seem to be known to each other.*

Plaintive/प्लेन्टिव *(adjective)* – दुःखपूर्ण, कातर sounding sad and mournful. *Why are you sounding so plaintive after receiving the phone call?*

P

Plait/प्लेट *(noun)* – चोटी, बालों की चोटी बनाना a single length of hair, rope, or other material made up of three or more interlaced strands. *The rope has been plaited strongly around the box.*

Plan/प्लान *(noun)* – योजना, विचार (किसी काम को करने के लिए) a detailed proposal for doing or achieving something. a scheme for the regular payment of contributions towards a pension, insurance policy, etc, a personal pension plan. *What is your plan for the future of your children?*

Plane/प्लेन *(noun)* – हवाई जहाज, रंदा a tool consisting of a black with a projecting street blade, used to smooth a wooden surface by paring shavings from it. *I cannot finish the varnish today as the plane is broken. (verb)* smooth with a plane. *The best and smoothest finish will be achieved only after we plane the surface.*

Planet/प्लैनेट् *(noun)* – ग्रह a celestial body moving in an elliptical orbit round a star. the earth. [chiefly astrology & historical] a celestial body distinguished from the fixed stars by having an apparent motion of its own. *The hunt for planets outside the solar system has been on for centuries.*

Plank/प्लैंक *(noun)* – पटरा a long, thin, flat piece of timber, used in building and flooring. *If you do not place the plank properly, the entire work will fail.*

Plant/प्लांट *(noun)* – पौधा लगाना, कारखाना लगाना a living organism of the kind exemplified by trees, shrubs, grasses, ferns, and mosses, typical growing in a permanent site, absorbing water and inorganic substances though the roots, and synthesizing nutrients in the leaves by photosynthesis using the green pigment chlorophyll. a small plant, as distinct from a shrub or tree. *Plants help maintain a balance in nature.*

Plantation/प्लांटेशन *(noun)* – बाग-बगीचा, पौधा लगाना a large estate on which crops such as coffee, sugar, and tobacco are grown. *The bride comes from a family that owns several coffee plantations.*

Plaque/प्लाक *(noun)* – स्मृति-पट, दाँतों पर जमी परत an ornamental tablet fixed to a wall in commemoration of a person or event. *He always placed his victory plaques on the walls of his study.*

Plaster/प्लास्टर *(noun)* – दीवार आदि को चिकना करना, हड्डी जोड़ने के लिए लगायी गयी औषधि पट्टिका a soft mixture of lime with sand or cement and water for spreading on walls and ceilings to form a smooth hard surface when dried. *Clay plaster on two walls adds a delicate contrast to concrete and redwood elements.*

Plastic/प्लास्टिक *(noun)* – एक चिकना पदार्थ जिसे आसानी से मोड़ा जा सके या भिन्न आकार दिया जा सके a synthetic material made from a wide range of organic polymers such as polyethylene, PVC, nylon, etc., that can be moulded into shape while soft, and then set into a rigid or slightly elastic form. *We need to reduce the use of plastic as much as possible to save planet earth from further poisoning.*

Plate/प्लेट *(noun)* – तश्तरी, भोजन की थाली, धातु की चद्दर धातु-पट्टिका a flat dish, typically circular, form which food is eaten or served. [north American] a main course of a meal, austral a plate of food contributed by a guest to a social gathering. *Please clean your own plates after you have eaten your meals.*

Plateau/प्लैटो *(noun)* – पठार an area of fairly level high ground. *The Deccan plateau is one of the largest plateaus in Asia.* a state or period of little or no change following a period activity or progress. *The manager of the retail company is deeply concerned about the plateau in the sales graph over the last few months.*

Platform/प्लैटफॉर्म *(noun)* – चबूतरा a raised level surface on which people or things can stand. *A platform was raised for the political leader to address the big gathering.* a raised structure along the side of a railway track where passengers get on and off trains. *Many of the railway platforms are still not disabled person friendly.*

Platinum/प्लैटिनम् *(noun)* – गहनों और उद्योग में प्रयुक्त एक रसायन a precious silvery white metal, the chemical element of atomic number 78. used in jewellery, electrical contacts, laboratory equipment, and industrial catalysts. *Platinum wedding rings are in vogue today.*

Platonic/प्लैटॉनिक *(adjective)* – वासनारहित प्रेम और मैत्री of or associated with the Greek philosopher Plato or his ideas. *Many of the platonic ideas are so very relevant in today's world too.*

Platoon/प्लाटून *(noun)* – सेना की टुकड़ी a subdivision of a company of soldiers, usually commanded by a subaltern or lieutenant and divided into three sections. *The platoon serving in the East Coasts had highly decorated soldiers amongst them.*

P

Plausible/प्लाजिबल् *(adjective)* – तर्कसंगत apparently reasonable or probable, without necessarily being so. *The story narrated by the apprehended thief sounded plausible to the cops.*

Play/प्ले *(verb)* – खेलना, वाद्य बजाना, अभिनय करना engage in games or other activities for enjoyment rather than for a serious or practical purpose. amuse oneself by engaging in imaginative pretence. treat inconsiderately for one's own amusement: *She likes to play with people's emotions.* tamper with something so as to damage it: *Has somebody been playing with these taps?*

Player/प्लेअर *(noun)* – खिलाड़ी a person taking part in a sport or game. *She got the best player's award at the Sports Day function.*

Playful/प्लेफुल *(adjective)* – प्रसन्नचित, विनोदपूर्ण found of games and amusement. *Children are best in their playful age.*

Playmate/प्लेमेट *(noun)* – खेल का साथी a friend with whom a child plays. *She is my playmate and I have grown up with her.*

Plaything/प्लेथिंग *(noun)* – खिलौना a toy. *The child asked her father to find her a plaything as she was bored.*

Plea/प्ली *(noun)*- दलील, अपना पक्ष रखना law a formal statement by or on behalf of a defendant or prisoner, stating guilt or innocence in response to a charge, offering an allegation of fact, or claiming that a point of law should apply. an excuse or claim of mitigating circumstances. *The criminal wanted to file a plea for mercy to save himself from the noose.*

Plead/प्लीड् *(verb)* – सफाई देना, याचना करना present and argue for a position, especially in court or in another public context. law address a court as an advocate on behalf of a party. law state formally in court whether one is guilty or not guilty of the offence with which one is charged. law invoke as an accusation or defense. offer or present as an excuse for doing or not doing something. *She pleaded self-defence.*

Pleasant/प्लेजेंट् *(adjective)* – प्रसन्न कर देने वाला, रमणीय, सुखकर, मैत्रीपूर्ण giving a sense of happy satisfaction or enjoyment. and considerate; likeable. *He had a pleasant nature and was easily lovable.*

Please/प्लीज् *(verb)* – प्रसन्न करना cause to feel happy and satisfied. *He was pleased at her social etiquettes.*

Pleasure/प्लेजर *(noun)* – आनन्द a feeling of happy satisfaction and enjoyment. enjoyment and entertainment, as opposed to necessity. an event or activity from which one derives enjoyment. intended for entertainment rather than business: pleasure boats. sensual gratification. *She derives great pleasure from feeding others.*

Pleat/प्लीट् *(noun)* – चुनट, कपड़े की चुनट a double or multiple fold in a garment or other item made of cloth, held by stitching the tip or side. *The pleats on her skirt had to be rearranged.*

Plebicite/प्लेबिसाइट *(noun)* – जनमत संग्रह direct vote by all electorates on any specific issue. *After the plebiscite, the state was left in a pathetic condition.*

Pledge/प्लेज् *(noun)* – प्रतिज्ञा, वचन a solemn promise or undertaking. a promise of a donation to charity. a solemn undertaking to abstain from alcohol. *The amount pledged for the child had actually increased after the advertisement.*

Plenty/प्लेंटि *(pronoun)* – बहुतायत में, प्रचुरता a large or sufficient amount or quantity; more than enough. *There was plenty of food left for the others.* *(noun)* a situation in which food and other necessities are available in sufficiently large quantities. *Food was available in plenty.* *(adverb)* [informal] fully; sufficiently. *She had plenty of clothes to give away.*

Pliable/प्लाइएबल् *(adjective)* – लचीला easily bent; flexible. *The wires were pliable and therefore could be adjusted easily.*

Pliant/प्लाइअन्ट् *(adjective)* – बिना टूटे आसानी से मुड़ने वाला pliable. *The tool kit was rather fancy as it even had a pliant with the plier for a sample.*

Pliers/प्लाइअर्स *(plural noun)* – एक प्रकार की सँड़सी, तार आदि को काटने का औज़ार pincers

P

with parallel, flat, serrated jaws, used for gripping small objects or bending wire. *I bought him a new plier for his tool kit.*

Plight/प्लाइट *(noun)* – दुःख स्थिति a dangerous, difficult, or otherwise unfortunate situation. *You must consider the plight of the needy when you walk past them.*

Plinth/प्लिंथ *(noun)* – नींव, नींव का ऊपरी भाग a heavy base supporting a stature or vase. *When the plinth started cracking, we knew the tremors had started.*

Plod/प्लॉड *(verb)* – कठिनाई से धीरे-धीरे चलना walk doggedly and slowly with heavy steps. work slowly and perseveringly at a dull. task. *we were plodding through the task to get the best results.* *(noun)* a slow, heavy walk. *After running across half the city, we were now plodding through the street near his house.*

Plop/प्लॉप *(noun)* – छप-छप, छप-छपाक a short sound as of a small, solid object dropping into water without a splash. *The snail fell into the puddle with a plop.* *(verb)* fall or drop with such a sound. *There was a plop where it landed.*

Plot/प्लॉट *(noun)* – छोटा भूमिखण्ड, कथानक, कुचक्र a plan made in secret by a group of people to do something illegal or harmful. *They had devised a sinister plot to kill the minister.*

Plough/प्लाउ *(noun)* – हल, हल जोतना a large farming implement with one or more blades fixed in a frame, drawn over soil to turn it over and cut furrows in preparation for the planting of seeds. *The land that has been ploughed will give a better crop.*

Ploy/प्लाय *(noun)* – लाभ हेतु सुनियोजित कथन a cunning plan or action designed to turn a situation to one's own advantage. *He had devised a cunning ploy to rob the bank.*

Pluck/प्लक *(verb)* – चुनना, बिनना, हटाना take hold of and quickly remove if from its place. catch hold of and pull quickly. *She plucked her eyebrows before setting out for the party.*

Plug/प्लग *(noun)* – छिद्र बन्द करने का रबर या धातु, बिजली संचालन के लिए प्रयुक्त यन्त्र a piece of solid material fitting tightly into a hole and blocking it up. a mass of solidified lava filling the neck of a volcano. *I put the plug into the hole so it won't leak any more.*

Plumb/प्लम्ब *(verb)* – सीधा करना install a bath, washing machine, etc. and connect it to water and drainage pipes. install and connect pipes in a building or room. *It was a new house so we had a lot of plumbs to fix.*

Plumber/प्लम्बर *(noun)* – नल का कारीगर a person who fits and repairs the pipes and fitting of water supply, sanitation, or heating systems. *The plumber came to fix the pipes in our house.*

Plumb line/प्लमलाइन *(noun)* – साहुल a line with a plumb attached to it. *The leak was found to have started from the plumb below the sink.*

Plume/प्लूम *(noun)* – बड़ा, पंख, पंखनुमा वस्तु a long, soft feather or arrangement of feathers used by a bird for display or worn on a hat or helmet as decoration. *The bird's plumes were shining in the sun's rays.*

Plummet/प्लमेट *(verb)* – रस्सी की छोर पर लगाया गया वजन fall or drop straight down at high speed. decrease rapidly in value or amount. *The value of the shares was plummeting.*

Plump/प्लम्प *(adjective)* – गोल-मटोल full and rounded in shape. rather fat. *I was meeting her after a long time and realized she had grown plump.* *(verb)* make or become full and round. *She had turned plump over the years.*

Plunder/प्लंडर *(verb)* – लूटपाट, लूट का सामान forcibly steal goods from, especially in time of war or civil disorder. *The enemies had plundered the whole state.* *(noun)* the action of plundering. property acquired in this way. *Property acquired by plundering will not yield profits for a long time.*

Plunge/प्लंज *(verb)* – जबरदस्ती घुसाना fall or move suddenly and uncontrollably. jump or dive quickly and energetically. *With a deep breath, he plunged into the water.*

Plural/प्लुरल *(adjective)* – बहुवचन move than one in number. [grammar] denoting more than one, or more than two. *Unfortunately, you may not have to consider the number of students appearing for the blood donation* camp in plural. (noun) [grammar] a plural word or form. the plural number. *The teacher asked the students the list out the plural forms of the given words.*

Plus/प्लस (noun) – जोड़ा का चिह्न (+) with the addition of. [informal] together with. *When you make icing, chocolates are indeed a plus.* (adjective) at least: $500,000 plus. *The cheque amounts to $500,000 plus.*

Plush/प्लश (noun) – मखमल a rich fabric of silk, cotton, or wool, with a long, soft nap. *Let us not live a plush life when we cannot afford it.* (adjective) [informal] richly luxurious and expensive. *I bought her a plush cushion to sleep on.*

Pluto/प्लूटो (noun) – सूर्य से अति दूर एक ग्रह the most remote known planet of the solar system, ninth in order from the sun. *Pluto is no longer considered a planet belonging to the solar system.*

Plutonium/प्लूटोनियम (noun) – परमाणु अभिक्रिया का एक तत्त्व the chemical element of atomic number 94, a dense silvery radioactive metal of the actinide series, used as a fuel in nuclear reactors and as an explosive in nuclear fission weapons. *Every since they discovered plutonium in the land behind his ancestral house, several government agencies have been flocking the place.*

Ply/प्लाइ (noun) – लकड़ी की परत, ऊन की लड़ी नियमित रूप से वाहन का परिचालन a thickness or layer of a folded or laminated material. *There were several layers of ply spread on the carpenter's table.* each of a number of multiple layers or strands of which something is made: four-ply. *The table had a four-ply structure.*

Pneumatic/न्यूमेटिक (adjective) – हवा से भरा हुआ containing or operated by air or gas under pressure. *We realized that the instrument he bought was not working because it was pneumatic.*

Pnemonia/न्यूमोनिया (noun) – फेफड़े में सूजन a lung infection in which the air sacs full with pus. *Unlike the earlier times, today there is a positive treatment available for pneumonia.*

Poach/पोच (verb) – अण्डे का पकवान, जानवर चुराना cook by simmering in a small amount of liquid. cook without its shell in or over building water. *Poached egg is extremely healthy and a good option for losing weight.*

Pocket/पॉकेट (noun) – जेब, पृथक् क्षेत्र a small bag sewn into or on clothing so as to form part of it, used for carrying small articles. a pouch like compartment providing separate storage space. [informal] one's financial resources. *I bought her a bag with several pockets so she could keep it neat and organized.*

Pod/पॉड (noun) – फली a small herd or school of marine animals, especially whales. *The friends were like peas in a pod.*

Podium/पोडिअम् (noun) – चबूतरा a small platform on which a person may stand to be seen by an audience. [north American] a lectern. *The chief guest was invited to the podium to say a few words to the audience.*

Poem/पोएम (noun) – कविता a literary composition that is given intensity by particular attention to diction rhythm, and imagery. *Her diary was full of poems.*

Poet/पोएट (noun) – कवि a person who writes poems. a person possessing special powers of imagination or expression. *Her beauty could turn anyone into a poet.*

Poetic/पोएटिक (adjective) – काव्यात्मक relating to or of the nature of poetry. *The prose he wrote was more poetic than like prose.*

Poetry/पोएट्रि (noun) – काल, कवित्व, कालात्मकता poems collectively or as a genre of literature. a quality of beauty and intensity of emotion regarded as characteristic of poetry. *She wanted to attend the poetry convention that would start soon.*

Poignant/पॉइनन्ट (adjective) – हृदय विदारक, दहला देने वाला evoking a keen sense of sadness or regret. *It was a poignant theme to write a play on.*

Point/पॉइन्ट (noun) – बिन्दु, नोक, नक्शे या चित्र पर स्थिति किसी की ओर इशारा करना the tapered, sharp end of a tool, weapon, or other object. archaeology a pointed flake or blade. ballet another term for Pointe. boxing the tip of a

P

person's chin as a spot for a blow. the prong of a deer's antler. *The spear was shining at its point so much that it would make any man shiver.*

Point-blank/पाँइन्ट ब्लैंक *(adjective & adverb)* – बहुत समीप से fired from very close to its target. *The shots were fired at point blank range.*

Pointer/पॉइन्टर *(noun)* – इंगित करने के लिए छड़ी a long, thin piece of metal on a scale or dial which moves to give a reading. a rod used for pointing to features on a map or chart. computing a link. *Do not depend on the pointer too much to get your results.*

Pointless/पॉइन्टलेस *(adjective)* – व्यर्थ, निरर्थक having little or no sense purpose. *It is pointless shedding tears before me, my father told me.*

Poise/पॉइज *(noun)* – सन्तुलित रहना [physics] a unit of dynamic viscosity, such dignity of manner. *He was somehow precariously poised at a 45 degree angle.*

Poison/पॉइजन *(noun)* – जहर, विष a substance that causes death or harm when introduced into or aborted by a living organism. *The poison was gradually spreading in the rest of his body.*

Poke/पोक *(noun & verb)* – प्रहार, कोंचना, कुरेदना to push, thrust. *He poked the stick down the hole to see how deep it was to push, to thrust.*

Poker/पोकर *(noun)* – धातु की कुरेदनी, ताश का एक खेल a metal rod with a handle, used for prodding and stirring an open fire. *She took the poker out of the fire and shoved it at the boy as if to scare him away.*

Polar/पोलर *(adjective)* – ध्रुव प्रदेशीय of or relating to a pole or poles, in particular, of the north or south pole or their adjacent area. *News has been doing the rounds that the polar ice caps are melting.*

Polaroid/पोलरॉइड् *(noun)* – शीघ्र तैयार चित्र का तकनीक trademark a composite material with the property of polarizing light, produced in thin plastic sheets. sunglasses a finished print rapidly after each exposure. a photograph taken with such a camera. *Father bought me a Polaroid camera this birthday.*

Pole/पोल *(noun)* – ध्रुव, पोलैण्ड का निवासी a native or national of Poland, or a person of polish descent. *There were people from several countries in our boat, including an American, two Indians, a Chinese couple and a Pole.*

Police/पॅलीस् *(noun)* – आरक्षी a civil force responsible for the prevention and detection of crime and the maintenance of public order. members of such a force. *Right from childhood, he has dreamt of joining the police force.* *(verb)* control and maintain law and order in an area, with or as with a police force. *The guards were asked to police the area for a few days.*

Policy/पॉलिसी *(noun)* – शर्त और नियम, बीमा course or principle of action adopted or proposed by an organization or individual. *The government introduced several policies in the agricultural sector this year.*

Polio/पोलिओ *(noun)* – एक रोग, सन्तुलित वृद्धि का अभाव short for poliomyelitis. *He had polio when he was an infant.*

Polish/पॉलिश *(noun)* – चमकाना, चमकाने वाला रंग, परिष्कृत साधारण the western Slavic language of Poland. *Initially I mistook his language for French but later I realized it was Polish.* *(adjective)* of or relating to Poland, its inhabitants, or their language. *He made a typical Polish gruel for dinner.*

Polite/पोलाइट *(adjective)* – विनम्र, शिष्ट respectful and considerate of other people. cultured and refined: polite society. *I had met her only once but she always came out as extremely polite.*

Political/पॉलिटिकल *(adjective)* – राजनीतिक of or relating to the government or public affairs of a country. interested in or active in politics. *That he had political ambitions was evident from the message he conveys in all his movies.*

Politician/पॉलिटिसिअन *(noun)* – राजनीतिज्ञ a person who is professionally involved in politics, especially as a holder of an elected office. *He made an excellent politician for the country.*

P

Politics/पॉलिटिक्स *(plural noun)* – राजनीति the activities associated with the governance of a country or area. a particular set of political beliefs or principles. *The politics of our country is beyond my understanding.*

Poll/पोल *(noun)* – मतदान, जनमत सर्वेक्षण, प्राप्त मत the process of voting in an election. a record of the number of votes cast in an election. an opinion poll. *The results of the opinion poll were in favour of the Democrats.*

Pollen/पॉलेन *(noun)* – पराग a powdery substance discharged from the male gamete that can fertilize the female ovule. *There is a heavy concentration of pollen grains in the air here.*

Pollute/पॉल्यूट *(verb)* – दूषित करना, गन्दा करना, प्रदूषण फैलाना contaminate water; the air, etc. with harmful or poisonous substances. *We were asked to get used to waste segregation and stop polluting the environment.*

Polo/पोलो *(noun)* – चौगान, एक प्रकार का खेल a game of eastern origin with rules similar to hockey, played on horseback with a long-handled mallet. *My cousin is a State level Polo player.*

Poly/पॉलि *(noun)* – बहु का प्रत्यय polyester. *She had found a rare sari made of polyester fabric.*

Polyandry/पॉलिएन्ड्रि *(noun)* – एक से अधिक पति where a woman has more than one husband. Compare with polygyny. *There are several instances of polyandry in our scriptures.*

Polyester/पॉलिएस्टर *(noun)* – कृत्रिम, कपड़ा a synthetic resin in which the polymer units are linked by ester groups, used chiefly to make textile fibers. *She wore a lovely polyester sari for her friend's wedding.*

Polygamy/पॉलिगैमि *(noun)* – बहुविवाह practice or custom of having more than one wife or husband at the same time. *In the ancient times, polygamy was actually forgiven.*

Polygon/पॉलिगॉन *(noun)* – पंचकोण geometry a plane figure with at least three straight sides and angles, and typically five or more. *I can never draw a perfect polygon.*

Polytechnic/पॉलिटेक्निक *(noun)* – वैज्ञानिक तथा तकनीकि शिक्षालय an institution offering higher education in vocationed subjects. *She has taken admission in civil engineering in government polytechnic.*

Polythene/पालिथिन *(noun)* – एक पारदर्शी लचीली वस्तु chiefly British a tough, light, flexible synthetic resin made by polymerizing ethylene, chiefly used for packaging. *The poor cow died because of the polythene bag that it accidentally ate and that got stuck in its throat.*

Pomp/पॉम्प *(noun)* – तड़क-भड़क, आडम्बर ceremony and splendid display. *The wedding will be celebrated with great pomp and show.*

Pompous/पॉम्पस *(adjective)* – आडम्बरपूर्ण affectedly grand, solemn, or self-important. *He read it out in a pompous voice.*

Pond/पॉन्ड *(noun)* – तालाब, ताल-तलैया a fairly small body of still water. *I asked the horticulturist to design a small pond for our garden.*

Ponder/पॉन्डर *(verb)* – गम्भीतापूर्वक विचार consider carefully. *The notices were passed to all of us to ponder over.*

Ponderous/पॉन्डरस *(adjective)* – नीरस, ऊबाऊ, बोझिल slow and clumsy because of great weight. *He strolled about with a ponderous heavy gait.*

Pony/पॉनि *(noun)* – टट्टू a horse of a small breed. *The hill station had ponies at every nook and corner.*

Pooh/पूह – घृणा, तिरस्कार का उद्गार *exclamatory* expressing disgust at an unpleasant smell. *"Pooh Pooh!" said Richard Parker, "and how could I know who did it?"*

Pool/पूल *(noun)* – जलजमाव, एक खेल, संसाधन एकत्र करना a small area of still water, typically one formed naturally. a deep place in a river. an artificial pool for swimming in. *We had a pool in our ancestral house where we all learnt swimming as kids.*

Poor/पूअर *(adjective)* – गरीब, निर्धन lacking sufficient money to live at a standard considered comfortable or normal. *Studies say that there are more poor people in our country than in any other country in the world.*

Poorly/पूअरलि *(adverb)* – दीनता के साथ, किसी तरह in a poor manner. *She did poorly in the* exams once again. *(adjective)* chiefly unwell. *I have been feeling poorly ever since we had dinner at that Dhaba the other day.*

Pop/पॉप *(noun)* – बोतल खुलने की आवाज, तड़ाक commercial popular music, in particular accessible, tuneful music of a kind popular since the 1950. *Michael Jackson is known as the king of pop music*

Popcorn/पॉपकार्न *(noun)* – मकई का लावा maize of a variety with hard kernels that swell up and burst open when heated and are then eaten as a snack. *She could never imagine watching a movie without popcorn.*

Pope/पोप *(noun)* – सर्वोच्च धर्म गुरु the bishop of Rome as head of the roman catholic church. *Everyone hoped that the next pope would be a great peacemaker.*

Poplin/पॉपलिन *(noun)* – चमकदार पतला सूती कपड़ा a plain woven fabric, typically a very light-weight cotton, with a corded surface. *She was prettily dressed in gray poplin, trimmed with gray velvet and a deep red sash around her trim waist.*

Poppy/पॉपि *(noun)* – अफीम, खसखस a plant having showy flowers, typically red or yellow, and rounded seed capsules. *Bengalis use a lot of poppy seeds in their cooking.*

Populace/पॉप्युलेस *(noun)* – जनसाधाररण the general public. *A large proportion of the populace was against the idea of breaking down the structure.*

Popular/पॉप्युलर *(adjective)* – प्रचलित, प्रसिद्ध, प्रशंसित liked or admired by many or by a particular person or group. *She was easily the most popular girl in school.*

Populate/पॉप्युलेट *(verb)* – बस्ती बसाना form the population of a place. cause people to settle in a place. *North America was largely populated by Europeans.*

Population/पॉप्युलेशन *(noun)* – जनसंख्या, आबादी all the inhabitants of a particular place. a particular group within this. the action of populating an area. *The population of our country has doubled over the last few years.*

Porcelain/पॉर्सिलेन *(noun)* – चीनी मिट्टी, चीनी मिट्टी की वस्तुएँ a white vitrified translucent ceramic; china. See also macro-paste, soft-paste. articles made of this. *Porcelain makes for some of the most beautiful and affordable cutlery.*

Porch/पोर्च *(noun)* – प्रवेश द्वार a covered shelter projecting in front of the entrance of a building. *Every villa in the complex had a designer car porch.*

Porcupine/पॉरक्युपाइन *(noun)* – शाही a large rodent with defensive spines or quills on the body and tail. *The population of porcupines had reduced over the years.*

Pore/पोर *(noun)* – रोमकूप, रोएँ के छिद्र, ध्यान से अध्ययन a minute opening in the skin or other surface through which gases, liquids, or microscope particles may pass. *The dermatologist advised me to wash my face frequently so the pores of my skin would not be closed.*

Pork/पॉर्क *(noun)* – सूअर का माँस the flesh of a pig used as food, especially when uncured. *Home cooked pork vindaloo was his favourite dish whenever he was at home.*

Pornography/पॅर्नॅग्राफी *(noun)* – कामुक चित्र, चलचित्र, पुस्तक आदि printed or visual material intended to stimulate sexual excitement. *The government was intending to put a censor on pornography in the internet as well.*

Porous/पोरस *(adjective)* – छिद्रवाला, छिद्रदार of a rock or other material having minute interstices through which liquid or air may pass. *Local limestone is extremely porous.*

Porpoise/पोर्पॅस *(noun)* – सूईस, सूँस, समुद्री जीव a small toothed whale with a low triangular dorsal fin and a blunt rounded snout. *The island was known for an occasional sighting of the porpoise.*

Porridge/पॉरिज *(noun)* – खीर, दलिया a dish consisting of oatmeal or another cereal boiled with water or milk. *My parents prefer having porridge for breakfast since its easy to cook.*

Port/पोर्ट *(noun)* – बन्दरगाह, द्वार, लाल शराब a town a city with a harbour or access to navigable water where ships load or unload. *Tuesday morning was a typical day at the port with all the hustle bustle and chaos of the fishermen, sailors and travellers.*

P

Portable/पोर्टेबल *(adjective)* – हल्का सामान, आसानी से ढोया जाने वाला able to be easily carried or moved. *I bought her a portable music player that she could take with her wherever she travels.*

Porter/पोर्टर *(noun)* – कुली, सामान वाहक British an employee in charge of the entrance of a hotel, block of flats, or other large building. *The manager signalled to the porter to take the customer's luggage to his room.*

Portfolio/पोर्टफोलिओ *(noun)* – चमड़े का बस्ता, निवेश, मन्त्री का विभाग large, thin, flat case for carrying drawings, maps, etc. *He had a portfolio in the almirah in which he keeps all his pictures and drawings.*

Porthole/पोर्टहोल *(noun)* – छोटी गोल खिड़की a small window on the outside of a ship or an aircraft. *He clung to the frame of the porthole as the airship swung and swayed in all directions.*

Portion/पोर्सन *(noun)* – हिस्सा, भाग, अंश a part or a share. an amount of food suitable for or served to one person. law the part or share of an estate given or descending by law to an heir. *The dietician advised us to take only one portion of meal at a time.*

Portly/पोर्टली *(adjective)* – स्थूलकाय rather fat. *Men are portly and women are stout.*

Portrait/पोर्ट्रेट *(noun)* – ऊपरी भाग का चित्र an artistic representation of a person, especially one depicting only the face or head and shoulders. *I asked the painter to paint my portrait.*

Portray/पोट्रे *(verb)* – पुस्तक या चित्र में दर्शाना depict in a work of art or literature. *The actress's life was portrayed in a beautiful manner in the movie.*

Pose/पोज *(verb)* – विशेष ढंग से बैठना या खड़ा होना [archaic] perplex with a question or problem. *The teacher was dumbfound at the question the student posed.*

Posh/पॉश *(adjective)* – उत्कृष्ट और महँगा elegant or stylishly luxurious. *He always had a tendency to live a posh life.*

Position/पोजिशन *(noun)* – स्थिति, विशेष जगह, ठिकाना a place where someone or something is located or has been put. the correct place. a place where part of a military force is posted for strategic purposes. *The paratroops had been given positions in such a way that the terrorists could not see where they were being attacked from.*

Positive/पॉजिटिव *(adjective)* – निश्चित, रचनात्मक, पक्का consisting in or characterized by the presence rather than the absence of distinguishing features, expressing or implying affirmation, agreement, or permission. *I look forward to a positive reply from you.*

Possess/पॅजेस *(verb)* – स्वामित्व रखना, अधिकार में रखना have as belonging to one. law have possession of as distinct from ownership. *He is said to possess a huge forturne.*

Possession/पॅजेशन् *(noun)* – स्वामित्व the state of possessing something. law visible power or control, as distinct from lawful ownership. temporary control of the ball by a player or team. *The home team was in possession during most of the fourth quarter.*

Possessive/पॅजेसिव *(adjective)* – अधिकार में रखने को आतुर demanding someone's total attention and love. *She had a tendency to be extremely possessive of her loved ones.*

Possibility/पॉसिबिलिटि *(noun)* – सम्भावना a thing that is possible. *There is a good possibility it may rain today.*

Possible/पॉसिबल् *(adjective)* – सम्भव capable of existing, happening, or being achieved. that may be so, but that is not certain or portable. *It is not possible to finish this in two weeks.*

Post/पोस्ट *(noun)* – खूँटा, ठिकाना, पद, स्थान, डाक a job. *She had applied for an interview for the post of manager,* a place where someone is on duty or where an activity is carried out. [north American] a force stationed at a permanent position or camp. *A soldier manned the entrance post.*

Postage/पोस्टेज *(noun)* – डाकटिकट, डाकव्यय the sending of letters and parcels by post. the amount required to send something by post. *I bought a dozen postage stamps so I don't need to run to the post office every time I need one.*

P

Postal/पोस्टल *(adjective)* – डाक से सम्बन्धित of or relating to the post. *The one postal delivery in our locality was in the morning.*

Postdate/पोस्टडेट *(verb)* – बाद की तारीख affix or assign a date later than the actual one to a document or event. *I gave her a postdated cheque.*

Poster/पोस्टर *(noun)* – प्रदर्शित सूचना a large printed picture or notice used for decoration or advertisement. *The police arrested the goons for pasting posters on the wall in spite of the warning not to.*

Posterity/पॅस्टेरिटि *(noun)* – भावी पीढ़ियाँ all future generation. *A photographer recorded the scene for posterity.*

Postgraduate/पोस्टग्रैड्युऍट *(adjective)* – स्नातकोत्तर relating to or denoting a course of study undertaken after completing a first degree. *She did her Post graduation in Applied Operation Analysis. (noun)* a person engaged in postgraduate study. *"I am a post graduate, so I should be allowed for the seminar."*

Posthumous/पॅस्ट्यूमस् *(adjective)* – मरणोपरान्त occurring awarded, or appearing after the death of the originator. *He was given a posthumous award and title for his bravery.*

Post-mortem/पोस्टमॉर्टम् *(noun)* – शव परीक्षा an examination of a dead body to determine the cause of death. *They took the body from the accident site for a post mortem.*

Postpone/पोस्टपोन *(verb)* – स्थगित करना arrange for to take place at a time later than that first scheduled. *Never postpone for tomorrow the work that you can finish today.*

Postscript/पोस्टस्क्रिप्ट *(noun)* – पत्र आदि के अंत में जोड़ा गया अतिरिक्त अंश, सूचना या संदेश an additional remark at the end of a letter, following the signature. *He had added a note as postscript in his mail saying the balance money is attached.*

Postulate/पॉस्ट्युलेट *(verb)* – पहले ही मान लेना suggest or assume the existence, fact, or truth of as a basis for reasoning, discussion, or belief. *He postulated several theories in his lifetime.*

Posture/पॉस्चर *(noun)* – शरीर की मुद्रा a particular position of the body. the way in which a person holds their body. *You must sit upright on a chair in order to have a good posture.*

Pot/पॉट *(noun)* – बरतन, गमले, गोली दागना an attempt to score a goal with kick *He took a pot-shot at the bird on the fence. (verb)* score a goal. *"What a pot he scored!"*

Potable/पोटेबल् *(adjective)* – पीने योग्य drinkable. *Wine and other potables were kept in a different bunker.*

Potato/पोटैटो *(noun)* – आलू a starchy plant tuber which is one of the most important food crops, cooked and eaten as a vegetable. *Boiled potatoes with cheese and ham are a common dish Europeans eat for breakfast.*

Potent/पोटेंट *(adjective)* – शक्तिशाली, गुणकारी, प्रभावशाली having great power; influence, or effect. *The drug is extremely potent but can have extreme side effects.* able to achieve an erection or to reach an orgasm. *The boy was pleased to know he was potent.*

Potential/पॅटेनशल् *(adjective)* – संभाव्य, विकसित होने का सम्भावना having the capacity to develop into something in the future. *Your ideas have potential, I have to admit. (noun)* latent qualities or abilities that may be developed and lead to future success or useful ability of something happening or of someone doing something in the future. *He has a huge potential to become someone great when he grows up.*

Pothole/पॉटहोल *(noun)* – गड्ढे, बारिस का गड्ढा a deep natural underground cave formed by the eroding action of water. a deep circular hole in a river bed formed by the eroding action of stones in an eddy. *Warnings were issued as the rain had caused several pot holes on the roads.*

Potter/पॉटर *(noun & verb)* – कुम्हार, भटकना occupy oneself in a desultory but pleasant manner. *She was pottering around the whole place all day.*

Potty/पॉटी *(adjective)* – छोटे बच्चे का मल त्याग पात्र foolish, crazy. *"Are you going potty?"*

Pouch/पॉउच *(noun)* – थैली, पुड़िया, आँखों के नीचे लटकता त्वचा a small flexible bag. a lacks able bag for mail or dispatches. *I carried all my junk jewellery in a pouch.*

P

Poultry/पाउल्ट्री *(noun)* – मुर्गीपालन chickens, turkeys, ducks, and geese; domestic fowl. *Most of the poultry was being culled because of the rumours of bird flu.*

Pounce/पाउन्स *(verb)* – अचानक आक्रमण, दबोचना spring or swoop suddenly to catch or as if to catch prey. *The tiger ran after the deer and pounced on its neck.*

Pound/पाउन्ड *(noun)* – ब्रिटेन की मुद्रा, चूर-चूर कर देना, धड़कना a place where strays may officially be taken and kept until claimed. a place where illegally parked motor vehicles removed by the police are kept until the owner pays a fine. *I visited the pound down the street to buy a pet.*

Pour/पोर *(verb)* – डालना, धारा में गिराना flow or cause to flow in a steady stream. fall heavily. prepare and serve. *Pour the curry into the serving bowl.*

Pout/पाउट *(verb)* – मुँह बिचकाना push one's lips or bottom lip forward as an expression of petulant annoyance or in order to make oneself look sexually attractive. *The actress tried pouting during the photo shoot but it didn't help her at all.* *(noun)* a pouting expression. *Her pout was not really of much help.*

Poverty/पावर्टि *(noun)* – गरीबी, निर्धनता the state of being extremely poor. the renunciation of the right to individual ownership of property as part of a religious vow. *The leaders of our country dreamt of achieving a state of no poverty in the country.*

Powder/पावडर *(noun)* – चूर्ण, चूरा, बारूद fine dry particles produced by the grinding, crushing, or disintegration of a solid substance. *Coffee beans need to be powdered to make instant coffee.*

Power/पॉवर *(noun)* – शक्ति, योग्यता the ability to do something or act in a particular way. *The power of his love saved her.*

Powerful/पॉवरफुल *(adjective)* – शक्तिशाली, योग्य, समर्थ having power. *The ruling party is one of the most powerful we have ever had till date.*

Powerless/पॉवरलेस *(adjective)* – अशक्त, अयोग्य, असमर्थ without ability, inflvence, power. *The cat was left powerless in front of the dog.*

Practicable/प्रैक्टिकेबल् *(adjective)* – व्यावहारिक, व्यवहार्य able to be done or put into practice successfully. *Teachers can only be expected to do what is practicable.*

Practical/प्रैक्टिकल *(adjective)* – व्यावहारिक of or concerned with practice. *He gained practical experience of sailing as a deck hand.*

Practice/प्रैक्टिस *(noun)* – अभ्यास the actual application or use of a plan or method, as opposed to the theories relating to it. *We tried putting the diet into practice but it was very difficult.*

Practise/प्रैक्टिस *(verb)* – अभ्यास करना perform or exercise repeatedly or regularly in order to acquire, maintain, or improve proficiency in it. *Practise constantly to gain knowledge in maths.*

Practitioner/प्रैक्टिश्नर *(noun)* – व्यवहार में लाने वाला a person actively engaged in an art, discipline, or profession, especially [medicine]. *He has been a practitioner of Ayurvedic medicine for the last ten years.*

Pragmatic/प्रैग्मेटिक *(adjective)* – व्यावहारिक, यथार्थ dealing with things in a way that is based on practical rather than theoretical considerations. *He gave a pragmatic perspective to the problem at hand.*

Prairie/प्रेरि *(noun)* – घास के पेड़हीन मैदान a large open area of grassland. *With global warming, even the prairies were disappearing.*

Praise/प्रेज *(verb)* – प्रशंसा, सराहना, स्तुति, गुणगान express warm approval of or admiration for. *She received lots of praise from her peers and teachers for being an all rounder.*

Pram/प्रैम *(noun)* – बच्चा गाड़ी British a four-wheeled carriage for a baby. pushed by a person on foot. *He was so excited about the baby coming home, he bought five different kinds of prams.*

Prance/प्रैंस *(verb)* – इठलाकर चलना move with high springy steps. *She was prancing around like a rooster in a hen house.*

Prank/प्रैंक *(noun)* – शरारत, नटखटपन a practical jokes or mischievous act. *The actor was known for the pranks he would play on the sets.*

Prattle/प्रैटल *(verb)* – बड़बड़ाना talk at length in a foolish or inconsequential way. *She prattled on till I wanted to scream.* *(noun)* foolish or inconsequential talk. *I had had enough of his mindless prattle.*

Prawn/प्रॉन *(noun)* – झींगा a marine crustacean which resembles a large shrimp. *Prawn sandwiches are her favourite indeed.*

Pray/प्रे *(verb)* – प्रार्थना, प्रार्थना करना, स्तुति करना address a prayer to god or another deity. *I have been taught from childhood to pray before I sleep at night.* wish or hope earnestly for a particular outcome. *I prayed incessantly for his speedy recovery.* *(adverb)* formal used in polite requests or questions. *"Pray continue."*

Prayer/प्रेअर *(noun)* – प्रार्थना, स्तोत्र-पाठ a solemn request for help or expression of thanks addressed to god or another deity. *The doctor told us that only prayer could save her now.*

Pre/प्री – एक उपसर्ग, पूर्व *prefix* before in time, place, order, degree, or importance: pre-adolescent. *She has entered her pre-adolescent years now.*

Preach/प्रीच *(verb)* – उपदेश देना deliver a religious address to an assembled group of people. publicly proclaim. *The father preached the gospel.*

Preamble/प्रिएम्बल *(noun)* – प्रस्तावना, आमुख a preliminary statement; an introduction. *The Preamble of our Constitution contains the Directive Principles of State Authority.*

Precarious/प्रिकेरिअस *(adjective)* – खतरे में, असुरक्षित not securely held or in position; likely to fall. *He was standing in a precarious position, and I feared anyone could easily catch him.*

Precaution/प्रिकॉशन *(noun)* – पूर्व से रखी जाने वाली सावधानी, पूर्व उपाय a measure taken in advance to prevent something undesirable from happening. *You must take proper precautions before you go for the adventure trip.*

Precede/प्रिसिड *(verb)* – पहले होना come or go before in time, order, or position. preface something with. *Stone tools precede bronze tools.*

Precedence/प्रिसिडेंस *(noun)* – वरीयता, प्राथमिकता the condition of preceding others in importance, order, or rank. an acknowledged or legally determined right to such precedence. *Recipients of military honour were called in order of precedence—higher ranking officers first.*

Precedent/प्रिसिडेंट *(noun)* – पूर्व पीठिका, स्थापित नियम या परम्परा an earlier event or action serving as an example or guide. law a previous case or legal decision that may be or must be followed in subsequent similar cases. *The trial could set an important precedent for similar cases.* *(adjective)* preceding in time, order, or importance. *The President followed historical precedent in forming the Cabinet.*

Precept/प्रीसेप्ट *(noun)* – नियम, नीतिवचन a general rule regulating behavior or thought. *He believed and followed all the precepts of Buddhism.*

Precinct/प्रीसिंक्ट *(noun)* – निर्धारित क्षेत्र the area within the walls or perceived boundaries of a particular place. an enclosed or clearly defined area of ground around a cathedral, church, or college. British an area in a town designated for specific or restricted use, especially one closed to traffic. *Hunting is not allowed within the precincts of the estate.*

Precious/प्रेशस *(adjective)* – बहुमूल्य, अमूल्य having great value. *She has kept all her precious jewels safely in the locker.*

Precipice/प्रेसिपिस *(noun)* – खड़ी चट्टान a tall and very steep rock face or cliff. *The path had sheer rock on one side and a precipice on the other.*

Precipitate/प्रेसिपिटेट *(verb)* – अचानक घट जाना, समय से पूर्व घटित होना cause to happen unexpectedly or prematurely. *The killings in the city have precipitated the worst crisis ever.*

Precis/प्रेसिस *(noun)* – संक्षेपण a summary of a text or speech. *We were asked to present a précis before the actual presentation.* *(verb)* make a précis of. *His précis invited a huge applause, so I won't be surprised if his presentation was a runaway success.*

P

Precise/प्रिसाइस् *(adjective)* – सावधानी पूर्वक कहा हुआ, सही ढंग से कहा हुआ marked by exactness and accuracy of expression or detail. very attentive to detail; careful in the expression of detail. exact; particular. *I want the precise details of the project that the rival company is taking up.*

Preision/प्रिसिजन *(noun)* – सावधानी, संक्षिप्तता, यथार्थता the quality, condition, or fact of being precise. *He handled it with the precision of an automated machine.*

Precocious/प्रिकोशस *(adjective)* – अवस्था से पूर्व योग्यता अर्जित करना having developed certain abilities or inclinations at an earlier age than usual. *Radhika has always been a precocious child.*

Preconceived/प्रिकन्सिव्ड *(adjective)* – पहले से धारित अवधारणा formed prior to having evidence for its truth or usefulness. *Do not enter into the experiment with any preconceived notions in your mind.*

Preconception/प्रिकन्सेप्शन *(noun)* – पहले से बनी अवधारणा a preconceived idea or prejudice. *He did not even try to confirm his preconceptions before he passed the news.*

Predator/प्रिडेटर *(noun)* – जीव भक्षी जानवर, हिंसक जानवर an animal that preys on others. *Life in the jungle follows the prey-predator format.*

Predecessor/प्रिडिसेसर *(noun)* – पूर्ववर्ती, पूर्व अधिकारी, पूर्व से प्रचलित a person who held a job or office before the current holder. *The new manager should learn a thing or two about management from his predecessor.*

Predicament/प्रिडिकमेंट् *(noun)* – अप्रिय स्थिति, परेशानी, द्विविधा a difficult situation. *You would definitely never understand my predicament unless you were in my shoes.*

Predicate/प्रिडिकेट *(noun)* – आधार पर निर्णय, भविष्यवाणी-सी घोषणा [grammar] the part of a sentence or clause containing a very and stating something about the subject. *The question was: Identify the predicate in "The child is very sleepy".*

Predicative/प्रिडिकेटिव *(adjective)* – विधेयात्मक [grammar] forming or contained in the predicate, as old in the dog is old. contrasted with attributive. denoting a use of the verb to be to assert something about the subject. *Identify the predicative word in : Jane opened the door.*

Predict/प्रिडिक्ट *(verb)* – भविष्यवाणी state that a specified event will happen in the future. *Nostradamous predicted the world to come to an end in 2012.*

Predictable/प्रिडिक्टेबल् *(adjective)* – जो भविष्यवाणी करने योग्य हो able to be predicted. derogatory always behaving or occurring in the way expected. *She has a predictable nature.*

Predominant/प्रिडॉमिनैन्ट् *(adjective)* – अधिकार और प्रभाव में दूसरों से प्रबल present as the strongest or main element. having or exerting the greatest control or power. *He played a predominant role in shaping the constitution of our country.*

Predominance/प्रिडॉमिनैन्स *(noun)* – प्राधान्य state or condition of being greater in number. *An interesting note was the predominance of London club players.*

Predominate/प्रिडॉमिनेट *(verb)* – प्रबल होना, प्रमुखता रखना be the strongest or main element. have or exert control or power. *Good predominates over evil in most of our scriptural epics.*

Pre-eminent/प्रिएमिनेंट *(adjective)* – सर्वश्रेष्ठ surpassing all others. *We were honoured to have a pre-eminent scholar amongst us.*

Preen/प्रीन *(verb)* – आत्म सन्तुष्ट, पक्षी का पंख सँवारना tidy and clean its feathers with its beak. *The birds were preening themselves in the sun.*

Preface/प्रेफेस् *(noun)* – भूमिका, प्रस्तावना, आमुख an introduction to a book, typically stating its subject, scope, or aims. *The preface explains how to use a dictionary.*

Prefect/प्रिफेक्ट *(noun)* – छात्रों पर शासक छात्र, शासनाधिकारी [chiefly British] a senior pupil authorized to enforce discipline in a school. *Right from primary school, I dreamt of being a prefect when I reached High School.*

Prefer/प्रिफर *(verb)* – दूसरो से ज्यादा महत्त्व देना like better than another or others; tend to choose. *I prefer gravy over a dry curry.*

P

Preference/प्रिफरेंस *(noun)* – मनपसन्द, अधिक मान, कृपा दृष्टि a greater liking for one alternative over another or others. a thing preferred. favour shown to one person over another or others. *She has a greater preference for literature.*

Preferential/प्रिफरेंसिअल *(adjective)* – प्राथमिता प्राप्त, अधिक मान of or involving preference or partiality. *The employer was given an earful by the Chief for giving preferential treatment to his secretary.*

Prefix/प्रिफिक्स *(noun)* – उपसर्ग, किसी शब्द के पूर्व जोड़ा जाने वाला a word, letter, or number placed before another. an element placed at the beginning of a word to adjust or qualify its meaning as an inflection. a title placed before a name. *A numerical prefix implies how many places to rotate the text.* *(verb)* add as a prefix or introduction. add a prefix or introduction to. *I thought it agreeable to prefix your name before them in both English and Latin.*

Pregnant/प्रेग्नेन्ट *(adjective)* – गर्भवती of a woman or female animal having a child or young developing in the uterus. *I gave the pregnant woman my seat as she looked very tired.*

Prehistoric/प्रिहिस्टॉरिक *(adjective)* – प्रागै-तिहासिक of or relating to prehistory. [informal] very old or out of date. *I wanted to sell of my mother's prehistoric cooker which she held on to for so long.*

Prejudice/प्रेजुडिस *(noun)* – पूर्वाग्रह preconceived opinion that is not based on reason or actual experience. unjust behavior formed on such a basis. *Her unjust prejudice towards children with better marks was leading to a rebellious attitude developing among other children.*

Preliminary/प्रिलिमिनरी *(adjective)* – प्रारम्भिक preceding or done in preparation for something fuller or more important. *Preliminary talks began yesterday.*

Prelude/प्रिल्यूड *(noun)* – पूर्वाभास, पूर्वमंचन, पूर्वरंग an action or event serving as an introduction to something more important. *Training is a necessary prelude to employment.*

Premature/प्रिमैच्यूर *(adjective)* – अवयस्क, अपूर्ण, अधूरा occurring or done before the proper time. *A 24-year old man was suffering from premature balding.*

Premeditated/प्रिमेडिटेटेड *(verb)* – पूर्वनिर्धारित think out or plan beforehand. *The murder was definitely premeditated.*

Premiere/प्रॅम्येअर *(noun)* – प्रथम प्रदर्शन the first performance of a musical or theatrical work or the first showing of a film. *The premiere of the film was a gala event attended by the who's-who of the industry.* *(verb)* give the premiere of. *He is organizing a special premiere of our movie specially for me.*

Premise/प्रेमिस *(noun)* – तर्क सम्मत विचार logic a previous statement from which another is inferred. an underlying assumption. *The judgment was based on the premise that men and women share equal space in society.*

Premises/प्रेमिसेस *(plural noun)* – भवन, अहाता a house or building, together with its land and outbuildings, occupied by a business or considered in an official context. *Smoking is not allowed within the office premises.*

Premium/प्रीमिअम् *(noun)* – किस्त an amount paid for a contract of insurance. *This month my account balance is low as I had to fill in a premium of an insurance I had applied for last year.*

Premonition/प्रीमॉनिशन् *(noun)* – पूर्वाभास a strong feeling that something is about to happen. *I had a strong premonition that one of us would die.*

Preoccupation/प्रीऑक्युपेशन् *(noun)* – कर्मरत the state of being preoccupied. a matter that preoccupies someone. *Post retirement men ought to find some or the other preoccupation to keep their mind busy.*

Preoccupy/प्रीऑक्युपाइ *(verb)* – पूर्व से ही कर्मबद्ध dominate or engross the mind of to the exclusion of other thoughts. *I had asked my son to study but he was preoccupied with something else.*

Preparation/प्रिपरेशन *(noun)* – तैयारी the action or process of preparing or being prepared. something done to get ready for an event of undertaking. *Behind any successful event lies several months of preparation.*

P

394

Preparatory/प्रिपेरेटरि *(adjective)* – आरम्भिक, शुरुआती serving as or carrying out preparation. [British] relating to education in a preparatory school. *Now she has turned four, her parents wanted to send her to preparatory school.*

Prepare/प्रिपेअर *(verb)* – बनाना, तैयार करना make ready for use of consideration. make ready for cooking or eating. *What are you preparing for dinner tonight?*

Prepay/प्रिपे *(verb)* – पूर्व भुगतान pay for in advance. *I applied for a prepaid connection for my mobile phone.*

Preposition/प्रिपोजिशन *(noun)* – कारक [grammar] a word governing, and usually preceding, a noun or pronoun and expressing a relation to another word or element, as in she arrived after dinner and what did you do it for. *We were being given a class on how to use prepositions effectively in essays.*

Preposterous/प्रिपॉस्टरस *(adjective)* – तर्कहीन, मूर्खतापूर्ण utterly absurd or ridiculous. *The idea she gave was more preposterous than obnoxious.*

Prerequisite/प्रिरिक्विजिट *(adjective)* – आवश्यक आधार required as a prior condition. *Competence is prerequisite to promotion.* *(noun)* a prerequisite thing. *Crossing the age bar of 18 years is a prerequisite to vote.*

Prerogative/प्रिरॉगेटिव *(noun)* – विशेषाधिकार a right or privilege exclusive to a particular individual or class. *It was the prinicipal's prerogative to suspend a student.*

Prescribe/प्रिस्क्राइब *(verb)* – नियत करना advise and authorize the use of especially in writing. *The doctor prescribed antibiotics for her lung infection.*

Prescription/प्रिस्क्रिप्शन *(noun)* – डॉक्टर का लिखा दवा का पर्चा an instruction written by a medical practitioner that authorizes a patient to be issued with a [medicine] or treatment. *She took the doctor's prescription to another doctor to seek a second opinion.*

Presence/प्रेजेन्स *(noun)* – उपस्थिति the state or fact of being present. a person or thing that is present but not seen. *Her presence was missed greatly during the family get-togethers.*

Present/प्रेजेन्ट *(noun)* – वर्तमान, उपहार, विद्यमान a thing given to someone as a gift. *I thought it bad etiquette to arrive at the party without a present for the host.*

Presentable/प्रेजेन्टेबल *(adjective)* – प्रस्तुत होने, करने योग्य clean, smart, or decent enough to be seen in public. *I asked Ram if I was looking presentable enough for the party.*

Presentation/प्रेजेन्टेशन *(noun)* – समपर्ण, मंचन, प्रस्तुति the action or an instance of presenting or being presented. the manner or style in which something is presented. a formal introduction. *The presentation was grand but the content was poor.*

Presently/प्रेजेन्टलि *(adjective)* – अभी, कुछ देर में after a short time; soon. *The management are presently discussing the matter.*

Preservation/प्रिजर्वेशन *(noun)* – रक्षा, सुरक्षा, संरक्षित a legal obligation laid on an owner to preserve a historic building, valuable natural habitat, etc. *Our school taught us the importance of preservation of natural resources.*

Preside/प्रिजाइड *(verb)* – अध्यक्षता करना, सभापतित्व करना, संचालन करना be in a position of authority in a meeting, court, etc. be in charge of a situation. *The Prime Minister presided over the meeting.*

Presidency/प्रेसिडेंसी *(noun)* – अध्यक्षीय, राष्ट्रपतित्व the office or status of president, the period of this. *Things were peaceful during the Eisenhower presidency.*

President/प्रेसिडेंट *(noun)* – राष्ट्रपति, अध्यक्ष, सभापति, संचालक the elected head of a republican state. the head of a society, council, college, or other organization. *The President likes to go for a jog every morning.*

Press/प्रेस *(verb)* – समाचार संस्था, मुद्रक, दबाना put to a specified use, especially as a temporary or makeshift measure. *This is a pressing problem.*

Pressure/प्रेसर *(noun)* – दबाव the continuous physical force exerted on or against an object by something in contact with it. the force per unit area exerted by a fluid against a surface. *The pressure of his fingers had relaxed.*

P

Pressurize/प्रेसराइज *(verb)* – दबाव का प्रयोग करना produce or maintain raised pressure artificially in. *The airplane cabin is pressurized.*

Prestige/प्रेस्टिज *(noun)* – प्रतिष्ठा widespread respect and admiration attracted through a perception of high achievements or quality. *His work gained him international prestige.*

Prestigious/प्रेस्टिजिअस *(adjective)* – लब्ध प्रतिष्ठ having high status. *He was given a prestigious award by the Prime Minister last year.*

Presumably/प्रिज्यूमेब्लि *(adverb)* – अनुमानतः as may reasonably be presumed. *Presumably, the culprit was one of the millions that died in the blast.*

Presume/प्रिज्यूम *(verb)* – अनुमान करना, मानकर चलना suppose that something is the case on the impertinent enough to do something. unjustifiably regard as entitling one to privileges. *I presume that you would have done some preliminary research before taking on the project.*

Presumption/प्रिजम्प्शन *(noun)* – परिकल्पना, अवधारणा, अनुमान an act or instance of presuming something to be the case. an idea that is presumed to be true. chiefly law an attitude adopted towards something in the absence of contrary factors. *He prepared a rough analysis after going through the various presumptions.*

Presumptuous/प्रिजम्प्ट्युअस *(adjective)* –निर्भीक, आत्मविश्वास से पूर्ण failing to observe the limits of what is permitted or appropriate. *Your presumptuous behavior is not going too well with your friends, I can see.*

Presuppose/प्रिसपोज *(verb)* – पूर्व अवधारणा, अनुमान require as a precondition of possibility or coherence. tacitly assume to be the case. *All your arguments presuppose that he is a rational man.*

Pretence/प्रिटेंस *(noun)* – बहाना, ढोंग an act of pretending. *He betrayed him under the pretence of friendship.*

Pretend/प्रिटेंड *(verb)* – स्वाँग भरना, बहाना बनाना, ढोंग करना act so as to make it appear that something is the case when in fact it is not. engage in an imaginative game or fantasy. simulate an emotion or quality. *I cannot pretend to say that you are wrong.*

Pretension/प्रिटेंसन *(noun)* – बहानेबाजी, मिथ्या अभिमान a claim or aspiration to something. *One of the few designers who doesn't have the pretensions to be an artist.*

Pretentious/प्रिटेंसस *(adjective)* – अभिमान से भरा attempting to impress by affecting greater importance or merit than is actually possessed. *He talked a lot of pretentious twaddle about modern art.*

Pretext/प्रिटेक्स्ट *(noun)* – बहाना an ostensible or false reason used to justify an action. *He excused himself on the pretext of a stomachache.*

Pretty/प्रिटी *(adjective)* – सुन्दर, मनोरम, आकर्षक, अत्यधिक attractive in a delicate way without being truly beautiful. *She is a charming and pretty girl.*

Prevail/प्रिवेल *(verb)* – हावी होना prove more powerful; be victorious. be widespread or current. *We hoped that common sense would prevail.*

Prevalent/प्रेवलेन्ट *(adjective)* – प्रचलित widespread in a particular area at a particular time. [archaic] predominant; powerful. *Smoking is becoming increasingly prevalent among younger women.*

Prevent/प्रिवेंट *(verb)* – रोकना keep from happening or arising. make unable to do something. *The state took several steps to prevent the strike.*

Preventable/प्रिवेंटेबल *(adjective)* – निवारण योग्य keep something form happenig. *It is sad that preventable diseases kill half of our population.*

Prevention/प्रिवेंशन *(noun)* – रोकथाम, निवारण keep somethig from occurring. *Prevention is better than cure.*

Preventive/प्रिवेंटिव *(adjective)* – रोकने वाला designed to prevent something from occurring. *They accused the police of failing to take enough preventive measures.* *(noun)* a preventive [medicine] or other treatment. *Cabbage is a preventive against stomach ulcers.*

P

Preview/प्रिव्यू *(noun)* – पूर्व दर्शन, पूर्व समीक्षा a viewing or display of something before it is acquired or becomes generally available. a publicity article, review, or trailer of a forthcoming film, book, etc. *They were releasing previews of the forthcoming movie before show in the movie hall.* *(verb)* provide or have a preview of a product, film, etc. *We will preview this season's collection from Paris.*

Previous/प्रिवियस *(adjective)* – पूर्वता, पूर्ववर्ती, पिछला existing or occurring before in time or order. *She had two children from a previous marriage.*

Prey/प्रे *(noun)* – शिकार, शिकार करना an animal hunted and killed by another for food. a victim or quarry. [archaic] plunder or a prize. *The muggers recognized their prey.* *(verb)* hunt and kill or for food. *The larvae preyed on small aphids.*

Price/प्राइस *(noun)* – मूल्य, दाम the amount of money expected, required, or given in payment for something. something expended or endured in order to achieve an objective. the odds in betting. [archaic] value; worth. *Rice is sold at a lower price in the kirana store near my house.* *(verb)* decide the price of. *I spent the day pricing dresses.*

Prick/प्रिक *(verb)* – चुभाना press briefly or puncture with a sharp point. draw or decorate by making small holes in a surface. *She gave a prick and the ball burst.*

Prickle/प्रिकल *(noun)* – काँटा a short spine or pointed outgrowth on the surface of a plant or on the skin of an animal. *A hedgehog is covered with prickles.*

Prickly/प्रिकलि *(adjective)* – काँटेदार covered in or resembling prickles. having or causing a prickling sensation. *I had a prickly sensation in my foot.*

Pride/प्राइड *(noun)* – अभिमान, गर्व, अहंकार, अहं a feeling of deep pleasure or satisfaction derived from achievements, qualities, or possessions that speciousness of one's own dignity. the quality of having an excessively high opinion of oneself. poetic the prime of something. *She felt a sense of pride rising in her when she saw her project report.*

Priest/प्रिस्ट *(noun)* – पुरोहित, पुजारी an ordained minister of the catholic, orthodoxs or Anglican church, authorized to perform certain rite and administer certain sacraments. a person who performs ceremonies in a non-Christian religion. *He became a priest after dropping out of school.*

Prim/प्रिम *(adjective)* – अतिव्यावहारिक feeling or showing disapproval of anything improper; stiffly correct. *The new teacher was prim and proper in her attire.* *(verb)* pursue into a prim expression. *She primmed her lips after every bite of food.*

Primafacie/प्राइमाफेसी *(adjective & adverb)* – प्रथम दृष्टि में law at first sight; accepted as so until proved otherwise. *Primafacie evidence showed the culprit trying to flee from the scene of crime.*

Primary/प्राइमरी *(adjective)* – प्रारम्भिक, मूलभूत of chief importance; principal. *Your health is primary to dieting.*

Prime/प्राइम *(adjective)* – मूलभूत, महत्त्वपूर्ण, उत्कृष्ट of first importance; main; primary. *Political stability was of prime concern.*

Primer/प्राइमर *(noun)* – प्रथम, रंगने के पूर्व का रंग a substance painted on wood, metal, etc. as a preparatory coat. *I put a coating of primer on the walls before applying the paint.*

Primitive/प्रिमिटिव *(adjective)* – आदिम of, relating to, or denoting the earliest times in history or stages in evolution or development. of or denoting a preliterate, (noun)-industrial society of simple organization. biology undeveloped; rudimentary. *All credits go to primitive man for discovering fire, for all the technological development that followed.*

Primrose/प्रिमरोज *(noun)* – पीले रंग का एक जंगली फूल a woodland and hedgerow plant which produces pale yellow flowers in early spring. *She had primroses in her garden, in full bloom.*

Prince/प्रिंस *(noun)* – राजकुमार a son, grandson, or other close male relative of a monarch. a male monarch of a small state, actually or nominally subject to a king or emperor: a nobleman, usually ranking next below a duke. *The kingdom rejoiced as the prince was born.*

P

Principal/प्रिंसिपल *(adjective)* – प्रधान, प्रमुख, प्राचार्य, प्रधानाचार्य first in order of importance; main. *Their principal concern is of winning the election.* denoting an original sum of money invested or lent. *Nowadays they have even introduced a loan on the principal amount.*

Principle/प्रिंसिपल *(noun)* – सिद्धान्त a fundamental truth or proposition serving as the foundation for belief or action a rule or belief governing one's personal behavior. morally correct behavior and attitudes: a man of principle. *He is known for being a man of principle.*

Print/प्रिंट *(verb)* – मुद्रण, मुद्रित produce by a mechanical process involving the transfer of text or designs to paper. produce in such a way. publish. produce in such a way. publish. produce a paper copy of information stored on a computer. *This news should not be printed.*

Prior/प्रायर *(adjective)* – पहले का, पहले से existing or coming before in time, order or importance. *The promotion came prior to his taking on the project.* *(noun)* [north American informal] a previous criminal conviction. *Prior to joining the new job and marriage, he had been convicted and had spent a few years in jail.*

Priority/प्रायरिटी *(noun)* – प्रमुखता the fact or condition of being regarded as more important. a thing regarded as more important than others. *She gave priority to her home over her job.*

Prison/प्रिजन *(noun)* – कारागार a building for the confinement of criminals or those awaiting trial. *She was born in a prison.* *(verb)* poetic imprison. *He was imprisoned for his crime.*

Prisoner/प्रिजनर *(noun)* – बन्दी a person legally committed to prison. a person captured and kept confined. a person trapped by a situation or circumstances. *The princess was kept prisoner in a tower far far away.*

Pristine/प्रिस्टाइन *(adjective)* – मूल दशा में in its original condition. spotless. *At the hill station, we saw nature in its pristine glory.*

Privacy/प्राइवैसि *(noun)* – एकान्त, एकान्तता, हस्तक्षेप विहीन a state in which one is not observed or disturbed by others. freedom form public attention. *The employer instructed the secretary not to disturb him as he wanted some privacy for the next few hours.*

Private/प्राइवेट *(adjective)* – निजी, व्यक्तिगत, गुप्त for or belonging to one particular person or group only. not to be shared or revealed. not choosing to share their thoughts and feelings. secluded. alone and undisturbed by others. *The actor was known for being a very private person.*

Privatize/प्राइवेटाइज *(verb)* – निजीकरण transfer from public to private ownership. *Several public sector organizations are being privatized these days.*

Privilege/प्रिविलेज् *(noun)* – विशेष सुविधा a special right, advantage, or immunity for a particular person. a special benefit or honour. *Shareholders have several privileges in the company.*

Privy/प्रिवि *(adjective)* – गोपनीय sharing in the knowledge of something secret. *His wife was privy to his official confidential information.*

Prize/प्राइज *(noun)* – पुरस्कार a thing given as a reward to a winner or in recognition of an outstanding achievement. something won in a game of chance. something of great value that is worth struggling to achieve. *The winners were awarded a prize of Rs 2000.*

Pro/प्रो *(preposition)* – वास्ते, नियमित an advantage or argument in favour of something. *Those who were against and pro the motion were grouped separately.*

Probability/प्रॉबबिलिटि *(noun)* – सम्भावना the extent of which something is probable. a probable or most probable event. *There is a probability she may take voluntary retirement from her service.*

Probable/प्रोबेबल *(adjective)* – सम्भावित, अपेक्षित likely to happen or be the case. *War seemed probable in 1938.* *(noun)* person likely to become or do something. *Chances of her promotion are highly probable.*

Probation/प्रोबेशन *(noun)* – परिवीक्षा law the release of an offender from detention, subject to a period of good behavior under supervision. *He was kept under probation until his crime was proved.*

P

Probationary/प्रोबेशनरी *(adjective)* – परिवीक्षा में शामिल a process of testing and observing the abilities of a new person. *She joined the bank as a probationary officer.*

Probe/प्रोब *(noun)* – जाँच, खोज, अन्वेषण a blunt-ended surgical instrument for exploring a wound or part of the body. *The probe helped to bring out the shrapnel stuck deep in his shoulder.*

Problem/प्रॉब्लम *(noun)* – समस्या an unwelcome or harmful matter needing to be dealt with and overcome. a thing that is difficult to achieve. *We need an urgent solution for the problem at hand.*

Procedure/प्रॉसीड्योर *(noun)* – औपचारिक प्रक्रिया an established or official way of doing something. a series of actions conducted in a certain order or manner. *Stick to the procedure and you will surely arrive at the solution.*

Proceed/प्रोसीड् *(verb)* – जारी रखना, बढ़ना, आगे बढ़ना begin a course of action go on to do something. carry on or continue. *Please proceed with your work without a break.*

Proceedings/प्रोसीडिंग् *(plural noun)* – कानूनी कारवाई an event or a series of activities with a set procedure. *The monkey perched up on the tree watched the fishermen below and their proceedings.*

Proceeds/प्रोसिड्स *(plural noun)* – राशि, लाभ, आय money obtained from an event or activity. *The proceeds of the show will go to charity.*

Process/प्रॉसेस *(verb)* – प्रणाली, प्रक्रिया walk in procession. *Leaves and plants follow the process of photosynthesis to breathe and live.*

Procession/प्रॅसेशन *(noun)* – जुलूस, जुलूस निकालना a number of people or vehicles moving forward in an orderly fashion, especially as part of a ceremony. the action of moving in such a way. a relentless succession of people or things. *Processions should be forbidden during peak traffic hours.*

Proclaim/प्रक्लेम *(verb)* – पोषण करना announce officially or publicly. declare to be. indicate clearly. *He was proclaimed king.*

Procrastinate/प्रोक्रैस्टिनेट *(verb)* – टाल-मटोल delay or postpone action. *You should stop procrastinating and start acting.*

Procure/प्रक्योर् *(verb)* – प्राप्त करना obtain. as a prostitute for someone else. *The minister asked the pimp to procure a woman for him the following night.*

Procurement/प्रक्योरमेन्ट् *(noun)* – प्राप्ति, सरकारी खरीद the action of obtaining something. *He was waiting for his procurement to arrive.*

Prod/प्रॉड *(verb)* – कोंचना, छेड़ना poke with a finger pointed object, etc. *Her ceaseless prodding got on his nerves.*

Prodigal/प्रॉडिगल *(adjective)* – व्ययी wastefully extravagant. *His prodigal habits will lead him to his own doom.*

Prodigious/प्रॅडिजॅस *(adj)* – अनोखा, विशाल surprising and very large. *He seemed to have a prodigious amount of energy.*

Prodigy/प्रॅडिजी *(noun)* – विलक्षण प्रतिभा a person, especially a young one, with exceptional abilities. an outstanding example of a quality. an amazing or unusual thing. *The child was growing into a prodigy.*

Produce/प्रोड्यूस *(verb)* – उत्पन्न करना, पैदा करना, उत्पादन करना make, manufacture, or create. or form as part of a physical, biological, or chemical process. *The yield produced a huge profit this year.*

Producer/प्रोड्सर *(noun)* – उत्पादक, निर्माता a person, firm or country that makes goods for sale. *They are producers of high quality wine.*

Product/प्रोड्क्ट *(noun)* – पैदावार, उपज, उत्पादन an article or substance manufactured or refined for sale. a substance produced during a natural, chemical, or manufacturing process. a result of n action or process. *Try to get the best products at the lowest price.*

Production/प्रोड्क्शन *(noun)* – पैदावार, उपज, उत्पादन the action or process of producing or being produced. the amount of something produced. denoting a vehicle manufactured in large numbers, as opposed to a prototype or other special version. *Production and manufacture at the factory had reduced by*

P

at least three times ever since the company went bankrupt.

Productive/प्रोड्क्टिव *(adjective)* - उपज देने वाला, लाभकारी, परिणाम देने वाला producing or able to produce large amounts of goods, crops, etc. relating to or engaged in the production of goods, crops, etc. *The crop has been highly productive ever since we started using the new fertilizers.*

Productivity/प्रोड्क्टिविटि *(noun)* - उपजाऊपन, उत्पादकता, उत्पादनशक्ति the state or quality of producing something. *Productivity had increased five times this year.*

Profane/प्रोफेन *(adjective)* - विधर्मी, सांसारिक काम में रमा secular rather than religious. not initiated into religious rites. *I encouraged her to listen to more sacred and profane music.*

Profess/प्रोफेस *(verb)* - दावा करना, घोषित करना claim that one has a quality or feeling. *She professes peace but her actions prove otherwise.*

Profession/प्रोफेशन *(noun)* - जीविका, पेशा, व्यवसाय a paid occupation, especially one involving training and a formal qualification a body of people engaged in a profession. *She has taken up stitching for a profession.*

Professional/प्रोफेशनल *(adjective)* - व्यासायिक of, relating to, or belonging to a profession. worthy of or appropriate to a professional person. *The event was attended by several professionals such as doctors, engineers, lawyers, and the like.*

Professor/प्रोफेसर *(noun)* - आचार्य a university academic of the highest rank; the holder of a university chair. [north American] a university teacher. *She works as a professor of English literature at the university now.*

Proficient/प्रॉफिशॅन्ट *(adjective)* - कुशल, दक्ष, प्रवीण, निपुण competent; skilled. *She is proficient in Spanish language.*

Proficiency/प्रॉफिशॅन्सि *(noun)* - कुशलता, दक्षता, प्रवीणता, निपुणता a high degree of skill or expertise. *She has established her proficiency in the language.*

Profile/प्रोफाइल *(noun)* - पार्श्व का दृश्य, रूपरेखा, वर्णन an outline of something, especially a face, as seen from one side. *She asked the photographer to click a side profile.*

Profit/प्रॉफिट *(noun)* - लाभ, फायदा, लाभ पाना financial gain, especially the difference between an initial outlay and the subsequent amount earned. *The company had made a profit of US$ 200,000000 this year.*

Profitable/प्रॉफिटेबल *(adjective)* - लाभप्रद, लाभदायक yielding profit or financeal gain. *Drug manufacturing the most profitable business in the US.*

Profound/प्रोफाउन्ड *(adjective)* - गहरा, गम्भीर very great or intense: profound social changes. severe. *The book was indeed profound.*

Profundity/प्रोफन्डिटी *(noun)* - गहराई, गम्भीता great depth of knowledge. *The profundity of this book had baffled.*

Profuse/प्रोफ्यूज *(adjective)* - प्रचुर, अत्यधिक plentiful; abundant. *He was bleeding profusely by the time the doctor arrived.*

Profusion/प्रोफ्यूज़न *(noun)* - प्रचुरता, अधिकता *We came across a delightful river with a profusion of flowers growing along its banks.*

Progeny/प्रॉजिनि *(noun)*- बच्चे, संतान offspring. *They set aside funds for the welfare of their progeny.*

Programme/प्रोग्रैम् *(noun)* - कार्यक्रम, योजना, कर्म में उत्प्रेरित a planned series of events. a set of related measures or activities with a long-term aim. *He was admitted to a new programme at the university.*

Progress/प्रोग्रेस *(noun)* - प्रगति, विकास, उन्नति forward or onward movement towards a destination. *The road was too rough to make any progress in the car.*

Progression/प्रोग्रेसन *(noun)* - क्रम, शृंखला, विकास क्रम में a gradual movement or development towards a destination or a more advanced state. a succession. music a passage or movement from one note or chord to another. *Both the drugs slow the progression of the virus.*

Progressive/प्रोग्रेसिव *(adjective)* - प्रगतिशील, विकासमान proceeding gradually or in stages: a progressive decline in popularity. increasing in severity. increasing as a proportion of the sum taxed as that sum increases. *He has been experiencing a progressive decline in popularity in the last few months.*

Prohibit/प्रोहिबिट *(verb)* – प्रतिबन्ध लगाना, निषेध करना formally forbid by law, rule, etc. *She was prohibited from leaving the country till a judgement was passed.*

Prohibitive/प्रोहिबिटिव *(adjective)* – निषेधात्मक, प्रतिबन्धकारी serving to forbid, restrict, or prevent. *Prohibitive regulations were set up for the welfare of the animals.*

Project/प्रोजेक्ट *(noun)* – परियोजना, योजना, शोध कार्य an enterprise carefully planned to achieve a particular aim. a proposed or planned undertaking. *The children were working on a community clean-up project.*

Projectile/प्रोजेक्टाइल *(noun)* – प्रक्षेपास्त्र a missile fired or thrown at a target. *At the museum we saw an ancient enormous artillery gun used to fire a huge projectile.*

Projection/प्रोजेक्शन *(noun)* – भाव स्थिति का आकलन, प्रदर्शन an estimate or forecast based on present trends. *The meeting involved a presentation on the company's sales projections for the next year.*

Projector/प्रोजेक्टर *(noun)* – प्रक्षेपक a device used to project rays of light, especially an apparatus for projecting slides or film on to a screen. *My colleague showed me how to use the projector for the presentation scheduled for the next day.*

Proletariat/प्रोलेटरिऑट *(noun)* – श्रमजीवी वर्ग, सर्वहारा वर्ग workers or working-class people often used with reference to Marxism. *Karl Marx's philosophy led to a war between the bourgeoisie and the proletariat.*

Proliferate/प्रॅलिफरेट *(verb)* – प्रजनन एवं वृद्धि करना reproduce rapidly; increase rapidly in number. *A certain section of the population fears that nuclear weapons might proliferate.*

Prolific/प्रॅलिफिक *(adjective)* – उर्वर, प्रचुर मात्रा में सृजन, उत्पादन producing much fruit or foliage or many offspring. *Closer planting will give you a more prolific crop.*

Prologue/प्रोलॉग *(noun)* – मंगलाचरण, प्रस्तावना, भूमिका a separate introductory section of a literary or musical work. an introductory scene in a play. *The prologue of the book was written in the form of a newspaper account.*

Prolong/प्रोलांग *(verb)* – विस्तृत अवधि तक, समय बढ़ाना extend the duration of. *We should not prolong the appointment with the doctor any more.* [technical] extend in spatial length. *The foreign military aid was prolonging the war.*

Prominent/प्रॉमिनेन्ट *(adjective)* – महत्त्वपूर्ण, प्रसिद्ध, प्रमुख important; famous. *We had to invite a prominent personality as a chief guest for the event.*

Promiscuous/प्रोमिस्क्युअस *(adj)* – व्यभिचारी having many brief sexual relationship. *She is promiscuous by nature.*

Promise/प्रॉमिस *(verb)* – वचन, प्रतिज्ञा, वचन देना assurance that one will do something or that something will happen. an indication that something is likely to occur: the promise of spring. *I promise never to hurt you again.*

Promote/प्रमोट *(verb)* – बढ़ावा देना, समर्थन देना further the progress of; support or encourage. publicized. attempt to ensure the passing of a private act of parliament. *He wishes to promote this appeal.* raise to a higher position or rank. *The boss announced that he will promote the boy in a month's time.*

Promotion/प्रमोशन *(noun)* – प्रचार, प्रसार, पदोन्नति activity that supports or encourages. *The actors were present for the promotion of their movie.* the publicizing of a product or venture so as to increase sales or public awareness; a publicity campaign. the activity or business of organizing such publicity. *We need to keep an amount separately for promotions.*

Prompt/प्रॉम्प्ट *(verb)* – सील, बिना बिलम्ब, प्रेरित करना, प्रोत्साहित करना, नेपथ्य से सहायता cause or bring about. cause someone to take a course of action. *I wonder what prompted her to reply so caustically.*

Promulgate/प्रमल्गेट *(verb)* – लागू करना, औपचारिक घोषणा करना promote or make widely known. put into effect by official proclamation. *The decree was promulgated across the town.*

P

Prone/प्रोन *(adjective)* – पीड़ित होने की प्रबल सम्भावना likely or liable to suffer from, do, or experience. *She has always been prone to accidents.*

Prong/प्रॉन्ग *(noun)* – कांटा, शूल each of two or more projecting pointed parts on a fork or other device. *I think she will need to use prongs here.*

Pronoun/प्रोनाउन *(noun)*– सर्वनाम a word used instead of a noun to indicate someone or something already mentioned or known, e.g. I, she, this. *Translate this sentence and underline any pronouns it might contain.*

Pronounce/प्रोनाउन्स *(verb)* – उच्चारण करना, घोषणा करना make the sound of a word or part of a word. *The kid can now pronounce some basic words.* declare or announce. pass judgement or make a decision on. *How do you pronounce your surname.*

Pronunciation/प्रननुसिएशन *(noun)* – उच्चारण, उच्चारण शैली the way in which a word is pronounced. *She is good at writing but her pronunciation is really bad.*

Proof/प्रूफ *(noun)* – प्रमाण, सुरक्षा देने वाला evidence establishing a fact or the truth of a statement. law the evidence in a trial. the proving of the truth of a statement. [archaic] a test or trial. a trial or a civil case before a judge without a jury. *I cannot believe all this without seeing any proof.*

Prop/प्रॉप *(noun)* – टेक लगाना, पर्दा, पोशाक a portable object used on the set of a play or film. *This was supposed to be an important prop for tonight's show.*

Propaganda/प्रॉपगैन्डा *(noun)* – प्रचार, दुष्प्रचार information, especially of a biased or misleading nature, used to promote a political cause or point of view. the dissemination of such information. *The people opposed such shocking propaganda by the leaders.*

Propogate/प्रॉपगेट *(verb)* – फैलाना प्रसारित करना, प्रजनन करना breed by natural processes from the parent stock. cause to increase in number or amount. *The new species could propagate without the drug.*

Propel/प्रॅपेल *(verb)* – धकेलना, धक्का, उत्प्रेरक drive or push for wards. drive into a particular situation. *Be careful not to propel the decision into the opposite direction.*

Propensity/प्रॅपेन्सिटि *(noun)* – कुछ करने की प्रवृति (प्राय: अनुचित) an inclination or tendency. *He had a propensity for violence.*

Proper/प्रॉपर *(adjective)* – उचित truly what something is said or regarded to be; genuine: she's never had a proper job. strictly so called: the world cup proper. *He is exhibiting proper depression tendencies.*

Property/प्रॉपटी *(noun)* – सम्पति, जायदाद, भूमि, भवन, गुण a thing or things belonging to someone. *Do not eye another's property.* a building and the land belonging to it. ownership. *He owns atleast four properties across the country.*

Prophecy/प्रॉफेसि *(noun)* – भविष्यवाणी a prediction the faculty or practice of prophesying. *The Mayan prophesy dictates that the Earth will perish in less than a month from today.*

Prophet/प्रॉफेट *(noun)* – सिद्ध, भविष्यवक्ता an inspired teacher or proclaimed of the will of god Muhammad. Joseph smith or one of his successors. *They read the teachings of the Prophet every morning.*

Prophetic/प्रॉफेटिक *(adjective)* – भविष्य सूचक accurately predicting the future. *sometimes she seems so prophetic.*

Propitiate/प्रॅपिशिएट *(verb)* – क्रोध शान्त करना, मना लेना appease. *The tribes believed their dance would propitiate their gods.*

Proponent/प्रॅपोनेन्ट *(noun)* – जन्मदाता विचारक, समर्थक विचारक a person who had vacates a theory, proposal, or project. *He is the proponent of this principle.*

Proportion/प्रॅपोर्शन *(noun)* – मात्रा में, मात्रा, अनुपात, आकार a part, share, or number considered in relation to a whole. the ratio of one thin to another. the correct or pleasing relation of things or between the parts of a whole. *take only in proportion to what others should take. A large proportion of the earth's surface is coverred by Sea.*

Proportional/प्रॉपोर्शनल *(adjective)* – समुचित अनुपात में corresponding in size or amount to

P

something else. *Keep the weights on one side, proportional to the weight of goods required.*

Proportionate/प्रपोर्शनेट *(adjective)* – समानुपाती another term for proportional. *If the bricks are placed proportionate to the height, they will hold on for a longer period of time.*

Proposal/प्रॅपोजॅल *(noun)* – प्रस्ताव a plan or suggestion. the action of proposing something. *There have been many proposals for this construction site in the past few months.*

Propose/प्रपोज *(noun* – प्रस्ताव रखना put forward an idea or plan for consideration by others. nominate for an office or position. put forward to a legislature or committee. *I propose we meet after you complete your exams.*

Proposition/प्रॉपॅजिशन *(noun)* – सुझाव, अर्थ a statement expressing a judgement or opinion. logic a statement expressing a concept that can be true or false. mathematic a formal statement of a theorem or problem. *This proposition needs to be proved using the right formula.*

Propound/प्रॅपाउण्ड *(verb)* – सिद्धान्त प्रस्तुत करना put forward an idea, theory, etc. for consideration. *He wishes to propound a new plan of action.*

Proprietor/प्रोप्राइटर *(noun)* – स्वामी, मालिक, व्यवस्थापक the owner of a business. *I wish to have a meeting with the proprietor.*

Propriety/प्रोप्राइटी *(noun)* – औचित्य, मर्यादा correctness concerning standards of behaviour or morals. the details or rules of conventionally accepted behavior. appropriateness; rightness. *She believes in maintaining propriety*

Propulson/प्रॅपल्सन *(noun)* – उत्तेजक बल, प्रणोदित बल the action of driving or pushing forward. *The right amount of propulsion will help the rocket take off into the sky.*

Prosaic/प्रोजेइक *(adjective)* – गद्यात्मक having the style or diction of prose. *That poet had a prosaic style of writing.*

Prose/प्रोज *(noun)* – गद्य ordinary written or spoken language, without metrical structure. *He loved speaking in prose.*

Prosecute/प्रॉसिक्यूट *(verb)* – अभियोग चलाना, कानूनी कारवाई institute legal proceedings against, institute legal proceedings in respect of a claim or focused or sued in a lawsuit. *Trespassers will be legally prosecuted.*

Prosecution/प्रॉसिक्यूशन *(noun)* – अभियोग, अभियोग की प्रक्रिया the prosecuting of someone in respect of a criminal charge. the party prosecuting someone in a lawsuit. *:Your prosecution shows selfish motives.*

Prospect/प्रॉस्पेक्ट *(noun)* – प्राप्ति की सम्भावना, प्रत्याशी the possibility or likelihood of some future event occurring. a mental picture of a future or anticipated event. chances or opportunities for success. *What are her prospects at winning tournament.*

Prospective/प्रॉस्पेक्टिव *(adjective)* – भावी, सम्भावित expected or likely to happen or be in the future. *He looks like a prospective son-in-law.*

Prospectus/प्रॉस्पेक्टस *(noun)*– विवरणिका, सूचना a printed booklet advertising a school or university or giving details of a share offer. *The application form will be provided along with the college prospectus.*

Prosper/प्रॉस्पर *(verb)* – समृद्धि, समृद्धि प्राप्त करना, फलना-फूलना succeed or flourish, especially financially. thrive. make successful. *I want you to prosper beyond anyone's imagination.*

Prosperity/प्रॉस्परिटि *(noun)* – समृद्धि, वैभव the condition of being prosperous. *Wishing you prosperity and happiness as you embark upon the journey.*

Prosperous/प्रॉस्परस *(adjective)* – समृद्धि की ओर अग्रसर bringing wealth and success. *It is a joy to see him become so prosperous today.*

Prostitute/प्रॉस्टिट्यूट *(noun)* – वेश्या a person, typically a woman, who engages in sexual activity for payment.

Protagonist/प्रटैगॅनिस्ट *(noun)* – नायक, मुख्य पात्र the leading character in a drama, film, or novel. a prominent figure in real situation. *You can never guess who the actual protagonist turns out to be.*

Protect/प्रॅटेक्ट *(verb)* – सुरक्षा देना, रक्षा करना keep safe from harm or injury. aim to preserve by legislating against collecting or hunting. *Wear woollens to protect yourself from the harsh winds.*

P

Protection/प्रॅटेक्शन *(noun)* – रक्षा, सुरक्षा the action or state of protecting or being protected. a person or thing that protects. a document guaranteeing safety to the person specified in it. *She left me under their protection.*

Protective/प्रॅटेक्टिव *(adjective)* – सुरक्षा देने वाला serving, intended, or wishing to protect. *I feel very protective of her.*

Protector/प्रॅटेक्टर *(noun)* – रक्षा देने वाला व्यक्ति a person or thing that protects. *I have always seen my father as my protector.*

Protein/प्रोटीन *(noun)* – वसा, एक पौष्टिक तत्व any of a class of nitrogenous organic compounds forming structural components of body tissues and constituting an important part of the diet. *You should include less proteins and more carbohydrate in your diet for the next few months.*

Protest/प्रोटेस्ट *(noun)* – विरोध, प्रतिवाद करना, असहमति जताना a statement or action expressing disapproval of or objection to something. an organized public demonstration objecting to an official policy or course of action. law a written declaration, typically by a notary public, that bill has been presented and payment or acceptance refuse. *The streets are filled with people who want to protest against the new law.*

Protestant/प्रॅटेस्टॅन्ट *(noun)* – ईसाई धर्म का एक विभाजन a member of follower of any of the western Christian churches that are separate from the roman catholic church in accordance with the principles of the information. *The protestant Christians of this town have always been a tolerant group.*

Protocol/प्रोटॅकॉल *(noun)* – व्यवस्था नियम, नियम की व्यवस्था the official procedure or system of rules governing affairs of state or diplomatic occasions. the accepted code of procedure or behavior in a particular situation. *I cannot breach the protocol followed in such situations.*

Prototype/प्रोटॅटाइप *(noun)* – आदिम रूप का नमूना a first or preliminary form from which other forms are developed or copied. *Bacteria is considered to be a prototype to all animal forms.*

Protracted/प्रोट्रैक्टेड *(adjective)* – दीर्घकालिक lasting for a period longer than expected. *They just ended a much protracted divorce.*

Protrude/प्रॅट्रूड *(verb)* – बाहर निकला हुआ extend beyond or above a surface. cause to do this. *The broken long protruded out of the top floor window.*

Proud/प्राउड *(adjective)* – घमण्डी, गौरवान्वित feeling pride or satisfaction in one's own or another's achievements. poetic imposing; splendid. *He made us all proud of him today.*

Prove/प्रूव *(verb)* – प्रमाधा, प्रमाणित करना demonstrate by evidence or argument the truth or existence of. law establish the genuineness and validity of a will. *I will believe only if you can prove this.*

Proven/प्रूवन *(verb & adjective)* – प्रमाणित, सिद्ध, जाँच द्वारा परखा हुआ demonstrate the existence of a thing. *He will be treated as a convict until proven otherwise.*

Proverb/प्रॉवर्ब *(noun)* – कहावत, लोकोक्ति a short pithy saying in general use, stating a general truth or piece of advice. *"Making hay while the sun shines" is a very popular proverb.*

Proverbial/प्रॉवर्बिअल *(adjective)* – कहावत की बात, लोकयुक्ति के आधार पर referred to in a proverb or idiom. *This feels like the proverbial catch-22 situation.*

Provide/प्रॉवाइड *(verb)* – उपलब्ध करना make available for use; supply. equip or supply someone with. *Please provide me with the raw materials.*

Provided/प्रवाडेड *(conjunction)* – यदि, इस शर्त पर on the condition or understanding that. *She agreed to go and work abrouad provided (that) her family could go with her.*

Providence/प्रॉविडेंस *(noun)* – विधाता का विधान, ईश्वरीय नियम the protective care of god or of nature as a spiritual power. god or nature as providing such care. *I certainly believe providence to be the reason for his success.*

Provident/प्रॉविडेंट *(adjective)* – भविष्य के प्रति जागरूक making or inductive of timely preparation for the future. *He prefers to invest in provident funds.*

P

Providential/प्रॉविडेंसियल *(adjective)* – सौभाग्य-पूर्ण occurring at a favourable time; opportune. *Your appearing in the morning seems to be providential.*

Province/प्रॉविंस *(noun)* – प्रदेश, प्रान्त a principal administrative division of a country or empire. British northern Ireland. Christian church a district under an archbishop or a metropolitan. a territory outside Italy under a roman governor. *I do not recognize which province he belongs to.*

Provincial/प्रॉविंसियल *(adjective)*– प्रादेशिक, प्रान्तीय, प्रदेशीय of or concerning a province of a country or empire. *This battalion belongs to the provincial army.*

Provision/प्रॉविजन *(noun)* – उपलब्ध कराने की क्षमता the action of providing or supplying something supplied or provided. arrangements for future eventualities or requirements. *Please make the necessary provisions for their stay.*

Provisional/प्रॉविजनल *(adjective)* – अस्थायी, कामचलाऊ arranged or existing for the present, possibly to e changed later. *This is just a provisional certificate and you will get the final document soon.*

Proviso/प्रॉवाइज़ें *(noun)* – शर्त, प्रतिबन्ध, प्रतिबन्ध के शर्त a condition attached to an agreement. *This has been clearly mentioned in the proviso, I sent in the morning.*

Provocation/प्रॉवॅकेशन *(noun)* – उत्तेजित करने की क्रिया, छोड़-छाड़ the action of provoking. action or speech that provokes. law action or speech held to be likely to prompt physical retaliation. *You should never hit children, even under extreme provocation.*

Provocative/प्रॉवॅकेटिव *(adjective)* – उत्तेजक causing annoyance, anger, or another strong reaction, especially deliberately. *Everyone avoids the provocative neighbour on the street.*

Provoke/प्रॉवोक *(verb)* – उकसाना stimulate in someone. *Do not provoke unnecessarily or the dog will bite you.*

Prow/प्राउ *(noun)* – मथनी the pointed front part of a ship; the bow. *The prow was the last bit to be seen slowly drowning into the waters.*

Prowess/प्राउएस् *(noun)* – पराक्रम, योग्यता skill or expertise in a particular activity of field. *He not only plays the piano, but his prowess is also in writing stories.*

Proximity/प्रॉक्सिमिटी *(noun)* – समीपता, निकटता nearness in space, time, or relationship. *The rumbling sound assured us that the vehicle was in our proximity.*

Proxy/प्रॉक्सि *(noun)* – प्रतिनिधित्व, दूसरे का मुख बनना the authority to represent someone else, especially in voting. a person authorized to act on behalf of another. *John would like to give proxy for his father William.*

Prude/प्रूड *(noun)* – अतिपाखण्डपूर्ण, विनीत स्त्री, कपटी a person who is easily shocked by matters relating to sex or nudity. *She is a prude.*

Prudent/प्रूडेन्ट *(adjective)* – विवेकपूर्ण acting with or showing care and thought for the future. *He is a prudent and miserly fellow.*

Prune/प्रून *(noun & verb)* – सूखा आलू-बुखारा, पौधे काँटना a plum preserved by drying and having a black, wrinkled appearance. *She stared at the giant prunes strewn all over the backyard.*

Pry/प्राइ *(verb)* – हस्तक्षेप, ताक-झाँक, खोलना, विलगाना enquire too intrusively into a person's private affairs. *I do not intend to pry, but if ever you need anything please let me know.*

Psalm/साम् *(noun)* – भजन, कीर्तन, स्तोत्र-पाठ a sacred song or hymn, in particular any of those contained in the biblical book of psalms. a book of the bible comprising a collection of religious verses, sung or recited in both Jewish and Christian worship. *We have to memorize five psalms for the function on Sunday.*

Pseudo/स्यूडे *(pref.)* – छद्म, नकली not genuine; fake, pretentious, or insincere. *i fired him as he was a pseudo at work.* *(noun)* a pretentious or insincere person. *I will not stand to tolerate any pseudo workers at my firm.*

Pseudonym/स्यूडॅनिम *(noun)* – छद्मनाम, उपनाम a fictitious name , especially one used by an author. *Many letters are sent to the editors under pseudonyms.*

P

Psych/साइक् *(verb)* – आत्मविश्वास कम कर देना [informal] mentally prepare for a testing takes or occasion. intimidate an opponent or rival by appearing very confident or aggressive. *His confidence sometimes looks like a plan to psych the opponent before the duel.*

Psyche/साइकि *(noun)* – मानस, चित्र the human soul, mind, or spirit. *Tom loves to study the psyche of his fellow team mates.*

Psychiatry/साइकाइअट्रि *(noun)* – मनोरोग अध्ययन और चिकित्सा the branch of [medicine] concerned with the study and treatment of mental illness, emotional disturbance, and abnormal behavior. *Psychiatry is a never ending study.*

Psychiatrist/साइकिअट्रिस्ट *(noun)* – मनोरोग चिकित्सक a medical practitioner specializing in the diagnosis and treatment of mental illness. *Please show her to a good psychiatrist soon.*

Psychic/साइकिक *(adjective)* – पारलौकिक relating to or denoting facilities or phenomena that are apparently inexplicable by natural laws, especially involving telepathy or clairvoyance. appearing or considered to be telepathic or clairvoyant. *Ever since she has been meditating, she has become increasingly psychic.*

Psychoanalysis/साइकोएनालिसिस *(noun)* – मनोविश्लेषण a system of psychological theory and therapy which aims to treat mental disorders by investigating the interaction of conscious and unconscious elements in the mind and bringing repressed fears and conflicts into the conscious mind. *The company policies call for a psychoanalysis of each new recruit.*

Psychology/साइकोलॉजी *(noun)* – मनोविज्ञान the scientific study of the human mind and its functions, especially those affecting behavior in a given context. *A parent always understands the psychology of the child.*

Psychopath/साइकोपैथ *(noun)* – मनोचिकित्सा शास्त्र a person suffering from chronic mental disorder with abnormal or violent social behavior. *The police declared the man a psychopath and warned his friends to be careful around him.*

Psychatherapy/साइकोथिरैपी *(noun)* – मनोचिकित्सा the treatment of mental disorder by psychological rather tan medical means. *She has trained in psychotherapy treatment under the guidance of this professor.*

Pub/पब *(noun)* – शराब खाना an establishment for the sale and consumption of beer and other drinks, often also serving food. *He often heads to the nearest pub after work.*

Puberty/प्यूबर्टि *(noun)* – यौवन का आरम्भ (स्त्रियों में) the period during which adolescents reach sexual maturity and become capable of reproduction. *Most of the female chimpanzees seem to have crossed their puberty years.*

Public/पब्लिक *(adjective)* – जनता of, concerning, or open to the people as a whole. involved in the affairs of the community, especially in government or entertainment: a public figure. *This is her first public performance in two years.*

Publication/पब्लिकेशन *(noun)* – प्रकाशन the action or process of publishing something. *Which publication house have you approached?*

Publicity/पब्लिसिटी *(noun)* – प्रचार notice or attention given to someone or something by the media. the giving out of information for advertising or promotional purposes. material or information used for such a purpose. *There has been a lot of publicity for this film.*

Publicize/पब्लिसाइज *(verb)* – प्रचार करना make widely known. *Be careful not to publicize the issue any further.*

Publish/पब्लिश *(verb)* – प्रकाशित करना prepare and issue for public sale. print in a book or journal so as to make generally known. *How many copies have been published so far?*

Pucker/पकर *(verb)* – सिकन पड़ना, सिकन डालना tightly gather or contract into wrinkles or small folds. *The child puckered under his mother's angry eyes.*

Pudding/पुडिंग *(noun)* – खीर a cooked sweet dish served after the main course of a meal. chiefly the dessert course of a meal. [north American] a dessert with a soft or creamy consistency. *My favourite dessert is chocolate pudding.*

P

Puddle/पड्ल (noun) – जलजमाव a small pool of liquid, especially of rainwater on the ground. *The children loved sailing their paper boats in the puddle.*

Puff/पफ् (noun) – धुँए या भाप की फूँक, कश लेना a short burst of breath or wind. a small quantity of vapour or smoke emitted in one blast. an act of drawing quickly on a pipe, cigarette, or cigar. [informal] berth. *The man huffed and puffed as he walked up the alley.*

Puffin/पफिन (noun) – एक पक्षी a hole-nesting northern bird with a large head and a massive brightly coloured triangular bill. *My friend sent me this photograph of a beautiful puffin stuttering around in their yard.*

Puke/प्यूक (verb & noun) – उल्टी करना [informal] vomit. *This stench makes me want to puke.*

Pull/पुल (verb) – खींचना, घसीटना exert force on so as to cause movement towards oneself or the origin of the force. be attached to the front and be the source of forward movement of a vehicle. remove by pulling. [informal] bring out for use. British draw from a barrel to serve. inhale deeply while drawing on a cigarette. damage by abnormal strain. *Try pulling the door knob towards you.*

Pulley/पुलि (noun) – घिरनी a wheel with a grooved rim around which a cord passes, used to raise heavy weights. a wheel or drum fixed on a shaft and turned by a belt, used to increase speed or power. *I can haul this rock to the upper landing with the pulley.*

Pulp/पल्प (noun) – गूदा, निकृष्ट साहित्य a soft, wet, shapeless, mass of material. the soft fleshy part of a fruit. a soft wet mass of fibers derived from rags or wood, used in papermaking. *The pulp is kept out in the sun to harden up.*

Pulpit/पुल्पिट (noun) – चर्च का मंच a raised enclosed platform in a church or chapel from which the preacher delivers a sermon. *The churchgoers waited patiently for the Bishop to step on to the pulpit.*

Pulsate/पल्सेट (verb) – फैलना-सिकुड़ना, धड़कना expand and contract with strong regular movements. *The doctor exclaimed that the body still pulsated feebly.*

Pulse/पल्स (noun) – नाड़ी, धड़कन, दाल the edible seeds of various leguminous plants, e.g. lentils. the plant or plants producing such seeds. *Pulses are a rich source of proteins in our diet.*

Pulverize/पल्वराइज (verb) – चूर करना, पीस देना reduce to fine particles. *The aliens pulverised the entire building into a huge heap of rubble.*

Pump/पम्प (noun) – निकालने-भरने का यन्त्र, एक प्रकार का जूता a machine of raising water, a kind of light shoe. *He refused to come jogging with us as he couldn't find his pumps.*

Pumpkin/पम्पकिन (noun) – कद्दू a large rounded orange-yellow fruit with a thick rind and edible flesh. *We have a pumpkin farm in the backyard.*

Pun/पन (noun) – श्लेष, द्वै-अर्थक a joke exploiting the different meanings of a word or the fact that there are words of he same sound and different meanings. *He loves to include pun in his speech.*

Punch/पंच (verb) – घूँसा मारना, छेद करना strike with the fist to make a hole in something with a special tool. *He punched the air when he heard the good news.*

Punctual/पंक्चुअल (adjective) – नियत समय पर happening or doing something at the appointed time. *She believes in being punctual to the last second.*

Punctuate/पंकचुएट (verb) – विरामचिह्न लगाना occur at intervals throughout. interrupt an activity with. *His rhythmic snoring seemed to punctuate the silence of the night.*

Punctuation/पंकचुएशन (noun) – विरामचिह्न the marks, such as full stop, comma, and brackets, used in writing to separate sentences and their elements and to clarify meaning. the use of such marks. *I wish you re-write this sentence by changing the punctuation marks.*

Puncture/पंक्चर (noun) – छिद्र करना, आत्मविश्वास तोड़ना a small hole caused by a sharp object, especially one in tyre. *Where can I get my punctured tyre mended?*

Pungent/पंजेण्ट (adjective) – तीखा, तिक्त having a sharply strong taste or small. *The kitchen had a pungent smell of rotten eggs.*

P

Punish/पनिश *(verb)* – दण्ड देना inflict a penalty on as retribution for an offence. inflict a penalty on someone for an offence. *His father would certainly punish him today.*

Punishable/पनिशेबल *(adjective)* – दण्डनीय subject to punishment. *Littering the streets is a punishable offence.*

Punishment/पनिशमेंट *(noun)* – दण्ड the action of punishing or the state of being punished. the penalty inflicted. *He deserves the harshest punishment possible for this crime.*

Punitive/प्यूनिटिव *(adjective)* – दण्ड विषयक inflicting or intended as punishment. *This is such a punitive remark from you.*

Punk/पंक *(noun)* – तीव्र संगीत a loud, fast-moving, and aggressive form of rock music, popular in the late 1970s. an admirer or player of such music. *My Parents loved punk during their college days.*

Puny/प्यूनि *(adjective)* – दुर्बल small and weak. *I am not affected by your puny threats.*

Pupil/प्यूपिल *(noun)* – शिष्य, विद्यार्थी, पुतली a person who is taught by another, especially a schoolchild. *The teacher observed the pupil sleeping in the last row.*

Puppet/पपेट *(noun)* – कठपुतली a movable model of a person or animal, typically moved either by strings or by a hand inside it. used to entertain. *The charlatan pretended to belong to the puppet show party.*

Puppetry/पपेट्रि *(noun)* – कठपुतली का खेल करना a movable model by strings of a person or animal used for entertainment. *She is holding a workshop on traditional puppetry this Saturday.*

Puppy/पपि *(noun)* – पिल्ला a young dog. *The children promised to take good care of the puppy.*

Purchase/परचेज *(noun & verb)* – खरीद, खरीदना, खरीदी वस्तु buy. *He just purchased the painting to gift his wife.* nautical haul up by means of a pulley or lever. *The captain ordered a purchase as the wind changed course.*

Pure/प्योर *(adjective)* – शुद्ध not mixed or adulterated with any other substance or material, unmixed origin or descent. *She was dressed in pure white.*

Purge/पर्ज *(verb)* – शुद्ध करना, स्वच्छ करना rid of an unwanted feeling or condition. *I wish to purge myself of this emotional baggage.*

Purify/प्योरिफाइ *(verb)* – शुद्ध करना, साफ करना remove contaminants from; make pure. *Camphor is considered to purify the surroundings.*

Purification/प्योरिफिकेशन *(noun)* – शोधन, शुद्धीकरण remove contaminants from. *The temple priests demanded a purification ceremony.*

Puritan/प्यूरिटन *(noun)* – नैतिकतावादी a member of a group of English protestants who regarded the reformation of the church under Elizabeth I as incomplete and sought to simplify and regulate forms of worship. *The puritans always were a bane to the church.*

Purity/प्योरिटी *(noun)* – शुद्धि the state of being pure. *The goldsmith rubbed the ring on his stone to check for its purity.*

Purl/पर्ल *(adjective)* – उल्टी सिलाई made by putting the needle through the front of the stitch from right to left. compare with plain. *(verb)* knit with a purl stitch. *The new sewing machine has facilities of doing the purl stitch.*

Purple/पर्पल *(noun)* – बैंगनी रंग का a colour intermediate between red and blue. *The sky turned a dark shade of purple in the setting sun.*

Purpose/पर्पस् *(noun)* – प्रयोजन, उद्देश्य the reason for which something is done of for which something exists. *What is the purpose of studying all night if you end up sleeping during the exam.*

Purr/पर्र *(verb)* – घुरघुराहट make a low continuous vibratory sound expressing contentment. *The cat purred contentedly as she lazed around in the winter sun.*

Purse/पर्स *(noun)* – बटुआ, उपलब्ध धन, होंठ सिकोड़ना a small pouch of leather of plastic used for carrying money. *The lady let out a scream as the thief ran off with her purse.*

Pursue/पर्स्यू *(verb)* – पीछा करना, जारी रखना follow in order to catch or attack. *Do not try to pursue him or you might get hurt.*

Pursuit/पर्स्यूट *(noun)* – पुरुषार्थ, खोज, पाने की चेष्टा धन्धा the action of pursuing. *The police gave pursuit to the escaping convicts.*

P

Purview/पर्व्यू *(noun)* – सीमा the scope of the influence or concerns of something. *What is the purview of this brand on the market?*

Push/पुश् *(verb)* – ढकेलना, ठेलना, आक्रमण exert, force on in order to move them away from oneself. hold and exert force on so as to cause it to move in front of one. move one's body or a part of it forcefully into a specified position. exert pressure with an oar etc. so as to move a boat out form a bank. *Push the table back into the corner.*

Pushy/पुशि *(adjective)* – महत्त्वाकांक्षी, बिल्ली excessively self-assertive or ambitious. *No one likes the pushy kid in her class.*

Put/पुट *(verb)* – रखना move to or place in a particular position. proceed in a particular direction: the boat put out to sea. *Please put the books back in the right order.*

Putrefy/प्यूट्रिफाइ *(verb)* – सड़ना, सड़ाना decay or rot and produce a fetid smell. *The abandoned flat had a putrefied odour to it.*

Putty/पटि *(noun)* – धुरकिली, जोड़ने का मसाला a malleable paste, made from whiting and raw linseed oil, that gradually hardens and is used chiefly for sealing glass in window frames. a malleable substance used as a filler, modeling material, etc. *The architect suggested using the latest brand of putty instead of the usual brand.*

Puzzle/पज़ल *(noun & verb)* – पहेली, चकरा देना confuse because difficult to understand. *Do not try to puzzle me with your riddled speech.*

Puzzled/पज़ल्ड *(adjective)* – घबड़ाया हुआ unable to understnd. *He looked puzzled as the police asked him to show his licence.*

Pygmy/पिग्मि *(noun)* – बौना a member of certain peoples of very short stature in equatorial Africa or parts or SE asia. *Consider yourself lucky that you were not caught by the indigenous pygmy clan in the jungle.*

Pyjamas/पाइजामज *(plural noun)* – पायजामा, सलवार a jacket and loose trousers for sleeping in. *Whatever I may forget, I can never forget to carry my pyjamas during any trip.*

Pylon/पाइलॅन *(noun)* – ऊँचा खम्भा a tall tower-like structure for carrying electricity cables. *The electrician needed a pylon to carry all the cables.*

Pyramid/पिरामिड *(noun)* – त्रिकोणीय स्तम्भ a monumental stone structure with a square or triangular base and sloping sides that meet in a point at the top, especially one built as a royal tomb in ancient Egypt. *Who built the pyramids in Egypt is still a mystery waiting to be solved.*

Pyre/पायर *(noun)* – चिता a heap of combustible material, especially one for burning a corpse as part of funeral ceremony. *Matt was inconsolable as he lit his father's pyre.*

Python/पाइथॅन *(noun)* – अजगर a large non-venomous snake which kills prey by constriction. *The highlight of our safari trip was a python we found lying on the side of the road.*

P

Qq

Q/क्यू *(noun)* – अंग्रेजी वर्णमाला का सत्रहवाँ वर्ण the seventeenth letter of the English alphabet.

1. denoting the next after P in a set of items, categories, etc.

Q-boat/क्यू-बोट *(noun)* – व्यवसायी पोत का रूप धारण किये लड़ाकू पोत a boat used by Germany during WWII. *Germany had used q-boats to chase boats and ships of allied forces.*

Qua/क्वे *(conjunction)* – योग्यता से या योग्यता के रूप में in the capacity of. *Equity holders qua members must attend the meeting called by the mompany.*

Quack/क्वैक *(noun)* – कुवैद्य, बत्तख की बोली an empth pretendor of skill in medicine, the characteristic harsh sound made by a duck. *Ducks make the sound of quack, quack!*

Quackery/क्वैकरी *(noun)* – चिकित्सा का ढोंग या अभ्यास a person who claims to have special skills but is not. *Quackery is the cause of many deaths.*

Quackish/क्वैकिश *(adjective)* – बुरे वैद्य के समान in the manner of a quack. *Quackish treatment leads to medical complications.*

Quadragesimal/क्वाड्राजेसिमल *(adj)* – चालीस दिन का व्रत belonging or appropriate to the period of Lent. *During lent, many Christians observe fast to repent for wrong doing they may have commiteed.*

Quadrangle/क्वाड्रैंगल *(noun)* – चतुर्भुज क्षेत्र a four sided geometrical figure, especially a square or rectangle. *He has a quadrangle courtyard at the back of his house.*

Quadrangular/क्वाड्रैंगुलर *(adjective)* – चतुष्कोण having four sides. *Quadrangular teams were playing against one another in a big playground.*

Quadrant/क्वाड्रैंट *(noun)* – वृत्त का चतुर्थ भाग, इस प्रकार का यन्त्र जो कोण नापने में काम आता है each of four parts of a circle, plane, body, etc. divided by two lines or planes at right angles. *A quadrant is used for measuring angles.*

Quadrate/क्वाड्रेट *(noun)* – चतुर्भुज a squarish bone in the skull of a bird or reptile, with which the jaw articulates. (adjective) roughly square or rectangular. *This plot seems quadrate.*

Quadrennial/क्वाड्रेनियल *(adjective)* – प्रत्येक चौथे वर्ष होने वाला lasting for or recurring every four years. *The term of my computer course is quadrennial.*

Quadrilateral/क्वाड्रिलैटरल *(noun)* – चतुर्भुज क्षेत्र a four sided figure. *I want to buy a quadrilateral plot.*

Quadrumanous/क्वाड्रुमेनस *(adjective)* – चतुर्भुजी having all four feet modified as hands, i.e. having opposable digits. *This figure seems quadrumanous.*

Quadruple/क्वाड्रुपल *(adjective)* – चतुर्गुण consisting of four parts or elements. *Four teams formed a quadruple alliance.*

Quadruplicate/क्वाड्रुप्लिकेट *(verb)* – चतुर्गुण करना consisting of four parts or elements. *Please quadruplicate this document.*

Quag/क्वैग *(noun)* – दलदल a marshy or boggy place. *The animal fell in a quag.*

Quagmire/क्वैगमायर *(noun)* – धँसाव a soft boggy area of land that gives way underfoot. *His downfall was to get trapped in the quagmire of dirty politics.*

Quail/क्वेल *(noun)* – साहस छोड़ना a small short tailed game bird. *While in jungle, he shot some quails.*

Quaint/क्वेंट *(adjective)* – पुराने ढंग का attractively unusual or old fashioned. *It is a quaint little piece of art.*

Quake/क्वेक *(verb)* – काँपना shake or tremble. *His legs quaked with fear as a violent crowd confronted him.*

Qualifiable/क्वालिफाइएबल *(adj)* - अनुकूल करने योग्य minimum acceptable level. *Qualifiable speeds for 100 metres race have been announced.*

Qualified/क्वालिफाइड *(adjective)* - योग्य certified as being trained to perform a job. *He is fully qualified for this job.*

Qualifier/क्वालिफाइअर *(noun)* - योग्य बनने या बनाने वाला a person or a team that qualifies for a competition. *He was the sixth and the last qualifier for one-mile race.*

Qualitative/क्वालिटेटिव *(adjective)* - जाति स्वभाव of, concerned with, or measured by quality. often contrasted with quantitative. *The difference is qualitative and not quantitive.*

Quality/क्वालिटि *(noun)* - विशेषता, गुण the standard of something as measured against other things of a similar kind. general excellence. high social standing. *Although rude, he has many qualities.*

Quandary/क्वान्डेरी *(noun)* - व्याकुलता a state of uncertainty over what to do in a difficult situation. *He was in a quandary as he found no place in the hostel.*

Quantitative/क्वान्टिटेटिव *(adjective)* - परिमाण सम्बन्धी of, concerned with, or measured by quantity. often contrasted with qualitative. *It is not the qualitative but the quantitative value of these things that counts.*

Quantity/क्वांटिटी *(noun)* - परिमाण a certain amount or number. a considerable number or amount. *Our success depends upon the quantity of goods that we produce.*

Quarrel/क्वॉर्ल् *(noun)* - कलह, विवाद an angry argument or disagreement. *He picked up a quarrel with his neighbour.*

Quarry/क्वैरी *(noun)* - खदान a place, typically a large pit, from which stone or other materials may be extracted. *The mining mafia is extracting lots of minerals from illegally dug quarries.*

Quart/क्वार्ट *(noun)* - चौथाई गैलन a unit of liquid capacity equal to a quarter of a gallon or two pints, equivalent in Britain to approximately 113 litres and in US to approximately 0.94 litre. a unit of dry capacity equivalent to approximately 110 litres. *I bought two quarts of milk.*

Quarterage/क्वार्टरेज *(noun)* - भुगतान a sum paid or received quarterly. *The quarterage sum is only rupees tour thousand.*

Quarterly/क्वार्टर्लि *(adjective)* - त्रैमासिक produced or occurring once every quarter of a year. *The installments are quarterly payable.*

Quartern/क्वार्टन *(noun)* - पाइन्ट का चौथाई भाग a quarter of a pint. *He drank a quarter of beer.*

Quartz - *(noun)* a hard mineral consisting of silica, typically occurring as colourless or white hexagonal prisms. *Quartz watches are quite popular.*

Quasi/क्वेसाइ (क्वाजी) *(comb. form)* - जो जैसा लगे वैसा वस्तुत: हो न अर्थात् seemingly: quasi scientific. *Think this statement is quasi scientific.*

Quaternary/क्वाटर्नरि *(adjective)* - चार भाग का fourth in order or rank. *He is a quaternary officer.*

Quaternion/क्वाटरनियन *(noun)* - चतुष्क a complex number of the form $w + xi + yj + zk$, where w, x, y, z are real numbers and I, j, k are imaginary units that satisfy certain conditions. *Quaternion is a theory in identities in algebra.*

Quatrain/क्वाट्रेन *(noun)* - चतुष्पदी श्लोक a stanza of four lines, typically with alternate rhymes. *It is a poem in quatrain.*

Quatre-foil/क्वाट्रफायल (कैटरफॉइल्) *(noun)* - इमारत में चौपतिया छिद्र an ornamental design of four lobes or leaves, resembling a flower or clover leaf. *The flowers were arranged in quatre-foil.*

Quaver/क्वेवर *(verb)* - काँपना tremble. *He quavered as he ran.*

Quean/क्वीन *(noun)* - वेश्या, पतुरिया an impudent girl or woman. *She is a quean and as such not worth talking to.*

Queasiness/क्वीजिनेस *(noun)* - सुकुमारता in the manner of feeling sick. *Queasiness overwhelmed me and I threw up.*

Queasy/क्वीजि *(adjective)* - रोगी होने वाला nauseous. inducing nausea. *The smell is the kitchen was queasy.*

Queer/विवअर *(adjective)* - विचित्र, झक्की strange; odd. slightly ill. *His face was a queer pink colour.*

Q

Quench/क्वेंच *(verb)* – बुझाना, दबाना satisfy by drinking. *He quenched his thirst by drinking a few glasses of water.*

Quenelle/क्वेनेल *(noun)* – पीसा हुआ माँस का लोंदा a small seasoned ball of fish or meat. *Quenelle is being cooked.*

Querist/क्वेरिस्ट *(noun)* – प्रश्न पूछने वाला a questioner. *Here is a querist for you to answer.*

Quern/क्वर्न *(noun)* – जाँता, चक्की a simple hand mill for grinding grain, typically consisting of two circular stones. *Querns may still be in use in villages.*

Querulous/क्वेर्युलस *(adjective)* – सर्वदा शिकायत करने वाला, विलापी complaining in a petulant or whining manner. *She became querulous as her husband rebuked her.*

Quest/क्वेस्ट *(noun)* – खोज a long or arduous search. *Quest for pyramids had begun in early twentieth century.*

Questionable/क्वेस्चनेब्ल *(adjective)* – संदिग्ध अनिश्चित open to doubt. *Your behaviour is questionable.*

Questionnaire/क्वेस्चनेअर *(noun)* – उत्तर देने के लिए प्रश्नों का समूह a set of printed questions, usually with a choice of answers, devised for a survey or statistical study. *Kindly fill this questionnaire, a survey is going on.*

Quibble/क्विबल् *(noun)* – वाक्छल, वक्रोक्ति a slight objection or criticism. *Quibble started after his talk to the press.*

Quick/क्विक *(adjective)* – सजीव, फुर्तीला moving fast or doing something in a short time. lasting a shot time. prompt. *He is a quick fellow and acts immediately.*

Quicken/क्विकेन *(verb)* – सचेत करना make or become quicker. *As she approached me, my heart beat quickened.*

Quick-eyed/क्विकआइड *(adj)* – तीव्र दृष्टिवाला having sharp sight. *Crow is a quick-eyed bird.*

Quicklime/क्विकलाइम *(noun)* – बिना बुझाया हुआ चुना a white caustic alkaline substance consisting of calcium oxide, obtained by heating limestone. *Quicklime is obtained from limestone.*

Quickly/क्विकली *(adjective)* – झटपट promptly. *He quickly jumped into water to save her from drowning.*

Quicksand/क्विकसैंड *(noun)* – कछारी बालू loose wet sand that sucks in anything resting on it. *He was pulled out timely from being sucked into quicksand.*

Quickset/क्विकसेट *(noun)* – हरी वनस्पति hedging, especially of hawthorn, grown from slips or cuttings. *Quickset was thick and nobody could enter.*

Quick-silver/क्विकसिल्वर *(noun)* – पारा liquid mercury. *His moods change rapidly like quick-silver.*

Quick-witted/क्विकविटेड *(adjective)* – हाजिर दिमाग वाला showing an ability to think or respond quickly. *Birbal was a quick-witted courtier of Akbar.*

Quid/क्विड *(noun)* – अशर्फी one pound sterling. *He used to save one quid every day.*

Quiddity/क्विडिटी *(noun)* – तत्त्व, पाखण्ड the inherent nature or essence of a person or thing. *Quiddity of a person hardly changes.*

Quiscent/क्विसेंट *(adjective)* – निश्चल, स्थिर in a state or period of inactivity. *He is quiescent these days, recovering from illness.*

Quiet/क्वायट *(adjective)* – शान्ति, आनन्द making little or no noise. free from activity, disturbance, or excitement. undisturbed; uninterrupted. *I like this quiet place.*

Quietus/क्वाइ-ईटस् *(noun)* – अन्तिम निर्णय death or a cause of death, regarded as a release from life. *The man is dead, we have to find the quietus.*

Quinate/क्विनेट *(noun)* – पंचपतिया a salt in chemistry. *Easter of quinic acid is known as quinate.*

Quince/क्विंस *(noun)* – शरीफा a hard, acid, pear shaped fruit used in preserves or as flavouring. *Quince a fruit, grows on shrubs in Asia and is used for flavouring.*

Quinine/क्विनाइन *(noun)* – कुनेन की दवा a bitter crystalline compound present in cinchona bark, used as a tonic and formerly as an antimalarial drug. *Quinine used to be taken against malaria.*

Q

Quin-quennium/क्विन-क्वेनियम *(noun)* – पाँच वर्ष की अवधि a period of five years. *It is a quin-quennium course of computer training.*

Quinsy/क्विन्सी *(noun)* – कण्ठमाला inflammation of the throat, especially an abscess near the tonsils. *He had pain in throat as he suffered from quinsy.*

Quintal/क्विंटल *(noun)* – एक सौ किलोग्राम का वजन a unit of weight equal to a hundred weight or, formerly, 100 IB. *He purchased a quintal of wheat grain.*

Quintessential/क्विन्टेसेंशल *(adj)* – सारयुक्त representing the most perfect or typical example. *She is a quintessential of beauty.*

Quintet/क्विंटेट *(noun)* – पंचक a group of five people playing music or singing together. a composition for such a group. *The band was played by a quintet.*

Quintuple/क्विंट्युपल *(adj)* – पंचगुना consisting of five parts or elements. *Ten is the quintuple of two.*

Quintuplicate/क्विंट्युप्लिकेट *(verb)* – पाँच तह करना fivefold. *You need to have quintuplicate. Copies of this document.*

Quintuply/क्विंट्युप्लाई *(adverb)* – पंचगुने रूप में increase five times. *The companie's profits quintuplied last year.*

Quip/क्विप *(noun)* – ताना a witty remark. *A quip is usually on his lips.*

Quirk/क्वर्क *(noun)* – व्यवहार में छल a peculiar behavioural habit. *A quirk of fate destroyed his career.*

Quit/क्विट *(verb)* – त्यागना leave, especially permanently. *He has quit smoking.*

Quite/क्वाइट *(adverb)* – सर्वथा absolutely; completely. US very; really. *You are quite right in saying this.*

Quittable/क्विटेबल *(adj.)* – खाली करने लायक *This assignment is not quittable.*

Quitter/क्विटर *(noun)* – छोड़ने वाला a person who gives up easily. *He is a quitter and never stays in one job.*

Quits/क्विट्स *(adjective)* – चुकती two people disagreeing to work together. *We are quits now, there should be no longer any grudge.*

Quiver/क्विवर *(noun)* – तरकस an archer's portable case for arrows. *All archers carry quivers on their back.*

Quivevingly/क्विविंगली *(adverb)* – काँपते हुए trembling with a visible rapid motion. *He quiveringly told us about her horror dream.*

Quivive/क्विवाइव *(noun)* – सचेत on the alert or lookout. *Every soldier has to be very quivive on border.*

Quixotic/क्विकसॉटिक *(adjective)* – अद्भूत, विलक्षण impractically idealistic or fanciful. *His quixotic behaviour amused her.*

Quixotism/क्विकसॉटिज़्म *(noun)* – विवेकहीन विलक्षण विचार being extremely idealistic. *Sometimes his quixotism is very upsetting.*

Quixotry/क्विकसॉट्रि *(noun)* – विवेकहीन कल्पना attitude of being unrealistic. *We are tired of his quixotry in seaching for clean hotels.*

Quiz/क्विज *(noun)* – पहेली, मसखरा, झक्की आदमी a test of knowledge, especially as a competition for entertainment. *Can you solve this quiz?*

Quizzically/क्विजिकली *(adverb)* – ठिठोलियापन से amusingly strange. *He answered all my questions quizzically.*

Quod/क्वॉड् *(noun)* – जेल prison. *He spent five years in quod.*

Quoin/क्वॉइन् *(noun)* – इमारत का बाहरी कोना an external angle of a wall or building. *Most building in the hills were made with coloured quoins.*

Quoit/क्वॉइट *(noun)* – लोहे का चक्र जो निशाने पर फेंका जाता हैं a ring if iron, rope, or rubber thrown in a game to encircle or land as near as possible to an upright peg. a game of aiming and throwing quoits. *He won a many prizes in the game of quoit.*

Quota/क्वोटा *(noun)* – अंश, भाग a limited quantity of a product which may be produced, exported, or imported. *There is only 30 p.c. quota fixed for the export of these goods.*

Quotable/क्वोटेबल् *(adjective)* – उद्धरण योग्य suitable for or worth quoting. *There are many quotable words in his speech. It is a quotable quote.*

Quotation/क्वोटेशन् *(noun)* – किसी पदार्थ का प्रचलित मूल्य a group of words from a text or speech repeated by someone other than the originator. a short musical passage or visual image taken from one piece of music or work of art and used in another. the action of quoting from a text, work of art, etc. *Let us buy this book of famous quotations.*

Quote/क्वोट *(verb)* – पहले कही या लिखी गयी बात को सही से दोहराना repeat or copy out, repeat a passage or statement from. *He quoted Gandhiji many times in his speech.*

Quotient/क्वोशन्ट *(noun)* – भजनफल, भागफल a result obtained by dividing one quantity by another. *Four divided by two has the quotient two.*

Q

Rr

R/आर *(noun)* – अंग्रेजी वर्णमाला का 18वाँ वर्ण the eighteenth letter of the English alphabet.
1. denoting the next after Q in a set of items, categories, etc.

Rabbi/रैबाइ *(noun)* – यहूदियों का धर्मगुरु, यहूदी विद्वान a Jewish scholar or teacher, especially of Jewish [law]. *There was a Rabbi among the rebels who were against anti-abortion laws in Ireland.*

Rabbit/रैबिट् *(noun)* – खरगोश, शशक a burrowing gregarious plant-eating mammal, with long ears, long hind legs, and a short tail. the fur of the rabbit. [north American] a hare. *There were cute little rabbits running around on the farm.*

Rabble/रैबल् *(noun)* – भीड़ a disorderly crowd. *A rabble of uncouth young men greeted the minister outside the court.*

Rabid/रैबिड *(adjective)* – अनांतक रोग से पीड़ित, उग्र, प्रचण्ड extreme; fanatical. *She is a rabid feminist, known for her scathing remarks to the ministers and politicians.*

Race/रेस *(noun)* – दौड़, प्रतियोगिता, आपाधापी, घुड़दौड़ each of the major divisions of humankind, having distinct physical characteristics. racial origin or distinction. an ethnic group. a group descended from a common feature. *People of all races, colour and creed are welcome to our country.*

Racial/रेसियल *(adjective)* – जाति, मानव प्रजाति, नस्ल, आनुवांशिक, जातिगत, जातीय of or relating to a race. *Racial minority is a one of the reasons why the Blacks are still suffering today.*

Racism/रेसिज्म *(noun)* – जातिवाद the belief that there are characteristics, abilities, or qualities specific to each race. *We were taught theories of racism in Sociology class today.*

Rack/रैक *(noun)* – खण्डदार खुला अलमारी, तबाह होना (लापरवाही से) हल्ला a horse's gait between a trot and a canter. *The horse's rack had everyone smiling.*

Racket/रैकेट *(noun)* – अवैध ढंग से पैसा बनाने का काम a bat with a round or oval frame strung with catgut, nylon, etc., use especially in tennis, badminton, and squash. *The rackets are out and the players are ready!*

Radar/रडार *(noun)* – रेडियो तरंग वाला एक उपकरण a system for detecting the presence, direction, and speed of aircraft, ships, etc. by sending out pulses of radio waves which are reflected back of the object. *The ship was frantically sending radar messages hoping someone will respond.*

Radial/रेडिअल *(adjective)* – किरणों की तरह क्रम में रखी हुई of or arranged like rays or the radial of a circle; diverging in lines from a common centre. running form a town centre to an outlying district. *Four mosaics having a radial arrangement were placed on a mat.*

Radiant/रेडिएण्ट *(adjective)* – चमकदार, प्रकाश करने वाला shining or glowing brightly. emanating great joy, love, or health. emanating powerfully. *We met a radiant sage at the hermitage in the forest today.*

Radiate/रेडिएट *(verb)* – चमकना, स्पष्ट अभिव्यक्ति emit in the form of rays or waves. be emitted in such a way. emanate a strong feeling or quality. *The stars radiate energy.*

Radiation/रेडिएश्न *(noun)* – विकिरण, हानिकारक तरंग बिखरना the action or process of radiating. *The boy suffering from cancer has been exposed to high level radiation.*

Radical/रेडिकल *(adjective)* – आमूल, मूलभूत, आधार से of, relating to, or affecting the fundamental nature of something. innovative or progressive. *We need a radical transformation of the existing legal system.*

Radio/रेडिओ *(noun)* – रेडियो the transmission and reception of radio waves, especially those

R

carrying audio messages. *Radio stations were demanding the eviction of the RJ from the Big Brother show.*

Radioactive/रेडियोएक्टिव *(adjective)* – परमाणु की हानिकारक किरणें निकलना emitting or relating to the emission of ionizing radiation or particles. *The water was radioactive.*

Radiography/रेडियोग्राफी *(noun)* – एक्सरे द्वारा चित्र लेने की प्रक्रिया the process of taking x-ray photograph. *He worked in the radiography department of the hospital.*

Radish/रेडिश *(noun)* – मूली a pungent-tasting edible root, typically small, spherical, and red, and eaten raw. *There were radishes of all kinds in the farm.*

Radium/रेडियम *(noun)* – एक प्रकार का धातु the chemical element of atomic number 88, a radioactive metal of the alkaline earth series. *Radium was used on clocks to make dials.*

Radius/रेडियस *(noun)* – त्रिज्या की लम्बाई, गोलाकार क्षेत्र a straight line from the centre to the circumference of a circle or sphere. a radial line from the focus to any point of a curve. *The radius of a circle is half its circumference.*

Raffle/रैफल *(noun)* – कुछ बेंच कर सद्कार्य हेतु धन एकत्रित करना a lottery with goods as prized. *I bought a raffle ticket at the mall.*

Raft/रैफ्ट *(noun)* – लकड़ी का बेड़ा, रबड़ की हवा भरी नाव a flat buoyant structure of timber or other materials fastened together, used as a boat or floating platform. a small inflatable boat. *Pi was stranded on a raft in the middle of the sea for 200 days.*

Rafter/रैफ्टर *(noun)* – शहतीर a beam forming part of the internal frame-work of a roof. *The rafters above the bed were falling off.*

Rag/रैग *(noun)* – पुराना कपड़ा, चिथड़ा, लत्ता, मजाक से तंग करना a piece of old cloth, especially one torn from a larger piece. old or tattered clothes. *I wiped my hands on a rag after cleaning the walls.*

Rage/रेज *(noun)* – अतिशय क्रोध violent uncontrollable anger. violent anger associated with conflict arising form a particular context: air rage. the violent action of a natural agency. *He was trembling with rage.*

Ragged/रैगड् *(adjective)* – फटा-पुराना वस्त्र, कटा-पिटा old and torn, wearing such clothes. *The tramp wore ragged clothes on his body and a radiant smile on his face.*

Raid/रेड *(noun)* – धावा a rapid surprise attack on people or premises. *A bombing raid was carried out in the desert.*

Rail/रेल *(verb)* – छड़, पटरी, गाली देना complain or protest strongly. *She railed at the police inefficacy in the high profile murder case.*

Railing/रेलिंग *(noun)* – घेरा a fence or barrier made of rails. *The thief jumped over the railing and escaped.*

Railway/रेलवे *(noun)*– पटरी का मार्ग [chiefly British] a track made of rails along which trains run. *The railway tracks badly needed maintenance.*

Rain/रेन *(noun)* – बर्षा, बौछार the condensed moisture of the atmosphere falling visibly in separate drops. falls of rain. *I love dancing in the rain.*

Rainbow/रेनबो *(noun)* – इन्द्रधनुष an arch of colours visible in the sky. caused by the refracting and dispersion of the sun's light by water droplets in the atmosphere. *There was a beautiful rainbow visible from my window.*

Rainy/रेनी *(adjective)* – बरसाती having or characterized by considerable rainfall. *It is going to be a rainy month now.*

Raise/रेज *(verb)* – उठाना, उभारना, एकत्र करना, सम्मुख रहना, फसल उगाना, लालन-पालन करना lift or move to a higher position or level. set upright. *Raise the curtain rod a bit higher.*

Raisin/रेजिन *(noun)* – किशमिश a partially dried grape. *I bought raisins for the cake.*

Rake/रेक *(noun)* – पाँचा, समतल करना, उखाड़ना a fashionable or wealthy man of dissolute habits. *He is known for being a merry Restoration rake.*

Rally/रैली *(verb)* – एकत्रित होना, एकत्रित करना [archaic] tease. *I've been rallied throughout high school for my funny hair.*

Ram/रैम *(noun)* – भेड़ा an uncastrated male sheep. *There were scores of rams on the farm.*

R

Ramble/रैम्बल *(verb)* – भ्रमण करना, बहक जाना, विषयान्तर करना walk for pleasure in the countryside. *I wanted a vacation where I can ramble aimlessly among trees in the woods.*

Ramification/रैमिफिकेशन् *(noun)* – जटिलता, विषमता the action or state of ramifying or being ramified. *His angiogram showed a ramification of the right coronary artery.*

Ramp/रैम्प *(noun)* – ढलान a sloping surface joining two different levels. *They had built a wheelchair ramp to make the hospital disabled-friendly.*

Rampage/रैम्पेज *(verb)* – रूक्षता का व्यवहार कना *(noun)* क्रोध का उन्माद rush around in a violent and uncontrollable manner. *The protestors rampaged around the whole city.*

Rampant/रैम्पैंट *(adjective)* – उच्छृंखला, अनियंत्रित flourishing or spreading unchecked. *Corruption is rampant in our country.*

Ramshackle/रैम्शैक्ल् *(adjective)* – जर्जर in a state of severe disrepair. *I was shocked to see the ramshackle cottage, he lived in.*

Ranch/रैंच *(noun)* – खेती-बाड़ी a large farm, especially in the western US and Canada, where cattle or other animals are bred. *She has been living in a ranch for several years now.*

Rancid/रैंसिड *(adjective)* – बासी, खट्टा smelling or tasting unpleasant as a result of being stale. *We could smell the rancid meat from outside.*

Rancour/रैंकर *(noun)* – वैमनस्य bitterness; resentment. *He spoke without rancour.*

Random/रैंडम *(adjective)* – क्रमहीन made, done, or happening without method or conscious decision. *It was evident from the result that she had made a random decision.*

Range/रेंज *(noun)* – एक ही प्रकार की विभिन्न वस्तुएँ, सीमा क्षेत्र, मार करने की अधिकतम दूरी, अँगीठी the area of variation between limits on a particular scale. *The cost for this house will range between Rs 25 lakh to Rs 35 lakh.*

Rangefinder/रेंजफाइन्डर *(noun)* – गोली आदि का पता लगाने वाला an instrument for estimating the distance of an object, especially for use with a camera or gun. *She bought a new fancy rangefinder to be attached to her camera.*

Rank/रैंक *(adjective)* – पद-स्तर, श्रेणी, बदबूदार growing too thickly. *There were clumps of rank grass in her garden.*

Rankle/रैंकल *(verb)* – दूषित करना, निरंतर कष्ट देना cause annoyance or resentment. chiefly annoy or irritate. *His mannerisms still rankle.*

Ransack/रैन्सैक *(verb)* – खोज-बीन, तोड़-फोड़ go hurriedly through stealing things and causing damage. *The thieves had ransacked every house in the whole village.*

Ransom/रैंसम *(noun)* – फिरौती a sum of money demanded or paid for the release of a captive. *The kidnappers had demanded a ransom of Rs 15 lakh.*

Rant/रैंट *(verb)* – प्रलाप करना speak or shout at length in a wild, impassioned way. *The politician was ranting about the opposition's demonstrations outside his house.*

Rap/रैप *(noun)* – छोटा टुकड़ा, खटखटाहट the smallest amount. *He doesn't care a rap.*

Rapacious/रपेशस् *(adjective)* – अति लोभी aggressively greedy. *Rapacious landlords are ruling the countryside to this day.*

Rape/रेप *(verb)* – बलात्कार करना a plant of the cabbage family with bright yellow flowers, especially a variety grown for its oil-rich seed and as stock feed. *There were rape seeds in the nursery.*

Rapid/रैपिड *(adjective)* – शीघ्रगामी, तेजी से बार-बार happening in a short time or at great speed. *The rapid economic decline of the country brought huge changes in its people's lifestyles.*

Rapids/रैपिड्स *(noun)* – नदी की तीव्र धारा, झरना, प्रपात, क्षिप्रिका *The raft was stuck in one of the rapids.*

Rapport/रैपार्ट *(noun)* – घनिष्टता a close and harmonious relationship in which there is common understanding. *I share a good rapport with my colleagues and employer.*

Rapt/रैप्ट *(adjective)* – तन्मय fully absorbed and intend; fascinate. *The therapist had a rapt teenage audience at his introduction speech.*

Rapture/रैप्चर *(noun)* – आनन्द-विह्वल, अत्यधिक आनंद a feeling of intense pleasure or joy. *My daughter listened to my stories with rapture.*

R

Rare/रेअर *(adjective)* – विरला occurring very infrequently. *The bird is rarely seen during this time of the year.*

Rarefied/रेअरिफायड *(adjective)* – कम वायु दबाव of lower pressure than usual; thin. *Trudging uphill in rarefied air can turn out to be the most difficult task.*

Raring/रेअरिंग *(adjective)* – आतुर [informal] very eager to do something. *She was raring to go.*

Rarity/रेअरिटी *(noun)* – दुर्लभता the state or quality of being rare. *Honesty and integrity are a rarity in people today.*

Rascal/रॉस्कल *(noun)* – नटखट, बेईमान a mischievous or cheeky person, especially a child. *Dennis is such a rascal!*

Rash/रैश *(adjective)* – फोड़े-फुन्सी, अविवेकी, जल्दीबाज acting or done impetuously, without careful consideration. *Please refrain from making a rash assumption.*

Rasher/रैशर *(noun)* – सूअर के माँस का टुकड़ा a thin slice of bacon. *She placed two rashers on his plate.*

Rasp/रैस्प *(noun)* – मोटी रेती, किरकिराहट, कर्कश ध्वनि a coarse file for use on metal, wood, or other hard material. *She tried rubbing on the table with a rasp.*

Raspberry/राज़बेरि *(noun)* – रसबरी an edible soft fruit related to the blackberry, consisting of a cluster of reddish-pink drupes. *I bought a kilo of raspberries from the fruit market.*

Rat/रैट *(noun)* – चूहा a rodent resembling a large, long-tailed mouse, typically considered a serious pest. *There has been a rat menace in the colony of late.*

Rate/रेट *(verb)* – मूल्य, कीमत, दर, मूल्यांकन [archaic] scold angrily. *She berated her daughter for forgetting her values.*

Rather/रैदर *(adverb)* – किसी हद तक, काफी हद तक indicating one's preference in a particular matter. *Would you like chocolate or would you rather stick to a sugar-free sweet?*

Ratify/रैटिफाई *(verb)* – संपुष्टि करना give formal consent to; make officially valid. *Both the parties have to ratify the treaty in a few days.*

Rating/रेटिंग *(noun)* – श्रेणी, श्रेणी में विभाजन a classification or ranking based on quality, standard, or performance. *The company retained its five star rating.*

Ratio/रेसियों *(noun)* – अनुपात the quantitative relation between tow amounts showing the number of times one value contains or is contained within the other. *The sex ratio in the state has dipped in favour of males.*

Ration/रैशन *(noun)* – राशन a fixed amount of a commodity officially allowed to each person during a time of shortage, as in wartime. *The bread ration had reduced during battle times.*

Rational/रैशनल *(adjective)* – बौद्धिक based on or in accordance with reason or logic. *There has to be a rational explanation to your action.*

Rationalism/रैशनलिज़्म *(noun)* – बुद्धिवाद the practice of principle of basing opinions and actions on reason and knowledge rather than one religious belief or emotional response. *Scientific rationalism has its own limitations.*

Rationalise/रैशनलाइज *(verb)* – तर्कसम्मत करना attempt to justify with logical reasoning. *You cannot rationalize your urge to eat sweets.*

Rattle/रैटल *(verb)* – खड़खड़ाहट make or cause to make a rapid succession of short, sharp knocking or clinking sounds. *The tiles on the roof were rattling in the strong wind.*

Ravage/रैवेज *(verb)* – उजाड़ना cause extensive damage to; devastate. *The town was ravaged by the tornado.*

Rave/रेव *(noun)* – प्रलाप a framework added to the sides of a cart to increase its capacity. *The raves were bending under the weight of the load.*

Raven/रैवेन *(noun)* – काला कौवा a large heavily built black crow. *The farm had more ravens than common crows.*

Ravenous/रैवेनस *(adjective)* – भुक्खड़ voracious; rapacious. *He had a ravenous appetite.*

Ravine/रैविन *(noun)* – खड्ड a deep, narrow gorge with steep sides. *The car plunged into the deep ravine.*

Ravishing/रैविशिंग *(adjective)* – मनमोहक causing intense delight; entrancing. *She was a ravishing beauty.*

Ray/रे *(noun)* – किरण, एक मछली a broad flat cartilaginous fish with wing like pectoral fins

R

and a long slender tail. *The marine researcher died when he was bitten by a ray.*

Raze/रेज *(verb)* – पूर्णत: नष्ट कर देना tear down and destroy. *Villages were razed to the ground.*

Razor/रेजर *(noun)* – उस्तरा an instrument with a sharp blade, used to shave unwanted hair from the face or body. *I bought an electric razor from the shop.*

Reach/रिच *(verb)* – पहुँचना stretch out an arm in a specified direction in order to touch or grasp something. stretch out one's hand or arm. stretch upwards to pick something up and bring it down to a lower level. hand to. *I tried to reach up to the loft to take out the suitcase.*

React/रिएक्ट *(verb)* – प्रतिक्रिया दिखाना या व्यक्त करना respond to something in a particular way or with particular behaviour. *She reacted angrily at the news of the break up.*

Reaction/रिएक्शन *(noun)* – प्रतिक्रिया an instance of reacting to or against something. *My immediate reaction was to throw something at him.*

Reactor/रिएक्टर *(noun)* – प्रतिक्रिया कराने का यन्त्र an apparatus or structure in which fissile material can be mad to undergo a controlled, self-sustaining nuclear reaction releasing energy. *The nuclear reactor is under threat.*

Read/रिड *(verb)* – पढ़ना look at and comprehend the meaning of by interpreting the characters symbols of which it is composed. speak aloud. contain or consist of specified words; have a certain wording. *It is the best story she had ever read.*

Reader/रिडर *(noun)* – पाठक, आचार्य a person who reads. *She is a voracious reader.*

Readership/रिडरशीप *(noun)* – आचार्य का पद, पाठकों की संख्या the readers of a newspaper or magazine regarded collectively. *The readership of the daily had gone down.*

Reading/रिडिंग *(noun)* – पढ़ने की क्रिया, वाचन, माप the action or skill of reading. *It was time for reading the will.*

Ready/रेडी *(adjective)* – तैयार, उपलब्ध in a suitable state for an activity or situation; fully prepared. *Get ready for the party quickly.*

Real/रिअल *(noun)* – वास्तविक, यथार्थ genuine. *This is a real silk.*

Realism/रिअलिज्म *(noun)* – यथार्थवाद the practice of accepting a situation as it is and dealing with it accordingly. *Try and ground yourself in realism instead of getting deluded.*

Reality/रिअलिटी *(noun)* – वास्तविकता the state of things as they actually exist, as opposed to an idealistic or notional idea of them. *Try and face the reality now.*

Realize/रिअलाइज *(verb)* – स्वीकार करना, उगाही करना, अनुभूति करना become fully aware of as a fact; understand clearly. *He realized his mistake when I pointed out.*

Really/रिअलि *(adverb)* – वस्तुत:, निस्सन्देह in reality; in actual fact. *The pie is really good.*

Realm/रेल्म *(noun)* – राज्य, क्षेत्र [archaic], poetic a kingdom. *He was banished from the realm.*

Ream/रीम *(noun)* – 20 जिस्ते कागज की गड्डी 500 sheets of paper. *She bought several reams of paper for her business.*

Raep/रीप *(verb)* – फल पाना, फसल काटना cut or gather a crop or harvest the crop from land. *We've been reaping a rich crop this year.*

Reappear/रिअपिअर *(verb)* – फिर से दिखना appear again. *Where did you just reappear from?*

Rear/रिअर *(noun)* – पिछला, पिछला हिस्सा, पालन-पोषण करना the back or hindmost part of something. *I will be waiting at the rear side of the building.*

Rearrange/रिअरेंज *(verb)* – क्रम परिवर्तित कर सजाना arrange again in a different way. *I was in a mood to rearrange our furniture.*

Reason/रिजन *(noun)* – कारण, हेतु, तर्क a cause, explanation, or justification. good or obvious cause to do something. logic a premise of an argument in support of a belief, especially a minor premise given after the conclusion. *She didn't give a reason for her decision.*

Reasonable/रिजनेबल् *(adjective)* – विवेक, विवेकपूर्ण fair and sensible. *It is only reasonable to allow him to present his side of the argument.*

Reassure/रिअश्योर् *(verb)* – आश्वासन देना, निश्चित करना allay the doubts and fears of. *She gave me a reassuring smile.*

R

Rebate/रिबेट *(noun)* – छूट a partial refund to someone who has paid too much for tax, rent, or a utility. *Rebates will be given in the first year alone.*

Rebel/रिबेल *(noun)* – विद्रोही a person who rebels. *She has been a rebel ever since her teenage days.*

Rebellion/रिबेलिअन *(noun)* – विद्रोह armed resistance to an established government or ruler. *The army took the rebellion to the streets to rebel against the ruling government.*

Rebound/रिबाउण्ड *(verb)* – टकरा कर लौटना bounce back after hitting a hard surface. *The ball hit the post and rebounded right on to his face.*

Rebuff/रिबफ *(verb)* – दो टूक जवाब reject in an abrupt or ungracious manner. *She rebuffed my offer in no mean terms.*

Rebuild/रिबिल्ड *(verb)* – पुनर्निमार्ण build again. *The house will be rebuilt in the same way.*

Rebuke/रिब्यूक *(verb)* – डॉट-फटकार करना criticize or reprimand sharply. *She was rebuked for sporting the wrong look at the theme party.*

Recall/रिकॉल् *(verb)* – याद करना, वापस बुलाना remember. cause one to remember or think of. bring back the memory of someone or something to. *I do recall meeting your friends long back.*

Recapitulate/रिकैपिट्यूलेट *(verb)* – मुख्य बिन्दु दोहराना summarize and state again the main points of. *He was trying to recapitulate his arguments before stepping into the courtroom.*

Recede/रिसिड *(verb)* – पीछे हटना, वापस लौटना move back or further away. *The sea had receded after the tsunami.*

Receipt/रिसीद् *(noun)* – रसीद, प्राप्ति-स्वीकृति the action of receiving something or the fact of its being received. a written acknowledgement of this. an amount of money received over a period by an organization. *I requested the shopkeeper to give a receipt of the commodities bought.*

Receive/रिसिव *(verb)* – पाना, प्राप्त करना be given, presented with, or paid. take delivery of. buy or accept. *She received an advance of Rs 10,000 for her project.*

Receiver/रिसिवर *(noun)* – चोंगा, प्राप्तकर्ता a person or thing that receives something. *Did you check the receiver before mailing the courier?*

Recent/रिसेंट *(adjective)* – हाल-फिलहाल का having happened or been done. *She is the most recent employee to have joined the company.*

Receptackle/रिसेप्टेक्ल् *(noun)* – थैला, सन्दूक an object or space used to contain something. *We got the food packed in the receptacle.*

Reception/रिसेप्शन *(noun)* – स्वागत, स्वागत कक्ष, स्वागत समारोह the action or process of receiving someone or something. the way in which something is received. *She received a warm reception at the event.*

Receptive/रिसेप्टिव *(adjective)* – ग्रहणशील able or willing to receive something. willing to consider new suggestion and ideas. *My appraisal says I am quite receptive to criticism.*

Recess/रिसेस *(noun)* – मध्यावकाश a small space set back in a wall. a hollow in something. remote, secluded, or secret places. *The table has a recess in its base.*

Recession/रिसेसन *(noun)* – मन्दी a temporary economic decline during which trade and industrial activity are reduced. *It was IT that was least affected in the recession.*

Recipe/रेसपि *(noun)* – निर्देश, नुस्खा a set of instructions for preparing a dish. *I learnt the typical South Indian recipe for pancakes.*

Recipient/रेसिपिएण्ट *(noun)* – पाने वाला a receiver of something. *She was the recipient of my gift.*

Reciprocal/रेसिप्रोकल *(adjective)* – पारस्परिक given, felt, or done in return. *I was hoping for some reciprocal action from him.*

Recital/रिसाइटल *(noun)* – पाठ the performance of a programme of music by a soloist or small group. *I bought passes for the sitar recital this weekend.*

Reckless/रेक्लेस् *(adjective)* – लापरवाह without thought or care for the consequences of an action. *He was a reckless driver.*

Reckon/रेकॅन् *(verb)* – गणना करना, समझना calculate. *Her bank balance was reckoned to be around 5 crore.*

R

Reckoning/रेकनिंग *(noun)* – गिनती, हिसाब, गिनती में the action of calculating or estimating something. *By my reckoning, we are at least 5 miles away.*

Reclaim/रिक्लेम *(verb)* – पुनः अधिकार जताना retrieve or recover. *You must reclaim your lost money.*

Recline/रिक्लाइन *(verb)* – आराम के साथ (सहारा लेते हुए), बैठना या लेटना lean or lie back in a relaxed position. *She was reclining on her beach chair.*

Recluse/रेक्लूज *(noun)* – संत, एकांतवासी a person who avoids others and lives a solitary life. *The actress became a recluse after the death of her husband.*

Recognition/रिकॉग्निशन *(noun)* – पहचान, मान्यता पाना the action or process of recognizing or being recognized. *He has been working towards a recognition from his workplace.*

Recognize/रिकॉग्नाइज *(verb)* – पहचानना, मान्यता देना, स्वीकृति देना identify as already known; know again. identify and respond correctly to a sound, character, etc. *I recognized her at the market.*

Recoil/रिकॉइल *(verb)* – लपेटा जाना, पीछे हटना suddenly spring back or flinch in fear, horror, or disgust. feel such emotions at the thought of something. *She recoiled at the memories of that accident.*

Recollect/रिकलेक्ट *(verb)* – याद करना, स्मृति में लाना remember. *I do recollect certain episodes of that drama.*

Recollection/रिकलेक्शन *(noun)* – याद करने की क्रिया, अनुस्मरण the action or faculty of remembering. *To my recollection, he has never given a reason to complain.*

Recommend/रिकमेंड *(verb)* – अनुशंसा करना put forward with approval as being suitable for a purpose or role. advise as a course of action. advise to do something. *She recommended me for the post.*

Recompense/रिकमपेन्स *(verb)* – पुरस्कृत करना, हर्जाना देना, क्षतिपूर्ति करना compensate. pay or reward for effort or work. make amends to or reward someone for loss, harm, or effort. *Victims should be recompensed by their culprits.*

Reconcile/रेकनसाइल *(verb)* – विवाद हल करना, सामंजस्य बैठाना, मेल कराना restore friendly relations between, settle a quarrel. *The two warring actors had reconciled.*

Recondition/रिकन्डिशन *(verb)* – फिर से ठीक करवाना, पुनः कार्य के योग्य बनाना condition again. *The car needs to be reconditioned.*

Reconnaissance/रिकॉनिसन्स *(noun)* – पता लगाना, टोह लेना the study of a place or arch for military reason. *The plan was shot down while on a reconnaissance mission over enemy territory.*

Reconsider/रिकन्सिडर *(verb)* – फिर से विचार करना consider again. *Would you like to reconsider your decision?*

Reconstruct/रिकनस्ट्रक्ट *(verb)* – फिर से निर्मित करना construct again. *The ship was being reconstructed.*

Record/रेकॉर्ड *(noun)* – अभिलेख, विवरण a piece of evidence about the past, especially a written or other permanent account of something. [law] an official report of the proceeding and judgements in a court. *They had a record of the proceedings of the court.*

Recorder/रिकॉर्डर *(noun)* – रिकार्ड करने की मशीन an apparatus for recording sound, pictures, or data. *I bought a recorder from the market.*

Recount/रिकाउन्ट *(verb)* – यादकर बताना give an account of something. *The police asked her to recount the sequence of events.*

Recoup/रिकूप *(verb)* – क्षतिपूर्ति regain. reimburse or compensate for money spent or lost. regain recover. *The companies are trying to recoup the money they lost in the recession.*

Recourse/रिकोर्स *(noun)* – अन्य स्रोत a source of help in a difficult situation, demand compensation or payment. *A surgery may be the only recourse.*

Recover/रिकवर *(verb)* – शान्त होना, धन या स्वास्थ्य वापस पाना return to a normal state of health, mind or strength. *She has recovered well from her trauma.*

Recovery/रिकवरी *(noun)* – पुनः प्राप्ति, वसूली, स्वास्थ्य लाभ an act or the process of recovering. the action of taking a vehicle that has broken down or crashed for repair. *I phoned a recovery vehicle to come and help immediately.*

R

Recreation/रिक्रिएशन *(noun)* – मन बहलाव, मनोरंजन enjoyable leisure activity. *There are few options for recreation here.*

Recruit/रिक्रूट *(verb)* – रंगरूट enlist in the armed forces. enroll as a member or worker in an organization. [informal] persuade to do or help with something. *Our toughest soldiers are recruited from the desert.*

Rectangle/रेक्टैंगल *(noun)* – आयताकार a plane figure with four straight sides and four right angles, especially one with unequal adjacent sides. *She bought me a curio that was a rectangular marble piece.*

Rectify/रेक्टिफाइ *(verb)* – सुधारना, परिशोधन put right; correct. convert to direct current. *Statements made now cannot be rectified later.*

Rector/रेक्टर *(noun)* – पुरोहित, अध्यक्ष the incumbent of a parish where all tithes formerly passed to the incumbent. a member of the clergy in charge of a parish. a priest in charge of a church or a religious institution. *He is a rector at the parish nearby.*

Rectum/रेक्टम *(noun)* – मलाशय the final section of the large intestine, terminating at the anus. *The doctor broke the news to the patient that he had been diagnosed with rectum cancer.*

Recuperate/रिक्यूपरेट *(verb)* – स्वास्थ्य लाभ recover from illness or exertion. *She is still recuperating from her illness.*

Recur/रेकर *(verb)* – बार-बार होना occur again. come back to one's mind. go back to in thought or speech. *This phenomenon has been seen to be recurring in her body ever few years.*

Recurrence/रेकरेंस *(noun)* – पुनरावृत्ति occur again. *The recurrence of this phenomenon can be a source of worry.*

Recycle/रिसाइकल् *(verb)* – गलाकर ढालना, पुनश्चक्रण convert into reusable material, use again. *Water recycling is a good option to follow in our future.*

Red/रेड *(adjective)* – लाल of a colour at the end of the spectrum next to orange and opposite violet, as of blood, fire, or rubies. of a reddish-brown colour. red due to embarrassment, anger, or heat. dated or offensive having reddish skin. *She was bright red with embarrassment as soon as she saw her boyfriend entering the show.*

Redden/रेडेन *(verb)* – लाल करना, लाल होना make or become red. *She was reddened and tanned after the whole week she spent at the beach.*

Redeem/रिडीम् *(verb)* – गुणों की क्षतिपूर्ति compensate for the faults or bad aspects of. make up for one's poor past performance or behaviour. save from sin, error, or evil. *It was a disappointing competition redeemed only by the exceptional performance of the winner.*

Redemption/रिडेम्पशन *(noun)* – उद्धार the action of redeeming someone or something, or of being redeemed. *The terms of redemption were not very attractive.*

Red-handed/रेड-हैंडेड *(adjective)* – रंगे हाथ in or just after the act of doing something wrong. *We hatched a plan to catch the thief red-handed.*

Redistribute/रिडिस्ट्रिब्यूट *(verb)* – पुनर्वितरण distribute again or differently. *The products were redistributed among the teammates.*

Redouble/रिडबल *(verb)* – दोगुना करना make or become much greater, more intense, or more numerous. *I thought it was over, but it was back redoubled!*

Redress/रिड्रेस *(verb)* – सुधारना remedy or set right. *The onus was on the government now to set policies to redress racist issues.*

Reduce/रिड्यूस *(verb)* – घटाना make or become smaller or less in amount, degree, or size. boil so that it becomes thicker and more concentrated. chiefly lose weight. photography make less dense. *They reduced the workforce by 10,000.*

Reduction/रिडक्शन *(noun)* – कटौती the action of reducing something. the amount by which something is reduced. *Talks on arms reduction have resumed.*

Redundent/रिडन्डेन्ट *(adjective)* – निष्क्रिय, अनुपयोगी, निरर्थक, पालतू no longer needed or useful; superfluous. able to be omitted without loss of meaning or function. engineering not strictly necessary but included in case another component fails. *Microsoft Windows 2 is redundant.*

R

Reed/रीड *(noun)* – सरकंडा, नई, बाँसुरी a tall, slender-leaved plant, of the grass family, growing in water or one marshy ground. *Reeds had grown and spread all around the pond.*

Reef/रीफ *(noun)* – पाल का हिस्सा, समुद्री चट्टान a ridge of jagged rock, coral, or sand just above or below the surface of the sea. *The coral reef of the Australian coast is endangered.*

Reek/रीक् *(verb)* – दुर्गन्ध, तीव्र दुर्गन्ध have a foul smell. [archaic] give off smoke, steam, or fumes. *He was reeking, so I knew where he was coming from.*

Reel/रील *(noun & verb)* – चरखी, लिपटा धागा, लिपटे चलचित्र, चक्कर खाना, डगमगाकर चलना a cylinder on which film, wire, thread, etc. can be wound. a length of something wound on a reel. *I bought a cotton reel from the thread shop.*

Refectory/रिफेक्टरी *(noun)* – भोजनालय, संस्था का भोजनालय a room used for communal meals, especially in an educational or religious institution. *The monk took his bowl of gruel and made his way towards the refectory.*

Refer/रेफर *(verb)* – उल्लेख, उद्धृत करना mention or allude to. direct the attention of someone to. *She never referred to him again.*

Referee/रेफरी *(noun)* – निर्णायक an official who watches a game or match closely to ensure that the rules are adhered to. *The referee showed the red card at the player.*

Reference/रेफरेंस *(noun)* – सन्दर्भ कथन, सन्दर्भ सूची the action of mentioning something. a mention or citation of a source of information in a book or article. *Please use the Chicago style of reference in the Bibliography.*

Referendum/रेफरेन्डम *(noun)* – जनमत संग्रह a general vote by the electorate on a single political question which has been referred to them for a direct decision. *The parliament was discussing a referendum.*

Refill/रिफिल *(verb)* – फिर से भरना act of refilling or a glass that is refilled. *Could you please refill my glass?*

Refine/रिफाइन *(verb)* – शुद्ध करना, शुद्धीकरण, सुधारना remove impurities or unwanted elements from. *Please refine the liquid twice before consuming it.*

Refinement/रिफाइन्मेंट *(noun)* – शोधन, परिष्कार, परिशोधन a small change that improves something. *The model has electric windows and other refinement.*

Refit/रिफिट *(verb)* – मरम्मत करना, ठीक करना replace or repair machinery, equipment, and fittings in a ship, building, etc. *I'm taking up a contract to refit the factory equipment.*

Reflect/रिफ्लेक्ट *(verb)* – परावर्तित करना throw back without absorbing it. show an image of. *The light was reflected off the box's surface.*

Reflection/रिफ्लेक्शन *(noun)* – परावर्तन, प्रतिबिम्ब the fact or phenomenon of light, heat, sound, etc. being reflected. something reflected or an image so formed. *The teacher showed us how reflection of light occurs.*

Reflective/रिफ्लेक्टिव *(adjective)* – विचारशील, परावर्तनीय providing or capable of providing a reflection. produced by reflection. *She bought some reflective clothing.*

Reflex/रिफ्लेक्स *(noun)* – सहज क्रिया, सहज प्रतिक्रिया an action performed without conscious thought as a response to a stimulus. a response in a part of the body to stimulation of a corresponding point on the feet, hands, or head. *I thought you would have basic reflexes.*

Reform/रिफॉर्म *(verb)* – सुधार, सुधार लाना, परिवर्तन make changes in to relinquish an immoral or criminal lifestyle. *We need to reform this society.*

Reformation/रिफॉर्मेशन *(noun)* – सुधार की प्रक्रिया the action or process of reforming. *The philosopher is responsible for the Reformation that has taken the society by surprise.*

Reformer/रिफॉर्मर *(noun)* – सुधारक a disputant who advocates reform.

Refrain/रिफ्रेन *(verb)* – आत्मनियन्त्रण, स्थायी-टेक, स्फूर्ति लाना stop oneself from doing something. *Please refrain from taking a hasty decision.*

Refresh/रिफ्रेश *(verb)* – तरो-ताजा करना, ताजगी लाना give new strength or energy to. *The old lady brought out some lemonade to refresh the spirits of the construction workers.* jog by going over previous information. *He refreshed his memory by going through his class notes.*

R

Refreshing/रिफ्रेशिंग *(adjective)* – स्फूर्तिदायक, ताजगी लाने वाला serving to refresh. *A refreshing shower helps out tremendously on a hot sweaty day.*

Refreshment/रिफ्रेशमेंट *(noun)* – जलपान, अल्पाहार, ताजगी a light snack or drink. *The refreshments at the party were delicious.*

Refrigerate/रेफ्रिजरेट *(verb)* – शीतल-ताजा रखना subject food or drink to cold in order to chill or preserve it. *Please refrigerate the chicken until further use.*

Refrigerator/रेफ्रिजरेटर *(noun)* – शीत-यन्त्र an appliance or compartment which is artificially kept cool and used to store food and drink. *Cold meat straight from the refrigerator should not be put into a hot pan.*

Refuge/रिफ्यूज *(noun)* – सुरक्षित स्थान, शरण स्थल a place or state of safety from danger or trouble. *A number of people took refuge from the storm in their basements.* [british] a traffic island. *Refuges are necessary to provide safety for pedestrians.*

Refugee/रिफ्यूजी *(noun)* – शरणार्थी a person who has been forced to leave their country in order to escape war, persecution, or natural disaster. *A large percentage of refugees suffer from depression.*

Refund/रिफण्ड *(verb)* – लौटाना, धन वापस करना pay back money to. *Customers will be refunded if the device is found faulty.*

Refusal/रिफ्यूजल *(noun)* – अस्वीकृति, इनकार, अस्वीकृत करना act of refusing something. *My request for more chocolate was met with outright refusal.*

Refuse/रिफ्यूज *(verb)* – अस्वीकार करना, नकारना indicate unwillingness. indicate unwillingness to accept or grant something offered or requested. decline to jump a fence or other obstacle. *The dessert was too good to refuse.*

Refute/रिफ्यूट *(verb)* – खण्डन करना, गलत प्रमाणित करना prove a statement or the person advancing it to be wrong. *He refutes any hint that he behaved badly.*

Regain/रिगेन *(verb)* – पुन: पाना, दोबारा प्राप्त करना, खोया हुआ स्थान, धन प्राप्त करना obtain possession or use of something again after losing it. *She regained her strength after a week of rest.*

Regal/रिगल *(adjective)* – राजसी, राज्योचित of, resembling, or fit for a monarch, especially in being magnificent or dignified. *The regal gesture of the queen left the commoners in awe.*

Regale/रिगेल *(verb)* – कथा, चुटकुला से मनोरंजन entertain with conversation. *The sailor regaled the boys with stories of his old days.*

Regard/रिगार्ड *(verb)* – मानना, समझना, सम्मान देना consider in a particular way. *She regards herself as a dog lover.*

Regency/रिजेन्सी *(noun)* – संरक्षक पद, संरक्षण का अधिकार the office or period of government by a regent. a commission acting as regent. the period of a particular regency, especially from 1811 to 1820 and from 1715 to 1723 adjective relating to or denoting a broadly neoclassical style of [British] architecture, clothing, and furniture of the late 18th and early 19th centuries. *The wealth of the kingdom was restored during his regency.*

Regenerate/रेजेनरेट/रिजेनरिट *(verb)* – पुन: शक्ति संचार करना, पुनर्जीवित करना regrow new tissue. regrow. *Salamanders are remarkable for their ability to regenerate limbs.*

Regent/रिजेन्ट *(noun)* – संरक्षक a person appointed to administer a state because the monarch is a minor or is absent or incapacitated. *The regent represented the King of Denmark as sovereign of Iceland until the country became a republic.*

Regime/रेजिम *(noun)* – शासन a government, especially an authoritarian one. *Hitler's regime showed early signs of army fascism.*

Regimen/रेजिमेन *(noun)* – आहार-व्यायाम निदेश, हिदायतें a therapeutic course of medical treatment, often including recommendations as to diet and exercise. *The new regimen will surely make her lose weight.*

Regiment/रेजिमेंट *(noun)* – सैन्यदल a permanent unit of an army, typically divided into several smaller units and often into two battalions. *The British army has an armoured regiment.*

Region/रीजन *(noun)* – क्षेत्र an area of a country or the world having definable characteristics but not always fixed boundaries. an administrative district of a city or country. *The river flows downstream along the northern region of the city.*

R

Regional/रीजनल *(adjective)* – क्षेत्रीय characteristic of a region. *His accent has a regional.*

Register/रजिस्टर *(noun)* – पंजी, पंजिका, पंजीकरण, सूचीबद्ध करना an official list or record. a record of attendance, for example of pupils in a class. *The teacher always carried her attendance register.*

Registrar/रजिस्ट्रार *(noun)* – प्रशासक, पंजीकरण-अधिकारी an official responsible for keeping a register of official records. *The Commissioner is the Registrar of Births and Deaths in some corporations.*

Registration/रजिस्ट्रेशन *(noun)* – पंजीकरण the action or process of registering or of being registered. *The newly-married couples are eager for their marriage registration.*

Registry/रजिस्ट्री *(noun)* – पंजीकृत, पंजीकरण की प्रक्रिया a place where registers are kept. *Windows maintains a hefty registry of files.*

Regret/रिग्रेट *(verb)* – दुःख प्रकट करना, खेद प्रकट करना, खेद, अनुताप, उदासी, खिन्नता feel or express sorrow, repentance, or disappointment over. *I regret not reaching the venue on time.*

Regular/रेगुलर *(adjective)* – नियमित, व्यवस्थित, सामान्य arranged in a constant of definite pattern, especially with the some space between individual instances. recurring at short uniform intervals. *The plants in the lawn were placed at regular intervals.*

Regulate/रेगुलेट *(verb)* – व्यवस्थित, नियन्त्रित control or maintain the rate or speed of a machine or process. *The green button regulates the tension in the sewing machine.*

Regulation/रेगुलेशन *(noun)* – नियम, नियमन, व्यवस्था a rule or directive made and maintained by an authority. in accordance with regulations. [informal] of a familiar or predictable type. *The new regulations were too tough.*

Rehabilitate/रिहैबिलिटेट *(verb)* – पुनः स्वास्थ्य लाभ, जीवन सामान्य करना restore to health or normal life by training and therapy after imprisonment, addiction, or illness. *The sensible doctor successfully rehabilitated the alcoholic.*

Rehearse/रिहर्स *(verb)* – अभ्यास करना, दुहराना practice for later public performance. *The dance troupe rehearsed their act many times.*

Reign/रेन *(verb)* – राज्य-काल, शासन rule as monarch. *The cruel king reigned for decades.*

Reimburse/रिइम्बर्स *(verb)* – पुनर्भुगतान करना, प्रतिपूर्ति करना repay a person who has spent or lost money. repay a sum of money that has been spent of lost. *My company reimburses my travel expenses.*

Rein/रेन *(noun)* – राज, बागडोर, नियन्त्रण a long, narrow strap attached at one end to a horse's bit, typically used in Paris to guide or check a horse in riding or driving. a similar device used to restrain a young child. *The new rider pulled the reins too hard.*

Reindeer/रेनडियर *(noun)* – बड़ा हिरन a deer with large branching antlers, native to the northern tundra and subarctic and domesticated in parts of Eurasia. *The herd of reindeers grazed on the sparse grasses.*

Reinforce/रिइनफोर्स *(verb)* – अतिरिक्त शक्ति देना, अतिरिक्त सेना भेजना strengthen with additional personnel or material. *After the threat, the government reinforced the security at crowded places.*

Reinstate/रिइनस्टेट *(verb)* – पुनः पद देना, पूर्व अवस्था में लाना restore to a former position or state. *The law and order situation was reinstated with some tough actions.*

Reiterate/रिइटरेट *(verb)* – बार-बार दुहराना, जोर देकर कहना say something again or repeatedly. *The principal reiterated her points regarding importance of discipline.*

Reject/रिजेक्ट *(verb)* – अस्वीकार, अस्वीकार करना dismiss as inadequate or faulty. refuse to consider or agree to. *The manufactured goods were rejected by the inspection department.*

Rejoice/रिज्वॉयस *(verb)* – हर्ष प्रदर्शित करना, उल्लास दिखाना feel or show great joy. [archaic] cause joy to. *The children rejoiced upon hearing about the unexpected holidays.*

Rejuvenate/रिजुविनेट *(verb)* – पुनर्नवा, पुनः युवा होना, तरुणाई पाना make or cause to appear younger or more vital. *The morning walks have rejuvenated me.*

Relapse/रिलैप्स *(verb)* – पुनर्पतन, सुधरने के बाद बिगड़ना deteriorate after a period of improvement. *The conditions of the patient relapsed.*

R

Relate/रिलेट (verb) - वर्णन करना, विवरण देना give an account of. *The child related the details of the family vacations to all his friends.*

Relation/रिलेशन (noun) - सम्बन्ध, नातेदार, सम्बन्धी, रिश्तेदारी the way in which two or more people or things are connected or related. the way in which two or more people or groups feel about and behave towards each other. *The relation between them demanded respect.*

Relationship/रिलेशनशीप (noun) - सम्बन्धी the way in which two or more people or things are connected, or the state of being connected. the way in which two or more people or groups regard and behave towards each other. *The relationship between hard work and success cannot be denied.*

Relative/रिलेटिव (adjective) - सम्बन्धी, नातेदार, रिश्तेदार considered in relation or in proportion to something else. existing or possessing a characteristic only in comparison to something else. *He admired his elder brother for his relative success in the sad economic environment.*

Relax/रिलैक्स (verb) - विश्राम करना, शिथिलता लाना, नरमी make or become less tense or anxious. cause to become less rigid. *Her face relaxed and broke into a smile.*

Relay/रिले (verb) - संकेत या संदेश को (प्राप्त कर) आगे भेजना to receive and trhen pass on a signal or message. *Instructions were relayed to us by phone.*

Release/रिलिज (verb) - मुक्त करना, छोड़ देना, खोल देना set free. *The policeman released the little pickpocket.*

Relegate/रेलिगेट (verb) - पीछे ढकेल देना, निम्न पद देना assign an inferior rank or position to. *The general relegated the officer.*

Relent/रिलेण्ट (verb) - नरम पड़ना, दया दिखाना abandon or mitigate a harsh intention or cruel treatment. *The teacher relented when the student told her the reason.*

Relentless/रिलेण्टलेस (adjective) - बिना सुस्ताए, लगातार, अनवरत oppressively constant. *The relentless winds damaged the seaside houses.*

Relevant/रेलिवन्ट (adjective) - प्रासंगिक, सम्बद्ध, संगत युक्त closely connected or appropriate to the matter in hand. *The audience asked all the relevant questions.*

Reliable/रिलाइअबल् (adj.) - विश्वनीय, भरोसेमन्द able to be relied on. *My car is pretty reliable.*

Reliance/रिलायन्स (noun) - विश्वास, विश्वसनीयता dependence on or trust in someone or something. *It was a question of reliance.*

Relic/रेलिक (noun) - स्मृति-अवशेष, स्मृति-शेष, अवशेष an object of interest surviving from an earlier time. a surviving but outdated object, custom, or belief. *The archaeologists were thrilled to find the relic.*

Relief/रिलिफ (noun) - राहत, आराम महसूस करना, नक्कासी का उभार the alleviation or removal of pain, anxiety, or distress. a feeling or cause of relief. a temporary break in a generally tense or tedious situation. *She felt some relief after taking the painkillers.*

Relieve/रिलिव (verb) - चिन्ता-मुक्ति, कार्यभार से निवृत्ति, चिन्तामुक्त alleviate or remove cause to stop duty by taking their place. *The morning guard relieved the night guard late today.*

Religion/रिलिजन (noun) - धर्म, ईश्वर में आस्था the belief in and worship of a superhuman controlling power, especially a personal God or gods. a particular system of faith and worship. *There are many religions in the world.*

Religious/रिलिजियस (adjective) - धार्मिक, धर्मपरायण of, concerned with, or believing in a religion. belonging or relating to a monastic order or other group united by their practice of religion. *This is a congregation of religious people.*

Relequish/रेलिंक्विश (verb) - त्याग देना, अधिकार छोड़ना voluntarily cease to keep or claim; give up. *I relinquished my claim on the property.*

Relish/रेलिश (noun) - रसास्वाद, आस्वाद, अत्यन्त आनन्द great enjoyment. pleasurable anticipation. *I wish the relish lasts forever.*

Relive/रिलिव (verb) - पुन: अनुभव करना, दुहराना live through an experience or feeling again in one's imagination. *I relived my college life during the reunion.*

Reluctant/रिलक्टैंट (adjective) - अनिच्छुक, चाहत की कमी unwilling and hesitant. *I took my reluctant dog to the vet.*

R

Rely/रिलाइ *(verb)* – विश्वास करना, निर्भर रहना depend on with full trust. *I rely upon you for quality work.*

Remain/रिमेन *(verb)* – बाकी रहना, बने रहना be in the same place or condition during further time. continue to be: he remained alert. *She remained in her seat even after all the students had left.*

Remainder/रिमेन्डर *(noun)* – बचा हुआ, शेष a part, number, or quantity that is left over. the number which is left over in a division in which one quanityty does not exactly divide another. *She calculated the remainder wrong.*

Remains/रिमेंस *(plural noun)* – अवशेष, मृत शरीर, बचा भाग things remaining. *The remains of the fight still make me angry.*

Remand/रिमान्ड *(verb)* – हवालात में डालना, भेजना place a defendant on bail or in custody, especially when a trial is adjourned. *The court remanded the suspect.*

Remark/रिमार्क *(verb)* – टिप्पणी say as a comment; mention. *He remarked about the quality of the thesis.*

Remedy/रेमिडि *(noun)* – उपचार, दवा, चिकित्सा a medicine or treatment for a disease or injury. *It was an effective remedy.*

Remember/रिमेम्बर *(verb)* – याद रखना, याद करना, स्मरण में रखना have in or be able to bring to one's mind someone or something form the past. bear in mind by making them a gift, making provision for them, or mentioning them in prayer. recover one's manners after a lapse. *Do you remember our first meeting?*

Remembrance/रिमेम्ब्रैन्स *(noun)* – स्मृति चिह्न, निशानी, स्मरण the action of remembering a memory. a thing kept or given as a reminder or in commemoration of someone. *Please keep this ring as a remembrance of our relationship.*

Remind/रिमाइन्ड *(verb)* – स्मरण दिलाना, याद दिलाना cause to remember something or to do something. cause someone to think of something because of a resemblance. *It was good of you to remind me of this association.*

Reminder/रिमाइन्डर *(noun)* – स्मरण-पत्र a thing that causes someone to remember something.

a letter sent to remind someone to pay a bill. *Did you get a reminder from the company?*

Reminiscent/रेमिनिसेंट *(adjective)* – स्मरण कराने वाला tending to remind one of something. *Your voice is reminiscent of someone I knew.*

Remiss/रिमिस *(adjective)* – काहिल, लापरवाह, कामचोर lacking care or attention to duty. *It would be remiss of me not to convey this information to students.*

Remission/रिमिसन *(noun)* – माफी, क्षमा, दण्ड कम करना the cancellation of a debt, charge, or penalty. [british] the reduction of a prison sentence, especially as a reward for good behavious. *The poor family was glad to have received a remission.*

Remit/रेमिट *(verb)* – ऋण या सजा माफ करना, डाक से धन भेजना refrain from exacting or inflicting. theology pardon a sin. *Will God remit my sin?*

Remittance/रेमिटैंस *(noun)* – रुपये भेजने की क्रिया a sum of money remitted. the action of remitting money. *Have you received the notification about the remittance?*

Remnant/रेमनन्ट *(noun)* – अवशेष, शेष a small remaining quantity. a piece of cloth left when the greater part has been used or sold. *These few trees are the remnant of a huge forest.*

Remonstrate/रिमॉन्सट्रेट *(verb)* – प्रतिवाद करना, विरोध करना make a forcefully reproachful protest. *The students remonstrated against the new rules.*

Remorse/रिमोर्स *(noun)* – पश्चाताप deep regret or guilt for a wrong committed. *I was touched by his genuine feelings of remorse.*

Remote/रिमोट *(adjective)* – दूर का, दूर से for away in space or time. situated far from the main centres of population. *The remote village didn't have any electricity supply.*

Remove/रिमुव *(verb)* – हटाना take off or away from the position occupied. abolish or get rid of. dismiss from a p0sot. dated relocate to another place. *The guard was removed after he was found sleeping.*

Remunerate/रिम्यूनरेट *(verb)* – पारिश्रमिक देना pay for services rendered or work done. *The company promised to remunerate him well for his services.*

R

Remuneration/रिम्यूनरेशन *(noun)* – पारिश्रमिक money paid for some work. *Diana agreed to work overtime if her firm promised to pay her extra remuneration.*

Renaissance/रिनेसन्स *(noun)* – पुनर्जागरण the revival of art and literature under the influence of classical models in the 14th-16th centuries. *Shakespeare and Ben Jonson are writers that belonged to the Renaissance age.*

Render/रेन्डर *(verb)* – करना, देना, हिसाब भेजना, प्रदर्शित करना provide or give a service, help, etc. submit for inspection, consideration, or payment. poetic hand over; surrender. *Sheela wished to be adequately paid for the services rendered by her.*

Rendezvous/रेन्डवू *(noun)* – निश्चित मिलन-स्थली, संगम a meeting that you have arranged with somebody. *Sameer had a secret randezvous with Deeya.*

Renew/रिन्यू *(verb)* – नवीकरण, नवीनीकरण resume or re-establish after an interruption. *The sisters renewed their love and affection for each other after the fight.*

Renounce/रिनाउन्स *(verb)* – त्यागना, अधिकार त्याग, संन्यास formally declare one's abandonment of a claim, right, or possession. [law] refuse or resign a right or position, especially one as an heir or trustee. *The priest renounced all his worldly possessions for a life of piety.*

Renovate/रिनोवेट *(verb)* – पुनः उद्धार, पुनरुद्धार restore something old to a good state of repair. *The old house was renovated last month.*

Renown/रिनॉउन *(noun)* – यश पाना, प्रसिद्धि पाना the state of being famous. *Dancers of great renown were present at the party last night.*

Renowned/रिनाउन्ड *(adjective)* – यशस्वी, प्रसिद्ध famous. *Vineet is renowned the world over for his talent of tap dancing.*

Rent/रेंट *(noun)* – किराया, भाड़ा, भाड़े पर लगाना a tenant's regular payment to a landlord for the use of property or land. *Fiona was ready to pay the exorbitant monthly rent for the seaside apartment.*

Renunciation/रिनन्सिएशन *(noun)* – त्याग देना the action of renouncing. *The promise to celibacy demands the renunciation of marriage.*

Reorganize/रिऑर्गनाइज *(verb)* – पुनर्गठन, पुनः संगठित करना order again. *The General reorganized the ranks to suit the interest of the army.*

Repair/रिपेअर *(verb)* – मरम्मत करना restore something damaged, worn, or faulty to a good condition. *Cindy repaired her bike for the new year at college.*

Repartee/रिपार्टी *(noun)* – श्लेष, व्यंग्यपूर्ण चतुर उत्तर conversation or speech characterized by quick, witty comments or replies. *Seema is popular all over the college campus for the witty repartee.*

Repast/रिपास्ट *(noun)* – भोज formal a meal. *We had a sumptuous repast during the morning celebration.*

Repatriate/रिपैट्रिएट *(verb)* – स्वदेश वापस भेजना send back to their own country. *After the war ended, trucks were repatriating the enemy soldires to their country.*

Repay/रिपे *(verb)* – वापस लौटाना pay back a loan. pay back money owed to someone. *Fiona repaid her car loan in just about six months time.*

Repeal/रिपील *(verb)* – रद्द करना revoke or annul a [law] or act of parliament. *The law was repealed after the mass murder.*

Repeat/रिपीट *(verb)* – दुहराना say or do again. say or do the same thing again. *Ben decided to repeat himself in order to get his point through to the audience at the workshop.*

Repel/रिपेल *(verb)* – पीछे धकेल देना, घृणा drive or force back or away. *Oil and water repel each other.*

Repent/रिपेंट *(verb)* – पछताना, पश्चाताप करना feel or express sincere regret or remorse. [archaic] feel regret or penitence about. *It is futile to repent one's actions after the damage has been done.*

Repentance/रिपेंटैंस *(noun)* – पछतावा, पश्चाताप sorrow, grief. *The capacity of repentance is impossible in the heart of an egotist.*

Repercussion/रिपरकसन *(noun)* – परिणाम, प्रभाव, प्रतिक्रिया a consequence of an event or action. *The political agenda can have multiple repercussions.*

Repertoire/रिपरट्वार *(noun)* – अभिनय संग्रह, रंग पटल the body of pieces known or regularly performed by a performer push back. *Jim is renowned all over the city for his performances and impeccable repertoire.*

Repetition/रेपिटिशन *(noun)* – दुहराई हुई, पुनरावृत्ति, प्रतिकृति the act or an instance of repeating or

R

being repeated. a thing that repeats another. *Any concept can be learned and internalized by the process of repetition.*

Replace/रिप्लेस (verb) – स्थानापन्न होना, स्थान ग्रहण करना take the place of. *We will replace any goods that are damaged.*

Replacement/रिप्लेसमेंट (noun) – स्थानापन्न replacing something or someone. *Ted found a suitable replacement for his secretary who has gone on a maternity leave.*

Replay/रिप्ले (verb) – फिर से खेलना, फिर से चलाना play back a recording. *Danny requested his wife to replay the song on the recorder at the party.*

Replenish/रिप्लेनिश (verb) – परिपूर्ण कर देना, हरा-भरा कर देना fill up again. *Europe turns to India in order to replenish all their resources.*

Replete/रिप्लीट (adjective) – परिपूर्ण, भरा-पूरा, ठसाठस भरा filled or well-supplied with something. *Our trip to Egypt was replete with incidents that reminded us of the yester years.*

Replica/रेप्लिका (noun) – प्रतिकृति, समान आकृति, नकल, दूसरे जैसा an exact copy or model of something, especially. *The museum of Madame Tussaud has on display exact replicas of famous personalities from all over the world.*

Reply/रिप्लाइ (verb) – उत्तर देना say or write something in response to something said or written. *I hope my mother replied to the Principal's letter.*

Report/रिपोर्ट (verb) – विवरण, विवरण देना, जानकारी देना give a spoken or written account of something. convey information about an event or situation. *All the new cadets reported their daily schedules to the manager on duty.*

Repose/रिपोज (verb) – आराम करना, लेटना, आस्था रखना place something, especially one's confidence or trust, in. *Tina succumbed to her fate of loneliness with quiet repose.*

Represent/रिप्रेजेंट (verb) – प्रतिनिधित्व करना, वर्णन करना be entitled or appointed to act or speak for. be an elected member of parliament of member of a legislature for. act as a substitute for. *Dan surprised the judge when he chose to represent the guilty party.*

Representation/रिप्रेजेंटेशन (noun) – प्रतिनिधित्व the action or an instance of representing or being represented. *The theatre group was present at the court for representation purpose only.*

Representative/रिप्रेजेंटेटिव (adjective) – प्रतिनिधि typical of a class or group. containing typical examples of many or all types. *Anna Hazare is a proper representative of the working class in India.*

Repress/रिप्रेश (verb) – दबाना, कुचलना, दमन करना subdue by force. *Celibacy demands the repressing of all sexual desires.*

Reprieve/रिप्रीव (verb) – सजा रोकना, सजा निरस्त करना, परेशानी से थोड़ी राहत देना cancel or postpone the punishment or demise of. *The new policy allowed the punishment of all wrong doers to be reprieved.*

Reprimand/रेप्रिमैन्ड (noun) – फटकारना, भर्त्सना करना a formal expression of disapproval. *To reprimand is to teach control and manners.*

Reprisal/रिप्राइजल (noun) – प्रतिशोध, बदला an act of retaliation. *The British government was shocked by the Indian reprisal.*

Reproach/रिप्रोच (verb) – असफलता, भूल जाने के लिए फटकार, धिक्कार, उलाहना भरा express to someone one's disapproval of or disappointment in their actions. *Tina was strongly reproached by her mother for her indecent behaviour.*

Reproachful/रिप्रोचफुल (adjective) – उलाहना पूर्ण, निन्दात्मक expresseing disapproval disappoitment. *Tia was reproachful of her husband's behaviour towards her relatives.*

Reproduce/रिप्रोड्यूस (verb) – दुबारा करना, दुबारा बना देना, नकल प्रति तैयार करना, पुनः उत्पादन की प्रक्रिया produce a copy or representation of. create something in a different medium or context that is very similar to. *The play was to reproduce in the original art form.*

Reproof/रिप्रूफ (noun) – भर्त्सना, दोष निकालना, निन्दा a rebuke or reprimand. *Tim strongly disapproved of his public reproof by his boss.*

Reprove/रिप्रूव (verb) – कड़ी भर्त्सना, कड़ी निन्दा rebuke or reprimand. *Tina was strongly reproved by her husband at the party last night.*

Reptile/रेप्टाइल (noun) – सरीसृप, रेंगने वाले जीव a cold-blooded vertebrate animal of a class that includes snakes, lizards, crocodiles, turtles,

R

and tortoises, typically having a dry scaly skin and laying soft-shelled eggs on land. *Lizard is a reptile.*

Republic/रिपब्लिक् *(noun)* – गणतन्त्र a state in which supreme power is held by the people and their elected representatives, and which has an elected or nominated president rather than a monarch. *He was unanimously elected President of the Republic of Kenya.*

Republican/रिपब्लिकन् *(adjective)* – गणतन्त्र राज्यीय, गणतन्त्र समर्थक belonging to or characteristic of a republic. *Every nation ought to have democratic as well as republican attributes.*

Repudiate/रिप्यूडिएट *(verb)* – नकारना, अस्वीकार करना refuse to accept or be associated with. *Tina repudiated the gender sensitization policies of the firm that she was working with.*

Repugnant/रिपग्नैंट *(adjective)* – अरुचिकर, जुगुप्सा extremely distasteful; unacceptable. *Domestic violence is a repugnant act.*

Repulse/रिपल्स *(verb)* – पीछे ढकेलना, हमले को निष्फल करना, घृणा उत्पन्न करना drive back by force. rebuff or refuse to accept. *Ned's repulsive behaviour was the main cause of his banishment from the Sunday meet group.*

Repulsion/रिपल्सन *(noun)* – अत्यधिक घृणा, अरुचि, प्रतिकर्षण a feeling of intense distaste or disgust. *The estranged husband and wife shared a mutual feeling of repulsion towards each other.*

Repulsive/रिपल्सिव *(adjective)* – घृणास्पद, प्रतिकर्षक arousing intense distaste or disgust. *A repulsive odour emanated from the cupboard.*

Reputable/रिप्यूटेबल् *(adjective)* – प्रतिष्ठित, ख्याति प्राप्त having a good reputation. *The company can bank upon its reputable owners.*

Reputation/रिप्यूटेशन *(noun)* – ख्याति, प्रसिद्धि, प्रतिष्ठा the beliefs or opinions that are generally held about someone or something. a widespread belief that someone or something has a particular characteristic. *The company's reputation depends upon its employees as well as its employers.*

Repute/रिप्यूट *(noun)* – ख्याति, नाम, प्रतिष्ठा the opinion generally held of someone or something. *Lack of public safety can lead to a bad repute for the government.*

Reputed/रिप्यूटेड *(adj)* – यशस्वी, लब्धप्रतिष्ठ, नामी, ख्याति प्राप्त generally regarded. *He's reputed to be the highest paid sportsman in the world.*

Request/रिक्वेस्ट *(noun)* – निवेदन, अनुरोध, प्रार्थना an act of asking politely or formally for something. a thing that is asked for in such a way. *Tim's plea to his father regarding the mowing down of their family home was more of a humble request.*

Require/रिक्वायर *(verb)* – निर्भरता, आवश्यक, जरूरत होना need or depend on. wish to have. *The orphanage required a great amount of donation to provide proper education for its inmates.*

Requisite/रेक्विजिट *(adjective)* – आवश्यक, जरूरी made necessary by particular circumstances or regulations. *The divorce proceedings will not be forwarded until the requisite fee is paid.*

Requisition/रेक्विजिशन *(noun)* – सामान की माँग an official order laying claim to the use of property or materials. *Heidi was required to make various requisitions to hire the office area.*

Rescue/रेस्क्यू *(verb)* – मुक्त कराना, छुड़ाना save from a dangerous or distressing situation. *The stray dogs were rescued by the shopkeepers.*

Research/रिसर्च *(noun)* – अन्वेषण, अनुसंधान the systematic investigation into and study of materials and sources in order to establish facts and reach new conclusion. *Field work is an important part of any scientific research.*

Researcher/रिसर्चर *(noun)* – अन्वेषण, अनुसंधान कर्ता one who conducts research. *Tim is employed as a researcher at the University of California.*

Resemble/रिजेम्बल *(verb)* – एकसा, समान, सदृश होना to look alike or similar in appearance. *John greatly resembles his grandfather.*

Resemblance/रिजेम्ब्लेंस *(noun)* – समानता, सादृश्यता the state of resembling. a way in which two or more things resemble each other. *The resemblance between Tim and his father is uncanny.*

Resent/रिजेंट *(verb)* – नाराज होना, बुरा मानना, क्रोध उपजना feel bitterness or indignation at. *Sam resents having betrayed his girlfriend for another woman.*

R

Resentment/रिजेंटमेंट *(noun)* – मनोमालिन्य, रोष, नाराजगी bitterness; indignation. *The resentment that Gill has towards her estranged husband is very visible.*

Reservation/रिजर्वेशन *(noun)* – आरक्षण the action of reserving. an arrangement whereby something has been reserved. *Tim made reservations in a popular restaurant to surprise his wife on her birthday.*

Reserve/रिजर्व *(verb)* – बचाकर, संचित, अतिरिक्त शक्ति retain for future use. *Tina believes in reserving her money for the rainy day.*

Reserved/रिजर्व्ड् *(adjective)* – आरक्षित, अल्पभाषी slow to reveal emotion or opinions. *Tina's reserved nature is her only drawback.*

Reservoir/रिजरवायर *(noun)* – जलाशय a large natural or artificial lake used as a source of water supply. a supply or source of something. *Fiona's mother is a reservoir of information where their family history is concerned.*

Reshuffle/रिशफल *(verb)* – फेंटना, पत्ते फेंटना, फेर बदल करना interchange the positions of members of a team, especially government ministers. *Coach Ned decided to reshuffle the team for better productivity.*

Reside/रिजाइड *(verb)* – निवास करना, रहना have one's permanent home in a particular place. *The family has been residing in the same locality for over five decades now.*

Residence/रेजिडेंस *(noun)* – निवास, निवास स्थान the fact of residing somewhere. *The company owner needed a residence in the city to open an office.*

Resident/रेजिडेंट *(noun)* – निवासी a person who lives somewhere on a long-term basis. a bird, butterfly, or other animal of a species that does not migrate. [British] a guest in a hotel who stays for one or more nights. US a pupil who boards at a boarding school. *American residents are investing in property in india.*

Residential/रेजिडेंसियल *(adjective)* – आवासीय designed for people to live in. providing accommodation in addition to other services. occupied by private houses. *John was given a residential apartment by his company upon relocation to another city.*

Residue/रेजिड्यू *(noun)* – अवशेष, बचा हुआ भाग a small amount of something that remains after the main part has gone or been taken or sued a substance that remains after a process such as combustion or evaporation. *The washing powder left a white residue on the clothes.*

Resign/रिजाइन *(verb)* – त्याग, पद-त्याग करना voluntarily leave a job or position of office. *Tina's improper behaviour with her co-workers forced her to resign from her job.*

Resignation/रेजिग्नेशन *(noun)* – त्याग-पत्र an act of resigning. a document conveying an intention to resign. *Fiona made her resignation public after being accused of being unethical.*

Resilient/रिजिलिअन्ट *(adj)* – सहने में समर्थ, सहनशील able to recoil or spring back into shape after bending, stretching, or being compressed. *She won accolades all over campus for her resilient behaviour and forbearance.*

Resist/रिजिस्ट *(verb)* – प्रतिरोध, सबलता से रोकना, विरोध करना withstand the action or effect of. *She strongly resisted his favours.*

Resistance/रिजिस्टन्स *(noun)* – प्रतिरोधक क्षमता, सहनशीलता the action of resisting. *The boys showed resistance when confronted by the school authorities.*

Resistant/रिजिस्टन्ट *(adj)* – प्रतिरोधक not tarmed or affected by something. *This watch is water-resistant.*

Resolute/रेजोल्यूट *(adjective)* – दृढ़निश्चयी, कृतसंकल्प, संकल्पवान determined; unwavering. *Nina's resolute behaviour is her greatest strength.*

Resolution/रेजल्यूशन *(noun)* – दृढ़ता, निश्चय, संकल्पबद्ध the quality of being resolute. *Tina listed her New Year resolutions on a piece of paper.*

Resolve/रिजॉल्व *(verb)* – दृढ़ निश्चय, पक्का इरादा, पारित प्रस्ताव settle or find a solution to. medicine cause to heal or disappear. *The medicine is said to resolve my problem in a month.*

Resonant/रेजनॅन्ट *(adjective)* – गूंज, गूंजित, अनुगूँज की ध्वनि deep; clear, and continuing to sound or ring. tending to reinforce or prolong sounds especially by synchronous vibration. filled or resounding with a sound. *His resonant voice charmed the ladies.*

Resonance/रेजनन्स *(noun)* – अनुगूंज, निनाद, प्रतिध्वनित the quality of sound being clear and continuing for a long time. *The audience was*

R

mighty impressed with the resonance of the speaker's voice.

Resort/रिजॉर्ट *(noun)* – सैरगाह स्थल, आश्रय the place where a lot of people for vacation. *The bride and groom decided to book the entire resort for their honeymoon.*

Resound/रिजाउन्ड *(verb)* – गूँजना, प्रतिध्वनित to fill a place with voice sound. *The palace resounded with a distinct echo of the yester year charm that the place once enjoyed.*

Resource/रिसोर्स *(noun)* – स्रोत, संसाधन, सम्पदा, युक्ति a stock or supply of materials or assets. *Sheena wanted to take full advantage of her estranged husband's resources even after their divorce.*

Respect/रिस्पेक्ट *(noun)* – आदर, आदर भाव, आदर भावना, आदर देना a feeling of deep admiration for someone elicited by their qualities or achievements. polite greetings. *We should respect our elders.*

Respectable/रिस्पेक्टेबल् *(adjective)* – आदरणीय, सम्मानीय, सम्मान योग्य regarded by society as being proper, correct, and good. *Ria wanted to be married into a respectable family.*

Respectful/रिस्पेक्टफुल *(adjective)* – आदरपूर्ण showing respect. *Children should be taught to be respectful of elders.*

Respective/रिस्पेक्टिव *(adjective)* – क्रमश: अपना-अपना belonging or relating separately to each of two or more people or things. *All the candidates were requested to talk about their respective personal lives as part of the interview process.*

Respiration/रिस्पिरेशन *(noun)* – श्वास, श्वास लेने की क्रिया the action of breathing. a single breath. *The doctors decided to monitor the patient's respiration for a day or so.*

Respire/रेस्पायर *(verb)* – श्वास लेना, साँस लेना breathe. carry out respiration. *Plants respire throughout the day.*

Respite/रेस्पाइट *(noun)* – राहत, आराम a short period of rest or relief from something difficult or unpleasant. *The prisoners of war sought respite from the Pakistan government.*

Resplendent/रेस्प्लेन्डेन्ट *(adjective)* – चमकता-दमकता, भव्य attractive and impressive through being richly colourful or sumptuous. *The peacock's resplendent plumage is a sight to behold.*

Respond/रिस्पॉन्ड *(verb)* – उत्तर देना, प्रतिक्रिया दिखाना say or do something *in* reply or as a reaction. *The court responded to her pleas.*

Response/रिस्पॉन्स् *(noun)* – उत्तर, अनुक्रिया, प्रतिक्रिया an instance of responding; an answer or reaction. *It is impossible to elicit a positive response from an intolerant person.*

Responsibility/रिस्पॉन्सिबिलिटि *(noun)* – उत्तरदायित्व the state or fact of being responsible. *It is the responsibility of children to take care of their parents.*

Responsible/रिस्पॉन्सिबल् *(adjective)* – उत्तरदायी, जबावदेह having an obligation to do something, or having control over or care for someone. *Diana relies a lot on her responsible son.*

Responsive/रिस्पान्सिव् *(adjective)* – रुचि लेन वाला, अनुकूल, उत्तरदावी responding readily and positively. *A well defined organization is responsive to any misdemeanours in society.*

Rest/रेस्ट *(noun)* – विश्राम, आराम, स्थिर, शेष, सहारा the remaining party of something. the remaining people or things; the others. *He was unable to convince the rest of the group.*

Restaurant/रेस्टरान्ट *(noun)* – भोजनालय a place where people pay to sit and eat meals that are cooked and served on the premises. *He made reservations at the restaurant for lunch.*

Restitution/रेस्टीट्यूशन *(noun)* – खोई या चुराई हुई वस्तु की उसके मालिक को वापसी the restoration of something lost or stolen to its proper owner. *Restitution of the documents was vital for the reputation of the institution.*

Restive/रेस्टिव *(adjective)* – बैचेन, नियन्त्रण से बाहर unable to keep still or silent; restless. *A restive wife causes strife.*

Restless/रेस्टलेस *(adj)* – अधीर, बेचैन unable to stay calm or be happy where you are because a feeling of boredom. *She was feeling rather restless after lunch.*

Restoration/रेस्टोरेशन् *(noun)* – पुनर्स्थापना, पुनर्रचना the action or process of restoring. a model or drawing representing the supposed original form of an extinct animal, ruined building, etc. *Restoration is definitely needed in our building.*

Restore/रिस्टोर *(verb)* – पुरानी स्थिति पर, वापसी bring back a previous right, practice, or situation; reinstate. return to a former condition

R

or position. *The government restored peace in the war struck area.*

Restrain/रिस्ट्रेन *(verb)* – रोकना, नियन्त्रित करना, नियन्त्रण में रहना prevent from doing something; keep within limits. deprive of freedom of movement or personal liberty. *The child had to be restrained from walking out of the house.*

Restrict/रिस्ट्रिक्ट *(verb)* – रोकना, सीमित करना, सीमा में रखना put a limit on; keep under control. *Entry to the museum was restricted.*

Result/रिजल्ट *(noun)* – फल, परिणाम a consequence, effect, or outcome. a satisfactory outcome: persistence guarantees results. *His poverty was result of his carelessness.*

Resume/रिज्यूम *(verb)* – पुनः कार्यारम्भ, फिर से शुरू करना begin again or continue after a pause or interruption. take or put on again. *We shall resume our work after a short break.*

Resurgent/रिसर्जेन्ट *(adjective)* – उत्साह के साथ उठना, पुनः सक्रियता increasing or reviving after a period of little activity; popularity, or occurrence. *Resurgent communalism is a result of intolerant religious factions of society.*

Resurrect/रिजरेक्ट *(verb)* – फिर से प्रयोग में लाना, पुनर्जीवन restore to life. *The mummy was resurrected from his sarcophagus.*

Resuscitate/रिससिटेट *(verb)* – चेतना में लाना revive from unconsciousness. *The man tried to resuscitate his wife using his mouth to blow air directly into her mouth.*

Retail/रिटेल *(noun)* – फुटकर, खुदरा the sale of goods to the public for use or consumption rather than for resale.

Retailer/रिटेलर *(noun)* – फुटकर विक्रेता, खुदरा बेंचने वाला a person or business that sells goods to public. *My brother is a retailer of sports goods.*

Retain/रिटेन *(verb)* – रखना, अधिकार में रखना continue to have; keep possession of. not abolish, discard, or alter. keep in one's memory. *Katherine decided to retain her mother's jewellery.*

Retaliate/रिटैलिएट *(verb)* – प्रत्याक्रमण, प्रतिकार करना make an attack or assault in return for a similar attack. *Tina retaliated violently to her husband's accusations.*

Retaliation/रिटैलिएशन *(noun)* – बदले की कार्रवाई, प्रतिकार का प्रयास *The terrorist group* said that the shooting was in retaliation for the murder of one of its member.

Retard/रिटार्ड *(verb)* – विकास में रुकावट, बाधा, बाधित delay or hold back in terms of development or progress. *Bad weather conditions retard the growth of plants.*

Retarded/रिटार्डेड *(adj)* – मन्दबुद्धि, अर्द्धविकसित less advanced in mental, physical, or social development than is usual for one's age. *The progress of the Indian economy is retarded owing to slow implementation of laws.*

Retention/रिटेंशन *(noun)* – स्वामित्व बनाये रखना, अधिकार रखना स्मृति में रखने की शक्ति, याददास्त the act of retaining or state of being retained. *The state government ordered the retention of all landed property even after the buyout by the multinational company.*

Rethink/रिथिंक *(verb)* – पुनर्विचार, पुनःचिन्तन assess or consider a policy or course of action again. *I am rethinking my decision of buying a sedan car.*

Reticent/रेटिसेंट *(adjective)* – अल्पभाषी not revealing one's thoughts or feelings readily. *His reticence adds to his charming personality.*

Retina/रेटिना *(noun)* – पुतली, दृष्टिपटल a layer at the back of the eyeball that contains cells sensitive to light, which trigger nerve impulse that pass via the optic nerve to the brain, where a visual image is formed. *The optician informed her that her blurred vision was a result of her torn retina.*

Retinue/रेटिन्यू *(noun)* – परिजन, मातहत a group of advisers or assistants accompanying an important person. *The judge always travels with his retinue of lawyers.*

Retire/रिटायर *(verb)* – अवकाश प्राप्त, सोने जाना, निवृत्त, सेवा निवृत्त होना leave one's job and cease to work, especially because one has reached a particular age. of a sports player cease to play competitively. *My father retired from job last year.*

Retirement/रिटायरमेंट *(noun)* – सेवानिवृत्ति के पश्चात the action or fact of retiring. *He was given a farewell party post retirement by his office people.*

Retort/रिटॉर्ट *(verb)* – मुँहतोड़ जवाब देना, समुचित प्रत्युत्तर देना say something sharp, angry, or

R

witty in answer to a remark or accusation. *She retorted to her sister's accusatory tone.*

Retouch/रिटच *(verb)* – लघु संशोधन करना improve or repair a painting, photograph, etc. by making slight additions or alternations. *The marble sculptures needed a retouch before being reinstalled to the hotel lobby.*

Retrace/रिट्रेस *(verb)* – वापसी, लौटना, दूसरे का मार्ग खोलना go back over the same route that one ahs just taken. discover and follow a route or course taken by someone else. *She retraced her footsteps to get out of the jungle safely.*

Retract/रिट्रैक्ट *(verb)* – समेटना, पलटना, मुकरना draw or be drawn back or back in. *The snail retracted into its shell on being disturbed.*

Retreat/रिट्रिट *(verb)* – पीछे हटना, वापस लौटना withdraw from confrontation with enemy forces. move back from a difficult or uncomfortable situation. withdraw to a quiet or secluded place. *The lion retreated back to his cave after having ravished his prey.*

Retrench/रिट्रेंच *(verb)* – खर्च कम करना, कर्मचारी हटाना, कटौती करना reduce costs or spending in response to economic difficulty. chiefly make redundant in order to reduce costs. *Several people lost their jobs because their companies retrenched.*

Retrenchment/रिट्रेंचमेंट *(noun)* – कटौती करना, छँटनी करना to reduce costs or work force. *Numerous companies were forced to undergo retrenchment following the global economic slowdown.*

Retribution/रिट्रिब्यूशन *(noun)* – प्रतिफल, बदला, प्रतिकार punishment inflicted in the spirit of moral outrage or personal vengeance. *The thieves were pelted to death by the public as retribution for their heinous crime.*

Retrieve/रिट्रीव *(verb)* – वापस पाना, दोबारा पाना, खोज निकालना get or bring back. find and bring back. *The emperor sent his general to retrieve his imperial sword.*

Retrograde/रिट्रोग्रेड *(adjective)* – अधोगामी, अवनति की ओर directed or moving backwards. the order of something reversed; inverse. *To act negatively would be a retrograde step.*

Retrospect/रिट्रॉस्पेक्ट *(noun)* – सिंहावलोकन, स्मृति फलक पर देखना a survey or review of a past course of events or period of time. *In retrospect, war can be considered a mass murder.*

Retrospective/रिट्रॉस्पेक्टिव *(adjective)* – विगत तिथि से, अतीत में झाँकना looking back on or dealing with past events or situations. of an exhibition or compilation showing the development of an artist's work over a period of time. *His paintings were retrospective in nature.*

Return/रिटर्न *(verb)* – लौटना, लौटने की क्रिया come or go back to a place. go back to a particular state or activity. come back after a period of absence. golf play the last nine holes in round of eighteen holes. give or send back or put back in place. *He promised to return after his project.*

Reunion/रियूनियन *(noun)* – पुनर्मिलन the process or an instance of reuniting. *All classmates decided to meet at the school reunion.*

Reunite/रियूनाइट *(verb)* – पुन: मिल जाना come together or cause to come together again after a period of separation or disunity. *The refugee camp ensured that all refugees were reunited with their family members.*

Revalue/रिवैल्यू *(verb)* – पुनर्मूल्यांकन करना value again. *He revalued his property before the final sell off.*

Reveal/रिविल *(noun)* – प्रकट करना, रहस्य खोलना disclose previously known or secret information. make known to humans by divine or supernatural means. *Jesus revealed his presence to his followers on the 40th day.*

Revel/रेवल *(verb)* – मौज, आमोद-प्रमोद, शोरगुल-प्रमोद समारोह engage in lively and noisy festivities. *They revelled themselves eating and dancing at the picnic yesterday.*

Revelry/रेवलरि *(noun)* – रंगरलियाँ, गुलछर्रे noisy fun involving eating dancing drinking. *Carnival ensures a night of revelry and joy.*

Revelation/रेवलेशन *(noun)* – प्रकटन, रहस्योद्घाटन a surprising disclosure. the revealing of something previously unknown. a surprising or remarkable thing. *Suddenly, he had a revelation that life was not just about monetary benefits, but also about love and brotherhood.*

Revenge/रिवेंज *(noun)* – प्रतिशोध retaliation for an injury or wrong. the desire to inflict this.

R

Revenge is a vice that ought to be avoided under all circumstances.

Revenue/रेवेन्यू *(noun)* – राजस्व income, especially when of a company and which public expenses are met. items or amounts constituting revenue. the department of the civil service collecting revenue. *The government body in villages is responsible for collecting revenue from the villages every year.*

Reverberate/रिवरवरेट *(verb)* – गूँजना, अनुगूँज of a loud noise be repeated as an echo. [archaic] return or re-echo a sound. *Diana's screaming reverberated through the entire hall and took everyone by surprise.*

Revere/रिवीअर *(verb)* – आदर, श्रद्धा रखना respect or admire deeply. *Good teachers are always revered by their students.*

Reverence/रेवरेंस *(noun)* – श्रद्धा deep respect. *Everybody stood up as the retired teacher entered the classroom as a mark of reverence.*

Reverend/रेवरेंड *(adjective)* – श्रद्धेय a title or form of address to members of the clergy. *The reverend jury members were requested to attend the court hearing.*

Reverent/रेवरेंट *(adjective)* – श्रद्धालु showing reverence. *The students were taught the importance of being reverent in class today.*

Reverie/रेवरि *(noun)* – दिवास्वप्न a daydream. [archaic] a fanciful idea or theory. *Leela pinched Tim on the arm in order to snap him out of his reverie.*

Reversal/रिवर्सल *(noun)* – विपरीत, विपरीत, पृष्ठ भाग, पलटना a change to an opposite direction, position, or course of action. [law] an annulment of judgement made by a lower court or authority. an adverse change of fortune. *The judge ordered a reversal of the court proceedings in order to ensure justice.*

Revert/रिवर्ट *(verb)* – पूर्वदशा में आना, पुरानी आदत पकड़ना return to a pervious state, condition, etc. [biology] return to a former or ancestral type. *The teacher reverted back with the results within a day.*

Review/रिव्यू *(noun)* – सर्वेक्षण, समीक्षा, निरीक्षण a formal assessment of something with the intention of instituting change if necessary. [law] a reconsideration of a judgement or sentence by a higher court or authority. *The government plans to review certain laws for the betterment of the society.*

Reviewer/रिव्यूअर *(noun)* – समीक्षक, सर्वेक्षक a person who writes reviews of books, films etc. *The student hired two reviewers to review her paper.*

Revile/रिवाइल *(verb)* – गाली देना, कटु शब्द कहना criticize abusively. *The teacher reviled the student who had abused his classmate.*

Revise/रिवाइज *(verb)* – संशोधन, पुनर्निरीक्षण examine and improve or amend something, especially written matter. reconsider and later an opinion or judgement. *I want to read the revised version of this play.*

Revision/रिविजन *(noun)* – पुनर्पाठ, संशोधन, पुन: देखना the action or revising. a revised edition or form. *Preeti is a travel editor who heads the revisions team.*

Revival/रिवाइवल *(noun)* – नवजागरण, पुनर्जीवन, पुनरुत्थान an improvement in the condition or strength of something. *The Celtic revival is a defining moment in the history of English Literature.*

Revive/रिवाइव *(verb)* – पहले-सी शक्ति पाना, पुन: स्फूर्ति पाना, पुनर्जीवित करना restore to or regain life, consciousness, or strength. restore interest in or the popularity of. restore or improve the position or condition of. *The doctor managed to revive the patient by injecting coramin.*

Revoke/रिवोक *(verb)* – रद्द करना, वापस लेना end the validity or operation of a decree, decision, or promise. *I am revoking all your powers.*

Revolt/रिवोल्ट *(verb)* – विद्रोह करना rise in rebellion. refuse to acknowledge someone or something as having authority. [archaic] having rebelled. *The Indian Army revolted on realizing what the British troops had done.*

Revolting/रिवोल्टिंग *(adj)* – अरुचिकर, विद्रोह जगाने वाला rebellious. *The filth strewn all over the house was a revolting sight.*

Revolution/रिवोल्यूशन *(noun)* – विद्रोह, क्रान्ति a forcible overthrow of a government or social order, in favour of a new system. the class struggle expected to lead to political change and the triumph of communism. *The Marxist leaders demanded a revolution to change the existing order.*

Revolutionary/रिवोल्यूशनरी *(adjective)* – क्रान्तिकारी, विद्रोही involving or causing dramatic change

R

or innovation. *His revolutionary spirit can land him into trouble with the authorities.*

Revolutionize/रिवोल्यूशनाइज *(verb)* – विद्रोह जगाना, क्रान्ति उत्पन्न करना change radically or fundamentally. *Liberal thinking leads to a revolutionized society.*

Revolve/रिवॉल्व *(verb)* – गोल घूमना, चक्कर खाना, परिक्रमा करना treat as the most important point or element. *The earth revolves around its own axis.*

Revolver/रिवॉल्वर *(noun)* – तमंचा a pistol with revolving chambers enabling several shots to be fired without reloading. *Sam carries a licensed revolver for his personal safety.*

Revulsion/रिवल्सन *(noun)* – घृणा, जुगुप्सा a sense of disgust and loathing. *Gia felt a sense of revulsion after meeting her sister's husband.*

Reward/रिवार्ड *(noun)* – पुरस्कार, पारितोषिक a thing given in recognition of service, effort, or achievement. a fair return for good or bad behaviour. a sum offered for the detection of a criminal, the restoration, of lost property, etc. *A reward acts as motivation to perform better.*

Rewarding/रिवार्डिंग *(adjective)*– पुरस्कार, पारितोषिक providing satisfaction. *Sid's rewarding work brought him laurels at his workplace.*

Rewind/रिवाइन्ड *(verb)* – विडियो कैसेट या टेप को पीछे करना या उल्टा घुमाना to make a video or cassette tape go backward. *Please rewind the tape at the end of the film.*

Rewrite/रिराइट *(verb)* – किसी बात को दो बार लिखना (भिन्न रूप से या बेहतर तरीके से) write again in an altered or improved form. *Mandy was asked to rewrite the essay by his teacher.*

Rhetoric/रेटरिक *(noun)* – शब्द-पटुता, शब्दालंकार, शब्दाडम्बर the art of effective or persuasive speaking or writing. language with a persuasive or impressive effect, but often lacking sincerity or meaningful content. *Rhetoric and prosody is an essential subject in literature.*

Rheumatic/रूमेटिक *(adjective)* – गठिया, गठिया से सम्बन्धित of, relating to, caused by, or suffering from rheumatism. *Sid's rheumatic legs made it tough for him to run swiftly.*

Rheumatism/रूमेटिज्म *(noun)* – गठिया any disease marked by inflammation and pain in the joints, muscles, or fibrous tissue,

especially rheumatoid arthritis. *Rheumatism is an affliction of the bones.*

Rhinoceros/राइनॉसरस *(noun)* – गैंडा a large, heavily built plant-eating mammal with one or two horns on the nose and thick folded skin, native to Africa and south Asia. *Rhinoceros is one of the endangered species.*

Rhombus/रॉम्बस *(noun)* – समचतुर्भुज geometry a parallelogram with oblique angles and equal sides. *Tom learned about geometrical shapes such as the rhombus today.*

Rhyme/राइम *(noun)* – तुक, तुकान्त कविता, तुक मिलना correspondence of sound between words or the endings of words, especially when used in poetry. a word with the same sound as another. *It is easier to remember songs that have words that rhyme.*

Rhythm/रिद्म *(noun)* – लय, ताल a strong, regular, repeated pattern of movement or sound. the systematic arrangement of musical sounds, according to duration and periodical stress. a type of pattern formed by this. *Tim's tutor realized that his pupil's music was in perfect rhythm and that he was nothing short of a prodigy.*

Rib/रिब *(noun)* – पसली each of a series of slender curved bones articulated in pairs to the spine, protecting the thoracic cavity and its organs. an animal rib with meat adhering to it used as food. *Eve is said to have been created from Adam's rib.*

Ribbon/रिबन *(noun)* – फीता a long, narrow strip of fabric, used for tying something or for decoration. a ribbon of a special colour or design awarded as a prize or worn to indicate the holding of an honour. *Sia ties a pretty red ribbon to her plait.*

Rice/राइस *(noun)* – चावल a swamp grass which is cultivated as a source of food, especially in Asia. the grains of this cereal used as food. *Rice is the staple food in India.*

Rich/रिच *(adjective)* – धनी, बहुलतापूर्ण, ऊर्वर having a great deal of money or assets having valuable natural resources or a successful economy. of expensive materials or workmanship. *Tom's rich relative offered to finance his university education.*

Riches/रिचेज *(plural noun)* – धन-दौलत, सम्पति material wealth valuable natural resources.

R

He lost all his riches due to his incompetence and misdemeanour.

Rickety/रिकेटी *(adjective)* – जर्जर, डाँवाँडोल poorly made and likely to collapse. *The rickety bullock cart was unable to pull through the course of the entire journey.*

Ricochet/रिकॅचेट *(verb)* – टकराकर वापस लौटना rebound off a surface. move or appear to move in such a way. *The ball ricocheted across the room due to the forceful impact of the thump.*

Rid/रिड *(verb)* – पिंड छुड़ाना, पीछा छुड़ाना make someone or something free of an unwanted person or thing. be freed or relieved of. *Tina wished to be rid of all her financial troubles by Christmas.*

Riddance/रिडंस *(noun)* – छुटकारा, राहत the action of getting rid of someone of something. *Doing away with meaningless superstitions is good riddance.*

Ridden/रिडेन – वशीभूत past participle of ride. *Nightmares are often ridden with mental imbalance.*

Riddle/रिडल *(noun)* – पहेली, बुझौवल a question or statement phrased so as to require ingenuity in ascertaining its answer or meaning. a person or thing that is difficult to understand. *This is complex riddle.*

Ride/राइड *(verb)* – सवारी, झूला पर चढ़ना, बैठना sit on and control the movement of a horse, bicycle, or motorcycle. travel in or on a vehicle or horse. compete in on a horse, bicycle, or motorcycle. [north American] travel in a lift or vehicle. *He rides his bicycle to work.*

Rider/राइडर *(noun)* – सवार a person who rides a horse, bicycle, motorcycle, etc. *She is an expert rider.*

Ridge/रिज *(noun)* – पहाड़ का लम्बा तंग ऊँचा भाग a long narrow hilltop, mountain range, or watershed. *I am going to the ridge.*

Ridicule/रिडिक्यूल *(noun & verb)* – खिल्ली उड़ाना, उपहास mockery or derision. *Your ridicule doesn't help anyone.*

Ridiculous/रिडिक्यूलस *(adjective)* – हास्यास्पद, बेतुका inviting ridicule; absurd. *Your ridiculous idea spoilt everything.*

Rife/राइफ *(adj)* – छितराया हुआ wide spread. *The rife violence was a cause of worry.*

Rifle/राइफल *(noun)* – बन्दूक a gun, especially one fired from shoulder level having a long spirally grooved barrel to make a bullet spin and thereby increase accuracy over a long distance. *The hunter carried a rifle on his shoulder.*

Rift/रिफ्ट *(noun)* – फटन, दरार, मतभेद, मनमुटाव a crack, split, or break in something. *The rift in the rock was dangerous.*

Rig/रिग *(verb)* – धांधली (अपने अनुकूल परिणाम के लिए किसी गतिविधि को अनुचित रूप से प्रभावित करना) manage or conduct fraudulently so as to gain an advantage. *He rigged the records to his benefit.*

Rigging/रिगिंग *(noun)* – जहाज के रस्से पाल इत्यादि the system of ropes or chains supporting a ship's masts and controlling or setting the yards and sails. *The rigging was old and needed to be replaced.*

Right/राइट *(adjective)* – सही, उचित, अधिकार, सही दशा में, दाहिना morally good, justified, or acceptable. *She says that my views are right.*

Righteous/राइट्यस *(adjective)* – नैतिक, नैतिक रूप से सही morally right or justifiable. *I sometimes find your righteous approach tiresome.*

Rightful/राइटफुल *(adjective)* – यथोचित having a legitimate right to something legitimately claimed; fitting. *You are the rightful owner of the estate.*

Rightfully/राइटफुली *(adverb)* – उचित तौर पर in the manner of ownership. *This estate is rightfully yours.*

Rigid/रिजिड *(adjective)* – कड़ा, अड़ियल, न मुड़ने वाला unable to bend or be forced out of shape. of a person stiff and unmoving. *You have a rigid personality.*

Rigidity/रिजिडिटि *(noun)* – कठोरता, दृढ़ता the physical property of being stiff and resisting bending. *Your rigidity will cause problems for you in your life.*

Rigmarole/रिग्मरोल *(noun)* – अनर्थक कथा, बिना अर्थ की बातचीत a meaningless or incoherent talk. *When will this rigmarole end!*

R

Rigour/रिगर *(noun)* – कड़ाई, संयम a sudden feeling of cold accompanied by shivering and a rise in temperature, especially at the onset or height of a fever. *The rigour lasted only a few minutes.*

Rigorous/रिगरस *(adjective)* - कष्टसाध्य, श्रमसाध्य extremely thorough, exhaustive, or accurate. *He hurt his back while doing some rigorous exercise.*

Rim/रिम *(noun)* – पहिया का घेरा the upper or outer edge of something, typically something circular. the outer edge of a wheel, on which the tyre is fitted. the part of a spectacle frame surrounding the lenses. *The rim of the spectacle was bent.*

Rind/रिन्ड *(noun)* – छिलका a tough outer layer or covering, especially of fruit, cheese, or bacon. the bark of a tree. *Some people consume the rind of an orange.*

Ring/रिंग *(noun)* – अँगूठी, छल्ला, घेरा, अखाड़ा, नाथना, बजना, बजाना, गूँजना, बजने की ध्वनि a small circular band, typically of precious metal, worn on a finger as an ornament or as a token of marriage or engagement. *He gave her a ring.*

Rinse/रिन्स *(verb)* - खंगालना wash with clean water to remove soap or dirt. remove by rinsing. *Please rinse this bottle properly.*

Riot/राइअट् *(noun)* – दंगा, बलवा a violent disturbance of the peace by a crowd. rowdy behaviour. *The riots went out of control.*

Rip/रिप *(verb)* - चीरना, काटना tear or pull forcibly away from something or someone. tear something into small pieces. *The bully ripped the toy away from the child.*

Ripe/राइप *(adjective)* - पका, पूर्ण विकसित ready for harvesting and eating. fully matured. *The fruit was ripe.*

Ripen/राइपेन *(verb)* - पकना, पकाना become or make ripe. *The fruits ripen by February.*

Ripple/रिपल् *(noun)* – तरंग, तरंगाचित a small wave or series of waves. [physics] a small wave in which the dominant force is surface tension rather than gravity. *Ripple look beautiful on the surface of water.*

Rise/राइज *(verb)* - उठना, वृद्धि, चढ़ाव, जगना, उन्नति, स्रोत come or go up reach a higher social or professional position. succeed in not being constrained by. *He rose up the corporate ladder.*

Risk/रिस्क *(noun)* – जोखिम, खतरा a situation involving exposure to danger. the possibility that something unpleasant will happen. *This investment is a huge risk.*

Rite/राइट *(noun)* – अनुष्ठान, संस्कार a religious or other solemn ceremony or event, e.g. marriage, marking an important stage in someone's life. *They left as soon as all the rites completed.*

Ritual/रिचुअल *(noun)* – कर्मकाण्ड, अनुष्ठान a religious or solemn ceremony involving a series of actions performed according to a prescribed order. a prescribed order of performing such a ceremony. *Hindu marriages involve many rituals.*

Rival/राइवल् *(noun)* – प्रतिद्वन्दी a person or thing competing with another for superiority or the same objective. a person or thing equal to another in quality. *The two rivals fought a bitter battle.*

Rivalry/राइवलरि *(noun)* – प्रतिद्वन्दिता competition between people, groups, etc. *There was a lot of rivalry between the sisters.*

River/रिवर *(noun)* – नदी a large natural flow of water travelling along a channel to the sea, a lake, or another river. used in names of animals and plants living in or associated with rivers, e.g. river dolphin. *The river has carved a passage for itself across the centuries.*

Rivet/रिवेट *(noun)* – कील, आँख गड़ाना a short metal pin or bolt for holding together two metal plates, its headless end being beaten out or pressed down when in place. *Watch out for the rivet.*

Rivulet/रिव्युलेट् *(noun)* – छोटी धारा a very small stream. *Several rivulet flow into the river.*

Road/रोड *(noun)* – सड़क, मार्ग a wide way between places, especially one surfaced for use by vehicles. *The road was wide and smooth.*

Roam/रोम् *(verb)* - घूमना, निरुद्देश्य घूमना travel aimlessly over a wide area. wander over, through, or about. pas lightly over. *He roamed all across the world when he was young.*

Roar/रोर् *(noun)* – दहाड़, गर्जन, दहाड़ना, गरजना a full, deep, prolonged sound as made by a lion, natural force, or engine. a loud, deep sound uttered by a person, especially as an expression of pain, anger, or great amusement. *The lion's roar could be heard miles away.*

Roast/रोस्ट *(verb)* – सेंकना, भूनना cook or be cooked by prolonged exposure to heat in an oven or over a fire. process by subjecting it to intense heat. *Please roast the meat.*

Rob/रॉब *(verb)* – लूटना, डाका डालना take property unlawfully from a person or place by force or threat of force. [informal] overcharge. *She robbed the man at gunpoint.*

Robbery/रॉबरी *(noun)* – डकैती, लूट the action of robbing a person or place. [informal] unashamed swindling or overcharging *The police were able to crack the case of robbery.*

Robe/रोब *(noun)* – लबादा, ढीला बाहरी वस्त्र a long, loose outer garment reaching to the ankles. such a garment worn, especially on formal or ceremonial occasions, as an indication of the wearer's rank, office, or profession. *She wore a beautiful robe over her dress.*

Robin/रॉबिन *(noun)* – लाल छाती वाली गाने वाली एक छोटी चिड़िया, एक पक्षी a small singing bird with red breast. *Robins flitted around in the sky.*

Robot/रोबोट् *(noun)* – मशीनी मानव, यन्त्र मानव a machine capable of carrying out a complex series of actions automatically, especially one programmable by a computer. *My sister gifted me a robot for my birthday.*

Robust/रोबस्ट *(adjective)* – तगड़ा, हृष्ट-पुष्ट sturdy or resilient. strong and healthy. *The robust laptop didn't need any repairs for many years.*

Rock/रॉक *(noun & verb)* – चट्टान, डुलाना, हिलना, तेज संगीत the hard mineral material of the earth's crust, exposed on the surface or underlying the soil. a mass of this projecting out of the ground of water. a boulder. [north American] a stone of any size. *The rock from moon was placed in a museum.*

Rocket/रॉकेट *(noun & verb)* – अग्निबाण, तीव्र वेग से बढ़ना a cylindrical projectile that can be propelled to a great height or distance by the combustion of its contents. a missile or spacecraft propelled by an engine providing thrust on the same principle. *We saw the rocket launch.*

Rod/रॉड *(noun)* – छड़, छड़ी, (लकड़ी या धातु की) a thin straight bar, especially of wood or metal. *Rods of iron were used to give strength to the structure.*

Rodent/रोडेन्ट् *(noun)* – कुतरने वाले जीव a mammal of an order that includes rats, mice, squirrels, and porcupines, distinguished by strong constantly growing incisors and no canine teeth. *I don't think rodents make good pets.*

Roe/रो *(noun)* – मछली का अण्डा (जो खाये जाते हैं) the eggs of a fish that we eat. *Roe is a delicacy in many parts of the world.*

Rogue/रोग *(noun)* – दुष्ट, दुर्जन, खतरनाक a dishonest or unprincipled man. a mischievous but likeable person. *He is such a rogue.*

Role/रोल *(noun)* – भूमिका an actor's part in a play, film, etc. *Can you tell me more about your role in the movie?*

Roll/रोल *(noun & verb)* – लपेटा, लपेटी वस्तु, लुढ़कना move by turning over and over on an axis, ship, aircraft, or vehicle sway on an axis parallel to the direction of motion *The ship rolled towards the port.*

Roller/रोलर *(noun)* – बेलन, बेलना, तरंग, लहर a cylinder that rotates about a central axis and is used in various machines and devices to move, flatten, or spread something. *Use a roller to roll the cotton.*

Romance/रोमैंस *(noun)* – रोमांचक अनुभव, रोमांचकारी घटना, प्रेम कथा the group of Indo-European language descended from Latin, principally French, Spanish, Portuguese, Italian, Catalan, Occitan. and Romanian. *I know several romances.*

Romantic/रोमैन्टिक *(adjective)* – प्रेम-विषयक, रूमानी inclined towards or suggestive of romance. relating to love, especially in a sentimental or idealized way. *This is a romantic poem.*

Romp/रॉम्प *(verb)* – खेलना, खिलवाड़ करना, उछलना-कूदना play about roughly and energetically. *The children romped around.*

Roof/रूफ *(noun)* – छत the structure forming the upper covering of a building or vehicle. the top inner surface of a covered area or space. *The ladder almost touched the roof.*

R

Rook/रूक् *(noun)* – कौवे की प्रजाति, शतरंज का हाथी a gregarious crow with black plumage and a bare face, nesting in colonies in treetops. *A rook was making a lot of noise around the tree.*

Room/रूम *(noun)* – कमरा, स्थान space viewed in terms of its capacity to accommodate contents or allow action: she was trapped without room to move. *There was no room to move.*

Roomy/रूमि *(adjective)* – लम्बा-चौड़ा having plenty of room; spacious. *This is a roomy house.*

Roost – *(noun)* a tidal race. *These waters are risky because of the tidal race.*

Rooster/रूस्टर *(noun)* – मुर्गा a male domestic fowl. *I bought a rooster yesterday.*

Root/रूट *(noun & verb)* – जड़, शोर, स्रोत, स्थिर करना, जमा देना turn up the ground with its snout on search of food. rummage. *The antelopes rooted around.*

Rope/रोप् *(noun)* – रस्सी a length of stout cord made by twisting together strands of hemp, sisal, nylon, etc. the ropes enclosing a boxing or wrestling ring. execution by hanging. *The rope was very strong.*

Rosary/रोज़री *(noun)* – सुमिरनी, जपमाला in the Roman catholic church a form of devotion in which five or fifteen decades of hail marys are repeated, each decade preceded by an our father and followed by those assembled there. *I love the sound of rosary.*

Rose/रोज *(noun)* – गुलाब a prickly bush or shrub that typically bears red, pink, yellow, or white fragrant flowers, native to north temperate regions and widely grown as an ornamental. used on names of other plants with similar flowers, e.g. a stylized representation of a rose in heraldry or decoration. *I planted a rose in my garden.*

Rostrum/रोस्ट्रम *(noun)* – चबूतरा a raised platform on which a person stands to make a public speech, play music, or conduct an orchestra. a similar platform for supporting a film or television camera. *The rostrum had been set up well.*

Rosy/रोज़ी *(adjective)* – गुलाबी, स्वस्थ rose red or pink, typically as an indication of health or youthfulness: rosy cheeks. *She is very proud of her rosy cheeks.*

Rot/रॉट *(verb)* – सड़ना decompose by the action of bacteria and fungi; decay. *The vegetables had started rotting.*

Rota/रोटा *(noun)* – कार्य-सूची a list showing times and names for people to take their turn to undertake certain duties. *No one seems to be following the rota.*

Rotate/रोटेट *(verb)* – धूरी पर घूमना move or cause to move in a circle round an axis. *The ball rotated for quite some time.*

Rote/रोट *(noun)* – रट्टा मारना, रटना mechanical or habitual repetition: a poem learnt by rote. *I am trying to break out of my rote.*

Rotor/रोटर *(noun)* – धूरी पर घूमने वाला the rotating part of a turbine, electric motor, or other device. *The rotor needs cleaning.*

Rotten/रॉटन *(adjective)* – सड़ा-गला suffering from decay. *The tomato is rotten.*

Rotund/रोटण्ड *(adjective)* – गोल-मटोल large and plump. round; spherical. *The rotund man went to the dietician for advice.*

Rouble/रूबल *(noun)* – रूस की मुद्रा the basic monetary unit of Russia and some other former republics of the USSR, equal to 100 kopeks. *This costs 100 Roubles.*

Rouge/रूज *(noun)* – लाली a red powder or cream used as a cosmetic for colouring the cheeks or lips. *She applied rouge with perfection.*

Rough/रफ *(adjective)* – खुरदरा, आरम्भिक, कर्णकटु, रूक्ष having an uneven or irregular surface; not smooth or level. having many obstacles; difficult or cross. *The rough terrain is making the ride uncomfortable.*

Roughly/रफली *(adverb)* – रूक्ष व्यवहार in a rough or harsh manner. *He was punished for handling the patient roughly.*

Roughage/रफेज *(noun)* – पाचक अंश fibrous indigestible material in vegetable foodstuffs which aids the passage of food and waste products through the gut. coarse, fibrous fodder. *You need to increase the amount of roughage in your diet.*

Roughen/रफन *(verb)* – खुरदुरा करना, रूखा बनाना make or become rough. *The ride roughened as the quality of the roads went down.*

R

Roulette/रूलेट *(noun)* – जुए का एक खेल a gambling game in which a ball is dropped on to a revolving wheel with numbered compartments, the players betting on the number at which the ball comes to rest. *She was delighted to have won the roulette.*

Round/राउन्ड *(adjective)* – गोल, चारों ओर, घूमते हुए, फेरा, बारी, दौरा, गोली दागना, अनुमोदन shaped like a circle or cylinders. *I liked the round logo better than the square one.*

Roundabout/राउन्डएबाउट *(noun)* – चक्करदार a road junction at which traffic moves in one direction round a central island to reach one of the roads converging on it. *There was an accident on the roundabout.*

Rouse/राउज *(verb)* – नींद से जागना, प्रेरित होना, क्रोधित करना bring out of sleep; awaken. cease to sleep; wake up. *The noise of the boxes falling roused the sleeping family.*

Rout/राउट *(noun)* – पूर्णहार a disorderly retreat of defeated troops. a decisive defeat. *The rout was intercepted by the enemy.*

Route/रूट *noun)* – रास्ता, मार्ग (a way or course taken in getting from a starting point to a destination. the line of a road, path, railway, etc. *What route should I take to the railway station?*

Routine/रूटीन *(noun)* – दिनचर्या, विकरणी a sequence of actions regularly followed; a fixed unvarying programme. *I finished my daily routine well in time.*

Rove/रोव *(verb)* – मटरगस्ती करना travel constantly without a fixed destination; wander. travel for one's work, having no fixed base: a roving reporter. *She roves around the world.*

Row/राउ *(noun)* – पंक्ति, कतार a number of people or things in a more or less straight line. *I sat in the third row.*

Royal/रॉयल *(adjective)* – राजकीय, राजर्षी of, relating to, or having the status of a king or queen or a member of their family. *The royal family travelled to the hills for vacations.*

Rub/रब *(verb)* – रगड़ना apply firm pressure against the surface of, using a repeated back and forth motion. move to and fro against a surface. apply with a rubbing action: she rubbed some cream on her nose. blend or mix ingredients together using a rubbing action: rub in the fat. dry, smooth, or clean something by rubbing. erase pencil marks with a rubber. be transferred by contact or association. *He rubbed her back to ease her backache.*

Rubber/रबर *(noun)* – चिपकाउ स्राव, मिटाने वाला पदार्थ a tough elastic polymeric substance made from the latex of a tropical plants or synthetically. *This unusual dress is made of rubber.*

Rubbish/रबिश *(noun)* – कूड़ा-कचरा, रद्दी waste material; refuse or litter. *There was rubbish everywhere.*

Rubble/रब्ल् *(noun)* – मलवा waste or rough fragments of stone, brick, concrete, etc. especially as the debris from the demolition of buildings. *Some people rummaged through the rubble.*

Ruby/रूबि *(noun)* – माणिक्य, गहरा लाल रंग a precious stone consisting of corundum in colour varieties varying from deep crimson or purple to pale rose. *I like wearing rubies.*

Rucksack/रकसैक *(noun)* – पीठ का थैला a bag with two shoulder straps which allow it to be carried on the back, used by hikers. *My rucksack is too heavy.*

Rudder/रडर *(noun)* – पतवार a flat piece hinged vertically near the stern of a boat for steering. a vertical aerofoil pivoted from the tailplane of an aircraft, for controlling movement about the vertical axis. application of the rudder in steering a boat or aircraft. *The rudder can be used to decide the direction of the boat.*

Ruddy/रडि *(adjective)* – लालिमा, लालिमापूर्ण having a healthy red colour. *She has a ruddy complexion.*

Rude/रूड *(adjective)* – रूखा, उग्र offensively impolite or ill mannered. referring to sex in a way considered improper and offensive. *His rude language made him very unpleasant to work with.*

Rudiments/रूडिमेंट्स *(noun)* – आधारभूत सिद्धान्त, आरम्भिक the first principles of a subject. an elementary or primitive form of something. *You don't even seem to know the rudiments.*

Rudimentary/रूडिमेंटरि *(adj)* – प्रारम्भिक,अविकसित involving or limited to basic principles. *It is important to follow the rudimentary practices.*

R

Ruffian/रफिअन *(noun)* – गुण्डा, बदमाश a violent or lawless person. *The ruffian turned out to be the king in disguise.*

Rug/रग *(noun)* – कालीन, कम्बल a small carpet. a thick woollen blanket. *The rug had gathered dust.*

Rugged/रगेड् *(adjective)* – ऊबड़-खाबड़ having a rocky and uneven surface. *The terrain is rugged.*

Ruin/रूइन *(noun)* – तबाह, बरबाद, तबाह करना, बरबाद करना physical destruction or collapse. *No one knows what led to the ruin of the civilization.*

Ruinous/रूइनस *(adjective)* – बरबाद करने वाला disastrous or destructive. *His ruinous tendencies are bound to land him in trouble.*

Rule/रूल *(noun)* – नियम, आदत, शासन, रेखा खींचना a regulation or principle governing conduct or procedure within a particular sphere. *The new rule wasn't acceptable to the students.*

Ruler/रूलर *(noun)* – शासक, पैमाना a person or agent exercising government or dominion. *The ruler of this country is tough but just.*

Ruling/रूलिंग *(noun)* – अधिकारिक आदेश, प्रभावशाली an authoritative decision or pronouncement. *The court issued the ruling without any delay.*

Rum/रम *(noun)* – गन्ने की शराब, अजीब, अनोखा an alcoholic spirit distilled from sugar cane residues or molasses. any intoxicating liquor. *He drank rum with water.*

Rumble/रम्बल *(verb)* – धड़धड़ाना, धड़धड़ाते हुए चलना make a continuous deep, resonant sound. move with such a sound. *The thunder rumbled throughout the night.*

Ruminate/रूमिनेट *(verb)* – चिन्तन करना think deeply about something. *I would like to ruminate over this matter for some time.*

Rummage/रमेज *(verb)* – ढूँढ़ने के लिए चीजों को छितराना search unsystematically and untidily for something. make a thorough search of a vessel. *They rummaged through the cabinets.*

Rumour/रूमर *(noun)* – उड़ती खबर, अफवाह a currently circulating story or report of unverified or doubtful truth. *Rumour has it that they are going to marry soon.*

Run/रन *(verb)* – दौड़ना, चालू करना, बहना, दौड़, दौड़ की संख्या move at a speed faster than a walk, never having both or all feet on the ground at the same time. enter or be entered in a race. chase or hunt their quarry. sail straight and fast directly before the wind. go upriver from the sea in order to spawn. *The thief ran as soon as he saw the police.*

Rung/रंग *(noun)* – सीढ़ी का डंडा, जिस पर पैर रखते हैं a horizontal support on a ladder for a person's foot. a strengthening crosspiece in the structure of a chair. *The rung broke as I was climbing up the ladder.*

Runner/रनर *(noun)* – धावक a person or animal that runs. a horse that runs in a particular race. a messenger, collector, or agent for a bank, bookmaker, or similar. an orderly in the army. *He is a fast runner.*

Running/रनिंग *(noun)* – दौड़ना, धावन the activity or movement of a runner. *The running in the race today was exceptional.*

Runny/रनि *(adjective)* – सामान्य स्तर पर आशा से अधिक तरल more liquid in consistency than is usual or expected. *The cake batter is too runny.*

Runway/रनवे *(noun)* – पथ a strip of hard ground along which aircraft take off and land. *A deer strolled on to the runway.*

Rupee/रूपी *(noun)* – भारतीय मुद्रा the basic monetary unit of India, Pakistan, Sri Lanka, Nepal, Mauritius, and the Seychelles, equal to 100 paise in India, Pakistan, and Nepal, and 100 cents in Sri Lanka, Mauritius, and the Seychelles. *I spent Rupees 300 on this dress.*

Rupture/रप्चर *(verb)* – सम्बन्ध-विच्छेद break or burst suddenly. cause to break or burst suddenly. suffer an abdominal hernia. *She had to be operated upon immediately when her appendix ruptured.*

Rural/रूरल *(adjective)* – ग्रामीण in, relating to, or characteristic of the country. side rather than the town. *I am very fascinated by the rural lifestyle.*

Ruse/रूज *(noun)* – धोखा, छल a stratagem or trick. *The ruse was very clever.*

R

Rush/रश *(noun)* – तालाब आदि के पास उगने वाला एक प्रकार का पौधा a marsh or waterside plant with slender stem like pith filled leaves, some kinds of which are used for matting, baskets, etc. *This basket is made of rush.*

Russet/रसद् *(adjective)* – गेरूआ रंग का reddish brown. *The russet dress is my favourite.*

Rust/रस्ट *(noun)* – जंग (लोहे आदि में लगने वाला), मोरचा a reddish or yellowish brown flaking coating of iron oxide that is formed on iron or steel by oxidation, especially in the presence of moisture. *The rust made the rod unusable.*

Rustic/रस्टिक *(adjective)* – देहाती, ग्रामीण of or characteristic of life in the country. having a simplicity and charm that is considered typical of the countryside. *He had a rustic home.*

Rustle/रसल *(verb)* – सरसराहट make a soft, muffled crackling sound like that caused by the movement of dry leaves or paper. move with such a sound. *Her dress rustled in the wind.*

R

Ss

S/एस – अंग्रेजी वर्णमाला का 19वाँ वर्ण the nineteenth letter of the English alphabet.
1. Any object shaped like S.
2. Roman numeral for 70 or 70,000.

Sabbath/सैबथ *(noun)* – प्रार्थना, विश्राम, प्रार्थना दिवस a day of religious observance and abstinence from work, kept by Jews from Friday evening to Saturday evening, and by most Christians on Sunday. *I will visit my grandmother on Sabbath.*

Sable/सेबल *(noun)* – रोएँदार खाल a marten with a short tail and dark brown fur, native to Japan and Siberia. *I believe I saw a sable take a flight at dawn.*

Sabotage/सैबॅटाज् *(verb)* – तोड़-फोड़, क्षतिग्रस्त करना deliberately destroy. or obstruct, especially for political or military advantage. *The athlete who had sabotaged the practice session was suspended.*

Sabre/सेबर *(noun)* – तेग, तलवार a heavy cavalry sword with a curved blade and a single cutting edge. historical   a cavalry soldier and horse. *Even though the sabre was old, it was still sharp.*

Saccharin/सैकरिन *(noun)* – अति मीठी टिकिया a sweet-testing synthetic compound used as a substitute for sugar. *She added saccharin to her porridge.*

Sachet/साशे *(noun)* – पुड़िया, लिफाफा [chiefly British] a small sealed bag or packet containing a small quantity of something. *Companies use sachets to promote their consumer products.*

Sack/सैक *(noun)* – बोरा, बोरी a large bag made of a material such as hessian or thick paper, used for storing and carrying goods. *The social workers gathered the garbage in sacks.*

Sacrament/सैक्रमेंट *(noun)* – शुद्धीकरण संस्कार (ईसाई धर्म में) a religious ceremony or ritual regarded as imparting diving grace, such as baptism, the Eucharist, and penance and the anointing of the sick. *During the sacrament, everyone's face was lit with joy.*

Sacred/सैक्रेड *(adjective)* – पवित्र, पावन connected with a deity and so deserving veneration; holy. embodying the doctrines of a religion. sacrosanct. *All sacred objects were collected from the antique dealer and installed in the temple.*

Sacrifice/सेक्रिफाइस *(noun)* – उत्सर्ग, त्याग, बलिदान the practice or an act of killing an animal or person or surrendering a possession as an officering to a deity. an animal, person, or object offered in this way. *She offered all her jewellery as a sacrifice for her husband's health.*

Sacrilege/सैक्रिलेज् *(noun)* – अपवित्र करना, अपमान violation or misuse of something regarded as sacred or as having great value. *He was punished severely for the sacrilege he had committed.*

Sad/सैड *(adjective)* – उदास feeling sorrow; unhappy. causing or characterized by sorrow or regret. *She felt very sad when her cousin had to go back home after vacations.*

Sadden/सैडेन *(verb)* – उदास कर देना cause to feel sad. *The news of the delay in his parents arrival saddened him.*

Sadness/सैडनेस *(noun)* – उदासी the feeling of sorrow. *However hard she tried, she couldn't explain the sadness in her heart.*

Saddle/सैड्ल *(noun)* – जीन a seat with a raised ridge at the front and back, fastened on the back of a horse for riding. *The saddle was made of pure leather.*

Safari/सफारी *(noun)* – वन्य पशु दर्शन या आखेट के लिए सैर an expedition to observe or hunt animals in their natural habitat, especially in east Africa. *The science students were very excited about going on a safari.*

Safe/सेफ *(adjective)* – सुरक्षित, निरापद, तिजोरी protected from or not exposed to danger or risk; not likely to be harmed or lsot. not causing or leading to harm or injury. affording security or protection. *He believed that he was at a safe place.*

Safeguard/सेफगार्ड *(noun)* – बचाव, सुरक्षा a measure taken to protect or prevent something. *Construction of the new fence around the house prove to be an effective safeguard.*

Safe-keeping/सेफकीपिंग *(noun)* – देख-भाल, संरक्षण preservation in a safe place. *My father left his car with his brother for safe-keeping.*

Safety/सेफ्टि *(noun)* – सुरक्षा the condition of being safe. denoting something designed to prevent injury or damage: a safety barrier. *They stayed indoors for safety.*

Safety net – *(noun)* a net placed to catch an acrobat in case of a fall. *It was fortunate that the trapeze artist fell on the safety net.*

Saffron/सैफ्रन् *(noun)* – केसर, जाफरानी an orange-yellow spice used for flavouring and colouring food, made from the dried stigmas of a crocus. *The flavour of the saffron overwhelmed the other flavours of the dish.*

Sag/सैग *(verb)* – धँसना sink, subside, or bulge downwards gradually under weight or pressure or through lack of strength. hang down loosely or unevenly. *The roof of the house sagged dangerously.*

Saga /सागा *(noun)* – बहुत लम्बी कहानी a long story of heroic achievement, especially a medieval prose narrative in old Norse or old Icelandic. *I was touched by the sheer courage of the hero of the medical saga.*

Sage/सेज *(noun)* – एक प्रकार की सुगंधित वनस्पति an aromatic plant with grayish-green leaves used as a culinary herb, native to southern Europe and the Mediterranean. used in names of similar aromatic plants, e.g. wood sage. *I love the fragrance of sage.*

Sagittarius/सैगिटेरियस *(noun)* – धनुर्धारी, धनु राशि the Archer, the ninth sign of the zodiac. *The students tried but weren't able to locate Sagittarius.*

Sail/सेल *(noun)* – पाल, पाल के सहारे, समुद्री यात्रा a piece of material extended on a mast to catch the wind and propel a boat or ship. a wind-catching apparatus attached to the arm of a windmill. the broad fin on the back of a sailfish or of some prehistoric reptiles. a structure by which an animal is propelled across the surface of water by the wind, e.g. the float of a Portuguese man-of-war. *The boat could be identified easily by its bright sails.*

Sailor/सेलर *(noun)* – नाविक a person who works as a member of the crew of a commercial or naval ship or boat, especially one who is below the rank of officer. a person who sails as a sport or recreation. a person who rarely becomes sick at sea in rough weather. *The actress was smitten by the handsome sailor.*

Saint/सेंट *(noun)* – सन्त, धर्मात्मा a person who is acknowledged as holy or virtuous and regarded in Christian faith as being in heaven after death. a person of exalted virture who is canonized by the church after death and who may be the object of veneration and prayers for intercession. [informal] a very virtuous person. *There is no doubt that he was a saint.*

Sake/सेक *(noun)* – चावल की बनी हुई जापानी मदिरा a Japanese alcoholic drink made from fermented rice. *The boss shamed his company by getting drunk on Sake.*

Salad/सैलड् *(noun)* – खीरा, प्याज आदि का मिश्रित खाद्य a dish consisting of a mixture of raw vegetables or other cold ingredients, typically served with a dressing. *Her diet consisted mostly of salads.*

Salary/सैलरि *(noun)* – वेतन a fixed regular payment made usually on a monthly basis by an employer to an employee, especially a professional or white-collar worker. *The employees were overjoyed to receive bonus with their salary.*

S

Sale/सेल *(noun)* – बिक्री the exchange of a commodity for money; the process of selling something. a quantity or amount sold. *The family is very happy with the sale of the flat.*

Saleable/सेलेब्ल *(adjective)* – विक्री हेतु, बिकाऊ fit or able to be sold. *The mirror was very old but saleable.*

Salesman/सेल्समैन *(noun)* – पुरुष बिक्रेता a person whose job involves selling or promoting commercial products. *The door-to-door salesman managed do good business.*

Salesmanship/सेल्समैनशीप *(noun)* – बिक्रय कला the technique of selling a product. *The experienced businessman delivered a valuable lecture on salesmanship.*

Saleswoman/सेल्सवुमन *(noun)* – बिक्री करने वाली स्त्री a woman whose job involves selling or promoting commercial products. *The saleswoman made a very strong sales pitch to sell her product.*

Salient/सेलिएन्ट *(adjective)* – प्रमुख most noticeable or important. *Her shapely nose was the salient feature of her face.*

Saline/सेलाइन *(adjective)* – रासायनिक नमक वाला, नमकीन containing or impregnated with salt. *The saline solution tasted horrible.*

Saliva/सलाइवा *(noun)* – लार a watery liquid secreted into the mouth by glands, providing lubrication for chewing and swallowing, and aiding digestion. *He swallowed his own saliva because he was thirsty.*

Sallow/सैलो *(adjective)* – पीला तथा अस्वस्थ of a yellowish or pale brown colour. *The student's sallow skin was a reminder of her long illness.*

Salmon/सैमन *(noun)* – एक मछली, रोहू सी मछली a large edible fish that matures in the sea and migrates to freshwater streams to spawn. any of various unrelated marine fish resembling this. the flesh of such a fish as food. *I enjoyed watching the salmon jump.*

Saloon/सैलून *(noun)* – कमरा, बैठका a public room or building used for a specified purpose. *They entered the saloon expecting splendour.*

Salt/साल्ट *(noun)* – नमक, लवण sodium chloride, a white crystalline substance which gives seawater its characteristic taste and is used for seasoning or preserving food. poetic something which adds freshness or piquancy. *I added salt to my bland salad.*

Salty/साल्टी *(adjective)* – नमकीन tasting of, containing, or preserved with salt. *The fish was salty.*

Salubrious/सल्यूब्रिअस *(adjective)* – स्वास्थवर्धक health-giving; healthy. *My mother's salubrious potion has always worked for me.*

Salutary/सैल्यूटरी *(adjective)* – हितकर, अच्छा प्रभाव डालने वाला beneficial in providing an opportunity for learning from experience. *The salutary interview will prove to be very helpful for the new gradates.*

Salute/सैलूट *(noun)* – अभिवादन, सलाम a gesture of respect and recognition. *The children offered salutes to everyone who passed them that day.*

Salvage/सैल्वेज् *(verb)* – नष्ट हुए से आंशिक बचाव rescue from loss at sea. *The rescue team salvaged the precious jewel just before the ship sank.*

Salvation/सैल्वेशन् *(noun)* – मुक्ति, मोक्ष theology deliverance from sin and its consequences, believed by Christians to be brought about by faith in Christ. *My grandfather prays for salvation every day.*

Same/सेम *(adj)* – एक तरह का, वही, वैसा ही, उसी तरह का identical; uncharged. *The twins had the same taste in food.*

Sample/सैम्पल *(noun)* – नमूना a small part or quantity intended to show what the whole is like. *The artist showcased a sample of his work.*

Sanatorium/सैनटोरिअम *(noun)* – स्वास्थ्य केन्द्र, पागलखाना an establishment for the treatment of people who are convalescing or have a chronic illness. *The family sent the woman to a sanatorium to recover.*

Sanctify/सैंक्टिफाइ *(verb)* – पवित्र करना consecrate. *The priests sanctified the piece of land.*

Sanctimonious/सैंक्टिमोनिअस *(adjective)* – पाखण्डी derogatory making a show of being morally superior. *Her sanctimonious attitude is the reason why no one wants to talk to her.*

S

Sanction/सैंक्शन *(noun)* – अनुमति, अनुज्ञप्ति, दण्ड a threatened penalty for disobeying a law or rule. measures taken by a state to coerce another to conform to an international agreement or norms of conduct. ethics a consideration operating to enforce obedience to any rule of conduct. *The community imposed sanctions against the family for disobeying the law.*

Sanctity/सैंक्टिटी *(noun)* – पवित्रता holiness; saintliness. *No one can question his sanctity.*

Sanctuary/सैंक्ट्युअरि *(noun)* – शरणस्थान, अभयारण्य a place of refuge or safety. immunity form arrest. *Even though the criminal was in the sanctuary, he never felt secure.*

Sand/सैंड *(noun)* – बालू, रेत loose granular substance, typically pale yellowish brown, resulting from the erosion of siliceous and other rocks and forming a major constituent of beaches, river beds, the seabed, and deserts. an expanse of sand. technical sediment whose particles are larger than silt. *The sand sparkled in the sun.*

Sandpaper/सैंडपेपर *(noun)* – सरेस paper with sand or another abrasive stuck to it, used for smoothing wooden or other surfaces. *It was good that I had the sandpaper handy.*

Sandstone/सैंडस्टोन *(noun)* – बलुआ पत्थर sedimentary rock consisting of sand or quartz grains cemented together, typically red, yellow, or brown in colour. *The spectacular formations of sandstone mesmerized the onlookers.*

Sandy/सैंडि *(adjective)* – रेतीला, बालू से भरा covered in or consisting of sand. *The sandy beach was abandoned during the day.*

Sandal/सैंडल *(noun)* – चप्पल a light shoe with an openwork upper or straps attaching the sole to the foot. *I prefer sandals over the other types of footwear.*

Sandwich/सैंडविच *(noun)* – ब्रेड के दो टुकड़े जिनके बीच में खाद्य वस्तु हो two slices of bread with food betwen then. *One sandwich is enough for me.*

Sane/सेन *(adjective)* – विवेकपूर्ण, स्वस्थचित्त of sound mind; not mad. *The lawyer proved in the court that the accused was a sane person.*

Sanguine/सैंग्विन *(adjective)* – विश्वासयुक्त, आशावान cheerfully optimistic. *The naughty boy remained sanguine even when he was on his way to the principal's office.*

Sanitary/सैनिटरी *(adjective)* – स्वच्छ, स्वस्थकर of or relating to conditions affecting hygiene and health. *The sanitary conditions of the market were horrible.*

Sanitation/सैनिटेशन *(noun)* – सफाई-व्यवस्था conditions relating to public health. *At last, the department woke up to the sanitation.*

Sanity/सैनिटी *(noun)* – उत्तेजना रहित, मानसिक सन्तुलन the condition of being sane. reasonable and rational behaviour. *I was thankful of my sanity through the tough times.*

Sap/सैप *(noun)* – रस, रस निचोड़ना, दुर्बल करना the fluid, chiefly water with dissolved sugars and mineral salts, circulating in the vascular system of a plant. *The sap of the tree was sweet.*

Sapling/सैपलिंग *(noun)* – पौधा, कलम a young, slender tree. *The sapling looked healthy.*

Sapphire/सैफायर *(noun)* – नीलमणि a transparent precious stone, typically blue, which is a form of corundum. *The large sapphire on her engagement finger confused everyone.*

Sarcasm/सरकाज्म *(noun)* – कटाक्ष the use of irony to mock or convey contempt. *His sarcasm irritated me during our fight.*

Sardine/सार्डिन *(noun)* – छोटी मछली a young pilchard or other young or small herring-like fish. *The preserved sardines tasted nice.*

Sash/सैश *(noun)* – कमरबन्द a long strip or loop of cloth worn over one shoulder or round the waist. *She wore her sash with pride.*

Satan/सेटन *(noun)* – शैतान the devil; Lucifer. *The family was accused of worshipping Satan.*

Satanic/सेटैनिक *(adjective)* – शैतान सा, दुष्टतापूर्ण of or characteristic of Satan. *His satanic ideas were rejected by his friends.*

Satchel/सैचल *(noun)* – बस्ता a shoulder bag with a long strap, used especially for school books. *He picked his satchel reluctantly and started walking towards the school.*

Satellite/सैटलाइट *(noun)* – उपग्रह an artificial body placed in orbit round the earth or

S

another planet to collect information or for technology. satellite television. *The satellite was visible to naked eyes on clear nights.*

Satiate/सैटिएट *(verb)* – तृप्त करना, अघा जाना another term for sate. *The generous helping satiated the poor man's hunger.* *(adjective)* [archaic] fully satisfied. *The girl's satiated curiosity was apparent on her face.*

Satin/सैटिन *(noun)* – साटन a smooth, glossy fabric, usually of silk, produced by a weave in which the threads of the warp are caught and looped by the weft only at certain intervals. *She planned to wear satin for the awards ceremony.*

Satire/सैटायर *(noun)* – व्यंग्य, व्यंग्य रचना the use of humour, irony, exaggeration, or ridicule to expose and criticize people's stupidity or vices. *The satire managed to move many people.*

Satisfaction/सैटिस्फैक्शन *(noun)* – सन्तोष the state of being satisfied. *Satisfaction made his life peaceful.*

Satisfactory/सैटिस्फैक्टरी *(adj)* – सन्तोषजनक fulfilling expectations or needs; acceptable. *His work was satisfactory.*

Satisfy/सैटिस्फाई *(verb)* – सन्तुष्ट करना meet the expectations, needs, or desires of. fulfil a desire or need. *The quality of the student's work satisfied the teachers.*

Saturate/सैच्युरेट *(verb)* – संतृप्त होना, संतृप्त करना soak thoroughly with water or other liquid. *The sponge was saturated and therefore left a trail of water when used for wiping.*

Saturday/सैटरडे *(noun)* – शनिवार the day of the week before Sunday and following Friday. *I promise I will complete the work by this Saturday.*

Saturn/सैटर्न *(noun)* – शनि a planet of the solar system, sixth in order from the sun and circled by broad flat rings. *Saturn has several rings of different colours.*

Satyr/सैटर *(noun)* – अर्द्धमानव देवता Greek one of a class of lustful, drunken woodland gods, represented as a man with a horse's ears and tail or in roman representations with a goat's ears, tail, legs, and horns. *The image of the Satyr frightened my son.*

Sauce/सॉस *(noun)* – चटनी thick liquid served with food to add moistness and flavour. *He ate pizza with sauce.*

Saucepan/सॉसपैन *(noun)* – डेकची a deep cooking pan, typically round, made of metal, and with one long handle and a lid. *My saucepan broke when it fell from the stove.*

Saucer/सॉसर *(noun)* – तश्तरी a shallow dish, typically with a central circular indentation, on which a cup is placed. *The saucer looked more beautiful than the cup.*

Sauna/सौना *(noun)* – भाप-स्नान a small room used as a hot-air or steam bath for cleaning and refreshing the body. *I enjoyed being in the sauna.*

Saunter/सॉन्टर *(verb)* – चहलकदमी, चहलकदमी करना walk in a slow, relaxed manner. *The doctor leisurely sauntered through the wards*

Sausage/सॉसेज *(noun)* – लंगोचा a short cylindrical tube of minced pork, beef, etc. encased in a skin, typically sold raw and grilled or fried before eating. a cylindrical tube of minced meat seasoned and cooked or preserved, sold mainly to be eaten cold in slices. *The sausages were excellently cooked.*

Savage/सैवेज *(adjective)* – जंगली, असभ्य fierce, violent, and uncontrolled. cruel and vicious. *The savage eyes of the accused convinced the jury that he could have committed the crime.*

Save/सेव *(preposition & conjunction)* – बचाना, सुरक्षित रखना formal except; other than. *I'm saving up for a new bike.*

Saving/सेविंग *(noun)* – बचत an economy of or reduction in money, time, etc. *The saving proved to be timely.*

Saviour/सेव्य्र *(noun)* – रक्षक, मुक्तिदाता a person who saves someone or something from danger or harm. *My boss proved to be my saviour when I made a mistake in the presentation.*

Savour/सेवर *(verb & noun)* – सुगन्ध, रस-स्वाद US spelling of savour. *I savoured cardamom-flavoured cookies.*

Savoury/सेवरि *(adjective)* – नमकीन भोजन salty or spicy rather than sweet. *I prefer savoury dishes to sweet ones.*

S

Saw/सॉ *(noun)* – आरा past of see. *I saw several animals in the zoo.*

Saxophone/सैक्सॉफोन *(noun)* – एक बाजा a member of a family of metal wind instruments with a reed like a clarinet, used especially in jazz and dance music. *He played saxophone like an expert.*

Say/से *(verb)* – कहना, दुहराना utter words so as to convey information, an opinion, an instruction, etc. convey information or instructions. of a clock or watch indicate a time. be asserted or reported. recite a speech or formula. *Please do as I say.*

Saying/सेइंग *(noun)* – लोकोक्ति, कहावत a short, commonly known expression containing advice or wisdom; an adage or maxim. *The little girl is well versed with many common sayings.*

Scab/स्कैब *(noun)* – घाव की पपड़ी a dry, rough protective crust that forms over a cut or wound during healing. *The little boy kept scratching his scab.*

Scabbard/स्कैबर्ड *(noun)* – म्यान a sheath for the blade of a sword or dagger. a sheath for a gun or other weapon or tool. *The museum had only the scabbard, not the sword.*

Scabies/स्केबिज *(noun)* – खाज, खुजली a contagious skin disease marked by itching and small raised red spots, caused by the itch mite. *He had a bad case of scabies.*

Scaffold/स्कैफॉल्ड *(noun)* – फाँसी का फन्दा a raised wooden platform used formerly for public executions. *The crowd was relieved when the execution was called off and the scaffold dismantled.*

Scald/स्कॉल्ड *(noun & verb)* – जला अंग, झुलसाना injure with very hot liquid or steam. *The hot water scalded my hand.*

Scale/स्केल *(noun)* – माप, सरगम, स्वर क्रम, कवच, तराजू, तुला के पल्ले an instrument for weighting, originally a simple balance but now usually a device with an electronic or other internal weighing mechanism. either of the dishes on a simple balance. *The vegetable vendor's scale didn't give correct results.*

Scalp/स्कॉल्प *(noun)* – सिर की खाल the skin covering the tip and back of the head. *His hair had thinned so much that his scalp was visible through them.*

Scalpel/स्कैल्पेल् *(noun)* – नस्तर a knife with a small sharp blade, as used by a surgeon. *I was petrified by the sight of the surgeon holding the scalpel.*

Scam/स्कैम *(noun)* – घोटाला [informal] a dishonest scheme; a fraud. *The rich businessman lost a lot of respect after the scam came to light.*

Scamp/स्कैम्प *(noun)* – शरारती [informal] a mischievous person, especially a child. *The teacher scolded the scamp after he was caught trying to jump the school gate.*

Scamper/स्कैम्पर *(verb)* – चौकड़ी भरना run with quick light steps, especially through fear or excitement. *The children scampered away as soon as the gate of the haunted house opened.*

Scan/स्कैन *(verb)* – निरीक्षण, परीक्षण करना look at quickly in order to identify relevant features or information. *My brother scanned the store and saw the laptop he would like to buy.*

Scandal/स्कैन्डल *(noun)* – अफवाह an action or event regarded as morally or legally wrong and causing general public outrage. outrage, rumour, or gossip arising from this. *The coalgate scam was a scandal that people talked about for months.*

Scant/स्कैन्ट *(adjective)* – अल्प, अपर्याप्त barely sufficient or adequate. barely amounting to the amount specified: a scant two pounds. *The scant food barely satisfied anyone's hunger.*

Scanty/स्कैन्टी *(adjective)* – अल्प मात्रा में small or insufficient in quantity or amount. revealing; skimpy. *The beggar's scanty clothes hardly protected him from cold.*

Scapegoat/स्केपगोट *(noun)* – बलि का बकरा a person who is blamed for the wrongdoing or mistakes of others. *The employee was made a scapegoat when the scam came to light.*

Scar/स्कार *(noun)* – दाग, निशान a mark left on the skin or within body tissue after the healing of a wound or burn. a mark left at the point of separation of a leaf, frond, or other part from

S

a plant. *Even though the burn had healed, the scars would take some time to go.*

Scarce/स्केअर्स *(adjective)* – बिरला of a resource insufficient for the demand. *The scarce vegetables worried everyone.*

Scarcely/स्केअर्सलि *(adj)* – बहुत ही कम, मुश्किल से only just; almost not. *There was scarcely a car on sight.*

Scare/स्केअर *(verb)* – भयभीत करना, डराना cause great fear or nervousness in; frighten. drive or keep someone away by fear. become scared. *The old man scared the children with his stories of ghosts.*

Scarecrow/स्केअरक्रो *(noun)* – बिजूका, चिड़ियों को डराने का पुतला a figure made to look and dressed like a person to frighten birds away.*The scarecrow looked like a man from a distance.*

Scarf/स्कार्फ *(verb)* – बल्ले के छोरों को जोड़ना join the ends of by bevelling or notching them so that they fit together. make an incision in the blubber of a whale. *I scarfed the strip of leather.*

Scarlet/स्कारलेट *(noun)* – सिन्दूरी a brilliant red colour. *Her scarlet dress complemented her fair complexion.*

Scathing/स्केदिंग *(adjective)* – कठोर witheringly scornful; severely critical. *His mother-in-law often gave him scathing looks.*

Scatter/स्कैटर *(verb)* – तितर-बितर, बिखेरना throw in various random directions. separate or cause to separate and move off in different directions. occur or be found at various places rather than all together. physics deflect or diffuse. *The decorators scattered the rose petals on the carpet.*

Scavenge/स्केवेंज *(verb)* – कूड़े-कबाड़ में ढूँढ़ना search for and collect from discarded waste. search for as food. *The hungry dog scavenged for food in the garbage.*

Scenario/शेनारिओ *(noun)* – दृश्यावली पटकथा a written outline of a film, novel, or stage work giving details of the plot and individual scenes. a setting, in particular for a work of art of literature. *The scenario the writer had presented interested the publisher.*

Scenery/सीनरि *(noun)* – दृश्य, मंच सज्जा the natural features of a landscape considered in terms of their appearance, especially when picturesque. *The scenery took my breath away.*

Scenic/सेनिक/सीनिक *(adjective)* – सुरम्य of or relating to impressive or beautiful natural scenery: the scenic route. *I am so glad we took the long but scenic route to the desert.*

Scent/सेंट *(noun)* – सुगन्ध a distinctive smell, especially one that is pleasant. *The scent of the roses attracted bees to the garden.*

Sceptic/स्केप्टिक *(noun)* – संशयवादी a person inclined to question or doubt accepted opinions. a person who doubts the philosophy a philosopher who denies the possibility of knowledge, or even rational belief, in certain spheres. *I am a sceptic by nature.*

Sceptre/सेप्टर *(noun)* – राजचिह्न a staff carried by rules on ceremonial occasions as a symbol of sovereignty. *The king carried a beautifully ornated sceptre.*

Schedule/शेड्यूल् *(noun)* – कार्य-सूची, समय-सारणी a plan for carrying out a process or procedure, giving lists of intended events and time. a timetable. *The secretary couldn't find even one empty slot in the boss's schedule.*

Scheme/स्कीम *(noun)* – योजना a systematic plan or arrangement for attaining some particular object or putting a particular idea into effect. a particular ordered system or arrangement: a classical rhyme scheme. *We were interested in the scheme as it seemed to offer considerable profit.*

Schizophrenia/सिजोफ्रेनिआ *(noun)* – भ्रम से पीड़ित a long-term mental disorder of a type involving a breakdown in the relation disorder of a type involving a breakdown in the relation between thought, emotion, and behaviour, leading to faulty perception, inappropriate actions and feelings, and withdrawal from reality into fantasy and delusion. *Several members of his family were suffering from Schizophrenia.*

Scholar/स्कॉलर *(noun)* – विद्यार्थी, विद्वान a specialist in a particular branch of study, especially the humanities; a distinguished academic. chiefly a person who is highly

S

educated or has an aptitude for study. *The students were highly impressed by the knowledge of the history scholar.*

Scholarly/स्कॉलर्लि *(adjective)* – पाण्डित्यपूर्ण spending a lot of time studying and having a lot of knowledge about academic subject. *The boy's scholarly approach to everything has enabled him to learn a lot from life.*

Scholarship/स्कॉलर्शिप *(noun)* – छात्रवृत्ति, विद्वता academic achievement; learning of a high level. *The learned man has a series of scholarships to his credit.*

Scholastic/स्कॉलैस्टिक *(adjective)* – पण्डिताऊ, शैक्षिक of or concerning schools and education. *The organization's concerns were mostly scholastic.*

School/स्कूल *(noun)* – विद्यालय, पाठशाला, the place where children go to be educated. *Their children are still at school.*

Science/साइंस *(noun)* – विज्ञान the intellectual and practical activity encompassing the systematic study of the structure and behaviour of the physical and natural world through observation and experiment. *The young scientist revealed that she had become interested in science when she was very young.*

Scientist/साइंटिस्ट *(noun)* – वैज्ञानिक a person who is studying or has expert knowledge of one or more of the natural or physical sciences. *The scientist changed the world by his new discovery.*

Scientific/साइंटिफिक *(adjective)* – विज्ञान से सम्बन्धित involving science. *We need to be more scientific in agriculture production.*

Scissors/सिजर्स *(plural noun)* – कैंची an instrument used for cutting cloth and paper, consisting of two crowing blades pivoted in the middle and operated by thumb and fingers inserted in rings at each end. *The children's mother took the scissors away from them.*

Scoff/स्कॉफ *(verb)* – ताना मारना, खिल्ली उड़ाना speak about something in a scornfully derisive way. *His friends scoffed at his new hairstyle.*

Scold/स्कोल्ड *(verb)* – डाँटना, फटकारना angrily remonstrate with or rebuke. *My mother often scolds me for not studying.*

Scone/स्कोन *(noun)* – एक नरम खाद्य a small unsweetened or lightly sweetened cake made from flour, fat, and milk. *I had a scone with my tea.*

Scoop/स्कूप *(noun)* – कलछी, बेलचा, खबर a utensil resembling a spoon, having a short handle and deep bowl, used for extracting liquids or substances from a container. the bowl-shaped part of a digging machine or dredger. a long-handled spoon-like surgical instrument. *The ice-cream vendor used the scoop with perfection.*

Scooter/स्कूटर *(noun)* – दो चक्के की छोटी गाड़ी a light two-wheeled motorcycle. *He loved his new scooter.*

Scope/स्कोप *(noun)* – क्षेत्र, व्याप्ति, गुंजाइश the extent of the area or subject matter that something deals with or to which it is relevant; these complex matters are beyond the scope of this book. *This topic is beyond the scope of this discussion.*

Scorch/स्कॉर्च *(verb)* – किसी वस्तु को झुलसाना become burnt or cause to become burnt on the surface or edges. cause to become dried out and withered as a result of extreme heat. *The extreme heat scorched all the leaves of the tree.*

Score/स्कोर *(noun)* – प्राप्त अंक, कोड़ी, बीस की संख्या the number of points, goals, runs, etc. achieved in a game or by an individual. a mark or grade. *Everyone was eagerly watching the score.*

Scorn/स्कार्न् *(noun)* – घृणा, तिरस्कार, घृणा दिखाना contempt or disdain expressed openly. *No one could ignore the persistent scorn she expressed throughout the party.*

Scorpio/स्कॉर्पिओ *(noun)* – वृश्चिक राशि astrology the eighth sign of the zodiac which the sun enters about 23 October. *I have many good friends whose zodiac sign is Scorpio.*

Scorpion/स्कॉर्पिअन *(noun)* – बिच्छू an arachnid with lobster-like pincers and a poisonous sting at the end of its tail. used in names of similar arachnids and insects, e.g. false scorpion. *A poisonous scorpion was hiding in the bathroom.*

S

Scot-free/स्कॉटफ्री *(adj.)* – बिना दण्ड पाये without suffering any punishment or injury. *He went scot-free even though he had committed the crime.*

Scoundrel/स्काउन्ड्रल *(noun)* – दुष्ट, घृणित व्यक्ति a dishonest or unscrupulous person; a rogue. *The scoundrel ran away after cheating all of his neighbours.*

Scour/स्काउर *(verb)* – माँजना, रगड़कर चमकना clean or brighten by vigorous rubbing, typically with an abrasive or detergent. remove by rubbing in such a way. *I watched with amazement as the man scoured age-old dust off the antique tray.*

Scourge/स्कर्ज *(noun)* – कोड़ा historical a whip used as an instrument of punishment. *I can't imagine from where he found the old scourge.*

Scout/स्काउट *(noun)* – बालचर, भेदिया chiefly US a fast armoured vehicle used for military reconnaissance and liaison. *People were amazed to see the scouts on the streets.*

Scowl/स्काउल *(noun)* – त्यौरी, बल पड़ना an angry or bad-tempered expression. *The teacher's scowl made him think that he had said something wrong.*

Scrabble/स्क्रैबल *(verb)* – खुरचना, टटोलना scratch or grope around with one's fingers to find, collect, or hold on to something. *She scrabbled inside her purse for money.*

Scraggy/स्क्रैगि *(adjective)* – मरियल scrawny. *The little boy was scraggy as compared to the rest of his classmates.*

Scramble/स्क्रैम्बल *(verb)* – रेंगना, छीना-झपटी move or make one's way quickly and awkwardly, typically by using one's hands as well as one's feet. [informal] act in a hurried, disorderly, or undignified manner: firms scrambled to win public-sector contracts. *All of them scrambled out of the room as soon as the angry teacher looked at them.*

Scrap/स्क्रैप *(noun)* – कतरन, टुकड़ा, झगड़ा a small piece or amount of something, especially one that is left over after the greater part has been used. bits of uneaten food left after a meal. *The scraps were delivered to the merchant.*

Scrape/स्क्रेप *(verb)* – घिसकर चिकनाना, खरोचना drag or pull a hard or sharp implement across. use a sharp or hard implement to remove. *The cupboard was scraped across the room.*

Scratch/स्क्रैच *(verb)* – कुरेदना, खुरचना, नोचना score or mark with a sharp or pointed object make a long, narrow superficial wound in the skin of. rub with one's fingernails to relieve itching. rake the ground with the beak or claws in search of food. make a living of find resources with difficulty. *I scratched my skin with the hard wooden board.*

Scrawl/स्क्रॉल *(verb)* – जल्दी में लिखना write in a hurried, careless way. *The students scrawled the notes as the professor spoke.*

Scream/स्क्रीम् *(verb)* – चीखना make a long, loud, piercing cry or sound, especially expressing extreme emotion or pain. *My mother screamed when she saw the fat rat.*

Screech/स्क्रीच् *(noun)* – कर्कश, चीख a loud, harsh, piercing cry or sound. *The screech startled me out of my sleep.*

Screen/स्क्रीन् *(noun)* – परदा, ओट an upright partition used to divide a room, give shelter, or provide concealment. a windscreen of a motor vehicle. a frame with fine wire netting used to keep out flying insects. *The screen effectively divided the huge room into two.*

Screw/स्क्रू *(noun & verb)* – पेंच, पेंच से कसना a short, slender, sharp-pointed metal pin with a raised helical thread running around it and a slotted head, used to join things together by being rotated in under pressure. a cylinder with a helical ridge or thread running round the outside that can be turned to seal an opening, apply pressure, adjust position, etc. historical an instrument of torture acting in this way. *The screws held the dilapidated cupboard together.*

Scribble/स्क्रिब्ल *(verb)* – जल्दीबाजी में लिखा हुआ write or draw carelessly or hurriedly. *I like to scribble important information when I am talking on the phone. .*

Scribbe/स्क्राइब *(noun)* – मुंशी, लिपिक historical a person who copied out documents. [informal] a writer, especially a journalist. *The scribe maintained the records very diligently.*

S

Scrip/स्क्रिप *(noun)* – पावती a provisional certificate of money subscribed to a bank or company, entitling the holder to a formal electively. finance an issue of additional of this type collectively. finanace an issue of additional shares to shareholders in proportion to the shares already held. *The shareholders were pleasantly surprised to receive the scrip.*

Script/स्क्रिप्ट *(noun)* – लिपि, मुद्रण, पटकथा handwriting as distinct from print: written characters. writing using a particular alphabet: Russian script. *Hindi has a script different from English.*

Scriptures/स्क्रिप्च्वर्स *(noun)* – धर्मग्रन्थ the sacred writings Christianity contained in the Bible. the sacred writings of another religion. *My mother likes to read scriptures of all religions.*

Scroll/स्क्रोल् *(noun)* – लिखने या रंगसाजी के लिए लिपटे हुए कागज का मुट्ठा a roll of parchment or paper for writing or painting on. a *The scroll was so fragile that it looked as if it will crumble at the slightest touch.*

Scrub/स्क्रब *(noun)* – साफ करना, झाड़-झंखाड़ vegetation consisting mainly of brushwood or stunted forest growth. land covered with such vegetation. *The scrub was vast and deserted.*

Scruff/स्क्रफ *(noun)* – गर्दन का पिछला भाग the back of a person's or animal's neck. *The magician held the rabbit by its scruff.*

Scruple/स्क्रूप्ल *(noun)* – धर्मभीरुता a feeling of doubt or hesitation with regard to the morality or propriety of an action. *He has no scruples against stealing.*

Scrupulous/स्क्रूप्युलस *(adjective)* – अति सावधान या ब्योरों पर अधिक ध्यान देने वाला very careful or paying great attention to detail. *I need a very scrupulous person for this job.*

Scrutinize/स्क्रूटिनाइज् *(verb)* – जाँच करना examine or inspect closely and thoroughly. *You need to scrutinize all evidences thoroughly before the court case.*

Scrutiny/स्क्रूटिनि *(noun)* – जाँच critical observation or examination. *There was no cheating in the examination hall because of the scrutiny.*

Scuffle/स्कफ्ल *(noun)* – हाथापाई a short, confused fight or struggle at close quarters. *I came running out of my room when I heard the scuffle.*

Scull/स्कल *(noun)* – चप्पू, नौका-दौड़ each of a pair of small oars used by a single rower. an oar placed over the stern of a boat to propel it with a side to side motion a light, narrow boat propelled with a scull or a pair of sculls. a race between boats in which each participant uses a pair of oars. *(verb)* propel a boat with sculls. *The rower felt so weak that he wasn't even able to hold the sculls.*

Scullery/स्कलरि *(noun)* – वर्तन माँजने का स्थान a small kitchen or room at the back of a house used for washing dishes and other dirty household work. *The maid worked in the scullery after clearing the table.*

Sculptor/स्कल्प्टर *(noun)* – मूर्तिकार an artist who makes sculptures. *I couldn't believe I was meeting the famous sculptor in person.*

Sculpture/स्कल्प्चर् *(noun)* – मूर्तिकला the art of making three-dimensional representative or abstract forms, especially by carving stone or wood or by casting metal or plaster. a work of such a kind. *The sculpture was true to life.*

Scum/स्कम् *(noun)* – झाग, फेन a layer of dirt or froth on the surface of a liquid. *They cleared the scum off the surface of the lake.*

Scurrilous/स्करिलस् *(adjective)* – अभद्र, अपमान जनक making scandalous claims about someone with the intention of damaging their reputation. humorously insulting. *When I joined my job, my father warned me of scurrilous colleagues.*

Scurry/स्करि *(verb)* – छोटे-छोटे तेज कदमों से आगे बढ़ना move hurriedly with short quick steps. *The little man scurried to take cover as soon as the rain started.*

Scurvy/स्कर्वि *(noun)* – एक प्रकार का रक्त रोग a disease caused by a deficiency of vitamin C, characterized by swollen bleeding gums and the opening of previously healed wounds. *Many people are suffering from scurvy and they don't even know it.*

S

Scuttle/स्कटल *(noun)* – टोकरा, छेद करना, असफल करना, भागना a metal container with a sloping hinged lid and a handle, used to fetch and store coal for a domestic fire. *Mother noticed just in time that the scuttle was almost empty.*

Scythe/साइद *(noun & verb)* – हँसिया, हँसिया से काटना a tool used for cutting crops such as grass or corn, with a long curved blade at the end of a long pole attached to one or two short handles. *The old scythe was rusty and blunt.*

Sea/सी *(noun)* – समुद्र the expanse of water that covers most of the earth's surface and surrounds its land masses. a roughly definable area of this: the black sea. waves as opposed to calm sea. *The sunset at the sea was mesmerizing.*

Seal/सील *(noun)* – मोहर, मुहर बन्द करना, समुद्री पशु a fish-eating aquatic mammal with a streamlined body and feet developed as flippers. *The young seal was barely able to swim. (verb)* hunt for seals. *The family hunted for seals everyday.*

Seam/सीम *(noun)* – सिलाई, सीवन a line where two pieces of fabric are sewn together in a garment or other article. a line where the edges of two pieces of wood or other material touch each other. *I was about to leave for office when I noticed that my dress was torn at the seam.*

Search/सर्च *(verb)* – खोज try to find something by looking or otherwise seeking carefully and thoroughly. examine thoroughly in order to find something. *I searched through my bag to find my keys.*

Searchlight/सर्चलाइट *(noun)* – खोजी प्रकाश a powerful outdoor eclectic light with a concentrated beam that can be turned in the required direction. *The rescue services were using searchlights to look for the ship.*

Season/सीजन *(noun)* – ऋतु, मौसम each of the four divisions of the year marked by particular weather patterns and daylight hours. the time of year when a particular fruit, vegetable, etc. is plentiful and in good condition. *This is not the season for mango trees to produce fruit.*

Seasonal/सीजनल *(adjective)* – मौसमी relating to or characteristic of a particular season of the year. fluctuating according to the season. *Apple is a seasonal fruit.*

Seasoned/सीजन्ड *(adjective)* – अनुभवी having lot of experience in a particular field. *She has become a seasoned lawyer over time.*

Seat/सीट *(noun)* – आसन, सभा, बैठना a thing made or used for sitting on, such as a chair or stool. the roughly horizontal part of a chair. a sitting place for a passenger in a vehicle or for a member of an audience. *It was uncomfortable sitting there because the seats were hard.*

Secede/सीसिड *(verb)* – अलग होना withdraw formally from membership of a federal union or a political or religious organization. *After giving it a good thought, I seceded my membership in the union.*

Seclude/सिक्लूड *(verb)* – स्वतन्त्र हो जाना keep away from other people. *The family secluded themselves from everyone.*

Secluded/सिक्लूडेड *(adjective)* – एकान्त, निर्जन not seen or visited by many people; sheltered and private. *Not many people enter the secluded part of the forest.*

Second/सेकंड *(noun)* – पल, दूसरा, समर्थन a sixtieth of a minute of time, which as the SI unit of time is defined in terms of the natural periodicity of the radiation of a casesium-133 atom. [informal] a very short time. *He was up and ready to go in seconds.*

Secondary/सेकंडरि *(adjective)* – माध्यमिक coming after, less important than, or resulting from something primary. *Studies were secondary to the tennis player.*

Secrecy/सीक्रेसि *(noun)* – छिपाव, गोपनीयता the fact of making sore nothing gets leaked about something. *I can't understand the secrecy around this issue*

Secret/सीक्रेट *(adjective)* – गोपनीय, रहस्यमय, भेद, गूढ़ not known or seen or not meant to be known or seen by others. fond of having or keeping secrets; secretive. *I formed a secret society with my friends when I was young.*

Secretive/सिक्रीटिव् *(adjective)* – गोपनीय inclined to conceal feelings and intentions or not to disclose information. *The actress was very secretive about her real identity.*

Sect/सेक्ट *(noun)* – पंथ, सम्प्रदाय, मत a religious group or faction regarded as heretical or as deviating from orthodox tradition. often a group that has separated from an established church; a nonconformist church. *A sect has often broken away from a larger group.*

Sectarian/सेक्टेरिअन् *(adjective)* – साम्प्रदायिक denoting, concerning, or deriving from a sect or sects. carried out on the grounds of membership of a sect, denomination, or other group: sectarian killings. *They passed a sectarian judgment for the man's sins.*

Section/सेक्शन *(noun)* – अंश, टुकड़ा, हिस्सा, खण्ड, परिच्छेद any of the more or less distinct parts into which something is or may be divided or from which it is made up. [north American] a measure of land, equal to one square mile, [chiefly north American] a particular district of a town. a building plot. *You need to fill all sections of the form*

Sector/सेक्टर *(noun)* – क्षेत्र अंचल, युद्धस्थल an area or portion that is distinct from others. a distinct part of an economy, society, or sphere of activity. a subdivision of an area for military operations. *Our sector mostly has apartments.*

Secular/सेक्युलर *(adjective)* – धर्मनिरपेक्ष not religious, sacred, or spiritual. *India is a secular country.*

Secure/सिक्योर *(adjective)* – सुरक्षित, निश्चिंत fixed or fastened so as not to give way. become loose, or be lost. *The door was secured properly.*

Security/सिक्यूरिटि *(noun)* – सुरक्षा, प्रतिभूति, जमानत the state of being or feeling secure. *Security made him very generous.*

Sedate/सिडेट *(adjective)* – सौम्य, नींद हेतु दवा calm and unhurried. *The sedate Congressman had a huge fan following.*

Sedative/सिडेटिव *(noun)* – नींद या आराम की औषधि promoting calm or inducing sleep. *The sedative properties of the medicine kept me from taking it during office hours.*

Sediment/सेडिमेंट *(noun)* – बहाकर लाये गये टुकड़े matter that settles to the bottom of a liquid. *The sediment was a proof of the dirtiness of water.*

Sedimentary/सेडिमेंटरि *(adjective)* – टुकड़े-टुकड़े में जमा of or relating to sediment. geology that has formed from sediment deposited by water or wind. *The sedimentary rock formations were breathtaking.*

Sedition/सिडिशन *(noun)* – राजद्रोह conduct or speech inciting rebellion against the authority of a state or monarch. *Even though he was punished for sedition, his speech inspired many.*

Seduce/सिड्यूस *(verb)* – प्रलोभन देना persuade to do something inadvisable. *Special offers seduce customers into spending their money.*

Seduction/सिडक्शन *(noun)* – प्रलोभन देकर राजी करना the act of persuading someone to have sex with you. *Several people fell prey to her seduction.*

Seductive/सिडक्टिव *(adjective)* – प्रलोभनपूर्ण tempting and attractive. *People often tell her that she has a very seductive voice.*

Seductiveness/सिडक्टिवनेस *(noun)* – प्रलोभन देने की कला/क्रिया attractiveness shown to someone in a way that makes you want to do or have something. *People often compliment her on the seductiveness of her eyes.*

See/सी *(noun & verb)* – देखना the place in which a cathedral church stands, identified as the seat of authority of a bishop or archbishop. *The see was surrounded by dense forest.*

Seed/सीड *(noun)* – बीज, कारण, उद्गम a flowering plant's unit of reproduction, capable of developing into another such plant. a quantity of these. *The seed sprouted almost immediately.*

Seedy/सीडी *(adjective)* – बीज से भरा हुआ, मैला, अस्वस्थ sordid or squalid. *The place looked very seedy.*

Seek/सीक *(verb)* – प्राप्त करने का प्रयत्न, खोजना attempt to find, search for and find someone or something. *I seek a good friend in you.*

Seem/सीम *(verb)* – प्रतीत होना give the impression of being. *He made it seem so simple.*

S

Seemly/सीमली *(adjective)* – उपयुक्त conforming to propriety or good taste. *Her dress was quite seemly.*

Seep/सीप *(verb)* – टपकना, रिसना flow or leak slowly through porous material or small holes. *Water seeped in through the concrete.*

Seer/सीअर *(noun)* – मनीषी, भविष्यद्रष्टा a person of supposed supernatural insight who sees visions of the future. *The seer foretold that the businessman would do very well.*

See-saw/सी-सा *(noun)* – एक झूला, ढेंकी a long plank balanced on a fixed support, on each end of which children sit and move up and down by pushing the ground alternately with their feet. *My nephew was desperate to go to the see-saw but there was no other child to play with him.*

Seethe/सीद् *(verb)* – खौलकर बुदबुदाना boil or be turbulent as if boiling. [archaic] cook by boiling. *I seethed the vegetables so that they could be cooked in a short time.*

Segment/सेग्मेंट *(noun)* – टुकड़ा, हिस्सा, खण्ड, फाँक each of the parts into which something is or may be divided. *That segment of the crowd is much more disciplined than this segment.*

Segregate/सेग्रिगेट *(verb)* – छाँटना, पृथक् करना set apart from or relating to the division of speech into segments. *The teacher segregated the children into two groups based on their heights.*

Segregation/सेग्रिगेशन *(noun)* – अलग-अलग करना the act of setting something apart from others. *The teacher does not believe in any kind of segregation.*

Seismic/साइज्मिक *(adjective)* – भूकम्प से सम्बन्धित of or relating to earthquakes or other vibrations of the earth and its crust. relating to or denoting geological surveying methods involving vibrations produced artificially by explosions. *The geologists predicted heavy seismic activities during the day.*

Seize/सीज *(verb)* – छीनना, कब्जा में लेना take hold of suddenly and forcibly. take forcible possession of by warrant or legal right. *The thugs seized my uncle's property.*

Seizure/सीजर *(noun)* – जब्ती, मिरगी का दौरा the action of seizing. *They called the police after the unauthorized seizure.*

Seldom/सेल्डम *(adverb)* – कभी-कभार, यदा-कदा not often. *I seldom visit the city park.* *(adjective)* dated infrequent. *The father's seldom visits left the child confused.*

Select/सिलेक्ट *(verb)* – चुनना, पसन्द करना carefully chose as being the best or most suitable. *The teacher selected the tallest students for the dance.*

Selection/सिलेक्शन *(noun)* – चुनाव, चयन, चुने हुए the action of fact of selecting. a number of selected things. a range of things from which a choice may be made. a horse or horses tipped as worth bets in a race or meeting. *Even though the selection appeared random, it had an unseen logic to it.*

Selective/सिलेक्टिव *(adjective)* – चयनित, पसंदीदा relating to or involving selection. tending to choose carefully. *The film star claims that he is very selective about his roles.*

Self/सेल्फ *(noun)* – आत्म, स्वत्व, स्वार्थ, स्वयं a person's essential being that distinguishes them from others, especially considered as the object of introspection or reflexive action. a person's particular nature or personality. one's own interests or pleasure. *He doesn't understand the concept of self.*

Self-centred/सेल्फसेंटर्ड *(adjective)* – आराम-केन्द्रित preoccupied with oneself and one's affairs. *The man was very self-centred.*

Self-conscious/सेल्फकॉन्सस् *(adj)* – आत्मचेतन nervous or awkward because unduly aware of oneself or one's actions. *The self-conscious student forgot his lines during the play.*

Self-control/सेल्फकन्ट्रोल *(noun)* – आत्म नियन्त्रण the ability to control one's emotions or behaviour, especially in difficult situation. *Everyone commended his self-control in the face of loss.*

Self-defence/सेल्फडिफेंस *(noun)* – आत्मरक्षा the defence of one's person or interests, especially through the use of physical force, which is permitted in certain cases as an answer to a charge of violent crime. *The crime was committed in self-defence.*

S

Selfish/सेल्फिश *(adjective)* – स्वार्थी concerned chiefly with one's own personal profit or pleasure at the expense of consideration for others. *His actions appeared selfish to the others.*

Selfishly/सेल्फिश्लि *(adverb)* – स्वार्थवश [chiefly] concerned with one's own pleasure. *He selfishly ate all the food.*

Selfless/सेल्फलेस *(adjective)* – निःस्वार्थ concerned more with the needs and wished of others than with one's own._No one can question a mother's selfless love.*

Selfmade/सेल्फमेड *(adjective)* – आत्मनिर्भर having become successful or rich by one's own efforts. *My father is a self-made man.*

Self-respect/सेल्फरिस्पेक्ट *(noun)* – आत्मसम्मान, आत्म गौरव pride and confidence in oneself. *The matter became a question of self-respect for her.*

Self-sufficient/सेल्फसफिश्यन्ट *(adj)* – स्वयं में पूर्ण able to satisfy one's basic needs without outside help, especially with regard to the production of food. *The island dwellers were self-sufficient in their agricultural needs.*

Self-willed/सेल्फविल्ड *(adjective)* – जिद्दी obstinately pursuing one's own wishes. *At times, he regretted his self-willed attitude.*

Sell/सेल *(verb)* – बेचना hand over in exchange for money. be subject to a specified demeand on the market: the book didn't sell well. sell all of one's stock of something. have sex in exchange for money. *I sold my painting for good money.*

Seller/सेलर *(noun)* – विक्रेता a person who sells. *The vegetable seller lived a honest life.*

Selvage/सेल्वेज *(noun)* – सिला, किनारी an edge produced on woven fabric during manufacture that prevents it from unravelling. *The selvage of the fabric was very ornate.*

Semantic/सिमैंटिक *(adjective)* – शब्द शास्त्र relating to meaning in language or logic. *I have never understood the semantic behind the usage of some words.*

Semblance/सेम्ब्लन्स *(noun)* – सादृश्य the outward appearance or apparent form of something. *The friendship they shared had the semblance of love.*

Semi/सेमि *(pref.)* – अर्द्ध, आंशिक [British] a semi-detached house. *The boy and his father lived in a semi-decorated house.*

Semicolon/सेमिकोलन *(noun)* – अर्द्ध विराम का चिह्न a punctuation mark (;) indicating a more pronounced pause than that indicated by a comma. *I asked the teacher to explain me the usage of a semi-colon.*

Semifinal/सेमिफाइनल *(noun)* – अन्त के पूर्व a match or round immediately preceding the final. *The semifinal match was very exciting.*

Seminar/सेमिनार *(noun)* – विचार गोष्ठी, गोष्ठी a conference or other meeting for discussion or training. *Some very relevant topics were covered in the seminar.*

Senate/सिनेट *(noun)* – सदन, शासीनिकाय the smaller upper assembly in the US, US states, France, and other countries. the governing body of a university or college. *The senate is meeting tonight to discuss the bilateral ties between the two countries.*

Send/सेंड *(verb)* – भेजना cause to go or be taken or delivered to a particular destination. arrange for someone to attend. *I requested my father to send me some books.*

Senior/सीनिअर *(adjective)* – वरिष्ठ, ज्येष्ठ of a more advanced age. [British] of, for, or denoting schoolchildren above a certain age, typically eleven. US of the final year at a university or high school. denoting the elder of two with the same name in a family. *Show respect to senior people.*

Seniority/सीनिऑरिटि *(noun)* – वरीयता, वरिष्ठता the state of being higher or older in rank or status than someone else. *He never took advantage of his seniority.*

Sensation/सेंसेशन *(noun)* – अनुभूति उत्पादक सनसनी a physical feeling or perception resulting from something that happens to or comes into contact with the body. the capacity to have such feeling or perceptions. *I had a sensation of pain in my arm.*

Sense/सेंस *(noun)* – ज्ञान, ज्ञानेन्द्रिय, बोध a faculty by which the body perceives an external

S

stimulus; one of the faculties of sight, smell, hearing, taste, and touch. one's sanity. *Dogs have a powerful sense of smell.*

Senseless/सेंसलेस *(adjective)* – बेहोश, अचेत, मूर्खतापूर्ण unconscious or incapable of sensation. *The drunkard lay senseless on the footpath.*

Sensibility/सेंसिबिलिटि *(noun)* – भावुकता, संवेदना, संवेदनशीलता the ability to appreciate and respond to complex emotional or aesthetic influences; sensitivity. a person's tendency to be offended or shocked. *The artist had the sensibility to judge a good work of art.*

Sensible/सेंसिब्ल *(adj)* – विवेकी, विवेकपूर्ण wise and prudent; having or showing common sense. practical and functional rather than decorative. *My father is a very sensible man.*

Sensitive/सेंसिटिव *(adjective)* – भावुक quick to detect, respond to, or be affected by slight changes, signals, or influences. photographic materials responding rapidly to the action of light. *The blind man is very sensitive to the changes in the intensity of light.*

Sensual/सेंसुअल *(adjective)* – दैहिक आनन्द, भोग-विलास of or relating to the physical senses, especially as a source of pleasure. *The artist was very proud of his sensual paintings.*

Sensuous/सेंसुअस *(adjective)* – इन्द्रियजनित, इन्द्रिय सम्बन्धी relating to or affecting the senses rather than the intellect. *The movie was very sensuous.*

Sentence/सेन्टेंस *(noun)* – वाक्य a set of words that is complete in itself conveying a statement, question, exclamation, or command and typically containing a subject and predicate. logic a series of signs or symbols expressing a proposition in an artificial or logical language. *The child has started talking in complete sentences.*

Sentiment/सेंटिमेंट *(noun)* – भावुकता, संवेदना a view, opinion, or feeling. general feeling or opinion. *I express my sentiments very openly.*

Sentimental/सेंटिमेंटल *(adjective)* – भावुक, संवेदनशील deriving from feelings of tenderness, sadness, or nostalgia. having or arousing such feelings in an exaggerated and

self-indulgent way. *The sentimental actress started crying for real during the scene.*

Sentinel/सेंटिनल *(noun)* – पहरेदार a soldier or guard whose job is to stand and keep watch. *The sentinel came running to announce the approach of the enemy.*

Sentry/सेन्ट्रि *(noun)* – पहरेदार, संतरी a soldier stationed to keep guard or to control access to a place. *The sentry was doing his job well.*

Separable/सेपरेब्ल *(adjective)* – अलग करने योग्य able to be separated or treated separately. *The hair-dryer has separable attachments.*

Separate/सेपरेट *(adjective)* – अलग या पृथक् करना forming or viewed as a unit apart or by itself; not joined or united with others. different; distinct. *Both friends run separate businesses.*

Separation/सेपरेशन *(noun)* – विभाजन, पृथक्करण, बँटवारा the action or state of separating or being separated. the state in which a husband and wife remain married but live apart: a trial separation. *Their separation was very traumatic for their children.*

September/सेप्टेम्बर *(noun)* – सितम्बर the ninth month of the year. *My niece was born in September.*

Septic/सेप्टिक *(adjective)* – विषाक्त infected with bacteria. *The septic wound needed to be treated immediately.*

Sepulchre/सेपल्कर *(noun)* – समाधि a small room, cut in store in which a dead person is buried. *The children were scared to go near the Sepulchre.*

Sequel/सीक्वेल *(noun)* – परिणाम, उत्तरकथा a published, broadcast, or recorded work that continues the story or develops the theme of an earlier one. *I loved the movie so much that I was desperately waiting for the sequel.*

Sequence/सीक्वेन्स *(noun)* – क्रमबद्ध, संबद्ध, संबद्धता a particular order in which related events, movements, etc. follow each other. music a repetition of a phrase or melody at a higher or lower pitch. biochemistry the order in which amino-acid or nucleotide residues are arranged in a protein, DNA, etc. *The* *piano sequence in the musical left everyone in awe.*

Seraph/सेरफ *(noun)* – स्वर्गीय दूत an angelic being associated with light, ardour, and purity. *The seraphs floating around in her dream made a beautiful picture.*

Serene/सिरीन् *(adjective)*- शान्त, गम्भीर calm, peaceful, and untroubled; tranquil. *The serene look on the saint's face was worth noticing.noun* [archaic] clear sky or calm sea. *The serene inspired many poets.*

Serenely/सिरीन्लि *(adverb)* – शान्ति से calmly, peacefully. *My mother listened to my problem serenely before giving me advice.*

Serf/सर्फ *(noun)* – दास an agricultural labourer who was tied to working on a particular estate. *In earlier times serfs were made to work without wages.*

Sergeant/सर्जेंट *(noun)* – एक पद नाम a rank of noncommissioned officer in the army or air force, above corporal and below staff sergeant. *The sergeant ordered his platoon to gather in the grounds for a warm-up.*

Serial/सीरिअल *(adjective)* – क्रमबद्ध, क्रमवार, धारा, वाहिक consisting of, forming part of, or taking place in a series. *The class was asked to stand according to their serial numbers.*

Series/सीरीज *(noun)* – श्रृंखला, श्रृंखलाबद्ध, श्रेणीबद्ध, विद्युतधारा a number of similar or related things coming one after another. a set of books, periodicals, etc. published in a common format. a set of stamps, banknotes, or coins issued at a particular time. *The kidnapper was caught with the series of banknotes that had been marked out by the police.*

Serious/सीरिअस *(adjective)* – गम्भीर, विचारमग्न demanding or characterized by careful consideration or application. solemn or thoughtful. *Are you serious about starting your own business?.*

Seriously/सीरिअस्लि *(adverb)* – गम्भीरता से in a serious manner or to a serious extent. *We need to think seriously about the problem of beggars in our country.*

Sermon/सर्मन *(noun)* – उपदेश, प्रवचन a talk on a religious or moral subject, especially one given during a church service and based on a passage from the bible. *During the Sunday church service the sermon lasts for over an hour.*

Sermonise/सर्मनाइज *(verb)* – भाषण झाड़ना deliver an opinionated lecture to someone. *Nowadays children feel that every time their parents tell them something, they are sermonizing*

Serpent/सर्पेंट *(noun)* – साँप chiefly a large snake. a dragon or other mythical snake-like reptile. a biblical name for satan. a sly or treacherious person. *There is a serpent in the tree trunk.*

Serpentine/सर्पेंटाइन *(adjective)* – कुण्डलीनुमा मुड़ा हुआ of or like a serpent or snake. winding and twisting. complex, cunning, or treacherous. *Many people suffer from motion sickness while travelling to the hills due to the serpentine roads.*

Serrated/सेरेटेड *(adjective)* – दाँतेदार आरी जैसे दाँत वाला having or denoting a jagged edge; saw like. *The serrated blade of the knife was very sharp.*

Servant/सर्वेंट *(noun)* – नौकर, कर्मचारी a person employed to perform duties for others, especially in a house on domestic duties or as a personal attendant. a person employed in the service of a government. a devoted and helpful follower or supporter. *Guru Nanak looked upon himself as a servant of God.*

Serve/सर्व *(verb)* – सेवा करना, नौकरी करना, लेन-देन करना, तामील करना, आराम करना a person or thing that serves. [north American] a waiter or waitress. *To serve the poor is the service of God.*

Service/सर्विस *(noun)* – नौकरी, सेवा the action of process of serving. an act of assistance. a period of employment with a company or organization: he retired after 40 year's service. pose. employment as a servant. *He was in government service for 21 years.*

Serviette/सर्विएट *(noun)* – खाने के समय प्रयुक्त नैपकिन [British] a table napkin. *I asked the waiter for a serviette.*

S

Servile/सर्वाइल *(adjective)* – दासोचित excessively willing to serve or please others. *Sam has a servile attitude when interacting with his boss.*

Sesame/सेसमि *(noun)* – तिल a tall annual herbaceous plant of tropical and subtropical areas of the old world, cultivated for its oil-rich seeds. *My uncle grows sesame in his fields.*

Session/सेशन *(noun)* – सत्र a period devoted to a particular activity: a training session. [informal] a period of heavy or sustained drinking. a period of recording music in a studio. *I had a session with the dietician today.*

Set/सेट *(verb)* – रखना, तैयार करना, गाड़ना, स्थापित करना, समूह, समुच्चय put, lay, or stand in a specified place or position. be situated in a specified place or position. represent as happening at a specified time or in a specified place. mount a precious stone in a piece of jewellery. printing arrange as required. prepare for a meal by placing cutlery, crockery, etc., on it. add to a written work. sailing put up in position to catch the wind. *The stage was set for the play.*

Settee/सेटी *(noun)* – आराम कुर्सी a long upholstered seat for more than one person, typically with a back and arms. *Most of the guests preferred to sit on the settee.*

Setting/सेटिंग *(noun)* – मंचसज्जा, सुसज्जित the surroundings of a place or the location where an event happens. the place and time at which a story is represented as happening. *The author used the town of his birth as the setting.*

Settle/सेटल *(noun)* – समझौता द्वारा निर्णय करना, स्थिर होना, धँसना a wooden bench with a high back and arms. typically incorporating a box under the seat. *The settle has broken down because of disrepair.*

Settlement/सेटलमेंट *(noun)* – समझौता, निपटारा, बस्ती, उपनिवेश the action or process of setting. *The settlement was taking a long time.*

Settler/सेटलर *(noun)* – नया बसने वाला a person who settles in an area, especially one with nor or few previous inhabitants. *The settlers soon began to cultivate crops.*

Seven/सेवेन *(cardinal number)* – सात equivalent to the sum of three and four; one more than six, or three less than ten; 7. *There were seven children in the balcony.*

Seventh/सेवेन्थ *(ordinal number)* – सातवाँ constituting number seven in a sequence; 7th. *He stood seventh in the queue.*

Seventeen/सेवेन्टीन *(noun)* – सत्रह a number. *There were a total of seventeen pigeons in the tree.*

Seventy/सेवेन्टि *(cardinal number)* – सत्तर the number equivalent to the product of seven and ten; ten less than eighty; 70. *The class had 70 students.*

Sever/सेवर *(verb)* – विभाजित करना, कटना divide by cutting or slicing. *The workmen severed the ropes.*

Several/सेवरल *(pronoun)* – अनेक more than two but not many. *Several of the guests left very early.*

Severe/सिविअर *(adjective)* – तीव्र, कठोर, प्रचण्ड very great; intense. *I had a severe headache.*

Sew/सियू *(verb)* – सीना, सिलाई join, fasten, or repair by making stitches with a needle and thread or a sewing machine. *I sewed the torn rim of my skirt.*

Sewing/सियूंग *(noun)* – सिलाई करना the action or activity of sewing. *My mom loves sewing.*

Sewage/सिवेज *(noun)* – मल-नाली waste water and excrement conveyed in sewers. *The smell of the sewage made it difficult to stand there.*

Sewer/सिवर *(noun)* – भूमिगत नाला an underground conduit for carrying off drainage water and waste matter. *The road was dug up because the sewer was being laid.*

Sex/सेक्स *(noun)* – लिंग, सम्भोग either of the two main categories into which humans and most other living things are divided on the basis of their reproductive functions. the fact of belonging to one of these categories. the group of all members of either sex. *The lion cub belonged to female sex.*

Sexism/सेक्सिज्म *(noun)* – लिंगवाद prejudice, stereotyping, or discrimination, typically against women, on the basis of sex. *Sexism isn't healthy in workplaces.*

S

Sexual/सेक्सुअल *(adjective)* – यौन विषयक relating to the instincts, physiological processes, and activities connected with physical attraction or intimate physical contact between individuals. *The photographer was working on a documentary about the sexual behaviour of tigers.*

Shabby/शैबि *(noun)* – जीर्ण-शीर्ण, फटेहाल, कमीना worn out or dilapidated. dressed in old or worn clothes. *The shabby man roamed around in the streets late at night.*

Shack/शैक *(noun)* – फूहड़, झोपड़ी a roughly built hut of cabin. *We were glad to find the shack when we got lost in the forest. (verb)* [informal] live with someone as a lover. *The man shacked with the girl he loved.*

Shackle/शैकल *(noun)* – बेड़ी, हथकड़ी a pair of fetters connected by a chain, used to fasten a prisoner's wrists or ankles together. restraints or impediments. *The man in the shackles was very menacing.*

Shade/शेड *(noun)* – छाया comparative darkeness and coolness caused by shelter from direct sunlight. *The shade was such a relief in the blazing sun.*

Shadow/शैडो *(noun)* – साया, परछाई, छाया the dark area or shape produced by a body coming between light rays and a surface. partial or complete darkness. a dark patch or area. *The dog chased its shadow.*

Shadowy/शैडोवि *(adj)* – धुँधला, अस्पष्ट difficult to see because there is not much light. *A shadowy figure was coming towards me.*

Shady/शेडि *(adjective)* – छायादार, अवैध situated in or full of shade. *Let us move to a shady part of the park.*

Shaft/शैफ्ट *(noun)* – भाले आदि का डण्डा a long, narrow part of section forming the handle of a toll or club, the body of a spear or arrow, or similar. an arrow or spear. a column, especially the part between the base and capital. a long cylindrical rotating rod for the transmission of motive power in a machine. each of the pair of poles between which a horse is harnessed to a vehicle. *He was hit by the shaft of the spear.*

Shaggy/शैगि *(adjective)* – उलझे बाल, मैल-कुचैले बाल long, thick, and unkempt. having shaggy hair or fur. of or having a covering resembling shaggy hair. *The dog had shaggy hair.*

Shake/शेक *(verb)* – थरथराना, हिलना, हिलाना tremble or vibrate or cause to do so. tremble uncontrollably with strong emotion. *The entire building shook with the impact.*

Shaky/शेकि *(adjective)* – अस्थिर, हिलता हुआ, कमजोर shaking or trembling. *The shaky man narrated his horrible tale of fear.*

Shall/शैल *(modal verb)* – सहायक क्रिया expressing a strong assertion or intention. *I shall get the work done*

Shallow/शैलो *(adjective)* – छिछला सतही, छिछोरा of little depth. *The lake was shallow but dangerous.*

Sham/शैम *(noun)* – स्वाँग भरना a person or thing that is not what they are purported to be. *His love was just a sham.*

Shambles/सैम्बल्ज़ *(noun)* – अव्यवस्थित [informal] a chaotic state. *No one wanted to visit the shambles.*

Shame/शेम *(noun)* – लज्जा, शर्म a feeling of humiliation or distress caused by the consciousness of wrong of foolish behaviour. *He experienced a lot of shame when he was caught cheating.*

Shameful/शेमफुल *(adjective)* – शर्मनाक, लज्जाजनक worthy of or causing shame. *Her actions were seen as shameful by her relatives.*

Shameless/शेमलेस *(adjective)* – बेशर्म, निर्लज्ज showing a lack of shame. *The thief was absolutely shameless even when he was caught by the police.*

Shampoo/शैम्पू *(noun)* – बालों को धोने का तरल पदार्थ a liquid preparation for washing the hair. a similar substance for cleaning a carpet, car, etc. *I prefer using a herbal shampoo.*

Shape/शेप *(noun)* – आकृति, निर्धारित करना the external form or appearance of someone or something; the outline of an area or figure. a specific form or guise assumed by someone or something. a piece of material, paper, etc. made or cut in a particular form. *I could see the shape of a man behind the curtains.*

S

Shapeless/शेपलेस *(adjective)* – आकृतिहीन lacking definite or attractive shape. *The dress is decidedly shapeless.*

Shapely/शेपली *(adjective)*- आकर्षक आकृति having an attractive or well-proportioned shape. *It is important for a model to have a shapely body.*

Share/शेअर *(noun)* – हिस्सेदारी, भाग, हिस्सा a part of portion of a larger amount which is divided among or contributed by a number of people. any of the equal parts into which a company's capital is divided. part-ownership of property. *Everyone was happy with their share in the property.*

Shavings/शेविंग्स *(noun)*- कतरन a thin strip cut off a surface. *My friend collected pencil shavings.*

Shawl/शॉल *(noun)* – ऊनी चादर a piece of fabric worn by women over the shoulders or head or wrapped round a baby. *I loved her pashmina shawl.*

She/शी *(pronoun)* – स्त्री वाचक 'वह' used to refer to a woman, girl, of female animal previously mentioned or easily indentified. *Ruby is the only daughter of her parents, and she is her father's favourite.*

Sheaf/शीफ़ *(noun)* – धान का पूल, गट्ठर a bundle of grain stalks laid lengthways and tied together after reaping. *The farmer's wife carried the sheaf of wheat on her head.*

Shear/शिअर *(verb)* – ऊन काटना, भेंड़ का बाल काटना cut the wool off a sheep or other animal. cut off with scissors or shears. have something cut off. *The men sheared the unwilling sheep.*

Shears/शिअर्स *(plural noun)* – घास, पौधे काटने की कैंची cutting instrument in which two blades move past each other, like very large scissors. *The shears were very sharp and dangerous.*

Sheath/शीथ *(noun)* – म्यान, आवरण, निषेध a cover for the blade of a knife or sword. *The sheath was very ornate.*

Sheathe/शीद् *(verb)* – म्यान में रखना put a knife or sword into a sheath. *The warrior sheathed the sword.*

Shed/शेड *(noun)* – छतदार, जानवरों की झोपड़ी गिराना, उतारना, छुटकारा पाना a simple roofed structure, typically of wood and used for storage or to shelter animals. a larger structure, typically with one or more sides open, for storing vehicles or machinery. *The tractor rolled out of the shed.*

Sheen/शीन *(noun)* – चमक, तड़क-भड़क a soft luster on a surface. *The new car had a beautiful sheen.*

Sheep/शीप *(noun)* – भेंड़ a domesticated ruminant mammal with a thick woolly coat, kept, in flocks for its wool or meat. a wild mammal related to this, e.g. a bighorn. *I love to see the sheep on the rolling green hills.*

Sheepish/शीपिश् *(adjective)* – भेंड़ के सदृश, लज्जालू, डरपोक showing embarrassment from shame. *The boy was caught because he was acting sheepish.*

Sheer/शिअर *(adjective)* – पूरा का पूरा, बारीक nothing other than; unmitigated: sheer hard work. *He owed his success to sheer hard work.*

Sheet/शीट *(noun)* – चादर, (कपड़ा, शीशा, कागज, लोहा) a rope attached to the lower corner of a sail. *The sailor desperately pulled the sheet.* the space at the bow or stern of an open boat. *They kept some luggage in the sheet.*

Shelf/शेल्फ *(noun)* – खाना, टाँड़, कगार a flat length of wood or rigid material attached to a wall or forming part of a piece of furniture, providing a surface for the storage or display of objects. *All my books are displayed on the shelf.*

Shell/शेल *(noun)* – कोश, छिलका, आवरण, सीप, सीपी a hard covering that protects eggs, nuts and some animals. *Some children were collecting shells on the beach.*

Shelter/शेल्टर *(noun)* – शरणस्थली a place giving protection from bad weather or danger. *The storm shelter proved to be very helpful when the tornado hit.*

Shelve/शेल्व *(verb)* – स्थगित करना abandon or defer a plan or project. *Our project was shelved after the product manager declared that the product will not sell.*

S

Shepherd/शेफर्ड *(noun)* – गड़ेरिया a person who tends sheep. *The shepherd sat near the sheep and played his flute.*

Sheriff/शेरिफ *(noun)* – शासकीय पद the chief executive officer of the crown in a country, having administrative and judicial functions. an honorary officer elected annually in some English towns. *The sheriff ordered the men to be arrested immediately.*

Shield/शील्ड *(noun)* – कवच, ढाल, खेल का पुरस्कार, रक्षक a broad piece of armour held by straps or a handle on one side, used for protection against blows or missiles. hardly a stylized representation of a shield used for displaying a coat of arms. *His shield protected him from the enemy's sword.*

Shift/शिफ्ट *(verb)* – खिसकना, खिसकाना, बदलाव, पाली move or change or cuause to move or change from one position to another. move one's body slightly due to discomfort. *The passengers shifted themselves slightly to accommodate the old man.*

Shifty/शिफ्टी *(adjective)* – अविश्वनीय deceitful or evasive. *I did not trust the man because he looked shifty.*

Shilling/शिलिंग *(noun)* – ब्रिटेन का सिक्का a former [British] coin and monetary unit equal to one twentieth of a pound or twelve pence. *The child had a huge collection of Shillings.*

Shimmer/शिमर *(verb)* – झिलमिल करना, झिलमिलाना shine with a soft tremulous light. *(noun)* a light with such qualities. *The water shimmered in the sun.*

Shin/शिन *(noun)* – टाँग the front of the leg below the knee. a cut of beef from the lower part of a cow's leg. *Her dressed came down to the middle of her shins.* *(verb)* climb quickly up or down by gripping with one's arms and legs. *He shinned up the drainpipe to avoid his professor.*

Shine/शाइन *(verb)* – चमकना, चमकाना, श्रेष्ठ या यशस्वी होना give out a bright light; glow with reflected light. direct somewhere. be bright with the expression of emotion. *Her eyes seemed to shine with excitement.*

Shingle/शिंगल *(noun)* – कंकड़ों का ढेर (समुद्र तट पर) small pieces of stone lying in a mass on a beach. *Several shingles fell from the roof.*

Ship/शिप *(noun)* – जहाज, पोत a large seagoing boat. a sailing vessel with a bowsprit and three or more square-rigged masts. *The ship was huge but didn't have enough lifeboats.*

Shipmate/शिपमेट *(noun)* – सहनाविक a fellow member of a ship's crew. *The young sailor got along well with his shipmates.*

Shipment/शिपमेंट *(noun)* – जहाज पर लादा जाने वाला माल the action of shipping goods. *The shipment has happened an hour back.* a consignment of goods shipped. *The shipment arrived yesterday.*

Shipshape/शिपशेप *(adjective)* – सुव्यवस्थित, साफ orderly and neat. *The shipshape cabin was such a relief.*

Shipwreck/शिपरेक *(noun)* – जहाज का टूटना, डूबना the destruction of a ship at sea by sinking or breaking up. a ship so destroyed. *The shipwreck happened miles from the shore.* *(verb)* suffer a shipwreck. *The shipwrecked passengers held on to the lifeboats.*

Shipyard/शिपयार्ड *(noun)* – जहाज बनाने का कारखाना enclosed area where ships are made or repaired. *The shipyard was full so we had to move ahead.*

Shirk/शर्क *(verb)* – कठिन या अप्रिय काम से जी चुराना avoid or neglect a duty or responsibility. *Only irresponsible people shirk their responsibilities.*

Shirker/शर्कर *(noun)* – कामचोर neglecting responsibility. *The shirker got scolded by his boss regularly.*

Shirt/शर्ट *(noun)* – कमीज a garment for the upper body, with a collar and sleeves and buttons down the front. a similar garment of stretchable material without full fastenings, worn for sports. *The pattern of his shirt was very tropical.*

Shiver/शिवर *(verb)* – काँपना, ठिठुरना shake slightly an uncontrollably as a result of being cold, frightened, or excited. *I shivered because of fear.* *(noun)* a momentary trembling movement. a spell or

S

attack of shivering. *In spite of layers and layers of warm clothes, the shivers refused to stop.*

Shoal/शोल *(noun)* – मछलियों का झुंड large number of fish swimming together. *The shoal was getting bigger and bigger.*

Shock/शॉक *(noun)* – आघात, आघात पहुँचाना a group of twelve sheaves of grain placed upright on supporting each other to allow the grain to dry and ripen. *The shock is a very effective arrangement. (verb)* arrange in shocks. *The farmer whistled as he shocked the grain.*

Shoddy/शॉडी *(noun)* – घटिया, रद्दी badly made or done. *The sticking was very shoddy.*

Shoe/शू *(noun)* – जूता a covering for the foot having a sturdy sole and not reaching above the ankle. a horseshoe. *He likes leather shoes.*

Shoelace/शूलेस *(noun)* – जूते का फीता a cord or leather strip passes through eyelets or hooks on opposite sides of a shoe and pulled tight and fastened. *His shoelaces had come undone.*

Shoot/शूट *(noun & verb)* – गोली चलाना, गोली मारना, अंकुर, शिकार kill or wound with a bullet or arrow. cause to fire. hunt game with a gun. bring down an aircraft or person by shooting. *He shot the dummy thrice.*

Shop/शॉप *(noun)* – दुकान a building or part of a building where goods or services are sold. [informal] an act of going shopping. *The shop is closed today.*

Shopping/शॉपिंग *(noun)* – खरीदारी the purchasing of goods from shops. *Shopping is my favourite activity.*

Shore/शोर *(noun)* – तट, किनारा a prop or beam set obliquely against something weak or unstable as a support. *Workers were worried because the shore had started splintering. (verb)* support or hold up with shores. *We shored the damaged door and called the carpenter for repairs.*

Short/शॉर्ट *(adjective)* – छोटा, नाटा, संक्षिप्त, कम, अचानक of a small length or duration. travelling only a small distance before bouncing. *We took the short journey to home.*

Shortage/शॉर्टेज *(noun)* – अभाव a state of situation in which something needed cannot be obtained in sufficient amounts. *The shortage of water caused a lot of worry amongst the residents.*

Shorten/शॉर्टेन *(verb)* – छोटा करना make or become shorter. *The orator shortened his speech as the time was running out.*

Shortly/शॉर्टली *(adverb)* – शीघ्र in a short time, soon. *I will be there shortly.*

Shorts/शार्ट्स *(plural noun)* – जांघिया, निकर short trousers that reach only to the knees or thighs. *No one was allowed to wear shorts at the workplace.*

Shot/शॉट *(adjective)* – गोली की आवाज woven with a warp and weft of different colours, giving a contrasting effect when looked at from different angles. interspersed with a different colour. *The shot fabric brought out the beauty of the dress.*

Should/शुड *(modal verb)* – क्रिया रूप used to indicate obligation, duty, or correctness. used to give or ask advice or suggestions. *You should make a schedule for your studies.*

Shoulder/शोल्डर *(noun)* – कंधा, स्कंध, भार उठाना the joint between the upper arm or forelimb and the main part of the body. the part of a bird or insect at which the wing is attached. *My shoulder started aching when I lifted the heavy suitcase.*

Shout/शाउट *(verb)* – चीखना, पुकारना speak or call out very loudly. reprimand loudly. prevent someone form speaking or being heard by shouting. *The teacher shouted at the students.*

Shove/शोव *(verb)* – धकेलना push roughly. *The girl shoved her friend away.*

Shovel/शॅवॅल *(noun)* – बेलचा a tool resembling a spade with a broad blade and upturned sides, used for moving coal, earth, snow, etc. *They bought a shovel to prepare for the winters.*

Show/शो *(noun & verb)* – दिखाना, प्रदर्शन, कार्यक्रम be, allow, or cause to be visible. exhibit or produce for inspection. present on a screen for viewing. represent or depict in art. allow oneself to be seen; appear in public. [informal] arrive for an appointment

S

or at a gathering. *He showed the film in his home theatre.*

Shower/शॉवर *(noun)* – बौछार, फुहारा-स्नान a mass of small things falling or moving at once. a large umber of things happening or given at the same time: a shower of awards. a group of particles produced by a comic-ray particle in the earth's atmosphere. *The meteor shower was a spectacular sight.*

Shred/श्रेड *(noun)* – धज्जी, धज्जियाँ उड़ाना a strip of material that has been torn, cut, or scraped from something larger. *The shred was too small to be used as a patch.*

Shrewd/श्रूड *(adjective)* – चतुर, समझदार, सयाना having or showing sharp powers of judgement; astute. *Her shrewd observations were very helpful for the company.*

Shriek/श्रीक *(verb)* – चीख मारना, चीख utter a high-pitched piercing sound, cry, or words. *She shrieked when she saw the shadow.*

Shrill/श्रिल *(adjective)* – तीखी, कर्णभेदी ध्वनि high-pitched and piercing. derogatory loud and forceful. *Stop the shrill sound immediately.* *(verb)* make a shrill noise. *"Close the door behind you," she shrilled.*

Shrimp/श्रिम्प *(noun)* – झींगा मछली a small free-swimming edible crustacean with ten legs, mainly marine. *The shrimps swam away.*

Shrine/श्राइन *(noun)* – समाधि a place regarded as holy because of its associations with a divinity or a sacred person. *The shrine received millions of visitors each year.*

Shrink/श्रिंक *(verb)* – सिकुड़न, सिकुड़ना become or make smaller in size or amount; contract. become smaller as a result of being immersed in water. *The t-shirt shrank considerably after the first wash.*

Shrivel/श्रिवेल *(verb)* – झुर्री, शिकन, कुम्हलाना US wrinkle and contract, or cause to wrinkle and contract, through loss of moisture. *The long exposure to water shrivelled her hands.*

Shroud/श्राउड् *(noun)* – कफन a length of cloth or an enveloping garment in which a dead person is wrapped for burial. *The holy man was wrapped in a saffron shroud.*

Shrub/श्रब *(noun)* – झाड़ी, झाड़-झंखाड़ a woody plant which is smaller than a tree and has several main stems arising at or near the ground. *The thorny shrub had to be removed.*

Shrug/श्रग् *(verb)* – कंधे झटकाना raise slightly and momentarily to express doubt, ignorance, or indifference. dismiss something as unimportant. *He shrugged away the opinions of his subordinates.*

Shudder/शडर *(verb)* – हिलना, काँपना, भय से काँपना tremble or shake convulsively, especially from fear or repugnance. *(noun)* act of shuddering. *I shudder at the memory of those tough times.*

Shuffle/शफल *(verb)* – घिसते हुए चलना walk by dragging one's feet along or without lifting fully from the ground. restlessly shift one's position. get out of or avoid a responsibility or obligation. *The lazy boy shuffled away.*

Shun/शन् *(verb)* – बचना persistently avoid, ignore, or reject. *I shunned his views on traditional education.*

Shunt/शन्ट *(verb)* – मार्ग बदलना, दुरस्थ करना slowly push or pull so as to make up or remove from a train. push or shove direct or divert to a less important place or through which some of the current may be diverted. *The extra carriages were shunted to another route.*

Shut/शट *(verb)* – बन्द करना move or cause to move into position to block an opening. confine or exclude by closing something such as a door. prevent an opponent from scoring in a game. [informal] stop or cause someone to stop talking. *I shut the door as it was very windy outside.*

Shutter/शटर *(noun)* – दुकान का लोहे का दरवाजा each of a pair of hinged panels fixed inside or outside a window that can be closed for security or privacy or to keep out the light. *The shutter was opened by the helper.*

Shuttle/शट्ल *(noun)* – जाना-आना, फेरा करना a form of transport that travels regularly between two places. *The shuttle from the office to the train station isn't running today.*

S

Shy/शाइ *(noun & verb)* – संकोची, झेंपू, हया से भरा fling or throw at a target. *He shied his shoe at the rat.* (noun) an act of shying. *His shy missed its target.*

Sibling/सिब्लिंग *(noun)* – सहोदर each of two or more children or offspring having one or both parents in common; a brother or sister. *I have one sibling.*

Sick/सिक *(adj)* – स्वस्थ नहीं, बीमार affected by illness. *Half of my staff were sick.*

Sicken/सिकेन *(verb)* – ऊबना, ऊबा देना become disgusted or appalled. [informal] very irritating or annoying. [archaic] disgust or horror. *The stench in the abandoned house sickened me.*

Sickle/सिकल *(noun)* – हंसिया a short-handled farming tool with a semicircular blade, used for cutting corn, lopping, or trimming. *We needed to buy a new sickle as the old one was broken.*

Sickly/सिक्ली *(adjective)* – दुर्बल, अस्वस्थ रहने वाला often ill; in poor health. causing, characterized by, or indicative of poor health. *She was a sickly child.*

Sickness/सिक्नेस् *(noun)* – बीमारी the state of being ill. a particular type of illness or disease. *Doctors are yet to diagnose my aunt's sickness.*

Side/साइड *(noun)* – बगल, पार्श्व, भुजाएँ, पक्ष, दल a position to the left or right of an object, place, or central point. *Please move to the other side.*

Sidle/सिड्ल् *(verb)* – दबकर चलना walk in a furtive or stealthy manner, especially sideways or obliquely. *She sidled up to her to surprise her.*

Siege/सीज *(noun)* – घेराबन्दी a military operation in which enemy forces surround a town or building, cutting off essential supplies, with the aim of compelling the surrender of those inside. *The siege was successful after seven days.*

Sieve/सिव *(noun)* – चलनी, छाननी a utensil consisting of a wire or plastic mesh held in a frame, used for straining solids, from liquids, for separating coarser from finer particles, or for reducing soft solids to a pulp. *I bought a new sieve today.*

Sift/सिफ्ट *(verb)* – चालना, छानना put through a sieve so as to remove lumps or large particles. *He sifted the beach sand to look for small snails.*

Sigh/साइ *(verb)* – आह भरना, ठण्डी साँस खींचना a long, deep, audible exhalation expressing sadness, tiredness, relief, etc. *She repressed a sigh at the sight.*

Sight/साइट *(noun)* – दृश्य, दृष्टि, देखना the faculty or power of seeing. *Her sight is perfect.*

Signal/सिग्नल *(adjective)* – चेतावनी, संकेत से सूचना, संकेत के उपकरण striking; outstanding. *The article describes the signal historical events of the city.*

Signature/सिग्नेचर *(noun)* – हस्ताक्षर a person's name written in a distinctive way as a form of identification or authorization. *The papers were cancelled as her signatures were missing.*

Significance/सिग्निफिकॅन्स *(noun)* – महत्त्व, तात्पर्य the quality of being significant; importance. *The significance of her contribution was recognized by everyone.*

Significant/सिग्निफिकॅन्ट *(adjective)* – महत्त्वपूर्ण, अर्थवान having an unstated meaning; indicative of something. *She gave her a significant glance.*

Signify/सिग्निफाइ *(verb)* – अर्थ रखना, महत्त्व रखना be an indication of. *The gathering signified the importance of the event.*

Silence/साइलेंस *(noun & verb)* – चुप्पी, मौन, मौन कर देना complete absence of sound. *She likes to study in silence.*

Silent/साइलेंट *(adjective)* – चुप, मौन, मूक, अल्पभाषी not making or accompanied by any sound. without an accompanying soundtrack. *They presented a silent act.*

Silhoutte/सिलुएॅट *(noun)* – छायाचित्र, परछाई का चित्र the dark shape and outline of someone or something visible in restricted light against a brighter background. *She identified them from their silhouette only.*

S

Silicon/सिलिकॉन *(noun)* – एक रसायन the chemical element of atomic number 14, a shiny grey crystalline non-metal with semiconducting properties, used in making electronic circuits. *She presented a paper on the different uses of silicon.*

Silk/सिल्क *(noun)* – रेशम, रेशमी वस्त्र a fine, strong, soft lustrous fibre produced by silkworms in making cocoons. *Silk fibre is quite expensive.*

Silky/सिल्कि *(adjective)* – रेशमी of or resembling silk. *The fabric was silky soft.*

Sill/सिल *(noun)* – जंगला का कोण a shelf or slab of stone, wood, or metal at the foot of a window or doorway. *She kept the flowers on the window sill.*

Silver/सिल्वर *(noun)* – चाँदी, चाँदी के सामान, रजत पदक a precious shiny grayish-white metal, the chemical element of atomic number 47. *She gifted her friend a silver pendant.*

Similar/सिमिलर *(adjective)* – समान, समतुल्य of the same kind in appearance, character, or quantity, without being identical. *She bought similar gifts for all the kids.*

Similarity/सिमिलैरिटी *(noun)* – सादृश्यता, समानता the state or fact of being similar. *They were asked to list the similarities.*

Simile/सिमिलि *(noun)* – उपमा, उपमा–अलंकार a figure of speech involving the comparison of one thing with another thing of a different kind. *He used too many similes in his essay.*

Simmer/सिमर *(verb)* – उबलता हुआ stay or cause to stay just below boiling point while bubbling gently. *The soup smelled wonderful after it started simmering.*

Simple/सिम्पल *(adjective)* – साधारण, सादा, सहज, सरल easily, understood or done. *She taught them simple calculations.*

Simplicity/सिम्प्लिसिटि *(noun)* – सादगी, सहजता the quality or condition of being simple. *Everyone was impressed by his simplicity.*

Simplify/सिम्प्लिफाइ *(verb)* – सरल करना make more simple. *She simplified the problem for him.*

Simulate/सिम्युलेट *(verb)* – नकल करना, स्वांग करना imitate or reproduce the appearance, character, or conditions of. *They were asked to simulate the experiment.*

Simultaneous/सिमल्टेनिअस् *(adjective)* – एक ही समय में occurring, operating, or done at the same time. *Both of them were burning crackers in simultaneous interval.*

Sin/सिन *(noun)* – पाप, गम्भीर अपराध an immoral act considered to be a transgression against divine law. *Immortality is considered a sin.*

Sinful/सिनफुल *(adjective)* – पापयुक्त immoral, committing sins. *His actions were sinful.*

Sinfully/सिनफुल्लि *(adverb)* – पापमय activity sinful. *It was sinfully delicious.*

Sinfulness/सिनफुलनेस *(noun)* – पापकर्म in the manner of commetting sins. *The sinfulness of their act is unforgiveable.*

Since/सिन्स *(preposition)* – के बाद से in the intervening period between and the time under consideration. *They have been fighting since morning.*

Sincere/सिन्सिअर *(adjective)* – सच्चा, निष्कपट proceeding from or characterized by genuine feelings; free from pretence or deceit. *Their sincere work won them the first prize.*

Sincerity/सिन्सिअरिटि *(noun)* – निश्छलता, यथार्थता the absence of pretence, deceit or high procrisy. *Her sincerity was recognized by the administration.*

Sing/सिंग *(verb)* – गाना, चहचहाना make musical sounds with the voice, especially words with a set tune. perform in this way. sing in accompaniment to a song or piece of music. *All gathered to hear her sing.*

Singer/सिंगर *(noun)* – गायक, गायिका a person who sings, especially professionally. *She's my favourite singer.*

Singe/सिन्ज *(verb)* – झुलसना, झुलसाना burn or be burnt lightly or superficially. *He singed his hair in the lab.*

Single/सिंगल *(adjective)* – एक, अकेला only one; not one of several. regarded as distinct from others in a group. even one use for emphasis: they didn't receive a single reply. designed or suitable for one person. *He didn't eat a single cookie.*

S

Singly/सिन्ग्लि *(adverb)* - अकेले one at a time; separately or individually. *The teacher talked to each student singly.*

Singular/सिंगुलर *(adjective)* - एक वचन, असाधारण exceptionally good or great; remarkable strange or eccentric in some respect. *He is a singular performer.*

Sinister/सिनिस्टर *(adjective)* - अनर्थकारी suggestive of evil or harm. *He acted out his sinister ideas. There is another more sinister possibility.*

Sink/सिन्क *(noun & verb)* - डूबना, धंसान, क्षीण होना, बर्तन या हाथ धोने का स्थान a fixed basin with a water supply and outflow pipe. *The sink broke yesterday.*

Sinner/सिनर् - *(noun)* पाप करने वाला a person who sins. *He was termed a sinner by the society.*

Sinus/साइनस *(noun)* - नाक से जुड़ा खाली स्थान anatomy & zoology a cavity within a bone or other tissue, especially one in the bones of the face or skull connecting with the nasal cavities. *His sinus troubles him in the winters.*

Sip/सिप *(verb)* - चुस्की, घूँट drink by taking small mouthfuls. *He sipped the tea slowly.*

Siphon/साइफन *(noun)* - खंगालना, निकास नली से दूसरे में लाना a tube used to convey liquid upwards from a container and then down to a lower level, the flow being forced initially by suction and maintained by atmospheric pressure. *It worked as a siphon.*

S

Sir/सर *(noun)* - महाशय, महोदय, श्रीमान् a polite or respectful form of address to a man. *They all call him 'sir'.*

Siren/साइरन *(noun)* - भोंपू-भोंपू की आवाज a device that makes a loud prolonged signal or warning sound. *The siren woke him up.*

Sissy/सिसि *(noun)* - स्त्री स्वभाव वाला a person regarded as feeble or effeminate. *He was angry when they called him sissy.*

Sister/सिस्टर *(noun)* - बहन, अस्पताल की सेविका a woman or girl in relation to other daughters and sons of her parents. *He has two sisters.*

Sister in law/सिस्टर इन लॉ *(noun)* - साली, ननद the sister of one's wife or husband. *He hates his sister-in-law.*

Sit/सिट *(verb)* - बैठना be or cause to be in a position in which one's weight is supported by one's buttocks rather than one's feet and one's back is upright. rest with the hind legs bent and the body close to the ground. *He sat down immediately after the race.*

Site/साइट *(noun)* - स्थान, स्थल, भवन-निर्माण स्थल an area of ground an which something is constructed. *This is the site for proposed metro station.*

Sitting/सिटिंग *(noun)* - बैठक a period or spell of sitting. *He was bored in the sitting.*

Situate/सिचुएट *(verb)* - स्थित होना, स्थिति place in a particular location or context. *He situated the new comers in perfect roles.*

Situation/सिचुएशन *(noun)* - स्थिति, हालत a set of circumstances in which one finds oneself. *He got caught in a bad situation.*

Six/सिक्स *(cardinal number)* - छः equivalent to the product of two and three; one more than five, or four less than ten; 6. *I have six pens in my bag.*

Sixteen/सिक्सटीन *(cardinal number)* - सोलह equivalent to the product of four and four; one more than fifteen, or six more than ten; 16. *She has won 16 races so far.*

Sixty/सिक्स्टि *(cardinal number)* - साठ the number equivalent to the product of six and ten; ten more than fifty; 60. *There are 60 chairs in that room.*

Size/साइज *(noun)* - वस्तु का आकार (छोटी व बड़ी) a thing's overall dimension. *Russia is six times the size of India.*

Sizzle/सिजल *(verb)* - कड़कड़, कड़कड़ाहट make a hissing sound when frying or roasting. *The meat is sizzling on the grill.*

Sizzling/सिजलिंग *(adjective)* - उत्तेजना, सनसनी very hot. *She heard the sizzling sound.*

Skate/स्केट *(noun)* - चक्के वाले जूते, चक्के पर चलना an edible marine fish of the ray family with a diamond-shaped body. *I cooked skate last night.*

Skeleton/स्केलिटन् *(noun)* - कंकाल, ढाँचा, रूपरेखा framework of bone cartilage supports the body or other structure. *I saw skeletons of dinosaurs in the museum.*

Sketch/स्केच *(noun)* – रेखाचित्र, खाका a rough or unfinished drawing or painting. *He drew an impressive sketch of the couple.*

Skewer/स्क्यूअर *(noun)* – सीक, सेंका कबाव a long piece of wood or metal used for holding pieces of food together during cooking. *She poked him with a skewer. (verb)* fasten together or pierce with a pin or skewer. *My little niece likes skewer.*

Ski/स्की *(noun)* – फिसलने की पट्टी each of a pair of long, narrow pieces of hard flexible material fastened under the fee for travelling over snow. a similar device attached beneath a vehicle or aircraft. *My brother gifted me a new pair of skis.*

Skid/स्किड *(verb)* – फिसलना slide, typically sideways, on slippery ground or as a result of stopping or turning too quickly. slip; slide. *He skidded on the ice.*

Skill/स्किल *(noun)* – कुशलता, निपुणता the ability to do something well; expertise or dexterity. *She has the skill to drive heavy trucks. (verb)* train to do a particular task. *She skilled him in carpentry.*

Skim/स्किम *(verb)* – मलाई निकालना remove from the surface of liquid. *He skimmed the milk.*

Skimp/स्किम्प *(verb)* – कम खर्च में प्रबन्ध expend fewer resources on something than are necessary in an attempt to economize. *They skimped the farewell lunch.*

Skin/स्किन *(noun)* – चमड़ा, त्वचा, चर्म the thin layer of tissue forming the natural outer covering of the body of a person or animal. the skin of a dead animal used as material for clothing or other items. a container made fro the skin of an animal, used for holding liquids. *She used moisturizer to soften her dry skin.*

Skip/स्किप *(noun)* – बीच में छोड़ना, उछलना, कूद जाना, चूक जाना [British] a large transportable open-topped container for bulky refuse. *The skip needed to be emptied.*

Skipper/स्किपर *(noun)* – अगुआ, नेता, संचालक the captain of a ship, boat, or aircraft. the captain of a side in a game or sport. *The skipper is down with fever. (verb)* act as captain of. *She knows how to skipper small yatchs.*

Skirmish/स्करमिश *(noun)* – भिड़ंत, मुठभेड़, कटु विवाद an episode of irregular of unpremeditated fighting, especially between small or outlying parts of armies. *The skirmishes were tiring and fruitless. (verb)* engage in a skirmish. *They skirmished with the king's army.*

Skirt/स्कर्ट *(noun)* – घघरा, लहंगा a woman's outer garment fastened around the waist and hanging down around the legs. the part of a coat or dress that hangs below the waist. women regarded as objects of sexual desire. *She wore a black skirt.*

Skittle/स्किटल *(noun)* – एक प्रकार का खेल a game played with wooden pins, typically nine in number, set up at the end of an alley to be bowled down with a wooden ball or disc. a game played with similar pins set up on a board to be knocked down by swinging a suspended ball. *He didn't win even a single game of skittles.*

Skulk/स्कल्क *(verb)* – छिपकर चलना hide or move around secretly, typically with a sinister or cowardly motive. *The spy skulked around the colony. (noun)* a group of foxes. *The skulk only came out at night.*

Skull/स्कल *(noun)* – खोपड़ी, कपाल a bone framework enclosing the brain of a vertebrate. a person's head or brain. *I bought a model of a skull.*

Sky/स्काइ *(noun)* – आकाश, आसमान the region of the atmosphere and outer space seen from the earth. *The sky is clear today.*

Skyline/स्काइलाइन *(noun)* – क्षितिज an outline of land and buildings defined against the sky. *It's a beautiful skyline.*

Slab/स्लैब *(noun)* – पटिया, पटरी a large, thick, flat piece of solid material, in particular stone, concrete, or heavy food. *The slab fell down and broke.*

S

Slack/स्लैक (noun) – ढीला, ढीला ढाला, मन्दा, सुस्त coal dust or small pieces of coal. *He cleaned the slack off the floor.*

Slacken/स्लैकेन (verb) – ढीला, मन्दा या सुस्त होना reduce or decrease in intensity. *The children slackened their pace to let others catch up.*

Slacks/स्लैक्स (noun) – पतलून, ढीला अधोवस्त्र casual trousers. *She had outgrown her pair of slacks.*

Slake/स्लेक (verb) – प्यास बुझाना quench. satisfy. *The athletes slaked their thirst after the long run.*

Slam/स्लैम (noun) – धमाके से, धमाकेदार जीत a grand slam or small slam, for which bonus points are scored if bid and made. *He won the slam.*

Slander/स्लैंडर (noun) – झूठी निन्दा, दोषारोपरण, बदनाम करना the action or crime of making a false spoken statement damaging to a person's reputation. compare with libel. a false and malicious spoken statement. *He sued the company for slander.* (verb) make such statements about. *He slandered the government.*

Slang/स्लैंग (noun)– केवल बोलचाल में प्रयुक्त शब्द [informal] language that is more common in speech than in writing and is typically restricted to a particular context or group. *He has learned the language but still faces problem with local slang.* (verb) attack using abusive language. *He slanged the other driver.*

Slant/स्लैंट (verb) – तिरछा, ढालुआ, तोड़-मरोड़कर पेश करना diverge from the vertical or horizontal; slope or lean. *The building slanted dangerously.*

Slap/स्लैप (verb) – थप्पड़, थप्पड़ मारना hit or strike with the palm of one's hand or a flat object. hit against with athe sound of such an action. reprimand someone forcefully. *The older child slapped the younger one.*

Slapdash/स्लैपडैश (adjective & adverb) – लापरवाही का काम done too hurriedly and carelessly. *It was a slapdashed project.*

Slapstick/स्लैपस्टिक (noun) – दोहरी पट्टी comedy based on deliberately clumsy actions and humorously embarrassing events. *He enjoys slapstick humour.*

Slash/स्लैश (verb) – छपाक से काटना, चर्र से चीरना cut with a violent sweeping movement. *The tiger slashed the sheet with its claws.*

Slat/स्लैट (noun) – पट्टी a thin, narrow piece of wood or other material, especially one of a series which overlap or fit into each other, as in a venetian blind. *The slats were left piled up on the wet floor.*

Slate/स्लेट (noun) – तख्ती a fine grained grey, green, or bluish purple metamorphic rock easily split into smooth, flat plates. a flat plate of such rock used as roofing material. *The slate formed spectacular scenery in the hills.*

Slaughter/स्लॉटर (noun & verb) – हत्या, काट देना the killing of farm animals for food. *The slaughter was a grisly sight to see.*

Slave/स्लेव (noun) – गुलाम, दास a person who is the legal property of another and is forced to obey them. a person who is excessively dependent upon or controlled by something: a slave to fashion. *She was a slave to fitness.*

Slavish/स्लैविश (adjective) – नकल showing no attempt at originality. *The slavish writer churned out manuscript after manuscript of unsuccessful writing.*

Slay/स्ले (verb) – काट देना, हत्या करना kill in a violent way. murder someone. *The criminal slayed the victim mercilessly.*

Sleazy/स्लीजि (adjective) – गन्दी जगह sordid, corrupt, or immoral. squalid and seedy. *His sleazy actions are bound to land him in trouble one day.*

Sledge/स्लेज (noun) – बर्फ पर चलने वाली गाड़ी a vehicle on runners for travelling over snow or ice, either pushed, pulled, or allowed to slide downhill. a toboggan. *My father bought me a new sledge.* (verb) ride or carry on a sledge. *I sledged down the snow-covered hill.*

Sledge-hammer/स्लेज हैमर (noun) – लम्बे हत्थे वाला बड़ा और भारी हथौड़ा a large, heavy hammer used for breaking rocks, driving in posts, etc. *The sledge-hammer was too heavy for me to carry.*

S

Sleek/स्लीक *(adjective)* - चिकना-चुपड़ा, देखने में स्वस्थ्य smooth, glossy, and healthy looking. *She has sleek hair.*

Sleep/स्लीप *(noun)* - नींद, निद्रा a regularly recurring condition of body and mind in which the nervous system is inactive, the eyes closed, the postural muscles relaxed, and consciousness practically suspended. *I went to sleep really late in the night.*

Sleepless/स्लीपलेस *(adjective)* - निद्रारहित experiencing lack of sleep. *I spent many sleepless nights worrying about my exam results.*

Sleeper/स्लीपर *(noun)* - तख्ती, सोने के लिए तख्ती a sleeping car or a train carrying sleeping cars. *The sleeper was very comfortable.*

Sleepy/स्लीपि *(adjective)* - निद्राग्रस्त, नींद से भरा needing or ready for sleep. *I am very sleepy.*

Sleet/स्लीट *(noun)* - बर्फीली वर्षा rain containing some ice, or snow melting as it falls. US a thin coating of ice formed by sleet or rain freezing on coming into contact with a cold surface. *The sleet made the roads slippery. (verb)* sleet falls. *It sleeted in the morning.*

Sleeve/स्लीव *(noun)* - आस्तीन, बाँह the part of a garment that wholly or partly covers a person's arm. *The sleeves of his pullover were too tight.*

Sleigh/स्ले *(noun)* - बर्फगाड़ी a vehicle without wheels that is used for travelling on snow and that is usually pulled by horses. *I enjoyed sleigh ride in Kashmir.*

Slender/स्लेन्डर *(adjective)* - छरहरा, पतला-लम्बा gracefully thin. *The athletic girl was very slender.*

Slice/स्लाइस *(noun)* - फाँका, कतरा, हिस्सा a thin, broad piece of food cut from a larger portion. a portion or share. *I would love to have a slice of cake.*

Slick/स्लिक *(adjective)* - दक्षता, निपुणता, फिसलाऊ done or operating in an impressively smooth and efficient way. glibly assured. *His slick operating the computer impressed the interviewer.*

Slide/स्लाइड *(noun & verb)* - फिसलना, खिसकना, काँच की पट्टी move along a smooth surface, especially downwards, while maintaining continuous contact with it. *Children slid down the slides.*

Slight/स्लाइट *(adjective)* - छरहरा, हल्का, मामूली, उपेक्षा small in degree; inconsiderable. not profound or substantial. *Even a slight drop in the temperature now will make it uncomfortably cold.*

Slim/स्लिम *(adjective)* - दुबला-पतला gracefully thin; slenderly built. small in width and long and narrow in shape. *The slim girl looked like a model.*

Slime/स्लाइम *(noun)* - कीचड़ कीचड़ में लिप्त an unpleasantly moist, soft, and slippery substance. *The porridge was covered with slime and had a horrible smell.*

Sling/स्लिंग *(noun)* - जख्मी हाथ, कलाई आदि को सहारा देने के लिए प्रयुक्त पट्टी a sweetened drink of spirits, especially gin, and water. *A good sling is enough to make him happy.*

Slink/स्लिंक *(verb)* - लुक-छिपकर आना जाना move quietly with gliding steps, in a stealthy or sensuous manner. come or go unobtrusively or furtively. *(noun)* an act of slinking. *The thief slinked through the kitchen door and headed towards the safe.*

Slip/स्लिप *(noun)* - कागज का छोटा टुकड़ा, पर्ची a small piece of paper for writing on or that gives printed information. *He gave the waiter a slip, instructing him to bring the surprise birthday cake.*

Slipper/स्लिपर *(noun)* - चप्पल, चट्टी a comfortable slip on shoe that is worn indoors. a light slip on shoe, especially one used for dancing. *(verb)* beat with a slipper. *I don't mind wearing my slippers even when I am stepping out.*

Slippery/स्लिपरि *(adjective)* - फिसलन भरा difficult to hold firmly or stand on through being smooth, wet, or slimy. *The surface was slippery because of the rain.*

Slipshod/स्लिपशॉड *(adjective)* - फूहड़ lacking in care, thought, or organization. *She had a slipshod way of working.*

Slit/स्लिट *(noun)* - चीरा, दरार, चीर देना a long, narrow cut or opening. *The slit was getting longer by the minute.*

S

Slither/स्लिदर *(verb)* – फिसल जाना, फिसलते हुए चलना move smoothly over a surface with a twisting or oscillating motion. slide or slip unsteadily on a loose or slippery surface. *The snake slithered around in the enclosure.*

Slob/स्लॉब *(noun)* – आलसी a lazy and slovenly person. *He was such a slob when it came to keeping his workplace clean.*

Slog/स्लॉग *(verb)* – कठिन या उबाऊ काम को लम्बे समय तक करना work hard over a period of time. walk or move with difficulty or effort. *I slogged the entire last year.*

Slogan/स्लोगन *(noun)* – नारा a short memorable phrase used in advertising or associated with a political party or group. *The brand had a catchy slogan.*

Slop/स्लॉप *(noun)* – छलक जाना, रसोई या स्नान का गन्दा पानी a workman's loose outer garment. *The slop was so dirty by the end of the day that it had to be discarded.*

Slope/स्लोप *(noun & verb)* – ढलान, ढलुआ बनाना a surface of which one end or side is at a higher level than another. a difference in level or sideways position between two ends or sides. a part of the side of a hill or mountain, especially as a place for skiing. *The skiers skied down the slope.*

Sloppy/स्लॉपि *(adjective)* – गीला, अतिभावुक containing too much liquid; watery. *The sloppy curry was tasteless.*

Slot/स्लॉट *(noun)* – खाँचा, खाका, कार्यक्रम, सूची the track of a deer, visible as slotted footprints in soft ground. *The curious child followed the slot.*

Sloth/स्लॉथ *(noun)* – सुस्ती, आलस्य reluctance to work or make an effort; laziness. *He is such a sloth when it comes to work.*

Slovenly/स्लॉवनलि *(adjective)* – लापरवाह untidy and dirty. *Her slovenly hair needed washing.*

Slow/स्लो *(adjective)* – धीमा, सुस्त moving or capable of moving only at a low speed. lasting or taking a long time. *My car was stuck behind the slow bullock cart.*

Sludge/स्लज *(noun)* – गाढ़ा कीचड़ thick, soft, wet mud or a similar viscous mixture. dirty oil or industrial waste. *The sludge spoiled the entire scenery.*

Slug/स्लग *(verb)* – घोंघा-सा strike with a hard blow. settle a dispute or contest by fighting or competing fiercely. *The wrestler slugged the opponent.* *(noun)* a hard blow. *The slug made him fall down.*

Sluggish/स्लगिश *(adjective)* – सुस्ती, सुस्त slow moving or inactive. lacking energy or alertness. *The sluggish movement of the traffic was very frustrating.*

Slum/स्लम *(noun)* – घनी गन्दी बस्ती a squalid and overcrowded urban area inhabited by very poor people. a house in such a place. *(verb)* voluntarily spend time in uncomfortable conditions or at a lower social level than one's own. *Several plans were formulated for the betterment of the slum dwellers.*

Slumber/स्लम्बर *(noun)* – सोना, निद्रा a sleep. *The deep slumber refreshed me.* *(verb)* sleep. *The woodcutter slumbered beneath the tree he was planning to cut.*

Slump/स्लम्प *(verb)* – धम से बैठना, मन्दी sit, lean, or fall heavily and limply. *Don't slump. Sit straight.*

Slur/स्लर *(verb)* – अस्पष्ट उच्चारण articulate or be articulated indistinctly. *He slurred under anaesthesia.*

Slurp/स्लर्प *(verb)* – आवाज करते हुए कुछ पीना eat or drink with a loud sucking sound. *He slurped his tea.*

Slush/स्लश *(noun)* – पिघलता बर्फ़, भावुकता partially melted snow or ice. *The slush made walking around very inconvenient.* watery mud. *His trousers got dirty when he walked through the slush.*

Slut/स्लट *(noun)* – फूहड़ स्त्री, बदतमीज औरत a slovenly or promiscuous woman. *She played the role of a slut in the movie.*

Sly/स्लाइ *(adjective)* – चालाकी, छल having a conning and deceitful nature. *She is a sly woman.*

Smack/स्मैक *(noun)* – थप्पड़, थप्पड़ मारना, नशीला पदार्थ a single masted sailing boat used for coasting or fishing. *His smack is in urgent need of repair.*

S

Small/स्माल *(adjective)* – नन्हा, छोटा, मामूली of a size that is less than normal or usual. *When I was small we lived in a big old house.*

Smallpox/स्मॉलपॉक्स *(noun)* – चेचक, शीतला an acute contagious viral disease, with fever and pustules usually leaving permanent scars. *They claim that smallpox has been eradicated.*

Smart/स्मार्ट *(adjective)* – आकर्षक, साफ़-सुथरा, बना-ठना clean, tidy, and stylish. *Her room is smart.*

Smash/स्मैश *(verb)* – तोड़ना, पटककर तोड़ना, हरा देना break or cause to break violently into pieces. violently knock down. *The mirror smashed into a hundred pieces.*

Smattering/स्मैटरिंग *(noun)* – किसी वस्तु की छोटी मात्रा a small amount. *A smattering of raindrops was enough to make the children happy.*

Smear/स्मिअर *(verb)* – पोतना, धब्बा लगाना coat or mark with a greasy or sticky substance. *The smear didn't go away even after getting the dress dry-cleaned.*

Smell/स्मेल *(noun)* – सूँघना, गन्ध आना the faculty of perceiving odours by means of the organs in the nose. *She lost her sense of smell in the accident.*

Smelt/स्मेल्ट *(noun)* – पिघलाना, गलाना a small silvery fish of both marine and fresh water. *The smelt quickly swam away.*

Smile/स्माइल *(noun & verb)* – मुस्कान, मुस्काना form one's features into a pleased, friendly, or amused expression, with the corners of the mouth turned up. *They smiled at each other.*

Smirk/स्मर्क *(verb)* – व्यंग्यात्मक हँसी हँसना smile in an irritatingly smug or silly way. *He smirked at our low marks.*

Smith/स्मिथ *(noun)* – लोहार a worker in metal. short for blacksmith. *The smith repaired the spade.*

Smock/स्मॉक *(noun)* – ढीला आराम देह वस्त्र a loose dress or blouse having the upper part closely gathered in smocking. *She wore a blue smock.*

Smooth/स्मुद *(adjective)* – चिकना, महीन, मधुर, प्रवाहमय having an even and regular surface; free from projections or indentations. having an even consistency; without lumps. *The smooth batter will rise beautifully when baked.*

Smother/स्मॉदर *(verb)* – दम घोंटकर मारना, suffocate by covering the nose and mouth. *The thief tried to smother the servant but failed.*

Smoulder/स्मोल्डर *(verb)* – सुलगना burn slowly with smoke but no flame. *The coal smouldered for a long time.*

Smudge/स्मज *(noun & verb)* – धब्बा लगाना cause to become messy, smeared. *You have smudged the picture. We could see the low smudge of the mountain during winter nights.*

Smug/स्मग *(adjective)* – सुन्दर आकृति का, अपने में प्रसन्न irritatingly pleased with oneself; self satisfied. *The student's smug attitude irritated everyone else.*

Smuggle/स्मगल *(verb)* – तस्करी करना move illegally into or out of a country. *The smugglers smuggled many paintings and artifacts out of the country.*

Snack/स्नैक *(noun)* – हल्का नास्ता a small quantity of food or a light meal, eaten between meals or in place of a meal. *We just had snacks at the party.*

Snag/स्नैग *(noun)* – छिपा हुआ, अप्रत्याशित रुकावट a sausage. *The snag tasted stale.*

Snail/स्नेल *(noun)* – घोंघा a slow moving mollusc with a spiral shell into which the whole body can be withdrawn. *I saw several snails in my garden.*

Snake/स्नेक *(noun)* – साँप, सर्प a predatory reptile with a long slender limbless supple body, many kinds of which have a venomous bite. *My brother was excited to see the snake in the zoo.*

Snap/स्नैप *(verb)* – फोटो खींचना, टूट जाना break or cause to break with a sharp cracking sound. *The stick snapped.*

Snare/स्नेअर *(noun)* – जाल, फन्दा, चूहेदानी a trap for catching small animals, consisting of a loop of wire or cord that pulls tight. a wire loop for severing polyps or other growths. *The snare failed to catch anything.*

Snarl/स्नार्ल *(verb)* – गुर्राना growl with bared teeth. *The dog snarled at me.*

S

Snatch/स्नैच *(verb)* - झपट लेना seize quickly and deftly. [informal] steal or kidnap by seizing suddenly. quickly secure or obtain. *The child snatched my pencil.*

Sneak/स्नीक *(verb)* - गलतियाँ बताना, चोरी से घुसना move, go, or convey in a furtive or stealthy manner. stealthily acquire or obtain: she sneaked a glance at her watch. *She sneaked into the house late at night.*

Sneer/स्निअर *(noun & verb)* - मुँह बिचकाना, उपहास करना a contemptuous or mocking smile, remark, or tone. *Her sneer was quite unnecessary.* *(verb)* smile or speak in a contemptuous or mocking manner. *The senior sneered at the juniors.*

Sneeze/स्निज *(verb)* - छींकना make a sudden involuntary expulsion of air from the nose and mouth due to irritation of one's nostrils. *He sneezed loudly.* *(noun)* an act or the sound of sneezing. *His loud sneeze alarmed the entire class.*

Snide/स्नाइड *(adjective)* - अप्रिय बातें कहना derogatory or mocking in an indirect way. *This is no time for making snide remarks.*

Sniff/स्निफ *(verb)* - सूँघना draw air audibly through the nose. *My friend sniffed the air.*

Sniffle/स्निफल *(verb)* - सों-सों करना sniff slightly or repeatedly, typically because of a cold or fit of crying. *He was sniffling by the time he reached home.*

Snigger/स्निगर *(noun)* - ही-ही करना, खी-खी करना a smothered or half-suppressed laugh. *The girls didn't know that everyone could hear their sniggers.*

Snip/स्निप *(verb)* - कैंची से काटना cut with scissors or shears, with small, quick strokes. *The barber snipped the locks off.*

Snipe/स्नाइप *(noun)* - एक प्रकार की दलदल की चिड़िया a kind of game bird found in marshes. *I saw a snipe near the pond.*

Snippet/स्निपट *(noun)* - छोटा-सा सूचना-अंश a small piece or brief extract. *This is a snippet from the story she wrote.*

Snivel/स्निवल *(verb)* - खीझना cry and sniffle. *She snivelled after the fall.*

Snob/स्नॉब *(noun)* - दंभी a person who has an exaggerated respect for high social position or wealth and who looks down on those regarded as socially inferior. a person with a similar respect for tastes considered superior in a particular area: a wine snob. *At times, you sound like a snob.*

Snooker/स्नूकर *(noun)* - एक खेल a game played with cues on a billiard table in which the players use a white cue ball to pocket the other balls in a set order. *She is a good player of snooker.*

Snoop/स्नूप *(verb)* - ताक-झाँक investigate or look around furtively in an attempt to find out something. *The detective snooped around the crime scene for clues.*

Snooty/स्नूटी *(adjective)* - दंभी [informal] showing disapproval of or contempt towards others, especially those considered to be socially inferior. *She is such a snooty employer.*

Snooze/स्नूज *(noun)*- झपकी, झपकी लेना a short, light sleep. *I took a snooze in the afternoon.* *(verb)* have a snooze. *She snoozed in the class.*

Snore/स्नोर *(noun & verb)* - खर्राटा, खर्राटा भरना a snorting or grunting sound in a person's breathing while they are asleep. *His snores made it difficult for me to sleep.* *(verb)* make such a sound while asleep. *She snores at times.*

Snorkel/स्नोरकेल *(noun)* - एक उपकरण a tube for a swimmer to breathe through while under water. *He forgot to carry his snorkel.*

Snort/स्नार्ट *(noun)* - फुफकारना an explosive sound made by the sudden forcing of breath through the nose. *He laughed with a snort.*

Snot/स्नॉट *(noun)* - नाक का कफ mucus from the nose. *Please wipe the snot off your nose.*

Snout/स्नाउट *(noun)* - थूथून the projecting nose and mouth of an animal, especially a mammal. the projecting front or end of something such as a pistol. *The alligator hurt its snout*

Snow/स्नो *(noun)* - बर्फ, हिम, हिमपात atmospheric water vapour frozen into ice crystals and falling in lgith white flakes or lying on the ground as a white layer. falls of snow. *Pure white sheet of snow covered the landscape.*

S

Snub/स्नब *(verb)* – अवज्ञापूर्ण ignore or spurn disdainfully. *She snubbed me in the party.*

Snuff/स्नफ *(verb)* – सूँघनी, मोमबत्ती बुझाना extinguish a candle. *Please snuff the candles.*

Snug/स्नग *(adj)* – हल्का गरम और आरामदेह warm and confortable. *Adjust the safety belt to give a snugfit.*

Snuggle/स्नग्ल *(verb)* – छाती से चिपकाकर सोना settle into a warm, comfortable position. *The puppies snuggled together to keep warm.*

So/सो *(adverb & conj.)* – ऐसा, इतना, अत:, इसालिए variant spelling of soh. *She thanked me so much.*

Soak/सोक *(verb)* – तरबतर make or become thoroughly wet by immersion in liquid. *I soaked my clothes overnight.*

Soap/सोप *(noun)* – साबुन a substance used with water for washing and cleaning, made of a compound of natural oils or fats with sodium hydroxide or another strong alkali, and typically perfumed. *I ran to the market as I had run out of soap.*

Soar/सोर *(verb)* – मँडराना fly or rise high into the air. glide high in the air. *The eagle soared through the sky.*

Sob/सॉब *(verb)* – सिसकी, सिसकना, सिसकी लेना cry making loud, convulsive gasps. say while sobbing. *The little girl sobbed when she thought she was lost.* *(noun)* an act or sound of sobbing. *His sobs were heard by some men passing by.*

Sober/सोबर *(adjective)* – संयत, सन्तुलित not affected by alcohol; not drunk. *The drunk was sober today.*

Sobriety/सॉब्राइटि *(noun)* – संयत, गम्भीरता the state of being sober. *Everyone was curious about his sobriety.*

Soccer/सॉकर *(noun)* – गेंद का खेल a form of football played by two teams of eleven players with a round ball which may not be handled during play except by the goalkeepers, the object of the game being to score goals by kicking or heading the ball into the opponents goal. *The game of soccer was very exciting.*

Sociable/सोशएबल/सोशॅबॅल *(adj)* – सामाजिक, मिलनसार engaging readily with other people. marked by friendliness. *She is a sociable person.*

Social/सोशल *(adjective)* – सामाजिक of or relating to society or its organization. of or relating to rank and status in society: a woman of high social standing. *This is a social gathering.*

Socialism/सोशलिज्म *(noun)* – समाजबाद a political and economic theory of social organization which advocates that the means of production, distribution, and exchange should be owned or regulated by the community as a whole. a transitional social state between the overthrow of capitalism and the realization of communism. *He believed in socialism.*

Society/सोसाइटी *(noun)* – समाज, समिति, संगठन the aggregate of people living together in a more or less ordered community. a particular community of people. who are fashionable. wealthy, and influential, regarded as forming a distinct group. *They were very protective about their society.*

Sociology/सोशिऑलजि *(noun)* – समाजशास्त्र the study of the development, structure, and functioning of human society. the study of social problems. *He took up sociology in college.*

Sock/सॉक *(noun)* – मोजा a knitted garment for the foot and lower part of the leg. *The sock was torn.*

Socket/सॉकेट *(noun)* – छिद्रदार विद्युत उपकरण a hollow in which something fits or revolves. the part of the head of a golf club into which the shaft is fitted. *The socket was too tight for the shaft.*

Soda/सोडा *(noun)* – क्षार carbonated water. chiefly [north American] a sweet carbonated drink. *I want to have a soda with my pizza.*

Sofa/सोफा *(noun)* – आराम कुर्सी a long upholstered seat with a back and arms, for two or more people. *She sat on the sofa.*

Soften/सॉफ्टेन *(verb)* – नरम बनाना make or become soft or softer. *My mom softened the dough.*

S

Software/सॉफ्टवेअर *(noun)* – जिसे उपकरण पर देखा जाना जाए programmes and other operating information used by a computer. compare with hardware. *Software are usually very expensive.*

Softy/सॉफ्टी *(noun)* – नरम, कमजोर variant spelling of softie. *I want to eat a softy after dinner.*

Soggy/सॉगी *(adjective)* – गीला, दलदली very wet and soft. *The bread was soggy.*

Soil/सॉइल *(noun)* – मिट्टी the upper layer of earth in which plants grow, a black or dark brown material typically consisting of organic remains, clay, and rock particles. *The soil was very fertile.*

Sojourn/सॅजर्न *(noun)* – अस्थायी निवास a temporary stay. verb stay temporarily. *I loved my little sojourn to the hills.*

Solace/सॅलेस् *(noun)* – सान्त्वना comfort or consolation in time of distress. *Her solace really helped me in my grief.*

Solar/सोलर *(adjective)* – सौर, सूर्य से सम्बन्धित of, relating to, or determined by the sun or its rays. *Solar energy is green energy.*

Solder/सोल्डर *(noun)* – टाँका लगाना a low-melting alloy, especially one based on lead and tin, used for joining less fusible metals. *The electrician forgot to bring the solder with himself.* *(verb)* join with solder. *The electrician soldered two ends of the wire together.*

Soldier/सोल्जर *(noun)* – सिपाही a person who serves in an army. *The soldier was very brave.*

Sole/सोल *(noun)* – तलुआ, तल्ला, एक मछली, अकेला the underside of a person's foot. the section forming the underside of a piece of footwear. the underside of a tool or implement, e.g. a plane or the head of a golf club. *His soles hurt after the long run.*

Solemn/सॉलेम *(adjective)* – सौम्य, गम्भीर formal and dignified: a solemn procession. *The funeral was a solemn procession.*

Solemnity/सॉलेम्निटी *(noun)* – सौम्यता, गम्भीरता the state of quality of being solemn. *Her solemnity was noticed by everyone.*

Solemnize/सॉलेम्नाइज *(verb)* – विधिवत संस्कार करना duly perform a ceremony, especially that of marriage. mark with a formal ceremony. *Their marriage was solemnized in a church.*

Solicit/सॉलिसिट *(verb)* – माँगना ask for or try to obtain from someone ask for something from. *I solicited his advice.*

Solicitor/सॉलिसिटर *(noun)* – वकील a member of the legal profession qualified to deal with conveyance and draw up wills, advise clients and instruct barristers, and represent clients in lower courts. compare with barrister. [north American] the chief law officer of a city, town, or government department. *They called a solicitor for advice.*

Solicitous/सॉलिसिटस *(adjective)* – उत्कंठित showing interest or concern. [archaic] eager or anxious to do something. *She was very solicitous about his situation.*

Solicitude/सॉलिसिट्यूड *(noun)*– उत्कण्ठा, उत्सुकता care or concern. *His solicitude was very evident.*

Solid/सॉलिड *(noun)* – ठोस, पक्का, पुष्ट firm and stable in shape: solid fuel. strongly built or made. *He had a solid body.*

Solidarity/सॉलिडैरिटि *(noun)* – एकात्मकता unity or agreement of feeling or action, especially among individuals with a common interest. *Their solidarity was quite evident.*

Solidify/सॉलिडिफाइ *(verb)* – ठोस करना, पक्का करना make or become hard or solid. *The liquid solidified under certain conditions.*

Soliloquy/सॉलिलॅक्विे *(noun)* – स्वगत भाषण an act of speaking one's thoughts aloud when alone or regardless of hearers, especially by a character in a play. *The soliloquy was very touching.*

Solitary/सॉलिटरि *(adjective)* – अकेला, सुनसान done or existing alone. not social or colonial. *She was a solitary person.*

Solitude/सॉलिट्यूड *(noun)* – एकान्त, अकेलापन the state of being alone. a lonely or uninhabited place. *He loved his solitude.*

Solo/सोलो *(noun)* – एकल, संगीत-रचना a piece of music, song, or dance for one performer. *His solo was touching.*

S

Soluble/सॉल्युब्ल *(adjective)* – घुलनशील able to be dissolved, especially in water. *The substance was soluble.*

Solution/सॉल्यूशन *(noun)* – हल, समाधान निकालना a means of solving a problem. the correct answer to a puzzle. *Can you tell me the solution to this problem?*

Solve/सॉल्व *(verb)* – हल करना, समाधान निकालना find an answer to, explanation for, or way of dealing with a problem or mystery. *I was able to solve the puzzle.*

Sombre/सॉम्बर *(adjective)* – धुँधला, निराशाजनक dark or dull. *The movie was very sombre.*

Some/सम् *(adj & pron. & adv.)* – कुछ, थोड़ा an unspecified amount or number of. *Some people were talking.*

Somebody/सम्बॉडि *(pronoun)* – कोई व्यक्ति, एक आदमी someone. *Somebody needs to do this work.*

Someday/सम्डे *(adverb)* – एक दिन, किसी दिन in some way. for an unknown or unspecified reason. *I will do this someday.*

Somehow/सम्हाउ *(adverb)* – किसी तरह in some way. for an unknown or unspecified reason. *I will complete this somehow.*

Somersault/समरसाल्ट *(noun)* – हवा में कलैया खाना, कलाबाजी an acrobatic movement in which a person turns head over heels in the air or on the ground and finishes on their feet. *The somersault was perfect.*

Something/सम्थिंग *(pronoun)* – कुछ an unspecified or unknown thing. *Something is moving upstairs.*

Sometime/सम्टाइम *(adverb)* – कभी at some unspecified or unknown time. [archaic] formerly. *I will do this sometime.*

Somewhat/सम्ह्वाट *(adverb)* – कुछ–कुछ, किसी तरह to some extent. *I find this somewhat disturbing.*

Somewhere/सम्ह्वेअर *(adverb)* – कहीं in or to some place. *I am going somewhere.*

Somnolent/सॉम्नॅलेन्ट *(adjective)* – निद्रा लाने वाला, नींद से भरा sleepy; drowsy. inducing drowsiness. *I was somnolent after the sleepless night.*

Son/सन *(noun)* – पुत्र a boy or man in relation to his parents. a male descendant. a man regarded as the product of a particular influence or environment. *They are very proud of their son.*

Sonata/सॅनाटा *(noun)* – एक प्रकार का संगीत a classical composition for an instrumental soloist, often with a piano accompaniment. *The audience enjoyed the sonata.*

Song/सांग *(noun)* – गीत, गाना a short poem or other set of words set to music. singing or vocal music. a musical composition suggestive of a song. *The song was very beautifully composed.*

Sonic/सोनिक *(adjective)* – ध्वनि सम्बन्धी relating to or using sound waves. *The sonic waves carried the sound far.*

Son-in-law/सन इन लॉ *(noun)* – दामाद the husband of one's daughter. *She invited her daughter and son-in-law for dinner.*

Sonnet/सॉनेट *(noun)* – कविता का प्रकार a poem of fourteen lines using any of a number of formal rhyme schemes, in English typically having ten syllables per line. *The sonnets were beautifully written.*

Soon/सून *(adverb)* – तत्क्षण, तत्काल, तुरन्त in or after a short time. early. *I will work on this soon.*

Soot/सूट *(noun)* – कालिख a black powdery or flaky substance consisting largely of amorphous carbon, produced by the incomplete burning of organic matter. *The young boy was covered with soot.*

Soothe/सूद *(verb)* – शान्त करना, शमन करना gently calm. reduce pain or discomfort, in. relieve pain. *His mom's hand on his head soothed his headache.*

Sooty/सूटि *(adjective)* – कालिख से भरा covered with or coloured like soot. *The sooty chimney needed to be cleaned.*

Sop/सॉप *(noun)* – घूस, मँहगाई a thing given or done to appease or bribe someone. *It was a sop for the cop.*

Sophisticated/सफिस्टिकेटेड *(adj)* – परिष्कृत, जटिल highly complex. aware of and able to interpret complex issues. *It was a sophisticated piece of machinery.*

S

Soppy/सॉपी *(adjective)* – अतिभावुक self-indulgently sentimental. *Her soppy behaviour often irritated her friends.*

Soprano/सॅप्रानो *(noun)* – पंचम सुर the highest singing voice. a singer with such a voice. *The soprano's voice was very soothing.*

Sorcerer/सोर्सरर् *(noun)* – जादूगर, जादू-टोना करने वाला a person believed to have magic powers. *Everyone thought that he was a sorcerer.*

Sordid/सॉर्डिड *(adjective)* – फटेहाल, गन्दा involving ignoble actions and motives. *It was a sordid affair.*

Sore/सोर *(adjective)* – दुखने वाला, दर्दीला, क्रोधित painful or aching. suffering pain. *I have a sore throat.*

Sorrow/सॉरो *(noun)* – व्यथा, उदासी a feeling of deep distress caused by loss or disappointment. a cause of sorrow. the outward expression of grief. *His sorrow was written all over his face.*

Sorry/सॉरि *(adjective)* – शोकाकुल, खिन्न, उदास, दु:खद feeling distress, especially through sympathy with someone else's misfortune. filled with compassion for. *I was sorry for her.*

Sort/सार्ट *(noun & verb)* – वर्ग, विशेष प्रकार, छाँटना a category of people or things with a common feature. [informal] a person with a specified nature. *He is the sort of person who plays to win.*

SOS/एसओएस *(noun)* – संकट सन्देश an international coded signal of extreme distress, used especially by ships at sea. an urgent appeal for help. [British] a message broadcast to an untraceable person in an emergency. *The ship sent out an SOS.*

Soul/सोल *(noun)* – आत्मा the spiritual or immaterial part of a human, regarded as immortal. one's moral or emotional nature or sense of identity. emotional or intellectual energy or intensity. *The solitude appealed to my soul.*

Soulful/सोल्फुल *(adjective)* – भावपूर्ण expressing deep and typically sorrowful feeling. *His soulful voice mesmerized the audience.*

Sound/साउन्ड *(noun)* – ध्वनि, स्वस्थ, ध्वनि उत्पन्न करना a narrow stretch of water forming an inlet or connecting two larger bodies of water. *I love visiting the sound when I want to be alone.*

Soundproof/साउन्डप्रूफ *(adjective)* – ध्वनि निरोधक preventing the passage of sound. *The room is soundproof.*

Soup/सूप *(noun)* – शोरबा, झोल a savoury liquid dish made by boiling meat, fish, or vegetables in stock or water. *The soup was very tasty.*

Sour/सावर *(adjective)* – खट्टा having an acid taste like lemon or vinegar. *The sour orange was very difficult to eat.*

Source/सोर्स *(noun)* – उद्गम, स्रोत a place, person, or thing from which something originates. a spring or fountain head from which a river or stream issues. *He was a source of inspiration for many youngsters.*

South/साउथ *(noun)* – दक्षिण the direction towards the point of the horizon 90 degree clockwise from east. *There is a park towards the south.*

Southwards/साउथवर्ड्स *(adverb)* – दक्षिण की ओर towards the south. *The train was southwards bound.* *(noun)* the direction or region to the south. *The colony stood southwards to the park.*

Southern/साउदर्न *(adjective)* – दक्षिणी situated in the south or directed towards south. *The southern hemisphere has more water.*

Souvenir/सूवनिर् *(noun)* – स्मारिका a thing that is kept as a reminder of a person, place, or event. *She kept the ticket as a souvenir.*

Sovereign/सॉव्रेन *(noun)* – सम्प्रभुता, प्रभुसत्ता, सत्तासम्पन्न a supreme, ruler, especially a monarch. *He was a well-loved sovereign.*

Sow/सो *(verb)* – बीज बोना to plant seeds in the ground. *They sowed tomato seeds.*

Spa/स्पा *(noun)* – खनिज जल वाला झरना a mineral spring considered to have health giving properties. a place or resort with such a spring. a commercial establishment offering health and beauty treatment. *I would love to visit a spa.*

Space/स्पेस *(noun)* – जगह, स्थान, अन्तरिक्ष, आकाश a continuous area or expanse which is free or unoccupied. a gap between printed

S

or written words or characters. pages in a newspaper, or time between broadcast programmes, available for advertising. the freedom and scope to live and develop as one wishes. one of two possible states of a signal on certain systems. the opposite of mark. *The space was empty for a long time.*

Spacecraft/स्पेसक्राप्ट *(noun)* – अन्तरिक्ष यान a vehicle used for travelling in space. *The spacecraft started its journey today.*

Spaceman/स्पेसमैन *(noun)* – अन्तरिक्ष यात्री a male astronaut. *The spaceman described his adventures.*

Spacious/स्पेशस *(adjective)* – लम्बा-चौड़ा having plenty of space. *They had a spacious house.*

Spade/स्पेड *(noun)* – कुदाल, फावड़ा a tool with a sharp edged, rectangular metal blade and a long handle, used for digging. *The spade was broken.*

Spadework/स्पेडवर्क *(noun)* – श्रमसाध्य कार्य hard o routine preparatory work. *Do some spadework before the presentation.*

Spaghetti/स्पेगेटि *(plural noun)* – एक पश्चिमी भोजन pasta made in solid strings, between macaroni and vermicelli in thickness. *I love spaghetti.*

Span/स्पैन *(noun)* – बीता, अवधि, दूरी, आर-पार a rope with its ends fastened at different points in order to provide a purchase. *The span was broken.*

Spank/स्पैंक *(verb)* – थप्पड़ मारना, थप्पड़ slap with one's open hand or a flat object, especially on the buttocks as a punishment. *His mother spanked him.* (noun) a slap or series of slaps of this type. *He still remembered the spanking.*

Spanner/स्पैनर *(noun)* – एक उपकरण a tool with a shaped opening or jaws for gripping and turning a nut or bolt. *The spanner was missing from his toolkit.*

Spare/स्पेअर *(adjective)* – अतिरिक्त, खाली additional to what is required for ordinary use. not currently in use or occupied. *The spare tyre was flat.*

Spark/स्पार्क *(noun)* – चिंगारी a lively person. *He was the spark of the party.* (verb) engage in courtship. *They sparked together.*

Sparkle/स्पार्कल *(verb)* – झिलमिलाना, चिंगारी फेंकना shine brightly with flashes of light. *The stage sparkled.*

Sparrow/स्पैरो *(noun)* – गौरैया a small, typically brown and grey finch like bird related to the weaver birds. used in names of many other birds which resemble this, especially American birds of the bunting family, e.g. java sparrow, song sparrow. *Sparrows chirped outside my house.*

Sparse/स्पार्स *(adjective)* – छितराया हुआ, बिखरा हुआ thinly dispersed. *He had sparse hair on his head.*

Spartan/स्पार्टन *(noun)* – सादा और कठोर a Canadian apple dessert of a variety with crisp white flesh and maroon flushed yellow skin. *I ate a Spartan after lunch.*

Spasm/स्पैज्म *(noun)* – मरोड़, ऐंठन, दौरा a sudden involuntary muscular contraction or convulsive movement. *His body went into spasms during the fit.*

Spate/स्पेट *(noun)* – बाढ़, अचानक वृद्धि a large number of similar things or events coming in quick succession. *Children were overwhelmed with a spate of tests.*

Spatial/स्पेशल् *(adjective)* – स्थानिक of or relating to space. *I find the spatial discussions very interesting.*

Spatter/स्पैटर *(verb)* – छिड़कन cover with drops or spots. splash or be splashed over a surface. *The child spattered the table with milk.*

Spawn/स्पॉन *(verb)* – अण्डे देना, मछली के अण्डे release or deposit eggs. produce off spring. *The frog spawned in the pond.*

Speak/स्पीक् *(verb)* – बोलना say something. make a speech. communicate in or be able to communicate in a specified language. express the views or position of. express one's opinions frankly and publicly. speak more loudly. hail and hold communication with at sea. *I was glad I heard him speak.*

Spear/स्पिअर *(noun)* – भाला, बरछी a metal weapon with a pointed tip and a long shaft, used for thrusting or throwing. *The ancient spear was very valuable*

S

Spearhead/स्पिअरहेड *(noun)* – अभियान का नेतृत्व the point of a spear. *Archaeologists found several spearheads on the site of the ancient battle.*

Special/स्पेशल *(adjective)* – विशिष्ट, असाधारण better, greater, or otherwise different from what is usual. *The special occasion deserves to be celebrated.*

Speciality/स्पेशिअल्टि *(noun)* – विशेषता, कौशल a pursuit, area of study, or skill to which someone has devoted themselves and in which they are expert. a product for which a person or region is famous. *Chicken curry was the chef's speciality.*

Specialize/स्पेशलाइज *(verb)* – विशेषज्ञता प्राप्ता करना concentrate on and become expert in a particular skill or area. make a habit of engaging in. adapt or set apart to serve a special function. *I specialize in growing flowering plants.*

Species/स्पीशीज् *(noun)* – जाति, किस्म a group of living organisms consisting of similar individuals capable of exchanging genes or interbreeding, considered as the basic unit of taxonomy and denoted by a Latin binomial, e.g. homo sapiens. *New species are being discovered every day.*

Specific/स्पेसिफिक *(adjective)* – निश्चित, निर्दिष्ट, निर्धारित clearly defined or identified. precise and clear: when ordering goods be specific. of or relating uniquely to a particular subject. *Her instructions were quite specific.*

Specification/स्पेसिफिकेशन *(noun)* – विस्तृत सूचना the action of specifying. a detailed description of the design and materials used to make something. a description of an invention accompanying an application for a patent. *I have brought the specifications of design for the meeting.*

Specify/स्पेसिफाइ *(verb)* – निश्चित उल्लेख, विस्तृत उल्लेख identify clearly and definitely. *They specified their choice of the dish clearly.*

Specimen/स्पेसिमेन *(noun)* – नमूना an individual animal, plant, object, etc. used as an example of its species or type for scientific study or display. an example of something regarded as typical of its class or group: a specimen signature. used to refer humorously to a person or animal. *He is a fine specimen of human species.*

Speck/स्पेक *(noun)* – धूल कण a tiny spot. a small particle. *Don't worry it is just a speck.* *(verb)* mark with small spots. *The child specked the wall with paint.*

Spectacle/स्पेक्टकल *(noun)* – दर्शनीय दृश्य, भव्य, तमाशा a visually striking performance or display. *The ballet was a spectacle.*

Spectacles/स्पेक्टकल्स *(plural noun)* – चश्मा, ऐनक [British] a pair of glasses. *The spectacles suited him very well.*

Spectacular/स्पक्टैक्युलर *(adjective)* – शानदार very impressive, striking, or dramatic. *The spectacular firework show is about to begin.*

Spectator/स्पेक्टेटर *(noun)* – दर्शक a person who watches at a show, game, or other event. *The spectators applauded his performance.*

Spectre/स्पेक्टर *(noun)* – भूत, पिशाच (बेताल) an apparition, a ghost. *The spectre floated around in the old building.*

Spectrum/स्पेक्ट्रम *(noun)* – कार्यक्रम, रंगक्रम, रंग-पट्टी a band of colours produced by separation of the components of light by their different degrees of refraction according to wavelength, e.g. in a rainbow. the entire range of wavelengths of electromagnetic radiation. a characteristic series of frequencies of electromagnetic radiation emitted or absorbed by a substance. the components of a sound or other phenomenon arranged according to frequency, energy, etc. *The whole spectrum of colours was visible in the rainbow.*

Speculate/स्पेक्युलेट *(verb)* – अन्दाजा करना, सट्टा लगाना from a theory or conjecture without firm evidence. *The team was speculating the change.*

Speculation/स्पेक्युलेशन *(noun)* – अन्दाज, अटकलबाजी, सट्टेबाजी theory or conjecture without firm evidence. *His speculation proved to be accurate.*

Speech/स्पीच *(noun)* – वाणी, भाषण the expression of or the ability to express thoughts and feelings by articulate sounds. *The child developed speech very early.*

S

Speechless/स्पीचलेस *(adjective)* – अवाक रह जाना, बोल न पाना unable to speak, especially as the temporary result of shock or strong emotion. *The teacher's response left me speechless.*

Speed/स्पीड *(noun)* – गति, चाल, रफ्तार the rate at which someone or something moves or operates or is able to move or operate. rapidity of movement or action. *They were moving at a high speed.*

Speedy/स्पीडि *(adjective)* – द्रुतगामी, शीघ्र done or occurring quickly. *That was a speedy recovery.*

Spell/स्पेल *(noun)* – छोटी समयावधि, दौर a short period of time. a period of rest from work. *There was a short spell of silence.*

Spellbound/स्पेलबाउंड *(verb)* – मन्त्रमुग्ध, मोहित hold the complete attention as if by magic. *The little girl left the crowd spellbound with her poetry.*

Spend/स्पेंड *(verb)* – खर्च करना pay out in buying or hiring goods or services. *He spends a lot of money in buying clothes.*

Spendthrift/स्पेंडथ्रिफ्ट *(noun)* – फिजूलखर्च a person who spends money in an extravagant, irresponsible way. *She was a spendthrift.*

Spew/स्पिउ *(verb)* – तेज प्रवाह से बहना या प्रवाहित करना expel or be expelled in large quantities rapidly and forcibly. *The volcano spewed ash.*

Sphere/स्फिअर *(noun)* – क्षेत्र, कार्यक्षेत्र, गोल a round solid figure, with every point on its surface equidistant from its centre. *The sphere of light became bigger by the day.*

Spherical/स्फेरिकल *(adjective)* – गोलीय, गोलाकार shaped like a sphere. of or relating to the properties of spheres. formed inside or on the surface of a sphere. *The scientists discovered a spherical asteroid heading towards the comet.*

Sphinx/स्फिंक्स *(noun)* – सिंह के धड़ की मानव मूर्ति an ancient Egyptian stone figure having a lion's body and a human or animal head. *The Sphinx is located near the pyramids.*

Spice/स्पाइस *(noun & verb)* – मसाला, उत्तेजना, छौंकना an aromatic or pungent vegetable substance used to flavor food, e.g. pepper. *The dish had all the spices in the correct proportion.*

Spider/स्पाइडर *(noun)* – मकड़ा an eight legged predatory arachnid with an unsegmented body consisting of a fused head and thorax and a rounded abdomen, most kinds of which spin webs in which to capture insects. used in names of other arachnids, e.g. sea spider. *I am afraid of spiders.*

Spike/स्पाइक *(noun)* – नोक, नुकिला भाग botany a flower cluster formed of many flower heads attached directly to a long stem. *The colourful spikes made the garden beautiful.*

Spill/स्पिल *(noun & verb)* – छलकना, जलाने का टुकड़ा a thin strip of wood or paper used for lighting a fire, pipe, etc. *The campers used a spill to light a fire.*

Spin/स्पिन *(verb)* – चक्कर खाना, चक्कर खिलाना turn or cause to turn round quickly. give a sensation of dizziness. move or cause to move through the air with a revolving motion. shape by pressure applied during rotation on a lathe. *All planets spin on their axes.*

Spinach/स्पिनैक् *(noun)* – पालक an edible Asian plant of the goosefoot family, with large dark green leaves which are eaten as a vegetable. *Spinach is good for health.*

Spinal/स्पाइनल *(adjective)* – रीढ़ सम्बन्धी of or relating to the spine. *Her spinal injury took a long time to heal.*

Spine/स्पाइन *(noun)* – रीढ़ की हड्डी a series of vertebrae extending from the skull to the small of the back, enclosing the spinal cord and providing support for the thorax and abdomen; the backbone. *It is important to sit with your spine in the correct position.*

Spinster/स्पिन्स्टर *(noun)* – अविवाहित महिला an unmarried woman, typically an older woman beyond the usual age for marriage. *The spinster didn't want to get married.*

Spiral/स्पाइरल *(adjective)* – घुमावदार, कुण्डलीनुमा winding in a continuous and gradually widening curve around a central point or axis. winding in a continuous curve of constant diameter about a central axis, as though along

S

a cylinder; helical. denoting galaxies in which the stars and gas clouds are concentrated mainly in spiral arms. *The spiral staircase was very risky.*

Spire/स्पार *(noun)* – मीनार zoology the upper tapering part of the spiral shell of a gastropod mollusc. *The snail had a beautiful spire.*

Spirit/स्पिरिट *(noun)* – आत्मा, चित्र, प्रेतात्मा, भूत, उत्साह the non physical part of a person which is the seat of emotions and character. this regarded as surviving after the death of the body, often manifested as a ghost. a supernatural being. *People say his spirit still haunts the building.*

Spiritual/स्पिरिचुअल *(adjective)* – आध्यात्मिक of, relating to, or affecting the human spirit as opposed to material or physical things. *My sister enjoys spiritual discussions.*

Spit/स्पिट *(noun & verb)* – थूक, पीक, थूकना, मांस भूनने का सीकंचा a long, thin metal rod pushed through meat in order to hold and turn it while it is roasted over an open fire. *The spit was too hot to touch.*

Spite/स्पाइट *(noun)* – दोष, दुर्भावना a desire to hurt, annoy, or offend. *She let go of her spite against her opponent.*

Spiteful/स्पाइटफुल *(adjective)* – द्वेषी showing or caused by malice. *She is very spiteful.*

Splash/स्प्लैश *(verb)* – छपाका, छपछपाना, छींटा, धब्बा make strike or fall on something in drops. strike or move around in water, causing it to fly about. land on water. *Children splashed around in water.*

Splashdown/स्प्लैशडाउन *(noun)* – समूह में उतरना alighting of a returning spacecraft on the sea. *The splashdown was successful and the crew were all fine.*

Splatter/स्प्लैटर *(verb)* – छिड़कना, उछालना splash with a sticky or viscous liquid. splash. *The child splattered the glue over the sheet.*

Splay/स्प्ले *(verb)* – फैलाना spread or be spread out or further apart. *They splayed the dummy's arms.*

Spleen/स्प्लीन *(noun)* – प्लीहा, तिल्ली an abdominal organ involved in the production and removal of blood cells and forming part of the immune system. *I had a pain in my spleen.*

Splendid/स्प्लेन्डिड *(adjective)* – भव्य, शानदार magnificent; very impressive. *The valley was a splendid sight.*

Splendour/स्प्लेंडर *(noun)* – भव्य, शानदार, वैभवपूर्ण splendid appearance. *The audience were blinded by all the splendour.*

Splice/स्प्लाइस *(verb)* – टुकड़े जोड़ना join by interweaving the strands at the ends. join at the ends. join or insert. *The sailors spliced the rope ends.*

Splint/स्प्लिंट *(noun)* – खपची a strip of rigid material for supporting a broken bone when it has been set. *He had to get a splint for his broken arm.*

Splinter/स्प्लिन्टर *(noun)* – लकड़ी, धातु या कांच के छोटे नुकीले टुकड़े a small, thin, sharp piece of wood, glass, etc. broken off from a larger piece. *A splinter pierced my skin.* (verb) break or cause to break into splinters. *The blow splintered the log of wood.*

Split/स्प्लिट *(verb)* – विभाजित, विभाजन करना, चीरना, पकड़ना break or cause to break forcibly into parts. cause the fission of. *The cell split into two.*

Spoil/स्पॉइल *(verb)* – बिगाड़ना, खराब करना, बेकार करना to change something good into something bad. *Our holiday was spoilt by bad weather.*

Sprit – *(noun)* a small spar reaching diagonally from a mast to the upper outer carner of the sail. *The sprit broke in the rough weather.*

Spoke/स्पोक *(noun)* – पहिए की तीली या आरा each of the bars or wire rods connecting the centre of a wheel to its rim. *The spokes of the wheel were broken.*

Spokesman/स्पोक्समैन *(noun)* – प्रवक्ता a person who makes statements on behalf of a group. *He was born to be a spokesman.*

Sponge/स्पंज *(noun)* – समुद्री जीव, सोखना, छिद्रदार a sedentary aquatic invertebrate with a soft porous body supported by a framework of fibres or sickles. *The wreck was covered with sponges.*

S

Spongy/स्पंजी *(adjective)* – छिद्रदार, रसीला like a sponge, especially in being porous, compressible, or absorbent. *The creature had a spongy feel to it.*

Sponsor/स्पॉन्सर *(noun)* – प्रायोजक, प्रवर्तक, खर्चवाहक a person or organization that pays for or contributes to the costs of a sporting or artistic event or a radio or television programme in return for advertising. *The sponsors wanted their product to be featured at a prominent place.*

Spontaneous/स्पॉन्टेनिअस *(adjective)* – स्वत:, अनियोजित सहज performed or occurring as a result of an unpremeditated inner impulse and without external stimulus. occurring without apparent external cause. instinctive or involuntary. *His spontaneous help was well appreciated.*

Spooky/स्पूकि *(adjective)* – डरावना sinister or ghostly. *The spooky mansion has always been an attraction for the children.*

Spoon/स्पून *(noun)* – चम्मच, चमचा an implement consisting of a small, shallow oval or round bowl on a long handle, used for eating, stirring, and serving food. a pair of spoons held in the hand and beaten together rhythmically as a percussion instrument. *The man used a spoon to eat rice.*

Spoonful/स्पूनफुल *(noun)* – चम्मचभर the contents in a spoon. *The child ate only a spoonful of rice.*

Sporadic/स्परैडिक *(adjective)* – कभी-कभार, कहीं-कहीं occurring at irregular intervals or only in a few places. *The city was under curfew because of reports of sporadic violence.*

Sport/स्पोर्ट *(noun)* – खेल, जी बहलाना, उदारता दिखाना an activity involving physical exertion and skill in which an individual or team competes against another or others for entertainment. success or pleasure derived from an activity such as hunting. *I love sports.*

Sportsmen/स्पोर्ट्समैन *(noun)* – खिलाड़ी men who take part in a sport, especially as a professional. *The sportsmen gathered to discuss the improvements in the stadium.*

Sporty/स्पोर्टि *(adjective)*– आकर्षक, खेल-कूद में रुचि रखने वाला fond of or good at sport. *The athlete was sporty even when he was a child.*

Spot/स्पॉट *(noun)* – चित्ती, किसी सतह पर छोटा गोल निशान a small round mark on a surface. *The spots on one cheetah were darker than the spots on the others.*

Spotless/स्पॉटलेस *(adjective)* – बेदाग, दागहीन absolutely clean or pure. *His spotless white shirt was visible amongst the crowd.*

Spotlight/स्पॉटलाइट *(noun)* – केन्द्रित प्रकाश a lamp projecting a narrow, intense beam of light directly on to a place or person. *She couldn't believe it when the spotlight fell on her.*

Spouse/स्पाउज *(noun)* – पति या पत्नी a husband or wife. *He introduced his spouse in the party.*

Spout/स्पाउट *(noun)* – चायदानी आदि की नली या टोंटी a projecting tube or lip through or over which liquid can be poured from a container. *The spout of the kettle was dirty.*

Sprain/स्प्रेन *(verb)* – मोच, मोच आना wrench the ligaments of violently so as to cause pain and swelling but not dislocation. *I sprained my arm.* *(noun)* the result of such a wrench. *The sprain in my arm was very painful.*

Sprawl/स्प्रॉल *(verb)* – पसर कर बैठना sit, lie, or fall with one's limbs spread out in an ungainly way. *My father scolded me when he found my friends sprawled all over the drawing room.*

Spray/स्प्रे *(noun)* – फुहारा सा छिड़काव, फुहारा देना a stem or small branch of a tree or plant, bearing flowers and foliage. *The sprays were weighed down by the flowers.*

Spread/स्प्रेड *(verb)* – हाथ-पैर फैलाकर बैठना या लेटना open out so as to increase in surface area, width, or length. stretch out so that they are far apart. *The spilt milk spread out all over the floor.*

Spree/स्प्री *(noun & verb)* – रंगरलिया (मनाना) a spell of unrestrained activity of a particular kind. *I went on a shopping spree after receiving my salary.* *(verb)* dated take part in a spree. *I spreed with rest of the participants.*

S

Sprightly/स्प्राइटलि *(adjective)* – प्रसन्नचित्त, जिन्दादिल lively; energetic. *She is a sprightly young girl.*

Spring/स्प्रिंग *(verb)* – कमानी, झरना, लोच, बसंत, उछलना move suddenly or rapidly upwards or forwards. cause to rise from cover. *The cat sprung forwards on the mouse.*

Springy/स्प्रिंगि *(adjective)* – लचीला springing back quickly when squeezed or stretched. *The springy couch was very comfortable to sit on.*

Sprinkle/स्प्रिंकल *(verb)* – छिटकाव, छिड़कना scatter or pour small drops or particles over. scatter or pour over an throughout. *I sprinkled salt over my salad.*

Sprint/स्प्रिंट *(verb)* – तेज दौड़ run at full speed over a short distance. (noun) an act or spell of sprinting. a short, fast race run over a distance of 400 metres of less. a short, fast race in cycling, horse racing, etc. *He sprinted through the market to catch the rickshaw.*

Sprout/स्प्राउट *(verb)* – अंकुरित होना, अँखुआना produce shoots. grow plant shoots or hair. start to grow or develop. *My tamarind plant sprouted branches.*

Spruce/स्प्रूस *(verb)* – साफ-सुथरा produce shoots. grow start to grow or develop.

Spur/स्पर *(noun)* – घुड़सवार का एँड़ (काँटा) उत्प्रेरक, प्रेरणा, प्रेरणा स्रोत a device with a small spike or a spiked wheel, worn on a rider's heel or urging a horse forward. *The rider fell down from the horse and broke the spur.*

Spurious/स्पुरिअस *(adjective)* – जाली, नकली false or fake. *The text claimed to be ancient was of spurious origin.*

Spurn/स्पर्न *(verb)* – तिरस्कार करना, ठुकराना reject with contempt. *She spurned his attention.*

Spurt/स्पर्ट *(verb)* – अचानक फूटना, फुहारा छोड़ना gush out suddenly in a forceful way. *The water gushed forwards in a spurt.*

Spy/स्पाइ *(noun)* – भेदिया, गुप्तचर, जासूस a person employed to secretly gather information about someone or something. *The spy kept an eye on the suspect.*

Squabble/स्क्वाब्ल *(noun)* – तू-तू मैं-मैं a trivial noisy quarrel. *The noise of their squabble disturbed the neighbours.* (verb) engage in a squabble. *They squabbled frequently.*

Squad/स्क्वॉड् *(noun)* – दल, दस्ता, टुकड़ी a small number of soldiers assembled for drill or assigned to a particular task. *The squad worked together as a good team.*

Squadron/स्क्वाड्रन *(noun)* – दल, दस्ता an operational unit in an air force consisting of two or more flights of aircraft. *The squadron performed a spectacular stunt.*

Squalid/स्क्वालिड *(adjective)* – गन्दा, घिनौना extremely dirty and unpleasant. *The squalid shop hardly ever got any customers.*

Squall/स्क्वाल *(noun)* – वायु का झोंका, बर्फीली आँधी a sudden violent gust of wind or localized storm, especially one bringing rain, snow, or sleet. *The squall lasted only for about half an hour.*

Squalor/स्क्वालर *(noun)* – गन्दगी the state of being squalid. *I am tired of your squalor.*

Squander/स्क्वान्डर *(verb)* – अपव्यय करना waste in a reckless or foolish manner. *He squandered his father's money.*

Square/स्क्वेअर *(noun)* – वर्ग, वर्गाकार, ईमानदार, सन्तोषप्रद, सीधा a plane figure with four equal straight sides and four right angles. *The child drew a square on the paper.*

Squash/स्क्वैश *(noun)* – कुचलना, एक शरबत, एक खेल a gourd with flesh that can be cooked and eaten as a vegetable. *I don't like squash much.*

Squat/स्क्वाट *(verb)* – उकड़ूँ, बैठना, कब्जा करना, ठिगना crouch or sit with the knees bent and the heels close to or touching the buttocks or thighs. *The homeless people squatted on the pavement.*

Squawk/स्क्वाक *(verb)* – पक्षी का कलख, बत्तख की आवाज make a loud, harsh noise. *The parrot squawked.*

Squeak/स्क्विक *(noun & verb)* – चूँ-चूँ, चूँ-चूँ करना, चरमराना a short, high-pitched sound or cry. a single remark or communication. *I didn't hear a squeak out of them.*

Squeal/स्क्विल *(noun & verb)* – किलकारी, किलकारी मारना a long, high-pitched cry or noise. *The squeal rang through the hall.*

Squeeze/स्क्विज *(verb)* – कसकर दबाने की क्रिया firmly press from opposite or all sides, typically with the fingers. extract from something by squeezing. *I squeezed the water out of the sponge.*

Squib/स्क्विब *(noun)* – फुलझड़ी, पलीता a small firework that hisses before exploding. *My nephew didn't find the squib exciting.*

Squid/स्क्विड *(noun)* – समुद्री जीव an elongated, fast swimming cephalopod mollusk with eight arms and two long tentacles. the flesh of this animal as food. an artificial fishing bait resembling a squid. *The squid swam away quickly.*

Squiggle/स्क्विगल *(noun)* – टेढ़ी-मेढ़ी रेखा a short line that curls and loops irregularly. She makes squiggles while talking on the phone. *(verb)* [chiefly north American] wriggle; squirm. squeeze from a tube so as to make squiggles on a surface. *The little girl squiggled on the paper.*

Squint/स्क्विंट *(verb)* – अधखुली आँखों से देखना, भेंगापन look at someone or something with party closed eyes. partly close. *He squinted in the sun.*

Squire/स्क्वायर *(noun)* – जमींदार a country gentleman, especially the chief landowner in an area. US [archaic] a title given to a magistrate, lawyer, or judge in some rural districts. *The squire walked with a lot of poise.*

Squirm/स्क्वर्म *(verb)* – ऐंठना, छटपटाना wriggle or twist the body from side to side, especially due to nervousness or discomfort. be embarrassed or ashamed. *The man squirmed in pain.* *(noun)* a wriggling movement. *The squirm proved that he was in a great pain.*

Squirrel/स्क्विरल् *(noun)* – गिलहरी an agile tree-dwelling rodent with a bushy tail, typically feeding on nuts and seeds. used in names of other rodents of the same family e.g. ground squirrel. *The squirrel was running up and down the tree.*

Squirt/स्क्वर्ट *(verb)* – पिचकारी मारना be or cause to be ejected in a thin jet from a small opening wet with a jet of liquid. *The water squirted out of the pipe suddenly.*

Stab/स्टैब *(verb)* – चाकू भोंकना, घोंपना, विश्वासघात करना thrust a knife or other pointed weapon into. *I stabbed the pumpkin with the knife.*

Stable/स्टेबल *(adj. & noun)* – स्थिर, हठ, स्थिर चित, अस्तबल not likely to give way or overturn; firmly fixed. *The scaffolding was very stable.*

Stability/स्टेबिलिटि *(noun)* – स्थिरता, दृढ़ता the state of being stable. *You can be sure of the programme's stability.*

Stack/स्टैक *(noun & verb)* – अंबार, एक के ऊपर एक सजा हुआ ढेर लगाना, चिमनी a pile, especially a neat one. *The clothes were all arranged in a stack.*

Stadium/स्टेडियम *(noun)* – खेल का घिरा मैदान an athletic or sports ground with tiers of seats for spectators. *The stadium was being prepared for the games.*

Staff/स्टाफ *(noun)* – कर्मचारी, सेना अधिकारी, डण्डा, लाठी a mixture of plaster of Paris, cement, etc. used for temporary building work. *The construction workers had run out of staff.*

Stag/स्टैग *(noun)* – हिरण a fully adult male deer. *The stag was a magnificent creature.*

Stage/स्टेज *(noun)* – मंच, रंगमंच, अवस्था, मंजिल, पड़ाव a point, period, or step in a process or development. a section of a journey or race. *We have reached the second stage in the building project.*

Stagger/स्टैगर *(verb)* – लड़खड़ाना, डगमगाना, धक्का पहुँचाना walk or move unsteadily, as if about to fall. [archaic] cause to stagger. *The drunk man staggered across the street.*

Stagnant/स्टैग्नन्ट *(adjective)* – ठहरा हुआ, गतिहीन motionless and often having an unpleasant smell as a consequence. showing little activity. *The stagnant water needed to be drained.*

Stagnate/स्टैग्नेट *(verb)* – ठहर जाना, उन्नति-अवरोध become stagnant. *The decisions have stagnated our growth in the company.*

Staid/स्टेड *(adjective)* – नीरस respectable and unadventurous. *The staid gentleman didn't have too many friends.*

S

Stain/स्टेन *(verb)* – धब्बा, दाग, दाग पड़ना, दाग लगाना mark or discolour with something that is not easily removed. *The turmeric stained my white dress.*

Stair/स्टेअर *(noun)* – सीढ़ी each of a set of fixed steps. a set of such steps leading from one floor of a building to another. *The child climbed down the stairs carefully.*

Staircase/स्टेअरकेस *(noun)* – सीढ़ियाँ, सीढ़ी a set of stairs and its surrounding structure. [British] a part of a large building containing a staircase. *The staircase was antique and beautifully ornate.*

Stake/स्टेक *(noun)* – खूँटा, खम्भा, दाँव, नियोजित धन a strong post with a point at one end, driven into the ground to support a tree, form part of a fence, etc. *I used a stake to support my tomato plant.*

Stale/स्टेल *(adjective)* – बासी, घिसा-पिटा no longer fresh or pleasant to eat. *The potatoes were stale.*

Stalemate/स्टेलमेट *(noun)* – गतिरोध, बराबर की बाज़ी chess a position counting as a draw, in which a player is not in check but can only move into check. *The experienced player soon placed the opponent in a stalemate.*

Stalk/स्टॉक *(noun & verb)* – डण्ठल, डण्डी, पीछा करना, अकड़ना the main stem of a herbaceous plant. the attachment or support of a leaf, flower, or fruit. *The stalk was still strong even though the plant had shed all its leaves.*

Stall/स्टॉल *(noun & verb)* – छोटी दुकान, टाल देना a stand, booth, or compartment for the sale of goods in a market. *The stall was selling some interesting bags.*

Stallion/स्टैलिअन् *(noun)* – वयस्क घोड़ा an uncastrated adult male horse. *The magnificent stallion trotted around the field.*

Stamina/स्टैमिना *(noun)* – दम-खम, शक्ति the ability to sustain prolonged physical or mental effort. *The athlete was asked to work on his stamina.*

Stammer/स्टैमर *(verb)* – हकलाना speak with sudden involuntary pauses and a tendency to repeat the initial letters of words. utter in such a way. *She stammered while addressing the public.* *(noun)* a tendency to stammer. *She went to the speech therapist to consult regarding her stammer.*

Stamp/स्टाम्प *(noun & verb)* – टिकट, पैर पटकना, पैर पटक कर चलना, छापना, मोहर लगाना, छल, दबाना bring down heavily on the ground or an object. crush, flatten, or remove with a heavy blow from one's foot. crush or pulverize. *The horse stamped the ground.*

Stampede/स्टैम्पीड *(noun & verb)* – भगदड़, भगदड़ मचाना a sudden panicked rush of a number of horses, cattle, etc. a sudden rapid movement or reaction of a mass of people due to interest or panic. *Several people were injured in the stampede.*

Stance/स्टैंस *(noun)* – मुद्रा, अंदाज, खड़े होने का तरीका the way in which someone stands, especially when deliberately adopted. *He copied my stance.*

Stand/स्टैंड *(verb)* – खड़ा होना, खड़ा रहना, खड़ा करना, खड़ा होने का निश्चित स्थान be in or rise to an upright position, supported by one's feet. move in this position to a specified place or be situated in a particular position. remain stationary. remain on a specified course. *They stand in the queue every day.*

Standard/स्टैन्डर्ड *(noun)* – स्तर, स्तरीय, औसत, मान्य, नियमित a level of quality or attainment. a required or agreed level of quality or attainment. [British historical] a grade of proficiency tested by examination. a class or year in a high school. *He met all the requirements demanded by a standard.*

Standardise/स्टैंडर्डाइज *(verb)* – मानक बनाना cause to conform to a standard. adopt as one's standard. determine the properties of by comparison with a standard. *The company standardized its processes.*

Standing/स्टैंडिंग *(noun)* – स्थिति, स्तर, स्थायी position, status, or reputation. *He has a standing in the community.*

Standpoint/स्टैंडपाइन्ट *(noun)* – दृष्टिकोण, आधार an attitude towards a particular issue. *I understand your standpoint.*

Standstill/स्टैन्ड-स्टिल *(noun)* – रुकावट, गतिरोध a situation or condition without movement or activity. *Due to an accident the traffic came to a standstill.*

Stanza/स्टैंजा *(noun)* – काव्य-पंक्तियों की इकाई, पद a group of lines forming the basic recurring metrical unit in a poem. a group of four lines in some ancient Greek and Latin meters. *The third stanza of the poem was the most powerful.*

Staple/स्टेप्ल *(noun & verb)* – बाँधना, बाँधने का तार a small flattened U-shaped piece of wire used to fasten papers together. *We need to buy more staples.*

Star/स्टार *(noun)* – तारा, श्रेष्ठ, तारा चिह्न a fixed luminous point in the night sky which is a large, remote incandescent body like the sun. *Many stars were visible in the pollution-free sky.*

Starry/स्टारि *(adjective)* – तारों भरा full of or lit by stars. *The starry sky was treat for the eyes.*

Starboard/स्टारबोर्ड *(noun)* – दाहिना भाग the side of a ship or aircraft on the right when one is facing forward. the opposite of port. *The starboard looked clear.*

Starch/स्टार्च *(noun)* – आलू चावल और डबल रोटी में पाया जाने वाला श्वेत पदार्थ, माँडी लगाना an odourless, tasteless carbohydrate which is obtained chiefly from cereals and potatoes and is an important constituent of the human diet. *I am off starch for some time.*

Stardom/स्टारडम *(noun)* – उच्च का दर्जा the status of being very famous. *He was largely unaffected by stardom.*

Stare/स्टेअर *(verb)* – घूरना, टकटकी लगाकर देखना look fixedly at someone or something with the eyes wide open. look fixedly at someone until they feel forced to look away. *If you stare at someone, you may offend them.*

Stark/स्टार्क *(adjective)* – कड़ा, कठोर severe or bare in appearance. *The stark boat was much older than the other more ornate ones.*

Starling/स्टार्लिंग *(noun)* – सारिका a gregarious songbird typically with dark lustrous or iridescent plumage. *The starling sang throughout the day.*

Start/स्टार्ट *(noun & verb)* – आरम्भ, शुरुआत strategic arms reduction talks. *The Start did not lead to any conclusions.*

Starter/स्टार्टर *(noun)* – आरम्भ करने वाला, पहला दौर [chiefly British] the first course of a meal. *I was full after eating the starters.*

Startle/स्टार्टल *(verb)* – चिहुँकना, चौंकना, चौंका देना cause to feel sudden shock or alarm. *You startled me.*

Starve/स्टार्व *(verb)* – भूखा रहना, भूखा रखना suffer or die or cause to suffer or die from hunger. force someone out of or into by starving them. deprive of. fee; very hungry. *It is a shame that many poor people still starve to death every year.*

State/स्टेट *(noun)* – अवस्था, दशा, स्थिति, राज्य, प्रदेश, व्यक्त करना, विचार कर कहना the condition of someone or something. a physical condition as regards internal or molecular from or structure. [informal] an agitated, disorderly, or dirty condition. *He was in a very shocked state.*

Stately/स्टेटली *(adjective)* – राजसी, वैभवशाली dignified, imposing, or grand. *Everyone was in awe of her stately figure.*

Statement/स्टेटमेंट *(noun)* – कथन, पंक्ति, ब्योरा a definite or clear expression of something in speech or writing. a formal account of facts or events, especially one given to the police or in court. *The witness gave his statement to the police.*

Stateroom/स्टेटरूम *(noun)* – विशेष कमरा a large room in a palace or public building, for use on formal occasions. *The stateroom was prepared for the meeting.*

Statesman/स्टेट्समैन *(noun)* – राजकीय पुरुष, राजनेता a skilled, experienced, and respected political leader or figure. *The statesman addressed the crowd and pacified them.*

Static/स्टेटिक *(adjective)* – गतिहीन, थमा हुआ lacking movement, action, or change. *His career had been static for a really long time.*

Station/स्टेशन *(noun)* – ठहराव, केन्द्र a place where passenger trains stop on a railway line, typically with platforms and buildings. *The station was crowded.*

S

Stationary/स्टेशनरी *(adjective)* - स्थिर, अचल, गतिहीन not moving. *The turtle was stationary for a long time.*

Stationer/स्टेशनर *(noun)* - लेखन-सामग्री विक्रेता a seller of stationery. *The stationer was well stocked.*

Stationery/स्टेशनरि *(noun)* - लेखन-सामग्री paper and other materials needed for writing. *I love buying stationery.*

Statistics/स्टैटिस्टिक्स *(noun)* - आँकड़ा, सांख्यिकी a fact or piece of data obtained from a study of a large quantity of numerical data. *Statistics say that the number of boys in the country is much larger than the number of girls.*

Statistical/स्टैटिस्टिकल *(adjective)* - आँकड़े से सम्बन्धित, सांख्यिकी से सम्बन्धित of or relating to statistics. *The statistical analysis of the situation revealed some interesting developments.*

Statue/स्टैचू *(noun)* - प्रतिमा, मूर्ति a carved or cast figure of a person or animal, especially one that is life size or larger. *The statue had stood there for centuries.*

Stature/स्टेचर *(noun)* - योग्यता, सामाजिक वाद, कद a person's natural height when standing. *He was of a tall stature.*

Status/स्टेटस *(noun)* - प्रतिष्ठा, पद, उच्चता relative social or professional standing. high rank or social standing. the official classification given to a person, country, etc. determining their rights or responsibilities. *He was very much aware of his status while talking to the others.*

Status symbol /स्टेटस सिम्बल *(noun)* - वैभव का प्रतीक a possession taken to indicate a person's wealth or high status. *The expensive watch was a status symbol.*

Status quo /स्टेटस को *(noun)* - यथास्थिति the existing state of affairs. *The status quo is very volatile.*

Statute/स्टैट्यूट *(noun)* - संविधि, अधिनियम a written law passed by a legislative body. a rule of an organization or institution. a law or decree made by a sovereign or by god. *The statute helped restore law and order in the city.*

Statutory/स्टैट्यूटरि *(adjective)* - नियमित, निर्धारित, कानूनी required, permitted, or enacted by statute. *The statutory warning is displayed at the beginning of the movies at times.*

Staunch/स्टॉन्च *(adjective)* - निष्ठावान, दृढ़निश्चयी very loyal and committed. *He was a staunch supporter of Gandhian views.*

Stay/स्टे *(noun)* - स्थगित करना, ठहरना, निश्चित स्थिति में a large rope, wire, or rod used to support a ship's mast. *The stay needed to be tightened.*

Stead/स्टेड *(noun)* - स्थान विशेष पर the place or role that someone or something should have or fill: appointed in his stead. *The vice-principal was appointed in the principal's stead.*

Steadfast/स्टेडफास्ट *(adjective)* - जिद्दी, अटल, पक्का resolutely or dutifully firm and unwavering. *He was steadfast in his views.*

Steadfastness/स्टेडफास्टनेस *(noun)* - जिद्दीपन, अकड़पन, अक्खड़पन state of being resolutely firm and unwavering. *His steadfastness bordered on stubbornness.*

Steady/स्टेडि *(adjective)* - समानगति से, नियमित, सन्तुलित, संयमित firmly fixed, supported, or balanced. *They had a steady relationship.*

Steak/स्टेक *(noun)* - टिक्की, टिक्का, मोटा टुकड़ा high quality beef taken from the hindquarters of the animal, typically cut into thick slices for grilling or frying. a thick slice of other meat or fish. *He liked his steak well done.*

Steal/स्टील *(verb)* - चोरी करना take without permission or legal right and without intending to return it. dishonestly pass off as one's own. *The thieves stole the diamond.*

Stealth/स्टेल्थ *(noun)* - गुप्तरूप से, चोरी-चुपके cautious and surreptitious action or movement. *He used stealth to win the game.*

Stealthily/स्टेल्थिलि *(adverb)* - चोरी-चुपके से in a cautious and surreptitious manner, so as not to be seen or heard. *He approached the base stealthily.*

Steam/स्टीम *(noun)* - भाप, भाप निकलना the hot vapour into which water is converted when heated, which condenses in the air into a mist

S

of minute water droplets. *Steam was coming out of the boiling water.*

Steamy/स्टीमि *(adjective)* – भापयुक्त, कामुकता पूर्ण producing, filled with, or clouded with steam. *I love steamy hot soup.*

Steel/स्टील *(noun)* – इस्पात a hard, strong grey or bluish grey alloy of iron with carbon and usually other elements, used extensively as a structural and fabricating material. *The utensils were made of steel.*

Steep/स्टीप *(verb)* – खड़ा, कठिन, अनुचित soak or be soaked in water or other liquid. *I steeped the sponge in soap and wiped the slab.*

Steeple/स्टीप्ल *(noun)* – मीनार a church tower and spire. a spire on the top of a church tower or roof. *Beautiful ringing of the bell issued from the steeple.*

Steer/स्टीअर *(noun & verb)* – परिचालन, परिचालित करना, चलाना another term of bullock. *The cart was being pulled by two steers.*

Stem/स्टेम *(noun & verb)* – डण्ठल, डण्डी, तना, रोकना, बाँधना stop or restrict. *I tried to stem the growth of weeds in my garden.*

Stench/स्टेन्च *(noun)* – बदबू a strong and very unpleasant smell. *The stench was getting stronger by the hour.*

Stencil/स्टेन्सिल *(noun)* – छापने के लिए कटा प्रारूप a thin sheet of card, plastic, or metal with a pattern or letters cut out of it, used to produce the cut design on the surface below by the application of ink or paint through the holes. *The child used a stencil to label the chart.*

Stenographer/स्टेनोग्राफर *(noun)* – आशुलिपिक one who takes notes in short hand and transcribes the same on a typewriter. *The stenographer took notes during the meeting.*

Step/स्टेप *(noun)* – कदम, डग भरना, चरण, सोपान, an act or movement of putting one leg in front of the other in walking or running. the distance covered by such a movement. a short and easily walked distance. *She walked in small steps.*

Stereo/स्टेरिऑ *(noun)* – ध्वनि यन्त्र stereophonic sound. *The stereo was very pleasant on the ears.*

Stereotype/स्टेरिऑटाइप *(noun)* – रूढ़ि, परम्पराबद्ध an image or idea of a particular type of person or thing that has become fixed through being widely held. *One should not judge based on stereotypes.*

Sterile/स्टेराइल *(adjective)* – बाँझ, नपुंसक, अनुर्वर, बंजर not able to produce children or young. not able to produce fruit or seeds. too poor in quality to produce crops. *The sterile seeds were thrown away.*

Sterility/स्टेरिलिटि *(noun)* – बाँझपन, बंध्यापन the quality or condition of being sterile. *He was ashamed of his sterility.*

Sterilize/स्टेरिलाइज *(verb)* – बाँझपन, बंध्या बनाना, जीवाणुहीन बनाना make sterile. *They sterilized the milk before packing it.*

Sterling/स्टर्लिंग *(noun)* – ब्रिटिश मुद्रा, खरा, विश्वसनीय [British] money. *I paid in Sterlings for this gift.* *(adjective)* excellent; of great value. *The toy turned out to be a sterling gift.*

Stern/स्टर्न *(noun)* – सख्त, कठोर, गम्भीर, पिछला भाग the rearmost part of a ship or boat. *The crew tied the stern of the boat to the pontoon.*

Stethoscope/स्टेथॉस्कोप *(noun)* – चिकित्सक का यन्त्र विशेष a medical instrument for listening to the action of someone's heart or breathing having a small disc shaped resonator that is placed against the chest and two tubes connected to earpieces. *The child started crying as soon as the doctor put on the stethoscope.*

Stew /स्ट्यू *(noun)* – दमपुख्त, तालाब, पोखर a pond or large tank for keeping fish for eating. *The stew was full of fish.*

Steward/स्टिवार्ड *(noun)* – कारिन्दा, भण्डारी a person who looks after the passengers on a ship or aircraft. *The steward did his job well.*

Stick/स्टिक *(noun)* – छड़ी, खेलों में प्रयुक्त छड़ी, चुभाना, चिपकना, चिपकाना, कायम रहना a thin piece of wood that has fallen or been cut off a tree. a stick used for support in walking or as a weapon. *My nephew gathered sticks and used them in his games.*

Sticker/स्टिकर *(noun)* – चिपकने वाला लेबल an adhesive label or notice. *I love collecting stickers.*

S

Stickler/स्टिकलर *(noun)* – अपेक्षित व्यवहार चाहने वाला a person who insists on a certain quality or type of behaviour. *He was such a stickler for propriety.*

Sticky/स्टिकि *(adjective)* – चिपचिपा, गन्दा tending or designed to stick; adhesive. glutinous; viscous. *The sticky substance was difficult to wash off with soap.*

Stiff/स्टिफ *(adjective)* – सख्त, कड़ा न मुड़ने वाला, दुस्साहाय, रूखा not easily bent; rigid. not moving freely; difficult to turn or operate. unable to move easily and without pain. *Her stiff back made it difficult for her to move.*

Stiffness/स्टिफनेस *(noun)* – कड़ापन, रूखड़ापन the state of not easily bent or changed in shape. *His stiffness is his strength as well as his weakness.*

Stiffen/स्टिफन *(verb)* – कड़ा या सख्त होना make or become stiff. *The body stiffened by the hour.*

Stifle/स्टिफल *(noun & verb)* – दमन करना, दबा देना, बुझाना a joint in the legs of horses, dogs, and other animals, equivalent to the knee in humans. *The dog hurt his stifle.*

Stigma/स्टिग्मा *(noun)* – लांछन, दाग, कलंक eighteenth letter of Greek alphabet. *The children hadn't been taught how to write the symbol of stigma yet.*

Still/स्टिल *(noun)* – शान्त, निश्चेष्ट, अब तक, तब भी an apparatus for distilling alcoholic drinks such as whisky. *The still needed to be sterilized.*

Stillborn/स्टिलबॉर्न *(adjective)* – मृत नवजात failing to accomplish an intended result. *A stillborn plot to assassinate the President.*

Stilt/ स्टिल्ट *(adjective)* – खम्भा, ऊँचा बाँस, मदारी का बाँस stiff and self conscious or unnatural. *The stilted conversation yielded no results.*

Stimulant/स्टिम्युलन्ट *(noun)* – उत्तेजक, प्रेरक, भेषज, उद्दीपक a substance that acts to increase physiological or nervous activity in the body. *The athlete was accused of taking a stimulant just before the race.*

Stimulate/स्टिम्युलेट *(verb)* – प्रेरित कर, उत्तेजित करना apply or act as a stimulus to. *Their discussion stimulated the revolution.*

Stimulus/स्टिम्युलस *(noun)* – उद्दीपक, प्रेरक, प्रेरणा a thing that evokes a specific functional reaction in an organ or tissue. *The change in the intensity of light was a stimulus for the pupil.*

Sting/स्टिंग *(noun & verb)* – डंक, डंक मारना, टीस, टीसना a small sharp pointed organ of an insect, plant, etc. capable of inflicting a painful wound by injecting poison. *The sting of a scorpion is located in its tail.*

Stingy/स्टिन्जि *(adjective)* – नीच, कृषण, लोभी mean; ungenerous. *He is so stingy that he doesn't ever dine outside.*

Stink/स्टिंक *(verb)* – दुगन्ध, दुर्गन्धि देना have a strong unpleasant smell. fill a place with such a smell. *The rotten tomatoes in the refrigerator has started to stink.*

Stint/स्टिंट *(noun)* – अवधि a very small short legged northern sandpiper. *They claimed that they sighted a stint.*

Stipend/स्टाइपेंड *(noun)* – निर्धारित राशि, शुल्क, वेतन a fixed regular sum paid as a salary or as expenses to a clergyman, teacher, or public official. *He says the reason he can't afford a better establishment is because he doesn't get a good stipend in his current job.*

Stipulate/स्टिप्युलेट *(verb)* – अन्दाजा करना demand or specify as part of a bargain or agreement. *All clauses of the agreement were stipulated in the deed.*

Stir/स्टर *(noun)* – चम्मच आदि से किसी तरल पदार्थ को चलाना, बिलोड़ना to move a liquid using a spoon etc. *She stirred her coffee with a teaspoon.*

Stirrup/स्टिरप *(noun)* – रकाब each of a pair of devices attached at either side of a horse's saddle, in the form of a loop with a flat base to support the rider's foot. *After getting off the horse, the rider lost his balance for a moment, so he grasped the stirrup to gain control.*

Stitch/स्टिच *(noun & verb)* – टाँका, सिलना, टाँका लगाना, सिलाई करना a loop of thread or yarn resulting from a single pass or movement of the needle in sewing, knitting, or crocheting. a method of sewing, knitting, or crocheting producing a particular pattern: an embroidery stitch. *The stitch of this dress seems fine.*

S

Stock/स्टॉक *(noun)* – भण्डार, माल, पशुधन, वंशधन, कुंदा, कलम-पौध, भण्डार में होना a supply of goods or material available for sale or use. *The stock available in the warehouse has been below mark for the past few weeks.*

Stockbroker/स्टॉकब्रोकर *(noun)* – दलाल a broker who buys and sells securities on a stock exchange on behalf of clients. *It is worth wondering why during any natural disaster activity of stockbrokers increases manifold.*

Stocking/स्टॉकिंग *(noun)* – लम्बा मोजा a woman's garment that fits closely over the foot and leg, typically made of fine knitted nylon yarn, held up by suspenders or an elasticated strip at the upper thigh. a cylindrical bandage or other medical covering for the leg resembling a stocking. *A fine pair of stockings with a skirt is what some woman prefer to wear when stepping out for a formal meeting.*

Stocky/स्टॉकि *(adjective)* – नाटा परन्तु गठीला especially of a person short and sturdy. *I would describe the accused as being a middle-aged man with a stocky figure.*

Stoke/स्टोक *(verb)* – झोंकना, बढ़ावा देना add coal to. *Stoke the fire well so that it keeps us warm all night in this freezing temperature.*

Stolid/स्टॉलिड *(adjective)* – भावशून्य calm, dependable, and showing little emotion or animation. *The man seemed to be having a stolid appearance.*

Stomach/स्टमक *(noun & verb)* – आमाशय, पेट, सहन करना an internal organ in which the first part of digestion occurs, being a pear shaped enlargement of the alimentary canal linking the oesophagus to the small intestine. each of four such organs in a ruminant. *It takes about two hours for the stomach to digest a full meal.*

Stomp/स्टॉम्प *(verb)* – भारी कदमों से चलना tread heavily and noisily, typically in order to show anger. *After being disobeyed his wife, he stomped about the room in anger.*

Stone/स्टोन *(noun)* – पत्थर, पत्थर का टुकड़ा, गुठली hard, solid non metallic matter of which rock is made. a small piece of stone found on the ground. a piece of stone shaped for purpose, especially one of commemoration or demarcation. a meteorite made of rock, as opposed to metal. *Protesters were dispersed just when they started throwing stones at the advancing troop of policemen.*

Stonemason/स्टोनमेशन *(noun)* – मिस्त्री, संगतराश a person who cuts, prepares, and builds with stone. *After losing his job as an architect, the last that I heard about him was that he was working as a stonemason somewhere.*

Stony/स्टोनि *(adjective)* – पथरीला, कठोर हृदय full of stones. *The ground here is generally stony.*

Stool/स्टूल *(noun)* – तिपायी a seat without a back or arms, typically resting on three or four legs or on a single pedestal. *The envelope was lying on a small stool in a corner of the room.*

Stoop/स्टूप *(noun)* – झुकना, झुकाव [north American] a porch with steps in front of a house or other building. *The stoop in front of that house is lined with pots of freshly bloomed purple orchids.*

Stop/स्टॉप *(verb)* – ठहरना, ठहराव, रोकना, रुका हुआ, गतिहीन come or cause to come to an end. discontinue an action, practice, or habit. *"Stop this evil practice!" cried the tribal leader.*

Stopgap/स्टॉपगैप *(noun)* – कामचलाऊ a temporary solution or substitute. *Shifting into that attic room was just a stopgap arrangement till we found something better.*

Stoppage/स्टॉपेज *(noun)* – ठहराव, बाधा, विराम, विराम स्थल an instance of stopping or being stopped. an instance of industrial action. *Agitated at the lack of heed paid by the management to their demands, the workers called for work stoppage.*

Stopper/स्टॉपर *(noun)* – डाट a plug for sealing a hole, especially in the neck of a bottle. *The stopper was broken and the bottle was lying in a pool of the spilled ketchup.*

Stopwatch/स्टॉपवाच *(noun)*- विराम घड़ी a special watch with buttons that starts, stops, and then zero the display, used to time races.

S

Jim won the race with a record time of 56.65 seconds, strictly by the stopwatch.

Store/स्टोर *(noun & verb)* – भण्डार, गोदाम, भण्डार गृह, गोदाम में रखना a quantity or supply kept for use as needed. supplies of equipment and food kept for use by members of an army, navy, or other institution. *The store of cereals is fast depleting and we need an urgent refill.*

Storey/स्टोरी *(noun)* – तल्ला, मंजिल a part of a building comprising all the rooms that are on the same level. *Three storeys of that building are dedicated to car parking.*

Stork/स्टॉर्क *(noun)* – सारस, लकलक a very tall long-legged bird with a long heavy bill and typically white and black plumage. *Well, we didn't come across any tigers in the jungle safari, but definitely saw a stork.*

Storm/स्टॉर्म *(noun)* – तूफान, आँधी, वेगवान a violent disturbance of the atmosphere with strong winds and usually rain, thunder, lighting, or snow. *There was a storm last evening.*

Story/स्टोरी *(noun)* – कथा, कहानी, घटना का वर्णन an account of imaginary or real people and events told for entertainment. a storyline. *The manuscript has a good story line.*

Stout/स्टाउट *(adjective)* – मजबूत, शक्तिशाली rather fat or heavily built. *He had a stout figure.*

Stove/स्टोव *(noun)* – अँगीठी, चूल्हा past and past participle of stave. *I guess all that we did to stave off the worse all this while was not enough.*

Stow/स्टो *(verb)* – माल सजाना pack or store tidily in an appropriate place. *Stow the oars away in a dry place when on shore.*

Strafe/स्ट्राफ *(verb)* – गोलियों से हमला attack with machine-gun fire or bombs from low-flying aircraft. *Strafe the jungle on the territorial border so that we are sure none of the militants have survived.*

Straggle/स्ट्रैग्ल *(verb)* – पिछड़ जाना, भटक जाना move along slowly so as to trail behind the person or people in front. *We straggled slowly ahead in the march against inflation.*

Straight/स्ट्रेट *(adjective)* – सीधा, सरल, व्यवस्थित, ईमानदार extending uniformly in one direction

only; without a curve or bend. flat-topped. *The queue went straight ahead at the bus stop.*

Straightforward/स्ट्रेटफॉरवार्ड *(adjective)* – स्पष्टवादी, सीधा-सादा easy to do or understand. *It was a straightforward question.*

Strain/स्ट्रेन *(noun)* – तनाव, परिश्रम, थकान, तान, शैली a distinct breed, stock, or variety of an animal, plant, or other organism. *This strain of bacteria is multi-drug resistant.*

Strait/स्ट्रेट *(noun)* – जल-संयोजी, जल-डमरूमध्य a narrow passage of water connecting two seas or other large areas of water. *The Palk Strait lies between India and Sri Lanka.*

Straitened/स्ट्रेटेंड *(adjective)* – तंगहाली characterised by poverty. *After losing his job, his means were straitened.*

Strand/स्ट्रैंड *(noun)* – कपास, ऊन आदि का एक अकेला तार या धागा a single piece of cotton, wool, hair, etc. *There was a loose strand of rope that needed to be tied in.*

Strange/स्ट्रेंज *(adjective)* – अनोखा, निराला unusual or surprising. *It was a strange incident.*

Stranger/स्ट्रेंजर *(noun)* – अनजाना a person whom one does not know. *He is a stranger to me.*

Strangle/स्ट्रैंग्ल *(verb)* – दम घोंटना squeeze or constrict the neck of, especially so as to cause death. *Based on prima facie evidence, the police said he had been strangled to death.*

Strangulation/स्ट्रैंग्युलेशन *(noun)* – दम घोंटना the action of strangling so as to stop supply of blood. *There were strangulation marks on his neck.*

Strap/स्ट्रैप *(noun)* – फीता, पट्टा, पट्टी बाँधना a strip of leather, cloth, or other flexible material, used for fastening, securing, carrying, or holding on to. *A pair of leather straps kept the shoe fastened.*

Strategic/स्ट्रेटेजिक *(adjective)* – व्यूह, व्यूह सम्बन्धी forming part of a long-term plan or aim to achieve a specific purpose. *This measure is part of our strategic planning.*

Strategy/स्ट्रेटेजि *(noun)* – व्यूह, व्यूह रचना a plan of action designed to achieve a long term aim. *We must have a plausible strategy in place for our firm for the next ten years.*

S

Straw/स्ट्रॉ *(noun)* - भूसा, पुआल, सूखी घास dried stalks of grain, used especially as fodder of for thatching, packing, or weaving. *There was a heap of straw kept in the backyard.*

Strawberry/स्ट्रॉबेरि *(noun)* - झरबेरी a sweet soft red fruit with a seed studded surface. *Strawberries are often used in desserts.*

Stray/स्ट्रे *(verb)* - पथहीन, भटका हुआ, छिट-पुट move away aimlessly from group or from the right course or place. moveably in a specified direction. *The man strayed away from his companions in the jungle.*

Streak/स्ट्रीक *(noun)* - लगातार चलती अवधि, धारी, परत a long, thin mark of a different substance or colour from its surroundings. *The streak of red on the rock was an evidence of recent violence.*

Streaky/स्ट्रीकि *(adjective)* - धारीदार having streaks. [British] form the belly, thus having alternate strips of fat and lean. *The streaky animal was difficult to spot.*

Stream/स्ट्रीम *(noun)* - नदी, प्रवाह a small, narrow river. *The stream merged into the river.*

Streamline/स्ट्रीमलाइन *(verb)* - प्रभावशाली व्यवस्था करना design or provide with a form that presents very little resistance to a flow of air or water. *The engineers streamlined the boat.*

Street/स्ट्रीट *(noun)* - सड़क, गली a public road in a city, town, or village, typically with buildings on one or both sides. *I walked down the street to reach the café.*

Strength/स्ट्रेंथ *(noun)* - शक्ति, बल, गुण the quality or state of being strong. *They tested the wrestler's strength before letting him fight the professional.*

Strengthen/स्ट्रेंग्थेन *(verb)* - शक्तिवर्धक, ताकतवर होना make or become stronger. *Unity strengthened their small country.*

Strenuous/स्ट्रेन्युअस *(adjective)* - श्रमसाध्य requiring or using great exertion. *Strenuous exercise left him feeling drained.*

Stress/स्ट्रेस *(noun)* - दबाव, तनाव pressure or tension exerted on a material object. physics the magnitude of this measured in units of force per unit area. *The rope gave way to the stress.*

Stressful/स्ट्रेसफुल *(adj)* - तनाव बढ़ाने वाला causing worry and pressure. *This is a stressful exercise.*

Stretch/स्ट्रेच *(verb)* - लहराना, खींचकर बड़ा करना, तानना, अंगड़ाई लेना, फैलकर सोना, फैलाव be made or be able to be made longer or wider without tearing or breaking. pull tightly form one point to another or across a space. *They stretched the rope to as far as it could go.*

Stretcher/स्ट्रेचर *(noun)* - मरीजवाहक a framework of two poles with a long piece of canvas slung between them, used for carrying sick, injured, or dead people. *The stretchers came in very handy when the ambulance crashed into a tree.*

Strew/स्ट्रियू *(verb)* - विखेरना scatter untidily over a surface or area. cover a surface or area with untidily scattered things. *The little girls strewed flower petals across the road.*

Striken/स्ट्रिकेन *(adj.)* - आक्रान्त, पीड़ित [north American or archaic] past participle of strike. *People were stricken with grief at the news of the mishap.* *(adjective)* seriously affected by an undesirable condition or unpleasant feeling. showing great distress. *His stricken face told a different story.*

Strict/स्ट्रिक्ट *(adjective)* - कठोर, सख्त demanding that rules concerning behaviour are obeyed. demanding total compliance; rigidly enforced. *The strict principal scolded the students.*

Stride/स्ट्राइड *(noun)* - डग, कदम walk with long, decisive steps. *She strided across the floor.*

Strife/स्ट्राइफ *(noun)* - झगड़ा, अनबन angry or bitter disagreement, conflict. *The strife left them stressed.*

Strike/स्ट्राइक *(verb)* - मारना, प्रहार करना, हड़ताल, हड़ताल करना deliver a blow to. accidentally hit against something. come into forcible contact with. hit or kick so as to score a run, point, or goal. ignite by rubbing it briskly against an abrasive surface. bring into being. *We watched him strike the ball across the stadium.*

Striker/स्ट्राइकर *(noun)* - गोल करने वाला, हड़ताली the player who is to strike the ball in

S

a game; a player considered in terms of ability to strike the ball. a forward of ability to strike the ball. a forward or attacker. *The team was relying upon the striker to help them win.*

Striking/स्ट्राइकिंग *(adjective)* – विशिष्ट, आकर्षक noticeable. *The striking building was an identifying feature of the city's skyline.*

String/स्ट्रिंग *(noun)* – डोरी, फीता, तार material consisting of threads of cotton, hemp, etc. twisted together to form a thin length. a piece of such material. *The string broke and the basket fell.*

Stringent/स्ट्रिन्जेन्ट *(adjective)* – सख्त, कड़ा strict, precise, and exacting. *His stringent action made the students work harder.*

Strip/स्ट्रिप *(noun)* – धारी, धज्जी, पट्टी, आवरण a long, narrow piece of cloth, paper, etc. steel or other metal in the form of narrow flat bars. *The children decorated the room with colourful strips of paper.*

Stripe/स्ट्राइप *(noun)* – धारी, रंगीन a long narrow band or strip of a different colour or texture from the surface on either side of it. *The stripes were visible from a distance.*

Strive/स्ट्राइव *(verb)* – प्रयत्न करना, प्रयास करना, संघर्ष करना make great efforts. fight vigorously against. *We saw them strive to bring about the change.*

Stroke/स्ट्रोक *(noun)* – मार, निशान, रंग की लकीर, प्रहार, पक्षाघात an act of hitting: he received three strokes of the cane. an act of hitting the ball with a club, as a unit of scoring. a sound made by a striking clock. *The clock's strokes were quite alarming.*

Stroll/स्ट्रॉल *(verb)* – टहलना, सैर walk in a leisurely way. *I strolled through the park.*

Strong/स्ट्रांग *(adjective)* – शक्तिशाली, हृष्ट-पुष्ट, टिकाऊ, तीव्र physically powerful. *He is a strong man.*

Stronghold/स्ट्रांगहोल्ड *(noun)* – प्रभाव क्षेत्र a place that has been fortified against attack. *The palace was a stronghold of the kingdom.*

Structure/स्ट्रक्चर *(noun)* – बनावट, रचना, ढाँचा, संरचना the arrangement of and relations between the parts of something complex. *The structure of the organization was difficult to understand.*

Structural/स्ट्रक्चरल *(adjective)* – संरचनात्मक of, relating to, or forming part of a structure. *The building had a structural weakness.*

Struggle/स्ट्रगल *(verb)* – संघर्ष, जूझना make forceful efforts to get free. *The captives struggled against the ropes.*

Strum/स्ट्रम *(verb)*– बजाना play by sweeping the thumb or a plectrum up or down the strings. play casually or unskilfully on a stringed instrument. *The guitarist strummed along with the music. (noun)* an instance or the sound of strumming. *The strum was not unpleasant.*

Strut/स्ट्रट *(noun & verb)* – अकड़ की चाल, अकड़कर चलना a bar forming part of a framework and designed to resist compression. *The strut was the most reliable part of the structure.*

Stub/स्टब *(noun)* – घिसने या जलने के बाद बचा छोटा हिस्सा the truncated remnant of a pencil, cigarette, or similar shaped object after use. *The stub of the pencil was of no use to the child.*

Stubble/स्टबल *(noun)* – फसल की खूँटी, जड़ the cut stalks of cereal plants left in the ground after harvesting. *The stubble was attacked by parasites.*

Stubborn/स्टबॉर्न *(adjective)*– जिद्दी, अड़ियल determined not to change one's attitude or position. *He was a stubborn man.*

Stubby/स्टबि *(adjective)* – ठूँठ short and thick. *She wriggled her stubby fingers. (noun)* a small squat bottle of beer. *He emptied the stubby in no time.*

Stud/स्टड *(noun)* – बढ़िया नस्ल के घोड़े या अन्य पशु के प्रजनन के लिए प्रयुक्त स्थान an establishment where horses or other domesticated animals are kept for breeding. *The stud produced some excellent racehorses.*

Student/स्टूडेन्ट *(noun)* – विद्यार्थी, छात्र a person studying at a university or other place of higher education. a school pupil. denoting someone who is studying to enter a particular profession: a student nurse. *He has been a student for 30 years now.*

Studio/स्टूडिओ *(noun)* – चित्रांकन या प्रसारण का कमरा a room where an artist works or where dancers practice. *His studio was his home.*

Studious/स्ट्यूडिअस *(adjective)* – अध्ययनशील, परिश्रमी spending a lot of time studying or reading. *He is a studious boy but he also enjoys sports a lot.*

Study/स्टडि *(noun)* – अध्ययन, परीक्षण the devotion of time and attention to acquiring knowledge, especially from books. *The man devoted a lot of time to studies.*

Stuff/स्टफ *(noun & verb)* – सामग्री, भरना, तुच्छ पदार्थ, भकोसना matte, material, articles, or activities of a specified or indeterminate kind. drink or drugs. one's area of expertise. *The scientists were trying to determine the stuff of which the alien craft was made.*

Stuffing/स्टफिंग *(noun)* – पूर्ति या भराव की वस्तु a mixture used to stuff poultry or meat before cooking. *The stuffing was too rich for my taste.*

Stuffy/स्टफि *(adjective)* – रुचिहीन lacking fresh air or ventilation. *The stuffy room made me feel sick.*

Stumble/स्टम्बल *(verb)* – ठोकर खाना, लड़खड़ाना trip or momentarily lose one's balance. walk unsteadily. *He stumbled towards his home.*

Stump/स्टम्प *(noun)* – पेड़ का ठूँठ भाग the part of a tree trunk left projecting from the ground after the rest has fallen or been felled. *Several stumps rose from the ground.*

Stumpy/स्टम्पि *(adjective)* – छोटा और मोटा short and thick; squat. *The dog has a stumpy tail.*

Stun/स्टन *(verb)* – बेहोश करना, हक्का-बक्का करना knock unconscious or into a dazed or semi conscious state. *She was stunned after falling from her bed.*

Stunning/स्टनिंग *(adjective)* – चकित करने वाला extremely impressive or attractive. *Our hotel room has a stunning view of the lake.*

Stunt/स्टन्ट *(noun & verb)* – कलाबाजी, करतब, कठिन कमाल, वृद्धि रोकना an action displaying spectacular skill and daring. something unusual done to attract attention. *My brother likes to perform stunts on his bike.*

Stupefy/स्टुपिफाइ *(verb)* – मति मंद करना make unable to think or feel properly. *She was stupefied after the ride on the roller coaster.*

Stupenduous/स्ट्यूपेन्डस *(adjective)* – विस्मयकारी extremely impressive. *The kids gave a stupendous performance on the occasion of diwali.*

Stupid/स्टुपिड *(adjective)* – मूर्ख, नासमझ lacking intelligence or common sense. used to express exasperation or boredom: stop messing about with your stupid paintings! *It was stupid of him to try and finish the whole cake at once.*

Stupidity/स्टुपिडिटी *(noun)* – मूर्खता, गलती *His stupidity made him lose the race.*

Stupor/स्ट्यूपर *(noun)* – अर्द्धबेहोशी a state of near unconsciousness or insensibility. *After the 14 hour-long journey, all of us were in a stupor.*

Sturdy/स्टर्डि *(adjective)* – ठोस, स्वस्थ, सुदृढ़ strongly and solidly built or made. confident and determined: a sturdy independence. *My father gifted me a sturdy study table on my birthday.*

Stutter/स्टटर *(verb)* – हकलाना talk with continued involuntary repetition of sounds, especially initial consonants. produce a series of short, sharp sounds. *He often stutters when he is afraid.*

Sty/स्टाइ *(noun)* – सूअर-बाड़ा, गन्दा स्थान a pen or enclosure for swine. *She visits the pig in the sty daily.*

Style/स्टाइल *(noun)* – शैली, आकृति, प्रचलित विशिष्ट शैली a manner of doing something. a way of painting, writing, etc. characteristic of a particular period, person, etc. *The Roman style of architecture fascinates me.*

Stylish/स्टाइलिश *(adjective)* – सजीला having or displaying a good sense of style. fashionably elegant. *She prepared a stylish bouquet of flowers.*

Stylus/स्टाइलश *(noun)* – ग्रामोफोन की सूई a hard point, typically of diamond or sapphire, following a groove in a gramophone record and transmitting the recorded sound for reproduction. *On my grandmother's birthday, I replaced the stylus of her gramophone.*

S

Suave/स्वेव *(adjective)* – शिष्ट charming, confident, and elegant. *The Hatter in Alice and the Wonderland was very suave and entertaining.*

Sub/सब *(noun)* – उप a submarine. *We are going to take the sub ride to see the underwater features of Grand Cayman next month.*

Subconscious/सबकांशस *(adjective)* – अवचेतन मन of or concerning the part of the mind of which one is not fully aware but which influences one's actions and feelings. *She took a subconscious decision to teach in a village.*

Subcontinent/सबकंटिनेन्ट *(noun)* – उपमहादेश a large distinguishable part of a continent, such as north America or southern Africa. *He visits the Indian subcontinent every year.*

Subdivide/सबडिवाइड *(verb)* – उपविभाजित divide something that has already been divided or that is a separate unit. *The term syllabus was subdivided into three sections.*

Subdue/सब्ड्यू *(verb)* – नियन्त्रित करना, हराना, शान्त करना overcome, quieten, or brig under control. bring under control by force. *It took a long time for the police to subdue the crowd protesting against the price hike.*

Subject/सबजेक्ट *(noun)* – विषय, कर्ता, प्रजा a person or thing that is being discussed or dealt with or that gives rise to something. the part of a proposition about which a statement is made. a person who is the focus of scientific or medical attention or experiment. *Many believe it is cruel to use animals as test subjects for different new treatments.*

Subjective/सबजेक्टिव *(adjective)* – व्यक्तिगत based on or influenced by personal feelings, tastes, or opinions. *His review of the book was very subjective.*

Subjudice/सबज्युडिस *(adjective)* – न्यायालय में, विचाराधीन under judicial consideration and therefore prohibited from public discussion elsewhere. *The media could not provide much about the murder case as it was still sudjudiced.*

Sabjugate/सबजुगेट *(verb)* – नियन्त्रण में लाना bring under domination or control, especially by conquest. *Alexander the Great subjugated many states in a relatively short time.*

Sublet/सबलेट *(verb)* – किरायेदार द्वारा किराये पर देना lease to a subtenant. *She is subletting the second floor of the house as she doesn't need so much space.*

Sublime/सब्लाइम *(adjective)* – उदात्त, लोकोत्तर of such excellence, grandeur, or beauty as to inspire great admiration or awe. *The experience of successfully scaling a high mountain is sublime.*

Submarine/सबमेरिन *(noun)* – पनडुब्बी a streamlined warship designed to operate completely submerged in the sea for long periods. *I built a model submarine for my science project.*

Submerge/सब्मर्ज *(verb)* – पानी के अन्दर cause to be under water. descend below the surface of water. *The legendary city of Dwarka is believed to have been submerged after Lord Krishna's death.*

Submission/सब्मिशन् *(noun)* – सहिष्णुता, परवशता, प्रस्तुतीकरण, हार की स्वीकृति the action or fact of submitting. an act of surrendering to a hold by one's opponent. *The labour were forced into submission and made to end the strike.*

Submissive/सब्मिसिव *(adjective)* – विनम्र, मिलनसार meekly obedient or passive. *The hotel staff is very submissive.*

Submit/सब्मिट *(verb)* – प्रस्तुत करना accept or yield to a superior force or stronger person. *They submitted to the demands of the workers.*

Subnormal/सब्नॉर्मल *(adjective)* – सामान्य से नीचे not number that can be divided exactly into a specified number. *We learnt the function of subnormal in our computer class today.*

Subordinate/सबॉर्डिनेट *(adjective)* – कनिष्ठ, मातहत, अधीनस्थ lower in rank or position. of less or secondary importance. *The subordinate counsellors handled the meeting very well.* *(noun)* a person under the authority or control of another. *Her subordinate is very efficient.* *(verb)* treat or regard as subordinate. make subservient or dependent. *The playtime of the class was subordinated to train them in disaster management.*

S

Subscribe/सब्सक्राइब *(verb)* – ग्राहक बनना, आवेदन देना, समर्थन देना arrange to receive something, especially a periodical, regularly by paying in advance. contribute or undertake to contribute a sum of money to a project or cause. apply to participate in. apply for an issue of shares. apply for an issue of shares. agree before publication to take a certain number of copies of a book. *I subscribe to two food magazines.*

Subsequent/सब्सिक्वेंट *(adjective)* – बाद का, परवर्ती coming after something in time. *He won the first round but could not participate in subsequent rounds due to a minor injury.*

Subsequently/सबसिक्वेंटलि *(adverb)* – बाद में after a particular thing has happened. *Many wanted to cancel the picnic but they subsequently changed their mind.*

Subservient/सबसर्विएन्ट *(adjective)* – सम्मान देते हुए, कम महत्त्वपूर्ण prepared to obey others unquestioningly; obsequious. *The new domestic help is very subservient.*

Subside/सब्साइड *(verb)* – शान्त होना, बैठ जाना become less intense, violent, or severe. give way to an overwhelming feeling. *The comic act made even the sulkiest child to subside to laughter.*

Subsidiary/सब्सिडियरी *(adjective)* – पूरक, अन्य से नियंत्रित, सहायक less important than but related or supplementary to. controlled by a holding or parent company. *The subsidiary groups meet every month to get directives for the coming months.*

Subsidy/सबसिडि *(noun)* – आर्थिक सहायता a sum of money granted from public funds to help an industry or business keep the price of a commodity or service low. a sum of money granted to support an undertaking held to be in the public interest. a grant or contribution of money. *The Indian government provides subsidy on railway service.*

Subsidize/सब्सिडाइज *(verb)* – आर्थिक सहायता देना support financially. pay part of the cost of producing to reduce its price. *Our school provides us subsidized food in the canteen.*

Subsist/सब्सिस्ट *(verb)* – जारी रहना, अस्तित्व बनाये रहना maintain or support oneself, especially at a minimal level. [archaic] provide substances for. *She subsists by giving dance lessons after her classes.*

Subsistence/सब्सिस्टेंस *(noun)* – जीविका, जीविकोपार्जन the action or fact of subsisting. the means of doing this denoting or relating to production at a level sufficient only for one's own use or consumption, without any surplus for trade: subsistence agriculture. *Despite the subsistence provided, there was a shortage of medicines at the camp.*

Substance/सब्स्टैन्स *(noun)* – सारतत्व, अर्थ a particular kind of matter with uniform properties. an intoxicating or narcotic drug. *The toxic substance from the factory is polluting the river.*

Substandard/सब्स्टैण्डर्ड *(adjective)* – सामान्य से नीचे, मानदण्ड से नीचे below the usual or required standard. *The food is usually good at the mess but it was substandard last night.*

Substantial/सब्टैंशल् *(adjective)* – कीमती, मूल्यवान, महत्त्वपूर्ण of considerable importance, size, or worth. strongly built or made. important in material or social terms; wealthy. *We collected a substantial amount in the annual bake sale.*

Substantiate/सब्स्टैन्शिएट *(verb)* – प्रमाणित करना, सिद्ध करना, सबूत देना provide evidence to support or prove the truth of. *She substantiated her report with facts and figure from multiple cases.*

Substitute/सब्स्टिट्यूट *(noun)* – स्थानापन्न, दूसरे की जगह पर a person or thing acting or serving in place of another. *The class was given to a substitute till the teacher got back from her leave.*

Substitution/सबस्टिट्यूशन *(noun)* – स्थानापन्न, बदलाव replacing something someone with another or person. *The substitution of the LPG with natural gas would be cheap and environment-friendly.*

Subterranean/सब्टर्रनिअन् *(adj)* – भूमिगत existing, occurring, or done under the earth's surface. *Earthquakes and volcanoes are caused by subterranean movements and pressures.*

S

497

Subtitle/सबटाइटल *(noun)* – उपशीर्षक, उपनाम captions displayed at the bottom of a cinema or television screen that translate or transcribe the dialogue or narrative. *We could not really enjoy the French movie that we saw last week as the subtitles were not in sync.*

Subtle/सट्ल *(adjective)* – सूक्ष्म so delicate or precise as to be difficult to analyse or describe: a subtle distinctin. capable of making fine distinctions. delicately complex and understated: subtle lighting. *There is a subtle taste of saffron in the dish.*

Subtlety/सट्ल्टि *(noun)* – सूक्ष्मता से, चतुराई से the quality of being subtle. *She has mastered the subtleties of this crochet design.*

Subtract/सबट्रैक्ट *(verb)* – घटाना take away from another to calculate the difference. remove a part of something. *She subtracted the fancy envelopes to save money for the return gifts.*

Subtraction/सबट्रैक्शन *(noun)* – घटाव the process of taking away one number away from another. *I got all the answers right in the subtraction exercise.*

Suburb/सबर्ब *(noun)* – उपनगर an outlying district of a city, especially a residential one. *I am searching for a flat in the suburbs.*

Suburban/सबर्बन *(adjective)* – उपनगरीय, बाहरी बस्तियों से सम्बन्धित of or characteristic of a suburb. *The suburban locations often have better residential facilities.*

Subversive/सबवर्सिव *(adjective)* – विनाशक seeking or intended to subvert an established system or institution. *The writer's article against the government was taken as subversive material.*

Subvert/सबवर्ट *(verb)* – समाप्त करने की चेष्टा, विश्वासघात करना undermine the power and authority of an established system or institution. *Teenagers often try to subvert their parents' authority.*

Subway/सबवे *(noun)* – सुरंग-पथ, भूमिगत पथ, उपपथ a tunnel under a road for use by pedestrians. *The authorites made a subway to help pedestrians cross the busy road.*

Succeed/सक्सीड *(verb)* – सफल होना, परवर्ती होना, बाद में होना achieve an aim or purpose.

attain fame, wealth, or social status. *Work hard to succeed in life.*

Success/सक्सेस *(noun)* – सफलता the accomplishment of an aim or purpose. the attainment of fame, wealth, or social status. a person or thing that achieves success. *The soft drink is a huge success all over the world.*

Successful/सक्सेसफुल *(adjective)* – सफल accomplishing an aim or purpose. having achieved fame, wealth, or social status. *She is a successful entrepreneur.*

Succession/सक्सेसन *(noun)* – उत्तराधिकार, अनुक्रम, अनवरतता a number of people or things following one after the other. *I was so hungry that I ate three bananas in succession.*

Successive/सक्सेसिव *(adjective)* – क्रमिक, बाद के following one another or following others. *The team was happy at winning three successive tournaments.*

Successor/सक्सेसर *(noun)* – उत्तराधिकारी a person or thing that succeeds another. *The captain finally named his successor.*

Succint/सक्सिंक्ट *(adjective)* – संक्षिप्त और स्पष्ट briefly and clearly expressed. *I will always keep your succinct words in mind.*

Succumb/सकम *(verb)* – झुक जाना, हार मानना, मर जाना fail to resist. *The government succumbed to the pressure of the business community.*

Such/सच *(det.)* – ऐसा predet., & pronoun of the type previously mentioned. *People think they can get away with any crime, but such people should be punished severely.*

Suck/सक *(verb)* – चूसना draw into the mouth by contracting the muscles of the lip and mouth to make a partial vacuum. hold in the mouth and draw at it by contracting the lip and cheek muscles. draw in a specified direction by creating a vacuum. make a gurgling sound as a result of drawing air instead of water. *Many children suck their thumbs.*

Suction/सक्शन *(noun)* – चूसने वाला चूषक, चुसाव the production of a partial vacuum by the removal of air in order to force fluid into a vacant space or procure adhesion. *Suction helped clear the drain.*

Sudden/सडेन *(adjective)* – अचानक occurring or done quickly and unexpectedly. *He felt a sudden pain in his leg.*

Suds/सड्ज *(plural noun)* – झाग, फेन froth made from soap and water. *The child played with the suds.*

Sue/सू *(verb)* – मुकदमा करना institute legal proceedings against, typically for redress. *He stole my patent so I am going to sue him.*

Suede/स्वेड *(noun)* – मुलायम चमड़ा या कपड़ा leather, especially the skin of a young goat, with the flesh side rubbed to make a velvety nap. *The rain muddied my nice new boots made of suede.*

Suffer/सफर *(verb)* – कष्ट उठाना, भुगतना experience or be subjected to something bad or unpleasant. be affected by or subject to an illness or ailment. become or appear worse in quality. undergo martyrdom or execution. *The farmers might suffer some losses but no one will starve.*

Suffering/सफरिंग *(noun)* – पीड़ा, वेदना the stae of undergoing pain or wardship. *Painkilling drugs were not enough to relieve her suffering.*

Suffice/सफाइस *(verb)* – पर्याप्त होना be enough or adequate. meet the needs of. *They thought that two meals a day would suffice an old man.*

Sufficient/सफिसिएन्ट *(adjective & det.)* – पर्याप्त, जरूरत के बराबर enough; adequate. *We have sufficient funds for this trip.*

Suffix/सफिक्स *(noun)* – प्रत्यय a morpheme added at the end of a word to form a derivative. *He used the suffix incorrectly.*

Suffocate/सफोकेट *(verb)* – दम घुटना, घुटने से मरना Die or cause to die from lack of air or inability to breathe. have or cause to have difficulty in breathing. *Because of faulty respirator the patient suffocated to death.*

Suffocation/सफोकेशन *(noun)* – घुटन feeling of lack of air or inability to breathe. *Because of the suffocation in the crowded carriage, several people felt sick.*

Suffrage/सफ्रेज *(noun)* – मतदान का अधिकार the right to vote in political elections. [archaic] a vote given for a person or in assent to a proposal. *I am going to practise my suffrage this year.*

Sugar/सुगर *(noun)* – चीनी, शक्कर a sweet crystalline substance obtained especially from sugar cane and sugar beet, consisting essentially of source and used a sweetener in food and drink. *She added sugar to her tea.*

Sugary/सुगरी *(adjective)* – भरपूर मिठास resembling, or containing much, sugar. *He eats too much sugary food.*

Suggest/सजेस्ट *(verb)* – सुझाव देना put forward for consideration. come into one's mind. *There is strong evidence to suggest that she is telling the truth.*

Suggestion/सजेशन *(noun)* – सुझाव an idea or plan put forward for consideration. the action of suggesting. *We like your suggestion.*

Suicide/सूइसाइड *(noun)* – आत्महत्या the action of killing oneself intentionally. a person who does this. relating to or denoting a military operation carried out by people who do not expect to survive it: a suicide bomber. *Several charities work towards preventing suicides.*

Suicidal/सूइसाइडल *(adjective)* – आत्महत्या जैसा deeply unhappy or depressed and likely to commit suicide. *The psychologist cured the man's suicidal tendencies.*

Suitable/सूटेबल *(adjective)* – अनुकूल, उचित, उपयुक्त right or appropriate for a particular person, purpose, or situation. *This is a suitable dress for the occasion.*

Suitcase/सूटकेस *(noun)* – बक्सा a case with a handle and a hinged lid, used for carrying clothes and other personal possessions. *He dragged his heavy suitcase across the railway station.*

Suite/सूइट *(noun)* – जोड़ा कमरा a set of rooms for one person's or family's use or for a particular purpose. *We booked a suite for the family.*

Suitor/सूटर *(noun)* – प्रार्थी, विवाहयोग्य a man who pursues a relationship with a woman with a view to marriage. a prospective buyer of a business or corporation. *She had a long queue of suitors to choose from.*

S

Sulk/सल्क *(verb)* – उदासीन (उद्विग्न) होना be silent, morose, and bad tempered through annoyance or disappointment. *The child sulked when his mom scolded him.*

Sulky/सल्कि *(adjective)* – चिड़चिड़ा morose, bad tempered, and resentful. *She doesn't have too many friends because of her sulky nature.*

Sullen/सलेन *(adjective)* – उदास, चिड़चिड़ा bad tempered and sulky. *She is in a sullen mood again.*

Sulphur/सल्फर *(noun)* – गन्धक an element in chemistry. *The bottle containing sulphur fell and broke.*

Sultry/सल्ट्रि *(adjective)* – उमस भरा hot and humid. *The sultry weather makes me want to bathe again and again.*

Sum/सम *(noun)* – धनराशि, योग, मुख्यतः a particular amount of money. *Please pay me the entire sum.*

Summary/समरि *(noun)* – सारांश, संक्षिप्त a brief statement of the main points of something. *The summary of our discussion will reach you in a minute.*

Summarize/समराइज *(verb)* – सारांश प्रस्तुत करना briefly or give main points. *Please summarize your speech.*

Summer/समर *(noun)* – गरमी, ग्रीष्म a horizontal bearing beam, especially one supporting joists or rafters. *The summer was old and unstable.*

Summon/समन् *(verb)* – उपस्थित होने का आदेश authoritatively call on to be present, especially to appear in a law court. *The witness was summoned by the court.*

Sumptuous/सम्प्चुअस *(adjective)* – भव्य, शानदार, कीमती splendid and expensive looking. *He organized a sumptuous meal for his guests.*

Sun/सन *(noun)* – सूर्य the star round which the earth orbits. any similar star, with or without planets. *The sun was hidden behind a blanket of fog.*

Sunny/सनि *(adjective)* – चमकीली, प्रसन्न bright with or receiving much sunlight. *The sunny morning was a welcome change from the foggy days.*

Sunblind/सनब्लाइंड *(noun)* – झिलमिली a window blind used to exclude the sun. *The sunblinds made the room dark.*

Sunburn/सनबर्न *(noun)* – तापित, धूप-झुलस inflammation of the skin caused by over exposure to the ultraviolet rays of the sun. *The sunburn was very painful. (verb)* suffer from sunburn. *I sunburnt myself.*

Sunlit/सनलिट *(adjective)* – धूप से भरा, प्रकाशित lighted by sunlight. *violet valleys and the sunlit ridges.*

Sunrise/सनराइज *(noun)* – सूर्योदय the time in the morning when the sun rises. the colours and light visible in the sky at sunrise. *I saw a beautiful sunrise today.*

Sunset/सनसेट *(noun)* – सूर्यास्त the time in the evening when the sun sets. the colours and light visible in the sky at sunset. *The sunset was spectacular today.*

Suntroke/सनस्ट्रोक *(noun)* – लू, लू की लपट heatstroke brought about by excessive exposure to the sun. *Sunstroke can be a dangerous to life.*

Sunday/सन्डे *(noun)* – रविवार the day of the week before Monday and following Saturday, observed by Christians as a day of rest and religious worship. *This Sunday, I will spend the time with my family.*

Sundry/सन्ड्रि *(adjective)* – फुटकर, विविध of various kinds. *They bough sundry stuff from the store.*

Super/सुपर *(adjective)* – असाधारण excellent. *You just gave me a super idea.*

Superannuate/सुपर्आन्युऍट् *(verb)* – सेवानिवृत्त retire with a pension. belonging to a superannuation scheme. *My father superannuated 12 years ago.*

Superannuation/सुपर्आन्युशन् *(noun)* – सेवानिवृत्ति regular payment made into a fund by an employee towards a future pension. *The pension from superannuation is a helpful scheme.*

Superb/सुपर्ब *(adjective)* – श्रेष्ठ, सर्वोत्तम excellent. *The superb food was very difficult to resist.*

Supercilious/सुपरसिलिअस *(adjective)* – घमण्डी, दंभी having an air of contemptuous superiority. *Her supercilious attitude does not go down too well with her friends.*

S

Superficial/सुपरफिसिअल *(adjective)* – सतही, छिछला existing or occurring at or on the surface. *The burns were just superficial.*

Superfluity/सुपरफ्लुइटि *(noun)* – अधिक an unnecessary large number of anything. *Superfluity is not recommended in the current economic scenario.*

Superfluous/सुपरफ्लुअस *(adjective)* – सतही, अतिसामान्य unnecessary, especially through being more than enough. *The superfluous kindness appeared fake.*

Superimpose/सुपरइम्पोज *(verb)* – किसी पदार्थ के ऊपर रखने की क्रिया, अध्यारोपण place or lay over another, typically so that both are evident. *I superimposed the transparent sheet of printed paper over the painted wall.*

Supritend/सुपरिन्टेंड *(verb)* – प्रबन्ध, निरीक्षण, नियन्त्रण करना act as superintendent of. *She superintends the girls' hostel.*

Superitendent/सुपरिन्टेंडेंट *(noun)* – अधीक्षक, संचालक a person who supervises or is in charge of an organization, department, etc. *Everyone ran to their seats as soon as they heard the superintendent arriving.*

Superior/सुपिरिअर *(adjective)* – उच्च, श्रेष्ठ, वरिष्ठ higher in rank, status, or quality. of high standard or quality. greater in size or power. *He is superior to us in rank.*

Superiority/सुपिरिअरिटी *(noun)* – उच्चता, श्रेष्ठता, वरिष्ठता state of being superior. *He often made his superiority clear.*

Superlative/सुपरलेटिव *(adjective)* – अन्यतम, उच्चतम, सर्वश्रेष्ठ of the highest quality or degree. *His superlative power of speech was very evident.* expressing the highest or a very high degree of a quality. contrasted with positive and comparative. *"Best" is the superlative of "Good".*

Supermarket/सुपरमार्केट *(noun)* – एक भवन में सीमित बाजार a large self service shop selling foods and household goods. *I went to the supermarket to buy groceries.*

Supernatural/सुपरनेचुरल *(adjective)* – अलौकिक attributed to some force beyond scientific understanding or the laws of nature. *People claimed that they felt a supernatural force in the house.*

Supersede/सुपरसिड *(verb)* – किसी का पद पाना, पद स्थापना take the place of; supplant. *The director's instructions superseded the ones issued by the HR department.*

Supersonic/सुपरसॉनिक *(adjective)* – तीव्रध्वनि एवं गति involving or denoting a speed greater than that of sound. *The jet moved at a supersonic speed.*

Superstar/सुपरस्टार *(noun)* – अतिप्रसिद्ध an extremely famous and successful performer or sports player. *He enjoyed being the superstar.*

Superstition/सुपरस्टिशन *(noun)* – अन्धविश्वास excessively credulous belief in and reverence for the supernatural. a widely held but irrational belief in supernatural influences, especially as bringing good or bad luck. *Our society is plagued by superstitions.*

Superstitious/सुपरस्टिशस *(adj)* – अन्धविश्वासी having belief in superstitions. *She is a superstitious girl.*

Supervise/सुपरवाइज *(verb)* – निगरानी करना observe and direct the execution of or the work of a person. *I supervised the arrangements for the party.*

Supervisor/सुपरवाइजर *(noun)* – निरीक्षक a person who supervises a person or activity. *I was the supervisor of the party arrangements.*

Supper/सपर *(noun)* – रात्रि भोजन a light or [informal] evening meal. *I go for a walk after the supper.*

Supplant/सप्लान्ट *(verb)* – स्थानापन्न करना supersede and replace. *The boss supplanted the instructions issued by the manager.*

Supple/सपल *(adjective)* – लचीला, सुरम्य flexible or pliant. *She had a supple body. (verb)* make more flexible. *He suppled the iron rod.*

Supplement/सप्लिमेंट *(noun)* – अनुपूरक, परिशिष्ट a thing added to something else to enhance or complete it. *The sugar supplement made the sugar-free dessert edible.*

Supplementary/सप्लिमेंटरी *(adjective)* – पूरक completing or enhancing something. *She took some supplementary diets to help her recover.*

S

Supply/सप्लाई *(adj)* – आपूर्ति, आपूर्ति करना to provide or give something. *The farmer supplies eggs to the surrounding villages.*

Support/सपोर्ट *(verb)* – समर्थन, सहायता, थामना, संभालना, भरण-पोषण करना bear all or part of the weight of. *He supports himself well on the stick.*

Supporter/सपोर्टर *(noun)* – समर्थक, सहायक a person who supports a sports team, policy, etc. *The team had many supporters.*

Supportive/सपोर्टिव *(adj)* – सहायता जनक giving help or spport to somebody in a difficult situation. *Her family was very supportive of her decision to go back to studies.*

Suppose/सपोज *(verb)* – मानना, कल्पना करना, अटकल करना think or assume that something is true or probable, but without proof. assume or require that something is the case as a precondition. used to introduce a suggestion. *I suppose that you lead a busy life.*

Supposition/सपोजिशन *(noun)* – अनुमान, अटकल an assumption or hypothesis. *The supposition became invalid when the assumption proved to be incorrect.*

Suppress/सप्रेश *(verb)* – दबाना, कुचलना, गुप्त रखना forcibly put an end to. *The police suppressed the protests.*

Supreme/सुप्रीम *(adjective)* – सर्वोच्च, सर्वश्रेष्ठ highest in authority or rank. *The President's word is supreme in some countries.*

Supremacy/सुप्रेमैसि (स्युप्रेमॅसि) *(noun)* – शासन, श्रेष्ठता, उच्चता the condition of being superior in authority. *No one could question her supremacy.*

Supreme Being/सुप्रीम बिइंग *(adjective)* – ब्रह्म, ईश्वर highest in authority. *There are several schools of thoughts regarding the Supreme being.*

Surcharge/सरचार्ज *(noun)* – अतिरिक्त कर an additional charge or payment. an amount in an official account not passed by the auditor and having to be refunded by the person responsible. the showing of an omission in an account for which credit should have been given. *There were many surcharges apart from the regular ones.*

Sure/शूअर् *(adjective)* – निश्चित, आश्वस्त, अचूक completely confident that one is right. *She is very sure of herself.*

Surely/शूअर्लि *(adverb)* – निश्चित रूप से unlikely to stumble or slip. *She treaded the red carpet surely.*

Surety/शूअर्टि *(noun)* – जमानत, जमानती a person who takes responsibility for another's undertaking, e.g. the payment of a debt. *He stood as a surety for his friend.*

Surf/सर्फ *(noun)* – फेन the mass or line of foam formed by waves breaking on a seashore or reef. *The surf was tossed high in the air as the waves became steeper.*

Surfing/सर्फिंग *(noun)* – खोजना, खेलना the sport of riding waves towards the shore while standing on a surfboard, the activity of moving from site to site on the internet. *I enjoy surfing.*

Surface/सर्फेस *(noun)* – सतह, बाहरी परत, ऊपरी हिस्सा, सतह पर आना, सतह पर लाना the outside part or uppermost layer of something. the area of this. *The surface of the sphere was smooth.*

Surfeit/सर्फिट *(noun)* – पूर्ण आहार, अधिकता an excess. *The surfeit of her emotions disgusted me after a point.*

Surge/सर्ज *(noun)* – लहराना, लहर-सदृश a sudden powerful forward or upward movement: tidal surges. *The surge uprooted the tree.*

Surgeon/सर्जन *(noun)* – शल्यचिकित्सक a medical practitioner qualified to practise surgery. *He was a respected surgeon.*

Surgery/सर्जरी *(noun)* – शल्यचिकित्सक the branch of medicine concerned with treatment of bodily injuries or disorders by incision or manipulation, especially with instruments. *He was undergoing surgery for the stones in his kidney.*

Surly/सर्लि *(adjective)* – उजड्ड, अक्खड़ bad tempered and unfriendly. *People stayed away from him because of his surly temper.*

Surmise/सर्माइज *(verb)* – अन्दाजा लगाना, अनुमान करना suppose without having evidence. *I surmise that they don't care for the cause.*

S

Surmount/सरमाउंट *(verb)* – कठिनाइयों पर विजय पाना, बाधा पार करना overcome a difficulty or obstacle. *He surmounted his bad finances to become a doctor.*

Surname /सरनेम *(noun)* – कुलनाम, उपनाम a hereditary name common to all members of a family, as distinct from a forename. *My surname says a lot about my heritage.*

Surpass/सरपास *(verb)* – आगे निकलना, मात देना be greater or better than. incomparable or outstanding. *You surpass me in intelligence.*

Surplus/सरप्लस *(noun)* – अतिरिक्त, ज्यादा an amount left over when requirements have been met. an excess of income or assets over expenditure or liabilities in a given period. the excess value of a company's assets over the face value of its stock. *The company didn't know what to do with the surplus.*

Surprise/सरप्राइज *(noun & verb)* – आश्चर्य, आश्चर्यजनक a feeling of mild astonishment or shock caused by something unexpected. *I was surprised to see all my friends at my place.*

Surrender/सरेंडर *(verb)* – समर्पण, परित्याग करना cease resistance to an opponent and submit to their authority. *The terrorists surrendered before the army.*

Surrogate/सरोगेट *(noun)* – स्थानापन्न, एवज में a substitute, especially a person deputizing for another I a specific role or office. a bishop's deputy who grants marriage licences. a judge in charge of probate, inheritance, and guardianship. *She acted as a surrogate to the child's mother.*

Surround/सराउन्ड *(verb)* – चारों ओर से घिरा/घेरना be all round; encircle. *They surrounded their leader eagerly.*

Surroundings/सराउन्डिंग्स *(plural noun)* – आस-पास, पास-पड़ोस the conditions or area around a person or thing. *I was happy with my surroundings.*

Surveillance/सर्वेलन्स *(noun)* – निगरानी close observation, especially of a suspected spy or criminal. *She was put under surveillance.*

Survey/सर्वे *(verb)* – सर्वेक्षण look carefully and thoroughly at. *The police surveyed the crime scene thoroughly.*

Surveyor/सर्वेअर *(noun)* – सर्वेक्षक a person who surveys land, buildings, etc. as a profession. *The surveyor did a good job.*

Survival/सर्वाइवल *(noun)* – जीवित रहना, अस्तित्व में रहना the state or fact of surviving. *Doctors raised serious doubts on her survival.*

Survive/सर्वाइव *(verb)* – बचना, अस्तित्व में होना continue to live or exist. continue to live or exist in spite of. remain alive after the death of. *Gandhi ji's philosophy will survive for a long time.*

Susceptible/ससेप्टिबल *(adjective)* – शीघ्र प्रभावित, सरलता से प्रभावित likely to be influenced or harmed by a particular thing. easily influenced by feelings or emotions. *The hut was susceptible to tornadoes.*

Suspect/सस्पेक्ट *(noun & verb)* – सन्देह करना, संदिग्ध व्यक्ति believe to be probable or possible. believe to be guilty of a crime or offence, without certain proof. *I suspect that what you are telling me is your own story, not your friend's.*

Suspend/सस्पेंड *(verb)* – स्थगित करना, कार्य से रोकना halt temporarily. *I suspended my work to take a break.*

Suspense/सस्पेंस *(noun)* – दुविधा, आसमंजस, अनिश्चय a state or feeling of excited or anxious uncertainty about what may happen. *I couldn't stand the suspense any longer.*

Suspension/सस्पेंशन *(noun)* – निलंबन, स्थगन, अधर में the action of suspending or the condition of being suspended. *The suspension was cancelled at the last moment.*

Suspicion/सस्पिशन *(noun)* – सन्देह, शक a feeling or belief that something is wrong. *She was arrested on suspicion of murder.*

Suspicious/सस्पिशस *(adjective)* – सन्देहास्पद, शक के घेरे में, शंका showing a cautious distrust of something or someone. *The police arrested him for his suspicious activities.*

Sustain/सस्टेन *(verb)* – सहजाना, बचा रहना, अस्तित्व बनाये रखना strengthen or support physically or mentally. bear. *The rope sustained the sails well.*

Sustenance/सस्टिनन्स् *(noun)* – पोषण, आहार, अड़े रहने की शक्ति food and drink regarded as

S

sustaining life. *Everyone needs sustenance to survive.*

Swab/स्वॉब *(noun & verb)* – मुलायम कपड़ा, रूई से पोंछना an absorbent pad used in surgery and medicine for cleaning wounds or applying medication. a specimen of a secretion taken with a swab. *They cleaned the wound with a swab.*

Swagger/स्वैगर *(verb)* – इठलाना, इतराना, अकड़कर चलना walk or behave arrogantly or self importantly. *He swaggered through the party, acting snooty and snobbish.*

Swallow/स्वॉलो *(noun & verb)* – निगलना, लीलना, फिरगिजी या अबाबील पक्षी a migratory swift flying insectivorous songbird with a forked tail. *The swallows were welcome visitors in our city.*

Swamp/स्वॉम्प *(noun)* – दलदल a area of waterlogged ground; a bog or marsh. *I squelched my way through the swamp.*

Swampy/स्वॉम्पी *(adjective)* – दलदली, दलदल से भरा characteristic of a swamp. *The swampy ground was dangerous in foggy conditions.*

Swan/स्वान *(noun)* – हंस a large water bird, typically all white, with a long flexible neck, short legs, and webbed feet. *Several beautiful swans lived near the lake.* *(verb)* move or go in a casual, irresponsible, or ostentatious way. *The young man swanned through the streets.*

Swarm/स्वार्म *(noun)* – झुण्ड a large or dense group of flying insects. a large number of honeybees that leave a hive with a queen in order to establish a new colony. *A swarm of locusts descended upon the fields.*

Swat/स्वैट *(verb)* – चपटी चीज से मारना hit or crush with a sharp blow from a flat object. *I swatted the fly.*

Swathe/स्वेथ *(verb)* – पट्टी बाँधना, लपेटना wrap in several layers of fabric. *She swathed the baby to protect it from chill.*

Sway/स्वे *(verb)* – डोलना, झूलना, शासन, प्रभाव move slowly or rhythmically backwards and forwards or from side to side. *The trees swayed in the gentle breeze.*

Swear/स्वेअर *(verb)* – शपथ लेना, कोसना, श्रापना state or promise solemnly or on oath. admit someone to a position or office by directing them to take a formal oath. compel to observe a certain course of action: I am sworn to secrecy. give an assurance that something is the case. promise to abstain from. have or express great confidence in. US law obtain the issue of a warrant for arrest by making a charge on oath. *The spy swore that she would lay down her life before being caught.*

Swear-word/स्वेअरवर्ड *(noun)* – अपशब्द, गाली an offensive or obscene word. *You should not use swear-words.*

Sweat/स्वेट *(noun)* – पसीना, पसीना बहाना moisture exude through the pores of the skin, especially as a reaction to heat, physical exertion, or anxiety. *I hate the smell of sweat.*

Sweaty/स्वेटि *(adjective)* – पसीने से लथपथ exuding, soaked in, or inducing sweat. *She was sweaty after the exercise.*

Sweater/स्वेटर *(noun)* – ऊनी वस्त्र a pullover with long sleeves. *I bought a new pullover from the store.*

Sweeper/स्वीपर *(noun)* – सफाई करने वाला, बहारने वाला, मेहतर a person or device that cleans by sweeping. *The sweeper worked hard to keep the school clean.*

Sweeping/स्वीपिंग *(adjective)* – व्यापक, सामान्य, बहाले जाने वाला extending or performed in a long, continuous curve. *She gestured with sweeping movements of her arms.*

Sweet/स्वीट *(adjective)* – मीठा, रोचक, सुन्दर, आकर्षक, मधुर, मिठाई, मीठा भोजन having the pleasant taste characteristic of sugar or honey; not salt, sour, or bitter. *I love sweet porridge.*

Sweeten/स्वीटेन *(verb)* – मीठा करना, मना लेना, ठण्डा करना make or become sweet or sweeter. *She sweetened the tea.*

Swell/स्वेल *(verb)* – फूलना, फुलाना, बढ़ जाना become larger or rounder in size, especially as a result of an accumulation of fluid. *Her injured leg swelled up.*

Swelling/स्वेलिंग *(noun)* – सूजन an abnormal enlargement of a part of the body as a result of an accumulation of fluid. a natural rounded protuberance. *He cold-pressed the swelling on his injured leg.*

S

Swelter/स्वेल्टर *(verb)* – उमस, कड़ी गरमी be uncomfortably hot. *All of us sweltered in the sun.* *(noun)* an uncomfortably hot atmosphere. *The swelter was getting very difficult to deal with.*

Swerve/स्वर्व *(verb)* – अचानक दिशा बदलना, तीव्र गति abruptly diverge or cause to diverge from a straight course. *The speeding vehicle swerved to the right.*

Swift/स्विफ्ट *(adjective)* – तेज, शीघ्र, तीव्र, द्रुत happening quickly or promptly. *I spied a swift movement from the corner of my eye.*

Swig/स्विग *(verb)* – जल्दी से, तेजी से drink in large draughts. *He quickly swigged his drink and left.*

Swill/स्विल *(verb)* – पानी डालना, बहाना, ज्यादा पीना wash or rinse out by pouring large amounts of water over or into it. cause to swirl round I a container or cavity. *She swilled the curry out into the sink.*

Swim/स्विम *(verb)* – तैरना, उतराना propel oneself through water by bodily movement. cross in this way. float. *I swam the length of the swimming pool.*

Swimmer/स्विमर *(noun)* – तैराक one who swing in water using limbs. *She is a brilliant swimmer.*

Swindle/स्विंडल *(verb)* – ठगना, ऐंठ लेना, ठगी use deception to deprive of money or possessions. obtain fraudulently. *The company swindled the customers' funds.*

Swine/स्वाइन *(noun)* – सूअर a pig. *The swine grew very fat.*

Swing/स्विंग *(verb)* – झूला, झूलना, झुलाना, झूमना most or cause to move back and forth or from side to side while or as if suspended. be executed by hanging. *The father swung the child around.*

Swipe/स्वाइप *(verb)* – तीव्र गति से घुमाकर मारना hit or try to hit with a swinging blow. *The cricketer swiped the ball.*

Swirl/स्वर्ल *(verb)* – गेंद की भाँति चक्कर खाते हुए move or cause to move in a twisting or spiralling pattern. *The dancers swirled gracefully.*

Swish/स्विश *(verb)* – सरसराना, सरसराहट move or cause to move with a hissing or rushing sound. *She swished across the hall.*

Switch/स्विच *(noun)* – विद्युत परिचालन यन्त्र, परिवर्तन, परिवर्तक a device for making and breaking an electrical connection. a program variable which activates or deactivates a function. *I could hear sparking in the switch.*

Swivel/स्विवल *(noun)* – घुमाऊ, घूमना a coupling between two parts enabling one to revolve without turning the other. *The canon could swivel to change directions.* *(verb)* turn on or as if on a swivel. *The dancer swivelled for one whole minute.*

Swoon/स्वून *(verb)* – मूर्छित होना, अचेत होना faint, especially from extreme emotion. *She swooned upon receiving his letter.*

Sword/सोई *(noun)* – तलवार, कटार a weapon with a long metal blade and a hilt with a handguard, used for thrusting or striking and often worn as part of ceremonial dress. military power, violence. *The warrior drew the sword and entered the fight.*

Swot/स्वॉट *(noun & verb)* – खूब पढ़ना, पढ़ाकू, परिश्रमी छात्र study assiduously or intensively. *He swotted for days.*

Sycophant/सिकफैन्ट *(noun)* – चापलूस, चाटुकार a toady; a servile flatterer. *The sycophant wasn't really liked much.*

Syllable/सिलेबल *(noun)* – मात्रा, एक ध्वनि के वर्ण-समूह a unit of pronunciation having one vowel sound, with or without surrounding consonants, and forming all or part of a word. *She pronounced each syllable clearly.*

Syllabus/सिलेबस *(noun)* – पाठ्यक्रम the subjects in a course of study or teaching. *The teacher followed the syllabus closely.*

Symbol/सिम्बल *(noun)* – प्रतीक, प्रतीक चिह्न, चिह्न, निशान a thing that represents or stands for something else, especially a material object representing something abstract. *A white dove is a symbol of peace.*

Symbolic/सिम्बलिक *(adj.)* – प्रतीकात्मक, लाक्षणिक the use of symbols to represent ideas or qualities. symbolic meaning. *She often uses symbolic images in her writings.*

S

Symbolism/सिम्बलिज्म *(noun)* – प्रतीकवाद be a symbol of. represent by means of symbols. *The imparting of a symbolic meaning of an object or action is called symbolism.*

Symmetrical/सिमेट्रिकल *(adjective)* – एक सा, समान और एक सा made up of exactly similar parts facing each other or around an axis; showing symmetry. *Symmetrical designs are out of fashion as of now.*

Symmetry/सिमेट्रि *(noun)* – समानता the quality of being made up of exactly similar parts facing each other or around an axis. correct or pleasing proportion of parts. similarity or exact correspondence. the property of being unchanged by a given operation or process. *He was very particular about the symmetry of things.*

Sympathetic/सिम्पथेटिक *(adjective)* – सहानुभूतिपूर्ण, सहृदयता से भरा feeling, showing, or expressing sympathy. showing approval of an idea or action. *His sympathetic feelings did not appeal to everyone.*

Sympathy/सिम्पथि *(noun)* – संवेदना, सहानुभूति feelings of pity and sorrow for someone else's misfortune. condolences. *My sympathies are with you.*

Symphony/सिम्फनि *(noun)* – लिपिबद्ध स्वर, स्वर संगति, सुरीलापल an elaborate musical composition for full orchestra, typically I four movements with at least one in sonata form. an orchestral interlude in a large scale vocal work. short for symphony orchestra. *The symphony was beautifully composed.*

Symposium/सिम्पोजियम *(noun)* – विचार-गोष्ठी, वैचारिक सम्मेलन a conference or meeting to discuss a particular academic or specialist subject. a collection of related papers by a number of contributors. *The symposium turned out to be an interesting event.*

Symptom/सिम्पटम *(noun)* – लक्षण, रोग के लक्षण a feature which indicates a condition of disease, in particular one apparent to the patient, compare with sign. an indication of an undesirable situation. *She showed all symptoms of a viral infection.*

Synagogue/सिनगॉग *(noun)* – प्रार्थना भवन a building where a Jewish assembly or congregation meets for religious observance and instruction. such an assembly or congregation. *There was a huge crowd outside the synagogue.*

Synchronize/सिन्क्रनाइज *(verb)* – एक साथ बजाना, चलाना या करना cause to occur or operate at the same time or rate. *Please synchronize your steps with the rest of the troop.*

Synchronous/सिन्क्रनस *(adjective)* – साथ घटित होने वाला, समकालिक existing or occurring at the same time. *I cannot attend both the synchronous events.*

Syndicate/सिंडिकेट *(noun)* – व्यवसायी संघ, सदन, परिषद् a group of individuals or organizations combined to promote some common interest. an agency supplying material simultaneously to a number of news media. a committee of syndics. *The syndicate's cause was to spread peace and tolerance amongst people.*

Syndrome/सिन्ड्रोम *(noun)* – लक्षण, एक ही विशेषता a group of symptoms which consistently occur together. *She suffers from Down's Syndrome.*

Synonym/सिननिम *(noun)* – पर्यायवाची शब्द a word or phrase that means the same as another word or phrase in the same language, e.g. shut and close. *"Help" is a synonym for "aid".*

Synonymous/सिननिमस *(adjective)* – समानार्थी शब्द having the same meaning as another word or phrase in the same language. closely associated with something: his name was synonymous with victory. *Her name was synonymous with success.*

Synopsis/सिनॉप्सिस *(noun)* – शोध का प्रारूप, सारांश a brief summary of something. *The synopsis was too long.*

Syntax/सिन्टैक्स *(noun)* – वाक्य रचना the system of rules for the structure of a sentence in a language. *The grammatical and due arrangement of words in a sentence is called syntax.*

Synthesis/सिन्थेसिस *(noun)* – संयोजन, संश्लेषण, सम्मिलित the combination of components to form a connected whole. often contrasted with analysis. *This school of philosophy was a result of the synthesis of various thoughts.*

S

Synthetic/सिन्थेटिक *(adjective)* – कृत्रिम made by chemical synthesis, especially to imitate a natural product. not genuine; unnatural. *Synthetic fibres are often used to make clothes.*

Syringe/सिरिन्ज *(noun)* – प्लास्टिक या काँच से बनी सूई से युक्त एक नली a plastic or glass tube with a needle that is used for taking a small amount of blood out of the body or putting drugs into the body. *The syringe needed to be sterilized.*

Syrup/सिरप *(noun)* – शीरा, चाशनी, मीठा घोल a thick sweet liquid made by dissolving sugar in boiling water, used for preserving fruit. a thick sweet liquid containing medicine or used as a drink. a thick, sticky liquid obtained from sugar cane as part of the processing of sugar. *The syrup was too sweet.*

System/सिस्टम *(noun)* – प्रणाली a complex whole; a set of things working together as a mechanism or interconnecting network. the human or animal body as a whole. *The entire system failed when a small fault was introduced during the testing.*

S

Tt

T/टी (noun) – अंग्रेजी वर्णमाला का बीसवाँ वर्ण the twentieth letter of the English alphabet.
1. Denoting the next after S in a set of items, categories, etc.

Tab/टैब (noun) – पहचान चिह्न, कुंजी पटल की सारणी a small flap or strip of material attached to something, for holding, manipulation, identification, etc. a collar marking distinguishing an officer of high rank. north American term for ring pull. *The can will opened only if you pull the tab.*

Table/टेबल (noun) – मेज, तालिका, सारिणी, सामने रखना a piece of furniture with a flat top and one or more legs, proving a level surface for eating, writing, or working at. food provided in a restaurant or household. *The newest addition to our house is the fancy dining table.*

Tablecloth/टेबलक्लॉथ (noun) – मेजपोश a cloth spread over a table, especially during meals. *I bought a bright and flowery tablecloth for our new dining table.*

Tablespoon/टेबलस्पून (noun) – बड़ी चम्मच a large spoon for serving food. the amount held by such a spoon, in the UK considered to be 15 milliliters when used as a measurement in cookery. *You need to add exactly a tablespoon of milk in the batter.*

Tabletennis/टेबलटेनिस (noun) – गेंद का एक खेल an indoor game based on tennis, played with small bats and a small, hollow ball bounced on a table divided by a net. *Being a state level table tennis champion helped her get a seat in the best college.*

Tableau/टैब्लो (noun) – नाटकीय, झाँकी, प्रभावशाली दृश्य a group of models or figores repoesenting a scene from history. *The movie was a tableau of a warrior's life.*

Tablet/टैबलेट (noun) – गोली, अंकित पट्टी a flat slab of stone, clay, or wood, used especially for an inscription. another term for table. *They put up a marble tablet in the memory of his father.*

Tabloid/टैब्लाइड (noun) – लोकप्रिय a newspaper having pages half the size of those of the average broadsheet, typically popular in style and dominated by sensational stories. *The news of the actress's breakup was fodder for all the tabloids in town.*

Taboo/टैबू (noun) – निषिद्ध वस्तु, वर्जित कार्य a social or religious custom placing prohibition or restriction on a particular thing or person. *There was a time in our country when widow remarriage was considered a taboo.*

Tabular/टैब्यूलर (adjective) – सारिणी, तालिका of data consisting of or presented in columns or tables. *We were asked to arrange all the information in a tabular form.*

Tabulate/टैब्युलेट (verb) – सारिणी या तालिका में क्रमबद्ध करना arrange data in tabular form. *Tabulating all the data would be an efficient way of recording it.*

Tacit/टैसिट (adjective) – मौन, अनकहा, उपलक्षित understood or implied without being stated. *The boss gave a tacit approval to his employee's plan.*

Taciturn/टैसिटर्न (adjective) – चुप्पा, अल्पभाषी reserved or uncommunicative in speech; saying little. *A taciturn man, he replied to my queries in monosyllables.*

Tack/टैक (noun) – सामान्य प्रवृत्ति, चपटी कील equipment used in horse riding, including the saddle and bridle. *She straightened the tack and sat upright on the horse.*

Tackle/टैकल (noun) – एक यन्त्र the equipment required for a task or sport. *I had to buy better fishing tackle to go for the competition.*

Tact/टैक्ट (noun) – व्यवहार कुशलता adroitness and sensitivity in dealing with others or with difficult issues. *You must use your tact while dealing with such issues.*

Tactic/टैक्टिक *(noun)* – दाँव-पेंच, युक्ति, चाल an action or strategy carefully planned to achieve a specific end. *The teacher knew the student was using some tactic to achieve something.*

Tadpole/टैडपोल *(noun)* – मेढक का बच्चा the tailed aquatic larva of an amphibian, breathing through gills and lacking legs until the later stages of its development. *The pond needed urgent cleaning as I could easily spot the tadpoles and the weeds.*

Tag/टैग *(noun & verb)* – नत्थी, पुर्जा नत्थी करना, शब्द जोड़ना a children's game in which one chases the rest, and anyone who is caught then becomes the pursuer. *As soon as we reached the park the children ran and started playing tag.*

Tail/टेल *(noun)* – पूँछ, दुम, पिछला भाग limitation of ownership, especially of an estate or title limited to a person and their heirs. *When she went to demand her rights in the property, his sons told her that the estate was in tail.*

Tailor/टेलर *(noun)* – दर्जी, अनुकूलता a person whose occupation is making clothes, especially men's outer garments for individual customers. *I searched and searched and finally found a good tailor to stitch his shirts.*

Taint/टेंट *(noun)* – दूषित वस्तु का दूषकारी प्रभाव, छूत, दूषित a trace of a bad or undesirable quality or substance. a contaminating influence or effect. *The government could not shake off the taint of corruption.*

Take/टेक *(verb)* – लेना, ले जाना, स्वीकार करना, सहन करना lay hold of with one's hands; reach for and hold. consume as food, drink, medicine, or drugs. occupy a place or position. buy, rent, or subscribe to. ascertain by measurement or observation. capture or gain possession of by force or military means. of illness suddenly strike or afflict. have sexual intercourse with. *We took over the enemy fortress in no time.*

Takings/टेकिंग्स *(noun)* – दुकान, थिएटर आदि को माल टिकट आदि बेचने से हुई आमदनी the amount of money that a shop theatre, etc gets from selling goods, tickets, etc. *He knew he would have to analyse the takings of his department thoroughly before giving the presentation.*

Talcum-powder/टैल्कम-पाउडर *(noun)* – मुलायम, सुगन्धित, महीन a preparation for the body and face consisting of the mineral talc in powdered form. *The talcum powder she uses was quite visible over her clothes.*

Tale/टेल *(noun)* – कहानी, किस्सा, अफवाह a fictitious or true narrative or story, especially one that is imaginatively recounted. a lie. *She spun a tale around the whole incident that she could boast to her friends about.*

Talent/टैलेंट *(noun)* – प्रतिभा, आन्तरिक योग्यता natural aptitude or skill. people possessing such aptitude or skill. people regarded as sexually attractive or as prospective sexual partners. *Both her children have a talent for cooking and music right from childhood.*

Talismant/टैलिस्मन *(noun)* – कवच, ताबीज an object thought to have magic powers and to bring good luck. *The Tantric gave the woman a talisman to be hung around her neck for the next ten days till her desire was fulfilled.*

Talk/टॉक *(noun & verb)* – बातचीत, वार्ता, बातचीत करना, बोलना, चर्चा, अफवाह, भाषण speak in order to give information or express ideas or feelings; converse or communicate by speech. have the power of speech. discuss something thoroughly. reply defiantly or insolently. speak patronizingly or condescendingly to. convince someone that they should adopt a particular point of view. persuade or dissuade someone to or from. *We were forbidden from talking inside the seminar hall.*

Talkative/टॉकेटिव *(adjective)* – बातूनी, बक-बक करने वाला fond of or given to talking. *Her daughter was more talkative than her.*

Tall/टॉल *(adjective)* – औसत से अधिक लम्बा of great or more than average height. measuring a specified distance from top to bottom. *Her daughter was taller than her father.*

Tallow/टैलो *(noun)* – चरबी a hard fatty substance made from rendered animal fat, used in making candles and soap. *The butcher was trying to break the lump of tallow in half.*

Tally/टैलि *(noun & verb)* – मेल, मेल खाना, मेल कराना a current score or amount. a record of a score or amount. *Their tally was exact with the list.*

T

Talon/टैलॅन *(noun)* – पंजा, चंगुल, पकड़ a claw, especially one belonging to a bird of prey. *The bird dug its talons into the skin of the prey.*

Tamarind/टैमरिन्ड *(noun)* – इमली sticky brown acidic pulp, from the pod of a tree of the pea family, used as a flavoring in Asian cookery. *Add tamarind extract to the cooked lentil to make the sambhar perfect.*

Tame/टेम *(adj. & verb)* – पालतू, घरेलू, पालतू बनाना of an animal not dangerous or frightened of people; domesticated. of a person willing to cooperate. *The pigeon in my balcony was quite tame.*

Tamper/टैम्पर *(verb)* – छेड़छाड़ करना, बिना अधिकार बदलना interfere with something without authority or so as to cause damages. *I warned my brother not to tamper with my project.* (noun) a machine or tool for tamping down earth or ballast. *She used the tamper to flatten the ground coffee.*

Tan/टैन *(noun)* – प्रभावित त्वचा, चर्म शोधन a yellowish brown colour. *She bought a tan dress for the party.*

Tanner/टैनर *(noun)* – चर्म शोधक a person employed to tan animal hides. *He sold his leather piece to the tanner.*

Tannery/टैनरि *(noun)* – चर्म शोधन स्थान a place where animal hides are tanned. *He arrived at the tannery early today.*

Tang/टैंग *(noun)* – तीखा स्वाद या गन्ध a strong taste, flavor, or smell. *She could smell the salty tang of the sea.*

Tangent/टैन्जेन्ट *(noun)* – स्पर्श रेखा, विषय-व्यवहार बदलना a straight line or plane that touches a curve or curved surface at a point, but if extended does not cross it at that point. *The teacher showed how to draw a tangent to three given lines.*

Tangible/टैन्जिबल् *(adjective)* – स्पष्ट, निश्चित, वास्तविक perceptible by touch. *Just because emotions are not tangible does not mean they are insignificant.*

Tangle/टैंग्ल *(verb)* – उलझा हुआ, उलझन, उलझाना twist strands together into a confused mass. *The ropes were too tangled to undo.*

Tank/टैंक *(noun)* – हौज, बड़ा पात्र a large receptacle or storage chamber, especially for liquid or gas. the container holding the fuel supply in a motor vehicle. a reservoir. *We ran to switch off the motor when we saw the tank overflowing.*

Tantalize/टैंटलाइज *(verb)* – ललचाना, तरसाना torment or tease with the sight or promise of something that is unobtainable or with held. *The stripper tantalized her customers at the bar.*

Tantamount/टैंटामाउंट *(adjective)* – तुल्य, समतुल्य, बराबर equivalent in seriousness to; virtually the same as. *His statement was tantamount to an admission of guilt.*

Tantrum/टैन्ट्रम *(noun)* – आवेश, क्रोध, झोंक में आना an uncontrolled outburst of anger and frustration, typically in a young child. *The mother lost her temper when the child threw tantrums in the movie hall.*

Tap/टैप *(noun & verb)* – नल, टोंटी, सुनने का उपकरण, चीरा लगाना, थपकी, थपथपाना, खटखटाना a device by which a flow of liquid or gas from a pipe or container can be controlled. *The water wouldn't stop as the washer was broken.*

Tape/टेप *(noun)* – पट्टी, पट्टी पर अंकित करना, चिपकाना light, flexible material in a narrow strip, used to hold, fasten, or mark off something. also adhesive tape a strip of paper or plastic coated with adhesive, used to stick things together. *When the vase cracked, I applied tape on it temporarily till I could get a better adhesive.*

Taper/टेपर *(verb)* – संकरा होता जाना diminish or reduce in thickness towards one end. *The spire tapers towards the end.*

Tapestry/टैपिस्ट्रि *(noun)* – कपड़े पर ऊन से बिनावट a piece of thick textile fabric with pictures or designs formed by weaving coloured weft threads or by embroidering on canvas. *Huge tapestries hung on the wall.*

Tar/टार *(noun)* – तारकोल a dark, thick flammable liquid distilled from wood or coal, used in road making and for coating and preserving timber. a similar substance formed by burning tobacco or other material. *The newly spread tar on the road was making it impossible for vehicles to pass.*

T

Tardy/टार्डि *(adjective)* – धीमी मंद गति से, सुस्त delaying or delayed beyond the right or expected time; late. slow in action or response; sluggish. *Mother asked me why I have been so tardy with my appointment with the dentist.*

Target/टार्गेट *(noun)* – लक्ष्य, निशाना, उद्देश्य, लक्ष्य बनाना a person, object, or place selected as the aim of an attack. around or rectangular board marked with concentric circles, aimed at in archery or shooting. *He's a good sportsman who has never missed his target in the game.*

Tariff/टैरिफ *(noun)* – दर की सूची, शुल्कदर a tax or duty to be paid on a particular class of imports or exports. *India is trying to do away with tariff on items such as electronics.*

Tarmac/टार्मैक *(noun)* – पक्की सड़क material used for surfacing roads or other outdoor areas, consisting of broken stone mixed with tar. a runway or other area surfaced with such material. *The plane was waiting on the tarmac. (verb)* surface with tarmac. *The airport had a new runway where new tarmac had been applied.*

Tarnish/टार्निश *(verb)* – दागदार बनाना, धब्बा लगाना lose or cause to lose luster, especially as a result of exposure to air or moisture. *The old statue of Buddha had tarnished over the years.*

Tarpaulin/टार्पालिन *(noun)* – तिरपाल heavy duty waterproof cloth, originally of tarred canvas. a sheet or covering of this. *The storm blew away the tarpaulin on the terrace.*

Tarry/टैरि *(adjective)* – ज्यादा देर ठहरना, आने-जाने में बिलंब of, like, or covered with tar. *The road was still a bit tarry, so we didn't risk driving on it.*

Tart/टार्ट *(noun)* – खट्टा, कटु-व्यंग्यात्मक, एक खाद्य an open pastry case containing a sweet or savoury filling. *I am making tarts for tea today.*

Task/टास्क *(noun)* – काम, दिया गया काम a piece of work. *He was given the task of breaking the news to the patient's family.*

Taskmaster/टास्कमास्टर *(noun)* – कठोर अधिकारी a person who imposes an onerous workload on someone. *Your new boss is known for being a hard taskmaster.*

Tassel/टैसल *(noun)* – फूँदना, झब्बा a small piece of stone or wood supporting the end of a beam or joist. *On his body, the cord and the tassel hung loosely in the wind.*

Taste/टेस्ट *(noun)* – स्वाद, चखने की शक्ति, चखना, स्वाद लेना the sensation of flavor perceived in the mouth on contact with a substance. the faculty of perceiving this. *She loved the tangy taste of the curry put on display.*

Tasteless/टेस्टलेस *(adjective)* – स्वादहीन lacking in aesthetic judgment or constituting inappropriate behaviour. *He gave a rather tasteless remark about her performance.*

Tasty/टेस्टि *(adjective)* – स्वादिष्ट of food having a pleasant, distinct flavor. *The snacks were tasty at the party.*

Tattered/टैटर्ड *(adjective)* – फटा-पुराना, चिथड़ा old and torn; in poor condition. *I saw a tattered old man begging outside the temple.*

Tattoo/टैटू *(verb)* – गोदना mark with an indelible design by inserting pigment into punctures in the skin. *The couple had tattooed their names on each other's arms.*

Taunt/टान्ट *(noun)* – ताना, ताना मारना a jeering or mocking remark made in order to wound or provoke. *Her taunts fell on deaf ears this time.*

Taurus/टॉरस *(noun)* – वृष राशि a constellation the bull, said to represent a bull tamed by Jason a hero of Greek mythology. *The boy was born under the Taurus constellation.*

Taut/टॉट *(adjective)* – तना हुआ, खींचा हुआ stretched or pulled tight. of muscles or nerves tense. *Her nerves were taut with anxiety.*

Tavern/टैवर्न *(noun)* – सराय an inn or public house. *I'll meet you in the evening over a drink at the tavern 200.*

Tawdry/टॉड्रि *(adjective)* – भड़कीला, कुत्सित showy but cheap and of poor quality. *She wore some tawdry costume at the party.*

Tax/टैक्स *(noun)* – कर, माँग, बोझ a compulsory contribution to state revenue, levied by the government on personal income and business profits or added to the cost of some goods, services, and transactions. *It was time to file our tax returns.*

T

Taxable/टैक्सेबल *(adjective)* – कर योग्य liable to be imposed tax. *The gain from an option is taxable as soon as the shares are acquired.*

Taxing/टैक्सिंग *(adjective)* – थकाने वाला physically or mentally demanding. *The whole trip was quite taxing to the nerves.*

Taxation/टैक्सेशन *(noun)* – कर पद्धति the levying of tax. money paid as tax. *We had a class on taxation scheduled for this evening.*

Taxi/टैक्सि *(noun)* – भाड़े की गाड़ी, जहाज के पहिए पर चलना a motor vehicle licensed to transport passengers in return for payment of a fare. *I took an airport taxi and rushed to catch my flight.*

Tea/टी *(noun)* – चाय, चायपत्ती a hot drink made by infusing the dried, crushed leaves of the tea plant in boiling water. the dried leaves used to make tea. a similar drink made from the leaves, fruits, or flowers of other plants. *She makes tea really well.*

Teach/टीच *(verb)* – अध्यापन करना impart knowledge to or instruct someone in how to do something, especially in a school or as part of a recognized programme. give instruction in a subject or skill. cause to learn by example or experience. *It takes a knack of dealing with children, to be able to teach well.*

Teacher/टीचर *(noun)* – शिक्षक, अध्यापक a person who teaches in a school. *I had the best teacher in the school to give me maths tuitions.*

Teak/टीक *(noun)* – सागौन hard durable wood used in shipbuilding and for making furniture. *I bought some teak furniture for my guest room.*

Team/टीम *(noun)* – दल a group of players forming one side in a competitive game or sport. *The team had to use a unique strategy this time to win.*

Teamwork/टीमवर्क *(noun)* – संगठित प्रयत्न the combined effective action of a group. *Nothing succeeds like teamwork.*

Tear/टीअर *(noun & verb)* – आँसू, चीरना, फाड़ना, खींच a drop of clear salty liquid secreted from glands in a person's eye when they are crying or when the eye is irritated. *I could make out from her tears that there was something deeply disturbing on her mind.*

Tearful/टीअरफुल *(adjective)* – अश्रुपुरित crying or inclined to cry. *She stood tearful at the station as the train passed by.*

Tease/टीज *(verb)* – छेड़ना, चिढ़ाना playfully make fun of or attempt to provoke. tempt sexually. *The young girl bashfully asked the boy to stop teasing her in front of her friends.*

Technical/टेक्निकल *(adjective)* – तकनीकी of or relating to a particular subject, art, or craft, or its techniques. requiring special knowledge to be understood. *One needs technical knowledge of the product before sitting for an exam.*

Technician/टेक्निशन *(noun)* – दक्ष, विशेषज्ञ a person employed to look after technical equipment or do practical work in a laboratory. *We need to recruit a new lab technician.*

Technique/टेक्निक *(noun)* – तकनीक a way of carrying out a particular task, especially the execution of an artistic work or a scientific procedure. a procedure that is effective in achieving an aim. *She used a special technique of mixing the icing with the cream and the batter and then frosting the cake.*

Technology/टेक्नॉलॉजि *(noun)* – प्रायोगिक विज्ञान the application of scientific knowledge for practical purposes. machinery and equipment based on such knowledge. the branch of knowledge concerned with applied sciences. *The information technology boom was the greatest leap in industrial development our country could take.*

Teddybear/टेडिबियर *(noun)* – खिलौनों वाला भालू soft toy bear. *I still have the teddy bear I used to sleep with as a baby.*

Tedious/टीडिअस् *(adjective)* – कठिन ऊबाऊ कार्य too long, slow, or dull. *I had a long tedious day at work today.*

Teem/टीम *(verb)* – बड़ी संख्या में उत्पन्न करना, उड़ेलना, भरपूर होना be full of or swarming with. *The hall was teeming with people of all castes, regions and race.*

Teenager/टीनेजर *(noun)* – युवा होते लड़के-लड़कियाँ a person aged between 13 and 19 years. *She has turned 13 and is now a teenager.*

Teens/टीन्स *(plural noun)* – किशोरावस्था the years of a person's age from 13 and 19. *Smoking and drugs are most common among teens today.*

Teethe/टीद् *(verb)* – दाँत निकलना cut one's milk teeth. *She has been feeling a lot of pain ever since she teethed.*

Teetotaller/टिटोटलर *(noun)* – जिसने कभी शराब नहीं पिया हो/पीता हो a person who never drinks alcohel. *Though he was a drunkard five years back, he is now a teetotaller.*

Telecast/टेलिकास्ट *(noun)* – प्रसारित करना a television broadcast. *They were showing a live telecast of the royal wedding.*

Telecommunication/टेलिकम्युनिकेशन *(noun)* – दूर-संचार communication over a distance by cable, telegraph, telephone, or broadcasting. the branch of technology concerned with this. *She joined BSNL as a telecommunication engineer.*

Telegram/टेलिग्राम *(noun)* – तार a message sent by telegraph and delivered in written or printed form, used in the UK only for international messages since 1981. *She rushed to her hometown as soon as she got the telegram about her grandmother's demise.*

Telegraph/टेलिग्राफ *(noun)* – तार भेजने का उपकरण a system or device for transmitting messages from a distance along a wire, especially one creating signals by making and breaking an electrical connection. *If only there was a telegraph service on the ship, help would have reached on time and the passengers would have survived the wreck.*

Telepathy/टेलिपैथी *(noun)* – अन्त: संवेदन, अन्त: बोध the supposed communication of thoughts or ideas by means other than the known senses. *I was alarmed at the telepathy, as she called just when I was thinking of her.*

Telephone/टेलिफोन *(noun)* – दूरभाष a system for transmitting voice over a distance using wire or radio, by converting acoustic vibrations to electrical signals. *Did you get the message on telephone or internet?*

Telescope/टेलिस्कोप *(noun)* – दूरबीन an optical instrument designed to make distant objects appear nearer, containing an arrangement of lenses, or of curved mirrors and lenses, by which rays of light are collected and focused and the resulting image magnified. *He took out his toy telescope and tried to see if he could spy on the girl next door.*

Television/टेलिविजन *(noun)* – दूरदर्शन a system for converting visual images with sound into electrical signals, transmitting them by radio or other means, and displayed them electronically on a screen. *We bought a new television transmitter for our audio visual system.*

Telex/टेलेक्स *(noun)* – दूर-संदेश an international system of telegraphy with printed messages transmitted and received by teleprinters using the public telecommunications network. *The telex system is finally being phased out after nearly 30 years.*

Tell/टेल *(verb)* – कहना, बताना, सुनाना in the middle east a mound formed by the accumulated remains of ancient settlements. *Abu Hureyra is a tell, excavated near the Euphrates valley in Syria.*

Temper/टेम्पर *(noun)* – मनोदशा, क्रोधी स्वभाव a person's state of mind in terms of their being angry or calm. *He is known for his short temper.*

Temperament/टेम्परामेंट *(noun)* – स्वभाव a person's nature with regard to the effect it has on their behaviour. *He was known for his temperament in his social circle.*

Temperance/टेम्परेंस *(noun)* – संयम abstinence from alcoholic drink. *I was overwhelmed when I saw a reformed alcoholic, rejoicing in the joys of temperance.*

Temperate/टेम्परेट *(adjective)* – संयमी, समशीतोष्ण, सहज (जलवायु) relating to or denoting a region or climate characterized by mild temperatures. *We are now in the temperate region.*

Temperature/टेम्परेचर *(noun)* – तापमान the degree or intensity of heat present in a substance or object. a body temperature above the normal: he was running a temperature. *He has been running a temperature for the last two days.*

Tempest/टेम्पेस्ट *(noun)* – तूफान, अति उत्तेजित a violent windy storm. *The ship caught in the tempest never made it to the shore.*

T

Template/टेम्पलेट (noun) – साँचा a shaped piece of rigid material used as a pattern for processes such as cutting out, shaping, or drilling. *The boss asked me to follow the template that he had mailed me for the presentation.*

Temple/टेम्पल (noun) – मन्दिर, कनपटी a building devoted to the worship of a god or gods. a synagogue. *A new temple had come up down the street.*

Tempo/टेम्पो (noun) – रफ्तार, ताल-लय the speed at which a passage of music is played. *The crowd was up on its feet as soon as he increased the tempo.*

Temporal/टेम्पोरल (adjective) – सांसारिक of or relating to time. *Specific acts are related to a spatial and temporal context.*

Temporary/टेम्पॉररि (adjective) – अस्थायी lasting for only a limited period. *Everything in life is temporary, the wise sage said.* (noun) a person employed on a temporary basis. *He joined on a temporary contract and is on probation now.*

Tempt/टेम्प्ट (verb) – प्रलोभन देना entice someone to do something against their better judgment. *Do not tempt me with sweets as I'm trying to lose weight.*

Temptation/टेम्प्टेशन (noun) – प्रलोभन the state or quality of being tempted; a desire to do something. a tempting thing. *The first rule for losing weight is to stop fighting your temptations.*

Ten/टेन (cardinal number) – दस equivalent to the product of five and two; one more than nine; 10 roman numeral: x or X. *There were ten children in a row.*

Tenth/टेन्थ (number) – दसवाँ constituting number ten in sequence. *I was talking to the tenth child in the row.*

Tenacious/टिनेशस् (adjective) – दृढ़ संकल्प का holding fast or keeping a firm hold of. *I had to face a persistent and tenacious interviewer once.*

Tenant/टेनन्ट् (noun) – किरायेदार a person occupying rented land or property. a person holding real property by private ownership. *The new tenants in our house are a nice family.*

Tend/टेंड (verb) – रखवाली करना, सेवा-शुश्रूषा करना, प्रवृत्त होना, विशेष दिशा की ओर care for or look after. wait on as an attendant or servant. *We were given the responsibility to tend wounded soldiers.*

Tendency/टेन्डेन्सी (noun) – प्रकृति, झुकाव, रूझान an inclination towards a particular characteristic or type of behaviour. *She has a tendency to go off track during her lectures.*

Tender/टेंडर (verb) – कोमल, संवेदनशील, सदय, ठेका offer or present formally. make a formal written offer to carry out work, supply goods, etc. for a stated fixed price. *She tendered her resignation this evening.*

Tendon/टेंडन (noun) – हड्डी और माँसपेशी जोड़ने वाले नस a flexible but inelastic cord of strong fibrous tissue attaching a muscle to a bone. the hamstring of a quadruped. *He damaged a tendon in his leg in the games.*

Tendril/टेंड्रिल (noun) – लताओं में पतले धागे या सूत का अंश (जिसके सहारे वही दीवार आदि पर चढ़ती है) a long thin part that grows from a climbing plant. *A plant uses tendrils to fasten itself to wall.*

Tenement/टेनिमेंट (noun) – अहाता, चाल especially in Scotland or the US a separate residence within a house or block of flats. a house divided into several separate residences. *He gazed at the tenements across the wall, dreaming of having a roof above his head some day.*

Tenet/टेनेट (noun) – मत, सिद्धान्त, धारणा a principle or belief. *Increasing intrusion of scientists has challenged some of the basic tenets of aboriginal life.*

Tennis/टेनिस (noun) – एक खेल a game in which two or four players strike a hollow rubber ball with rackets over a net stretched across a grass or clay court. see also real tennis. *Leander Paes is one of our country's best tennis players.*

Tenor/टेनर (noun) – दस्तूर, दिशा, स्वभाव, स्वर a singing voice between baritone and alto or countertenor, the highest of the ordinary adult male range. *His tenor could not be matched.*

Tense/टेन्स (noun) – तनावग्रस्त, बेचैन, काल a set of forms taken by a verb to indicate the time and something the continuance or comspleteness of the action in relation to the time of the utterance. *In English class today, the teacher taught us the application of tenses.*

Tension/टेन्शन् *(noun)* – तनाव the state of being tense. a strained state or condition resulting from forces acting in opposition to each other. *I have noticed that she has been under some sort of tension for the last few days.*

Tent/टेन्ट *(noun)* – तंबू, खेमा, शिविर a deep red sweet wine chiefly from Spain, used especially as sacramental wine. *As soon as we reached the farm, we took out and fixed our tents.*

Tentacle/टेन्टकल् *(noun)* – कीड़ों के सूँड़ a long slender flexible appendage of an animal, used for grasping or moving about, or bearing sense organs. *The jelly fish seemed to be coming nearer with its tentacles almost touching me.*

Tentative/टेन्टेटिव *(adjective)* – अनिश्चित, अंतरिम provisional. hesitant. *The college administration has released the tentative timetable for the exams.*

Tenuous/टेनुअस *(adjective)* – नाजुक जोड़, कमजोर तर्क very weak or slight. very slender or fine. *She was holding on to life by a tenuous thread.*

Tenure/टेन्युर *(noun)* – कार्यकाल, अवधि the conditions under which land or buildings are held or occupied. *Lack of security of tenure has led to more unemployment among the youth.*

Tepid/टेपिड *(adjective)* – गुनगुना lukewarm. *He hates the tepid bath water.*

Term/टर्म *(noun)* – पद, पदबंध, शब्द, अवधि a word or phrase used to describe a thing or to express a concept. a way of expressing oneself. a word or words that may be the subject or predicate of a proposition. *She used some difficult words to comprehend terms in her lecture.*

Terminal/टर्मिनल *(adjective)* – अन्त, आखिरी, मरणांतक लाइलाज of, forming, or situated at the end of something. of or forming a transport terminal. *I was waiting for her at the bus terminal.*

Terminate/टर्मिनेट *(verb)* – समाप्त करना bring to an end. end a pregnancy before term by artificial means. of a train or bus service end its journey. *The journey was terminated halfway because of the bomb threat in the area.*

Terminology/टर्मिनॉलॉजि *(noun)* – शब्दावली the body of terms used in a subject of study, profession, etc. *The terminology the lecturer used in the class was beyond the comprehension of the students.*

Terminus/टर्मिनस *(noun)* – अन्तिम स्टेशन a railway or bus terminal. an oil or gas terminal. *There was a huge traffic jam at the railway terminus.*

Termite/टर्माइट *(noun)* – दीमक a small, pale soft bodied social insect, typically making large nests of earth and feeding on wood. *All our furniture was being eaten up by termites.*

Terracotta/टेराकोटा *(noun)* – पथरी मिट्टी के बरतन या मूर्ति unglazed, typically brownish red earthenware, used chiefly as an ornamental building material and in modeling. *She works in a boutique where they make terracotta items.*

Terrestrial/टेरेस्ट्रिअल *(adjective)* – थलचर of, on, or relating to the earth or dry land. of an animal or plant living on or in the ground. of a planet resembling the earth. *I gave the teacher a list of terrestrial birds, just as she had asked.*

Terrible/टेरिब्ल *(adjective)* – संगीन, गम्भीर, भयानक extremely bad, serious, or unpleasant. *She came from the room with a grim face and revealed the terrible news of the death of her parents.*

Terrier/टेरिअर *(noun)* – छोटे नस्ल का कुत्ता a small dog of a breed originally used for turning out foxes and other animals from their earths. *I spotted a fox terrier at the kennel the other day.*

Terrific/टेरिफिक *(adjective)* – विशाल, श्रेष्ठ, भयानक of great size, amount, or intensity. excellent. *Listening to songs in our speakers has a terrific effect.*

Terrify/टेरिफाई *(verb)* – भयभीत करना cause to feel terror. *Children were terrified of going to the Dark House.*

T

Territory/टेरिटरि *(noun)* – सीमा an area under the jurisdiction of a ruler or state. *The Congress Party ruled most of the territories in India.*

Terror/टेरर *(noun)* – भय, आतंक extreme fear. the use of terror to intimidate people. a cause of terror; the period of the French revolution when the ruling Jacobin faction ruthlessly executed anyone considered a threat to their regime. *Hitler was a terror the world had to live with for a long long time.*

Terrorism/टेररिज्म *(noun)* – आतंकवाद unauthorised use of violence in pursuit of any political objective. *Terrorism is an evil our world has been facing for a long time now.*

Terrorist/टेरेरिस्ट *(noun)* – आतंकवादी a person who uses violence and intimidation in the pursuit of political aims. *Three terrorists were caught in the recent bomb attacks.*

Terse/टर्स *(adjective)* – कठिन, रूखा sparing in the use of words; abrupt. *She explained her role to the subordinates in a rather terse manner.*

Tertiary/टरशरि *(adjective)* – तीसरे क्रम या दर्जे का third in order or level. relating to or denoting education at a level beyond that provided by schools. *Tertiary education follows secondary education.*

Test/टेस्ट *(noun)* – जाँच परीक्षण, परीक्षण the shell or integument of some invertebrates and protozoans. *We had to break the test to know what the body composition of the sea urchin was like.*

Testament/टेस्टामेंट *(noun)* – प्रमाण a person' will. *She wrote a testament giving all rights to her property to her husband, before she died.*

Testify/टेस्टिफाइ *(verb)* – गवाही देना give evidence as a witness in a law court. *Bill Clinton was the only President in the USA to have testified for an embarrassing case.*

Testimonial/टेस्टिमोनिअल *(noun)* – संस्तुति प्रमाण पत्र a formal statement testifying to someone's character and qualifications. a public tribute to someone and to their achievements. *She didn't expect him to give testimonials on her skill.*

Testimonny टेस्टिमनि *(noun)* – प्रमाण, गवाही something that shows that something else exists or is true.

Tetanus/टेटनस *(noun)* – धनुषटंकार a bacterial disease causing rigidity and spasms of the voluntary muscles. *We had to get a tetanus vaccination done before the disease spreads.*

Tether/टेदर् *(noun)* – पशुओं को बाँधा गया पगहा (रस्सी) आदि a rope or chain with which an animal is tied to restrict its movement. *The cow was pulling at the string, trying to break the tether to which it was tied.*

Text/टेक्स्ट *(noun)* – मूल पाठ a written or printed work regarded in terms of content rather than form. the original words of an author or document. data corresponding to a body of writing. *There were more than a thousand words of text to study and analyse.*

Textile/टेक्सटाइल *(noun)* – वस्त्र, बुना हुआ वस्त्र a type of cloth or woven fabric. *She has been into textile business for quite some time now.*

Texture/टेक्सचर *(noun)* – रंग-आस्वाद the feel, appearance, or consistency of a surface or a substance. the character of a textile fabric as determined by its threads. *The dress had a rough texture making it itchy when you wear.*

Than/दैन *(conjunction & preposition)* – तुलना हेतु प्रयुक्त introducing the second element in a comparison. *She is a better athlete than I.*

Thatch/थैच *(noun)* – छप्पर, फूस की छत a roof covering of straw, reeds, or similar material. material used for such a covering. *Thatch roofs are a common sight in houses in South India.*

Thaw/थॉ *(verb)* – पिघलना of ice, snow, or a frozen thing become liquid or soft as a result of warming up. the weather becomes warmer and causes snow and ice to melt. cause to thaw. *It was time to thaw the ice.*

The/द *(det.)* – निश्चित सूचक शब्द denoting one or more people or things already mentioned or assumed to be common knowledge; the definite article. used to refer to a person, place, or thing that is unique. with a unit of time the present. used instead of a possessive. used with a surname to refer to a family or married couple. *The river was flowing in the wrong territory, apparently.*

Theatre/थीऐटर् *(noun)* – रंगशाला, नाट्यशाला a building in which plays and other dramatic performances are given. a cinema. *I got a list of movies running at the theatre nearby.*

T

Theft/थेफ्ट *(noun)* – चोरी the action or crime of stealing. *There has been a theft in my neighbourhood.*

Their/देअर *(possessive det.)* – उनका belonging to or associated with the people or things previously mentioned or easily identified. *The principal read out their accomplishments at the end of his speech.*

Them/देम *(pronoun)* – वे used as the object of a verb or preposition to refer to two or more people or things previously mentioned or easily identified. used after the verb 'to be' and after 'than' or 'as'. *We saw them at the party.*

Theme/थीम *(noun)* – सार, विषय वस्तु a subject or topic on which a person speaks, writes, or thinks. the first major constituent of a clause, indicating the subject matter. contrasted with rheme. *The theme of their speech was world peace.*

Then/देन *(adverb)* – तब at that time. *Back then, there were no cars, only horse carriages.*

Thence/देन्स *(adverb)* – वहाँ से from a place or source previously mentioned. *We flew to Norway and thence to Denmark.*

Thenceforward/देन्सफॉरवार्ड *(adverb)* – उस समय के बाद thenceforth. *With a significant nod of the head, he left the scene, and thenceforward, the world was a happy place to live in.*

Theology/थिऑलजि *(noun)* – धार्मिक विश्वास the study of the nature of god and religious belief. religious beliefs and theory when systematically developed. *She wanted to do her post graduate studies in theology.*

Theorem/थिअरेम *(noun)* – प्रमेय, साध्य a general proposition not self evident but proved by a chain of reasoning. a rule in algebra or other branches of mathematics expressed by symbols or formulae. *He proved the theorem he postulated.*

Theoretical/थिअरेटिकल *(adjective)* – सैद्धान्तिक concerned with or involving theory rather than its practical application. based on or calculated through theory. *After scoring well in the practical exam, it was now time to prepare for the theoretical exam.*

Theory/थिअरि *(noun)* – सिद्धान्त a supposition or a system of ideas intended to explain something, especially one based on general principles independent of the thing to be explained. an idea accounting for or justifying something. *She postulated a theory and was asked to prove it.*

Therapeutic/थेरप्यूटिक *(adjective)* – स्वास्थ और चिकित्सा सम्बन्धी of or relating to the healing of disease. having a good effect on the body or mind. *The spa treatment had a therapeutic effect on her.*

There/देअर *(adverb)* – वहाँ in, at, or to that place or position. in that respect; on that issue. *We were asked to sit there.*

Thereabouts/देअरएबाउट्स *(adverb)* – लगभग near that place. *Thereabouts lay the haunted house.*

Thereby/देअरबाइ *(adverb)* – इस तरह by that means; as a result of that. *She knocked the jug, thereby staining the tablecloth.*

Thereupon/देअरअपॉन *(adverb)* – फलस्वरूप immediately or shortly after that. *Thereupon the whole class gave a standing ovation to their favourite professor.*

Therm/थर्म *(noun)* – ऊष्मा की इकाई a unit of heat, especially as the former statutory unit of gas supplied in the UK equivalent to 100.000 British thermal units or 1055*10/8 joules. *1 therm of gas produces 100,000 B.T.U.*

Thermal/थर्मल *(adjective)* – ऊष्मा से सम्बन्धित of or relating to heat. another term for geothermal. relating to or denoting particles in thermodynamic equilibrium with their surroundings: thermal neutrons. *The scientists were working on discovering a new source of bio-thermal energy.*

Thermometer/थर्मामीटर *(noun)* – तापमान मापक यन्त्र an instrument for measuring and indicating temperature, typically consisting of a graduated glass tube containing mercury or alcohol which expands when heated. *The thermometer showed that she was running a temperature of 107.*

Thermostat/थर्मस्टैट *(noun)* – ताप नियन्त्रक a device that automatically regulated temperature or activates a device at a set temperature. *Turn down the thermostat, its getting hot!*

Thesaurus/थीसॉरॅस *(noun)* – पर्यायवाची शब्दकोश a book that lists words in groups of synonyms and related concepts. *I had to repeatedly refer to the thesaurus to be able to get synonyms for the words.*

These/दिज – ये plural form of this. *These chocolates are mine.*

Thesis/थीसिस *(noun)* – सिद्धान्त, शोध-प्रबन्ध a statement or theory that is put forward as a premise to be maintained or proved. a proposition forming the first stage in the process of dialectical reasoning. compare with antithesis, synthesis. *Now that you've presented the thesis, kindly explain the antithesis and the synthesis.*

They/दे *(pronoun)* – वे used to refer to two or more people or things previously mentioned or easily identified. people on general. people in authority regarded collectively. *They had gathered at the ground for a demonstration.*

Thick/थिक *(adjective)* – मोटा, घना, काफी with opposite sides or surfaces relatively far apart. made of heavy material. *I had to get a thick board that wouldn't fall off easily.*

Thickness/थिकनेस *(noun)* – मोटाई the distance through an object, as distinct from width or height. a layer of material. a thicker part of something. *The thickness of her hair was every hair stylists' dream.*

Thick-skinned/थिक-स्किन्ड *(adj)* – अपमान से अप्रभावित *Your words would have no effect on this thick-skinned man.*

Thicket/थिकेट *(noun)* – झाड़ी, झुरमुट a dense group of bushes or trees. *The voice seemed to be coming from the thicket at a distance.*

Thief/थिफ *(noun)* – चोर a person who steals another person'. *We ran and caught the thief.*

Thigh/थाइ *(noun)* – जाँघ the part of the human leg between the hip and the knee. the corresponding part in other animals. *He had cut a deep wound in his thigh that needed urgent treatment.*

Thimble/थिम्बल *(noun)* – अंगुस्ताना, अँगुलित्राण a metal or plastic cap with a closed end, worn to protect the finger and push the needle in sewing. any short metal tube or ferrule. *She could not stitch unless she had her thimble replaced.*

Thin/थिन *(adjective)* – पतला, दुबला, महीन, कमजोर having opposite surfaces or sides close together. having become less thick as a result of wear. *I gave her a thin book to read.*

Thin-skinned/थिनस्किन्ड *(adjective)* – अपमान से शीघ्र प्रभावित sensitive to criticism. *He is too thin-skinned to survive the competition.*

Thing/थिंग *(noun)* – वस्तु, परिस्थिति, शर्त an object that one need not, cannot, or does not wish to give a specific name to. personal belongings or clothing. *The sword had a black thing on it.*

Think/थिंक *(verb)* – विचारना, सोचना, धारणा बनाना have a particular opinion, belief, or idea about someone or something. *She thought good of him.*

Thinker/थिंकर *(noun)* – विचारक *Paul Brunton is a famous thinker.*

Thinking/थिंकिंग *(adjective)* – विचार, सोचने की क्रिया, सोच using thought or rational judgment; intelligent. *I thought he is a thinking man.* *(noun)* a person's ideas or opinions. thoughts; meditations. *She told me I need to change my thinking and consider a different perspective.*

Third/थर्ड *(ordinal number)* – तृतीय, तिहाई constituting number three in a sequence; 3rd. *Look at the third boy in the row.*

Third-rate/थर्डरेट *(adjective)* – घटिया किस्म का of inferior or very poor quality. *The sun glasses you bought were a third rate commodity.*

Thirst/थर्स्ट *(noun)* – प्यास, जिज्ञासा a feeling of needing or wanting to drink. lack of the liquid needed to sustain life. *We were dying of thirst in the desert.*

Thirsty/थर्स्टि *(adjective)* – प्यासा feeling thirst. in need of water; dry or parched. consuming a lot of fuel or water. *I felt sad for the thirsty plants.*

Thirteen/थर्टीन् *(cardinal number)* – तेरह equivalent to the sum of six and seven; one more than twelve, or seven less than twenty. *There were thirteen children in the room.*

Thirty/थर्टि *(cardinal number)* – तीस *(cardinal number)* the number equivalent to the product of three and ten; ten less forty; 30. *At least thirty people died in the bomb blast.*

T

Thirtieth/थर्टियथ *(number)* – तीसवाँ constituting number thirty in sequence. *Yesterday was his thirtieth birthday.*

This/दिस *(pronoun & det.)* – यह used to identify a specific person or thing close at hand or being indicated or experienced. referring to the neared of two things close to the speaker. *This is the tree I was talking about.*

Thistle/थिसल *(noun)* – गोखरू a widely distributed herbaceous plant of the daisy family, typically with a prickly stem and leaves and rounded heads of purple flowers. *Thistles were growing in abundance in her garden.*

Thistledown/थिस्लडाउन *(noun)* – गोखरू के बीज the light fluffy down of thistle seeds, enabling them to be blown about in the wind. *Like a ball of thistledown, it kissed the sea.*

Thorax/थोरैक्स – वक्ष, छाती, कीट के शरीर का मध्य भाग the middle part of your body between your neck and your waist, the middle section of an insect's body. *Thorax is a part of body between the neck and the stomach.*

Thorn/थॉर्न *(noun)* – काँटा a stiff, sharp pointed woody projection on the stem or other part of a plant. *The thorn in the plant pierced into my skin.*

Thorny/थॉर्नि – काँटेदार *(adjective)* having many thorns or thorn bushes. *We had to cut and remove the thorny bush that was growing in the garden.*

Thorough/थॉरो *(adjective)* – सभी प्रकार से complete with regard to every detail. performed with or showing great care and completeness. *She was thoroughly ready for the exam.*

Thoroughbred/थॉरोब्रेड *(adjective)* – असली नस्ल का of pure breed, especially of a breed of horse originating from English mares and Arab stallions. *One look at the horse and I knew it was a thoroughbred.*

Thorughfare/थॉरोफेअर *(noun)* – आम रास्ता a road or path forming a route between two places. *It was a busy thoroughfare.*

Those/दोज – वे, उन plural form of that. *Those were the people who should have been punished.*

Thought/थाट – विचार, चिन्तन past and past participle of think. *You spend too much time in thought.*

Thousand/थाउजैन्ड *(cardinal number)* – हजार the number equivalent to the product of a hundred and ten; 1,000. *I received a thousand rupees as prize.*

Thrash/थ्रैश *(verb)* – पीटना beat repeatedly and violently with or as with a stick or whip. *I will thrash him if he behaves like this again.*

Thread/थ्रेड *(noun)* – धागा, तारा, सूत, सूई में तारा डालना a long, thin strand of cotton, nylon, or other fibres used in sewing or weaving. *The thread on the fabric was standing up.*

Threat/थ्रेट *(noun)* – आशंका, खतरा a statement of an intention to inflict injury, damage, or other hostile action as retribution. a menace of bodily harm, such as may restrain a person's freedom of action. *We received a threat call this evening and immediately informed the police.*

Threaten/थ्रेटेन *(verb)* – धमकी देना make or express a threat to or to do something. *The kidnappers threatened to kill the boy if their ransom was not paid.*

Three/थ्री *(cardinal number)* – तीन equivalent to the sum of one and two; one more than two; 3 *Three men made their way on a horse towards Jerusalem.*

Thresh/थ्रेस *(verb)* – कूट-पीटकर अनाज निकालना, दँवनी separate grain from typically with a flail or by the action of a revolving mechanism. *I found a new technique for threshing.*

Threshold/थ्रेसोल्ड *(noun)* – देहरी, द्वार, प्रवेश-निकास मार्ग a strip of wood or stone forming the bottom of a doorway and crossed in entering a house or room. *She stood at the threshold, waiting for everyone to come out of their shock of seeing her.*

Thrice/थ्राइस *(adverb)* – तीन बार three times. *Shake the bottle thrice before consuming the medicine.*

Thrift/थ्रिफ्ट *(noun)* – कमखर्च the quality of being careful and not wasteful with money and other resources. *Save money and be thrift.*

Thrill/थ्रिल *(noun)* – पुलक, रोमांच a sudden feeling of excitement and pleasure. an experience that produces such a feeling. a wave or nervous tremor of emotion or sensation. *She felt the thrill rising and adrenaline pumping her blood as the rollercoaster started.*

T

Thrive /थ्राइब *(verb)* - फलना-फूलना grow or develop well or vigorously. prosper; flourish. *Virus thrives on garbage.*

Throat/थ्रोट *(noun)* - गला, कंठ the passage which leads from the back of the mouth of a person or animal. the front part of the neck. *She has been having severe throat pain for the last four days.*

Throb/थ्राब *(verb)* - धड़कन, धड़कना, स्पंदन beat or sound with a strong, regular rhythm; pulsate. *I could feel my heart throbbing through my veins.*

Throes/थ्रोज *(plural noun)* - प्रसव वेदना, व्यथा, वेदना intense or violent pain and struggle. *He convulsed in his death throes.*

Throne/थ्रोन *(noun)* - सिंहासन, राजगद्दी a ceremonial chair for a sovereign, bishop, or similar figure. the power or rank of a sovereign. *The prince would be the heir to the throne.* (verb) place on a throne. *The prince was throned on June 25th.*

Throng/थ्राँग *(noun)* - भीड़ a large, densely packed crowd. *He made his way through the throng of people.* (verb) gather in large numbers in. flock or be present in great numbers. *A crowd thronged the station.*

Throttle/थ्रॉटिल *(noun)* - गला घोंटना a device controlling the flow of fuel or power to an engine. *The devices were at full throttle.*

Through/थ्रू *(preposition & adverb)* - आर-पार moving in one side and out of the other side of. so as to make a hole or passage in. expressing the position or location of something beyond. expressing the extent of changing orientation. *The sword went right through his heart.*

Throw/थ्रो *(verb)* - फेंकना, फेंकने की दूरी propel with force through the air by a rapid movement of the arm and hand. send to the ground in wrestling, judo, etc. unseat. bowl with an illegitimate bent arm action. *She threw the newspaper into the window.*

Thrush/थ्रश *(noun)* - सारिका, गायिका पक्षी a small or medium sized songbird, typically with a brown back and spotted breast. *The patient called the sad looking doctor a singing thrush.*

Thrust/थ्रस्ट *(verb)* - धकेलना, घुसेड़ना, आगे की ओर push suddenly or violently in the specified direction. *She thrust her hand into his box and it got stuck there!*

Thud/थड *(noun)* - धम की आवाज, धब-धब a dull, leaden sound, such as that made by a heavy object falling to the ground. *I heard a thud from somewhere downstairs, around midnight.*

Thug/थग *(noun)* - आक्रामक, हिंसात्मक, अपराधी a violent and uncouth man, especially a criminal. *The thugs were convicted without much delay.*

Thumb/थम्ब *(noun)* - अँगूठा the short, thick first digit of the hand, set lower and apart from the other four and opposable to them. *She broke her thumb in the accident.*

Thump/थम्प *(verb)* - टोकना, खटखटाना, आघात hit heavily, especially with the fist or a blunt implement. put down forcefully, noisily, or decisively. beat or pulsate strongly. *My heart was thumping so loud I thought everyone would hear.*

Thunder/थंडर *(noun & verb)* - कड़क, गरज, कड़कना, गरजना a loud rumbling or crashing noise heard after a lightning flash due to the expansion of rapidly heated air. *There was thunder and lightning all night.*

Thunderbolt/थंडरबोल्ट *(noun)* - बिजली, वज्र a flash of lightning with a simultaneous crash of thunder. a supported bolt or shaft believed to be the destructive agent in a lightning flash, especially as an attribute of a god such as Jupiter. *The news hit her like a thunderbolt.*

Thunderstorm/थंडरस्टॉर्म *(noun)* - गरजता तूफान a storm with thunder and lightning and typically also heavy rain or hall. *The town was struck by a thunderstorm.*

Thunderstruck/थंडरस्ट्रक *(adjective)* - हक्का-बक्का, जड़, हो जाना extremely surprised or shocked. *They stood thunderstruck when they heard the news.*

Thursday/थर्सडे *(noun)* - गुरुवार the day of the week before Friday and following Wednesday. *I look forward to our Thursday-parties.*

Thus/दस *(adverb)* - इस प्रकार, इसलिए as a result or consequence of this; therefore. *She killed him, thus landing up in jail.*

T

Thwart/थ्वार्ट *(verb)* – निष्फल करना, बाधा डालना prevent from succeeding in or accomplishing something. *Their plans were thwarted by the teacher who had always an eye on them.*

Tick/टिक *(noun)* – टिक-टिक a fabric case stuffed with feathers or other material to form a mattress or pillow. short for ticking. *The sound of the clock ticking was actually comforting.*

Ticket/टिकेट *(noun)* – यात्रा का, दर्शन का अनुमति पत्रक a piece of paper or card giving the holder a right to admission to a place or event or to travel on public transport. *She ran to get the tickets before the movie starts.*

Tickle/टिकल *(noun & verb)* – गुदगुदी, चुनचुनी, गुदगुदाना lightly touch in a way that causes itching or twitching and often laughter. catch a trout by lightly rubbing it so that it moves backwards into the hand. *She tickled me so badly I was rolling on the floor.*

Tidal/टाइडल *(adjective)* – ज्वार-भाटा सम्बन्धी having to do with rise flow of river or sea water. *The river here is not tidal.*

Tide/टाइड *(noun)* – ज्वार-भाटा the alternate rising and falling of the sea due to the attraction of the moon and sun. *We were asked to stay away from the beach as the tide was higher than usual.*

Tiding/टाइडिंग *(singular noun)* – समाचार news; information. *If the tiding ever reached her, there would be nothing to save her from dishonour.*

Tidy/टाइडि *(adjective)* – सुव्यवस्थित arranged neatly and in order. inclined to keep things or one's appearance neat and in order. not messy; neat and controlled. *She keeps her cupboard quite neat and tidy.*

Tie/टाइ *(verb)* – बन्ध, फीता, गला बन्ध, बाँधना attach or fasten with string, cord, etc. form into a knot or bow. restrict someone's movement by binding their arms or legs or binding them to something. bring something to a satisfactory conclusion. *The thief tied the hands of the lady with a string.*

Tier/टीयर *(noun)*- ऊँचे-नीचे खाने में सोने की व्यवस्था, स्तर one of a series of rows or levels stacked one above the other. *We were travelling on a three-tier AC compartment.*

Tiff/टिफ *(noun)* – दोस्ताना झगड़ा a quarrel. *The couple were caught in a tiff.*

Tiger/टाइगर *(noun)* – बाघ a very large solitary cat with a yellow brown coat striped with black;s native to the forests of Asia. *The number of tigers in the country has dwindled.*

Tight/टाइट *(adjective)* – कसा हुआ, चुस्त, तंग, दृढ़, सख्त fixed or fastened firmly; hard to move, undo, or open. close fitting, especially uncomfortably so. very firm. well sealed against something such as water or air. *Her shawl was twisted into a tight knot.*

Tighten/टाइटन *(verb)* – कस देना having to do with fastened firmly. *The noose was tightened around the neck of the culprit.*

Tight-fisted/टाइटफिस्टेड *(adjective)* – हाथ दाब लेना, कम खर्च not willing to spend or give much money; miserly. *He is extremely tight-fisted with his finances.*

Tight-lipped/टाइटलिप्ड *(adjective)* – होठ सी लेना, कम बोलना with the lips firmly closed, especially as a sign of suppressed emotion or determined reticence. *Everyone was instructed to be tight-lipped about the incident.*

Tights/टाइट्स *(plural noun)* – चुस्त कपड़े a close fitting garment made of a knitted yarn, covering the legs, hips, and bottom. *She wore tights under her skirt.*

Tigress/टाइग्रेस *(noun)* – बाघिन, शेरनी a female tiger. *The tigress roared at the trembling goat.*

Tile/टाइल *(noun)* – पत्थर का खपड़ा या पट्टी a thin square or rectangular slab of baked clay, concrete, etc., used in overlapping rows for covering roofs. a similar slab of glazed pottery or other material for covering floors or walls. *She was using vitrified tiles for her house.*

Till/टिल *(prep. noun & verb)* – तब तक, दराज, हल जोतना drawer for money in a shop, bank, or restaurant. *There were long queues at the till.*

Tiller/टिलर *(noun)* – पतवार का डण्डा a horizontal bar fitted to the head of a boat's rubber post and used for steering. *The tiller was swinging with the ship completely out of control.*

T

Tilt/टिल्ट *(verb)* – झुकना, झुकाना, तिरछी move or cause to move into a slopping position. move in a vertical plane. *The windows tilted slightly.*

Timber/टिम्बर *(noun)* – इमारती लकड़ी wood prepared for use in building and carpentry. trees grown for such wood. a wooden beam or board used in building and shipbuilding. *They had a timber plantation in their estate.*

Time/टाइम *(noun)* – समय, काल, अवधि the indefinite continued progress of existence and events in the past, present, and future, regarded as a whole. *He dreamt of travelling through space and time.*

Timeless/टाइमलेस *(adjective)* – समय से अप्रभावित not affected by the passage of time or changes in fashion. *Some of Kishore Kumar's songs are timeless melodies.*

Timely/टाइमलि *(adjective)* – समय पर done or occurring at a favourable or appropriate time. *Thanks to the doctor's timely arrival, her father was saved.*

Timid/टिमिड *(adjective)* – कायर, भीरु lacking in courage or confidence. *She was rather timid when she was new to the city.*

Timorous/टिमॅरस *(adjective)* – कायर और भ्रान्त lacking in courage or confidence; nervous. *A timorous voice spoke from the last bench.*

Tin/टिन *(noun)* – डिब्बा a silvery white metal, the chemical element of atomic number 50. *She bought a tinplate for some lab work.*

Tinge/टिन्ज *(noun & verb)* – हल्का रंग, आभा, झलक, हल्का रंग देना colour slightly. *The pink-tinged cloud was a picture worth being framed.*

Tingle/टिंगल *(noun & verb)* – झुनझुनी, सनसनाहट महसूस करना a slight prickling or stinging sensation. *She was tingled all over with joy.* *(verb)* experience or cause to experience a tingle. *A tingle went down my spine at the mere thought of going to that house.*

Tinker/टिंकर *(noun)* – अकुशल कारीगर an itinerant mender of pots, kettles, etc. *I met a tinker once in one of my trips.*

Tinkle/टिंकल *(verb)* – घण्टा ध्वनि make or cause to make a light, clear ringing sound. *The tinkling of the cycle bells seemed too loud in this quite town.*

Tinsel/टिंसेल *(noun)* – सजावटी धागा, पट्टी a form of decoration consisting of thin strips of shiny metal foil attached to a length of thread. *I decorated her room with tinsels and party lights.*

Tint/टिंट *(noun)* – रंग की आभा, झलक a shade or variety of colour. a trace of something. *The sky had a grey tint to it.*

Tiny/टाइनि *(adjective)* – नन्हा, लघु very small. *A tiny little insect was nibbling at my feet.*

Tip/टिप *(noun & verb)* – नोक, उलट देना, झुकाना, इनाम देना, सूचना the pointed or rounded extremity of something slender or tapering. a small part fitted to the end of an object. *What we saw before us was just the tip of the ice berg.*

Tipsy/टिप्सि *(adjective)* – सरूर में slightly drunk. *I asked the others to ignore her as she is tipsy.*

Tiptoe/टिपटो *(verb)* – पंजों के बल चलना walk quietly and carefully with one's heels raised and one's weight on the balls of the feet. *We tip-toed through the hall and stealthily entered the kitchen.*

Tirade/टिरेड *(noun)* – उत्तेजक भाषण a long speech of angry criticism or accusation. *As soon as I entered, I was welcomed with a tirade of complaints.*

Tire/टायर *(verb)* – थक जाना, ऊब जाना become or cause to become in need of rest or sleep. exhaust the patience or interest of. become impatient or bored with. *I was tired of hearing her complaints everyday.*

Tiresome/टायरसम *(adjective)* – ऊबाऊ, कष्टकर causing one to feel bored or impatient. *Her tantrums were indeed getting quite tiresome.*

Tissue/टिशू *(noun)* – ऊतक, कागज का रूमाल any of the distinct types of material of which animals or plants are made, consisting of specialized cells and their products. *She had a tear in the tissue near her elbow.*

Tit/टिट *(noun)* – एक छोटी चिड़िया a titmouse. *There was a tit mouse in the attic.*

Titbit/टिटबिट *(noun)* – चटपटे आहार का टुकड़ा a small piece of tasty food. *The little mouse was hunting around for titbits.*

T

Title/टाइटल *(noun)* – नाम, शीर्षक, उपाधि, पदवी, अधिकार the name of a book, musical composition, or other artistic work. a caption or credit in a film or broadcast. *The title of the book had to be mentioned in bold caps.*

Title-page/टाइटलपेज *(noun)* – मुखपृष्ठ first cover page of a book, film documentary. *The author had unreasonable demands for even the title page.*

To/टू *(preposition)* – तक, वहाँ तक expressing direction or position in relation to a particular location, point, or condition. in telling the time before the hour specified. *We were on the way to the station when the accident happened.*

Toad/टोड *(noun)* – मेढक a tailless amphibian with a short stout body and short legs, typically having dry warty skin that can exude poison. *A rather big toad jumped in front of our vehicle.*

Toadstool/टोडस्टूल *(noun)* – कुकुरमुत्ता the spore bearing fruiting body of a fungus, typically in the form of a rounded cap on a stalk, especially one that is inedible or poisonous. *Learn to distinguish between a mushroom and a toadstool.*

Toast/टोस्ट *(noun)* – सेंकना, सेंकी हुई दोहरी रोटी, शुभकामना घूँट bread baked and browned on open fire. *I like toast and tea in the morning.*

Tobacco/टॅबैको *(noun)* – तम्बाकू a preparation of the dried and fermented nicotine rich leaves of an American plant, used for smoking or chewing. *There is too much tobacco in this particular brand of cigars.*

Tobacconist/टॅबैकोनिस्ट *(noun)* – तम्बाकू बेंचने वाला a shopkeeper who sells cigarettes and tobacco. *He worked as a tobacconist for 15 years down the road.*

Today/टुडे *(adverb)* – आज on or in the course of this present day. at the present period of time; nowadays. *The effect of the radiation that spread 50 years ago continues even today.*

Toddle/टॉडल *(verb)* – छोटे बच्चे का चलना move with short unsteady steps while learning to walk. walk or go in a casual or leisurely way. *The baby has started toddling.*

Toe/टो *(noun)* – पैर की अँगुली any of the five digits at the end of the human foot. any of the digits of the foot of a quadruped or bird. the part of an item of footwear that covers a person's toes. *She had sharp toe nails.*

Toffee/टॉफी *(noun)* – एक मिठाई a kind of firm or hard sweet which softens when sucked or chewed, made by boiling together sugar and butter. *She was planning to make toffees for Christmas.*

Together/टुगेदर *(adverb)* – साथ में, सम्मिश्रण with or in proximity to another person or people. so as to touch or combine. in combination; collectively. into companionship or close association. married or in a sexual relationship. so as to be united or in agreement. *My parents have been together for 35 years now.*

Toil/टॉयल *(verb)* – श्रम, कड़ा परिश्रम work extremely hard or incessantly. move somewhere slowly and with difficulty. *He has been toiling away at the farm for days now.*

Toilet/टॉयलेट *(noun)* – शौचालय a large bowl for urinating or defecating into, typically plumbed into a sewage system. *The public toilet was in desperate need for maintenance.*

Token/टोकन *(noun)* – सिक्के जैसा साक्ष्य a thing serving to represent a fact, quality, feeling, etc. a badge or favour worn to indicate allegiance to a person or party. a word or object conferring authority on or serving to authenticate the speaker or holder. a device given to a train driver on a single track railway as authority to proceed. *She was given a bonus as a token of appreciation for her hard work.*

Tolerate/टॉलरेट *(verb)* – सहन करना allow the existence or occurrence of without interference. *I will not tolerate this disobedience any more.*

Tolerance/टॉलरन्स *(noun)* – सहनशक्ति, सहिष्णुता the ability, willingness, or capacity to tolerate something. *Gandhiji is known for his great level of tolerance.*

Tolerant/टॉलरन्ट *(adjective)* – सहिष्णु showing tolerance. *We must learn to be tolerant of others.*

Toll/टॉल *(noun)* – मार्ग कर, मृतको की संख्या, लय में a charge payable to use a bridge or road.

T

a charger for a long distance telephone call. *The toll for this road was increased twice in the last few months.*

Tomato/टॅमैटो *(noun)* – टमाटर a glossy red or yellow edible fruit, eaten as a vegetable or in salads. *I like tomato sandwiches better than onion.*

Tomb/टॅम्ब *(noun)* – समाधि a burial place, especially a large underground vault. a monument to a dead person, erected over their burial place. *The Taj Mahal is the greatest tomb of love.*

Tomboy/टॉम्बॉय *(noun)* – लड़कानुमा लड़की a girl who enjoys rough, noisy activities traditionally associated with boys. *She grew up as a tomboy but transformed into a lovely lady later.*

Tombstone/टूमस्टोन *(noun)* – समाधि लेख a large, flat inscribed stone standing or laid over a grave. *Her tombstone mentioned her name differently, I noticed.*

Tommorow/टुमॉरो *(adverb)* – अगला दिन on the day after today. *The dress will be delivered tomorrow.*

Ton/टन *(noun)* – तोल की एक माप measure of weight. *I have got tones of homework to do.*

Tone/टोन *(noun)* – स्वर-शैली, स्वभाव, आभा a musical or vocal sound with reference to its pitch, quality, and strength. *They were talking in hushed tones.*

Toneless/टोनलेस *(adjective)* – नीरस, फीका, निर्जीव lacking experssion in a vocie or musical sound. *I wonder why he is singing in a toneless voice.*

Tongs/टॉग्स *(plural noun)* – चिमटा, सँड़सी a tool with two movable arms that are joined at one end, used for picking up and holding things. *She moved the barbecue away from the fire with the tongs.*

Tongue/टंग *(noun)* – जीभ, भाषा, बोली, बोलने की शैली the fleshy muscular organs in the mouth, used for tasting, licking, swallowing, and articulating speech. the tongue of an ox or lamb, as food. *The ox has a really long tongue that reaches almost till its eyes.*

Tonic/टॉनिक *(noun)* – स्फूर्तिदायक a medicinal substance taken to give a feeling of vigour or well being. *You should take this tonic as it will give you energy.*

Tonight/टुनाइट *(adverb)* – आज की रात या शाम on the present or approaching evening or night. *Let's go for a drink tonight.*

Tonnage/टनेज *(noun)* – कुल भार weight in tons. *Trucks carry more tonnage than tractors.*

Tonne/टन *(noun)* – माप की इकाई another term for metric ton. *Six tonnes of iron were being transported.*

Tonsil/टॉन्सिल *(noun)* – गले की ग्रन्थि, गलसुआ either of two small masses of lymphoid tissue in the throat, one on each side of the root of the tongue. *He had to have his tonsils taken out.*

Tonsure/टॉन्सर *(noun)* – मुंडन a part of a monk's or priest's head left bare on top by shaving off the hair. *At this rate, he'll soon have a tonsure like a monk.*

Too/टू *(adverb)* – भी, इसके अतिरिक्त, अधिक to a higher degree than is desirable, permissible, or possible. very. *I'm sorry, you're too late.*

Tool/टूल *(noun)* – औजार a device or implement, typically hand held, used to carry out a particular function. *I bought him a tool kit for his birthday.*

Toot/टूट *(noun & verb)* – भोंपू, सीटी, भोंपू बजाना a short, sharp sound made by a horn, trumpet, or similar instrument. *I could hear the toot of the school bus from down the street.*

Tooth/टूथ *(noun)* – दाँत, दाँतनुमा hard bonelike structures in the jaws of vertebrates; used for biting and chewing or for attack and defence. *My one tooth was broken in an accident.*

Toothache/टूथ-एॅक *(noun)* – दाँत का दर्द pain in a tooth or teeth. *She has been having a toothache for the last few days now.*

Top/टॉप *(noun)* – चोटी, शिखर, पराकाष्ठा, लट्टू, ऊपरी भाग, ऊपरी वस्त्र, ऊँचा, सर्वोपरि a conical, spherical, or pear shaped toy that may be set to spin. *The top was her favourite toy throughout her childhood.*

Topaz/टोपाज *(noun)* – पुखराज a precious stone, typically colourless, yellow, or pale blue, consisting of a fluorine containing aluminium silicate. *She has been wearing a topaz ring for the last few years now.*

Topic/टॉपिक *(noun)* – विषय, विचार, प्रकरण, वार्ता a subject of a text, speech, conversation, etc. *What exactly is the topic of discussion here?*

Topical/टॉपिकल *(adjective)* – सामयिक relating to or dealing with current affairs. *One of my favorite topical affairs programme was We The People.*

Topography/टॅपॅग्राफि *(noun)* – स्थान की आकृति, स्थान का विवरण the arrangement of the natural and artificial physical features of an area. a detailed description or representation on a map of such features. *I could see the topography change as the train went from the North to the South.*

Topple/टॉपल *(verb)* – गिराना, लुढ़कना, लुढ़काना overbalance or cause to overbalance and fall. *I laughed at the story of Humpty Dumpty toppling off the wall.*

Topsy-turvy/टॉप्सिटर्वि *(adjective & adverb)* – अव्यवस्थित, उल्टा-पुल्टा upside down. *Why is the whole house topsy-turvy today?*

Torch/टॉर्च *(noun)* – प्रकाश यन्त्र, मशाल, आग लगाना a portable battery powered electric lamp. *I took the torch when I left her house last night as it was really dark outside.*

Torment/टॉर्मेंट *(noun)* – सताना, वेदना, यातना severe physical or mental suffering. a cause of torment. *She has been the chief cause of my torment.*

Tornado/टॉर्नेडो *(noun)* – बवंडर, तूफान, समुद्री तूफान a mobile, destructive vortex of violently rotating winds having the appearance of a funnel shaped cloud. *The entire state was devastated by the twin tornadoes that struck yesterday.*

Torpedo/टॉर्पीडो *(noun)* – एक प्रकार की मछली a cigar shaped self propelled underwater missile designed to be fired from a ship, submarine, or an aircraft and to explode on reaching a target. *The torpedo attack was started by the US first.*

Torrent/टॉरेंट *(noun)* – बौछार a strong and fast moving stream of water of other liquid. *It was pouring in torrents in the neighbouring state.*

Torrid/टॉरिड *(adjective)* – गरम और सूखा, तीव्र very hot and dry. *The torrid heat of the desert was getting to me.*

Torso/टॉर्सो *(noun)* – धड़ the trunk of the human body. *His torso was visible in the night.*

Tortoise/टॉर्टस (टार्टिज) *(noun)* – कछुआ a slow moving land reptile of warm climates, enclosed in a scaly or leathery domed shell into which it can retract its head and legs. *The zoo kept different kinds of tortoise.*

Tortuous/टार्ट्युअस *(adjective)* – चक्करदार, वक्र, टेढ़ा-मेढ़ा full of twists and turns. *The route is remote and tortuous.*

Torture/टॉर्चर *(noun)* – यन्त्रणा, कष्ट देना the action or practice of infliction severe pain as a punishment or a forcible means of persuasion. *The prisoners have been through immense torture.*

Toss/टॉस *(verb)* – उछालना, झटका देना throw lightly or casually. throw off its back. throw into the air so as to make a choice, based on which side of the coin faces uppermost when it lands. *She tossed her bag on to the sofa.*

Total/टोटल *(adjective)* – समग्र, पूर्ण, सब comprising the whole number or amount. *The total figure amounts to $5,000.*

Totalitarian/टोटलिटेरियन *(adjective)* – एक का पूर्ण अधिकार of or relating to a centralized and dictatorial system of government requiring complete subservience to the state. *The country was experiencing a totalitarian regime.*

Totter/टॉटर *(verb)* – लड़खड़ाना, डगमगाना move in an unsteady way. *The old lady came tottering towards the train.*

Touch/टच *(verb)* – छूना, स्पर्श करना come into or be in contact with. come or bring into mutual contact. bring one's hand or another part of one's body into contact with. strike lightly in a specified direction. *The child was glad when his feet touched the ground.*

Touching/टचिंग *(adjective)* – मर्मस्पर्शी, कारुणिक arousing strong emotion; moving. *The scene was indeed touching.* preposition concerning. *Several discoveries touching the lost traditions of the Andamanese tribes, have been made.*

T

Touchy/टचि *(adjective)* – तुनुक मिजाज quick to take offence; over sensitive. *He is a touchy guy when it comes to his race.*

Tough/टफ *(adjective)* – कड़ा, कठिन, दुर्भाग्यपूर्ण strong enough to withstand wear and tear. difficult to cut or chew. *The bread you made was too tough.*

Tour/टूर *(noun)* – दौरा, यात्रा, यात्रा करना a journey for pleasure in which several different places are visited. *Guided tours may limit your scope for discovering unknown places.*

Tourism/टूरिज्म *(noun)* – पर्यटन the commercial organization and operation of holidays and visits to places of interest. *The movie has promoted tourism in the state.*

Tourist/टूरिस्ट *(noun)* – पर्यटक a person who travels for pleasure. *Tourists receive a lot of special attention in this restaurant.*

Tournament/टूर्नामेंट *(noun)* – खेल प्रतियोगिता a series of contests between a number of competitors, competing for an overall prize. *The tournament was organized to improve the relations between the two countries.*

Tow/टो *(noun & verb)* – खींचकर ले जाना, खिंचाई करना the coarse and broken part of flax or hemp prepared for spinning. *The tow was ready for spinning.*

Towards/टुवाईस *(preposition)* – की ओर in the direction of. *We drove towards the beach.*

Towel/टॉवेल *(noun)* – तौलिया a piece of thick absorbent cloth or paper used for drying. *There were clean and fresh towels in the cupboard.*

Tower/टॉवर *(noun)* – मीनार, ऊँचा a tall, narrow building, either free standing or forming part of a building such as a church or castle. *The bell on the church tower rang non-stop.*

Town/टाउन *(noun)* – नगर a built up area with a name, defined boundaries, and local government, that is larger than a village and generally smaller than a city. the chief city or town of a region. *There were seven towns in the province.*

Town hall/टाउन हॉल *(noun)* – नगर भवन a building used for the administration of local government. *The protestors gathered at the town hall to conduct their demonstration.*

Toxic/टॉक्सिक *(adjective)* – विषाक्त, जहरीला poisonous. of, relating to, or caused by poison. *There have been reports of toxic water in certain areas.*

Toxin/टॉक्सिन *(noun)* – नशा उपजाने वाला, बीमार करने वाला a poison produced by a microorganism or other organism and acting as an antigen in the body. *The doctor could clearly spot harmful toxins in the patient's bloodstream.*

Toy/टॉय *(noun)* – खिलौना, गम्भीरताहीन an object for a child to play with, typically a model or miniature replica of something. a gadget or machine regarded as providing amusement for an adult. *She had a room overflowing with toys.*

Trace/ट्रेस *(noun & verb)* – अवशेष, चिह्न, थोड़ी मात्रा, खोज निकालना each of the two side straps, chains, or ropes by which a horse is attached to a vehicle that it is pulling. *The traces were wearing off and the horse was revolting too.*

Track/ट्रैक *(verb)* – चिह्न, पदचिह्न, लीक, दिशा, पटरी tow a canoe along a waterway from the bank. *He was trying to track the canoe up the rapids.*

Tract/ट्रैक्ट *(noun)* – भूभाग, बड़ा क्षेत्र, नलिका a short treatise in pamphlet form, typically on a religious subject. *I read out the tract we received from the Church.*

Traction/ट्रैक्शन *(noun)* – खींचना, खींचने की शक्ति the action of pulling a thing along a surface. the motive power used for pulling, especially on a railway. *There was a primitive vehicle used for animal traction at the museum.*

Tractor/ट्रैक्टर *(noun)* – खेत जोतने वाली गाड़ी a powerful motor vehicle with large rear wheels, used chiefly on farms for hauling equipment and trailers. *She worked in a factory that manufactures tractors.*

Trade/ट्रेड *(noun)* – व्यापार, लेन-देन, व्यवसाय, पेशा the buying and selling of goods and services. a business of a particular kind. *All kinds of trade between the two countries have been stopped.*

Trademark/ट्रेडमार्क *(noun)* – व्यावसायिक चिह्न a symbol, word, or words legally registered or established by use as representing a company or product. *The invention got the trademark of the company.*

T

Tradition/ट्रेडिशन *(noun)* – परम्परा the transmission of customs or beliefs from generation to generation, or the fact of being so passed on. a long established custom or belief passed on in this way. *Traditions were made by man and therefore are liable to be changed.*

Traditional/ट्रेडिशनल *(adjective)* – पारंपरिक relating to, or following tradition. *The traditional festivities of Onam were all set to begin.*

Traffic/ट्रैफिक *(noun)* – यातायात, वाहन-संचालन, अवैध व्यापार vehicles moving on a public highway. *The traffic was being diverted to let the VIPs pass.*

Tragedy/ट्रेजिडि *(noun)* – दु:खद, दु:खान्त, त्रासदी an event causing great suffering. destruction, and distress. *The family was struck by a tragedy three years ago.*

Trail/ट्रेल *(noun)* – पीछा करना, पदचिह्न, अवशेष a mark or a series of sign or objects left behind by the passage of someone or something. a track or scent used in following someone or hunting an animal. *The police found a trail of blood at the site of crime.*

Trailer/ट्रेलर *(noun)* – साथ खींची जाने वाली गाड़ी, लघु अंश an unpowered vehicle towed by another. the rear section of an articulated truck. a caravan. *He has been living in a trailer for the last few months.*

Train/ट्रेन *(noun & verb)* – रेलगाड़ी, कतार, पंक्तिबद्ध, ताँता, सिलसिला, प्रशिक्षण देना, सिखाना teach a particular skill or type of behaviour through regular practice and instruction. be taught in such a way. *The students were being trained to become good professionals.*

Trainer/ट्रेनर *(noun)* – प्रशिक्षक a person who trains people or animals. an aircraft or simulator used to train pilots. *He enrolled at the farm as a horse trainer.*

Training/ट्रेनिंग *(noun)* – प्रशिक्षण the action of teacing a person or animal a particular skill. *She is undergoing rigorous training for the event.*

Trait/ट्रेट *(noun)* – विशेष गुण a distinguishing quality or characteristic, a genetically determined characteristic. *She did show instances of self denigration typical to her family trait.*

Tram/ट्राम *(noun)* – पटरी पर चलने वाली गाड़ी a passenger vehicle powered by electricity conveyed by overhead cables, and running on rails laid in a public road. *There have been terror attack threats to the local trams.*

Tramp/ट्रैम्प *(verb)* – धब-धब करते चलना, लम्बी पद यात्रा walk heavily or noisily. *The little girl was tramping around the whole house.*

Trample/ट्रैम्प्ल *(verb)* – रौंदना, कुचलना tread on and crush. *The child trampled all over the ants on the doorway.*

Trance/ट्रांस *(noun)* – बेहोशी, समाधि, गहन ध्यान, मग्न a half conscious state characterized by an absence of response to external stimuli, typically as induced by hypnosis or entered by a medium. *The patient entered into a state of trance as directed by the hypnotist.*

Tranquil/ट्रैन्क्विल *(adjective)* – शान्त, प्रशान्त, निस्तब्ध free from disturbance; calm. *The sea was as tranquil as a sleeping baby.*

Tranquillity/ट्रैन्क्विलिटी *(noun)* – शान्ति, स्तिब्धता scene of peacefulness. *We went to the monastery in the hills seeking tranquility and peace of mind. We went to the monastery in the hills seeking tranquillity and peace of mind.*

Trans/ट्रांस *(prefix)* – उस पार का across; beyond: transcontinental. on or to the other side of: transatlantic. *Their transatlantic journey had just begun.*

Transact/ट्रैन्ज़ैक्ट *(verb)* – कारोबार करना, सौदा करना to do business with a person or organisation. *Be careful while transacting on the phone.*

Transaction/ट्रैन्ज़ैक्शन *(noun)* – कारोबार, सौदा करना an instance of buying or selling. the action of conducting business. *Transactions on the phone are extremely risk prone.*

Transcend/ट्रांसेंड *(verb)* – सीमा से ऊपर जाना be or go beyond the range or limits of. *The monk had transcended the limits of phenomenal life.*

Transcendent/ट्रांसेन्डेन्ट *(adjective)* – उत्कृष्ट, अति उत्तम transcending normal or physical human experience. existing apart from and not subject to the limitations of the material universe. often contrasted with immanent.

T

Philosophy is about the search for a transcendent level of knowledge.

Transcribe/ट्रान्सक्राइब *(verb)* – उतारना, प्रतिलेखन, मुद्रित या लिखित रूप में बदलना write out from speech, notes, etc.

Transcription/ट्रांसक्रिप्शन *(noun)* – प्रतिलेखन, अभिलेख a transcript. *They produced a complete transcription of the journal.*

Transfer/ट्रांसफर *(verb)* – स्थानान्तरण, हस्तान्तरण move from one place to another. *Your money is being transferred from the headquarters to the home branch.*

Transfix/ट्रांसफिक्स *(verb)* – स्तंभित make motionless with horror, wonder, or astonishment. *He was transfixed with the sorrow in her eyes.*

Transform/ट्रान्सफॉर्म *(verb)* – परिवर्तित होना, परिवर्तित करना, रूपान्तरित subject to or undergo transformation. change the voltage of by electromagnetic induction. *We have learnt that energy can be transformed to light.* *(noun)* the product of a transformation. a rule for making a transformation. *Your transformation needs rules to be implemented.*

Transfusion/ट्रांसफ्यूजन *(noun)* – खून चढ़ाना act of transferring blood or other fluid into a person or animal. *Blood transfusion was the only option she had for a treatment.*

Transgress/ट्रांसग्रेस *(verb)* – उल्लंघन करना go beyond the limits set by a moral principle, standard, law, etc. *You will be punished if you transgress the rules I have laid out for this house.*

Transient/ट्रांजिएण्ट *(adjective)* –अस्थिर, कुछ समय के लिए lasting only for a short time. *Fame is transient, so don't hold on to it.*

Transistor/ट्रांजिस्टर *(noun)* – ध्वनि प्रसारक यन्त्र a semiconductor device with three connections, capable of amplification and rectification. *The mechanical professor explained how to fix a transistor connection.*

Transit/ट्रांजिट *(noun)* – गमन, गति the carrying of people or things from one place to another. the conveyance of passengers on public transport. *His instrument was damaged in transit.*

Transition/ट्रांजिशन *(noun)* – संक्रमण the process of changing from one state or condition to another. a period of such change. *The girl has been through a phase of transition and has come out way more mature and sensible than she was.*

Transitive/ट्रांजिटिव *(adjective)* – सकर्मक able to take a direct object e.g. saw in he saw the donkey. the opposite of intransitive. *The English Grammar teacher explained the significance and application of transitive (verb)s in language.*

Translate/ट्रांसलेट *(verb)* – अनुवाद express the sense of in another language. be expressed or be capable of being expressed in another language. *She works as a translator at the Embassy.*

Translucent/ट्रांसल्यूसेंट *(adjective)* – पारभासी, अर्ध-पारदर्शक allowing light to pass through partially; semi transparent. *She kept a translucent sheet of cloth over the window.*

Transmission/ट्रांसमिशन *(noun)* – प्रसारण the action or process of transmitting or the state of being transmitted. *The transmission of the virus is facilitated by the rains.*

Transmit/ट्रांसमिट *(verb)* – प्रसारित करना cause to pass on from one place or person to another. communicate. *The sages of ancient Indian transmitted their knowledge to their students who in turn went to on to transmit it down the generations.*

Transparent/ट्रांसपैरेन्ट *(adjective)* – पारदर्शी allowing light to pass through so that objects behind can be distinctly seen. *There was a transparent sheet on the table.*

Transparency/ट्रांसपैरेन्सी *(noun)* – पारदर्शिता the condition of being transparent. *The masses were seeking transparency from the government.*

Transplant/ट्रांसप्लांट *(verb)* – दूसरी जगह पौधा हटाना, प्रतिरोपण transfer to another place or situation. replant in another place. *The club was transplanted from its current location to the erstwhile community centre.*

Transport/ट्रांसपोर्ट *(verb)* – ढोना, ले जाना, दूरस्थ भेजना, परिवहन take or carry from one place to another by means of a vehicle, aircraft, or ship. send to a penal colony. *Arrangements were being made to transport the criminal to the jail in the outskirts of the city.*

Transpose/ट्रांसपोज *(verb)* – स्थान परिवर्तित करना cause to exchange places. *You will realize the truth of the situation only if you and the opposing party were transposed.*

Transverse/ट्रांसवर्स *(adjective)* – आड़ा, तिरछा situated or extending across something. *From the transverse hall, the stairway ascends.*

Trap/ट्रैप *(noun)* – फँसाना, पकड़ना, फन्दा basalt or a similar dark, fine grained igneous rock. *There have been sightings of trap in the mines here.*

Trapese/ट्रैपीज *(noun)* – कलाबाजी का झूला a horizontal bar hanging by two ropes and free to swing, used by acrobats in a circus. *The trapeze artist is my favourite sight at the circus.*

Trash/ट्रैश *(noun)* – रद्दी, बेकार waste material; refuse. *The trash was accumulating and the garbage van was late.*

Trauma/ट्रॉमा *(noun)* – आघात, सदमा, चिन्ता a deeply distressing experience. *She has been through the trauma of losing her parents.*

Travail/ट्रैवेल *(noun)* – अप्रिय अनुभव painful or laborious effort. labour pains. *The woman in travails was really loud. (verb)* undergo such effort. *The travails of life sometimes lead to happy endings.*

Travel/ट्रैवल *(verb)* – यात्रा, यात्रा करना, चलना make a journey. journey along or through a region. *I will be travelling across the country next month.*

Traveller/ट्रैवलर *(noun)* – यात्री a person who is travelling or who often travels. *I made friends with random travellers during my journey.*

Traverse/ट्रैवर्स *(verb)* – तानना travel or extend across or through. cross a rock face by means of a series of sideways movements from one practicable line of ascent or descent to another. ski diagonally across losing only a little height. *He traversed the hills and the forests.*

Travesty/ट्रैवेस्टि *(noun)* – नकल, तमाशा an absurd or grotesque misrepresentation. *A travesty of the trial will not be dealt with benignly. (verb)* represent in such a way. *By travestying the situations of his family in the play, he has distanced himself from them even more.*

Trawl/ट्रॉल *(verb)*– छान डालना, खंगाल डालना fish or catch with a trawl net or seine. *The boat was out in the sea trawling for big fish.*

Tray/ट्रे *(noun)* – तश्तरी, किश्ती, खाद्य व पेय पदार्थों को ले जाने के लिए प्रयुक्त बर्तन a flat, shallow container with a raised rim, typically used for carrying or holding things. *The girl brought a tray of tea to be served to the guests.*

Treacherous/ट्रेचरस *(adjective)* – विश्वासघाती, धोखेबाज guilty of or involving betrayal or deception. *The treacherous minister was banished from the kingdom.*

Treachery/ट्रेचरि *(noun)* – विश्वासघात, धोखा betrayal of trust, faith. *The king accused the minister of indulging in treachery.*

Treacle/ट्रीकल *(noun)* – शीरा, राब, अतिभावुक molasses. golden syrup. *I bought some treacle syrup from the grocer's and stored it in my larder.*

Tread/ट्रेड *(verb)* – कुछ पर से चलना, कुचलना, मार्ग बनाना walk in a specified way. walk on or along. *Tread carefully on the path as its pebbled and may hurt your tender feet.*

Treadle/ट्रेडल *(noun)* – पायदान a lever worked by the foot and imparting motion to a machine. *I made a treadle for him to complete his school project. (verb)* operate by a treadle. *He was treadling the machine made for his school project.*

Treason/ट्रेजन *(noun)* – विश्वासघात the crime of betraying one's country, especially by attempting to kill or overthrow the sovereign or government. *The party leader was arrested on charges of treason and corruption.*

Treasure/ट्रेजर *(noun)* – कोष, खजाना, मूल्यवान वस्तु अतिप्रिय a quantity of precious metals, gems, or other valuable objects. a very valuable object. *Legend says that there is a pirate's treasure down in the wreck.*

Treasurer/ट्रेजरर *(noun)* – खजांची, कोषाध्यक्ष कोषपाल a person appointed to manage finance of a company, society or other body. *He has been working as the party's treasurer for five years now.*

Treasury/ट्रेजरि *(noun)* – कोष, राजकोष, कोषागार, सरकारी खजाना the funds or revenue of a

T

state, institution, or society. the government department responsible for the overall management of the economy. *The party leader wondered how he would tell the party that the treasury was almost empty.*

Treat/ट्रीट *(verb)* – विशेष व्यवहार, समझना, मानना, दावत behave towards or deal with in a certain way. present or discuss a subject. *You must learn to treat your elders with respect.*

Treatise/ट्रीटिस् *(noun)* – ग्रन्थ, शोध ग्रन्थ, उत्तम ग्रन्थ a written work dealing formally and systematically with a subject. *She wrote a treatise on Indian political theory.*

Treatment/ट्रीटमेंट *(noun)* – चिकित्सा, समाधान, व्यवहार the process or manner of treating someone or something in a certain way. the presentation or discussion of a subject. *The bill declared equal treatment for men and women in the issue of remarriage.*

Treaty/ट्रीटि *(noun)* – सन्धि, सुलह, सन्धि-पत्र a formally concluded and ratified agreement between states. *The two countries signed a treaty regarding the distribution of oil.*

Treble/ट्रेब्ल *(noun)* – तिगुना करना, उच्च स्तर a high pitched voice, especially a boy's singing voice. *The boy had a brilliant treble that got everybody's notice.*

Tree/ट्री *(noun)* – पेड़, वृक्ष a woody perennial plant typically with a single stem or trunk growing to a considerable height and bearing lateral branches. *We had different kinds of trees in our garden.*

Trek/ट्रेक *(noun)* – लम्बी यात्रा a long arduous journey, especially one made on foot. a leg or stage of a journey. *She is planning a trek up the mountains for sometime end of the month.* *(verb)* go on a trek. migrate or journey by ox wagon. draw a vehicle or pull a load. *We've been trekking for five hours now.*

Tremble/ट्रेम्बल *(verb)* – काँपना, कँपकँपी, उदिग्नता shake involuntarily, typically as a result of anxiety, excitement, or frailty. be in a state of extreme apprehension. shake or quiver slightly. *She was trembling with fever.*

Tremendous/ट्रेमेन्डस *(adjective)* – विशाल, भयंकर आकार वाला very great in amount, scale, or intensity. inspiring awe or dread. *Scaling that peak was a tremendous achievement by the team.*

Tremor/ट्रेमर *(noun)* – कँपकँपी, कंप, उत्तेजित तरंग an involuntary quivering movement. a slight earthquake. *Tremors have been felt in the nearby areas of the epicentre.*

Tremulous/ट्रेम्युलस *(adjective)* – उत्तेजना या आशंका से काँपना shaking or 1quivering slightly. timid, nervous. *She gave a tremulous smile.*

Trench/ट्रेन्च *(noun)* – खाई a long, narrow ditch. a ditch of this type dug by troops to provide shelter from enemy fire. *The car was parked at the tip of the trench.*

Trend/ट्रेन्ड *(noun)* – झुकाव, प्रचलन, प्रचलित a general direction in which something is developing or changing. *A trend towards part time jobs has begun in the East.*

Trepidation/ट्रेपिडेशन *(noun)* – आशंका, घबड़ाहट a feeling of fear or agitation about something that may happen. *There was trepidation in the air about the impending blow.*

Trespass/ट्रेस्पास *(verb)* – अनधिकार प्रवेश enter someone's land or property without their permission. make unfair claims on or take advantage of something. *There was a board outside the boundary wall stating that trespassers will be prosecuted.*

Tresses/ट्रेसेस *(noun)* – लट, महिला के लम्बे बाल long lock of a woman's hair. *Many men have been victims of the charm of her eyes, her long tresses.*

Tri/ट्राइ *(prefix)* – तीन *form* three; having three: triathlon. containing three atoms or groups of a specified kind: trichloroethane. *Today's experiment was using tri-chloroethylene.*

Trial/ट्रायल *(noun)* – मुकदमा, साक्ष्य की जाँच, परीक्षण, परख a formal examination of evidence in order to decide guilt in a case of criminal or civil proceedings. *The trial for her case is scheduled sometime early next month.*

Triangle/ट्राइऐंगल *(noun)* – त्रिकोण, त्रिकोण की आकृति a plane figure with three straight sides and three angles. *The teacher taught us equilateral triangles today.*

Tribe/ट्राइब *(noun)* – जनजाति a social division in a traditional society consisting of linked families or communities with a common culture and dialect. each of several political divisions. a distinctive close knit social or political group. large numbers of people. *Relief has been sent to the tribes on the island affected by the tsunami.*

Tribal/ट्राइबल *(adjective)* – जनजातीय of or characteristic of a tribe or tribes. characterized by a tendency to form groups or by strong, group loyalty. (noun) members of tribal communities, especially in the Indian subcontinent. *There was tribal jewellery exhibited at the fair.*

Tribulation/ट्रिब्युलेशन *(noun)* – विपत्ति a state of great trouble or suffering. a cause of this. *They have been through trials and tribulations all their life.*

Tribunal/ट्रिब्यूनल *(noun)* – विशेष न्यायालय a body established to settle certain types of dispute. *The case of the insurance claim was taken to the tribunal.*

Tributary/ट्रिब्यूटरी *(noun)* – सहायक नदी a river or stream flowing into a larger river or lake. *The tributary was as big as the river itself.*

Tribute/ट्रिब्यूट *(noun)* – श्रद्धांजलि, प्रशंसा an act, statement, or gift that is intended to show gratitude, respect, or admiration. something resulting from and indicating the worth if something else. *His victory was a tribute to his persistence.*

Trick/ट्रिक *(noun)* – चाल, छल-कपट, दाँव-पेच a cunning or skilful act or scheme intended to deceive or outwit someone. a mischievous practical joke. a skilful act performed for entertainment. an illusion. intended to mystify or create an illusion: a trick question. liable to fail; defective: a trick knee. *The magician performed a trick of the light.*

Trickery/ट्रिकरि *(noun)* – छल, धोखा the practice of deception. *His trickery cannot escape the eyes of the warden.*

Trickle/ट्रिकल *(verb)* – बूँद-बूँद टपकना flow in a small stream. *Water was trickling from the roof.*

Tricky/ट्रिकि *(adjective)* – जटिल, कपटपूर्ण requiring care and skill because difficult or awkward. *The question was tricky and needed careful analysis.*

Tricycle/ट्राइसिकल *(noun)* – तीन पहिया साइकिल a vehicle similar to a bicycle, but having three wheels, two at the back and one at the front. a three wheels motor vehicle for a disabled driver. *I asked the little girl to first be confident of riding a tricycle before moving on to a grown-up's cycle.* (verb) ride on a tricycle. *She has caught on to tricycling big time!*

Trident/ट्राइडेन्ट *(noun)* – त्रिशूल a three pronged spear. *The trident stood proudly on the mast of the pirate ship.*

Trifle/ट्राइफल *(noun)* – तुच्छ, नगण्य a thing of little value or importance. a small amount. *Don't trouble mother with such trifles when she is working.*

Trigger/ट्रिगर *(noun)* – बन्दूक का घोड़ा, यन्त्र को चालू करने का पुर्जा a device that releases a spring or catch and so sets off a mechanism, especially in order to fire a gun. *The thief's finger was on the trigger, all set to shoot.*

Trigonometry/ट्रिगॅनॅमेट्रि *(noun)* – त्रिकोणमिति the branch of mathematics concerned with the relations of the sides and angles of triangles and with the relevant functions of any angles. *Trigonometry is one of my favourite topics in mathematics.*

Trillion/ट्रिल्यन् *(cardinal number)* – एक लाख करोड़ large number or amount. *The fraud was of a whopping six trillion dollars.*

Trilogy/ट्राइलॅजि (ट्रिलॅजि) *(noun)* – तीन का समूह a group of three related novels, plays, films, etc. a series of three tragedies performed one after the other. *The Lord of the Rings trilogy is one of Hollywood's best made movies.*

Trim/ट्रिम *(verb)* – काट-छाँट करना, संवारना, सुव्यवस्थित make neat by cutting away irregular or unwanted parts. cut off irregular or unwanted parts. reduce the size, amount, or number of. *I will pay you to trim the hedges.*

Trinity/ट्रिनिटि *(noun)* – त्रिकक, तीन वस्तुओं का समूह, ब्रह्म, विष्णु और महेश the three persons of the Christian godhead; father, son, and holy spirit. *We were taught many stories about the Holy Trinity.*

Trio/ट्रायो *(noun)* – तीन समूह a set or group of three. a group of three musicians. a

T

composition written for three musicians. the central section of a minuet, scherzo, or march. a set of three aces, kings, queens, jacks, or tens held in one hand. *The trio set out to try their luck in the jungle.*

Trip/ट्रिप *(verb)* – लड़खड़ाना, पतन, भेद खोलना, भूल करना catch one's foot on something and stumble or fall. make a mistake. *She tripped and fell flat on her face.*

Triple/ट्रिपल *(adjective)* – तीन, त्रिपक्षीय, तिगुना consisting of or involving three parts, things, or people. *Having eggs ensure triple benefits.*

Triplet/ट्रिप्लेट *(noun)* – तीन, तीन का समूह, तीन बच्चे one of three children or animals born at the same birth. *We never knew Mary was one of triplets.*

Tripod/ट्राइपॉड *(noun)* – तीन टाँगों वाला a three legged stand for supporting a camera or other apparatus. *She set the camera on the tripod and waited.*

Trite/ट्राइट *(adjective)* – घिसा-पिटा, मौलिकताहीन lacking originality or freshness; dull on account of overuse. *I couldn't read through the trite story.*

Triumph/ट्राइअम्फ *(noun)* – विजय, सफलता, जीत a great victory or achievement. the state of being victorious or successful. joy or satisfaction resulting from a success or victory. a highly successful example: the arrest was a triumph of international co operation. *He has led his side to many a triumphs.*

Triumphant/ट्राइअम्फ़न्ट *(adjective)* – विजयी having won a battle or contest; victorious. jubilant after a victory or achievement. *We heard their triumphant shouts for a mile around.*

Trivia/ट्रिविआ *(plural noun)* – तुच्छ, महत्त्वहीन unimportant details or pieces of information. *Do not waste time on such trivia.*

Trivial/ट्रिविअल *(adj)* – नगण्य, तुच्छ of little importance, not worth considering. *It is a trivial matter.*

Trolley/ट्रालि *(noun)* – हाथगाड़ी a large wheeled metal basket or frame used for transporting heavy or unwieldy items such as luggage

or supermarket purchases. a small table on wheels or castors, used especially to convey food and drink. *Take the luggage on this trolley to the train.*

Trombone/ट्रॉम्बोन *(noun)* – तुरही a large brass wind instrument having an extendable slide with which different notes are made. *She couldn't stand her son playing the trombone at night.*

Troop/ट्रूप *(noun)* – सेना दल soldiers or armed forces. *Lead this troop safely.*

Trophy/ट्रॉफि *(noun)* – विजयोपहार, विजय प्रतीक a cup or other decorative object awarded as a prize for a victory or success. a souvenir of an achievement, especially a head of an animal taken when hunting. *She needs an entire room to exhibit all her trophies.*

Tropic/ट्रॉपिक *(adjective)* – समशीतोष्ण क्षेत्र relating to, consisting of, or exhibiting tropism. *This plant exhibits tropic behaviour against the sun.*

Trot/ट्रॉट *(noun)* – दुलकी a Trotskyism or supporter of extreme left wing views. *Do not get into an argument with that trot.*

Trouble/ट्रबल *(noun)* – चिन्ता, परेशानी, कठिनाई difficulty or problems. malfunction; failure to work property. effort or exertion. a cause of worry or inconvenience. a situation in which one is liable to incur punishment or blame. *I blame you for all out troubles.*

Trough/ट्रफ *(noun)* – नाद, मन्दी का दौर a long, narrow open container for animals to eat or drink out of. a similar container, e.g. one for growing plants. *Plant the seeds in a trough and place it on the window sill.*

Trounce/ट्राउन्स *(verb)* – हराना, हराकर बाहर करना defeat heavily in a contest. rebuke or punish severely. *He will never forget this trounce.*

Trousers/ट्राउजर्स *(plural noun)* – पतलून an outer garment covering the body from the waist to the ankles, with a separate part for each leg. *He walked in completely drenched in shirt and trousers.*

Trousseau/ट्रूसो *(noun)*– दुल्हन का सामान the clothes, linen, and other belongings collected by a bride for her marriage. *Have you finalized your wedding trousseau?*

T

Trout/ट्राउट(noun)- कतला, मछली का एक प्रकार an edible fish of the salmon family, chiefly inhabiting fresh water. *Let us serve them trout this evening.* (verb) fishing for trout. *This is your night to go fishing for trout.*

Trowel/ट्रावेल (noun) – करनी a small hand held tool with a flat, pointed blade, used to apply and spread mortar or plaster. *The mason used his trowel to flatten the mud.*

Truant/ट्रूअन्ट (noun) – पलायनवादी, भगोड़ा a pupil who stays away from school without leave or explanation. *He may be a truant so keep an eye on him.* (verb) stay away from school without leave or explanation. *You will be punished for being truant all week.* (adjective) wandering; straying: her truant husband. *She is unaware of having such a truant husband.*

Truce/ट्रूस (noun) – शान्ति, युद्धविराम an agreement between enemies to stop fighting for a certain time. *The king offered a truce in order to avoid a war.*

Truck/ट्रक (noun) – खुली गाड़ी, खुला डिब्बा, ठेला गाड़ी barter. the payment of workers in kind or with vouchers rather than money. *This truck is over-loaded.*

Trudge/ट्रज (verb) – थकावट के कारण धीरे-धीरे चलना, धीमी गति walk slowly and with heavy steps, typically because of exhaustion or harsh conditions. *He trudged up the steep path.* (noun) a difficult or laborious walk. *I cannot trudge any further.*

True/ट्रू (adjective) – सच्चा, वास्तविक in accordance with fact or reality. rightly or strictly so called; genuine: true love. real or actual. *This is a true story.*

Truly/ट्रूलि (adverb) – सच ही in a truthful way. *This is a truly beautiful scene.*

Trumpet/ट्रम्पेट (noun) – तुरही a brass musical instrument with a flared bell and a bright, penetrating tone. an organ stop with a quality resembling that of a trumpet. *Go out and practise your trumpet someplace else.*

Truncate/ट्रंकेट (verb) – सिरा छोटा करना shorten by cutting off the top or the end. *Truncate the ends and fit the pipe into the slot.* (adjective) ending abruptly as if truncated. *The long scene needs to be truncated to fit into the film.*

Truncheon/ट्रंशन (noun) – हथियार रूपी छड़ी a short thick stick carried as a weapon by a police officer. *The robber stared at the police's truncheon.*

Trundle/ट्रंडल (verb) – लुढ़कना, लुढ़काना move slowly and unevenly on or as if on wheels. *The drunk trundle out of the bar every night.* (noun) an act of trundling. *Stop trundling or you will lose balance and fall on the road.*

Trunk/ट्रंक (noun) – तना, धड़ा, वक्सा, सूँड़ the main woody stem of a tree as distinct from its branches and roots. the main part of an artery, nerve, or other structure from which smaller branches arise. *This tree has the softest trunk in the world.*

Trust/ट्रस्ट (noun & verb) – विश्वास, भरोसा, न्यास, सौंपना firm belief in someone or something. acceptance of the truth of a statement without evidence or investigation. *I trust your decision.*

Trustee/ट्रस्टी (noun) – न्यासी an individual or member of a board given powers of administration of property in trust with a legal obligation to administer it solely for the purposes specified. *He was selected into the board of trustees on account of hard work.*

Trusting/ट्रस्टिंग (adjective) – विश्वासी showing trust in or tending to trust others; not suspicious. *His trusting nature will harm him in the long run.*

Trustworthy/ट्रस्टवर्दि (adjective) – विश्वास योग्य able to be relied on as honest, truthful, or reliable. *He is a trustworthy employee.*

Truth/ट्रूथ (noun) – सत्य the quality or state of being true. that which is true as opposed to false. a fact or belief that is accepted as true. *I want to hear the whole truth.*

Truthful/ट्रूथफुल (adjective) – सत्यवादी telling or expressing the truth; honest. *This is an example of a truthful man.*

Try/ट्राइ (verb) – प्रयत्न या कोशिश करना, परखना make an attempt or effort to do something. test in order to see if it is suitable, effective, or pleasant. attempt to operate, open contact, etc.: I tried the doors, but they were locked. put on an item of clothing to see if it fits or suits one. *Did you try out each and every shirt?*

T

Tryst/ट्राइस्ट *(noun)* – मिलनस्थल a private, romantic rendezvous between lovers. *There were rumours of their trysts. (verb)* keep or arrange a tryst. *She asked him to arrange a tryst next week.*

Tub/टब *(noun)* – नाद a low, wide, open container with a flat bottom used for holding liquids, growing plants, etc. a similar small plastic or cardboard container for food. a bath. a container for conveying ore, coal, etc. *Pour the water into the tub.*

Tube/ट्यूब *(noun)* – नली a long, hollow cylinder used for conveying or holding liquids gases. a flexible metal or plastic container sealed at one end and having a cap at the other. material forming tubes; tubing. *The doctor passed a tube into the patient's throat.*

Tuber/ट्यूबर *(noun)* – कन्द a much thickened underground part of a stem or rhizome, e.g. in the potato, serving as a food reserve and bearing buds from which new plants arise. a thickened fleshy root, e.g. of the dahlia. *He has been advised to stay off any tuber.*

Tuberous/ट्यूबरस *(adjective)* – कन्द वाला resembling, forming, or having a tuber or tubers. *You can identify this root by its tuberous appearance.*

Tuberculosis/ट्यूबरक्यूलोसिस *(noun)* – यक्ष्मा, क्षयरोग an infectious bacterial disease characterized by the growth of nodules in the tissues, especially the lungs. *Tuberculosis was considered to be incurable till the last century.*

Tuck/टक *(verb)* – सुरक्षित स्थान पर रखना, समेटना, लपेटना push, fold, or turn under or between two surfaces or into a confined space. store something in a secure place. settle someone in bed by pulling the edges of the bedclothes firmly under the mattress. *Her mother tucked her to bed every night and read her a story.*

Tuesday/ट्यूजडे *(noun)*– मंगलवार the day of the week before Wednesday and following Monday. *(adverb)* on Tuesday. on Tuesdays; each Tuesday. *They hold a market here every Tuesday.*

Tug/टग *(verb)* – प्रयत्न से खींचना pull hard or suddenly. *Please stop tugging at the other end.*

Tugged/टग्ड *(p.t. of tug)* – झटका दिया pull something hard or suddenly. *The little girl tugged at her pigtails nervously.*

Tuition/ट्यूशन *(noun)* – शिक्षण, अध्यापन teaching or instruction, especially of individuals or small groups. a fee charged for this. *She wants to take tuitions in mathematics.*

Tulip/ट्यूलिप *(noun)* – फूल का एक प्रकार a bulbous spring flowering plant of the lily family, with boldly coloured cup shaped flowers. *I suggest you gift her a bunch of tulips.*

Tumble/टम्बल *(verb)* – लुढ़कना, गिरना fall suddenly, clumsily, or headlong. perform acrobatic feats, typically handsprings and somersaults. *The clown tumbled down from the staircase.*

Tumbler/टम्बलर *(noun)* – गिलास a drinking glass with straight sides and no handle or stem. *The giant drinks milk from that huge tumbler.*

Tumour/ट्यूमर *(noun)* – गाँठ, घाव, रसौली a swelling of a part of the body, generally without inflammation, caused by an abnormal growth of tissue, whether benign or malignant. *She was shocked to discover a tumour in her stomach.*

Tumult/ट्यूमल्ट *(noun)* – हंगामा, उत्पात, शोर-शराबा a loud, confused noise, as caused by a large mass of people. *The shouting was growing really tumult with each passing minute.*

Tumultuous/ट्यूमल्ट्युअस *(adjective)* – उत्पाती, कोलाहलपूर्ण very loud or uproarious. *She always gets her way by being tumultuous with her demands.*

Tuna/ट्यूना *(noun)* – समुद्री मछली a large and active predatory schooling fish of warm seas, extensively fished commercially. *She loves tuna sandwiches.*

Tune/ट्यून *(noun)* – धुन, राग, स्वर-संगीत a melody, especially one which characterizes a certain piece of music. *This was a truly haunting tune.*

Tuneful/ट्यूनफुल *(adjective)* – मधुर having a pleasing tune; melodious. *Can you please repeat the tuneful melody?*

Tunic/ट्यूनिक *(noun)* – चोंगा, लबादा a loose sleeveless garment reaching to the thigh or knees. a gymslip. *I loved the colour of her tunic.*

Tunnel/टनल *(noun)* – सुरंग, सुरंग खोदना an artificial underground passage, as built through a hill or under a building or by a burrowing animal. *This is the longest tunnel in the country.*

Turban/टर्बन *(noun)* – पगड़ी, साफा a man's headdress, consisting of a long length of material wound round a cap or the head, worn especially by Muslims and Sikhs. *She thinks she knows the man wearing the blue turban.*

Turbine/टर्बाइन *(noun)* – एक यन्त्र a machine for producing continuous power in which a wheel or rotor, typically fitted with vanes, is made to revolve by a fast moving flow of water, steam, gas, air, or other fluid. *The deafening roar of the turbines could be heard for miles.*

Turbulent/टर्ब्युलेंट *(adjective)* – अव्यवस्थित, अशान्त disorderly or confused; not calm or controlled. *The sea turned turbulent within a matter of minutes.*

Turf/टर्फ *(noun)* – घास, गोबर या कृत्रिम मैदान grass and the surface layer of earth held together by its roots. a piece of such grass and earth cut from the ground. *The architect has designated a small patch of turf in the front of the house.*

Turkey/टर्की *(noun)*– एक पक्षी a large mainly domesticated game bird native to north America, having a bald head and red wattles. *Have you seen the turkey at the zoo?*

Turmoil/टर्मॉइल *(noun)* – तूफानी अस्त-व्यस्तता a state of great disturbance, confusion, or uncertainty. *I could sense he was in a great turmoil within.*

Turn/टर्न *(verb)* – मोड़ना, मुड़ना, घूमना, घुमाना, क्रम, बारी move or cause to move in a circular direction wholly or partly around an axis. move or cause to move into a different position, especially so as to face the opposite direction. change or cause to change direction. change from flood to ebb or vice versa. pass round so as to attack from the side or rear. twist or sprain. bend back so as to make it blunt. *Please turn your face away from the bonfire.*

Turnip/टर्निप *(noun)* – शलजम around root with white or cream flesh which is eaten as a vegetable and also has edible leaves. *The rabbit loves chewing on turnip leaves.*

Turpentine/टर्पेन्टाइन *(noun)* – तारपीन, तारपीन का तेल an oleoresin secreted by certain pines and other trees and distilled to make rosin and oil of turpentine. *Just apply oil of turpentine and the scar will heal quickly.*

Turquoise/टरक्वाइज *(noun)* – फिरोजा, फिरोजी रंग a semi precious stone, typically opaque and of a greenish blue colour, consisting of a hydrated phosphate of copper and aluminium. *Her turquoise gown was the talk of the evening.*

Turret/टरेट *(noun)* – कंगूरा, बुर्ज a small tower at the corner of a building or wall, especially of a castle. *The turret of the medieval era castle was stinking due to neglect.*

Turtle/टर्टल *(noun)* – कछुआ a marine or freshwater reptile with a bony or leathery shell and flippers or webbed toes. the flesh of a sea turtle, used chiefly for soup. *You can see the migratory turtles on the beach next month.*

Tusk/टस्क *(noun)* – दाँत, हाथी दाँत a long, pointed tooth, especially one which protrudes from the closed mouth, as in the elephant, walrus, or wild boar. *The tusk itself weighed nearly 2 kilos.*

Tussel/टसल *(noun)* – संघर्ष, हाथापाई a vigorous struggle or scuffle. *Freedom always comes after a tussle.* *(verb)* engage in a tussle. *The teacher suspended the students who participated in the tussle.*

Tutor/ट्यूटर *(noun)* – निजी शिक्षक a private teacher, typically one who teaches a single pupil or a very small group. a university or college teacher responsible for assigned students. an assistant lecturer in a college or university. *He will be your tutor for this semester.*

Tutorial/ट्यूटोरिअल *(noun)* – शिक्षकीय a period of tuition given by a university or college tutor. an account or explanation of a subject, intended for private study. (adjective) of or relating to a tutor or a tutor's tuition. *He attends tutorial classes after work.*

Tweak/ट्वीक *(verb)* – झटके से खींचना, चिकोटी काटना twist or pull with a small but sharp movement. *The nail will come off if you tweak it.*

T

Tweed/ट्वीड (noun) – खुरदरी-सी सतह वाला मोटा गरम कपड़ा a rough surface woolen cloth, typically of mixed flecked colours, originally produced in Scotland. clothes made of tweed. *I love wearing my father's tweed coat during winters.*

Tweezers/ट्वीजर्स (plural noun) – चिमटा, चिमटी a small instrument like a pair of pincers for plucking out hairs and picking up small objects. *The lab assistant used the tweezers to pick the tiny particles from the bowl.*

Twelve/ट्वेल्व (cardinal number) – बारह equivalent to the product of three and four; two more than ten; 12. *There were twelve packets arranged on the bed.*

Twelfth/ट्वेल्फ्थ (number) – बारहवाँ constituting number twelve in a sequence. *Which is the twelfth alphabet in Latin?*

Twenty/ट्वेन्टि (cardinal number) – बीस the number equivalent to the product of two and ten; ten less than thirty; 20. *I wish to buy twenty books for the class.*

Twentieth/ट्वेन्टिअथ (number) – बीसवाँ constituting number twenty in sequence. *This is his twentieth attempt so far.*

Twice/ट्वाइस (adverb) – दुगुना two times. *Playing with the kids was twice the fun.*

Twiddle/ट्विडल (verb) – बेचैनी में कुछ करना play or fiddle with, typically in a purposeless or nervous way. turn or move in a twirling way. *The boy twiddled his way through the crowded market.*

Twig/ट्विग (noun) – टहनी a slender woody shoot growing from a branch or stem of a tree or shrub. a small branch of a blood vessel or nerve. *They saw many dry twigs lying below the tree.*

Twilight/ट्वाइलाइट (noun) – संध्या का प्रकाश, गोधूलि, झुटपुटा the soft glowing light from the sky when the sun is below the horizon, caused by the reflection of the sun's rays from the atmosphere. *The twilight gave the entire hill an eerie glow.*

Twin/ट्विन (noun) – जुड़वा one of two children or animals born at the same birth. *You two look like twins.*

Twinge/ट्विन्ज (noun) – टीस, हूक a sudden, sharp, localized pain. *The boy twinged as the doctor took an injection.*

Twinkle/ट्विंकल (verb) – टिमटिमाना, चमकना, चमक shine with a gleam that changes constantly from bright to faint. sparkle, especially with amusement. *I could detect a twinkle in his eyes.*

Twirl/ट्विर्ल (verb) – चक्कर खिलाना, घुमाना spin quickly and lightly round. *The girl twirled and her skirt formed a neat circle around her.* (noun) an act of twirling. a spiralling or swirling shape, especially a flourish made with a pen. *She always ends her signature with a twirl.*

Twist/ट्विस्ट (verb) – ऐंठना, लपेटना, बटना, मरोड़ना, ऐंठन, मरोड़ form into a bent, curled, or distorted shape. turn or bend round or into a different direction. force or be forced out of the natural position by a twisting action: he twisted his ankle playing tennis. *The woman twisted the towel to drain the water.*

Twitch/ट्विच (verb) – फड़कन, फड़कना, खिंचाव make or cause to make a short, sudden jerking movement. *The boy's arm twitched as the lighted matchstick fell on his palm.*

Twitter/ट्विटर (verb) – चहचहाना, चहकना, चहचहाहट make a series of light tremulous sounds. *I woke up hearing the twittering of birds on my window sill.*

Two/टू (cardinal number) – दो equivalent to the sum of one and one; one less than three. *There were two eggs in the basket.*

Tycoon/टाइकून (noun) – व्यावसायिक बादशाह, पूँजीपति a wealthy, powerful person in business or industry. *He recognized the man to be a business tycoon.*

Type/टाइप (noun) – जाति, प्रारूप, नमूना, प्रकार, मुद्रण के अक्षर a category of people or things having common characteristics. a person or thing considered as a representative of such a category. a person of a specified character of nature: two sporty types in tracksuits. an abstract category or class of linguistic item or unit. contrasted with token. *The scientists have never see this type of organism till date.*

T

Typhoid/टाइफाइड *(noun)* – एक प्रकार का ज्वर an infectious bacterial fever with an eruption of red spots on the chest and abdomen and severe intestinal irritation. *The student missed his examinations as he was suffering from typhoid.*

Typhoon/टाइफून *(noun)* – तूफ़ान a tropical storm in the region of the Indian or western pacific oceans. *We expect the typhoon to hit the coast before tomorrow noon.*

Typical/टिपिकल *(adjective)* – नमूना, विशेष प्रकार का, विशेष लक्षणों वाला, प्रतिनिधि लक्षण having the distinctive qualities of a particular type. characteristic of a particular person or thing. *Feigning innocence is typical of her.*

Typify/टिपिफाइ *(verb)* – प्रतीकात्मक, प्रतीक लक्षण be typical of. *Snow will typify the winter season in this land.*

Tyranny/टिरॅनि (टिरैनि) *(noun)* – तानाशाही, प्रजा का उत्पीड़न cruel and oppressive government or rule. a state under such rule. *Our country ruled under tyranny during the last decade.*

Tyrannical/टिरैनिकल *(adjective)* – अत्याचार पूर्ण exercising power in a cruel way. *The government formed by Talibans was believed to be tyrannical in nature.*

Tyrant/टाइरैंट *(noun)* – तानाशाह, अत्याचारी a cruel and oppressive ruler. *He will always be known as a tyrant in this country.*

Tyre/टायर *(noun)* – पहिए का बाहरी खोल a rubber covering, typically inflated or surrounding an inflated inner tube, placed round a wheel to form a soft contact with the road. *The cycle wobbled as the tyre moved on the rocky surface.*

T

Uu

U/यू – अंग्रेजी वर्णमाला का इक्कीसवाँ वर्ण the fifth Vowel and the twenty first letter of the English alphabet.

Udder/अडर *(noun)* – थन, थान an organ shaped like a bag, produces milk and hangs underneath. *Udder is an organ shaped like a bag that produces milk and hangs underneath the body of a cow, goat etc.*

Ugly/अग्लि *(adjective)* – कुरूप unpleasant or repulsive in appearance. *She has an ugly face.*

Ulcer/अल्सर *(noun)* – फोड़ा, घाव an open sore in an external or internal surface of the body, caused by a break in the skin or mucous membrane which fails to heal. *Harish is suffering from stomach ulcer.*

Ulterior/अल्टिरिअर *(adjective)* – परोक्ष, परवर्ती, घातक other than what is obvious or admitted: *Sachin claims he just wants to help Aman but I suspect he has an ulterior motive.*

Ultimate/अल्टिमेट *(adjective)* – चरम, परम being or happening at the end of a process. The ultimate decision about who to employ lies with Bob. *Infidelity is considered the ultimate betrayal.*

Ultimatum/अल्टिमेटम *(noun)* – चेतावनी a final demand or statement of terms, the rejection of which will result in retaliation or a breakdown in relations. *Shweta has given Sachin an ultimatum – she could either stop seeing him and come back to him.*

Ultra/अल्ट्रा *(noun)* – परा, सूक्ष्म a person who holds extreme views, especially in politics. *Ultra violet rays can darken our skin when exposed to the sun.*

Ultrasonic/अल्ट्रासॉनिक *(adjective)* – परा ध्वनि से सम्बन्धित, पराश्रव्य of or involving sound waves with a frequency above the upper limit of human hearing. *At normal condition our ears can't hear ultrasonic sound.*

Ultrasound/अल्ट्रासाउण्ड *(noun)* – अन्तःचित्र का तकनीक sound or other vibrations having an ultrasonic frequency, particularly as used in medical imaging. *Doctors use ultrasound to monitor ovaries to see if they're responding to the treatment.*

Umbilical cord/अम्बिलिकल कॉर्ड *(noun)* – नाल, जनमोती नाल, मातृ सम्पर्क नाल a flexible cord like structure containing blood vessels, attaching a fetus to the placenta during gestation. *He asked the doctor if he could cut his wife's umbilical cord.*

Umbrage/अम्बरेज *(noun)* – अपमानित offence or annoyance. *She'll take umbrage if she isn't invited to the wedding.*

Umbrella/अम्ब्रेला *(noun)* – छाता, छतरी a device consisting of a circular fabric canopy on a folding metal frame supported by a central rod, used as protection against rain. *Gauri used to carry her umbrella while walking to school.*

Umpire/अम्पायर *(noun)* – संचालक, नियन्त्रक in certain sports an official who watches a game or match closely to enforce the rules and arbitrate on matters arising from the play. *Umpires play a significant part in a cricket match.*

Umpteen/अम्पटीन – अनेक, लम्बा very, many: *She has told this story upteen times.*

Un/अन *prefix* – विपरीत added to adjectives, participles, and their derivatives denoting the absence of a quality or state; not: *unacademic.* the reverse of: *unselfish.*

Unable/अनेबल *(adjective)* – असमर्थ, अयोग्य lacking the skill, means, or opportunity to do something. *My father is unable to get to town without a car.*

Unacceptable/अनएक्सेप्टबॅल *(adjective)* – अस्वीकार्य not satisfactory or allowable. *The coach told the players that defeat was unacceptable.*

Unaccompanied/अनएकम्पनिड *(adj)* – बिना साथी having no companion or escort. *The baby stayed home unaccompanied.*

Unanimous/यूनैनिमस *(adjective)* – एकमत, सर्वसम्मति से fully in agreement. *The owner of the house wants a unanimous decision.*

Unanimity/यूनॅनिमिटि *(noun)* – सर्वसम्मत full agreement between a number of people. *People always look for unanimity.*

Unanimously/यूनैनिमसली *(adverb)* – सर्वसम्मति से of one mind; without dissent. *The Parliament unanimously approved the bill.*

Unarmed/अॅन्-आर्म्ड *(adjective)* – बिना हथियार, नि:शस्त्र, शस्त्रहीन not equipped with or carrying weapons. *Unarmed peasants were shot down in the valley.*

Unashamed/अॅनशेम्ड *(adjective)* – बेशर्म, बिना संकोच के He is a sinner and an unashamed man.

Unassuming/अनॅस्यूमिंग *(adjective)* – अहंकारहित, विनम्र not pretentious or arrogant. *Unassuming to a fault, Vinay is unassuming about the value of his work.*

Unattached/अनटैच्छ *(adjective)* – अविवाहित, असम्बद्ध not working for or belonging to a particular organization. *He is unattached to his office.*

Unattended/अनॅटेन्डिड *(adjective)* – बिना देखभाल के not dealt with. *He dashed out leaving the bar unattended.*

Unauthorised/अनआथराइज्ड *(adjective)* – अवैध, अनधिकृत not having official permission or approval. *The employees go for an unauthorized strike.*

Unavoidable/अनएवायडेबल *(adjective)* – जिससे बचा न जा सके, टाला न जा सके not able to be avoided or prevented; inevitable. *According to eye witness the accident was unavoidable.*

Unaware/अनवेअर *(adjective)* – अनजान, अनभिज्ञ having no knowledge of a situation or fact. *Unaware of the danger they entered the room.*

Unawares/अनवेअर्स *(adverb)* – अनजाने में, औचक में so as to surprise. *Rain caught the family unawares.*

Unbalanced/अनबैलंस्ड *(adj)* – असंतुलित upset the mental equilibrium of; derange. *A man who had gone unbalanced is very difficult to manage.*

Unbearable/अन्बेयरेबल *(adjective)* – असह्य not able to be endured or tolerated. *Raju suffers an unbearable degree of sentimentality.*

Unbelievable/अनबिलिवेबल *(adj)* – अविश्वसनीय unlikely to be true. *The matter is unbelievable to many.*

Unborn/अनबॉर्न *(adjective)* – अजन्मा of a baby not yet born. *Please do something good for unborn generations.*

Unbreakable/अनब्रेकेबल *(adjective)* – अटूट not liable to break or able to be broken. *Raju gifted her unbreakable plastic dinnerware.*

Unbroken/अनब्रोकन *(adjective)* – अटूट, बाधारहित, बिना टूटे not broken; intact. *Fortunately the other lens is unbroken.*

Unburden/अनबर्डेन *(verb)* – भारहीन, भाररहित, हल्का relieve of a burden; be relieved of cause of anxiety or distress through confiding in someone. *She unburdened the family from giving her economical support.*

Uncalled-for/अॅनकॉल्ड-फॉर *(adjective)* – बिन बुलाये not required or requested. *Ramesh is not interested in uncalled-for suggestions.*

Uncanny/अनकैनी *(adjective)* – आन्तरिक विचित्रता, असामान्य strange or mysterious. *The new born baby had uncanny shapes as of monstrous creatures.*

Uncertain/अन्सर्टेन *(adjective)* – अनिश्चित not known, reliable, or definite. *He is facing an uncertain recollection of events.*

Uncharacteristic/अनकैरेक्टरिस्टिक *(adjective)* – अस्वाभाविक not typical of a particular person or thing. *The prize goes to a book uncharacteristic of its author.*

Uncle/अंकल *(noun)* – चाचा, काका, मामा, फूफा, मौसा the brother of one's father or mother or the husband of one's aunt; an unrelated adult male friend of a child. *Sachin loves his uncle very much.*

Uncomfortable/अनकम्फ़्टॅबॅल *(adjective)* – अस्थिर-चित, बेचैन not physically comfortable. uneasy or awkward. *We spent an uncomfortable day in the hot sun.*

U

Uncommon/अन्कॉमॅन *(adjective)* - असामान्य out of the ordinary; unusual. remarkable great: an uncommon amount of noise. . *Frost and floods are uncommon during these months in many countries.*

Uncompromising/अनकम्प्रोमाइजिंग *(adj)* - हठी unwilling to make concessions; resolute. harsh or relentless. *The minister of state took an uncompromising stance in the peace talks.*

Unconcerned/अनकर्सन्ड *(adjective)* - उदासीन, रुचिहीन, बिना परवाह lacking in interest, care or feeling. *He seemed unconcerned during the entire process of negotiation.*

Unconditional/अनकन्डिशनल *(adjective)* - बिना शर्त not subject to any conditions. *Police want unconditional surrender of the criminals.*

Unconscious/अनकांशस *(adjective)* - अचेत, बेहोश, बेसुध, सुध-बुधहीन not awake and aware of and responding to one's environment. *He is lying unconscious on the floor.*

Uncontrollable/अनकंट्रोलॅबॅल *(adj)* - अनियन्त्रित जो नियन्त्रित न हो not controllable. *He is facing uncontrollable pain.*

Unconventional/अनकन्वेंशनल *(adj)* - अपारम्परिक, परम्परा से अलग not based on or conforming to what is generally done or believed. *People look at her unconventional dress and hair style.*

Uncountable/अनकाउन्टॅबॅल *(adjective)* - अगणित, अनेक, अनगिनत too many to be counted. *There are uncountable people present in the meeting.*

Uncouth/अनकूथ *(adjective)* - असभ्य, अपरिष्कृत lacking good manners, refinement, or grace. *Don't behave like an untutored and uncouth human being.*

Uncover/अनकवर *(verb)* - उघाड़ना, भेद खोलना, प्रत्यक्ष करना remove a cover or covering from. discover something previously secret or unknown. *Summer uncovers bright clothes in nature.*

Undecided/अनडिसाइडेड *(adjective)* - अनिर्णित, जिस पर निर्णय न हुआ हो not having made a decision; uncertain. not settled or resolved. *Our position on this bill is still undecided which affects the case significantly.*

Undeniable/अॅनडिनाइअॅबॅल *(adj)* - अखण्डनीय unable to be denied or disputed. *There are undeniable consequences to their actions.*

Under/अण्डर *(preposition)* - नीचे, आच्छन्न, दबा हुआ extending or directly below. below or behind so as to cover or protect. planted with. *A book is lying under the table.*

Undercover/अण्डरकवर *(adjective & adverb)* - छिपकर, छिपा हुआ, गुप्त रूप से involving secret work for investigation or espionage: an undercover operation. *Police want an undercover operation to catch the culprits.*

Undercurrent/अण्डरकरेंट *(noun)* - जल के तल के नीचे की धारा, गुप्त प्रभाव a current of water below the surface and moving in a different direction from any surface current. *The undercurrent of the river is very strong.*

Undercut/अण्डरकट *(verb)* - कम दाम पर बेचना, नीचे प्रहार करना offer goods or services at a lower price than a competitor. *The local exporter will actually undercut the foreign dealer by very nearly the whole difference.*

Underdog/अण्डरडॉग *(noun)* - जिसे श्रेष्ठ न माना जाए a competitor thought to have little chance of winning a fight or contest. a person who has little status in society. *Our sympathies were always with the underdog.*

Underdone/अण्डरडन *(adjective)* - अधपका of food insufficiently cooked. *The old lady served us underdone rice and burnt bread.*

Underestimate/अंडरएस्टिमेट *(verb)* - कम करके आँकना estimate something to be smaller or less Important than it really is. *Don't underestimate the value of this land, you could get more than what you think.* regard someone as less capable than they really are. *You should not underestimate his capabilities.*

Undergo/अण्डरगो *(verb)* - सहना, भुगतना experience or be subjected to something unpleasant or arduous. *Suddenly his behaviour undergoes a strange change.*

Undergraduate/अण्डरग्रेजुएट *(noun)* - स्नातक पूर्व, स्नातक से नीचे a student at a university who has not yet taken a first degree. *Only undergraduate students can apply for the post.*

Underground/अण्डरग्राउण्ड *(adjective & adverb)* - भूमिगत beneath the surface of the ground. *Underground caverns.*

Undergrowth/अण्डरग्रोथ *(noun)* - निम्नविकास, घास-पात a dense growth of shrubs and other

U

plants, especially under trees. *The ferny undergrowth covers the road to the temple.*

Underhand/अण्डरहैण्ड *(adjective)* – गुप्त बेईमानी से acting or done in a secret or dishonest way. *Anurag achieved success in business by underhand methods.*

Underlie/अण्डरलाइ *(verb)* – के नीचे पड़ा होना lie or be situated under. *The mobile underlies the bed.*

Underline/अण्डरलाइन *(verb)* – रेखांकित करना, महत्त्व देना draw a line under a word or phrase to give emphasis or indicate special type. *The teacher advises the students to underline the important sentences.*

Undermine/अण्डरमाइन *(verb)* – महत्त्व घटाना, क्षीण करना, जड़ खोदना to make somebody's confidence or authority, gradually weaker or less effective. *Our confidence in the team has undermined by their recent defeat.*

Underneath/अण्डरनिथ *(preposition & adverb)* – तल में नीचे situated directly below. *The floor underneath the table.*

Underpay/अण्डरपे *(verb)* – वेतन कम देना pay too little to someone or for something. *The labourers have been underpaid since the inception of the factory.*

Underplay/अण्डरप्ले *(verb)*– कम कर देना perform a role or part in a restrained way. *The experienced actor underplayed his role brilliantly.*

Underprivileged/अण्डरप्रिविलेज्ड *(adjective)*– कम अधिकार वाले not enjoying the same rights or standard of living as the majority of the population. *The church brought gifts to the underprivileged children of the neighbourhood.*

Underrate/अण्डररेट *(verb)* – कम आँकना underestimate the extent, value, or importance of. *She underrated the work that went into the renovation.*

Underscore/अण्डरस्कोर *(verb)* – रेखांकित करना Give extra weight to (a communication) *His gesture underscored his words.*

Undersigned/अण्डरसाइन्ड *(adjective)* – अधो हस्ताक्षरी appending one's signature to the document in question. *He has to bear the responsibility as the undersigned person.*

Understand/अण्डरस्टैंड *(verb)* – समझना perceive the intended meaning of words, a language, or a speaker. *I understand what he means*; *She understands French*. perceive the significance, explanation, or cause of; interpret or view in a particular way. *You don't need to explain-I understand.*

Understandable/अंडरस्टैंडेबॅल *(adjective)* – समझने योग्य able to be understood. *The students weren't getting the simple and understandable lesson.*

Understatement/अण्डरस्टेटमेंट *(noun)* – बात हल्की करना a statement that makes something less important than it really is. *To say that he is pleased, is an understatement.*

Understudy/अण्डरस्टडि *(noun & verb)* – स्थानापन्न अध्येता an actor who learns another's role in order to be able to act in their absence. Ramesh is considered *(verb)* study a role or actor as an understudy. *He understudied the role of the most experienced actor of their troupe.*

Undertake/अण्डरटेक *(verb)* – भार लेना, बीड़ा उठाना commit oneself to and begin an enterprise or responsibility; take on. *The social worker undertakes the responsibity of opening an English medium school in the village.*

Undertaking/अण्डरटेकिंग *(noun)* – वचन a formal pledge or promise to do something; a task that is taken on; an enterprise. *The youth organisation is preparing for great undertakings.*

Undertaker/अण्डरटेकर *(noun)* – अन्त्येष्टि का प्रबंधक a person whose business is preparing dead bodies for burial or cremation and making arrangements for funerals. *The oldest undertaker is suffering from some grave diseases and there is a little time left in him.*

Undertone/अण्डरटोन *(noun)* – मंद स्वर a subdued or muted tone of sound or colour. *The doctor spoke in undertones.*

Underwater/अण्डरवाटर *(adjective & adverb)* – जलमग्न situated or occurring beneath the surface of the water. *Many ships get wrecked after colliding underwater rocks.*

Underwear/अण्डरवियर *(noun)* – जाँघिया clothing worn under other clothes next to the skin. *Always wear good quality underwears.*

U

Underweight/अण्डरवेट *(adj)* – कम वजन below a weight considered normal or desirable. *He is underweight to his age.*

Underworld/अण्डरवर्ल्ड *(noun)* – छिपा हुआ, अपराधलोक the world of criminals or of organized crime. *The Underworld is notorious for demanding money from celebrities and kill innocent people for ransom.*

Underwrite/अण्डरराइट *(verb)* – बीमा करना, जिम्मा लेना sign and accept liability under an insurance policy. accept a liability or risk in this way. *The insurance companies underwrite all the damage caused by the devastating fire.*

Undesirable/अन्डिजाइअरॅबॅल *(adjective)* – अवांछित not wanted or desirable because harmful, objectionable, or unpleasant. *It is important to separate the undesirable impurities in steel.*

Undivided/अन्डिवाडिड *(adjective)* – अविभाजित not divided, separated, or broken into parts. *All the three brothers keep an undivided interest in the property.*

Undo/अन्डू *(verb)* – खोलना unfasten, untie, or loosen. *The child requests to undo the shoelace.*

Undoubted/अनडाउटिड *(adjective)* – असंदिग्ध not questioned or doubted by anyone. *The schoolmaster is the undoubted judge of the entire village.*

Undress/अन्ड्रेस *(verb)* – वस्त्र उतारना take off one's clothes. take the clothes off someone else. *The mother requests the child not to undress in front of everybody.*

Undue/अन्ड्यू *(adjective)* – उचित से अधिक, अनुचित unwarranted or inappropriate because excessive or disproportionate. *Please don't show undue excitement in that matter.*

Undulate/अन्ड्यूलेट *(verb)* – लहराना to go or move gently. *The crops undulate pleasantly in the country side.*

Unearth/अन्अर्थ *(verb)* – खोज निकालना find in the ground by digging; *The police unearthed the town to capture the criminals.* discover by investigation or searching. *The CBI unearthed a plot to kill the Prime Minister.*

Unearthly/अन्अर्थलि *(adjective)* – अलौकिक unnatural or mysterious, especially in a disturbing way. *He somehow believes in unearthly love which is quite strange for others.*

Uneasy/अॅनईजी *(adjective)* – बेचैन causing or feeling anxiety; troubled or uncomfortable. *The shy girl is feeling uneasy in the crowded marriage reception.*

Uneconomical/अन्इकोनॉमिकल *(adjective)* – खर्चीला, अलाभकर wasteful of money or other resources; not economical. *The main issue is whether a firm would ever operate in the uneconomical region.*

Uneducated/अॅनएड्यूकेटिड *(adjective)* – अशिक्षित poorly educated. *Only an uneducated person behaves like this.*

Unemployed/अनइम्प्लाइड *(adjective)* – बेरोजगार without a paid job but available to work. *The unemployed workers marched on the capital city.*

Unemployment/अनइम्प्लाइमेन्ट *(noun)* – बेरोजगारी the state of being unemployed. the number or proportion of unemployed people. *Unemployment is considered as serious social evil in alomost all countries in the world.*

Unending/अन्एन्डिन्ग *(adjective)* – अन्तहीन having or seeming to have no end. countless or continual. *I am tired of his unending demands.*

Unequal/अनुईक्वॅल *(adjective)* – असमान not equal in quantity, size, or value. not fair, evenly balanced, or having equal advantage. *The proposed human resource is unequal to the project.*

Unequivocal/अनइक्विवॅकॅल *(adjective)* – स्पष्ट, एकार्थक leaving no doubt; unambiguous. *It is not very difficult to understand the plain and unequivocal language of the presentation.*

Unerring/अन्एनरिंग *(adjective)* – अचूक always right or accurate. *He is believed to be an unerring shooter.*

Unethical/अनएथिकल *(adjective)* – अनैतिक not morally correct. *Many social organisations fight to remove unethical business practices.*

Uneven/अनईवन *(adjective)* – असमतल not level or smooth. *An uneven colour.*

U

Uneventful/अनइवेंटफुल *(adjective)* - घटनारहित not marked by interesting or exciting events. *The journey was pleasant and uneventful.*

Unexpected/अनएक्सपेक्टेड *(adj)* – अप्रत्याशित not expected or regarded as likely to happen. He *was shocked after hearing the unexpected news.*

Unexplained/अनएक्सप्लेन्ड *(adjective)* – अस्पष्ट not made clear or accounted for. *It is not possible to accomplish the task with some unexplained process.*

Unfair/अनफेअर *(adjective)* – अन्यायपूर्ण not based on or showing fairness; unjust. contrary to the rules of a game. *It was an unfair trial.*

Unfaithful/अनफेथफुल *(adjective)* – अविश्वासी not faithful; disloyal. *She is suffering for his unfaithful lover.* engaging in sexual relations with a person other than one's lover or spouse. *Her husband was unfaithful.*

Unfamiliar/अनफैमिल्यर *(adjective)* – अपरिचित not known or recognized; uncharacteristic. *His name is unfamiliar to the most of the people of this country.*

Unfashionable/अनफैशनेबॅल *(adjective)* – अप्रचलित not fashionable or popular. *He wears unfashionable clothes.*

Unfasten/अनफास्रॅन *(verb)* - खोलना open the fastening of; undo. *The airhostess requests the passengers to unfasten their belts.*

Unfavourable/अनफेवरेबॅल *(adjective)* – प्रतिकूल expressing lack of approval or support. *He will suffer for his unfavourable comments.*

Unfit/अनफिट *(adjective)* – अयोग्य unsuitable or inadequate for something. *The manager thinks all the project members are unfit for the new challenging project.*

Unfold/अनफोल्ड *(verb)* - खोलना, रहस्य बताना open or spread out from a folded position. *He unfolded the report to have a comprehensible idea.*

Unforeseen/अनफोर्सीन *(adjective)* - अदृश्य not anticipated or predicted. *The poor people are preparing to face the unforeseen circumstances.*

Unforgettable/अनफर्गेटॅबॅल *(adj)* – अविस्मरणीय highly memorable. *Rajesh has recorded all the unforgettable moments of his baby's life on video.*

Unforgiving/अनफॉर्गिविंग *(adjective)* – क्षमाहीन not willing to forgive or excuse faults.*His mother is surely an unforgiving old woman.*

Unfortunate/अनफॉरट्यूनेट *(adjective)* – दुर्भाग्यपूर्ण having bad fortune; unlucky. inauspicious. *An unfortunate night for all concerned.*

Unfounded/अनफाउन्डेड *(adjective)* – निराधार having no foundation or basis in fact. *He has been facing unfounded suspicion from various people.*

Ungainly/अनगेनलि *(adjective)* – अभद्र clumsy; awkward. *What an ungainly creature a giraffe is!*

Ungratful/अनग्रेटफुल *(adjective)* – कृतघ्न not feeling or showing gratitude. *He left behind all his possession to some ungrateful heirs.*

Unguarded/अनगार्डेड *(adjective)* – असुरक्षित without protection or a guard. *The unguarded queen of Mysore was open to attack.*

Unhappy/अनहैप्पि *(adjective)* – अप्रसन्न not happy; unfortunate. *After the argument all the members lapsed into an unhappy silence.*

Unhealthy/अनहेल्दि *(adjective)* – अस्वस्थ in poor health. *He seems to be unhealthy.* not conducive to health. *He frequently takes an unhealthy diet of fast foods.*

Unheard/अनहॅर्ड *(adjective)* – अनसुना not heard or listened to. *The teacher will ask questions from the chapters which is unheard to all the students.*

Unicorn/यूनिकॉर्न *(noun)* - एकसिंहा a mythical animal represented as a horse with a single straight horn projecting from its forehead. a heraldic representation of this, with a twisted horn, a deer's feet, a goat's beard, and a lion's tail. *He always dreams of riding a unicorn.*

Unidentified/अनॲइडेन्टिफाइड *(adj)* – अनपहचाना not recognized or identified. *The prosecutor is talking about an unidentified witness.*

Uniform/यूनिफॉर्म *(adjective)* – एकरूपता, वर्दी not varying; the same in all cases and at all times. *We are passing through a street of uniform tall white buildings.*

Unify/यूनिफाइ *(verb)* - एकीकरण करना make or become united or uniform. *We should unify our resources.*

Unilateral/यूनिलैटॅरॅल *(adjective)* – एकपक्षीय, एकतरफा, एकात्मक performed by or affecting

U

only one person, group, etc. *A unilateral decision was taken.*

Union/यूनियन *(noun)* – संघ the action or fact of uniting or being united. a state of harmony or agreement. *There is strength in union.*

Unique/यूनिक *(adjective)* – अजूबा, विचित्र, असामान्य being the only one of its kind. *We have seen a unique copy of an ancient manuscript*; unlike anything else. unique to belonging or connected to one particular person, group, or place. remarkable or unusual. *He spoke with a unique accent.*

Unison/यूनिसॅन *(noun)* – एक स्वर से simultaneous action or utterance. *The army is marching in unison.*

Unit/यूनिट *(noun)* – इकाई an individual thing or person regarded as single and complete; each of the individual components making up a larger whole. a device or part with a specified function. *The word is a basic linguistic unit.*

Unite/यूनाइट *(verb)* – संयुक्त करना to join together in an agreement. *Unless we unite, our enemies will defeat us.*

Universal/यूनिवर्सल *(adjective)* – सार्वभौमिक of, affecting, or done by all people or things in the world or in a particular group. *Universal experience*; applicable to all cases. *The movie opened to universal acclaim.*

Universe/यूनिवर्स *(noun)* – विश्व, ब्रह्माण्ड all existing matter and space considered as a whole; the cosmos. *They wish to study the evolution of the universe.*

University/यूनिवर्सिटी *(noun)* – विश्वविद्यालय a high level educational institution in which students study for degrees and academic research is done. *His daughter is a university professor.*

U

Unjust/अन्जस्ट *(adjective)* – अन्यायपूर्ण not just; unfair. *He used unjust methods to earn material gain.*

Unkempt/अनकेम्प्ट *(adjective)* – मैला-कुचैला untidy or dishevelled. *wild unkempt hair.*

Unkind/अन्काइन्ड *(adjective)* – निर्दयी inconsiderate and harsh. *The teacher made a thoughtless and unkind remark of the students.*

Unknown/अन्नोन *(noun)* – अज्ञात an unknown person or thing. an unknown quantity or variable. *an unknown island; an unknown amount; an unknown poet.*

Unlawful/अन्लॉफुल *(adjective)* – अवैध not conforming to or permitted by the law or rules. *People are engaged in unlawful banking practices.*

Unleaded/अन्लेडिड *(adjective)* – बिना शीशे का especially of petrol without added lead. *They use unleaded petrol.*

Unless/अन्लेस *(conjunction)* – जब तक नहीं except when; if not. *The new rules shall not have effect unless they have been approved.*

Unlike/अन्लाइक *(preposition)* – असमान different from; not like. in contrast to. uncharacteristic of. *He is very friendly, unlike his father.*

Unlikely/अन्लाइकलि *(adjective)* – असंभावित not likely; improbable. *It is unlikely to question the legislation.*

Unlimited/अन्लिमिटेड *(adjective)* – असीमित not limited or restricted; infinite. *He wants a internet connection with unlimited downloading.*

Unload/अन्लोड *(verb)* – उतारना, निकालना remove a load from. remove goods from a vehicle, ship, etc. *The manager ordered the labourers to unload the truck.*

Unlock/अन्लॉक *(verb)* – ताला खोलना, खोलना undo the lock of something using a key. *She quickly unlocked the door.*

Unlucky/अन्लॅकि *(adjective)* – अभागा having, bringing, or resulting from bad luck. *The unlucky prisoner was put in prison again.*

Unmarried/अन्मैरिड *(adjective)* – अविवाहित not married; single. *He invited only unmarried men and women to the function.*

Unmistakable/अन्मिस्टेकॅबॅल *(adjective)* – सुस्पष्ट not able to be mistaken for anything else. *His guide's opposition to slavery was unmistakable.*

Unnatural/अन्नैचुरल *(adjective)* – अप्राकृतिक contrary to nature; abnormal. *His unnatural behaviour is dangerous to the society.*

Unnecessary/अन्नेसेसॅरि *(adjective)* – अनावश्यक not necessary; more than is necessary. *Remove the unnecessary stuff from the car.*

Unnerve/ॲन्नॅर्व *(verb)* – हिम्मत जबाब देना deprive of courage or confidence. *The incident shouldn't unnerve him at all.*

Unnoticed/ॲन्नोटिस्ड *(adj)* – अनदेखा, अलक्षित not noticed. *He has crossed the road unnoticed.*

Unobtrusive/ॲन्बट्रूसिव *(adjective)* – कठिनाई से दिखने वाला not conspicuous or attracting attention. *He is living an unobtrusive life of self-denial.*

Unofficial/अन्ऑफिशॅल *(adjective)* – अन-अधिकारिक, गैर सरकारी not official authorized or confirmed. *He announced an unofficial declaration to the members.*

Unpack/ॲन्पैक *(verb)* – सामान खोलना open and remove the contents of a suitcase or container. remove from a packed container. *The child's mother unpacks the birthday presents.*

Unpaid/ॲन्पेड *(adjective)* – बिना अदायगी of a debt not yet paid. *He notices the unpaid bill.*

Unpleasant/ॲन्प्लेजॅन्ट *(adjective)* – अप्रिय not pleasant; disagreeable. *She can't tolerate his unpleasant personality.*

Unplug/ॲन्प्लग *(verb)* – सम्बन्ध-विच्छेद, विद्युत-विच्छेद disconnect an electrical device by removing its plug from a socket. *She unplugged the hair drier after using it.*

Unpopular/ॲन्पाप्यूलॅर *(adjective)* – अप्रसिद्ध, अनचाहा not liked or popular. *The country is ready to wage an unpopular war.*

Unprecedented/अन्प्रेसिडेंटेड *(adj)* – अभूतपूर्व, अघटित never done or known before. *Our generation is witnessing an unprecedented expansion in population and industry.*

Unpredictable/ॲन्प्रिडिक्टॅबॅल *(adj)* – जिसकी भविष्यवाणी न हो सके not able to be predicted; changeable. *His sudden outburst is completely unpredictable.*

Unprepared/ॲन्प्रिपेअर्ड *(adjective)* – तैयार नहीं होना not ready or able to deal with something. *He is unprepared for today's exam.*

Unpretentious/ॲन्प्रिटेन्शॅस *(adjective)* – अहंकार रहित, विनम्र not pretentious; modest. *His quiet unpretentious demeanour attracts all.*

Unprofessional/ॲन्प्रॅफेशनल *(adj)* – अव्यावसायिक below or contrary to the standards expected in a particular profession. *His unprofessional behabviour surprises all.*

Unprovoked/ॲन्प्रॅवोक्ड *(adjective)* – बिना भड़काये of an attack, crime, etc. not directly provoked. *The army is not prepared for the unprovoked and dastardly attack.*

Unqualified/ॲन्क्वॉलिफाइड *(adjective)* – मान्यताहीन, योग्यताविहीन not having the necessary qualifications or requirements. *Raj is unqualified for the post applied for.*

Unquestionable/ॲन्क्वेस्च्नॅबॅल *(adj)* – निर्विवाद, निस्संदेह not able to be disputed or doubted. *He upholds his unquestionable authority.*

Unravel/अनरैवल *(verb)* – सुलझाना undo twisted, knitted, or woven threads; unwind. become undone. *His old grandmother asks him to unravel the thread.*

Unreal/ॲन्रिअॅल *(adjective)* – अवास्तविक imaginary; not seeming real. *She is desirous of unreal success.*

Unreasonable/ॲन्रीजनॅबॅल *(adjective)* – अनुचित not guided by or based on good sense. *The young man's unreasonable attitude distracts all from the goal.*

Unreliable/ॲन्रिलाइअबल *(adjective)* – अविश्वसनीय not able to be relied upon. *People consider our generation unreliable.*

Unremitting/ॲन्रिमिटिंग *(adjective)* – निरन्तर never relaxing or slackening. *We couldn't go out for picnic because of unremitting rain.*

Unrest/ॲन्रेस्ट *(noun)* – अशान्ति a state of rebellious dissatisfaction and agitation in a group of people: civil unrest. a state of uneasiness or disturbance. *I feel a bit unrest today.*

Unripe/ॲन्राइप *(adjective)* – कच्चा not ripe. *The vendor is ready to sell unripe fruits to the customers.*

Unrivalled/ॲन्राइवल्ड *(adjective)* – अद्वितीय, प्रतिद्वन्द्री विहीन surpassing all others. *Her unrivalled mastery of art suppresses all others.*

Unroll/ॲन्रोल *(verb)* – खोलना open or cause to open out from a rolled up state. *The activist unrolls the banner before the followers.*

U

Unruly/अॅन्रूलि (adjective) – बेकाबू, उपद्रवी disorderly and disruptive; difficult to control. *The teachers find his attitude unruly.*

Unsafe/अॅन्सेफ (adjective) – असुरक्षित not safe; dangerous. *People think their fortune was increasingly unsafe.*

Unsaid/अॅन्सेड (adjective) – अनकहा not said or uttered. *Many things left unsaid.*

Unsatisfactory/अॅन्सैटिस्फैक्टरी (adjective) – असन्तोषप्रद Unacceptable; not good enough. *Life is becoming increasingly unsatisfactory.*

Unsavoury/अॅन्सेवरि (adjective) – आक्रामक, अनचाहा स्वाद unpleasant. *I cannot eat such unsavoury food.*

Unscathed/अॅन्स्केद्ड (adjective) – बिना घायल हुए without suffering any injury, damage, or harm. *The young man survived unscathed.*

Unscrew/अॅन्स्क्रू (verb) – पेंच खोलना with reference to a screw, lid, etc. unfasten or be unfastened by twisting. *He is asked to unscrew the outlet plate.*

Unscrupulous/अनस्क्रूप्युलस (adj) – कपटी without moral scruples. *Unscrupulous politicians are destroying our country.*

Unsettle/अॅन्सेटॅल (verb) – अस्थिर करना cause to be anxious or uneasy; disturb. *Don't unsettle them.*

Unshaven/अनशेवेन (adjective) – बिना दाढ़ी बनाये not having shaved or been shaved. The young *man looked unshaven but energetic.*

Unsightly/अॅन्साइटलि (adjective) – घिनावना, घृणित, नहीं देखने योग्य unpleasant to look at; ugly. *There were unsightly seenes on the road last night.*

Unskilled/अॅन्स्किल्ड (adjective) – अकुशल not having or requiring special skill or training. *He is unskilled in the art of rhetoric.*

Unsound/अनसाउण्ड (adjective) – अस्वस्थ, कमजोर not safe or robust; in poor condition. *The new organization is based on an unsound foundation.*

Unspeakable/अॅन्स्पीकेबॅल (adj) – अकथनीय not able to be expressed in words. *He can't express unspeakable happiness in words.* too bad or horrific to express in words. *Never dare to utter the unspeakable name of the witch.*

Unstable/अॅन्स्टेबॅल (adjective) – अस्थिर prone to change or collapse; not stable. *We are witnessing the worst unstable political conditions of the country.*

Unsteady/अॅन्स्टेडी (adjective) – अस्थिर, हिलने वाला liable to fall or shake; not firm. *His hand was unsteady as he poured the wine.*

Unsuccessful/अॅन्सक्सेसफुल (adjective) – असफल not successful. *Ramesh was unsuccessful in his first attempt.*

Unsuitable/अन्सूटेबल (adjective) – अनुपयुक्त not fitting or appropriate. *The college authority forms new rules unsuitable to students.*

Unsure/अन्श्यूर (adjective) – अनिश्चित lacking confidence. *His father thinks him to* be *a very unsure young man.*

Unsuspecting/अॅन्ससपेक्टिंग (adjective) – संदेह से परे not aware of the presence of danger; feeling no suspicion. *The politicians are deceiving the unsuspecting public.*

Untamed/अॅन्टेम्ड (adjective) – न दबने वाला not tamed or controlled. of land wild or uncultivated: *The man is fond of the untamed wilderness.*

Untangle/अॅन्टैंगल (verb) – सुलझाना free from tangles. *Untangle the thread.*

Unthinkable/अॅन्थिंकेर्बॅल (adjective) – कल्पनातीत, विचार से परे too unlikely or undesirable to be considered a possibility. *The unthinkable usually remains the unmentionable.*

Unthinking/अॅन्थिंकिंग (adjective) – विचारहीन, अविचारी without proper consideration. *The unthinking activities of the young prince will bring the doomsday to the kingdom soon.*

Untidy/अॅन्टाइडि (adjective) – गन्दा, तितर-बितर, अव्यवस्थित not arranged tidily. of a person not inclined to be neat. *He lives in an untidy living room.*

Untie/अॅन्टाइ (verb) – खोलना undo or unfasten something tied. *The people untied the prisoner.*

Until/अॅन्टिल (preposition & conjunction) – तक up to the point in time or the event mentioned. *He sleeps until it gets light.*

U

Untimely/अन्टाइम्लि *(adjective)* – कुसमय happening or done at an unsuitable time; inappropriate. *He makes an untimely remark.* of a death or end happening too soon or sooner than normal. *Alcohol brought him to an untimely end.*

Unto/अन्टु *(preposition)* – तब तक [archaic] term for to. *The Lord said unto Moses.*

Untold/अनटोल्ड *(adjective)* – अनकहा too much or too many to be counted; indescribable: *Thieves caused untold damage to the family.*

Untouchable/अन्टचेबल *(adjective)* – अछूत not able to be touched or affected. *He is untouchable for the critics.*

Untoward/अनटुवार्ड *(adjective)* – अप्रत्याशित unexpected and inappropriate or adverse. *They made a place for themselves under the most untoward conditions.*

Untrue/अनटू *(adjective)* – असभ्य false or incorrect. *The statement was simply untrue.*

Untruth/अनटूथ *(noun)* – असत्य, झूठा a lie. His story is bitter untruth. *Don't tell me a untruth story to save your life.*

Unused/अन्यूज़्ड *(adjective)* – अप्रयुक्त, अनुभवहीन *He has seen an unused envelope.*

Unusual/अन्यूजुअल *(adjective)* – असामान्य not habitually or commonly done or occurring. *Nuclear families are no longer unusual.*

Unutterable/अन्अटरेब्ल *(adjective)* – अकथनीय too great or awful to describe. *The small girl can't describe the unutterable incident.*

Unveil/अन्वेल *(verb)* – परदा हटाना, घूँघट उठाना remove a veil or covering from. *Women are not allowed to unveil themselves in public in Islamic societies.*

Unwanted/अन्वांटेड *(adjective)* – अनचाहा not wanted. *The family is scared of unwanted guests.*

Unwelcome/अन्वेलकम *(adjective)* – अवांछित not welcome. *He is unwelcome in the function.*

Unwell/अन्वेल *(adjective)* – अस्वस्थ ill. *He is severely unwell.*

Unwieldy/अन्वील्डि *(adjective)* – बोझिल hard to move or manage because of its size, shape, or weight. *The person almost dropped the unwieldy parcel.*

Unwilling/अन्विलिंग *(adjective)* – अनिच्छुक not willing. *She is unwilling the do the homework.*

Unwind/अन्वाइन्ड *(verb)* – लपेट खोलना undo or be undone after winding or being wound. *Unwind a ball of yarn.*

Unwitting/अन्विटिंग *(adjective)* – अनजाना not aware of the full facts: *He is going to encounter an unwitting accomplice.*

Unwrap/अन्रैप *(verb)* – खोलना, अनाकृत करना remove the wrapping from. *Let's unwrap the gifts!*

Up/अप *(adverb)* – ऊपर, पूरी तरह, उठना towards a higher place or position. to or at a place perceived as higher: *a walk up to the shops.* of the sun visible in the sky. towards the north. towards or in the capital or a major city. at or to a university, especially oxford or Cambridge. *I am up and about here.*

Upbeat/अप्बिट *(noun)* – प्रसन्न और उत्साहित in music an unaccented beat preceding an accented beat. *His wishes are considered upbeat.*

Upbraid/अप्ब्रेड *(verb)* – झिड़कना, डाँटना scold or reproach. *The president upbraided the minister for his irresponsible behaviour.*

Upbringing/अप्ब्रिंगिंग *(noun)* – पालन-पोषण the treatment and instruction received from one's parents throughout childhood. *His behaviour reflects his upbringing.*

Update/अप्डेट *(verb)* – अद्यतन करना make more modern. *We updated the bedroom in the old house.*

Upgrade/अप्ग्रेड *(verb)* – स्तर बढ़ाना raise to a higher standard or rank. *The teacher upgraded the most brilliant student to the next class.*

Upheaval/अप्हीवल *(noun)* – उथल-पुथल a violent or sudden change or disruption. *The industrial revolution was a period of great upheaval in the world.*

Uphill/अप्हिल *(adverb)* – कठिन towards the top of a slope. *He moves uphill.*

Uphold/अप्होल्ड *(verb)* – अनुमोदन करना confirm or support. *He upholds the conditions put forward by the suffering family*; maintain a custom or practice. *The man is trying to uphold the family tradition.*

U

Upholster/अॅपहोल्स्टर *(verb)* – गद्दा लगाना provide furniture with a soft, padded covering. cover the walls or furniture in a room with textiles. *There are many chair companies that import all types of upholstery, frames.*

Upholstery/अॅपहोल्स्टरि *(noun)* – गद्दा soft, padded textile used to upholster furniture. *The family is doing the business of importing upholstery for many decades.*

Upkeep/अॅपकीप *(noun)* – रख-रखाव the process of keeping something in good condition. *His upkeep of maintaining the museum is commendable.*

Upland/अॅपलैंड *(noun)* – ऊच्चभूमि, ऊँचासी also uplands an area of high or hilly land. *Upland agriculture may bring good result.*

Uplifting/अॅपलिपिंटग *(noun)* – ऊपर खींचना The rise of something. *The uplifting of the clouds revealed the blue of a summer sky.*

Upon/अॅपॉन *(preposition)* – पर, किसी पर more formal term for on. *The man balanced upon one leg well.*

Upper/अपर *(adjective)* – ऊपरी the topmost one of two. *The small tree is located in the upper centre of the picture.*

Uppermost/अपरमोस्ट *(adjective)* – सबसे ऊपर also upmost highest in place, rank, or importance. *Please bring me the uppermost book in the pile.*

Upright/अॅपराइट *(adjective)* – सीधा, ईमानदार vertical; erect. of a piano having vertical strings. *He is a man of upright nature.*

Uprising/अॅपराइजिंग *(noun)* – विद्रोह an act of resistance or rebellion. *The security has been stepped up since the recent uprising in the city.*

Uproar/अॅपरोर *(noun)* – हंगामा a loud and impassioned noise or disturbance. a public expression of outrage. *There is a sudden uproar in the city due to a terrorist threat.*

Uproot/अॅपरूट *(verb)* – उखाड़ना, जड़ से उखाड़ना pull a plant, tree, etc. out of the ground. *Uproot the vine that has spread all over the garden.*

Upset/अॅपसेट *(verb)* – गड़बड़ी करना, हड़बड़ी होना make unhappy, disappointed, or worried. *The hostile talks upset the peaceful situation in the room.*

Upshot/अॅपशॉट *(noun)* – निष्कर्ष the eventual outcome or conclusion. *The recent incidents are the upshot of various happenings occurred two decades ago.*

Upside-down/अॅपसाइड-डाउन *(adjective & adverb)* – उलटा-पुलटा with the upper part where the lower part should be. *The box was lying on the floor upside down.*

Upstairs/अॅपस्टेअर्स *(adverb)* – ऊपरी मंजिल on or to an upper floor. *The younger son lives upstairs.*

Upstart/अॅपस्टार्ट *(noun)* – नवधनाढ्य a person who has risen suddenly to prominence, especially one who behaves arrogantly. *The man who was so poor one year back is considered an upstart in the city.*

Upstream/अॅपस्ट्रीम *(adjective & adverb)* – प्रतिकूल दिशा में situated or moving in the direction opposite to that in which a stream or river flows. *He went upstream to look at a sure-enough fish wheel.*

Uptake/अॅपटेक *(noun)* – उद्ग्रहण the action of taking up or making use of something. *The machine makes paper napkins with a greater uptake of liquids.*

Uptight/अॅपटाइट *(adjective)* – भयभीत, आशंकित nervously tense or angry. *For some unknown reasons these animals are more laid back than their uptight counterparts.*

Up-to-date/अॅप-टू-डेट *(adj)* – आधुनिक, अद्यतन incorporating or aware of the latest developments and trends. *People are discussing an up-to-date issue of the magazine.*

Upward/अॅपवार्ड *(adverb)* – ऊपर की ओर also upwards towards a higher point or level. *The cards are faced upward. (adjective)* moving or leading towards a higher point or level. *The team moves upward.*

Urban/अर्बन *(adjective)* – नागरी, नगरीय, शहरी of or relating to a town or city. *The urban property owners behvave very rudely to students.*

Urbane/अर्बेन *(noun)* – सुसभ्य especially of a man suave, courteous, and refined. *The director maintained an urbane tone in his letters.*

U

Urchin/अर्चिन *(noun)* – गन्दा, नटखट a mischievous child, especially a raggedly dressed one. *The urchin makes the family members' life very difficult with his mischievous deeds.*

Urge/अर्ज *(verb)* – सुझाव देना, प्रेरणा देना encourage or entreat earnestly to do something. *Father urged me to finish my studies.* strongly recommend. encourage to move more quickly. *The leader urges the team members to wind up things quickly.* encourage someone to continue. *The teacher urges the students to continue study even if they face difficult situations.*

Urgent/अर्जेन्ट् *(adjective)* – अति आवश्यक requiring immediate action or attention. *The old bridge requires an urgent need of repair.*

Urine/यूरिन *(noun)* – मूत्र a pale yellowish fluid stored in the bladder and discharged through the urethra, consisting of excess water and substances removed from the blood by the kidneys. *There was blood in her urine.*

Urn/अर्न *(noun)* – पात्र, अस्थि कलश a tall, rounded vase with a stem and base, especially one for storing a cremated person's ashes. *The son kept his father's ashes in an urn.*

Us/अस *(pronoun)* – हम, हमें used by a speaker to refer to himself or herself and one or more others as the object of a (verb) or preposition. used after the verb to be and after than or as. *Give the football to us.*

Usage/यूजेज *(noun)* – प्रयोग, व्यवहार the action of using something or the fact of being used. *The Police warned against the usage of narcotic drugs.*

Use/यूज *(verb)* – उपयोग, उपयोग करना take, hold, or deploy as a means of accomplishing or achieving something. take an illegal drug. *Don't use illegal drugs.*

Used/यूज्ड *(adjective)* – पुरानी, प्रयोग में लायी हुई, अभ्यस्त having already been used. Second hand. *He bought a used car.*

Used to/यूज्ड टु – आदी, आदत, करने की आदत In the habit. *I am telling you, you'll get used to the idea.*

Useful/यूजफुल *(adjective)* – उपयोगी able to be used for a practical purpose or in several ways. *The servant is useful to the owner.*

Useless/यूजलेस *(adjective)* – अनुपयोगी, बेकार serving no purpose. *He is useless in an emergency.*

User/यूजर *(noun)* – उपभोक्ता a person who uses or operates something. He is a very careful user. *The user exploits his employee.*

Usher/अशर *(noun)* – उपयोक्ता a person who shows people to their seats in a theatre or cinema or at a wedding. *The usher is doing his job properly in the marriage reception.*

Usual/यूजुअल *(adjective)* – सामान्य, अधिकतर होने वाला habitually or typically occurring or done. *Mother knows the child's usual bedtime.*

Usurp/यूजर्प *(verb)* – हड़प लेना, हड़पना take a position of power illegally or by force. *He usurped my rights.*

Usury/यूजरी *(noun)* – सूदखोरी the practice of lending money at unreasonably high rates of interest. interest at such rates. *Usuries are done by very rich persons.*

Utensil/यूटेंसिल *(noun)* – बरतन, रसोई के वर्तन a tool or container, especially for household use. *Use of utensils should be minimum.*

Utilitarian/यूटिलिटेरिअन *(adjective)* – उपयोगितावाद useful or practical rather than attractive. *She prefers utilitarian steel tables.*

Utility/यूटिलिटी *(noun)* – उपयोगिता, उपयोग the state of being useful, profitable, or beneficial. in game theory or economics the value of that which is sought to be maximized in any situation involving a choice. *The utility of a computer is known to all people in today's era.*

Utilize/यूटिलाइज *(verb)* – प्रयुक्त, उपयोग करना, सदुपयोग make practical and effective use of. *Do you know how do you utilize this tool?*

Utmost/अटमोस्ट *(adjective)* – परम, सर्वाधिक most extreme; greatest. *He endures to the utmost measure of human endurance.* *(noun)* the greatest or most extreme extent or amount. *She tried her utmost.*

Utopia/यूटोपिया *(noun)* – कल्पना जगत्, काल्पनिकश्रेष्ठ स्थान an imagined perfect place or state of things. *Some people still think India to be a Utopia.*

U

Utter/अटर *(adjective & verb)* – पूरा, निरा, कहना, बोलना, उच्चारण करना complete; absolute: utter amazement. *His behaviour shows utter nonsense.*

Utterance/अॅटॅरॅन्स *(noun)* – अभिव्यक्ति, कथन, उद्गार a word, statement, or sound uttered. the action of uttering. an uninterrupted chain of speech or writing. *The sudden utterance of the speech of the political leader disturbs the peaceful environment of the school.*

U-turn/यू-टर्न *(noun)* – पीछे मुड़ना, छोड़कर हट जाना the turning of a vehicle in a U shaped course so as to face the opposite way. *He takes a U-turn as he has mistaken the road to be the right one.*

U

V v

V/वी *(noun)* – अंग्रेजी वर्णमाला का 22वाँ वर्ण the twenty second letter of the English alphabet.

1. Denoting the next after U in a set of items, categories, etc. *V-shaped sweaters are quite popular during winter.*
2. The Roman numeral for five. *He is a student of class V.*
3. Denoting an internal combustion engine with a number of cylinders arranged in two rows at an angle to each other. *A V-engine is an internal combustion engine used to convert fuel into energy to run motor car.*

Vacancy/वेकेन्सि *(noun)* – शून्यता, रिक्त स्थान an unoccupied position or job. *There is a vacancy for a DTP operator in our office.*

Vacant/वैकेन्ट *(adjective)* – रिक्त not occupied; empty. of a position not filled. *Nearly half of the offices are still vacant.*

Vacate/वैकेट *(verb)* – खाली करना, परित्याग करना leave a place. give up a position or job. *Hotel room must be vacated by noon on the last day of the month.*

Vaccinate/वैक्सिनेट *(verb)* – शीतला का टीका लगाना treat with a vaccine to produce immunity against a disease. *All the children of this school were vaccinated against tuberculosis.*

Vaccinia/वैक्सिनिया *(noun)* – चौपायों का विस्फोटक रोग cowpox or the virus causing it. *The virus that causes small pox is known as vaccinia.*

Vacillate/वैसिलेट *(verb)* – डगमगाना waver between different opinions or actions. *He vacillated between teaching and writing.*

Vacuity/वैक्युइटि *(noun)* – खालीपन lack of thought or intelligence; empty-headedness: *He spoke on the subject of frivolity or vacuity in modern day literature.*

Vacuole/वैक्ओल *(noun)* – गर्त a space or vesicle within the cytoplasm of a cell, enclosed by a membrane and typically containing fluid. *The small cavity developed in nervous tissue as the result of disease is known as vacuole.*

Vacuous/वैक्युअस *(adjective)* – खाली showing a lack of thought or intelligence. *The vacuous smile he gave out was quite inappropriate at such a serious discussion session.*

Vagabond/वैगाबांड *(noun)* – आवारा, फालतू आदमी a vagrant. *He is a vagabond, here today, there tomorrow.*

Vagary/वैगरि *(noun)* – मनजौज an unexpected and inexplicable change. *Vagaries of nature are difficult to predict and hard to control.*

Vagina/वजाइना *(noun)* – योनि, संगम-पथ the muscular tube leading from the vulva to the cervix in women and most female mammals. *Vagina is the passage in the body of a woman or female animal between the outer sex organs and womb.*

Vagrancy/वेग्रन्सि *(noun)* – आवारापन, आपन the state of living as a vagrant; homelessness: *Drug abuse may lead to descent into vagrancy.*

Vagrant/वेग्रन्ट *(noun)* – घुमक्कड़ a person without a home or job. a wanderer. *A person without a settled home or regular work who wanders from place to place and lives by begging is known as a vagrant.*

Vague/वेग *(adjective)* – अस्थिर of uncertain or indefinite character or meaning. *There are many patients who suffer from vague symptoms.* imprecise in thought or expression. *She has been very vague about her life and activities.*

Vale/वेल *(noun)* – घाटी valley (used in place names). *The Vale of Glamorgan as a poetic term is popular all over the literary world.*

Valentine/वैलेन्टाइन *(noun)* – प्रेमी, प्रेमिका, प्रेम-पत्र a card sent, often anonymously, on St valentine's day 14 February to a person one loves or is attracted to. a person to whom one sends such a card. *Radha is my valentine, I send her a card but without putting my name on it.*

V

Valetudinarian/वैलेट्यूडिनेरियन *(noun)* – रोगी a person who is unduly anxious about their health. *People suffering from poor health are commonly known as valetudinarian.*

Valiance/वैलिअन्स *(noun)* – पराक्रम great courage or determination. *He always demonstrates great courage and valiance in all battles.*

Valid/वैलिड *(adjective)* – प्रबल actually supporting the untended point or claim: *The article carried a valid criticism just below the story.*

Valley/वैलि *(noun)* – घाटी a low area between hills or mountains, typically with a river or stream flowing through it. *There are many valleys between the mountains in Himachal Pradesh.*

Valorous/वैलरस *(adjective)* – साहसी great courage in the face of danger. *The medal was awarded to the Colonel for his valorous act in the battle area.*

Valuable/वाल्युऍबल (वैल्यूऑबॅल) *(adjective)* – मूल्यवान worth a great deal of money. *She bought a valuable antique in London.* extremely useful or important. *I respect my time as highly valuable.*

Value/वैल्यू *(noun)* – सारता, मूल्य the regard that something is held to deserve; importance or worth. *Your support would be of great value during election campaigning.* material or monetary worth. *The value of products seldom remains constant.* the worth of something compared to its price: *At Rs.1000/- it is good value for this mobile phone.*

Valve/वैल्व *(noun)* – कपाट a device for controlling the passage of fluid through a pipe or duct, especially an automatic device allowing movement in one direction only. *This valve will shut off the flow from the boiler when the water is hot enough.*

Vampire/वैम्पायर *(noun)* – प्रेत in folklore a corpse supposed to leave its grave at night to drink the blood of the living. *In TV serials, we see that vampires have long pointed sharp teeth.* a person who exploits others

ruthlessly. *The members who oppose money spent on welfare measures are no less than a blood sucking vampire.*

Vanadium/वैनेडियम *(noun)* – चाँदी जैसा एक धातुतत्त्व the chemical element of atomic number 23, a hard grey metal used to make alloy steels. *Vanadium is a soft poisonous silver-grey metal that is added to some type of steel to make it stronger.*

Vanguard/वैनगार्ड *(noun)* – सेनामुख the foremost part of an advancing army or naval force. *Vanguards have reported sighting enemy forces near the border.*

Vanish/वैनिश *(verb)* – लुप्त हो जाना disappear suddenly and completely. *The ship vanished into the sea without a trace.* gradually cease to exist. *The environment is under threat since large trees are vanishing due to rising temperature.*

Vanishing Point/वैनिशिंग पॉइंट *(noun)* – अदृश्य होने वाला the point at which something has been decreasing disappears altogether. *The rates of interest have dwindled to vanishing point.*

Vantage/वैन्टेज *(noun)* – सुविधा a place or position affording a good view. *From my vantage point, I could see the whole of Delhi.*

Vaporable/वेपरेब्ल *(adjective)* – वाष्प में बदलने योग्य possible to convert into vapour. *Water is vaporable liquid.*

Varicosity/वैरिकोसिटि *(noun)* – शिरा की सूजन something to do regarding vein, especially in the leg. *Following the accident, he has been diagnosed as suffering from varicosity due to poor circulation of blood in the leg.*

Varied/वैरिड *(adjective)* – बदला हुआ incorporating a number of different types or elements; showing variation or variety. *His bio data reflects a long and varied career.*

Variety/वेराइटी *(noun)* – परिवर्तन the quality or state of being different or diverse. *It's the variety that makes my job so enjoyable.*

Variform/वैरिफॉर्म *(adjective)* – विभिन्न आकार का of a group of things differing from one another in form. *India has a variform*

V

of languages. of a single thing or a mass consisting of a variety of forms or things. *Variform education is necessary to succeed in present day competitive world.*

Variola/वेराइऑला *(noun)* – चेचक technical term for smallpox. *In 18th century, smallpox was known as variola.*

Varlet/वारलेट *(noun)* – सेवक an unprincipled rogue. *Dishonest people go by the name of varlet.*

Varletry/वारलेट्रि *(noun)* – भीड़-भक्कड़ practice of being a varlet. *Practice of varletry was fairly in vogue about a century ago.*

Varnish/वार्निश *(noun)* – रोगन, चमक a substance consisting of resin dissolved in a liquid, applied to wood to give a hard, clear, shiny surface when dry. *The cupboard was coated with several coats of varnish.*

Vary/वैरि *(verb)* – पलटना differ in size, degree, or nature from something else of the same general class. *The properties here vary in size and price.*

Vascular/वैस्कुलर *(adjective)* – वाहक नलियों से सम्बन्धित relating to or denoting the system of vessels for carrying blood or in plants sap, water, and nutrients. *Overweight and lack of physical activity have started affecting his vascular system.*

Vasculum/वैस्क्युलम *(noun)* – बटुआ a collecting box for plants, typically a flattened cylindrical metal case with a lengthwise opening. *Vasculum is a metallic container botanists use to collect plants.*

Vase/वेस *(noun)* – बर्तन a decorative container without handles, typically made of glass or china and used as an ornament or for displaying cut flowers. *Porcelain vases containing cut flowers make drawing rooms a showpiece.*

Vaseline/वेसलिन *(noun)* – मिट्टी के तेल से निकाला गया तैलीय पदार्थ a type of petroleum jelly used as an ointment and lubricant. *The doors glide open as if their rails have been vaselined.*

Vassal/वैसल *(noun)* – प्रजा a holder of land by feudal tenure on conditions of homage

and allegiance. a person or country in a subordinate position to another. *Macedonia was a vassal state of the Ottoman Empire.*

Vast/वास्ट *(adjective)* – विशाल of very great extent or quantity; immense. *Tired of walking we decided to rest at a vast plain full of orchards.* *(noun)* an immense space. *India is a vast country in terms of area and population.*

Vastitude/वास्टिट्यूड *(noun)* – विशालता quality of being vast. *Many neighbouring countries are fearful due to Chinese assertiveness and vastitude.*

Vastly/वास्टलि *(adverb)* – विपुलता से the state of being vast. *He vastly exaggerated the inconveniences he faced during training.*

Vaticinate/वैटिसिनेट *(verb)* – भविष्य कहना foretell the future. *The lady spent much of her time vaticinating on learned political panels.*

Vaulter/वॉल्टर *(noun)* – कूदने वाला one who vaults *He is the only vaulter who could jump over twenty feet in the first attempt.*

Vegetable/वेजिटेब्ल *(noun)* – शाक a plant or part of a plant used as food. *Cauliflower, cabbage, potato, turnip, and bean are vegetables.*

Vegetal/वेजिटल *(adjective)* – वनस्पति-सम्बन्धी of or relating to plants. *A vegetal aroma was coming out strongly when cooking was under way.*

Vegetarian/वेजिटेरिअन *(noun)* – शाकाहारी a person who does not eat meat for moral, religious, or health reasons. *I would like to order a vegetarian lunch today.* *(adjective)* eating or including no meat. *We decided to go to a vegetarian restaurant.*

Vegetate/वेजिटेट *(verb)* – उत्पन्न होना, नीरस जीवन बिताना live or spend a period of time in a dull, inactive, unchallenging way. *If left alone, he would become inactive, sit in front of a TV and vegetate.*

Vehicle/वीइकल *(noun)* – वाहन, गाड़ी, साधन a thing used for transporting people or goods on land, e.g. a car, truck, or cart. *Mercedes has launched a new series of premium*

V

passenger vehicles in India. Heavy vehicles are not allowed to enter the city limit during day time.

Velarium/विलेरियम *(noun)* – छत के नीचे तानी हुई चाँदनी a large awning used in ancient Rome to shelter an amphitheatre. *Velariums are still used overhead to protect tennis courts from vagaries of weather.*

Velleity/वेलेइटी *(noun)* – इच्छा a wish or inclination not strong enough to lead to action. *The outlandish speech angered me, but I chose to remain a velleity.*

Velocity/विलॉसिटि *(noun)* – गति the speed of something in a given direction. *There are high-tech machines to increase the velocity of the emitted particles.* in general use speed. *The rocket blasted off with an incredible velocity.*

Velvet/वेल्वेट *(noun)* – मखमल a closely woven fabric of silk, cotton, or nylon with a thick short pile on one side. *The armchair we bought is covered in velvet.*

Venal/वीनल *(adjective)*– घूसखोर, उत्कोची showing or motivated by susceptibility to bribery. *The customs officers at air and seaports are notoriously venal.*

Vend/वेन्ड *(verb)* – बेचना offer small items for sale, especially from a slot machine. *There was a woman vending cakes and panties at the cinema hall.*

Vender/वेन्डर *(noun)* – बेंचने वाला, ठेले पर सामान बेंचने वाला a person offering something for sale, especially in a street. *We buy vegetables from the vendor, he comes here each evening.*

Vendee/वेन्डी *(noun)* – खरीददार a buyer, especially of property. *The real estate developer invited all vendees to lunch and showed them their flats.*

Vendue/वेनड्यू *(noun)* – नीलाम द्वारा बिक्री a public auction. *Dutch used to call sale by auction as vendue during 18th century.*

Venerability/वेनरेबिलिटि *(noun)* – आदर respect given due to age, character, knowledge. *He is known for great wisdom and, therefore, his venerability is not in doubt.*

Venereal/विनीरिअल *(adjective)* – मैथुन-सम्बन्धी of or relating to venereal disease. *There has been a steady increase in venereal infection in South Africa.*

Venery/वेनरि *(noun)* – शिकार exercise of hunting. *All but a few of them engaged in venery.*

Vengeance/वेन्जिएन्स *(noun)* – बदला punishment inflicted or retribution exacted for an injury or wrong. *In the ensuing election, voters are ready to wreak vengeance on all politicians.*

Venial/वीनिअल *(adjective)* – क्षम्य denoting a sin that is not regarded as depriving the soul of divine grace. *Everything they have disclosed up to now can be seen as venial.*

Venter/वेन्टर *(noun)* – गर्भाशय relating to abdomen. *The underside of the belly of animal is known as venter.*

Ventiduct/वेन्टिडक्ट *(noun)* – वायु मार्ग an air passage, especially one for ventilation. *The ventiduct of the air conditioner is not working.*

Ventricle/वेन्ट्रिकल *(noun)* – प्रवेश each of the two larger and lower cavities of the heart. *Each of the two main chambers of the heart, left and right, that pump blood to the body are called a ventricle.*

Ventricular/वेन्ट्रिक्यूलर *(adjective)* – कोष्ठक सम्बन्धी something to do with a hollow part or cavity of an organ *An x-ray was done to determine the ventricular positioning of the heart.*

Verdancy/वरडैन्सी *(noun)* – हरापन the state of greenery with grass or other rich vegetation *We stayed for a few hours enjoying the alluring verdancy of the hills in Kodaikanal.*

Verderer/वर्डेरर *(noun)* – जंगलों का रक्षक a judicial officer of a royal forest. *The verderer arrested the poachers who were trying to kill elephants for their tusk.*

Verdict/वर्डिक्ट *(noun)* – न्याय a decision on an issue of fact in a civil or criminal case or an inquest. *The jury returned a verdict of not guilty.*

V

Verdure/वर्ड्योर *(noun)* – हरियाली से टँका हुआ lush green vegetation. *Fresh green colour of lush vegetation is called verdure.*

Verifiable/वेरिफाइएबल *(adj)* – प्रमाणित करने योग्य anything that can be substantiated, proved correct or otherwise. *This matter is verifiable.*

Verily/वेरिलि *(adverb)* – अवश्य truly; certainly. *Verily, what these people are doing is nothing but madness.*

Veritable/वेरिटेबल *(adjective)* – सत्य genuine; actual; properly so called used to qualify a metaphor: a veritable price explosion. *The meal that followed was a veritable feast.*

Vermicelli/वर्मिसेलि *(plural noun)* – सेवई pasta made in long slender threads. *Fine wheat flower converted into long thin threads is known as vermicelli.*

Vermicide/वर्मिसाइड *(noun)* – कीड़ा मारने वाला पदार्थ a substance that is poisonous to worms. *Vermicides are used to kill worms in sewerage lines.*

Vermicular/वर्मिक्युलर *(adjective)* – कीड़े के समान like a worm in form or movement; vermiform. *Medical tests confirmed some vermicular movement in his stomach.*

Vermilion/वर्मिलिअन *(noun)* – सिन्दूर a brilliant red pigment made from mercury sulphide cinnabar. *Married Indian women put vermilion on their head between the partings of hair.* a brilliant red colour. *They coated the outer portion of their house using vermillion coloured paint.*

Vermination/वर्मिनेशन *(noun)* – कीड़े की संख्या बढ़ने की क्रिया the state of breeding or becoming infected with vermin. *Vermination in this area must be curbed.*

Vernacular/वर्नाकुलर *(noun)* – प्राकृत the language or dialect spoken by the ordinary people of a country or region. *He writes in the vernacular to reach a larger audience.* the specialized terminology of a group or activity. *When talking to the gardener, I used the gardening vernacular.*

Vernal/वर्नल *(adjective)* – वासन्तिक of, in, or appropriate to spring. *The vernal freshness of the land was very alluring.*

Vernier/वर्नियर *(noun)* – अंको में अंकित, एक स्केल (वर्नियर) a small movable graduated scale for obtaining fractional parts of subdivisions on a fixed main scale of a barometer, sextant, or other measuring instrument. *Vernier calliper is used to make small measurements in the laboratory.*

Versant/वर्सन्ट *(noun)* – परिचित, ढाल a region of land sloping in one general direction. *We came down the mountain by using the low gradient eastern versant.*

Versify/वर्सिफाइ *(verb)* – कविता बनाना turn into or express in verse. *It was never suggested that Wordsworth should simply versify Coleridge's ideas.*

Version/वर्सन *(noun)* – वर्णन, कथन a particular form of something differing in certain respects from an earlier form other forms of the same type of thing. *The revised version of the paper was produced for a later meeting.*

Versus/वर्सस *(preposition)* – विपरीत, के विरुद्ध especially in sporting and legal use against. *England versus Australia cricket test match starts today.* as opposed to; in contrast to. *The company is weighing up the pros and cons of organic versus inorganic produce.*

Vertebra/वर्टिब्रा *(noun)* – पृष्ठवंश each of the series of small bones forming the backbone. *The needle was inserted between two of the vertebrae.*

Vertical/वर्टिकल *(adjective)* – लम्बरूप at right angles to a horizontal plane. *The y-axis is at right angle to the x-axis.* having the top directly above the bottom. *Don't move, please keep your back in vertical position.*

Vertiginous/वर्टिजिनस *(adjective)* – घूमता हुआ causing vertigo, especially by being extremely high or steep. *We encountered a vertiginous drop to the valleys below.*

Vertigo/वर्टिगो *(noun)* – चक्कर a sensation of whirling and loss of balance, caused by looking down from a great height. *Be warned that looking down from the mountain can bring about vertigo leading to fall.*

Vertu/वर्टू *(noun)* – कला की विशिष्टता variant spelling of virtu. *Literary speaking, the good*

V

qualities inherent in a person or thing is referred as vertu.

Verve/वर्व *(noun)* – उत्साह vigour, spirit, and style. *Shakira sings with supreme verve and flexibility.*

Very/वेरी *(adverb)* – सच्चा, ठीक in a high degree. *A very large amount of money was deposited yesterday.* without qualification: the very best quality. *He decided to donate his very own car.*

Vesical/वेसिकल *(adjective)* – मूत्राशय सम्बन्धी relating to or affecting the urinary bladder. *The tests confirm that his vesical artery is functioning properly.*

Vesicant/वेसिकैंट *(adjective)* – फफोला उत्पन्न करने वाला लेप tending to cause blistering. *Rubbing hands on a stone may be vesicant.* *(noun)* an agent that causes blistering. *Even dilute hydrochloric acid is a vesicant; you must wear hand gloves for protection.*

Vessel/वेसल *(noun)* – पात्र, नाव a ship or large boat. *Titanic was the largest sea-going passenger vessel during 1910s.*

Vestal/वेस्टल *(adjective)* – पवित्र of or relating to the Roman goddess Vesta. *Romans even today go to vestal temple to seek blessings of Goddess Vesta.*

Vestiary/वेस्टिअरि *(adjective)* – अँगरखा of or relating to dress. *Gender equality demands one to stay away from vestiary.* *(noun)* a room in a monastery in which clothes are kept. *Vestiary is a place similar to a vestibule to keep coats and hats.*

Veteran/वेटरन *(noun)* – अभ्यासवृद्ध a person who has had long experience in a particular field. *Sachin Tendulkar is a veteran Indian cricketer.*

Veterinary/वेटरिनरि *(adjective)* – पशुचिकित्सा सम्बन्धी of or relating to the diseases, injuries, and treatment of farm and domestic animals. *There are not enough veterinary doctors to take care of animals in India.*

Vex/वेक्स *(verb)* – पीड़ा देना cause to feel annoyed or worried. *Food security is proving to be a vexed issue defying solution at World Trade Organisation meetings.* *(adjective)*

angry; annoyed. *Price rise is the most vexing questions for policymakers.*

Vexatious/वेक्सेशस *(adjective)* – दुःखदायी causing annoyance or worry. *Her behaviour is vexatious to others.*

Vexing/वेक्सिंग *(adjective)* – सन्तापकर annoying, worrying. *Solution to India-Pakistan border issues is a vexing problem.*

Via/वाया *(preposition)* – मार्ग से travelling through a place en route to a destination. *We came to India via Bangladesh.* by way of; *Many people buy a home with a mortgage via a housing society.* through. by means of. *We have a file sent via electronic mail.*

Viaticum/वियाटिकम *(noun)* – यात्रा सामग्री the Eucharist as given to a person near or in danger of death. *Viaticum is an occasion when Christian people eat and drink in memory of last Supper Jesus had with his disciples.*

Vibrancy/वाइब्रंसि *(noun)* – कम्पन youthfulness. *During Christmas time you will find the whole city flirting with vibrancy.*

Vibrant/वायब्रैंट *(adjective)* – काँपने वाला full of energy and enthusiasm. *We went around the vibrant cosmopolitan city.* of colour or sounds bold and strong. *The huge ball room was decorated in vibrant blues and greens.*

Vibrissa/वाइब्रिस्सा *(noun)* – गलमुच्छा long stiff hairs growing around the mouth or elsewhere on the face of many mammals; *Vibrissae is one of the characteristics to differentiate animals into kinds.* whiskers. coarse bristle like feathers growing around the gape of certain insectivorous birds that catch insects in flight. *There are many birds that make use of their characteristic of vibrissae to survive.*

Viceregal/वाइसरिगल *(adjective)* – राज-प्रतिनिधि सम्बन्धी of or relating to a viceroy. *The viceregal carriage moved out drawn with eight horses.*

Vicious/विशस *(adjective)* – दुराचारी cruel or violent. *As a result of vicious assault, the person had to be hospitalized with multiple fracture.* of an animal wild and dangerous. *The dog was vicious and likely to bite.*

Victor/विक्टर *(noun)* – विजयी a person who defeats an enemy or opponent in a battle, game, or competition. *The president congratulated the victors.*

Victorious/विक्टोरिअस *(adjective)* – जयप्राप्त having won a victory; triumphant. of or characterized by victory. *The victorious team was accorded a red carpet welcome on arrival at the airport.*

Victual/विट्ल *(verb)* – रसद जुटाना food or provisions. *Meat, chicken, fish and other savoury victuals were served at the party.*

Vide/वाइड *(verb)* – देखो see; consult used as an instruction in a text to refer the reader elsewhere. *Vide your comments I have to state the following.*

Videlicet/वाइडिलिसेट *(adverb)* – अर्थात् more formal term for viz. *Instead of 'videlicet', people are better aware of its short form 'viz'.*

Vie/वाइ *(verb)* – स्पर्धा करना compete eagerly with others in order to do or achieve something. *Both finalists are vying with each other to win the trophy.*

Vigneron/विनेरॉन *(noun)* – अंगूर की खेती करने वाला a person who cultivates grapes for winemaking. *He is the most trusted vigneron for suppling grapes to wine manufacturers.*

Vignette/विनेट *(noun)* – छोटा a brief evocative description, account, or episode. *The function was organized to witness the classic vignette of embassy life.*

Vigour/विगर *(noun)* – शक्ति physical strength and good health. *His physique reflected a sign of vigour and health.* effort, energy, and enthusiasm. *He set about executing the new task with vigour.*

Village/विलेज *(noun)* – गाँव a group of houses situated in a rural area, larger than a hamlet and smaller than a town. *The coastal areas in Kerala consist essentially of pretty fishing villages.* a self contained district or community within a town or city: *A Olympic village was built for participants to live comfortably.* a small municipality with limited corporate powers. *The village sarpanch ensured that construction of two wells near the dwelling area was completed at the earliest.*

Vim/विम *(noun)* – बल energy; enthusiasm. *You should go out and play the game with vim, vigour and energy.*

Vindicable/विन्डिकेब्ल *(adjective)* – समर्थन करने योग्य state of clearing someone of suspicion. *More sober views expressed by respectable citizens were vindicable of proper action taken by police.*

Vindicator/विन्डिकेटर *(noun)* – रक्षक step that removes suspicion. *Immediate action taken by police was vindicator of its seriousness to arrest the criminals.*

Vindictive/विन्डिक्टिव *(adjective)* – बदला लेने वाला having or showing a strong or unreasoning desire for revenge. *The barrage of criticism was both vindictive and personalized.*

Vinegar/विनेगर *(noun)* – सिरका a sour tasting liquid containing acetic acid, obtained by fermenting dilute alcoholic liquids, typically wine, cider, or beer, and used as a condiment or for pickling. *Most pickles served at hotels and restaurants are made with the help of vinegar.*

Viol/वाइअल *(noun)* – एक प्रकार की वायलिन a musical instrument of the renaissance and baroque periods, typically six stringed, held vertically and played with a bow. *Shaped like a violin, early type of musical instrument that produced similar kind of music was known as viol.*

Violate/वाइअॉलेट *(verb)* – तोड़ना break or fail to comply with a rule or formal agreement. *Those who violate the agreement, would be punished.*

Violet/वायलेट *(noun)* – बैंगनी रंग a small plant typically with purple, blue, or white five petalled flowers. *Violet is a small garden plant that grows in spring with purple or white flowers.* used in names of unrelated plants with similar flowers, e.g. African violet. *She came dressed in violet.*

Violin/वायलिन *(noun)* – सारंगी, बेला, चिकारा a stringed musical instrument of treble pitch,

V

having for strings and a body narrowed at the middle and with two shaped sound holes, played with a horsehair bow. *Violin is one of the most popular musical instruments.*

Viper/वाइपर *(noun)* – सर्प, साँप a venomous snake with large hinged fangs, typically with dark patterns on a lighter background. *Russel viper is one of the most deadly snakes in the world.*

Virgate/वर्गेट *(noun)* – डण्डे के आकार का a varying measure of land, typically 30 acres. *He purchased in the suburban area a land measuring a virgate for constructing farmhouse.*

Virgo/वर्गो *(noun)* – कन्या राशि a large constellation the virgin, said to represent a maiden or goddess associated with the harvest. *Virgo is a large constellation of bright stars, largest of which is Spica.*

Virility/विरिलिटि *(noun)* – मनुषत्व, पुरुषत्व quality of having strength, energy, sex drive, manliness. *This club lays great importance on a man's virility.*

Virtuosity/वर्चुऑसिटी *(noun)* – ललित कला के प्रेमी great skill in music or another artistic pursui. *The auditorium vibrated with high performance of considerable virtuosity.*

Virtuous/वर्चुअस *(adjective)* – सदाचारी having or showing high moral standards. *She considered herself virtuous because she neither drank nor smoked.*

Virulence/विरयुलेंस *(noun)* – प्रचण्डता extremely severe disease. *The virulence of influenza is causing concern among medical fraternity.*

Virus/वाइरस *(noun)* – विषैला तत्व a submicroscopic infective particle, typically consisting of nucleic acid coated in protein, which is able to multiply within the cells of a host organism. *The tests have confirmed existence of hepatitis B virus in the sample.*

Visage/विसेज *(noun)* – चेहरा a person's face, with reference to the form of the features. *The candidate selected for this position has an elegant, angular visage.* a person's facial expression. *There was lurking sadness behind his visage of cheerfulness.*

Viscera/विसरा *(plural noun)* – आँत the internal organs in the main cavities of the body, especially those in the abdomen, e. g. the intestines. *The large organs inside the body, such as the heart, lungs and stomach are known as viscera.*

Viscous/विस्कस *(adjective)* – चिपचिपा having a thick, sticky consistency between solid and liquid; having a high viscosity. *Diesel is more viscous than petrol or kerosene.*

Viscus/विस्कस – आँत singular form of viscera. *The viscus has been sent for medical examination.*

Visibility/विजिबिलिटि *(noun)* – प्रत्यक्षता the state of being able to see or be seen. *A reduction in police presence helped improve visibility of people on the streets.* the distance one can see as determined by light and weather conditions. *All trains are running slow because the visibility, because of fog, is down to 15 yards.*

Visible/विजिबल *(adjective)* – दृष्टिगोचर able to be seen. *The temple spire is clearly visible from miles away.* of light within the range of wavelengths to which the eye is sensitive. *Silhouette of a man hiding behind the bush was visible even in that dark night.* able to be perceived or noticed easily. *Improvement in cleanliness in the city is clearly visible.* in a position of public prominence. *A highly visible member of the visiting delegation met the President today.*

Vision/विजन *(noun)* – दृष्टि, नजर, परिकल्पना the faculty or state of being able to see. *She has a defective vision.*

Visit/विजिट *(verb)* – देखने जाना, मिलना go to see and spend some time with socially or as a guest. *He went to visit his grandmother.* go to see and spend some time in a place as a tourist or guest. *He went out to visit Qutub Minar in Delhi with his friends.* go to see for any specific purpose, such as to receive or give professional advice. *She visited a doctor for a thorough check-up of her well-being.*

Visor/वाइजर *(noun)* – घूँघट a movable part of a helmet that can be pulled down to cover the face. *He purchased a plastic safety helmet with a transparent visor.*

Vista/विस्टा *(noun)* – तरुपर्पंक्ति a pleasing view, especially one seen through a long, narrow opening. *The telescope allowed us to see the vista of bright stars.*

Visual/विजुअल *(adjective)* – नेत्रीय of or relating to seeing or sight. *You should have a visual perception of the landscape before shooting the film. (noun)* a picture, piece of film, or display used to illustrate or accompany something. *The music should fit the visuals.*

Vital/वाइटल *(adjective)* – अति आवश्यक absolutely necessary; essential. *It is vital that the system is regularly checked.* indispensable to the continuance of life: *Her vital organs were showing signs of improvement.*

Vitamin/विटामिन *(noun)* – खाद्योज any of a group of organic compounds which are essential for normal growth and nutrition and are required in small quantities in the diet because they cannot be synthesized by the body. *Most people generally don't get all the vitamins they need from a regular diet.*

Viticulture/विटिकल्चर *(noun)* – अंगूर की खेती the cultivation of grapevines. *The study of grape cultivation is known as viticulture.*

Vitreous/विट्रिअस *(adjective)* – काँचमय likes glass in appearance or physical properties. *A coarse-grained rock with much grey vitreous quartz was available for sale at a premium..* of a substance derived from or containing glass. *This dinner-set is made of vitreous china.*

Vitriol/विट्रिओल *(noun)* – निन्दा के योग्य sulphuric acid. in names of metallic sulphates, e.g. blue vitriol copper sulphate and green vitriol ferrous sulphate. *It was as if his words were spraying vitriol right in front of her.*

Vituperate/विट्युपरेट *(verb)* – रोचक blame or insult in strong or violent language. *For no fault of hers, she was at the centre of vituperative sarcasm.*

Vivacious/वाइवेशस *(adjective)* – उत्साह especially of a woman or child attractively lively and animated. *We were amused with the vivaciousness of a little girl jumping all over the park.*

Vivacity/वाइवैसिटि *(noun)* – प्रफुल्लता quality, especially in a woman, of being attractively lively. *He was struck by her vivacity, sense of humour and charm.*

Viva-voce/वाइवा-वॅवि *(adjective)* – मौखिक, जबानी especially of an examination oral rather than written. *The viva voce examination has been scheduled for today itself. (adverb)* orally rather than in writing. *(noun)* full form of viva. *We had better discuss this viva voce.*

Vivarium/विवेरिअम *(noun)* – जीवशाला an enclosure prepared so as to give animals a feeling of semi-natural conditions. *In most zoological parks, at least one vivarium is built to keep animals under observation, when required.*

Viviparous/विविपेरस *(adjective)* – सजीव बच्चा देने वाली of an animal bringing forth live young which have developed inside the body of the parent. *Animals that produce live babies from their body rather than eggs are known as viviparous.*

Vixen/विक्सन *(noun)* – मादा लोमड़ी, कर्कशा औरत a spiteful or quarrelsome woman. *She is a kind of outrageous little shaven-headed vixen who is always ready to get into a tiff with anyone.*

Vogue/वोग *(noun)* – प्रचलित, व्यवहार often in phr. in/out of vogue the prevailing fashion or style at a particular time. *Child-centred education is quite in vogue these days.*

Voice/वॉइस *(noun)* – वाणी, ध्वनि the sound produced in a person's larynx and uttered through the mouth, as speech or song. *She raised her voice so that everyone present in the hall could hear her speech.* the ability to speak or sing. vocal condition for singing or speaking: *The soprano is in good voice.*

Volition/वॉलिशन *(noun)* – इच्छा often in phr. of one's own volition the faculty or power of using one's will. *She went to the carnival on her own volition.*

V

Voltage/वोल्टेज *(noun)* – विद्युत शक्ति, वोल्टों की नाप an electromotive force or potential difference expressed in volts. *Electric trains are powered by high voltage traction wires.*

Volubility/वाल्युबिलिटि *(noun)* – वाचालता the quality of talking fluently, readily, or incessantly; talkativeness. *Her legendary volubility deserted her at the time of making first public speech.*

Volume/वॉल्यूम *(noun)* – पुस्तक, अलग भाग a book forming part of a work or series. *We have published a biography of Rabindranath Tagore in three volumes.*

Voluptuous/वॅलप्ट्युअस *(adjective)* – विषयी, भोगी relating to or characterized by luxury or sensual pleasure. *We bought long curtains for our bedroom in voluptuous crimson red.*

Volution/वल्यूशन *(noun)* – घुमौवा माला a rolling or revolving motion. *A single turn of a spiral or coil is defined as a volution.*

Volvulus/वॅल्व्युलस *(noun)* – आँतों का ऐंठन an obstruction caused by twisting of the stomach or intestine. *The doctor advised surgery for caecal volvulus.*

Vomit/वॅमिट *(verb)* – वमन द्वारा निकला हुआ पदार्थ eject matter from the stomach through the mouth. *She used to vomit every time she took solid food.* emit in an uncontrolled stream or flow. *The newspaper press vomited fold after fold of paper.* *(noun)* matter vomited from the stomach. *The children's ward smelled of vomit and urine.*

Vowel/वॉवेल *(noun)* – स्वर a speech sound which is produced by comparatively open configuration of the vocal tract and which is capable of forming a syllable. *He spoke with deep-vowelled German accent.* a letter representing such a sound. *In the English alphabet there are five vowels, namely, A, E, I, O and U.*

Vowelled/वॉवेल्ड *(adjective)* – स्वरपूर्ण speech which is capable of being formed into a syllable. *A man with heavy vowelled voice came to the restaurant.*

Voyage/वॉयेज *(noun)* – समुद्रयात्रा a long journey involving travel by sea or in space. *He has decided to go on a voyage to Spain.* *(verb)* go on a voyage. sail over or along a sea or river. *He spent substantial part of his life voyaging along the Latin American coast.*

Vulcan/वल्कन *(noun)* – अग्नि देवता God of fire. *In Roman mythology, Vulcan is a name given to the God of fire.*

Vulgarian/वल्गेरियन *(noun)* – असभ्य व्यवहार वाला धनी मनुष्य an unrefined person, especially one with newly acquired power or wealth. *Due to enormous ancestral wealth coming his way, he has become a sort of jumped-up vulgarian.*

Vulpine/वल्पाइन *(adjective)* – धूर्त of, relating to, or reminiscent of a fox or foxes. *She gave a vulpine smile while plotting next course of action.*

V

Ww

W/डब्ल्यू *(noun)* – अंग्रेजी वर्णमाला का 23वाँ वर्ण the twenty third letter of the English alphabet.

1. Denoting the next after V in a set of items, categories, etc.

Waddle/वैडल *(verb)* – डगमगाते चलना, हंस के समान चलना walk with short steps and a clumsy swaying motion. *Two geese have waddled across the road.*

Wade/वेड *(verb)* – पानी में हेलकर चलना walk through a liquid or viscous substance. *He waded through the knee-deep water.*

Wafer/वेफर *(noun)* – मालपुआ (पतली रोटी) a very thin light, crisp sweet biscuit. *We purchased a wafer packet with a layer of chocolate.*

Waft/वैफ्ट *(verb)* – तैरने वाला पदार्थ pass easily or gently through the air. *The smell of stale food wafted out from the kitchen. (noun)* a gentle movement of air. a scent carried in the air. *A waft of roasting chicken was coming out from the kitchen.*

Wag/वैग *(verb)* – हिलाना move rapidly to and fro. *The dog was wagging its tail.*

Wages/वेजेज *(noun)* – मजदूरी, वेतन a fixed regular payment for work, typically paid on a daily or weekly basis. *The factory workers were struggling to get better wages.*

Waggery/वैगरि *(noun)* – ठिठोली jocular behavior or remarks. *You can expect such pranks and waggery only from the older boys.*

Waggish/वैगिश *(adjective)* – मसखरा humorous, playful, or facetious. *Don't try out waggish tales on every occasion.*

Wagonette/वैगनेट *(noun)* – आमने-सामने की गद्दी की चौपहिया हल्की गाड़ी a four wheeled horse drawn pleasure vehicle with facing side seats and one or two seats arranged crosswise in front. *Wagonettes are hardly in use today, they have given way to modern sleek cars.*

Wagtail/वैगटेल *(noun)* – खंजन पक्षी a slender songbird with a long tail that is frequently wagged up and down. *Wagtails are found wagging up and down over rivers only in Siberia.*

Waif/वेफ *(noun)* – फेंका हुआ बालक a homeless and helpless person, especially a neglected or abandoned child. *She is foster-mother to various waifs who have nowhere to go.*

Wail/वेल *(noun)* – विलाप करना a prolonged high pitched cry of pain, grief, or anger. *Harish let out a wail as soon as lights went out.* a sound resembling this. *The wail of air siren made them a worried lot.*

Wainscot/वेन्स्कॉट *(noun)* – दीवार से लकड़ी की पट्टियों का जड़ाव an area of wooden panelling on the lower part of the walls of a room. *It has been decided to wainscot the interior to a height of 6 feet.*

Waist/वेस्ट *(noun)* – कमर the part of the human body below the ribs and above the hips. *He put his arm around her waist.*

Waken/वेकन *(verb)* – जगाना wake from sleep. *She wakened the child and dressed him.*

Waking/वेकिंग *(noun)* – जागृत अवस्था the period of being awake. *I was in waking state when all were asleep.*

Wall/वाल *(noun)* – दीवार a continuous vertical brick or stone structure that enclose or divides an area of land. *It was difficult to jump over the garden wall.* a side of a building or room. *We entered the drawing room having tapestries on the walls.*

Walled/वाल्ड *(adjective)* – दीवार से घिरा हुआ to block or seal something by erecting a barrier. *One doorway has been completely walled up.*

W

Wall-eyed/वाल-आइड *(adjective)* – कंजी आँख वाला an eye squinting outwards. *Pikeperch is a wall-eyed fish.*

Wall-flower/वाल-फ्लाउअर *(noun)* – एक प्रकार का फूल a southern European plant with fragrant flowers that bloom in early spring. *Wall-flower is a garden plant with yellow, orange or red flowers.*

Wallet/वैलेट *(noun)* – झोला a pocket sized, flat, folding holder for money and plastic cards. *He took out money from his wallet.*

Wallop/वॉलॅप *(verb)* – कोड़ा मारना strike or hit very hard. heavily defeat. *He walloped the back of her head with a flexible stick.*

Walnut/वाल्नट *(noun)* – अखरोट an edible wrinkled nut enclosed by a hard shell, produced inside a green fruit. *Walnut is a good source of high quality protein.*

Wan/वैन *(adjective)* – पीला pale and giving the impression of illness or exhaustion. *He was disappointed when she gave him a wan smile.*

Wander/वान्डर *(verb)* – घूमना walk or move in a leisurely, casual, or aimless way. *He wandered aimlessly around the park.* move slowly away from a fixed point or place. move slowly through or over. *The child was found wandering in the streets all alone.* *(noun)* an act or instance of wandering. *Her thoughts wandered back to her college days.*

Wane/वेन *(verb)* – कम होना have a progressively smaller part of its visible surface illuminated, so that it appears to decrease in size. *Confidence in dollar has waned considerably around the world markets.*

Wang/वैंग *(noun)* – दाद की हड्डी the jaw bone. *His wang is broken in the accident.*

Want/वान्ट *(verb)* – कमी have a desire to possess or do something; wish for. *We want to go to the beach party. I want to speak to her immediately.*

Wanted/वान्टेड *(adjective)* – इच्छित, जिसकी खोज हो being searched for by police. *He is wanted by the police in connection with robberies.*

Wanton/वॉन्टॅन *(adjective)* – लम्पट, मर्यादाहीन, चंचल deliberate and unprovoked. *Properties were destroyed due to sheer wanton vandalism.*

Warble/वार्बल *(verb)* – कूकना sing softly and with a succession of constantly changing notes. *Birds were warbling in the trees.* sing in a trilling or quavering voice. *He warbled in an implausible baritone voice. (noun)* a warbling sound or utterance. *Through the wall we could hear a faint warble.*

Warbler/वार्बलर *(noun)* – गाने वाला a small, actives songbird, typically living in trees and bushes and having a warbling song. *These are a few warblers that catch insects with the help of their melodious songs.*

Ward/वार्ड *(noun)* – 'दिशा' सूचक प्रत्यय a room in a hospital, typically one allocated to a particular type of patient. *Hospitals designate different wards for different diseases.*

Warden/वार्डेन *(noun)* – संरक्षक a person responsible for the supervision of a particular place or procedure. *The warden came down heavily on the boys creating nuisance in the hostel.*

Warder/वार्डर *(noun)* – पहरेदार a prison guard. *Warders have been cautioned to be in a state of high alert in the face of intelligence reports.*

Ware/वेअर *(noun)* – सौदा, पण्य, द्रव्य pottery, typically that of a specified type. *These are the cooking wares recently excavated from this area.* manufactured articles of a specified type. *These wares are of Italian make.*

Warehouse/वेअरहाउस *(noun)* – गोदाम a large building where raw materials or manufactured goods may be stored. *Before sending to the distributors, we sent all our products from the factory to our warehouse.*

Wares/वेअर्स *(noun)* – माल-असबाव pottery of specified type. *All aluminum wares were on display.*

Warily/वेअरिलि *(adverb)* – सावधानी से cautiously, carefully. *He walk warily down the street, afraid of being caught.*

Wariness/वेअरिनेस *(noun)* – सावधानी caution about possible dangers or problems. *I seldom*

W

use computer at night because of my mother's wariness. lack of trust, suspicion. *They had all regarded her presence with wariness.*

Warlock/वारलॉक *(noun)* – जादूगर a man who practises witchcraft. *Stay away from him, he is a warlock.*

Warner/वार्नर *(noun)* – सावधान करने वाला informer of something in advance. *He acted like a warner that police were searching for him.*

Warning/वार्निंग *(noun)* – चेतावनी, प्रबोधन a statement or event that warns or serves as a cautionary example. *The police issued a warning about fake Rs 100 notes.*

Warren/वॉरिन (वॉरन) *(noun)* – खरहों के पालने का बाड़ा a densely populated or labyrinthine building or district. *At the end of this lane is a warren of narrow gas-lit streets.*

Warrior/वॉरिअर *(noun)* – योद्धा a brave or experienced soldier or fighter. *Warriors have been decorated with medals recently.*

Warship/वॉरशिप *(noun)* – युद्ध का जहाज a ship equipped with weapons and designed to take part in warfare at sea. *Indian Navy has more than 100 warships.*

Wary/वेअरि *(adjective)* – होशियार cautious about possible dangers or problems. *I am quite wary of going to that place again.*

Wasp/वास्प *(noun)* – बर्रे a social insect with a narrow waisted, typically black and yellow striped body, which carries a sting and builds elaborate nests from wood pulp. *Wasp is a yellow and black flying insect that can sting.*

Wastage/वेस्टेज *(noun)* – क्षय से हानि use action or process of wasting. *This is a sheer wastage of natural resources.* an amount wasted. *The government is trying to cut wastage of food grains by 20 per cent.*

We/वी *(pronoun)* – हम लोग used by a speaker to refer to himself or herself and one or more other people considered together or regarded as in the same category. *Nobody knows kids better than we teachers do. May we have a drink now?* people in general. *We should eat as well-balanced a diet as possible.*

Weak/वीक *(adjective)* – दुर्बल lacking physical strength and energy. *He was recovering from flu, and was very weak.*

Weal/वील *(noun)* – सुख a red, swollen mark left on flesh by a blow or pressure. a temporarily raised and reddened area of skin, usually accompanied by itching. *He slapped her cheek and a bright red weal sprang up on it.*

Wealth/वेल्थ *(noun)* – ऐश्वर्य an abundance of valuable possessions or money. *Many industrialists use their wealth to bribe officials.* the state of being rich. *Many people buy bungalows and cars to display their wealth.*

Weasel/वीजल *(noun)* – नकुल a small slender carnivorous mammal related to, but smaller than, the stoat. Irish term for stoat. *Siberian weasels have stormed the city.*

Wednesday/वेनेज़्डे *(noun)* – बुधवार the day of the week before Thursday and following Tuesday. *We are going on a picnic next Wednesday. (adverb)* on Wednesday. *Parents-teachers meeting is held the first Wednesday of each month.*

Wee/वी *(adjective)* – छोटा little. *The lyrics of the song are a wee bit too sweet and sentimental.*

Weeds/वीड्स *(noun)* – विधवा का शोक-वस्त्र, घास a wild plant growing where it is not wanted and in competition with cultivated plants. *The garden was overgrown with weeds.*

Week/वीक *(noun)* – सप्ताह a period of seven days. *The training programme lasts twenty six weeks.* the period of seven days generally reckoned from and to midnight on Saturday night. *She has dance classes twice a week.*

Ween/वीन *(verb)* – विचारना think or suppose. *Don't ween too much on the matter.*

Weep/वीप *(verb)* – रोना shed tears. *He wept over his poor result.* mourn for. *A grieving son wept over the body of his father.* shed tears over. *A young woman is weeping her lost lord.*

Weir/वेअर *(noun)* – नदी का बाँध a low dam built across a river to raise the level of water upstream or regulate its flow. *The government has built a weir on the western side of the river to prevent flood water entering the city.*

W

Welkin/वेल्किन *(noun)* – आकाश the sky or heaven. *The crew made the welkin ring with their hurrahs.*

Well/वेल *(adverb)* – हितकर in a good or satisfactory way. *The whole team played very well.* in a condition of prosperity or comfort. *They lived well and were generous with their money.*

Wellington/वेलिंगटन *(noun)* – जूता a knee length waterproof rubber or plastic boot. *Wellington boots are hardly used these days.*

Welsh/वेल्श *(verb)* – ऋण दिये बिना भाग जाना fail to honour a debt or obligation. *I am not in the habit of welshing on my promises.*

Wen/वेन *(noun)* – माँस की गाँठ a boil or other swelling or growth on the skin. *A sebaceous cyst is generally known as a wen.*

Wench/वेंच *(noun)* – दुष्टा स्त्री a girl or young woman. *In the new film about Shaley, she plays the token buxom wench.*

Wend/वेंड *(verb)* – जाना go slowly or by an indirect route. *He wended his way home through bylanes and not straight.*

Went/वेंट – गया past of go. *We went to a party last night.*

Wept/वेप्ट – रोया past and past participle of weep. *He literally wept on seeing the poor workmanship.*

Wet/वेट *(adjective)* – भीगा हुआ covered or saturated with liquid. *He followed the leader, slipping on the wet rock in the process.* of the weather rainy. *We had nothing for protection on that wet, windy evening.* involving the use of water or liquid. *He is yet to learn the wet methods of photography.*

Wetness/वेटनेस *(noun)* – गीलापन, भींगा होना liquid that makes something wet. *The child caught cold due to wetness of his body.*

What/व्हाट *(pronoun)* – क्या asking for information specifying something. *What's the time?* asking for repetition of something not heard or confirmation of something not understood. *What did you say?*

Wheat/व्हीट *(noun)* – गेहूँ a cereal widely grown in temperate countries, the grain of which is ground to make flour for bread, pasta, etc. *Wheat is a staple food in India.*

Wheaten/व्हीटेन *(adjective)* – गेहूँ का बना हुआ made of wheat. *The content of these packets are wheaten products.*

Wheedle/व्हीडल *(verb)* – फुसलाना employ endearments or flattery to persuade someone to do something. *He had wheedled us into employing his sister.*

Wheen/व्हीन *(noun)* – थोड़ा-सा a considerable number or amount. *She carried a when of small changes.*

Wheeze/व्हीज *(verb)* – कष्ट से साँस लेने का शब्द breathe with a whistling or rattling sound in the chest, as a result of obstruction in the air passages. *The sickness often leaves her wheezing.* make an irregular rattling or spluttering sound. *The engine of the motor car coughed, wheezed, and came to a standstill.* *(noun).* a sound of a person wheezing. *'Don't worry my child,' he wheezed.*

Whelk/व्हेल्क *(noun)* – दिदोरा a predatory marine mollusc with a heavy pointed spiral shell. *Only a few whelks are edible.*

Whelp/व्हेल्फ *(noun)* – पिल्ला a puppy. a cub. *The lioness was suckling her whelps.*

When/व्हेन *(interrogative adverb)* – जबकि at what time. *When are you reaching?* how soon. *When can you make it to the station, the train is about to depart?*

Whence/व्हेन्स *(interrogative adverb)* – कहाँ से from what place or source. *The Andes Mountains, whence the ore is procured.* *(adverb)* from which; from where. *Whence does our Parliament derive this power?* to the place from which. *She would be sent back whence she came.* as a consequence of which. *Whence it followed that the strategies were quite obsolete.*

Whenever/व्हेनएवर *(conjunction)* – जब कभी at whatever time. *You can seek help whenever you need it.* every time that. *The springs in the chair creak whenever I change my position.* *(interrogative adverb)* used for emphasis instead of when in questions. *Whenever shall we get to the top of the mountain?*

W

Where/ह्वेअर *(interrogative adverb)* – कहाँ in or to what place or position. *Where are we going?* in what direction or respect. *Where does the argument lead?*

Wherewithal/ह्वेअरविदल *(noun)* – जिस किसी के साथ the money or other resources needed for a particular purpose: *They lacked the wherewithal to pay the dues.*

Wherry/ह्वेरि *(noun)* – छिछली नाव a light rowing boat used chiefly for carrying passengers. *We enjoyed a short sea trip on a wherry.*

Whether/ह्वेदर *(conjunction)* – हो न हो expressing a double or choice between alternatives. *She appeared undecided whether to go or stay at home.* expressing an enquiry or investigation. *I'll see whether she's at home.* indicating that a statement applies whichever of the alternatives mentioned is the case. *The only issue arising would be whether or not the publication was defamatory.*

Whew/ह्यू – आश्चर्यसूचक अव्यय *(exclamatory)* used to express surprise, relief, or a feeling of being very hot or tired. *Whew—and I thought it was a serious matter!*

Whey/ह्वे *(noun)* – मट्ठा the watery part of milk that remains after the formation of curds. *Whey is very good for health if taken in the morning or afternoon.*

Which/ह्विच – कौन asking for information specifying one or more people or things from a definite set. *Which way is the wind blowing?* used referring to something previously mentioned when introducing a clause giving further information. *It was a crisis for which he was completely unprepared.*

Whiff/ह्विफ *(noun & verb)* – फूँक, फूत्कार, फूँकना a smell that is smelt only briefly or faintly. *I caught a whiff of Lakme perfume.*

Whilst/ह्वाइलस्ट *(adverb)* – जब तक while. *The captain was in the pool whilst other players were toying in the field.*

Whimper/ह्विम्पर *(verb)* – तुनकना, धीमा शब्द करना make a series of low, feeble sounds expressive of fear, pain, or discontent. *Being alone, the child in a bed nearby began to whimper. (noun)* a whimpering sound. *Her first appearance on the stage ended with a whimper rather than a bang.*

Whimsey/ह्विमजी *(noun)* – लहर, जोश playfully quaint or fanciful behavior or humour. *The movie we watched was an awkward blend of whimsy and moralizing.* a thing that is fanciful or odd. *The stone carvings and whimsies.*

Whinny/ह्विन्नि *(verb)* – प्रसन्नता से हिनहिनाना make such a sound. *The horse whinnied and tossed his head happily.*

Whippy/ह्विपि *(adjective)* – लम्बा एवं लचीला flexible; springy. *This stick is whippy.*

Whisky/ह्विस्कि *(noun)* – जव से बनी हुई मदिरा a spirit distilled from malted grain, especially barley or rye. *Bottles of whisky were ordered for the party.*

Whisper/ह्विस्पर *(verb)* – कानाफूसी करना speak very softly using one's breath rather than one's throat. *She was whispering in his ear.* be rumoured. *It was whispered that he would soon join the opposition party. (noun)* a whispered word or phrase, or a whispering tone of voice. *She spoke to him in a whisper.* a soft rustling or murmuring sound. *The thunder became a muted whisper.* a rumour or piece of gossip. *We heard the whispers of their blossoming romance.*

Whither/ह्विदर *(interrogative adverb)* – जिधर to what place or state. *They asked people whither they would emigrate.* what is the likely future of. *Whither modern architecture.*

Whittle/ह्विटल *(verb)* – जेब की छोटी छुरी carve by repeatedly cutting small slices from it. *He was sitting at the door, whittling a piece of wood with a knife.*

Whiz/ह्विज *(verb)* – सनसनाहट का शब्द move quickly through the air with a whistling or whooshing sound. *The missiles whizzed past us.* move or cause to move or go fast. *The weeks whizzed by and the time arrived to go back to hostel.*

Who/हू *(pronoun)* – किसने what or which person or people. *I wonder who that letter was from.* introducing a clause giving further information

W

about a person or people previously mentioned. the person that *Aron plays the cat who caught the mouse* ; whoever. *Who was I to object?*

Whoa/ह्वो *(exclamatory)* – ठहरो! used as a command to a horse to stop or slow down. *Whoa! That's a huge bargain.*

Whop/ह्वॉप *(verb)* – एकाएक गिराव hit hard. *Tony whopped him on the nose. (noun)* a heavy blow or its sound. *The loud whop of the helicopter echoed in the still air.*

Whopper/ह्वॉपर *(noun)* – अति विलक्षण पदार्थ a thing that is extremely large. *The novel is nearly 2000 page whopper.*

Whoso/ह्वसो *(pronoun)* – जो कोई [archaic] term for whoever. *The word whoso is an archaic word.*

Wicked/विकेड *(adjective)* – पापी evil or morally wrong. *There is no dearth of wicked and unscrupulous politicians.*

Wicker/विकर *(noun)* – कमाची pliable twigs, typically of willow, plaited or woven to make items such as furniture and baskets. *We went to the market looking to buy a set of wicker chairs.*

Wide/वाइड *(adjective)* – चौड़ा of great or more than average width. *At last we reached a wide road.* from side to side. *This page measures 15 cm long by 12 cm wide.* open to the full extent. *Her eyes were wide with fear.*

Width/विड्थ *(noun)* – विस्तार the measurement or extent of something from side to side; the lesser of two or the least of three dimensions of a body. a piece of something at its full extent from side to side. *The cricket pitch was about seven feet in width.*

Wig/विग *(noun)* – कृत्रिम केश a covering for the head made of real or artificial hair. *She wore an auburn coloured wig.*

Wigeon/विजन *(noun)* – एक प्रकार का बत्तख a dabbling duck with mainly reddish brown and grey plumage, the male having a whistling call. *Penelope and Americana ducks are two prominent species of wigeon.*

Wiggle/विगल *(verb)* – शरीर को आगे पीछे घुमाना move or cause to move with short movements up and down or from side to side. *My teeth*

were *wiggling about due to fear. (noun)* a wiggling movement. *The dancer tantalizingly wiggled her hips.*

Wile/वाइल *(noun)* – कपट a devious or cunning stratagem. *He is a wily politician. (verb)* lure; entice. *She could be neither driven nor wiled into flaunting her physical assets.*

Will/विल *(modal verb)* – गा, गी, गे expressing the future tense. *You will regret it as you become older.* expressing a strong intention or assertion about the future. *I will succeed, come what may.*

Willy-nilly/विलि-निलि *(adverb)* – अनिच्छापूर्वक whether one likes it or not. *The management has been forced to accept labour union's terms willy-nilly.*

Windbag/विन्डबैग *(noun)* – निरर्थक शब्द बोलने वाला मनुष्य a person who talks a lot but says little of any value. *You can discount 90 percent of anything that windbag says.*

Winder/विन्डर *(verb)* – ओसाना to remove chaff from grain. *The farmer is windering.*

Windling/विन्डलिंग *(noun)* – घुमावा a twisting movement or course. *The windings of the stream pass through the valleys of that mountain.*

Window/विन्डो *(noun)* – झरोखा, खिड़की an opening in a wall or roof, fitted with glass in a frame to admit light or air and allow people to see out. *Thieves smashed a window and took all jewellary and cash.*

Windpipe/विन्डपाइप *(noun)* – वायुप्रणाली the trachea. *Something has got stuck in his windpipe.*

Wind-up/विन्डअप *(noun)* – परिणाम [British informal] an attempt to tease or irritate someone. *Surely this was a wind-up.*

Wine/वाइन *(noun)* – सुरा an alcoholic drink made from fermented grape juice. *They decided to celebrate the success by opening a bottle of red wine.* a fermented alcoholic drink made from other fruits or plants. *He ordered a glass of seine wine of France.*

Winsome/विनसम *(adjective)* – मनोहर attractive or appealing. *She fell for his winsome behaviour.*

W

Wire/वायर *(noun)* – तार metal drawn out into a thin flexible thread or rod. *We purchased a coil of aluminum wire.* a length or quantity of wire used for fencing, *We have decided to wire our compound to prevent animals from getting near our house.* to carry an electric current, etc. *Stay away from these wires, they carry electric current.*

Wise/वाइज *(noun)* – चतुर manner, way, or extent. *It would only be wise to discuss the matter with the director.*

Wish/विश *(verb)* – आकांक्षा, इच्छा करना desire something that cannot or probably will not happen. *Every one wished for peaceful election.*

Wit/विट *(noun & verb)* – बुद्धि, चातुरी, अवगत होना the capacity for inventive thought and quick understanding. *She needed all her wits to figure out the way back.* keen intelligence. *I had the wit to realize that the only way out was up.*

Witch/विच *(noun)* – डाइन a woman thought to have evil magic powers. *Witches are popularly depicted as wearing a black cloak and pointed hat casting spell on unsuspecting people.*

Withal/विदल *(adverb)* – साथ-साथ in addition. *She gave him a grateful smile, but rueful withal.* preposition with. *They sat with little to nourish themselves withal but vile water.*

Wither/विदर *(verb)* – सुखा देना become dry and shrivelled. *The grass had withered to an unappealing brown.*

Within/विदिन *(preposition)* – बीच में inside. *The fire spread fast within the building.* inside the range of. *All illegal buildings within the green belt have been demolished.* inside the bounds set by. *Each member nation extended full cooperation within the terms of the treaty.*

Without/विदाउट *(preposition)* – बाहर not accompanied by or having the use of. *She went to England without him.*

Witness/विटनेस *(noun)* – प्रमाण a person who sees an event taking place. *I was a witness in a murder case.*

Witticism/विटिसिज्म *(noun)* – हँसी a witty remark. *His witticism was remarkable and harmless.*

Wive/वाइव – विवाह करना to wed, to marry. *He has two wives.*

Wo/वो *(exclamatory)* – ठहरो! variant spelling of whoa.

Woe/वो *(noun)* – दु:ख, शोक, शाप great sorrow or distress. *To add to automobile company's woes, customers have been spending less.*

Wold/वोल्ड *(noun)* – खुला मैदान especially in [British] place names a piece of high, open, uncultivated land or moor. *There are many Wolds in England that have hardly ever been cultivated.*

Wolf/वुल्फ *(noun)* – भेड़िया, हुँड़ार a carnivorous mammal which is the largest member of the dog family, living and hunting in packs. *Tasmanian and Maned wolves are an endangered species.*

Woman/वुमन *(noun)* – औरत, नारी an adult human female. *The court was composed of seven women and five men.*

Won/वन् – जीत लिया past and past participle of win. *India had won five medals at the London Olympic Games in 2012.*

Wonder/वन्डर *(noun)* – आश्चर्य a feeling of surprise and admiration, caused by something beautiful, unexpected, or unfamiliar. *She observed the intricacy of the woodwork with the wonder of a child.*

Wondrous/वन्डरस *(adjective)* – आश्चर्यजनक inspiring wonder. *Mumbai is a wondrous city.* (adverb) wonderfully. *She is grown into a wondrous pretty.*

Wood/वुड *(noun)* – चाल-ठाल the hard fibrous material forming the main substance of the trunk or branches of a tree or shrub, used for fuel or timber. *We use only best quality woods in furniture making.*

Worry/वरि *(verb)* – चिन्तित होना feel or cause to feel troubled over actual or potential difficulties. *I began to worry whether I had done the right thing.* expressing anxiety. *She was worried about his soldier son in the war.*

W

Worst/वर्स्ट *(adjective)* – सबसे बुरा of the poorest quality or the lowest standard. *The speech was the worst he had ever made.* most severe or serious. *At least 25,000 people died in Bhopal's worst industrial accident.*

Worsted/वर्स्टेड *(noun)* – सुलझाया हुआ ऊन a fine smooth yarn spun from combed long staple wool, fabric made from such yarn, having a close textured surface with no nap. *He came to the party wearing a worsted three-piece suit.*

Wort/वर्ट *(noun)* – एक प्रकार की वनस्पति a kind of herb, the sweet infusion of ground malt or other grain before fermentation, used to produce beer and distilled malt liquors. *The manufactures add yeast to the wort for production of malted liquor.*

Wound/वुण्ड *(noun)* – घाव an injury to living tissue caused by a cut, blow, or other impact. *She slipped and suffered chest wounds.*

Wove/वोव *(verb)* – धुना हुआ past of weave. *He wove a story to escape punishment.*

Woven/वोवेन *(verb)* – बुना हुआ past participle of weave. *He came again with woven stories to convince us about his sincerity.*

Wow/वॉऊ *(interj.)* – आश्चर्यसूचक अव्यय expressing astonishment or admiration. *'Wow!' she cried enthusiastically! (noun)* a sensational success. *Your speech was a real wow. (verb)* impress and excite greatly. *The audiences wowed her thunderous lecture.*

Wraith/रेथ *(noun)* – भूत, प्रेत a ghost or ghostly image of someone, especially one seen shortly before or after their death. *Constant chest pains had reduced his father to a wraith.*

Wrangle/रैंगल *(noun)* – लड़ाई, झगड़ा a long and complicated dispute or argument. *The compensation was held up due to an insurance wrangle.*

Wrap/रैप *(verb)* – लपेटना, ढाँकना cover or enclose in paper or soft material. *She wrapped up the marriage gifts attractively.* arrange paper or soft material round something, as a covering or for warmth or protection. *She wrapped herself with a pashmina shawl.* place around so as to encircle. *Please wrap the bandage around the injured finger.*

Wrath/रॉथ *(noun)* – क्रोध, गुस्सा extreme anger. *The students faced the wrath of the professor for bunking the class.*

Wreak/रीक *(verb)* – बदला लेना, नुकसान करना cause a large amount of damage or harm. *The environmental damage wreaked by years of industrial pollution.*

Wreath/रीद *(noun)* – माला, हार an arrangement of flowers, leaves, or stems fastened in a ring and used for decoration or for laying on a grave. *The visiting president laid a wreath at the Mahatma Gandhi's Samadhi at Rajghat.*

Wreathe/रीद *(verb)* – लपेटना, लिपटाना envelop, surround, or encircle. *She sits wreathed in smoke.* twist or entwine round or over something. *Should I once more wreathe my arms about Anita's waist?*

Wreck/रेक *(noun)* – पोतभंग the destruction of a ship at sea; a shipwreck. *A naval ship brought ashore the survivors of the wreck.* a ship destroyed in such a way. *Another ship was dispatched for salvaging of treasure from wrecks.* brought ashore by the sea from a wreck. *The profits of wreck were deposited with the government.*

Wrest/रेस्ट *(verb)* – छीन लेना forcibly pull from a person's grasp. *She tried to wrest her arm from robber's hold.* take power or control after considerable effort or resistance. *They wanted to wrest control of their lives from irresponsible bureaucracy.*

Wrestle/रेसलॅ *(verb)* – कुश्ती लड़ना take part in a fight that involves close grappling with one's opponent, either as sport or in earnest. *A shot rang out as the policeman wrestled with the gunman.* force into a particular position in such a way. *The security guards wrestled the ruffians to the ground.* extract or manipulate an object with difficulty and some physical effort. *He wrestled the keys out of the lock after a considerable time.*

Wretch/रेच *(noun)* – अभागा an unfortunate person. *Can the poor wretch's corpse tell us anything about his death?* a contemptible person. *Ungrateful wretches of the society.*

W

Wriggle/रिगल *(verb)* – छटपटाना twist and turn with quick writhing movements. *She kicked and wriggled to free herself from his hold.* move with wriggling movements. *She wriggled to come out of her tight dress.*

Wright/राइट *(noun)* – कारीगर, बढ़ई a maker or builder. *Carpenters in Scotland are usually called a wright.*

Wring/रिंग *(verb)* – निचोड़ना, मरोड़ना squeeze and twist to force liquid from. *She wrung the cloth out in the tub.* extract in this way. *She wrung out the excess water from the cloths.*

Wrinkle/रिंकल *(noun)* – झुर्री a slight line or fold, especially in fabric or the skin of the face. *She ironed out the wrinkles from her shirt.*

Wrist/रिस्ट *(noun)* – कलाई the joint connecting the hand with the forearm. *She fell down and sprained her wrist.* also wrist pin in a machine a stud projecting from a crank as an attachment for a connecting rod. *The parts have elastic wrists and ankles.*

Writ/रिट *(noun)* – कानूनी दस्तावेज, आज्ञापत्र a form of written command in the name of a court of other legal authority to do or abstain from doing a specified act. *The reinstated employee issued a writ for libel against the applicants.* one's power to enforce compliance or submission. *You have business here which is out of my writ and competence.*

Wrong/राँग *(adj.)* – अशुद्ध not correct or true. mistaken. *That is the wrong answer.*

Wrote/रोट *(verb)* – लिखा (past tense of write). *He wrote the article last night.*

Wroth/रॉथ *(adjective)* – अति क्रुद्ध archaic angry. *The professor is majestically wroth with the students.*

Wrung/रंग *(verb)* – ऐंठा हुआ past and past participle of wring. *The confession wrung by the police was rejected in the court.*

Wye/वाइ *(noun)* – बैशाखी a crutch, name of a river. *Wye is the river which forms part of the border between Wales and England.*

Wynd/वाइन्ड *(noun)* – पतली गली narrow street or alley. *Fleet Street is a wynd where leading newspapers have offices.*

W

Xx

X/एक्स *(noun)* - अंग्रेजी वर्णमाला का 24वाँ वर्ण the twenty fourth letter of the English alphabet.

1. Denoting the next after W in a set of items, categories, etc.
2. Denoting an unknown or unspecified person or thing. *In mathematics we use the symbol 'X' to denote an unknown number quantity.*

Xangti/जैन्ग्टि *(noun)* - चीन देश के पुराणों में ईश्वर का नाम the Supreme being of Chinese mythology. *Xangti is the name of God.*

Xanthic/जैन्थिक *(adj.)* - चमड़े के रंग के पीला पड़ जाने की क्रिया pertaining to yellow colour. *Yellow coloured products are also known as xanthic.*

Xanthium/जैन्थियम *(noun)* - गेंदा के समान एक फूल Coarse herbs having small heads of greenish flowers followed by burrs with hooked bristles. *Xanthium is a small flower.*

Xanthoma/जैन्थोमा *(noun)* - पीले रंग की रचना an irregular yellow patch or nodule on the skin, caused by deposition of lipids. *People who are suffering from Xanthoma should take proper care and consult doctor immediately.*

Xanthophyll/जैन्थोफिल *(noun)* - पीत a yellow or brown carotenoid plant pigment which causes the autumn colours of leaves. *Xanthophyll is a natural pigment that causes leaves to turn yellow.*

Xanthosis/जैन्थॅसिस *(noun)* - पीले रंग की रचना An abnormal yellow discolouration of the skin. *Xanthosis makes skin colour yellow.*

Xanthous/जैन्थस *(adjective)* - पीत, पीले रंग का of the colour intermediate between green and orange in the colour spectrum; of something resembling the colour of an egg yolk. *Xanthous is a shade of colour that looks like the colour of egg yolk.*

Xebec/जीबेक *(noun)* - तीन मस्तूल का चौकोर पालों का छोटा जहाज a small three masted Mediterranean sailing ship with lateen and square sails.

Xenarthral/जेनार्थ्रल *(noun)* - पीठ के रीढ़ के सदृश जुटा हुआ joined like a vertebrae American anteaters; sloths. *Xenarthral is a strange looking mammal largely due to its odd shaped vertebrae.*

Xenial/जेनियल *(adjective)* - आतिथेय सम्बन्धी pertaining to hospitality or relations with friendly visitors. *His xenial attitude attracts all.*

Xenogamy/जेनोगैमि *(noun)* - वृक्षों में गर्भधारण की क्रिया fertilization of a flower by pollen from a flower on a genetically different plant. *Xenogamy is a process of fertilization of flower.*

Xenogenesis/जेनोजेनेसिस *(noun)* - माता-पिता से भिन्न सन्तति की उत्पत्ति The alternation of two or more different forms in the life cycle of a plant or animal. *Xenogenesis is a name given to those plants that can produce hydrogen cyanide.*

Xenomania/जेनोमैनिया *(noun)* - परदेशी वस्तुओं पर उत्कट प्रेम undue love for foreign goods. *I do not suffer from xenomania.*

Xenon/जेनन *(noun)* - एक धातु विशेष the chemical element of atomic number 54, a member of the noble gas series, obtained by distillation of liquid air and used in some specialized electric lamps. *Xenon is a gas used in manufacturing specialised electric lamps.*

Xerophilous/जेरोफायलस *(adjective)* - सूखा चाहने वाला adapted to a dry climate or habitat. *To stay in a desert you need to be Xerophilous.*

Xerophyle/जेरोफायल *(noun)* - सूखी भूमि का पौधा a plant which needs very little water. *Xerophyle grows in desert.*

Xerophytic/जेरोफायटिक *(adjective)* - सूखी स्थिति के योग्य Adapted to a xeric (or dry) environment. *Cacti are xerophytic plants.*

Xerostomia/जेरॉस्टोमिया *(noun)* - मुख सूखने का रोग Abnormal dryness of the mouth resulting from decreased secretion of saliva. *In hot summer days people normally suffer from xerostomia.*

Xerotes/जेरॉटस *(noun)* – शरीर का सूखापन The condition of not containing or being covered by a liquid. *In xerotes condition fishes die in rivers.*

X-ray/एक्स-रे *(noun)* – अदृश्य किरण जो भीतर की तस्वीर खींचे an electromagnetic wave of very short wave length. able to pass through many materials opaque to light. denoting an apparent or supposed faculty for seeing beyond an outward form: *X-ray eyes are required to see what is going in the godown of the merchant.*

Xylem/जाइलम *(noun)* – वनस्पति का लकड़ी का भाग the vascular tissue in plants which conducts water and dissolved nutrients upwards from the root and also helps to from the woody element in the stem. *Xylem tissue is responsible for passing water and nutrients from roots to the whole tree.*

Xylocarp/जाइलोकार्प *(noun)* – कड़ी लकड़ी के समान फल Life Sciences & Allied Applications/Botany) *Botany* a fruit, such as a coconut, having a hard woody pericarp. *Xylocarp is a coconut like fruit that some people eat.*

Xylograph/जाइलोग्राफ *(noun)* – लकड़ी पर खुदाई का काम An engraving on wood. *Xylograph should be avoided as it reduces the life of three.*

Xylographic/जाइलोग्राफिक *(noun)* – लकड़ी की नक्काशी से सम्बन्धित Wood engraving, especially of an early period. *Xylographic art was practised widely in older times.*

Xylol/जाइलॉल *(noun)* – लकड़ी से निकाला गया तेल A colourless flammable volatile liquid hydrocarbon used as a solvent. *Xylol is used as solvent in washing powder.*

X

Yy

Y/वाइ *(noun)* – अंग्रेजी वर्णमाला का 25वाँ वर्ण the twenty fifth letter of the alphabet.

1. Denoting the next after X in a set of items, categories, etc.
2. Denoting an unknown or unspecified person or thing.
3. The second unknown quantity in an algebraic expression, usually the dependent variable. denoting the secondary or vertical axis in a system of coordinates. *Vertical axis in co-ordinate geometry is known as 'Y' axis.*

Yacca/याका *(noun)* – एक प्रकार का सर्वदा हरा रहने वाला वृक्ष West Indian evergreen with medium to long leaves. *Yacca looks very pretty during summer.*

Yahoo/याहू *(noun)* – जंगली असभ्य मनुष्य a rude, coarse, or brutish person. *People hate yahoo.*

Yak/याक *(noun)* – याक, सुरागाय, चमर a large ox with shaggy hair, humped shoulders, and large horns, used in Tibet as a pack animal and for its milk, meat, and hide. *In Tibet yak is domesticated.*

Yam/यैम *(noun)* – अरुई the edible starchy tuber of a climbing plant, widely distributed in tropical and subtropical countries. *Have you ever tested yam? People say it is very tasty.*

Yank/यैन्क *(noun & verb)* – झटका, झटके से खींचना to pull something quickly and suddenly. *Naresh yanked at my arm. She gave a yank to the rope.*

Yap/यैप *(verb)* – कुत्ते की तरह भौंकना give a sharp, shrill bark. *The puppies yapped.*

Yapok/यापक *(noun)* – एक चौपाया जीव a semiaquatic carnivorous opossum with dark banded grey fur and webbed hind feet, native to tropical America. *Yapok is generally found in tropical America.*

Yardarm/यारडर्म *(noun)* – पाल के डण्डे का सिरा the outer extremity of a ship's yard. *People are resting and enjoying the evening sitting in the yardarm.*

Yare/येअर *(adjective)* – उत्सुक moving lightly and easily; easily manageable. *Don't be in hurry, move yare.*

Yarn/यार्न *(noun)* – सूत, तन्तु spun thread used for knitting, weaving, or sewing. *She uses sharp yarn to sew. Her yarn was hesitant.*

Yarrow/यैरो *(noun)* – एक प्रकार का पौधा a plant with feathery leaves and heads of small white or pale pink aromatic flowers, used in herbal medicine. *Yarrow is a very useful medicine for many diseases.*

Yataghan/याॅटगैन *(noun)* – कटार a long Turkish knife with a curved blade having a single edge. *Don't allow children to use the yatoghan.*

Yaup/याउप *(verb)* – बच्चे की तरह चिल्लाना emit long loud cries. *Please don't yaup.*

Yaw/या *(verb)* – विचलना, विचलन twist or oscillate about a vertical axis. *The yawing motion of the ship.*

Yawl/यावल *(noun)* – मछली पकड़ने की नाव a two masted fore and aft rigged sailing boat with the mizzenmast stepped far aft so that the mizzen boom overhangs the stern. *Many yawls are lying in the vacant space of the ship.*

Yawn/याॅन *(verb)* – उबासी लेना involuntarily open one's mouth wide and inhale deeply due to tiredness or boredom. *The cute child yawned during the long performance.*

Yaws/याॅज *(plural noun)* – एक बीमारी a contagious tropical disease caused by a bacterium that enters skin abrasions and causes small crusted lesions which may develop into deep ulcers. *Yaws is considered a very dangerous disease by doctors.*

Yea/ये *(noun)* – हाँ an affirmative answer. *Yea, I will surely meet you in the function.*

Yean/यीन *(verb)* – ब्याना [archaic] of a sheep or goat give birth to a lamb or kid. *The goat yeaned two yeanlings.*

Year/यीअर *(noun)* – वर्ष the time taken by the earth to make one revolution around the sun. *Our planet earth takes a year to complete one revolution around the sun.*

Yearn/यर्न *(verb)* – इच्छा करना have an intense feeling of loss and longing for something. HH*He yearned for a cigarette badly.*

Yeast/यीस्ट *(noun)* – खमीर, यीस्ट a microscopic single celled fungus capable of converting sugar into alcohol and carbon dioxide. *Have you ever seen yeast through microscope?* a grayish yellow preparation of this obtained chiefly from fermented beer, used as a fermenting agent, to raise bread dough, and as a food supplement. *Yeast is used as food supplement.*

Yell/येल *(noun)* – चीत्कार a loud, sharp cry, especially of pain, surprise, or delight. *He uttered a yell of pain.*

Yellow/येलो *(adjective)* – सुनहला of the colour between green and orange in the spectrum, a primary subtractive colour complementary to blue; coloured like ripe lemons or egg yolks. *My mother wants to know the reason for the yellow tinge on my teeth.*

Yen/येन *(noun)* – शिलिंग मूल्य का सिक्का the basic monetary unit of Japan. *Yen is of the highly rated currencies in the world.*

Yeoman/योमॅन *(noun)* – किसान a man holding a small landed estate; a freeholder. a person qualified for jury duties, electoral rights, etc. by virtue of possessing free land. *Yeomen are very respectable persons in society.*

Yes/येस (यस) *(exclamatory)* – हाँ, हूँ used to give an affirmative response. *Yes! I will do the job for you.*

Yesterday/यस्टरडे *(noun)* – गत दिवस the day immediately before today; it was in yesterday's newspapers. *Yesterday's solutions are not good enough.*

Yew/यू *(noun)* – हरा रहने वाला वृक्ष a coniferous tree with poisonous red berry like fruit and dense, springy wood. *Never dare to try the fruit of yew tree.*

Yiddish/यिडिश *(noun)* – परदेशी यहूदियों का भाषा a language used by Jews in or from central and eastern Europe, originally a German dialect with words from Hebrew and several modern languages. *The Yiddish language is almost no longer in use now a days.*

Yoke/योक *(noun)* – जुआ a wooden crosspiece that is fastened over the necks of two animals and attached to a plough or cart that they pull in unison. *Experienced farmers know well how to use a yoke properly.* a pair of yoked animals. the amount of land that one pair of oxen could plough in a day. *The small oxen pair can only plough yoke of land each day.* something that represents a bond between two parties: *The yoke of marriage that lasted for almost three years.*

Yokel/योकल *(noun)* – अज्ञानी an unsophisticated country person. *The yokel behaved very rudely with the woman.*

Yolk/योक *(noun)* – पीतक, जरदी the yellow internal part of a bird's egg, which is rich in protein and fat and nourishes the developing embryo. *It is very good for health to have yoke every day as breakfast.*

Yon/यॉन *(adjective)* – सामने का distant but within sight; *He asks me what is my yon place.*

Yonder/यॉन्डॅर *(adverb)* – वहाँ, उधर at some distance in the direction indicated; over there. *Ramesh visited the yonder valley last year.*

You/यू *(pronoun)* – तुम लोग used to refer to the person or people that the speaker is addressing. used to refer to the person being addressed together with other people regarded in the same class. *I love you are listening?*

Younker/यंकर *(noun)* – लड़का a youngster. *He is proud to be a younker.*

Yowl/याउल *(noun)* – भौंकना a loud wailing cry of pain or distress. *The old lady's yowl filled the hallway.*

Yucca/यका *(noun)* – कुमुदनी के प्रकार की वनस्पति a plant of the agave family with sword like leaves and spikes of white bell shaped flowers, native to warm regions of the US and Mexico. *Yucca is native to warm regions like US and Mexico.*

Yuck/यक *(noun)* – छि:, गंदा, घिनौना *exclamatory* used to express strong distaste or disgust. *Yuck, that's really gross!(noun)* something messy or disgusting. *The environment of the restaurant is yuck to me.*

Yurt/यर्ट *(noun)* – ध्रुवदेश के निवासियों के रहने का खेमा a circular tent of felt or skins used by nomads in Mongolia, Siberia, and Turkey. *Yurt is normally used in Mongolia and Turkey.*

Y

Zz

Z जेड *(noun)* – अंग्रेजी वर्णमाला का 26वाँ वर्ण the twenty sixth letter of the English alphabet.
1. Denoting the next after Y in a set of items, categories, etc.
2. The third unknown quantity in an algebraic expression. denoting the third axis in a three dimensional system of coordinates. *Third unknown quantity in the co-ordinate geometry.*

Zabrus/जैब्रस *(noun)* – एक प्रकार का बड़ा झींगुर या गुबरैला a kind of large beetle. *Have seen a Zabrus*

Zadkiel/जैड्किअल *(noun)* – इस नाम का प्रसिद्ध ज्योतिष पंचांग a popular almanac of this name. *I have no knowledge of Zadkiel almanac.*

Zaffre/जैफर *(noun)* – एक प्रकार का खनिज विशेष impure cobalt oxide formerly used to make small and blue enamels. *In today's world zaffre is rarely used.*

Zamia/जामिया *(noun)* – एक प्रकार का ताड़ का वृक्ष Any of various cycads of the genus Zamia; among the smallest and most verdant *cycads*

Zarf/जार्फ *(noun)* – कहवा पीने का सुन्दर पात्र an ornamental metal cup-shaped holder for a hot coffee cup. *Rajesh is very fond of having his morning coffee in a zarf.*

Zebu/जीब्यू *(noun)* – पलुआ साँड़ an ox of a humped breed originally domesticated in India. *Zebu is rarely found to see in India now a days.*

Zephyr/जेफायर *(noun)* – पश्चिमी वायु a soft gentle breeze. *The zephyr was cooled by the river.*

Zeppelin/जेपेलिन *(noun)* – बेलन के आकार का हवाई जहाज a large German dirigible airship of the early 20th century. *Zeppelin aircraft were used by German Forces during First World War.*

Zero/जीरो *(cardinal number)* – शून्य the figure 0; nought; nothing. a temperature of 0 degree c., marking the freezing point of water. a worthless or insignificant person. *The number zero was invented in India.*

Zeus/ज्यूस *(noun)* – ग्रीस देश-निवासियों का सबसे बड़ा देवता (Greek mythology) the Supreme God of ancient Greek mythology; son of Rhea and Cronus whom he dethroned; husband and brother of Hera; brother of Poseidon and Hades; father of many gods; counterpart of Roman Jupiter. *The state of Zeus at Olympic is one of the seven wonders of the world.*

Zither/जिथर *(noun)* – एक प्रकार का सितार a musical instrument consisting of a flat wooden sound box with numerous strings stretched across it, placed horizontally and played with the fingers and a plectrum. *I have a desire to listen to the music of zither once in my life time.*

Zizania/जिजैनिया *(noun)* – एक प्रकार की सेवार wild rice. *People from different parts of the world are still using zizania.*

Zoetrope/जोइट्रूप *(noun)* – एक प्रकार जिसमें तस्वीर चलती देख पड़ती है a cylinder with a series of pictures on the inner surface that, when viewed through slits with the cylinder rotating, give an impression of continuous motion. *Collection of zoetrope is found in many renowned museums in the world.*

Zonal/जोनल *(adjective)* – कटिबन्धों से सम्बन्धित relating to or of the nature of a zone. *Krish will reach the zonal frontier tomorrow.* associated with or divided into zones. *The Railway department has ordered to divide the east wing in zonal division.*

Zonula/जोन्युला *(noun)* – छोटी मेंखला small beltlike zone. *The zonal is divided into many zonulas.*

Zoo/जू *(noun)* – पशु वाटिका an establishment which keeps wild animals for study, conservation, or display to the public. *Kamal's parents and children visited the zoo yesterday.*

Zooide/जूआइड *(noun)* – जीवित प्राणि की आकृति का an animal arising from another by budding or division, especially each of the individuals which make up a colonial organism. *Research is going on to find out the advantages and disadvantages of development of zooid.*

Z

Zoolatry/जूलेट्री *(noun)* – पशु पूजा the worship of animals. *The tradition of zoolatry is still in practice in many countries.*

Zoology/जूलॉजि *(noun)* – जीव विज्ञान the scientific study of the behaviour, structure, physiology, classification, and distribution of animals; the animal life of a particular region or geological period. *Patrick is doing his research in Zoology.*

Zoomorphism/जूमॉरफिज्म *(noun)* – देवता या मनुष्य को पशु रूप में दिखाने की कला the attribution of animal forms or qualities to a god. *The concept of Zoomorphism reflects the conducts and behaviour of some societies.*

Zoophyte/जूफाइट *(noun)* – जन्तु तथा उद्भिज दोनों का गुण रखने वाला तत्त्व a plant like animal, especially a coral, sea anemone, sponge, or sea lily. *The life cycle of zoophytes is being telecast in many documentaries in discovery channel.*

Zopilote/जोपाइलोट *(noun)* – अमेरिका देश का छोटा गिद्ध American black vulture. *People could see Zopilote in many American Zoos.*

Zoroastrian/जोरोस्ट्रियन *(adjective)* – पारसी धर्म का अनुयायी of or pertaining to Zoroaster or the religion he founded *(noun)* follower of Zoroaster and Zoroastrianism. *Zoroastrians live in many countries in the world and their population is recognisable in those countries.*

Zoster/जॉस्टर *(noun)* – एक प्रकार का चर्म रोग Eruptions along a nerve path often accompanied by severe neuralgia. *People suffering from zoster have to take proper medication.*

Zulu/जूलू *(noun)* – दक्षिणी अफ्रीका की एक जाति a member of a south African people living mainly in Kwaza/Natal province. *Zulu people are said to be very adventurous.*

Zwieback/स्वीबैक *(noun)* – एक प्रकार का मीठा बिस्कुट slice of sweet raised bread baked again until it is brown and hard and crisp. *American people like to have zwieback in their breakfast.*

Zygomatic/जिगॅमैटिक *(adj.)* – गाल की हड्डी का of or relating to the cheek region of the face. *(noun)* the arch of bone beneath the eye that forms the prominence of the cheek. *The zygomatic bone is very delicate, it needs proper care.*

Zymogen/जाइमॅजेन *(noun)* – उफान लाने वाला पदार्थ an inactive substance which is converted into an enzyme when activated by another enzyme. *Scientists use various methods to convert zymogen into enzymes.*

Zymoid/जाइमॉइड *(adjective)* – उफान के सदृश resembling an enzyme. *You won't be able to see zymoid with normal eyes.*

Zymotic/जाइमॅटिक *(adjective)* – उफान सम्बन्धी relating to or denoting contagious disease regarded as developing after infection, like the fermenting of yeast. *Sachin is now recovering from Cancer, but doctor has advised him to be careful of zymotic diseases.*

Zymurgy/जाइमर्जि *(noun)* – आसव बनाने का रसायन the study or practice of fermentation in brewing, winemaking, or distilling. *Mr. Sharma's younger daughter is very much interested in studying zymurgy.*

Z

Appendix-1/परिशिष्ट–1
Means of Transport
यातायात के साधन

Aeroplane	एयरोप्लेन	हवाई जहाज
Airbus	एअरबस	हवाई गाड़ी
Airship	एअरशीप	हवाईजहाज
Aircraft	एअरक्राफ्ट	विमान
Ambulance	एम्बुलेंस	मरीज वाहक
Auto rickshaw	ऑटो रिक्शा	ऑटो
Bike	बाइक	साइकिल (मोटर साइकिल)
Boat	बोट	नाव
Bus	बस	बस
Ballon	बैलून	गुब्बारा
Bomber plane	बम्बर प्लेन	बमवर्षक विमान
Bullock cart	बुलॉक कार्ट	बैलगाड़ी
Bicycle	बाइसिकल	साइकिल
Cart	कार्ट	गाड़ी
Car	कार	कार
Cycle rickshaw	साइकिल रिक्शा	रिक्शा
Camel cart	कैमेल कार्ट	ऊँटगाड़ी
Double decker bus	डबल डेकर बस	दो मंजिला बस
Engine	इंजिन	इंजन
Fire engine	फायर इन्जिन	अग्निशमक
Fighter plane	फाइटर प्लेन	लड़ाकू विमान
Helicopter	हेलिकॉप्टर	हेलिकॉप्टर
Jeep	जीप	जीप
Motor bike	मोटरबाइक	मोटर बाइक
Motor	मोटर	मोटर गाड़ी
Motor cycle	मोटर साइकिल	मोटर साइकिल
Moped	मोपेड	मोपेड
Metro rail	मेट्रो रेल	भूमिगत रेल
Parachute	पैराशूट	पैराशूट
Pram	प्राम	शिशुगाड़ी

Plane	प्लेन	विमान
Rail	रेल	पटरी
Railway	रेलवे	पटरी मार्ग
Roller	रॉलर	मार्ग बेलन
Rocket	रॉकेट	अन्तरिक्षयान
Rickshaw	रिक्शा	रिक्शा
Ship	शीप	जहाज
Scooter	स्कूटर	स्कूटर
Scooty	स्कुटी	स्कुटी
Space craft	स्पेस क्राफ्ट	अन्तरिक्ष यान
Shuttle	शटल	दो स्थानों के बीच की गाड़ी
Satellite	सेटेलाइट	उपग्रह
Tram	ट्राम	ट्राम
Trolley	ट्रॉली	ट्रॉली
Track	ट्रैक	मार्ग
Train	ट्रेन	रेलगाड़ी
Tyre	टायर	चक्का
Tonga	टाँगा	तांगा
Tractor	ट्रैक्टर	खेत जोतने की गाड़ी
Truck	ट्रक	मालवाहक, ट्रक, माल ठोने वाली गाड़ी
Tempo	टेम्पो	टेम्पो
Tricycle	ट्रॉइसिकल	तीन पहिया साइकिल
Tank	टैंक	युद्ध की गाड़ी
Tanker	टैंकर	तरल वाहक
Van	वान	वान
Wheel	ह्विल	चक्का
Yatch	याच	नाव
Brake	ब्रेक	ब्रेक
Pedal	पैडल	पायडिल
Pump	पम्प	पम्प
Rim	रिम	चक्का

Appendix-2/परिशिष्ट−2
Travel and Transport
यात्रा और यातायात के शब्द

Accelerator	एक्सिलेरेटर	गतिउत्पादक यन्त्र
Axle	एक्सल	धूरा, धुरी
Brake	ब्रेक	गति नियन्त्रक
Bonnet	बॉनेट	बॉनेट
Battery	बैटरी	बैटरी
Bumper	बम्पर	बम्पर
Booking-office	बुकिंग ऑफिस	टिकट घर
Carrier	केरियर	सामान ठोने का जगह
Carburattor	कारब्यूरेटर	कारबोरेटर
Crossroad	क्रॉसरोड्स	चौराहा
Clutch	कल्च	क्लच
Compartment	कम्पार्टमेंट	डिब्बा
Coach	कोच	विलासी डिब्बा
Footboard	फुटबोर्ड	पायदान
Freight	फ्रेट	भाड़ा
Guard	गार्ड	गाड़ी रक्षक
Gear	गिअर	गेअर
Helmet	हेलमेट	शिरस्त्राण
Horn	हॉर्न	भोंपू
Harness	हार्नेश	नियन्त्रित करना
Hub-cap	हब-कैप	सायकिल के चलने का एक यन्त्र
Headlight	हेडलाइट	अग्रप्रकाश
Hand brake	हैंड ब्रेक	हस्त नियंत्रक
Jack	जैक	गाड़ी उठाने वाला
Level crossing	लेवल क्रॉसिंग	लाइन पार करने का स्थान
Left turn	लेफ्ट टर्न	बायें मुड़ना
Luggage rack	लगेज रैक	सामान स्टैंड
Lever	लिवर	लिवर
Light	लाइट	बत्ती

Mudguard	मडगार्ड	कींच से बचाने वाला
Milo meter	मायलोमीटर	दूरी सूचक निर्देशक
Number plate	नम्बर प्लेट	गाड़ी संख्या पट्टिका
No parking	नो पार्किंग	गाड़ी खड़ी करना प्रतिबंधित
Passenger	पैसेंजर	यात्री
Plateform	प्लेटफॉर्म	यात्री स्थान
Parking place	पार्किंग प्लेस	गाड़ी खड़ी करने का स्थान
Pedal	पैडल	पायडिल
Pump	पम्प	पम्प
Rear mirror	रीअर मिरर	पृष्ठदर्शक
Right turn	राइट टर्न	दाहिने मुड़ना
Refreshment room	रिफ्रेशमेंट रूम	अल्पाहार कक्ष
Sleeper car	स्लिपर	शयनयान
Station	स्टेशन	विराम-स्थान
Stand	स्टैंड	विराम-स्थान
Signal	सिग्नल	निर्देशिका
Speed limit	स्पीड लिमिट	गतिसीमा
Speed braker	स्पीड ब्रेकर	गतिनियन्त्रक
Steering wheel	स्टियरिंग व्हील	गाड़ी नियंत्रक
Sparking plug	स्पार्किंग प्लग	विद्युत संचालक
Speedo-meter	स्पीडोमीटर	गतिसूचक
Tyre	टायर	चक्का
Tool bag	टूल बैग	औजार का थैला
Traffic light	ट्रैफिक लाइट	नियन्त्रक बत्ती
Traffic sign	ट्रैफिक साइन	नियन्त्रक चिह्न
Traffic police	ट्रैफिक	यातायात पुलिस आरक्षी
Waggon	वैगन	मालडिब्बा
Wind screen	विन्ड स्क्रीन	वायु नियन्त्रक
Wind wiper	विन्ड वायपर	पोंछने वाला
Wheel brake	व्हिल ब्रेक	चक्का नियन्त्रक
Wheel	व्हिल	चक्का
Zigzag	जिग्जैग	घुमावदार

Appendix-3/परिशिष्ट–3
Animal Sound
जानवरों की आवाजें

Cry	क्राई	चिल्लाना, रोना
Bark	बर्क	भूँकना
Neigh	नाइ	हिनहिनाना
Howl	हाउल	फें करना, हुआँ-हुआँ करना
Yowl	याॅल	भूँकना
Wail	वेल	रोना, कलपना
Ululu	उलुलु	हुलकना
Whine	ह्वाइन	हेंकरना
Blat	ब्लैट	भेंकरना
Bleat	ब्लीट	मिमियाना
Moo	मू	हेंकरना
Low	लो	रंभाना
Squeak	स्क्वीक	चूँ-चूँ करना
Squeal	स्क्वील	चीं-चीं करना
Grunt	ग्रन्ट	गुर्राना, बुरबुराना
Hiss	हिस	फुफकारना, फुसकरना
Blow	ब्लो	पीं-पीं बजना
Rattle	राॅटल	खड़खड़ाना, खड़खड़ाहट
Bay	बे	साँय-साँय करना
Yap	याप	केंकियाना
Yelp	येल्प	कें-कें करना
Yip	यिप	हेंकरना
Whinny	ह्विन्नी	हिनहिनाहट
Whieker	ह्विकर	खी-खी करना
Snort	स्नाॅर्ट	घुँ-घुँ करना
Bray	ब्रे	रेंकना
Mew	मियू	म्याऊँ करना
Miau	मिआऊँ	म्याऊँ करना
Purr	पर्र	पड़पड़ाना
Roar	रोर	गीजना

Bellow	बेलो	डकरना
Trumpet	ट्रम्पेट	चिंघाड्ना
Growl	ग्रॉल	गुर्राना
Snarl	स्नार्ल	घुघुआना
Yarr	यर्र	केंकिचाना
Troat	ट्रॉट	हिरनी सा कामोत्तेजक आवाज
Bell	बेल	घंटी की आवाज
Chirp	चर्प	चहचहाना
Sing	सिंग	गाना
Trill	ट्रिल	टिहकारी भरना
Call	कॉल	पुकारना
Chip	चिप	चिहुकना
Chirrup	चर्प	चहचहाना
Chirr	चर्र	चहचहाना
Chitter	चिटर	किटकिटाना
Twitter	ट्विटर	चहचहाना
Tweet	ट्विट	चहकना
Cheep	चीप	चींचीं करना
Chuck	चक	चहकना
Churr	चउर	चहचहाना
Chatter	चैटर	कटकटाना
Coo	कू	गुटरू गूँ करना
Curr	कर्र	करकराना
Whistle	ह्विस्टल	सीटी सी आवाज करना
Pipe	पाइप	बाँसुरी सी आवाज
Crow	क्रो	कुकड़ूँ कूँ करना
Cock-a-doodle	कॉक-ए-डूडल	कुकड़ूँ कूँ
Cluck	क्लक	कूँ-कूँ करना
Cackle	कैकल	कूँ-कूँ करना
Chuckle	चकल	चिहकना
Gabble	गैबल	गिलगिलाना
Quack	कैक	कों-कों करना
Gobble	गोबल	गिलगिलाना, भकोसना
Hiss	हिस	फुफकारना
Clang	क्लैंग	सीत्कार भरना

Honk	हॉन्क	बुबुआना
Scream	स्क्रीम	चीखना
Screech	स्क्रीच	चिल्लाना
Squawk	स्क्वीक	कोलाहल
Squall	स्क्वैल	चिल्लाहट
Hoot	हूट	बुड़कना
Tuwhit	टुहिट	टिहकारी भरना
Tuwhoo	टुहू	टहकना
Whoop	हूप	फटाक करना
Boom	बूम	भड़ाम करना
Crock	क्रॉक	टर्-टर् करना
Caw	कॉ	काँव-काँव करना
Plunk	पलंक	पुटपुटाना
Croank	क्रोंक	कूँ-कूँ करना
Buzz	बज	भनभनाना
Hum	हम	गुनगुनाना
Drone	ड्रून	मसकबाजे सी आवाज
Stridulate	स्ट्रिड्युकेट	कर्कश आवाज, चिल्लाहट
Creak	क्रीक	चर्-चर् करना
Crick	क्रिक	करकराना
Bellow	बेलो	हकरना, गरजना
Whir	ह्वर	किर्न-घिर्न करना
Whir	ह्वर्	घिर्न-घिर्न करना
Whirl	ह्वर्ल	गलगलाना
Clulk	क्लक	कुक-कुक करना
Hoot	हूट	बुबुआना
Whiff	ह्विफ	फुत्कार करना, फू-फू करना

Appendix-4/परिशिष्ट–4
Sound of Objects
वस्तु की आवाजें

Aeroplane zoom	एअरोप्लेनन्स	जूम हवाई जहाज गरजते हुए उड़ते हैं
Bells ring	बेल्स रिंग	घंटी टनटनाती हैं
Boots creak	बूट्स क्रीक	जूते चरमराते हैं
Bugles blow	बगल्स ब्लो	बिगुल बजाता है
Coins gingle	क्वायन्स	सिक्के जिंगल खनकते हैं
Clocks tick	क्लॉक्स	घड़िया टिक खड़खड़ाती है
Clouds thunder	क्लाउड्स थंडर	बादल गरजते हैं
Dishes rattle	डिशेज रैटल	थालियाँ खड़खड़ाती हैं
Fire crachles	फायर क्रैकल्स	अग्नि पटपटाती है
Guns boom	गन्स बुम	बन्दूकें गरजती है
Steam hiss	स्टीम हिस	भाप फदफदाता है
Engines whistle	इन्जिन व्हिस्ल्स	गाड़ियाँ सीटी देती हैं
Cooker whistle	कूकर व्हिस्ल्स	कूकर सीटी देती है
Feet patter	फीट पैटर	पाँव पटपटाते हैं
Hinges creak	हिन्जेस क्रीक	कब्जे चरमराते हैं
Hands clap	हैन्डस क्लैप	हाथ ताली बजाती है
Hoofs clatter	हुफ्स क्लैटर	खुर खटपटाते हैं
Dry leaves clatter	ड्राइ लिव्ज क्लैटर	सूखे पत्ते खड़खड़ाते हैं
Leaves rustle	लिव्ज रस्ल	पत्तियाँ सरसराती हैं
Metals ring	मेटल्स रिंग	धातु टनटनाते हैं
Raindrops patter	रेनड्रॉप्स पैटर	वर्षा की बूँदें पटपटाती हैं
Rifles report	रायफल्स रिपोर्ट	रायफल धमाके करते हैं
Shoes creak	सूज क्रीक	जूते चरमराते हैं
Weapons clatter	विपन्स क्लैटर	हथियार खड़खड़ाते हैं
Wind howl	विन्ड हाउस	हवा हू-हूकर बहती है
Wind whistle	विन्ड व्हिसल	हवा सनसनाती है
Spinning wheels whirr	स्पिनिंग व्हिल्स ह्वर	चरखा घरघराता है

Appendix-5/परिशिष्ट–5
Professionals
पेशेवर

Announcer	एनाउन्सर	उदघोषक
Auctioneer	ऑक्शनियर	नीलामी करने वाला
Acrobat	एक्रोबैट	नट
Artist	आर्टिस्ट	कलाकार
Artisan	आर्टिजन	कारीगर, शिल्पकार
Astrologer	एस्ट्रोलोजर	ज्योतिषी
Agent	एजेन्ट	प्रतिनिधि, कारिन्दा
Author	ऑथर	लेखक
Advocate	एडवोकेट	वकील
Barber	बारबर	हजाम, नाई
Blacksmith	ब्लैक स्मिथ	लोहार
Butcher	बुचर	कसाई
Butler	बटलर	भण्डारी
Boatman	बोटमैन	नाविक, मल्लाह
Brasier	ब्रेसिलर	ठठेरा
Baker	बेकर	नानबाई
Broker	ब्रोकर	दलाल
Binder	बाइन्डर	जिल्दसाइज
Barrister	बैरिस्टर	वकील
Beggar	बेगर	भिखारी
Betel-seller	बिटल सेलर	तमोली
Bookseller	बुक सेलर	पुस्तक विक्रेता
Carrier	कैरियर	सामान ठोने वाला
Clerk	कल्र्क	किएनी
Cobbler	कॉबलर	मोची
Chemist	केमिस्ट	दवा विक्रेता
Cashier	कैशियर	खजांची, रोकड़िया
Cook	कुक	रसोइया
Coolie	कुली	कुली, मोटिया
Carder	कार्डर	धुनिया

Contractor	कॉन्ट्रैक्टर	ठीकेदार
Compositer	कम्पोजिटर	प्रेस में शब्द बिठाने वाला, कम्पोजिटर
Coachman	कोचमैन	कोचवान
Confectioner	कन्फेक्सनर	हलवाई
Cleaner	क्लिनर	खलासी, सफाई करने वाला
Constable	कांस्टेबल	सिपाही
Counsellor	काउन्सेलर	सन्मतिदाता
Conductor	कन्डक्टर	गाड़ी नियन्त्रक
Carpenter	कारपेन्टर	बढ़ई
Compounder	कम्पाउन्डर	डाक्टर का सहायक
Chanffeur	शोफर	कार चालक
Cartman	कार्टमैन	गाड़ीवान
Dentist	डेन्टिस्ट	दाँत-निर्माता
Doctor	डाक्टर	चिकित्सक
Dramatist	ड्रेमेस्टि	नाटककार
Draper	ड्रेपर	जबाज
Dancer	डांसर	नर्तका, नर्तकी
Druggist	ड्रगिस्ट	दवा-विक्रेता
Draftsman	ड्राफ्ट्समैन	चित्र बनाने वाला
Dyer	डायर	रंगरेज
Brummer	ब्रमर	तबला वादक, तबलवी
Decorator	डेकोरेटर	सज्जाकार
Docker	डॉकर	गोदी-मजदूर
Engineer	इन्जिनियर	अभियन्ता
Engraver	इन्ग्रवेर	नक्काशी करने वाला
Enchanter	इन्चैन्टर	जादूगर
Enchantress	इन्चैन्ट्रेस	जादूगरनी
Editor	एडिटर	सम्पादक
Enameller	इनामेलर	मीनाकार
Examiner	एक्जामिनर	परीक्षक
Employee	इम्पलाई	नौकरी-पेशा कला, कर्मचारी
Fisherman	फिशमैन	मछुआरा
Farmer	फारमर	किसान
Fireman	फायरमैन	अग्निशमक

Fitter	फिटर	यन्त्र संयोजक
Foreman	फोरमैन	प्रधान कर्मचारी
Gardener	गार्डेनर	माली
Goldsmith	गोल्ड स्मिथ	सोनार
Greem grosser	ग्रीन ग्रोसर	सब्जी विक्रेता
Hawker	हॉकर	फेरीवाला
Inkman	इंकमैन	रोशनाई वाला
Inn-keeper	इनकीपर	धर्मशाला वाला
Inspector	इन्सेपेक्टर	निरीक्षक
Janitor	जैनीटर	द्वारपाल
Jeweller	ज्वेलर	जौहरी
Judge	जज	न्यायाधीश
Lawyer	लायर	वकील
Mason	मेसन	राजमिस्त्री
Milkman	मिल्कमैन	ग्वाला
Middleman	मिड्लमैन	दलाल
Magician	मैजिसियन	जादूगर
Minor	माइनर	खनिक
Mechanic	मेकेनिक	यान्त्रिक
Musician	म्यूजिशियन	गायक, संगीतज्ञ
Merchant	मरचेंट	सौदा व्यापार
Midwife	मिडवाइफ	दाई
Messenger	मेसेन्जर	दूत, धावक
Manager	मैनेजर	प्रबंधक
Milkmaid	मिल्कमेड	अहीरिन, ग्वालिन
Newsreader	न्यूजरीडर	समाचार वाचक
Newspaper vandor	न्यूजपेपर वेन्डर	अखबार वाला
Nurse	नर्स	नर्स, धाय, दाई
Novelist	नोवेलिस्ट	उपन्यासकार
Nun	नन	भिक्षुणी
Oilman	वायलमैन	तेली
Operator	ऑपरेटर	मशीन चालक
Order-supplier	ऑर्डर सप्लायर	आदेश आपूरक
Orderly	ऑर्डरली	अर्दली
Potter	पॉटर	ठठेरा, कुम्हार

English	Hindi (pronunciation)	Hindi (meaning)
Pupil	पुपिल	शिष्य, छात्र
Printer	प्रिंटर	मुद्रक
Publisher	पब्लिशर	प्रकाशक
Priest	प्रिस्ट	पादरी
Painter	पेंटर	चित्रकार
Postman	पोस्टमैन	डाकिया
Photographer	फोटोग्राफर	तस्वीर उतारने वाला
Proprietor	प्रोप्राइटर	मालिक
Proprietress	प्रोप्राइट्रेस	मालकिन
Pleader	प्लीडर	वकील
Procurer	प्रोक्यूरर	कुटना
Player	प्लेयर	खिलाड़ी
Policeman	पुलिसमैन	सिपाही
Packer	पैकर	सामान बाँधने वाला
Pager	पेजर	दूत
Pawner	पावनर	बंधक रखने वाला
Peddler	पेडलर	फेरी वाला
Perfumer	परक्यूमर	इत्र बेचने वाला
Repairer	रिपेअरर	मरम्मत करने वाला
Retailer	रिटेलर	खुदरा विक्रेता
Sculptor	स्कल्पटर	मूर्तिकार, संगतराश
Seedsman	सीड्समैन	बीज बिक्रेता
Sailor	सेलर	मांझी, नाविक
Sweeper	स्वीपर	मेहतर, मंगी
Surgeon	सर्जन	शल्य-चिकित्सक
Sanitary inspector	सैनिटरी इन्सिपेक्टर	निरीक्षक
Shopkeeper	शॉपकीपर	दुकानदार
Salesman	सेल्समैन	विक्रेता
Shoemaker	शूमेकर	मोची
Student	स्टुडेंट	छात्र
Scientist	साइन्टिस्ट	वैज्ञानिक
Soldier	सोल्डर	सैनिक
Teacher	टीचर	शिक्षक

Tailor	टेलर	दर्जी
Ticket collector	टिकट कलक्टर	टिकट जमाकर्ता
Tabla player	टबला प्लेयर	तबला वादक, तबलची
Treasurer	ट्रेजरर	खजांची
Turner	टर्नर	खरादने वाला
Trainer	ट्रेनर	प्रशिक्षक
Typist	टाइपिस्ट	टंकक
Vegetable seller	वेजिटेब्ल सेलर	सब्जी विक्रेता
Washerman	वाशर मैन	धोबी
Weaver	वीवर	बुनकर
Waiter	वेटर	बेयरा

Appendix-6/परिशिष्ट—6
Cereals/अनाज/उपज/अन्न

Grain/	ग्रेन-अन्न, दाना, अनाज	
Pea	पी	मटर
Pigeon pea	पिजिअन पी	अरहर
Field pea	फिल्ड पी	गोल मटर
Pulse	पल्स	दाल, दलहन
Gram	ग्राम	चना
Phaseolies mungo	फेजलीज मंगो	उड़द
Coffee	कॉफी	कहवा
Cluster bean	कलस्टर बीन	ज्वार
Wheat	ह्विट	गेहूँ
Paddy	पैडी	धान
Rice	राइस	चावल
Millet	माइलेट	बाजरा
Oat	ओट	जई
Barley	बार्ली	जौ
Great millet	ग्रेट माइलेट	ज्वार, चोलम
Sesame	सिसेम	तिल
Pear millet	पर्ल माइलेट	बाजरा
Poppy	पॉपी	पोस्ता दाना
Corn	कॉर्न	मकई
Corn ear	कॉर्न ईअर	मकई के बाल
Maize	मेज	मकई
Lentil	लेंटिल	मसूर
Kidney bean	किडनी बीन	मूँग
Buck wheat	बक ह्विट	मेथी
Mustard	मस्टर्ड	तोरी, राई, सरसों
White mustard	ह्वाइट मस्टर्ड	सफेद सरसों
Castor seed	कस्टर सीड	रेंड़ी

Appendix-7/परिशिष्ट—7
Eatables/खाद्य पदार्थ

Rice	राइस	चावल
Flour	फ्लोर	आटा
Arrowroot	एरोरूट	अरारूट
Pickle	पिकल	अचार
Grain	ग्रेन	अनाज
Comfit	कमफिट	इलायचीदाना
Curry	करी	शोरबा, रसा
Coffee	कॉफी	कहवा
Meat	मीट	मांस
Mutton	मटन	बकरे का मांस
Minced meat	माइसिड मीट	कीमा
Beaf	बीफ	गाय का मांस
Pork	पोर्क	सूअर का मांस
Kulfi	कुल्फी	कुल्फी
Ice-cream	आइसक्रीम	आइसक्रीम
Butter	बटर	मक्खन
Clarified butter	क्लैरिफायड	घी बटर
Ghee	घी	घी
Cheese	चीज	पनीर
Sweets	स्वीट्स	मिठाईयाँ
Confectionary	कंफेक्सनरी	मिठाईयाँ
Pulse	पल्स	दाल
Fried	फ्रायड	भूना हुआ
Cooked	कुक्ड	पकाया हुआ
Sauce	सॉस	चटनी
Tomato sauce	टोमैटो सॉस	टमाटर की चटनी
Bread	ब्रेड	रोटी
Sliced bread	स्लाइस ब्रेड	पावरोटी
Chapati	चपाती	चपाती
Beaten paddy	बिटेन पैडी	चिउड़ा
Beaten rice	बिटेन राइस	चिउड़ा

Baked grain	बेकड ग्रेन	भूजा
Tea	टी	चाय
Broth	ब्रॉथ	रस, शोरबा
Vegetable	बेजटेब्ल	सब्जी
Fruit	फ्रुट्स	फल
Salad	सलाद	सलाद
Gruel	ग्रुएल	दलिया, माँड़
Oil	आयल	तेल
Refined oil	रिफाइन्ड आयल	फैटरहित तेल
Curd	कर्ड	दही
Milk	मिल्क	दूध
Vinegar	वाइनेगर	सिरका
Semolina	सेमोलिना	सूजी
Tomato ketchup	टोमैटो केचप	टमाटर की चटनी
Loaf	लोफ	फूली हुई रोटी
Bun	बन	गोल फूला हुआ रोटी
Biscuit	बिस्कुट	बिस्कुट
Baked corn	बेक्ड कार्न	भुट्टा
Corn flake	कॉर्न फ्लेक	कुटा हुआ मकई
Whey	ह्वे	मट्ठा
Cream	क्रीम	मलाई
Sugar	सुगर	चीनी
Sugar candy	सुगर कैंडी	मिश्री
Murabba	मुरब्बा	मुरब्बा
Papar	पापड़	पापड़
Mixture	मिक्सचर	मसालेदार भूना हुआ दाना
Maida	मैदा	मैदा
Syrup	सिरप	मीठा रस
Sorbet	शर्बत	शरबत
Treacle	ट्रिकल	चाशनी
Wine	वाइन	शराब
Beer	बिअर	बिअर
Whisky	ह्विस्की	ह्विस्की
Honey	हनी	शहद, मधु
Drinks	ड्रिंक्स	पेय
Cold-drinks	कोल्ड ड्रिंक्स	शीतल पेय
Mathari	मठरी	मठरी

Puri	पुरी	पुड़ी
Pua	पुआ	पुआ
Breakfast	ब्रेकफास्ट	नास्ता
Lunch	लंच	दिन का भोजन
Snax	स्नैक्स	हल्का नास्ता
Luncheon	लंचिअन	हल्का नास्ता
Dinner	डिनर	रात का भोजन, भोज
Supper	सपर	रात का भोजन
Feast	फीस्ट	भोज
Food	फुड	भोजन
Chew	चिउ	चबाना
Swallow	स्वैलो	निगलना
Digest	डायजेस्ट	पचाना
Vomit	वोमिट	उगलना
Jelly	जेली	जेली
Jam	जैम	जैम
Pizza	पिज्जा	पिज्जा
Toast	टोस्ट	टोस्ट
Sausage	सौसेज	सॉसेज
Hamburger	हैम्बरगर	हैम्बरगर
Egg	एग	अण्डा
Cake	केक	केक
Pancake	पैनकेक	पैनकेक
Soup	सूप	सूप
Dessert	डेजर्ट	मीठा पकवान
Pie	पाइ	अदौरी, तिलौरी
Chicken	चिकेन	मुर्गा
Fish	फिश	मछली
Honey	हनी	शहद
Maeggrone	मारजेरिन	सेवई
Samosa	समोसा	समोसा
Noodle	नूडल	नमकीन पेठा
Toffee	टॉफी	टॉफी
Chocolet	चॉकलेट	चॉकलेट
Pudding	पुडिंग	खीर
Chips	चिप्स	चिप्स
Croquette	क्रोक्वेट	आलूचप

Appendix-8/परिशिष्ट–8
Spices/मसाले

Vitriol	विटरियोल	तूतिया
Musk	मस्क	कस्तुरी
Nigella	नाइजेला	कलौंजी
Salt	साल्ट	नमक
Coriander	कोरिएण्डर	धनिया
Cinnamon	सिनामॉन	दालचीनी
Cassia	कैसिया	तेजपात
Basil	बेसिल	तुलसी
Niger	नायगर	तिल
Cumin seed	क्यूमिन सीड	जीरा
Mace	मैस	जावित्री
Nutmeg	नटमेग	जायफल
Chirota	चिराटा	चिरैता
Sandal	सैंडल	चंदन
Menthol	मेन्थॉल	पोदीना
Indian madder	इन्डियन मैडर	मजीठ
Gall nut	गॉलनट	माजूफल
Red pepper	रेड पिपर	लाल मिर्च
Chili	चिली	मिर्च
Licorice	लिकोराइस	मुलैठी
Black pepper	ब्लैक पिपर	गोल मिर्च
Pseudo-alum	स्यूडो एलम	फिटकिरी
Saffron	सेफ्रॉन	केसर
Cocain	कोकीन	कोकीन
Feast	ईष्ट	खमीर
Aloe	एलो	मुसब्बर
Parsley	पार्सलि	अजवाइन खुरासानी
Caraway	कारावे	अजवाइन
Thymol	थायमल	अजवाइन का सत
Ginger	जिंजर	अदरख
Linseed	लिनसीड	अतली

Phyllanthus embhica	फाइलेथंस इम्बिलंक	आँवला
Cardamom	कारडामॉम	इलाइची (छोटी)
Catechu	कैटेचु	काथ
Camphor	कैम्फर	कपूर
Nitre	नाइटर	शोरा
Opium	ओपिअम	अफीम
Cubeb	क्यूबेब	कबाबचीनी
Ruddle	रडल	गेरू
Copper sulphate	कॉपर सल्फेट	तूतिया
Bitumen	बिटुमेन	राल
Soapnut	सोपनट	रीठा
Benzoin	बेन्जोयाइन	लोहबान
Arsenic	आर्सेनिक	संखिया
Alkali	अलकलि	सज्जीखार
Litharge	लिथार्ज	सफेदा
Sago	सैगो	साबूदाना
Cinnabar	सिनाबार	सिंगरिफ
Betel-nut	बिटलनट	सुपारी
Vinegar	वाइनेगर	सिरका
Albaster	एलबास्टर	सेतखली
Dry ginger	ड्राइ जिंजर	सोंठ
Borex	बोरैक्स	सोहागा
Turmeric	टरमेरिक	हल्दी
Myrobalan	मायरोबलान	हर्रे
Asafoctida	एसफोएटिडा	हींग
Curcuma	करक्यूमा	हल्दी
Clove	क्लोव	लवंग
Mado saffron	मैडो सेफरॉन	शरत केसर
Pistil	पिस्टिल	केसर
Origanum	ऑरिगेनम	शिकाकाई

Appendix-9/परिशिष्ट—9
Fruits/फल

Apple	एप्पल	सेव
Pine apple	पाइनएप्पल	अनानास
Stone apple	स्टोन एप्पल	बेल
Crab apple	क्रैब एप्पल	जंगली सेव
Custard apple	कस्टर्ड एप्पल	शरीफा
Melon	मेलन	तरबूज
Water melon	वाटरमेलन	खरबूजा
Musk melon	मस्क मेलन	फूट
Cucumber	ककम्बर	खीरा, ककड़ी
Berry	बेरी	बैर
Black berry	ब्लैक बेरी	जामुन
Sweet berry	स्वीटबेरी	लसलसा
Mul berry	मलबेरी	शहतूत
Rose berry	रोजबेरी	गुलाब जामुन
Nut	नट	कड़े छिलके का फल
Betel nut	बिटलनट	सुपारी
Chest nut	चेस्ट नट	अखरोट
Cashew nut	कैशियू नट	काजू
Ground nut	ग्राउण्ड नट	बादाम
Water nut	वाटरनट	सिंघाड़ा
Coconut	कोकोनेट	नारियल
Kernel	करनेल	कड़े फल का खाने योग्य बाग
Pomegranate	पॉमग्रेनेट	अनार
Grapes	ग्रेप्स	अंगूर
Fig	फिग	अंजीर
Mango	मैंगो	आम
Sugar cane	सुगरकेन	ईख
Jack fruit	जैकफ्रूट	कटहल
Currant	क्यूरेंट	किशमिश
Plantain	प्लेंटेन	केला
Banana	बनाना	केला
Guava	ग्वावा	अमरूद
Date	डेट	खजूर
Apricot	एप्रिकॉट	खूबानी
Carrot	कैरॉट	गाजर

English	Hindi (transliteration)	Hindi
Euryle forex	यूराइल फोरेक्स मखाना	
Sweet potato	स्वीट पोटैटो	शकरकन्द
Lichi	लिची	लिची
Cifrus fruit	साइट्रस फ्रूट	खट्टे-रसीले फल
Orange	ऑरेंज	नारंगी
Mausambi	मौसमी	मौसमी
Lemon	लेमन	नींबू
Pear	पीअर	नाशपाती
Peach	पीच	सतालू
Papaya	पपाया	पपीता
Mountain papaya	माउन्टेन पपाया	पहाड़ी पपीता
Pistalhio	पिस्टैचियो	पिस्ता
Plum	प्लम	बेर
Almond	आल्मन	बादाम
Yam	याम	रतालू
Stone	स्टोन	गुठली
Pulp	पल्प	गुदा
Skin	स्किन	छिलका
Juice	जूस	रस
Sap	सैप	रस
Seed	सीड	बीज
Sapling	सैप्लिंग	कलम
Plant	प्लांट	पौधा
Gerom	जर्म	अंकुर
Graft	ग्राफ्ट	कलम
Bud	बड	कली
Rind	रिंड	छिलका
Fibre	फायबर	रेशा
Cherry	चेरी	चेरी
Sour cherry	सावर चेरी	खट्टी चेरी
Sopodilla	सैपोडिला	चीकू
Sugar beet	सुगर बीट	चुकन्दर
Gravia	ग्राविया	फालसा
Raspberries	रैस्पबेरीज	रसीलेबेर
Kivi fruit	किवीफ्रूट	किवीफल
Strawberry	स्ट्रॉबेरी	स्ट्रॉबेरी
Jambu	जैम्बु	जैम्बु

Appendix-10/परिशिष्ट–10
Flowers/फूल

Oleander	ओलिएण्डर	कनेर
Lotus	लोटस	कमल
Lily	लिलि	कमलिनी, कुमुदनी
Pandanus	पैन्डेनस	केतकी, केवड़ा
Chrysanthemum	क्राइसथेंमम	गुलदाऊदी
Touch-me-not	टचमी नॉट	गुल मेंहदी
Daisy	डेजी	गुलबहार
Marogold	मेरीगोल्ड	गेंदा
Jasmine	जेस्मिन	चमेली
Magnolia	मैग्नोलिया	चम्पा
Amaranthus	एमरैन्थस	चौलाई
Prickly amaranthus	प्रिकली एमरैन्थस	कटीली चौलाई
Belladona	बेलाडोना	धतूरा
Narassus	नारसिसस	नरगिस
Cactus	कैक्टस	नागफनी, सेहुड़
Prickly pear	प्रिकली पिअर	नागफनी, कटीले फूल
Cobra flower	कोबरा फ्लावर	नागफनी, नागमिका
Lilac	लाइलैक	बकाइन
Pyrus malus	पायरस मेलस	वंगूगोशा
Violet	वायलेट	बनफशा
Sweet violet	स्वीट वायलेट	सुगन्धित बनफशा
Mogra	मोगरा	बेला
Allamanoa	एलामानोआ	एलामानोआ
Periwinkle	पेरिविंकल	पेरिविंकल
Balsam	बाल्सम	गुलहजारा
Creeper	क्रीपर	लता
Rose	रोज	गुलाब, चुवती
Ivory	आइवरी	दूधिया फूल
Cosmos	कॉसमॉस	कॉसमॉस
Blue bell	ब्लूबेल	ब्लूबेल
Dog flower	डॉग फ्लावर	कुत्ता फूल
Petunia	पिटुनिया	पिटुनिया
Platonica	प्लेटोनिका	दसबजिया

Agastya	अगस्त्य	अगस्त्य
Kanak	कनक	कनक
Aparajita	अपराजिता	अपराजिता
Shami	शमी	शमी
Poppy	पॉपी	अफीम
Desert blue bell	डेजर्ट ब्लूबेल	जंगली ब्लूबेल
Pensy	पैंजी	पैंजी
Dahlia	डालिया	डालिया
Zinnia	जिनिया	जिनिया
Carnation	कारनेशन	कारनेशन
Blue carnation	ब्लू कारनेशन	नीला कारनेशन
Morning glory	मार्निंग ग्लोरी	आभा
Night queen	नाइट क्विन	रात की रानी
Rajnigandha	रजनीगंधा	रजनीगंधा
Hibiscus	हिबिसकस	हिबिसकस
Tulip	ट्यूलिप	ट्यूलिप
Gandhraj	गंधराज	गंधराज
Mountain lotus	माउन्टेन लोटस	इन्द्रकमल
10 O' clock	टेन ओ क्लॉक	दसबजिया
4 O' clock	फोर ओ क्लॉक	चरबजिया
Root	रूट	जड़
Stem	स्टेम	तना
Leaf	लिफ	पत्ता
Branch	ब्रांच	डाली
Hair root	हेअर रूट	महीन रेशा
Flower	फ्लावर	फूल
Fruit	फ्रूट	फल
Seed	सीड	बीज
Sapling	सैप्लिंग	बीचड़ा
Plantation	प्लांटेशन	रोपना
Grafting	ग्राफ्टिंग	एक में दूसरा पौधा जोड़ना
Seedling	सिडलिंग	बीचड़ा
Harsingoor	हरसिंगार	हरसिंगार
Kamini	कामिनी	कामिनी
Rakhi	राखी	राखी (कौरव-पांडव)
Shivling	शिवलिंग	शिवलिंग
Kachnar	कचनार	कचनार

Appendix-11/परिशिष्ट–11
Vegetables/सब्जियाँ

Bulbous	बलबस	कन्द
Ginger	जिंजर	अदरक
Potato	पोटैटो	आलू
Tomato	टोमैटो	टमाटर
Tamarind	टेमरिंड	इमली
Cucumber	ककम्बर	खीरा, ककड़ी
Jack fruit	जैक फ्रुट	कटहल
Pumpkin	पम्पकिन	कोहड़ा
Gourd	गावर्ड	कद्दू
Carambola	कैरमबोला	कमरख
Bitter gourd	बिटर गावर्ड	करेला
Jhigune	झिंगुनी	झिंगुनी
Ghiya	घिया	घिया
Red pumpkin gourd	रेड पम्पकिन गोवर्ड	काशीफल
Mushroom	मशरूम	कुकुरमुत्ता
Banana	बनाना	केला
Cucurbit gourd	ककरबिट गावर्ड	फूट, कोहड़ा
Lime	लाइम	नींबू
Carrot	कैरॉट	गाजर
Knol khol	नोलखोल	गाँठ गोभी
Cabbage	कैबेज	बन्द गोभी
Cauliflower	कावलीफ्लावर	फूलगोभी
Luffa	लुफा	तुरई, तोरी
Snake gourd	स्नेक गावर्ड	चिचड़ी
Luffa gourd	लुफा गावर्ड	चिकनी चुरई, तोरी
Pinus geradiana	पायनस जेराडियाना	चिलगोजा
Sapodilla	सैपोडिला	चीकू
Beetroot	बीटरूट	चुकन्दर
Sugar beet	सुगर बीट	चुकन्दर
Yam	याम	रतालु
Coriandor	कोरिएण्डर	धनिया

Papaya	पपाया	पपीता
Trichosanths dioica	ट्रिकोसेन्थस डियोइका	परवल
Parval	परवल	परवल
Brassica campestrice	ब्रासिका केम्पेस्ट्राइस	पत्तागोभी
Spinch	स्पिनैच	पालक
Mint	मिन्ट	पुदीना
Onion	ओनियन	प्यास
Brinjal	ब्रिंजल	बैगन
Lady finger	लेडीफिंगर	भिण्डी
Pea	पी	मटर
Nightshade	नाइटशेड	मकोय
Chilli	चिली	मिर्च
Raddish	रैडिश	मूली
Turnip	टरनिप	शलजम
Bean	बीन	सेम
Lettuce	लेट्यूस	सलाद
Green leaves	ग्रीन लिव्स	साग
Garlic	गारलिक	लहसुन

Appendix-12/परिशिष्ट–12
Birds/पक्षी

Swallow	स्वैलो	अबाबील
Owl	आउल	उल्लू
Woodpecker	बुडपेकर	कठफोड़वा
Pigeon	पिजन	कबुतर
Cockatoo	कोकाटू	काकतुआ
Crow	क्रो	कौवा
Raven	रैवेन	डोमकौवा
Cuckoo	ककू	कोयल
Nightingale	नाइटिंगेल	बुलबुल
Stanglin	स्टारलिंग	सारिका
Mynah	मैना	मैना
Eagle	ईगल	गरूड़
Lark	लार्क	लवा
Kite	काइट	चील
Skylark	स्काईलार्क	बाज
Vulture	वल्चर	गिद्ध
Sparrow	स्पैरो	गोरैया
Bat	बैट	चमगादड़
Thrush	थ्रश	सारिका
Falcon	फैल्कॉन	बाज
Bulbul	बुलबुल	बुलबुल
Partridge	पार्ट्रिज	तीतर
Magpie	मैजपी	नीलकंठ
Dove	डोव	पैन्डुक
Drake	ड्रोक	बत्तख
Duck	डक	बत्तख
Duckling	डकलिंग	बत्तख का बच्चा
Weaverbird	विवरवर्ड	बयाँ
Quail	क्वेल	बटेर
Hawk	हॉक	बाज, मुसैचा
Fowl	फॉल	मुर्ग
Cock	कॉक	मुर्गा
Hen	हेन	मुर्गी
Chicken	चिकेन	मुर्गी का बच्चा
Peacock	पीकॉक	मोर

Peahen	पीहेन	मोरनी
Ostrich	ऑस्ट्रिच	शुतुरमुर्ग
Crane	क्रेन	सारस
Parrot	पैरोट	तोता
Macaw	मकाव	हीरामन तोता
Swan	स्वान	हंस
Stork	स्टॉर्क	सारस, बगुला
Golden oriole	गोल्डेन ओरियोल	सुनहला पक्षी
Swift	स्विफ्ट	उड़नछू
Painter bird	पेन्टर बर्ड	चित्रकार पक्षी
Albatross	अल्बट्रॉस	अल्बाट्रॉस
Condor	कॉन्डर	कॉन्डर
Humming bird	हम्मिंग बर्ड	गाने वाला पक्षी
Kiwi	किवी	किवी
Hornbill	हॉर्नबिल	लम्बे चोंच वाला पक्षी
Goose	गूज	हंसिनी
Gander	गैंडर	हंस
Gosling	गॉस्लिंग	हंस का बच्चा
Flamingo	फ्लेमिंगो	फ्लेमिंगो
Turkey	टर्की	टर्की
Canary	कैनरी	कैनरी
Dragon	ड्रेगन	ड्रेगन
Toucan	टॉकन	मोटे चोंच वाला पक्षी
Kingfisher	किंगफिशर	टिटहरी
Penguin	पेन्गुइन	पेन्गुइन
Pelican	पेलिकन	पेलिकन
Hoopoe	हूपो	मथबन्हनी
Emu	इमू	इमू
Puffin	पफिन	पफिन
Robin	रॉबिन	रॉबिन
Gold finch	गोल्डफिंच	गोल्डफिंच
Wing	विंग	डैना
Feather	फिदर	पैख
Claw	क्ला	पंजर
Beak	बिक	चोंच
Bill	बिल	चोंच
Nest	नेस्ट	घोंसला

Appendix-13/परिशिष्ट–13
Animals/जानवर

Antelop	एन्टिलोप	बारहसिंगा
Ape	एप	लंगूर
Ass	आस	गदहा
Beast	बीस्ट	पशु
Bitch	बिच	कुतिया
Boar	बोअर	जंगली सूअर
Bear	बिअर	भालू
Buffallow	बुफैलो	भैंस
He-buffallow	ही-बुफैलो	भैंसा
Bull	बुल	साँड़
Bison	बायसन	जंगली बैल
Cat	कैट	बिल्ली
Cattle	कैटल	मवेशी
Kitten	किटन	बिल्ली का बच्चा
Claw	क्ला	पैजा
Chimpanzee	चिम्पैंजी	बनमानुष
Colt	कोल्ट	बछड़ा
Cow	काउ	गाय
Calf	काफ	बछड़ा
She calf	शी काफ	बछिया
Chipmon	चिप्मान	गिलहरी
Camel	कैमल	ऊँट
Deer	डिअर	हिरण, मृग
Dog	डॉग	कुत्ता
Bull-dog	बुलडॉग	मुँह काला कुत्ता
Ewe	इयू	भेड़ी
Elephant	एलिफैंट	हाथी
Filly	फिली	बछेड़ी
Fox	फॉक्स	लोमड़ी
Fawn	फॉन	हिरण का बच्चा
Foal	फोल	फोल

Giraffe	जिर्राफ	जिर्राफ
Guinea-pig	गिनी पिग	एक पूँछहीन वाला जानवर
Goat	गोट	बकरी
He-goat	ही-गोट	बकरा
She-goat	शी-गोट	बकरी
Hound	हाउंड	शिकारी कुत्ता
Hind	हिन्ड	बारहसिंगी
Heifer	हीफर	बछिया
Hyena	हायना	लकड़बग्घा
Horn	हॉर्न	सींग
Hare	हेअर	खरगोश
Hoop	हूप	खुर
Hog	हॉग	सुअर
Pig	पिग	सुअर
Swine	स्वाइन	सुअरी
Hanster	हैंस्टर	चूहा सा जानवर, हैंस्टर
Jackal	जैकाल	सियार
Jaguar	जगुआर	अमेरिकन चीता, जगुआर
Kid	किड	बकरी का बच्चा, बच्चा जानवर
Koala bear	कोयला बीअर	भालू जाति का छोटा भालू
Kangaroo	कंगारू	कंगारू
Lion	लायन	शेर
Lioness	लायनेस	शेरिनी
Leo	लियो	शेर का बच्चा
Lamb	लैम्ब	मेमना
Leopard	लेपर्ड	तेंदुआ
Moose	मुज	डालिदार सींगो वाला हिरण
Mole	मोल	छछुन्दर
Mouse	माउस	चूहा
Mice	माइस	चूहे
Musk deer	मस्क डिअर	कस्तूरी मृग
Mule	म्यूल	खच्चर
Mare	मेअर	घोड़ी
Monkey	मंकी	बन्दर
Mongoose	मोन्गुज	नेवला

Orangutan	ओरंगुटन	बनमानुष
Ox	ऑक्स	बैल
Oxen	ऑक्सेन	बैलों की जोड़ी
Oxyx	ऑक्सिक्स	आक्सिक्स
Otter	ओटर	जलमार्जर, ऊदबिलाव
Poreupone	पॉर्क्यूपाइन	साही
Paw	पॉ	पंजा
Panther	पैन्थर	चीता
Pony	पोनी	टट्टू
Puppy pup	पपी पप	पिल्ला, छोटा कुत्ता
Porporise	पोरपोआयज	सुईंस
Polar bear	पोलर बिअर	ध्रुवीय भालू
Panda	पंडा	पंडा, चीनी नाटा भालू
Pointer	पोआयन्टर	शिकारी कुत्ता
Piglet	पिगलेट	छोटा सुअर
Pigling	पिगलिंग	सुअर का बच्चा
Rabbit	रैबिट	खरगोश
Reindeer	रेइन्डियर	मृग
Doe	डो	मृगी
Rhinoceros	रीनोसॉर्स	रीनो
Ram	रैम	भेंड़
Swine	स्वाइन	सुअरी
Spaniel	स्पैनियल	झबरा कुत्ता
Stag	स्टैग	बारहसिंगा
Sheep	शीप	भेंड़
Mammoth	मेमॉथ	ऐरावत हाथी
Billy-goat	बिल्ली गोट	बकरा
Tusker	टस्कर	बड़ा हाथी
Hedgehog	हेजहॉग	जंगली चूहा
Cub	कब	जंगली जानवर के बच्चे
Catling	कैअलिंग	बिल्ली का बच्चा
Gibbon	गिबॉन	बन्दर का प्रकार
Gorilla	गोरिल्ला	बनमानुष का प्रकार
Frog	फ्रॉग	मेढक
Tadpole	टैडपोल	मेढक का बच्चा

Appendix-14/परिशिष्ट–14
Reptiles and Insects
सरीसृप एवं कीड़े

Raptiles	रेप्टाइल्स	सरीसृप, रेंगने वाले जानवर
Raptileen	रेप्टायलिन	सरीसृप सम्बन्धी
Saurian	सॉरियन	सॉरियन
Dragon	ड्रेगॉन	चीनी दैत्य
Dinosaur	डायनोसोर	डायनोसोर
Ichthyosaur	इचथायोसोर	इचथाओसोर
Snake	स्नेक	साँप
Cobra	कोबरा	नाग
Boa	बोआ	अजगर
Python	पायथन	अजगर
Serpent	सर्पेंट	साँप
Ophidian	ओफिडियन	सर्प सम्बन्धी
Eel	ईल	सर्प सी मछली
Viper	वाइपर	जहरी साँप
Crocodile	क्रोकोडायल	मगरमच्छ
Alligator	एलिगेटर	घड़ियाल
Turtle	टरटल	कछुआ
Newt	न्यूट	गोह
Tortoise	टोरट्वाएज	कछुआ
Terrapin	टेरापिन	कछुआ
Lizard	लिजार्ड	छिपकली
Chameleon	चेमेलियन	गिरगिट
Eft	इफ्ट	इफ्ट
Geeko	गेको	घरेलू छिपकली
Horned	हार्नेड	सिंगदार मेढक
Iguana	इगुआना	छिपकली का एक प्रकार
Gila monster	गिला मॉनस्टर	गिला मॉनस्टर
Slough	सल्फ	केंचुली
Insects	इन्सेक्ट्स	कीड़े
Bug	बग	खटमल

Centipede	सेन्टिपेड	गोजर
Earwig	इअरविग	कनगोजर
Millipede	मिलिपेड	गोजर
Nit	निट	लीख
Maggot	मेजॉट	कृमि
Maggoty	मेगॉटी	कीड़ों से भरा हुआ
Blight	ब्लाइट	पौधों का कीड़ा
Pest	पेस्ट	पौधे का कीड़ा
Vermin	वरमिन	अन्न का कीड़ा
Louse	लाउस	जूँ
Leech	लीच	जोंक
Flea	फ्ली	देहिक
Bedbug	बेड्बग	खटमल
Bee	बी	मधुमक्खी
Honeybee	हनी	बी मधुमक्खी
Queen bee	क्वीन बी	रानी मधुमक्खी
Drone	ड्रॉन	नर मधुमक्खी
Wasp	वास्प	बर्रे
Ant	एण्ट	चींटी
White ant	ह्वाइट एण्ट	दीमक
Teronite	टरमाइट	दीमक
Grass hopper	ग्रास हॉपर	टिड्डा, फतिंगा
Pismire	पिसमायर	पिसमायर
Spider	स्पाइडर	मकड़ा
Scorpion	स्कॉरपियन	बिच्छू
Fly	फ्लाई	मक्खी
Fire fly	फायर फ्लाइ	जुगनूँ
Mosquito	मॉस्क्विटो	मच्छर
Butterfly	बटरफ्लाइ	तितली
Moth	मॉथ	कपड़े का कीड़ा
Beetle	बीटल	गोबरैला
Weevil	विविल	पौधा खाने वाला झींगुर
Locust	लोकस्ट	टिड्डे
Cricket	क्रिकेट	झींगुर
Cockroach	कॉक्रोच	तिलचट्टा

Pupa	प्यूपा	तीसरी अवस्था का कीड़ा
Chrysalis	क्राइसेलिस	तितली, कीड़े की पहली अवस्था
Aurelia	एउरेलिया	सुनहरे रंग का कीड़ा
Nymph	निम्फ	मत्स्य कन्या
Larva	लार्वा	मच्छर का अण्डा
Grub	ग्रब	कीड़ा, कोआ
Oyster	वायस्टर	सीप
Bivalve	बाइवॉल्ब	द्विकोशिय
Clam	क्लैम	क्लैम
Mussel	मसेल	मसेल
Mollusk	मोलुस्क	मोलुस्क
Snail	स्नेल	घोंघा
Slug	स्लग	स्लग
Whelk	व्हेल्क	व्हेल्क
Univalve	यूनिवॉल्व	एककोषीय
Scallop	स्कैलॉप	स्कैलैप
Lobster	लोबस्टर	केंकड़ा
Shrimp	श्रृम्प	श्रृम्प
Crab	क्रेब	केकड़ा
Dolphin	डॉलफिन	डालफिन
Porporise	पॉरपोअएज	सुईस
Seal	सील	सील मछली
Sea-lion	सीलायन	सागरीय शेर
Walrus	वालरस	दरियाई घोड़ा
Whale	व्हेल	व्हेल
Conch	कोंच	शंख
Worm	वर्म	बीमारी के कीड़े
Angleworm	एंगलवर्म	केंचुआ
Earthworm	अर्थवर्म	केंचुआ
Tapeworm	टेपवर्म	फीताकृमि
Leech	लीच	जोंक
Roundworm	राउन्डवर्म	राउन्डवर्म
Flatworm	फ्लैटवर्म	फ्लैटवर्म
Silkworm	सिल्क वर्म	रेशम का कीड़ा

Appendix-15/परिशिष्ट–15
Relations/सम्बन्ध और रिश्ते

Guest	गेस्ट	अतिथि, यजमान
Teacher	टीचर	अध्यापक, गुरु
Mother	मदर	माता
Tenant	टिनैंट	किरायेदार
Mistress	मिस्ट्रेस	उप–पत्नी
Preceptor	प्रिसैप्टर	गुरु
Customer	कस्टमर	ग्राहक
Uncle	अंकल	चाला
Aunt	ऑन्ट	चाची
Disciple	डिसाइपल	चेला
Land lord	लैंड लॉर्ड	जमींदार
Sister in law	सिस्टर-इन-लॉ	साली, जेठानी, देवरानी, ननद
Adopted daughter	ऐडॉप्टिड डॉटर	दत्तक कन्या
Adopted son	ऐडॉप्टिड सन	दत्तक पुत्र
Grand father	ग्रैण्ड फादर	दादा
Grand mother	ग्रैण्ड मदर	दादी
Son in law	सन इन लॉ	दामाद
Friend	फ्रैंड	दोस्त, मित्र
Maternal grand father	मैट्रनल ग्रैण्ड फादर	नाना
Maternal grand mother	मैट्रनल ग्रैण्ड मदर	नानी
Husband	हसबैंड	पति
Wife	वाइफ	पत्नी
Daughter in law	डॉटर इन ला	पतोहू, बहू
Father	फादर	पिता
Son	सन	बेटा
Daughter	डॉटर	बेटी
Lover	लवर	प्रेमी
Brother	ब्रदर	भाई
Sister	सिस्टर	बहन
Brother in law	ब्रदर इन लॉ	बहनोई
Nephew	नेफ्यू	भतीजा, भांजा

English	Hindi (transliteration)	Hindi
Niece	नीस	भतीजी, भांजी
Maternal uncle	मैटर्नल अंकल	मामा
Maternal aunt	मैटर्नल ऑन्ट	मामी
Client	क्लाइंट	मुवक्किल
Mother's sister	मदर्स सिस्टर	मौसी
Keep	कीप	रखैल
Patient	पेशेंट	रोगी
Heir	एयर	वारिस
Pupil	प्यूपिल	शिष्य
Own	ऑन	सगा
Father in law	फादर इन लॉ	ससुर
Mother in law	मदर इन लॉ	सास
Relative	रिलेटिव	सम्बन्धी
Step daughter	स्टेप-डॉटर	सौतेली कन्या
Step son	स्टेप सन	सौतेला पुत्र
Step father	स्टेप फादर	सौतेला पिता
Step sister	स्टेप सिस्टर	सौतेली बहन
Step brother	स्टेप ब्रदर	सौतेला भाई

Appendix-16/परिशिष्ट–16
Colours/रंग

White	ह्वाइट	सफेद
Milky white	मिल्की ह्वाइट	दुधिया सफेद
Sea green	सी ग्रीन	हल्का हरा
Parrot green	पैरॉट ग्रीन	गहरा हरा
Sky blue	स्काई ब्लू	हलका नीला
Navy blue	नेवी ब्लू	गहरा नीला
Royal blue	रॉयल ब्लू	मद्धिम नीला
Blue	ब्लू	नीला
Green	ग्रीन	हरा
Bottle green	बोट्ल ग्रीन	गहरा हरा
Yellow	येलो	पीला
Mustard	मस्टर्ड	पीला
Off white	ऑफ ह्वाइट	गाढ़ा सफेद
Silver white	सिल्वर ह्वाइट	चाँदी से धवल
Golden	गोल्डेन	सुनहरा
Orange	ऑरेंज	संतरा, नारंगी रंग
Black	ब्लैक	काला
Cream	क्रीम	गाढ़ा सफेद
Gray	ग्रे	भूरा
Grayish	ग्रेयिश	भूरा सा
Greenish	ग्रीनिश	हरा सा
Whitish	ह्वाइटिश	सफेद सा
Bluish	ब्लूयिश	नीला सा
Yellowish	येलोयिश	पीला सा
Blackish	ब्लैकिश	काला सा
Red	रेड	लाल
Reddish	रेडिश	लाल सा
Purple	परपल	बैंगनी
Violet	वायलेट	बैंगनी
Maroon	मारून	गाढ़ा नीला

Lemon	लेमन	हल्का पीला
Brick red	ब्रिक रेड	सुर्ख लाल
Scarlet	स्कार्लेट	गहरा गुलाबी
Pink	पिंक	गुलाबी
Brown	ब्राउन	भूरा
Dark brown	डार्क ब्राउन	गहरा भूरा
Light brown	लाइट ब्राउन	हल्का भूरा
Chocolate	चॉकलेट	कत्थई
Saffron	सेफ्रॉन	केसरिया
Pale	पेल	पीला
Mauve	मॉव	चमकीला गुलाबी
Natural	नेचुरल	प्राकृतिक
Artificial	आर्टिफिसल	बनावटी, कृत्रिम
Mixed	मिक्सड	मिश्रित
Matabi	मटाबी	मटमैला
Gold bulsh	गोल्डबल्श	सुनहरा पीला
Skin colour	स्कीन कलर	चमड़ी सा हल्का भूरा रंग
Coffee colour	कॉफी कलर	गहरा भूरा रंग
Snow white	स्नो ह्वाइट	बर्फ सा श्वेत
Baby pink	बेबी पिंक	हल्का गुलाबी
Crimson	क्रिमसन	गहरा लाल
Blood red	ब्लड रेड	रक्तिम
Paint	पेंट	उड़ा हुआ रंगा
Copper	कॉपर	ताँबे सा भूरा
Jet black	जेट ब्लैक	गहरा काला

Appendix-17/परिशिष्ट–17
Household Articles
घेरलू सामान

Almirah	अलमिरा	अल्मारी
Ash	एश	राख
Attache	एटैची	एटैची
Ash-tray	एशट्रे	राख झाड़ने का बर्तन
Bed	बेड	बिछावन
Bed-sheet	बेड सीट	चादर
Bucket	बकेट	बाल्टी
Brush	ब्रश	ब्रश
Bottle	बोटल	बोतल, शीशी
Broom	ब्रूम	झाड़ू
Bolster	बोल्स्टर	मसनद, तकिया
Box	बॉक्स	बक्शा
Bowl	बॉउल	कटोरा
Balance	बैलेंस	तराजू
Basket	बास्केट	टोकरी
Blanket	ब्लैंकेट	कम्बल
Bundle	बंडल	गट्ठर
Bale	बेल	गाँठ, गट्ठर
Button	बटन	बटन
Cover	कवर	खोल
Cot	कॉट	चारपाई
Chair	चेअर	कुर्सी
Comb	कम्ब	कंघी
Canister	कैनिस्टर	कनस्तर
Cauldron	कॉलड्रॉन	कड़ाही
Cylander	सिलेंडर	सिलेंडर
Cinder	सिंडर	अंगार, राख
Casket	कास्केट	श्रृंगारदान
Candle	कैंडल	मोमबत्ती
Calender	कैलेंडर	पंचांग, तिथि-पत्र
Cup	कप	कप
Chandelier	शैनडिलियर	झाड़-फानूस

Container	कन्टेनर	बर्तन
Dish	डिश	थाली
Door-mat	डोर-मैट	पाँवदान
Electric lamp	इलेक्ट्रिक लैम्प	बिजली का दीप
Earthen lamp	अर्थेन लैम्प	दीया
Earthen pot	अर्थेन पॉट	मिट्टी का बर्तन
Earthen vessel	अर्थेन वेसल	मिट्टी का बड़ा बर्तन
Electric stove	इलेक्ट्रिक स्टोव	बिजली का चूल्हा
Flagon	फ्लगन	सुराही
Flower vase	फ्लावर वेस	फूलदान
Flower pot	फ्लावर पॉट	गमला
Funnel	फनेल	कीप
Fork	फॉर्क	काँटा
Fuel	फुएल	जलावन
Grate	ग्रेट	चूल्हे आदि की जाली
Hearth	हर्थ	अंगीठी, बड़ा चूल्हा
Harp	हार्प	बाजा
Hardware	हार्थवेअर	लोहे के सामान
Hubble-bubble	डबल-बबल	हुक्का
Ice	आइस	बर्फ
Ice-cream	आइस क्रीम	क्रीमयुक्त बर्फ
Ice-tray	आइस ट्रे	बर्फ का ट्रे
Ice-pot	आइस पॉट	बर्फ का बर्तन
Ice-box	आइस बॉक्स	बर्फ की पेटी
Ice-cube	आइस क्यूब	चौकोर बर्फ
Iron	आयरन	इस्त्री, प्रेस
Jar	जार	मर्तबान, गगरा, बड़ा बर्तन
Knit yarn	निट यार्न	बुनाई का धागा
Knitting needle	निटिंग नीड्ल	सलाई
Key	की	चाभी
Lamp	लैम्प	बत्ती
Lantern	लैन्टर्न	लालटेन
Lock	लॉक	ताला
Ladle	लैड्ल	करछुल
Mace	मैस	मुगदर
Mirror	मिरर	ऐनक
Mirror stand	मिरर स्टैंड	ऐनक रखने का उपकरण

Mat	मैट	चटाई
Match	मैच	माचिस
Match box	मैच बॉक्स	माचिस की डिबिया
Match stick	मैच स्टिक	माचिस की तीली
Mortar	मोरटार	खरल
Mosquito net	मॉस्क्विटो नेट	मच्छरदानी
Mosquito spray	मॉस्क्विटो स्प्रे	मच्छरमार छिड़काव
Mosquito coil	मॉस्क्विटो क्वायल	मच्छर अगरबत्ती
Needle	नीड्ल	सूई
Needle box	नीड्ल बाक्स	सूई की पेटी
Nut cracker	नट क्रेकर	सरौता
Nail-cutter	नेल कटर	नाखून काटने वाला
Nail sharpner	नेल शार्पेनर	नाखून चिकना करने वाला
Nail file	नेल फाइल	नाखून की रेती
Nail paint	नेल पैंट	नाखून का रंग
Oil	ऑयल	तेल
Oven	ओवेन	चूल्हा, तन्दूर
Pincers	पिंसर्स	चिमटा
Pencil	पेन्सिल	पेन्सिल
Pen	पेन	कलम
Pencil cutter	पेन्सिल कटर	पेन्सिल छिलने वाला
Perambulator	पेरैम्बुलेटर	शिशु-गाड़ी
Plate	प्लेट	थाली
Powder	पावडर	पावडर
Palanquin	पैलेंक्विन	पलंग, पालकी
Pestle	पेसल	मूसल
Pastry-board	पेस्ट्री-बोर्ड	चकला
Pillow	पिलो	तकिया
Pillow cover	पिलो कवर	तकिया का खोल
Rolling pin	रॉलिंग पिन	बेलन
Rope	रोप	रस्सी
Rack	रैक	सामान रखने के लिए फर्निचर
Spittoon	स्पिटून	पीकदान
Safe	सेफ	तिजोरी
Sack	सैक	बोरा
String	स्ट्रिंग	रस्सी
Soap	सोप	साबुन

Soap case	सोप केस	साबुनदानी
Soap cake	सोप केक	साबुन की टिकिया
Sieve	सीव	चलनी
Spoon	स्पून	चम्मच
Spoon stand	स्पून स्टैंड	चम्मच धारक
Stove	स्टोव	चूल्हा (लोहे या पीतल का)
Stick	स्टिक	छड़ी
Swing	स्विंग	झूला
Saucer	सॉसर	तश्तरी, छोटा प्लेट
Sundry	सनड्राइ	फुटकर वस्तुएँ
Sprayer	स्प्रेअर	छिड़कने वाला
Tooth paste	टूथपेस्ट	दाँतों का मंजन
Tooth powder	टूथपाउडर	दंतपाउडर
Tooth prick	टूथपिक	दाँत खोदनी
Table	टेबल	मेज
Tablet	टेबलेट	टिकिया
Table cloth	टेबल क्लाथ	मेज पोश
Table spoon	टेबल स्पून	बड़ा चम्मच
Table mat	टेबल मैट	भोजन वस्त्र
Thread	थ्रेड	कपड़ा, धागा
Tap	टैप	नल
Tray	ट्रे	सामान ठोने का बड़ा बर्तन
Thimble	थिम्बल	अंगुश्ताना
Tong	टांग	चिमटा
Taper	टैपर	छोटी मोमबत्ती
Tapestry	टैपेस्ट्री	खोल
Tassel	टैसल	रेशमी गुच्छा, फुंदना
Tankard	टैंकार्ड	चषक, जल ढोने का बड़ा बर्तन
Umbrella	अम्ब्रेला	छाता
Utensils	यूटेन्सिल्स	बर्तन
Vase	वेस	बर्तन
Wardrobe	वार्डरोब	वस्त्रधारक
Wire	वायर	तार
Wick	विक	बत्ती, बतिहर
Wool	वुल	ऊन

Appendix-18/परिशिष्ट–18
Jewels/गहने और आभूषण

Chain	चेन	कड़ी, कड़ीदार हार
Coral	कोरल	मूँगा
Cat's eye	कैट्स आई	लहसूनिया पत्थर
Crown	क्रॉन	मुकुट
Clip	क्लिप	चिमटा जैसा पकड़ने वाला
Hair clip	हेअर क्लिप	बालों का क्लिप
Pin	पिन	नुकीला पहनने का गहना
Nose pin	नोज पिन	लवंग, नाक गहना
Ear pin	इअर पिन	कान का लवंग जैसा गहना
Ring	रिंग	अँगूठी, छल्ला
Ear ring	इअर रिंग	कान का गोल गहना
Nose ring	नोज रिंग	नथिया
Toe ring	टो रिंग	पाँव की अँगुलियों का छल्ला
Sari pin	साड़ी पिन	साड़ी का काँटा
Sari clip	साड़ी क्लिप	साड़ी को पकड़ने वाला गहना
Broach	ब्रूच	साड़ी का काँटा
Tops	टॉप्स	कर्णफूल, कान का फूलदार गहना
Bangle	बैंगल	चूड़ी
Jewellery	ज्वेलरी	आभूषण, जवाहिरात
Head locket	हेड लॉकेट	माँग टीका
Ear stud	इअर स्टड	कान का तल्ला
Nose stud	नोज स्टड	नाक का तल्ला
Bracelet	ब्रैसलेट	कंगन, कड़ा
Wristlet	रिस्टलेट	तोड़ा, पहुँची
Belt	बेल्ट	कमरबन्द
Anklet	एंकलेट	पायजेब
Armlet	आर्मलेट	बाजूबंद
Neckless	नेकलेस	गले का हार
Garland	गारलैंड	माला
Tiara	टिआरा	माँग टीका, मुकुट

English		Hindi
Diamond	डायमण्ड	हीरा
Mother of pearl	मदर ऑफ पर्ल	सीप
Pearl	पर्ल	मोती
Ruby	रूबी	माणिक
Quartz	क्वार्टज	बिल्लौर
Torquois	टरकॉयज	फीरोजा
Opal	ओपल	दूधिया पत्थर
Zircon	जिरकॉन	गोमेद
Gold	गोल्ड	सोना
Silver	सिल्वर	चाँदी
Bronze	ब्राँज	ताँबा
Sapphire	सेफायर	नीलम
Emerald	इमरॉल्ड	पन्ना
Topaz	टोपाज	पुखराज

Appendix-19/परिशिष्ट–19
Musical Instruments
वाद्य-यंत्र

Veena	वीणा	वीणा
Sitar	सितार	सितार
Sarod	सरोद	सरोद
Ektara	एकतारा	एकतारा
Mridang	मृदंग	मृदंग
Corch	कोंच	शंख
Tabor	टेबर	तबला
Tomtom	टॉमटॉम	ढोलक
Drum	ड्रम	ढोल, नगाड़ा
Clorionet	क्लेरियोनेट	शहनाई
Guitar	गिटार	गिटार
Harp	हार्प	चंग, सारंगी
Symbol	सिम्बल	करताल, छैना
Tambourine	टैम्बरीन	डफ, डफली
Bugle	बगल	बिगुल, सिंघा, तुरही
Jew's harp	जिउज हार्प	मुरचंग
Flute	फ्लूट	बाँसुरी
Piano	पियानो	पियानो
Violin	वायलिन	वायलिन
Bagpipe	बैगपाइप	मशक
Bell	बेल	घंटी
Dumet	डमेट	डुगडुगी
String instrument	स्ट्रिंग इन्स्ट्रूमेंट	तारवाद्य
Brass	ब्रास	ताम्बे के वायुवाद्य
Woodwind instrument	वुडविंड इन्स्ट्रूमेंट	लकड़ी के वायु वाद्य
Jazz instrument	जाज इन्स्ट्रूमेंट	जाज के सेट
Percussion	परक्यूशन	पीटकर बजाने वाले वाद्य
Bango	बैंगो	बैंगो
Congo	कौंगो	कौंगो
Timpani	टिम्पानी	टिम्पानी

Bass drum	बास ड्रम	बड़ा ढोल
Drum stick	ड्रम स्टिक	ठोल बजाने का डंडा
Keyboard	की बोर्ड	पटरी युक्त बोर्ड
Reed	रीड	पटरी
Saxophone	सेक्सोफोन	एक मोटी आवाज का पीतल का बाजा
Acoustic guitar	एकॉस्टिक गिटार	गिटार का एक प्रकार
Electric guitar	इलेक्ट्रिक गिटार	गिटार का एक प्रकार
Drum kit	ड्रम किट	ढोलों का समूह
Triangle	ट्रिंगल	तिकोना बाजा
Bassoon	बैसुन	बैसुन
Piccolo	पिकोलो	पिकोलो
Tuba	ट्यूबा	ट्यूबा
French horn	फ्रेंच हॉर्न	फ्रेंच हॉर्न
Trombone	ट्रॉम्बॉन	ट्राम्बॉन
Trumpet	ट्रम्पेट	तुरही
Viola	वायला	बेला या वायलिन का एक प्रकार
Xylophone	जाइलोफोन	जाइलोफोन
Banjo	बेंजो	बेंजो
Harmonica	हारमोनिका	माउथ आरगन
Mouth organ	माउथ ऑर्गन	मुँह से बजाने का बाजा
Harmonium	हारमोनियम	हारमोनियम
Whistle	ह्विसल	सीटी
Bell	बेल	घंटी

Appendix-20/परिशिष्ट–20
Classified Vocabulury (वर्गीकृत शब्दावली)

Parts of Body
शरीर के अंग

Ring finger	रिंग फिंगर	अनामिका
Toe	टो	अँगुली पैर की
Finger	फिंगर	अँगुली हाथ की
Thumb	थम	अँगूठा
Eye	आई	आँख
Intestine	इन्टेस्टाइन	आँत, अंतड़ी
Cartilage	कार्टिलिज	उपास्थि
Lip	लिप	ओंठ
Heel	हील	एड़ी
Shoulder	शोल्डर	कंधा
Temple	टैम्पल	कनपटी
Waist	वेस्ट	कमर
Eardrum	ईयरड्रम	कर्णपटल
Wrist	रिस्ट	कलाई
Ear	ईयर	कान
Little finger	लिटिल फिंगर	छोटी अँगुली
Armpit	आर्मपिट	काँख, बगल
Elbow	एल्बो	कोहनी
Skull	स्कल	खोपड़ी
Neck	नैक	गर्दन, ग्रीवा
Womb	वूम	गर्भाशय
Uterus	यूटेरस	गर्भाशय
Whiskers	व्हिस्कर्स	गालमुच्छ
Throat	थ्रोट	गला
Cheeks	चीक्स	गाल
Anus	ऐनस	गुदा
Kidney	किडनी	गुर्दा, वृक्क
Lap	लैप	गोद

English		Hindi
Knee	नी	घुटना
Skin	स्किन	चमड़ा
Nipple	निप्पल	चूचुक
Rump	रम्प	चूतड़
Face	फेस	चेहरा
Chest	चैस्ट	छाती पुरुष की
Breast	ब्रैस्ट	छाती स्त्री की
Stomach	स्टोमक	आमाशय
Jaw	जॉ	जबड़ा
Thigh	थाइ	जाँघ
Liver	लिवर	जिगर
Tongue	टंग	जीभ
Bun	बन	जूड़ा बालो का
Ankle	ऐंकल	टखना
Joint	जाएंट	जोड़
Chin	चिन	ठुड्डी
Index finger	इंडैक्स फिंगर	तर्जनी
Sole	सोल	तलवा
Palate	पैलेट	तालू
Snout	स्नाउट	थूथन
Molar teeth	मोलर टीथ	चबाने वाला दाँत
Beard	बिअर्ड	दाढ़ी
Tooth	टूथ	दाँत
Brain	ब्रेन	दिमाग
Artery	आर्टरी	धमनी
Nail	नेल	नाखून
Nostril	नॉस्ट्रिल	नथुना
Vein	वेन	नस
Nose	नोज	नाक
Pulse	पल्स	नाड़ी
Navel	नेवल	नाभि
Gullet	गलेट	निगल नली
Eyelid	आइलिड	पलक
Rib	रिब	पसली
Spleen	स्प्लिन	प्लीहा

Calf	काफ	पिंडली
Bile	बाइल	पत्ति
Back	बैक	पीठ
Belly	बैली	पेट बाहरी
Abdomen	ऐब्डोमेन	पेट
Eyeball	आइबॉल	पुतली आँख की
Muscle	मस्ल	मांसपेशी
Foot	फुट	पैर
Lung	लंग	फेफड़ा
Armpit	आर्मपिट	बगल
Eyelash	आइलैश	बरौनी
Hair	हेयर	बाल, रोंवा
Arm	आर्म	बाँह
Vagina	वजिना	भग, योनि
Glans clitoris	गलैन्स क्लिटोरिस	भगनास
Embryo	एम्ब्रयो	भ्रूण
Eyebrow	आइब्रो	भौंह, भृकुटि
Middle finger	मिड्ल फिंगर	मध्यमिक
Gum	गम	मसूड़ा
Brain	ब्रेन	मस्तिष्क
Fist	फिस्ट	मुट्ठी
Mouth	माउथ	मुख
Urinary bladder	यूरिनरी ब्लेडर	मूत्राशय
Moustache	मास्टेच	मूँछ
Nerve	नर्व	रग
Pore	पोर	रोमकूप
Forehead	फोरहेड	ललाट
Saliva	सेलिवा	लार
Penis	पेनिस	लिंग
Blood	ब्लड	लहू, रक्त, खून
Trunk	ट्रंक	मध्य धड़
Bone	बोन	हड्डी
Palm	पाम	हथेली
Collar bone	कालर बोन	हसुली की हड्डी
Heart	हॉर्ट	हृदय

Ailments & Body Conditions
रोग और शारीरिक दशाएँ

Pericardium	पेरीकार्डियम	हृदयावरण
Acidity	एसिडिटी	अम्ल पित्त, गैस
Diarrhoea	डायरिया	अतिसार
Hernia	हर्निया	आँत उतरना
Tears	टिअर्स	आँसू
Eczema	एग्जिमा	उकवत
Yawn	यॉन	उबासी
Stature	स्टैचर	कद
Vomit	वौमिट	कै करना
Indigestion	इंडाइजैशन	बदहजमी
Blind	ब्लाइंड	अन्धा
Jaundice	जॉन्डिस	कामला, पीलिया
Typhus	टाइफस	काला ज्वर
Bronchitis	ब्रॉनकाइटिस	कास
One eyed	वन आइड	काना
Hunchback	हन्चबैक	कुबड़ा
Leprosy	लेप्रोसी	कोढ़, कुष्ठ
Constipation	कांस्टिपेशन	कब्ज
Worm	वर्म	कृमि
Measles	मीजल्स	खसरा
Scabies	स्कैबीज	खाज
Cough	कफ	खाँसी
Itch	इच	खुजली
Anaemia	एनेमिया	खून की कमी
Bleeding	ब्लीडिंग	खून का बहना
Rheumatism	रूमेटिज्म	रूठिया
Abortion	एबॉर्शन	गर्भपात
Syphilis	सिफलिस	गरमी
Sore throat	सोर थ्रोट	गलदाह
Hoarseness	होर्सनैस	गला बैठना
Tonsil	टॉन्सिल	गलसुआ

Tumour	ट्यूमर	गाँठ
Gland	ग्लैंड	गिल्टी
Dumb	डम	गूँगा
Bald	बॉल्ड	गंजा
Wound	वून्ड	घाव
Giddiness	गिडीनैस	चक्कर आने की स्थिति
Obesity	ओबेसिटी	चर्बी बढ़ना
Hurt	हर्ट	चोट
Sneezing	स्नीजिंग	छींकना
Cancer	कैंसर	जहरबाद
Dropsy	ड्राप्सी	जलोदर
Coryza	कोरिजा	जुकाम
Ague	ऐग्यू	शीतज्वर
Yawning	यॉनिंग	जंभाई
Fever	फीवर	ज्वर, बुखार
Chill	चिल	ठंड
Belching	वैल्चिंग	डकार
Health	हैल्थ	तन्दरुस्ती
Spittle	स्पिटल	थूक
Asthma	एस्थमा	दमा
Pain	पेन	दर्द
Headache	हैडेक	दर्द सिर का
Stomachache	स्टमकएक	दर्द पेट का
Loose stool	लूज स्टूल	दस्त
Motion	मोशन	दस्त
Ring worm	रिंगवर्म	दाद
Lean	लीन	दुबला
Psychosis	साइकोसिस	दुस्साध्य उन्माद
Long- sightedness	लांग साइटिडनैस	दूरदृष्टि
Bronchitis	ब्रानकाइटिस	श्वासनली शोध
Epistaxis	एपिसटैक्सिस	नकसीर
Sprain	स्प्रेन	मोच
Narcolepsy	नार्कोलैप्सी	निद्रा रोग
Sleep	स्लीप	नींद
Insomnia	इन्सोम्निया	नींद न आना

Stone	स्टोन	पथरी
Sweat	स्वैट	पसीना
Mad	मैड	पागल
Lunacy	ल्यूनेसी	पागलपन, उन्माद
Pus	पस	पीव
Dysentery	डाइसेंट्री	पेचिश
Leucorrhoea	लिकोरिया	प्रदर
Thirst	थर्स्ट	प्यास
Plague	प्लेग	प्लेग, महामारी
Pimple	पिम्पल	फुंसी, मुहांसा
Boil	बॉयल	फोड़ा
Phlegm	फ्लेग	बलगम, कफ
Piles	पाइल्स	बवासीर
Diabetes	डायबिटीज	मधुमेह
Sore	सोर	वृण
Dwarff	डवार्फ	बौना
Fistula	फिस्टुला	भगन्दर
Lack of appetite	लैक ऑफ एपिटाइट	मन्दाग्नि
Griping	ग्राइपिंग	मरोड़
Wart	वॉर्ट	मस्सा
Epilepsy	एपिलैप्सी	मिरगी
Acne	एक्नि	मुंहासे का रोग
Urine	यूरिन	मूत्र
Cataract	कैटेरेक्ट	मोतियाबिन्द
Typhoid	टायफायड	मोतीझरा
Hepatitis	हेपाटिटिस	यकृत शोध
Sun stroke	सनस्ट्रोक	लू लगना
Stool	स्टूल	विष्टा
Tuberculosis	ट्यूबर कुलोसिस	राजयक्ष्मा
Disease	डिजीज	रोग
Lame	लेम	लंगड़ा
Dengue	डेंगू	लंगड़ा बुखार
Influenza	इन्फ्लुएन्जा	शीतज्वर
Small pox	स्माल पॉक्स	शीतला
Leucoderma	ल्यूकोडेर्मा	श्वेत कुष्ठ

Breath	ब्रेथ	साँस
Swelling	स्वैलिंग	सूजन
Albino	एल्बिनो	सूरजमुखी
Gonorrhoea	गोनोरिया	सूजाक
Hiccup	हिक्कप	हिचकी
Cholera	कॉलरा	हैजा
Pericarditis	पैरिकार्डिटिस	हृदय झिल्ली शोध
Consumption	कनसम्पशन	क्षय
Anorexia	ऐनोरेक्सिया	अरुचि

Dress
वेशभूषा

Lining	लाइनिंग	अस्तर
Sleeve	स्लीव	आस्तीन
Bodice	बॉडिस	चोली, अंगिया
Hat	हैट	अंग्रेजी टोपी
Wool	वूल	ऊन
Cloth	क्लॉथ	कपड़ा
Belt	बैल्ट	कमरबन्द
Shirt	शर्ट	कमीज
Shirting	शर्टिंग	कमीज का कपड़ा
Blanket	ब्लैंकेट	कम्बल
Cap	कैप	टोपी
Cashmere	कैशमीर	कश्मीरा
Diaper brocade	डिआपर ब्रोकेड	कामदानी
Border	बॉर्डर	किनारा
Canvas	कैनवास	किरमिच
Coat	कोट	कोट
Suit	सूट	कोट-पतलून
Mattress	मैट्रेस	गद्दा
Suspenders	सस्पैंडर्स	गैलिस
Muffler	मफलर	गुलूबन्द
Skirt	स्कर्ट	घाघरा

Veil	वेल	घूँघट
Sheet	शीट	चादर
Chints	चिंट्स	छींट
Socks	सॉक्स	छोटा मोजा
Damask	डैमस्क	रेशमी वस्त्र
Gauze	गॉज	जाली
Underwear	अंडरवियर	जांघिया
Drill	ड्रिल	जीन
Pocket	पॉकेट	जेब
Trimming	ट्रिमिंग	झालर
Cap	कैप	टोपी
Scarf	स्कार्फ	दुपट्टा
Laces	लेसिस	तसमे
Thread	थ्रैड	तागा
Towel	टॉवेल	तौलिया
Gloves	ग्लव्स	दस्ताने
Shawl	शॉल	दुशाला
Lace	लेस	पट्टा
Trousers	ट्राउजर्स	पतलून
Pyjama	पाजामा	पाजामा
Jacket	जैकेट	फतुही
Flannel	फ्लैनेल	फलालीन
Tape	टेप	फीता
Button	बटन	बटन
Overcoat	ओवरकोट	बड़ा कोट
Velvet	वेल्वेट	मखमल
Border	बॉर्डर	मगजी
Linen	लिनेन	मलमल
Stockings	स्टॉकिंस	मोजे
Oil-cloth	आइल क्लॉथ	मोमजामा
Quilt	क्विल्ट	रजाई
Darning	डार्निंग	रफू
Cotton	कॉटन	रूई
Handker chief	हैंडकर-चीफ	रूमाल
Silk	सिल्क	रेशम

Gown	गाउन	चोगा
Long cloth	लांग क्लाथ	लट्ठा
Long skirt	लांग स्कर्ट	लहंगा
Uniform	यूनिफार्म	वर्दी
Satin	सैटेन	साटन
Turban	टर्बन	साफा
Yarn	यार्न	सूत
Bright colour	ब्राइट कलर	चटख रंग
Light colour	लाइट कलर	हल्का रंग

Appendix-21/परिशिष्ट—21
Antonyms/विपरीतार्थक शब्द

Above	ऊपर	Below	नीचे
Aceept	स्वीकारना	Deny	नकारना
Acquire	कमाना	Lose	गंवाना
Ancient	प्राचीन	Modern	नवीन
Agree	सहमत होना	Differ	असहमति होना
Alive	जीवित	Dead	मृत
Admire	प्रशंसा	Despise	निन्दा
Big	बड़ा	Small	छोटा
Blunt	कुंद	Sharp	तेज
Bold	साहसी	Timid	कायर
Bright	चमकीला	Dim	धुंधला
Broad	चौड़ा	Narrow	पतला
Civilised	सभ्य	Savage	असभ्य
Care	देखभाल	Neglect	लापरवाही
Clean	साफ	Dirty	गंदा
Confess	स्वीकारना	Deny	इनकार करना
Cool	ठंडा	Warm	गर्म
Cruel	क्रूर	Kind	दयालु
Domestic	पालतू	Wild	जंगली
Difficult	कठिन	Easy	आसान
Danger	खतरा	Safety	सुरक्षा
Dark	अंधेरा	Bright	उजाला
Death	मृत्यु	Birth	जन्म
Debit	उधार	Credit	जमा
Early	जल्दी	Late	बिलम्ब
Earn	कमाना	Spend	खर्च करना
Empty	खाली	Full	भरा हुआ
Enjoy	मौज मनाना	Suffer	तकलीफ रहना
Freedom	स्वतंत्रता	Slavery	गुलामी
Fierce	निर्दय	Gentle	नम्र
False	झूठ	True	सच
Fine	महीन	Coarse	मोटा
Foolish	मूर्ख	Wise	बुद्धिमान

Fresh	ताजा	Stale	बासी
Fear	भय	Courage	साहस
Guilty	दोषी	Innocent	निर्दोष
Gain	लाभ	Loss	हानि
Good	अच्छा	Bad	बुरा
Handsome	सुन्दर	Ugly	कुरूप
High	ऊँचा	Low	नीचा
Humble	विनम्र	Proud	घमंडी
Honour	सम्मान	Dishonour	अपमान
Joy	हर्ष	Sorrow	विषाद
Knowledge	ज्ञान	Ignorance	अज्ञान
Lie	झूठ	Truth	सच
Little	थोड़ा	Much	ज्यादा
Masculine	पुल्लिंग	Feminine	स्त्रीलिंग
Make	बनाना	Break	तोड़ना
Natural	प्राकृतिक	Artificial	कृत्रिम
Noise	शोर	Silence	मौन
Oral	मौखिक	Written	लिखित
Permanent	स्थायी	Temporary	अस्थायी
Presence	उपस्थिति	Absence	अनुपस्थिति
Profit	लाभ	Loss	हानि
Prose	गद्य	Poetry	काव्य
Quick	तेज	Slow	धीमा
Receive	पाना	Give	देना
Reject	अस्वीकार	Accept	स्वीकार
Ripe	पका	Raw	कच्चा
Rough	खुरदुरा	Smooth	चिकना
Remember	याद करना	Forgot	भूल जाना
Rich	धनी	Poor	गरीब
Superior	बढ़िया	Interior	घटिया
Thick	मोटा	Thin	दुबला
Tragedy	दुःखान्त	Comedy	सुखान्त
Universal	सर्वजनीय	Particular	व्यक्तिगत
Victory	विजय	Defeat	हार
Weak	कमजोर	Strong	मजबूत
Wisdom	बुद्धिमान	Folly	मूर्खता
Youth	युवा	Aged	अधेड़

Appendix-22/परिशिष्ट–22
Synonyms /समानार्थक शब्द

Aid	सहायता	Assistance, help, relief, support
Apology	क्षमायाचना	Pardon, excuse, regret, amends
Adversity	मुसीबत	Misery, calamity, misfortune
Ability	योग्यता	Capacity, capability, skill, talent
Anger	क्रोध	Fury, rage, wrath
Answer	उत्तर	Reply, response, respond
Attack	आक्रमण	Onslaught, assault, aggression, invasion
Actual	वास्तविक	Current, real, effectual
Bane	शाप	Curse, scourge, mischief, harm
Barbarous	असभ्य	Cruel, uncivilized, savage, illiterate
Bear	सहन करना	Tolerate, endure
Belief	आस्था	Confidence, faith, trust, credence
Beautiful	सुन्दर	Gratifying, delighting, lovely, charming
Brave	साहसी	Fearless, courageous, bold, valiant
Busy	व्यस्त	Engaged, occupied, preoccupied, employed
Capture	पकड़ना	Arrest, apprehend, seize, nab
Clever	चालाक	Ingenious, skilful
Confess	दोष स्वीकारना	Avow, acknowledge, own, admit
Coquer	जीतना	Vanquish, overcome, win, triumph
Crown	ताज	Skull, dignity, tiara
Convict	अपराधी	Prisoner, criminal, captive
Command	आदेश	Control, order, restrain
Cunning	धूर्त	Strewed, witty, sly, crafty
Decide	निर्णय लेना	Determine, settle, fix, finalize
Decent	शानदार	Proper, modest, tolerable
Defeat	पराजय	Frustrate, foil, reject
Delightful	आनन्ददायक	Enjoyable, pleasing, charming, alluring
Desolate	निर्जन	Lonely, forlorn, barren, solitary
Despise	घृणा करना	Disdain, dislike, hate, scorn
Destroy	नष्ट करना	Demolish, devastate, ruin, ravage
Devotee	भक्त	Worshipper, votary, disciple

Disaster	बरबादी	Misfortune, calamity, tragedy
Discover	अन्वेषण	Find, reveal, disclose, discern
Dispute	विवाद	Controversy, argument, quarrel
Distribute	वितरण	Scatter, divide, classify
Divine	स्वर्गिक	Celestial, godlike, holy
Doubt	सन्देह	Hesitate, suspense, uncertainly
Dull	मूर्ख	Blunt, stupid, boring
Earnest	गम्भीर	Solemn, serious, determined
Effert	प्रयत्न	Endeavour, attempt, venture, trial
Enemy	शत्रु	Adversary, opponent, foe, antagonist
Enoronous	विशाल	Huge, tremendous, stupendous
Enthusiasm	उत्साह	Force, spirit, zest, fervour
Eternal	अनन्त	Immortal, everlasting, endless
Fade	धुंधला	Vanish, dim, pale, languish
Fatal	घातक	Deadly , lethal, fateful, mortal
Fierce	भयंकर	Savage, ferocious, aggressive
Forbod	प्रतिबंधित	Ban, prohibit, check
Fury	रोष	Rage, excitement, anger
Gloom	निराशा	Dejection, shadow, darkness
Glory	कीर्ति	Fame, pride, splendor
Grief	दुःख	Sorrow, distress, tribulation
Hard	कठिन	Rough, difficult, solid, firm
Haven	शरण	Refuge, protection, settler
Holy	पवित्र	Godly, pious, blessed, saintly
Hope	आशा	Desire, anticipation, expectation
Horror	भय	Terror, dread, disgust
Humble	विनम्र	Modest, meek, submissive
Ideal	आदर्श	Model, example, perfect, paragon
Idle	आलसी	Unemployed, inactive, futile, useless
Immortal	अमर	Divine, everlasting, eternal
Industrious	परिश्रमी	Hardworking, assiduous, diligent
Infinite	अनन्त	Limitless, boundless, endless, timeless
Jealous	ईर्ष्यालु	Envious, suspicious
Kill	मारना	Assassinate, murder, behead
Lack	कमी	Shortage, deficiency, need, want

Lazy	आलसी	Indolent, sluggish, slothful
Lusture	चमक	Shining, brilliance, brightness
Marvel	आश्चर्य	Surprise, wonder, miracle
Mourn	शोक	Bewail, aggrieve, lament, bemoan
Naughty	शरारती	Mischievous, troublesome, disobedient
Obstacle	बाधा	Barrier, hindrance, obstruction
Obvious	स्पष्ट	Plain, manifest, evident, clear
Outlaw	अपराधी	Criminal, bandit, fugitive
Outstanding	विशिष्ट	Eminent, prominent, exceptional
Overcome	विजय	Conquer, overthrow, surmount
Pain	दुःख	Suffering, misery, distress
Peak	चोटी	Apex, top, summit, pinnacle
Pledge	प्रतिज्ञा	Security, promise, vow, oath
Pray	प्रार्थना	Beg, request, revere
Precious	मूल्यवान	Priceless, costly, invaluable, dear
Pressure	दबाव	Force, urgency, affection
Prevent	रोकना	Restrain, hinder, check, stop
Proficient	कुशल	Skilful, expert, adept
Prominent	प्रसिद्ध	Distinguished, notable, eminent
Protect	रक्षा करना	Guard, defend, save, shield
Quarrel	झगड़ा	Controversy, dispute, wrangle
Question	प्रश्न	Inquiry, interrogation, doubt
Regard	सम्मान	Respect, esteem, worship
Soothe	शान्ति देना	Console, comfort, assuage
Splendid	शानदार	Glorious, magnificent, gorgeous
State	बासी	Musty, tasteless, decayed, insipid
Struggle	संघर्ष	Try, endeavour, fight, strive
Understanding	समझ	Insight, perception, comprehension
Unique	विचित्र	Matchless, singular, unequalled
Vice	पाप	Wickedness, sin, degradation
Victory	विजय	Success, conquer, triumph, win
View	दृश्य	Sight, scene, display
Vigour	शक्ति	Energy, force, power
Wisdom	बुद्धिमान	Prudence, intelligence, foresight
Wretched	दुःखी	Unfortunate, miserable, deplorable

Appendix-23/परिशिष्ट–23
One word Substitute
अनेक शब्दों के बदले एक शब्द

Alien	विदेशी नागरिक	A citizen of another country
Ambassador	राजदूत	An official person sent to another country
Antidote	विषहर	A medicine to counter the effect of a disease
Antiseptic	घाव नियन्त्रक	A medicine which prevents decay
Antibiotic	जीवाणुनाशक	A medicine which destroys bacteria
Atheist	नास्तिक	A man who does not believe in God
Audience	श्रोता	A group of listeners
Bigot	कट्टरपंथी	A person who holds strongly to an opion
Biography	आत्मकथा	Life story of a person written by somebody else
Bankrupt	दीवालिया	A person who is incapable of paying his debts
Cosmetics	प्रसाधन	The things used to increase physical beauty
Credible	विश्वसनीय	That can be believed
Deaf	बहरा	One who is incapable of listening a sound
Democracy	प्रजातन्त्र	A government by the people
Drought	सूखा	Lack of rain
Edible	खाने योग्य	Fit to eat or consume
Eligible	योग्य	Fit to be chosen
Epidemic	महामारी	A disease which spreads over a large area
Export	निर्यात	Things sent to another country
Fatal	घातक	Which may cause death
Foreigner	विदेशी	A person of another country
Glutton	पेटू	An over eating person
Honorary	अवैतनिक	An office without pay or emolument
Ignorant	अनभिज्ञ	A person who lacks in knowledge
Illegal	अवैधानिक	Contrary to law

Invincible	अजेय	That which cannot be conquered
Inavdible	आश्रव्य	That which cannot be heared
Inedible	अखाद्य	A thing unfit for eating
Inflammable	प्रज्वलनशील	That which catches fire easily
Illigible	अपठनीय	Which cannot be read
Illiterate	अनपढ़	A person who can neither read not write
Indelible	अमिट	Which cannot be effaced
Invincible	अजेय	He who can not be defeated
Laboratory	प्रयोगशाला	A place where experiments are performed
Library	पुस्तकालय	A place where various books are kept
Optimist	आशावादी things	One who looks at the bright side of
Orphan	अनाथ	A child whose parents are dead
Patriot	देशभक्त	One who has great love for his country
Pedestrian	पदयात्री	One travels on foot
Pilgrim	तीर्थयात्री place	One who goes on a journey to a holy
Spokesman	प्रवक्ता	A person who speaks on behalf
Theist	आस्तिक	One who believes in God
Vegetarian	शाकाहारी	One who lives on vegetative food
Widow	विधवा	A woman whose husband is dead
Zoo	चिड़ियाघर	A place where animals are kept

Appendix-24/परिशिष्ट–24
Homophones Pairs of Words
श्रुतिसम भिन्नार्थक शब्द

Accede	सहमत होना	Exceed	अधिक होना
Accept	स्वीकार करना	Except	सिवाय
Adapt	समायोजित होना	Adept	प्रवीण
Affect	प्रभाव होना	Effect	प्रभाव
Alien	विदेशी	Align	सीध में रहना
All ready	सब तैयार	Already	पहले से ही
Altar	वेदी	Alter	बदलना
Amiable	मधुर	Amicable	मैत्रीपूर्ण
Artist	कलाकार	Artiste	पेशेवर कलाकार
Ascent	चढ़ाई	Assent	स्वीकृति
Berth	सीट	Birth	जन्म
Beside	निकट पास में	Besides	के अतिरिक्त
Bonne	अच्छा	Bone	अस्थि
Chase	पीछा करना	Chess	शतरंज
Chaste	पवित्र	Chest	छाती
Chord	वाद्ययन्त्र का तार	Cord	डोरी
Check	रोकना, जाँच करना	Cheque	धनादेश
Cite	उदाहरण देना	Site	स्थान
Coarse	मोटा, भद्दा	Course	पाठ्यक्रम
Complement	पूरक	Compliment	सम्मान, शुभकामनाएँ
Confidant	विश्वासपात्र	Confident	आश्वस्त
Corps	सेना की शाखा	Corpse	मानक शव
Deference	सम्मान	Difference	अन्तर
Deprecate	असहमति	Depreciate	कम करके आँकना
Decent	विनीत, शानदार	Descent	नीचे उतरना
Die	मरना	Dye	रंगना
Draught	हवा का झोंका	Drought	सूखा
Dual	दोहरा	Duel	द्वन्द्व युद्ध
Egoist	स्वार्थी	Egotist	अहंकारी
Eligible	योग्य	Illegible	अपठनीय
Eminent	प्रसिद्ध	Imminent	शीघ्र घटित होने वाली

Ensure	सुनिश्चित करना	Insure	बीमा करना
Expense	व्यय	Expanse	विस्तार
Fair	मेला	Fare	किराया
Feat	साहसिक कार्य	Feet	पैर
Flea	पिस्सू	Flee	भाग जाना
Gaol	जेल	Goal	लक्ष्य
Groan	कराहना	Grown	प्रौढ़
Human	मानव	Humane	सहृदय
Idle	आलसी	Idol	मूर्ति
Incite	उकसाना	Insight	अन्तर्दृष्टि
Jealous	ईर्ष्यालु	Zealous	उत्साही
Lessen	कम करना	Lesson	पाठ
Lose	खोना, गंवाना	Loose	ढीला
Marry	विवाह करना	Merry	प्रसन्नता
Meter	मीटर, यन्त्र	Metre	इकाई
Miner	खनिज खोदने वाला	Minor	लघु, पुच्छ
Need	आवश्यकता	Knead	गूँथना
Peace	शान्ति	Piece	टुकड़ा
Pray	प्रार्थना करना	Prey	शिकार
Rage	तीव्र क्रोध	Raise	उठाना
Rest	विश्राम	Wrest	ऐंठना
Root	जड़	Route	मार्ग
Sale	बिक्री	Sell	बेचना
Siege	घेरा डालना	Seize	जब्त कर लेना
Storey	मंजिल	Story	कहानी
Soar	उड़ना	Sore	पीड़ा युक्त
Soar	खट्टा	Shore	समुद्र तट
Stationary	स्थिर	Stationery	लेखन सामग्री
Tail	पूँछ	Tale	कहानी
Taste	स्वाद	Test	परीक्षण
Troop	सेना की टुकड़ी	Troupe	मण्डली
Umpire	निर्णायक	Empire	साम्राज्य
Urban	नगरीय	Urbane	सुसंस्कृत
Vacation	छुट्टी	Vocation	व्यवसाय
Vale	घाटी	Veil	घूँघट
Vain	व्यर्थ	Vein	नस
Waste	बर्बाद करना	Waist	कमर

Appendix-25/परिशिष्ट—25
Designations/कुछ पदनाम

Chairman & Managing Director	अध्यक्ष एवं प्रबन्ध निदेशक
Executive Director	कार्यपालक निदेशक
General Manager	महाप्रबन्धक
Joint-general Manger	संयुक्त महाप्रबन्धक
Deputy General Manager	उपमहाप्रबन्धक
Secretary	सचिव
Manager	प्रबन्धक
Chief Manager	मुख्य प्रबन्धक
Branch Manager	शाखा प्रबन्धक
Divisional Manager	मण्डल प्रबन्धक
Chief Officer	मुख्य अधिकारी
Accountant	लेखाकार
Security Officer	सुरक्षा अधिकारी
Medical Mfficer	चिकित्साधिकारी
Law Officer	विधि अधिकारी
Investigation Officer	जाँच अधिकारी
Head Clerk	प्रधानलिपिक
Translator	अनुवादक
Typist	टंकण
Cashier	खजांची
Bill Collector	बिल संग्राहक
Publication	प्रकाशन
Publisher	प्रकाशक
Publishing	प्रकाशन व्यवसाय
Author	पुस्तक लेखक/रचयिता
Writer	लेखक
Editor	सम्पादक
News Editor	समाचार सम्पादक
Chief Sub-editor	मुख्य उप-सम्पादक
Sub Editor	उप-सम्पादक
Proof Reader	लेख त्रुटि शोधक
Printer	मुद्रक
Superintendent of Police	पुलिस अधीक्षक

Appendix-26/परिशिष्ट—26
Occupation/व्यवसाय

News-agent–अखबार वाला

Professor–अध्यापक

Milkmaid–अहिरिन

Milkman–अहीर

Engineer–इंजीनियर

Butcher–कसाई

Artist–कारीगर

Farmer–किसान

Book-seller–किताब फरोश

Coolie–कुली

Coachman–कोचवान

Banker–कोठीवाल

Treasurer–खजांची

Turner–खरादने वाला

Retailer–खुदरा विक्रेता

Perfumer–गन्धी

Coachman–गाड़ीवान

Author–ग्रन्थकार

Postman–चिट्ठीरसाँ

Surgeon–जर्राह

Sailor–जहाजी

Magician–जादूगर

Book-binder–जिल्दसाज

Weaver–जुलाहा

Shoe-maker–जूता बनाने वाला

Jeweller–जौहरी

Compositor–टाइप बैठाने वाला

Brasier–ठठेरा

Contractor–ठीकेदार

Doctor–डाक्टर

Drummer–तबलची

Betel-seller–तमोली

Oil-man–तेली

Sorcerer–तान्त्रिक

Tailor–दर्जी

Broker–दलाल

Druggist–दवा विक्रेता

Midwife–दाई

Dentist–दाँत बनाने वाला

Shopkeeper–दुकानदार

Nurse–धाय

Carder–धुनियाँ

Washerwoman–धोबिन

Washerman–धोबी

Baker–नानबाई

Waterman–पनभरा

Examiner–परीक्षक

Watchman–पहरेदार

Publisher–प्रकाशक

Manager–प्रबन्धकर्ता

Hawker–फेरी वाला

Photographer–फोटो वाला

Carpenter–बढ़ई

Draper–बजाज

Barrister–बारिस्टर

Seeds-man – बीच–विक्रेता

Beggar–भिक्षुक

Parcher–भूँजा

Butler–भंडारी

Fisherman–मछुवा

Repairer–मरम्त करने वाला

Boatman–मल्लाह

Proprietor–मालिक

Gardener–माली

Enamellet–मीनाकार

Agent–मुनीम

Printer–मुद्रक

Clerk–मुंशी

Sweeper–मेहतर

Cobbler–मोचो

Grocer–मोदी

Writer–लेखक

Chemist–रसायनी

Cook–रसोइयादार

Cashier–रोकड़िया

Inkman–रोशनाई वाला

Painter–रंगसाज

Dyer–रंगरेज

Carrier–लादने वाला

Writer–लेखक

Blacksmith–लोहार

Pleader–वकील

Physician–वैद्य

Teacher–शिक्षक

Groom–साईस

Vaccinator–सीतला छापने वाला

Glazier–सिकलीगर

Goldsmith–सोनार

Sculptor–संगतराश

Editor–सम्पादक

Barber–हज्जाम

Confectioner–हलवाई

Appendix-27/परिशिष्ट—27
English and Hindi Equivalents of terms used in Indian Constitution
भारतीय गणतन्त्र के संविधान में प्रयुक्त अंग्रेजी और हिन्दी के पारिभाषिक शब्द

Abandonment	परित्यजन	Administrative	प्रशासनीय
Abandonment	परित्याग	Administrative functions	प्रशासनीय कृत्य
Abridgement	न्यूनन		
Abrogate	निराकरण करना	Admiralty	नावाधिकरण
Access	प्रवेश	Admiralty	नौकाधिकरण
Accession	प्रवेशन	Admissible	ग्राह्य
Account	लेखा	Adoption	दत्तक ग्रहण
Accretion	प्रोद्भवन	Adoption	दत्तक स्वीकरण
Accrue	प्राप्त होना	Adult suffrage	वयस्क मताधिकार
Accrued	उपार्जित	Adulteration	अपमिश्रण
Accrued	प्रोद्भूत	Advance	अग्रिम धन
Accusation	अभियोग	Advance	पेशगी
Accused	अभियुक्त	Advice	मन्त्रणा
Acquisition	अर्जन अर्जी	Advice	सलाह
Act	अधिनियम	Advice, Instruction	उपदेश
Acting	कार्यकारी	Advise	मन्त्रणा देना
Actionable wrong	अभियोज्य दोष	Advisory Council	मन्त्रणा परिषद्
Ad hoc	तदर्थ	Advocate	अधिवक्ता
Adaptation	अनुकूलन	Advocate General	महाधिवक्ता
Additional Judge	अतिरिक्त न्यायाधीश	Affect prejudicially	प्रतिकूल असर डालना
Additional Judge	अपर-न्यायाधीश	Affect prejudicially	प्रतिकूल प्रभाव डालना
Addressed	सम्बोधित	Affirmation	प्रतिज्ञान
Adherence	अनुशक्ति	Agency	अभिकरण
Adjourn	अवधिदान	Agent	अभिकर्त्ता
Administered	प्रशासित	Agreement	करार
Administration	प्रशासन	Agreement	चुकती

Air Force	विमान बल	Arbitrator	मध्यस्थ
Air navigation	विमान परिवहन	Arbitrator Tribunal	मध्यस्थ न्यायाधिकरण
Air traffic	विमान यातायात	Area	क्षेत्र
Airway	वायु-पथ	Armed forces	सशस्त्र बल
Alienate	अन्य-संक्रामण	Arrest	प्रग्रहण
Alienation	अन्य-संक्रामण	Article	अनुच्छेद
Alienation	परकीकरण	As the case may be	यथास्थिति
Aliens	अन्यदेशीय	Assemble	समवेत होना
Allegation	अभिकथन	Assembly	सभा
Allegation	आरोप	Assent	अनुमति
Allegiance	निष्ठा	Assessment	निर्धारण
Allocation	बटवारा	Assign, Entrust	सौंपना
Allot	वंटन	Association	संस्था
Allotment	बाँट	Assurances of	संपत्ति हस्तांतरण पत्र
Allowance	भत्ता	transfer of property	
Amendment	संशोधन	Attachment	कुर्की
Amnesty	सर्वक्षमा	Attorney General	महान्यायवादा
Amount	राशि	Audit	लेखा परीक्षा
Annual	वार्षिक	Auditor General	महालेखापरीक्षक
Annual financial	वार्षिक वित्त विवरण	Authentication	प्रमाणीकरण
statement		Authorised	प्राधिकृत
Annuities	वार्षिकी	Authority	प्राधिकरण
Annulment	रद्द करना	Authority	प्राधिकारी
Appeal	अपील	Autonomy	स्वायत्तता
Appear	उपस्थित होना	Auxiliary	सहायक
Appended	संरक्षक संलग्न	Award	पंचाट्ञा
Application	लागू होना	Bail	जामिन
Application exercise	प्रयोग	Bank	बैंक
Appointment	नियुक्ति	Banking	महाजनी
Appropriation	विनियोग	Bankruptcy, insolvency	दिवाला
Appropriation bill	विनियोग विधेयक	Bar	रुकावट
Approval	अनुमोदन	Bet	पण लगाना
Arbitration	मध्यस्थ निर्णय	Betting	पण क्रिया

Bicameral	द्विगृही	Bureau	विभाग
Bill	बिल	Certificate	प्रमाण पत्र
Bill	विधेयक	Certiorarl	उत्प्रेषण लेख
Bill of exchange	विनिमय पत्र	Cess	उपकर
Bill of Indemnity	क्षतिपूर्ति बिल	Charge	अभियुक्ति
Bill of indemuity	परिहार विधेयक	Charge	दोषारोप
Board	बोर्ड	Charge	भार
Body	निकाय	Charities	दातव्य
Body, Corporate	निगम निकाय	Cheque	चेक
Borrowing	उधार ग्रहण	Chief	मुख्य
Broadcasting	प्रसारण	Chief Commissioner	मुख्य आयुक्त
Business	कारबार	Chief Election	मुख्य निर्वाचन आयुक्त
Business	कार्य	Commissioner	
Bye-election	उपनिर्वाचन	Chief Judge	मुख्य न्यायाधीश
Bye-law	उपविधि	Chief Justice	मुख्य न्यायाधिपति
Calculation	गणना	Chief Minister	मुख्यमन्त्री
Callings	आजीविका	Citizenship	नागरिकता
Callings tax	आजीविका कर	Civil	असैनिक
Camp	शिविर	Civil	दीवानी
Candidate	अभ्यर्थी	Civil	व्यवहार
Candidate	उम्मीदवार	Civil Court	दीवानी अदालत
Cantonment	छावनी	Civil power	असैनिक शक्ति
Capital	पूँजी	Claim	दावा
Capital	मूलधन	Clarification	स्पष्टीकरण
Capital value	मुलधन मुल्य	Clause	खण्ड
Capitation tax	प्रतिव्यक्ति कर	Code	संहिता
Casting vote	निर्णायक मत	Colonization	उपनिवेशन
Cattle pound	काँजी हौस	Commerce	वाणिज्य
Cattle pound	पशु अवरोध	Commercial	वाणिज्य सम्बन्धी
Cause	वाद	Commercial Tax	व्यापार कर
Cause of action	वादमूल	Commission	आयोग
Census	जनगणना	Commissioner	आयुक्त
Central Intelligence	केन्द्रीय गुप्तवार्ता	Common good	सार्वजनिक व्यवस्था

Common seal	सामान्य मुहर	Context	प्रसंग
Common seal	सार्वजनिक अभिसूचना	Contingency Fund	आकस्मिकता निधि
Communicate	संचार करना	Contract	संविदा
Communication	संचार	Contravention	उल्लंघन
Community	लोक समाज	Contravention	प्रतिकूलता
Community	समुदाय	Contribution	अंशदान
Commute	लघुकरण	Control	नियन्त्रण
Company	कम्पनी	Controller & Auditor	नियन्त्रक महालेखा
Company	समवाय	General	परीक्षक
Compensation	प्रतिकर	Controversy	वाद प्रतिवाद
Competent	क्षमताशाली	Convention	अभिसमय
Competent	सक्षम	Convicted	अभिशस्त
Complaint	फरियाद	Convicted	दोष–प्रमाणित
Computation	संगणना	Convicted	सिद्ध दोष
Concurrence	सहमति	Conviction	अभिशस्ति
Concurrent list	समवर्ती सूची	Conviction	दोष सिद्धि
Condition	शर्त	Co-operative society	समवाय संस्था
Condition of service	सेवा की शर्त	Co-operative Society	सहकारी संस्था
Conference	सम्मेलन	Copy	प्रतिकृति
Conscience	अन्त:करण	Copy	प्रतिलिपि
Consent	सम्मति	Corporation	निगम
Consideration	विचार	Corporation sole	एकल निगम
Consolidated Fund	संचित निधि	Corporation tax	निगम कर
Constituency	निर्वाचन क्षेत्र	Corrupt	भ्रष्ट
Constituent Assembly	संविधान सभा	Cost	खर्च
Constitution	संविधान	Cost	परिव्यय
Construe	अर्थ–दण्ड	Cost	लागत
Consul	वाणिज्यदूत	Council	परिषद्
Consultation	परामर्श	Council of Ministers	मन्त्रि परिषद्
Consumption	उपभोग	Council of States	राज्य परिषद्
Contact	सम्पर्क	Countervailing duties	प्रति शुल्क
Contempt	अवमान	Court	न्यायालय
Contempt of Court	न्यायालय अवमान	Court Martial	सेना न्यायालय

Court of Appeal	अपील न्यायालय	Deliberate	पर्यालोचन
Court of Appeal	पुनर्विचार न्यायालय	Delimitation	परिसीमन
Court of record	अभिलेख न्यायालय	Demand	अभियाचना
Court of Wards	प्रतिपालक अधिकरण	Demand	माँग
Credit	पत	Demarcation	सीमांकन
Crime, offence	अपराध	Demobilization	सैन्य वियोजन
Criminal	अपराधी	Deprive	वियुक्त करना
Criminal	आपराधिक	Deprive	वंचित करना
Criminal	दंड सम्बन्धी	Deputy Chairman	उपसभापति
Criminal Court	दंड न्यायालय	Deputy Commissioner	उपायुक्त
Criminal Law	दंड विधि	Deputy Speaker	उपाध्यक्ष
Current	प्रचलित	Derogation	अल्पीकरण
Custody	अभिरक्षा	Descent	उद्भव
Custody	कावल	Design	रूपांकन
Custom	आचार	Detrimental	अहितकारी
Custom	रूढ़ि	Diplomacy	राजनय
Custom duty	बहि:शुल्क	Direct election	प्रत्यक्ष निर्वाचन
Custom duty	सीमा शुल्क	Direction	निर्देश
Customs duty	शुल्क सीमान्त	Disability	नियोग्यता
Dealing	व्यवहार	Discharge	निर्वहन
Dealings	लेना-देना	Disciplinary	अनुशासन-सम्बन्धी
Death duty	मरण शुल्क	Discipline	अनुशासन
Debate	वाद-विवाद	Discover	प्रकट करना
Debenture	ऋणपत्र	Discretion	स्वविवेक
Debt	ऋण	Discrimination	विभेद
Decision	विनिश्च	Discussion	चर्चा
Declaration	घोषणा	Dismiss	पदच्युत करना
Decree	आज्ञप्ति	Dispersion	विसर्जन
Decree	डिक्री	Dispute	विवाद
Dedicate	समर्पण	Disqualification	अनर्हता
Deed	विलेख	Disqualification	अनर्हीकरण
Defamation Validity	मानहानि मान्यता	Dissent	विमति
Defence	प्रतिरक्षा	Dissolution	विघटन

Distribution	वितरण	Electoral rolls	निर्वाचक नामावली
Distribution	विभाजन	Eligibility	पात्रता
District	जिला	Eligible	पात्र
District Board	जिलागण	Emergency	आपात
District Board	जिला मंडली	Emergent	आपाती
District Council	जिला परिषद्	Emigration	उत्प्रवास
District Court	जिला न्यायालय	Emolument	उपलब्धि
District Fund	जिला निधि	Employer's liability	नियोजक उत्तरवादिता
District Magistrate	जिलाधीश	Employer's Liability	नियोजक दात्व्य
Dividend	लाभांश	Employment	उपायोजन
Divorce	विवाह-विच्छेद	Employment	नौकरी
Document	दस्तावेज	Employment	सेवा नियोजन
Document	लेख्य	Employment tax	नौकरी कर
Domicile	अधिवास	Enactment	अधिनियमन
Domiciled	अधिवासी	Encumbered estate	भारग्रस्त संपदा
Due, Payable	देय	Endorsed	अंकित
Dullness	मतिमान्द्य	Endorsed	पृष्ठांकित
During the pleasure of the President	राष्ट्रपति प्रसाद पर्यन्त	Endorsement	अंकन
		Endorsement	पृष्ठांकन
During good behaviour	सदाचरण पर्यन्त	Endowment	धर्मस्व
Duty	कर्तव्य	Engagement	वचन बन्ध
Duty	शुल्क	Engineering	यन्त्र शास्त्र
Economic	आर्थिक	Enquiry	परिप्रश्न
Efficiency of administration	प्रशासन कार्यपटुता	Enterprise	उद्यम
		Entitled	हक्क
Efficiency of administration	प्रशासन कार्यक्षमता	Entitled	हक्क होना
		Entrust	न्यस्त करना
Elected	चुने हुए	Entry	दाखिला
Elected	निर्वाचित	Entry	प्रविष्टि
Election	निर्वाचन	Equal protection of law	विधियों का समान संरक्षण
Election Commissioner	निर्वाचन आयुक्त		
Election Tribunal	निर्वाचन अधिकरण	Equality	समता
Electoral rolls	निर्वाचक गण	Establish	स्थापित करना

Establishment	संस्थापन	Fare	भाड़ा
Establishment	स्थापना	Federal Court	फेडरल न्यायालय
Estate	सम्पदा	Fees	फीस
Estate duty	सम्पदा शुल्क	Finance	वित्त
Estimate	आकलन	Finance bill	वित्त विधेयक
Estimate	आँक	Finance Commission	वित्तायोग
Estimate	प्राक्कलन	Financial	वित्तीय
Evidence	साक्ष्य	Financial obligation	वित्तीय भार
Excess profit	अतिरिक्त लाभ	Financial statement	वित्तीय विवरण
Excise duty	उत्पादन शुल्क	Fined	जुर्माना किया
Exclude	अण्वर्जन करना	First reading	प्रथम पठन
Exclusion	अपवर्जन	Fishery	मीन क्षेत्र
Exclusive jurisdiction	अनन्य क्षेत्राधिकार	Fleet	निर्वाचन (करना)
Executive	कार्यपालिका	Forbid	निषेध
Executive power	कार्यपालिका शक्ति	Forbidden	निषिद्ध
Exempt	मुक्त	Forces	बल
Exercise	अनुष्ठान	Foreign affairs	विदेशीय कार्य
Ex-officio	पदेन	Foreign exchange	विदेशीय विनिमय
Expenditure	व्यय	Form	प्रपत्र
Explanation	स्पष्टीकरण	Form	फारम
Explosive	विस्फोटक	Form	रूप
Export	निर्यात	Formula	सूत्र
Export duty	निर्यात शुल्क	Formulated	सूत्रित
Export Tax	निर्यात कर	Freedom	आजादी
Extent	विस्तार	Freedom	स्वतंत्रता
External affairs	वैदेशिक कार्य	Freedom	स्वातंत्र्य
Extradition	प्रत्यर्पण	Freedom of speech	वाक्स्वातंत्र्य
Extraterritorial operation	राज्य क्षेत्रातीत प्रवर्त्तन	Freight	वस्तु भाड़ा
		Frontiers	सीमान्त
Factory	कारखाना	Function	कृत्य
Faith	धर्म	Fund	निधि
Faith	श्रद्धा	Future market	वायदा-बाजार
Fare	किराया	Gambling	जुआ

Gambling	द्यूत	Incidental	प्रासंगिक
Gazette	गजट	Incidental, Ancillary	आनुषंगिक
General election	साधारण निर्वाचन	Income Tax	आयकर
Govern	शासन करना	Incompetency	अक्षमता
Governance	शासन	Incompetent	अक्षम
Governing body	शासी निकाय	Incorporation	निगमन
Government	सरकार	Incumbent of an office	पदधारी
Government of India	भारत सरकार	Indebtedness	ऋणग्रस्तता
Governor	राज्यपाल	Indirect election	परोक्ष निर्वाचन
Grant	अनुदान	Industry	उद्योग
Grants-in-aid	सहायक अनुदान	Ineligibility	अपात्रता
Gratuity	उपदान	Ineligible	अपात्र
Guarantee	प्रत्याभूति	Infant	शिशु
Guidance	मार्ग प्रदर्शन	Infectious	सांक्रामिक
Habeous Corpus	बन्दी प्रत्यक्षीकरण	Influence	प्रभाव
Handicraft	दस्तकारी	Inheritance	दाय
Handicraft	हस्त शिल्प	Injury	क्षति
Hazardous	संकटमय	Inland waterway	अन्तर्देशीय जलपथ
Headman	मुखिया	Inoperative	अप्रवृत्त
High Court	उच्च न्यायालय	Inquire	जाँच करना
Honorarium	मानेदय	Inspection	पर्यवेक्षण
Illegal	अवैध	Institution	संस्था
Illegal practice	अवैधाचरण	Instruction	अनुदेश
Immunity	उन्मुक्ति	Instruction, Education	शिक्षा
Impeachment	महाभियोग	Instructions	हिदायतें
Implement	परिपालन	Instrument	लिखित
Import duty	आयात शुल्क	Insurance	बीमा
Impose	आरोपण करना	Intercourse	समागम
Impose	लगाना	Interest	वृद्धि
Imprisoament	कारावास	Interest	सूद
Imprisonment	कैद	International	अन्तर्राष्ट्रीय
Improvement Trust	सुधार प्रन्यास	Interpretation	निर्वचन
Incapacity	असमर्थता	Intestacy	इच्छा पत्रहीनत्व

Intestacy	निर्वसीयता	Legislative	विधान मण्डल
Intestate	इच्छा पत्रहीन	Legislative Assembly	विधान सभा
Intestate	निर्वसीयत	Legislative Council	विधान परिषद्
Introduction	पुर:स्थापना	Legislative power	विधायिनी शक्ति
Invalid	अमान्य	Levy	आरोपण
Invalidity pension	असमर्थता निवृत्ति वेतन	Levy	उगाहना
Investigation	अनुसंधान	Levy	उद्ग्रहण
Involved	अन्तर्ग्रस्त	Liability	उत्तरवादिता
Involvement	अन्तर्ग्रसन	Liability	दायित्व
Irregularity	अनियमितता	Libel	अपमान लेख
Irrelevant	विसंगत	Liberty	स्वाधीनता
Issue	वाद-पद	Licence	अनुज्ञप्ति
Joint-family	अवभिक्त कुटुम्ब	License	लाइसेन्स
Joint-family	अविभक्त परिवार	Lieutenant, Governor	उपराज्यपाल
Judge	न्यायाधीश	Limitation	परिसीमा
Judgment	निर्णय	Livelihood	जीविका
Judicial power	न्यायिक शक्ति	Living-wage	निर्वाह मजूरी
Judicial proceeding	न्यायिक कार्यरीति	Loan	उधार
Judicial proceeding	न्यायिक कार्यवाही	Local area	स्थानीय क्षेत्र
Judicial stamp	न्यायिक मुद्रांक	Local Authority	स्थानीय प्राधिकारी
Judiciary	न्यायपालिका	Local Board	स्थानीय मण्डली
Jurisdiction	क्षेत्राधिकार	Local body	स्थानीय निकाय
Justice	न्यायाधिपति	Local Government	स्थानीय शासन
Labour	श्रम	Lok Sabha	लोकसभा
Labour Union	श्रमिक संघ	Lunacy	उन्माद
Land records	भू-अभिलेख	Lunatic	उन्मत्त
Land revenue	भू-राजस्व	Magistrate's Court	दंडाधिकारी न्यायालय
Lapse	व्यपयत होना	Maintain	पोषण करना
Laws of Nations	राष्ट्रों की विधि	Maintain	बनाये रखना
Legal	कानून सम्बन्धी	Maintenance	पोषण
Legal	विधि सम्बन्धी	Major	वयस्क
Legal tender	विधि मान्य	Majority	बहुमत
Legislation	विधान	Mandamus	परमादेश

Manufacture	निर्माण	Municipal area	नगर क्षेत्र
Maritime shipping	समुद्र नौवहन	Municipal Committee	नगर समिति
Mark	चिह्न	Municipal Corporation	नगर निगम
Maternity relief	प्रसूति साहाय्य	Municipal tramway	नगर ट्रामवे
Maternity relief	प्रसूति सहायता	Municipality	नगर पालिका
Means of Communications	संचार साधन	Nation	राष्ट्र
		National highway	राष्ट्रीय राजपथ
Memo	ज्ञापक	Naturalization	देशीयकरण
Memorandum	ज्ञापन	Naval	नौसेना सम्बन्धी
Memorial	स्मारक	Navigation	नौ–परिवहन
Mental deficiency	मनोवैकल्य	Nomination	नाम निदर्शन
Mental weakness	मनोदौर्बल्य	Nomination	मनोनयन
Merchant marine	वणिक पोत	Notice in writing	लिखित सूचना
Migration	प्रव्रजन	Notification	अधिसूचना
Military	सैनिक	Obligation	आभार
Mineral	खनिज	Occupation	उपजीविका
Mineral resources	खनिज सम्पत	Occupation	धंधा
Minister	मन्त्री	Octroi	चुंगी
Minor	अवयस्क	Office	पद
Minority	अल्पसंख्यक वर्ग	Officer	पदाधिकारी
Misbehaviour	कदाचार	Official residence	पदावास
Modification	रूपभेद	Opinion	अभिप्राय
Money	धन	Opinion	राय
Money lender	साहूकारी	Order	आदेश
Money lending	सांसर्गिक	Order	व्यवस्था
Money-bill	धन विधेयक	Order-in-Council	परिषद् आदेश
Morality	सदाचार	Ordinance	अध्यादेश
Mortgage	बन्धक	Own	स्वामी होना
Motion	प्रस्ताव	Owner	स्वामी
Motion for consideration	विचारार्थ प्रस्ताव	Ownership, Royalty	स्वामित्व
Motion of confidence	विश्वास प्रस्ताव	Pardon	क्षमा
Motion of no-confidence	अविश्वास प्रस्ताव	Parliament	संसद
		Partnership	भागिता

Party	पक्ष	Preamble	प्रस्तावना
Passed	पारित	Preference	अधिमान
Passport	पार पत्र	Prejudice	प्रतिकूल प्रभाव
Patent	एकस्व	Preside	अध्यासीन होना
Pay, Salary	वेतन	Preside	पीठासीन होना
Peace	शान्ति	President	राष्ट्रपति
Pecuniary Jurisdiction	आर्थिक क्षेत्राधिकार	Presiding officer	अधिष्ठाता
Penalty	शास्ति	Presiding Officer	पीठासीन पदाधिकारी
Pending	लम्बमान	Prevention	निरोध
Pending	लम्बित	Preventive detention	निवारक निरोध
Pension	निवृत्ति वेतन	Previous consent	पूर्व सम्मति
People	लोक	Previous sanction	पूर्व मंजूरी
Permit	अनुज्ञा	Prime Minister	प्रधानमन्त्री
Permit	परमिट	Prison	कारागार
Perpetual succession	शाश्वत उत्तराधिकार	Prison	जेल
Perquisite	परिलब्धि	Prisoner	कारबन्दी
Person	व्यक्ति	Prisoner	कैदी
Personal law	स्वीय विधि	Privilege	विशेषाधिकार
Petition	अर्थ करना	Procedure	प्रक्रिया
Petition	याचिका	Process	आदेशिका
Piracy	जलदस्युता	Proclamation	उद्घोषणा
Plead	वकालत करना	Proclamation of emergency	आपातकाल उद्घोषणा
Pleader	वकील		
Police	आरक्षक	Production	उत्पादन
Police force	आरक्षक बल	Profession	पेशा
Police Station	थाना	Profession	वृत्ति
Police Station Officer	थानेदार	Profession Tax	वृत्ति कर
Policy of insurance	बीमा पत्र	Profit	लाभ
Port quarantine	पत्तन निरोध	Prohibited	प्रतिषिद्ध
Possession	कब्जा	Prohibition	प्रतिषेध
Post	जगह	Promissory note	प्रामिसरी नोट
Post	पद	Promissory note	वचन पत्र
Power	शक्ति	Promulgation	प्रख्यापन

Propagate	प्रचार करना	Receipt (Paper)	पावती
Proportional representation	अनुपाती-प्रतिनिधित्व	Record	अभिलेख
		Record of rights	अधिकार अभिलेख
Proposal	प्रस्थापना	Recruitment	भर्ती
Prorogue	सत्रावसान	Recurring	आवर्त्तक
Prosecution	अभियुक्ति	Redemption	विमोचन
Prosecution	अभियोजन	Redemption charges	विमोचन भार
Provided	परन्तु	Reference	निर्देश
Provident Fund	भविष्य निधि	Reformatory	सुधारालय
Province	प्रान्त	Regional Commissioner	प्रादेशिक आयुक्त
Provision	उपबन्ध	Regional Council	प्रादेशिक परिषद्
Proxy	प्रतिपत्री	Regional Fund	प्रादेशिक निधि
Public debt	राष्ट्र ऋण	Register	पंजी
Public demand	सरकारी अभियाचना	Registered	निबद्ध
चइसपब कमउंदक	सार्वजनिक कल्याण	Registered	पंजीबद्ध
Public health	लोक स्वास्थ्य	Registration	निबन्धन
Public notification	लोक अधिसूचना	Registration	पंजीबन्धन
Public notification	सार्वजनिक अभियाचना	Registration	पंजीयन
Public order	साहूकार	Regulate	विनियमन करना
Public Service Commission	लोक सेवा आयोग	Regulation	विनियम
		Relevancy	सुसंगति
Public Services	लोक सेवाएँ	Relevant	सुसंगत
Publication	प्रकाशन	Remedy	उपचार
Punish	दंड देना	Reminder	अनुस्मारक
Purporting to be done	कर्तुमभिप्रेत	Remission	परिहार
Qualification	अर्हता	Removal	हटाना
Question of law	विधि प्रश्न	Remuneration	पारिश्रमिक
Quo warranto	अधिकार-पृच्छा	Rent	लगान
Quorum	गणपूर्ति	Repeal	निरसन
Railway	रेल	Report	प्रतिवेदन
Ratification	अनुसमर्थन	Representation	प्रतिनिधित्व
Receipt	प्राप्ति	Representative	प्रतिनिधि
Receipt	रसीद	Reprieve	प्रविलम्बन

Republic	लोकतंत्रात्मक गणराज्य	Scheduled tribe	अनुसूचित-जनजाति
Repugnance	विरोध	Seal	मुद्रा
Repugnancy	विरोध	Second reading	द्वितीय पठन
Repugnant	विरुद्ध	Security	प्रतिभूति
Requisition	अधिग्रहण	Select Committee	प्रवर समिति
Research	गवेषणा	Self Governmen	स्थानीय स्वशासन
Research	शोध, शोधना	Sentence	दंडादेश
Reservation	रक्षण	Service	सेवा
Reserved forest	रक्षित वन	Service charges	सेवा भार
Resignation	पदत्याग	Session	सत्र
Resolution	संकल्प	Sessions Court	सत्र न्यायालय
Respite	विराम	Share	अंश
Restriction	निर्गन्धन	Sheriff	शेरीफ
Retire	निवृत्त होना	Single transferable vote	एकल संक्रमणीय मत
Retirement	निवृत्ति	Sinking Fund	निक्षेप निधि
Return	विवरणी	Sitting	उपवेशन
Revenue	राजस्व	Sitting	बैठक
Revenue Court	राजस्व न्यायालय	Slander	अपमान-वचन
Review	पुनर्विलोकन	Social custom	सामाजिक रूढ़ि
Revision	पुनर्निरीक्षण	Social insurance	सामाजिक बीमा
Revoke	प्रतिसंहरण	Social service	सामाजिक मुद्रा
Reward	पारितोषिक	Sovereign	प्रभु
Right	अधिकार	Sovereign democratic	सम्पूर्ण प्रभुत्व सम्पन्न
Rule	नियम	Sovereignty	प्रभुता
Rule of the road	पथ कर	Speaker	अध्यक्ष
Ruler	शासक	Staff	कर्मचारी वृन्द
Safeguard	परित्राण	Stamp duty	मुद्रांक शुल्क
Safeguard	रक्षाकवच	Standing Committee	स्थायी समिति
Sales tax	विक्रय कर	Standing Orders	स्थायी करना
Sanction	मंजूरी	State	राज्य
Schedule	अनुसूची	State Fund	राज्य निधि
Scheduled area	अनुसूचित-क्षेत्र	State-list	राज्य सूची
Scheduled caste	अनुसूचित जाति	Sub-division	उपविभाग

Subject	अधीन	To initiate	उपक्रमण करना
Subject	विषय	To introduce	पुर:स्थापन करना
Subject matter	वाद-विषय	To suspend	निलम्बन करना
Subordinate Court	अधीन-न्यायालय	Toll	पथ नियम
Subordinate Officer	अधीन-अधिकारी	Trade	व्यापार
Succession	उत्तराधिकार	Trade association	व्यापार संघ
Succession duty	उत्तराधिकार शुल्क	Trade mark	व्यापार चिह्न
Successor	उत्तराधिकारी	Trade union	कार्मिक संघ
Suffrage	मताधिकार	Trademark	पण्य चिह्न
Summoned	आहूत	Traffic	यातायात
Summons	आह्वान	Traffic in human beings	मानवी पण्य
Superintendence	अधीक्षण		
Superintendent	अधीक्षक	Training	प्रशिक्षण
Supplementary	अनुपूरक	Tram car	ट्रामगाड़ी
Supplementary grant	अनुपूरक अनुदान	Tramway	ट्राम
Supreme Command	सर्वोच्य समादेश	Tranquillity	प्रशान्ति
Supreme Court	उच्चतम न्यायालय	Transfer	स्थानान्तरण
Surcharge	अधिभार	Transfer	हस्तांतरण
Suspension	निलम्बन	Transition	संक्रमण
Tax	कर	Transport	परिवहन
Technical training	शिल्पी प्रशिक्षण	Transportation	निर्वासन
Tenant	किसान	Treasure trove	निखात निधि
Tenure	पदावधि	Treaty	सन्धि
Term	निबंधन	Tribal area	जनजाति क्षेत्र
Terminal Tax	सीमाकर	Tribal Council	जनजाति परिषद्
Territorial Charges	प्रादेशिक भार	Tribe	जनजाति
Territorial jurisdiction	प्रादेशिक क्षेत्राधिकार	Tribunal	अधिकरण
Territorial waters	जल प्रांगण	Tribunal	न्यायाधिकरण
Territory	राज्य क्षेत्र	Triennial	त्रैवार्षिक
Third reading	तृतीय-पठन	Trust	न्यास
Tidal water	ज्वार जल	Typewriting	टंगण
To arrest	बन्दी करना	Undischarged	अनुन्मुक्त
To charge	भारित करना	Undue influence	अयुक्त प्रभाव

Unemployment	बेकारी	Vocation	व्यवसाय
Union	संघ	Void	शून्य
Union List	संघ-सूची	Vote	मत
Unit	अंग	Voter	मतदाता
Unit	एकक	Votes on accounts	लेखानुदान
Unit	एकांश	Voting	मतदान
Unsound mind	विकृत चित्त	Wage	मजूरी
Unsoundness of mind	चित्त विकृति	Want of confidence	विश्वास का अभाव
Vacancy	रिक्तता	Warrant	अधिपत्र
Vacancy	रिक्त स्थान	Will	इच्छा पत्र
Vacancy	रिक्ति	Will	वसीयत
Vagrancy	आवारागर्दी	Winding up	समापन
Vice President	उपराष्ट्रपति	Writ	लेख
Village Council	ग्राम परिषद्	Writ of prohibition	प्रतिषेध लेख
Violation	अतिक्रमण		

Appendix-28/परिशिष्ट–28
Terms used in Government Notifications
शासकीय शब्दावली

A fee in cash	नकद फीस	Abutment	तोरणाधार
A vain Tuberculosis test	पक्षियों की यक्ष्मा परीक्षा	Academy	विद्यापरिषद्
Abate	शांत होना	Acceleration	वेगवृद्धिकर
Abatement	घटना (घटाया जाना)	Access	पहुँच
Abatement of rent	लगान में कमी	Accessories	सहायक वस्तुएँ
Abbreviated	संक्षिप्त	Accessory, Subsidiary	सहायक
Abduction, Kidnapping	अपहरण	Accord	एकमत्य
Abetment	दुरुत्साहन	Account	लेखा (गणना)
Abide by	पालन करना	Accountant	कणनाध्यक्ष
Abnormal, Irregular	नियम विरुद्ध	Accountant General	महालेखाकार
Abolition	उन्मूलन	Accounts officer	गणनाधिकारी
Above par	अधिक मूल्य पर	Accoutrement	आकल्प (सज्जा)
Above standard	प्रमाण से ऊपर	Accrual increment	संभूत वेतन वृद्धि
Absconder	भगोड़ा	Accusation	अभियोग (दोषण)
Absconding	फरार	Accused	अभियुक्त
Absentee statement	अनुपस्थिति विवरणपत्र	Acknowledgment	प्राप्ति स्वीकार
Absolute order	अबाधित करना	Acknowledgment due	पावती-पावनी
Absorption	खपत	Acknowledgment, Receipt	पावती
Abstract	उपसंक्षेप	Acknowledgment, Sanction, Approval	स्वीकृति
Abstract book	उपसंक्षेप पुस्तक	Acoustics	ध्वनि शास्त्र
Abstract of cost	परिव्यय उपसंक्षेप	Acquisition	अधिगमन

Acquisition	प्राप्ति	Adjustment	समाधान
Acquittal	दोष मुक्ति	Administration	प्रशासन
Acquittance roll	निष्क्रियवर्ति, (वेतन चिट्ठा)	Administrative	प्रशासकीय
Acreage	एकड़ों में क्षेत्रफल	Administrative bond	प्रशासकीय प्रतिज्ञापत्र
Act	अधिनियम	Administrative department	प्रशासकीय विभाग
Act	विधान	Administrator	प्रशासक
Acting appointment	कार्यवाह नियुक्ति	Administrator General	महा प्रबंधक
Actinomycosis	अंशुक वकीय (रोग)	Admissibility in evidence	साक्ष्य में ग्राहिता
Active allowance	सक्रिय भत्ता	Admissible	ग्राह्य
Actual travelling allowance	वास्तविक यात्रा व्यय	Admission board	प्रवेश परिषद्
Actuals	वास्तविक आँकड़े	Admitted for hearing	सुनवाई के लिए स्वीकृत
Acute angle	न्यूनकोण	Admonition	डाँट-फटकार
Ad Hoc	एतदर्थ	Adoption deed	दत्तक पत्र
Ad valorem	मूल्यानुसार	Adulteration	मिलावट
Addendum	क्षप (क)	Adumbrated	छायांकित
Addendum	जोड़पत्र	Advance, Taqavi-advance.	अग्र ऋण
Additional	उपाधिक	Advice of Credit Transfer	नाम संक्रम सूचना
Additional entry	अतिरिक्त प्रविष्टि	Advisory officer	मंत्रणा अधिकारी
Additional grant	अतिरिक्त अनुदान	Advocate	अधिवक्ता
Adequate	यथोचित	Advocate General	महाअधिवक्ता
Adhesive stamp	श्लेष्क मुद्रांक	Affect	प्रभावित करना
Adjacent	समीपस्थ (आसन्न)	Affected	ग्रस्त (प्रभावित)
Adjournment	स्थगन	Affidavit	शपथ पत्र
Adjudication	दिवालिया ठहराना	Affiliation	संबद्धता
Adjudication	न्यायिक निर्णय		

Affinity	रुझान	Allegation, Imposition	आरोप
Affirmation	प्रतिज्ञा, प्रतिज्ञान	Allocation	नियतन
Affirmative	स्वीकारात्मक	Allocation	विभाजन
Aflux	बहाव	Allocation of fund	रुपये का बँटवारा
Against	विरुद्ध	Allotment	दिष्टि
Age limit	वयस प्रतिबंध	Allotment	निर्दिष्ट भाग
Agenda	कार्यावली	Allowance	भत्ता
Agent	अभिकर्ता	Alluvial	नदमट (कछार)
Aggregate	योग	Alluvion	कछार
Aggregate	सकल	Amalgamation, Coordination	एकीकरण
Agreement for service	सेवानियम पत्र	Amendment Act	संशोधक विधान
Agricultural	कृषि विषयक	Ammunition	गोला–गारूद
Agricultural implements	कृषि उपकरण	Ammunition	गोली
Agricultural lease	कृषि पट्टा	Amnesty	राजक्षमा
Agriculturists Loan Act	कृषक ऋण एक्ट	Amortization	ऋणशोधन (किशतों में)
Aide-de-camp	परिधिस्थ	Amphistome worm	द्विमुखी कृमि
Air force	हवाई बेड़ा	Anachronism	कालव्यतिक्रम (तारीख की गलती)
Air gun	वायुसंचालित बन्दूक		
Air-force	नभ–सेना	Analysis	विश्लेषण
Alienatipn	हस्तांतरण	Analyst	विश्लेषक
Alien's branch	विदेशी शाखा	Ancestral property	पैतृक संपत्ति
Alignment	पंक्ति	Anchor bolt	लंगर
Alignment	पंक्तिकरण	Angle of repose	विश्रामकोण
Alimony	दारा–भूति	Animal Husbandry Department	पशुपालन विभाग
Alimony pendentilite	विचारकालिक दाराभृति	Ankle, Ring	कड़ा

Annexure	नत्थी	Apparatus (as a whole)	यन्त्रजाल (यन्त्र कलाप)
Annotated	सटीक	Apparatus (for a particular experiment)	यन्त्रजात
Annuling	अभिशून्यन		
Annulled	निरर्थक किया हुआ (मंसूख किया हुआ)	Appeal	अपील
Annulment of Marriage	विवाह का रद्द किया जाना	Appear	उपस्थित होना
		Appearance	उपस्थिति
Anomalous	अनैयमिक	Appearance slips	न्यायालय उपस्थितिपत्र
Anomaly	अनियम		
Anonymous	अनामक	Appellant	अपीलकर्ता
Ante	पूर्व	Appellate	अपीली
Antecedent, precedent	पूर्व दृष्टांत	Appendix	परिशिष्ट
		Appliance	यन्त्र (औजार)
Anthrax	विसहारिया	Applicant	प्रार्थी
Anticipated	प्रत्याशित	Apportionment	संविभाग
Anticipated excess and savings	प्रत्याशित अधिक व्यय और बचत	Appraisement	कनकत
		Appreciation	अधिमूल्यन
Anticipation	प्रत्याशा	Apprehend	बन्दी करना
Anticipator	प्रत्याशिक	Apprehension	बन्दीकरण
Antidote	विषमार	Apprentice	शिक्ष्यमाण
Anti-inflatory	मुद्रास्फीतिरोधक	Appropriate	उपयुक्त
Antiquities	प्राचीन अवशेष	Appropriation	पर्यादान
Anti-rabies treatmerit	जलांतक चिकित्सा	Approval	अनुमति
		Approved candidate	स्वीकृत उम्मीदवार
Antiseptic fluid	सड़न रोक रस		
Apathy	उदासीनता	Approved service	अनुमोदित सेवा
Aperture	छेद	Approver	राजसाक्षी
Apex	सिरा (चोटी)	Approximate	उपसन्न
Apparatus	यन्त्र-कलाप		

Approximate areas	लगभग क्षेत्रफल
Apron	पिटवा
Aquaduct	जलनियन्त्रक पुल
Arbitration	पंचायत
Arbitration, Tribunal	पंचमंडल
Arbitrator	पंच (मध्यस्थ)
Arboriculture	वृक्षरोपण विद्या
Arcade	छत्ता
Archaeological department	पुरातत्त्व विभाग
Architect	स्थपति
Architecture	वास्तु विद्या (स्थापत्य)
Argument	तर्क
Armed guard	सशस्त्र रक्षकगण
Armourer	आयुधक
Armourer	आयुधकार
Arrear claims	अवशिष्ट के प्राप्य
Arrears	अवशिष्ट
Arrows	सूजा
Art gallery	कलादीर्घा
Arterial road	नगर योजक सड़क
Artery	धमनी
Article, Bench	अधिकरण
Artisan	शिल्पकार
Arts college	साहित्यादि विद्यालय
Asbestos	अदह
Ashman	राखिया
Asphalt	डामर
Assault	आक्रमण
Assess	आँकना
Assessment, Assess	कर निर्धारण
Assets	परिसम्पत (संपत्ति)
Assets (as opposed to liability)	आदेय
Assignee	अभिहस्तांकिती
Assignee	सुपुर्दगी लेने वाला
Assignment (of land)	अभिहस्तांकन (बेंची)
Assignment (of Property)	संकल्प
Asstt. Inspector General	सहायक महानिरीक्षक
Asstt. Supdt. fo Police	सहायक पुलिस अधीक्षक
Assumed rent	माना हुआ लगान
Assurance	आश्वासन
Asterisk	तारा चिह्न
At a discount	बट्टे पर (से)
At a premium	बढ़ती पर (से)
At your earliest convenience, As early as possible	यथाशीघ्र
Athletic	खेल-कूद
Attach (Legal Term)	कुड़क करना
Attendant	परिचर
Attendant	परिचारक
Attestation	साक्षीकरण

Attested	साक्षीकृत	Award	पंच निर्णय
Auction	घोष विक्रय (नीलाम)	Axis	अक्षधुरी
Audit	लेखा परीक्षा	Axis of a cone	शंकुकक्ष
Audit objection	लेखा परीक्षा आपत्ति	Bacteriological examination	कीटाणु परीक्षा
Audit officer	लेखा परीक्षा अधिकारी	Bail bond, Security bond	प्रतिभू पत्र
Audit report	गणना परीक्षा विवरण	Bailable	प्रतिभाव्य
Auditor	लेखा परीक्षक	Bailment	निक्षेपण
Auditor General	लेखा महापरीक्षक	Ballast	गिट्टी
Auditorium	सभाभवन	Ballot	गुप्तमत
Auger	बरमा	Balustrade	कटहरा
Aural education	कर्ण शिक्षा	Bamboo measuring rod	गट्ठा
Authentic	आप्त (प्रामाणिक)	Ban	प्रतिबन्ध
Authentication of power of attorney	दत्तक ग्रहण का अधिकारपत्र	Bank	अधिकोष (धनागार)
Authorise	अधिकृत	Bank draft	बैंक की हुंडी
Authorised agent	प्राधिकृत अभिकर्ता	Banquet	जेवनार
Authority	प्राधिकारी वर्ग	Bar (as in efficiency bar), Bolt, Latch	अर्गल
Authority of consideration	विचाराधिकार	Bar Association, Bar	अभिभाषक संघ
Authority, Officer	अधिकारी	Bar Council	अभिभाषक परिषद्
Authrax	बिसहरिया	Bar-fetters	डंडा बेड़ी
Automatic	स्वयंचल	Barometer	वायुभार मापक
Automatically	स्वत:	Barrack	योधागार
Available	उपलब्ध	Barrack	सहतावारिक
Average	औसत	Barred by limitation	अवधि बाधित
Average emoluments	औसत परिलाभ	Barren	ऊसर
Average pay	माध्य वेतन		

Barrister, Advocate, Lawyer	विधि वक्ता	Bifurcation	द्विविभाजन
Barrow	हाथ गाड़ी (ठेला)	Bilious fever (horse)	पैत्तिक ज्वर (अश्व)
Base line	आधार-रेखा	Bill	विधेयक
Basement	नींव	Bill of lading	वहन पत्र
Basic coupon	मूलकूपन	Bit, Bit-Head, Bit-Rims	लगाम (दहाना)
Batch	जत्था	Biting	डाँस
Battalion	बटालियन	Bitumen	राल
Batten	पुश्तीवान	Black quarter	लँगड़िया
Bay window	निकासा	Blight	तुषार
Bayonet	संगीन	Blue fringe	झालर (नीली)
Bearing, (Direction)	दिक स्थिति	Blue Vitriol	नीला थोथा (तूतिया)
Beet (Patrolling), Patrol	गश्त	Bluk	थोक
Belief	विश्वास	Board of revenue	माल बोर्ड
Bellows	भस्त्रका	Boiler	पिठर (बायलर)
Below par	अंकित मूल्य से कम	Boiler	भबका
Bench mark	स्तरांक	Bond	प्रतिज्ञापत्र
Bench of magistrates	अधिकरणिक वर्ग	Bond	बंध (बमस्सुक)
Beneficiary	हिताधिकारी	Bond of indemnity	क्षतिपूरक बंध
Benevolent trust	पर हितकारी प्रन्यास	Bone marrow	अस्थि-मज्जा
Benevolent trust	हितकारी ट्रस्ट	Bonus	लाभांश
Berth	ढूला (नौशय्या)	Book craft	गत्ताकारी
Beyond time	समय के बाहर	Book transfer	पुस्त संक्रम
Bib cock, Cock stop	टोंटी	Books of reference	संदर्भ ग्रन्थ
Biennial	द्विवर्षीय	Bots & warble	उदरकीट का विरु
Biennial	द्विवार्षिक	Bottle-neck	संकीर्णनिगम मार्ग

Bottle-neck	संकेत लिपिक	Burglar Alarm	चोर घंटी
Boulders	महाशिला	Burglary	सेंध लगाना
Brace	अढ़वाल (कसनी)	Business statement	कार्यविवरण पत्र
Bracket	दीवारगीर	By order of the Court	न्यायालय की आज्ञा से
Brake speed	रुढ़गति	By virtue of	कारण से
Branch depot	शाखाकोठार	Bye-laws	उपनियम
Branded portion	दग्ध भाग	Cable Crossing	तार काट
Branding Gertificate	गग्धांकन प्रमाणपत्र	Cable jointers	तार जोड़
Breach of law	विधि भंग	Cadet	बालबीर (सेनाछात्र)
Breach of peace	शांति-भंग	Cadre	मूल रचना
Breach of rule	नियम भंजन	Calamity, Distress	विपत्ति
Breast wall	आवक्ष भित्ति	Calculation	गणना
Breeder	ढोर पालक	Calendar month	पंचांग मास
Breeding operation	पशु प्रवर्धन क्रिया	Calendar year	पत्री वर्ष
Bressummer	सरदल	Calibre	क्षमता
Brick	इष्टिका	Calibre	छिद्र व्यास
Buck ammunition	छर्रा	Calling for the record	कागजात तलब करना
Budget	आयति	Camp	शिविर
Budget	आयव्ययक (बजट)	Camp equipage	निवेश संभार
Budget manual	आयव्ययक सारसंग्रह	Camp equipment	निवेश सज्जा
Bulletin	बुलेटिन	Canal irrigation	नहर की सिंचाई
Bullet-proof	गोली रोक	Cancellation	विलापन
Bullion	सोना-चाँदी	Cancelled	रद्द किया गया
Bully	गुंडा	Cancelling officer	रद्द करने वाला
Bundle Lifter	बस्ताबरदार	Cantonment Act	छावनी कानून
Burden of proof	प्रमाण भार	Cap	फौजी टोपी
Bureau	कार्य पीठ		

Capital sentence	प्राणदण्ड
Capital, Cash	पूँजी परिव्यय
Capitalized	पूँजीकृत
Capitation charges	प्रतिव्यक्ति प्रभार
Carbine bucket	कड़ाबीन आधार
Care (attention)	प्रणिधि
Care (regard)	अवेक्षा
Care Protection	संरक्षा
Cargo	नौभार
Cash balance	रोकड़ बाकी
Cash book	रोकड़ बही
Cash chest	रोकड़ की पेटी
Cash Outlay	नगदी लगान
Cash payment	नकद भुगतान
Cash rents	नकदी लगान
Castration	बधिया करना
Casual (As in casual prisoner)	इकबारा
Casual Leave	आकस्मिक छुट्टी
Catchment	पोषक क्षेत्र
Category	श्रेणी
Cattle Breeding farm	पशुओं की नसलकशी का फार्म
Cattle house	काजी हाउस
Cattle killer	पशुवध यन्त्र
Cattle prioplasmose, or Red water	लालमूत्र रोग
Caution	सतर्कता
Caveat	उच्चदारी (इत्तलानामा)
Caveat	सावधान
Ceased	समाप्त
Cellular	कोष्ठीय
Censure	निन्दा
Census	जनगणना
Central division	केन्द्रीय विवरणपत्र
Central Excise & Salt	केन्द्रीय उत्पादकर और नमक
Central Record Office	केन्द्रीय अभिलेखालय
Central Revenue Stamp	केन्द्रीय राजस्व मुद्रांक
Centrifugal	केन्द्रायग
Centripetal	केन्द्राभि
Certified extract	प्रमाणित अवतरण
Cess	अतिरिक्त कर
Cess	उपकर
Chain (measuring)	जरीब
Character of rainfall	वर्षा की दशा
Character-roll	चरित्रवर्ति (चरित्रावली)
Charge	अभियोग
Charge	प्रभार
Charge certificate	कार्यभार प्रमाणपत्र
Charge of office	पदभार
Charge sheet	अभियोग फलक
Charge, Expenditure	व्यय

Chargeable	देय	Claimant	अधियाचक
Charter party	जहाज का किराया नाम	Claimant	दावेदार
Check against fraud	धोखादेही से बचाने की रोकथाम	Clamp	सिकिजा
		Classification	वर्गीकरण
Check of discount	बट्टे की जाँच पड़ताल	Clause	वाक्य खण्ड
Check of stamp register	स्टाम्प रजिस्टरों की जाँच-पड़ताल	Cleaner	परिमार्जक
		Cleaning losses	फटकन
Cheque	धनादेश	Cleaning register	सफाई का रजिस्टर
Chevron, Badge, Stripe	बिल्ला	Clearing agent	चेक चुकाई एजेन्ट
		Clearing office	चेक चुकाई कार्यलय
Chief Commissioner	मुख्य आयुक्त	Clemency	राजदया
		Client	मुवक्किल
Chief controlling revenue authority	मुख्य नियन्त्रक राजस्व प्राधिकारी	Clinical	रोग विषयक
		Clinically affected	प्रत्यक्ष रोगग्रस्त
Chief Justice	मुख्य न्यायाधीश	Closing balance	अंतिम शेष
Chord	जीवा	Coat of arms	कुल चिह्न
Chronological order	ऐतिहासिक क्रम	Coccidiosis	बदरावण रोग
		Code	संहिता
Circle	हलका	Codicil	क्रोड़पत्र
Circle officer	चक्राधिकारी	Co-efficient	बारद्योतक
Circular (letter)	परिपत्र	Coercion	अनुचित दबाव
Cistern	हौज (टंकी)	Cognate	सगोत्र
Citation	उपस्थिति के लिए सफीना	Cognizable	अनुसंधेय
		Cognizable	हस्तक्षेप्य
Citations	नजीर का हवाला	Coinage	टंकन
Civil	नागरिक (दीवानी)	Collaboration	सहयोग
Civil employee	असैनिक कर्मचारी	Collateral agreement	अतिरिक्त नियमपत्र
Civil list	अधिकारवर्ग सूची		
Claim	अधियाचन (दावा)		

Collecting government	समाहरणकारी सरकार
Collection	समाहरण
Collective subscription	सामूहिक चन्दा
Collector	समाहर्ता
Colonial service	उपनिवेशी सेवा
Combination	मवषय
Combustion	दहन
Combustion chamber	दहनागार
Command	समादेश
Commandant	समादेशक
Commanded area	अधिक्षेत्र
Commander	सेनापति
Commemoration volume	स्मारक ग्रन्थ
Commencement	आरंभ
Commencement and transitory	आरंभ और क्षणिक
Comment	आलोचना
Commercial	वाणिज्य सम्बन्धी
Commercial department	वाणिज्य विभाग
Commission	आयोग
Commission of inquiry	जाँच आयोग
Commissioner	आयुक्त
Commitment	समर्पण (कारागार भेजना)
Committal	सौंप
Committee	समिति
Common contingent charges	सामान्य प्रासंगिक व्यय
Commutation	पलटा करना
Commutation	संराशिदान
Commutation of pension	पेंशन का संराशिकरण
Commuted value	संराशि
Compass (pair of)	परकार
Compassionate	दयामूलक
Compassionate Gratuity	अनुग्रह-धन
Compensation	प्रतिकर (क्षतिपूर्ति)
Compensatory allowance	प्रतिकर भत्ता
Competency	योग्यता
Competent	योग्य (समर्थ)
Competent authority	शक्त प्राधिकारी
Competent court	समर्थ न्यायालय
Competitive examination	प्रतियोगिता परीक्षा
Compilation	संकलन
Compilation of statistics	आँकड़े का संकलन
Complainant	अभियोक्ता
Complainant	अभियोगी
Complaint	परिदेवना
Completion	समापन
Compliance	पालनादेश
Component parts	अवयव
Composition deed	निपटारा पत्र

Compoundable offences	समाधेय अपराध
Compounder, Mixer	मिश्रक
Compression	संपीड़न
Compulsory retirement	अनिवार्य निवृत्ति
Computation of fees	शुल्क गणना
Computer	गणनाकार
Concentration camp	कारा शिविर
Concessions	रियायतें
Concurrence	सहमति
Concurrent	समकालिक
Concurrent	सहवर्ति (संगामी)
Concurrent judgment	एकमत निर्णय
Condemned	फाँसी का (कैदी)
Condition	दशा
Condition	शर्त
Condition of qualifying service	योग्यकारी सेवा की शर्त
Condition of service	नौकरी की शर्त
Conditional long settlements	सोपाधिक दीर्घकालीन बन्दोबस्त
Conditional Order	औपाधिक आदेश
Conditional release	सोपाधिक मुक्ति
Conditional sale	सप्रतिबन्धक विक्रय
Condonation	क्षमा
Conduct	आचरण
Conduction	संवाहन
Conduit	बम्बा (पटी हुई नाली)
Cone	शंकु
Confederacy	प्रसंधि
Confederacy	राजसंघ
Confidential	गोप्य
Confinement	बंधन (कैद)
Confirmation	पक्का करना
Confiscation	राजसात्करण
Confiscation, Forfeiture	जब्ती
Conformity	अनुरूपता
Conjugal right	वैवाहिक अधिकार
Connivance	गजनिमीजिका
Conscription	अनिवार्य भर्ती
Consecutive	निरंतर
Consequential	पारिणामिक
Consignee	परेषणी
Consignment	प्रेषण
Consignment	सौंप पत्र
Consistent	संगत
Consolidated	एकस्थीकृत
Consolidated forecast	एकीकृत पूर्वानुमान
Consolidated pay	एकीकृत वेतन
Consolidation	एकस्थीकरण
Consolidation of holdings	चकबंदी
Consolidation Officer	चकबंदी अधिकारी

Consolidator	चकबंदीकर्ता	Convener	संयोजक
Constable	रक्षी (तिलंगा)	Conventionally	प्रथानुसार
Constitution	संविधान	Conversion	पलट
Consultation	संमन्त्रण	Conveyance	सवारी
Consumer	उपभोक्ता	Conveyance	हस्तांतरण पत्र
Contact	सम्पर्क	Convict	आधर्षित
Contagious disease	संक्रामक रोग	Conviction	आधर्षण
Contempt of Court	न्यायालय अपमान	Co-operation	सहकारिता (सहयोग)
Content	अंतर्वस्तु	Co-operative	सहकारी
Context	प्रसंग	Co-operative societies	सहकारी समितियाँ
Contingencies	आकस्मिक व्यय		
Contingency	प्रासंगिक व्यय	Co-ordinate	आसजन
Contingent	प्रासंगिक	Co-owner	सहस्वामी
Contingent Reserve	आकस्मिक घृतदल	Co-parcener	अंशी
Continuous active service	अविरत सक्रिय सेवा	Copy stamped papers	प्रतिलिपि मुद्रित पत्र
Continuous service	अविरत सेवा	Copying Department	प्रतिलिपि विभाग
Contraband	व्यासिद्ध (विनिषिद्ध)	Copyist	प्रतिलिपिक
Contract	ठेका	Corbel	भारधारक बढ़ाव
Contract allowance	नियत भत्ता	Cornice	सीका (कगार)
Contract of sale	नियमबद्ध विक्रय	Coroner	अपमृत्यु-मीमांसक
Contractual relation	संविद्जनित सम्बन्ध	Corporal punishment	शारीरिक दण्ड
Contribution	अंश दान	Corpuscles	अणु-कण
Control over expenditure	व्यय पर नियन्त्रण	Correction	शोधन (सुधार)
Controller of stamps	मुद्रांक नियन्त्रक	Correction slip	शुद्धि पर्ची
		Corrigendum	शुद्धिपत्र
Controlling Officer	नियन्त्रक अधिकारी	Corrosive sublimate	रसकपूर

Corrugated	नालीदार	Covering farm	गाभिन फार्म
Corruption	भ्रष्टाचार	Covering return	गाभिन विवरण पत्र
Cost outstanding	गैर वसूल लागत	Creamery	मक्खन-मलाई शाला
Cost realized	वसूल लागत	Creation (of post)	पद स्थापन
Co-tenant	सहकृषक	Creative	रचनात्मक
Cotton balls	कपास का गोला	Credit	ऋण (उधार)
Council of State	राज्य परिषद्	Credit	जमा
Council, Board	परिषद्	Credit	साख
Counsel	मंत्रण	Credit advice	जमा की सूचना
Counter affidavit	प्रतिशपथ पत्र	Crest	शिखर
Counter balance	बराबर करना	Crime police	अपराध रोधक पुलिस
Counter claim	मुकाबिल दावा	Crime, Offence	अपराध
Counter signature	प्रतिहस्ताक्षर	Criminal conspiracy	आपराधिक षड्यन्त्र
Counterfoil	प्रतिपर्ण (मुसन्ना)	Criminal offence	दंडअपराध
Counterpart	प्रतिरूप	Criminal procedure	जाब्ता फौजदारी
Counterpart, Copy	प्रतिलिपि (मुसन्ना)	Criminal Procedure Code	दंड विधि संग्रह
Course of law	विधि प्रक्रम	Crop prospects	फसल की प्रत्याशा
Courses of training	शिक्षण पाठचर्या	Cropped area	बोया हुआ क्षेत्रफल
Court fee label	न्याय शुल्क चिप्पी	Cross examination	जिरह
Court fees	न्याय शुल्क	Cross examination	प्रतिपरीक्षा
Court fees act	न्याय शुल्क विधान	Cross mark	कर्तनी चिह्न
Court of law	न्यायालय	Cross objection	प्रति आपत्ति
Covenant	संविदा	Cross objection	प्रत्याक्षेप
Covenanty	पारस्परिक संविदा	Cross, bar, fetter	कैंची, डंडा, बेड़ी
Cover	आवरक	Crossing	चतुष्पथ
Cover	छद (आवरण)	Crosssection	अनुप्रस्थ छेद
Cover glass preparation	काचावृत रचनाएँ		

Crown of an arc	तोरण शीर्ष
Crown post	शिखर खण्ड
Cube	घन
Cube-root	घनमूल
Culinarv	पाक विषयक
Culpable	दंडनीय (अपराध)
Cultivator	कृषक
Culturable waste	कृषि योग्य बंजर
Culture medium	पोषक माध्यम
Curative measure	रोगहर उपाय
Current	चालू
Current duty	चालू कर्तव्य
Current fallow	वर्तमान पड़ती
Curve	वक्र
Cusecs	प्रतिसेकंड घनफुट
Custodian of museum	संग्रहालय संरक्षक
Custody	संरक्षण
Custody & Supply of forms	फार्मों का संरक्षण और दिया जाना
Custody of stamp	स्टाम्प का संरक्षण
Custody of wills	रिक्थपत्रों का संरक्षण
Cut, Deduction	कटौती
Cutaneous	चर्मीय
Cyclostyle	साइक्लोस्टाइल
Cylinder	बेलन
D. O. letter	अर्ध सरकारी पत्र
Dacoity	बटमारी
Daily labour return	श्रमिकों का दैनिक नकशा
Dairy	दुग्धशाला
Dairy farm	डेरी फार्म
Dak	डाक
Dam	संवर (बाँध)
Damage	हरजाना
Damages suit	क्षतिपूर्ति का वाद
Data	दी हुई बात
Date of institution	दायर करने की तारीख
Day scholar.	अनावासिक छात्र
De jure	विधानत:
De Novp	नये सिरे से
Deal thoroughly	पूरी तरह उपचार करना
Debenture	ऋणपत्र
Debit	विकलन
Debit advice	नाम की सूचना
Debit and Credit	नाम और जमा
Decay	क्षय
Decentralization	विकेन्द्रीकरण
Decentralization committee	विकेन्द्रीकरण (समिति)
Decided	निर्णीत
Decimal fraction	दशमलव भिन्न
Decision, Finding, Judgment	निर्णय
Declaration of trust	प्रन्यास घोषणा

Declaratory decree	अधिकार घोषक न्यायपत्र	Demand, Requisition	माँग
Decorations	सैनिक चिह्न	Demi-official	अर्धसरकारी
Decree	डिग्री	Demodectic scabies	खुजली
Decree	न्याय पत्र	Denaturalised	स्वभाव विकृत
Decree absolute	अंतिम डिगरी	Denial of execution	निष्पादन की इन्कारी
Decree nisi	प्रतिबन्धित न्यायपत्र		
Decree-holder	न्याय पत्रग्राही (डिगरीदार)	Denomination	मूल्यवान
		Departmental	वैभागिक
Deed (Sale, Lease)	विक्रयपत्र, पट्टा	Departmental account	वैभागिक लेखा
Deed of agreement	नियम पत्र	Deportation	निर्वासन (देश निकाला)
Deed of gift	दानपत्र		
Defalcation	व्ययहरण	Depose	राजच्युत करना
Defamation, Contempt	मानहानि	Depose	शपथपूर्वक साक्ष्य देना
Default	अनुपस्थान	Deposit	उपनिधान
Default	दोष	Deposit	धरोहर
Defence	उत्तर पक्ष	Deposition	सशपथ कथन
Defence	प्रतिरक्षा	Deposition	साक्षी का बयान
Defence Department	प्रतिरक्षा विभाग	Depreciation	अवलूल्यन
		Deputation	अभिप्रेषण
Defence witness	प्रतिवाद साक्षी	Deputation	प्रतिनियुक्ति (प्रतिनिधि मण्डल)
Defendant	प्रतिवादी		
Deferred pay	आस्थगित वेतन	Deputation (duty) allowance	प्रतिनियुक्ति भत्ता
Delegation	प्रत्यायुक्ति		
Delegation	शिष्टमडण्ल	Depute	प्रत्यायुक्त
Deletion	अपमार्जन	Derogatory	लाघवकारक
Delinquent	दोषी (अपराधी)	Descriptive roll	वर्णनवर्ति
Delivered	समर्पित	Deserter	दलत्यागी

Design	परिकल्पना	Discharge of duties	कर्तव्य पालन
Designate	मनोनीत	Discharge of water	निकासी
Designation	पदनाम, ओहदा	Discharged	अभियोग मुक्त
Designed	परिकल्पित	Discharged	कार्यत्यक्त
Designer	परिकल्पक	Discharged	दोष मुक्त
Despatch Rider	डाक सवार	Disciplinary action	अनुशासनात्मक कार्यवाही
Despatcher	संप्रेषक	Disciplinary action	अनुशासन की कार्यवाही
Detailed bill	ब्योरेवार बिल	Discipline	अनुशासन
Detention	अवरोध	Disciplined	अनुशासित
Detenue	अवरुद्ध	Disclaimer	दावा छोड़ने वाला
Development minister	विकास मन्त्री	Discount	बट्टा
Deviate	रास्ते से हटना	Discredited document	अमान्य लेख
Devolution	अवक्रमण	Discredited document	रद्द किया हुआ लेखपत्र
Diary	दैनंदिनी (दिन पंजी)	Discrepancy	असंगति
Diet money	भोजन व्यय	Discrepancy	भिन्नता
Difference of opinion	मतभेद	Discrepancy memo	कमी का स्मृतिपत्र
Digest	संक्षिप्त संग्रह	Discretion	विवेक
Direct charge	प्रत्यक्ष व्यय	Discretional registration	विवेकाधीन रजिस्टरी
Direct supervision	सीधी देखभाल	Disinfectant	कीटाणु नाशक
Direction	निर्देश	Disinfectant	रोगाणु नाशक
Directory	निर्देशिनी	Disinherit	दाय वंचित करना
Disability leave	अशक्तता छुट्टी	Dismiss, Weed out, Set side	खारिज करना
Disappearance	लोप	Dismissal	पदच्युति
Disbursement, Distribution	वितरण		
Disbursing authority	भुगतान प्राधिकारी		
Disbursing officer	भुगतानकारी अधिकारी		

Dismissed summarily	सरसरी तौर पर खारिज	Dress	वेष, वस्त्र
Display	प्रदर्शन	Dress regulation	वेष नियमावली
Disposal	निवर्तन	Drought	अनावृष्टि
Disposed off	निबटाया	Dryage	सूख
Disputed	विवादास्पद	Ductility	नरमी (तार खींचे जाने की क्षमता)
Disqualification	अयोग्यता	Dues	प्राप्य
Dissolution of partnership	साझाभंग पत्र	Duly	यथावत्
Distemper	दीवार पकड़ रंग	Duly approved	यथाविधि स्वीकृति
Distinguishing letter	विभेदक अक्षर	Duly stamped	यथोचित टिकट लगा हुआ
Distrain	कुड़क कराना	Duplicate	दुहरा
Distress warrant	अभिहरण अधिपत्र	Dust-proof	धूलरोक
Distributory	रजबहा	Duty	शुल्क
Diversity factor	भंदगुणक	Duty allowance	कर्तव्य भत्ता
Division of holdings	जोत का बँटवारा	Duty of transfer	हस्तांतरण शुल्क
Divisional canal Officer	नहर डिविजन अधिकारी	Duty on counterpart or duplicate	प्रतिलिपि पर शुल्क
Document	लेखपत्र (लेख्य)	Duty on release	अधिकार त्यागपत्र
Documentary	लेख्यात्मक	Dying declaration	मरणासन्न कथन
Domicile	स्थायी निवास	Dynamics	गतिशास्त्र
Dotted line	विन्दु रेखा	Earmark	निर्दिष्ट करना
Double shift system	द्विपारी प्रथा	Earnest money	सत्यकार (बयाना)
Dourine Act	उपदंश कानून	East coast fever	पूर्वतटीय ज्वर
Draft	आलेख (नक्शा)	Eaves	अलोनी
Draft	पांडुलेख (मसविदा)	Ebony	आबनूस
Draftsman	आलेखक	Eccentric	उत्केन्द्र
Drainage	जलोत्सारण	Ectozoa	बहिःपरजीवी
		Effective capacity	वास्तविक क्षमता

Effective span	कारगर चौड़ाई	Enactment	विधिकरण, विधि निर्माण
Efficiency bar	प्रगुणता अर्गल	En-camera trial	गुप्त अक्ष विचार
Egress	निष्कास	Encamping ground	निवेश स्थल
Ejectment	निर्मुक्ति (बेदखली)	Encampment	निवेशन (छावनी)
Ejectment	बेदखली	Encasing	कोष
Election Campaign	चुनाव आन्दोलन	Enclosure	अनुपत्र
Electrical equipment	विद्युत् सज्जा	Enclosure	अंतर्गतपत्र
Electrical installation	विद्युत् प्रतिष्ठापन	Encroachment	जमीन बढ़ाना
Electrician	वैद्युतिक	Encroachment	प्रत्यधिकार
Eligibility	पात्रता	Encroachment	सीमा-भंजन
Eligibility	वरणीयता	Encumbered	ऋणग्रस्त
Eligible	योग्य पात्र	Endorsement	पृष्ठ लेख
Eliptic and curved figures	अंडाकार क्षेत्र तथा वक्र क्षेत्र	Endorsement	पृष्ठांकन
Ellipse	अण्डवृत्त	Endorsement, Approval	अनुमोदन
Embankment	पंकार (बंध)	Endowment	अग्रहार-दान
Embezzlement	अपहार	Energy	शक्ति
Embezzlement	गबन	Enfacement	बिगाड़ना
Embezzlement	छल (हरण, गबन)	Enhancement	वृद्धि
Emergency	आकस्मिक	Enrolment	नाम निवेश
Emergency	संकटकाल (आपत्, विपत्ति)	Entozoa	अंतर्परजीवी
Emergency	संकट कालीन	Entry	प्रविष्टि
Emergency (Police)	संकट (पुलिस)	Epidemic	व्यापक संक्रामक रोग (मनुष्य)
Emoluments	परिलाभ	Epidemic disease	महामारी
Emulsion	दूधा	Epizootic	व्यापक संक्रामक रोग (पशु)
Enactment	विधायन (कानून)	Equilibrium	समतोल

Equipage	संभार	Exchange of compensation allowance	विनिमय क्षतिपूरक भत्ता
Equipment	सज्जा	Excise department	आबकारी विभाग
Equipment catalogue	सज्जा सूची	Excise duty	उत्पाद कर
Equipment table	सज्जा सारणी	Excreta	पुरीप (विष्ठा)
Equity	न्यायता	Executable	निर्वर्तन योग्य
Errata list	अशुद्धि-सूची	Executed document	लिखा-पढ़ा गया लेखपत्र
Erratic	अनिश्चित	Execution	तामील
Escape (for surplus water)	परिवाह	Execution	फाँसी
Escapee	अपसृत	Execution (as of decree)	निष्पादन
Escheat	अस्वाभाविक धन	Executive	निर्वाही
Escheat	साजसात् किया माल	Executor	इच्छापत्र साधक
Escort	गारद	Executor of will	रिक्थ साधक
Escort	रक्षक वर्ग	Exemplify	उदाहृत करना
Establishing	सिद्ध करना	Exemption	मुक्ति (छूट)
Establishment	स्थापना	Ex-gratia relief	अनुग्रह रूप सहायता
Estimate	आगणन	Exhaust	तली
Estopped	उत्तर रोध	Exhibit	प्रदर्शित वस्तु
Evasion of registration	सकपट रजिस्ट्री को बचा लेना	Ex-officio	पद कारणात्
Evidence	साक्ष्य	Ex-officio	पदेन
Evolution	उद्विकास	Ex-officio Sub-Registrar	पदकारणात् उपपंजीयक
Excepted	वर्जित	Ex-officio vendor	देन विक्रेता
Exception	अपवाद	Exoneration	छुटकारा
Excessive	अत्यधिक	Exparte	एकपक्षीय
Exchange	विनिमय	Experimental	प्रयोगात्मक
Exchange deed	विनिमय पत्र	Expert	विशेषज्ञ
Exchange instrument	विनिमयकरण पत्र		

Explanatory supplement	व्याख्यानात्मक अनुपूरक	Famine-duty	दुर्भिक्ष कर्तव्य
Export	निर्यात	Farcy	जहरबाद
Exposure	खुला रखना	Fatigue	दलेल
Express	आशु	Federation, Union	संघ
Express letter	आशुपत्र	Feeder	पोषक
Ex-proprietary	गतस्वामित्व	Fellowship	परिषद्यता
Ex-tenant	भूतपूर्व असामी	Fenestra	गवाक्ष
Extension	अवधि वद्धि	Ferries	घाट
Extension of leave	छुट्टी बढ़ाना	Ferries Act	घाट विधान
Extension of load	भार-वृद्धि	Ferrule	छल्ला
Extortion	बलात ग्रहण	Fertiliser, manure	खाद
Extract	अवतरण (उद्धरण)	Fetter	गेड़ी
Extract	उद्धरण	Fibrin	रक्त तन्तु
Extradition	विदेशी अपराधी का प्रत्यर्पण	Field-book	खसरा
Extraneous duties	अतिरिक्त कर्तव्य	Figures, Statistics	आँकड़े
Extraordinary leave	असाधारण छुट्टी	File	नत्थी (मिसिल, नस्ती)
Extremist	उग्रवादी	File register	नस्ती पंजी
Exudation	स्राव	Filing of document	मुकदम में कागजात दाखिल करना
Eye and hook	तुकमा और हुक	Fillet	फीता
Factor	गुणक	Finality	पूर्णता (अंतिमता)
Faculty	शाखा	Finally disposed of (decided)	अंतिम रूप से निर्णीत
Faecal discharge	मलत्याग	Finance Minister	अर्थमन्त्री
Fair copy	विशुद्ध प्रतिलिपि	Financial hand book	अर्थ पुस्तिका
Family arrangement	पारितोषिक व्यवस्थापन	Fine	अर्थदण्ड
		Finger Print	अँगुली छाप
		Finial	कलश (शिखर)
Famine-code	दुर्भिक्ष संहिता	Fire brigade	दमकल

Fire service	दमकल भृत्या	Flush latrine	धवनी
Fire-brick.	अग्नि-इष्टिका	Fly-proof	मक्खी रोक
Fireman, Fire-extin	अग्नि प्रशामक	Focus	नाभि
Fire-place	अलाव	Folio	पर्ण
Fire-proof safe.	अग्नि सुरक्षित तिजोरी	For consideration	विचारार्थ
First aid	प्रथमोपचार	Forced labour	बेगार
First Information Report	प्रारंभिक सूचना रपट	Forecast	पूर्वानुमान
Fiscal	राजस्व विषयक	Foreclosure of mortgage	बंधक मोक्षण प्रतिरोध
Fish ladder	मत्स्यारोह सीढ़ी	Foreign currency	विदेशी मुद्रा
Fish plate	मत्स्य पट्टिका	Foreigner	पर राष्ट्रिक
Fitness certificate	काग्र योग्यता प्रमाणपत्र	Foreman of the Jury	जूरी पंच
Fitness certificate	निरोगिता प्रमाणपत्र	Foremost	अग्रतम (प्रमुख)
Fitness for further advance	अधिकतम उन्नति के लिए योग्यता	Fore-noon	पूर्वाह्न
Fixed deposit	स्थिर जमा	Forensic	न्यायालय सम्बन्धी
Fixed for hearing	सुनवाई के लिए नियत की गयी	Forfeit	जब्त करना
Fixed point duty	एक स्थानीय चौराहा ड्यूटी	Forfeiture	अपहरण
Flag staff	पताका दंड	Forgery	कूटकरण (बाल कल्पना)
Flake	पापड़ (पपड़ी)	Forgery	कूट रचना
Flange	अग्रीव	Form	रूपपत्र (फार्म)
Flat charge	समान प्रभार	Forma pauperis.	अकिंचनता का मद
Fleas	पिस्सू	Formal	यथाचार
Floating debt	अल्पकाल ऋण	Formal (superficial)	ऊपरिक
Florescence	बसन्त (ऋतुराज)	Formal warning	यथानियम चेतावनी
Fluctuation	उतार-चढ़ाव	Formula	सूत्र
Flush	उद्धावन	Forthcoming	आगामी
		Forwarded	प्रेषित

Foundry	संघानी	Gazetted Officer	राजपत्रित अधिकारी
Framing of issues	विवाद प्रश्नों को स्थिर करना	General Provident fund	सामान्य पूर्वोपायी कोष
Fraud	कपट (कूट, छल, धोखा)	General rules	सामान्य नियम
Freight	अनुतर	General Rules, Civil	दीवानी के सामान्य नियम
Frequency	वारंवारता	Generating station	विद्युत उत्पादन संस्थान
Frontis piece	मुखचित्र		
Fugitive criminal	पलायित दोषी	Generator	जनित्र (जनक)
Fulcrum	आलंब (टक)	Geological survey	भूगर्भ अनुदर्शन
Full Bench	न्यायाधीश गण	Girder	गार्टर
Full particulars	सारा वृत्तान्त	Girth	तंग
Function	कृत्य	Glue	सरेस
Function	पद कर्तव्य	Good behaviour	सदाचार
Functus officio	समाप्ताधिकार	Good Faith	सद्भाव
Fund	निधि	Goods	भंडक (माल)
Fundamental	आधारभूत	Governed	शासित
Fundamental	मौलिक	Government order	सरकारी आज्ञा
Fundamental guide book	मौलिक पथप्रदर्शनी	Government pleader	सरकारी अधिवक्ता
Fundamental rule	मौलिक नियम	Government pleader	सरकारी अभिभावक
Furnish security	जमानत दाखिल करना	Government, Crown	सरकार
Furniture	उपस्कर	Governor	राज्यपाल
Fuse	दहन वर्ति	Gradation	कोर्ट साहिब
Gallery	दीर्घा	Gradation list	कोटिक्रम
Gallows	वधस्थान	Grand total	पूर्णयोग
Galvanized	जस्ता चढ़ी	Grant	अनुदान
Gauge	आमान	Grant-in-aid	सहायक अनुदान
Gazette	राजपत्र (गजट)	Graph	विन्दुरेख

Gratification	परितोष	Hand grenade	हथगोला
Gratings	जाली (झँझरी)	Hand slip	हथचिट्ट
Gratuity	सेवोपहार	Hand writing	हस्तलिपि
Gravel	रोड़ा (कंकड़)	Harness	काठी
Gravity	गुरुत्व	Hasp	कुन्दा कब्जा
Gravity canal	ढाल चालित नहर	Head and Sub-head	शीर्षक और उपशीर्षक
Grease free	चर्बी रहित	Head of account	लेखा शीर्षक
Gridiron	तवा (लपरी)	Head of the department	विभागाध्यक्ष
Grind-stone	सान		
Gross load	सकल भार	Head Regulator	शीर्षस्तर नियामक
Gross negligence	भारी प्रमाद	Head rope	शिररज्जु
Gross salary	सकल वेतन	Head works	उद्गम कार्यजात
Ground water supplied	पाताल जलपुंज	Headquarter	मुख्य स्थान
Grounds of appeal	अपील के आधार	Headquarters	मुख्यालय
Group	गुट (समूह)	Headway	प्रगति
Group leader	टोली नायक	Health certificate	स्वास्थ्य प्रमाणपत्र
Groyne	जलतोड़	Hearing	सुनवाई
Guarantee letter	सुरक्षापत्र	Heel file	एड़ी जोड़ा
Guards & Escorts	गादद और कमान	Helmet	शिरस्त्राण
Guilty	दोषी (दोष प्राप्त)	Hereditary	पारंपरीय (पैतृक)
Gunpowder	बारूद	Heritage, Inheritance	दाय (बपौती)
Guts, Water course	गूल		
Gymnasium	व्यायामशाला	High Court	उच्च न्यायालय
Habitual offender	आभ्यासिक अपराधी	High flood level	महाप्लवस्तर चिह्न
Half-margin	अर्धोपान्त	Higher authority	उच्च अधिकारी
Halt	निवेशन	Highway	राजमार्ग
Halting (allowance)	निवेशन (भत्ता)	Hindu reversioner	हिन्दू उत्तरभोगी
		Hindu widow's	हिन्दू विधवा का

Hip rafter	शीर्ष शहतीर	Illustrated, Illustrate	उदाहृत
Hire purchase	भाड़ाक्रय	Imminent	प्रत्यासन्न
His Excellency	महामान्य (महामहिम)	Immoral traffic	अनैतिक पण
History sheet	अपराध वृत्त	Immovable property	अचल सम्पत्ति
Holding cost	रोक रखने की लागत	Immovable property	स्थावर सम्पत्ति
Home guard	होमगार्ड	Impersonation, False personation	छद्मव्यक्तिता
Homogeneous	सजातीय (समाधान)	Impervious	अप्रवेश्य
Honorarium	मानदेय	Implement, Tools	उपकरण
Honorary	अवैतनिक	Implementation	कार्यान्वयन
Horse power	अश्व-शक्ति	Import	आयात
Horse stallion	बीजाश्व (घुड़साँड़)	Impound	निरोध करना
Hot-pursuit	तीव्र अनुधावन	Impounded documents	जब्त किये हुए लेख पत्र
House rent allowance	मकान किराया भत्ता	Impressed stamp	मुद्रांकित स्टाम्प
human resources department	नियुक्ति विभाग	Impression	छाप
Humane cattle killer	अनिर्दय पशुवध-यन्त्र	Impression (copy)	निवेश
Hundi, Stamp	हुंडी मुद्रांक	Imprest	अग्रधन
Hydraulic	जल चालित	Improved	सुधरा हुआ
Hydro	जल	In Camera	कक्षस्थ (गुप्त)
Hydro-electric grid	जल विद्युत तारजाल	In compliance with	पालन करते हुए
Hypotenuse	कर्ण	In consequence	परिणामस्वरूप
Hypothecation	आड	In due course	यथासमय
Hypothesis	कल्पना	In furtherance of a common cause	सार्वजनिक हितोन्नति
Identical	अनन्य	In moderate excess	कुछवाजिबी अधिक
Identification	पहचान	In pursuit of	अनुशीलन
Identification mark	चिह्न		
Illegal	अवैध		
Illegible copy	दुर्वचनीय कापी		

In supersession of.	अकारण करते हुए	Indigent	निर्धन
In toto	बिलकुल	Indiscriminate	अविवेकी, अविवेकपूर्ण
Inadequate	अपर्याप्त	Indivisible transaction	अविभाज्य लेन–देन
Inadmissible claims	अग्राह्य दावा	Indoor patient	भरती रोगी
Inaugural	प्रतिष्ठापनिक	Inducement	प्रेरणा (प्रलोभन)
Incidence	आपात	Industrialization	औद्योगीकरण
Incidental charge	आनुषंगिक व्यय	Industry, Labour	परिश्रम
Inclined	झुका	Inefficiency	अप्रगुणता
Incognizable	अहस्तक्षेप्य	Inertia	जड़ता
Income-tax	आयकर	Infanticide	शिशुवध
Increment	वेतन वृद्धि	Infantry	पदाति
Incumbency	पद धारणा	Infections, Jaundice of the dogs	कुत्ते का संक्रामक पाण्डुरोग
Indemnification	तावान देना		
Indemnity bond	क्षतिपूरक प्रतिज्ञापत्र	Inferior staff	अवर कर्मचारी वर्ग
Indemnity bond	हानिपूरक नियमपत्र	Infinitesimal	अत्यन्त छोटा
Indemnity, Compensation	क्षतिपूर्ति	Infirm	अशक्त
Index	अनुक्रमणिका	Infirmary	आतुरालय
Indian Arms Act	भारतीय शस्त्र विधान	Infirmity	असमर्थता
Indian Army Act	भारतीय सेना विधान	Inflation	मुद्रास्फीति
Indian Civil Service	भारतीय जनपद भृत्या	Influence line	प्रभाव रेखा
		Infra	नीचे
Indian Divorce Act	भारतीय विवाह विच्छेद विधान	Infringement	भंग करना
Indian Evidence Act	भारतीय साक्ष्य विधान	Infringement, Contravention	उल्लंघन
Indian Penal Code	भारतीय दण्ड संहिता	Ingredient	अंश (घटक द्रव्य)
Indian Succession Act	भारतीय उत्तराधिकार विधान	Ingress, Inlets	प्रवेश (द्वार)
		Initial pay	आरंभिक वेतन
Indicator	देशित	Initialled	लघुहस्ताक्षरित

Injunction	निषेधाज्ञा	Insulation layer	विसंवाहकस्तर
Injured stamp	क्षत मुद्रांक	Insulator	विसंवाहक
Injury	आघात	Intangible property	अमूर्त सम्पत्ति
Injury to records	कागजात का नुकसान	Integrity	सत्यशीलता
Inoculation, Comments, Notes	टीका	Intensity	प्रगाढ़ता
Inscription	शिलालेख	Intercourse	संसर्ग
Insemination	गर्भाधान	Interest-free	बेब्याज
Insertion	अंतर्न्यास	Interim	अंतर्कालीन (अंतरिम)
Insignificant	तुच्छ	Interim	मध्यवर्ती
Inspection	निरीक्षण	Interim stay	मध्वर्ती स्थगन
Inspection fee	निरीक्षण शुल्क	Interlination	पंक्तिमध्य लेख
Inspector General	महानिरीक्षक	Inter-lineation	लाइन के बीच में लिखना
Inspector General of Prisons	महाकारानिरीक्षक	Intermediary, Intermediate	अंत:स्थायी
Inspectorate of stamp	स्टाम्प निरीक्षणाधिकारी वर्ग	Intermediate	माध्यमिक
Installation	प्रतिष्ठापन	Intermediate forecast	बीच का पूर्वानुमान
Institute	ज्ञानमन्दिर (ज्ञानालय)	Intermittent cultivation	अतिरिक्त खेती
Instruction	अनुदेश	Interpolating	कोई शब्द छल से लिख देना
Instrument (in writing)	करणपत्र	Interpretation	व्याख्या
Instrument of dowery	दहेहकारणपत्र	Interrogation, Inquiry	प्रच्छना
Instrument of furthep charge	अधिक भार का कारण पत्र	Interval	अंतराल
Instrument of gift	प्रदान पत्र	Intimation	सूचना
Instrument of Settlement	व्यवस्थापत्र	Intoxicating drug	मादक द्रव्य
Instruments creating interest	स्वार्थोत्पादक करणपत्र	Intrados	महराब
		Intramural	भित्ति भीतर
		Introduction	पुर: स्थापना

Inventory	सूची	Judicial	न्याय सम्बन्धी
Inverse rate	प्रतीप दर	Judicial authority	न्यायालयिक प्राधिकारी
Investigation	अनुसंधान	Judicial Department	न्याय विभाग
Investment	रुपये का लगाना	Judicial investigation	न्यायिक विचारण
Invidious	द्वेषजनक	Judicial proceeding	न्यायिक कार्यवाही
Invoice	बीजक	Judiciary	न्यायाधिकारी वर्ग
Ipso facto	स्वत: सिद्ध	Junction	संगम
Irksome	अप्रिय (थकाऊ)	Jurisdiction	अधिकार क्षेत्र
Irrecoverable	अप्रतिलक्ष्य	Jurisdiction Act	विचाराधिकार विधान
Irregularity	अनियमता	Justice of the peace	शांति-रक्षा दण्डनायक
Irrelevant	असंगत	Justice of the Peace	शांति रक्षा आधिकरणिक
Isometric	चित्रसम (प्रक्षेप)	Juvenile offender	अल्पवयस्क अपराधी
Issue Price	निर्गम मूल्य	Juvenile offender	किशोर अपराधी
Issue, Code	जारी करना	King post	खड़ा लम्ब
Issues	निर्गमन	Kink	अलपेट
Item	मद	Lack, Want	अभाव
Jail premises.	कारोपान्त	Land record manual	भूअभिलेख सार संग्रह
Jailor	कारापाल	Land Improvement loan	भूमि सुधारार्थ ऋण
Jambs	छिद्र पक्ष	Land Improvement Loans Act	भूमि सुधार ऋण विधान
Jet	नाल (टोंटी)	Land record	भू लेखा
Job	काम (ठेके का)	Land record clerk	भूअभिलेख लेखक
Joining time	कार्यग्रहण अवधि	Land record department	भू लेखा विभाग
Joint family property	अविभक्त परिवार सम्पत्ति		
Joint holding	अविभक्त जोत		
Joist	धरणी		
Judgment writer	निर्णय लेखक		
Judgment-debtor	निर्णीत ऋणी		
Judicature	न्यायाधिकार		

Land revenue	भू राजस्व	Legitimate (as in legitimate child)	औरस
Land revenue	मालगुजारी	Legitimate dues	न्यायोचित दातव्य
Landed property, Estate	भूसम्पत्ति	Lessee	पट्टेदार
Landlord	भूस्वामी	Lessor	पट्टा करने वाला
Lapse	अतिवृत्त	Letter of administration	उत्तराधिकार (विरासत) का प्रमाणपत्र
Lapsed	कालातीत	Letter of administration	प्रबंधाधिकार पत्र
Larder	खाद्य सामग्री भण्डार	Letter of credit	प्रत्ययपत्र
Lathe	कुन्द	Letters patent appeal	राजदया अपील
Lathe	खराद	Letting	जमीन का उठाना
Lawful assembly	विधि अनुकूल सभा	Levelling staff	स्तरमापक दण्ड
Lay out	समहिति	Levy	लगान उगाहना
Lease	पट्टा	Liability	दायित्व
Lease hold	पट्टे की भूमि	Liable	उत्तरदायी
Leases	पट्टे	Licence	अनुज्ञा-पत्र
Leave preparatory to retirement	निवृत्ति पूर्व छुट्टी	Licencing authorities	अनुज्ञा पत्र दायक
Leave salary	छुट्टी वेतन	Licensee	अनुज्ञाधारी
Leaves of door	द्वारपट	Lien	ग्रहणाधिकार
Ledger	बहीखाता	Lien suspended	स्थगित ग्रहणाधिकार
Legal	वैधिक	Lieutenant Governor	उपराज्यपाल
Legal practitioner	विध्युपजीवी अभिभाषक	Life-tenure	आजीवन पट्टा
Legal Rememberancer	वैध उद्बोधक	Lightning conductor	तड़ित संवाहक
Legatee	रिक्थी	Limitation	अवधि
Legislative assembly	व्यवस्थापिका सभा	Linear	लकीरी
Legislative department	व्यवस्थापिका विभाग	Link	कड़ी
Legitimate	न्याय्य	Lintel	पटीरन

Liquidation	अपाकरण (दिवाला)	Lump-sum	पिंडराशि
Listing of cases	मुकदमों को सूचीगत करना	Lunatic criminal	विक्षिप्त दोषी
		Lymphatic glands	लसीका ग्रन्थि
Litigation	विवाद	Magazine	शस्त्रागार
Live stock	पशुधन	Maggot	कोट (कृषि)
Indent	माँग पत्र	Magistrate	अधिकरणिक
Inquest	मृत्यु विचारणा	Magistrate	दंडनायक
Loaded	भारित	Main wall (Jail ward), Baton, Bludgeon	डंडा
Lobby	सभाकक्ष		
Lobby, Chaupal	चौपार (डेवढ़ी)	Maintenance	अनुपालन
Local	स्थानिक (स्थानीय)	Maintenance	रखरखाव
Local allowance	स्थानीय भत्ता	maintenance	जीवन निर्वाह
Local bodies	स्थानीय निकाय	Maintenance officer	रखरखाव निरीक्षक
Local cess	स्थानीय कर	Maintenance officer	रखरखाव अधिकारी
Local depot	स्थानीय कोठार		
Local funds	स्थानीय संस्थाकोष	Major	वयस्क
Local government	स्थानीय सरकार	Major head	बड़ा शीर्षक
Lock-up	हवालात	Majority	बहुमत
Locus standi	स्थानाधिकार	Make restoration, Compensate	टोटा भरना
Locust	टिड्डी	Malignant growth	रोगज वृद्धि
Logarithm	छेदा	Manager	प्रबंधक
Long section	अन्वायाम काट	Mandatory	आदेशात्मक
Longitude	देशांतर (लंबान)	Manifesto	घोषणापत्र
Loose cotton	खुली हुई रूई	Manual (books)	सार-संग्रह
Louvre	झिलमिली	Manual of Irrigation Order	सिंचाई आदेश सारसंग्रह
Lower	अधस्तन		
Lump	पिंड	Manual of orders	आज्ञासार संग्रह
Lump sum	एकराशि	Manufacturing process	निर्माण क्रिया

Manufiicture	निर्माण
Margin	उपात
Marginal	औपान्तिक
Marginal heading	उपांत शीर्षक (पार्श्व शीर्षक)
Marginally noted	उपांत लिखित
Marine Officer	समुद्री अधिकारी
Maritime policy	समुद्री पालिसी
Market	विपणी (आपण)
Marketable security	क्रयविक्रय योग्य सरकारी हुण्डी
Marriage (Dissolution of)	विवाह भंग
Marriage certificate	विवाह प्रमाणपत्र
Mask	मुखावरण
Mason	राज
Masonry	राजगीरी
Master of ship	पोतपति
Material change	मुख्य परिवर्तन
Material injustice	वास्तविक अन्याय
Maternity hospital	प्रसूति चिकित्सालय
Maternity leave	प्रसूति छुट्टी
Matrimonial reader	विवाह विषयक पेशकार
Matron	मातृका
Mature	प्रौढ़ (परिपक्व)
Maturity	परिपक्वता
Maximum demand indicatory	अधिकतम माँग-सूचक
Mean	माध्य (औसत)
Measurement book	नाप पुस्तक
Medical leave	चिकित्सकीय छुट्टी
Medium pressure	मध्यम भार
Member (Roof)	अंग
Memo of appearance	उपस्थिति का स्मृतिपत्र
Memorandum	स्मृतिपत्र
Memorialist, Applicant	आवेदक
Mensuration	क्षेत्रमिति
Mercy petition	दया की अभ्यर्थना
Merger	समावेश
Mesh	जाल (जालि का छेद)
Mesne profit	अपलाभ (जरे वासलात)
Metalled (Road)	पक्की (सड़क)
Meteorological observatory	अंतरिक्ष विज्ञान मान-मन्दिर
Meter	मापक (मीटर)
Meter reader	मीटर वाचक
Microscopical examination	सुक्ष्मदर्शकीय परीक्षा
Military officer	सैनिक अधिकारी
Military service	सैनिक सेवा
Military stores	सैनिक कोषागार
Miniature	सूक्ष्माकार (लघुचित्र)
Minister of food	खाद्य मन्त्री
Minor	अल्पवयस्क

Minute book	कार्यवाही का रजिस्टर	Mortgagor	बन्धक कर्ता
Minutes	कार्यवाही	Mould	खाँचा
Misappropriation	अपाहरण	Mound	टीला
Misbehaviour	अविनय	Mounted police	घुड़सवार पुलिस
Miscarriage	गर्भपात	Movable property, Movable effect	चल सम्पत्ति
Miscarriage of Justice	न्याय वैफल्य	Mud mortar	गारा
Miscellaneous	प्रकीर्ण (विविध)	Mufti	साधारण वेष
Mis-description	अशुद्ध वर्णन	Multifarious (suit)	अनेकार्थ (वाद)
Mitigation	शमन (न्यूनीकरण)	Multifarious suit	बहुविधवाद
Mobile squad	गश्ती दस्ता	Municipality	नगरपालिका
Modification, Amendment	संशोधन	Muster	गिनती (हाजिरी)
Modified grant	संशोधित अनुदान	Muster-roll	गिनती की किताब
Modulus	माप	Mutation register	दाखिल खारिज रजिस्टर
Moiety fees	अल्पशुल्क	Mutatis Mutandis	आवश्यक परिवर्तनों सहित
Moment of inertia	जड़ता प्रवृत्ति	My Lord	धर्म-मूर्ति
Momentum	झोंक	Narrative	वृत्तान्त
Monetary allotment	आर्थिक दिष्टि	National Service	राष्ट्रीय सेवा
Monopoly	एकाधिकार	Nationalization	राष्ट्रीयकरण
Monthly abstract	मासिक उपसंक्षेप	Native of India	भारतवासी
Monthly return	मासिक विवरणपत्र	Naturalization	देशीकरण (नागरिकीकरण)
Morbid material	विकृत कायिक पदार्थ	Nature of the case	मुकदमे का प्रकार
Mortgage	बंधक	Naval Force	नाविक सेना
Mortgage	रेहन बन्धक	Navigation	नौचालन
Mortgage bond	बंधक पत्र	Negative	ऋणात्मक
Mortgagee	बन्धक ग्राही	Negligence	असावधानी

Net	शुद्ध	Normal, General	सामान्य
Net assets	वास्तविक सम्पत्ति	Northern India	उत्तरी भारत
Net emoluments	शुद्ध परिलाभ	Notary public	लेख्यप्रमाणक
Net profit	शुद्ध लाभ	Notch	दान्ता
Neutral axis	क्लीवाक्ष	Noter and Drafter	टिप्पणी लेखक तथा पाण्डु लेखक
New fallow	नई परती		
Nomenclature	नामकरण	Notes and orders	टीपें और आज्ञाएँ
Nominal roll	नाम सूची	Notification, Communique	विज्ञप्ति
Non Judicial	न्यायालयेत्तर		
Non Judicial Stamp	न्यायेतर स्टाम्प	Nozzle	नाक (टोंटी)
		Nuisance	कंटक (बाधा)
Non-commissioned officer	अनायुक्त अधिकारी	Null and void	निष्प्रभाव और निरर्थक
		Numbered	संख्यात
Non-compliance	न पालन करना	Numerator, Share	अंश
Non-contract	अनियत	Nursery	पौधशाला
Non-food crops	अखाद्य फसल	Oath of allegiance	राज्य निष्ठा शपथ
Non-gazetted (officer)	अराजपत्रित (अधिकारी)	Object	उद्देश्य
Non-labouring	अपरिश्रमी	Objection	आपत्ति
Non-occupancy tenant	गैरदखिलकारी असामी	Objection (statement)	अवक्षेपण (विवरण पत्र)
		Objector	आपत्तिकर्ता
Non-official	अनाधिकारिक	Obligation instrument	दायरा का करणपत्र
Non-porous	असोख		
Non-recurring expenditure	अनावर्ती व्यय	Obligation of residence	निवास प्रतिबंध
Non-residential	अनावासिक	Oblique	तिर्यक्
Non-scheduled	अपरिगणित	Oblong	आयत (याताकार)
Non-testamentary	असम्बन्धित इच्छापत्र	Obscure	अस्पष्ट (अप्रसिद्ध)
Normal	साधारण	Observation	आलोचन

Obsolete stamp	अप्रचलित स्टाम्प	Option	रुचि
Occupancy right	भोगोधिकार (दखीलकारी)	Option, Alternative	विकल्प
Occupancy tenant	दखील असामी	Oral evidence	मौखिक साक्ष्य
Occupation	वृत्ति, पेशा	Orbit	अक्षिकप
Occupiers' rate	किरायेदार की दर	Orbit	कक्ष (ग्रहपथ)
Octroi duty	चुंगीकर	Order book	आज्ञा पुस्तक
Odd	विषम	Order file	आज्ञा नस्ती
Offer	उपदान	Order sheet	आज्ञा फलक
Officer under training	शिक्षणाधीन अधिकारी	Order-book	आदेश-पंजी
Officer on special duty	विशेष कार्याधिकारी	Ordinance (law)	अध्यादेश
		Ordinate, Grade	कोटि
Official	कर्मचारी	Organisation	संगठन
Official Assignee	सरकारी अधिहस्तांकिती	Organisation	संघटन
		Organiser	आयोजक
Official trustee	सरकी प्रन्यासी	Organiser	संघटनकर्ता
Officiating appointment	स्थानापन्न नियुक्ति	Oriental	पूर्वी
Officiating, Substitute	स्थानापन्न	Original	मूल
		Original award	आरंभिक निर्णय
Offset piece	गुनिया	Outlay	लागत
Old fallow	पुरानी परती	Outlet	निकास
On parole	संगर-बद्ध	Outpost (Police)	चौकी
On special duty	विशेष कार्यार्थ	Oval or rounded creature	वर्तुलाकार जीव
Ooze	चूना (टपकना)	Overcharge	अधिक व्यय
Opening balance	आरंभिक	Overcharge, Surcharge	अधिभार
Operator	चालक		
Opposite party	प्रतिपक्ष	Overhead charges	उपरिव्यय
Opposite party	विपक्ष	Overpayment	अधिक भुगतान

Overseas pay	समुद्र पार का वेतन	Pass-book	ग्राहक–पुस्तिका (पासबुक)
Overseer	अवेक्षक	Passport	पारपत्र
Overstay	अत्वस्थान	Patch repairs	थोप चेप मरम्मत
Overtime	समयोत्तर (काम)	Patent medicine	एकस्व भेषज
P. T. Instructor	व्यायाम शिक्षक	Pathological specimens	रोग विषयक नमूने
P.W. (Prosecution witness)	अभियोग साक्षी	Pathology	रोगशास्त्र
Painter	रंजक	Patron, Custodian	संरक्षक
Panel (architecture)	दिलाहा	Pattern	प्रतिमान
Pantographer	प्रतिलिपिक यन्त्र	Pauper appeal.	अकिंचन अपील
Pantry	खाद्य कोष्ठ	Pauper suit.	अकिंचन वाद
Par	समता	Pawn, Pledge	आधि (गिरवी)
Para	अनुच्छेद	Pay	वेतन
Parallel	समान्तर	Pay account	वेतन लेखा
Parapet	कमरकोटा (मुँडेर)	Payment	भुगतान
Paraphernalia	सामान	Peace	शांति
Parcel	पोट्टलिका (पार्सल)	Pebble	रोड़ी (छान)
Park	उद्यान	Pecuniary, Monetary	आर्थिक
Parlour	बैठक (बरोठा)	Pedestrian	पदिक
Parole	संगर	Penal	दंड विषयक
Part performance, Part supply	आंशिक पूर्ति	Penalty	डाँड़
Part time	अंश कालिक	Pencil	अंकनी
Part-heard	सुना भाग	Pendant, Hanger	लटकन (झुमका)
Particular	विशिष्ट (सविशेष)	Pendency	लम्बमानता
Particular, Statement	विवरण	Pending	अम्बमान
		Penology	दंडशास्त्र
Parties	उभयपक्ष	Pension	निवृत्ति वेतन
Passage (voyage by sea)	संयात्रा	Pensioner	निवृत्ति वेतनी

Perforator	वेधनी	Pier	पाया (संभा)
Perimeter	परिमाप	Pile bridge	भूमि प्रविष्ट पुल
Period of limitation	अवधिताकाल	Pilot scheme	पथदर्शक योजना
Periodical	सामयिक	Pivot	चूल (जिस पर कोई वस्तु घूमे)
Permanent advance	स्थायी अग्रधन	Plaint	वाद, अर्जीदावा
Permanent alimony	स्थायी दाराभूति	Plaint	वादपत्र (अर्जी दावा)
Permanent post	स्थायी पद	Plaintiff	वादी
Permanent tenure holder	स्थायी भू भुक्तिधारी	Plan	मानचित्र
Permanently settled	स्थायी बन्दोबस्ती	Plane	समतल
Permissible	अनुज्ञेय	Plant and machinery	स्थिर यन्त्र और मशीनें
Permit	अनुमतिपत्र	Plate	पट्टिका
Perpetration, Delinquency	अपराध (बुरा काम)	Pleader	अभिभाषक
Perpetual allowance	शाश्वत भत्ता	Plinth	पीठभू (कुर्सी)
Personal appearance	व्यक्तिगत उपस्थिति	Plumb (mason)	संबक
Personal law	स्वधर्म शास्त्र	Plumber	सीसागर
Personal ledger	वैयक्तिक प्रपंजी	Plus & minus memo	धन तथा ऋण का स्मृति पत्र
Personal pay	वैयक्तिक वेतन	Polygon	बहुभुज
Pertain	सम्बन्ध रखना	Pool	पल्वल (पोखर)
Petition	अभ्यर्थना (याचिका)	Portable	सुवहनीय
Petitioner	अभ्यर्थी	Positive	धनात्मक
Petty contingent expenditure	क्षुद्र प्रासंगिक व्यय	Post	रास्ता
Petty establishment	लघु स्थापना	Post, Rank	पद (ओहदा)
Physical assets	भौतिक परिसम्पत्	Posting	तैनाती
Piece work	ठेके का काम	Post-mortem	शवपरीक्षा
		Postscript	अनुलेख

Posture	मुद्रा (आसन)	Preventive	निवारक
Post-war	युद्धोत्तर	Prima facie	पहली दृष्टि में
Power	अधिकार	Prima facie	प्राम दृष्टि सिद्ध
Power of attorney	अभिकर्तापत्र	Primary unit	प्राथमिक इकाई
Power of attorney	प्रतिनिधि पत्र	Prime mover	प्रधान प्रेरक
Power-vested	संप्राप्त अधिकार	Principal money	मूलधन
Preamble, Introduction	प्रस्तावना	Principal rafter	मुख्य धरणी
Precaution	पूर्वोपाय	Priority	आदिता (पूर्वता)
Precedence	पूर्वता (आदिता)	Privilege	विशेषाधिकार
Pre-censorship	पूर्वदोष वेंचन	Privilege leave	रियायती छुट्टी
Predecessor-in-title	स्वत्वाधिकार पूर्ववर्ती	Privy Council	प्रिवी कौंसिल
Predication	उपाधि प्राप्ति	Prize bonds	पारितोषिक प्रतिज्ञापत्र
Pre-emption, Right of pre-emption	पूर्वक्रयाधिकार (हकशफा)	Probate	इच्छापत्र की प्रमाणित प्रतिलिपि
Preference	अधिमान	Probation	परीक्षण
Prejudice	पक्षपात	Probationer	परीक्ष्यमाण
Preliminary	प्रारंभिक	Procedure	कार्य पद्धति
Premises	गृहोपान्त	Procedure	कार्यविधि
Preponderance	प्रधान	Procedure	प्रक्रम
Prescribed	नियत	Procedure	विधि
Prescribed	विहित (निर्धारित)	Proceedings, Action	कार्यवाही
Prescribed form	नियत फारम	Process	रीति
Presented, Submitted	प्रस्तुत	Process fees	आह्वान शुल्क
Preservation	परिरक्षा	Process server	आदेश पत्र वाहक
Presiding officer	निर्वाचनाध्यक्ष	Proclamation, Declaration	घोषणा
Presumptive (pay)	अनुमानिक (वेतन)	Procuress	दूती (संचारिका)
		Production	उत्पादन
		Production (as a document)	प्रस्तुति

Profession	वृत्त (व्यवसाय)	Prosecution	अभियोग
Proficient	प्रवीण	Prosecution	अभियोग पक्ष
Pro-forma	नियमानुरूप	Prospective	भावी
Proforma respondent	यथानियम उत्तरवादी	Protected land	सुरक्षित भूमि
Proforma-defendant	गौण प्रतिवादी	Protection	रक्षा
Proforma-respondent	गौण उत्तरवादी	Protector of emigrants	उत्प्रवासी संरक्षक
Progressive pay	वर्धमान वेतन	Pro-vice-chancellor	प्रति उपकुलपति
Prohibition	निषेध	Provident	दूरदर्शी
Prohibition	मद्यनिषेध	Provident fund	पूर्वापायी कोष
Project, Scheme	योजना	Provision (Budget)	व्यवस्था
Projection	प्रक्षेपण	Provision, Instructions (law)	आदेश
Promotion	पदोन्नति	Provisional	अस्थायी
Pronote	बचन पत्र	Provisional substantive	अस्थायी मूल
Pronote	रुक्का	Proviso	प्रतिबन्धात्मक वाक्य खण्ड
Propaganda	प्रचार		
Proportion	अनुपात	Proxy, Locum tenens	प्रतिपुरुष
Proportion	समानुपात		
Proportionate	आनुपातिक	Public Prosecution	सरकार-चालित मुकदमा
Proposition statement	प्रस्तावित नकशा	Public affairs	सार्वजनिक मामले
Proposition statement	प्रस्तावित विवरण	Public conveyance	किराये की गाड़ी
Proprietor	स्वामी	Public debt	सार्वजनिक ऋण
Propulsion charges	चालान-व्यय	Public Officer	सार्वजनिक अधिकारी
		Public safety	जन-सुरक्षा
Pro-rata	अनुपातत:	Public servant	जन-सेवक
Prosecute	अभियोग (चलान)	Public utility	सार्वजनिक उपयोगिता
Prosecuting inspector	कोषस्थीकरण	Public works Department	सार्वजनिक निर्माण विभाग

Publicity	प्रकाशना (प्रख्यापना)	Re-appropriation	पुन: पर्यादान
		Re-armament	पुन: शस्त्रीकरण
Punishment, Penalty	दंड	Rebate	अवहार (छूट)
Purview	अधिकार सीमा	Recall from leave	छुट्टी से वापस बुलाना
Pyramid (ancient world)	सूची		
		Receipt book	रसीद बही
Quadrant	पाद	Receipt register	प्राप्ति पंजी
Quadratic equation	वर्ग समीकरण	Receiver	प्रतिग्राहक
		Receptacle	भाजन (आधान)
Quadrennial	चौसाला	Recess	विश्राम (छुट्टी)
Quantity, Volume	परिमाण		
Quarantine	स्पर्शवर्जन	Recess, Vacation	अवकाश
Quarantine leave	स्पर्शवर्जन छुट्टी	Recipient	आदाता
Quarterly statement	त्रैमासिक विवरण	Reciprocity	पारस्परिकता
		Recognised agent	मान्यता प्राप्त अभिकर्ता
Quasi-permanent	अर्थ स्थायी		
Questionnaire	प्रश्नावली	Recognition	मान्यता
Quinquennial	पंचवर्षीय	Recognizance	मुचलका
Rafter	कड़ी (धरणी)	Reconnaissance	पूर्वानुदर्शन
Railings, Rack	करघटा	Re-constitution	पुन: रचना
Rain gauge	वर्षामापक	Record	अभिलेख
Rake	पाँचा	Record of service	सेवाभिलेख
Random	अव्यवस्था	Record operation	अभिलेख संशोधन
Rank	आस्पद (पदवी)	Record-in-charge	अभिलेखाधिकृत
Rank and file	साधारण सैनिक वर्ग	Record-keeper	अभिलेख पाल
Ratchet	कुत्ता	Recovery	प्रतिलब्धि
Rate of exchange	विनिमय दर	Recruitment	भरती
Raw material	कच्चा माल	Rectification of error	अशुद्धि शोधन
Realization	उगाही (वसूली)	Rector	अधिष्ठाता

Recurring	आवर्ती	Relaxation	शैथिल्य
Redemption	विमोचन	Relaxed	शिथिलीकृत
Redemption of mortgage	बंधकमोचन	Relief (Carving)	उभार
Reduction	पदावनति	Relinquishment	परित्याग दस्तबरदारी
Re-employed	पुनर्नियुक्त	Relinquishment of land	भूमि का अधिकारत्याग
Re-employment	पुनर्नियंक्ति	Relinquishment, Abandonment, Surrender	त्याग
Re-establishment, Re-instatement	पुन: स्थापन		
Reference	अभ्युद्देश	Remain at large	अबन्धित आज्ञा
Reflection	प्रतिकाश	Remarks	अभ्युक्ति (कैफियत)
Reflector	प्रतिकाशक	Reminder	अनुस्मारक
Refresher's course	नवीकर कोर्स	Reminder	स्मारकपत्र
Refugee	शरणार्थी	Remission	छूट
Refund	रुपये की वापसी	Remittance	विप्रेषित धनराशि
Region	प्रदेश	Remuneration	पारिश्रमिक
Regional	प्रादेशिक	Renewal	नवीकरण
Register	पंजी	Renort	प्रतिवेदन
Register of duty	ड्यूटी का रजिस्टर	Renovation	पुनर्नवीकरण
Registered	पंजीयित	Rent statement	किराये का नक्शा
Registrar	पंजीयक	Rent statement	लगान का नक्शा
Registration	पंजीयन	Rental	मालियत जमाबन्दी
Regulation	आनियम (नियमन)	Re-organisation	पुन: संगठन
Regulator	नियामक	Repatriation	स्वदेशार्पण
Reinforcement	अधिक बलन	Repeal	मंसूखी
Rejoinder	प्रत्युत्तर	Repeal	विखंडन करना
Relaxation	शिथिलता	Replacement	प्रतिस्थापन
Relaxation	शिथिलीकरण	Report	रपट
		Report	विवरण प्रतिवेदन

Representation	आवेदन पत्र	Retardation	वेगक्षय
Representative	प्रतिनिधि	Retention	प्रतिधारण
Representative fraction	नमना	Retirement	निवृत्ति
		Re-totalling	पुनर्योग
Repugnant	विपरीत	Retrenchment	छटनी
Requisition	अपेक्षण	Retrograde (Motion)	वक्र (पीछे को, उलटा)
Re-registration	पुन: पंजीयन		
Rescue Home	तारण गृह	Retrospective effect	पूर्व प्रभाव
Reserve	रक्षित		
Reservists	धृतदल रक्षिगण	Return	प्रबंधक विवरण पत्र
Reservoir	जलाशय (टंकी, हौज)	Return (Statistics)	विवरण पत्र
		Returning	प्रतिदान
Residence, Quarter	आवास	Revenue	माल
		Revenue	राजस्व
Resident	आवासिक	Revenue administration report	माल विभाग की रिपोर्ट
Residue	अवशेष		
Resignation	त्यागपत्र	Revenue administrator	माल प्रशासक
Resistance	प्रतिरोध		
Res-Judicata	प्राङ्ग्न्याय	Revenue Establishment	मालस्थापना
Resolution	संकल्प		
Resolution, Proposal	प्रस्ताव	Revenue stamp	माल का स्टाम्प
		Reverend	परम पूज्य
Respondent	उत्तरदायी	Reverend	पूज्य
Respondent and Co-respondent	उत्तरवादी और सहोत्तरवादी	Reversion	प्रत्यावर्तन
		Review	पुनर्दर्शन
Restitution	यथापूर्व कर देना	Review	पुनरवलोकन
Restraint by Court	न्यायालय द्वारा रोक	Review of judgment	निर्णय का पुनर्निरीक्षण
Resumption	पुनर्ग्रहण		
Resumption	प्रत्यादान	Revised	संशोधित
Retainer	आयुधपाल	Revised estimate	संशोधित आगणन
		Revision	पुनरावृत्ति

Revision of scale of pay	वेतन क्रम का संशोधन	Satisfactory	संतोषजनक
Revision Officer	संशोधक अधिकारी	Savings	संचय
Revocation of licence	अनुज्ञप्ति खण्डन	Scabbard	मियान
Revocation, Cancellation	निरसन (मंसूखी)	Scale of pay	वेतन क्रम
Revoke	निरस्त करना	Scale prescribed	निर्धारित वेतन क्रम
Rib of an arc	डाट का पार्श्व	Scarbutic	खुजीला
Ribands (of decorations & medals), Sash and banner	मानचित्र	Scene of outbreak	रोग फैलाने का स्थान
		Schedule	अनुसूची
Rinderpest	बेदन	Schedule of rates	दरअनुसूची
Rolled (steel)	पीड़ित	Scheduled	परिगणित
Rotten	पूतिक	Scrap	छीलन
Rule of proportion	समानुपात नियम	Script	लिपि
Ruling	व्यवस्था (नजीर)	Scrum	चर्भसार (पन्छा)
Run off, Gradient	ढाल	Scrutiny	सूक्ष्म परीक्षा
Runner	धावक (हरकारा)	Sculpture	मूर्तिकर्म
Running statement	चलता विवरण	Seal	मुहर
Rupture	फटाव	Secant	छेदिका
Rural	ग्राम्य	Secret service Charges	गुप्त सेवा व्यय
Rust	मंडूर (जंग)	Secretary	सचिव
Saddle	पर्याण	Secretary of state	राजमन्त्री
Safety factor	अरिष्ट गुणक	Section	उपविभाग
Sale certificate	विक्रय प्रमाणपत्र	Section	धारा
Sale proposal	विक्री का प्रस्ताव	Section (Cross & long)	काट (खाड़ी और खंबानी)
Sanctioned estimate	स्वीकृत आगणन	Sector (Radius Vector)	ओरी कोल
Sanctioned grant	स्वीकृत अनुदान	Security	सरकारी ऋण पत्र
Satchel	खलीता	Security	अरिष्टि

Security (of a person) Bail order	प्रतिभू	Set off	घटोत्तरी
Security, Bail, Surety	प्रतिभूति	Settlement	भूव्यवस्था
Sedition	राजद्रोह	Settlement	व्यवस्थान
Segment	कट्टा	Settlement, revocation of	व्यवस्था खण्डन पत्र
Segregation	अलगाव	Severality	संपत्ति का पृथक् पूर्ण अधिकार
Seizure, Attachment	कुड़की	Sewer	गंदा नाला
Select committee	प्रवर समिति	Sextant	षटक
Selection	वरण	Shade	रंगमान (रंग)
Selection post	चुनावपद	Shaft	दंड (धुरा)
Self-explanatory	स्वत: व्याख्यात्मक	Shank	बारंग (डंडी)
Seniority	ज्येष्ठता	Share warrant	अंशाधिपत्र
Sentencing authority	दंड आज्ञा देने वाले प्राधिकारी	Sharp curve, Hairpin	तंग मोड़
Sentry	प्रहरी	Shingle	कंकड़ी (छोटी-छोटी)
Serial	क्रमिक	Shrivelled grain	पतला अनाज
Serpentine	सर्पीली (सँपेनी)	Side wall	पार्श्व भित्ति
Served	तामील किया गया	Sieve test	छलनी परीक्षा
Service roll	सेवावर्ति	Sight	बन्दूक की मक्खी
Service-book	सेवा पुस्तिका	Silt	चहला (कीचड़)
Service-rules	सेवा नियमावली	Silt	पंककिट्ट
Servitude	दंडात्मक श्रम	Sink	मलकूप
Sessions	दौरा	Sinking fund	ऋण चुकाव कोष
Sessions House	दौरा न्यायगृह	Site	आस्थान
Sessions Judge	दौराजज	Site plan	स्थल चित्र
Sessions trial	दौरा अदालत में मुकदमा	Sizarship	फीसमाफी
		Skeleton form	रूप (ढाँचा)
Set aside	पराकृत (करना)	Skilled labour	प्रवीण श्रम

Sliding scale	चढ़ता	Sphere	गोला
Slip book	पर्चीपुस्त	Spill way	जल निर्गमन मार्ग
Small Causes Court	अल्पवाद न्यायालय	Splinter	छिपटी (खपच्ची)
		Sport	आखेट (खेल)
Small Causes Court	लघुवाद न्यायालय	Spring level	स्रोतस्तर
Smuggling	चौर्यपण	Spur	काँटा (ठोकर)
Soil classifier	भूमि वर्गीकारक	Square	चौक (चबूतरा, बाजार, कचहरी)
Solitary confinement, Dungeon	कालकाठरी	Stabilization	स्थिरीकरण
		Stable	गोष्ठ
Solution (chemistry)	घोल	Stable gear	सामान अस्तबल
Solution (Math)	सुलझान	Staff	कर्मचारी वर्ग
Space	आकाश (रिताई)	Stamp defalcation	स्टाम्प व्यवहरण
Space Science	अंतरिक्ष विद्या	Stamp duty	स्टाम्प शुल्क
Spare	फालतू	Stamp vendor	स्टाम्प विक्रेता
Special duty	विशेष कार्य	Standard	प्रमाण
Special messenger	विशेष दूत	Standard at work	कार्यस्तर
Special pay	विशेष वेतन	Standard of work	कार्यसमिति
Special prosecuting officer	विशेष अभियोग अधिकारी	Standard, Bonafide	प्रामाणिक
Specific	आपेक्षिक	Standardization	प्रामणिक करना
Specific	निर्दिष्ट	Standing counsel	स्थायी वकील
Specific area	विशिष्ट क्षेत्र	Standing Order	स्थायी आदेश
Specific performance	विशिष्ट अनुष्ठान	Statement	वर्णन
Specification	व्यौरा	Statement of expenditure	व्यय विवरण
Speculative reference	अनुमानित अभ्युद्देश	Station	संस्थान
Speed limit	गति सीमा	Station officer	थानेदार (बड़े)
Spelling	अक्षरोटी	Stationary	स्थिर
		Stationed	संस्थापित

Stationery	लेखन सामग्री	Strut	रोक
Statistics	संख्याशास्त्र	Stud buck	बीज छाग
Statistical assistant	संख्या शास्त्रीय सहायक	Stud ram	बीजाज
Statuary	वैधानिक	Study-leave	अध्ययन-छुट्टी
Statuary Responsibility	वैधानिक उत्तरदायित्व	Sub-committee	उपसमिति
Statute	कानून-व्यवस्था	Sub-division	उपभाग
Statutory form	विधिविहित फार्म	Sub-head	उपशीर्षक
Stave	पटरी (पाया)	Sub-Inspector	थानेदार
Stay application	स्थगन प्रार्थनापत्र	Submerged	जलमग्न
Stay of suit	वाद स्थगन	Submission	उपस्थापन
Stay order	स्थगन आज्ञा	Subordinate	अधीनस्थ
Stear	पिचक	Subordinate Veterinary service	अधीनस्थ पशुचिकित्सा सेवा
Stencil	निकृन्त (स्टेन्सिल)	Sub-paragraph	उप अनुच्छेद
Stenographer	संकेन्द्र	Sub-proprietor	उपस्वामी
Stimulus	प्रोत्साहन	Subscription for the loan	कर्जे में दिया गया रुपया
Stipendiary	वैतनिक	Sub-section	उपधारा
Stirrup	रकाब	Subsequent proceeding	बाद की कार्यवाही
Stock	निचय	Subsidiary rule	सहायक नियम
Stock-in-hand	वर्तमान स्टाक	Subsistance grant	निर्वाह अनुदान
Storage	संचयन	Subsistence	उपजीवन (निर्वाह)
Storage losses	संचयन में माल की हानियाँ	Subsistence allowance	निर्वाह भत्ता
Storeman	भांडागारिक	Substitution application	प्रतिस्थानी बनने के लिए प्रार्थनापत्र
Strain	आतान	Substantive	स्वनिष्ठित
Stream gauging observation	प्रवाहमान ईक्षण	Substantive pay	मूल वेतन
Stretcher	तानक	Substantive post	मूलपद
Strong room	दृढ़ कोष्ठ	Sub-station	उपसंस्थान

Subtraction	घटाव	Supra	ऊपर
Sub-voucher	उप प्रमाणक	Surgeon	शल्यवैद्य (सर्जन)
Succession	अनुक्रम (परम्परा)	Surplus	अतिरेक (वचत)
Succession certificate	उत्तराधिकार प्रमाणपत्र	Surrender of lease	पट्टा समर्पण पत्र
Successor	उत्तराधिकारी	Surveillance, Revision	निगरानी
Suction	चूसण	Survey	अनुदर्शन (जाँच)
Suffix	प्रत्यय	Survey and Settlement	भूमाप और भूव्यवस्था
Suit	वाद (नालिश)		
Suit for maintenance	रोटी कपड़े का दावा	Survey instructor	भूमाक शिक्षक
Suit of easement	सुखाधिकार का वाद	Survey sheet	भूमाप फलक
Suit Valuation Act	वादमूल्य विधान	Suspect, Suspected	संदिग्ध
Suit, case	वाद	Suspend	स्थगित करना
Suits clerk	दायरा क्लर्क	Suspense	उचन्त (अवर्गित)
Suits for guardianship	संरक्षतावाद	Suspension	निलंबन
		Suspension	प्रलंबन
Summary Judgement	सरसरी निर्णय	Suspension	स्थगन
Summon dasti	हाथ समन	Switch-board	पिजापट्ट
Summons	आह्वान पत्र	Sword knot	असिग्रन्थि
Summons	सम्मन	Symptoms	लक्षण
Superannuation	पचपन साला	Syphon	निनाल
Superannuation (date of)	पचपन साले की तारीख	Syringe	पिचकारी
		Table	सारिणी
Superior staff	प्रवर स्थापना	Tack	बिरंजी
Supervisor	पर्यवेक्षक	Tag	नस्या (टग)
Supplemental deed	पूरक लेख्य	Taking up execution proceedings	इजरा की कार्रवाई करना
Supplementary	अनुपूरक	Tallow	पीट्ट (चरबी)
Supporating lesion	मवाद पड़ा हुआ घाव	Tariff	मांडकशुल्क

Tariff, Customs-duty.	आयात-निर्यात कर	Terminal tax	सीमाकर
Tarpaulin	तरपल (तिरपाल)	Termination, Abolition	समाप्ति
Taxing Judge	करनिर्धारक जज	Territorial application	प्रादेशिक ढंग पर लागू होना
Tear-smoke squad	अश्रु-धूम टुकड़ी	Testator	इच्छापत्र कर्ता
Technical	औद्योगिक	Tetanus	धनुर्वाद
Technical	प्राविधिक	The charge should be debited to the head	प्रभार शीर्षक पर डाला जाये
Technical pay	विशेष विषयक वेतन		
Technical sanction	प्राविधिक स्वीकृति	Theorem	प्रमेय (साध्य)
Technique	प्रविधि	Theory	सिद्धान्त
Telephone	दूरभाष (टेलीफोन)	Thermometer	तापमापक
Temporary post	अस्थायी पद	Thorax	वक्षस्थल
Tenancy	कब्जा आराजी	Tillage, Holdings	जोत
Tenancy	भूमि अधिकार	Time barred	समय सार्गल
Tenant at will	कच्चा काश्तकार	Time Scale	कालक्रम
Tenant-in-chief	असली काश्तकार	Time scale of pay	वेतन कालक्रम
Tender	निविदा (टेंडर)	Time table	समय विभाग
Tenement	भवन भाग (घर)	Time-barred	कालतिरोहित
Tensile	तन्य	Time-keeper	समय लेखक
Tension	आतति (तनाव)	Title	स्वत्वाधिकार
Tenure in perpetuity	पट्टा इस्तमरारी	Title-deed	आगमपत्र
Tenure in severality	पट्टीदारी	To be recouped from time to time	समय-समय पर पूरा किया जाय
Tenure of post	सार्वधिक पद	To cover	गाभिन करना (या कराना)
Tenure, Land tenure	मिल्कियत अमीन	To defend the case	मुकदम की पैरवी करना
Term of Sentence	दंड विधि	To execute decree	डिग्री इजरा करना
Terminal	आवधिक	To serve notice on	पर नोटिस तामील करना
Terminal	सीमांकित		

Toe wall	अंगुष्ठ भित्ति	Transitory	क्षणिक
Token	प्रतीक	Transmission	पारेषण
Topography	पृष्ठ विवरण	Transmit	पारप्रेषण
Torch	चोरबत्ती	Transport	वाहन
Torsion	मरोड़ (ऐंठन)	Trans-shipment	नावन्तरण
Totalling register	योग पंजी	Trapezium (with only two sides parallel)	समलम्ब चतुर्भुज
Tour programme	दौरा का प्रोग्राम		
Tracer	अनुचित्रक	Trapezoid (with no sides parallel)	असलम्ब चतुर्भुज
Tracings	अनुरेखण		
Tract	भूमि खण्ड	Travelling allowance	यात्रा भत्ता
Trade mark	व्यापार चिह्न	Tread of steps	सीढ़ी
Trade pay	व्यवसाय वेतन	Treasure vault	खजाना
Traffic Police	व्यवस्था पुलिस	Treasury, bill	सरकार द्वारा जारी की हुई हुंडी
Traffic, Communication	यातायात		
		Trial court	विचार न्यायालय
Training	उपशिक्षा	Tribe	जनजाति
Transaction	पणायन (लेनदेन)	Tripod	त्रिपाद
Transaction	व्यवहार (लेनदेन)	Troops	फौज, फौजी दस्ते
Transcription	प्रतिलेखन	Troops	सेना
Transfer	बदली	Truncheon	लाठी
Transfer	स्थानान्तरण	Trust endowment	प्रन्यास वृत्तिदान
Transfer charge	हस्तांतरहण व्यय	Trust property	प्रन्यास सम्पत्ति
Transfer of control	नियन्त्रण परिवर्तन	Tube well	नलकूप
Transfer of share	अंश हस्तांतरण	Tubercular	क्षय रोग सम्बन्धी
Transfer, Transit	संक्रम	Tuberculin test	यक्ष्मा परीक्षा
Transferee	क्रेता	Tumour	फोड़ा
Transformation	रूपान्तर	Turban	कुलाह
Transformer	रूपपरिवर्तक	Turbine	परिवर्त
Transition	संक्रमण	Turbine mistri	वरीवत मिस्त्री

Turn down collar	लौटकालर	Unmanageable	असाध्य
Turn over	पूर्ण बिक्री	Unnatural	अस्वाभाविक
Turner	कुन्दकार	Unproductive	अनुत्पादक
Turpitude	हीनता	Unserviceable	निकम्मा
Type writing	मुद्रलेखन	Unskilled	अप्रवीण
Typist	मुद्रलेखक	Unsound	अस्वस्थ
Unclaimed	अस्वामिक	Unwholesome	अस्वास्थ्यकर
Unclaimed documeat	अस्वामिक लेखपत्र	Up-to-date	आतिथि
Unclassified	अवगीकृत	Urban	शहरी
Uncurrent coin	अप्रचलित मुद्रा	Urgent	आत्ययिक
Under consideration	विचाराधीन	Urgent slip	आत्ययिक पर्ची
Under cultivation	काश्त में	Vacancy	रिक्त स्थान
Under section	धारा के अधीन	Vacancy	रिक्ति
Under the auspices	तत्वावधान में	Vaccinal lymph	वैक्सीन लसीका
Under-secretary	अनुसविच	Vaccine	मसूरी, मसूरी लाल
Undertaking	समारम्भ	Vaccine depot	वैक्सीन भण्डार
Undertrial prisoner	विचाराधीन बन्दी	Vacuum	शून्यक (रिक्त)
Undertrial prisoner	हवालाती	Vagrancy	आवारगर्दी
Unexpired	शेष	Vagrant	आवारागर्द
Unhealthiness	अस्वास्थ्यकरदा	Validity	वैधता
Uniform	इकसार	Valuation	मालीयत्त
Uniform	एक सार (वर्दी)	Value	मूल्य
Uniform	गणवेश	Variation	घटबढ़
Uniform	वर्दी	Various	विभिन्न
Uniform procedure	समान कार्यविधि	Vault	गुंबज
Unlawful assembly	अवैध समुदाय	Velocity	वेग
		Ventilation	वायु संचार
		Ventilation	संवातन

Ventricle	हृदय संपुट	Visa	दृष्टांत
Verbal	मौखिक	Viscosity	संलग्नशीलता
Verification	जाँच	Visitation	भेंट
Verification	सत्यापन (जाँच)	Visitor, Inspector	निरीक्षक
Verification, Authentication, Certification	प्रमाणीकरण	Visitors' book	निरीक्षण पुस्तक
Vernacular Department	देशी भाषा विभाग	Visual signalling Section	द्राष्टिक संकेत उप. विभाग
Versus	प्रति (बनाम)	Viva voce	मौखिक परीक्षा
Vertex	शीर्ष	Vocation	व्यवसाय
Vesting	प्रदान	Vocational	व्यावसायिक
Veteran	ज्ञान वृद्ध	Void	शून्य
Veterinary Assistant Surgeon	पशुचिकित्सा सहायक सर्जन	Volatile	बाप्प शील
		Volley	बौछार
Veterinary College	पशुविज्ञान महाविद्यालय	Volume	आयतन (खंड)
Veto	निषेधाधिकार	Volume, Bay (division of roof)	खंड
Viaduct	सेतु	Voluntary contribution	स्वेच्छापूर्ण चंदा
Vice versa	विलामतः	Voted allotment	मतदत्त दिष्टि
Vicinity	पड़ोस	Voucher	प्रमाणक
Vide	देखिए	Wage	भृति
Vigil	जागरण	Wage earner	मजदूर
Vigilance	चौकसी	Wage earning scheme	भृति अर्जन योजना
Vigilant control	जागर नियन्त्रण	Waive the recovery	वसूली छोड़ देना
Village defence society	ग्राम रक्षा समिति	Walking stick gun	बन्दूकदार छड़ी
Violate	तोड़ना (भंग करना)	Waqf	वक्फ
Violence	हिंसा	Warder	वार्डर
Violent	झगड़ालू	Warder reserve	धृतवार्डर
Virulent	प्रचंड		

Warning	चेतावनी	Welder	संधाता
Warrant	अधिपत्र	Welding	पिघलाकर जोड़ना
Warrant for goods	माल अधिपत्र	Welfare centre	कल्याण-केन्द्र
Warrant of arrest	आसेध	Well boring	कूट वेधन
Warrant of commitment	सुपुर्दगी का अधिपत्र	Whistle	सीटी
Warrant of precedence	पूर्वता अधिपत्र	Whole	सम्पूर्ण
Warrant-officer	अधिपत्र-अधिकारी	Wholesale price	थोक भाव
Watch & ward (Police)	चौकी पुलिस	Will	रिक्थ (वसीयत)
Water carrier	भिश्ती	Wireless operator	बेतार तार चालक
Water closet	संडास	With retrospective effect	पूर्व प्रभाव सहित
Water proof	बरसाती	Withdrawal	वापसी
Water-logged land	चोपे की भूमि	Withdrawal of amount	निकाली हुई धनराशि
Wear and tear	टूट-फूट	Withhold	रोकना
Wedge	फन्नी	Witness	साक्षी
Weeding	निराई	Workman	कामगर
Weeding	निर्दान (निराई)	Workshop	कर्मशाला
Weeding label	निर्दान चिप्पी	Writ	आज्ञापत्र (फरमाना)
Weeding list	निर्दान सूची	Write-off	बट्टे खाते डालना
Weeding slip	निर्दान पर्ची	Written statement	लिखित उत्तरवाद
Weeviling	घुन लगना	Yield	उपज
Weighment	बोझ	Yield	दावा छोड़ देना
Weir, Barrage	बाँध	Yours truly, Yours sincerely, faithfully	भवन्निष्ठ

Appendix-29/परिशिष्ट–29
Terms defined in English and their Hindi Equivalents in the Indian Constitution
भारतीय गणतन्त्र के संविधान में प्रयुक्त अंग्रेजी के पारिभाषिक शब्दों और पदों के हिन्दी समानार्थक शब्द व पद

Abandonment	परित्यजन, परित्याग	Adulteration	दत्तक ग्रहण, दत्तक स्वीकरण
Abridgement	न्यूनन		
Abrogate	निराकरण	Adulteration	अपमिश्रण
Access	प्रवेश	Adult suffrage	वयस्क मताधिकार
Account	लेखा, गणना	Advance	अग्रिम धन, पेशगी
Accrue	प्रापण, प्रोद्भवन	Advice	मन्त्रणा, उपदेश, सलाह
Accrued	प्राप्त, प्रोद्भूत उपार्जित	Advise	मन्त्रणा देना
Accusation	अभियोग	Advisory Council	मन्त्रणा परिषद्
Accused	अभियुक्त	Advocate	अधिवक्ता
Acquisition	अर्जन	Advocate General	महाधिवक्ता
Act	अधिनियम	Affect prejudicially	प्रतिकूल प्रभाव डालना
Acting	कार्यकारी	Affirmation	प्रतिज्ञान
Actionable wrong	अभियोज्य दोष	Agency	अभिकरण
Adaptation	अनुकूलन	Agent	अभिकर्त्ता
Addressed	सम्बोधित	Agreement	करार
Adherence	अनुषक्ति	Air Force	विमान बल
Ad hoc	तदर्थ	Air navigation	विमान परिवहन
Adjourn	स्थगन, स्थापित करना, अवधिदाब, कालदान	Air traffic	विमान यातायात
		Air ways	वायु पथ
Administer	प्रशासन करना	Alien	अन्यदेशीय
Administration	प्रशासित	Alienate	अन्य संक्रामण करना
Administrative	प्रशासन	Alienation	अन्य संक्रामण, परकीयकरण
Administrative function	प्रशासकीय		
		Allegation	अभिकथन, आरोप
Admiralty	नौसेना प्रमुख	Allegiance	निष्ठा
Admissible	स्वीकार्य	Allocation	बँटवारा
Adoption	ग्राह्य	Allot	बाँट लगाना

Allotment	बाँट	Assurance of property	संपत्ति हस्तांतरण पत्र
Allowances	भत्ता	As the case may	यथास्थिति, यथाप्रसंग
Amendment	संशोधन	Attach	कुर्की
Amnesty	सर्वक्षमा	Attorney General	महा-न्यायवादी
Amount	राशि	Audit	लेखा परीक्षा
Annual	वार्षिक	Auditor-General	महालेखा परीक्षक
Annual financial statement	वार्षिक वित्त-विवरण	Authentication	प्रमाणीकरण
		Authorize	प्राधिकृत करना
Annuity	वार्षिकी	Authority	प्राधिकारी
Annulment	रद्द करना	Autonomous	स्वायत्त
Appeal	अपील	Autonomy	स्वायत्तता
Appear	उपस्थित होना	Award	पंचाज्ञा
Appended	संलग्न	Bail	प्रतिभू, जमानत
Application	प्रयुक्ति, लागू होना, आवेदन पत्र	Ballot	मतपत्र
		Bank	बैंक
Appointment	नियुक्ति	Banking	महाजनी
Appropriation	विनियोग	Bankruptcy	दिवाला
Appropriation bill	विनियोग-विधेयक	Bar	रुकावट
Approve	अनुमोदन करना	Benefit	हित
Approval	अनुमोदन	Betting	पण लगाना, पण क्रिया
Arbitral Tribunal	मध्यस्थ न्यायाधीशकरण	Bicameral	दोघरा, द्विगृही
		Bill	विधेयक, बिल
Arbitration	मध्यस्थ निर्णय	Bill of exchange	विनिमय पत्र
Arbitrator	मध्यस्थ	Bill of indemnity	परिहार-विधेयक, क्षतिपूर्ति बिल
Area	क्षेत्र		
Armed Forces	सशस्त्र बल	Bill of lading	वहन पत्र
Arrest	बन्दी करना	Board	परिषद्
Article	अनुच्छेद	Body	निकाय
Assemble	समवेत होना, सम्मिलित होना	Body, Corporate	निगमनिकाय
		Body governing	शासीनिकाय
Assembly	सभा	Borrowing	उधार ग्रहण
Assent	अनुमति	Boundary	सीमा
Assessment	निर्धारण	Broadcasting	प्रसारण
Assignment	सौंपना	Business	कारबार
Association	संस्था	Bye-election	उपनिर्वाचन

Bye-law	उपनियम	Chief Minister	मुख्यमन्त्री
Calling	आजीविका	Citizenship	नागरिकता
Camp	शिविर	Civil	व्यवहारिक, असैनिक
Candidate	अभ्यर्थी, उम्मीदवार	Civil Court	दीवानी अदालत
Cantonment	छावनी	Civil power	असैनिक शक्ति
Capacity	सामर्थ्य	Claim	दावा
Capital	मूलधन, पूँजी	Clarification	स्पष्टीकरण
Capital Value	मूलधन-मूल्य	Clause	खण्ड
Capitation tax	प्रतिव्यक्ति कर	Code	संहिता
Carriage	परिवहन	Coinage	टंकण
Casting vote	निर्णायक मत	Colonization	उपनिवेशन
Cattle pound	पशु अवरोध, कांजीहौस	Commerce	वाणिज्य
Cause	वाद	Commercial	वाणिज्य सम्बन्धी
Cause of Action	वादमूलक	Commission	आयोग
Census	जनगणना	Commissioner	आयुक्त
Central Bureau of Intelligence	केन्द्रीय जाँच ब्यूरो विभाग	Committee	समिति
Certificate	प्रमाण पत्र	Committee, Select	प्रवर समिति
Certiorari	उत्प्रेषण-लेख	Committee, Standing	स्थायी समिति
Cess	उपकर	Common good	सार्वजनिक कल्याण
Chairman	सभापति	Common Seal	सामान्य मुद्रा, सामान्य मुहर
Charge	दोषारोप, अभियुक्ति	Communicate	संचार करना
Charge	भार, भारित करना	Communication, Means of	संचार साधन
Charity	पूर्त, दातव्य	Community	लोकसमाज समुदाय
Charitable and endowments	दातव्य तथा धार्मिक धर्मस्व	Commute	लघुकरण
Charitable institution	दातव्य संस्था	Company	कम्पनी
Cheque	चेक	Compensation	प्रतिकर
Chief	मुख्य	Competent	सक्षम
Chief Commissioner	मुख्य आयुक्त	Complaint	फरियाद
Chief Election-Commissioner	मुख्य निर्वाचन आयुक्त	Comptroller and Auditor General	नियंत्रक महालेखा परीक्षक
Chief Judge	मुख्य न्यायाधीश	Compute	संगणना
Chief Justice	मुख्य न्यायाधिपति	Concurrence	सहमति
		Concurrent list	समवर्ती सूची

Condition	शर्त	Co-operative	सहकारी संस्था
Conditions of service	सेवा की शर्तें	Copy	प्रतिलिपि, प्रतिकृति
Conference	सम्मेलन	Copyright	प्रकाशनाधिकार
Confidence, want of	विश्वास का अभाव	Corporation	निगम
Conscience	अन्तःकरण	Corporation, Sole	एकल निगम
Consent	सम्मति	Corporation Tax	निगम-कर
Consent, Previous	पूर्व सम्मति	Corresponding	तत्स्थानी
Consequential	आनुषंगिक	Corrupt	भ्रष्ट
Consideration	विचार	Cost	परिव्यय, खर्च, लागत
Consolidated Fund	संचित निधि	Council	परिषद्
Constituency	निर्वाचन क्षेत्र	Council of Ministers	मन्त्रिपरिषद्
Constituency, territorial	प्रादेशिक निर्वाचन क्षेत्र	Council of State	राज्यपरिषद्
		Council Regional	प्रादेशिक परिषद्
Constituent Assembly	संविधान सभा	Council, Tribal	जनजाति-परिषद्
Constitution	संविधान	Countervailing duty	प्रति शुल्क
Consul	वाणिज्य-दूत	Court	न्यायालय
Consultation	परामर्श	Court of Appeal	पुनर्विचार न्यायालय
Construe	अर्थ करना	Court, Civil	दीवानी अदालत
Consumption	उपभाग	Court, District	जिला न्यायालय
Contact	सम्पर्क	Court, High	उच्च-न्यायालय
Contagious	सांसर्गिक	Court, Magistrate	दंडाधिकारी न्यायालय
Contempt	अवमान	Court, Martial	सेना न्यायालय
Contempt of Court	न्यायालय अवमान	Court of Wards	प्रतिपालक अधिकरण
Context	संदर्भ, प्रसंग	Court, Revenue	राजस्व न्यायालय
Contingency-Fund	आकस्मिकता निधि	Court, Sessions	सत्र न्यायालय
Contract	संविदा	Court, Subordinate	अधीन न्यायालय
Contravention	प्रतिकूलता, उल्लंघन	Court, Supreme	उच्चतम न्यायालय
Contribution	अर्थदान	Credit	प्रत्यय, साख, पत्त
Control	नियंत्रण	Crime	अपराध
Controversy	प्रतिवाद	Criminal	अपराधी, आपराधिक, दण्ड सम्बन्धी
Convention	प्रथा, परम्परा		
Conveyance	सम्पत्ति हस्तांतरण	Criminal Law	दण्ड-विधि
Convicted	दोषसिद्ध, अभिशस्त, दोष प्रमाणित	Currency	प्रचलित मुद्रा
		Custody	अभिरक्षा
Conviction	दोषसिद्धि, अभिशस्ति	Custom duty	सीमा शुल्क

Customs duty	शुल्क, सीमान्त	Dismiss	पदच्युत करना
Custom	रूढ़ि, आचार	Disperse	विसर्जन करना
Dealing	व्यवहार, लेना-देना	Dispute	विवाद
Debate	वाद-विवाद	Disqualification	अनर्हता
Debenture	ऋण-पत्र	Disqualify	अयोग्य ठहराना
Debt	ऋण	Dissent	विमति
Decision	विनिश्चय	Dissolution	विघटन
Declaration	घोषणा	Distribution	वितरण, विभाजन
Decree	आज्ञप्ति, डिगरी	District	जिला
Dedicate	समर्पण	District Board	जिला परिषद्
Deed	विलेख	District Council	जिलापरिषद्
Detamation	मानहानि	District Fund	जिलानिधि
Defence	प्रतिरक्षा	Dividend	लाभांश
Deliberation	पर्यालोचन	Divorce	विवाह-विच्छेद
Demand	माँग, अभियाचना	Documents	लेख्य, दस्तावेज
Demarcation	सीमांकन	Domicile	अधिवास
Demobilisation	सैन्य-वियोजन	Domiciled	अधिवासी
Deprive	वंचित करना	Dullness	प्रतिमान्द्य
Deputy Chairman	उपसभापति	During good behaviour	सदाचारपर्यन्त
Deputy Commissioner	उपायुक्त	During the pleasure of the President	राष्ट्रपति-प्रसाद पर्यन्त
Deputy Speaker	उपाध्यक्ष		
Descent	उद्भव	Duty	शुल्क, कर्तव्य
Derogation	अल्पीकरण	Duty, Custom	सीमा-शुल्क
Design	रूपांकरण	Duty, Death	मरण शुल्क
Detrimental	अहितकारी	Duly, Estate	सम्पत्ति शुल्क
Diplomacy	राजनय	Duty, Excise	उत्पादन शुल्क
Direction	निर्देश	Duty, Export	निर्यात शुल्क
Disability	नियोग्यता	Duty, Import	आयात शुल्क
Discharge	निर्वहन	Duty, Stamp	मुद्रांक शुल्क
Discipline	अनुशासन	Duty, Succession	उत्तराधिकार शुल्क
Disciplinary	अनुशासन सम्बन्धी	Economic	आर्थिक
Discovery	अन्वेषण, खोज	Education	शिक्षा
Discretion	स्वविवेक	Efficiency of administration	प्रशासन कार्य क्षमता
Discrimination	विभेद		
Discussion	चर्चा	Elect	निर्वाचित करना
		Elected	निर्वाचित चुने हुए

Election	निर्वाचन	Evidence	साक्ष्य
Election Commissioner	निर्वाचन आयुक्त	Excess profit	अतिरिक्त लाभ
		Exclude	अपवर्जन करना
Election, Direct	प्रत्यक्ष निर्वाचन	Exclusion	अपवर्जन
Election, General	साधारण निर्वाचन	Exclusive jurisdiction	अनन्य क्षेत्राधिकार
Election, Indirect	परोक्ष निर्वाचन	Executive	कार्यपालिका
Election Tribunal	निर्वाचन अधिकरण	Executive power	कार्यपालिका शक्ति
Electoral roll	निर्वाचन नामवली	Exempt	मुक्त
Eligibility	पात्रता	Exercise	प्रयोग, अनुष्ठान
Eligible	पात्र होना	Ex-officio	पदेन
Emergency	आपात	Expenditure	व्यय
Emergent	आपाती	Explanation	व्याख्या, स्पष्टीकरण
Emigration	उत्प्रवास	Explosives	विस्फोटक
Emoluments	उपलब्धियाँ	Export	निर्यात
Employer's liability	नियोजक दात्व्य, नियोजक उत्तरवादिता	Extent	विस्तार
		External Affairs	वैदेशिक कार्य
Enact	अधिनियम	Extradition	प्रत्यर्पण
Encumbered estate	भारग्रस्त सम्पदा	Extra territorial operations	राज्य क्षेत्रातीत प्रवर्तन
Endorse	पृष्ठांकन		
Endorsed	पृष्ठांकित	Factory	कारखाना
Endowment	धर्मस्व	Faith	धर्म–श्रद्धा
Engagements	वचनबद्ध	Fare	भाड़ा, किराया
Engineering	यन्त्र शास्त्र	Finance Bill	देय शुल्क
Enterprise	उद्यम	Finance	वित्त
Entitled	हक्क होना	Financial bill	वित्त विधेयक
Entrust	सौंपना	Financial Commission	वित्तायोग
Entry	प्रविष्टि, दाखला	Financial	वित्तीय
Equality	समता	Financial obligation	वित्तीय भार
Equal protection of laws	विधियों का समान संरक्षण	Finance statement	वित्तीय विवरण
		Fine	अर्थदण्ड
Escheat	राजगामी	Fishery	मीन क्षेत्र, मीन पण्य
Establishment	स्थापना, संस्थापन, स्थापना करना	Forbid	निषेध
		Forbidden	निषिद्ध
Estates	संपदा	Forces	बल
Estimates	आँक, प्राक्कलन	Foreign affairs	विदेशीय कार्य

Foreign exchange	विदेशीय विनिमय	Honorarium	मानदेय
Form	रूप, प्रपत्र, फारम	House	सदन
Formula	सूत्र	House of People	लोकसभा
Formulated	सूत्रित	Illegal	अवैध
For the time being	तत्समय	Illegal practice	अवैधाचरण
Freedom	स्वतंत्रता, स्वातंत्र्य, आजादी	Immunity	उन्मुक्ति
		Impeachment	महाभियोग
Freight	वस्तु भाड़ा	Implementing	परिपालन
Frontiers	सीमान्त	Impose	आरोपण लगाना
Function	कृत्य	Imprisonment	कारावास, कैद
Function, Administrative	प्रशासकीय कृत्य	Improvement Trust	सुधार प्रन्यास
		Incapacity	असमर्थता
Fund	निधि	Incidental	प्रासंगिक
Fund sinking	निक्षेप निधि	Incompetency	अक्षमता
Future market	वायदा बाजार	Incompetent	अक्षम
Gambling	द्यूत, जुआ	Incorporation	निगमन
Gaztte	सूचना-पत्र, राजपत्र	Incumbent of an office	पदधारी
General election	साधारण निर्वाचन		
Govern	शासन करना	Indebtedness	ऋणग्रस्तता
Governance	शासन	Industry	उद्योग
Government	सरकार, शासन	Ineligibility	अपात्रता
Government of State	राज्य की सरकार	Ineligible	अपात्र
Government of India	भारत सरकार	Infectious	सांक्रामिक
Governor	राज्यपाल	Inheritance	दाय
Grant	अनुदान	Initiate	उपक्रमण करना, दीक्षा देना
Grant-in-aid	सहायक अनुदान		
Gratuity	उपदान	Injury	क्षति
Guarantee	प्रत्याभूति	Inland waterways	अन्तर्देशीय जलपथ
Guardian	संरक्षक	Inoperative	अप्रवृत्त
Guidance	मार्ग प्रदर्शन	Inquiry	परिप्रश्न, जाँच
Habeas Corpus	बन्दी प्रत्यक्षीकरण	Insolvency	दिवाला
Handicrafts	हस्तशिल्प, दस्तकारी	Inspection	पर्यवेक्षण
Hazardous	संकटमय	Institution	संस्था
Headman	मुखिया	Instruction	शिक्षा, अनुदेश, हिदायत
High Court	उच्च न्यायालय		

Instrument	संविदा, विलेख, उपकरण, साधन	Land revenue	भू-राजस्व
		Land tenures	भू-धृति
Insurance	बीमा	Law	विधि
Intercourse	समागम	Law of Nations	राष्ट्रों की विधि
Interest	ब्याज, सूद	Legal	विधि सम्बन्धी
International	अन्तर्राष्ट्रीय	Legislation	विधान
Interpretation	निर्वचन, व्याख्या	Legislative power	विधायिनी शक्ति
Intestacy	इच्छापत्र-हीनत्व, निर्वसीयत	Legislative Assembly	विधान सभा
		Legislative Legislature	विधान परिषद्
Intestate	इच्छापत्र-हीनत्व, निर्वसीयता	Legislature	विधान-मण्डल
		Letters of credit	प्रत्ययपत्र
Introduce	पुर:स्थापन करना	Levy	आरोपण, उद्ग्रहण, उगाहना
Introduction	पुर:स्थापना		
Invalid	अमान्य, असमर्थ	Liability	दायित्व
Invalidity pension	असमर्थता निवृत्ति वेतन	Libel	अपमान लेख
Investigation	अनुसंधान	Liberty	स्वाधीनता
Involve	अन्तर्ग्रस्त	Licence	अनुज्ञप्ति, लाइसेन्स
Involved	अन्तर्ग्रस्त	Lieutenant Governor	उप राज्यपाल
Irregularity	अनियमितता	Limitation	परिसीमा
Issue	बाद-पद	List	सूची
Joint family	अवभक्त कुटुम्ब, अविभक्त परिवार	List, Concurrent	समवर्ती सूची
		List, State	राज्य सूची
Judge	न्यायाधीश	List, Union	संघ सूची
Judge, Additional	अतिरिक्त न्यायाधीश	Livelihood	जीविका
Judgement	निर्णय	Loan	उधार, ऋण
Judicial power	न्यायिक शक्ति	Local area	स्थानीय क्षेत्र
Judicial proceeding	न्यायिक कार्यवाही, न्यायिक कार्यरीति	Local authorities	स्थानीय प्राधिकारी
		Local Board	स्थानीय मण्डली
Judicial stamp	न्यायिक मुद्रांक	Local body	स्थानीय निकाय
Judiciary	न्यायपालिका	Local Government	स्थानीय शासन
Jurisdiction	क्षेत्राधिकार	Local Self Government	स्थानीय स्वशासन
Justice, Chief	मुख्य न्यायाधीश		
Labour	श्रम	Lock up	बन्दीखाना
Labour union	श्रमिक संघ	Maintain	पोषण, बनाये रखना
Land records	भू-अभिलेख	Maintenance	पोषण

Major	वयस्क	Newspaper	समाचार-पत्र
Majority	बहुमत	Nominate	नामनिर्देशन, मनोनयन
Mandamus	परमादेश	Notice in writing	लिखित सूचना
Manufacture	निर्माण	Obligation	अधिसूचना
Maritime shipping	समुद्र-नौवहन	Occupation	आभार
Maternity relief	प्रसूति सहायता, प्रसूति साहाय्य	Official residence	उपजीविका, धंधा
		Officer	पदाधिकारी
Member	सदस्य	Official residence	पदावास
Memo	ज्ञाप, स्मृति पत्र	Opinion	अभिप्राय, राय
Memorandum	ज्ञापन	Order in Council	परिषद्-आदेश
Memorial	स्मारक	Order, Standing	स्थायी आदेश
Mental deficiency	मनोवैकल्प	Ordinance	अध्यादेश
Mental weakness	मनोदौर्वल्य	Organization	संघटन
Merchandise marks	पण्य-चिह्न	Owner	स्वामी
Merchant Ship	वणिक-पोत	Parliament	संसद
Migration	प्रव्रजन	Partnership	भागिता
Mind, unsound	विकृतचित्त	Pass	पारण, आदेश, परिचयपत्र
Mineral	खनिज		
Mineral resources	खनिज-सम्पत्	Passed	पारित
Minor	अवयस्क	Passport	पारपत्र
Minority	अल्पसंख्यक वर्ग	Patent	एकस्व
Misbehaviour	कदाचार	Pecuniary jurisdiction	आर्थिक क्षेत्राधिकार
Modification	रूपभेद	Penalty	शास्ति, दण्ड
Money bill	धन-विधेयक	Pending	रुका हुआ
Morality	सदाचार	Pension	निवृत्ति वेतन
Motion of confidence	विश्वास-प्रस्ताव	Permission	अनुज्ञा
Motion of no-confidence	अविश्वास-प्रस्ताव	Perpetual succession	शाश्वत उत्तराधिकार
		Perquisite	परिलब्धि
Municipal area	नगर-क्षेत्र	Personal law	स्वीय विधि
Municipal Committee	नगर-समिति	Piracy	जल-दस्युता
Municipal Corporation	नगरनिगम	Plead	वकालत करना
National highways	राष्ट्रीय राजपथ	Police	आरक्षक, पुलिस
Naturalization	देशीयकरण	Police Force	आरक्षक बल
Naval	नौसेना-सम्बन्धी	Policy of insurance	बीमा-पत्र
Navigation	नौ-परिवहन	Port-quarantine	पत्तन-निरोधा

Possession	स्ववश, कब्जा	Quarantine	निरोधा
Preamble	प्रस्तावना	Question of Law	विधि प्रश्न
Preference	अधिमान	Quorum	गणपूर्ति
Prejudice	प्रतिकूल प्रभाव	Quo warranto	अधिकारपृच्छा
Preside	पीठासीन होना, सभापतित्व करना	Ratification	अनुसमर्थन
President	राष्ट्रपति	Reading first	प्रथम वाचन
Presiding Officer	पीठाधीश	Receipt (paper)	पावती रसीद
Preventive detention	निवारक निरोध	Recommend	सिफारिश करना
Prisoner	बन्दी, कैदी	Recommendation	सिफारिश
Privileges	विशेषाधिकार	Records, Court of	अभिलेख न्यायालय
Process	आदेशिका	Record of rights	अधिकाराभिलेख
Proclamation	उद्घोषणा	Recruitment	भर्ती
Proclamation of emergency	आपतकाल उद्घोषण	Recurring	आवर्तक
		Redemption charges	विमोचन भार
		Reference	निर्देश
Prohibited	प्रतिषिद्ध	Reformatory	सुधारालय
Prohibition	प्रतिषेध, निषेध	Refundable to	लौटाई जाने वाली
Promulgation	प्रख्यापन	Regional Commissioners	प्रादेशिक आयुक्त
Proportional representation	अनुपाती प्रतिनिधित्व		
		Regional Councils	प्रादेशिक परिषद्
Proposal	प्रस्ताव	Regional Fund	प्रादेशिक निधि
Prorogue	सत्रावसान	Registered	पंजीबद्ध, निबद्ध
Provided	परन्तु	Registration	पंजीयन, पंजी-बन्धन, निबन्धन
Proxy	प्रतिपत्री		
Publication	प्रकाशन	Regulation	विनिमय
Public debt	राष्ट्र-ऋण	Relevancy	सुसंगति
Public demand	सार्वजनिक अभियाचना	Relevant	सुसंगत
Public health	लोक-स्वास्थ्य	Remission	परिहार
Public notification	सार्वजनिक अधिसूचना, लोक-अधिसूचना	Remuneration	पारिश्रमिक
		Repeal	निरसन
Public order	सार्वजनिक व्यवस्था	Representation	प्रतिनिधित्व
Public Service Commission	लोक सेवा आयोग	Representative	प्रतिनिधि
		Reprieve	प्रविलम्बन करना
Public service	लोक सेवा	Repugnancy	विरोध
Qualification	अर्हता	Repugnant	विरुद्ध

716

Requisition	अधिग्रहण	State Funds	राज्य-निधि
Reservation	रक्षण	Stock exchange	श्रेष्ठि-चत्वर
Reserved forest	रक्षित वन	Subject matter	वाद-विषय
Respite	विराम	Subordinate officer	अधीन अधिकारी
Restriction	निबन्धन	Succession	उत्तराधिकार
Retire	निवृत्त होना	Successor	उत्तराधिकारी
Retirement	निवृत्ति	Sue	व्यवहार लाना
Review	पुनर्विलोकन	Suffrage	मताधिकार
Revoke	प्रतिसंहरण	Suit, Civil	दीवानी मुकदमा
Reward	पारितोषिक	Summon	आह्वान
Rule of the road	पथ-नियम	Superintendence	अधीक्षण
Ruler	शासक	Supplementary grant	अनुपूरक अनुदान
Safeguard	रक्षा	Supreme Command	सर्वोच्च समादेश
Sale	विक्रय	Suspend	निलम्बन
Sanction, previous	पूर्व मंजूरी	Tax, Callings	आजीविका कर
Savings	बचत	Tax, Capitation	प्रतिव्यक्ति कर
Security	प्रतिभूति	Tax, Corporation	निगम कर
Sentence	दण्डादेश	Tax, Employment	नौकरी कर
Service charges	सेवा भार	Tax, Entertainment	मनोरंजन कर
Session	सत्र	Tax, Export	निर्यात कर
Single transferable vote	एकल संक्रमणीय मत	Tax, Profession	वृत्तिकर
		Tax, Income	आयकर
Sinking Fund	निक्षेप निधि	Tax, Sale	विक्रयकर
Slander	अपमान वचन	Tax, Terminal	सीमा कर
Social custom	सामाजिक रूढ़ि	Tax, Commercial	व्यापार कर
Social insurance	सामाजिक बीमा	Technical training	शिल्पी प्रशिक्षण
Social service	सामजिक सेवा	Tenant	किसान
Sovereign	प्रभु	Tender, Legal	विधि मान्य
Sovereign Democratic Republic	सम्पूर्ण प्रभुत्व-संपन्न लोकतन्त्रात्मक गणतन्त्र	Tenure	पदाविधि
		Term	अवधि
Speaker	अध्यक्ष	Territorial charges	प्रादेशिक भार
Speech, Freedom of	वाक्स्वातन्त्र्य	Territorial Jurisdiction	प्रादेशिक क्षेत्राधिकार
Staff	कर्मचारी-वृन्द	Territorial waters	जल-प्रांगण
Stamp duties	मुद्रांक-शुल्क	Territory	राज्य-क्षेत्र
Standing orders	स्थायी आदेश	Tidal waters	वेला-जी, ज्वार-जी

Tolls	पथ-कर	Union	संघ
Trade marks	व्यापार चिह्न	Unity	एकता
Trade Union	कार्मिक-संघ	Unsoundness of mind	चित्त-विकृति
Traffic	यातायात	Vacancy	रिक्ति, रिक्तता
Traffic (human)	मानव-पणन	Vagrancy	अवारागर्दी
Training	प्रशिक्षण	Validity	मान्यता
Transfer	स्थानान्तरण, हस्तान्तरण	Vice-President	उप-राष्ट्रपति
Transition	संक्रमण	Village Council	ग्राम-परिषद्
Transport	परिवहन	Violation	अतिक्रमण
Transportation	निर्वासन	Vocation	व्यवसाय
Treasure troves	निखात निधि	Vote, Casting	निर्णायक-मत
Treaty	धि	Voter	मतदाता, वोटदाता
Tribal area	जनजाति क्षेत्र	Votes on account	लेखानुदान
Tribe	जनजाति	Votes of credit	प्रत्ययानुदान
Tribunal	न्यायाधिकरण	Wage	मजूरी
Triennial	त्रैवार्षिक	Wage, Living	निर्वाह मजूरी
Trust	न्यास	Warrant	अधिपत्र
Undischarged	अनुन्मुक्त	Will	इच्छा-पत्र, बिल, वसीयत
Unemployment	बेकारी	Winding up	समापन
		Writ	लेख

Appendix-30/परिशिष्ट—30
Prefixes (उपसर्ग)

English Prefixes

A—signifies in, on, asleep, abroad, ashore, aside, away ; away from, far away: arise, awake, avert, abide, ago; in intensive meaning : athirst, afresh, aweary.

Al—all : altogether : almighty.

Be—identical with the meaning of by in the senses (1) adding intensive force to transitive verb : bedaub, besmear. (2) making intransitive verbs transitive : become. (3) when prefixed to transitive verbs, it changes the object of the transi¬tive relation : bethink, becalm, bespeak. (4) in the privative meaning : behead. (5) in conver¬ting nouns into transitive verbs : befriend. (6) in converting adjec¬tives into transitive verbs : bedim, becalm. (7) in forming adverbs and prepositions from nouns: beside, because. By—by, by the side of : bypath, bystander.

Em— form of en before p or b: if the sense of 'to make' enlighten, embitter.

For—through, completely, away, oppo¬site : forbear, forgive, forswear, forget, forbid.

Fore—in advance of : foretell, foresight.

Forth—forward: /forthcoming.

Fro—from, away: /reward.

Gain—against: gainsay.

In—into, in : inside, insight, incision.

Mis—in the sense of wrong, mistake, mislead.

Off—of Offspring, offshoot. Outt-beyond : outbreak, outside; denoting excess; outrun, outbid, outshine. Over—above, beyond : overhang, overflow, overhold, overdo.

Un—not : unnatural, untrue, unbro¬ken in sense of reversal : unloose, undress; against back : untie, undo, unwind.

Under—lower, below, beneath : under¬sell, underwear,' underlie, under-ground.

With—from, back, against : withdraw, withhold, withstand.

Appendix-31/परिशिष्ट–31
Suffixes (प्रत्यय)

English Suffixes
संज्ञा के अर्थ

-*ard*_r —*art*—to form nouns, one who; *drunkard,* braggart.

-*dom*—dominion, state or jurisdiction : martyrdom, kingdom, freedom.

-*er*—male agent : painter, gardener.

-*hood*—state or rank, nature: man-*hood;* likeli*hood,* false*hood,* neigh-bour*hood.*

-*head*—rank: godhead,

-*kin*—diminutive: napkin, lamb*kin,*

-*let*—diminutive: eyelet, streamlet.

-*ling*—diminutive: duckling, codling,

-*ledge,* lock—state: knowledge, wedlock.

-*ness*—state of: mildness, redness.

-*ock*—diminutive: *bullock,*

-*ow*—diminutive: shadow.

-*red*—state: kindred.

-*ship, -skip, -sc* condition : counsel-*ship,* land*skip,* land*scape.*

-*ster*—(one who), agent : spinster, huckster.

-*ther*—agent or instrument : *feather, father.*

-*wright*—a workman : wheelwright.

-*y*—state or quality, place of; smithy, dirty.

विशेषण के अर्थ

-*fast*—firm : steadfast.

-*fold*—repetition : manifold, twofold.

-*ish*—in sense of (1) like : *childish,* waspish (2) designating nationalities : *English* (3) joined to adjectives with weakened effect; yellow-*ish, sweetish.*

-*less*—without : shoeless, fearless.

-*ly*—like, in manner of: manly, silently.

-*some*—same, full of : gladsome, frolicsome.

-*wise*—manner or position : lengthwise.

क्रियापद के प्रत्यय

-*worth*—worth : stalworth.

-*ate*—to make : variegate, captivate, invalidate.

-*en, -er*—to make of: broaden, lighten, hinder, potter.

-*el, -le*—turning into frequentative verbs: grovel, nipple.

-*fy* (Fr.)—to make : clarify, mollify.

-*ize* (Gr.)–to make: patronize, monopolize, dogmatize, philoso-

Latin and Greek Suffixes
क्रियापद के प्रत्यय

phize, Christianize.

-*able, -ible*—able to : eatable, receivable, legible.

-*aceous*—distinguished by: herbaceous.

-*age*—collective sense: parsonage, assemblage.

-*ary, -ier, -eer, -er*—place or profession: seminary, parliamentary, -*ary, -ier, -eer, -er*—place or profession: seminary, parliamentary, grenad. *ier*, engineer, painter, falconer.

-ee—object of acquisition: examinee.

-ery, -ry—an art, collective: cookery poultry.

—ferous—producing: cupriferous.

-ic (Gr.)—art or science: Physic.

-ic—belonging to: metallic, sulphuric.

-icle—diminutive: particle.

-ism (Gr.)—state or doctrine: *egoism* barbarism, spiritualism.

-ist (Gr.)—agent: artist.

-ive—that which is operative: explosive, pensive.

-scle—diminutive : corpuscle.

-ment—*state* of: concealment, pavement.

-sque—like: picturesque.

-tery—condition: mastery.

-tive—able to: sensitive.

-tory, -sory—place: dormitory, illusory.

-ose, -ous—full of: bellicose, glorious.

Appendix-32/परिशिष्ट–32
Weights and Measures
भार, तौल तथा माप

अंग्रेजी चालू तौल
(Avoirdupois Weight)

27.32 grains make 1 dram.

16 drams	... 1 ounce.
16 ounces.	... 1 pound (1b.)
28 pounds	... 1 quarter (qr.)
4 quarters	... 1 hundred weight (cwt)

अंग्रेजी जौहरियों की तौल सोना, चाँदी और मणियों के लिए
(Troy Weight)

4 grains make 1 carat.

24 grains ...	1 penny weight (dwt).
20 dwts.	... 1 ounce troy
12 ounces troy	... 1 pound troy
25 lbs.	... 1 quarter.
100 lbs.	... 1 cwt.
20 cwts.	1 Ton of gold or silver

सूखी औषधियों की अंग्रेजी तौल
(Apothecaries Weight (Dry)

20 grains	make 1 scruple.
3 scruples	... 1 drachm.
8 drachms	... 1 ounce.
12 ounces.	... 1 pound (lb.)

तरल औषधियों की अंग्रेजी तौल
(Apothecaries Fluid Measure)

60 minims	(drops) make 1 dra fluid
8 dra fluid	... 1 fluid ounce.

16 ounces make	... 1 pint.
8 pints	...1 gallon.

भूमि के क्षेत्रफल का माप या वर्ग परिमाण
(Measurement of Area)

144 sq. inches = 1 sq. foot.
1296 sq. inches = 9 sq. ft. = 1 sq. yd.

काल या समय माप
(Measurement of Time)

60 seconds	= 1 minute.
60 minutes	= 1 hour.
24 hours	= 1 day.
7 days	= 1 week.
28 days	= 1 Lunar Month.
28 to 31 days	= 1 Calender Month.
12 Calender Months	= 1 Year.
365 ¼ days	= 1 Common Year.
366 days	= 1 Leap Year.

भारतीय लम्बाई का परिमाप
(Indian Measurement of Length)

72 बिन्दु या 3 लम्बे जव = 1 इंच

9 इंच = 1 बित्ता (Span) या बालिशत

2 बित्ता या 18 इंच = 1 हाथ

2 हाथ = 1 गज

भारतीय भूमि या धरती की लम्बाई नापने का परिमाण
(Indian Measurement of Area)

22 गज या चार पोप या लाठा = 1 जरीब या चेन

1 जरीब = 100 कड़ी (Links)

भारतीय काल या समय परिमाण
(Indian Measurement of Time)

60 अनुपल	= 1 विपल
60 विपल	= 1 पल या 24 सेंकड
60 पल	= 1 घड़ी या दण्ड या 24 मिनट
2।। घड़ी	= 1 घण्टा
7।। घड़ी	= 1 पहर (प्रहर)
8 पहर या 60 घड़ी	= 1 दिन (दिवस)

1 चन्द्र मास = 29 दिन, 31 घड़ी, 50 पल और 7 विपल

7 दिन	= 1 सप्ताह
15 दिन	= 1 पक्ष या पाख
30 दिन	= 1 मास या महीना
12 मास	= 1 युग
100 वर्ष	= 1 शताब्दी या सदी

भारतीय काल या समय परिमाण

12 units = 1 dozen या 12 इकाई = 1 दर्जन

12 dozen = 1 gross या 12 इकाई = 1 ग्रोस

20 units = kori या 12 इकाई = 1 कोड़ी

20 sheets of paper = quire
या 20 ताव कागज = 1 दस्ता या जिस्ता

20 qrires of paper = 1 ream
या 20 दस्ता = 1 रीम

10 reams of paper = 1 gattha
या 20 रीम = 1 गट्ठा

परिवर्तन सारिणी—बीच वाले कालम में मोटे अक्षरों में छपे अंक मीट्रिक या ब्रिटिश पैमाने के हैं। अतः 1 मीटर = 1.09 गज या 1 गज = 0.91 मीटर।

मीटर		गज	लीटर		पिन्ट्स	किग्रा		पाउंड
0.91	1	1.09	0.28	½	0.88	0.11	¼	0.55
1.83	2	2.19	0.57	1	1.76	0.23	½	1.10
2.74	3	3.28	1.14	2	3.52	0.45	1	2.20
3.66	4	4.37	1.70	3	5.28	0.68	1	3.31
4.57	5	4.47	2.27	4	7.04	0.91	2	4.41
			2.84	5	8.80	2.27	5	11.02
						2.72	6	13.23
						3.17	7	15.47

कि.मी		मील	सें.मी.		फा.हाइट	लिटर		गैलन
1.61	1	0.62	−18	0	32	4.55	1	0.22
3.22	2	1.24	−14	6	43	6.82	1½	0.33
4.83	3	1.86	−11	12	54	9.09	2	0.44
6.44	4	2.48	−4	24	75	11.36	2½	0.55
8.05	5	3.11	0	32	90	13.64	3	0.66
9.65	6	3.73	2	36	97	15.91	3½	0.77
11.26	7	4.35	9	48	118	18.18	4	0.88
12.87	8	4.97	16	60	140	20.46	4½	0.99
14.48	9	5.59	22	72	162	22.73	5	1.10
			29	84	183	27.28	6	1.32
			36	96	205	31.82	7	1.54
			38	100	212	36.37	8	1.76
						40.91	9	1.98

Appendix-33/परिशिष्ट–33
Roman Numerals/रोमन अंक प्रणाली

1	एक	I	31	इक्तीस	XXXI
2	दो	II	32	बत्तीस	XXXII
3	तीन	III	33	तैंतीस	XXXIII
4	चार	IV	34	चौंतीस	XXXIV
5	पाँच	V	35	पैंतीस	XXXV
6	छ:	VI	36	छत्तीस	XXXVI
7	सात	VII	37	सैंतीस	XXXVII
8	आठ	VIII	38	अड़तीस	XXXVIII
9	नौ	IX	39	उन्तालिस	XXXIX
10	दस	X	40	चालीस	XL
11	ग्यारह	XI	41	इकतालिस	XLI
12	बारह	XII	42	बयालिस	XLII
13	तेरह	XIII	43	तैतालिस	XLIII
14	चौदह	XIV	44	चौवालिस	XLIV
15	पन्द्रह	XV	45	पैंतालिस	XLV
16	सोलह	XVI	46	छियालिस	XLVI
17	सत्रह	XVII	47	सैंतालिस	XLVII
18	अठारह	XVIII	48	अड़तालिस	XLVIII
19	उन्नीस	XIX	49	उन्चास	XLIX
20	बीस	XX	50	पचास	L
21	इक्कीस	XXI	51	इक्यावन	LI
22	बाइस	XXII	52	बावन	LII
23	तेइस	XXIII	53	तिपन	LIII
24	चौबीस	XXIV	54	चौवन	LIV
25	पच्चीस	XXV	55	पचपन	LV
26	छब्बीस	XXVI	56	छप्पन	LVI
27	सत्ताइस	XXVII	57	सत्तावन	LVII
28	अट्ठाइस	XXVIII	58	अट्ठावन	LVIII
29	उन्तीस	XXIX	59	उनसठ	LIX
30	तीस	XXX	60	साठ	LX
			61	एकसठ	LXI

62	बासठ	LXII	87	सत्तासी	LXXXVII
63	तिरसठ	LXIII	88	अट्ठासी	LXXXVIII
64	चौंसठ	LXIV	89	नवासी	LXXXIX
65	पैंसठ	LXV	90	नब्बे	XC
66	छाछठ	LXVI	91	एक्यानबे	XCI
67	सड़सठ	LXVII	92	बानवे	XCII
68	अड़सठ	LXVIII	93	तिरानवे	XCIII
69	उनहत्तर	LXIX	94	चौरानबे	XCIV
70	सत्तर	LXX	95	पंचानबे	XCV
71	इकहत्तर	LXXI	96	छियानवे	XCVI
72	बहत्तर	LXXII	97	सत्तानबे	XCVII
73	तिहत्तर	LXXIII	98	अट्ठानवे	XCVIII
74	चौहत्तर	LXXIV	99	निन्यानवे	XCIX
75	पचहत्तर	LXXV	100	सौ	C
76	छिहत्तर	LXXVI	200	दो सौ	CC
77	सतहत्तर	LXXVII	300	तीन सौ	CCC
78	अठहत्तर	LXXIII	400	चार सौ	CD
79	उन्यासी	LXXIX	500	पाँच सौ	D
80	अस्सी	LXXX	600	छ: सौ	DC
81	एक्यासी	LXXXI	700	सात सौ	DCC
82	बयासी	LXXXII	800	आठ सौ	DCCC
83	तिरासी	LXXXIII	900	नौ सौ	CM
84	चौरासी	LXXXIV	1000	एक हजार	M
85	पचासी	LXXXV	2000	दो हजार	MM
86	छियासी	LXXXVI	3000	पाँच हजार	MMM

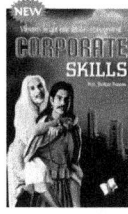

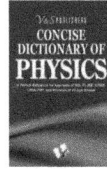

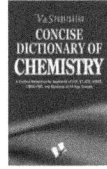

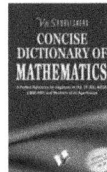

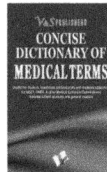

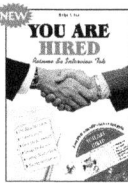

www.ingramcontent.com/pod-product-compliance
Lightning Source LLC
Chambersburg PA
CBHW060420100426
42812CB00030B/3246/J